The Annotated

Pickett's History of Alabama

The Annotated
PICKETT'S HISTORY OF ALABAMA

And Incidentally of Georgia and Mississippi, from the Earliest Period

BY

ALBERT JAMES PICKETT

EDITED, ANNOTATED, AND WITH AN INTRODUCTION BY JAMES P. PATE

NEWSOUTH BOOKS
Montgomery

2018

NewSouth Books
105 S. Court Street
Montgomery, AL 36104

Published in the United States by NewSouth Books, a division of NewSouth, Inc., Montgomery, Alabama.

Cataloging-in-Publication Data

Names: Pickett, Albert James (1810–1858), author; Pate, James P. (1942–), editor.

Title: The annotated Pickett's history of Alabama: and incidentally of Georgia and Mississippi, from the earliest period

Description: Montgomery, Alabama : NewSouth Books [2018] | Includes bibliographical references and index.

Identifiers: ISBN 9781588380326 (cloth : alk. paper) | ISBN 9781588383785 (ebook)

Subjects: United States—History. | Southern states—History. | Alabama—History. | Alabama—Civilization. |Native Americans—History. | Pickett, Albert J.—Biography. |

Library of Congress Control Number: 2018956007

Design by Randall Williams

Printed in the United States of America by Sheridan

Contents

Table of Illustrations

* *Reprinted from the 1896 edition (see page xxxvi).*

** *All other illustrations were taken from the 1851 two-volume edition, courtesy of the Alabama Department of Archives and History.*

Introduction to the Annotated Edition

James P. Pate

Writing his wife Sarah from the Pavilion Hotel in Charleston, South Carolina, on 5 May 1851, Albert James Pickett buoyantly announced the completion of the first volume of his *History of Alabama*. In a follow-up letter ten days later, after expressing concern for her health, and declaring his own, he enthused about his imminent homecoming when he would finally announce the completion of the opus that had consumed five years of his life in researching and writing. He assured Sarah he wanted "this disagreeable job off his hands." He echoed these sentiments in his preface in that completed first volume, writing: "I thought it would serve to amuse my leisure hours; but it has been the hardest work of my life."[1]

Pickett's journey to become Alabama's first historian began in North Carolina where he was born on 13 August 1810 in Anson County to William Raiford Pickett and Frances Dickson Pickett. Before immigrating to the Alabama Territory in 1818, the elder Pickett served as sheriff and as a North Carolina legislator for several years. During Albert's formative years in Autauga County, Alabama, his father, known as Colonel Pickett, was a prominent landowner, slave owner, and merchant. He operated a trading house for several years that served a diverse clientele, including early settlers, Indian countrymen, and Creek Indians. Young Albert's exposure to the culture and society of the Creeks, the reminiscences of Indian traders, and stories from the Revolutionary War era—related by Whigs and Tories—made a deep impression on him. Colonel Pickett was active in politics, serving thirteen years in the Alabama house, in the senate in the 1820s and 1830s, and on three occasions as a Democrat presidential elector. His

[1] AJP to Sarah Pickett, Charleston, S.C., 5 May 1851; AJP to Sarah Pickett, Charleston, S.C., 15 May 1851, Albert James Pickett Papers, Alabama Department of Archives and History, Montgomery, AL. [Hereafter cited as Pickett Papers, ADAH]

father's varied background in farming, business, and state politics allowed young Albert a rich education and enabled his unique contact with a social and cultural milieu that shaped his perception of early Alabama, its people, and its emerging institutions.[2]

Likewise, Albert Pickett's formal education was unique. Unlike his chief literary rival and foil, Alexander Beaufort Meek—whose matriculation at the University of Georgia culminated with two degrees from the University of Alabama—Albert was exposed to the basics of a classical education in "field schools" conducted by Neil Blue and Joseph Hall at Rocky Mount in Autauga County. In the spring of 1828—with the approval of his father and mother—Pickett traveled to Middletown, Connecticut, via North Carolina and New York City, to attend the American Literary, Scientific, and Military Academy conducted by Captain Alden Partridge, former superintendent of the United States Military Academy. When he arrived at Middletown, he learned Partridge had left the school over a misunderstanding, and young Pickett then traveled to Cambridge, where he attempted to enter Harvard College. However, a letter from his father advised him that he preferred his son attend Harwood Academy, a large boarding and day school at Mill Farm in Stafford County, Virginia. The Academy, founded by Charles Tackett, "a great disciplinarian," had an "able corps of assistants," and Pickett spent two years here with classmates from throughout Virginia and "from other states—North and South."[3]

After his return to Alabama in 1830, Pickett studied law for two years in Montgomery under the tutelage of his brother, William Dickson Pickett, judge of the Sixth Judicial Circuit. But he never practiced law. It seems a combination of factors, including his early experiences in Autauga, extensive travel, and educational pursuits in the East, had whetted his appetite for literature and political commentary. While working in his brother's law office, he had become exposed to courtroom procedure, document analysis, and legal discovery—skills that honed his historical research and writing. His legal study brought him into intimate contact with the hustle and bustle of Montgomery—Alabama's capital city after 1846—and its newspapers, especially the *Alabama Journal*, owned by his-brother-in-law Moseley Baker, and the *Planter's*

[2] Frank L. Owsley Jr., "Albert J. Pickett: Typical Southern Pioneer State Historian," (Ph.D. diss., University of Alabama, 1955), 4–5; Philip D. Beidler, *First Books: The Printed Word and Cultural Foundation in Early Alabama* (Tuscaloosa: University of Alabama Press, 1999), 64–65; Johanna Nicol Shields, *Freedom in a Slave Society: Stories from the Antebellum South* (New York: Cambridge University Press, 2012), 75–76.

[3] Michael Leonard Woods, "Personal Reminiscences of Col. Albert James Pickett," in *Transactions of the Alabama Historical Society, 1899–1903*, ed., Thomas McAdory Owen, vol. 4 (Montgomery: The Society, 1904), 597–99, 601; Mary Ann Neeley, ed., The *Works of Mathew Blue Montgomery's First Historian* (Montgomery: NewSouth Books, 2010), 336–40; Henry Barnard, "Alden Partridge," *The American Journal of Education* 23 (No. 28, 1872): 844–45; Strother Harding, "School History of Stafford County," *Virginia School Report, 1885, Fifteenth Annual Report of the Superintendent of Public Instruction for the Operating Year Ending July 31, 1885* (Richmond: Rush U. Derr, 1886), 278.

Gazette, which became outlets for many of his literary and political articles. Another turning point for Pickett was his marriage to Sarah Smith Harris in 1832, which added her dowry lands—Forest Farm, at Pickett Springs in Montgomery County—to his land holdings located near his father's lands in Autauga County. By 1837, the Picketts divided their primary residence between Forest Farm and Montgomery, and later added their retreat at Robinson Springs, where Pickett concentrated on writing his history of Alabama.[4]

Despite the demands of managing two plantations and a growing slave labor force, Pickett took an early interest in public affairs, which in that era were often factional. On 4 July 1832, there were three distinct Independence Day celebrations in Montgomery presided over by the "Union men, the Nullifiers, and the Mechanics," respectively. At the union celebration at the Washington Street theatre, Pickett delivered a stirring address—demonstrating his attachment to and support for President Andrew Jackson and his disdain for the nullification forces in South Carolina, Alabama, and elsewhere in the South. Three years later, he authored a report for a Montgomery grand jury—"Presentment Against the Abolitionists"—attacking northerners who might stir slave unrest following Nat Turner's violent revolt in 1831 and calling on the legislature to pass laws to inhibit the introduction of slaves from other states, to enforce strict slave patrols, and to remove persons who stirred unrest. Several months later, he authored a pamphlet—*An Address to the Democratic Republicans of Autauga, by the Committee of Correspondence*—calling on the friends of Jackson to hold the first statewide party convention in Tuscaloosa in December 1835. His loyalty to Jackson led him to write a series of articles published in the *Montgomery Advertiser* to combat the growing anti-Martin Van Buren forces in the Alabama legislature and to oppose the nomination of Hugh Lawson White. At this early date, his political activism and his writing had brought him in contact with influential members of Alabama's social and political elite.[5]

Whether in his speeches, anti-abolitionist activities, or promoting of Andrew Jackson, Pickett was never without a platform to air his strong beliefs on Alabama's economy in the Montgomery newspapers.

[4] Woods, "Personal Reminiscences," 601; Crawford Jackson, *Brief Biographical Sketch of the Late Col. Albert James Pickett of Alabama* (Montgomery: Barrett & Wimbish, 1859), 6; Thomas McAdory Owen, "Albert James Pickett," in *Library of Southern Literature,* ed., Edwin Anderson Alderman, et al, 17 vols. (Atlanta: Martin & Hoyt Company, 1907–1923), 4: 4017; Neeley, *The Works of Matthew* Blue, 103, 105; "Back in the Day: Parsonage Hosts Famous Writer," *Wetumpka Herald,* 20 June 2016.

[5] Pickett Scrapbook, Pickett Papers, ADAH; Albert James Pickett, *An Address to the Democratic Republicans of Autauga, by the Committee of Correspondence* (Montgomery: Belser & Child, 1835); Woods, "Personal Reminiscences," 603–04; Owsley, "Albert J. Pickett," 7–8; Shields, *Freedom in a Slave Society,* 137, 137 n. 6; J. Mills Thornton, *Politics and Power in a Slave Society: Alabama, 1800–1860* (Baton Rouge: Louisiana State University Press, 1978), 35.

He continued his attacks on Judge White's nomination and White's supporters in the Alabama legislature—a makeshift coalition of Whigs and dissident states' rights Democrats upset over Jackson's failure to quickly expunge the Creeks from Alabama. When not opposing White's quest of the presidency over Van Buren, Jackson's vice president and hand-picked successor, Pickett authored other articles on a variety of topics: "The French Question," "The Alabama Legislature," "The Speaker's Chair," "The Hon. William Smith," and "The Proposed Convention." He generally signed most of his articles "Reviewer," but this was not an effort to escape controversy. In "The Speaker's Chair" article, he openly attacked James White McClung from Madison County who sought election as speaker of the Alabama House of Representatives in 1835. Pickett accused him of being little more than a rabble-rouser—an obvious slam for his support of Hugh Lawson White. Despite Pickett's article, McClung won the speaker's chair and served as speaker during three legislative sessions in the 1830s.[6]

The Creek War of 1836 and the anti-bank fallout over the Panic of 1837 pulled Pickett, a political dilettante and editorialist, fully into Alabama's no-holds barred political arena. Clement Comer Clay, a fellow Jacksonian Democrat, was elected governor in 1835 and was soon confronted by Creek dissidents who violently opposed removal—a conflict known as the Creek War of 1836. Clay appointed Pickett as military aide-de-camp in 1836. Pickett took an active role during this brief conflict, writing military orders, requisitioning supplies, and lobbying support for Clay, who was roundly criticized for his leadership—or the lack of it—in rounding up the Creek dissidents. This short military stint appears to have earned Pickett his honorific title of "Colonel," and perhaps his later role in Governor Benjamin Fitzpatrick's bank reform efforts. Pickett, a friend and political confidant of Fitzpatrick, received an appointment as a bank examiner in September 1845. While in this position, he investigated the Montgomery branch of the State Bank of Alabama, whose charter had expired in January 1845. These two disparate experiences may have dissuaded Pickett from pursuing a political career and extending his *History of Alabama* beyond 1820, except for a few digressions

[6] Pickett Scrapbook, Pickett Papers, ADAH; Woods, "Personal Reminiscences," 603; Owsley, "Albert J. Pickett," 5–8; Shields, *Freedom in a Slave Society*, 137, 137 n. 6.; Thornton, *Politics and Power in a Slave Society*, 35; Willis Brewer, *Alabama: Her History, Resources, War Record, and Public Men; From 1540 to 1872* (Montgomery: Barrett & Brown, 1872), 359, 371.

[7] Pickett Scrapbook, Pickett Papers, ADAH; Owsley, "Albert J. Pickett," 9–15; Woods, "Personal Reminiscences," 602; Frank L. Owsley Jr., "Albert J. Pickett: Planter-Historian of the Old South," *Louisiana History* 8 (Summer 1969): 161–64; J. Mills Thornton, "Benjamin Fitzpatrick," in *Alabama Governors: A Political History of the State*, ed., Samuel L. Webb and Margaret Armbrester (Tuscaloosa: University of Alabama Press, 2001), 54–57.

in his narrative and the biographical sketches in the final chapter.[7]

In the summer of 1837, wedged in between political appointments and a statewide controversy, Pickett took his wife, seven-month-old daughter, Martha Raiford Pickett, and his sister-in-law, Mary Gatlin Harris, on an extended trip, traveling first to Hot Springs, North Carolina, at the confluence of the French Broad River and Spring Creek. Here they spent several days enjoying the cooler air of the Blue Ridge Mountains and taking in the mineral waters—believed to have healing properties. Then the family traveled west, over the Buncombe Pike and the Tennessee Road, to Nashville, where they visited Daniel Graham, Tennessee's state comptroller. Graham had traveled to Mobile in March 1836, and, on his return home, he stayed briefly in Montgomery. With Graham and a letter of introduction from Governor Clement Comer Clay, Pickett and his family enjoyed an extended visit with Andrew and Rachel Jackson at the Hermitage. Following this visit, Jackson sent Pickett an oil portrait; this painting and his conversations with Jackson confirmed Pickett's assessment of him: "The most extraordinary man that ever lived in any age or country, was Gen. Andrew Jackson."[8]

Ironically, Pickett's service on a Montgomery grand jury in 1845 may have persuaded him to withdraw from the public arena entirely and to launch his seminal writing project. Pickett served on a grand jury before Judge George W. Stone's Montgomery circuit court for the September 1845 term. He wrote the grand jury's report calling for legislative action to tax itinerant traders out of business, to prohibit the importation of slaves into the state, and to impose a general ban on interstate slave traders. Pickett's grand jury report—"Presentment of the Grand Jury"—and its recommendations circulated statewide in Alabama newspapers, receiving the endorsement of some county grand juries and opposition from others. While many newspapers supported the report, others vehemently attacked it, claiming the proposed legislation would limit free trade and prevent hard-working Alabamians from becoming slave owners and entering the planter class. The Mobile-based *Herald and Tribune* not only opposed the call for legislation but criticized Pickett as a wealthy aristocrat for promoting the proposal.[9]

[8] AJP to Governor C. C. Clay, 3 May 1836, Pickett Papers, ADAH; Woods, "Personal Reminiscences," 604; Daniel Graham to James K. Polk, Nashville, Tennessee, 5 May 1836, *Correspondence of James K. Polk: 1835–1836* (vols. 1–7; Nashville: Vanderbilt University Press, 1969–1989; vols. 8 - ; Knoxville: University of Tennessee Press, 1993—present), 3: 614–16; "History of Hot Springs, NC," http://hotspringsnc.org/about/history/; Albert J. Pickett, *Eight Days in New Orleans, In February, 1847* (Montgomery: n.p., 1847), 13. Note: James Patton bought the hot spring in 1837 and built the Warm Springs Hotel, and the area was referred to as Warm Springs until 1886. The portrait of Andrew Jackson by William Stewart Watson was consigned to Christies in 2001 by a great grandchild of Mary Pickett Harris and sold at auction in January 2010 for $32,000. https://new.liveauctioneers.com/item/6958439.

[9] Owsley, "Albert J. Pickett," 15–20; Woods, "Personal Reminiscences," 604–05; Shields, *Freedom in a Slave Society*, 138.

While this attack was at its height, including the impugning of Pickett's name, Pickett responded with a letter defending himself and his position. The letter, dated 20 October 1845, was published as a pamphlet—*A Continuation of the Views of Col. A. J. Pickett, on Negro Introduction*—and received support in the Wetumpka-based *Whig*, which had endorsed his original grand jury report. Although the timeline is not certain, a Montgomery County committee that supported Pickett's views published a second pamphlet—*A reply to the objections urged against a prohibitory law in relation to the introduction of negroes*. This pamphlet, published by Charles Yancey in Wetumpka, contained an expanded version of Pickett's original report. While the controversy swirled, causing statewide debate, the Alabama legislature met and adjourned without passing any new laws regarding the importation of slaves. The personal attacks from the newspapers and grand juries that questioned Pickett's involvement simply added more reasons for him to shun the political arena and eventually fuelled Pickett's decision to end his *History of Alabama* in 1820.[10]

Although Pickett had grown weary of this slavery proposal controversy, he continued to write articles on issues that touched on economic and commercial affairs in central Alabama. In early January 1847, he published a newspaper article—"Let the Planter Have Fair Play"—supporting the Winter and Company Bank of Montgomery, which had come under negative public scrutiny. While Pickett was careful not to take a side, he pointed out that Montgomery needed a bank. He emphasized the bank's contributions to the city's businesses and its policy of extending credit to area planters at reasonable rates. He contrasted the bank's practice with local merchants, who tended to charge high interest rates and accepted cotton as payment at a lower market price, causing area planters to ship their cotton to be sold in other markets to receive higher prices. He emphasized his support for a local bank, whether it was Winter and Company or another organized by local citizens.[11]

As one of the largest planters in Autauga and Montgomery counties, Pickett understood the challenges faced by Alabama's farmers, as revealed by his comments on the services provided by the Winter

[10] Pickett Scrapbook, Pickett Papers, ADAH; Owsley, "Albert J. Pickett," 18–20; Shields, *Freedom in a Slave Society*, 138, 138 n. 9; Albert J. Pickett, *A Continuation of the Views of Col. A. J. Pickett, on Negro Introduction* (Wetumpka: Wetumpka *Whig* Printing Office, 1845); Albert J. Pickett, *A reply to the objections urged against a prohibitory law in relation to the introduction of negroes* (Wetumpka: Charles Yancey, 1845).

[11] Miscellaneous newspaper article, Pickett Scrapbook, Pickett Papers, ADAH; Owsley Jr., "Albert J. Pickett: Planter-Historian," 166–67.

and Company Bank. His Forest Farm plantation produced an average of 150 bales of cotton annually in the 1840s, but he also raised hogs, dairy cattle, and large crops of corn, oats, rye and "fodder," sweet potatoes, peas, and beans—and a market garden valued at $2,500 in 1850. The *Alabama Journal* described his dairy as one of the finest in Montgomery County; it produced an average of $850 from 1842 to 1846. In many respects, he was a scientific farmer, as reflected in his diversified farming, and he frequently corresponded with Richard T. Brumby, a professor of chemistry, mineralogy, and geology at the University of Alabama, sharing information or seeking advice—such as eliminating weeds from his fields. In return, Brumby asked Pickett in December 1847 to examine his plantation operated with his brother and publish the results of his investigations in the *Southern Cultivator* or *Alabama Planter*. Obviously, Brumby, who was attempting to promote rice cultivation over cotton in south Alabama, was aware of Pickett's articles—"The Redlands of Alabama"—published in the January, February, and June 1847 issues of the *Southern Cultivator*. Using his research and analytical skills, Pickett detailed his production from 1842 to 1846 and described his rich soil, farming techniques—using certain plows and applying no fertilizers—and planting methods, especially for corn and cotton.[12]

As demonstrated above, Pickett's writings brought him statewide attention and contacts with newspaper editors, political elites, educators and scientists, and prominent business and community leaders. Although no clear documentation of his intention exists in his available correspondence or public utterances, he appears to have determined to write a history of Alabama by early 1846. Based on a cursory review of his writings from 1835 to 1845 and the subjects addressed after 1851, it is obvious that Pickett's voracious intellectual curiosity had transformed him into a dedicated bibliophile with an extensive library. His correspondence in 1847 and 1848 and his extensive book purchases from Bartlett & Welford, international book dealers in New York City, and George Templeman, a prominent bookseller in Washington, all demonstrate his commitment to supplement his research and to add critical sources on the Southwest and Alabama. We know he acquired

[12] Owsley, "Albert J. Pickett," 35–38; Richard T. Brumby to AJP, University of Alabama, 12 May 1847, Pickett Papers, ADAH; Richard T. Brumby to AJP, Tuscaloosa, 8 December 1847, ibid.; A. J. Pickett, "The Redlands of Alabama," *Southern Cultivator* 5 (January, February, and June 1847), 10, 25–26, 91–92. Note: Between 1842 and 1846, Pickett's Forest Farm plantation produced an average of 150 bales of cotton and yielded a total of 41,000 bushels of corn, 46,000 pounds of pork, and 190,000 pounds of "fodder" (i.e., oats, rye, etc.). He also declared that each year his plantation "made negro clothes"—further demonstrating how self-sufficiently it operated.

several journals, travel accounts, and memoirs published in French, a language he did not read, forcing him to employ Bowdoin College graduate Charles McDougal as a translator. We also learn from his correspondence that he received books, journals, diaries, and personal papers as gifts or loans. On the advice of William Gilmore Simms, he appears to have purchased books from John Russell's bookstore in Charleston and perhaps from others in Montgomery, Mobile, and New Orleans. However, a review of the Pickett Book Collection in the Alabama Department of Archives and History in Montgomery contains titles unrelated to Alabama's protohistoric and historic eras: *Arabian Nights*; *The English Theophrastus; or, The Manners of the Age*; Richard Lander, *Journal of an Expedition to Explore the Course and Termination of the Niger*; *Memoir of the Life of Richard Henry Lee*; and Mango Park, *Travels in the Interior of Africa*. The other fifty-plus titles are either cited by Pickett or have some connection to issues and/or events covered in *History of Alabama*, but these books account for less than a third of the works cited in his footnotes.[13]

As Pickett began to develop his plan to research and write his history, his list of potential contacts grew along with his sources for original documents, journals, papers, and memoirs. One such possible source, James Abercrombie, a veteran legislator of the 1820s and 1830s who lived in Girard, Alabama, received one of Pickett's earliest letters, dated 25 April 1846. In that letter, Pickett posed few questions, limiting his requests for information about the Creeks and Yuchis and the papers of Colonel John Crowell, a Creek Indian agent in Alabama and Georgia. Abercrombie responded on 10 May 1846, telling Pickett that he was "gratified" to find him "engaged" in writing a history of Alabama, but that he had no information in his possession that could be helpful to him. Like other Pickett correspondents over the next three years, he provided the names of men he thought could provide the information requested or access to manuscript sources.[14]

While he was engaged in extensive correspondence in 1846 and 1847, canvassing for material on early Alabama, Pickett made a trip to New Orleans that dramatically influenced the trajectory of his history of Alabama. He not only made several important contacts,

[13] Owsley, "Albert J. Pickett," 131; Pickett Book Collection, Pickett Papers, ADAH; Bartlett & Welford to AJP, New York, 16 September 1847, ibid.; Bartlett & Welford to AJP, New York, 19 November 1847, ibid; Bartlett & Welford to AJP, New York, 17 December 1847, ibid; Bartlett & Welford to AJP, New York, 22 March 1848, ibid; Bartlett & Welford to AJP, New York, 9 May 1848, ibid; George Templeman to AJP, 10 March 1848, ibid; George Templeman to AJP, 29 March 1848, ibid.

[14] James Abercrombie to AJP, Girard, Ala., 10 May 1846, Picket Papers, ADAH.

but his visit resulted in the publication of a series of articles—"A Late Visit to New Orleans"—in the Montgomery *Daily Alabama Journal.* The widespread statewide response in newspapers prompted Pickett to publish his sketches of New Orleans as a pamphlet in May 1847: *Eight Days in New Orleans, in February, 1847.* In his brief introductory note, Pickett states his intent to present his essay to "his friends at a distance" and share his first attempt at "descriptive and historic writing." While some might question the sincerity of his remarks, Pickett's trip to New Orleans, his original newspaper articles, and the pamphlet had far-reaching implications for his primary goal.[15]

After the appearance of his first four or five articles in the *Daily Alabama Journal,* the editors of the *Tri-weekly Flag and Advertiser* of Montgomery suggested that Pickett should consider writing a history of the state. On 27 March 1847, he declared that he would indeed write the history of Alabama and asked for help in pursuing his work. Pickett began sending copies of his newspaper articles in his letters requesting information and material for his history. Newspapers from across the state quickly spread the word and encouraged their readers to send Pickett material. Although the *Herald and Tribune* welcomed the news of a possible state history, it expressed regret that its author might not be Alexander Beaufort Meek, a well-known Mobile judge and writer. Another semi-negative response in the Marion *News* in April 1847 noted that it was aware that an unnamed writer was already working on a history of Alabama. *News* editor Samuel Townes openly taunted Pickett by expressing doubt that he would complete his history and giving him "a year and a day" to finish his work.[16]

Whether the unnamed historian was Meek or Judge Benjamin Porter, of Tuscaloosa, Pickett had written to both men in March and April 1847 after being alerted of their possible ambitions by friends or other sources. Meek had published his "Sketches of the history of Alabama, and, incidentally, of the adjacent States" in his literary journal—*The Southron: A Monthly Magazine and Review*—in January and March 1839, and he delivered an address on "The Southwest: Its history, character, and prospects" to the Erosophic Society of the University of Alabama in December 1839, which was printed as a pamphlet in

[15] Miscellaneous newspaper articles, Pickett Scrapbook, Pickett Papers, ADAH; Owsley, "Albert J. Pickett: Planter-Historian," 168–69; Shields, *Freedom in a Slave Society*, 139; Albert J. Pickett, *Eight Days in New Orleans, in February, 1847* (Montgomery: n.p., 1847).

[16] Miscellaneous newspaper articles, Pickett Scrapbook, Pickett Papers, ADAH; Owsley, "Albert J. Pickett: Planter-Historian," 168–70; Shields, *Freedom in a Slave Society*, 139–40.

1840. On 1 May 1847, Porter confirmed to Pickett that he had an interest in writing a school history but had deferred to Meek, and had only resumed when he determined that Meek's work was "coming out slowly." He agreed to "freely . . . give up the field to you" and added: "This is an affair about which we should have no jealousies; and it will afford me pleasure to see the History of Alabama rise under your pen." On 8 June, Meek responded to Pickett's letter of March 1847 with a curt offer to "be of service in the furtherance of your purposes . . . and shall be happy to hear from you." Before answering Pickett's letter, Meek had responded to a letter from William Gilmore Simms—his literary muse—and reported that he had a "History of Alabama" book manuscript of some 800 pages "which has been on my hands for nearly three years" and gave three reasons he had failed to complete it. He shared with Simms that Judge Porter had planned to write a history of the state but "has abandoned the idea" and that "Mr. A. J. Pickett has set about his design very earnestly . . . but I do not think he has sufficient ability for the undertaking."[17]

[17] **Benjamin F. Porter to AJP, Tuscaloosa, 1 May 1847, Pickett Papers, ADAH; A. B. Meek to AJP, Mobile, 8 June 1847, ibid; A. B. Meek to William Gilmore Simms, Mobile, 18 May 1847, Alexander Beaufort Meek Papers, ADAH; A. B. Meek, "Sketches of the history of Alabama, and, incidentally, of the adjacent States," *The Southron: A Monthly Magazine and Review* (January and March 1839), 17, 150; Alexander B. Meek, *The Southwest: Its History, Character and Prospects. A discourse for the eighth anniversary of the Erosophic Society of the University of Alabama. December 7, 1839* (Tuscaloosa: C. B. Baldwin, 1840).**

After his *Eight Days* pamphlet was published, Pickett dispatched copies to a long list of his correspondents and contacts to promote his forthcoming history and to seek their advice on writing and historiography. Upon receiving the sketches, Mississippi physician and historian John Wesley Monette responded by advising him to use "a blank book" with subject headings, placing events in chronological order, and, as he began writing, to leave "blank spaces" to add new material Eventually Pickett filled eight manuscript notebooks, from which he extracted his book manuscript by late 1850. In New Orleans, David Macaulay promised to review Pickett's *Eight Days* in the *Daily National* and to promote his "enterprise in bringing out a history of Alabama." A reviewer for the *Southern Quarterly Review* thought Pickett's first chapters of *Eight Days* suffered "from being too ambitious in style" but thought his observations of New Orleans showed "he is natural, and his sketches bear the marks of a good eye for observation." Following a three-month absence from Charleston, William Gilmore Simms acknowledged the receipt of Pickett's "graceful sketches" in October 1847 and added that he had enjoyed "perusing" his pamphlet. He also commented "you have suffered some grammatical errors . . . which should be carefully avoided in things of more elaborate character" and wished Pickett success with his "historical labors." Charles Gayarré, author of *Histoire de la Louisiane*, responded in early January 1848, acknowledged the receipt of "eight days in New Orleans," and promised to send Pickett a copy of "my romance of the history of Louisiana."[18]

Even as Pickett reached out to an array of prominent writers and historians for their assistance and guidance, his writing and publications began to garner attention and honors from Baltimore to New Orleans. Macaulay asked Pickett to consider being a contributor to the *New Orleans Literary and Scientific Miscellany* or grant him permission to "occasionally copy from your Eight Days." In June 1847, Israel Keech Tefft, secretary of the Georgia Historical Society, notified Pickett that he had been elected an honorary member of the Society and promised to send the first two volumes of the Society's *Collections* and a diploma of membership. James T. Killough, secretary of the Philomathic Society of the University of Alabama, informed Pickett by letter on 19 August 1847 that he had been elected to honorary membership in the Society. In April 1848, Pickett received a request to deliver a public lecture to the People's Lyceum—founded in 1841 and "which . . . has each year been favored with addresses from gentlemen of much talent and highest distinction." He received a letter in March 1849 notifying him of his unanimous election as an honorary member of the Reading Room Society of St. Mary's College in Baltimore. With support from President Basil Manly of the University of Alabama. Pickett became a founding member of the Alabama Historical Society in July 1850 and served as its first vice president. By 1850, Pickett had received increased recognition for his articles published in Montgomery newspapers and for two pamphlets—*Eight Days in New Orleans* and *Arrest of Aaron Burr in Alabama in 1807*. However, he published his most ambitious writing as a pamphlet in 1849: *Invasion of the Territory of Alabama, by One Thousand Spaniards, Under Ferdinand de Soto, in 1540*—which became chapter one of his *History of Alabama*.[19]

Not only did Pickett's voluminous correspondence produce research materials and spread the word about his work, but his letters to and

[18] John Wesley Monette to AJP, Washington, Miss., 9 June 1847, Pickett Papers, ADAH; David Macaulay to AJP, New Orleans, 29 July 1847, ibid; William Gilmore Simms to AJP, Charleston, 25 October 1847, ibid; Charles Gayarré to ASP, New Orleans, 7 January 1848, ibid; "*Eight Days in New Orleans, in February, 1847*. By Albert J. Pickett, of Montgomery, Ala.," *The Southern Quarterly Review* 12 (1847), 533–34; Owsley, "Albert J. Pickett: Planter-Historian," 168; Shields, *Freedom in a Slave Society*, 140. Note: Five of Pickett's original eight manuscript notebooks can be found in the Albert James Pickett Papers at the Alabama Department of Archives and History, Montgomery, Alabama.

from several prominent writers and historians yielded advice on critical research sources and writing. The exchanges between Pickett and William Gilmore Simms—one of the most prolific and widely respected writers in the pre-war South—covered writing style, research materials, booksellers, and printers. While Pickett adopted Monette's advice to start with "a blank book," it was Simms, author of an 1842 *History of South Carolina*, from whom Pickett most wanted to hear and attempted to emulate with his *History*. They exchanged eight or more letters between March and December 1847 before Pickett submitted a list of questions to Simms on writing style, structure, organization, format, length, and paper. Writing from his Woodlands Plantation on 18 March 1848, Simms commented, "It is not easy to respond to your questions." He added that it would be better if Pickett would come for a visit so he could show Pickett his process "and possibly counsel yours." Then he commented on Pickett's inquiries one by one, stating that "Style is not innate" and depends on the author's temperament, admonishing Pickett to polish and perfect his paragraphs, to avoid copying from an author, to rewrite "twice or thrice," and to write on one side of ruled paper, which printers preferred. He ended his writing instructions by urging Pickett to limit his history to one volume and observing: "I doubt you can find a better size for your purpose than my history of South Carolina." He closed his letter by telling Pickett how to reach Woodlands and that he would "be very glad to see you."[20]

Other letters arrived from Gayarré, Monette, and Porter offering assistance, advice, and lists of books and other sources. William Bacon Stevens and Jared Sparks also replied to Pickett's queries on writing and sources. Stevens, professor of belles-lettres, oratory, and moral philosophy at the University of Georgia, advised Pickett to collect every book and document that cast light on his subject, to become acquainted with "everything" written about Alabama from the days of Cabeza de Vaca, and to resolve not "to write until you have collected all the materials you require." Writing from Cambridge in November 1847, Sparks, a professor of ancient and modern history at Harvard, gave Pickett a beginner's seminar on primary sources related to Hernando de Soto's expedition, French colonizing efforts in East Florida, and the

[19] Israel Keech Tefft to AJP, Savannah, 22 June 1847, Pickett Papers, ADAH; David Macaulay to AJP, New Orleans, 10 July 1847, ibid; James T. Killough to AJP, Pickensville, Ala., 19 August 1847, ibid.; People's Lyceum to AJP, [Montgomery], 1 April 1848, ibid; E. H. Bartlett to AJP, Baltimore, 1 March 1849, ibid; Owsley, "Albert J. Pickett," 24.

[20] William Gilmore Simms to AJP, Woodlands, 14 April 1847, Pickett Papers, ADAH; William Gilmore Simms to AJP, Woodlands, 19 April 1847, ibid; William Gilmore Simms to AJP, Woodlands, 3 May 1847, ibid; William Gilmore Simms to AJP, 25 October 1847, Charleston, ibid; William Gilmore Simms to AJP, Woodlands, 18 March [1848], ibid. Note: The editors of *The Letters of William Gilmore Simms* have determined by internal evidence that Simms wrote his lengthy letter to Pickett on writing history in 1848, because it references his *The Life of Chevalier Bayard* which was published several months after 18 March 1847. See *The Letters of William Gilmore Simms* eds. Mary C. Simms Oliphant, et al, 6 vols. (Columbia: University of South Carolina Press, 1952–1982), 3: 398 n.1.

"doings of the French at Mobile" and in Louisiana—including Charles Gayarré's recently published *Histoire de la Louisiane*. Although Stevens had directed Pickett to the major sources on De Soto, Sparks specifically instructed Pickett on the value of the account of the Gentleman of Elvas over that of Garcilaso de la Vega—a book of "sheer romance from beginning to end"; this was advice Pickett failed to follow. Sparks closed by responding to Pickett's query "on the manner of writing your history," urging him to find his facts in original sources, perform thorough research, and "not be in a hurry to finish your work."[21]

Even before he received Sparks's insightful critique of Spanish, Portuguese, and French sources, Pickett took Simms's advice and contacted booksellers Bartlett & Welford, seeking an English translation of the "Portuguese eye witness" and "the narratives of Laudonnière." His invoice for books purchased in September 1847 included "Le Moyne's Florida," which Pickett used as a source and for six plates for his illustrations, and "Adair's American Indians," which informed Pickett's narrative on the Old Southwest frontier and Southern Indians. Attached to this invoice was a brief note advising Pickett: "Mr. Welford sailed for Europe having your list in his possession last week." Subsequent letters and invoices from Bartlett & Welford list memoirs, travel accounts, and multi-volume works cited in the footnotes of Pickett's *History*, especially volume one. They not only filled Pickett's book requests, but they also sent him lists of books that "our Mr. Welford" had found in London. In a letter of 9 May 1848, Bartlett & Welford offered Pickett the opportunity to purchase "books on America" that were also on "two applications" from Peter Force and Jared Sparks—"but as they are directly in your line, you have the first offer." In March 1848, Pickett received letters, books, and lists from George Templeman, a bookseller in Washington, which included Congressional documents related to the Creeks, Indian removal, and "hostilities with the Creeks." One Templeman letter fulfilled Pickett's request for three books, including General James Wilkinson's *Memoirs of My Own Times* and his *Burr's Conspiracy Exposed*, and Arsène Lacarrière Latour's *Historical Memoir of the War in West Florida and Louisiana in 1814–15*, and promised to find a fourth book in New York or Philadelphia.[22]

[21] William Bacon Stevens to AJP, Athens, 24 April 1847, Pickett Papers, ADAH; Jared Sparks to AJP, Cambridge, 29 November 1847, ibid.

As his library grew exponentially, Pickett received books, documents, papers, and "Notes" from prominent and not so prominent correspondents. Alfred Hennen, a highly successful New Orleans lawyer with an extensive private library, provided Pickett with letters written by Alexander McGillivray and an original copy of the secret treaty between George Washington and McGillivray in 1790. J. F. H. Claiborne, a lawyer-planter, newspaper editor, and historian who later published *The Life and Times of Sam Dale*, sent the papers of his father, General Ferdinand Leigh Claiborne, who commanded the Mississippi Territorial militia during the Creek War in 1813–1814. Although former Governor Clement Comer Clay and future Governor John Gill Shorter offered little more than a few "valuable contacts," they sent their best wishes for success with his *History of Alabama*. U.S. Senator Arthur P. Bagby, another former governor, offered to assist Pickett by writing a letter of introduction to George Strother Gaines. Writing from Mobile, Arthur Francis Hopkins, former Chief Justice of the Alabama Supreme Court, agreed to send Pickett a copy of his speech issued in a pamphlet and autobiographical material. He also urged Pickett to contact William Rufus King, recently resigned as U.S. minister to France, for information about the members of the 1819 constitutional convention. Pickett filed the letters from his correspondents as follows: "Letters from various distinguished and well informed persons answering enquiries made of them by Albert J. Pickett of Montgomery, Ala., in relation to the History of Alabama."[23]

Most of Pickett's letters to his correspondents requesting information included fairly specific questions regarding people, places and events, such as the siege of Fort Mims, Sam Dale's Canoe Fight, Indian attacks, Ellicott's line, early settlements, and Spanish occupation. Few examples of these letters survived, except for one written by Pickett on 22 August 1848 to Jeremiah Austill, an early settler and participant in Sam Dale's Canoe Fight, asking him to follow-up with questions of Hiram Mounger, an early resident on the Tombigbee River. In his letter to Austill, Pickett first posed twenty-three questions and then added six more in his postscript. Austill and Gerard Walthall Creagh, a witness to the Battle of Burnt Corn and Dale's Canoe Fight, responded

[22] Bartlett & Welford to AJP, New York, 16 September 1847, Pickett Papers, ADAH; Bartlett & Welford to AJP, New York, 119 November 1847, ibid; Bartlett & Welford to AJP, New York, 18 December 1847, ibid; George Templeman to AJP, Washington, 10 March 1848, ibid; Bartlett & Welford to AJP, New York, 22 March 1848, ibid; George Templeman to AJP, Washington, 29 March 1848, ibid; Bartlett & Welford to AJP, New York, 9 May1848, ibid.

[23] C. C. Clay to AJP, Huntsville, 12 April 1847, Pickett Papers, ADAH; Arthur P. Bagby to AJP, Washington, 14 April 1847, ibid; Arthur F. Hopkins to AJP, Mobile, 24 April 1847; Arthur P. Bagby to AJP, Washington, 2 August 1847, ibid; Alfred Hennen to AJP, Retreat Parish of St. Tammany, La., 26 September 1847, ibid; John Gill Shorter to AJP, Eufaula, 2 October 1847, ibid.

to Pickett's letters with detailed descriptions of engagements during the War of 1812 and the Creek War of 1813–1814, replete with forts, names of participants, military units, and the role of the Choctaws and Chickasaws. Pickett filed the responses from his twenty-three informants, such as Austill and Creagh, as follows: "Notes furnished by Col. G. W. Creagh of Clarke County, Alabama, In relation to the Battle of "Burnt Corn," the "Canoe Fight" and other engagements in which he was concerned in 1813–1814." In most instances, Pickett accepted these "Interesting Notes upon the History of Alabama" as completely factual, including dates, individual actions, and names, because he did not have access to a well-organized state archive or anything that resembled a research library to corroborate the content of the reminiscences and reports he received.[24]

Fully aware of the voracious amount of data needed to complete his work, Pickett aggressively and extensively networked with aging early settlers, military veterans, and public servants through his letters and personal interviews. Pickett described the interviews that he employed to glean this panoramic oral history: "I have taken many of the following notes down on paper in a great hurry, as fast as the people narrating would speak, and there are many mistakes in grammar, spelling & general arrangement. I wrote often under many disadvantages—frequently surrounded by intrusive people asking idle questions, often writing in fields, in swamps, on my knees, wherever I had an opportunity of meeting persons I desired to obtain information from—I have traveled much over South Alabama to complete my stock of historical information & was about twelve months engaged at it. I have seen many curious people, been in many curious houses, took all kinds of fare & lodging most cheerfully & was always enthusiastic & well satisfied if I obtained information. . . . As the reader of these notes will see I left no stone unturned to get all the information necessary or that was extant."[25]

Between June 1847 and spring 1848, Pickett made at least three trips to Mobile and Baldwin County to interview Dr. Thomas G. Holmes, a survivor of the bloody siege of Fort Mims, and George Strother Gaines, former factor of the Choctaw Trading House at St. Stephens. Pickett's

[24] Jeremiah Austill to AJP, Mobile, 12 April 1847, Pickett Papers, ADAH; Gerard W. Creagh to AJP, Suggsville, 5 May 1847, ibid; Jeremiah Austill to AJP, Clarke County, 4 August 1847, ibid.; Jeremiah Austill to AJP, Salt Works, Clarke County, 22 August 1847, ibid; Gerard W. Creagh to AJP, Suggsville, 23 August May 1847, ibid; Gerard W. Creagh to AJP, Suggsville, 7 October 1847, ibid; AJP to Jeremiah Austill, Montgomery, Ala., 22 August 1848, ibid.

[25] Albert J. Pickett, Interesting Notes upon the History of Alabama, Montgomery, 8 December 1848, Pickett Papers, ADAH.

first interview of Holmes occurred at his home, Poplar Grove, in Baldwin County "while he was talking on the subject of Fort Mims," the "Burnt Corn expedition," and other events in 1813–1814. In his second interview, Pickett recorded twenty-nine pages which he labeled: "Notes from the lips of Dr. Thos. G. Holmes in relation to various expeditions made by Capt. Blue, Col. Benton & others in 1814." Pickett's first interview of Gaines at his home in Spring Hill near Mobile may have been coordinated with his second interview with Holmes. At the end of this interview, "Notes taken from the lips of George S. Gaines," Pickett had again written twenty-nine pages of notes covering the Choctaws and the arrest of Aaron Burr. Pickett returned to Spring Hill in the spring of 1848 and conducted a second "Conversation" with Gaines covering several topics, including Pushmataha, the Colberts and Chickasaws, and Gaines's role in the Treaty of Dancing Rabbit Creek and the first Choctaw removal in 1831.[26]

Other than the arduous journeys themselves to south Alabama to interview Holmes and Gaines, Pickett encountered none of the challenges presented by Abram Mordecai, a resident of Dudleyville in Tallapoosa County, Alabama. Acknowledged as one the first residents of central Alabama, the nearly ninety-two year old Mordecai had settled among the Upper Creeks by 1783 where he was involved in the Indian trade. This aged Indian countryman of Jewish-German ancestry provided Pickett with unfiltered insights to the Muscogees, Indian affairs, Benjamin Hawkins, William Weatherford, and the Red Stick War. However, when Pickett sat down to interview him on 30 September 1847, he had failing eyesight and was so deaf that Pickett presented his questions in large printed characters so he could read them. Despite some bits of misinformation, Pickett was so impressed with Mordecai that he published part of his interview of "Old Mordecai" in the Montgomery *Flag and Advertiser* on 5 October 1847. After his interview with Mordecai, Pickett interviewed James Moore of Dudleyville, cited as seventy-two years old in one place, and as "a white man 78 years old" in his notes of his "Conversation with James Moore." Moore had spent most of his adulthood among the Creeks and talked at length about the tribe and also the death of William McIntosh.

[26] George S. Gaines to AJP, Spring Hill near Mobile, 27 July 1847, Pickett Papers, ADAH; George S. Gaines to AJP, Spring Hill near Mobile, 28 September 1847, ibid; Notes of Doctor Thomas G. Holmes and Notes taken from the lips of Dr. Thos. G. Holmes, ibid; Notes taken from the lips of Mr. George S. Gaines, ibid.; Thomas G. Holmes to AJP, Poplar Grove, Baldwin County, Alabama, 15 March 1848, ibid; "Conversation with George S. Gaines," in *The Reminiscences of George Strother Gaines: Pioneer and Statesman of Early Alabama and Mississippi, 1805–1843*, ed. James P. Pate (Tuscaloosa: University of Alabama Press, 1998), 131–145; "2nd Conversation with Geo. S. Gaines, Spring of 1848," ibid, 147–53.

He also told Pickett that a second group of Creek assassins had killed Benjamin Hawkins after McIntosh's assassination on 30 April 1825. However, in this instance, Pickett could easily separate this lapse in memory and faulty timeline, knowing that Hawkins had died nine years earlier in 1816. But there were other times when he did not have access to other sources to corroborate or refute faulty statements.[27]

Although he continued supplementing his voluminous material through December 1848, Pickett then turned his focus to writing for the next two years. To keep his name and his *History* before the general public—and possibly as a notice to his potential unnamed rivals—Pickett published two pamphlets in 1849–1850: *Invasion of the Territory of Alabama, by One thousand Spaniards, Under Ferdinand de Soto, in 1540* and *Arrest of Aaron Burr in Alabama, in 1807.* Both became chapters in his forthcoming book. The latter had appeared in the columns of the *Flag and Advertiser* as an "extra." However, the widely circulated first pamphlet was printed as a prospectus to advertise his *History* and to reach a broader audience in the South and beyond. While both publications received notice, the *Invasion* pamphlet received several favorable reviews, including the *Southern Quarterly Review* and *De Bow's Review of Southern and Western States.*[28]

The Southern Quarterly Review made some brief comments in its "Critical Notices" section of the April 1850 issue before a longer review appeared in the July 1850 issue. The reviewer first mentions Pickett's two other publications: *Aaron Burr* and *Eight Days in New Orleans,* but he focused his comments on *Invasion of the Territory of Alabama, by One thousand Spaniards.* He declared the "'De Soto' pamphlet is merely the introductory chapter of 'Pickett's History of Alabama' . . . which covers the period of 281 years, between 1540 and the close of 1820." He complimented Pickett on his "sly native humor" in certain dry passages of his narrative and the "methodical arrangement and a clear, perspicuous expansion." The reviewer commended Pickett on his pursuit of the truth and his exhaustive research and predicted that his fellow Alabamians would be proud of his forthcoming history of their state. In his "Alabama invaded by De Soto" review in January 1851, J. D. B. De Bow was equally complimentary, stating that Pickett had

[27] Notes taken from the lips Abram Mordecai, Also the Conversations of James Moore, Pickett Papers, ADAH.

[28] According to WorldCat.org, the *Invasion* pamphlet published in 1849 went through three editions and the *Arrest of Aaron Burr in Alabama* published in 1850 went through five editions. "Pickett, Albert James, 1810–1858," http://w.w.w.worldcat.org.

"written with great care and research" and had spared no means or labor on his work. He closed his review with the hope that "Colonel Pickett, will receive a generous response in the hearts of his countrymen."[29]

Pickett's *Invasion of the Territory of Alabama, by One thousand Spaniards* received attention far beyond Alabama's newspapers and the Southern monthly journals. A third acknowledgment of Pickett's De Soto pamphlet and his forthcoming book received a two-page article in the "Notices of New Books" in the July 1850 issue of the *United States Magazine and Democratic Review* published in New York City. The reviewer stated his "great pleasure" to receive notice of "a work so authentic, and at the same time so attractively written as this History of Alabama by Mr. Pickett, judging from the first chapter." Since this article quotes Pickett's complete introduction to the De Soto pamphlet, we can assume Pickett probably sent multiple copies of his pamphlet to several literary journals outside his beloved Southwest. Theodore Irving in the preface to the 1851 revised edition of his *The Conquest of Florida* also lauded Pickett's forthcoming work. He noted: "Col. Albert J. Pickett, a young author of reputation, at the South, has issued in pamphlet form the first chapter of a History of Alabama he is preparing for the press, and which promises to be a valuable addition to the historical literature of our country." Ironically, none of these reviews or book notices mentioned that Pickett refers to De Soto as Ferdinand and not as Hernando de Soto, which apparently came from his use of Richard Hakluyt's English translation of the Gentleman of Elvas—*Virginia Richly Valued*—from the original in Portuguese.[30]

By Christmas 1850, the *History of Alabama* now completed, Albert James Pickett finalized travel plans to New York and Charleston. He had already identified an engraver in New York City—perhaps through John Wesley Monette—to "execute" his maps and illustrations for his *History* and a printer, Walker and James, for his book in Charleston on the advice of William Gilmore Simms. On 12 February 1851, Pickett checked into the Astor House—reputedly the most famous hotel in the world—at the corner of Broadway and Vesey Street in Lower Manhattan. He reported to his wife Sarah that he was staying at the "most pleasant hotel I've ever was in." He was equally effusive about

[29] *Southern Quarterly Review*, [New Series] 1 (April 1850), 252; ibid, 1 (July 1850), 524–26; "De Soto in Alabama," *De Bow's Review*, 9 (January 1851), 19–21.

[30] "Notices of New Books," *United States Magazine and Democratic Review* 27 (July 1850), 92–93; Theodore Irving, *The Conquest of Florida, by Hernando De Soto* (New York: G. P. Putnam, 1851), xii.

the city, its cool weather, and his reception throughout his stay. Like all Victorians, he also noted in his letter of 13 February that his "health is good." On the same day, he had met with the engraver and confided to Sarah that his "pictures" would not be ready until 10 March, meaning a month-long stay in New York "and then two in Charleston." But three weeks languishing in his hotel room and abroad on the streets of the city dampened his spirits, as he witnessed the seamier side of New York. This, in turn, altered his views and his interaction with New Yorkers. Whether it was homesickness, loneliness, or his divergent political perspective, his wait for his engravings had caused Pickett to feel out of place, dramatically altering his views of the city and its social and economic stratification.[31]

[31] The Astor House had welcomed Henry Clay before Pickett and later Jefferson Davis and Abraham Lincoln. AJP to Sarah Pickett, New York, 13 February 1851, Pickett Papers, ADAH; AJP to Absalom Jackson, New York, 7 March 1851, ibid; Shields, *Freedom in a Slave Society*, 140–41; Christopher Gray, "Where Lincoln Tossed and Turned, *New York Times*, 24 September 2009.

Based on his letters to family members, Pickett arrived in Charleston, South Carolina, on or about 22 March 1851 and settled into his room at the Charleston Hotel—considered by many as the city's finest. He quickly dashed off a series of notes and letters to Sarah and four of their children on the 24th and 25th of March, letting them know he missed them but also expressing his delight with his hotel. He added in his letter to Sarah that he had been vaccinated for smallpox. Less than two weeks later, he reported to Sarah in his letter of 4 April that he had moved to the Pavilion Hotel, located at the corner of Meeting and Hassell streets, the much larger lodging affording him more comfort. He noted that the climate in Charleston was "most delightful" and asked Sarah to direct his letters to his printers, Walker and James. In his letter of 12 April, he confirmed that his *History* was being printed and he was busy proofreading the pages of his book as they came off the press. He also exhibited a touch of homesickness but wrote that he could not "break away for a trip home which would cost $50." In letters written on the 5th and 15th of May, he expressed his concern for Sarah's health—following the extraction of seven teeth—and reaffirmed his confidence in her handling issues related to the proper treatment and feeding of their slaves. While his letter on the 5th announced the completion of volume one, a letter ten days later assured her he was enjoying good health and was anxious to get the job of printing done. He emphasized he wanted to tell his fellow Alabamians that his

History of Alabama "is done" and to get "this disagreeable job off his hands." He closed by assuring her he would return to Montgomery by the 10th of June.[32]

The printing of Pickett's *History* had been completed by early July 1851, but the first copies did not arrive in Alabama until September. An advertisement on 1 September 1851 announced its arrival in Montgomery and subsequent notices directed Montgomerians and fellow Alabamians that they could purchase the two-volume set at Little and Bolling's and Armand Pfister's Book Store for three dollars.* A notice in the *Tri-Weekly Alabama Journal*—"Laudable State Pride"—on 5 September 1851 reported "Mr. Absalom Jackson, an intelligent planter of Autauga, has recently purchased twelve copies of Pickett's history of Alabama for his twelve children." James J. Donegan, a prominent Huntsville businessman, banker, and former city councilman, agreed to sell the book and received an order of four hundred copies. Governor Henry W. Collier convinced the Alabama legislature to appropriate funds to purchase copies of Pickett's history for all the state libraries in the United States. William Gilmore Simms advised Pickett to send one hundred and fifty copies to Thomas, Cowperthwaite and Company in Philadelphia and Charles Welford in New York City. The Philadelphia firm was not only an important retailer and regional distributor, but it may have been a national distributor with contacts in every state, including all the southern states but Florida. Pickett's previous publications, newspaper articles, and the positive press coverage touting his *History* appear to have generated an overwhelming public demand for his work, which subsequently went through three editions in 1851 to generally positive reviews.[33]

The reception for Pickett's book in Alabama was favorable, and most of the newspaper reviews were laudatory. The editor of the *Alabama Journal*, noting Pickett's long, arduous years of work, declared his history would be the foundation of all future histories of Alabama. He commented on the fine printing of the book and opined that every Alabamian should own a copy. Greensboro's *Alabama Beacon* and other papers expressed similar views and lauded Pickett for his excellent *History of Alabama*. As may have been expected, the Mobile

[32] AJP to Sarah Pickett, Charleston, S.C., 25 March 1851, Pickett Papers, ADAH; AJP to Sarah Pickett, Charleston, S.C., 4 April 1851, ibid; AJP to Sarah Pickett, Charleston, S.C., 12 April 1851, ibid; AJP to Sarah Pickett, Charleston, S.C., 5 May 1851, ibid; AJP to Sarah Pickett, Charleston, S.C., 15 May 1851, ibid.

[33] Shields, *Freedom in a Slave Society*, 141; "Armand P. Pfister," in Owen, *History of Alabama*, 4: 1355; Frank L. Owsley Jr., "Albert J. Pickett: Historian of Alabama," *Alabama Review* 11 (January 1958): 31; Ronald J. Zboray, *A Fictive People: Antebellum Economic Development and the American Reading Public* (New York: Oxford University Press, 1993), 60–62.

**Publisher's Note: This would equal $93.07 today, so the purchase price of this 2018 edition is a relative bargain.*

Herald and Tribune published a critical article—"The Early Times of Mobile"—taking issue with his "shadowy" sketches of Mobile and his portrayal of Mobile's unhealthy climate. It challenged the accuracy of his *History* regarding the impact of yellow fever on the British military and the growth of Mobile's population. Of course, this is the same paper that expressed the opinion that their favorite son—Alexander Beaufort Meek—should be the first to write a history of Alabama.[34]

As for Meek himself, in typical style, he added his cryptic review of Pickett privately in a letter of 23 November 1851 to William Gilmore Simms. He admitted that because of his own procrastination "mine must lie upon the shelf until [his] has run its career." He confessed to Simms he wanted to point out Pickett's "errors, blunders, fictions and shortcomings—but it would be attributed to jealousy; so I let the acid vinegar remain uncorked." Despite his smugness and backbiting, Meek never published his long-touted history of Alabama, and his unfinished manuscript can now be perused at the Alabama Department of Archives and History in Montgomery.[35]

Unlike the brief reviews of the state and regional newspapers, *De Bow's Review* and the *Southern Quarterly Review* published in-depth reviews of Pickett's *History of Alabama*. J. D. B. De Bow used two issues—January and February 1852—and twenty-seven pages to review the new two-volume history. In more than ten pages in the January issue, De Bow systematically reviewed volume one from De Soto through 1763. At the outset, he credited Simms, Gayarré, and Pickett for rescuing "southern literature from the charge of degrading subserviency and dependence upon that of other regions" and telling the "true poetry and romance of actual history, on the soil of the South." De Bow turned his attention to volume two in the February 1852 issue, tracing Alabama's history from the advent of the British through the election of William Wyatt Bibb. Although he did not consider Pickett's *History* a great literary masterpiece, he complimented Pickett on producing a worthwhile history "of truthful and minute narrative" with a "simplicity of style" and predicted that it "will be a prominent text." He closed his review by observing that a "historian must not be satisfied with chronicling 'wars and rumors of wars,' political maneuvering and

[34] Owsley, "Albert J. Pickett," 198–201; Miscellaneous newspaper clippings, Pickett Scrapbook, Pickett Papers, ADAH.

[35] Alexander B. Meek to William Gilmore Simms, Mobile, 23 November 1851, Alexander Beaufort Meek Papers, ADAH; Shields, *Freedom in a Slave Society*, 158; Michael O'Brien, *Conjectures of Order: Intellectual Life and the American South, 1810–1860*, 2 vols. (Chapel Hill: University of North Carolina Press, 2004), 2: 636.

[36] "The State of Alabama," *De Bow's Review* [New Series] 5 (January 1852), 56–66; "The State of Alabama," ibid, 5 (February 1852), 148–66.

[37] "Pickett's History of Alabama," *Southern Quarterly Review* [New Series] 5 (January 1852): 182–86, 187–88; William Gilmore Simms to James Henry Hammond, Charleston, 9 June 1851, *Letters of William Gilmore Simms*, 3: 125–27.

results." Expressing his "regret" for the "abrupt termination" of volume two, De Bow urged Pickett to write a third volume on the development of Alabama for "rising generations of Alabamians," including the subjects of commerce, manufacturing, and agriculture—and social and intellectual progress.[36]

On the heels of De Bow's January 1852 review of volume one, the *Southern Quarterly Review* printed a twenty-seven page review of Pickett's two-volume *History* in its January 1852 issue. Although the reviewer is not identified, no one but William Gilmore Simms could have written this long, introspective essay which begins with the historiography of the histories of the southern states from colonial times to the mid-nineteenth century. Before invoking Pickett's work—or even his name—the reviewer cataloged the writers who had produced state histories, ticking off their names and shortcomings, but never mentioning Simms's *History of South Carolina*. The reviewer mentioned "some glowing and very attractive sketches of Alabama . . . from the pen of Judge Meek" before "Mr. Pickett" is named on the ninth page of the review. Without naming Walker and James, the reviewer notes that these volumes come "from the press of our own publishers, afford as fine a sample of good printing and 'getting up,' as is often to be seen in this country." His litany of achievements included "presses . . . worked by steam," numerous operatives, and "an extensive bindery gives constant employment to a large number of intelligent and industrious girls." In his letter to James Henry Hammond, former governor of South Carolina, on 9 June 1851, Simms not only praised the local press but Pickett's book as well: "By the way, you could be well printed & sent forth in this city. Walker & James have accumulated all the means & appliances for good work. They are now doing a History of Alabama, by Pickett, one of the prettiest specimens of book making ever done in America." [37]

After acknowledging that Pickett, a wealthy planter, had written his *History* as a patriotic service to Alabama, the reviewer turned to his main task of evaluating Pickett's work—virtually chapter by chapter. Noting that Pickett was "not a practiced writer," he assessed his writing style as being "uneven and unequal" and observed that he did not appreciate the duty of the historian—by focusing on the facts and arranging them in a "clear manner" for his reader. Instead, the reviewer asserts that the historian "should be an artist" and that Pickett had included irrelevant material, such as his using twenty pages for "a detailed narrative of the arrest of Aaron Burr." He accused Pickett of not critically evaluating his sources and for a narrative style that reflected a chronicle "rather than a history." In his survey of Pickett's chapters, he questioned Pickett's use of certain accounts, such as Leclerc Milfort's memoir, but complimented him for his "keen research," his careful use of "his authorities," and for giving brief sketches, "personal as well as historical." In closing, the reviewer credited Pickett for producing "a very valuable" chronicle for the people of Alabama and making an important contribution to the state histories of the South.[38]

Pickett's aggressive effort to promote his *History* beyond his beloved Alabama garnered several reviews, including three reviews by literary journals in New York City. In a short review, the *Knickerbocker* found Pickett had written in a fresh style that was "absolutely enchanting." The reviewer commended Pickett for contributing a history of his state *"con amore"* and commented favorably on the narrative of Aaron Burr's arrest and the printing of the book. The *Literary World* in its November 1851 issue agreed with the *Knickerbocker* review that Pickett's section on Burr's arrest and the Indians were outstanding. Other than the surfeit of capital letters and exclamation points, the reviewer found Pickett's writing style agreeable and pleasant. While these reviews covered both volumes of Pickett's *History*, the article in the *International Monthly Magazine* for July 1851 only reviewed volume one but promised to cover the second volume when it arrived. Like the previous articles, this reviewer thought the Charleston printer had produced an elegant book "that would do credit to the best northern printers." He commended Pickett for using "great care" throughout his book, "his arduous and intelligently prosecuted labors," and "his important service to his state." This last review indicates that at least volume one of Pickett's *History of Alabama* had reached New York City well before the complete two-volume set arrived in Pickett's home state.[39]

While the reviews in *De Bow's Review* and the *Southern Quarterly*

[38] "Pickett's History of Alabama," 188, 191, 193, 197–98, 207, 209.

[39] Owsley, "Albert J. Pickett," 207–09; *Knickerbocker, or New York Monthly Magazine*, 38 (December 1851), 632; *Literary World, A Journal of Science, Literature, and Art*, 9 (November 1851), 362–63; *International Monthly Magazine of Literature, Science, and Art*, 3 (July 1851), 468–69.

Review found fault with Pickett's writing style, most early historians reacted favorably to his *History of Alabama*. J. F. H. Claiborne, a Pickett correspondent and admirer, commended Pickett's *History* for its accuracy and praised Pickett for his outstanding research and writing in his *Life of and Times of Gen. Sam Dale*. Claiborne's biography of Dale closely follows Pickett's narrative of the events in south Alabama during the Creek War of 1813–1814. Benjamin F. Riley, author of *Makers and Romance of Alabama History*, praised Pickett's work as "scrupulously written" and agreed that it "furnished a basis for all future historians," though finding the book poorly organized and occasionally disjointed. Henry Sale Halbert and Timothy Hall Ball in writing their book *The Creek War of 1813–1814* relied heavily on Pickett's work, citing his *History of Alabama* throughout their study and praising him as a leading Alabama historian. William Garrott Brown in his school textbook—*A History of Alabama, For Use in Schools*—published in 1900, praised Pickett's "admirable work," citing it in the early part of his book. Willis Brewer in his *Alabama: Her History, Resources, War Record and Public Men*, published in 1872, praised Pickett for his focus on original sources, calling his work "positively invaluable." However, as had many writers before and after, Brewer criticized Pickett's writing style and his "defective arrangement."[40]

While some writers questioned his style or pointed out certain inaccuracies, Thomas S. Woodward attacked Pickett on his perceived strength—his intimate knowledge of Alabama's Indian people. In a series of letters to the *Montgomery Mail* in 1858, Woodward, a *metis* Creek, cited several points of contention where he either outright disagreed with Pickett or questioned his accuracy. While Pickett has the Muscogees migrating into Alabama after De Soto, Woodward claimed that they had immigrated much earlier and resisted Spain's *entrada* under De Soto. Woodward also challenged Pickett's claims that Juan Ortiz, who lived several years among the Florida Indians, could speak all the languages of the Indians encountered by De Soto. He questioned Pickett's description of Choctaw burial practices, denying that the Choctaw placed the bones of their dead in boxes. Woodward also disagreed with Pickett's narrative of the Battle of Mabila, claiming

[40] J. F. H. Claiborne, *Life and Times of Gen. Sam Dale, The Mississippi Partisan* (New York: Harper & Brothers, 1860); Benjamin F. Riley, *Makers and Romance of Alabama History* (Birmingham: n.p., [1914]), 134, 135; Henry Sale Halbert and Timothy Hall Ball, *The Creek War of 1813–1814* (Chicago: Donohue & Henneberry, 1895); William Garrott Brown, *A History of Alabama, For Use in Schools; Based as to its Earliest Parts on the Work of Albert J. Pickett* (New York: University Publishing Company, 1900), 223; Brewer, *Alabama*, 453.

that De Soto actually fought Creeks and not Mabilians. Modern scholars—such as Frederick Hodge, John Swanton, Charles Hudson, Patricia Galloway, and others—agree that the Muscogees had arrived prior to De Soto's expedition, but they also point out that Pickett's Mabilians were Muskogean speakers with possible connections to the Creeks and Choctaws. Most scholars agree that Juan Ortiz may have mastered the Mobilian trade jargon which allowed him to communicate with several tribes in the Gulf South region. Furthermore, these same scholars confirm the Choctaw burial practices and similar mortuary practices of the Natchez and other early chiefdoms. However, Woodward's criticism of Pickett's account of William Weatherford's actions in the Red Stick War is generally more accurate because Woodward actually knew Weatherford. Pickett never met him.[41]

Despite its sundry inaccuracies, writing style peccadilloes, digressions, and overreliance on single sources, most modern Alabama historians hold Pickett's *History of Alabama* in high regard. Thomas Perkins Abernethy, in his *The Formative Period of Alabama,* noted Pickett's personal knowledge of the period prior to Alabama's statehood. Albert B. Moore, in his *History of Alabama,* used Pickett as a major source in the early sections of his textbook and found his style to be "lucid and lively." In his seminal work, *McGillivray of the Creeks,* John W. Caughey credited Pickett for writing the first significant work on Alexander McGillivray. While referring to Pickett as "Alabama's First Historian" in 1930, Marie Bankhead Owen declared that "No honest writer" could write about Alabama's history without acknowledging Albert James Pickett's *History*. Pickett biographer Frank L. Owsley Jr. wrote the most thorough assessment of Pickett as a prototypical early state historian, noting that, although influenced by the Southern Romantic writers of his era, Pickett's research methods, evaluation of available source material, and careful source citation are clearly indicative of his development as "a good historian." Despite the legitimate criticisms of Pickett's bias and digressions, most scholars agree with Owsley that Pickett made lasting contributions as Alabama's first historian. Leah Rawls Atkins, one of four nationally recognized authors of the most recent state history—*Alabama: The History of a Deep South*

[41] Owsley, "Albert J. Pickett," 217–25; Thomas S. Woodward, *Woodward's Reminiscences of the Creek or Muscogee Indians, Contained in Letters to Friends in Georgia and Alabama* (Montgomery: Barrett & Wimbish, 1859), 15–19, 22–23, 27, 29–30, 34, 39, 64–90, 102–03; John R. Swanton, *Early History of the Creek Indians and Their Neighbors,* Bureau of American Ethnology, *Bulletin 73* (Washington: GPO, 1922); 151–60, 191–94; Frederick Hodge, ed., *Handbook of the American Indians North of Mexico,* Bureau of American Ethnology, *Bulletin 30,* 2 parts (Washington: GPO, 1907–1910), 1: 916, 945–47; Charles Hudson, *The Southeastern Indians* (Knoxville: University of Tennessee Press, 1976), 24–25, 107–08, 334–35; Patricia Galloway, *Choctaw Genesis, 1500–1700* (Lincoln: University of Nebraska Press, 1995), 298–300, 337, 344, 358–59.

State, published in 1994—declared unequivocally that Pickett was the writer who made the "most historical contribution to Alabama" in the antebellum period. Although dated, neglectful of north Alabama, and "uneven in quality," she believes it remains "a valuable work."[42]

Pickett, his *History*, and his contributions have continued to come under scrutiny by several accomplished scholars and writers of the late twentieth century and early twenty-first century. One of the most remarkable commentaries on Pickett occurred when Harper Lee—Alabama's most consequential twentieth-century writer—made a rare appearance at the Alabama History and Heritage Festival in Eufaula in March 1983. Depicting Pickett's prose style as somewhere between Macaulay and Bulwer-Lytton, she praised his long digression to describe the native population in the region between Hernando de Soto's *entrada* and the French presence in the Gulf South. For this miniature social history alone, she asserts Pickett "deserves a place in American literature." She credits him for unfolding a story "more hair-raising" than found on American television and discussing the "small dramas" within the greater pageantry of America. She closes by assessing Pickett's *History of Alabama* as a "unique treasure" that "should be in every high school library" in Alabama. Another writer, Michael O'Brien, has written two penetrating essays, "The Lineaments of Antebellum Southern Romanticism" and "On Writing of History in the Old South," delineating the impact of Southern Romanticism on its writers and the writing of state and local history—"the historicist narrative"—by men like Pickett, John Wesley Monette, and Charles Gayarré. While acknowledging that Pickett and his ilk "struggled to understand and adopt the principles of historicism," O'Brien claims they demonstrated an understanding of the "layered quality of history," especially in the Southwest before historians on the eastern seaboard. Despite his Anglo-American ancestry, Pickett's early exposure to the Five Nations and smaller Southern tribes, his grasp of European settlement of the Gulf Coast by non-English speaking nations, and recognition of the discovery of Alabama by Hernando de Soto gave him a broader, less Anglo-Saxon context for understanding his region.[43]

Two other scholars provide a more critical, insightful deconstruction.

[42] Owsley, "Albert J. Pickett," 212–14; Thomas P. Abernethy, *The Formative Period in Alabama, 1815–1828* (Montgomery: Brown Printing Company, 1922); Albert B. Moore, *History of Alabama* (University, Ala.: University Supply Store, 1934); John W. Caughey, *McGillivray of the Creeks* (Norman: University of Oklahoma Press, 1938); Marie Bankhead Owen, "Alabama's First Historian," *Alabama Historical Quarterly* 1 (Spring 1930), 113; William Warren Rogers, et al., *Alabama: The History of a Deep South State* (Tuscaloosa: University of Alabama, 1994), 132.

[43] Harper Lee, "Romance and High Adventure," in *Clearings in the Thicket: An Alabama Humanities Reader*, ed. Jerry Elijah Brown (Macon, Ga.: Mercer University Press, 1985), 13–20; Michael O'Brien, "The Lineaments of Antebellum Southern Romanticism," in Michael O'Brien, *Rethinking the South: Essays in Intellectual History* (Baltimore: Johns Hopkins University Press, 1988), 40 44, 46, 47, 50; Michael O'Brien, "On Writing of History in the Old South" in *Rewriting the South: History and Fiction*, eds. Lothar Hönnighausen, et al (Tübingen: Francke, 1993), 144–47, 150–51.

In his essay "Antebellum Alabama History in the Planter Style: The Example of Albert J. Pickett," Philip D. Beidler provides an analysis of Pickett's "orotund narrative exposition" grounded in "gaudy dramatic spectacle," displaying his unremitting "regional patriotism" and class consciousness. He traces Pickett's personal life journey, his claims to "cultural authority," and his development as "the first epic historian of Alabama," albeit with some measure of literary talent, with a "voice of political authority." In Beidler's assessment, Pickett's *History* is little more than a panoply of colorful heroes and villains, products of a diverse cultural and social milieu—stirred by geopolitical conflict, bloody encounters, "Negro slavery," intrigues, and "sociopolitical tragedy." Finally, Beidler is certain that this "gentleman chronicler" ended his work in 1820 to avoid some mystical "fault line" connected to sectional conflict and slavery—not issues related to his family, his health, or his new manuscript on the Southwest. In a shorter, more succinct essay—"Southwestern Histories for A Divided Market: An Anxious Planter's History"—Johanna Nicol Shields dissects Pickett's actions beyond the actual process of writing his *History of Alabama*, including his controversial grand jury reports advocating tighter control of slaves and a ban on the interstate slave trade. She sees Pickett as a highly motivated, authoritarian figure and class-conscious planter-historian who aspired to write a history for "mostly southern readers" and "primarily about white people." She credits Pickett for including "all types of people"—a diverse cultural and social milieu "within a slave society"—but accuses him of obscuring causes, "focusing on heroic individuals," and highlighting his narrative with bloody, action-packed drama. Shields notes the random examples of Pickett's "anxieties about slavery"—digressions in defense of slavery—including his attacks on abolitionists and the role played by the French, English, and Puritans as purveyors of slaves. She also reveals Pickett's latent paranoia about young Alabamians and whether they would be stout warriors when called upon to defend their land. In her conclusion, she reiterates Pickett's class bias, loyalty to Democrats, kinsmen, and Autauga County, and his decision to end his *History* in 1819 instead of confronting the controversies facing his contemporary Alabama.[44]

[44] Beidler, *First Books*, 63–75; Shields, *Freedom in a Slave Society*, 133–46.

While most authorities end their connection with Pickett after the publication of his *History*, he himself continued his work as a speaker and lecturer before a variety of audiences. On 10 March 1852, he delivered an address in Montgomery—"A History of the City of Montgomery, Ala."—which was placed in the cornerstone of the Montgomery Baptist Church. In a less formal address on 17 September 1853, he talked to a gathering at the Asbury Church of Autaugaville about fulfilling his "duty" by completing his *History of Alabama* and his thorough satisfaction with "this achievement," a culmination of the "hardest work of my life." In July 1854, he delivered a paper at the annual meeting of the Alabama Historical Society at Tuscaloosa—"The Origin and Progress of History in the Eastern Hemisphere," later published in newspapers as "History of Historians" or as "Historians of all Ages." It may have been this visit to Tuscaloosa that prompted Pickett to write a series of letters and essays—"Hampden's Letters to a student at the University of Alabama"—ostensibly addressed to a student at the University of Alabama. These were published in the Montgomery *Mail* in the latter part of 1854 and expressed Pickett's concern for the young men of Alabama, urging them to study diligently and embrace learning.[45]

Pickett's son-in-law, Colonel Michael Leonard Woods, claims that after the publication of his *History* Pickett had turned "with great assiduity and increased energy" to writing a history of the Southwest. This may partially explain his trip to Texas in 1856 when he visited his brother-in-law General Moseley Baker, scouted out land for his family, and wrote glowing letters to Sarah and other family members about the prospects of moving to Texas. According to Woods, Pickett's health caused him to abandon plans to travel to France and Spain to collect material for his new work, and Woods questioned a report in the Montgomery *Mail* on 11 April 1857 that Pickett had completed "two-thirds of the necessary labor." Apparently Pickett's chronic ill-health prevented him from completing his contemplated history of the Southwest, but he continued to write articles and essays that appeared in the Montgomery newspapers, including a series of articles on "The Mystery of a Century"—expressing his opinion on the true identity of Junius, the writer and man. Concern over his health led him to travel

[45] Miscellaneous Newspaper Articles, Pickett Papers, ADAH; "A History of the City of Montgomery, Ala.," ibid; "The Origin and Progress of History in the Eastern Hemisphere," ibid.; "Address, Delivered at Asbury Church, in Autaugaville, Ala., on Saturday, September 17, 1853, by Col. A. J. Pickett," Autauga *Mercury*, 5 October 1853, ibid; Woods, "Reminiscences of Colonel Pickett," 606; Beidler, *First Books*, 149 n. 3; Shields, *Freedom in a Slave Society*, 146, 146 n. 25.

to Pensacola in the spring of 1857, and his letters describing his journey and the history of Pensacola were published in several Alabama newspapers in 1858.[46]

In the spring of 1858, Pickett, accompanied by Woods, traveled to Bladon Springs in modern Choctaw County, Alabama, for his health, where he sought relief in the mineral springs. The circuitous and nostalgic trip obviously fostered recollections of earlier times and caused Pickett to reflect on his life with Woods and those he encountered at the resort near the end of his life. On 24 June 1858, the Mobile *Register* reported that Pickett had arrived on the 23rd from Bladon Springs "and is en route for Point Clear, where he will pass some time enjoying the refreshing breezes and baths of that delightful resort." Sometime after his return to Montgomery, Pickett purchased the John Poston Figh house but never moved into it, though Sarah lived in it until her death in 1894. At the age of forty-eight, Albert James Pickett—"Alabama's First Historian," "Planter-Historian," and "gentleman chronicler"—died at his plantation Forest Farm on 28 October 1858 of dropsy or possibly a kidney ailment. The following day, the *Daily Confederation* in Montgomery published a short obituary: "With feelings of profound regret, we are compelled, this morning, to announce the death of Col. Albert J. Pickett, which occurred on yesterday in the neighborhood of this city. A hereditary disease, which only a few months since developed itself, has hurried to the grave a gentleman, distinguished alike for the virtues that ennobled, and the qualities which adorned his life—a life exemplary to so great a degree, as to have been almost blameless. Devoted as Col. Pickett has been for the last few years to literary pursuits, which had for their aim the discovery and publication of historical events connected with the early settlement and gradual of the great Southwest, his death will be rightly regarded as a public loss . . . ." He was buried at Forest Farm, but he was reinterred at Oakwood Cemetery in Montgomery in 1894 following the death of his wife Sarah on 9 July of that year.[47]

Whatever his shortcomings as a historian, Pickett's *History of Alabama* has generated comment and analysis since the first copies arrived in Montgomery in September 1851. His work inspired others

[46] AJP to Sarah Pickett, 5 December 1856, Pickett Papers, ADAH; AJP to Sarah Pickett, 10 December 1856, ibid; Woods, "Reminiscences of Colonel Pickett," 606–07; Owsley, "Albert J. Pickett," 34–35; Shields, *Freedom in a Slave Society*, 82.

[47] "A. J. Pickett Obituary," Montgomery *Daily Confederation*, 29 October 1858, in "Wood & Torbert Families—Albert James Pickett," http://www.woodvorwerk.com/wood/g8/p8333.htm; "Col. A. J. Pickett," Mobile *Register* article [24 June 1858] quoted in the *Daily Confederation*, 29 June 1858, ibid; Woods, "Reminiscences of Colonel Pickett," 607–10; Neeley, *The Works of Matthew Blue*, 241; James Frederick Sulzby, *Historic Alabama Hotels and Resorts* (Tuscaloosa: University of Alabama Press, 1960) 51–58. Note: Dropsy is an older term for generalized edema—collection of fluid in the tissues and often associated with heart failure or cardiac arrest. See Thomas Lathrop Stedman, *Stedman's Medical Dictionary for the Health Professions and Nursing* (Philadelphia: Wolters Kluwer Health/Lippincott Williams & Wilkins, 2012).

to emulate his efforts, such as Matthew Blue, who developed plans to write a history of Alabama for the schools, and his publisher announced the book would "embrace the important facts of Pickett's *History* but would bring material to a later date." His book, especially its sections related to the Southern Indians and the Red Sticks or Creek War of 1813–1814, has been cited by dozens of scholars. The rich primary resources he amassed—the papers of General Ferdinand Leigh Claiborne, his oral history interviews, and the "Interesting History Notes" he pried out of some thirty participants and eyewitnesses to events that shaped Alabama and the Gulf South—continue to be utilized by scholars. Despite references to an alleged 1878 edition of Pickett's *History*, and documentation of his wife's 1878 renewed copyright, this writer has found no creditable evidence that it was reprinted then. However, Robert Carter Randolph, Pickett's son-in-law, did publish the two-volume *History* in a one-volume edition in 1896 and added a portrait of Pickett as a frontispiece. Thomas McAdory Owen, founder and first director of the Alabama Department of Archives and History, published an "updated" Pickett's *History* in 1900 by appending his *Annals of Alabama, 1819–1900* and adding an index. In 1962, the Birmingham Book and Magazine Company reprinted the 1896 copy of Pickett's *History*, and subsequently numerous vendors have offered Pickett's *History of Alabama* as facsimile reprints of the 1962 edition or as e-books and on-demand editions; none of these versions of Pickett's *History of Alabama* were annotated or professionally indexed.[48]

[48] Albert James Pickett, *History of Alabama and Incidentally of Georgia and Mississippi, From the Earliest Period*, Republished by Robert C. Randolph of Sheffield, Ala. (Birmingham: Roberts & Son, 1896); Albert James Pickett, *History of Alabama and Incidentally of Georgia and Mississippi, From the Earliest Period*; *Annals of Alabama, 1819–1900*, Thomas McAdory Owen (Birmingham: Webb Book Company, 1900); Owen, "Albert James Pickett," 9: 4019–20; Blue, *The Works of Matthew Blue*, 10–11, 27.

Acknowledgments

First, I want to thank Suzanne La Rosa and Randall Williams, co-owners of NewSouth Books, for giving me the opportunity to edit and annotate Albert James Pickett's *History of Alabama* as part of Alabama's Bicentennial Celebration in 2018–2019. Second, I thank them for their respect and trust and for publishing this one-volume edition of Pickett's original two-volume work as published by Walker and James of Charleston, South Carolina, in 1851.

My journey with Pickett started over two decades ago when a prominent university press agreed to a contract to publish an annotated one-volume reprint of the 1962 edition of Pickett's *History*. When that press learned that a local specialty press planned to print a paperback edition of Pickett, the editor asked me to allow them to withdraw their contract, which I concurred with since they had published my first two books. When I received the offer to revisit my interest in AJP, I readily agreed to the opportunity, and it has been a pleasure getting reacquainted with Pickett, his early Alabama and his friends—correspondents, informants, critics, political cronies and other writers—who helped shape the first history of Alabama.

The work of editing and annotating Pickett's remarkable opus was made easier by the assistance that I received from colleagues at my last position in academe—the University of Mississippi-Tupelo. Sophie Houin, a student assistant in our writing center, produced a complete transcription of the 1962 edition of Pickett's *History,* which I tweaked using a third edition of the original 1851 *History*. When I encountered technical issues, I received incredible assistance from James Hamilton and Tim Moore, the distance-learning technicians and computer gurus at UM-Tupelo. I also received support from the interlibrary loan personnel at the University's J. D. Williams Library and from Anna Bedsole, User

Services/Interlibrary Loan Librarian in the Julia Tutwiler Library at the University of West Alabama.

I am also deeply grateful to the dedicated staff at NewSouth Books who assisted with formatting, editing, production, and promotion of this edition of Pickett's *History*: Matthew Byrne, Liyang Dong, Lisa Emerson, Lisa Harrison, Anna Jeffcoat, Beth Marino, and Brian Seidman. I owe special thanks to Meredith McDonough of the Alabama Department of Archives and History for providing high-resolution scans of several of the illustrations found in the following pages.

Much as Pickett did in his dedication page, I want to thank some truly incredible scholars whose work made the process of editing and annotating Pickett possible, including James Atkinson, Patricia Galloway, Robbie Ethridge, Kathryn E. Holland Braund, Tom Kanon, Robert Vincent Remini, John Sugden, Robert V. Haynes, Gregory A. Waselkov, and the late Charles Hudson and Frank Lawrence Owsley Jr. Their research and scholarship were invaluable to me in expanding and explaining Pickett's narrative of Alabama and the Old Southwest. Norwood Kerr and his colleagues at the Alabama Department of Archives and History provided immeasurable assistance and access to the Albert James Pickett Papers. Finally, I want to thank Jeff Conine of Bacon College and my wife, Betty Love Pate, for reading and critiquing my introduction.

The Annotated

Pickett's History of Alabama

A Note on Organization and Presentation

The pages that follow present Pickett's 1851 text as he published it except that typos have been corrected and some punctuation and spellings have been slightly modernized for ease of reading.

Pickett's original text runs in the wider inside column and is set in Caslon, a typeface that would have been quite at home in the "steam-power press" shop of Walker and James, publishers, in Charleston, South Carolina, in 1851. Pickett's footnotes are referenced in his text with the symbols * † ‡ § and ¶ and appear at the bottoms of the pages. For contrast, editor Jim Pate's contributions in the front matter and his annotations are set in a contemporary typeface, Warnock. The annotations are referenced within Pickett's running text with footnote numbers and appear in semibold and semibold italic in the narrower column running along the outsides of the pages.

Pickett's original layout used margin notations to indicate the date of the events being discussed on a given page. That reader convenience was not available in the present edition because the annotations occupy the side margins. Instead, running years are indicated at the inside margins of the page headers.

The four pages that immediately follow this one contain facsimiles of the original frontispiece, title page, copyright page, and dedication from volume one of Pickett's 1851 two-volume edition. Those pages are followed by the text of Pickett's original Preface, also annotated by Pate. Then comes the Volume One Table of Contents, as Pickett presented it, except for the page numbers, of course. Then the body of Volume One follows, then Volume Two, then Pickett's Bibliography and the editor's Suggestions for Additional Reading, and then a new Index.

INDIANS EMPLOYED IN PLANTING CORN. Drawn from life by Jacob le Moyne, in 1564.

HISTORY

OF

ALABAMA,

AND INCIDENTALLY OF

GEORGIA AND MISSISSIPPI,

FROM THE EARLIEST PERIOD.

BY

ALBERT JAMES PICKETT,
Of Montgomery.

IN TWO VOLUMES,

VOL. I.

THIRD EDITION.

CHARLESTON:
WALKER AND JAMES,
1851.

CHARLESTON:
STEAM POWER-PRESS OF WALKER AND JAMES,
No. 101 East-Bay.

DEDICATION.

As a token of my sincere esteem, and of the high respect I feel for their talents and character, as well as in consideration of the deep interest which they have taken in my literary enterprises,

I DEDICATE THESE VOLUMES TO

BENJAMIN FITZPATRICK, JOHN ARCHIBALD CAMPBELL,
ARTHUR FRANCES HOPKINS, THOMAS JAMES JUDGE,
WILLIAM LOWNDES YANCEY, EDMUND STROTHER DARGAN,
FRANCIS BUGBEE, THADDEUS SANFORD,
WILLIAM PARISH CHILTON, BURWELL BOYKIN,
JOSHUA LANIER MARTIN, ALEXANDER BOWIE, BASIL MANLY,
SILAS PARSONS, NICHOLAS DAVIS AND CLEMENT C. CLAY, JR.,
Of Alabama;

GEORGE M. TROUP AND JOHN M. BERRIEN,
Of Georgia;

JOHN H. F. CLAIBORNE AND JOHN W. MONETTE,
Of Mississippi;

LESLIE A. THOMPSON AND WALKER ANDERSON,
Of Florida;

CHARLES GAYARRE AND SAMUEL F. WILSON,
Of Louisiana;

DANIEL GRAHAM,
Of Tennessee;

ARTHUR P. HAYNE, FRANCIS W. PICKENS,
JAMES H. HAMMOND, W. GILMORE SIMMS, RICHARD YEADON,
MITCHELL KING AND HENRY W. CONNER,
Of South-Carolina.

A. J. PICKETT.

Preface to the 1851 Edition

In submitting my first book to the public, I refrain from making apologies in its behalf, and shall only briefly allude to my labors, in order to show how strenuously I have endeavored to ensure its authenticity. I have sought materials for a correct history of my country, wherever they were to be procured, whether in Europe or America, and without regard to cost or trouble. All the Atlantic states have historical societies, and books and manuscripts relating to those states have been collected. In addition to this, agents have been sent to Europe by different legislatures, who have transcribed the colonial records which relate to their history. I have had none of these aids. I have been compelled to hunt up and buy books and manuscripts connected with the history of Alabama, and to collect oral information in all directions. I rejoice, however, to know that a historical society has recently been formed at Tuscaloosa by some literary gentlemen, and it gives me pleasure to reflect that the authors who may appear after my day, will not be subjected to the labor which it has been my lot to undergo.[1] Believing that the historian ought to be the most conscientious of men, writing, as he does, not only of the present age but for posterity, I have endeavored to divest myself of all prejudices, and to speak the truth in all cases. If it should be found, by the most scrutinizing reader, that my statements are incorrect, let me say in advance, that when I penned those statements I believed them to be true. So anxious have I been to record each incident as it really occurred, that upon several occasions I have traveled over four hundred miles to learn merely a few facts.

About four years since, feeling impressed with the fact that it is the duty of every man to make himself, in some way, useful to his race, I looked around in search of some object, in the pursuit of which I could benefit my fellow-citizens; for, although much interested in agriculture, that did not occupy one-fourth of my time. Having no taste for politics, and never having studied a profession, I determined to write a history. I thought it would serve to amuse my leisure hours, but it has been the hardest work of my life. While exhausted by the labor of reconciling the statements of old authors, toiling over old French and Spanish manuscripts, traveling through Florida,

[1] The Alabama Historical Society was established by Basil Manly, president of the University of Alabama in 1850. Pickett served as its first vice president and continued as an active member until his death. Thomas M. Owen, "Dr. Basil Manly, The Founder of the Alabama Historical Society," in *Transactions of the Alabama Historical Society, 1899–1903,* ed. Thomas M. Owen (Montgomery: Alabama Historical Society, 1904), 4: 125–40; Frank Lawrence Owsley, Jr., "Albert J. Pickett, Planter-Historian of the Old South," *Louisiana Studies* 8 (Summer 1969): 173.

Alabama, and Mississippi for information, and corresponding with persons in Europe and elsewhere for facts, I have sometimes almost resolved to abandon the attempt to prepare a history of my state.

In reference to that portion of the work which relates to the Indians, I will state that my father removed from Anson County, North Carolina, and carried me to the wilds of the "Alabama Territory," in 1818, when I was a boy but eight years of age. He established a trading house, in connection with his plantation, in the present county of Autauga. During my youthful days, I was accustomed to be much with the Creek Indians—hundreds of whom came almost daily to the tradinghouse. For twenty years I frequently visited the Creek Nation. Their green corn dances, ball plays, war ceremonies, and manners and customs, are all fresh in my recollection. In my intercourse with them, I was thrown into the company of many old white men, called "Indian countrymen," who had for years conducted a commerce with them. Some of these men had come to the Creek Nation before the Revolutionary War, and others, being Tories, had fled to it during the war, and after it, to escape from Whig persecution. They were unquestionably the shrewdest and most interesting men with whom I ever conversed. Generally of Scotch descent, many of them were men of some education. All of them were married to Indian wives, and some of them had intelligent and handsome children. From these Indian countrymen I learned much concerning the manners and customs of the Creeks, with whom they had been so long associated, and more particularly with regard to the commerce which they carried on with them. In addition to this, I often conversed with the chiefs while they were seated in the shades of the spreading mulberry and walnut, upon the banks of the beautiful Tallapoosa. As they leisurely smoked their pipes, some of them related to me the traditions of their country. I occasionally saw Choctaw and Cherokee traders, and learned much from them. I had no particular object in view, at that time, except the gratification of a curiosity, which led me, for my own satisfaction alone, to learn something of the early history of Alabama.

In relation to the invasion of Alabama by De Soto, which is related in the first chapter of this work, I have derived much information in regard to the route of that earliest discoverer from statements of General McGillivray, a Creek of mixed blood, who ruled this country, with eminent ability, from 1776 to 1793. I have perused the manuscript history of the Creeks by Stiggins, a half-breed, who also received some particulars of the route of De Soto, during his boyhood, from the lips of the oldest Indians.[2] My library contains many old Spanish and French maps, with the towns through which De Soto passed correctly laid down. The sites of many of these are familiar

[2] George Stiggins (1788–1845) wrote his manuscript "A Historical Narrative of the Genealogy, Traditions and Downfall of the Ispocoga or Creek Indian Tribe of Indians by One of the Tribe" between 1835 and 1843. Lyman C. Draper, secretary of the Wisconsin Historical Society, acquired the unfinished manuscript from his widow in 1873, and it became the property of the Wisconsin State Historical Society following Draper's death in 1891. Despite the efforts of Thomas M. Owen and William Stokes Wyman (1830–1915), who produced a typed copy of the manuscript for the Alabama Department of Archives and History with "penciled notes" and an introduction, Stiggins's work was not published until 1989. See *Creek Indian History: A Historical Narrative of the Genealogy, Traditions and Downfall of the Ispocoga or Creek Indian Tribe of Indians by One of the Tribe,* ed. Virginia Pounds Brown with intro. and notes, William Stokes Wyman (Birmingham: Birmingham Public Library Press, 1989), 7–20.

[3] Other than this reference, Pickett identifies the De Soto narrative in his notes as "Portuguese Narrative"—an expression used by Theodore Irving in his preface to his *The Conquest of Florida, by Hernando De*

to the present population. Besides all these, I have procured, from England and France, three journals of De Soto's expedition.

One of these journals was written by a cavalier of the expedition, who was a native of Elvas, in Portugal. He finished his narrative on the 10th February, 1557, in the city of Evora, and it was printed in the house of Andrè de Burgos, printer and gentleman of the Lord Cardinal and the Infanta. It was translated into English by Richard Hakluyt in 1609, and is to be found in the supplementary volume of his voyages and discoveries; London, 1812. It is also published at length in the historical collections of Peter Force, of Washington City.[3]

Another journal of the expedition was written by the Inca Garcilaso de la Vega, a Peruvian by birth and a native of the city of Cuzco. His father was a Spaniard of noble blood, and his mother the sister of Túpac, one of the Indian sovereigns of Peru. Garcilaso was a distinguished writer of that age. He had heard of the remarkable invasion of Florida by De Soto, and he applied himself diligently to obtain the facts. He found out an intelligent cavalier of that expedition, with whom he had minute conversations of all the particulars of it. In addition to this, journals were placed in his hands, written in the camp of De Soto—one by Alonso de Carmona, a native of the town of Priego, and the other by Juan Coles, a native of Zafra. Garcilaso published his work, at an early period, in Spanish. It has been translated into French, but never into English. The copy in our hands is entitled *Histoire de la Conquete de la Floride: ou Relation, de ce qui s'est passé dans la Decouverte de ce païs, par Ferdinand De Soto, Composée en Espagnol, par L'Inca Garcillasso de la Vega, et traduite en François, par Sr. Pierre Richelet*, Nouvelle Edition, Divisee en deux tomes; A. Leide: 1731.[4]

I have still another journal, and the last one, of the expedition of De Soto. It was written by Biedma, who accompanied De Soto as his commissary. The journal is entitled, "Relation de ce qui arriva pendant le voyage du Capitaine Soto, et details sur la nature du pas qu'il parcourut; par Luis Hernandez de Biedma," contained in a volume entitled *Recueil de Pieces sur la Floride*, one of a series of *Voyages, relations et mémoires originaux pour servir à l'histoire de la découverte de l'Amérique, publiés pour la première fois en français*, par H. Ternaux-Compans, Paris, 1841.[5]

In Biedma there is an interesting letter written by De Soto, while he was at Tampa Bay, in Florida, which was addressed to some town authorities in Cuba. The journal of Biedma is much less in detail than those of the Portuguese Gentleman and Garcilaso, but agrees with them in the relation of the most important occurrences.

***Soto* (Philadelphia: Carey, Lea & Blanchard, 1835). The anonymous Gentleman of Elvas published his narrative of the De Soto expedition—*Relação verdadeira dos trabalhos que o Governador D. Fernando de Souto e certos fidalgos portugueses passaram no descobrimento da Província da Flórida*—at Évora, Portugal in 1557. Richard Hackluyt published the first English translation in London in 1609. Pickett used Richard Hackluyt's translation as printed in Peter Force's *Tracts and Other Papers, Relating Principally to the Origin, Settlement, and Progress of the Colonies in North America,* which had the title: "Virginia richly valued, by the description of the main land of Florida, her next neighbour: out of the foure years continuall travel and discoveries, for above one thousand miles East and West, of Don Ferinando de Soto, and sixe hundred able men in his companie." Peter Force, *Tracts and Other Papers, Relating Principally to the Origin, Settlement, and Progress of the Colonies in North America,* 4 vols. (Washington: William Q. Force, 1846), 4: 1–132.**

[4] Garcilaso de la Vega (1539–1616) published his account of Hernando de Soto's expedition—*La Florida del Inca*—in Lisbon in 1605. The title page of this

Our own accomplished writer and earliest pioneer in Alabama history—Alexander B. Meek, of Mobile—has furnished a condensed, but well written and graphic account of De Soto's expedition, contained in a monthly magazine, entitled *The Southron*, Tuscaloosa, 1839. He is correct as to the direction assumed by the Spaniards over our soil, as well as to the character of that extraordinary conquest.[6]

Theodore Irving, M. A., of New York, has recently issued a revised edition of his *Conquest of Florida*. Its style is easy and flowing, when the author journalizes in regard to marches through the country, and is exceedingly graphic, when he gives us a description of De Soto's battles. As I have closely examined the sources from which Mr. Irving has collated his work, I am prepared to state that he has related all things as they are said to have occurred. For the complimentary terms which Mr. Irving has employed in the preface, and also in many of the notes of his late edition, in relation to my humble efforts in endeavoring to throw new light upon the expedition of De Soto, I beg him to accept my profound acknowledgments.[7]

There are many gentlemen of talents and distinction, who have unselfishly, nobly and generously interested themselves in my behalf, while engaged in the arduous labors which are now brought to a close. I will name John A. Campbell and George N. Stewart, of Mobile; Alfred Hennen and J. D. B. DeBow, of New Orleans; the Rev. Francis Hawks, of New York; William H. Prescott and Jared Sparks, of Massachusetts; the Rev. William Bacon Stevens, of Philadelphia; W. Gilmore Simms, of South Carolina; and particularly, John H. F. Claiborne, of Mississippi, who placed in my hands the manuscript papers of his father, Gen. F. L. Claiborne, who commanded the southern wing of the army, during the Creek War of 1813 and 1814.[8] The son has requested me to present the manuscript papers of his father, as a contribution from him, to the Historical Society of Alabama. I shall comply with his request upon the first suitable occasion. There are many other persons who have manifested an interest in my behalf, to enumerate all of whom, would be extending this preface to an unreasonable length. While I omit the mention of their names, I shall ever cherish the memory of their attentions with the most grateful recollections.

The Author.

May 1851.

edition spelled his name as Garcilasso de la Vega. The 1731 French edition cited by Pickett spelled his name as Garcillasso in the title but spelled it Garcilasso in the "Advertissement." The first English translation was published in 1951. Pickett purchased the two-volume French edition listed as "Garcillasso de la Vega Histoire de la conquete de la Floride" by Bartlett & Welford, New York City booksellers, for $3.50 in December 1847. Bartlett & Welford to AJP, New York, 18 December 1847, Albert James Pickett Papers, Alabama Department of Archives and History, Montgomery, Alabama.

[5] Luís Hernández de Biedma, the royal factor on De Soto's expedition, kept a journal from his departure from Cuba in 1539 until 1543 when the expedition arrived at Panuco in New Spain, modern Mexico. His journal is the only surviving eyewitness account of the expedition and Henri Ternaux-Compans included it in volume twenty—*Recueil de Pieces sur la Floride*—of his collection of voyages, relations, and memories published in French between 1837 and 1841.

[6] Alexander Beaufort Meek (1814–1865) launched *The Southron: A Monthly Magazine and Review*, a literary magazine,

Albert James Pickett.

in January 1839 but it folded in 1840 after publishing six issues. Pickett references Meek's article "Sketches of the History of Alabama, and, incidentally of Adjacent States" published in the first issue of his magazine. Johanna Nicol Shields, *Freedom in a Slave Society: Stories from the Antebellum South* (New York: Cambridge University Press, 2012), 30–2, 32 n. 11.

[7] Theodore Irving (1809–1880) originally published *The Conquest of Florida by Hernando De Soto* in two volumes in 1835. In the preface to his 1851 edition, he acknowledged Pickett as "a young author of reputation" and noted that his forthcoming *History of Alabama* "promises to be a valuable addition to the historical literature of our country."

[8] In addition to receiving the papers of Brigadier General Ferdinand Leigh Claiborne (1773–1815), Pickett received significant encouragement, assistance and advice on the writing of his *History* from those cited here and on his dedication page.

CONTENTS OF VOLUME I.

CHAPTER I.

CHAPTER II.

CHAPTER X.

CHAPTER XI.

CHAPTER XII.

CHAPTER XIII.

Chapter I

DE SOTO IN ALABAMA, GEORGIA, AND MISSISSIPPI

The first discovery of Alabama was by Hernando De Soto, a native of Spain, and the son of a squire of Xerez of Badajos. When a youth he went to Peru, enlisted under Pizarro, and with no property but his sword, won distinguished military reputation. Returning to his native country, and making an imposing appearance at court, he was made governor of Cuba, and Adelantado of Florida.[1] In the unknown regions of the latter, he resolved to embark his vast wealth in a splendid expedition, designed to conquer a people whom he believed to possess more gold than he had yet beheld in South America. Young men of the best blood in Spain and Portugal, sold their houses and their vineyards and flocked to his standard. Soon he was surrounded by an army of six hundred chosen men, with whom he put to sea, over the bar of San Lúcar de Barremeda.[2] Arriving at Cuba, he consumed a year in arranging the affairs of his government, and in preparation for the great enterprise before him.* At the end of that period, he left his wife, Doña Isabel de Bobadilla, and the lieutenant governor in charge of the island, and sailed for the coast of Florida, with a fleet of nine vessels—five large ships, together with caravels and brigantines.

A prosperous voyage soon enabled De Soto to pitch his camp upon the shores of Tampa Bay, in Florida, with an army now increased to one thousand men. Sending out detachments to capture Indians, from whom he expected to learn something of the country, he found them skillful with the bow and too wily to be easily taken. In one of these sallies, the soldiers under Baltasar de Gallegos charged upon a small number of Indians. At that moment a voice cried out, "I am a Christian! I am a Christian!—slay me not." Instantly Alvaro Nieto, a stout trooper, drew back his lance, and lifting the unknown

* Portuguese Narrative, 695–700; Garcilaso de la Vega, 59–60.

[1] On 20 April 1537, the Holy Roman Emperor Charles V granted De Soto the governorship of Cuba and unrestricted power to "conquer, pacify, and people" La Florida as adelantado—a title granted to other conquistadores. He had recognized De Soto's service by making him a knight of the prestigious military Order of Santiago. Charles Hudson, *Knights of Spain, Warriors of the Sun: Hernando de Soto and the South's Ancient Chiefdoms* (Athens: University of Georgia Press, 1997), 44–46.

[2] The total number of people who departed with De Soto from San Lúcar, Spain, on 7 April 1538 was probably closer to 700, including several wives and slaves. Ignacio Avellaneda, *Los Sobrevivientes de la Florida: The Survivors of the De Soto Expedition.* Research Publications of the P. K. Yonge Library of Florida History, No. 2

man up behind him, pranced off to join his comrades.[3]

Panfilo de Narvaez had attempted to overrun this country with a large expedition; but after disastrous wanderings, he reached Apalachee without finding any gold, and from thence went to the site of the present St. Marks, where his famished troops embarked for Cuba, in rude and hastily constructed boats, which were soon swallowed by the waves.* Juan Ortiz, the person taken prisoner, and who now, in all respects, resembled a savage, was a native of the town of Seville, in Spain. When a youth, he came to this coast with some others in search of Narvaez, and was captured by the Indians, who were about to burn him to death, when he was fortunately saved through the entreaties of the beautiful daughter of Uzita, the chief.[4] In the earlier periods of his slavery he was treated with barbarity, and compelled to guard, night and day, a lonely temple, in which the dead were deposited. After having been twelve years a prisoner among these savages, he was joyfully hastening to the camp of De Soto, when the Castilian words, which he so imploringly uttered, arrested the terrible lance of Alvaro Nieto.†

Gratified at the appearance of Juan Ortiz, who became his interpreter, De Soto gave him clothes and arms, and placed him upon a good charger. The adelantado was now ready to penetrate the interior. His troops were provided with helmets, breastplates, shields, and coats of steel to repel arrows of the Indians; and with swords, Biscayan lances, rude guns called arquebuses, crossbows, and one piece of artillery.[5] His cavaliers, mounted upon two hundred and thirteen horses, were the most gallant and graceful men of all Spain. Greyhounds, of almost the fleetness of the winds, were ready to be turned loose upon the retreating savages; and bloodhounds, of prodigious size and ferocity, were at hand to devour them, if the bloody Spaniards deemed it necessary. To secure the unhappy Indian, handcuffs, chains, and neck collars abounded in the camp. Workmen of every trade, with their various tools, and men of science, with their philosophical instruments and crucibles for refining gold, were in attendance. Tons of iron and steel, and much other metal, various merchandise, and provisions to last two years, were provided by the munificence of the commander and

*A history of the expedition of Narvaez will be found in Barcia, volume 1, folio edition (Madrid: 1749), entitled "Naufragios de Álvar Núñez Cabeza de Vaca, y Relacion de la Jornada, que hizo a la Florida con el Ádelantado Pánfilo de Narváez." See also Herrera's *The General History of the Vast Continent and Islands of America, Commonly Call'd, the West-Indies*, 6 vols. (London: 1740), 4: 27–38 and 5: 91–105.

† Portuguese Narrative, 702–04; Garcilaso, 45–64.

(Gainesville: University of Florida Libraries, 1990), 6–15, 38–39, 68–73.

[3] Baltasar de Gallegos, a kinsman of Cabeza de Vaca, served as De Soto's chief constable and consoled him at his death in May 1542. Hudson, *Knights of Spain*, 80–81, 349.

[4] The Gentleman of Elvas refers to Ucita, but more recent scholars use Uzita when describing the sixteenth century chiefdom, town, and Indian captors of Juan Ortiz. The Uzita, part of the Safety Harbor culture, occupied a territory that extended from the Little Manatee River to Sarasota Bay. Jerald T. Milanich, "Early Groups of Central and South Florida," *Handbook of North American Indians: Southeast*, vol. 14, ed. Raymond D. Fogelson (Washington: Smithsonian Institution, 2004), 213–18.

[5] After the first year of the expedition, there is little evidence the arquebus—a rather primitive, heavy matchlock gun about three feet long—was used by De Soto's troops, perhaps indicating its effectiveness or an inadequate supply of gunpowder. The artillery piece—a wrought-iron, breach-loading hand cannon—was hauled on a mule pack and buried at Cofaqui in modern Georgia, demonstrating its impracticality during the first year. Greg Waselkov, "What Do Spanish Expeditionary Artifacts of Circa 1540 Look Like and How Often Are they Preserved?" in *The Search for Mabila:*

his followers. A large drove of hogs, which strangely multiplied upon the route, together with cattle and mules, was also attached to the expedition.[6] The establishment of the Catholic religion appears to have been one of the objects; for, associated with the army, were twelve priests, eight clergymen of inferior rank, and four monks, with their robes, holy relics, and sacramental bread and wine. Most of them were relatives of the superior officers. Never was an expedition more complete, owing to the experience of De Soto, who, upon the plains of Peru, had ridden down hundreds in his powerful charges, and had poured out streams of savage blood with his broad and sweeping sword! It is not within our scope to detail the bloody engagements which attended the wanderings of this daring son of Spain, upon the territory of the now state of Florida. Everywhere, but especially in narrow defiles, the natives showered clouds of arrows upon the invaders. Strong in numbers, and made revengeful by the cruelties inflicted by Narvaez, they had determined to fight De Soto until his army was destroyed or driven from their soil. Nowhere in Florida did he find peace. His gallant troops, however, were successful. The Indians, often put to flight, and as often captured, were laden with chains, while the ponderous baggage of the expedition was unfeelingly thrown upon their backs for transportation. When in camp, they were made to pound corn, and to perform the most laborious and servile drudgery.[7]

Cutting his way from Tampa, De Soto arrived at Anhaica Apalache, in the neighborhood of the modern Tallahassee.[8] Then, as it is yet, a fertile region, he drew from this town, and from others which surrounded it, breadstuffs to last him during the winter. The sea, only thirty miles distant, was explored by a detachment, and at the present St. Marks the bones of horses, hewn timbers, and other evidences of Narvaez, were discovered. During the winter all the detachments, in their various expeditions, were attacked by the Indians, and the main camp at Apalachee was harassed day and night, in the fiercest manner, and with the most sanguinary results. At length Captain Maldonado, who had been ordered to sail to the west in some brigantines, which arrived from Tampa Bay, in search of a good harbor, returned in February and reported the discovery of the bay of Ochuse, since called Pensacola, which had a spacious channel, and was protected from the winds on all sides.* Delighted at this good news,

* The Portuguese Narrative asserts that Maldonado was sent to the west, at the head of a detachment, by land; but I adopt the more reasonable statement of Garcilaso, especially as he is sustained by Biedma, De Soto's commissary. See "Relation de ce qui arriva pendant le voyage du Capitaine Soto, et details sur la nature du pays qu›il

The Decisive Battle between Hernando de Soto and Chief Tascalusa, **ed. Vernon James Knight, Jr. (Tuscaloosa: University of Alabama Press, 2009), 94–95, 98.**

6 Elvas talks about a large herd of pigs and reports that seven hundred hogs were auctioned off following De Soto's death. Luis Hernandez de Biedma recorded that three hundred hogs were killed at Chicaza in 1541. ***The De Soto Chronicles: The Expedition of Hernando de Soto to North America in 1539–1543,*** **ed. Lawrence A. Clayton, Vernon James Knight Jr., and Edward C. Moore, 2 vols. (Tuscaloosa: University of Alabama Press, 1993), 1: 138, 237.**

7 The most complete source for the De Soto expedition is ***The De Soto Chronicles: The Expedition of Hernando de Soto to North America in 1539–1543,*** **ed. Lawrence A. Clayton, Vernon James Knight Jr., and Edward C. Moore, 2 vols. (Tuscaloosa: University of Alabama Press, 1993). These two volumes present annotated English translations of the four primary accounts of the De Soto expedition by the Gentleman of Elvas, Luís Hernández de Biedma, Rodrigo Rangel, and Garcilaso de la Vega.**

8 The De Soto chroniclers use variations of Anhaica such as Iniahico and Iviahica while most modern scholars use Anhayca. See ***The De Soto Chronicles,*** **1: 190–91 n. 88 and John H. Hann, "The**

which enabled the governor to make a wide circuit in the interior, he now ordered Maldonado to put to sea in the brigantines which then lay in the Apalachee Bay, and to sail for Cuba.[9] He was commanded to sail from thence to Ochuse with a fleet of provisions, clothes, and military supplies, with which to recruit the expedition, when it should have met him at that point in October.*

Learning from an Indian slave that a country to the northeast abounded in gold, De Soto broke up his winter encampment, and set out in that direction. He entered the territory of the present Georgia at its southwestern border, and successively crossing the Ocmulgee, Oconee and Ogeechee,† finally rested upon the banks of the Savannah, immediately opposite the modern Silver Bluff. On the eastern side was the town of Cofitachequi,‡ where lived an Indian queen, young, beautiful and unmarried, and who ruled the country around to a vast extent.[10] She glided across the river in a magnificent canoe, with many attendants, and, after an interesting interview with De Soto, in which they exchanged presents, and passed many agreeable compliments, she invited him and his numerous followers over to her town. The next day the expedition crossed the Savannah upon log rafts and in canoes, and quartered in the wigwams and under the spreading shades of the mulberry. Many interesting things occurred at this place, which are mentioned at length by both of the journalists of De Soto, particularly by Garcilaso, but which are here reluctantly omitted in our anxiety to reach the borders of Alabama.[11]

parcourut, par Luis Hernandez de Biedma," 59.

* Portuguese Narrative, 709; Garcilaso, 211–14.

† Biedma states that De Soto crossed a river (while in this part of the country) called the Altapaha. The substitution of only one letter would make it the Altamaha. Biedma, 62.

‡ All Indian tradition locates this town at the modern Silver Bluff, which is situated on the east bank of the Savannah, in Barnwell District, South Carolina, and which is now the property of Governor [James Henry] Hammond. In 1736, George Galphin, then a young Irishman, established himself as an Indian trader at this point, and gave the old site of Cofitachequi the name of Silver Bluff. The most ancient Indians informed him that this was the place where De Soto found the Indian Princess; and this tradition agrees with that preserved by the other old traders, and handed down to me. Galphin became a very wealthy man, and was for many years one of the most influential persons in Georgia and South Carolina, as we will see hereafter. He left many descendants; among others, the wife of the late Governor [John] Milledge, was his daughter; Dr. Thomas G. Holmes, an intelligent man, of Baldwin County, Alabama, is his grandson. Bartram, in his *Travels*, on page 313, speaking of Silver Bluff, says: "The Spaniards formerly fixed themselves at this place in the hopes of finding silver."

Apalachee in the Historic Era," in *The Forgotten Centuries: Indians and Europeans in the American South, 1521–1704*, ed. Charles M. Hudson and Carmen Chaves Tesser (Athens: University of Georgia Press, 1994): 327–54.

9 De Soto gave Maldonado, captain of his infantry, and Gómez Arias explicit instructions to report news of the conquest in Havana and to collect critical supplies and provisions, including clothing, food, footwear, weapons, powder and lead. They sailed for Cuba on 26 February 1540, but they failed to contact De Soto when they returned in the fall of 1540 or the summer of 1541—despite sailing along the Gulf Coast from Pensacola to Mexico. In October 1543, they finally made contact with the survivors at Vera Cruz. Hudson, *Knights of Spain*, 56, 144–45, 220, 411–12.

10 Again Pickett uses the Gentleman of Elvas as his source over Biedma's Cofitachyque. Modern scholars use alternatives of Cofitachequi or Cofitachiqui, to reference the village near modern Camden, South Carolina where De Soto arrived on 31 April 1540. *De Soto Chronicles*, 1: 82–86; Hudson, *Knights of Spain*, 172–84.; Chester B. DePratter, "The Chiefdom of Cofitachequi," in *The Forgotten Centuries*, 197–226.

11 The Indians on the Savannah did not live in wigwams but constructed their temples or town houses

After a halt of several weeks at Cofitachequi, De Soto broke up his camp, and, in company with the beautiful young queen, whom he retained about his person as a hostage, to ensure obedience among her subjects, and who did not escape from him until the army had nearly accomplished its route through northern Georgia—marched up the Savannah to its headwaters, and rested, for a short time, at a town in present Habersham County, Georgia. From this place the expedition assumed a direct western course, across northern Georgia, until they struck the headwaters of the Coosa River, where they advanced upon the town of Guaxule, containing three hundred houses, and situated between streams which had their sources in the surrounding mountains.[12] The chief met De Soto with five hundred warriors clothed in light costume, after the fashion of the country, and conducted him to his own house—surrendered at the instance of his wife—which stood upon a mound, and was surrounded by a terrace wide enough for six men to promenade abreast.* Having but little corn for the famished troops, the natives collected and gave them three hundred dogs, which the Spaniards had been accustomed to eat in the pine barrens of lower Georgia, "esteeming them as though they had been fat wethers."† Gaining much information about the country, in conversations with the chief, conducted by the interpreter, Juan Ortiz, the governor, after the fourth day's sojourn at Guaxule, marched to the town of Conasauga, in the modern county of Murray, Georgia. Crossing the Conasauga Creek, and journeying down its western banks, the Spaniards found it to increase in size, and being joined by other streams, it presently grew larger than the Guadalquivir which passes by Seville.‡ This was the Oostanaula; and following its western side, De Soto, after a very slow march, advanced within seven miles of Chiaha, where he was met by fifteen Indians, laden with corn, bearing a message from the chief, inviting him to hasten to his capital, where abundant supplies awaited him. Soon the eager Spaniards stood before the town of Chiaha, which is the site of the modern Rome.[13]

The most ancient Cherokee Indians, whose tradition has been handed down to us through old Indian traders, disagree as to the precise place where De Soto crossed the Oostanaula to get over into the town of Chiaha—some asserting that he passed over that river seven miles above its junction with the Etowah, and that he marched from thence down to Chiaha, which, all contend, lay immediately at the confluence of the two

* Garcilaso, 294.

† Portuguese Narrative, 712.

‡ Garcilaso, 295.

and other structures of poles, cane, interwoven cane, and split-cane mats. Rodrigo Rangel reported seeing structures "covered, high and low, with very excellent and beautiful mats." Hudson, *Knights of Spain*, 178–79; *De Soto Chronicles*, 1: 280.

[12] Garcilaso de la Vega's "Guaxule" is identified as Guaquili near modern Hickory, North Carolina, by more recent scholars. See Hudson, *Knights of Spain*, 186–87, and H. Trawick Ward and R. P. Stephen Davis, *Time before History: The Archaeology of North Carolina* (Chapel Hill: University of North Carolina Press, 1999), 229–30.

[13] More recent scholarship identifies Conasauga as Canasoga, a town near the Nolichucky River in the Upper Tennessee River Valley and locate Chiaha, a fortified town on the French Broad River, near modern Dandridge, Tennessee—not Rome, Georgia. Hudson, *Knights of Spain*, 199–200; Robin A. Beck, Jr., "From Joara to Chiaha: Spanish Exploration of the Appalachian Summit Area, 1540–1568," *Southeastern Archaeology* 16 (Winter 1997): 162–69.

rivers; while other ancient Indians asserted that he crossed, with his army, immediately opposite the town. But this is not very important. Coupling the Indian traditions with the account by Garcilaso, and that by the Portuguese eye-witness, we are inclined to believe the latter tradition that the expedition continued to advance down the western side of the Oostanaula, until they halted in view of the mouth of the Etowah.[14]

De Soto having arrived immediately opposite the great town of Chiaha, now the site of Rome, crossed the Oostanaula in canoes and upon rafts made of logs prepared by the Indians, and took up his quarters in the town.* The noble young chief received De Soto with unaffected joy, and made him the following address: "Mighty chief: Nothing could have made me so happy as to be the means of serving you and your warriors. You sent me word from Guaxule to have corn collected to last your army two months. Here I have twenty barns full of the best which the country can afford. If I have not met your wishes, respect my tender age, and receive my good will to do for you whatever I am able."† The governor responded in a kind manner, and was then conducted to the chief's own house, prepared for his accommodation.

Chiaha contained a great quantity of bear's oil in gourds, and walnut oil as clear as butter and equally palatable; and for the only time upon the entire route were seen pots of honey.‡ The Spaniards, irregularly quartered in the fields, and scattered about at their will, reposed under trees and loitered upon the banks of the rivers. The horses, reduced in flesh and unfit for battle, grazed upon the meadows. Unaccustomed to allow such loose discipline, De Soto now winked at it, for the natives were friendly, and every soul in the camp needed repose. One day the chief presented the governor with a string of pearls, two yards in length, and as large as filberts, for which he received in return pieces of velvet and other cloth much esteemed by the Indians. He said that the temple of this town, where the remains of his ancestors were deposited, contained a vast quantity of these valuables. He invited his distinguished guest to take from it as many as he desired. But the latter declined, remarking that he wished to appropriate nothing to himself from so sacred a place.[15]

The chief, to gratify him in regard to the manner of obtaining these pearls,

[14] Without access to twentieth century historical and archaeological evidence, Pickett continues to track the De Soto expedition in central and north central Georgia rather than the Carolinas and East Tennessee. See Hudson, *Knights of Spain*, 455–81.

[15] Chiaha was the first fortified town encountered by the De Soto expedition, and archaeologists have identified this chiefdom with the Dallas culture which extended down the Tennessee River Valley to modern Chattanooga. Hudson, *Knights of Spain*, 199–201.

* Garcilaso, 295.

† Portuguese Narrative, 717.

‡ I have often been informed by old bee hunters and Indian countrymen, that after the territory of Alabama became partially settled by an American population, wild bees were much more abundant than they were in their earliest recollection. They were introduced into the country from Georgia and the Carolinas, and often escaping from their hives to the woods, became wild; hence De Soto found no honey in the country at the early period in which he invaded it, except at Chiaha.

immediately dispatched some of his subjects in four canoes, with instructions to fish all night for the oysters which contained them. In the morning he caused a fire to be made upon the bank. The canoes returned laden, and the natives throwing the oysters upon the glowing coals, succeeded in finding many pearls the size of peas, which De Soto pronounced beautiful, but for the fire, which had robbed them of some of their brilliancy. A soldier, in eating some of the oysters, or, rather, mussels, found one of great size uninjured, and offered it to the commander for Dona Isabel. He declined the kindness intended for his wife, and urged the generous fellow to keep it to buy horses with at Havana. Connoisseurs in camp valued it at four hundred ducats.* While here, a cavalier, named Luis Bravo de Xeres, walking one day upon the bank of the river, threw his lance at a dog, which suddenly disappeared under the bluff. Coming up to recover his weapon, he found, to his horror, that it had pierced the temple of Juan Mateos and had killed him. The poor man was quietly fishing on the margin of the stream, and little suspecting that death was at hand.[16] The accident caused deep regret in the camp, the deceased being much esteemed, and, having the only gray head in the army, was called, by way of pleasantry, Father Mateos.† About this time a principal Indian from Coste, a town below, informed De Soto that in the mountains to the north, at a place called Chisca, were mines of copper, and of a yellow metal, still finer and softer.[17] Having seen, upon the Savannah, copper hatchets supposed to be mixed with gold, his attention was deeply aroused upon the subject. Villalobos and Silvera, two fearless soldiers, volunteered to explore that region. Furnished with guides by the chief of Chiaha, they departed upon their perilous journey.[18]

The Spaniards had basked upon the delightful spot where now stands the town of Rome, for the space of thirty days. The horses had recruited, and the troops had grown vigorous and ready for desperate deeds. De Soto demanded

[16] Charles Hudson identifies the French Broad River as the place of this incident that claimed Juan Mateos's life, citing Garcilaso de la Vega but not Pickett. See Hudson, *Knights of Spain*, 202, 512 n.63.

[17] While Biedma refers to Costehe and Elvas calls the province Acoste, Pickett calls the province Costa. Modern scholars prefer Rangel's name of Coste—located downriver from Chiaha. *De Soto Chronicles*, 1: 89–91, 232, 283; Hudson, *Knights of Spain*, 203.

[18] Garcilaso de la Vega identifies the two volunteer explorers as Juan de Villalobos and Francisco de Silvera, respectively from Seville and Galicia, Spain. *De Soto Chronicles*, 2: 317.

* Garcilaso, 297. The oyster mentioned was the mussel to be found in all the rivers of Alabama. Heaps of mussel shells are now to be seen on our riverbanks wherever Indians used to live. They were much used by the ancient Indians for some purpose, and old warriors have informed me that their ancestors once used the shells to temper the clay with which they made their vessels. But as thousands of the shells lie banked up, some deep in the ground, we may also suppose that the Indians, in De Soto's time, everywhere in Alabama, obtained pearls from them. There can be no doubt about the quantity of pearls found in this state and Georgia in 1540, but they were of a coarser and more valueless kind than the Spaniards supposed. The Indians used to perforate them with a heated copper spindle, and string them around their necks and arms like beads—others made toy babies and birds of them.

† Garcilaso, 298.

[19] **Modern scholarship places the province or chiefdom of Chisca and the towns of Chiaha and Coste in the Upper Tennessee River Valley. Coste was an island town at the mouth of the Little Tennessee River near modern Lenoir City, Tennessee. Hudson, *Knights of Spain*, 199–209; Charles M. Hudson, "Conversations with the High Priest of Coosa," in *Lamar Archaeology: Mississippian Chiefdoms in the Deep South*, ed. Mark Williams and Gary Shapiro (Tuscaloosa: University of Alabama Press, 1990), 215.**

of the hospitable chief, through the persuasion of some of his unprincipled officers, a number of females to accompany them in their wanderings. That night the inhabitants quietly left the town and hid themselves in the bordering forests. The chief entreated the governor not to hold him responsible for their conduct, for, during his minority, an arbitrary uncle ruled them with a despotic will. With sixty troopers De Soto ravaged the surrounding country, and, provoked at not finding the fugitives, laid waste their flourishing fields of corn. When afterwards informed that men only would be required to bear the baggage, the Indians returned to Chiaha, apologized for their flight, and yielded to the last proposition.* De Soto then broke up his camp, re-crossed the Oostanaula, and marched down the west side of the Coosa, leaving the generous people of Chiaha well satisfied with presents. On the 2nd July, and after seven days slow march, he entered the town of Coste.† The Spaniards were now in Alabama, in the territory embraced in the county of Cherokee, and by the side of the Coosa, one of our noblest streams. Never before had our soil been trodden by European feet![19] Never before had our natives beheld white faces, long beards, strange apparel, glittering armor, and, stranger than all, the singular animals bestrode by the dashing cavaliers! De Soto had discovered Alabama, not by sea, but after dangerous and difficult marches had penetrated her northeastern border with a splendid and well equipped land expedition! The Atlantic states were quietly discovered by voyagers entering their harbors. Alabama was marched upon by an army, whose soldiers sickened with famine upon the barrens of Georgia, and left tracks of blood upon the soil of Florida!

Commanding his camp to be pitched two cross-bow shots from the town, De Soto, with eight men of his guard, approached the chief of Costa, who received him with apparent friendship. While they were conversing together, some unscrupulous footmen entered the town and plundered several of the houses. The justly incensed Indians fell upon them with their clubs. Seeing himself surrounded by the natives, and in great personal danger, the governor seized a cudgel, and, with his usual presence of mind, commenced beating his own men. The savages, observing that he took their part, became pacified for a moment. In the meantime, taking the chief by the hand, he led him, with flattering words, towards the camp, where he was presently surrounded by a guard and held as a hostage.‡ The Spaniards remained under arms all night. Fifteen hundred Indians, armed complete, often made dispositions to charge

* Portuguese Narrative, 718–19.
† Portuguese Narrative, 718–19.
‡ Portuguese Narrative, 718–19.

upon them, vociferating angry and insulting language. Averse to war since he had been so repeatedly attacked by the Floridians, De Soto restrained his anxious troops. His coolness, together with the influence of a prominent Indian who followed him from Chiaha, put an end to the serious affair.* Three days after this, Villalobos and Silvera returned from Chisca. They passed into the mountains, found no gold, but a country abounding with lofty hills and stupendous rocks. Dispirited, they returned to a poor town, where the inhabitants gave them a buffalo robe, which they supposed once covered a tremendous animal, partaking of the qualities of the ox and the sheep.† According to Garcilaso, the mines which they reached were of a highly colored copper, and were doubtless situated in the territory of the county of De Kalb. The sick, who were placed in canoes at Chiaha, had by this time arrived down the river. Furnished with the burden carriers by the chief, who was to the last hour held a prisoner, the governor left Costa on the 9th of July 1540, and crossed over to the east side of the Coosa upon rafts and canoes.[20] Proceeding down its eastern bank, he encamped the first night at the town of Talle. The chief came forth to receive him, and, in a formal speech, begged him to command his services. Here the Spaniards remained two days, sharing the hospitality of the natives. Upon their departure they were supplied with two women and four men. Indeed, De Soto brought from the forests of Florida over five hundred unhappy men and women, secured with chains, driven by keepers, and made to transport the effects of the expedition. When any of them became sick, died, or escaped, it was his policy to supply their places at the first town upon which he marched. He always, however, distributed among the principal Indians presents, which were gratifying to them, and left at many of the towns pairs of swine to stock the country.[21]

The expedition now began to enter the far-famed province of Coosa, the beauty and fertility of which were known to all the Indians, even upon the seaside. Garcilaso asserts that it extended three hundred miles, and other authors agree that it reached over the territory now embraced in the counties of Cherokee, Benton, Talladega, and Coosa. Continuing through the rich lands of Benton, the expedition passed many towns subject to the chief of Coosa. Every day they met ambassadors, "one going and another coming," by which De Soto was assured of a hearty welcome at the capital.‡ With joyful faces the Indians rushed to his lines every mile upon the route, furnishing supplies and assisting the troops from one town to another. The same generous

[20] De Soto's expedition spent eight days at Coste enjoying the largesse of the people, exploring the countryside, and waiting for his men left up river at Chiaha to rejoin him. Hudson, *Knights of Spain*, 205–07.

[21] The Gentleman of Elvas identifies this town as Tali in the province of Coça. Charles Hudson and other scholars refer to the town as Tali in the province or chiefdom of Coosa, stretching some three hundred miles from East Tennessee into central Alabama. Instead of crossing the Coosa River, De Soto's expedition probably crossed the Tellico River and traveled south to Tasqui, passing several smaller villages until they reached the town of Coosa on the Coosawattee River in northwest Georgia in mid-July 1540. *De Soto Chronicles*, 1: 91; Hudson, *Knights of Spain*, 207, 213–18; David J. Hally, "The Chiefdom of Coosa," in *The Forgotten Centuries*, 227–31; Robbie Franklyn Ethridge, *From Chicaza to Chickasaw: The European Invasion and the Transformation of the Mississippian World* (Chapel Hill: University of North Carolina Press, 2010), 62–64.

* Garcilaso, 300.

† Portuguese Narrative, 719.

‡ Portuguese Narrative, 719.

[22] **Pickett's Alabama route for De Soto through the Coosa chiefdom continues well ahead of modern scholarship which has located most of this chiefdom in northeast Georgia. Pickett's "barns . . . full of corn" were storehouses raised off the ground on four posts constructed of interwoven limbs or cane. The Spanish referred to these structures as *barbacoas*. Hudson, *Knights of Spain*, 156, 211, 455–72.**

reception attended him upon entering the soil of the county of Talladega. The hospitality of the Coosas surpassed that of any people whom he had yet discovered. The trail was lined with towns, villages and hamlets, and "many sown fields which reached from one to the other."* With a delightful climate, and abounding in fine meadows and beautiful little rivers, this region was charming to De Soto and his followers. The numerous barns were full of corn, while acres of that which was growing bent to the warm rays of the sun and rustled in the breeze. In the plains were plum trees peculiar to the country, and others resembling those of Spain. Wild fruit clambered to the tops of the loftiest trees, and lower branches were laden with delicious Isabella grapes.[22]

On the 26th of July 1540, the army came in sight of the town of Coosa. Far in the outskirts, De Soto was met by the chief, seated upon a cushion, and riding in a chair supported upon the shoulders of four of his chief men. One thousand warriors, tall, active, sprightly and admirably proportioned, with large plumes of various colors on their heads, followed him, marching in regular order. His dress consisted of a splendid mantle of martin skins, thrown gracefully over his shoulder, while his head was adorned with a diadem of brilliant feathers. Around him many Indians raised their voices in song, and others made music upon flutes.† The steel-clad warriors of Spain, with their glittering armor, scarcely equaled the magnificent display made by these natives of Alabama. The chief, receiving De Soto with the warmth of a generous heart, made him the following speech: "Mighty chief! above all others of the earth! Although I come now to receive you, yet I received you many days ago deep in my heart. If I had the whole world, it would not give me as much pleasure as I now enjoy at the presence of yourself and your incomparable warriors. My person, lands and subjects are at your service. I will now march you to your quarters with playing and singing."‡

De Soto responded in his best style, after which he advanced to the town, conversing with the chief, who rode in his sedan chair, while the lofty Spaniard sat upon his fiery steed. The royal house was set apart for the accommodation of the adelantado, and one half of the other houses were surrendered to the troops. The town of Coosa was situated upon the east bank of the river of that name, between the mouths of the two creeks, now known as Talladega and Tallaseehatchee, one of which is sometimes called Kiamulgee.§ It contained

* Portuguese Narrative, 719.

† Garcilaso, 300.

‡ Portuguese Narrative, 719–20.

§ In 1798, Col. Benjamin Hawkins, then Creek agent, visited the Coosa town, now embraced in the county of Talladega. He accurately describes the inhabitants and the location

five hundred houses, and was the capital of this rich and extensive province.[23]

The chief of Coosa was twenty-six years of age, well formed, intelligent, with a face beautifully expressive, and a heart honest and generous. He always dined with De Soto. One day he rose from the table, and, in an earnest manner, besought the governor to select a region anywhere in his dominions, and immediately establish upon it a large Spanish colony. De Soto had contemplated peopling some beautiful country, and was better pleased with this section than any other, but his imagination still pointed him to some gold region, like Peru. He returned the chief his profound thanks, adduced many reasons for declining the liberal offer, among others, that Maldonado's ships would await him at the bay of Pensacola. Yet, in the face of all the kindness, the politic and suspicious De Soto kept the chief about his person, as a hostage, to preserve peace among the Indians, and to exhort slaves and provisions. Enraged at the imprisonment of their chief, the Indians fled to the woods to prepare for war. Four captains, with their companies, were dispatched in different directions in pursuit, and returned with many women and men in chains.[24] Some of the principal of these were released at the entreaty of the chief, while others were carried off with the expedition, laden with irons and baggage, and those who were not destroyed at the battle of Mabila were conducted far beyond the Mississippi River.*

The Indians returned from the forest, and remained at peace with the Spaniards, but were still dissatisfied at the restrictions imposed upon the liberties of their chief. After twenty-five days had been passed at the capital of Coosa, De Soto marched in the direction of the Tallapoosa, leaving behind a Christian Negro, too sick to travel, whom the Indians desired to retain among them on account of his singular hair and sable complexion.[25] He recovered, and was doubtless the distant ancestor of the dark-colored

of the town, which he says was situated on the banks of the Coosa, between the mouths of two creeks, the Indian names of which were Natche and Ufaula. When the French expelled the Natchez from the Mississippi in 1730, some of that tribe sought refuge among the Talladegas—hence the name of one of these creeks in Hawkins's day. When the Americans, in 1832, began to settle this country, they changed the name of these creeks to Talladega, or Kiamulgee, and Tallaseehatchee. In addition to the testimony of Col. Hawkins, many old Indian countrymen have informed me that here was the site of the Coosa town, which was known by that name in their early days. Several ancient French and Spanish maps, in my possession, lay down the town of Coosa at the place described. See Hawkins, "A Sketch of the Creek Country, In the Years 1798–1799," published by the Historical Society of Georgia, Savannah, 1848.

* Portuguese Narrative, 720.

[23] The Creek town of Coosa visited by Benjamin Hawkins in the 1790s was not the same town reached by De Soto's expedition on 16 July 1540. The principal town of the Coosa chiefdom was excavated in the twentieth century and the site now lies beneath Carter's Lake, fed by the Coosawattee River that runs between Ellijay and Chatsworth, Georgia. Hudson, *Knights of Spain*, 214–19. See http://www.georgiatrails.com/gt/Carters_Lake.

[24] Rangel describes Coosa as "a great cacique with much land and most abundant that they found in Florida." He also confessed that seeing the Indians in iron and chains "was a thing of much pity to see it." *De Soto Chronicles*, 1: 284–85.

[25] De Soto's expedition left Coosa on 20 August 1540, traveled southward through heavy rain, and reached Itaba—Elvas and Pickett's Ytaua—near modern Cartersville, Georgia, on the Etowah River on 21 August. Nine days later he finally forded the Etowah and soon began to encounter men from Ulibahali towns along the Coosa River. Garcilaso identifies the Christian slave as Robles. Hudson, *Knights of Spain*, 220–24; *De Soto Chronicles*, 1: 94; ibid., 2: 326.

[26] **De Soto left the first Ulibahali town on 2 September 1540, stopped at a second town two days later near Foster's Bend on the Coosa River, and reached Tuasi on 5 September near the junction of Terrapin Creek and Nance's Creek in northeast Alabama. After resting for six days, he moved southward, stopped near Jacksonville, Alabama, on 13 September, and bivouacked two days later at a palisaded town near Talladega. On 16 September he reached a new village on the upper Tallaseehatchee Creek and on the 18th he arrived at Talisi—Pickett's Tallase—near modern Childersburg, Alabama. According to Rodrigo Rangel's account of De Soto's expedition, Manzano (Mansano) may have enjoyed looking for grapes but he also was probably a deserter—and certainly not the first. Hudson, *Knights of Spain*, 224–28; *De Soto Chronicles*, 1: 285, 288.**

savages seen in that region in more modern times.* The first day the army passed through the large town of Tallimuchase, within a few hours after it had been abandoned by its inhabitants. The next day the town of Ytaua was reached, where De Soto encamped six days, awaiting the abatement of the stream which ran by it, now violently swollen by incessant rains. As the expedition had not crossed any stream since leaving Coosa, it is probable the one alluded to was the modern Tallaseehatchee. The march was continued to Ulibahali, situated upon Hatchet Creek, which was called a "small river." The town was surrounded by a wall composed of two rows of posts driven deep in the ground, with poles laid horizontally between them, the inner and outside of the frame work neatly stuccoed with clay and straw. Portholes were left at proper distances, forming a defense "as high as a lance." Such was the character of the Indian fortifications from this place onward. In consequence of the duress of the chief of Coosa, whom De Soto carried along with him, but treated with respect and kindness, the Indians of Ulibahali were in arms. Before the Spaniards entered the suburbs, twelve principal men, armed with bows, and with lofty plumes upon their heads, advanced and volunteered to rescue their beloved chief by arraying a formidable force, but he dissuaded them from it. On the opposite side of the creek lived a sub-chief, who furnished De Soto with thirty women for slaves, and to carry burdens. Then the adelantado pursued his wanderings, leaving behind Manzano, a native of Salamanca, of noble parentage, who was lost while rambling in the hills for grapes, which were found in great abundance. The route lay along the modern Socapatoy region, in the county of Coosa. The expedition passed the town of Toase, and several others, subject to the chief of Tallase, and arrived at the great town of that name on the 18th September 1540.[26]

Tallase was an extensive town, the principal part of which was encompassed by a wall, similar to that just described, with the addition of terraces. It reposed upon a point of land "almost surrounded by a main river," which

* The Negro left at Coosa was not the only memorial of De Soto that remained with these people. George Stiggins, whose mother was a Natchez Indian, and whose father was a Scotchman, was born in the Talladega country. He was a fair English scholar, and a pretty good writer. He had been for years engaged in writing a history of the Creeks, and died some years ago, leaving it in an unfinished state. His son permitted me to peruse it one day. Stiggins asserts that the Talladegas had, at a late day, a brass kettle-drum and several shields which once belonged to the army of De Soto, and that he had often seen them. The Coosas used them as trophies in their annual festivals. Besides these, De Soto left hogs and sometimes cattle among the Alabama towns, and such is the origin of these animals among the Indians. Horses and mules were too valuable to be given away.

was the Tallapoosa.* Extensive fields of corn reached up and down the banks. On the opposite side were other towns, skirted with rich fields laden with heavy ears of maize. The beautiful river, rolling its silvery waters through these fertile lands, and the delightful climate, contributed to render the whole prospect most pleasing. But the reception of De Soto among those people was cool and scarcely civil. Some had abandoned their houses at his approach, and gone into the woods. However, the chief gave him forty Indians. After a few days, a noble-looking young savage, of gigantic proportions, and with a face extremely handsome and interesting, visited the marquee. He was the son of Tuscaloosa, a potent chief, whose domains commenced thirty miles below, and extended to the distant Tombigbee. He bore an invitation from his father to De Soto to hasten to his capital, where he was making preparations to receive him upon a magnificent scale, and then awaited him upon the eastern confines of his territory. The son was dispatched with a suitable reply, and presents for the father.[27]

Having remained at Tallase twenty days, De Soto dismissed the chief of Coosa, with whom he parted upon good terms, crossed the Tallapoosa in canoes and upon rafts, marched down the eastern side, and encamped the first night at Casista, probably the sight of the modern Autossee. Delayed in passing the river, he could not have advanced further that day. In the morning the march was resumed. During this day a large town was discovered, and at night the camp was pitched upon the borders of another. The next day, advancing within six miles of the temporary residence of Tuscaloosa, a halt was made in the woods. Luis de Moscoso, the camp master, with fifteen horsemen, was dispatched to inform the chief of the proximity of the governor. Moscoso found the proud Mabilian seated upon two cushions, placed on a large and elegant matting, upon an eminence which commanded a delightful prospect. His numerous attendants posted themselves around him, leaving space for the nearer position of his chief men. One of these held over his head a round deerskin shield, with a staff in the middle, resembling an umbrella. Painted with stripes of different colors, it was used as a banner in his wars, but was employed at present in protecting his head from the rays of the sun.

* Some years after De Soto passed through this country, the Muscogees or Creeks came from the Mexican empire of which they were subjects, and overrun all East Alabama and the greater portion of Georgia, killing and making slaves of many of the Alabamas, Ockmulgees, Oconees and Uchees, the latter of whom then lived near the modern city of Savannah. Upon the ruins of the Tallase discovered by De Soto, the Muscogees built the town of Tookabatcha [Tuckabatchee], but immediately opposite, across the river, the name of Tallase [Tallassee] was preserved until they moved to Arkansas in 1836. The ancient and extensive Indian settlement is now a large cotton plantation.

[27] Rodrigo Rangel reports that the expedition arrived in Talisi (Tallase) on a Saturday and found the "cacique and people gone" but that on 25 September 1540 the cacique gave De Soto all he had requested in supplies and women. Chief Tascaluza—Pickett's Tuscaloosa—sent his son to Talisi as a spy and to ascertain the strength of De Soto's forces and his plans. *De Soto Chronicles,* 1: 288; Hudson, *Knights of Spain,* 228–29.

[28] On 5 October 1540, De Soto left Talisi (Tallase), spent the night at Casiste (Casista), and continued his trek southward the next day—probably for the bay of Ochuse (i.e., Pensacola) and a meeting with his supply vessels commanded by Maldonado. The march carried them past a small village on Hatchet Creek and they camped on the Coosa River opposite Humati on the 7th. After an overnight stop at Uxapita, near modern Wetumpka, they crossed the Tallapoosa River on 9 October and bivouacked near Tascaluza's (Tuscaloosa's) new town of Atahachi (Piachi)—Pickett's Piache—near modern Montgomery. De Soto and Tascaluza exchanged messages and De Soto dispatched Luis de Moscoso to Atahachi to tell Tascaluza of his coming for a meeting. *De Soto Chronicles,* 1: 95, 288; Hudson, *Knights of Spain,* 229.

Tuscaloosa was forty years of age, of great stature, with immense limbs. He was spare around the waist, and his whole form was admirably proportioned. His countenance was handsome, but grave and severe. "He was lord of many territories and much people, and was feared by his neighbors and subjects." In vain did Moscoso endeavor to excite his curiosity, by prancing his horses before him. Sometimes he scarcely deigned to raise his eyes, and then, again, he bestowed upon the troopers the most contemptuous smiles.[28]

Even when De Soto arrived, he preserved the same haughty demeanor; but, in consideration of his position as commander-in-chief, he reluctantly advanced, and made the following address:

"Mighty chief: I bid you welcome. I greet you as I would my brother. It is needless to talk long. What I have to say can be said in a few words. You shall know how willing I am to serve you. I am thankful for the things which you have sent me, chiefly because they were yours. I am now ready to comply with your desires."[29]

The governor replied in true Spanish style, failing not to assure the chief that, even in distant Indian countries through which he had passed, he had heard of his greatness and power. This interesting scene occurred below Line Creek, in the present county of Montgomery. Both journalists agree that De Soto had advanced thirty-five miles below Tallase. Reposing at this town the space of two days, preparations were made to advance. An officer was sent among the horses, to find one large enough to sustain the great Indian. A large pack horse, the property of the governor, was selected. Appareled in a rich suit of scarlet, and a cap of the same, given to him by De Soto, the chieftain, who was a head taller than any of his attendants, mounted upon his horse, with his feet nearly trailing on the ground. Onward the lofty and graceful Mabilian rode, side by side with the governor.[30] Marching through the territory embraced in the present counties of Montgomery, Lowndes, and the southeastern part of Dallas, the expedition arrived at a town called Piache,[31] seated on a peninsula formed by the windings of a large river, "the same which runs by Tallase, but here grown much wider and deeper."* This was the Alabama. On the march hither, a distressing disease broke out among the Spaniards, from the want of salt. The death of several, together with the loathsome condition of the sufferers, spread alarm in the camp. Those who afterwards used ashes with their food, from a weed recommended by the Indians, escaped the dreadful malady.†

The town of Piache was strongly fortified. Its name is probably preserved

* Garcilaso, 310; Portuguese Narrative, 722.

† Garcilaso, 369–70.

[29] Pickett's version of Tascaluza's (Tuscaloosa's) welcome is a loose paraphrasing of the speech reported by the Gentleman of Elvas. Luís Hernández de Biedma, Garcilaso de la Vega, and Rodrigo Rangel do not mention a welcoming speech. *De Soto Chronicles,* 1: 96.

[30] In his original narrative, Pickett refers to Tuscaloosa (Tascaluza) as the Mobilian and his province and town as Maubila. For this chapter, this writer has chosen to use Mabila and Mabilians. Modern scholars have generally followed Rangel who used Mabila over Elvas's Mavilla and Biedma's Mavila. Ibid., 1: 98–104, 232–36, 291–948; Hudson, *Knights of Spain,* 232–49.

[31] Rodrigo Rangel described Piachi as a town "upon the bluff of a rocky river," characterized its cacique as "malicious" and reported that his warriors threatened to resist their crossing. Charles Hudson locates Piachi (Piache) on the Alabama River where it cuts through Selma chalk, possibly at Durant Bend or Selma. *De Soto Chronicles,* 1: 291–92; Hudson, *Knights of Spain,* 233–34.

in a large creek which flows into the Alabama on the northern side, called Chilatchee. The Indians having no canoes, soon constructed rafts of dry logs and cane, upon which the troops were wafted to the northern or western side of the Alabama—according to the conviction of the writer, in the upper part of the county of Wilcox.*

The expedition assumed a southern direction, and marched down the western side of the Alabama, over the soil of the present county of Wilcox. De Soto began to read the Mabilian chief. He was still proud and distant, and evidently felt that he was a prisoner. Upon the whole route he had been studiously engaged in consulting with his principal men, and in constantly sending runners to the capital with messages. De Soto suspected that he meditated schemes, which aimed at the destruction of the Spaniards. His suspicions were further awakened, when Villalobos and another cavalier were believed to have been killed by his subjects. When asked about them Tuscaloosa indignantly replied, "I am not their keeper." High words ensued between him and De Soto; but the latter restrained himself until an opportunity offered of taking deep revenge on the chief for his insolence and the death of the two Spaniards. On the third day of the march from Piache, they passed through many populous towns, well stored with corn, beans, pumpkins, and other provisions. In the meantime, Xaramillo and Vásquez, two able and discreet cavaliers, were dispatched in advance to discover if any conspiracy was going on at the capital. Before daylight, on the fourth morning, De Soto placed himself at the head of one hundred horse, and an equal number of foot, and marched rapidly in that direction with the chief, leaving Moscoso, the camp-master, to bring up the larger portion of the troops.[32] At eight o'clock the same morning, the 18th October 1540, De Soto and Tuscaloosa arrived at the capital, called Mabila. It stood by the side of a large river, upon a beautiful plain, and consisted of eighty handsome houses, each capacious enough to contain a thousand men. They all fronted a large public square. They were encompassed by a high wall, made of immense trunks of trees, set deep in the ground and close together, strengthened with cross-timbers, and interwoven with large vines. A thick mud plaster, resembling handsome masonry, concealed the wood work, while port-holes were abundant, together with towers, capable of containing eight men each, at a distance of fifty paces apart. An eastern and a western gate opened into the town. The writer is satisfied that Mabila

* Biedma says that De Soto occupied two days in passing the river; and he learned from the Indians that Narvaez's barques touched at the mouth of the river (the Alabama) in search of water, and that a Christian, named Teodoro, was still among the Indians below—and they exhibited to De Soto a dagger which they had obtained from him. Biedma, 72.

[32] Tascaluza's (Tuscaloosa's) reserve and open disdain for the Spanish reflected his position of power in the regions bordering his province. He accepted De Soto's gifts and agreed to accompany him to Mabila (also Mavila), but he did not meet all his demands at Piache (Piachi). According to Garcilaso de la Vega, the two men sent ahead to Mabila as spies were Gonzalo Quadrado Xaramillo and Diego Vásquez, but another source identifies them as Gonzalo Cuadrado and Diego Velazquez. *De Soto Chronicles*, 2: 330; Hudson, *Knights of Spain*, 230–32, 234–35. See Ignacio Avellaneda, *Los Sobrevivientes de la Florida: The Survivors of the De Soto Expedition*. Research Publications of the P.K. Yonge Library of Florida History, No. 2 (Gainesville: University of Florida Libraries, 1990).

[33] Tascaluza's (Tuscaloosa's) capital town of Mabila was surrounded by a palisaded wall constructed of thick posts with a covering of smaller posts interwoven with river cane and plastered over with mud and straw. Inside this stockade were several large houses with a large plaza in the center and two gates, one in the west wall and one in the east wall. However, there is no evidence that the houses could hold "a thousand men." Hudson,

was upon the north bank of the Alabama, and at a place now called Choctaw Bluff, in the county of Clarke, about twenty-five miles above the confluence of the Alabama and Tombigbee. The march from Piache, the time occupied, the distance from Mabila to the bay of Pensacola—computed by Garcilaso and the Portuguese Gentleman at eighty-five miles—and the representations of aged Indians and Indian countrymen, that here was fought the great battle between De Soto and the brave Mabilians, have forcibly contributed to make that impression upon his mind.[33]

De Soto and Tuscaloosa were ushered into the great public square of Mabila with songs, music upon Indian flutes, and the graceful dancing of beautiful brown girls. They alighted from their chargers, and seated themselves under a "canopy of state." Remaining here a short time, the chief requested that he should no longer be held as a hostage, nor required to follow the army any further. The adelantado hesitated in reply, which brought Tuscaloosa immediately to his feet, who walked off with a lofty and independent bearing, and entered one of the houses. De Soto had scarcely recovered from his surprise, when Juan Ortiz followed the chief and announced that breakfast awaited him at the governor's table. Tuscaloosa refused to return, and added, "If your chief knows what is best for him, he will immediately take his troops out of my territory." In the meantime, Xaramillo, one of the spies, informed the governor that he had discovered over ten thousand men in the houses, the subjects of Tuscaloosa and other neighboring chiefs; that other houses were filled with bows, arrows, stones and clubs; that the old women and children had been sent out of town, and the Indians were at that moment debating the most suitable hour to capture the Spaniards. The general received this startling intelligence with the deepest solicitude. He secretly sent word to his men to be ready for an attack. Then, anxious to avert a rupture, by regaining possession of the person of the chief, he approached him with smiles and kind words, but Tuscaloosa scornfully turned his back upon him, and was soon lost among the host of excited warriors.[34] At that moment a principal Indian rushed out of the same house, and loudly denounced the Spaniards as robbers, thieves and assassins, who should no longer impose on their great chief, by depriving him of a liberty with which he was born, and his fathers before him. His insolence, and the motions which he made to shoot at a squad of Spaniards with a drawn bow, so incensed Baltasar de Gallegos, that, with a powerful sweep of his sword, he split down his body and let out his bowels! Like bees in a swarm the savages now poured out upon the Spaniards. De Soto placed himself at the head of his men, and fought face to face with the enemy, retreating slowly and passing the gate into the plain. His cavalry

***Knights of Spain*, 236; *De Soto Chronicles*, 2: 330–31.**

[34] Biedma records that they initially encountered three to four hundred Indians who chatted with the Spaniards "in peace" but he estimated "a good five thousand Indians . . . hidden in the houses" around the plaza. While Juan Ortiz issued the invitation to Tascaluza to join De Soto for breakfast, it was Baltasar de Gallegos who barged into the house to demand that he join De Soto and observed the armed warriors around him. *De Soto Chronicles*, 1: 233; ibid., 2: 335; Hudson, *Knights of Spain*, 237–38.

[35] Biedma admits in his account that the first assault of the Mabilians forced the Spaniards "to leave, fleeing from the town." Outside the walls of the town, De Soto rallied his forces including a large number who had been slow in arriving and who found themselves thrown into an unexpected battle. *De Soto Chronicles*, 1: 235; ibid., 2: 336–38; Hudson, *Knights of Spain*, 238–39.

had rushed to rescue their horses, tied outside the walls, some of which the Indians came upon in time to kill. Still receding to get out of the reach of the enemy, De Soto at length paused at a considerable distance upon the plain. The Mabilians seized the Indian slaves, packed upon their backs the effects of the expedition, which had now arrived and lay scattered about, drove the poor devils within the walls, knocked off their irons, placed bows in their hands, and arrayed them in battle against their former masters. In the first sally, De Soto had five men killed and many wounded, himself among the latter number.[35] Having captured the baggage, the victors covered the ground in advance of the gate, and rent the air with exulting shouts. At that moment the governor headed his cavalry, and followed by his footmen, charged upon the savage masses; and, with a terrible slaughter, drove them back into the town. The Indians rushed to the portholes and towers, and shot upon the invaders clouds of arrows, compelling them again to retire from the walls. A small party of Spaniards were left in a perilous situation. Three cross-bow men, an armed friendly Indian, five of De Soto's guard, some servants and two priests, not having time to join the others when first attacked in the square, took refuge in the house set apart for their commander. The savages sought an entrance at the door, but the unhappy inmates bravely defended it, killing many of the assailants. Others clambered upon the roof to open the covering, but were as successfully repulsed. Separated from their friends by a thick wall, and in the midst of thousands of enemies panting to lap their blood, their destruction appeared inevitable. During the long struggle for existence, the holy fathers engaged in earnest prayer for their deliverance, while the others fought with a desperation which rose with the occasion.[36]

Seeing the Spaniards again retreat, the Indians rushed through the gates, and dropping down from the walls, engaged fiercely with the soldiers, seizing their sweeping swords and piercing lances! Three long hours were consumed in the terrible conflict, first one side giving way and then the other. Occasionally De Soto was strengthened by small squads of horsemen who arrived, and without orders, charged into the midst of the bloody melee. The governor was everywhere present in the fight, and his vigorous arm hewed down the lustiest warriors. That sword, which had often been dyed in the blood of Peruvians, was now crimsoned with the gore of a still braver race. The invincible Baltasar de Gallegos, who struck the first blow, followed it up, and was only equaled by the commander in the profuse outpouring of savage blood. Far on the borders of the exciting scene rode his brother, Fray Juan, a Dominican friar, who constantly beckoned him to quit the engagement on foot, and take the horse which he bestrode in order to fight the better. But Baltasar, gloating

[36] While Pickett's two sources—Garcilaso and Elvas—disagree on the members and the number of De Soto's party trapped inside one of the houses, Rangel intimates that some actually survived when "the Christians arrived with fire and brought them out." *De Soto Chronicles,* 1: 294.

[37] Baltasar de Gallegos's brother was Juan de Gallegos, a Dominican friar, who was wounded slightly while trying to get his brother on a horse. Hudson, *Knights of Spain,* 241; *De Soto Chronicles,* 2: 338.

on blood, heeded him not; when presently an Indian arrow, which made a slight wound upon the back of the worthy father, caused him to retire to a less dangerous distance. Indeed, during the whole battle the priests kept the plain, watched the awful carnage with intense anxiety, and often fell upon their knees, imploring Almighty God to give victory to the Spaniards.[37]

At length the matchless daring of De Soto and his troops forced the Indians to take a permanent position within Mabila, closing after them its ponderous gates. The sun began to lower towards the tops of the loftiest tress, when Moscoso and the last of the army arrived. He had strangely loitered by the way, allowing the soldiers to scatter in the woods and hunt at their leisure. His advanced guard heard at a distance the alarum of drums and the clangor of trumpets. With beating hearts they passed back the word along the scattered lines, from one to the other, and soon the hindmost rushed to the support of their exhausted and crimson-stained comrades. Joined by all his force, De Soto formed the best armed into four divisions of foot. Provided with bucklers for defense, and battle-axes to demolish the walls, they made a simultaneous charge, at the firing of an arquebus. Upon the first onset, they were assailed with showers of arrows and dreadful missiles. Repeated blows against the gates forced them open. The avenues were filled with eager soldiers, rushing into the square. Others, impatient to get in, battered the stucco from the walls and aided each other to climb over the skeleton works. A horrible and unparalleled carnage ensued. The horsemen remained on the outside to overtake those who might attempt to escape. The Indians fought in the streets, in the square, from the tops of the houses and walls. The ground was covered with their dead, but not one of the living entreated for quarters. The Spaniards were protected with bucklers and coats of mail, while the poor Indians were only covered with the thin shield which the Great Spirit gave them at the dawn of their existence. The troops entered the town in time to save the two priests and their companions, who had so long held out against such fearful odds.[38] The battle, which now waxed hotter and more sanguinary than ever, cannot be as graphically described as the heroic deeds on either side so justly deserve. Often the Indians drove the troops out of the town, and as often they returned with increased desperation. Near the wall lay a large pool of delicious water, fed by many springs. It was now discolored with blood. Here soldiers fell down to slake the intense thirst created by heat and wounds, and those who were able rose again, and once more pitched into a combat characterized by the most revolting destruction of human life. For some time the young females had joined in the fight, and they now contended side by side with the foremost warriors, sharing in the indiscriminate slaughter. Heated

[38] According to Rangel, Luis de Moscoso was inside the walls of Mabila "fighting like a knight" and called Baltasar de Gallegos "come forth, or I will have to leave you, for I cannot wait for you any longer." When Rangel made his escape outside the palisaded walls, De Soto removed twenty arrows from his armor, a quilted tunic made of thick cotton. *De Soto Chronicles,* 1: 292–93; Hudson, *Knights of Spain,* 239.

with excitement, smarting with his wounds, and provoked at the unsubdued fierceness of the natives, De Soto rushed out alone by the gate, threw himself into the saddle, and charged into the town. Calling, with a loud voice, upon "Our Lady and Santiago," he forced his charger over hundreds of fighting men and women, followed by the brave Nuño de Tovar. While opening lanes through the savage ranks and sprinkling his tracks with blood, he rose on one occasion to cast his lance into a gigantic warrior. At that instant, a powerful winged arrow went deep into the bottom of his thigh. Unable to extract it, or to sit in his saddle, he continued to fight to the end of the battle, standing in his stirrups. Everywhere, that mighty son of Spain now gorged upon Alabama blood! His fearless bounds filled the boldest soldiers with renewed courage. At length the houses were set on fire, and the wind blew the smoke and flames in all directions, adding horror to the scene. The flames ascended in mighty volumes! The sun went down, hiding himself from the awful sight! Mabila was in ruins, and her inhabitants destroyed![39]

The battle of Mabila had lasted nine hours. It was disastrous to De Soto. Eighty-two Spaniards were slain, or died in a few days after the engagement. Among these were Diego De Soto, the nephew of the governor; Don Carlos Enriquez, who had married his niece; and Men-Rodriquez, a cavalier of Portugal, who had served with distinction in Africa and upon the Portuguese frontiers. Other men of rank and blood lost their lives in the terrible conflict, some of whom died in great agony, being shot in the eyes and in the joints of their limbs. Forty-five horses were slain—an irreparable loss, mourned by the whole expedition. All the camp equipage and baggage were consumed in the house where the Indians had stored it, except that of Captain Andréde Vasconcelos, which arrived late in the evening. All the clothes, medicines, instruments, books, much of the armor, all the pearls, the relics and robes of the priests, their flour and wine, used in the holy sacrament, with a thousand other things which a wilderness could not supply, perished in the flames. The Mabilians were nearly all destroyed. Garcilaso asserts that above eleven thousand were slain. The Portuguese Gentleman sets down the number at two thousand five hundred killed within the walls alone. Assuming a point between the two estimates, it is safe to say that at least six thousand were killed in the town and upon the plains, or were afterwards found dead in the woods. These authors also disagree as to the fate of Tuscaloosa—the one contending that he was consumed in the flames, and the other that he decamped upon the arrival of Moscoso, at the solicitation of his people, attended by a small guard, and laden with rich Spanish spoils.[40] It is more probable that the Black Warrior remained

[39] While De Soto proved himself to be an inspiring and courageous leader in the fog of battle, he had an equally impressive band of fighting men, including Moscoso, Rangel, Baltasar de Gallegos, Don Carlos Enríquez, and Nuño de Tovar. In the heat of the battle and the air literally filled with arrows, Tovar had his lance "made of two pieces of ash . . . pierced by an arrow through the middle from side to side, like a drill, without splintering anything, and the arrow made a cross on the lance." *De Soto Chronicles,* 1: 294; Hudson, *Knights of Spain,* 242.

[40] Rangel reports killing three thousand Indians and "many others wounded." He also notes that they did not know the fate of Tuscaloosa (Tascaluza) "either dead or alive," but his "son was found lanced." While Garcilaso gives a greatly exaggerated death count, the two eyewitnesses—Elvas and Rangel—provide very similar death numbers for the total Indians killed in the battle. Rangel also records that many of the wounded were found "afterward dead in the huts and by the roads." *De Soto Chronicles,* 1: 104, 294; Hudson, *Knights of Spain,* 241.

in his capital, desiring not to survive the downfall of his people.*

Upon the ruins of Mabila the Spaniards passed the first night, in confusion and pain, sending forth groans and cries that fell upon the distant air like the ravings of the damned! In every direction a sickening and revolting sight was presented. In the slowly receding fire, piles of brave Mabilians cracked and fried upon the glowing coals! Upon the great square, pyramids of bodies, smeared with blood and brains, lay still unburnt. Outside the walls, hundreds lay in the sleep of death, still hot from their last desperate exertions, and copiously bleeding from the large orifices made by lances and swords, and discoloring the beautiful grounds upon which they had so often sported in their native games. All the Spaniards were wounded except the holy fathers, and were, besides, exhausted, famished, and intoxicated with the most fiendish desperation. Seventeen hundred dangerous wounds demanded immediate attention. It was often that a soldier had a dozen severe ones, with barbed arrows rankling in his flesh. But one surgeon of the expedition survived, and he was slow and unskilled. Everything, in his department, was devoured by the terrible element. Those who were slightly wounded, administered to those whom the Indians had pierced deepest. As the soldiers of Cortés did in Mexico, they opened the bodies of some of the savages, and with the fat obtained, bound up the wounds with bandages torn from the garments of the soldiers who were killed. Others rushed to the woods, obtained straw and boughs, and formed against the walls beds and imperfect covering for the wounded and dying. Although severely pierced himself with arrows, and bruised with missiles, yet the generous De Soto unselfishly gave his whole attention to his men. During that miserable night, many of the unhappy Spaniards joined the priests in fervent appeals to their Heavenly Father for the alleviation of their wretched condition.[41]

They remained within the walls eight days, and then removed to the Indian huts upon the plain. De Soto sent out foraging detachments, who found the villages abounding in provisions. In the woods and ravines, Indians were found dead, and others lay wounded. The latter were treated with kindness by the Spaniards, who fed them and dressed their wounds.[42] Females of incomparable beauty were captured upon these excursions, and added to those who were taken at the close of the battle. From them, the governor was astounded to learn the deep schemes which Tuscaloosa had planned to capture his army, weeks before his arrival at Mabila. To the Tallases, who complained to him

* In describing the battle of Mabila, I have carefully consulted the Portuguese Narrative and Garcilaso. I find that they are, in the main, sustained by Biedma. See Garcilaso, 312–31; Portuguese Narrative, 722–25; Biedma, 74–78.

[41] Rangel provides the most accurate report on the Spanish injuries and losses at Mabila: 22 Spaniards killed, and 148 wounded who received 688 arrow wounds. He also noted the loss of seven horses killed and twenty-nine others wounded. De Soto's nephew Captain Diego De Soto and Don Carlos Enríquez were found among the dead Spaniards. *De Soto Chronicles,* 1: 294.

[42] Both Biedma and Elvas confirm that the expedition remained at or near Mabila for twenty-eight days to heal the wounded and recuperate before resuming their march. De Soto had now lost one hundred and two members of his expedition since landing in Florida. *De Soto Chronicles,* 1: 104, 235–36; Hudson, *Knights of Spain,* 246–48.

that their chief had given their people to De Soto as slaves, he replied, "Fear nothing; I shall shortly send the Spaniards back from my country to Tallase in chains, led by your people whom they have enslaved."[43]

The priests, monks, and best informed laymen, went into convention to determine the propriety of substituting corn meal for flour in the celebration of Mass. They decided that bread made of pure wheat, and wine of the juice of the grape, were required for consecration. After this, the fathers, in lieu of the chalices, altar dresses, chasubles, and other sacred ornaments, which had been consumed by fire, made some robes of dressed deer skins, erected rude altars and read the *introitus* and other prayers of the Mass on Sundays and feasts, omitting the consecration. This unusual ceremony was denominated the Dry Mass.[44]

While referring to the religious exercises of the Spaniards, it is proper to allude to some of their vices. Upon the whole journey from Tampa Bay to this place, they had passed much of their leisure time in gambling. This vice was common to all classes; those of rank often bet high, staking their money, jewels, horses, effects, and even their female slaves! The fire of Mabila destroyed their cards. They now made others of parchment, painted them with admirable skill, and loaned these packs from one company to another, continuing to gamble under trees, upon the river banks, and in their rude huts.

The report which De Soto had received upon his first arrival at Mabila, that Maldonado and his vessels awaited him at the bay of Pensacola, was now fully confirmed by the females whom he had captured. Refreshed by this good news, which determined him to plant a colony in the wilderness, he dismissed a chief of that country whom Maldonado had brought into the camp, while at Anhaica Apalache. He had always treated him with kindness, and they parted upon the most friendly terms. The chief set out for Ochuse. When it became known in camp that the ships had arrived, joy succeeded the sadness which had universally prevailed. Some of the most distinguished cavaliers secretly talked of sailing from Ochuse to Spain, and others to Peru, each resolved upon quitting De Soto and his fortunes. He heard of the conspiracy with painful solicitude, and determined to ascertain if it was founded in seriousness. One dark night he disguised himself and cautiously moved about the camp. Approaching the hut of Juan Gaitan, the treasurer, he overheard an earnest conversation, which satisfied him of the truth of what had been intimated. De Soto was startled at the faithless schemers. It altered his plans. He now dreaded to march to Ochuse, for he well knew that some of these cavaliers had once deserted Pizarro, leaving him on the island of Gorgona. He reflected, that his means were exhausted, his hopes of finding a gold country, thus far,

[43] The Tuscaloosa (Tascaluza) quote and the "deep schemes" are found in Garcilaso's *La Florida* and not in the eyewitness accounts of Biedma, Elvas, and Rangel. *De Soto Chronicles*, 2: 352.

[44] Elvas confirms that all the religious "ornaments for saying Mass" were burned, but only Garcilaso discussed the ceremony and used the term "Dry Mass." Ibid., 1: 104; ibid., 2: 354.

blasted, and that he had nothing to tempt the cupidity of recruits; even the pearls, all he had to exhibit of his discoveries, having shared the fate of the other effects. These things, connected with a desire to thwart the plans of his conspirators, influenced him to turn his back upon his ships, laden with provisions, clothes, arms, and everything which the whole army needed.[45]

De Soto became gloomy and morose. Sometimes, in the midst of his desponding fits, a hope of yet finding a gold region shot across his mind, but, like a flashing meteor, it exploded in darkness, leaving him in deeper despair! He resolved, however, to strike into the wilderness. The wounded had recovered enough to march, and he gave orders to break up the camp. On Sunday, the 18th of November 1540, a direction was assumed to the north. The order fell like a clap of thunder upon the unwilling cavaliers. But they obeyed, for he threatened to put to death the first man who should even think of Maldonado and his ships.* The expedition traversed an extremely fertile, but uninhabited country, called Pafallaya, now embraced in the counties of Clarke, Marengo and Greene, and, at the expiration of five days, passed the town of Taliepataua, and reached another called Cabusto. This was "near a river, wide, deep, and with high bluffs."† The Spaniards had now arrived upon the Black Warrior, and near the modern town of Erie. Fifteen hundred Indians advanced in battle array, shouting that a war of "fire and blood" was what they desired. They remembered the destruction of their friends at Mabila, and they were determined to be revenged. Severe skirmishing ensued. The Spaniards drove the savages into the river; some crossed over in canoes and others swam, and on the opposite side they were joined by a force estimated at eight thousand. For six miles they stretched along the western bank to oppose the crossing of the army. De Soto occupied Cabusto, and was attacked every night by detachments of the enemy, who came over secretly in canoes from different directions, and sprang upon him. He at length caused ditches to be cut near the landings, in which he posted cross-bow men and those armed with arquebuses. After the Indians were repulsed three times from these entrenchments, they ceased to annoy the Spaniards at night.[46] In the meantime, one hundred men completed in the woods two large boats. They were placed upon sledges, and by the force of horses and mules, and with

* De Soto had no doubt determined to settle a colony in the province of Coosa. The desperate resolution, now formed, of again plunging into unknown regions, was unfortunate for him and his followers, and for the historians of Alabama. A colony in Alabama, at that early period, would have afforded many rich historic incidents.

† "Etoit sur un fleuve, grand, profond et haut de bord." Garcilaso, 348. The American rivers, of ordinary size, appeared large to the Spaniards, and do even now to all Europeans.

[45] Biedma reports that De Soto had learned "news of the brigantines" and that members of the expedition wanted "to go to the sea," but the onset of cold weather and finding sources of food "in order to be able to winter" caused the expedition to turn north away from the Gulf Coast. Elvas and Rangel do not provide any commentary on a "mutiny" or on De Soto's decision to turn north. Gorgona Island is located in the Pacific Ocean off the coast of Colombia. Ibid., 1: 236; Michael Wood, *Conquistadors* (Berkeley: University of California Press, 2000), 112–13.

[46] While the basic outline of the events are correct, Pickett relied too much on Garcilaso who seems to have combined two separate encounters, first at Apafalaya on the Black Warrior near Eutaw, Alabama, and the second at Chicaza on the Tombigbee—probably near modern Columbus, Mississippi. While Elvas refers to Cabusto, Pafallaya, and Taliepataua, Hudson and other scholars generally follow Rangel's place names, such as Chicaça, Taliepacana, Zabusta, and Apafalaya. *De Soto Chronicles*, 1: 105, 296; 2: 362; Hudson, *Knights of Spain*, 250, 256–59; Charles Hudson, Marvin T. Smith, and Chester DePratter, "The

the assistance of the soldiers, were conveyed to a convenient landing one and a half miles up the river, and launched before day. Ten cavalry and forty infantry entered each of these boats, the former keeping the saddle while the latter rowed rapidly across. Five hundred Indians rushed down the banks and overwhelmed the voyagers with arrows. However, the boats reached the shore, one of them coming to with great difficulty. The soldiers, all of whom were wounded, sprang out, and, headed by the impetuous Silvestre and Garcia, charged the Indians with great resolution. A severe conflict continued until the boats returned and brought over De Soto with eighty men, who, joining in the fight, forced the Indians to retreat to a distant forest. The advanced wing keeping off the enemy, the whole army soon crossed the river. When all were over, the Indians were driven to their first position, which they had strengthened with palisades, and from which they continually sallied, skirmishing with the invaders until the sun was lost behind the hills.* Upon the Warrior, De Soto found a delightful country, with towns and villages well supplied with corn, beans and other provisions. The next day he caused the boats to be broken up, for the iron which they contained, and the expedition marched in a northern direction, passing through a portion of Greene and Pickens.[47]

After five days they reached the Little Tombigbee, somewhere in the county of Lowndes, Mississippi. Here the Indians had collected to dispute the passage. Having recently suffered so severely in contentions with the natives of Alabama, De Soto felt unwilling to expose his army to further loss. Halting two days for the construction of a small boat, he dispatched in it an Indian, who bore a message to the chief, with offers of peace and friendship. Immediately upon reaching the opposite bank, the poor fellow was seized and barbarously killed, in the sight of the governor. His murderers then rent the air with terrific yells and dispersed. De Soto conducted his troops unmolested across the river, and marched until he arrived at the town of Chicazsa, in the province of that name. It consisted of two hundred houses, and reposed upon a hill extending towards the north, shaded by oak and walnut trees, and watered by several rivulets. The Spaniards had now reached the territory embraced in the county of Yalobusha. The region was fertile, well-peopled and dotted with villages. The cold weather set in with much severity. In the midst of the snow and ice, the army encamped upon the fields opposite the town, until houses could be erected; for here De Soto had determined to pass the winter. Foraging parties scoured the country, collected provisions, and captured

* Portuguese Narrative, 725; Garcilaso, 348–62.

Hernando de Soto Expedition: From Mabila to the Mississippi River," in *Towns and Temples Along the Mississippi*, ed. David H. Dye and Cheryl Anne Cox (Tuscaloosa: University of Alabama Press, 1990), 183–87, 192–93.

[47] Elvas reports the "piragua was built inside the town"—most likely at Mozulixa—in secrecy in four days, by 28 November 1540. Only Garcilaso names Diego Garcia and Gonzalo Silvestre as leaders or heroes in this fight. *De Soto Chronicles*, 1: 105; ibid., 2: 363–65; Hudson, *Knights of Spain*, 256–57.

[48] After dispensing with the warriors at Mozulixa, De Soto steadily marched his forces to Zabusta on 1 December—possibly at Moundville—crossed the Black Warrior and rested a week in a town under the command of Chief Apafalya, who became his captive. On 14 December 1540, they reached the Tombigbee—river of the Chicaza—and two days later Baltasar de Gallegos with thirty mounted men helped force a crossing with limited resistance. De Soto spent the Christmas season and the bitter winter of 1540–1541 in southwestern Monroe County, east-central Clay County, eastern Oktibbeha County, northern Noxubee County, or Lowndes County—not Yalobusha County. *De Soto*

Chronicles, 1: 105–06, 297; Hudson, *Knights of Spain,* 260.

[49] Elvas reports De Soto took "thirty horse and eighty foot" to subdue Saquechuma (also Sacchuma), which had been abandoned. He also recorded the Chicaza developed a taste for pork and began stealing De Soto's hogs at night and the thievery of the "four horsemen" and their escape from severe punishment. *De Soto Chronicles,* 1: 106–07.

Indians. The latter were invariably dismissed, with presents for their chief.[48]

The chief at length came to see De Soto, and offered him his lands, person and subjects. He returned, shortly after, with two neighboring chiefs—Alibamo and Nicalasa. The august trio gave the adelantado one hundred and fifty rabbits, besides mantles and skins. The chief of Chicaza became a frequent visitor, and De Soto often sent him home on one of the horses. Having besought the general to aid him in overcoming a prominent and rebellious subject, for the purpose of dividing and destroying the army, as was afterwards ascertained, De Soto marched, with thirty horsemen and two hundred Indians, upon Saquechuma, and destroyed that place by fire. Upon their return to the camp, the principal Indians were feasted upon the flesh of the swine. They were pleased with the first dish of an animal never before seen, and from that time the place where the hogs were kept was often broken in upon dark nights and many stolen. Three of the rogues were caught on one occasion and two of them put to death. The hands of the other were chopped off, and in that painful and helpless situation he was sent to his chief. On the other side, the Spaniards robbed the Indians. One day four horsemen, Francisco Osorio, a servant of the Marquis of Astorga, called Reynoso, Ribera, the page of the governor, and Fuentes, his chamberlain, entered a neighboring village and forcibly carried off some valuable skins and mantles. The enraged Indians forsook their town and went into the woods to prepare for war. The robbers were arrested, and Fuentes and Osorio were condemned to die. The priests and some of the most distinguished cavaliers pleaded, in vain, for the pardon of the latter. De Soto had them brought out to have their heads chopped off, when the Indians arrived with a message from the chief, informing him of the outrage upon his people. At the suggestion of Baltasar de Gallegos, the interpreter cunningly turned it to the advantage of the prisoners. He said to De Soto that the chief desired him not to execute the robbers, for they had not molested his subjects.[49] He said to the Indian ambassadors that they might return home well assured that the plunderers would be immediately put to death, according to the wishes of the chief. The prisoners, in consequence were all set at liberty, much to the joy of the army.*

* Poor Ortiz never reached his native country, but died in Arkansas. He was of great service as an interpreter. Understanding only the Floridian language, he conducted conversations through the Indians of different tribes who understood each other, and who attended the expedition. In conversing with the Chickasaws, for instance, he commenced with a Floridian, who carried the word to a Georgian, the Georgian to the Coosa, the Coosa to the Mabilian, and the latter to the Chickasaw. In the same tedious manner the answer was conveyed to him and reported to De Soto.

Upon the appearance of March 1541, the thoughts of the unhappy De Soto occasionally turned upon pursuing the journey. He demanded of the chief two hundred men for burden bearers. An evasive answer was given, and for several days the governor was apprehensive of an attack. He posted sentinels, under the supervision of Moscoso. One dark night, when the cold wind was howling awfully, the Chickasaws rushed upon the camp, in four squadrons, sending up yells the most terrific, and adding horror to the scene by the sound of wooden drums and the discordant blasts of conch shells. The houses of the town, in which the larger portion of the troops now lodged, were set on fire by arrows containing burning matches, made of a vegetable substance, which shot through the air like flashing meteors and fell upon the roofs! Constructed of straw and canc, thc wigwams were soon wrapped in flames. The Spaniards, blinded by the smoke, ran out of the houses half dressed, and, in their dismay, knew not the best way to oppose the assailants. Some of the horses were burned in the stables and others broke their halters, and running in all directions among the soldiers, increased the unparalleled confusion. De Soto and a soldier named Tapier, the first to mount, charged upon the enemy, the former being enveloped in an overcoat, quilted with cotton three inches thick, to shield him from the arrows. His saddle, which, in the haste, had not been girted, turned with him in one of his sweeping bounds, and he fell heavily to the ground, at the moment his lance had pierced a savage. The soldiers drove off the Indians, who had surrounded him with clubs, and adjusted his saddle. Vaulting into it, he charged in the thickest of the enemy, and reveled in blood![50]

The Spaniards were now seen in all directions, engaged in a dreadful fight. Many, however, had just awoke, and now crawled upon their hands and knees out of the devouring flames above them. In a house, at some distance, lay the sick, and those who had not recovered from the wounds which they had received at Mabila and Cabusto. Hordes of savages pressed upon the poor fellows, and, before they were rescued, several fell victims. In the meantime, the cavaliers, some without saddles and others without clothes, joined the intrepid De Soto; and now the awful wind, the flames, the yells and the clangor of arms, made the scene frightfully sublime, and the night one long to be remembered. Fifty infantry took flight, which was the first instance of cowardice upon the march. Nuño de Tovar, sword in hand, rushed before them, and with the assistance of a detachment of thirty men under Juan de Guzmán, arrayed them against the enemy. At that instant, André de Vasconcelos, at the head of twenty Portuguese hidalgos, most of whom had served as horsemen upon the African frontier, accompanied by Nuño de Tovar on foot, forced

[50] Elvas writes that De Soto and "a soldier called Tapia" got mounted and attacked the intruders who had spread fire throughout the campsite. Biedma records the soldier's name as Tapia de Valladolid. Ibid., 1: 108, 298.

the savages to retire on one side of the town. At length the Indians fled from the battlefield, and were pursued by De Soto and his troops as long as they could distinguish objects by the light of the burning town.[51]

Returning from the chase, the governor found that the engagement had resulted in considerable loss. Forty Spaniards were killed, and among them the only white woman in camp, the wife of a soldier, whom she had followed from Spain. Fifty horses were lost, either burned or pierced with arrows. Dreading these singular quadrupeds in war, the Indians aimed at their entire destruction, and many were found shot entirely through in the most vital parts. The swine, the increase of which had often kept the Spaniards from starving, when hard pressed for food, were confined in a roofed enclosure, and a number of them were consumed by the fire. De Soto surveyed the scene with deep mortification. He blamed Moscoso for the unfortunate attack. His negligence here, reminded him of his tardy advance upon Mabila, and, in his anger, he deposed his old brother in arms from the rank of camp-master, and bestowed it upon the bold Baltasar de Gallegos. A succession of losses had attended him since he crossed the Alabama at Piache. Indeed, from his first landing at Tampa Bay, over three hundred men had fallen by the assaults of the natives. The fire at Chicaza swept the few things saved at Mabila, together with half their wearing apparel. And now many of the unfortunate soldiers shivered in the cold, with scarcely a vestige of clothing.[52]

In the fit of deep despondency into which he was thrown, De Soto did not forget the duties which a commanding officer owes to his suffering troops. The dead were buried and the wounded properly attended. The Indians, thick upon the plain, and upon the ruined town, remained, a prey for the hungry wolves and birds of carrion. The Spaniards abandoned the sickening spot, and encamped three miles distant, at Chicazilla, or little Chicaza, where they erected a forge and tempered their swords, now seriously injured by the fire. They busied themselves in making shields, lances and saddles. The remainder of the winter was passed in great wretchedness. Intense cold and grievous wounds were not all they had to bear, but often the natives assailed them at night, with the agility and ferocity of tigers! At sunset they were compelled to evacuate the town, and take position in the field, for fear that fire might be applied to the houses. The ingenuity of one of the soldiers devised mattings, four inches in thickness, made of long soft grass, in which those who were not upon guard wrapped themselves, and were somewhat protected from the piercing air. Often De Soto sent forth detachments, who cut down every Indian they overtook; yet, in a few succeeding nights, the savages would return and attack the camp. Before daylight on Wednesday, the 15th March 1541,

[51] Biedma, Elvas, and Rangel do not give any of the detail cited here by Pickett regarding Guzmán, Tovar, and Vasconcelos. All of this action is described by Garcilaso, and it is possible that he gleaned these details from short narratives of Alonso de Carmona and Juan de Coles—who accompanied De Soto—but that only survive in the account written by Garcilaso de Vega. Ibid., 1: 406; ibid., 2: 106–07.

[52] The battle and fire at Chicaza on 4 March 1541 left the Spanish devastated. The three eyewitnesses give much lower death totals than Garcilaso: Biedma says thirteen or fourteen were killed; Elvas reports "eleven Christians and fifty horses died," and Rangel records twelve "killed or burned alive." At a conference in 1989, the Mississippi De Soto Trail Commission reached a consensus that Chicaza was probably located in the Tibbee Creek drainage area. Ibid., 1: 108, 237, 298; Hudson, *Knights of Spain*, 260, 475–76.

Captain Juan de Guzmán, a man of delicate form, but of indomitable courage, was seized by the collar by an athletic Indian, who carried a banner, and jerked from his horse. The soldiers, rushing up, cut the bold fellow to pieces. Others dashed after the main body of Indians, and deep revenge would have been taken, if a monk, fearful that they would be led into an ambush, had not arrested the charge by the cry of, "To the camp! To the camp!" Forty Indians fell, two horses were killed, and two soldiers wounded.[53]

On the 25th of April 1541, De Soto marched northwest, through a champaign country, thickly populated, and journeying twelve miles, halted in a plain not far from the town of Alibamo. Juan de Añasco, with a foraging party, came in sight of this fortress, which was garrisoned by a large number of savages, whose bodies were painted in stripes of white, black and red, while their faces were frightfully blackened. Red circles surrounded their eyes. These, with headdresses of feathers and horns, gave them a fantastic and ferocious appearance. The drums sounded alarums, and they rushed out of the fort with fearful whoops, forcing Añasco to retreat to the open fields. The enemy, scorning the inferiority of the detachment, pretended to knock one of the warriors in the head with a club, in front of the fort; and swinging him by the head and the heels near a fire, in insulting mockery, indicated the fate of the Spaniards who should fall into their hands. The irritated Añasco sent three troopers to the camp, who returned with De Soto at the head of a considerable force. The latter assaulted the fortress of the Alibamo, leading on his men in three squadrons, commanded by Guzmán, Avaro Romo de Cardeñosa, and the stout Gonzalo Silvestre. A hundred Alabamas poured out from each portal and met the Spaniards. Upon the first encounter, Diego de Castro, Luis Bravo, and Francisco de Figueroa fell, mortally wounded. An arrow struck the casque of the governor with such force that it made his eyes flash fire.[54]

The victorious Spaniards forced the Alabamas into the fort, pressing them to death by the united shock of cavalry and infantry—the passes of the gates admitting but few of the Indians at once. The soldiers remembered that they had united with the Chickasaws, and they knew no bounds to the revenge which they now sought. In the rear many savages escaped, by climbing over the walls and through the back portals, pitching into the river which ran by the fort, but far below its foundation. In a short time, De Soto held possession of the interior. Alibamo stood upon the Yazoo River, in the county of Tallahatchie.* It was built of palisades, in the form of a quadrangle, four

[53] Elvas claims "thirty or forty" Indians were killed at Chicazilla—Pickett's Chickasilla. Rangel reported an attack on three sides, but the Spaniards "showed themselves very valiant" and "not one failed to do his duty." Garcilaso appears to have used Alonso de Carmona for the details cited by Pickett for the battles at Chickasa (Chicaza) and Chickasilla (Chicazilla). De *Soto Chronicles,* 1: 109, 298; ibid., 2: 368–74.

[54] While Elvas calls the town Alimamu, Rangel records that the expedition "spent the night at Limamu (Alibamo)" and "were looking for corn." Biedma calls the province Alibamo and reports attacking a barricade defended by "about three hundred Indians" on 28 April 1541. Only Garcilaso comments on De Soto's role and the identity of the commanders of the three squadrons. Ibid., 1: 109, 237, 299; ibid., 2: 380–82.

* General Leclerc Milfort, an intelligent Frenchman, lived in the Creek Nation from

hundred paces long on either side. Inner walls divided it into separate parts, enabling the besieged to retreat from one to the other. The centre wall, on the backside, was immediately upon a perpendicular bluff, beneath which flowed a deep and narrow river, across which were thrown a few rude bridges. Portions of the fort appeared to have been recently constructed for defense against the horses. It was decidedly the best fortified place yet discovered, except Mabila, but the garrison was greatly inferior in numbers to that of the latter. The outside portals were too low and narrow for a cavalier to enter on his horse.[55]

De Soto crossed the river at a ford below the plain, and pursued the savages until twilight, leaving many of them in the sleep of death. Four days were consumed at Alibamo in attending to the wounded. Fifteen Spaniards died—among them the cavaliers first wounded, who were young, valiant, and of the best blood of Spain. So terminated the battle of Alibamo, the last one of the many De Soto fought, which it is within our province to describe. We have followed that extraordinary adventurer through our state into the heart of Mississippi. A few more words must close the account of his nomadic march, as far as it rests in our hands.[56]

The Spaniards reached the Mississippi River in May 1541, and were the first to discover it, unless Cabeza de Vaca crossed it twelve years before in wandering to Mexico with his four companions, which is not probable from the evidence afforded by his journal. De Soto consumed a year in marching over Arkansas, and returned to the "Father of Waters," at the town of Guachoya, below the mouth of the Arkansas River, on the last of May 1542. He here engaged in the construction of two brigantines to communicate with Cuba. That great man, whose

1776 until 1799. He wrote a history of the Muscogees or Creeks, and published his work in Paris in 1802. He married the sister of General Alexander McGillivray of the Creek tribe. When he arrived in France, Bonaparte made him a general of brigade, and in 1814 he was attacked in his house by a party of Russians, and rescued by some grenadiers. Shortly afterwards he died. Milfort states that the Alabamas wandered from the northern part of Mexico, and settled upon the Yazoo, and afterwards removed to the river which bears their name. This fact, connected with that of the Alibamo fort, mentioned by the journals of De Soto, establishes conclusively that they were the same people. The Alabamas, after De Soto's time, settled on the site of the modern Montgomery, Coosawda, and Washington, below the confluence of the Coosa and Tallapoosa. From these people the river and state took their name. *Mémoire ou coup d'oeil rapide sur mes différents voyages et mon séjour dans la nation Crëck, par Leclerc de Milfort*, 229–88.

[55] While Pickett locates Alibamo in Tallahatchie County, Mississippi, on the Yazoo River, Charles Hudson and others place Alibamo at alternate sites along the upper tributaries of Tibbee Creek near Lyon's Bluff in Oktibbeha County, Mississippi, or in the Chuquatonchee Creek or Houlka Creek locale in Chickasaw County, Mississippi. Hudson, *Knights of Spain*, 271; David H. Dye, "Reconstruction of the de Soto Expedition Route in Arkansas: The Mississippi alluvial Plain," in *The Expedition of Hernando de Soto West of the Mississippi, 1541–1543: Proceedings of the De Soto Symposia, 1988 and 1990*, ed. Gloria A. Young and Michael P. Hoffman (Fayetteville: University of Arkansas Press, 1999), 40; David Morgan, *The Mississippi De Soto Trail Mapping Project, Archaeological Report No. 26* (Jackson: Mississippi Department of Archives and History, 1996), 3–5.

[56] Biedma reports that they suffered "seven or eight" killed and "twenty-five or twenty-six" wounded in the Battle of Alibamo. While Rangel mentions "some casualties of dead and wounded," Elvas claims that De Soto had many wounded and fifteen of them died over the next few days. *De Soto Chronicles*, 1: 110, 237, 299.

spirits had long since forsaken him—who had met with nothing but disappointments—and who had, in his most perilous wanderings, discovered no country like Peru and Mexico—became sick with a slow and malignant fever. He appointed Moscoso to the command—bid his officers and soldiers farewell—exhorted them to keep together, in order to reach that country which he was destined never to see—and then closed his eyes in death! Thus died Hernando De Soto, one of the most distinguished captains of that or any age. To conceal his death and protect his body from Indian brutalities, he was placed in an oaken trough, and silently plunged into the middle of the Mississippi, on a dark and gloomy night. Long did the muddy waters wash the bones of one of the bravest sons of Spain! He was the first to behold that river—the first to close his eyes in death upon it—and the first to find a grave in its deep and turbid channel.[57]

Moscoso and the remaining troops again plunged into the wilderness west of the Mississippi, with the hope of reaching Mexico. Departing on the 1st of June 1542, he returned on the 1st of December to the Mississippi River, at a point fifty miles above where De Soto died. The Spaniards began the construction of seven brigantines, the building of which required the chains of the slaves, saddle-stirrups, and everything which contained a particle of iron, made into nails by the erection of forges, the Indian mantles stitched together for sails, and the inner bark of trees made into ropes. When these were completed, Governor Moscoso departed down the vast stream, the 2nd of July 1543. The once splendid army of one thousand men was reduced to three hundred and twenty! Five hundred slaves were left at the place of embarkation, and Moscoso took with him one hundred, among others the beautiful women of Mabila. Twenty-two of the best horses were embarked; the others were killed and dried for food, as were the hogs, a large number of which still remained. The Spaniards were attacked, in descending the river, by fleets of Indian canoes. In one of these engagements, the brave Guzman and eleven others were drowned, and twenty-five wounded.[58]

In sixteen days they reached the Gulf, and put to sea on the 18th July 1543. Having landed at Tampa Bay on the 30th of May 1539, they had consumed a little over four years in wandering through Florida, Georgia, Alabama, Mississippi and the vast regions of the Arkansas territory. Tossed by the waves, famished with hunger, parched with thirst, and several times wrecked by tornadoes, the poor Spaniards finally reached the mouth of the river Panuco, upon the Mexican coast,

[57] The expedition made a difficult march across the headwaters of the Yalobusha, Yocona, and Tallahatchie rivers in northwest Mississippi and first sighted the Mississippi River—the *Rio de Espiritu Santo*—between 9 May and 21 May 1541. De Soto ordered his men to cross the Mississippi south of modern Memphis, Tennessee on 18 June in four large piraguas under the command of Juan de Guzmán. The expedition wandered through Arkansas for the next ten months, returning to the Mississippi River in the chiefdom of Guachoya where De Soto died on 21 May 1542. Although he was given a Christian burial, his replacement Luis de Moscoso had his body secretly dug up and deposited in the Mississippi River. Dye, "Reconstruction," 41–44; Hudson, *Knights of Spain*, 345–50; *De Soto Chronicles*, 1: 136–38, 243.

[58] Biedma and Elvas report the meanderings west of the Mississippi, De Soto's death and the events that lead the expedition back to the Mississippi. Prior to his death, De Soto named Luís de Moscoso as his successor who made the decision to turn west to reach Mexico. In October 1542, Moscoso and his captains made the decision to return to the Mississippi where his men built seven boats at Aminoya between December 1542 and June 1543. When they started downriver, their vessels carried 322 Spaniards and a number of Indian slaves. *De Soto Chronicles*, 1: 147–54, 243–45; Hudson, *Knights of Spain*, 349, 373, 381–88.

on the 10th September 1543. From thence they went to the town of Panuco. Appareled in skins of deer, buffalo, bear and other animals—with faces haggard, blackened, shriveled, and but faintly resembling human beings—they repaired to the church and offered up thanks to God for the preservation of their lives. Repairing to the city of Mexico, the viceroy extended to them every hospitality.[59] So did the elegant Castilian ladies of his court, who were enraptured with the beauty of Mabilian females—the high-spirited daughters of Alabama.*

Maldonado, whom we left at Pensacola Bay, awaited, in vain, the arrival of De Soto. He and his distinguished associate, Gómez Arias, at length weighed anchor and sailed along the coast in different directions, hoping to meet the expedition at some point. They left signals upon the trees, and attached letters to the bark. Returning to Cuba, they again sailed in search of De Soto in the summer of 1541, and touched frequently upon the Floridian and Mexican coasts, but heard nothing of him. Again, in the summer of 1542, they made a similar voyage, with no better success. Determined not to give up the search for the lost Spaniards, Maldonado and Arias, in the spring of 1543, departed on a long voyage. On the 15th of October they touched at Vera Cruz, and learned that De Soto had died upon the Mississippi, and that three hundred of his army only had lived to reach Mexico. When this sad intelligence was conveyed to Havana, everyone grieved, and Doña Isabel, long racked with anxiety, died of a broken heart![60]

[59] Elvas reports that 311 arrived at Pánuco, Mexico on 10 September 1543. Ignacio Avellaneda in his 1990 work has accounted for 257 by name through his analysis of the available documents.

[60] De Soto's widow, Doña Isabel de Bobadilla, auctioned off their property in Cuba, returned to Spain in spring 1544, and became involved in a bitter lawsuit with De Soto's former business partner Hernán Ponce de León. While numerous works created the legend that Doña Isabel died shortly after De Soto of a broken heart, more recent studies and Spanish court documents indicate she lived a much longer life, into the 1550s. Hudson, *Knights of Spain,* 414–17; Paul E. Hoffman, "Hernando De Soto: A Brief Biography" in *De Soto Chronicles,* 2: 457; Sherry Johnson, "Introduction: Senores . . . no ordinaries," *Cuban Studies* 34 (2003): 1–4, 8 n.13.

* An interesting account of the expedition, from the battle of Alibamo to their entrance into the city of Mexico, which I have rapidly glanced at, may be found in the Portuguese Narrative, 728–62; Garcilaso de la Vega, 372–557.

Chapter II – Part I

THE ABORIGINES OF ALABAMA AND THE SURROUNDING STATES

The Indians of Alabama, Florida, Georgia, and Mississippi were so similar in form, mode of living and general habits, in the time of De Soto and of others who succeeded him in penetrating these wilds, that they will all be treated, on the pages of this chapter, as one people. Their color was like that of the Indians of our day. The males were admirably proportioned, athletic, active and graceful in their movements, and possessed open and manly countenances. The females, not inferior in form, were smaller, and many of them beautiful. No ugly or ill-formed Indians were seen, except at the town of Tula, west of the Mississippi.[1] Corpulency was rare; nevertheless, it was excessive in a few instances. In the neighborhood of Apalachee, in Florida, the chief was so fat that he was compelled to move about his house upon his hands and knees.[2]

The dress of the men consisted of a mantle of the size of a common blanket, made of the inner bark of trees, and a species of flax, interwoven. It was thrown over the shoulders, with the right arm exposed. One of these mantles encircled the body of the female, commencing below the breast and extending nearly to the knees, while another was gracefully thrown over the shoulders, also with the right arm exposed. Upon the St. John's River, the females, although equally advanced in civilization, appeared in a much greater state of nudity—often with no covering in summer, except a moss drapery suspended round the waist, and which hung down in graceful negligence. Both sexes there were, however, adorned with ornaments, consisting of pretty shells and shining pearls, while the better classes wore moccasins and buskins of dressed deer leather. In Georgia and Alabama the towns contained storehouses, filled with rich and comfortable clothing, such as mantles of hemp, and of feathers of every color, exquisitely arranged, forming admirable cloaks for winter; with a variety of dressed deer skin garments, and skins of the

[1] Garcilaso de la Vega talks about the Indians having been "handsome and graceful" until the Spaniards encountered the Tula, who had "ugly faces" and "deform themselves." Rangel simply writes that the Tula "were the best warriors the Christians came upon . . . with the greatest courage in the world." *De Soto Chronicles*, 1: 305; ibid., 2: 413; Hudson, *Knights of Spain*, 320–26.

[2] Pickett may have misinterpreted Garcilaso, who reports that the "cacique of Apalache"—Capafi—was a cripple and made his escape from his Spanish guards by crawling on his "all fours." *De Soto Chronicles*, 2: 215–26; Hudson, *Knights of Spain*, 142–44.

martin, bear and panther, nicely packed away in baskets.* Fond of trinkets, the natives collected shells from the seaside, and pearls from the beds of the interior rivers. The latter they pierced with heated copper spindles, and strung them around their legs, necks and arms.† The queen upon the Savannah took from her neck a magnificent cordon of pearls, and twined it round the neck of the warlike but courteous De Soto.‡ In the interior of the country, pearls were worn in the ears; but upon the coast, fish bladders, inflated after they had been inserted, were greatly preferred. § The chiefs and their wives, the prophets and principal men, painted their breasts and the front part of their bodies with a variety of stripes and characters.[3] Others, like sea-faring people, had their skins punctured with bone needles and indelible ink rubbed in, which gave them the appearance of being tattooed.¶ Juan Ortiz, so long a prisoner among the Floridians, when discovered by De Soto, was taken for an Indian, on account of his body being "razed" in this manner.** It will be remembered that the Alabamas, upon the Yazoo, painted in stripes of white, yellow, black and red, and "seemed as though they were dressed in hose and doublets."†† Lofty plumes of the feathers of the eagle, and other noted birds, adorned the heads of the warriors. At the Battle of Vitachuco, in Middle Florida, ten thousand warriors appeared in this magnificent native head-dress. They also punished and deformed themselves in the display of their more peculiar ornaments.[4] Upon an island in West Florida, they wore reeds thrust through their nipples and under lips.‡‡ Indian grandees were often seen promenad-

* Portuguese Narrative, 711.

† Portuguese Narrative, 701.

‡ Portuguese Narrative, 714.

§ Le Moyne's Florida plate 38. Renaud de Laudonnière, an admiral of France, made a second voyage to Florida, and landed upon its shore in 1564. Attached to this expedition was a Frenchman, named Jacques Le Moyne, who was an admirable painter. Laudonnière left some soldiers at a fort which he built upon the St. John's, and with them this accomplished artist. Le Moyne was frequently dispatched with small detachments along the coast, and at some distance in the interior, to make surveys of the rivers and to cultivate the friendship of the natives. During these excursions he made admirable drawings of the Indians, their houses, farms, games, amusements, manners, customs and religious ceremonies. Returning to France, he related his adventures to Charles IX, and exhibited to him his pictures. These, with his explanatory notes, were published by Theodore de Bry, in 1591, in the Latin language, at Frankfort. The copy in my possession, a most interesting book upon the ancient Indians of Florida and the adjoining states, contains forty-two plates, a few specimens of which are introduced in this volume.

¶ Le Moyne, plate 38.

**Portuguese Narrative, 702.

†† Portuguese Narrative, 727.

‡‡ Expedition of Narvaez contained in Herrera, *General History of the Vast Continent*

[3] Pickett cited Jacques le Moyne de Morgues as one of his main sources—specifically citing seventeen sketches—in this section of his original Chapter II. He also reproduced six sketches attributed to Le Moyne but actually engraved by Theodore de Bry, based on Le Moyne's watercolors and printed in his *Les Grand Voyages,* a multivolume work published between 1590 and his death in 1598. De Bry published *Brevis narratio eorum quœ in Florida Americœ provincia Gallis acciderunt* in Frankfort in 1591—volume two of ten volumes, most published after his death. This work is based on a narrative written by René Goulaine de Laudonnière and the papers and sketches and/or watercolors of Le Moyne that De Bry purchased from his widow in the 1580s. Pickett purchased a copy of "Le Moyne's Florida Folio" for $9 from Bartlett & Welford in September 1847. See Bartlett & Welford to AJP, New York, 16 September 1847, Albert James Pickett Papers, Alabama Department of Archives and History [Hereafter cited as Pickett Papers, ADAH]; Jacques le Moyne de Morgues, *Brevis narratio eorum quœ in Florida Americœ provincia Gallis acciderunt* (Frankfort: Johann Wechel and Theodor de Bry, 1591); and Miles

Chiefs, with their ornaments and war implements, upon their march against the enemy. Drawn from life by Jacques le Moyne in 1564.

ing, of an evening, enveloped in beautiful mantles of deerskins and of the martin, trailing behind them, and often held up by attendants. Among the prettiest ornaments were flat shells, of varied colors, which they suspended from girdles around their waists, and which hung down around their hips.

The bow, the most formidable weapon of the ancient Indians, was long, elastic, and exceedingly strong. The string was made of the sinews of the deer. The arrows, of strong young cane, hardened before the fire, were often tipped with buck horn, and invariably pointed either with palm or other hard wood, flints, long and sharp like a dagger, fish bones shaped like a chisel, or diamond flints.* The Spaniards soon ascertained that they pierced as deep as those which they themselves shot from the crossbow, and were discharged more rapidly.† The quiver which held them was made of fawn or some other spotted skin, and was cased at the lower end with thick hide of the bear or the alligator. It was always suspended by a leather strap, passing round the neck, which permitted it to rest on the left hip, like a sword. It was capable of holding a great many arrows. Shields were universal appendages in war, and were made of either wood, split canes strongly interwoven, alligator hide, and sometimes that of buffalo. The latter was often the case west of

and Islands of America, 4: 33.

* Garcilaso de la Vega, 266.

† Portuguese Narrative, 102.

Harvey, *Painter in a Savage Land: The Strange Saga of the First European Artist in North America* (New York: Random House, 2008).

[4] Garcilaso seems to be relying on Elvas for certain elements, but he quotes liberally from some remnants of Alonso de Carmona's manuscript that he refers to as his *Peregrination*—an eyewitness account that has been lost for centuries. Biedma refers to Elvas's Vitachuco as Yvitachuco. While Garcilaso writes several pages about the Spanish in Vitachuco, the chroniclers devote no more than a few sentences. *De Soto Chronicles*, 1: 71, 227; ibid., 2: 153–74, 178–83, 208–09.

the Mississippi. Of various sizes, but ordinarily large enough to cover the breast, these round shields were painted with rings and stripes, and suspended from the neck by a band. Sometimes a noted chief protected his breast and a portion of his abdomen with three of them.[5] These, with a piece of bark covering the left arm, to prevent the severe rebound of the bow-string, were all that shielded the natives in time of war. Wooden spears, of the usual length, pointed with excellent darts of fish-bone or flint, were, also, much used. And, strange to say, swords of a palm wood, of the proper shape, were often seen. A chief, in Georgia, seized one of this description, which was borne by one of his servants, and began to cut and thrust with it to the admiration of De Soto and his officers. The war clubs were of two kinds—one, small at the handle, gradually enlarging at the top in oval form; and the other, with two sharp edges at the end, usually employed in executions.[6] Decoration with plumes, appears to have been more common in general costume and pleasant excursions, than in war. In enterprises of the latter character, the natives sought to appear as ferocious as possible. The skins of the eagle, of the wolf and of the panther, with the heads of these animals attached, and well preserved, were worn by warriors, while the talons and claws were inserted as ear ornaments.*

When about to make war, a chief dispatched a party, who approached near the town of the enemy, and by night stuck arrows into the cross-paths and public places, with long locks of human hair waving from them.† After this declaration of war, he assembled his men, who, painted and decorated in the most fantastic and frightful manner, surrounded him on all sides. Excited with seeming anger, he rolled his eyes, spoke in guttural accents, and often sent forth tremendous war whoops. The warriors responded in chorus, and struck their weapons against their sides. With a wooden spear he turned himself reverentially towards the sun, and implored of that luminary victory over his enemies. Turning to his men, he took water from a vessel on his right and sprinkled it about, saying, "Thus may you do with the blood of your enemies." Then raising another vessel of water, he poured its entire contents on a fire which had been kindled on his left, and repeated, "Thus may you destroy your enemies and bring home their scalps."‡ Having marched his army within the vicinity of the enemy, he bid his prophet to inform him of their number and position, and in what manner it was best to bring on the attack. The old man, usually a hundred

* Le Moyne, plates 11, 12, 13, 14.

† Le Moyne, plate 33.

‡ Le Moyne, plate 11.

[5] Pickett seems to be describing the shields worn by the Timucuan Indians in De Bry's rendering of Le Moyne's plate number 14, "Order of March Observed by Outina on a Military Expedition." "Theodor de Bry's Engravings of the Timuca," https://www.floridamemory.com/collections/debry/.

[6] While the bow and arrow was the main weapon of quick strike raids and surprise attacks, the war club was used in close combat and was a symbol of war and masculinity for these Mississippian warriors. Biedma, Elvas, Garcilaso, and Rangel report the use of these weapons in the battles and skirmishes during De Soto's expedition. David H. Dye, "Warfare in the Protohistoric Southeast," in *Between Contacts and Colonies: Archaeological Perspectives on the Protohistoric Southeast,* ed. Cameron B. Wesson and Mark a. Rees (Tuscaloosa: University of Alabama Press, 2002), 128–32.

A chief addressing his warriors, who are armed, painted and plumed, and ready to march against the enemy. Drawn from life by Jacques le Moyne in 1564.

years of age, advanced, and a large circle was immediately formed around him. He placed a shield upon the ground, drew a ring around it five feet in diameter, in which he inscribed various characters. Then kneeling on the shield, and sitting on his feet, so as to touch the earth with no part of his body, he made the most horrible grimaces, uttered the most unnatural howls, and distorted his limbs until his very bones appeared to be flexible. In twenty minutes he ceased his infernal juggling, assumed his natural look, with apparently no fatigue, and gave the chief the information which he desired.* Some of our ancient natives marched in regular order, with the chief in the center, but it was their common habit to scatter in small parties, and take the enemy by surprise.[7] But in the arrangement of their camp, which was always made at sunset, they were exceedingly particular. They then stationed detachments around the chief, forming a compact and well-arranged defense.†

The women who had lost their husbands in battle, at a convenient time surrounded the chief, stooped at his feet, covered their faces with their hands, wept, and implored him to be revenged for the death of their companions. They entreated him to grant them an allowance during their widowhood, and to permit them to marry again when the time appointed by law expired. They afterwards visited the graves of their husbands and

[7] Pickett used the sketches attributed to Le Moyne—plates 11, 12, 13, 14, and 33—in De Bry's *Brevis narration eorum quœ in Florida Americœ provincia Gallis acciderunt* and the Laudonnière-Le Moyne narrative to discuss the Florida Indians—Timucuans—encountered by De Soto's expedition. However, modern scholars question the origin, authenticity, and accuracy of these sketches. See Christiane F. Feest, "Jacques Le Moyne Minus Four," *European Review of Native American Studies* 2, No. 1 (1988): 33–38; Miles Harvey, *Painter in a Savage Land: The Strange Saga of the First European Artist in North America* (New York: Random House, 2008), 84–85.

* Le Moyne, plate 12.
† Le Moyne, plate 14.

deposited upon them the arms which they used in hunts and wars, and the shells out of which they were accustomed to drink. Having cut off their long hair, they sprinkled it also over their graves, and then returned home. They did not marry until it had attained its ordinary length.*

The natives drank a tea, which, in modern times, was called black drink. It was made by boiling the leaves of the cassina plant until a strong decoction was produced. The chief took his seat, made of nine small poles, in the center of a semi-circle of seats; but his was the most elevated of all. His principal officers approached by turns, one at a time, and placing their hands upon the top of their heads, sung "*ha, he, ya, ha, ha*." The whole assembly responded, "*ha, ha*." After which they seated themselves upon his right and left. The women, in the meantime, had prepared the black drink, which was served up in conch shells and handed to certain men, who distributed it around. The warriors drank large portions of it, and presently vomited it with great ease.[8] It seemed to have been used at the early period of 1564, as it is at present, to purify the system, and also to fulfill a kind of religious rite.†

The punishments of that day were summary and cruel. For a crime deserving death, the criminal was conducted to the square and made to kneel with his body inclined forward. The executioner placed his left foot upon his back, and with a murderous blow with the sharp-sided club, dashed out his brains.‡ Juan Ortiz and his companions were stripped naked, and forced to run from corner to corner through the town while the exulting savages shot at them by turns with deadly arrows. Ortiz alone survived, and they next proceeded to roast him upon a wooden gridiron, when he was saved by the entreaties of a noble girl.§ Whenever they made prisoners of each other, those who were captured were often put to menial services.[9] To prevent them from running away, it was customary to cut the nerves of their legs just above the instep.¶

When a battle was fought, the victors seized upon the enemy and mutilated their bodies in the most brutal manner. With cane knives the arms and legs were cut around, and then severed from the body by blows upon the bones, from wooden cleavers. They thus amputated with great skill and rapidity. The head was also cut around, with these knives, just above the ears, and the whole scalp jerked off. These were then rapidly smoked over a fire, kindled in a small round hole, and borne off in triumph toward home, together with

* Le Moyne, plate 19.
† Le Moyne's Florida, plate 29.
‡ Le Moyne's Florida, plate 32.
§ Garcilaso de la Vega.
¶ Garcilaso de la Vega.

[8] The cassina tea or black drink was produced from roasted leaves of the yaupon holly and was used widely among southeastern Indians. Scholars generally agree that the Indians used it for three purposes: as a stimulating drink with a high caffeine content; as a medicine to improve their well-being; and as an emetic to induce vomiting. The most common ceremonial shell cup used has been identified as a lightning whelk (i.e., *Busycon perversum*). Charles M. Hudson, ed., *Black Drink: A Native American Tea* (Athens: University of Georgia Press, 1979), 1–5; Jerald T. Milanich, "Origins and Prehistoric Distribution of Black Drink and the Ceremonial Shell Drinking Cup," Ibid., 83–88.

[9] While Biedma and Rangel provide no details of Juan Ortiz's captivity, Elvas gives considerable insights on his lengthy imprisonment. Garcilaso romanticizes his captivity and embellishes it with his killing "a lion"—maybe a wolf or panther but not a lion. He gives credit to Alonso de Carmona as his source for details of Ortiz's story. *De Soto Chronicles,* 1: 60–62, 225, 255; ibid., 2: 102–19; *De Soto Chronicles,* 80–82.

Indians engaged in scalping and cutting up the enemy. Drawn from life by Jacques le Moyne in 1564.

the arms and legs, suspended upon spears.* The joyous and excited inhabitants now assembled upon the square and formed a large area, in which these trophies were hung upon high poles. An old prophet took a position on one side of the circle, held in his hand a small image of a child, and danced and muttered over it a thousand imprecations upon the enemy.[10] On the other side, and opposite to him, three warriors fell upon their knees. One of them, who was in the middle, constantly brought down a club, with great force, on a smooth stone, placed before him, while the others, on either side of him, rattled gourds filled with shells and pebbles, all keeping time with the prophet.†

The houses of the chiefs, with but few exceptions, stood upon large and elevated artificial mounds. When the Indians of 1540 resolved to build a town, the site of which was usually selected upon low, rich land, by the side of a beautiful stream, they were accustomed, first, to turn their attention to the erection of a mound from twenty to fifty feet high, round on the sides, but flat on top. The top was capable of sustaining the houses of the chief, and those of his family and attendants; making a little village by itself of from ten to twenty cabins, elevated high in the air. The earth to make this mound was brought to the spot. At the foot of this eminence a square was marked out, around which the principal men placed their houses. The inferior classes joined these with their wigwams. Some of these mounds had several stairways

[10] Pickett's description of the mutilated bodies of the Timucuans defeated enemies and the antics of the prophet are drawn from the De Bry renderings of Le Moyne's sketches and/or watercolors and the Laudonnière-Le Moyne narrative from the French colonizing effort in 1564—1565. De Bry, *Brevis narration eorum quæ in Florida Americæ provincia Gallis acciderunt*; Charles E. Bennett, *Laudonniere & Fort Caroline: History and Documents* (Gainesville: University Presses of Florida, 1964), 22–32.

* Le Moyne, plate 15.
† Le Moyne, plate 16.

to ascend them, made by cutting out incline-planes fifteen or twenty feet wide, flanking the sides with posts, and laying poles horizontally across the earthen steps—thus forming a kind of wooden stairway. But, generally, the lofty residence of the chief was approached by only one flight of steps. These mounds were perpendicular, and inaccessible, except by the avenues already mentioned, which rendered the houses upon them secure from the attacks of an Indian enemy.[11] Besides the motive for security, a disposition to place the chief and his family in a commanding position, and to raise him above his subjects, caused the formation of these singular elevations.*

Upon the coasts of Florida, the houses were built of timber, covered with palm leaves, and thatched with straw. Those of Toa, between Apalachee and the Savannah, and for some distance beyond, were covered with reeds in the manner of tiles, while the walls were extremely neat. In the colder regions of the territories of Georgia, Alabama and Mississippi, every family possessed a house daubed inside and out with clay, for a winter house, and another, open all around, for summer; while a crib and kitchen, also, stood nearby. The houses of the chiefs, much larger than the others, had piazzas in front, in the rear of which were cane benches of comfortable dimensions.[12] They contained, also, lofts, in which were stored skins, mantles, and corn, the tribute of the subjects.† Upon the headwaters of the Coosa, it will be recollected, that De Soto found the house of a chief standing upon a mound, with a piazza in front, "large enough for six men to promenade abreast."‡ The town of Ochile, in Middle Florida, contained fifty very substantial houses.[13] The chief's house was built in the form of a large pavilion, upwards of one hundred and twenty feet in length by forty in width, with a number of small buildings, connected like offices.§ Narvaez found a house large enough to contain three hundred men, in which were fishing nets and a tabor with gold bells.¶ The Indian grandeur and spacious dimensions of the houses of Mabila, in Alabama, have already been described. In the province of Palisema, west of the Mississippi,[14] the house of the chief was covered with deerskins, which were painted with stripes of various colors, and with animals, while the walls were hung, and the floor carpeted, with the same materials.**

In the first town which De Soto discovered, at Tampa Bay, was found a

* Garcilaso de la Vega, 136.

† Portuguese Narrative, 701.

‡ Garcilaso de la Vega, 294.

§ Garcilaso de la Vega, 101.

¶ Herrera, vol. 4.

** Portuguese Narrative.

[11] From their earliest contacts, the De Soto expedition encountered elevated artificial mounds with a chief's house and other structures that housed his extended family, retainers and guards. The De Soto chroniclers reported that the chiefdoms had mound and town centers that were often palisaded to provide for defense. Hudson, *Knights of Spain*, 69, 126, 162, 290–91.

[12] While Pickett uses Toalli from Elvas's writings, Rangel refers to the river and town as Toa which is the name used by modern scholars. Rangel reports that Toa was a large town, and more recent researchers locate Toa in the upper Flint River watershed. *De Soto Chronicles*, 1: 75–77, 269–70; Hudson, *Knights of Spain*, 152–57, 468, 475, 480.

[13] Pickett continues to rely on Garcilaso's narrative, which misplaced Vitachuco and Ochile, belonging to the Apalachee province—not the Timucuan chiefdom. Garcilaso's Ochile is the equivalent of Biedma's Aguacalecuen, Elvas's Caliquen, and Rangel's Aguacaleyguen. *De Soto Chronicles*, 1: 66–67, 189 n.76, 226, 263–65; ibid., 2: 153–57, 153 n. 4; John H. Hann, "De Soto, Dobyns, and Demography in Western Timucua," *Florida Anthropologist* 43 (March 1990): 5–6.

large temple, on the top of which was a wooden bird with gilded eyes.* The chief, Ucita, made Juan Ortiz keeper of the temple, situated in a lonely forest in the outskirts of the town. In this temple were deposited dead Indians, contained in wooden boxes, the lids of which, having no hinges, were kept down with weights.[15] The bodies and bones were sometimes carried off by panthers and wolves. In this horrible place was poor Ortiz stationed to watch, day and night, and threatened with instant death if he allowed a single body to be taken away. At length, constant anxiety and fatigue overcame him, and one night he fell asleep. The heavy falling of a coffin-lid awoke him. In his terror he seized a bow, and running out, heard the crackling of bones amid a dark clump of bushes! He winged a powerful arrow in that direction. A scuffle ensued, and then all was still! He moved towards the spot, and found an enormous panther, dead, by the side of the body of the child of a principal Indian. He replaced the latter in its box, exultingly dragged the animal into the town, and was from that time respected by the Indians.†

Narvaez, upon first landing in Florida, found a temple in which were chests, each containing a dead body, covered with painted deerskins. The commissary, Juan Xuárez,[16] considering it to be idolatrous, ordered them to be burned.‡ A remarkable temple was situated in the town of Talimeco, upon the Savannah River, three miles distant from Cofitachequi, now Silver Bluff. It was more than one hundred feet in length, and forty in width. The walls were high in proportion, and the roof steep and covered with mats of split cane, interwoven so compactly that they resembled the rush carpeting of the Moors. (The inhabitants of this part of the country all covered their houses with this matting.) Shells of different sizes, arranged in an ingenious manner, were placed on the outside of the roof. On the inside, beautiful plumes, shells and pearls were suspended in the form of festoons, from one to the other, down to the floor. The temple was entered by three gates, at each of which were stationed gigantic wooden statues, presenting fierce and menacing attitudes. Some of them were armed with clubs, maces, canoe-paddles, and copper hatchets, and others with drawn bows and long pikes. All these implements were ornamented with rings of pearls and bands of copper. Below the ceiling, on four sides of the temple, arranged in niches, were two rows of wooden statues of the natural size—one of men, with pearls suspended from their hands, and the other of women.[17]

On the side of the walls were large benches on which sat boxes containing

* Portuguese Narrative, 701.

† Garcilaso de la Vega, 274–82.

‡ Herrera, 4: 30.

[14] While Elvas uses Palisema and describes the interior of the cacique's house, Rangel calls this village Palisma and reports they reached it on Thursday, 8 September 1541. *De Soto Chronicles,* 1: 123, 208 n. 209, 304.

[15] Pickett and Garcilaso retell the Ortiz captivity saga based largely on Elvas's *La Florida.* While Rangel uses Oçita, modern scholars use variations of the spelling of Ucita, including Ecita, Ocita, and Uzita. *De Soto Chronicles,* 1: 57–61, 186 n. 48, 186 n. 51, 254; Ethridge, *From Chicaza to Chickasaw,* 53–54.

[16] Father Juan Xuárez served as commissary with the expedition led by Pánfilo de Narváez in 1527–1528. Alvar Núñez Cabeza de Vaca, *Chronicle of the Narváez Expedition,* trans. Fanny Bandelier; revised trans. Harold Augenbraum (1905; reprint, New York: Penguin Books, 2002), 14.

[17] Talimeco was part of the chiefdom of Cofitachequi in the vicinity of Camden, South Carolina—not near Augusta, Georgia, on the Savannah River. Rangel reports the "temple or oratory" contained breastplates, corselets, helmets, and "good shields," all made from "hides of cows." He was impressed with the "caney or house of the cacique" which was covered

the deceased chiefs and their families. Two feet below these were statues of the persons entombed, the space between them being filled with shields of various sizes, made of strong woven reeds, adorned with pearls and colored tassels. Three rows of chests, full of valuable pearls, occupied the middle of the temple. Deerskins, of a variety of colors, were packed away in chests, together with a large amount of clothing made of the skins of wildcat, martin, and other animals.[18] The temple abounded in the most splendid mantles of feathers. Adjoining was a store-house, divided into eight apartments, which contained long pikes of copper, around which rings of pearls were coiled, while clubs, maces, wooden swords, paddles, arrows, quivers, bows, round wooden shields, and those of reeds and buffalo hide, were decorated in like manner.* Everywhere upon the route through Alabama and the neighboring states, De Soto found the temples full of human bones. They were held sacred, but sometimes were wantonly violated by tribes at war with each other. On the west bank of the Mississippi, De Soto, joined by the Indian forces of the chief Casqui, sacked the town of Pacaha. The invading Indians entered the temple, threw down the wooden boxes containing the dead, trampled upon the bodies and bones, and wreaked upon them every insult and indignity.[19] A few days after the chief of Pacaha and his people came back to the ruined town, and gathering up the scattered bones in mournful silence, kissed and returned them reverentially to their coffins.†

The productions of the country were abundant. Peas, beans, squashes, pumpkins and corn grew as if by magic. Persimmons, formed into large cakes, were eaten in winter, together with walnut and bear's oil. A small pumpkin, when roasted in the embers, was delightful, and resembled, in taste, boiled chestnuts. Corn was pounded in mortars, but Narvaez saw stones for grinding it upon the Florida coast.‡ The Indians prepared their fields by digging up the ground with hoes made of fish bone. When the earth was leveled in this manner, others followed with canes, with which they made holes, certain distances apart. The women next came with corn, in baskets, which they dropped in the holes. The virginity and richness of the soil produced the crop without further labor. [See Frontispiece.] The granaries were sometimes erected in the woods, near navigable streams, and were constructed with stone and dirt, and covered with cane mats. Here were deposited corn, fruits, and all kinds of cured meat, for subsistence during the winter hunts in that part of the country. The universal honesty of the people was a guarantee that the

* Garcilaso de la Vega, 274–82.

† Portuguese Narrative, 701.

‡ Herrera, 4: 30.

with excellent and beautiful mats. Unlike Garcilaso, Rangel does not mention the wooden statutes in the temple or that Talimeco had been deserted due to a "recent pestilence." *De Soto Chronicles,* 1: 195 n. 118, 280; ibid., 2: 298–304; Hudson, *Knights of Spain,* 178–79.

[18] Elvas provides some additional details of the temple at Talimeco, and he also shares that "two years ago there had been a plague in the land." However, Garcilaso's detailed description here is based on his access to the lost works of Alonso de Carmona, Juan Coles, and an anonymous source—possibly Captain Gonzalo Silvestre. *De Soto Chronicles,* 1: 83, 406; Hudson, *Knights of Spain,* 178–79.

[19] The chiefdom of Casqui was located on the St. Francis River in Arkansas some twenty miles northwest of modern Memphis, Tennessee. The province of Pacaha and its principal town was located on Wapanocca Bayou, about twenty miles north of Memphis, in Crittenden County, Arkansas. Biedma and Rangel report that that these two chiefdoms were bitter enemies and often at war. Biedma describes Pacaha as "well palisaded and with a moat of water around it." Ethridge, *From Chicaza to Chickasaw,* 118; *De Soto Chronicles,* 1: 238,

Indians preparing meats to be deposited in their winter hunt houses. Drawn from life by Jacques le Moyne in 1564.

contents of these granaries would remain undisturbed, until consumed by the owners.[20]

Hunting and fishing occupied much of the time of the natives. The hunter threw over his body the skin of a deer, with the head, horns and legs admirably preserved. Round wooden hoops gave the body of the skin its proper shape, inside of which the Indian placed his body. Then, in a stooping position, so as to allow the feet to touch the ground, he moved along and peeped through the eye-holes of the deer's head, all the time having a drawn bow. When near enough to the deer, he let fly a fatal arrow.[21] The deer, in that day, unaccustomed to the noise of firearms, were gentle and numerous, and easily killed by a stratagem like this.*

At certain periods the Indians were a social people, and indulged in large feasts. At other times, they resorted to bow-shooting, ball-plays and dancing.†

The population was much greater when De Soto was in the country than it has been since. Large armies were frequently arrayed against him. In Patofa, Florida, he was even furnished with seven hundred burden bearers. In Ocute, Georgia, he was supplied with two hundred of these indispensable men. At Cofaqui, in the same state, four thousand warriors escorted him, while four thousand more transported the effects of his army. It has been seen what a

* Le Moyne's Florida, plate 25; Bossu, *Travels Through That Part of North America Formerly Called Louisiana*, 1: 259.

† Le Moyne, plate 28.

241, 301; Hudson, *Knights of Spain*, 293–95, 298–303.

[20] From Florida to the Mississippi River Valley, the De Soto chroniclers talk less about the farming techniques of the Mississippian peoples and more about the variety of foods and the abundance or lack of corn—maize. Elvas reported that the town of Coligua along the White River in Arkansas had such an abundance of "maize" that they threw out the old "in order to store the new." He also wrote that the beans and pumpkins were superior to those in Spain. *De Soto Chronicles*, 1: 81, 95, 122–23, 241, 304; Hudson, *Knights of Spain*, 123–24, 127, 315.

[21] Pickett's description of the stalking of deer comes directly from De Bry's rendering of a sketch or watercolor attributed to Jacques le Moyne. See plate number XXV in De Bry, *Brevis narration*.

numerous population was found in the province of Coosa, and what forces opposed him at Mabila, Chicaza and Alibamo.[22]

The ingenuity of the natives, displayed in the construction of mounds, arms, houses and ornaments, was by no means inconsiderable. At Chaguate, west of the Mississippi, earthenware was manufactured equal to that of Estremoz or Montemor.* At Tula, in Arkansas, salt was made from the deposits formed upon the shores of a lake; and again, at several saline springs.[23] The salt was made into small cakes, and vended among other tribes for skins and mantles.† The walls which surrounded the towns, with their towers and terraces, have already been mentioned in the preceding chapter. Entrenchments and ditches were also found over the country. The most remarkable of the latter was at Pacaha, west of the Mississippi. Here a large ditch, "wide enough for two canoes to pass abreast without the paddles touching," surrounded a walled town. It was cut nine miles long, communicated with the Mississippi, supplied the natives with fish and afforded them the privileges of navigation.[24]

The construction of canoes and barges, connected with the things which have already been enumerated, affords abundant proof that our aborigines were superior, in some respects, to the tribes who afterwards occupied Alabama, but who were also ingenious in the manufacture of articles. The queen of Savannah, borne out of her house in a sedan chair, supported upon the shoulders of four of her principal men, entered a handsome barge which had a tilted top at the stern—under which she took a seat upon soft cushions. Many principal Indians likewise entered similar barges, and accompanied her to the western side, in the style of a splendid water procession.[25] When De Soto first discovered the Mississippi, a chief approached from the other side with two hundred handsome canoes of great size, filled with painted and plumed warriors, who stood erect, with bows in their hands, to protect those who paddled. The boats of the chiefs and principal men had tops—like that of the Georgia queen—decorated with waving flags and plumes, which floated on the breeze from poles to which they were attached.[26] They are described by the journalists to have been equal to a beautiful army of galleys.‡

The natives worshipped the sun, and entertained great veneration for the moon, and certain stars. Whether they also believed in a Great

* Portuguese Narrative and Garcilaso.

† Portuguese Narrative and Garcilaso.

‡ Portuguese Narrative, 729.

[22] The De Soto expedition seized or requisitioned burden bearers or *tamemes*—loosely translated as porters or "carriers of loads on their backs"—from Florida to Arkansas. Pickett seems to have transposed some information, and the four thousand burden bearers cannot be documented by the De Soto chroniclers. Elvas records that the cacique of Ocute provided four hundred *tamemes* and the caciques at Ulibahali and Tallise gave the "necessary *tamemes*." Biedma reports that the cacique of Cofaqui "provided eight hundred Indians to carry our food and cloths" and others to serve as guides. *De Soto Chronicles*, 1: 77, 94–95, 194 n. 110, 229, 273.

[23] Not only did the people of Chaguate produce pottery of "refined clay," but Elvas reported that they presented the expedition with "a rich gift of blankets and skins." Both Elvas and Rangel report the Spaniards produced an abundance of salt at Tula, near modern Fort Smith, Arkansas. Ibid., 1: 140–41,149, 209 n. 213, 305; Hudson, *Knights of Spain*, 353–58.

[24] Biedma and Rangel confirm Elvas's description of Pacaha. Biedma notes that the town was heavily palisaded and surrounded by a moat "dug by hand." Rangel provides a more detailed comment, declaring Pacaha "very well palisaded, with towers on the walls, and with a ditch roundabout, and most filled with water, which enters through an irrigation ditch that flows from the river [Mississippi]." *De Soto Chronicles*, 1: 117–18, 239, 301; Hudson, *Knights of Spain*,

Spirit is not stated. When the Indian ambassadors crossed the Savannah to meet De Soto, they made three profound bows towards the east, intended for the sun; three towards the west, for the moon; and three to the governor.* Upon the east bank of the Mississippi, all the Indians approached him without uttering a word, and went through precisely the same ceremony; making, however, to him three bows much less reverential than those made to the sun and moon. On the other side of that river, he was surrounded by the chief and his subjects. Presently, his Indian majesty sneezed in a loud manner. The subjects bowed their heads, opened and closed their arms, and saluted the chief with these words, "may the sun guard you"—"may the sun be with you"—"may the sun shine upon you"—and "may the sun prosper and defend you."† About the first of March, annually, the natives selected the skin of the largest deer, with the head and legs attached. They filled it with a variety of fruit and grain, and sewed it up again. The horns were also hung with garlands of fruit. This skin, in all respects resembling a large buck, was carried by all the inhabitants to a plain. There it was placed upon a high post, and just at the rising of the sun, the Indians fell down on their knees around it, and implored that bright luminary to grant them, the ensuing season, an abundance of fruits and provisions, as good as those contained in the skin of the deer.‡ This was the practice upon the coast of East Florida, and, doubtless, it was observed all over the country. It was certainly a very practical mode of asking favors of the sun.

When a chief or prophet died upon the St. John, he was placed in the ground, and a small mound, of conical form, was erected over him. The base of this mound was surrounded with arrows, stuck in regular order. Some sat, and others kneeled around it, and continued to weep and howl for the space of three nights. Chosen women next visited the mound for a long time, every morning at the break of day, at noon, and at night.§ Indeed, great respect appears to have been paid to the chief when alive, and to him a cruel sacrifice was accustomed to be made. The first born male child was always brought out before the chief, who sat upon a bench on one side of a large circle. Before him was a block, two feet high, and near it stooped the young mother, weeping in great agony. The child was brought forward by a dancing woman, placed upon

* Garcilaso de la Vega, 256.

† Garcilaso de la Vega, 439–40.

‡ Le Moyne, plate 35.

§ Le Moyne, plate 40.

293–95.

[25] The De Soto chroniclers referred to Pickett's "queen of Savannah" as the "La Senora of Cofitachequi"—the Lady of Cofitachequi. At one point in his narrative, Rangel talks about De Soto's greed and how he wanted more than the "queen or cacica of Cofitachequi, lady of Talimeco, offered him." Garcilaso compares the meeting between De Soto and the Lady of Cofitachequi with when Cleopatra received Marc Antony on the "River Cydnus in Cilicia . . . though inferior in grandeur and majesty." More recent research places Cofitachequi in the valley of the Congaree-Broad River basin in South Carolina and near Columbia, South Carolina. *De Soto Chronicles,* 1: 82–83, 195 n. 118, 229, 290; ibid., 284–86; Hudson, *Knights of Spain,* 175.

[26] Elvas refers to the "great lord of Aquixo" who arrived with the "two hundred canoes full of Indians" with bows and arrows and shields to protect the paddlers. Although De Soto, walking along the bluff of the Mississippi, invited the cacique to land, he only sent three canoes to deliver fish "and loaves made of the pulp of plums in the shape of bricks." Rangel reports a confrontation on the Mississippi, but he does not mention Elvas's "beautiful galleys." The Spaniards finished their piraguas during their thirty-day stay south of Memphis and then crossed the Mississippi into Arkansas. *De Soto Chronicles,* 1: 111–13; 2: 389–90; Hudson, *Knights of Spain,* 284–87.

Indians bearing, in a chair, a young girl, who has been selected as one of the future wives of the king. Drawn from life by Jacques le Moyne in 1564.

the block, and a prophet dashed out its brains with a club; at the same time many females danced, and raised their voices in song.*

If a chief desired to marry, he was accustomed to send his principal men to select, from the girls of nobility, one of the youngest and most beautiful. Painted with various colors and adorned with shells and pearls, the chosen one was then placed in a sedan chair, the top of which formed an arch of green boughs. When placed by his side, on an elevated seat, great pomp and ceremony, an array of ornaments of all kinds, and music and dancing, characterized the affair, while she and her lord were fanned with beautiful feathers.

The treatment of diseases in that day were few and simple. The doctor sometimes scarified the patient with shells and fishes teeth, and sucked out the blood with his mouth. This he spurted in a bowl, and it was drunk by nursing women who stood by, if the patient was an athletic young man, in order to give their children the same vigor. It was customary, also, to smoke the patient with tobacco, and other weeds, until perspiration ensued and re-action was produced.†

* Le Moyne, plate 34.
† Le Moyne, plate 20.

Chapter II – Part II

THE MODERN INDIANS OF ALABAMA, GEORGIA AND MISSISSIPPI

It has been seen that the Indians living in that part of Alabama through which De Soto passed, were the Coosas, inhabiting the territory embraced in the present counties of Benton, Talladega, Coosa, and a portion of Cherokee; the Tallassee, living upon the Tallapoosa and its tributary streams; the Mabilians, extending from near the present city of Montgomery to the commercial emporium which now bears their name; the Pafallayas or Choctaws, inhabiting the territory of the modern counties of Greene, Marengo, Tuscaloosa, Sumter and Pickens; and, in the present state of Mississippi, the Chickasaws, in the valley of the Yalobusha; and the Alabamas, upon the Yazoo. It will, also, be recollected, that this remarkable Spaniard overrun the rich province of Chiaha, the territory of the present northwestern Georgia, and that he there found the Chalaques, which all writers upon aboriginal history decide to be the original name of the Cherokees.[1]

The invasion of De Soto resulted in the destruction of an immense Indian population, in all the territory through which he passed, except that of Georgia, where he fought no battles. The European diseases, which the natives inherited from the Spaniards, served, also, to thin their population. Again, the constant bloody wars in which they were engaged afterwards, among each other, still further reduced their numbers. And while the bloody Spaniards were wandering over this beautiful country, the Muscogees were living upon the Ohio.* They heard of the desolation of Alabama, and after

* Alexander McGillivray, whose blood was Scotch, French, and Indian, who was made a colonel in the British service, afterwards a Spanish Commissary with the rank and pay of colonel, then a brigadier general by Washington, with full pay—a man of towering intellect and vast information, and who ruled the Creek country for a quarter of a century—obtained the information that the Creeks were living upon the Ohio when De Soto was here in 1540. He was informed, upon the best traditional authority, that the Creek Indians then

[1] More recent archaeological, ethnographical, and historical data and studies question the presence of the Cherokee in their historic homeland prior to 1600. The name Chalaque was applied to a province encountered by De Soto's expedition, and its origin is probably from a Muskogean word—*tciloki* or "Chilokee"—meaning "people of another language." Thomas M. N. Lewis and Madeline D. Kneberg Lewis, *The Prehistory of the Chickamauga Basin in Tennessee*, comp. and ed. Lynne P. Sullivan, 2 vols. (Knoxville: University of Tennessee Press, 1995), 1: 247–48; John R. Swanton, *The Indians of the Southeastern United States*, Bureau of American Ethnology, Smithsonian Institution, *Bulletin 137* (Washington: GPO, 1946), 46, 217.

a long time came to occupy and re-people it. The remarkable migration of this powerful tribe, and that of the Alabamas, will now, for the first time, be related, and that, too, upon the authority of a reliable person, who must here be introduced to the reader.[2]

Le Clerc Milfort, a young, handsome, and well educated Frenchman, left his native country, sailed across the Atlantic, made the tour of the New England states, and came, at length, to Savannah. A love of adventure led him to the Creek Nation, and in May, 1776, he arrived at the great town of Coweta, situated on the Chattahoochee River, two miles below the present city of Columbus. There he became acquainted with Colonel McGillivray, the great chieftain of the nation, and accompanied him to the Hickory Ground, upon the banks of the Coosa. Fascinated with the society of this great man, the hospitality of the Indians, and the wide field afforded for exciting enterprise, Milfort resolved to become a permanent inmate of McGillivray's house, then situated at Little Tallassee, four miles above Wetumpka. He married his sister, was created Tustenuggee, or Grand Chief of War, and often led Indian expeditions against the Whig population of Georgia, during the American Revolution. A fine writer, and much of an antiquarian, he employed some of his leisure hours in preparing a history of the Creeks. Remaining in the nation twenty years, he resolved to return to France.[3] In 1796 he sailed from Philadelphia, and it was not long before he was among the gay people from whom he had so long been absent. Bonaparte, at length, heard of this adventurous man, and honored him with an audience. He desired to engage his services in forming alliances with the Alabama and Mississippi Indians, for the purpose of strengthening his Louisiana possessions. But, finally giving up these possessions, and turning his whole attention to the wars in which he was deeply engaged with the allied powers, he still retained Milfort, conferring upon him the pay and rank of general of brigade, but without active employment. In the meantime, General Milfort had published his work upon the Creek Indians.* In 1814 his home was attacked by a party of Russians, who had heard of his daring exploits in assisting to repel the allied invaders. He barricaded it, and defended himself with desperation. His French wife assisted him to load his guns. At length he was rescued by a troop of grenadiers. Shortly after this, General Milfort closed, by death, a career which had been full of event in

heard of De Soto, and the strange people with him; and that, like those whom they had seen in Mexico, they had "hair over their bodies, and carried thunder and lightning in their hands."

* Leclerc Milfort, *Mémoire, ou coup d'oeil rapide sur mes différents voyages et mon séjour dans la nation Crëck et général de brigade au service de la République Française* (Paris: Giguet et Michaud, 1802).

[2] The eighteenth century societies of the Cherokee, Chickasaw, Choctaw, Creeks or Muscogees emerged out of the collapse of the Mississippian chiefdoms caused by the encounters with the early Spanish explorers and subsequent European expeditions, colonization, and disease—the "Columbian exchange." See Robbie Ethridge, *Creek Country: The Creek Indians and Their World* (Chapel Hill: University of North Carolina Press, 2003), 22–31; Charles Hudson, *The Southeastern Indians* (Knoxville: University of Tennessee Press, 1976), 90–119.

[3] Although born as Jean Antoine Le Clerc (1752–1820), he used several alternatives and aliases during his lifetime, including Jean Leclerc Milfort, Louis Le Clerc Milfort, and Louis Milfort—and on occasion signed his name as Milford. After returning to France in 1796, he married Marie-Anne Beya and published his memoirs in 1802, which according to Darius Alexander Spieth were written by a ghostwriter. Darius Alexander Spieth, *Napoleon's Sorcerers: The Sophisians* (Plainsboro Township, NJ: Associated University Press, 2007), 153–54.

[4] The name Muscogee or Muscogees is the name used by the modern Creek

the savage as well as the civilized world. His wife, at an advanced age, was recently burned to death in her own house at Reims.*

When Milfort arrived among the Creeks, the old men often spoke of their ancestors, and they exhibited to him strands of pearls which contained their history and constituted their archives. Upon their arrangement depended their signification, and only principal events were thus preserved. One of their chaplets sometimes related the history of thirty years. Each year was rapidly distinguished by those who understood them. The old men, therefore, with the assistance of these singular records and strong memories, were enabled to impart to Milfort a correct tradition, the substance of which we give.† Hernando Cortez, with some Spanish troops, landed at Veracruz in 1519. He fought his way thence to the city of Mexico. In the meantime, Montezuma had assembled his forces from all parts of his empire to exterminate the invaders. The Muscogees then formed a separate republic on the northwest of Mexico.[4] Hitherto invincible in war, they now rallied to his aid, engaging in the defense of that greatest of aboriginal cities. At length Cortez was successful—Montezuma was killed, his government overthrown, and thousands of his subjects put to the sword. Having lost many of their own warriors, and unwilling to live in a country conquered by foreign assassins, the Muscogees determined to seek some other land. The whole tribe took up the line of march, and continued eastward until they struck the sources of the Red River. The route lay over vast prairies, abounding with wild animals and fruits, which afforded them all the means of subsistence. In journeying down the banks of the Red River, they discovered salt lakes and ponds, which were covered with fowl of every description. Consuming months upon the journey, they finally reached a large forest, in which they encamped. The young men, sent in advance to explore the country, returned in a month, and announced the discovery of a forest on the banks of the Red River, in which were beautiful subterranean habituations. Marching thither, they found these caves had been made by buffalos and other animals who came there to lick the earth, which was impregnated with salt. A town was here laid out, houses constructed, an extensive field enclosed, and corn, which they had brought with them, planted. Subsisting by the chase and the products of the earth, they passed here several years in health and tranquility. But even in this remote retreat they eventually found those who would molest them.[5]

The Alabamas, who seem also to have been wandering from the west,

* Extract from a Paris paper, published by Galignani.

† Milfort, 47.

or Muscogee Nation of Oklahoma to identify its polity and its citizens. It was not generally used to identify a particular tribe, province or chiefdom from the Mississippian era to the modern era. Linguistically the historic Creek or Muscogee spoke a variant of Muskogean, but there were non-Muskogean speakers who coalesced into the Creek or Muscogee Confederacy in the historic period. In addition, none of these native people of Alabama and Georgia called themselves Creeks, but it was a synecdochial figure of speech used by English traders to identify the American Indians on the western borders of South Carolina and Georgia. Ethridge, *Creek Country*, 21–31; Joel W. Martin, *Sacred Revolt: The Muskogees' Struggle for a New World* (Boston: Beacon Press, 1991), 6–8; Claudio Saunt, *A New Order of Things: Property, Power, and the Transformation of the Creek Indians, 1733–1816* (Cambridge, UK: Cambridge University Press, 1999), 13–14.

[5] Modern scholarship questions much of the migration legend of the Muscogees related by Louis Milfort and subsequent writers. The people of the Muscogee or Creek Confederacy in the eighteenth century did not refer to themselves as Muscogees

attacked a party of Muscogees, who were hunting, and killed several of them. The Muscogees abandoned their town, which they believed did not afford them sufficient protection from the buffalo and human foes. They resumed their march in the direction of the camps of the Alabamas, upon whom they had resolved to be revenged. Traversing immense plains, they reached a grove on the Missouri River, having shaped their course in a northern direction from their last settlement. Here they came upon the footprints of the Alabamas. The most aristocratic among the Muscogees, called the family of the Wind, passed the muddy river first. They were followed by the family of the Bear; then by that of the Tiger; and thus, till the humblest of the tribe had crossed over. Resuming the march, the young warriors and the chiefs formed the advanced guard; the old men were placed in the rear, and those of an age less advanced on the flanks, while the women and children occupied the center. Coming within the neighborhood of the enemy, the main party halted, while the Tustenuggee, or Grand Chief of War, at the head of the young warriors, advanced to the attack.[6] The Alabamas, temporarily dwelling in subterranean habitations, were taken by surprise, and many of them slain. Forced to abandon this place, and retreat from the victors, they did not rally again until they had fled a great distance down on the eastern side of the Missouri. After a time they were overtaken, when several bloody engagements ensued.

The Muscogees were triumphant, and the vanquished retreated in terror and dismay to the banks of the Mississippi. The enemy again coming upon them with invincible charges, precipitated many of them into the river. Thus, alternately fighting, constructing new towns, and again breaking up their last establishments, these two war-like tribes gradually reached the Ohio River, and proceeded along its banks almost to the Wabash.* Here, for a long time, the Muscogees resided, and lost sight of the Alabamas, who had established themselves upon the Yazoo, and were there living when De Soto, in 1541, attacked their fortress.† The Muscogees abandoned their home in the northwestern province of Mexico about the period of 1520, had consumed fifteen years in reaching the Ohio, and were there residing when the Spanish invasion occurred. How long they occupied that country Milfort does not inform us; but he states that they finally crossed the Ohio and Tennessee, and settled upon the Yazoo—thus continuing to pursue the unfortunate Alabamas. Delighted with the genial climate, the abundance of

* Milfort, 234–59.

† Other Indian traditions in my possession.

or Creeks. Instead they considered themselves as Alabamas, Chehaws, Coosas, Cowetas, Cussetas, Hitchitis, Oakfuskees, Tuckabatchees, Yuchis (Uchees/Euchees), or another group that had coalesced into a polity that emerged in west central-southwest Georgia and in central Alabama by the middle of the eighteenth century. Ethridge, *Creek Country*, 92–119.

[6] Tustenuggee, or *tastanagi*, loosely translates as "warrior," and as a warrior achieved greater status, his rank or title would change, such as Tustenuggee Thlucco, or "big warrior" or "grand warrior." Benjamin Hawkins wrote that *isti puccanchau thlucco* was the highest rank, meaning "great leader." Ethridge, *Creek Country*, 102–04; Michael Green, *The Politics of Indian Removal: Creek Government and Society in Crises* (Lincoln: University of Nebraska Press, 1982), 7–10. See J. Leitch Wright, *Creeks and Seminoles: The Destruction and Regeneration of the Muscogulge People* (Lincoln: University of Nebraska Press, 1986) for the Muskogean orthography, 29–30.

[7] In 1735, Chigellie and Antioche, both residents of Coweta at modern Columbus, Georgia, presented a written account in English on a buffalo skin of a migration legend. They related how their ancestors and their neighbors from Kashita

fruit and game with which it abounded, they established towns upon the Yazoo, constructed subterranean habituations, and for some years passed their time most agreeably. It is probable the Alabamas had fled before their arrival, for the Spaniards had so thinned the number of the latter that it was folly to resist the Muscogees, who had conquered them when they were much stronger. Milfort states that the Alabamas finally advanced to the river which now bears their name. Here, finding a region charming in climate, rich in soil, convenient in navigation, and remote from the country of their enemies, they made permanent establishments, from the confluence of the Coosa and Tallapoosa some distance down the Alabama.

Remembering how often they had been surprised by the Muscogees, and how insecure from their attacks was even a distant retreat, the Alabamas sent forth young warriors westward, to see if their foes were still wandering upon their heels. It happened that a party of the latter were reconnoitering eastward. They met, fought, and some of the Muscogees were killed. In the meantime, the latter tribe had learned what a delightful country was occupied by the Alabamas, and this new outrage, coupled with a desire to go further south-east, induced them to break up their establishments upon the Yazoo. Without opposition the Muscogee took possession of the lands upon the Alabama, and also those upon the Coosa and Tallapoosa. The Alabamas fled in all directions, seeking asylums among the Choctaws and other tribes.[7]

Gaining a firm footing in the new region, enjoying good health, and increasing in population, the Muscogees advanced to the Ocmulgee, Oconee, and Ogeechee, and even established a town where now reposes the beautiful city of Augusta. With the Indians of the present state of Georgia, they had combats, but overcame them. Pushing on their conquests, they reduced a warlike tribe called the Uchees,[8] lower down upon the Savannah, and brought the prisoners in slavery to the Chattahoochee.* In 1822, the Big Warrior, who then ruled the Creek Confederacy, confirmed this tradition, even going further back than Milfort, taking the Muscogees from Asia, bringing them over the Pacific, landing them near the Isthmus of Darien, and conducting them from thence to this country.[9] "My ancestors were a mighty people. After they reached the waters of the Alabama

* Milfort, 263–69; Bartram, *Travels,* 53, 54, 464. Also traditional MS notes in my possession.

emerged from a "mouth in the ground" and journeyed east. Subsequently three other peoples joined them, they crossed a "red bloody river," competed for scalps in a war with their enemies, and traveled further east until they encountered the Apalachicolas, who helped them find peace and unity. Their oral tradition was presented at a meeting with Georgia officials in Savannah, but the buffalo skin has been lost. Milfort may have used this legend in shaping his narrative of the Muscogees and Alabamas. Saunt, *New Order of Things,* 11–17; Amelia Bell Walker, "The Kashita Myth," *Anthropology Tomorrow* 12 (Spring 1979): 46–63; Steven C. Hahn, *The Invention of the Creek Nation, 1670–1763* (Lincoln: University of Nebraska Press, 2004), 10–12.

[8] The name for the Uchee is spelled differently in several primary and secondary sources, such as Euchee, Yuchee, Uchi, and Yuchi. Modern sources generally prefer Yuchi. The Uchees migrated from the Savannah River watershed around 1715 to the Lower Creek towns on the Chattahoochee, especially Cusseta and Yuchi Town. Their language separated them from the Muskogean speakers in the Muscogee or Creek Confederacy. Stephen Warren, "Reconsidering Coalescence: Yuchi and Shawnee Survival Strategies in the Colonial Southeast," in *Yuchi Indian Histories Before the Removal Era,* ed. Jason Baird Jackson (Lincoln: University of Nebraska Press, 2012), 156–87.

[9] Big Warrior (*Tustenuggee Thlucco*) of Tuckabatchee worked closely with Benjamin Hawkins and emerged as a prominent peace

leader in the Upper Creek towns prior to the Red Stick War. In 1816, he was paid $12,597.25 for "property destroyed by hostile Creek Indians," which included his inn on the Federal Road. Gregory A. Waselkov, *A Conquering Spirit: Fort Mims and the Redstick War of 1813–1814* (Tuscaloosa: University of Alabama Press, 2006), 89, 207; Green, *Politics of Indian Removal*, 38–42.

[10] Lee Compere's Muskogean language notes and the Lord's Prayer in Muskogean are found in Albert Gallatin's "A Synopsis of the Indian Tribes of North America," in *Archaeologia Americana, Transactions and Collections of the American Antiquarian Society*, (Cambridge: The Society, 1836), 11: 381–82, 386, 388, 390, 392, 394, 396, 405–06, 408, 410, 412, 421. See his brief biography—"Lee Compere"—at http://www.encyclopediaofalabama.org/article/h-1046.

[11] Eight Alabama chiefs from the Upper Creek towns participated in peace talks with French officials in Mobile in May 1702. The French peace overtures were focused on developing relations with the Indian people of the interior and to block the British expansion into the Gulf region. Verner W. Crane, *The Southern Frontier, 1670–1732*, new preface by Peter H. Wood (1956; reprint, New York: W. W. Norton & Company, 1981), 67–70.

and took possession of all this country, they went further—conquered the tribes upon the Chattahoochee, and upon all the rivers from thence to the Savannah—yes, and even whipped the Indians then living in the territory of South Carolina, and wrested much of their country from them." The Big Warrior concluded this sentence with great exultation, when Mr. Compere, to whom he was speaking, interposed an unfortunate question:[10] "If this is the way your ancestors acquired all the territory now lying in Georgia, how can you blame the American population in that state for endeavoring to take it from you?" Never after that could the worthy missionary extract a solitary item from the chieftain, in relation to the history of his people.*

Sometime after these conquests, the French established themselves at Mobile. The Alabamas, scattered as we have seen, and made to flee before superior numbers, became desirous to place themselves under their protection. Anxious to cultivate a good understanding with all the Indian tribes, and to heal old animosities existing among them, the French caused an interview between the chiefs of the Alabamas and those of the Muscogees, at Mobile. In the presence of M. Bienville, the commandant of that place, a peace was made, which has not since been violated.[11] The Alabamas returned to their towns, upon the river of that name, which were called Coosawda, Ecunchate, Pauwacta, Toowoossau and Attaugee, situated on both sides of the river, and embracing a country from the junction of the Coosa and Tallapoosa, for forty miles down. They consented to become members of the Muscogee Confederacy, and to observe their national laws, but stipulated to retain their ancient manners and customs.[12]

Not long afterwards, the Tuckabatchees, who had nearly been destroyed by the Iroquois and Hurons, wandered from the Ohio country, and obtained permission from the Muscogees to form a part of their nation.[13] They were willingly received by the cunning Muscogees, who were anxious

* Rev. Lee Compere's MS notes in my possession. This gentleman was born in England, on November 3, 1790. He came to South Carolina in 1817. The Baptist Missionary Board and that of the General Convention, sent him as a missionary to the Creek Nation in 1822. He and his wife, who was an English lady, resided at Tookabatcha [Tuckabatchee] (the capital) six years. Mr. Compere made but little progress towards the conversion of the Creeks, owing to the opposition of the chiefs to the abolition of primitive customs. He was a learned man and a respectable writer. He furnished the Indian Bureau, at Washington, with a complete vocabulary of the Muscogee language and also the Lord's Prayer, all of which is published in the 2nd volume of *Transactions and Collections of the American Antiquarian Society* (Cambridge: 1836), 2: 381–422. In 1821, I often heard Mr. Compere and his wife sing beautiful hymns in the Creek tongue. He lives in the state of Mississippi.

to gain all the strength they could, to prevent the encroachments of the English from South Carolina. Upon the ruins of the western Tallassee, where De Soto encamped twenty days, the Tuckabatchees built a town and gave it their name.*

The Tuckabatchees brought with them to the Tallapoosa some curious brass plates, the origin and objects of which have much puzzled the Americans of our day, who have seen them. Such information respecting them as has fallen into our possession, will be given. On the 27th July 1759, at the Tuckabatchee square, William Balsover, a British trader, made inquiries concerning their ancient relics, of an old Indian chief, named Brackett, near a hundred years of age. There were two plates of brass and five of copper.[14] The Indians esteemed them so much that they were preserved in a private place, known only to a few chiefs, to whom they were annually entrusted. They were never brought to light but once in a year, and that was upon the occasion of the Green Corn Celebration, when, on the fourth day, they were introduced in, what was termed the "brass plate dance." Then one of the high prophets carried one before him, under his arm, ahead of the dancers—next to him the head warrior carried another, and then others followed with the remainder, bearing aloft, at the same time, white canes, with the feathers of a swan at the tops.

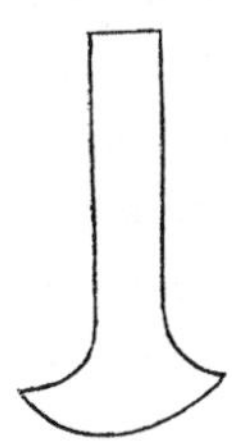

Shape of the five copper plates: One a foot and a half long, and seven inches wide; the other four a little shorter and narrower.

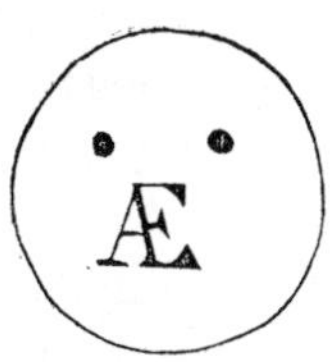

Shape of the two brass plates: Eighteen inches in diameter, about the thickness of a dollar, and stamped as exhibited upon the face.

Formerly, the Tuckabatchee tribe had many more of these relics, of different sizes and shapes, with letters and inscriptions upon them, which were given to their ancestors by the Great Spirit, who instructed them that they were only to be handled by particular men, who must at the moment be engaged in fasting, and that no unclean woman must be suffered to come near them or the place where they were deposited. Brackett further related, that several of these plates were then

* Milfort, 263–66.

[12] In the late seventeenth and early eighteenth centuries, the Alabamas, Abihkas, Tallapoosas, and Okfuskees with their towns on the Tallapoosa, Coosa and Alabama Rivers became known to the English as the Upper Creeks while the French continued to use tribal, province or town names. Ethridge, *Creek Country*, 26–28.

[13] While citing Milfort's *Mémoire*, published in 1802, Pickett refers to the "Tookabatchas" in his original narrative, but Milfort used "Tukabahchee" where he was named "Tastanegy." Modern scholars refer to them as Tuckabatchees. They migrated into central Alabama and established their town, which became the capital of the Tallapoosa province on the lower Tallapoosa River. By the mid-eighteenth century, their town had become the largest town of the Upper Creeks. Ibid., 27, 68–69; Wright, *Creeks and Seminoles*, 12–17. See Louis LeClerc de Milford [Milfort], *Memoir or A Cursory Glance at My Different Travels & Sojourn in the Creek Nation*, trans. Geraldine de Corcy and ed. John Francis McDermott (Chicago: R. R. Donnelley & Sons, 1956), 29, 184, 222.

[14] James Adair refers to the five copper plates and two brass plates at Tuckabatchee when discussing burial practices that included "medals, and other monuments of antiquity." He credits William Balsover for recording Old Brackett's account "of these

buried under the miccos' cabin in Tuckabatchee, and had lain there ever since the first settlement of the town; that formerly it was the custom to place one or more of them in the grave by the side of a deceased chief of the pure Tuckabatchee blood, and that no other Indians in the whole Creek Nation had such sacred relics.* Similar accounts of these plates were obtained from four other British traders, "at the most eminent trading house of all English America."† The town of Tuckabatchee became, in later times, the capital of the Creek Nation; and many reliable citizens of Alabama have seen these mysterious pieces at the Green Corn dances, upon which occasions they were used precisely as in the more ancient days.‡ When the inhabitants of this town, in the autumn of 1836, took up the line of march for their present home in the Arkansas Territory, these plates were transported thence by six Indians, remarkable for their sobriety and moral character, at the head of whom was the chief, Spoke-Oak Micco. Medicine, made expressly for their safe transportation, was carried along by these warriors. Each one had a plate strapped behind his back, enveloped nicely in buckskin.[15] They carried nothing else, but marched on, one before the other, the whole distance to Arkansas, neither communicating nor conversing with a soul but themselves, although several thousands were emigrating in company; and walking, with a solemn religious air, one mile in advance of the others.§ How much their march resembled that of the ancient Trojans, bearing off their household gods!

Another tradition is, that the Shawnees gave these plates to the Tuckabatchee, as tokens of their friendship, with an injunction that they would annually introduce them in their religious observances of the new corn season. But the opinion of Opothleyahola, one of the most gifted chiefs of the modern Creeks, went to corroborate the general tradition that they were gifts from the Great Spirit.¶

* Adair, *History of the American Indians*, 178–79.

† Adair, *American Indians*, 179.

‡ Conversations with Barent Dubois, Abraham Mordecai, James Moore, Capt. William Walker, Lachlan Durant, Mrs. Sophia McComb, and other persons who stated that these plates had Roman characters upon them, as well as they could determine from the rapid glances which they could occasionally bestow upon them, while they were being used in the "brass plate dance."

§ Conversations with Barent Dubois.

¶ Conversations with Opothleyahola in 1833.

important monuments of antiquity" that were buried under a cabin in "Tuccabatchy-square." James Adair, *The History of the American Indians*, ed. Kathryn Holland Braund (1775; reprint, Tuscaloosa: University of Alabama Press, 2005), 208–09, 505 n. 181, 506 n. 182.

[15] Old Brackett had been a prominent warrior and leader in Tuckabatchee, and according to a South Carolina agent, Daniel Pepper, he was a staunch ally of the British during the Seven Years' War. George Stiggins refers to "six brass or breastplates," three with hieroglyphics or Hebrew characters, and records that they were "handed down by the Giver or Taker of Breath." Adair, *American Indians*, 505 n. 181; George Stiggins, *Creek Indian History: A Historical Narrative of the Genealogy, Traditions and Downfall of the Ispocoga or Creek Indian Tribe of Indians*, ed. Virginia Pounds Brown (Birmingham: Birmingham Public Library, 1989), 45–46, 63, 149 n. 33; James Howard, *The Southeastern Ceremonial Complex and Its Interpretation*, Memoir Series No. 6 (Columbia: Missouri Archaeological Society, 1968), 64–74.

[16] Barent Dubois, a descendant of a prominent French Huguenot family from New Paltz, New York, was a trader at Tallassee and married Milly McQueen, a daughter of Peter McQueen. He assisted Col. John Crowell with the emigration of the Creeks and sold corn and other supplies to the emigrating officers. One source gives him credit for conducting an exploring party of prominent Creek leaders, including Opothleyahola (c. 1780–1863), in the winter of 1834–1835. Ralph Lefevre, *History of New Paltz, New York and Its Old Families* (Albany: Fort Orange Press, 1903), 117–18, 307; *Reports of Committees of the House of Representatives at the First*

It will be recollected that our aborigines, in the time of De Soto, understood the use of copper, and that hatchets and ornaments were made of that metal. The ancient Indians may have made them, and engraved upon their face hieroglyphics, which were supposed, from the glance only permitted to be given them, to be Roman characters. An intelligent New Englander, named Barent Dubois, who had long lived among the Tuckabatchee, believed that these plates originally formed some portion of the armor or musical instruments of De Soto, and that the Indians stole them, as they did the shields, in the Talladega country, and hence he accounts for the Roman letters on them.[16] We give no opinion, but leave the reader to determine for himself—having discharged our duty by placing all the available evidence before him.

The reputation which the Muscogees had acquired for strength and a warlike spirit, induced other tribes who had become weak to seek an asylum among them. The Tuskegees wandered down into East Alabama, were received with open arms, and permitted to occupy the territory immediately in the fork of the Coosa and Tallapoosa.[17] Upon the east bank of the former, a town was erected and called after the name of the tribe. Sometime after this, the French fort, Toulouse, was built here; and, one hundred years afterwards, Fort Jackson was placed upon the same foundation by the Americans.[18]

A tribe of the Oxiailles came at the same time,[19] and were located eighteen miles above, on a beautiful plain, through which meandered a fine creek.* A large tribe of Uchees, made prisoners and brought to Cusseta, upon the Chattahoochee, not long afterwards, were liberated and assigned residences upon the creeks which bear their name, flowing through the eastern portion of the county of Russell.[20] Or, upon the authority of Col. Hawkins, the Uchees, formerly living upon the Savannah in small villages at Ponpon, Saltketchers and Silver Bluff, and also upon the Ogeechee, were continually at war with the Creeks, Cherokees and Catawbas; but in 1729 an old chief of Cusseta, called Captain Ellick, married three Uchee women and brought them to Cusseta, which greatly displeased his friends. Their opposition determined him to move from Cusseta. With three of his brothers, two of whom also had Uchee wives, he settled upon the Uchee Creek.[21]

* Milfort, 267.

Session of the Twenty-Second Congress, 5 vols. (Washington: Duff Green, 1831), 5:73–75; "Barent DuBois," www.tallassee-al.gov/29-content-1/27-history-of-tallassee.

[17] The Tuskegees were non-Muskogean speakers who according to Benjamin Hawkins were among the most progressive people in the Creek Nation raising hogs and cattle. Wright, _Creeks and Seminoles,_ 112–13; Ethridge, _Creek Country,_ 84.

[18] By 1716 the French had determined to establish a military post on the Alabama River to maintain friendly relations with the Alabamas and to block the British. Lieutenant Vitral de La Tour led a French expedition that constructed Fort Toulouse in late summer 1717 on a bluff at the confluence of the Coosa and Tallapoosa Rivers. Daniel H. Thomas, _Fort Toulouse: The French Outpost on the Coosa,_ new introduction by Gregory A. Waselkov (1960; reprint, Tuscaloosa: University of Alabama Press, 1989), xxxii, 8–11; Ethridge, _Creek Country,_ 82–84.

[19] While Milfort refers to the "les Oxiailles" in his _Mémoire,_ the town was mentioned as Oaktchoy in 1791 and the old town site was located on Oakachoy Creek, a western tributary of the Tallapoosa River, in Coosa County, Alabama. Albert Samuel Gatschet, _A Migration Legend of the Creek Indians,_ Brinton's Library of Aboriginal American Literature, No. IV (Philadelphia: D. G. Britton, 1884), 141.

[20] Modern scholars refer to this tribe as Yuchis, but in the eighteenth century, these emigrants from Eastern Tennessee were called Uchees. They established villages primarily on the Flint and upper Chattahoochee Rivers, including Uchee Creek in Russell County, Alabama. The Yuchis claimed descent from the sun and their name

Afterwards he collected all that tribe, and with them formed there a distinct community, which, however, became amenable, nationally, to the government of the Muscogees.*

In 1729, the Natchez massacred the French at Fort Rosalie, now the site of the city of Natchez, and were in turn overpowered, and many of them made slaves, while others escaped to the Coosa. In the Talladega country they built two towns, one called Nauchee and the other Aubecooche.[22] Thus a branch of the Natchez also became members of the Muscogee Confederacy. At the close of the Revolutionary War, a party of Savannahs came from that river in company with some Shawnees, from Florida, and formed a town on the east side of the Tallapoosa, called Sauwanogee upon the ruins of which the Americans, in 1819, established the village of Augusta—no remains of which now exist.[23] Sauwanogee was laid out in conformity with their usages and habits,[24] which they retained; but they willingly came under the national government of the confederacy.†

Thus did the Muscogee Confederacy gain strength, from time to time, by the migration of broken tribes. When the English began to explore their country, and to transport goods into all parts of it, they gave all the inhabitants, collectively, the name of the "CREEKS," on account of the many beautiful rivers and streams which flowed through their extensive domain.‡ By that name they will, in the future pages of this history, be called.[25]

The Creek woman was short in stature, but well formed. Her cheeks were rather high, but her features were generally regular and pretty. Her brow was high and arched, her eye large, black and languishing, expressive of modesty and diffidence. Her feet and hands were small, and the latter exquisitely shaped. The warrior was larger than the ordinary race of Europeans, often above six feet in height, but was invariably well formed, erect in his carriage, and graceful in every movement. They were proud, haughty and arrogant; brave and valiant in war; ambitious of conquest; restless, and perpetually exercising their arms, yet magnanimous and merciful to a vanquished

* Benjamin Hawkins, "A Sketch of the Creek Country, In the Years 1798–1799," 61–66. Also, manuscript traditional notes in my possession, taken from the lips of aged Indian countrymen.

† Milfort, 282–83; Hawkins, "A Sketch of the Creek Country," 34. Also, conversations with Indian countrymen.

‡ Hawkins, 19.

for themselves was *coyaha* or *tsoyaha,* meaning "Children of the Sun." Wright, *Creeks and Seminoles,* 9; Ethridge, *Creek Country,* 28–30, 55.

[21] Captain Ellick of Cusseta was an influential leader and spokesman for the Cussitas, Chehaws, and Yuchis on the lower Chattahoochee River. He is a signatory on a letter to John Stuart, 16 September 1763, requesting clarification regarding a report that the governors of Georgia, North Carolina and South Carolina intended to use the conference in Augusta "to buy our lands." *The Colonial and State Records of North Carolina,* ed. William L. Saunders, Stephen B. Weeks, and Walter Clark, 26 vols. (Raleigh: P. M. Hale, 1886–1907), 11: 167–69 [Hereafter cited as *CSRNC*]; H. Thomas Foster, *Archaeology of the Lower Muskogee Creek Indians, 1715–1836* (Tuscaloosa: University of Alabama Press, 2007), 52–54.

[22] The Natchez refugees among the Creeks settled principally among the Abihkas in Aubecooche and Nauche in the vicinity of the present-day Tallaseehatchee Creek in Talladega County, Alabama. Ethridge, *Creek Country,* 88–89; Wright, *Creeks and Seminoles,* 10–11; James F. Barnett, Jr., *The Natchez Indians: A History to 1735* (Jackson: University Press of Mississippi, 2007), 132.

[23] As early as 1708, the Shawnee had three towns on the Savannah River and were often referred to as the Savannahs. By mid-century, the very mobile Shawnee may have had two towns among the Upper Creeks and possibly small numbers living in the Lower Creek towns on the Chattahoochee. Ethridge, *Creek*

Indian enemy who afterwards sought their friendship and protection.* Encountering fatigue with ease, they were great travelers, and sometimes went three or four hundred leagues on a hunting expedition. "Formerly they were cruel, but at the present day they are brave, yet peaceable, when not forced to abandon their character."†

Like all other Indians, they were fond of ornaments, which consisted of stones, beads, wampum, porcupine quills, eagles' feathers, beautiful plumes, and earrings of various descriptions. The higher classes were often fantastic in their wearing apparel. Sometimes a warrior put on a ruffled shirt of fine linen, and went out with no other garment except a flap of blue broadcloth, with buskins made of the same. The stillapica or moccasin, embroidered with beads, adorned the feet of the better classes. Mantles of good broadcloth, of a blue or scarlet color, decorated with fringe and lace, and hung with round silver or brass buttons, were worn by those who could afford them. When they desired to be particularly gay, vermillion was freely applied to the face, neck and arms. Again, the skin was often inscribed with hieroglyphics and representations of the sun, moon, stars and various animals.‡ This was performed by puncturing the parts with gar's teeth, and rubbing in a dye made of the drippings of rich pine roots. These characters were inscribed during youth, and frequently in manhood, every time that a warrior distinguished himself in slaying the enemy. Hence when he was unfortunately taken prisoner, he was severely punished in proportion to the marks upon his skin, by which he was known to have shed the blood of many of the kindred of those into whose hands he had fallen.§ The Creeks wore many ornaments of silver. Crescents or gorgets, very massive, suspended around the neck by ribbons, reposed upon the breast, while the arms, fingers, hats, and even sometimes the necks, had silver bands around them.[26]

The female wore a petticoat which reached to the middle of her leg. The waistcoat, or wrapper, made of calico, printed linen, or fine cloth, ornamented with lace and beads, enveloped the upper part of the body. They never wore boots or stockings, but their buskins reached to the middle of the leg. Their hair, black, long and rather coarse, was

* Bartram, *Travels*, 482, 500, 506.

† Milfort, 216–17.

‡ Bartram, *Travels*, 482–506.

§ Adair, *American Indians*, 389.

Country*, 97; Warren, "Reconsidering Coalescence," 169–71; John R. Swanton, *Early History of the Creek Indians and Their Neighbors*, Bureau of American Ethnology, *Bulletin 73* (Washington: GPO, 1922), 189–90, 317–20; Stephen Warren, *The Worlds the Shawnees Made: Migration and Violence in Early America* (Chapel Hill: University of North Carolina Press, 2014), 92–105, 208–12.

[24] While Hawkins spells the name of this Shawnee town, phonetically Sau-wa-no-gee, modern scholars use Sawanogi for this town located in the floodplain of the Tallapoosa River. Ethridge, *Creek Country*, 73, 81–83, 97; Warren, *Worlds the Shawnees Made*, 206–20.

[25] More recent scholarship reveals the Creeks—the Muskogean speakers—received their name through a combination of events. Sometime in the seventeenth century, Muscogees displaced the Hichitis on the Ocmulgee River and the Hitchiti name for these western intruders was Ochesee. Subsequently, the Carolinians opened up trade with the people living on Ochesee Creek on the upper Ocmulgee River, and the traders began to refer to these Indians as the Ochesee Creeks, or Ochesees, and finally as Creeks. The next step was to refer to those living on the upper reaches of the Alabama River as Upper Creeks and those living on the Chattahoochee and Flint Rivers as Lower Creeks. Wright, *Creeks and Seminoles*, 2–3.

[26] Pickett continues to paraphrase William Bartram, but Bartram also mentioned "silver and gold chains" as part of the men's ornamentation. See *William Bartram on the Southeastern Indians*, ed. Gregory A.

Waselkov and Kathryn E. Holland Braund (Lincoln: University of Nebraska Press, 1995), 120–22.

plaited in wreaths, and ordinarily turned up and fastened to the crown with a silver band. This description of dress and ornaments were worn only by the better classes. The others were more upon the primitive Indian order. They were fond of music, both vocal and instrumental; but the instruments they used were of an inferior kind, such as the tambour, rattle-gourd, and a kind of flute, made of the joint of a cane or the tibia of the deer's leg. Dancing was practiced to a great extent, and they employed an endless variety of steps.*

Their most manly and important game was the "ball play." It was the most exciting and interesting game imaginable, and was the admiration of all the curious and learned travelers who witnessed it. The warriors of one town challenged those of another, and they agreed to meet at one town, or the other, as may have been decided. For several days previous to the time, those who intended to engage in the amusement took medicine, as though they were going to war. The night immediately preceding was spent in dancing and other ceremonious preparations. On the morning of the play, they painted and decorated themselves. In the meantime, the news had spread abroad in the neighboring towns, which collected, at the place designated, an immense concourse of men, women, and children—the young and the gay—the old and the grave—together with hundreds of ponies, Indian merchandise, extra wearing apparel, and various articles brought there to stake upon the result.[27]

The players were all nearly naked, wearing only a piece of cloth called "flap." They advanced towards the immense plain upon which they were presently to exhibit astonishing feats of strength and agility. From eighty to a hundred men were usually on a side. They now approached each other, and were first seen at the distance of a quarter of a mile apart, but their war songs and yells had previously been heard. Intense excitement and anxiety were depicted upon the countenances of the immense throng of spectators. Presently the parties appeared in full trot, as if about to encounter fiercely in fight. They met and soon became intermingled together, dancing and stamping, while a dreadful artillery of noise and shouts went up and rent the air. An awful silence then succeeded. The players retired from each other, and fell back one hundred and fifty yards from the center. Thus they were three hundred yards apart. In the center were erected two poles, between which the ball must pass to count one. Every warrior was provided with two rackets or hurls, of singular construction, resembling a ladle or hoop-net with handles nearly three feet long. The handle was of wood, and the netting of the thongs of rawhide or the tendons of an animal. The play was commenced by a ball,

* Bartram, *Travels*, 482–506.

covered with buckskin, being thrown in the air. The players rushed together with a mighty shock, and he who caught the ball between his two rackets, ran off with it and hurled it again in the air, endeavoring to throw it between the poles in the direction of the town to which he belonged. They seized hold of each other's limbs and hair, tumbled each other over, first trampled upon those that were down, and did everything to obtain the ball, and afterwards to make him who had it, drop it, before he could make a successful throw. The game was usually from twelve to twenty. It was kept up for hours, and during the time the players used the greatest exertions, exhibited the most infatuated devotion to their side, were often severely hurt, and sometimes killed, in the rough and unfeeling scramble which prevailed.[28] It sometimes happened that the inhabitants of a town gamed away all their ponies, jewels, and wearing apparel, even stripping themselves, upon the issue of the ball play. In the meantime, the women were constantly on the alert with vessels and gourds filled with water, watching every opportunity to supply the players.*

[27] The ball play had nearly universal appeal among the southeastern Indians, and Bartram provides a vivid report on the preparations and ceremony followed by the Cherokee at Cowee in 1775. There is a Cherokee tradition that claims the Cherokee defeated the Creeks in a ball play and their victory gave them control of a large part of North Georgia. Bartram, *William Bartram on the Southeastern Indians*, 85–86; James Mooney, "The Cherokee Ball Play," *American Anthropologist* 3 (April 1890), 107.

If a Creek warrior wished to marry, he sent his sister, mother, or some female relation, to the female relations of the girl whom he loved. Her female relations then consulted the uncles, and if none, the brothers, on the maternal side, who decided upon the case. If it was an agreeable alliance, the bridegroom was informed of it, and he sent, soon after, a blanket and articles of clothing to the female part of the family of the bride. If they received these presents, the match was made, and the man was at liberty to go to the house of his wife as soon as he deemed it proper. When he had built a residence, produced a crop, gathered it in, made a hunt and brought home the game, and tendered a general delivery of all to the girl, then they were considered man and wife. Divorce was at the choice of either party. The man, however, had the advantage, for he could again marry another woman if he wished; but the woman was obliged to lead a life of celibacy until the Boosketau, or Green Corn Dance, was over.[29] Marriage gave no right to the husband over the property of the wife, or the control or management of the children which he might have by her.

Adultery was punished by the family of the husband, who collected together, consulted and agreed on the course to pursue. One-half of them then went to the house of the woman, and the other half to the residence of the guilty warrior. They apprehended, stripped, and beat them with long poles until they were insensible. Then they cropped off their ears, and sometimes

* *A Narrative of the Military Actions of Colonel Marinus Willett: Taken Chiefly From His Own Manuscript*, 108–10; Bartram, *Travels*, 482–506.

[28] Captain Basil Hall in his *Travels in North America in the Years 1827 and 1828* described a Lower Creek ball field as being "in the bosom of the forest" and measuring 20-by-200 yards. He also recounted, as a spectator, seeking refuge behind a tree when "a dozen or twenty Indians whizzed past" him in pursuit of the ball. Ethridge, *Creek Country,* 100–101.

[29] While most modern scholarship refers to the Green Corn Ceremony/Festival or Busk, Pickett continues to use Hawkins, who spelled this celebration as "Boos-ke-tau." This celebration of renewal and purification was generally celebrated in July or August as the corn began to mature by all the southeastern Indians. Ethridge, *Creek Country,* 94–95, 147; Bartram, *William Bartram on the Southeastern Indians,* 124–27; Hudson, *Southeastern Indians,* 365–75; Martin, *Sacred Revolt,* 37–42.

their noses, with knives, the edges of which were made rough and saw-like.[30] The hair of the woman was carried in triumph to the square. Strange to say, they generally recovered from this inhuman treatment. If one of the offenders escaped, satisfaction was taken by similar punishment inflicted upon the nearest relative. If both of the parties fled unpunished, and the party aggrieved returned home and laid down the poles, the offense was considered satisfied. But one family in the Creek Nation had authority to take up the poles the second time, and that was the Ho-tul-gee, or family of the Wind. The parties might absent themselves until the Boosketau was over, and then they were free from punishment for this and all other offenses, except murder, which had to be atoned for by death upon the guilty one or his nearest relative.* The Creeks buried their dead in the earth, in a square pit, under the bed where the deceased lay in his house. The grave was lined on the sides with cypress bark, like the curbing of a well. The corpse, before it became cold, was drawn up with cords, and made to assume a squatting position; and in this manner it was placed in the grave and covered with earth. The gun, tomahawk, pipe, and other articles of the deceased, were buried with him.†

In 1777, Bartram found, in the Creek Nation, fifty towns, with a population of eleven thousand, which lay upon the rivers Coosa, Tallapoosa, Alabama, Chattahoochee and Flint, and the prominent creeks which flowed into them. The Muscogee was the national language, although in some of these towns, the Uchee or Savannah, Alabama, Natchez and Shawnee tongues prevailed.[31] But the Muscogee was called, by the traders, the "mother tongue," while the others mentioned were termed the "stinkard lingo."‡

The general council of the nation was always held in the principal town, in the center of which was a large public square, with three cabins of different sizes in each angle, making twelve in all. Four avenues led into the square. The cabins, capable of containing sixty persons each, were so situated that from one of them a person might see into the others. One belonging to the grand chief fronted the rising sun, to remind him that he should watch the interests of his people. Near it was the grand cabin, where the councils were held. In the opposite angle, three others belonged to the old men, and faced the setting sun, to remind them that they were growing feeble, and should not go to war. In the two remaining corners were the cabins of the different chiefs of the nation, the dimensions of which were in proportion to the rank and services of those chiefs. The whole number in the square was painted red,

* Hawkins, "A Sketch of the Creek Country," 73–74.

† Bartram, *Travels,* 513–14.

‡ Bartram, *Travels,* 461–62.

except those facing the west, which were white, symbolical of virtue and old age. The former, during war, were decorated with wooden pieces sustaining a chain of rings of wood. This was a sign of grief, and told the warriors they should hold themselves in readiness, for their country needed their services. These chains were replaced by garlands of ivy leaves during peace.[32]

In the month of May, annually, the chiefs and principal Indians assembled in the large square formed by these houses, to deliberate upon all subjects of general interest. When they were organized they remained in the square until the council broke up. Here they legislated, eat and slept. During the session, no person, except the principal chiefs, could approach within less than twenty feet of the grand cabin. The women prepared the food, and deposited it at a prescribed distance, when it was borne to the grand cabin by the subordinate chiefs.[33] In the center of the square was a fire constantly burning. At sunset the council adjourned for the day, and then the young people of both sexes danced around this fire until a certain hour. As soon as the sun appeared above the horizon, a drum-beat called the chiefs to the duties of the day.*

Besides this national legislature, each principal town in the nation had its separate public buildings, as do the states of this American Union; and like them, regulated their own local affairs. The public square at Autossee, upon the Tallapoosa, in 1777, consisted of four square buildings, of the same dimensions and uniform in shape, so situated as to form a tetragon, enclosing an area of an half-acre. Four passages, of equal width at the corners, admitted persons into it. The frames of these buildings were of wood, but a mud plaster, inside and out, was employed to form neat walls; except two feet all around under the eaves, left open to admit light and air. One of them was the council house, where the micco (king), chiefs and warriors, with the white citizens, who had business, daily assembled to hear and decide upon all grievances, adopt measures for the better government of the people, and the improvement of the town, and to receive ambassadors from other towns. This building was enclosed on three sides, while a partition, from end to end, divided it into two apartments, the back one of which was totally dark, having only three arched holes large enough for a person to crawl into. It was a sanctuary of priestcraft, in which were deposited physic-pots, rattles, chaplets of deer's hoofs, the great pipe of peace, the imperial eagle-tail standard, displayed like an open fan, attached to which was a staff as white and clean as it could be scoured. The front part of this building was open like a piazza, divided into three apartments, breast high—each containing three rows of seats, rising

* Milfort, 206–08.

[30] William Bartram relates a serious but also humorous story of his role in assisting the young son of a trader from losing his ears and possibly his life because of his "amorous intrigue" with the wife of "a young chief" at the Upper Creek town of Mucclassee. He had been beaten by a dozen men using "knotty cudgels of green Hickory" and tearfully asked for Bartram to request the intercession by the principal trader George Galphin to save his life. Bartram, *William Bartram on the Southeastern Indians,* 101–02.

[31] Modern scholarship has determined that the eighteenth century towns of the historic Creek or Muscogee were divided along linguistic and/or ethnic lines. While the core Muscogee towns spoke Eastern Muskogean, others spoke a dialect of Muskogee—such as the Hitchitis. But the non-Muskogean speakers in other towns required interpreters at public meetings or relied on the Mobilian trade jargon to communicate. There is also evidence that non-Muscogee towns were viewed as inferior, and the term stinkards (*estenko* or *istinko*) was used to denote inferiority or non-Muskogean speakers. Ethridge, *Creek Country,* 30; Wright, *Creeks and Seminoles,* 5–13, 18, 77, 112–13.

[32] Each town (*talwa*) had a council house or rotunda and other structures related to hosting dignitaries and public meetings. William Bartram gives a detailed report on the council house and public square at Tuckabatchee during his visit in 1776. Bartram, *William Bartram on the Southeastern Indians*, 102–06.

[33] In December 1775, William Bartram attended a meeting of "venerable chiefs and warriors" at the council house in Autossee and confirmed Milfort's observation that "women and youth are never admitted." Bartram, *William Bartram on the Southeastern Indians*, 102.

one above the other, for the legislators. The other three buildings fronting the square were similar to the one just described, except that they had no sanctuary, and served to accommodate the spectators; they were also used for banqueting houses.[34]

The pillars and walls of the houses of the square abounded with sculptures and caricature paintings, representing men in different ludicrous attitudes; some with the human shape, having the heads of the duck, turkey, bear, fox, wolf and deer. Again, these animals were represented with the human head. These designs were not ill executed, and the outlines were bold and well proportioned. The pillars of the council house were ingeniously formed in the likeness of vast speckled snakes ascending—the Autossee being of the Snake family.*

Rude paintings were quite common among the Creeks, and they often conveyed ideas by drawings. No people could present a more comprehensive view of the topography of a country with which they were acquainted, than the Creeks could, in a few moments, by drawing upon the ground. Bernard Romans, a captain in the British Army, saw at Hoopa Ulla, a Choctaw town, not far from Mobile, the following drawing, executed by the Creeks, which had fallen into the possession of the Choctaws.[35]

This represents that ten Creek warriors, of the family of the Deer, went into the Choctaw country in three canoes; that six of them landed, and in marching along a path, met two Choctaw men, two women and a dog; that

* Bartram, *Travels*, 448–54.

the Creeks killed and scalped them. The scalp, in the deer's foot, implies the horror of the action to the whole Deer family.*

The great council house at Autossee, was appropriated to much the same purpose as the square, but was more private. It was a vast conical building, capable of accommodating many hundred people. Those appointed to take care of it, daily swept it clean, and provided canes for fuel and to give lights. Besides using this rotunda for political purposes, of a private nature, the inhabitants of Autossee were accustomed to take their "black drink" in it. The officer who had charge of this ceremony ordered the cassina tea to be prepared under an open shed opposite the door of the council house; he directed bundles of dry cane to be brought in, which were previously split in pieces of two feet long. "They were now placed obliquely across upon one another on the floor, forming a spiral line round about the great center pillar, eighteen inches in thickness. This spiral line, spreading as it proceeded round and round, often repeated from right to left, every revolution increased its diameter, and at length extended to the distance of ten or twelve feet from the center, according to the time the assembly was to continue." By the time these preparations were completed, it was night, and the assembly had taken their seats. The outer end of the spiral line was fired. It gradually crept round the entire pillar, with the course of the sun, feeding on the cane, and affording a bright and cheerful light.[36]

The aged chiefs and warriors sat upon their cane sofas, which were elevated one above the other, and fixed against the backside of the house, opposite the door. The white people and Indians of confederate towns sat, in like order, on the left—a transverse range of pillars, supporting a thin clay wall, breast high, separating them. The king's seat was in front; back of it were the seats of the head warriors, and those of a subordinate condition. Two middle-aged men now entered at the door, bearing large conch shells full of black drink. They advanced with slow, uniform and steady steps, with eyes elevated, and singing in a very low tone. Coming within a few feet of the king, they stopped, and rested their shells on little tables. Presently they took them up again, crossed each other, and advanced obsequiously. One presented his shell to the king, and the other to the principal man among the white audience.[37] As soon as they raised them to their mouths the attendants uttered two notes—"*a-hoo-ojah!*" and "*a-lu-yah!*"—which they spun out as long as they could hold their breath. As long as the notes continued, so long did the person drink or hold the shell to his mouth. In this manner all the assembly were served with the "black drink." But when the drinking begun, tobacco, contained in

* Barnard Romans, *A Concise Natural History of East and West Florida*, 102.

[34] Pickett uses Bartram's *Travels* as his primary source for his discussion of the events at Autossee. However, more recent study of Bartram's travel confirms that he made his visit to Autossee in December 1775, not 1777. By January 1777, he had returned to his home in Philadelphia. Francis Harper, ed., *The Travels of William Bartram; Naturalist's Edition* (1958; reprint, Athens: University of Georgia, 1998), xxviii, 422.

[35] Bernard Romans (c. 1720-c. 1784), an artist, surveyor, and naturalist, published his *A Concise Natural History of East and West Florida* in 1775. While working as a deputy surveyor in 1771, he and fellow surveyor David Taitt worked with John Stuart, British superintendent of Indian affairs for the Southern District, to develop a comprehensive map of the Southern Indian nations. Taitt surveyed the Creek country, and Romans covered West Florida which included the Choctaws and Chickasaws. Bernard Romans, *A Concise Natural History of East and West Florida*, ed. Kathryn E. Holland Braund (Tuscaloosa: University of Alabama Press, 1999), 4–8; A. F. Harley, "Bernard Romans's Map of Florida Engraved by Paul Revere, and Other Early Maps in the Library of the Florida

Historical Society," *Florida Historical Quarterly* 9 (July 1930): 47–57.

[36] More of Bartram's detailed report on his visit to Autossee in December 1775, not 1777. Harper, *Travels of William Bartram*, xxviii, 422; Bartram, *William Bartram on the Southeastern Indians*, 103.

[37] In addition to himself, Bartram identified the other whites present at this event in December 1775 at Autossee as traders "who are numerous in this town," and he reported that they "spent the evening and the greater part of the night together, drinking Cassine and smoking Tobacco." Bartram, *William Bartram on the Southeastern Indians*, 102.

pouches made of the skins of the wildcat, otter, bear and rattlesnake, was distributed among the assembly, together with pipes, and a general smoking commenced. The king began first, with a few whiffs from the great pipe, blowing it ceremoniously, first toward the sun, next toward the four cardinal points, and then toward the white audience. Then the attendants passed this pipe to others of distinction.[38] In this manner, these dignified and singular people occupied some hours in the night, until the spiral line of canes was consumed, which was a signal for retiring.*

Twenty-one years after the visit of Bartram to the Creek Nation, Col. Benjamin Hawkins, to whom Washington had confided important trusts in relation to the tribes south of the Ohio, penetrated these wilds. He found the public buildings, at that period similar to those already described, with, however, some exceptions, which may have been the result of a slight change of ancient customs.[39]

Every town had a separate government, and public buildings for business and pleasure, with a presiding officer, who was called a king, by the traders, and a micco, by the Indians. This functionary received all public characters, heard their talks, laid them before his people, and, in return, delivered the talk of his own town. He was always chosen from some noted family. The Micco of Tuckabatchee was of the Eagle tribe (Lum-ul-gee.) When they were put into office, they held their stations for life, and when dead, were succeeded by their nephews. The micco could select an assistant when he became infirm, or for other causes, subject to the approval of the principal men of the town. They generally bore the name of the town which they governed, as Cusseta Micco, Tuckabatchee Micco, etc.[40]

"Choo-co-thluc-co, (big house) the town house or public square, consists of four buildings of one story, facing each other, forty by sixteen feet, eight feet pitch; the entrance at each corner. Each building is a wooden frame supported on posts set in the ground, covered with slabs, open in front like a piazza, divided into three rooms, the back and ends clayed up to the plates. Each division is divided lengthwise into two seats. The front, two feet high, extending back half way, covered with reed mats or slabs; then a rise of one foot and it extends back, covered in like manner, to the side of the building. On these seats they lie or sit at pleasure.[41]

"THE RANK OF THE BUILDINGS WHICH FORM THE SQUARE.[42]

* Bartram, *Travels*, 448–54. The site of Autossee is now embraced in Macon County, and is a cotton plantation, the property of the Hon. George Goldthwaite, Judge of the Eighth Judicial Circuit. On the morning of the 29th of November 1813, a battle was fought here between the Creeks and the Georgians—the latter commanded by Gen. John Floyd.

"1st. Mic-ul-gee in-too-pau, the *Micco's cabin.* This fronts the east, and is occupied by those of the highest rank. The center of the building is always occupied by the Micco of the town, by the agent for Indian affairs, when he pays a visit to a town, by the Miccos of other towns, and by respectable white people.

"The division to the right is occupied by the Mic-ug-gee (Miccos, there being several so called in every town, from custom, the origin of which is unknown), and the councilors. These two classes give their advice in relation to war, and are, in fact, the principal councilors.

"The division to the left is occupied by the E-ne-hau-ulgee (people second in command, the head of whom is called by the trader's *second man*). These have the direction of the public works appertaining to the town, such as the public buildings, building houses in town for new settlers, or working in the fields. They are particularly charged with the ceremony of the ã-ce, (a decoction of the cassine yupon, called by the traders "black drink"), under the direction of the Micco.

"2nd. Tus-tun-nug-ul-gee in-too-pau, the *warrior's cabin.* This fronts the south. The head warrior sits at the end of the cabin, and in his division the great warriors sit beside each other. The next in rank sit in the center division, and the young warriors in the third. The rise is regular by merit from the third to the first division. The Great Warrior, for this is the title of the head warrior, is appointed by the Micco and councilors from among the greatest war characters.

"When a young man is trained up and appears well qualified for the fatigues and hardships of war, and is promising, the Micco appoints him a governor, or, as the name imports, a *leader* (Is-te-puc-cau-chau), and if he distinguishes himself they elevate him to the center cabin. A man who distinguishes himself repeatedly in warlike enterprises, arrives to the rank of the great leader (Is-te-puc-cau-chau-thlucco). This title, though greatly coveted, is seldom attained, as it requires a long course of years, and great and numerous successes in war.

"The second class of warriors is the *Tusse-ki-ul-gee.* All who go to war, and are in company when a scalp is taken, get a war-name. The leader reports their conduct and they receive a name accordingly. This is the *Tus-se-o-chif-co* or war name. The term leader, as used by the Indians, is a proper one. The war parties all march in Indian file, with the leader in front, until coming on hostile ground. He is then in the rear.

"3rd. Is-te-chaguc-ul-gee in-too-pau, the *cabin of the Beloved Men.* This fronts the north. There are a great many men who have been war leaders and

[38] Bartram made sketches of the chunky yards, council houses, public squares, rotundas and plans of towns and "private habitations" in his "Observations on the Creek and Cherokee Indians," which were not available to Pickett. He also made a drawing of a stone pipe bowl similar to those he encountered in the pipe ceremonies at Autossee and Cowee. Bartram, *William Bartram on the Southeastern Indians,* 121,157–59, 169–86.

[39] Benjamin Hawkins (1754–1816), a native of North Carolina and educated at Princeton, was appointed as the temporary agent to the Southern Indians by President George Washington in 1796. He had served as a treaty commissioner or as an unofficial observer at the 1785 Treaty of Hopewell with the Cherokees, the 1790 Treaty of New York with the Creeks, and the 1796 Treaty of Colerain with the Creeks. Florette Henri, *The Southern Indians and Benjamin Hawkins, 1796–1816* (Norman: University of Oklahoma Press, 1986), 32–33, 39–47, 51–63, 81–82.

[40] While Pickett relies heavily on Hawkins, ascendency to leadership positions among the Creeks or Muscogees was not as simple as Hawkins related in "A Sketch of the Creek Country." Laurels won in

war, clan membership, and autonomous town structure were transcendent forces in determining positions of leadership. Ethridge, *Creek Country*, 102–07, 109–11; Saunt, *New Order of Things*, 19–21; Green, *Politics of Indian Removal*, 4–10. See Benjamin Hawkins, "A Sketch of the Creek Country, In the Years of 1798 and 1799," in *Creek Confederacy and A Sketch of the Creek Country* (Savannah: Georgia Historical Society, 1848), 19–85.

[41] Pickett continues to quote directly from Hawkins' "A Sketch of the Creek Country." Bartram sketched a Creek public square with the four facing buildings and the council house or rotunda. Unfortunately, Bartram did not disclose whether his town plan represented a particular Creek town. Bartram, *William Bartram on the Southeastern Indians*, 168, 172–76, 180–83, 279 n. 80.

[42] Although he is quoting directly from Hawkins's "A Sketch of the Creek Country," Pickett actually deleted the final three paragraphs that describe the "Micco's cabin." Hawkins, "Sketch of the Creek Country," 69–70.

who, although of various ranks, have become estimable in long course of public service. They sit themselves on the right division of the cabin of the micco, and are his councilors. The family of the micco, and great men who have distinguished themselves occupy this cabin of the beloved men.

"4th. Hut-te-mau-hug-gee, the *cabin of the young people and their associates.* This fronts the west.

"THE CONVENTION OF THE TOWN.[43]

"The Micco, councilors and warriors meet every day in the public square, sit and drink of the black tea, talk of the news, the public and domestic concerns, smoke their pipes, and play Thla-chal-litch-cau (roll the bullet). Here all complaints are introduced, attended to and redressed.

"5th. Chooc-ofau-thluc-co, the *rotundo or assembly room*, called by the traders "*hot house*." This is near the square, and is constructed after the following manner: Eight posts are driven into the ground, forming an octagon of thirty feet in diameter. They are twelve feet high, and large enough to support the roof. On these five or six logs are placed, of a side, drawn in as they rise. On these, long poles or rafters, to suit the height of the building, are laid, the upper ends forming a point, and the lower-ends, projecting out six feet from the octagon, and resting on the posts, five feet high, placed in a circle round the octagon, with plates on them, to which the rafters are tied with splits. The rafters are near together and fastened with splits. These are covered with clay, and that with pine bark. The wall, six feet from the octagon, is clayed up. They have a small door, with a small portico curved round for five or six feet, then into the house.

"The space between the octagon and wall is one entire sofa, where the visitors lie or sit at pleasure. It is covered with reed, mat or splits.

"In the centre of the room, on a small rise, the fire is made of dry cane, or dry old pine slabs, split fine, and laid in a spiral line. This is the assembly room for all people, old and young. They assemble every night and amuse themselves with dancing, singing or conversation. And here, sometimes, in very cold weather, the old and naked sleep. "In all transactions which require secrecy, the rulers meet here, make their fire, deliberate and decide."*

A very interesting festival, common not only to the Creeks, but to many other tribes, will now be described. As Col. Hawkins was, in all respects, one of the most conscientious and reliable men that ever lived, his account, like the preceding, will be copied in his own style. Of the many descriptions of the Green Corn Dance, in our possession, that by the honest and indefatigable Creek agent is the most minute and most readily understood.

* Hawkins, "A Sketch of the Creek Country," 68–72.

"BOOS-KE-TAU.[44]

"The Creeks celebrate this festival in the months of July and August. The precise time is fixed by the Micco and councilors, and is sooner or later, as the state of affairs of the town or the early or lateness of their corn will suit. In Cusseta this ceremony lasts for eight days. In some towns of less note it is but four days.

"FIRST DAY.

"In the morning the warriors clear the yard of the square, and sprinkle white sand, when the black drink is made. The fire-maker makes the fire as early in the morning as he can, by friction. The warriors cut and bring into the square four logs, each as long as a man can cover by extending his two arms. These are placed in the center of the square, end to end, forming a cross, the outer ends pointed to the cardinal points; in the center of the cross the new fire is made. During the first four days they burn out these first four logs.

"The Pin-e-bun-gau (turkey dance) is danced by the women of the Turkey tribe, and while they are dancing the possau is brewed. This is a powerful emetic. It is drank from twelve o'clock to the middle of the afternoon. After this, Toc-co-yula-gau (tad-pole) is danced by four women and four men. In the evening the men dance E-ne-hou-bun-gau (the dance of the people second in command). This they dance till daylight.

"SECOND DAY.

"About ten o'clock the women dance Its-ho-bun-gau (gun dance). After twelve o'clock the men go to the new fire, take some of the ashes, rub them on the chin, neck and abdomen, and jump head foremost into the river, and then return into the square. The women having prepared the new corn for the feast, the men take some of it and rub it between their hands, then on their faces and breasts, and then they feast.

"THIRD DAY.

"The men sit in the square.

"FOURTH DAY.

"The women go early in the morning and get the new fire, clean out their hearths, sprinkle them with sand, and make their fires. The men finish burning out the first four logs, and they take ashes, rub them on their chin, neck and abdomen, and they go into the water. This day they eat salt, and they dance Obungauchapco (the long dance).

"FIFTH DAY.

"They get four new logs, and place them as on the first day, and they drink the black drink.

"SIXTH AND SEVENTH DAYS.

[43] Again Pickett here edits the quotes from Hawkins changing the spelling of "counsellors" to "councilors," dropping parts of sentences, and deleting the last sentences of the last paragraph of this extended quote. Hawkins, Ibid., 71–72.

[44] Pickett has edited the extended quote by Hawkins describing the "Boos-ke-tau" or Busk among the Creek towns, especially the format and wording of the first paragraph under "EIGHTH DAY." Ibid., 77.

"They remain in the square.

"EIGHTH DAY.

"They get two large pots, and their physic plants, the names of which are:

Mic-ca-ho-you-e-juh,	Co-hal-le-wau-gee,
Toloh,	Chofeinsack-cau-fuck-au,
A-che-nau,	Cho-fe-mus-see,
Cap-pau-pos-cau,	Hillis-hutke,
Chu-lis-sau (the roots),	To-te-cuh-chooe-his-see,
Tuck-thlau-lus-te,	Welau-nuh,
To-te-cul-hil-lis-so-wau,	Oak-chon-utch-co.

These plants are put in pots and beat up with water. The chemists, E-lic-chul-gee, called by the traders physic-makers, blow into it through a small reed, and then it is drank by the men and rubbed over their joints till the afternoon.

"They collect old corn cobs and pine burs, put them into a pot and burn them to ashes. Four very young virgins bring ashes from their houses and stir them up. The men take white clay and mix it with water in two pans. One pan of clay and one of the ashes are carried to the cabin of the Micco, and the other two to that of the warriors. They then rub themselves with the clay and ashes. Two men, appointed to that office, bring some flowers of tobacco of a small kind, Itch-au-chee-le-pue-pug-gee, or as the name imports, the old man's tobacco, which was prepared on the first day and put in a pan in the cabin of the Micco, and they gave a little of it to everyone present.

"The Micco and councilors then go four times around the fire, and every time they face the east they throw some of the flowers into the fire. They then go, and stand to the west. The warriors then repeat the same ceremony.

"A cane is stuck up at the cabin of the Micco, with two white feathers at the end of it. One of the fish tribe (Thlot-logulgee) takes it, just as the sun goes down, and goes off to the river, followed by all. When he gets half way down the river he gives the death whoop, which he repeats four times between the square and the water's edge. Here they all place themselves as thick as they can stand near the edge of the water. He sticks up the cane at the water's edge, and they all put a grain of the old man's tobacco on their heads and in each ear. Then, at a signal given four different times, they throw some into the river; and every man, at a signal, plunges into the river and picks up four stones from the bottom. With these they cross themselves on their breasts four times, each time throwing a stone into the river and giving the death whoop. They then wash themselves, take up the cane and feathers, return and stick it up in the square, and visit through the town. At night they dance *O-bun-gau-hadjo* (mad dance), and this finishes the ceremony.

"This happy institution of the *Boos-ke-tau* restores man to himself, to his family, and to his nation. It is a general amnesty, which not only absolves the Indians from all crimes, murder alone excepted, but seems to bring guilt itself into oblivion."*

With some slight variations, the Green Corn Dance was thus celebrated throughout the Creek Confederacy. At the town of Tuckabatchee, however, it will be recollected, that on the fourth day, the Indians introduced the "brass plates." At Coosawda, the principal town of the Alabamas, they celebrated a Boosketau of four days each, of mulberries and beans, when these fruits respectively ripened.†

James Adair, a man of learning and enterprise, lived more than thirty years among the Chickasaws, and had frequent intercourse with the nations of the Muscogees, Cherokees and Choctaws, commencing in 1735. He was an Englishman, and was connected with the extensive commerce carried on at an early period with these tribes. While among the Chickasaws, with whom he first began to reside in 1744, he wrote a large work on aboriginal history. When he returned to his mother country, he published this work, the *American Indians*, a ponderous volume of near five hundred pages, at London, in 1775. Well acquainted with the Hebrew language, and having, in his long residence with the Indians, acquired an accurate knowledge of their tongue, he devoted the larger portion of his work to prove that the latter were originally Hebrews, and were a portion of the lost tribes of Israel. He asserts, that at the Boosketaus of the Creeks and other tribes within the limits of Alabama, the warriors danced around the holy fire, during which the elder priest invoked the Great Spirit, while the others responded "*Halelu! Halelu!*" then "*Haleluiah, Haleluyah!*" He is ingenious in his arguments, and introduces many strange things to prove, to his own satisfaction, that the Indians were descendants of the Jews—seeking, throughout two hundred pages, to assimilate their language, manners and customs. He formed his beliefs that they were originally the same people, upon their division into tribes, worship of Jehovah, notions of a theocracy, belief in the ministration of angels, language and dialects, manner of computing time, their prophets and high priests, festivals, fasts and religious rites, daily sacrifices, ablutions and anointings, laws of uncleanliness, abstinence from unclean things, marriages, divorces, and punishments for adultery, other punishments, their towns of refuge, purification and ceremony preparatory to war, their ornaments, manner of curing the sick, burial of the dead, mourning for the dead, raising seed to a deceased brother, choice of names adapted to their circumstances and times, their own traditions, and the accounts of our English writers, and the testimony which the Spanish and other authors have given

* Hawkins, "A Sketch of the Creek Country," 75–78.

† Adair, *American Indians*, 97.

concerning the primitive inhabitants of Peru and Mexico.[45]

He insists that in nothing do they differ from the Jews except that rite of circumcision, which, he contends, their ancestors dispensed with, after they became lost from the other tribes, on account of the danger and inconvenience of the execution of that rite, to those engaged in a hunting and roving life. That when the Israelites were forty years in the wilderness, even then they attempted to dispense with circumcision, but Joshua, by his stern authority, enforced its observance.[46] The difference in food, mode of living and climate are relied upon by Adair, to account for the difference in the color, between the Jew and Indian, and also why the one has hair upon the body in profusion and the other has not.*

Adair is by no means alone in his opinion of the descent of the American Indians. Other writers, who have lived among these people, have arrived at the same conclusion. Many of the old Indian countrymen with whom we have conversed believe in their Jewish origin, while others are of a different opinion. Abram Mordecai, an intelligent Jew, who dwelt fifty years in the Creek Nation, confidently believed that the Indians were originally of his people, and he asserted that in their Green Corn dances he had heard them often utter in grateful tones the word "*yavoyaha! yavoyaha!*"[47] He was always informed by the Indians that this meant Jehovah, or the Great Spirit, and that they were then returning thanks for the abundant harvest with which they were blessed.†

Colonel Hawkins concludes his account of the religious and war ceremonies of the Creek Indians as follows:[48]

"At the age of from fifteen to seventeen, the ceremony of initiating youth to manhood is performed. It is called the Boosketau, in like manner as the annual Boosketau of the nation. A youth of the proper age gathers two handfuls of the Sou-watch-cau, a very bitter root, which he eats a whole day. Then he steeps the leaves in water and drinks it. In the dusk of evening he eats two or three spoonfuls of boiled grits. This is repeated for four days, and during this time he remains in a house. The Sou-watch-cau has the effect of intoxicating

* Adair, *American Indians*, 15–220.

† Conversations with Abram Mordecai, a man of ninety-two years of age, whom I found in Dudleyville, Tallapoosa County, in the fall of 1847. His mind was fresh in the recollection of early incidents. Of him I shall have occasion to speak in another portion of the work.

and maddening. The fourth day he goes out, but must put on a pair of new moccasins (stillapicas). For twelve moons he abstains from eating bucks, except old ones, and from turkey cocks, fowls, peas and salt. During this period he must not pick his ears or scratch his head with his fingers, but use a small stick. For four moons he must have a fire to himself to cook his food, and a little girl, a virgin, may cook for him. His food is boiled grits. The fifth moon any person may cook for him, but he must serve himself first, and use one pan and spoon. Every new moon he drinks for four days the possau (button snakeroot), an emetic, and abstains for three days from all food, except in the evening a little boiled grits (humpetuh hutke). The twelfth moon he performs, for four days, what he commenced with on the first. The fifth day he comes out of his house, gathers corncobs, burns them to ashes, and with these rubs his body all over. At the end of this moon he sweats under blankets, then goes into water, and thus ends the ceremony. This ceremony is sometimes extended to four, six or eight moons, or even to twelve days only, but the course is the same.

"During the whole of this ceremony the physic is administered by the Is-te-puc-cau-chau-thlucco (Great Leader), who, in speaking of the youth under initiation says, 'I am physicing him'– Boo-se-ji-jite saut li-to mise-cha. Or 'I am teaching him all that it is proper for him to know'– (nauk o-mul-gau e-muc-e-thli-jite saut litomise cha). The youth during this initiation does not touch any one except young persons, who are under a like course with himself. And if he dreams, he drinks the possau."*

Whenever Creeks were forced to take up arms, the Tustenuggee caused to be displayed in the public places a club, part of which was painted red. He sent it to each subordinate chief, accompanied with a number of pieces of wood, equal to the number of days that it would take that chief to present himself at the rendezvous. The war chief alone had the power of appointing that day. When this club had arrived, each chief caused a drum to be beat before the grand cabin where he resided. All the inhabitants immediately presented themselves. He informed them of the day and place where he intended to kindle his fire. He repaired to that place before the appointed day, and rubbed two sticks together, which produced fire. He kindled it in the

* Hawkins, 78–79.

[45] James Adair (c. 1709–1783) was born in County Antrim, Ireland, a Scottish Presbyterian community, in 1709 and arrived in South Carolina in 1735 and entered the Indian trade in the towns of the Catawba and Cherokee. By the 1740s he was deeply involved in the deerskin trade with the Chickasaw and Choctaws and referred to himself as an "English Chickasaw" and lived much of his life among the Chickasaw. He published his *History of the American Indians* in London in 1775 in which he presented twenty-three arguments that the American Indians were descendants of the Hebrews. His origin thesis was controversial and challenged immediately after the publication of his book. Adair, *American Indians,* xi, 1–53, 140–43, 447–48 n. 1, 449 n. 3.

[46] Modern research—including the most recent editor of Adair's *History,* Kathryn E. Holland Braund—provides evidence to refute Adair's claims regarding the lack of circumcision by American Indians from Romans' *Concise Natural History* and a work published in 1652. Mounting archaeological, anthropological, and historical data and research provide ample evidence to disprove Adair's twenty-three arguments and others who have embraced the theories surrounding the lost Israelites. Ibid., 75–241, 500 n. 138.

[47] Abraham Mordecai (1755–1850), an early Jewish migrant to Alabama, established a trade with Cusseta on the Alabama-Georgia border around 1783, married a Creek woman, and continued to expand his trade and influence after moving to Ecunchata in 1785. He worked closely with Benjamin Hawkins to implement the federal

government's "plan of civilization" by building a cotton gin on the Alabama River in present day Montgomery County, Alabama. He aided the U.S. war effort against the Creek Red Sticks and continued his business enterprises through the Creek removal era after 1836. In September 1847, Pickett interviewed Mordecai and published the interview in the Montgomery *Tri-Weekly Flag and Advertiser*. Albert James Pickett, "A Sketch of Old Mordecai," *Tri-Weekly Flag and Advertiser*, 5 October 1847; Matthew Blue, *The Works of Matthew Blue: Montgomery's First Historian*, ed. Mary Ann Neeley (Montgomery: NewSouth Books, 2010), 35, 308; "Abraham Mordecai," http://www.encyclopediaofalabama.org/article/h-3135.

[48] Hawkins subtitles this section "The Ceremony of initiating Youth into Manhood" and it is followed by "War Physic, Ho-ith-le Hil-lis-so-wau." Hawkins, "Sketch of the Creek Country," 78–79.

midst of a square, formed by four posts, sufficiently extended to contain the number of warriors he desired to assemble. As soon as the day dawned, the chief placed himself between the two posts which fronted the east, and held in his hand a package of small sticks. When a warrior entered the enclosure, which was open only on one side, he threw down a stick and continued until they were all gone, the number of sticks being equal to the number of warriors he required. Those who presented themselves afterwards could not be admitted, and they returned home to hunt, indicating the place where they could be found if their services should be needed. Those who thus tardily presented themselves were badly received at home, and were reproached for the slight desire they had testified to defend their country.[49]

The warriors who were in the enclosure remained there, and for three days took the medicine of war. Their wives brought them their arms, and all things requisite for the campaign, and deposited them three hundred yards in front of the square, together with a little bag of parched corn-meal, an ounce of which would make a pint of broth.* It was only necessary to mix it with water, and in five minutes it became as thick as soup cooked by a fire. Two ounces would sustain a man twenty-four hours. It was indispensable, for, during a war expedition, the party could not kill game.

The three days of medicine having expired, the chief departed with his warriors to the rendezvous appointed by the Grand Chief. Independently of this medicine, which was taken by all, each subordinate chief had his particular talisman, which he carefully carried about his person. It consisted of a small bag, in which were a few stones and some pieces of cloth which had been taken from the garments of the Grand Chief, in the return from some former war. If the subordinate chief forgot his bag, he was deprived of his rank, and remained a common soldier during the whole expedition. The Grand Chief presented himself at the rendezvous on the appointed day, and he was sure to find there the assembled warriors. He then placed himself at the head of the army, making all necessary arrangements, without being obliged to rendezvous on account of any one. Being certain that his discipline and orders would be punctually enforced, he marched with confidence against the enemy. When they were ready to march, each subordinate chief was compelled to be provided with the liquor which they called the medicine of war; and the Creeks placed it in such a degree of confidence that it was difficult for a war chief to collect his army if they were deprived of it. He would be exposed to great danger if he should be forced to do battle without having satisfied

* Called by the modern Creek traders "coal flour."

this necessity. If he should suffer defeat—which would certainly be the case, because the warriors would have no confidence in themselves, but be overcome by their own superstitious fears,—he would be responsible for all misfortunes.

There were two medicines, the great and the little, and it remained for the chief to designate which of these should be used. The warrior, when he had partaken of the great medicine, believed himself invulnerable. The little medicine served, in his eyes, to diminish danger. Full of confidence in the statements of his chief, the latter easily persuaded him that when he gave him only the little medicine it was because the circumstances did not require the other. These medicines being purgative in their nature, the warrior found himself less endangered by the wounds which he might receive. The Creeks had still another means of diminishing the danger of their wounds, which consisted in fighting almost naked, for it is well known that the particles of cloth remaining in wounds render them more difficult to heal. They observed during war the most rigorous discipline, for they neither eat nor drank without an order from the chief. They dispensed with drinking, even while passing along the bank of a river, because circumstances had obliged their chief to forbid it, under pain of depriving them of their medicine of war, or, rather, of the influence of their talisman. When an enemy compelled them to take up arms they never returned home without giving him battle, and at least taking a few scalps. These may be compared to the *colors* among civilized troops, for when a warrior had killed an enemy he took his scalp, which was an honorable trophy for him to return to his nation. They removed them from the head of an enemy with great skill and dexterity. They were not all of the same value, but were classed, and it was for the chiefs, who were the judges of all achievements, to decide the value of each. It was in proportion to the number and value of these scalps that a Creek advanced in civil as well as military rank. It was necessary, in order to occupy a station of any importance, to have taken at least seven of them. If a young Creek, having been at war, returned without a single scalp, he continued to bear the name of his mother and could not marry, but if he returned with a scalp, the principle men assembled at the grand cabin, to give him a name, that he might abandon that of his mother. They judged of the value of the scalp by the dangers experienced in capturing it, and the greater these dangers, the more considerable were the title and advancement derived from it, by its owner.

In time of battle, the Great Chief commonly placed himself in the center of the army, and sent reinforcements wherever danger appeared most pressing. When he perceived that his forces were repulsed and feared that they would yield entirely to the efforts of the enemy, he advanced in person, and

[49] While Pickett uses Milfort's *Mémoire* as his source to discuss Creek warfare, it parallels Adair's lengthy narrative on the Indian way of war. See Adair, *American Indians,* 375–92.

combated hand to hand. A cry, repeated on all sides, informed the warriors of the danger to which a chief was exposed. Immediately the *corps de reserve* came together, and advanced to the spot where the Grand Chief was, in order to force the enemy to abandon him. Should he be dead, they would all die rather than abandon his body to the enemy, without first securing his scalp. They attached such value to this relic, and so much disgrace to the loss of it, that when the danger was very great, and they were not able to prevent his body from falling into the hands of the enemy, the warrior who was nearest to the dead chief, took his scalp and fled, at the same time raising a cry, known only among the savages. He then went to the spot which the deceased chief had indicated, as the place of rendezvous, should his army be beaten. All the subordinate chiefs, being made aware of his death by this cry, made dispositions to retreat; and, this being effected, they proceeded to the election of his successor, before taking any other measures. The Creeks were very warlike, and were not rebuffed by defeat. On the morrow, after an unfortunate battle, they advanced with renewed intrepidity, to encounter their enemy anew.

When they advanced towards an enemy, they marched one after another, the chief of the party being at the head. They arranged themselves in such a manner as to place the foot of everyone in the track made by the first. The last one concealed even that track with grass. By this means they kept from the enemy any knowledge of their number. When they made a halt, for the purpose of encamping, they formed in a circle, leaving a passage only large enough to admit a single man. They sat cross-legged, and each one had his gun by his side. The chief faced the entrance of the circle, and no warrior could go out without his permission. At the time of sleeping he gave a signal, and after that no person could stir. Rising was performed at the same signal. It was ordinarily the Grand Chief who marked out positions, and placed sentinels to watch for the security of the army. He always had a great number of runners, both before and behind, so that an army was rarely surprised. They, on the contrary, conducted wars against the Europeans entirely by sudden attacks, and they were very dangerous to those who were not aware of them.*

When the Creeks returned from war with captives, they marched into their town with shouts and the firing of guns. They stripped them naked and put on their feet bearskin moccasins, with the hair exposed. The punishment was always left to the women, who examined their bodies for their war-marks.

* Leclerc Milfort, *Mémoire ou coup d'oeil rapide sur mes différens voyages et mon séjour dans la nation Crëck*, 218–19, 240, 252.

Sometimes the young warriors, who had none of these honorable inscriptions, were released and used as slaves. But the warrior of middle age, even those of advanced years, suffered death by fire. The victim's arms were pinioned, and one end of a strong grape vine tied around his neck, while the other was fastened to the top of a war-pole, so as to allow him to track around a circle of fifteen yards. To secure his scalp against fire, tough clay was placed upon his head. The immense throng of spectators were now filled with delight, and eager to witness the inhuman spectacle. The suffering warrior was not dismayed, but, with a manly and insulting voice, sang the war-song. The women then made a furious onset with flaming torches, dripping with hot, black pitch, and applied them to his back and all parts of his body. Suffering excruciating pain, he rushed from the pole with the fury of a wild beast, kicking, biting and trampling his cruel assailants under foot. But fresh numbers came on, and after a long time, and when he was nearly burned to his vitals, they ceased and poured water upon him to relieve him—only to prolong their sport. They renewed their tortures, when, with champing teeth and sparkling eyeballs, he once more broke through the demon throng to the extent of his rope, and acted every part that the deepest desperation could prompt. Then he died.[50] His head was scalped, his body quartered, and the limbs carried over the town in triumph.*

An enumeration of the towns found in the Creek Nation by Col. Hawkins, in 1798, will conclude the notice of the manners and customs of these remarkable people, though, hereafter, they will often be mentioned, in reference to their commerce and wars with the Americans.

TOWNS OF THE UPPER CREEKS.[51]

Tal-e-se, derived from Tal-o-fau, *a town*, and e-se, *taken*—situated in the fork of the Eufaube, upon the left bank of the Tallapoosa.

Took-a-batcha, opposite Tallase.

Auttose, on the left side of Tallapoosa, a few miles below the latter.

Ho-ith-le-waule—from ho-ith-le, *war*, and waule, *divide*—right bank of the Tallapoosa, five miles below Auttose.

Foosce-hat-che—fooso-wau, *a bird*, and hat-che, *tail* –two miles below the latter, on the right bank.

Coo-loo-me was below and adjoining the latter.

E-cun-hut-ke—e-cun-nau, *earth*, and hut-ke, *white*—below Coo-loo-me, on the same side of the Tallapoosa.

* Adair, 390–91.

Sou-van-no-gee, left bank of the river.

Mook-lau-sau, a mile below the latter, same side.

Coo-sau-dee, three miles below the confluence of the Coosa and Tallapoosa, on the west bank of the Alabama.

E-cun-chate—e-cun-na, *earth*, chate, *red*—(now a part of the city of Montgomery.)

Too-was-sau, three miles below, same side of the Alabama.

Pau-woe-te, two miles below the latter, on the same side.

Au-tau-gee, right side of the Alabama, near the mouth of the creek of the same name.

Tus-ke-gee—in the fork of the Coosa and Tallapoosa, on the east bank of the former—the old site of Forts Toulouse and Jackson.

Hoochoice and Hookchoie-ooche, towns just above the latter.

O-che-a-po-fau—o-che-ub, *hickory tree*, and po-fau, *in* or *among*—east bank of the Coosa, on the plain just below the city of Wetumpka.

We-wo-cau—we-wau, water, wo-cau, *barking* or *roaring*–on a creek of that name, fifteen miles above the latter.

Puc-cun-tal-lau-has-see—epuc-cun-nau, *may-apple*, tal-lau-has-see, *old town*—in the fork of a creek of that name.

Coo-sau, on the left bank of that river, between the mouths of Eufaula and Nauche (creeks now called Talladega and Kiamulgee).

Au-be-cho-che, on Nauche creek, five miles from the Coosa. Nau-che, on same creek, five miles above the latter.

Eu-fau-lau-hat-che, fifteen miles still higher up on the same creek.

Woc-co-coie—woc-co, *blow horn*, coie, *a nest*—on Tote-pauf-cau creek.

Hill-au-bee, on col-luffa-creek, which joins Hillaubee creek on the right side, one mile below the town.

Thla-noo-che-au-bau-lau—thlen-ne, *mountain*, ooche, *little*, au-bau-lau, over—on a branch of the Hillaubee.

Au-net-te-chap-co—au-net-te, *swamp*, chap-co, *long*—on a branch of the Hillaubee.

E-chuse-is-li-gau, *where a young thing was found* (a child was found here)—left side of Hillaubee creek.

Oak-tau-hau-zau-see—oak-tau-hau, *sand*, zau-see, *great deal*—on a creek of that name, a branch of the Hillaubee.

Oc-fus-kee—oc, *in*, fus-kee, *a point*, right bank of the Tallapoosa.

New-yau-cau, named after *New York*, when Gen. McGillivray returned from there in 1790, twenty miles above the latter, on the left side of the Tallapoosa.

Took-au-batche-tal-lau-has-se, four miles above the latter, right side of the river.

[50] Pickett provides a close paraphrasing of Adair's narrative of the treatment of captives based on his experiences among the Cherokee, Chickasaw, Choctaw, and Creek. Adair, *American Indians*, 384–85.

[51] While Hawkins provided more descriptive detail and history of the towns, Pickett used a listing of the towns with the phonetic spellings provided by Hawkins and with much briefer comments. Hawkins titled this subsection "A description of the towns on Coosau and Tal-la-poo-sa, generally called Upper Creeks." In several instances, Pickett used slightly altered spellings for several towns, including Aut-tos-se, Au-be-coo-che, and Nau-che, or the printer failed to follow his manuscript correctly. Hawkins, "Sketch of the Creek Country," 26–52.

Im-mook-fau, *a gorget made of a conch*, on the creek of that name.

Too-to-cau-gee—too-to, *corn-house*, cau-gee, *standing*—twenty miles above New-yau-cau, right bank of the Tallapoosa.

Au-che-nau-ul-gau—auche-nau, cedar, ul-gau, *all*—forty miles above New-yau-cau, on a creek. It is the farthest north of all the Creek settlements.

E-pe-sau-gee, on a large creek of that name.

Sooc-he-ah—sooc-cau, *hog*, he-ah, *here*—right bank of the Tallapoosa, twelve miles above Oc-fus-kee.

Eu-fau-lau, five miles above Oc-fus-kee, right bank of the river.

Ki-a-li-jee, on the creek of that name, which joins the Tallapoosa on the right side.

Au-che-nau-hat-che—au-che, *cedar*, hat-che, *creek*.

Hat-che-chub-bau—hat-che, *creek*, chub-bau, *middle* or *half way*.

Sou-go-hat-che—sou-go, *cymbal* (musical instrument), hatche, *creek*—joins the Tallapoosa on the left side.

Thlot-lo-gul-gau—thlot-lo, *fish*, gul-gau, *all*—called by traders "Fish Ponds," on a creek, a branch of the Ul-hau-hat-che.

O-pil-thluc-co—O-pil-lo-wau, *swamp*, thlucco, *big*—twenty miles from the Coosa, a creek of that name.

Pin-e-hoo-te—pin-e-wau, *turkey*, choo-te, *house*—a branch of the E-pee-sau-gee.

Po-chuse-hat-che—po-chu-so-wau, *hatchet*, hat-che, *creek*—(in Coosa County).

Oc-fus-coo-che, *little ocfuskee*, four miles above New-yau-caw.

TOWNS AMONG THE LOWER CREEKS.[52]

Chat-to-ho-che—chat-to, *a stone*, ho-che, *marked* or *flowered*. Such rocks are found in the bed of that river above Ho-ith-le-te-gau. This is the origin and meaning of the name of that beautiful river.

Cow-e-tough, on the right bank of the Chat-to-ho-che, three miles below the falls.

O-cow-ocuh-hat-che, *falls creek*, on the right side of the river at the termination of the falls.

Hatche-canane, *crooked creek*.

Woc-coo-che, *calf creek*.

O-sun-nup-pau, *moss creek*.

Hat-che-thlucco, *big creek*.

Cow-e-tuh Tal-hau-has-se—Cowetuh Tal-lo-fau, *a town*, hasse, *old*—three miles below Cowetuh, on the right bank of the Chattahoochee.

[52] Pickett again uses a listing of towns with much briefer commentary than provided by Hawkins in this subsection titled "The towns on the Chat-to-ho-che, generally called the Lower Creeks." Hawkins, Ibid., 52–66.

We-tum-cau—we-wau, *water*, tum-cau, *rumbling*—a main branch of the Uchee Creek.

Cus-se-tuh, five miles below Cow-e-tuh, on the left bank of the Chattahoochee.

Au-put-tau-e, a village of Cussetuh, on Hat-che-thluc-co, twenty miles from the river.

U-chee, on the right bank of the Chat-to-ho-che, ten miles below Cowetuh Tallauhassee, and just below the mouth of the Uchee Creek.

In-tuch-cul-gau—in-tuch-ke, *dam across water*—ul-gau, *all*; a Uchee village, on Opil-thlacco, twenty-eight miles from its junction with the Flint River.

Pad-gee-li-gau—pad-jee, *a pigeon*—li-gau, sit, *pigeon roost*—on the right bank of Flint River (a Uchee village).

Toc-co-qul-egau, *tadpole*, on Kit-cho-foone creek (a Uchee village).

Oose-oo-chee, two miles below Uchee, on the right bank of the Chattahoochee.

Che-au-hau, below and adjoining the latter.

Au-muc-cul-le, *pour upon me*, on a creek of that name, which joins on the right side of the Flint.

O-tel-who-yau-nau, *hurricane town*, on the right bank of the Flint.

Hit-che-tee, on the left bank of the Chattahoochee, one mile below Che-au-hau.

Che-au-hoo-chee, *Little Cheauhaw*, one mile and a half west from Hit-che-tee.

Hit-che-too-che, *Little Hitchetee*, on both sides of the Flint.

Tut-tal-lo-see, fowl, on a creek of that name.

Pala-chooc-le, on the right bank of the Chattahoochee.

O-co-nee, six miles below the latter, on the left bank of the Chattahoochee.

Sou-woo-ge-lo, six miles below Oconee, on the right bank.

Sou-woog-e-loo-che, four miles below Oconee, on the left bank of the Chattahoochee.

Eu-fau-la, fifteen miles below the latter, on the left bank of the same river.

From this town settlements extended occasionally to the mouth of the Flint.*

* Hawkins, "A Sketch of the Creek Country," 26–66. In addition to the published copy of this interesting pamphlet, sent to me by I. K. Tefft, Esq., of Savannah, the Hon. F. W. Pickens, of South Carolina, loaned me a manuscript copy of the same work, written by Col. Hawkins for his grandfather, Gen. Andrew Pickens, who was an intimate friend of Hawkins, and was associated with him in several important Indian treaties, and whose name will often be mentioned hereafter.

Chapter II – Part III

MOBILIANS, CHATOTS, THOMEZ AND TAENSAS

In 1718, the French West India Company sent, from Rochelle, eight hundred colonists to Louisiana. Among them was a Frenchman of intelligence and high standing, named Le Page Du Pratz, who was appointed superintendent of the public plantations. After a residence of sixteen years in this country, he returned to France, and published an interesting work upon Louisiana. Du Pratz was often at Mobile, and about the period of 1721 found living, in that vicinity, a few small tribes of Indians, whom we will now describe.[1]

The Chatots were a very small tribe, who composed a town of about forty huts, adjoining the bay and river of Mobile. They appear to have resided at or near the present city of Mobile. The Chatots were great friends of the French settlers, and most of them embraced the Catholic religion. North from Mobile, and upon the first bluffs on the same side of the river of that name, lived the Thomez, who were not more numerous than the Chatots, and who, also, had been taught to worship the true God. Opposite to them, upon the Tensaw River, lived a tribe of Taensas, whose settlement consisted of one hundred huts. They were a branch of the Natchez, and, like them, kept a perpetual fire burning in their temple.[2]

Further north, and near the confluence of the Tombigbee and Alabama, and above there, the Mobilians still existed. It was from these people, a remnant of whom survived the invasion of De Soto, that the city, river and bay derive their names.* They, also, kept a fire in their temple, which was never suffered for a moment to expire. Indeed, they had some pre-eminence in this particular—for, formerly, the natives obtained this holy light from their temples.† These small tribes were all living in peace with each other, upon

* Le Page Du Pratz, *History of Louisiana*, 308–09.

† Charlevoix, *Journal of a Voyage to North America*, 2: 273.

[1] Antoine Simon Le Page du Pratz (c. 1695–1775) published his *Histoire de la Louisiane Contenant la Decouverte de ce vaste pays* in 1758 which was based on his sixteen years in French Louisiana from 1718–1734. He may have been born in the Netherlands, but he received his education in France, graduating from a French *cours de mathematiques*. He considered himself French and a professional architect with skills as a hydraulic engineer. He arrived at Dauphin Island in 1718, settled on a four hundred acre plantation near Fort Rosalie in the Natchez District, and developed a friendship with the Natchez. In 1728, he moved to New Orleans, where he was recruited by the new governor, Etienne de Périer, and his commissary, Jacques de la Chaise, to operate a plantation owned by the Company of the Indies. The

the discovery of their country by the French, and continued so. Gradually, however, they became merged in the larger nations of the Choctaws and Chickasaws. They were all, sometimes, called the Mobile Indians, by the early French settlers.[3]

The Natchez once inhabited the southwestern portion of the Mexican empire, but on account of the wars with which they were continually harassed by neighboring Indians, they began to wander northeast. Finally they settled upon the banks of the Mississippi, chiefly on the bluff where now stands the beautiful city which bears their name.* They retained, until they were broken up by the French, many of the religious rites and customs of the Mexicans. Their form of government was distinguished from that of other tribes in Alabama and Mississippi, by its ultra-despotism, and by the grandeur and haughtiness of its chiefs. The grand chief of the Natchez bore the name of the sun. Every morning, as soon as that bright luminary appeared, he stood at the door of his cabin, turned his face toward the east, and bowed three times, at the same time prostrating himself to the ground.[4] A pipe, which was never used but upon this occasion, was then handed him, from which he puffed smoke, first toward the sun, and then toward the other three quarters of the world.[5] He pretended that he derived his origin from the sun, acknowledged no other master, and held absolute power over the lives and goods of his subjects. When he or his nearest female relation died, his body-guard was obliged to follow to the land of the spirits. The death of a chief sometimes resulted in that of an hundred persons, who considered it a great honor to be sacrificed upon his death. Indeed, few Natchez of note died without being attended to the other world by some of their relatives, friends or servants.[6] So eager were persons to sacrifice themselves in this way, that sometimes it was ten years before their turn came,

*Le Page Du Pratz, *Louisiana.*

Natchez revolt and its aftermath ended the Company's charter and Le Page du Pratz left Louisiana in 1734. Although he had an opportunity to purchase the three-volume *Histoire de la* Louisiane in 1848, Pickett apparently used the 1774 one-volume edition based on the incomplete two-volume English translation published in 1763. Antoine Simon Le Page du Pratz, *The History of Louisiana*, ed. Joseph G. Tregle, Jr. (1774; reprint, Baton Rouge: Louisiana State University Press, 1975), xviii-xxviii. See Bartlett & Welford to AJP, New York, 9 May 1848, Pickett Papers, ADAH.

2 The Chatot and Thomez or Tohome were small coastal Indian tribes and Muskogean speakers who found refuge on the upper Mobile River under the French early in the eighteenth century. The French first made contact with the Taensa living in northeastern Louisiana in the late seventeenth century. At the invitation of Bienville, they settled north of Mobile on the Tensaw River but returned to Louisiana in 1764 after the British occupied Mobile. Le Page du Pratz, *History of Louisiana*, 308; Swanton, *Indians of the Southeastern United States*, 107–08, 188–89, 196–97

3 Despite Pickett's assertion that the French referred to all the Indians in the Tombigbee and Alabama basins as Mobile Indians, the French learned very quickly to identify their Indian neighbors by tribal and town affiliation. See Le Page du Pratz, *History of Louisiana*, 304–27.

4 Le Page du Pratz reports that he convinced the "keeper of the temple" at the Grand Village of the Natchez to discuss how his people came to inhabit their lands and that he revealed that they had "lived yonder under the sun, (pointing with his finger nearly south-west, by which I understood that he meant Mexico) . . ." While the Natchezan speakers may have had a migration legend linking them to Mexico, more recent archaeological, anthropological, and historical data and study prove that the Natchez were a coalescent society of Natchezan and Timucuan speakers, including the Tiou and Grigra refugee groups. Le Page du Pratz, *History of Louisiana*, 291–98; Barnett, *Natchez Indians*, xiv-xv, 41–48.

5 The Great Sun gave a sunrise prayer offering with a calumet and tobacco each morning, and he

and those who obtained the favor, spun the cord with which they were to be strangled.*

The cabins of the Natchez were in the shape of pavilions, low, without windows, and covered with corn stalks, leaves and cane matting. That of the great chief, which stood upon an artificial mound, and fronted a large square, was handsomely rough-cast with clay, both inside and out. The temple was at the side of his cabin, facing the east, and at the extremity of the square. It was in an oblong form, forty feet in length and twenty in breadth. Within it were the bones of the deceased chiefs, contained in boxes and baskets. Three logs of wood, joined at the ends and placed in a triangle, occupied the middle part of the floor, and burned slowly away, night and day.[7] Keepers attended and constantly removed them.† The Great Sun informed Du Pratz, who had, in 1720, taken up his abode among them, that their nation was once very formidable, extending over vast regions and governed by numerous Suns and nobility; that one of the keepers of the temple once left it on some business, and while he was absent his associate keepers fell asleep; that the fire went out, and that, in the terror and dismay into which they were thrown, they substituted profane fire, with the hope that their shameful neglect would escape unnoticed. But a dreadful calamity was the consequence of this negligence. A horrible malady raged for years, during which many of the Suns, and an infinite number of people, died.‡ This fire was kept constantly burning in honor of the sun, which they seemed to worship and adore above everything else.[8] In the spring of 1700, Iberville, in company with a few of his colonial people, visited the Natchez. While there, one of the temples was consumed by lightning. The priests implored the women to cast their children in the flames to appease the anger of their divinity.[9] Before the French, by prayers

* Charlevoix, *Voyage to North America*, 2: 260–61.

† Charlevoix, *Voyage to North America*, 2: 256.

‡ Le Page Du Pratz, *Louisiana*, 333.

and his family were considered as living representatives of the physical sun. Lee Irwin, *Coming Down From Above: Prophecy, Resistance, and Renewal in Native American Religions* (Norman: University of Oklahoma Press, 2008), 36; John R. Swanton, *Indian Tribes of the Lower Mississippi Valley and Adjacent Coast of the Gulf of Mexico*, Bureau of American Ethnology, *Bulletin 43* (Washington: GPO, 1911), 174–75.

[6] Le Page du Pratz recorded the death of Stung Serpent, brother of the Great Sun, who died in 1725, and those who were to die at his interment, including his two wives and others, who were strangled. More recent research identifies the younger brother of the Great Sun as the Tattooed Serpent. Le Page du Pratz, *History of Louisiana*, 353–57. See James F. Barnett, Jr., *The Natchez Indians: A History to 1735* (Jackson: University Press of Mississippi, 2007), 54, 68–71, 86–99; and George Edward Milne, *Natchez Country: Indians, Colonists, and the Landscapes of Race in French Louisiana* (Athens: University of Georgia Press, 2015), 117–19.

[7] In his *History*, Le Page du Pratz reports that the temple was "about thirty feet square" and stood on a mound eight feet high near a small river. Pierre-François Xavier de Charlevoix's *Journal of a Voyage to North America* is presented as a series of letters, and in his "Letter XXX," he discusses the customs, manners, and religion of the Natchez. Le Page du Pratz, *History of Louisiana*, 351; Pierre-François Xavier de Charlevoix, *Journal of a Voyage to North America, Undertaken by Order of the French King*, trans. from the French of P. de Charlevoix. 2 vols. (London: R. and J. Dodsley, 1761), 2: 249–74.

[8] The Great Sun told Le Page du Pratz that they had not learned about the fire being allowed to burn out until the "guardian" of the temple confessed his culpability as he lay dying from the malady himself. Le Page du Pratz, *History of Louisiana*, 333.

[9] According to an entry in Pierre Le Moyne d'Iberville's journal, the temple destroyed by lightning was not at the Grand Village of the Natchez: "The night of the 16th to the 17th [March 1700] a thunderbolt fell on the temple of the Taensas and set fire to it which burned it entirely. These savages

and entreaties, could arrest this horrible proceeding, some of the innocent babes were already roasting in the flames.* At this time the Natchez, reduced by war and the death of the nobility, upon whose decease the existence of many others terminated, did not exceed a population of twelve hundred.[10]

Fort Rosalie, erected by the French in 1716, upon the bluff which sustains the city of Natchez, had a garrison of soldiers and numerous citizens.[11] On the morning of the 28th November 1729, the Great Sun and his warriors suddenly fell upon them, and before noon the whole male population were in the sleep of death. The women, children and slaves were reserved as prisoners of war. The consternation was great throughout the colony when this horrible massacre became known.[12] The French and Choctaws united, and drove the Natchez upon the lower Ouachita, just below the mouth of the Little River.[13] Here the latter erected mounds and embankments for defense, which covered an area of four hundred acres. In the meantime, having obtained assistance from France, the colonists marched against this stronghold, and, in January 1733, made a successful attack. They captured the Great Sun, several of the war chiefs and four hundred and twenty-seven of the tribe, who were sent from New Orleans to Santo Domingo as slaves. The remainder of the tribe made their escape.[14] Some of them sought asylum among the Chickasaws and Creeks, while others scattered in the far west.†

* Gayarré, *Histoire de la Louisiane*, 1: 73.

† The Natchez have been mentioned at length by a number of French authors, who were eyewitnesses of their bloody rites and ceremonies. See Bossu, *Travels Through . . . Louisiana*, 1: 32–67; Dumont de Montigny, *Mémoires historiques sur la Louisiane*, 1: 118–32; Charlevoix, *Voyage to North America*, 2: 252–74; Le Page Du Pratz, *Louisiana*, 79–95, 291–316. *Voyage en Amérique, suivi des Natchez; par m. le vicomte de Chateaubriand*—of this work 400 pages are taken up with the Natchez. *The Early Jesuit Missions in North America*—a recent publication. Many other works in my possession, upon Louisiana and Florida, allude briefly to that tribe.

to appease the Spirit . . . threw five little children in swaddling clothes into the fire of the temple." Quote in James F. Barnett, Jr., "The Yamasee War, the Bearded Chief, and the Founding of Fort Rosalie," ***Journal of Mississippi History*** **74 (Spring 2012): 12–13.**

[10] Bienville estimated that the Natchez numbered 1,200 men in 1699, but on 4 March 1700, Henri de Tonti reported the Natchez nation "counts 8 to 900 men." However, either number, using a multiplier of three or four to account for women and children, would yield a total population in the range of 3,200 to over 4,000—not Pickett's twelve hundred. Daniel H. Usner, Jr., ***American Indians in the Lower Mississippi Valley: Social and Economic Histories*** **(Lincoln: University of Nebraska Press, 1998), 49.**

[11] The French completed Fort Rosalie on 3 August 1716. The simple four-cornered palisaded fort—150 feet by 90 feet—was constructed on a prominent bluff. Barnett, ***Natchez Indians*****, 71.**

[12] Most contemporary observers—Du Pratz, Dumont, and Le Petit—blame the French commandant Chépart for the Natchez revolt that claimed 183 lives at Natchez, Terre Blanche, and the post of the Yazoos. "Data Concerning the

Natchez Massacre 1729–1730," *Louisiana Historical Quarterly* 1 (January 1918): 126–31; Jean-François-Benjamin Dumont de Montigny, *The Memoir of Lieutenant Dumont, 1715–1747: A Sojourner in the French Atlantic*, trans. Gordon M. Sayre, ed. Gordon M. Sayre and Carla Zecher, (Chapel Hill: University of North Carolina Press, 2012), 233–38; Le Page Du Pratz, *History of Louisiana*, 79–91; Barnett, *Natchez Indians*, 101–06.

[13] In his original narrative, Pickett frequently refers to the "lower Washita." The Natchez actually retreated to the Ouachita River, which flows out of west-central Arkansas in an east-southeastern direction into Louisiana, joining the Black and Red rivers in north-central Louisiana. The Washita River originates in Texas and flows into Oklahoma, terminating in Lake Texoma and the Red River. Glenn Gore, "Ouachita River," *The Encyclopedia of Arkansas History & Culture*, www.encyclopediaofarkansas.net. See also the U.S. Geological Survey Geographic Names Information System: Washita River.

[14] Between 27 January and 26 February 1730, a poorly coordinated assault by several hundred Choctaws and French forces under Henry de Louboëy gained the release of many French hostages but failed to stop the Natchez fighters from escaping across the Mississippi. In December 1730, Governor Etienne Périer launched a campaign that ended with the surrender and capture of some four hundred Natchez on 26 January 1731. While the captured Natchez ended up as slaves in Santo Domingo, the Natchez continued their resistance through 1734 before seeking asylum among the Chickasaw, Creeks, and Cherokee. Dumont de Montigny, *Memoir*, 238–39, 242–48, 250–54; Le Page Du Pratz, *History of Louisiana*, 91–96; Barnett, *Natchez Indians*, 109–31.

Chapter II – Part IV

THE CHOCTAWS AND CHICKASAWS

The Choctaws and Chickasaws descended from a people called the Chichimecas,who were among the first inhabitants of the Mexican empire. At an ancient period they began to wander towards the east, in company with the Chakchiumas. After a time they reached the Mississippi River and crossed it, arriving in this country with an aggregate force of ten thousand warriors. The Chakchiumas established themselves upon the headwaters of the Yazoo, the Chickasaws upon the northwestern sources of the Tombigbee, and the Choctaws upon the territory now embraced in southern Mississippi and southwestern Alabama. They thus gradually became three distinct tribes; but the Chickasaws and Chakchiumas were generally known by the name of the former,[1] while the Choctaws spoke the same language, with the exception of a difference produced by the intonation of the voice.*

Upon the first settlement of Mobile by the French, they found that the Choctaws and the remnant of the Mobilians employed the same language. Indeed, we have seen that the Mobilian chief, in 1540, had a name which was derived from two well-known Choctaw words—Tusca, *warrior*, and lusa, *black*. The Indians who fought De Soto at Cabusto, upon the Warrior, and who extended their lines six miles up and down its western banks to oppose his crossing, were the Pafallayas. They are believed to have been no other people than the Choctaws. There is a word in the language of the latter called falaya, *long*.† It is scarcely necessary to remind the reader that the Chickasaws were living in the upper part of Mississippi when De Soto invaded it, and that they fought him with great courage. Now, as the Choctaws, according to tradition, came with them into this country, and were a portion of the same family; it

[1] **In his original narrative, Pickett used James Adair's spelling of Chokchooma instead of Chakchiuma. Adair discounted the Spanish sources for linking the Chickasaw with the Chichimecas, who conducted a long resistance against the Spanish in modern northern Mexico known as the Chichimeca War (1550–1591). However, there is a source that claims the Choctaw migrated east to escape bondage under the Chichimeca and relates the story of "Chicameca's Head"—an upright bust-like stone near modern Louisville, Mississippi, standing three feet tall. The Chickasaw, Chakchiuma, and Choctaw were Muskogean speakers and often at war with each other. Adair, *American Indians*, 117, 354; Charlotte M. Gradie, "Discovering the Chichimecas," *The Americas* 51 (July 1994): 67–88; William Brecscia, Jr., "Choctaw Oral Traditions Relating to Tribal**

* Adair, *American Indians*, 5, 66, 352.

† *Transactions and Collections of the American Antiquarian Society*, 2: 105. (A paper read before the society by Albert Gallatin.)

is reasonable to suppose that the Pafallayas, the brave allies of Tuscaloosa, were the Choctaws—especially when taken in connection with the collateral evidence in our possession.[2] The tradition of the migration of the Chickasaws and Choctaws from the Mexican empire has been preserved by the former alone; while the latter, with few exceptions, have lost it.

On the road leading from St. Stephens, in Alabama, to the city of Jackson, Mississippi, was, some years ago, a large mound, embracing at the base about two acres, and rising forty feet high in a conical form, and enclosed by a ditch encompassing twenty acres. On the top of it was a deep hole, ten feet in circumference, out of which the ignorant portion of the Choctaws believed that their ancestors once sprung as thick as bees, peopling the whole of that part of the country. They had great regard for this artificial elevation, and called it Nanih Waiya, the signification of which is nanih, *hill*, and waiya, *mother*.[3] When hunting near this mound they were accustomed to throw into the hole the leg of a deer, thus feeding their mother. One day, in 1810, Mr. George S. Gaines, the United States Choctaw Factor, in going to the agency, rode up on this mound, which lay near the road. Presently a good many warriors passed by, and, after he had satisfied his curiosity, he rode on and overtook them. The chief, who was no less a personage than the celebrated Pushmataha, with a smile full of meaning and mischief, said: "Well, Mr. '*Gainis*,' I suppose you have been to pay our mother a visit; and what did she say?" Your mother, said the Factor, observed that her children were poor, had become too numerous to inhabit the country they were then occupying, and desired very much that they would sell their lands to the United States and move west of the Mississippi, to better and more extensive hunting grounds.* The old chief laughed immoderately, vociferating, "Holauba, holauba, feenah." (*It's a lie, it's a lie, it's a real lie.*) Our good mother never could have made such remarks."[4] On the journey he conversed much with Mr. Gaines upon the Indian traditions, and said that the true account was that his ancestors came from the west.†

In 1771, the population of the Choctaw Nation was considerable. Two thousand three hundred warriors were upon the superintendent's books at Mobile, while two thousand more were scattered over the country, engaged in hunting.[5] At that period Capt. Romans passed through seventy of their towns.‡ The eastern district of the nation was known as Oypat-oo-coo-la, or

* It was the policy of all the Indian agents to encourage the emigration of the Indians further west, and they never let an opportunity slip of alluding to it.

† Conversations with Mr. George S. Gaines. See also Bernard Romans, *Florida*, 71–90.

‡ Romans, 70–90.

Origin," in *The Choctaw Before Removal*, ed. Carolyn Keller Reeves (Jackson: University Press of Mississippi, 1985), 13–14.

2 While Rangel refers to the chiefdom of Apafalaya, Pickett continues to follow Elvas's etymology for the "province called Pafallaya" and applies it to the eighteenth century Choctaw. Modern scholars place the Apafalaya on the Black Warrior in western Alabama and refer to them as the historic Choctaw. *De Soto Chronicles*, 1: 105, 296; Hudson, *Knights of Spain*, 257–59, 480; Ethridge, *From Chicaza to Chickasaw*, 29–30.

3 Le Page Du Pratz and Romans recorded Choctaw origin legends that they "sprung out of the ground" and of them "coming out of a hole in the ground." Henry S. Halbert and Gideon Lincecum provide more descriptions of the Nanih Waiya mound and its connection to the Choctaw traditions. Le Page Du Pratz, *History of Louisiana*, 310; Romans, *Concise Natural History*, 129; Henry S. Halbert, "Nanih Waiya, The Sacred Mound of the Choctaw," *Publications of the Mississippi Historical Society*, vol. 2 (Oxford: The Society, 1898), 223–24; Gideon Lincecum, "Choctaw Traditions about Their Settlement in Mississippi and the Origin of Their Mounds,"

***Publications of the Mississippi Historical Society*, vol. 8 (Oxford: The Society, 1904), 521–42.**

[4] George Strother Gaines became the factor at the Choctaw Trading House at St. Stephens, Mississippi Territory, in 1806 and developed close friendships with the Choctaw, especially Pushmataha. Albert James Pickett, "2nd Conversation with Geo. S. Gaines, Spring of 1848," in *The Reminiscences of George Strother Gaines: Pioneer Statesman of Early Alabama and Mississippi, 1805–1843*, ed. James P. Pate (Tuscaloosa: University of Alabama Press, 1998), 147–48.

[5] Pickett misread Romans's text. He actually reported in 1771 "about two thousand men" in seventy villages and that he "heard of as many camps as could make no less than six hundred more men." In his 1726 memoir, Bienville falsely reported that the Choctaw had eight thousand warriors, and a second French source reported 3,610 warriors in forty-five villages. A devastating smallpox epidemic during the winter of 1764–1765 dramatically affected the Choctaw and their neighbors, making Romans's numbers credible. Romans, *Concise Natural History*, 131; Usner, *American Indians in the Lower Mississippi Valley*, 40–41, 43.

[6] Pickett is citing Romans in naming the political divisions of the Choctaw. Modern scholarship lists three divisions and some outlying towns: Western—Okla falaya (*people widely dispersed* or "*Long People*"); Eastern—Okla tannap (*people from the other side*); and Southern or Six Towns—Okla hannali (*people of the six towns*). Romans, *Concise Natural History*, 130–31; Patricia Galloway, "Choctaw Factionalism and Civil War, 1746–1750," in *The Choctaw Before Removal*, 124; Swanton, *Social and Ceremonial Life of the Choctaw Indians*, 55–75; Greg O'Brien, *Choctaws in a Revolutionary Age, 1750–1830* (Lincoln: University of Nebraska Press, 2002), 13–14.

[7] While Adair describes how the Choctaw achieved their flat "fore-heads," he failed to mention that it did not pertain to females but only male children. Both Romans and Bartram note that the practice only applied to males.

the *small nation*. The western was called Oocooloo-Falaya, Oocooloo-Hanalé, and Chickasawhays.[6]

These people were more slender in their form than other tribes. The men were raw-boned and astonishingly active. None could excel them in the ball play, or run as fast upon level ground.* Both sexes were well made, and the features of the females were lively and agreeable. They had the habit of inscribing their faces and bodies with a blue indelible ink, which appears to have been the practice of all the tribes to which it has been our province to allude. The Choctaws formed the heads of the infants into different shapes by compression, but it was chiefly applied to the forehead, and hence they were called, by traders, "flat heads."[7] The infant was placed in a cradle, with his feet elevated twelve inches above a horizontal position, while his head was bent back and rested in a hole made for the purpose. A small bag of sand was fixed upon the forehead, and as the little fellow could not move, the shape required was soon attained, for at that age the skull is capable of receiving any impression.†

The dress of the male Choctaw was similar to that of the Creeks, and was influenced in its style by his wealth or poverty. But they all wore the buck-she-ah-ma, *flap*, made of woolen cloth or buckskin. The female had usually only a petticoat reaching from the waist to the knees, while some of the richer classes wore a covering also upon the neck and shoulder, and little bells fastened to a buckskin garter, which clasped the leg just below the knee. They wore ornaments in their ears, noses and around the fingers, like the Creeks. They were not cleanly in their persons like the Creeks, who were eternally engaged in bathing; but, strange to relate of Indians, very few of the Choctaws could swim, a fact recorded by all early travelers among them.[8] As they seldom bathed, the smoke of their lightwood fires made their bodies assume a soot color.‡ Peculiarly fond of the taste of horse flesh, they preferred

* Adair.

† Adair, 8–9.

‡ Bossu, *Travels*, 298.

it to beef, even if the animal had died a natural death; and it was not uncommon for them to devour snakes when hard pressed for food.*

Yet, notwithstanding, they were, upon the whole, very agreeable Indians, being invariably cheerful, witty and cunning. The men, too, unlike the proud chiefs of other nations, helped the women to work, and did not consider it a degradation to hire themselves for that purpose to their constant friends, the French, and afterwards to the English.† No Indians, moreover, excelled them in hospitality, which they exhibited particularly in their hunting camps, where all travelers and visitors were received and entertained with a hearty welcome.[9] In regard to their habits in the chase, it may here be observed, that they excelled in killing bears, wild-cats, and panthers, pursuing them through the immense cane swamps with which their country abounded; but that the Creeks and Chickasaws were superior to them in overcoming the fleet deer. While hunting, the liver of the game was divided into as many pieces as there were campfires, and was carried around by a boy, who threw a piece into each fire, intended, it would seem, as a kind of sacrifice.

The Choctaws were superior orators.[10] They spoke with good sense, and used the most beautiful metaphors. They had the power of changing the same words into different significations, and even their common speech was full of these changes. Their orations were concise, strong and full of fire.‡ Excessive debauchery, and a constant practice of begging, constituted their most glaring faults; and it was amusing to witness the many ingenious devices and shifts to which they resorted to obtain presents.

Timid in war against an enemy abroad, they fought like desperate veterans when attacked at home. On account of their repugnance to invading the country of an enemy, in which they were unlike the Creeks and Chickasaws, they were often taunted by these latter nations with the charge of cowardice. Frequently, exasperated by these aspersions, they would boldly challenge the calumniators to mortal combat upon an open field. But the latter, feigning to believe that true Indian courage consisted in slyness and stratagem, rarely accepted the banter. However, in 1765, an opportunity offered in the streets of Mobile, when Hooma, at the head of forty Choctaws, fell

* Milfort, 290; Adair, 133.

† Romans, 71–90.

‡ Adair, 11.

Adair, *American Indians,* 71, 297; Romans, *Concise Natural History,* 129, 135–37; Bartram, *William Bartram on the Southeastern Indians,* 129.

[8] Bartram called the Choctaw men "remarkably slovenly and negligent" in their dress and noted that they failed to keep their hair trimmed. Romans found their women had "agreeable features and countenances" but thought "their nasty way of life" made them less attractive. Bartram, *William Bartram on the Southeastern Indians,* 129–30; Romans, *Concise Natural History,* 135.

[9] While descending the Tombigbee River on 8 January 1772, Romans recorded an encounter with a Choctaw hunting party on the west side of the river "who invited us on shore, treated us very kindly, and spared us some venison, bear's meat and oil." Romans, *Concise Natural History,* 279.

[10] At a public meeting of Choctaw "head-men and chief orators," James Adair heard an impassioned speech eulogizing Red Shoe, Shulush Homa—leader of the pro-British faction during the Choctaw Civil War of 1746–1750. Despite his death on 22 June 1747, his faction continued their opposition until entering into the Grand-Pré Treaty at Fort Tombecbé on 15 November 1750. Galloway, "Choctaw Factionalism and Civil War," 80–92, 94–97.

upon three hundred Creeks, and routed and drove them across the river, into the marsh. Hooma alone killed fifteen of them, and was then dispatched himself, by a retreating Creek. They were pursued no further, because the Choctaws could not swim.[11]

They did not torture a prisoner, in a protracted manner, like other tribes. He was brought home, dispatched with a bullet or hatchet, and cut up, and the parts burned. The scalp was suspended from the hot-house, around which the women danced until they were tired. They were more to be relied upon as allies than most other American Indians. The Creeks were their greatest enemies. In August 1765, a war began between them, and raged severely for six years.* Artful in deceiving an enemy, they attached the paws or trotters of panthers, bears and buffaloes to their own feet and hands, and wound about the woods, imitating the circlings of those animals. Sometimes a large bush was carried by the front warrior, concealing himself and those behind him, while the one in the extreme rear defaced all the tracks with grass. Most excellent trackers themselves, they well understood how to deceive the enemy, which they, also, effected by astonishing powers in imitating every fowl and quadruped. Their leader could never directly assume the command, but had, rather, to conduct his operations by persuasion.†

Gambling was a common vice, and even boys engaged in it by shooting at marks for a wager. In addition to the great ball play, which was conducted like that of the Creeks, already described, they had an exciting game called CHUNKE, or, by some of the traders, "running hard labor." An alley was made, two hundred feet long, with a hard clay surface, which was kept swept clean. Two men entered upon it to play. They stood six yards from the upper end, each with a pole twelve feet long, smooth, and tapering at the end, and with the points flat. One of them took a stone in the shape of a grind-stone, which was two spans round, and two inches thick on the edges. He gave it a powerful hurl down the alley, when both set off after it, and running a few yards, the one who did not roll, cast his pole, which was anointed with bear's oil, with a true aim at the stone in its flight. The other player, to defeat his object, immediately darted his pole, aiming to hit the pole of his antagonist. If the first one hit the stone he counted one, and if the other, by the dexterity of his cast, hit his pole and knocked it from its proper direction, he also counted one. If both of the players missed, the throw was renewed. Eleven was the game, and the winner had the privilege of casting the stone. In this manner the greater part of the day was passed, at half speed; the players and bystanders staking their ornaments, wearing apparel, skins, pipes

* Romans, 70–91.

† Adair, 309; Bossu, 297.

[11] Using Romans as his source, Pickett relates the story of Captain Hooma's successful skirmish with a superior Creek force in 1765 at Mobile, which claimed his life. Romans, *Concise Natural History*, 130.

[12] The game of chunke or chunky described by Romans was rather universal among the southeastern Indians. While William Bartram sketched chunky yards, James Adair declared "Chungke" a favorite game of warriors. Henry S. Halbert gives the name of the game in Choctaw as "*achahpih*" and the stone as "*tali chanah*." Romans, *Concise Natural History*, 134–35; Bartram, *William Bartram on the Southeastern Indians*, 168–71, 273 n. 38; Adair, *American Indians*, 394; Henry S. Halbert, "The Choctaw Game of Achahpih," *Journal of American Folklore* 10 (April-June 1897): 155–56.

[13] William Bartram contrasted the funerary practices of the Muscogees, who buried their dead, with the Choctaws, who placed their dead on scaffolds "eighteen or twenty feet high," followed by a prescribed ritual of placing the bones

and arms upon the result.[12] Sometimes, after a fellow had lost all, he went home, borrowed a gun, and shot himself. The women, also, had a game with sticks and balls, something like the game of battledore.*

The funeral ceremonies of the Choctaws were singular, and, indeed, horrible, but like those of nearly all the aborigines at the time of the invasion of De Soto. As soon as the breath departed from the body of a Choctaw, a high scaffold was erected, thirty-six feet from the dwelling where the deceased died. It consisted of four forks set in the ground, across which poles were laid, and then a floor made of boards or cypress bark. It was stockaded with poles, to prevent the admission of beasts of prey. The posts of the scaffold were painted with a mixture of vermillion and bear's oil, if the deceased was an Indian of note. The body, enveloped in a large bear skin, was hauled up on the scaffold by ropes or vines, and laid out at length. The relations assembled, and wept and howled with mournful voices, asking strange questions of the corpse, according to the sex to which it belonged. "Why did you leave us?" "Did your wife not serve you well?" "Were you not contented with your children?" "Did you not have corn enough?" "Did not your land produce?" "Were you afraid of your enemies?" To increase the solemnity and importance of the funeral of a noted Indian, persons were hired to cry, the males having their heads hung with black moss, and the females suffering their hair to flow loosely to the winds. These women came at all hours, for several weeks, to mourn around the scaffold; and, on account of the horrid stench, frequently fainted and had to be borne away.[13]

When the body had thus lain for three or four months, the BONE-PICKER made his appearance. In 1772 there were five of these hideous undertakers in the Choctaw Nation, who traveled about in search of scaffolds and the horrible work which will be described. The bone-picker apprised the relatives of the deceased that the time had arrived when dissection should take place. Upon the day which he had appointed, the relatives, friends, and others hired to assist in mourning, surrounded the scaffold. The bone-picker mounted upon it, with horrid grimaces and groans, took off the skin, and commenced his disgusting work. He had very long and hard nails growing on the thumb, fore and middle fingers of each hand. He tore off the flesh with his nails, and tied it up in a bundle. He cleaned the bones, and also tied up the scrapings. Leaving the latter on a scaffold, he descended with the bones upon his head. All this time the assembly moaned and howled most awfully. They then painted the head with vermilion, which, together with all the bones, was placed in a nice box with a loose lid. If the bones were those of a chief, the coffin also was painted red.[14]

* Romans, 70–91; Adair, 402; Bossu, 306.

in a "bone-house," and burial at a festival "called the feast of the dead." Bartram, *William Bartram on the Southeastern Indians*, 129.

[14] When George Strother Gaines was trying to relocate the Choctaw Trading House nearer to the Choctaw and Chickasaw, Pushmataha told him about a site on Etombaigaby or Box Maker's Creek, a tributary of the Tombigbee in Sumter County, Alabama—later renamed Factory Creek. He told Gaines that a celebrated box maker had lived on the creek who made boxes for the bones of their dead and that the Choctaws knew the path to the "Old Box Makers." Gaines, *Reminiscences*, 72–73.

[15] Jean-Bernard Bossu reported that the Choctaws trusted their "medicine men or seers," but he referred to them as "true charlatans" who took advantage of his patients who seemed to believe they were "oracles." Romans even admits to submitting himself to a "knowing Physician" to cure a violent fever but his prescription of "herbs and roots" brought him no relief. Jean-Bernard Bossu, *Travels in the Interior of North America, 1751–1762*, trans. and

Next, fire was applied to the scaffold, around which the assembly danced and frightfully whooped until it was consumed by the flames. Then a long procession was formed and the bones were carried, amid weeping and moaning, to the bone-house, of which every town of importance had several. These houses were made by four pitch pine posts being placed in the ground, upon the top of which was a scaffold floor. On this a steep roof was erected, like that of some modern houses, with the gables left open. There the box was deposited with other boxes containing bones. In the meantime a great feast had been prepared, and sometimes three horses were cooked up, if the deceased was wealthy. But the infernal bone-picker still was master of ceremonies, and having only wiped his filthy, bloody hands with grass, served out the food to the whole assembly.*

When the bone-house was full of chests, a general interment took place. The people assembled, bore off the chests in procession to a plain, with weeping, howling and ejaculations of Allelujah! Allelujah! The chests containing the bones were arranged upon the ground in order, forming a pyramid. Then they covered all with earth, which raised a conical mound. Then returning home, the day was concluded with a feast.†

The Choctaws entertained a great veneration for their medicine men or doctors, who practiced upon them constant frauds. Their fees were exorbitant, and required to be satisfied in advance. When a doctor had attended a patient a long time, and the latter had nothing more to give as payment, he usually assembled the relations in private, informed them that he had done all in his power, and had exhausted his skill in endeavoring to restore their friend; that he would surely die, and it was best to terminate his sufferings.[15] Reposing the blindest confidence in this inhuman declaration, two of them then jumped upon the poor fellow and strangled him. In 1782, one of these doctors thus began to consult with the relations upon the case of a poor fellow. While they were out of the house, he suspected their intentions, and making an unnatural effort, crawled to the woods which fortunately were near the house. It was night, and he succeeded in getting beyond their reach. The doctor persuaded them that he was certainly dead, and they erected a scaffold as though he were upon it and wept around it. Fortunately, laying his hands upon an opossum, the poor fellow eat of it from time to time, and gained strength, now that he had escaped the clutches of the doctor, who had nearly smoked and bled him into another world. At length, after much suffering, he

* Adair, 183–88; Romans, 71–90; Milfort, 293–98.
† Bartram, 514–15.

ed. Seymour Feiler (Norman: University of Oklahoma Press, 1962), 167; Romans, *Concise Natural History*, 133.

[16] The Jesuit priest, Father Mathurin Le Petit, started a mission at Chickasawhay in 1727, and he was succeeded by Father Michael Baudouin in 1729, who lived there for eighteen years. They marketed deerskins and corn in exchange for manufactured goods—beads, knives and other items—which fostered some disillusionment about their principal mission. Usner, *Indians, Settlers, and Slaves*, 253.

[17] The Chickasaw defeated two invading French and Indian armies commanded by Pierre d'Artaguette and Jean Baptiste Le Moyne de Bienville in two separate battles on 25 March and 26 May 1736. *Mississippi Provincial Archives: French Dominion [1701–1763]*, ed. and trans. Dunbar Rowland, Albert Godfrey Sanders, and Patricia Kay Galloway, 5 vols. (Jackson: Mississippi Department of Archives and History, 1927–1932; Baton Rouge: Louisiana State University Press, 1984–1985), 1: 294–320. [Hereafter cited as *MPA: FD*].

[18] Pickett's Bevist is probably Jean Baptiste Benoît de St. Clair, who served as commander at Fort Toulouse

made his way to the Creek Nation and threw himself upon the compassion of Colonel McGillivray, who had him restored to health by proper attention.

Again going back to his nation, at the expiration of three months, he arrived at the house from which he had escaped, at the very time that the people were celebrating his funeral by burning the scaffold and dancing around it. His sudden appearance filled them with horror and dismay. Some fled to the woods, others fell upon the ground. Alarmed himself, he retreated to the house of a neighbor, who instantly fell on his face, saying, "Why have you left the land of spirits if you were happy there? Why do you return among us? Is it to assist in the last feast which your family and your friends make for you? Go, return to the land of the dead for fear of renewing the sorrow which they have felt at your loss!" Shunned by all his people, the poor Choctaw went back to the Creek Nation, married a Tuskegee woman, and lived in that town the balance of his life. Before his door lay the four French cannon of old Fort Toulouse. When the Choctaws had become satisfied that he did not die, and was really alive, they killed the doctor who had deceived them. They often entreated the fellow to return home, but he preferred to remain among a people who would not strangle him when he was sick.*

The Choctaws had no other religion than that which attached to their funeral rites. The French, to whom they were warmly attached, sought in vain to convert them to Christianity. At Chickasawhay, they erected a chapel and gave the control of it to a Jesuit missionary. When the English took possession of this country, the Choctaws of that place would, for the amusement of their new friends, enter the old chapel, and go through the Catholic ceremonies, mimicking the priest with surprising powers. In 1771, Capt. Romans saw the lightwood cross still standing, but the chapel had been destroyed.[16]

The Chickasaws, although at the period of 1771 a small nation, were once numerous, and their language was spoken by many tribes in the western states. They were the fiercest, most insolent, haughty and cruel people among the Southern Indians. They had proved their bravery and intrepidity in constant wars. In 1541, they attacked the camp of De Soto in a most furious midnight assault, threw his army into dismay, killed some of his soldiers, destroyed all his baggage, and burnt up the town in which he was quartered. In 1736, they whipped the French under Bienville, who had invaded their country, and forced them to retreat to Mobile.[17] In 1753, MM. Bevist and Reggio encountered defeat at their hands. They continually attacked the boats of the French voyagers upon the Mississippi and Tennessee.[18] They were constantly

* Milfort, 298–304.

in 1733–1734, at Fort Tombecbé in 1737, at Fort Chartres in 1740 and again in 1749–1751, and at Natchez in 1752. After serving as commander at the Vincennes post on the Wabash, Captain Charles Marie de Reggio replaced Captain Paul Augustin Le Pelletin de La Houssaye in 1753 as commander of Arkansas Post on the Arkansas River. While the Chickasaw routinely harassed French boats on the Mississippi River, there is no evidence that Reggio was directly involved in any attacks against the Chickasaw. Romans, *Concise Natural History*, 122; *MPA: FD*, 1: 208–11; ibid., 4: 30 n. 12, 140, 143, 152; ibid., 5: 131, 138 n. 5, 147, 174; Morris S. Arnold, *Rumble of a Distant Drum: The Quapaws and Old World Newcomers, 1673–1804* (Fayetteville: University of Arkansas Press, 2000), 27–28.

[19] Romans, who referred to all Indians as "savages," shows unrestrained disdain for most things related to the Chickasaws. He found them to be the "most fierce, cruel, insolent, and haughty people, among the southern nations." Romans, *Concise Natural History*, 133.

[20] Edmund Atkin made a report to the British Board of Trade in 1755 in which he claimed that the Chickasaw lived in seven towns

at war with the Kickapoos and other tribes upon the Ohio, but were defeated in most of these engagements. But, with the English as their allies, they were eminently successful against the Choctaws and Creeks, with whom they were often at variance.

The Chickasaws were great robbers, and, like the Creeks, often invaded a country, killing the inhabitants and carrying off slaves and plunder. The men considered the cultivation of the earth beneath them; and, when not engaged in hunting or warfare, slept away their time or played upon flutes, while their women were at work. They were athletic, well-formed and graceful. The women were cleanly, industrious, and generally good-looking.[19]

In 1771, they lived in the center of a large and gently rolling prairie, three miles square. They obtained their water from holes, which dried up in summer. In this prairie was an assemblage of houses one mile and a half long, very narrow, and irregular, which was divided into seven towns, as follows:[20]

Melattaw—*hat and feather.*
Chatelaw—*copper town.*
Chukafalaya—*long town.*
Hikihaw—*stand still.*
Chuckalissa—*great town.*
Tuckahaw—*a certain weed.*
Ashuck hooma—*red grass.*

The last was once well fortified with palisades, and there they defeated D'Artaguette.[21] The nearest running water was two miles distant; the next was four miles off, to which point canoes could ascend from the Tombigbee in high tide. The ford, which often proved difficult of crossing, was called Nahoola Inalchubba—*the white man's hard labor.* Horses and cattle increased rapidly in this country. The breed of the former descended from importations from Arabia to Spain, from Spain to Mexico, and from thence to the Chickasaw Nation. Here they ran wild in immense droves, galloping over the beautiful prairies, the sun glittering upon their various colors. They were owned by the Indians and traders.[22]

The Chickasaws were very imperious in their carriage towards females, and extremely jealous of their wives. Like the Creeks, they punished adultery by beating with poles until the

"having each a Pallisade Fort with a Ditch." Little had changed when Bernard Romans visited these towns in 1771. Romans, *Concise Natural History*, 124–25; Walter R. Jacobs, ed., *The Appalachian Indian Frontier: The Edmond Atkin Report and Plan of 1755* (1954; reprint, Lincoln: University of Nebraska Press, 1967), 67.

21 Pierre d'Arteguette, commander at Fort Chartres, led the northern army against the Chickasaw in 1736. He suffered a devastating defeat at Chuckalissa (Ogoula Tchetoka) on 25 March 1736 before he could join Bienville. He was one of several French soldiers—dead and alive—burned by the Chickasaw. *MPA: FD*, 1: 201 n. 1, 311–13; James A. Atkinson, "The Ackia and Ogoula Tchetoka Village Locations in 1736 during the French-Chickasaw War of 1736 and 1740," *Mississippi Archaeology* 20 (1985): 53–72.

22 While some observers complimented the Chickasaw on their horses, Romans thought the Chickasaw had "so mixed them with meaner kinds, as to cause them to degenerate much." Romans, *Concise Natural History*, 125.

23 Pickett continues to rely heavily on Romans and loosely paraphrases his observations and commentary during his visit with the Chickasaw in 1771. Romans, *Concise Natural History*, 122–29.

24 Romans's estimate of Chickasaw gunmen in 1771 is probably low. Two years later, Georgia's Governor James Wright, with more resources, reported that the Chickasaw "have four hundred and fifty Effective or Gun men." He also reported the Choctaws had twenty-five hundred gunmen. "Report of Sir James Wright on the Condition of the Province of Georgia, on 20 September 1783," *Collections of the Georgia Historical Society*, vol. 3 (Savannah: Georgia Historical Society, 1873), 169.

25 Henry S. Halbert analyzed Romans's map, his phonetic spelling and misspelling

sufferer was senseless, and then concluded by cropping the ears, and, for the second offence, the nose or a piece of the upper lip. Notwithstanding they resided so far from large streams, they were all excellent swimmers, and their children were taught that art in clay holes and pools, which remained filled with water unless the summer was remarkably dry.

Of all the Indians in America, they were the most expert in tracking. They would follow their flying enemy on a long gallop over any kind of ground without mistaking, where perhaps only a blade of grass bent down told the footprint. Again, when they were leisurely hunting over the woods, and came upon an indistinct trail recently made by Indians, they knew at once of what nation they were by the footprints, the hatchet chops upon the trees, their camp- fires, and other distinguishing marks. They were also esteemed to be admirable hunters, and their extensive plains and unbroken forests afforded them the widest field for the display of their skill. In 1771 their grounds extended from middle Mississippi to the mouth of the Ohio, and some distance into the territory of the present state of Tennessee. But this extreme northern ground they visited with caution, and only in the winter, when their northern enemies were close at home. They were often surprised on the sources of the Yazoo, but below there, and as far east as the branches of the Tombigbee to Oktibbehaw, they hunted undisturbed. This last point they regarded as the boundary between them and the Choctaws. With the latter they had no jealousies in regard to the chase, and they sported upon each other's grounds when not at war. Although the country of the Chickasaws abounded with that valuable animal, the beaver, they left them for the traders to capture, saying, "Anybody can kill a beaver." They pursued the more noble and difficult sport of overcoming the fleet deer, and the equally swift and more formidable elk.[23]

The summer habitations of the Chickasaws were cabins of an oblong shape, near which were corn-houses. In the yard stood also a winter house of a circular form. Having no chimneys, the smoke found its way out of this "hot-house" wherever it could. These they entered and slept all night, stifled with smoke, and, no matter how cold the morning, they came forth naked and sweating as soon as the day dawned. These

of Choctaw words and place names in the early twentieth century, such as Bogue Hooma and Hoopa Ullah which, using correct Choctaw orthography, would be Bok Homma (*red creek*) and Opa aiola (*owl there hoots*—not *noisy owl*). Henry S. Halbert, "Bernard Romans' Map of 1772," *Publications of the Mississippi Historical Society*, vol. 6 (Oxford: The Society, 1902): 433, 435.

[26] Halbert says Oka Hullo (*Beloved Water*), Coosha or Kusha (*cane brake*), Hankha Aiola (*wild goose*), and Sukenatcha (*hog river*) more closely paralleled Choctaw orthography than Oku Ullah, Coosa, Haanka Ulla, and Sookhan-Hatcha. Although he accepted Romans's spelling of Coosa as an alternative form, he noted that Romans located the town on the wrong creek. Ibid., 415–18, 420, 437; John R. Swanton, *Source Material for the Social and Ceremonial Life of the Choctaw Indians*, Bureau of American Ethnology, *Bulletin 103* (Washington: GPO, 1931), 61, 65.

[27] Although it could be printer errors, Romans uses three different spellings of Abecka and Soukhan-Hatcha. Halbert states that Aiabeka (*unhealthy place*) was located on Straight Creek (Bok Apissali), which empties into the Sucarnoochee (*Sukenatcha*) River. The Sucarnoochee River originates in Kemper County, Mississippi, and winds east by southeast through Sumter County, Alabama, and enters the Tombigbee River above Black Bluff. Halbert, "Bernard Romans' Map," 425, 436; Swanton, *Social and Ceremonial Life of the Choctaw Indians*, 65; http://riversofalabama.org/Tombigbee/TB_Tributaries.htm.

[28] Halbert translates these towns using correct Choctaw orthography, as follows: Chooka Hoola (Chukka Hullo—*Beloved House*), Oka Hoola (Oka Hullo—*Beloved Water*), Hoola Tassa (Holitasha—*Fort Town*), Ebeetap Ocoola Cho (Ibetap okla

chitto—*Fountain-head Big People*), and Oka Attakkala (Oka Alhtakala—*between the waters*). Halbert, "Bernard Romans' Map," 424–26; Swanton, *Social and Ceremonial Life of the Choctaw Indians*, 63, 65, 67.

[29] Pickett's Bogue Fooka and Romans's Baguefouka (Bouckfouca) and Bogue Chitto Creek may have been transposed on his map or notes. There is a Bogue Chitto Creek located near the Neshoba-Kemper County lines that is part of the upper Pearl River watershed. While Bouckfouca may have been a small stream, Juan de la Villebeuvre negotiated a treaty with the Choctaws at Bouckfouca on behalf of Spain in 1793 that led to the construction of Fort Confederation on the site of the old Fort Tombecbé site in 1794. In 1795 he completed a census of the Choctaws and listed Bouckfouca near the Pearl River with a population of 103. http://kemper.msghn.org/rivers.html; Jack D. L. Holmes, "The Choctaws in 1795: A Choctaw Census of 1795, District of the Six Villages," *Alabama Historical Quarterly* 30 (Spring 1968): 33–48.

[30] Benjamin James (c. 1746–1803), a Virginian, was a licensed Georgia trader when Romans visited him in 1771. During the Revolutionary War, he became a licensed Spanish trader working with the Mobile trading company of Strother and Mather. He had a Choctaw wife and several métis children, and his oldest son, Benjamin James, was granted two sections of land under the supplementary articles of the Treaty of Dancing Rabbit Creek in 1830. Charles A. Weeks, *Paths to Middle Ground: The Diplomacy of Natchez, Boukfouka, Nogales, and San Fernando de las Barrancas, 1791–1795* (Tuscaloosa: University of Alabama Press, 2005), 52–54, 259 n. 21; Supplementary Articles, Treaty of Dancing Rabbit Creek, 1830, *Indian Affairs: Laws and Treaties*, comp. and ed. Charles J. Kappler, 2 vols. (Washington: GPO, 1904), 2: 317.

[31] While Pickett used Nashooba from Romans, he substituted Oktibbehaw (Oktibbeha) in place of Oka tebbe haw in Romans. Halbert gives us *Oka Nakshobi* (strong smelling) and *Okti abeha* (blocks of ice therein) as the correct Choctaw names. In the late 1880s, there were two streams in Mississippi with the name Oktibbeha: one north that

houses were used by the sick also, who, remaining in them until perspiration ensued, jumped suddenly into holes of cold water.

They dried and pounded their corn before it came to maturity, which they called Boota Copassa—*coal flour*. A small quantity of this thrown into water swelled immediately, and made a fine beverage. They used hickory nut and bear's oil, and the traders learned them to make the hams of the bear into bacon. In 1771 the whole number of gunmen in the Chickasaw Nation only amounted to about two hundred and fifty.[24] It is astonishing what a handful of warriors had so long kept neighboring nations of great strength from destroying them.

They buried their dead the moment vitality ceased, in the very spot where the bed stood upon which the deceased lay, and the nearest relatives mourned over it with woeful lamentations. This mourning continued for twelve moons, the women practicing it openly and vociferously, and the men silently.*

The modern reader may form some idea of the Chickasaw and Choctaw nations, as they once existed, by briefly tracing the route of Captain Romans through their country. He began his tour at Mobile, encamped at Spring Hill, passed the headwaters of Dog River, and again encamped at Bogue Hooma—*red creek*—the boundary between the English and the Choctaws. Pursuing his journey, the camp was pitched at Hoopa Ullah—*noisy owl*—where he saw the Creek painting described upon page 78.[25] Then passing Oku Ullah—*noisy water*—and the towns of Coosa, Haanka Ullah—*bawling goose*—he crossed a branch of the Sookhan-Hatcha River.[26] He reached a deserted town called Etuck Chukke—*Blue Wood*—passed through Abecka, an inhabited town, and there crossed another branch of the Sookhan-Hatcha, and arrived at Ebeetap Oocoola, where the Choctaws had erected a

* Bernard Romans, *Florida*, 59–71.

large stockade fort.[27] A southwestern direction was now assumed, and Capt. Romans passed through the following towns:[28] Chooka Hoola, Oka Hoola, Hoola Tassa, Ebeetap Oocoola Cho, Oka Attakkala, and crossing Bogue Fooka and Bogue Chitto, which runs into Bogue Aithe-Tannè,[29] arrived at the house of Benjamin James, at Chickasawhay.[30]

He set out from this place for the Chickasaw Nation, and crossed only two streams of importance—Nashooba and Oktibbehaw.[31] Without accident he arrived at the Chickasaw towns enumerated upon page 83 and lying within a few miles of Pontotoc. He proceeded east-by-south five miles and crossed Nahoola-Inal-chubba—*Town Creek*—and then assumed a southeast direction, and arrived at the Twenty Mile Creek, a large branch of the Tombigbee. At the mouth of Nahoola-Inal-chubba, Capt. Romans found a large canoe, in which he and his companions embarked and proceeded down the Tombigbee. One mile below, on the west bank, they passed a bluff on which the French formerly had a fortified trading post. Capt. Romans next saw the mouth of the Oktibbeha, the dividing line between the two nations, and passed the mouth of the Nasheba, on the east. Floating with rapidity down the river, he next came to the Noxshubby, on the west side, and then to the mouth of a creek called Etomba-Igaby—*Box Maker's Creek*—where the French had a fort.* From this creek, the name of which has been corrupted by the French to Tombecbé, and by the Americans to Tombigbee, the river takes its name. Upon it lived an Indian who made chests to hold the bones of the Choctaws.[32]

Romans came to the confluence of the

* Now Jones' Bluff.

is now called Tibbee Creek, which is a tributary on the upper Tombigbee; and one south, now called Okatibbee Creek, which joins the Chunky River near Enterprise, Mississippi, to create the Chickasawhay River. Halbert, "Bernard Romans' Map," 435–36; James Greenleaf, "Report on the Water Power of the Mississippi River and Some of its Tributaries," in *Statistics of Power and Machinery Employed in Manufactures: Reports on the Water Power of the United States*, ed. William P. Trowbridge, Department of the Interior, Part 2 (Washington: GPO, 1887), 144.

[32] Pickett's Oktibbehaw—now Tibbee Creek—was the historic dividing line between the Chickasaw and Choctaw in northeast Mississippi. While Pickett's Nasheba and Romans's "Nasbehaw river" cannot be identified, their Noxshubby is clearly the Noxubee River—*Oka Nakshobi* in Choctaw—that enters the Tombigbee at modern Gainesville, Alabama. While some form of "Etomba-Igaby" is often given for the source of the name of the Tombigbee River, the correct Choctaw orthography is *itumbi* (box) *ikbi* (maker)—Box Maker's Creek. Halbert, "Bernard Romans' Map," 435–36; William Bright, *Native American Placenames of the United States* (Norman: University of Oklahoma Press, 2004), 504.

[33] Chickasaw Gallery was renamed Ecor Blanc—White Bluff—by the French exiles who settled at modern Demopolis, Alabama, beginning in July 1817. Located below the confluence of the Black Warrior and Tombigbee Rivers, this chalk cliff—composed of a geological layer known as Demopolis chalk—stretches for nearly one mile along the east bank of the Tombigbee. Winston Smith, *Days of Exile: The Story of the Vine and Olive Colony in Alabama* (Tuscaloosa: W. B. Drake and Son, Printers, 1967), 19–21, 35, 38–39.

[34] According to James Adair, the Coosada and Okchai settlements mentioned by Pickett and Romans were established around 1763. Their occupants withdrew back eastward when they found themselves caught in the middle between warring parties of Choctaw and Creeks. Henry Halbert gives "*Sakti lusa*"—Black Bluff—as the correct Choctaw spelling for "Suctaloosa" in Pickett and Romans. Adair, *American Indians*, 201, 281–82, 521 n. 289; Halbert, "Bernard Romans' Map," 437.

[35] The correct Choctaw orthography for "Nanna Falaya" is nanih falaya—"*long hill*"—and near this site is a small village in modern Marengo County, Alabama, known as Nanafalaia. Halbert gives us Bachcha Chukka

Tombigbee and Black Warrior, and, a little below, passed some steep chalky bluffs, which the traders called the Chickasaw Gallery, because from this point they were accustomed to shoot at the French boats.[33] On the top of this bluff was a vast plain, with some remains of huts standing upon it.* Three miles below the mouth of the Sookhan-Hatcha, Romans came upon the old towns of the Coosadas and Okchai, commencing at Suctaloosa—Black Bluff[34]—and extending from thence down the river for some distance.† Next, passing a high bluff called Nanna Falaya, he reached Batcha Chooka, a bluff on the east side, where he encountered a desperate band of thieves, belonging to the town of Okaloosa, of the Choctaws.[35] He then came to some bluffs called Nanna Chahaws, where a gray flat rock, called Teeakhaily Ekutapa, rises out of the water. Here the people of Chickasawhay once had a settlement.[36] Lower down, the party saw a bluff upon the east side, called Yagna Hoolah—beloved ground—and encamped at the mouth of Sintabouge—Snake Creek—three miles below which was the English line separating them from the Choctaws.[37] Having entered the British settlements, Capt. Romans continued his voyage until he reached Mobile.‡

(*ridge houses*) for "Batcha Chooka" and Oka Lusa for Pickett's Okaloosa. William A. Read, *Indian Place Names in Alabama* (1937; revised edition, Tuscaloosa: University of Alabama Press, 1984), 44; Halbert, "Bernard Romans' Map," 420, 433.

[36] Neither John R. Swanton nor Henry Halbert provide any information about "Nanna Chahaws." However, Swanton, in his list of Choctaw villages, identifies "Teeakhaily Ekutapa" as "standing pine" and locates it on the lower Tombigbee. Swanton, *Social and Ceremonial Life of the Choctaw Indians*, 67.

[37] Halbert gives "*Yakni Hullo*" (beloved country) as the correct Choctaw for "Yagna Hoolah" and "*Sinti bok*" (Snake Creek) for "Sintabouge." Halbert, "Bernard Romans' Map," 437–38.

* Now the site of Demopolis.

† Some of the Alabamas living at the town of that name below the confluence of the Coosa and Tallapoosa, and some Creeks of the town of Oakchoy (Okchoy), to be nearer to the French, who were their friends, moved upon the main Tombigbee, and the deserted towns which Romans mentions were those in which they had formerly lived.

‡ Romans, *Florida.*

Chapter II – Part V

THE CHEROKEES

It has been seen that De Soto passed over a portion of the country of these Indians in the territory which embraces northern Georgia. The name Cherokee is derived from Chera, *fire*; and the prophets of this nation were called Cherataghge, *men of divine fire.*[1]

The first that we hear of the Cherokees, after the Spanish invasion, is their connection with the early British settlers of Virginia. A powerful and extensive nation, they even had settlements upon the Appomattox River, and were allied by blood with the Powhatan tribe.[2] The Virginians drove them from that place, and they retreated to the head of the Holston River. Here, making temporary settlements, the northern Indians compelled them to retire to the Little Tennessee River, where they established themselves permanently. About the same time, a large branch of the Cherokees came from the territory of South Carolina, near Charleston, and formed towns upon the main Tennessee, extending as far as the Muscle Shoals. They found all that region unoccupied, except upon the Cumberland, where resided a roving band of Shawnees. But the whole country bore evidence of once having sustained a large Indian population. Such is the origin of the first Cherokee settlements upon the main Tennessee, but the great body of the nation appears to have occupied northern Georgia and northwestern Carolina as far back as the earliest discoveries can trace them.[3]

But very little was known of these natives until the English formed colonies in the two Carolinas. They were first mentioned when some of their chiefs complained that the Savannas and Congarees attacked their extreme eastern settlements, captured their people and sold them as slaves in the town of Charles Town. Two years afterwards, Governor Archdale, of Carolina, arrested this practice, which induced the Cherokees to become friends of the English.[4] They joined the latter in a war against the Tuscaroras. But three years afterwards they became allies of the northern Indians and

[1] James Adair is Pickett's source for the name Chera-taghge. John R. Swanton and others speculate the name Cherokee may come from the Muskogean tciloki or chilo-kee—"*people of a different speech*." Swanton also believes this is the source of Chalaque cited by the Gentleman of Elvas in his narrative of De Soto's expedition. While the historic Cherokee referred to themselves as the ani-yunwi-ya, meaning "*real people*" or "*principal people*," they generally called themselves Tsalagi, and the modern Cherokee in their written language use Tsa-la-gi. Adair, *American Indians*, 247; Swanton, *Indians of the Southeastern United States*, 23, 46, 217; James Mooney, *Myths of the Cherokee and Sacred Formulas of the Cherokees* (1900; reprint, Nashville: Charles and Randy Elder—Booksellers, Publishers, 1982), 15; Russell Thornton, *The Cherokees: A*

once more fought their European friends.[5] At length Governor Nicholson concluded a peace with them, which was confirmed by Alexander Cuming, the British general superintendent of Indian affairs.[6] The Cherokees assisted the English in the capture of Fort Duquesne. When returning home, however, they committed some depredations upon the settlers of Virginia, which were resented. This, together with the influence of French emissaries, had the effect again to array them against the people of Georgia and the Carolinas. Various expeditions marched against them, and their country was finally invaded with success, by Colonel Grant. Having sued for peace, articles of amity and alliance were signed at Long Island, upon the Holston.[7] According to the traditions preserved by Judge Haywood, who wrote the *History of Tennessee*, the Cherokees originally came from the territory now embraced by the eastern states of the Union, in which they differ from the other tribes of whom it has been our province to speak, all of whom came from the west.[8]

When they began to be visited by the Carolina traders, their nation was powerful and warlike, and was divided into two parts. The Upper Cherokees lived upon the rivers Tellico, Great and Little Tennessee, the Holston and French Broad. The Lower Cherokees inhabited the country watered by the sources of the Oconee, the Ocmulgee and the Savannah.[9] The great Unaka or Smoky Mountains lay between and divided the two sections.* Their whole country was the most beautiful and romantic in the known world. Their springs of delicious water gushed out of every hill and mountain side. Their lovely rivers

* Haywood, *Natural and Aboriginal History of Tennessee*, 233–34; *Transactions and Collections of the American Antiquarian Society*, 2: 89–90; Adair, *American Indians.*

Population History* (Lincoln: University of Nebraska Press, 1990), 7–9.

[2] The Powhatan Indians lived in the Virginia tidewater from the Potomac River southward to the James River. While the Cherokee were Iroquoian speakers, the Powhatan were Algonquian speakers. Swanton, *Indians of the Southeastern United States*, 24, 31, 175, 241; Hudson, *Southeastern Indians*, 23–24.

[3] Modern scholars believe that the people who became the Cherokee came from the north, northeast, or northwest, and that they were driven into the southeast by the Iroquois—their linguistic kinsmen. However, migration legends of the Delawares and Wyandots (Hurons) involve conflicts or disputes over land, which caused them to expel or drive these people southward. Cherokee oral traditions and legends confirm some of this narrative but also embrace a westward migration toward the rising sun. Mooney, *Myths of the Cherokee*, 17–23.

[4] John Archdale (c.1642—c. 1717) was appointed the provincial governor of the Carolina colony by the proprietors in August 1694 and arrived in North Carolina in June 1695. He traveled to Charles Town in August where he focused on the affairs of South Carolina and ended his tenure a year later. Dennis F. Daniels, "John Archdale," http://ncpedia.org/biography.

[5] When the Tuscarora War broke out in September 1711, the Cherokee joined the North Carolinians and their other Indian allies to punish their old enemies and enhance their status as warriors. The fighting continued through 1715, but many of the Tuscarora began to migrate to New York in 1713 to escape their enemies, European and Indian, joining their kinsmen in the Iroquois Confederacy. Despite Pickett's assertion of an alliance with "northern Indians," the Cherokee were often at war with the Shawnee, Iroquois, and Creeks during the post-war period—not the Carolinians. Chapman J. Milling, *Red Carolinians* (1940; second edition, Columbia: University of South Carolina Press, 1969), 113–31.

[6] In 1721 South Carolina's Governor Francis Nicholson brokered a treaty of peace and friendship with the Cherokee to establish clearly defined boundaries and to protect the deerskin trade. He also convinced the representatives from thirty-seven Cherokee towns to recognize a prominent warrior, Wrosetasatow of Keowee, as their principal chief. Sir Alexander Cuming, a member of the Royal Society, undertook a personal tour of the Cherokee country, and convinced seven Cherokee to

meandered, now smoothly and gently, through the most fertile valleys, and then, with the precipitancy and fleetness of the winds, rushed over cataracts and through mountain gaps. The forests were full of game, the rivers abounded with fish, the vales teemed with their various productions, and the mountains with fruit, while the pure atmosphere consummated the happiness of the blest Cherokees.[10]

About the period of 1700, the Cherokee Nation consisted of sixty-four towns.[11] But the inhabitants of those situated in the upper district, were continually engaged in wars with the northern Indians, while those below were harassed by the Creeks. Then again, the Cherokees had to encounter, first, the French, and then the English. From these causes (added to which was the terrible scourge of the small pox, introduced into Charles Town by a slave ship, and thence carried into their country), the population had greatly decreased—so that, in 1740, the number of warriors was estimated at only five thousand.[12] That year fully one thousand of these were destroyed by that disease.*

The Cherokees were so similar to the Creeks in their form, color, general habits and pursuits, that the reader is requested to refresh his recollection in relation to our description of the latter, and will not be required, tediously, to retrace the same ground. Their ball plays, green corn dances, constant habit of indulging in the purifying black drink, their manner of conducting wars and of punishing prisoners, their council houses, their common apparel, and also their appearance during war, were all precisely like those of the Creeks. And, in addition, they played chunke, like the Choctaws.[13] However, a careful examination of

* *Collections of the Georgia Historical Society*, 2: 72.

accompany him back to England and to curry favor with King George II. He had no official role and never served as superintendent of Indian affairs. Ibid., 273–74; Crane, *Southern Frontier*, 277–80; Samuel C. Williams, ed., "Journal of Sir Alexander Cuming (1730)," in *Early Travels in the Tennessee Country, 1540–1800* (Johnson City, Tenn.: Watauga Press, 1928), 117–19, 122–28, 132–33; William R. Reynolds, Jr., *The Cherokee Struggle to Maintain Identity in the 17th and 18th Centuries* (Jefferson, NC: McFarland & Company, 2012), 38–39.

7 Several parties of Cherokee warriors led by Attakullkulla, Oconostota, Ostenaco, and others assisted the British in defeating the French and their Indian allies between 1757 and 1758, including their victory at Fort Duquesne in November 1758. Clashes occurred as these war parties traveled back and forth on the Virginia and Carolina frontier with blame equally shared. These skirmishes led to the first Cherokee War of 1760–1761. Two British armies led by Col. Archibald Montgomery in 1760 and Col. James Grant in 1761 invaded the Cherokee towns, causing great devastation and loss of life. The Cherokee signed peace treaties with Virginia at Long Island of the Holston in November 1761 and in Charles Town in December 1761. John Oliphant, *Peace and War on the Anglo-Cherokee Frontier, 1756–63* (Baton Rouge: Louisiana State University Press, 2001), 21, 31–45, 49–70, 114–38, 140–86, 189–90; David H. Corkran, *The Cherokee Frontier: Conflict and Survival, 1740–62* (Norman: University of Oklahoma Press, 1962), 112–62, 207–16, 247–55, 263–72.

8 John Haywood (1762–1826), a prominent jurist and historian, published two early histories of the state of Tennessee in 1823: *The Natural and Aboriginal History of Tennessee* and *The Civil and Political History of the State of Tennessee.* While Pickett cites the former work, it appears that he used both while discussing the Cherokee and other Southern Indians. "John Haywood," *Tennessee Encyclopedia of History and Culture* (online edition, Knoxville: University of Tennessee Press, 2009).

9 Geographically, the Cherokee settlement core in the Southern Appalachian Highlands, from about 1730 through the American Revolution, has been generally understood in four divisions: Lower Towns, Middle Towns, Valley Towns, and Overhill Towns. With the greater intrusion of American settlements in the 1780s and 1790s, the Cherokee gradually realigned their towns into two divisions—Upper Towns and Lower Towns. Ted L.

Gragson and Paul V. Bolstad, "A Local Analysis of Early-Eighteenth-Century Cherokee Settlement," *Social Science History* 32 (Fall 2007): 438–39, 441, 444, 446; Betty Anderson Smith, "Distribution of Eighteenth-Century Cherokee Settlements," in *The Cherokee Nation: A Troubled History*, ed. Duane H. King (Knoxville: University of Tennessee Press, 1979): 46–60.

[10] The Cherokee domain was bountiful, with its lush, forested mountains, sheltered abundant game, and food sources. In 2009, Ben Stout, a biologist, said: "There are more kinds of organisms living in the southern Appalachians than in any other forest ecosystem in the world." John McQuaid, "Mining the Mountains," *Smithsonian* 39 (January 2009), 80.

[11] Eighteenth century travel accounts, documents, and maps provide names and lists of towns from 62 to 39, in the Cherokee heartland, with an average population under 200. In his *History* published in 1775, James Adair wrote "Not above forty years ago, they had 64 towns and villages." While Reverend Francis Varnod reported 53 Cherokee towns in 1721, William Bartram developed a list of 43 towns and villages in his travels in the Cherokee country in May–June 1775. Adair, *American Indians*, 248; Bartram, *William Bartram on the Southeastern Indians*, 87–88; Gragson and Bolstad, "Early-Eighteenth-Century Cherokee Settlement," 438–39, 441, 444, 446, 454; Smith, "Distribution of Eighteenth-Century Cherokee Settlements," 47–57; Thornton, *The Cherokees*, 32.

[12] The Cherokee suffered a devastating smallpox epidemic in 1738–1739 which dramatically reduced the population as thousands died from the disease. Most modern estimates place the Cherokee population in a range of 8,000 to 12,000 and a warrior population of 3,000 to 4,000 after 1740. Thornton, *The Cherokees*, 29–31; Gary C. Goodwin, *Cherokees in Transition: A Study of Changing Culture and Environment Prior to 1775* (Chicago: Department of Geography, University of Chicago, 1977), 103, 110–11.

[13] Despite Pickett's assertions about the similarities of the Cherokee and Creeks, the

several authorities has unfolded a few peculiarities which will now be introduced.

Unlike other Indian nations, who once trod our soil, the Cherokees had no laws against adultery. Both sexes were unrestrained in this particular, and marriage was usually of short duration.[14]

On account of the pure air which they breathed, the exercise of the chase, the abundance of natural productions which the country afforded, and the delicious water which was always near, the Cherokees lived to an age much more advanced than the other tribes which have been noticed in this chapter.*

They observed some singular rules in relation to the burial of the dead. When a person was past recovery (to prevent pollution), they dug a grave, prepared a tomb, anointed the hair of the patient and painted his face; and when death ensued, interment was immediately performed. After the third day, the attendants at the funeral appeared at the council house and engaged in their ordinary pursuits, but the relatives lived in retirement and moaned for some time.† Such ceremonies, practiced upon a poor fellow in his last moments, and while in his senses, was certainly a cooler and less cruel method than that of the Choctaws, who, as we have seen, suddenly jumped down upon the patient and strangled him to death, after the doctor had pronounced his recovery impossible.[15]

It was formerly the habit of the Cherokees to shoot all the stock belonging to the deceased, and they continued to bury, with the dead, their guns, bows and household utensils. If one died upon a journey, hunt, or war expedition, his companions erected a stage, upon which was a notched log pen, in which the body was placed to secure it from wild beasts. When it was supposed that sufficient time had elapsed, so that nothing remained but the bones, they returned to the spot, collected these, carried them home, and buried them with great ceremony. Sometimes

* Adair, 226–28.

† Adair, 126.

heaps of stones were raised as monuments to the dead, whose bones they had not been able to "gather to their fathers," and every one who passed by added a stone to the pile.* Henry Timberlake, a lieutenant in the British service, was dispatched with a small command from Long Island, upon the Holston, to the Cherokee towns upon the Tellico and the Little Tennessee Rivers. His object was to cultivate a good understanding with these people, who had, indeed, invited him to their country. He descended the Holston in canoes to the mouth of the Little Tennessee, and thence passed up that stream to their towns.[16] Spending some weeks here, he returned to Charles Town with three Cherokee chiefs, and sailed for England.[17] Three years afterwards he published a book, from which we have been enabled to gain some information respecting the Cherokees.†

The Cherokees were of middle stature, and of an olive color, but were generally painted, while their skins were stained with indelible ink, representing a variety of pretty figures. According to Bartram, the males were larger and more robust than any others of our natives, while the women were tall, slender, erect, and of delicate frame, with features of perfect symmetry. With cheerful countenances, they moved about with becoming grace and dignity. Their feet and hands were small and exquisitely shaped. The hair of the male was shaved, except a patch on the back part of the head, which was ornamented with beads and feathers, or with a colored deer's tail. Their ears were slit and stretched to an enormous size, causing the persons who had the cutting performed to undergo incredible pain. They slit but one ear at a time, because the patient had to lay on one side forty days for it to heal. As soon as he could bear the operation, wire

* Adair and Bartram.

† *Memoirs of Lieutenant Henry Timberlake* (London: 1765).

narratives by James Adair, William Bartram, and Henry Timberlake provide evidence of differences regarding Cherokee social and cultural activities, such as their dances, farming, music, pipes, housing, town houses, horses and war ceremonies. Adair, *American Indians*, 134, 250–51, 412–13; Bartram, *William Bartram on the Southeastern Indians*, 74–80, 84–87; Henry Timberlake, *The Memoirs of Lt. Henry Timberlake: The Story of a Soldier, Adventurer, and Emissary to the Cherokees, 1756–1765*, ed. Duane H. King (Cherokee, NC: Museum of the Cherokee Indian, 2007), 15–21, 30–35, 39–46.

[14] While the Southern Indians generally operated as matrilineal societies, James Adair was especially critical of the Cherokee "petticoat-government" that allowed "their women full liberty . . . without fear of punishment." Adair, *American Indians*, 181–82.

[15] Adair talks about the Israelites becoming unclean "by touching their dead" and transposes his Hebrew theories on the Cherokee and the preparation of a tomb for their dead. He also noted that the Cherokee, under the "persuasion of the traders," had abandoned their custom of burying the personal "effects with the dead body." Adair, *American Indians*, 165–66, 208.

[16] Lieutenant Henry Timberlake, a Virginia militiaman, volunteered to visit the Cherokee at the end of peace negotiations in 1761, and journeyed into the nation by canoe in early 1762 with Sergeant Thomas Sumter and William Shorey, an interpreter. The Cherokee welcomed Timberlake as a visiting dignitary, and his mission as an ambassador of peace and reconciliation achieved a measure of success. However, suspicion and mistrust of Virginians and Carolinians did not evaporate. Timberlake, *Memoirs*, xxiv–xxvi, 8–9; John P. Brown, *Old Frontiers: The Story of the Cherokee Indians from Earliest Times to the Date of Their Removal to the West, 1838* (Kingsport, Tenn.: Southern Publishers, Inc., 1938), 116–17. Note: Pickett bought a copy of Timberlake's *Memoirs* from Bartlett & Welford for $3.00 in November 1847. See Bartlett & Welford to AJP, New York, 19 November 1847, Pickett Papers, ADAH.

[17] In March 1762, Timberlake traveled to Williamsburg with a large number of Cherokee warriors where Ostenaco voiced a desire to journey to England to see King George III. On 15 May 1762,

was wound around them to expand them, and when they were entirely well they were adorned with silver pendants and rings. Many of them had genius, and spoke well, which paved the way to power in council. Their language was pleasant. It was very aspirated, and the accents so many and various that one would often imagine them singing in their common discourse.[18]

They had a particular method of relieving the poor, which ought to be ranked among the most laudable of their religious ceremonies. The head men issued orders for a war dance, at which all the fighting men of the town assembled. But here, contrary to all their other dances, only one danced at a time, who, with a tomahawk in his hand, hopped and capered for a minute, and then gave a whoop. The music then stopped till he related the manner of his taking his first scalp. He concluded his narration, and cast a string of wampum, wire, plate, paint, lead, or anything he could spare upon a large bear skin spread for the purpose. Then the music again began, and he continued in the same manner through all his warlike actions. Then another succeeded him, and the ceremony lasted until all the warriors had related their exploits and thrown presents upon the skin. The stock thus raised, after paying the musicians, was divided among the poor. The same ceremony was used to recompense any extraordinary merit.[19]

The Cherokees engaged oftener in dancing than any other Indian population; and when reposing in their towns, almost every night was spent in this agreeable amusement. They were likewise very dexterous at pantomimes. In one of these, two men dressed themselves in bear-skins, and came among the assembly, winding and pawing about with all the motions of that animal. Two hunters next entered, who, in dumb show, acted in all respects as if they had been in the woods. After many attempts to shoot the bears, the hunters fired, and one of them was killed and the other wounded. They attempted to cut the throat of the latter. A tremendous scuffle ensued between the

Timberlake, Sumter, and Shorey departed for England with Ostenaco and two young warriors, Pouting Pigeon and Stalking Turkey. Timberlake, *Memoirs*, 14–54, 55–58, 130 n. 156, 132 n. 161; Brown, *Old Frontiers*, 118–19.

[18] In his *Memoirs*, Henry Timberlake not only expressed his appreciation for the Cherokee's public speaking skills, but he also noted their ability to recite "a sort of loose poetry," including war songs and love songs—"many composing both tunes and song off hand, according to the occasion." Bartram, *William Bartram on the Southeastern Indians*, 77–78, 85, 111–12, 150; Timberlake, *Memoirs*, 24–25, 30–31.

[19] Pickett's description of the Cherokee providing relief for the poor is loosely paraphrased from Henry Timberlake's *Memoirs*. Timberlake, *Memoirs*, 36.

[20] While both Bartram and Timberlake commented on the Cherokee love of dancing and other diversions, the narrative of the hunting pantomime and "pigeons at roost" is a loose paraphrase from Timberlake's *Memoirs*. Bartram, *William Bartram on the Southeastern Indians*, 85–86, 123, 125; Timberlake, *Memoirs*, 41.

[21] When William Bartram entered the Cherokee Lower Towns in May 1775, he knew that there was significant unrest among the Cherokee, and he made a quick tour of the towns east of the "Cherokee mountains." He developed a list of forty-three towns and villages before returning through the Lower Towns by mid-June 1775 and joining a "company of adventurers for West Florida." Bartram, *William Bartram on the Southeastern Indians*, 87–89.

[22] William Blount (1749–1800), a native of North Carolina and a prominent land speculator, was appointed governor of the Territory of the United States South of the River Ohio on 8 June 1790. John R. Finger, *Tennessee Frontiers: Three Regions in Transition* (Bloomington: Indiana University Press, 2001), 125–27.

[23] In March 1777, the Cherokee from the Overhill Towns of Great Island, Tellico, Toqua, and Chilhowie under the leadership of Dragging Canoe, a militant-nativist, moved southwest to Chickamauga Creek, north of present day Chattanooga,

wounded bruin and the hunters, affording the whole company a great deal of diversion. They also had other amusing pantomimic entertainments, among which was "taking the pigeons at roost."[20]

They were extremely proud, despising the lower class of Europeans. Yet they were gentle and amiable to those whom they thought their friends. Implacable in their enmity, their revenge was only completed in the entire destruction of the enemy. They were hardy, and endured heat, cold and hunger in a surprising manner. But when in their power to indulge, no people on earth, except the Choctaws, carried debauchery to greater excess.*

William Bartram, who penetrated the Cherokee nation, mentions the following towns. We use his orthography.[21]

ON THE LITTLE TENNESSEE RIVER, EAST OF THE SMOKY MOUNTAINS.

Echoe; Nucasse; Whataga; Cowe.

ON THE BRANCHES OF THAT RIVER.

Ticaloosa; Jore; Conisca; Nowe.

ON THE LITTLE TENNESSEE, NORTH OF THE SMOKY MOUNTAINS.

Tomothle; Noewe; Tellico; Clennuse; Ocunnolufte; Chewe; Quanuse; Tellowe.

INLAND TOWNS ON THE BRANCHES OF THAT RIVER, AND OTHERS NORTH OF THE SMOKY MOUNTAIN.

Tellico; Chatuga; Hiwasse; Chewase; Nuanha.

OVERHILL TOWNS ON THE TENNESSEE OR CHEROKEE RIVERS.

Tallase; Chelowe; Sette; Chote-great; Joco; Tahasse; Tamohle; Tuskege; Big Island; Nilaque; Niowe.

LOWER TOWNS, EAST OF THE MOUNTAINS.

Sinica; Keowe; Kulsage; Tugilo; Estotowe; Qualatche; Chote; Estotowe, great; Allagae; Jore; Naeoche.†

Governor Blount, of the Tennessee Territory, made a report to the Indian Department of the Federal Government, in which he described the other towns of the Cherokee Nation.[22] It appears that a portion of the Cherokees established themselves upon

* Timberlake, *Memoirs*, 49–80; Bartram, 368–69.

† Bartram, 371–72.

Tennessee. Following militia incursions into these towns, these militant Cherokee secessionists known as the Chickamauga established five towns in 1782 lower down the Tennessee which became known as the Five Lower Towns of the Chickamauga. James Paul Pate, "The Chickamauga: A Forgotten Segment of Indian Resistance on the Southern Frontier" (Ph.D. diss., Mississippi State University, 1969), 80–81, 93–95, 119, 125–26, 128–29; *American State Papers: Documents, Legislative and Executive of the Congress of the United States*, ed. Walter Lowrie and M. St. Clair Clarke, 38 vols. (Washington: Gales and Seaton, 1832–1861), Class 2, *Indian Affairs* [2 vols.], 1: 264, 277–78. [Hereafter cited as *ASP: IA*].

[24] Running Water, twelve miles below the whirl and suck of the Tennessee River, served as the capital of the Chickamauga with a council house measuring sixty feet in diameter. Dragging Canoe and several allied Indian delegations resided here. By 1794, it included some two hundred log houses with a population of approximately three to four hundred. Pate, "The Chickamauga," 129; *ASP: IA*, 1: 264.

[25] When Nickajack was destroyed in 1794, it had nearly two hundred houses and a population of three hundred people. Shawnee delegates lived here in 1789 and 1790. Pate, "The Chickamauga," 129; *ASP: IA*, 1: 264.

[26] The smallest of the Five Lower Towns "contained ten or twelve huts in 1790," and it was located at the Old Creek Crossing place on the Tennessee River near modern Bridgeport, Alabama. *ASP: IA*, 1: 264; William E. Myer, "Indian Trails of the Southeast," *Forty-Second Annual Report, 1924–1925*, Bureau of American Ethnology, (Washington: GPO, 1928), 733–34.

[27] Located thirty miles below the whirl and suck of the Tennessee near modern

Chickamauga Creek, one hundred miles below the mouth of the Holston, being averse to any terms of friendship with the English. But believing these new settlements to be infested with witches, they abandoned them, moved forty miles lower down the Tennessee, and there laid out the foundation of the "five towns" which they inhabited for many years afterwards, and until their final removal to Arkansas.[23] These towns were:

Running Water—on the south bank of the main Tennessee, three miles above Nickajack, containing one hundred huts, the inhabitants of which were a mixed population of Cherokees and Shawnees.[24]

Nickajack—on the south bank of the Tennessee, containing forty houses.[25]

Long Island Town—on the south side of the Tennessee, on an island of that name, containing several houses.[26]

Crow Town—on the north side of the Tennessee, half a mile from the river, up Crow Creek. This was the largest of the towns.[27]

Lookout Mountain Town—between two mountains, on Lookout Mountain Creek, fifteen miles from its confluence with the Tennessee.[28]

The first four of these towns were considerable Indian thoroughfares for a long period, being the crossing places of the Southern and Northern Indians during their wars with the Cumberland American settlements. Of these five towns, the sites of Nickajack and Long Island only are in Alabama, situated in the northeast part of De Kalb County. But still lower down, in the present state of Alabama, were Will's Town[29] and Turkey Town[30]—important Cherokee establishments. The former was named for a half-breed called Redheaded Will. At these towns lived the British superintendent (the celebrated Col. Campbell)[31] before and during the Revolutionary War.*

* *American State Papers: Indian Affairs*, 1: 264–89.

Stevenson, Alabama, Crow Town contained 50 huts in 1790. The Creeks and northward Indians often crossed the Tennessee River at this point. *ASP: IA*, 1: 264; John Norton, *The Journal of Major John Norton*, ed. Carl F. Klinck and James J. Talman (Toronto: The Champlain Society, 1970), 42 n. 2.

[28] Lookout Mountain Town was the residence of Richard Justice, a noted conjurer, and The Glass, a prominent war chief. One report states it had 80 huts, giving it a population of approximately 240. It was located near modern Trenton, Georgia. *ASP: IA*, 1: 264.

[29] Following the death of Dragging Canoe on 1 March 1792, John Watts Young Tassel), a métis Cherokee, became the leader of the Chickamauga and established his headquarters at Will's Town (also Willstown), located near modern Fort Payne, Alabama. Will Weber, a métis Cherokee, established the town, and he became known as Redhead Chief Will or simply Redheaded Will because of his thick mane of red hair. It was later referred to as Watt's Town because he established his headquarters there. *ASP: IA*, 1: 278, 289; Norton, *Journal*, 37, 37 n. 2, 42.Tyler Boulware, *Deconstructing the Cherokee Nation: Town, Region, and Nation among Eighteenth-Century Cherokees* (Gainesville: University Press of Florida, 2011), 166–67.

[30] Lower Cherokees under the leadership of Little Turkey established New Seneca or Turkey's Town on the upper Coosa River. Boulware, *Deconstructing the Cherokee Nation*, 162, 166; *ASP: IA*, 1: 276–77, 451.

[31] Pickett's "celebrated Col. Campbell" is a reference to Alexander Campbell, who served as a British agent and commissary to the Chickamauga in concert with Alexander Cameron and John McDonald. He first resided at Turkey Town, adjacent to modern Centre, Alabama, and later at Wills Town, near the community of Leonard, Alabama. *ASP: IA*, 1: 327, 434; Pate, "The Chickamauga," 146, 160; John L. Nichols, "Alexander Cameron, British Agent among the Cherokee, 1764–1781," *South Carolina Historical Magazine* 97 (April 1996): 111–13.

Chapter III

ANCIENT MOUNDS AND FORTIFICATIONS IN ALABAMA

In the southern and northwestern states mounds of various dimensions and descriptions are yet to be seen, and continue to elicit no little speculation in regard to the race of people who formed them, and the objects which they had in view.[1]

Mounds are most commonly heaps of earth, but in some instances they are made of fragments of rock. In Florida, Georgia, Alabama and Mississippi, they are of two classes. We will first treat of the large mounds, some of which are round, some elliptical, and others square. Many of them are flat on top, while others present conical forms. They ascend to the height of from forty to ninety feet, and some are eighteen hundred feet in circumference at the base. Especial contrivances appear to have been resorted to, to ascend these singular and imposing elevations, by means of steps cut in the sides, inclining at an easy angle, and reaching from the ground below to their tops.* During the invasion of De Soto, they were used as elevated platforms, sustaining the houses of the chief, his family and attendants, while the common people lived around the base. The writers upon that expedition describe the manner in which the natives brought the earth to the spot and formed these elevations. Garcilaso de la Vega states that the erection of a mound was the first object in building a new town, which was generally located upon some low alluvial ground. When completed, the chief's houses, from ten to twenty in number, were placed upon its top, and a public square laid out at the base, around which were the houses of the prominent Indians, while the humbler wigwams of the common people stood around the other side of the mound.[2]

Such, then, three hundred and ten years ago, was found to be the use of these mounds. By the writers of De Soto, they are repeatedly mentioned as

* See Chapter 2, 55–56.

[1] When Pickett was engaged in researching and writing his *History of Alabama,* he had no archaeological or scientific data sources available to him that would allow him to use the term Mississippian or differentiate Early Mississippian (1000–1200 CE), Middle Mississippian (1200–1400 CE), and Late Mississippian (1400–1500 CE). See John A. Walthall, *Prehistoric Indians of the Southeast: Archaeology of Alabama and the Middle South* (Tuscaloosa: University of Alabama Press, 1980) and Guy Gibbon, ed., *Archaeology of Prehistoric Native America: An Encyclopedia* (New York: Garland Publishing, 1998).

[2] Much of Pickett's narrative regarding the mounds—platform, burial or effigy—discovered by De Soto and other explorers and the descriptions by the various chroniclers is paraphrased from James Haines

being almost daily seen in all the territory through which that remarkable adventurer passed. Yet, many very learned and wise antiquaries have contended, in various works which they have published, that these mounds must have been constructed at a very ancient period, by a race far advanced in civilization—that the aborigines who were first discovered by Europeans were incapable of erecting such works on account of their ignorance of the arts and their want of sufficient population. Our readers have seen what a numerous population De Soto and other discoverers found here, and that they possessed much ingenuity in the building of boats, fortifications, temples, houses, etc. Of all people upon earth the American Indians had most time to engage in such works, for they were never accustomed to regard their time as of the least importance. Indeed, the American citizen of the present day, who has lived upon the Indian frontiers, knows that they often assembled together in great numbers and performed public works of all kinds.[3] But much later authority than that offered by the writers of De Soto will be presented. It will be recollected that when the French drove the Natchez tribe from the spot now occupied by the city of that name, that the latter established themselves upon the Lower Ouachita, where they "erected mounds and embankments for defense, which covered an area of four hundred acres." These mounds are still to be seen there, and some of them are very large. These Indians were driven from Natchez in 1730.[4] Two years afterwards the French defeated them upon the Ouachita, where they were protected by their embankments and mounds, which they had only been a little over two years in constructing.[5] Let it be borne in mind that this was about one hundred and ninety-one years after the invasion of De Soto; and the facts are attested by numerous Frenchmen and other authors, some of whom were eyewitnesses.*

Charlevoix and Tonti both mention that they found Indians a little south of Lake Michigan, who well understood the construction of mounds and fortifications.[6] Even during the administration of Jefferson, Lewis and Clark, who had been dispatched upon an overland route to Oregon, discovered the Sioux and other western Indians erecting earthen embankments around their camps and towns. Were it deemed necessary, other authorities could be adduced to overthrow the speculations of those antiquarians who endeavor to inculcate the

* See Chapter 2, Part 3, 98–99.

McCulloh, *Researches, Philosophical and Antiquarian, Concerning the Aboriginal History of America* (Baltimore: F. Lucas, Jr., 1829), see pages 503–17.

3 When De Soto's expedition came in contact with the Mississippian chiefdoms, they found structured societies and people making daily use of their platform and burial mounds and continuing to construct mounds. Hudson, *Knights of Spain*, 13–30, 425–27, 434–35; Patricia A. Galloway, *Choctaw Genesis, 1500–1700* (Lincoln: University of Nebraska Press, 1995), 27–74.

4 While the mounds mentioned by Pickett may have had a connection to the Natchez, they had not been constructed "a little over two years." Twentieth century archaeological investigations at the "Natchez Fort site" have identified Plaquemine and Coles Creek pottery shards, "including the Leland/Fatherland type." The Plaquemine culture (1200–1650 CE) is an indigenous development that emerged from Coles Creek, a Late Woodland culture, in the Lower Mississippi valley. Barnett, *Natchez Indians*, 120–22; Southeast Archaeological Center, National Park Service, http://www.nps.gov/history/seac/outline/04-woodland/index-2.htm.

5 As noted earlier, the Natchez defensive works were constructed near the Ouachita River that flows out of Arkansas into Louisiana, eventually joining the Black and Red Rivers. In his original narrative Pickett referred to the Washita River. which originates in Texas and flows into southwestern Oklahoma, where it terminates in Lake Texoma and the Red River.

belief that our country was once inhabited by an almost civilized race. We heartily concur in the opinion expressed by McCulloh, in his *Researches*, that the "mounds were sites for the dwellings of the chiefs, for council halls and for temples, which fancy and conceit have constructed into various shapes and variously situated, one to the other." This author has reference, of course, to the larger mounds.*

Bartram found, in East Florida, many peculiar mounds. He saw groups of square mounds surrounded by walls of earth, and pyramidal mounds of great height. "From the river St. John, southwardly to the point of the peninsula of Florida, are to be seen high pyramidal mounds, with spacious and extensive avenues leading from them out of the town to an artificial lake or pond of water." In another place he says: "At about fifty yards distance from the landing place stands a magnificent Indian mount. But what greatly contributed to the beauty of the scene, was a noble Indian highway, which led from the great mount, in a straight line three-quarters of a mile, through a forest of live-oaks, to the verge of an oblong artificial lake, which was on the edge of an extensive level savannah. This grand highway was about fifty yards wide, sunk a little below the common level, and the earth thrown on each side, making a bank of about two feet high."[7]

On the east side of the Ocmulgee, and a little below the city of Macon, in Georgia, are some large and interesting mounds. In the town of Florence, Lauderdale County, Alabama, is a very large and peculiar mound. Near Carthage, in the same state, there are many mounds of various sizes, some of which are large.[8]

Dr. Charles A. Woodruff—a native of Savannah, but now a resident of Alabama—a man of letters and research, who has travelled over Georgia, Mississippi, Florida, Louisiana, Arkansas and Alabama, engaged in geological researches—has called our attention to a very remarkable group of mounds on the lands of Judge Messier, twenty-one miles in a southeastern direction from Fort Gaines. A reference to the sketch which he has furnished us, and his description of it, which follows, will make the reader acquainted with these remarkable artificial elevations.

"No. 1. The large sacrificial mound, seventy feet in height and six hundred feet in circumference. This mound is covered with large

* J. H. McCulloh, Jr., *Researches, Philosophical and Antiquarian, Concerning the Aboriginal History of America* (Baltimore: 1829), 516.

[6] In 1721–1722, Pierre-François-Xavier de Charlevoix (1682–1761), a Jesuit priest, made a long journey from Canada through the Great Lakes, and down the Mississippi, arriving at the Natchez villages on Christmas Day 1721 and modern Ocean Springs, Mississippi, in February 1722. Henri de Tonty (ca. 1649–1704), an explorer, guide and trading post commander, spent twenty-six years in New France, traversing the interior of North America from Canada through the Illinois country to Mobile Bay. David M. Hayne, "Pierre-François-Xavier de Charlevoix," *Dictionary of Canadian Biography*, vol. 3, University of Toronto/Université Laval, 2003, http://www.biographi.ca/en/bio/ [Hereafter cited as *DCB* (online)]; E. B. Osler, "Henri Tonty," ibid., vol. 2.

[7] William Bartram made two trips up the St. Johns River in East Florida and repeatedly identified the mound sites he observed as works of American Indians—and not some "race of non-Indian mound builders." From his investigations at Mount Royal on the St. Johns River to his account of the Choctaw funerary mounds, Bartram demonstrated an innate understanding of the connection between American Indians and the construction and utilization of the mounds he observed from the Atlantic Coast to the Gulf of Mexico. Bartram, *William Bartram on the Southeastern Indians*, 45–46, 129, 131–32, 167–68, 176–80, 210–13, 240–41 nn. 31–32.

[8] The Ocmulgee mounds—Ocmulgee National Monument—near Macon, Georgia include a large group of mounds from the Early Mississippian period which were abandoned by 1200 CE. The mound at Florence, Alabama, was described

Ancient Indian fortifications and mounds, in Early County, Georgia, from a sketch by the visitor, Dr. C. A. Woodruff.

forest trees, from four to five hundred years old. A shaft has been sunk in the center to the depth of sixty feet, and at its lower portion a bed of human bones, five feet in thickness, and in a perfectly decomposed state, was passed.

"No. 2, 2. Like the former, have hearthstones on the summit, with charred wood around them, which would show that they, too, were used for sacrifices. They are thirty feet high.

"No. 3. A wall of earth enclosing these mounds.

"No. 4, 4, 4, 4. Mounds outside of the enclosure, twenty feet high, and probably used as watch towers.

"No. 5. Entrance to the enclosure.

"In the rear of these mounds is a creek, No. 6, and from the large mound there has been constructed an arched passage, three hundred yards in length, leading to the creek, and probably intended to procure water for religious purposes."[9]

The smaller mounds, to be found in almost every field upon the rivers Tennessee, Coosa, Tallapoosa, Alabama, Cahaba, Warrior and Tombigbee, will next be considered.

Many of these elevations are cultivated in cotton and corn, the plough ascending and descending from year to year, with more ease as they gradually wear away. They are usually from five to ten feet high, from fifteen to sixty feet in circumference at the base, and of conical forms, resembling haystacks. Where they have been excavated they have, invariably, been found to contain human

as a hexagonal mound surrounded by a wall in 1848, and in 2015, as being 43 feet high with a summit that is 145 feet by 94 feet. Carthage, Alabama, was founded in 1823, and its name was changed to Moundville in 1894 because of the nearby Middle Mississippian mound complex abandoned around 1400 CE. Mark Williams, "Ocmulgee Mounds," *New Georgia Encyclopedia*, http://www.georgiaencyclopedia.org/; Ephraim G. Squier and Edwin H. Davis, *Ancient Monuments of the Mississippi Valley*, Smithsonian Contributions to Knowledge, vol. 1 (Washington: Smithsonian Institution, 1848), 110; John H. Blitz, "Moundville Archaeological Park," http://www.encyclopediaofalabama.org/.

9 Pickett's informant, Dr. Charles A. Woodruff, provided him with a general description of the Kolomoki Mounds (250–950 CE) near Blakely, Early County, Georgia, one of the earliest and largest Early Woodland

bones, various stone ornaments, weapons, pieces of pottery, and sometimes ornaments of copper and silver, but of a rude manufacture, clearly indicating Indian origin. Layers of ashes and charcoal are also found in these mounds.

It will be recollected that the Spaniards, during the invasion of De Soto, discovered temples in all the chief towns, in which the dead were deposited in baskets and wooden boxes. At a late day this custom was found to exist only among the Choctaws, Natchez, and a few other tribes. The Muscogees and Alabamas, who came into the country after it had been overrun by De Soto, had, as we have seen, simple modes of burial, and hence knew nothing about the construction of these mounds. The bone houses of the Choctaws were miniature temples of the Indians of 1540. We have seen in what manner the Choctaws placed their dead upon scaffolds, and afterwards picked off all the flesh and fragments from the bones, and deposited the latter in bone-houses. It is positively asserted by Bartram that every few years, when these houses became full of bones, the latter were carried out upon a plain, buried in a common grave, and a mound raised over them.* According to Charlevoix, another conscientious author, the Six Nations and the Wyandot every eight or ten years disinterred their dead, who had been deposited where they had died, and carried all the bones to a certain place, where they dug a pit, thirty feet in diameter and ten in depth, which was paved at the bottom with stones.[10] In this the various skeletons, with the property which the deceased possessed, were thrown. Over the heap a mound was raised, by throwing in the earth they had dug out, together with rubbish of every kind. Much later authority will be adduced.

Lewis and Clark, whom, as we have said, Jefferson sent to explore Oregon, saw a mound twelve feet in diameter at the base, and six feet high, which had just been erected over the body of a Maha chief.[11] It appears to have always been the custom to erect a mound over a chief or person of distinction, and no other bodies were interred with him. Indeed, no practice has been more universal than that of erecting a mound or tumulus over the dead, not only in America, but over the world. Adair asserts that it was the practice of the Cherokees to collect the skeletons of those who had died far from home, and erect over them stone mounds, and every person who passed by was required to add a stone to the heap.† This, then, accounts for heaps of stones to be found in the northern part of Georgia and northeastern Alabama, resembling mounds in form. In North Alabama and Tennessee, skeletons have been

* Bartram, *Travels*, 516. See also Bossu, *Travels*, 1: 299.

† Adair, *American Indians*.

mound complexes in the Southeastern United States. Located on Kolomoki Creek in the Chattahoochee watershed, the complex included villages, two burial mounds, a temple mound, ceremonial plaza, and four ceremonial mounds representing the Swift Creek and Weeden Island cultures. Francine Weiss and Cecil McKithan, National Register of Historic Places Inventory-Nomination: Kolomoki Mounds (September 1981).

[10] Pierre-François Xavier de Charlevoix kept a journal of his exploration of the boundaries of Acadia lost to the British by the Treaty of Utrecht (1713) and his journeys to find a route to the Pacific, exploring from the St. Lawrence through the Great Lakes to the Mississippi River. He also wrote a history of New France published in 1744. Pickett appears to cite from his *Journal of a Voyage to North America,* translated from French and published in two volumes in 1761. See Pierre-François Xavier de Charlevoix, *Journal of a Voyage to North America, Undertaken by Order of the French King,* trans. from the French of P. de Charlevoix, 2 vols. (London: R. and J. Dodsley, 1761).

[11] Pickett's Maha chief was actually an Omaha chief named Blackbird who died of smallpox in 1800. The Lewis and Clark

found in caves.[12] In mountainous countries this may have been one of the modes of disposing of the dead, or, which is more probable, persons died there suddenly, and their bones were not afterwards gathered together, buried in a common grave, and a mound erected over them, as was the general custom of ancient times.

The small mounds in Alabama, which have been excavated, contained different strata. Beginning to dig at the top, the operators first pass through a strata of earth about two feet thick, then they come to a bed of ashes and charcoal, and then a bed of human bones mixed with pieces of pottery, pipes, arrow-heads and various Indian ornaments. Mussel shells are often mixed with these. Continuing to dig downwards, the excavators pass through a strata of earth, which is succeeded by stratas of bones, charcoal, pottery, Indian ornaments and arrow-points. Now, from all we have read and heard of the Choctaws, we are satisfied that it was their custom to take from the bone-houses the skeletons, with which they repaired in funeral procession to the suburbs of the town, where they placed them on the ground in one heap, together with the property of the dead, such as pots, bows, arrows, ornaments, curious shaped stones for dressing deer-skins, and a variety of other things. Over this heap they first threw charcoal and ashes, probably to preserve the bones, and the next operation was to cover all with earth. This left a mound several feet high. In the course of eight or ten years, when the bone-house again became full of skeletons, the latter were carried in the same manner to the mound, placed upon top of it, and covered with ashes and earth. When the mound became high enough to excite a kind of veneration for it, by depositing upon it heaps of bones, from time to time, another was made not far from it, and then another, as time rolled on. This accounts for the different stratas of bones to be found in the same mound, and for the erection of several mounds, often found near each other.[13]

As for the ancient ditches at Cahaba, and in other portions of Alabama, in which are now growing the largest trees of the forest, indicating the works to have been of very remote date, we have been unable, in our investigations, to ascribe

expedition encountered his gravesite at his village Ton-won-tonga near Homer, Nebraska, on the Upper Missouri River in 1804. Guillaume Delisle, a French cartographer, mapped the northern stretch of the Missouri in 1718 and labeled the tribe as "The Maha, a wondering nation." McCulloh, *Researches, Philosophical and Antiquarian*, 515–16; "Omaha Tribe Historical Research Project," http://omaha-nsn.gov/tribe/history/.

[12] Although Pickett does not name Russell Cave located near Bridgeport, Jackson County, Alabama, it is an archaeological site that was occupied in the Archaic and Woodland periods. This National Monument has been explored and excavated by archaeological teams since the 1950s and some of the earliest artifacts have been carbon-14 dated to around 6,500 years ago. The excavations have yielded human burials and thousands of artifacts. Jessica Fordham Kidd, "Russell Cave," http://www.encyclopediaofalabama.org/.

[13] Bernard Romans refers to the Choctaw scaffold for the dead as a stage and reports that the bones were placed in a "neatly made chest" and "deposited in the loft of a hut . . . called a bone house." William Bartram records that that the Choctaws placed their bones in a coffin and at an appointed time they were stacked "forming a pyramid" and covered with earth creating "a conical hill or mound." Another source claimed that the Choctaw continued to add on the same burial mound, with "each deposit being covered up with earth to the depth of three or four feet." Bossu, *Concise Natural History*, 166–67; Bartram, *William Bartram on the Southeastern Indians*, 129–30; Swanton, *Social and Ceremonial Life of the Choctaw*," 177.

[14] The French built Fort Louis de la Mobile in 1702 and replaced it with a more substantial structure in 1710. In 1717, the French started construction on a

them to European origin, as they are generally supposed to be. De Soto erected no forts, in passing through this country, and had no occasion to do so, for his army was competent to subdue the natives without such means of defense. It is true he cut some temporary ditches upon the Warrior, near Erie, to repel the savages, who were charging him constantly from the other side of the river. These were soon abandoned, and his journalists mention no other works of the kind which he made.* The French and Spaniards, who afterwards occupied Alabama, erected no forts, except those at Mobile, upon the Tensaw River, at St. Stephens, at Jones' Bluff upon the Tombigbee, and four miles above the confluence of the Coosa and Tallapoosa, upon the east bank of the former.[14]

The English, at an early period, constructed a fort at Okfuskee upon the Tallapoosa.[15] If any other forts or entrenchments were made by the Europeans who first established themselves upon our soil, we have not been so fortunate as to trace them. The conclusion, then, seems to us to be apparent, that these ancient entrenchments or fortifications were the works of the aborigines of the country. It will be recollected that De Soto, and the French authors who succeeded him, nearly two centuries afterwards, discovered towns which were well fortified with immense breastworks of timber, around which were cut large ditches. It was easy, within a short space of time, for a few hundred Indians to have cut an immense ditch, or to have thrown up a great mound. The same tools employed in the erection of the latter, certainly the work of the ancient Indians, could well have been used in the cutting of these entrenchments or ditches. Hence, we contend, that at the town of Cahaba there once existed a large Indian establishment, which was fortified with palisades, and that the ditch, which has produced so much modern speculation among the good people of that place, was cut around these palisades, or rather around the town, having the Alabama River open on

* "Had Hernando De Soto erected one-tenth of the works which have been ascribed to him, in the states bordering on the Gulf, in Tennessee, and even in Kentucky, he must have found ample demands on his time and exertions." E. G. Squier and E. H. Davis, *Ancient Monuments of the Mississippi Valley*, 112.

more permanent fortification of brick and stone and changed its name to Fort Condé in 1724. The French also had a fortification on Dauphin Island (1699–1719), but it may have been little more than a well-entrenched gun emplacement. They constructed Fort Toulouse—"Les Alibamons"—at the confluence of the Coosa and Tallapoosa Rivers in 1717 in Elmore County, near modern Montgomery. Bienville's campaign against the Chickasaw in 1736 led to the construction of Fort Tombecbé on the Tombigbee River near Epes, Sumter County, Alabama. The British rechristened Fort Condé as Fort Charlotte in 1764 following the Treaty of Paris of 1763 and the organization of the colony of West Florida. The British also occupied Fort Tombecbé in 1764, but they chose not to occupy Fort Toulouse. The Spanish seized Mobile in 1780 during the Revolutionary War, occupied Fort Charlotte, and in 1794 constructed Fort Confederation on the old Fort Tombecbé site. René Chartrand, *The Forts of New France: The Great Lakes, the Plains and Gulf Coast* (Oxford, UK: Osprey Publishing, 2010), 51–58; James P. Pate, "The Fort of the Confederation: Spain on the Upper Tombigbee," *Alabama Historical Quarterly* 44 (Fall—Winter 1982): 171–86; Robert R. Rea, "The Trouble at Tombeckby," *Alabama Review* 21 (January 1968): 21–39.

[15] Captain Patrick McKay, Georgia's Indian agent among the Upper Creeks, negotiated an agreement to build a fort at Okfuskee in May 1735. The fort was constructed by a contingent of Georgia rangers, and a small garrison remained at the fort until it was abandoned in 1743. Anthony Willey, Fort Okfuskee's commanding officer, worked to maintain the loyalty of the Upper Creeks to the Georgia trade and to blunt the efforts of the French at Fort Toulouse. When the Georgia garrison departed in 1743, South Carolina received permission to build a second fort at Okfuskee, but the South Carolina House

one side.[16] There is a ditch near the Talladega Springs, which formerly had trees growing in it, and which surrounds an elevation, embracing a few acres and taking in a beautiful spring, which gushes out of the rocks at the side of a hill.* No doubt, this, and all other works like it, now frequently seen over the territories of Alabama and Mississippi, are the works of our ancient Indians, for they invariably erected their defenses at those places which admitted of the encompassment of running water; while, on the other hand, the Europeans who came to this country at an early period, always dug wells within the fortifications which they made.

In the month of October 1850, we visited a remarkable place at the falls of Little River, situated in the northeastern corner of Cherokee County, Alabama, and very near the line of De Kalb County, in the same state. [See picture at the beginning of volume II.] What is rather singular, Little River has its source on the top of Lookout Mountain, and runs for many miles on the most elevated parts of it. In the winter and spring it is a stream of considerable size, affording a rapid and dangerous current of water; but when it was seen upon the present occasion, a very protracted drought had nearly dried it up. The river flows along the top of the mountain with very inconsiderable banks, until it reaches a precipice of solid rock, in the form of a half circle, over which it falls seventy feet, perpendicularly, into a basin. After being received in this rock basin, the river flows off without much interruption, and, in winding about, forms a peninsula about two or three hundred yards below the falls. The banks of the river bordering on this peninsula are the same unbroken rock walls which form the falls, and are equally high and bold. Across the neck of the peninsula are yet to be traced two ancient ditches, nearly parallel with each other, and about thirty feet apart in the middle of the curve which they form, though they commence within ten feet of each other upon the upper precipice, and when they have reached the lower precipice are found to run into each other. These ditches have been almost filled up by the effects of time. On their inner sides are rocks piled up and mixed with the dirt which was thrown up in making these entrenchments, indicating them to be of the simplest and rudest Indian origin.[17] The author has seen many such entrenchments in his travels over Alabama, Mississippi and Florida, and hesitates not to say that they are the works of the aborigines of the country.

On one side of the bend of the peninsula, and about ten feet below the top of the rock precipice, are four or five small caves, large enough, if square, to form rooms twelve by fourteen feet. They are separated from each other

* Formerly the property of Henry G. Woodward.

of Commons refused to continue funding the garrison in 1744. Joshua Piker, *Okfuskee: A Creek Indian Town in Colonial America* (Cambridge: Harvard University Press, 2004), 30–37, 124, 141.

[16] Archaeological excavations at Old Cahawba in the 1970s and 1980s have confirmed the site as a Mississippian site with a circular mound and palisaded village in the Lower Cahaba River near its confluence with the Alabama River. The site has not yielded enough artifacts to link it with the battle of Mabila. Hudson, *Knights of Spain*, 248–49; Amanda L. Regnier, *Reconstructing Tascalusa's Chiefdom: Pottery Styles and the Social Composition of Late Mississippian Communities along the Alabama River* (Tuscaloosa: University of Alabama Press, 2014), 65–68.

[17] The Little River is the nation's longest flowing mountaintop river, flowing 30 miles atop Lookout Mountain. Little River Falls plunges 45 feet into Little River Canyon, which drops 600 feet in 18 miles. The river and its canyon, with its thick sandstone bluffs and canyon walls, is the longest and deepest canyon and gorge system east of the Mississippi. The Little River Canyon National Preserve was established as part of the National Park

by strata of rock, two of which resemble pillars, roughly hewn out. Three of them communicate with each other by means of holes which can be crawled through. These caves open immediately upon the precipice, and from their floors it is at least seventy feet down to the surface of the river. Many persons who have visited this singular place, call these "De Soto's Rock Houses," and they have stretched their imagination to such an extent as to assert that they have distinctly traced his pickaxes in the face of the rocks. There can be no question, however, but that these caves have been improved, to a slight extent, in size and shape, by human labor. But it was the labor of the Red people. Occasionally we could see where they smoothed off a point, and leveled the floors by knocking off the uneven places. It was, doubtless, a strong Indian fortification, and long used as a safe retreat when the valleys below were overrun by a victorious enemy. The walls are black with smoke, and everything about them bears evidence of constant occupation for years. These caves or rock houses constituted a most admirable defense, especially with the assistance of the walls at the head of the peninsula. In order to get into the first cave, a person has to pass along a rock passage wide enough for only one man. Below him, on his right, is the awful precipice, and on his left, the rock wall reaching ten feet above his head. A few persons in the first rock house with swords or spears, could keep off an army of one thousand men; for, only one assailant being able to approach the cave at a time, could be instantly dispatched and hurled down the abyss below. In regard to the inner walls of the ditches, the author saw no cement among the rocks, although he had heard that that ingredient (never used by Indians) was to be found there.[18]

Upon creeks and rivers in Alabama, where they meander through mountainous regions, are occasionally seen cuttings upon rocks, which have also been improperly attributed to Europeans discoverers. In the county of Tallapoosa, not far below the mouth of the Saugahatchee, and a few miles east from the Tallapoosa River, are cliffs of a singular kind of gray rock, rather soft, and having the appearance of containing silver ore. The face of these cliffs is literally cut in pieces, by having round pieces taken out of them. The ancient Indians used to resort to this place to obtain materials for manufacturing pipes, of large and small sizes, and, more particularly, for bowls and other household vessels. They cut out the pieces with flint rocks fixed in wooden handles.[19] After working around as deep as they desired, the piece was prized out of the rock. Then they formed it into whatever vessel, toy or implement they pleased. Hence, bowls, small mortars, immense pipes, and various pieces

Service in 1992. Thomas V. Ress, "The Little River Canyon National Preserve," http://www.encyclopediaofalabama.org/; Little River Canyon, National Park Service, http://www.nps.gov/liri/learn/historyculture/index.htm.

[18] Pickett's caves became known as the "Welsh Caves" with a mythological connection to Prince Madoc and his Welsh colonists. The caves are located near De Soto Falls, which drops 104 feet into the west fork of the Little River. The rock pillars or walls have deteriorated over the years, and there is no archaeological connection to the De Soto expedition. Janice Price-Gattis, *The Legend of the Welsh Caves at De Soto Falls* (n.p.: Janice Price-Gattis, 2008), 14–30; Frank Emory, "Little River Canyon," http://www.frankemory.com/articles/lrcnp.html.

[19] The cliffs and rock formations in the Tallapoosa River valley include igneous and metamorphic stratigraphy that include granites, gneisses, syerites, schists, semi-crystalline slates, and phyllites. The Hog Mountain area of Tallapoosa County produced the largest amount of gold found in Alabama in 1839. Dorothy E. Raymond, et al., *Alabama Stratigraphy*, Geological Survey of Alabama, Circular 140 (Tuscaloosa: 1988), 655–56,

resembling wedges* in shape, are often ploughed up in the fields in Macon, Tallapoosa and Montgomery, and other counties in Alabama, of precisely the same kind of rock of which these cliffs are composed. The author is also sustained in this position by unquestionable Indian testimony, which has been procured by him.

A few miles from Elyton, in the county of Jefferson, the author is informed that there stands a large quadrangular mound, about fifty feet high, and flat on the top; that, near its base, are to be seen cuttings in the rock something like mortars, some of which would hold over a gallon. These were done by the Indians, for the limestone rock could easily be worked into any shape by means of flint picks.[20]

The reader has observed that we have often mentioned the published works of Bartram, the botanist, who was in our country just before the Revolutionary War. We now quote from his MS, never published entire, but occasionally introduced by Squier in his *Ancient Monuments of the Mississippi Valley*. Squier embodies in his work the following account, from Bartram's MS, of the "CHUNK YARDS" of the Creeks or Muscogees: "They are rectangular areas, generally occupying the centre of the town. The public square and rotunda, or great winter council house, stood at the two opposite corners of them. They are generally very extensive, especially in the large old towns. Some of them are from six hundred to nine hundred feet in length, and of proportionate breadth. The area is exactly level, and sunk two, and sometimes three, feet below the banks of terraces surrounding it, which are occasionally two in number, one behind and above the other, and composed of the earth taken from the area at the time of its formation. These banks or terraces serve the purposes of seats of spectators. In the center of this yard or area there is a low circular mound or eminence, in the middle of which stands the "*chunk pole*," which is a high obelisk, or four-square pillar, declining upward to an obtuse point. This is of wood, the heart of a sound pitch pine, which is very durable. It is generally from thirty to forty feet in height, and to the top is fastened some object which serves as a mark to shoot at with arrows, or the rifle, at certain appointed times."[21]

* These wedges, in appearance, were used by the Indians in dressing their deer-skins. They were also used as clubs in war, having handles fixed to them.

660, 663, 665–66; Lewis Dean, "Minerals of Alabama," http://www.encyclopediaofalabama.org/.

[20] Pickett's rock formation near Elyton—now part of modern Birmingham—cannot be located. There are numerous rock formations—mainly sandstone—in Shades Mountain that may have been his "large quadrangular mound" standing 50 feet high. The Indians of Alabama would have found chert and flint deposits in the limestone in Jefferson County and several areas of the state. Dean, "Minerals of Alabama," http://www.encyclopediaofalabama.org/.

[21] Ephraim G. Squier and Edwin H. Davis produced extracts of William Bartram's "Observations on the Creek and Cherokee Indians"—which was not printed in his *Travels* published in 1791—in their *Ancient Monuments of the Mississippi Valley* published in 1848. Squier also published a heavily edited copy of "Observations" as the third volume of the *Transactions* of the American Ethnological Society in 1853. All the iterations of Bartram's sketches of the "CHUNK YARDS" are available in *William Bartram on the Southeastern Indians*, ed. Gregory A Waselkov and Kathryn Holland Braund (Lincoln: University of Nebraska Press, 1995), including a complete copy of his "Observations." Bartram, *William Bartram on the Southeastern Indians*, 133–86.

Chapter IV

THE FRENCH IN ALABAMA AND MISSISSIPPI

After the Spanish invasion of De Soto, to which allusion has so often been made, our soil remained untrodden by European feet for nearly a century and a half. At the end of that long and dark period, it became connected with the history of the distant French possessions of Canada, which were contemporaneous with the oldest English colonies in America. For more than fifty years the French fur traders of Canada, associated with the enterprising Jesuit fathers, had continued to advance southwestward upon the Great Lakes, discovering new regions, different races of Indians, more abundant game, and wider and brighter waters. At length, from the tribes upon the southern shores of Lake Superior, Father Allouez heard some vague reports of a great western river.[1] Subsequently, Father Marquette was dispatched from Quebec with Joliet, a trader of that place, five other Frenchmen, and a large number of Indian guides, to seek the Mississippi, and thus add new regions to the dominion of France, and new missions of the empire of the Jesuits. Ascending Fox River to the head of navigation, and crossing the portage to the banks of the Wisconsin, with birch bark canoes, the adventurers again launched their tiny boats and floated down to the Mississippi River. Descending it to the mouth of the Arkansas, and encountering decided evidences of a southern climate, Marquette finally found himself among the Chickasaws, whose reports that hostile tribes thronged the banks from thence to the sea, served to arrest his progress. Reluctantly commencing his return up the stiff and turbid tide, he found the mouth of the Illinois River, ascended to its head, crossed the portage to Chicago, launched his canoes upon Lake Michigan, and paddled to Green Bay, where he resumed his missionary labors. Joliet proceeded to Quebec with the news of the discovery.[2]

The young and gifted La Salle, a native of Rouen, in France, educated as a Jesuit, went to Canada to acquire fortune and fame by finding an overland passage to China. Becoming fired at the discovery which Marquette had made,

[1] Claude Jean Allouez (1622-1689), a Jesuit missionary and French explorer, arrived in Quebec in 1658 and worked as a missionary among American Indian tribes from the St. Lawrence River through modern Wisconsin. Léon Pouliot, "Claude Allouez," *DCB* (online).

[2] In May-June 1673, Father Jacques Marquette (1637-1675), a Jesuit missionary; Louis Joliet (1645-1700), a fur trader; and five *voyageurs* traveled in canoes from the Great Lakes, down the Mississippi River, and reached modern Arkansas in June 1673. Their contact with the Quapaw confirmed that the Indians of the interior could become important allies to France and that the Mississippi flowed to the Gulf of Mexico. Despite Pickett's claim, they did not make contact with the Chickasaw. Galloway, *Choctaw Genesis*, 165-66; Jacques Marquette, "The Mississippi Voyage of

he returned to France and obtained a royal commission for perfecting the exploration of the Mississippi, for which he was granted a monopoly in the trade of the skins of the buffalo. Sailing back to Canada, with men and stores, and accompanied by the Chevalier Tonti, an Italian soldier, who acted as his lieutenant, La Salle proceeded, by way of the lakes, upon his important enterprise. Consuming over two years in exploring those vast sheets of water, in building forts and collecting furs, he at length rigged a small barge, in which he descended the Mississippi to its mouth. Here, upon a small marshy elevation, in full view of the sea, he took formal and ceremonious possession in the name of the King of France. The country received the name of Louisiana, in honor of Louis XIV, who then occupied the French throne; but the attempt to give the river the name of Colbert, in honor of his minister of finance, did not succeed, and it retained that by which the aborigines had designated it. Leaving the Chevalier Tonti in command of Fort St. Louis, which La Salle had established in the country of Illinois, the latter returned to France, where the report of his discoveries had already given rise to much excitement and joy.[3]

The government immediately furnished him with a frigate and three other ships, upon which embarked two hundred and eighty persons, consisting of priests, gentlemen, soldiers, hired mechanics and agricultural emigrants, for the purpose of forming a colony at the mouth of the Mississippi. But the fearless adventurer, having crossed the Atlantic, and being unable to find, from the Gulf, the entrance to that river, was forced to disembark upon the coast of Texas. Here, erecting Fort St. Louis, and leaving the larger portion of the colonists, he explored the surrounding country, with the hope of finding the Mississippi, but returned unsuccessful. Death had hovered over the colony, which was now reduced to thirty-six persons; and with sixteen of these, La Salle again departed, with the determination to cut his way to Canada by land. After three months' wanderings, he was murdered by two of his companions, in the prairies of Texas, near the western branch of the Trinity River. In the meantime the Chevalier Tonti, with twenty Canadians and thirty Indians descended from the Illinois to meet his old commander; but, disappointed in not finding the French fleet at the Balize, he returned to the mouth of the Arkansas, where he established a little post.4 The few colonists left upon the coast of Texas all perished obscurely, except the brother of La Salle and six others, who

Jolliett and Marquette," in *Early Narratives of the Northwest, 1634-1699*, ed. Louise P. Kellogg (New York: Charles Scribner's Sons, 1917), 223-57.

3 René-Robert Cavalier de la Salle (1643-1687) established French claims to the Mississippi River Valley from the Great Lakes to the Gulf of Mexico through his expedition in 1682 and named the vast interior Louisiana in honor of King Louis XIV. Unfortunately, his failed colonizing effort in 1685 led to his death in 1687 near Matagorda Bay on the Texas coast. Galloway, *Choctaw Genesis*, 173-75; Robert S. Weddle, "Rene Robert Cavelier, Sieur de la Salle," *Handbook of Texas Online*, http://tshonline.org/handbook/online/.

4 La Salle left Henri de Tonti (also Tonty) to hold on to their claims to the Lower Mississippi interior and to develop the fur trade from their trading house among the Quapaw. He developed important contacts with the Indians and became the first European to contact the Choctaw. Galloway, *Choctaw Genesis*, 175, 187, 204.

5 The Treaty of Ryswick in 1697 ended King William's War (War of the League of Augsburg), 1688-1697. Jack D. L. Holmes, "Pierre Lemoyne, Sieur d'Iberville et d'Ardillieres: Colonial Explorer, 1699-1702," in *The Louisiana Governors: From Iberville to Edwards*, ed. Joseph G. Dawson III (Baton Rouge: Louisiana State University Press, 1990), 1-4.

6 Iberville had two sisters and eleven brothers and he was the

made their way to Canada. Such was the melancholy termination of the first attempt to colonize Louisiana.*

Louis XIV of France, the most splendid sovereign whom Europe had yet seen, had long been engaged in a war with William III of England, which had extended to their respective colonies in North America. In consequence of these troubles, further efforts to colonize the Mississippi were not attempted until after the Peace of Ryswick. By the terms of the treaty each party was to enjoy the territories in America which they possessed before the war.[5] The attention of the French monarch was now once more turned to the new country which La Salle had discovered. A number of Canadians had been left upon the shores of France upon the conclusion of the war, and among them was a distinguished naval officer named Iberville, who had acquired great military renown by his exploits against the English on the shores of Hudson Bay and Newfoundland, and by the capture of Pemaquid. He was one of seven sons, all natives of Quebec, all men of ability and merit, and all engaged in the king's service.[6]

To Iberville was confided the project of peopling Louisiana. He sailed from Rochelle with the *Badine*, of thirty guns, of which he had the immediate command, and with the *Marin*, commanded by Count Surgères, together with two harbor boats, each of forty tons.[7] On board these vessels were his two young but gallant brothers, Bienville and Sauvole, and two hundred colonists, mostly Canadians, who had gone to France to assist in her defense. Among them were some women and children. Arriving at Cape Francois, in the island of Santo Domingo, he was joined by the Marquis Châteaumorand, with a fifty-two gun ship. There he received on board a famous buccaneer named De Grace, who had pillaged Vera Cruz some years before.[8] Leaving Santo Domingo, Iberville sailed for the coast of Florida, and after a prosperous voyage stood before the Island of St. Rosa, from which point he discovered two men-of-war at anchor in the harbor of Pensacola, at whose mast-heads floated the colors of Spain. One month previous to this Don Arriola,

* Hildreth, *History of the United States of America* (New York: 1849), 2: 81–99; Charles Gayarré, *Historie de la Louisiane,* 1: 23–61; Henri Joutel, *Journal Historique Du Dernier Voyage que feu M. de La Sale fit dans le golfe de Mexique, pour trouver l'embouchure, & le cours de la Riviere de Missicipi, nommeé à present la Riviere de Saint Loüis, qui traverse la Louisiane* (Paris: 1713), 386 pages; Francois Xavier Martin, *The History of Louisiana, From the Earliest Period* (New Orleans: 1827), 1: 59–121. Also many other authorities.

third oldest. He played a major role in the battles against France's enemies, especially the English in New England and the victory at Pemaquid in August 1696 at modern Bristol, Maine. Bernard Pothier, "Pierre Le Moyne d'Iberville et d'Ardillieres," *DCB* (online), vol. 2; Nellis M. Crouse, *Lemoyne d'Iberville: Soldier of New France* (1954; reprint, Baton Rouge: Louisiana State University, 2001), 6-7, 90-116.

7 François de la Rochefoucauld, Chevalier de Surgères (1664-1731), commander of the *Le Marin*, served as Iberville's second in command of his small fleet. Marcel Giraud, *A History of French Louisiana:* Volume 1, *The Reign of Louis XIV, 1698-1715*, trans. Joseph C. Lambert (1953; reprint, Baton Rouge: Louisiana State University Press, 1974), 1: 22-23.

8 Joseph-Charles Joubert la Bastide, marquis de Châteaumorand (also Château-Morand), joined Iberville's expedition at Saint-Domingue (Santo Domingo) and served as his escort in the *François*, a ship-of-the-line. He later served as governor of Saint-Domingue in 1717-1719. Pickett's De Grace was probably Laurent Cornelis Boudewijn de Graaf (c.1653-1704), a Dutch pirate and mercenary, who served as a naval officer in the French service in the late seventeenth and early eighteenth centuries. He served as Iberville's interpreter—"Lorencillo"—at Pensacola Bay in 1699, and he is listed under staff officers at Fort Maurepas in May 1700: "Le Sieur Graffe, clerk for the King." David F. Marley, *Pirates of the Americas*,

2 vols. (Santa Barbara: ABC-CLIO, 2010), 1: 113-14; John C. Rule, "Jérôme Phélypeaux, Comte de Pontchartrain, and the Establishment of Louisiana, 1696-1715," in *Frenchmen and French Ways in the Mississippi Valley*, ed. John Francis McDermott (Urbana: University of Illinois Press, 1969), 189-90.

[9] Andrés de Arriola y Guzmán founded a Spanish post in Pensacola Bay in November 1698 and served as its first governor (1698-1700). Irving Albert Leonard, "Don Andrés de Arriola and the Occupation of Pensacola Bay," in *New Spain and the Anglo-American West: Historical Contributions Presented to Herbert Eugene Bolton*, ed. Charles W. Hackett, et al., 2 vols. (Lancaster, PA: Lancaster Press, 1932), 1: 85, 89-92.

[10] Isle of Massacre (*Ile du Massacre*) was the name given to Dauphin Island near Mobile Bay because Iberville's crew discovered some sixty decomposed bodies. Pierre Le Moyne d'Iberville, *Iberville's Gulf Journals*, trans. and ed. Richebourg McWilliams (Tuscaloosa: University of Alabama Press, 1981), 38.

[11] After discovering the Spanish presence at Pensacola Bay, Iberville sailed along the coast to Mobile Bay, past Dauphin Island, and west into the Mississippi Sound, where he encountered the barrier islands, Petit Bois Island, Horn Island, Ship Island, and Cat Island. He later made contact with the Chandeleur Islands, a fifty-mile-long barrier island complex, while searching for the mouth of the Mississippi River. Ibid., 35-53.

[12] Father Anastase Douay was one of the 320 members of La Salle's colonizing venture that missed the Mississippi and ended up on the Texas coast at Matagorda Bay. He witnessed

with three hundred Spaniards, from Vera Cruz, had established a battery upon the site of the present town of Pensacola.[9]

A deputation sent by Iberville was received with much politeness, but the Don declined to permit the French vessels to enter the harbor, for fear of a treacherous surprise.* The French then made sail to the west, and presently cast anchor off an island, which, from the quantity of human bones discovered upon it by Midshipman Bienville, was called the Isle of Massacre.[10] The small vessels passed through the channel between two elevations, to which they gave the name of Cat and Ship Islands. The fifty-two gun ship sailed for Santo Domingo, while the frigates lay off a group of banks, which received the names of the Chandeleurs. Iberville dispatched two boats to the main land, the crews of which found seven recently abandoned canoes, and succeeded in capturing two sick old Indians, whom they left with presents. The next day, a woman being taken and likewise sent off with presents, returned with two of her people, who belonged to the Biloxi tribe, whose name was given by the French to the bay. Four savages of this nation were then carried on board of Iberville's ship, while his brother, Bienville, remained upon the beach as a hostage.[11] On the same evening, twenty-four Bayogoulas arrived upon the shore, being on their way to fight the Mobilians, who, they said, lived on the banks of a great river which flowed into the sea, not far to the east.†

When Iberville had caused some huts to be erected upon Ship Island, he entered a boat with thirty men, accompanied by his brother, Bienville and Father Anastase, a Franciscan friar, the companion of the unfortunate La Salle in his descent of the Mississippi, and at the time when he was killed upon the plains of Texas.[12] Upon the third day, Iberville made the Balize, and was the first to enter the great river from the sea. He ascended for the space of ten days, until he arrived at a town of the Bayogoula nation. There he found, preserved by these Indians, a prayer book which

*The Spaniards, who still claimed the whole circuit of the Gulf, had hastened to occupy the Pensacola harbor, the best upon it. The barrier thus formed, made the dividing line between Florida and Louisiana.

† Bénard de la Harpe, *Journal historique de l'établissement des Français à la Louisiane*, 4–8. La Harpe was one of the first French settlers in Mobile, and he kept a journal of all he witnessed in that place, at Dauphin, Biloxi, Ship Island, etc.

belonged to the first expedition of La Salle, some cloaks which the discoverer had given them, a coat of mail which had belonged to the troop of De Soto, and a letter written by the Chevalier Tonti to La Salle, whom he had been disappointed in not meeting, as we have already seen. All these things combined to dispel the doubts which Iberville had entertained, that this was really the Mississippi, and re-assured the convictions of Father Anastase. Continuing the voyage to a point which he named Portage de la Croix, Iberville turned his boat downstream and touched at Bayou Manchac. Here Bienville, who was placed in command of the main boat, presently descended the river to the sea, while Iberville passed through the bayou in birch-bark canoes, guided by a Bayogoula Indian. Entering the river Amite, he soon fell into Lakes Maurepas and Pontchartrain, which he named in honor of the two principal ministers of his king. Bienville joined him soon after he reached his shipping.[13]

At the eastern extremity of the Bay of Biloxi and within the limits of the present state of Mississippi, a fort, with four bastions and mounted with twelve pieces of artillery, was now erected, the command of which was given to Sauvole, the elder of the two brothers of Iberville, while Bienville, the youngest of the three, was made lieutenant.[14] After the colonists had built huts and houses around it, Iberville and the Count Surgères sailed in the two frigates for France. Sauvole dispatched a vessel to Santo Domingo for provisions, and Bienville, with a small command, to visit the neighboring tribes, with whom he desired to cultivate friendly relations. Visiting the Colapissas upon the northern shore of Lake Pontchartrain, and the Pascagoulas upon the river of that name, among whom he distributed presents, and going by land from Mobile Point to Pensacola, to observe the movements of the Spaniards, he returned to Fort Biloxi; but in a few days set off in a boat, again to explore the Mississippi River.[15] After having ascended it some distance, and while returning, he met, not far below the site of New Orleans, an English captain named Barr, in charge of a vessel of sixteen guns, who asserted that there was another vessel of the same class belonging to him at the mouth of the river, and that his intention was to establish an English colony upon the banks of the Mississippi. The ingenious Bienville turned him toward the Gulf, by telling him that France had already taken possession of the river in which he then was, and above there had

the murder of La Salle by Pierre Duhaut in April 1686. Henri Joutel, "Henri Joutel's Account of the Murder of La Salle, 1687," in *Interpreting a Continent: Voices from Colonial America*, ed. Kathleen Du Val and John Du Val (Lanham, MD: Rowman & Littlefield Publishers, 2009), 244-48; Jacques Valois, "Anastase Douay," *DCB* (online).

[13] Iberville named Lake Pontchartrain and Lake Maurepas for a father and son and two of most powerful men in King Louis XIV's court. Louis Phélypeaux, Comte de Pontchartrain (1643-1727), served as Chancellor of France (1699-1714), and his son Jérôme Phélypeaux, Comte de Pontchartrain et de Maurepas (1674-1747), served as the minister of the marine in charge of the colonies (1699-1715). Iberville, *Iberville's Gulf Journals*, 82-84; Guy Rowlands, *Dangerous and Dishonest Men: The International Bankers of Louis XIV's France* (London: Palgrave Macmillan, 2015), 17-18, 43-44, 132, 171-72, 183.

[14] Sieur de Sauvole had no family relationship to the Le Moyne brothers. He was a naval officer and a trusted confidant to Iberville who left him in command of Fort Maurepas at Biloxi Bay. He died in August 1700—possibly from yellow fever—and never formally served as governor of Louisiana. Iberville, *Iberville's Gulf Journals*, 97, 158; Patricia Kay Galloway, "Sieur de Sauvole: Colonial Governor, 1699-1700," *Louisiana Governors*, 4-7.

[15] Bienville encountered the Colapissas living up the Pearl River. While Bienville traveled west and up the Mississippi, Sauvole sent a small party up the Pascagoula River where they visited villages of the Pascagoulas, Biloxis, and Moctobis. Galloway, *Choctaw Genesis*, 185, 188.

occupied it with a fort and garrison, and furthermore, that the Mississippi River lay considerably to the west.[16]

In the meantime, Sauvole received two Canadian missionaries, who had sometime before established themselves among the Yazoos. These holy men dropped down the Mississippi, entered the lakes by the Bayou Manchac, and paid their brethren an unexpected but most pleasing visit. Upon a bluff on the Mississippi, the site of old Fort Adams, lived one of these men, Father Davion, who erected a cross in the open air, and kept his holy relics in the hollow of a large tree. Here he told the Indians who the true God was, and baptized those who were converted with the waters of the ancient Mississippi. Could a life so entirely solitary, and attended with so many dangers, have been influenced by any other motives than such as are prompted by the purest piety?[17]

At length, the roar of distant cannon at sea announced the arrival of two large ships of war, commanded by Iberville and the Count Surgères, direct from France, laden with provisions for the colony, and having on board thirty laborers and sixty Canadians, intended as military pioneers, with their commanders, St. Denis and Maltot, together with a person named Le Sueur, who had acquired some celebrity in his voyage to Canada. They brought the pleasing intelligence that Sauvole had been appointed Governor of Louisiana, and Bienville Lieutenant Governor. Boisbriant, who also came with the ships, was commissioned to take the command of Fort Biloxi.[18]

Dreading the advance of the British, and determined to secure the banks of the Mississippi from their grasp, Iberville sailed, with fifty Canadians, to a point eighteen leagues above the Balize, which had been selected by the indefatigable young Bienville, who had arrived for that purpose a few days before, by way of Manchac, with some Bayogoulas, who were acquainted with the inundations of the river. Here they immediately began the construction of a fort, and, after a short time, were joined by the aged Tonti, who came from Canada, down the Mississippi, with a few Frenchmen and Indians. This veteran pioneer was joyfully received by those who had so often heard of his intrepid and fearless adventures.[19]

In the meantime Sauvole wrote to the minister, regretting that he was not allowed to accompany Iberville upon the Mississippi, where he could have learned so much of the country, condemned

[16] On 6 September 1699, Bienville encountered a British frigate coming up the Mississippi under the command of Captain William Bond—Pickett's Barr. Iberville's brash nineteen-year old brother convinced Bond that the river was under French control, and he turned his ship around and descended the river. The point some eighteen miles below New Orleans became known as English Turn or *Détour des Anglais*. Iberville, *Iberville's Gulf Journals*, 107, 107 n. 2; Carl J. Ekberg, "The English Bend: Forgotten Gateway to New Orleans," in *La Salle and His Legacy: Frenchmen and Indians in the Lower Mississippi Valley*, ed. Patricia Kay Galloway (Jackson: University Press of Mississippi, 1982), 212-14.

[17] Father Francis Jolliet de Montigny and Father Antoine Davion were the two Jesuit missionaries who visited Sauvole at Biloxi. Montigny returned to his mission assignment among the Taensas and Natchez, and Davion went back up river to his chapel among the Tunicas where he placed a cross in a rock—a place known as *Roche á Davion*—later know as Loftus Heights and the site of Fort Adams. Iberville, *Iberville's Gulf Journals*, 109-10, 144; Galloway, *Choctaw Genesis*, 187-91.

[18] Louis Juchereau de St. Denis, François Maltot, Pierre-Charles Le Sueur, and Pierre Dugué (Du Guay) Boisbriant (Boisbriand) were Canadians who joined Iberville on his second expedition into Louisiana. St. Denis replaced Bienville at Fort de la Boulaye and later established the post at Natchitoches. Maltot also served briefly as commander at Fort de la Boulaye. Le Sueur was an experienced fur trader and explorer. Boisbriant was a cousin to the Le Moyne brothers and served as an aide-major to Bienville. Iberville, *Iberville's Gulf Journals*, 116-21, 132-37; Donald E. Pusch, "Iberville's

the location at Biloxi as too low, sterile and sickly, and gave it as his opinion that the country offered no inducement to enterprise, except in the solitary article of hides. He closed his letter by expressing the hope that some mines of precious metals would be discovered. About this time Governor Arriola, of Pensacola, advanced to Ship Island with a man-of-war and some smaller vessels, for the purpose of expelling the French; but, deterred by Iberville's fleet, he hastened back, leaving only a proclamation protesting against the settlement of any portion of the coast, the whole breadth of which, he contended, belonged to His Catholic Majesty's Mexican possessions.[20]

Taking with them the Chevalier Tonti, Iberville and Bienville left their new fort and ascended the Mississippi, visiting the different tribes upon its shores, and finally resting at the site of the present city of Natchez, where lived the Indians who bore that name, and whose manners and customs have already been described. Delighted with this place, and resolved to plant a settlement there, Iberville marked out a town, and called it Rosalie—the name of the Countess Pontchartrain. From this place the Chevalier Tonti went up the river, and Bienville and St. Denis, with twenty-two Canadians, started to the west, by an overland route, to reconnoiter the Spanish settlements, while Iberville floated down the river to rejoin his fleet.[21]

Returning from the west to Biloxi, Bienville was sent to take command of the new establishment upon the Mississippi, and then Iberville once more spread the sails of his ships for beloved France. Meanwhile the colony languished; the earth was not cultivated, and, relying for supplies from Santo Domingo, horrible famine and sickness reduced the number of inhabitants to one hundred and fifty souls! Sauvole himself died, leaving the cares of the colony to the more redoubtable Bienville. The latter, deploring the condition of his people, and seeing the necessity of tilling the earth, in a dispatch to the French government, urged them to send him laborers, rather than the vicious and the idle, who roamed the forests in search of mines and Indian mistresses.[22]

A delegation of Choctaws and Mobilians visited Fort Biloxi, and requested assistance in their war with the Chickasaws. These were succeeded by twenty other Mobilians, and the chief of the Alabamas, all of whom were dismissed with presents and

Canadians: Lists of the Canadians Participating in Iberville's Second Voyage to Louisiana, 1699-1700," https://www.scribd.com/doc/90821450/Iberville-s-Canadians, 5-6, 10, 15.

[19] The fort constructed on a plan drawn by Iberville—Fort de la Boulaye—was generally referred to as the "Fort of the Mississippi." Apparently François Maltot served temporarily as the commander with a small garrison of fifteen men to complete the building of the post. Giraud, *Reign of Louis XIV*, 39-40.

[20] Actually Governor Andres de Arriola y Guzmán arrived at Biloxi in March 1699 with four ships, but he was not looking to attack the French. Iberville had similar orders to seek peace at all costs, but he stated their resolve to maintain their post and to stop English intrusion into the Gulf. Arriola delivered a firm letter protesting the French post, and then he and his underfed men enjoyed the French hospitality and food. Iberville, *Iberville's Gulf Journals*, 135; Leonard, "Don Andrés de Arriola," 85, 99-101.

[21] In March 1700 Bienville led a small expedition—which included Louis Juchereau de St. Denis—up the Red River to renew ties with the Caddos. They smoked the peace pipe with the Natchitoches tribes—Doustionis, Yatasis, and Natchitoches—and their principal leader Chief Blanc at his village on the Red River. Some years later, St. Denis returned to make a lifetime commitment among the Caddo confederacies and at Fort St. Jean Baptiste des Natchitoches. H. Sophie Burton and F. Todd Smith, *Colonial Natchitoches: A Creole Community on the Louisiana-Texas Frontier* (College Station: Texas A & M University Press, 2008), 4-6.

[22] Before his death in late August 1701, Sauvole wrote a lengthy letter

dated 4 August 1701 to Pontchartrain detailing the challenges faced by the French colonizing efforts, including the lack of reliable food sources, weather and health challenges, uncertainty of supplies from France, and the general "unruliness" and "disobedience" of the Canadians. He reported on four Canadians who went to the Carolinas to trade furs: "It is certain that if these vagabonds and rebels once become accustomed to going to the English we shall not see them again soon in Canada or here." *MPA: FD*, 2: 9-18.

[23] From the visit by Governor Arriola in March 1700 forward, the French and Spanish on the Gulf Coast had cooperated and supported one another, sharing food and returning deserters. Francisco Martinez was second in command of the Spanish presidio on Santa Maria de Galve Bay during Arriola's many absences. After Arriola's final departure in August 1700, he apparently remained the acting commander until replaced by Sergeant Major and Interim Governor Don Sebastian de Moscoso. Iberville, *Iberville's Gulf Journals*, 157-58, 162; Leonard, "Don Andrés de Arriola," 94-101; William B. Griffin, "Spanish Pensacola, 1700-1763," *Florida Historical Quarterly* 37 (January-April 1959): 244-45, 247, 250-51.

[24] Iberville returned to the Gulf in the *Renommée* with colonists and with orders to establish a fort on Mobile Bay. The second vessel, the *Palmier*, was under the command of his brother, Joseph Le Moyne de Sérigny. *MPA: FD*, 2: 550 n. 3; Iberville, *Iberville's Gulf Journals*, 157-68.

[25] Nicolas de La Salle, commissary and colonial administrator, had responsibility for the royal warehouses and financial accounts for the operation in Louisiana. Following Iberville's departure from the colony and his death in 1706, he openly clashed with Bienville and fostered a lengthy investigation of Bienville for profiteering and exceeding his authority. In 1708, he coordinated the first census of the colony. *MPA: FD*, 2: 18-20, 31-32; Iberville, *Iberville's Gulf Journals*, 160-61; C. E. O'Neill, "Nicolas de la Salle," *DCB* (online).

[26] Pickett has the first Mobile fort—Fort Louis de la Louisiane (Mobile)—in the wrong location.

exhortations to remain at peace with each other. At this time, the Spaniards of Pensacola and the French colony were not only upon good terms, but of mutual assistance to each other; so much so that Bienville arrested eighteen Spanish deserters and sent them back to Don Martinez, the governor of Pensacola.[23]

Iberville and his brother, Serigny, arriving at Pensacola, direct from France on board two men-of-war, dispatched supplies to the colonists in smaller vessels, which were joyfully received, as a meager portion of corn had for a long time barely kept them alive. Having received orders to break up the colonial establishment at Biloxi, and to remove it upon the Mobile, Bienville left only twenty soldiers at the fort, under Boisbriant, and sailed with his people to Dauphin Island, to which, as we have seen, they first gave the name of Massacre.[24]

Here he met his brother, Serigny, and a person named La Salle. The latter had been sent out to perform the duties of marine commissary.[25] With forty sailors and some ship carpenters, Bienville began the construction of a warehouse on Dauphin Island. With a sufficient force of soldiers, artisans and laborers he then sailed up the bay of Mobile, and at the mouth of the Dog River, commenced the erection of a fort, a warehouse and other public buildings. This place received the name of Mobile, from the spacious bay upon which it was situated, which was called after the tribe of Indians who had so resolutely fought De Soto upon the field of Mabila. The fort itself was long designated as Fort Louis de la Mobile.* Here was the seat of government for the space of nine years, when, in 1711, as we shall see, the French moved up to the mouth of the Mobile River, where they founded the town of Mobile, which has since become the beautiful commercial emporium of the state of Alabama.[26] A few

* In 1777 Bartram, being on a voyage from Mobile to Pearl River, in a French trading boat, touched at the mouth of Dog River, and saw there the ruins of old Fort Louis de la Mobile, where lay some iron cannon and some immense iron kettles, formerly used by the French for boiling tar into pitch. Bartram, *Travels*, 416–17.

days of activity and bustle had scarcely been passed at the new place, at the mouth of Dog River, before it was made sad by the meeting of Bienville and Iberville, who wept for the loss of Sauvole while affectionately locked in each other's arms.[27]

Iberville had passed with his ship-of-war, the *Palmier*, over the bar of Mobile Point, finding at least twenty feet of water. It was not long before La Salle and his family came up to Mobile, which now presented the appearance of a settlement, with houses and shelters. Bienville, anxious to obtain the friendship of all tribes upon the Mobile River and its tributaries, and to institute friendly relations between the different savage nations themselves, had sent Tonti with a small command to the Choctaw and Chickasaw countries. They now returned, with seven chiefs of those tribes. The governor gave them handsome presents, and exhorted them to remain at peace with the French and with each other. The Iberville and his retinue dropped down the bay of Mobile, went to Pensacola, and from thence sailed for France.[28]

Mobile being now the seat of government, various delegations of chiefs, Spaniards from Veracruz, and Canadians from the northern lakes and rivers, constantly repaired there to see Governor Bienville upon business. Among others, a delegation of eight chiefs of the Alabamas arrived, whom his excellency treated with kindness, and dissuaded from making war upon the Mobilians, Thomez, and Chickasaws.[29] Don Robles came with a letter from the governor of Pensacola, requesting the loan of provisions for his famishing garrison, with which the generous Frenchman readily complied. Midshipman Beaucourt, commanding the colonial marine, made several trips to Veracruz and returned with provisions, the king of Spain having granted the French free access to his colonial ports. Father Davion, the missionary upon the Mississippi, and Father Limoges, a Jesuit, came by way of the Bayou Manchac, and reported that one of their companions and four other Frenchmen had been

The first fort was constructed in 1702 on the Mobile River above the modern city of Mobile near Twenty-Seven Mile Bluff. In 1711, the French abandoned this fort site due to flooding and moved south on the bay and built Fort Condé. *MPA: FD*, 3: 18 n. 2, 162; Iberville, *Iberville's Gulf Journals*, 167-68; Chartrand, *Forts of New France*, 53-56.

27 Actually Sauvole had died on 22 August 1701, leaving Bienville in command at Fort Maurepas, and Iberville learned about his death when he landed at Spanish Pensacola on 15 December 1701. Iberville, *Iberville's Gulf Journals*, 157-58; Ethridge, *From Chicaza to Chickasaw*, 195-96.

28 Contrary to Pickett's timeline, Iberville did not leave Mobile for France until 31 March 1702. On 25 March 1702, Iberville welcomed Tonti's party, which included three Choctaw headmen, five Chickasaw "notables, three Chickasaw women, and two burden bearers," to Fort Louis de la Mobile. Before addressing the peace conference the next day that also included representatives from the Mobile, Tohomé, and Little Tohomé, he displayed the gifts to be distributed to the emissaries, including guns, powder and ball, axes, knives, kettles, beads, and other gifts. He urged the nations to remain peaceful but issued a warning to the Chickasaw to expel the slave-trading English or he would declare the Chickasaw as enemies and arm the other nations. Iberville, *Iberville's Gulf Journals*, 171-77; Ethridge, *From Chicaza to Chickasaw*, 196-204.

29 The Alabama headmen arrived in Mobile in May 1702, and Bienville extracted a promise from the emissaries to remain at peace with the Choctaw, Mobilians, and Tohomés. He sent them home with gifts to secure their commitment. In October, Bienville hosted forty Alabama headmen who smoked the calumet with Bienville and gave promises of peace with the Choctaw, Apalachees and Pensacolas. Ethridge, *From Chicaza to Chickasaw*, 206; Jean-Batiste Bénard de La Harpe, "The Historical Journal of the Establishment of the French in Louisiana," in *Historical Collections of Louisiana*, ed. and trans. Benjamin. F. French, vol. 3 (New York: D. Appleton, 1851), 28.

killed by the Indians above the Yazoo River.[30] News also reached Bienville that St. Denis, at the head of the Canadian scouts, had wantonly made war upon and killed some Indians with whom they were at peace, for the purpose of obtaining slaves. Bienville, grieved at his conduct, endeavored, unsuccessfully, to have the slaves restored to their people.[31] Governor Martinez, of Pensacola, came to Mobile, with the information that France and Spain had gone to war with England, and his request to be furnished with arms and ammunition was granted by Bienville. He was succeeded by two Spanish officers from St. Augustine, with a letter from Cerda, governor of that place, requesting military supplies, as he had been blockaded by the English and Indians. Bienville sent to his assistance a liberal supply of powder and ball.[32]

The English of Carolina began to disturb the French colonies, by sending emissaries among the Muscogees and Alabamas. In a very short time two artful Alabamas came down the river, to decoy the French into the country. Having assured the governor that their homes abounded in corn, which would be furnished at the most reasonable price, the latter forthwith dispatched Labrie, with four Canadians in canoes, to procure some. They had not proceeded far, before they were all killed except one of the Canadians, who returned to Mobile with his arm nearly severed by a blow which he received from an axe. To avenge this outrage, Bienville began the ascent of the Mobile in seven canoes, in which were forty soldiers and Canadians. In fourteen days he arrived in the vicinity of the Alabamas, upon the river of that name, where he discovered ten canoes without occupants, but saw smoke floating upon the air and rising over the forest trees and cane, upon the bluff. St. Denis and Tonti advised him not to make the attack until night, to which he assented, contrary to his better judgment. The night was very dark, and the path which led to the Indian camp was full of weeds and briars. However, an engagement ensued, in which three Frenchmen were slain, and the savages dispersed. Capturing the canoes, which were laden with provisions, Bienville returned to Mobile.[33] But he did not relax in his efforts to be revenged, for he presently engaged parties of Chickasaws and Choctaws to pursue the Alabamas, who brought some of their scalps to Mobile, for which they received rewards.*

* Bénard de la Harpe, *Journal historique* de l›établissement des Français à la Louisiane, 35–83.

[30] Father Antoine Davion served as a missionary to the Tunicas from 1699 to 1716. Father Joseph de Limoges, a Jesuit from Canada, began preaching among the Houma in 1699. Galloway, *Choctaw Genesis*, 187, 189-90; Jay Higginbotham, *Old Mobile: Fort Louis de la Louisiane, 1702-1711* (Mobile: Museum of the City of Mobile, 1977), 97, 100-04, 206-09; Michelene E. Pesantubbee, *Choctaw Women in a Chaotic World: The Clash of Cultures in the Colonial Southeast* (Albuquerque: University of New Mexico Press, 2005), 65-66.

[31] Pickett's source may have conflated or transposed this slave raiding action by St. Denis. Bienville actually authorized an assault in 1707 on a Chitimacha village in retaliation for the murder of Father Saint-Cosme. St. Denis, commander at Fort de la Boulaye, led a combined Canadian and Indian force against the village and captured the man "who boasted . . . he killed the missionary." They also took a number of women and children as slaves and sold many to settlers in Biloxi and Mobile. Saint-Cosme's killer was "tomahawked in the square of the fort" after Bienville had consulted with his officers. *MPA: FD*, 3: 38, 115-16; Usner, *Indians, Settlers & Slaves*, 24.

[32] José de Zúñiga y la Cerda (1654-1725) served as governor at St. Augustine from 1699 to 1706. As second in command at Santa Maria de Galve Bay, Francisco Martinez served as interim governor of Pensacola after August 1700. Timothy Paul Grady, *Anglo-Spanish Rivalry in Colonial South-East America,*

An official dispatch represented the following to be the condition of the feeble colony of Louisiana at this period:[34]

"180 men capable of bearing arms.

2 French families, with three little girls and seven little boys.

6 young Indian boys, slaves, from fifteen to twenty years of age.

A little of the territory around Fort Louis (Mobile) has been cultivated.

80 wooden houses, of one story high, covered with palm leaves and straw.

9 oxen, five of which belonged to the King.

14 cows.

4 bulls, one of which belonged to the King.

6 calves.

100 hogs.

3 kids.

400 hens."

This account did not, of course, include the officers.

The colonists, suffering from severe famine, were temporarily relieved by the governor of Pensacola, but again became destitute of provisions; and, while forced to disperse themselves along the coast, procuring subsistence upon fish and oysters, a vessel of war from France, commanded by Chateaugué, another brother of Bienville, happily re-established abundance among them. This vessel was succeeded by the *Pélican*, another man-of-war, laden with provisions, and having on board seventy-five soldiers intended for the various posts, La Vente, of the foreign mission, sent as rector by the Bishop of Quebec, four priests, and four Sisters of Charity, together with four families of laborers.[35] But what created more novelty and excitement than all the rest of the arrivals were twenty-three girls, whom Bienville was informed, by the minister's dispatch, were all of spotless chastity, pious and industrious, and that his majesty had enjoined upon the Bishop of Quebec to send no females to Mobile who did not bear characters as irreproachable as these. He was instructed to have them married to Canadians and others, who were competent to support them. Only a few days rolled around, before they all found husbands.[36] These were the first marriages which were solemnized in old Mobile, or, indeed, upon any part of the soil of Alabama, by Christian marital rites.*

* "The first child born in the colony, and, consequently, the first 'Creole,' was named Claude Jousset, and was the son of a Canadian who carried on a small trading

_1650–1725_ (London: Pickering & Chatto, 2010), 108-29.

[33] Bienville launched two punitive expeditions against the Alabamas. His first effort with a force of 220 French and Indians was doomed by poor tactical decisions, illness, and desertions by his Indian forces who saw bad omens. On his second expedition, he took a force of forty-eight Frenchmen and struck a small Alabama hunting party, killing two and losing two men. He learned some valuable intelligence about the location of Indian towns and the influence of the English trade. _MPA: FD,_ 3: 19-21; Ethridge, _From Chicaza to Chickasaw,_ 211-13.

[34] Pickett is citing data from a census of Louisiana completed by Nicolas de la Salle, Commissary of the Navy, dated 31 August 1704 at Fort Louis de la Mobile. _MPA: FD,_ 2: 18-20.

[35] Henri Roulleaux de la Vente (c. 1655-1717), a fifty year old missionary priest, became the first curate of the first church in Mobile. La Vente and Bienville seem to have clashed over most everything, especially the construction of his parish church in 1708. _MPA: FD,_ 2:43; Higginbotham, _Old Mobile,_ 249-58.

[36] While one young woman died and a second procrastinated, twenty-one of the young women on board the _Pélican_ found suitors and husbands fairly quickly. Their marriages were confirmed by Father La Vente. In his report to Pontchartrain on 6 September 1704, Bienville confirmed that shortly after their arrival "the girls married the Canadians and

But sickness and disasters soon dispelled the joy which these arrivals had occasioned. Half the crew of the *Pélican* died. Tonti and Levasseur, invaluable officers—Father Dongé, a Jesuit—and thirty of the soldiers lately arrived, soon followed them to the grave.[37] The fort and out-houses at Pensacola were wrapped in flames. Lambert, with his Canadians, driven from the post of Washita by the Indians, had fled to Mobile, where the Chickasaws and Choctaws had begun a war with each other, which was exceedingly embarrassing to Bienville.[38] More than seventy of the former, of both sexes, being in Mobile, and imploring Bienville to have them safely conducted to their nation, the route to which lay over the country of their enemies, he dispatched twenty Canadians, under Boisbriant, with them. Arriving at one of the Choctaw towns, the inhabitants assembled in great numbers to put them to death, but Boisbriant interposing, they then fell upon a stratagem to accomplish their purposes. Pretending that they only desired to rebuke the Chickasaws for their conduct, while the chief was accordingly making his speech to them, he let a feather fall, which was a signal for attack. The Chickasaw warriors were all instantly put to death, and the women and children reserved for slaves. Boisbriant was accidentally wounded by a ball, which was exceedingly regretted by the Choctaws, three hundred of whom carried him on a litter to Mobile, in mournful procession. Bienville was shocked and mortified at the ruthless massacre, and saw, at a glance, that the Chickasaws would suspect him of decoying these unhappy people there to meet the fate which they received.[39]

When Boisbriant recovered from his wound, he was dispatched up the Alabama River, with sixty Canadians, to fight the Alabamas and Muscogees. After a long absence he returned with only two scalps and an Indian slave. In the meanwhile the Chickasaws and Choctaws continued their war, which raged with the most savage ferocity. The French unavoidably became implicated in these feuds. Being considered the exclusive friends of the Choctaws, on account of their proximity, they were often suddenly slain by skulking Chickasaws. Iberville wrote to the minister that famine again prevailed in the unhappy colony of Louisiana; that the Spaniards could afford them but little corn, which the men only had become accustomed

business at Mobile." Charles Gayarré, *Louisiana; Its Colonial History and Romance* (New York: 1851), 464–65.

others who are in a position to support them." *MPA: FD*, 3: 15-16, 24; Higginbotham, *Old Mobile*, 178-87.

[37] Charles Levasseur (Le Vasseur) and Henri Tonti (Tonty) had great knowledge of the French Gulf domain. Levasseur, a Canadian military engineer, played a major role in the design and construction of Fort Louis de la Mobile near Twenty-Seven Mile Bluff on the Mobile River. In May 1700, he explored Mobile Bay and the rivers that fed into the bay and traveled into the Lower Tombigbee. Through an Alabama informant at the village of Maugoulacho, he developed a list of thirty-six towns on the Coosa, Tallapoosa, and Alabama Rivers. Gregory A. Waselkov, "French Colonial Archaeology at Old Mobile: An Introduction," *Historical Archaeology* 36 (1 - 2002): 4-5, 7; Usner, *American Indians*, 40; Higginbotham, *Old Mobile*, 41, 47-52.

[38] Pickett is referring to a French post—Oüabache—on the Wabash River, not the Washita. Gabriel Philippe de St. Lambert, an ensign in François Juchereau de Vaulezard's company, served as second in command at the Oüabache (Wabash) post on the Ohio. Bienville reported his death in 1706—apparently in Mobile. *MPA: FD*, 2: 29; ibid., 3: 56, 166.

[39] Pickett used Jean-Baptist Bénard de la Harpe's version of this incident in 1705, which differs in several details of the same incident as reported by André Pénicaut. According to Pénicaut, a Choctaw mico told Boisbriant that the Chickasaw had burned a young man—Saint-Michel—sent by Bienville to learn their language in order to sow discord between the French and the

to eat, the Parisian women eschewing it, and blaming the Bishop for not telling them what they had to encounter in the "promised land"; that fifty men had come to make a settlement at Mobile from the Upper Mississippi; and that the colonists would not unite to resist the savages and combat famine, but quarreled among themselves.[40] At this period, Commissary General La Salle had commenced a series of vindictive and unprincipled assaults upon the character of Bienville, in his dispatches to the court. In one of these he said that "Iberville, Bienville and Chateaugué, the three brothers, are guilty of all kinds of malpractices, and are extortioners and knaves, who waste the property of his Majesty." Father La Vente, the rector of Mobile, a man of bad temper and sordid feelings, and unpopular with the priests over whom he was placed, became a willing coadjutor of La Salle in his indiscriminate abuse of the governor. He, too, wrote letters to the court, the burden of which was the corruption of Bienville's colonial government. He essayed to persuade the inhabitants that their sufferings were owing alone to the conduct of their governor, who too tardily ordered supplies from France. He attempted to buy up the sick soldiers who he visited by giving them (as his own) money which had been placed in his hands for charitable purposes. The Lady Superior also vented her spleen against Bienville, by writing to the minister that Boisbriant had intended to have *married* her, but had been prevented by the governor. Hence, she adds, "Bienville does not possess the qualities necessary for a Governor."[41]

The colonists continued to lead unpleasant lives; the Muscogees and Alabamas threatened their existence; their hearts were troubled with the Chickasaw and Choctaw war; while the quarrels among the authorities continued to increase. Father Gravier, a Jesuit, took up the cudgels for Bienville, and defended him in a letter which he addressed to the minister. But Bienville, disdaining these cabals, continued to discharge his duty faithfully to the government, as far as it could be done with his means and ability, and in his dispatches refrained from alluding to the animosities of the commissary and rector, except casually to mention that he encountered much opposition from the former. Iberville, the indefatigable founder of Louisiana and the devoted friend of the colonists, died of yellow fever at Havana, where he had touched with his fleet while on his way to attack Charleston and Jamaica. This was severe blow, added to the general sufferings of the colony, and seriously retarded its advance. About the same

Chickasaws. He also reported that Boisbriant was not wounded and that he left the Chickasaws' fate in the hands of the Choctaws. Ethridge, *From Chicaza to Chickasaw*, 214-15. See André Pénicaut, *Fleur de Lys and Calumet: Being the Pénicaut Narratives of French Adventure in Louisiane*, ed. Richebourg McWilliams (1953; reprint, Tuscaloosa: University of Alabama Press, 1988), 73, 78.

[40] Contrary to Pickett's timeline of February 1706, Iberville left French Louisiana on 31 March 1702 and never returned. With France deeply involved in the War of the Spanish Succession (1701-1714), he sailed from France in early 1706 into the Caribbean as commander of a twelve ship fleet, devastating the island of Nevis. He went to Havana and began planning an attack on Charles Town, South Carolina, when he died of yellow fever aboard his flagship *Pélican* on 9 July 1706. Crouse, *Lemoyne d'Iberville*, 240-62, 266.

[41] Apparently Nicolas de la Salle and Father La Vente developed an alliance in opposition to Bienville and started sending letters of complaint to French officials. Bienville countered by accusing La Vente of sowing discord with the Jesuit priests, within the Mobile community, and with the military. In 1706 Bienville wrote a series of letters to Pontchartrain on the status of Louisiana, including Indian affairs, construction of the parish church, and the pressing need for provisions. He also reported his own complaints about the conduct of La Vente who claimed to be "the vicar general of the Bishop of Quebec," allowed missionaries to conduct marriages of Frenchmen and Indian women, and

time, Bergier, Grand Vicar of the Lord of Quebec, came from the Illinois country to Mobile, and reported that Saint-Cosme, a missionary among the Natchez, with three other Frenchmen, had been murdered, while descending the Mississippi, by the Chitimachas.[42] This induced Bienville to send presents to all the nations of the Lower Mississippi, which would cause them to make war upon those savages. The English from Carolina, aided by troops from Great Britain, had continued to advance upon the Spanish settlements of the Floridas, assisted by large bands of Muscogee Indians, and had overrun the greater portion of middle and East Florida, laying waste the Spanish settlements, and forcing the inhabitants and friendly Indians almost to abandon the country. News reaching Bienville that they had besieged the fort of Pensacola, which had recently been rebuilt, he advanced from Mobile with one hundred and twenty Canadians; but, on reaching that place, he found that the thirteen Englishmen and three hundred and fifty Muscogees, who for two days had lain around the fort to attack it, becoming destitute of provisions, had already retired.[43]

In the meanwhile, Bienville, in a dispatch to the minister, urged the necessity of sending out more colonial supplies, as the inhabitants had not yet made plantations ample enough from which to derive a support. He stated that his lands were fertile up the Mobile River, but too unhealthy during the period of cultivating the crops. The want of Negroes, horses and oxen also contributed its share in embarrassing the feeble efforts of the Louisiana planter, and failures were often made. He informed the minister, further, that he had intended establishing a fort upon the Tombecbé, in the vicinity of the Chickasaws, in order to secure the friendship of those Indians, who were the most warlike of all, and who were daily tampered with by the English of Carolina, but that the distance to that point, and the general distress of the colony, had prevented it; that all the Indians were treacherous, and often assassinated the French, for whose strength they had begun to entertain a most contemptible opinion; that three-fourths of the soldiers were too young to prosecute a war, and constantly deserted, while the Canadians, whom he had declined to discharge, contrary to the orders of Bégon, Intendant of Rochefort, were the sole pillars of the colony.[44] In consequence of these things,

refused to approve the marriage of one of the young women sent on the *Pélican*. *MPA: FD*, 2: 20-9; ibid., 3: 40-45.

[42] Jean-François Buisson de Saint-Cosme (1667-1706) was traveling to Mobile when he was killed by a Chitimacha war party in December 1706. Father Louis-Marc Bergier (c.1667-1707) had responsibility for the missions in the Mississippi valley, and Saint-Cosme had served as his assistant among the Tamaroas in 1700-1703. Bergier came to Mobile in early 1707 for supplies and to calm the situation with La Vente and the other priests. Higginbotham, *Old Mobile*, 289-98, 303, 369-72; Swanton, *Indian Tribes of the Lower Mississippi Valley*, 20-21, 192.

[43] English-inspired attacks on the Pensacola presidio had continued in the summer of 1706. War parties of Tallapoosas, Abihkas, and Alabamas attacked Spanish soldiers in the spring of 1707, killing one and taking thirteen captives to Charles Town for rewards. While Bienville's relief force had apparently arrived during a brief lull, he reported a second assault in a letter dated 25 February 1708 that plundered the town, taking fifteen Spanish prisoners and killing eleven. *MPA: FD*, 3: 113-14; Higginbotham, *Old Mobile*, 307-13.

[44] Bienville continued to make detailed reports and requests to Jérôme Phélypeaux, Comte de Pontchartrain, who as Minister of the Marine had the administrative and management responsibilities of the French colonies in North America. Michel V. Bégon (1638-1710) served as intendant de la marine at the port of Rochefort and intendant of the généralité of La Rochelle. Bégon had financial oversight for the colonies, sent invoices for all cargoes—including the *Pélican* girls—and demanded detailed reports. As the king's principal accountant for the colonies, he had

he had been compelled to abandon the establishment upon the Mississippi.[45] In addition, he stated that La Salle had refused to pay the colonists their just dues, and had withheld payment from those who had been sent to a distance upon important duties.

The continued reports of the malpractices of Bienville, which reached the ears of the minister, induced the French government to order his arrest. De Muy was appointed governor of Louisiana, "to prove the facts charged against this person, to arrest him if they were true, and to send him a prisoner to France." Thus the unjust and singular position was assumed, of leaving to Bienville's *successor* to decide whether he was guilty or innocent! In the meantime, Bienville, hearing of his disgrace at court, demanded to be dismissed from his post, to enable him to return to France. This startled the inhabitants of Mobile, who were warmly attached to him, and who immediately petitioned the government that, if Bienville's request should be allowed, that he should immediately be sent back to them as their governor. But De Muy, his successor and his judge, died at Havana on his passage out.[46] Diron d'Artaguette was appointed commissary general in the place of the growling La Salle, whom the government had also removed. D'Artaguette, more fortunate than his companion, had reached Mobile in safety, and was directed to investigate the charges against Bienville, without letting him know what they were. However, fortunately for the cause of justice, and perhaps the future welfare of the colony, D'Artaguette, in the report of his investigations to the minister, was enabled to close by saying, that "all the accusations brought against Bienville were most miserable calumnies."[47] Subjoined to this statement was the attestation of Boisbriant, now major of the fort at Mobile. But the disappointed and vindictive La Salle renewed his accusations, in which he assured the minister that an understanding existed between Bienville and the new commissary, and that the report of the latter was not to be believed. At the same time he denounced Barrot, the surgeon of the colony, as "an ignorant man—a drunkard and a rogue, who sold, for his own profit, the medicines belonging to the King."[48]

The following is a statement of the condition of the colony of Louisiana at this period:[49]

GARRISON.

14 superior officers, comprising a midshipman attending on the commandant.

recently told Bienville to cut his expenses by dismissing his Canadians and using his soldiers and sailors. *MPA: FD*, 3: 15, 16, 24, 29, 38-39, 74, 112, 131.

45 Bienville ordered the evacuation of Fort de la Boulaye in 1707 to conserve supplies and men. Higginbotham, *Old Mobile*, 291-93.

46 Nicolas Daneau De Muy (1651-1708) received a letter from Minister of Marine Pontchartrain on conditions in Louisiana and an enclosed "memoir" of instructions and appointment as governor of Louisiana from King Louis XIV—both dated at Versailles on 30 June 1707. He sailed in the *Renommée* for his new post but died on 25 January 1708 near Havana. *MPA: FD*, 3: 46-60, 67-71, 111.

47 Diron d'Artaguette, in his capacity as Commissary General of Louisiana, conducted an impressive investigation of the charges lodged against Bienville, as disclosed in the abstract of documents that he sent to Pontchartrain. While Bienville did not escape totally from suspicion, Pontchartrain's 23 May 1710 letter to D'Artaguette directing him to return La Salle to France and Louis XIV's "memoir" to Lamothe Cadillac—Bienville's replacement as governor—stating his displeasure with Father La Vente's conduct dated 13 May 1710 must have given Bienville a degree of satisfaction. Ibid., 3: 78-110, 130-32, 150.

48 In his letter to Pontchartrain on 4 March 1708, La Salle reiterated many of his charges against Bienville and added a complaint against D'Artaguette: "Sieur d'Artaguette, the commissary, has taken his quarters in the house of Sieur de Bienville's brother and they all eat together." Ibid., 3: 125-27.

49 Data collected by La Salle as part of his census of the colony of Louisiana included "each sort of people" and the

76 soldiers, comprising four military officers.

13 sailors, comprising four naval officers.

2 Canadians, serving as clerks in the warehouses, by order of Bienville.

1 superintendent of the warehouses.

3 priests, comprising one rector.

6 workmen.

1 Canadian, serving as interpreter.

6 cabin boys, learning the Indian language, and intended to serve by land and sea as workmen.

INHABITANTS.

24 inhabitants who have no grants of land, which prevents the majority from working plantations.

28 women.

25 children.

80 slaves, men and women, of various Indian nations.

———

157

TOTAL.

279, of whom six are sick.

In addition to these there are more than 60 Canadians who live in the Indian villages on the Mississippi, without the permission of the Governor, and who destroy, by their evil and libertine life with the Indian women, all that the missionaries and others have instructed them in the mysteries of religion.

ANIMALS.

50 cows.

40 calves.

4 bulls.

8 oxen, four of which belong to the King.

1400 hogs and sows.

2000 hens, or thereabouts.

In consequence of the death of the recently appointed governor of Louisiana, and the complete overthrow of the charges brought against the old one, the French government permitted the latter to continue at his responsible and thankless post. Knowing that the colony could not prosper unless the earth was cultivated, Governor Bienville endeavored in vain to make the whites under him labor in the fields. On the other hand, the savages, whom the French had endeavored to enslave, would escape to their native woods, at the slightest appearance of coercion. In a dispatch to the minister, Bienville recommended that the colonists be allowed to send Indians to the West India Islands, and

"domestic animals of this colony." He enclosed the census data in his letter of 12 September 1708 to Pontchartrain. Ibid., 2: 31-32.

[50] While M. Robert remains unidentified, he wrote Pontchartrain on 26 November 1708 advising him that the proposal from Bienville and D'Artaguette to aid the colonists of Louisiana to exchange Indian slaves for Negroes could only occur when they were in position to pay for them with produce or money and "only when French vessels bring them for them." In his letter to Bienville on 10 May 1710, Pontchartrain acknowledged that he had "examined" his proposal "to introduce Negroes into Louisiana" for Indian slaves but found it was not practical. He reasoned that "unless the inhabitants are in a position to buy them in the same way as the English it will not be possible to introduce any there." Ibid., 2: 45-46; ibid., 3: 141

[51] Bienville, Father La Vente, Lamothe Cadillac, and others echoed Nicolas de la Salle's call to Pontchartrain to send women to Louisiana to stop the "extreme debauchery" and enslavement of Indian women by Frenchmen and Canadians. Ibid., 2: 49, 57, 68-69, 169; ibid., 3: 135, 140, 147.

[52] While Pickett writes "Indian corn,"

there to exchange them for Negroes, asserting that these islanders would give two Africans for three savages. His proposition was laid before M. Robert, one of the heads of the Bureau of the Minister of Marine, who pronounced against it, upon the ground that the inhabitants of the West Indies would not part with their good Negroes, and that the only way to obtain such was by purchases from Guinea.[50] Another idea of Bienville's seemed still more unreasonable. He had given orders to watch several inhabitants of Mobile, to prevent them from leaving the country. As they had "amassed considerable property in the colony, by keeping public-houses, it was but just," said he to the minister, "to compel them to remain."

Although discharged from office, La Salle, far from remaining quiet, continued to complain of the administration of the colony. He urged the minister to send thirty females to Mobile, to prevent, by marriage, the debauchery which was committed with Indian women. He said that such an importation would serve to keep at home a number of Canadians who roamed the country in search of female slaves.[51] He agreed in opinion with Bienville that Negroes were indispensable to the prosperity of the colony; and in this he was right, for experience has proved that neither South Carolina, Louisiana, nor any other southern state, with such low, rich lands, and with a humid atmosphere so destructive to the constitutions of the whites, could ever have been successfully brought into cultivation without African labor.

Commissary D'Artaguette, visiting the country lying between Lake Pontchartrain and the Mississippi River, now a portion of New Orleans, found there seven Frenchmen, who had each planted an acre of Indian corn, brought from the Illinois, and which grew most luxuriantly. He wrote to the minister, as Iberville and Bienville had often done before, urging the establishment of colonies upon that river, and for their protection against the floods, the erection of embankments along the margin.[52]

Although La Salle had died at Mobile early in the year 1710, a short time after the death of his second wife, who, like the first, had been reared in the hospitals, yet Bienville failed not to find those who were equally willing to comment, in the most illiberal manner, upon his administration.[53] Marigny, an officer of the garrison, in a dispatch to the minister, accused him with disregarding the interests of the colony.[54] La Vente, the curate, who appeared officiously desirous to attend to the temporal as well as the spiritual affairs of Louisiana, also abused him without measure, attributing to him every misfortune which attended the inhabitants of Mobile. He assured the minister, that if the permission of the government could be obtained, they had determined to form a colony upon Dauphin Island, where there were twenty fortified

D'Artaguette's letters to Pontchartrain discuss the planting of wheat and report he had promised "to have a mill built as soon as their crop is made." Even King Louis XIV acknowledges D'Artaguette's "information" about "five settlers" planting wheat on land between the Mississippi and Lake Pontchartrain in his letter to Lamothe Cadillac on 13 May 1710. Ibid., 2: 53, 59, 61; ibid., 3: 147.

[53] Nicolas de la Salle "died of the flux" on 31 December 1710, ending his feud with Bienville. Ibid., 2: 18 n.1; ibid., 3: 168.

[54] Francois Philippe du Hautmesnil de Mandeville, Sieur de Marigny (1682-1728), received a promotion from ensign to lieutenant and command of a company on Dauphin Island. He would later be further promoted to captain and command at Fort Condé. Ibid., 2: 29, 29 n.2, 46; ibid., 3: 129, 166; Higginbotham, *Old Mobile*, 271-72.

[55] Bienville's complaints regarding Father La Vente did not go unheeded. Both Pontchartrain and King Louis XIV voiced their concern and displeasure and requested first D'Artaguette and later Lamothe Cadillac to investigate Bienville's charges. *MPA: FD,* 2: 27; ibid., 3: 42-45, 117, 119, 134, 148.

houses, for the purpose of catching fish, and being more convenient to the supplies which might be sent to them from Pensacola and France. Under these repeated assaults, Bienville lost the dignity and patience which had formerly characterized his conduct, and now retorted upon his adversaries with considerable acrimony. In one of his dispatches, he said, that "the curate, La Vente, endeavored to excite everybody against him"; that the curate was "not ashamed to keep an open shop and sell like an avaricious Jew."[55] Verily, this father must have been a man who possessed too much malignity, avarice and bad temper, to have been a successful missionary in the holy cause in which he was ostensibly engaged.

Thus the year 1710 closed with such controversies, while Bienville had been obliged to distribute his men among the Indian towns to procure something to eat.* How unfortunate that the colonists, like mere children, should have depended upon the mother country for everything which went into their mouths, when moderate industry, bestowed higher up the Tombigbee and Alabama rivers, upon the more elevated and less sickly lands, would have ensured them an abundance.

* Charles Gayarré, *Historie de la Louisiane,* 1: 78–91.

Chapter V

THE COLONY OF LOUISIANA GRANTED TO CROZAT

The high floods having inundated the settlements around Fort Louis de la Mobile, Bienville determined to place his people upon more elevated ground. All the inhabitants, except the garrison of the fort, removed upon the Mobile River, where, upon the site of the present beautiful and wealthy commercial emporium of Alabama, they established themselves. Here Bienville built a new wooden fort, which, in a few years, was destroyed to give place to an extensive fortress of brick, called, in French times, Fort Condé, and in English and Spanish times, Fort Charlotte. The seat of government was permanently fixed here, and the leading characters of the colony made Mobile their headquarters. Only a small garrison was left at the old settlement at the mouth of the Dog River, which, however, continued to guard that point for several years after this period.[1]

The Chickasaws, having again engaged in a war with the Choctaws, at the instance of the English, and thirty of the former tribe being at Mobile at the time, implored Bienville to have them safely conducted home, through the country of their enemies. Desiring to acquire the confidence of the Chickasaws by acts of kindness that would induce them to break up their alliance with the Carolinians, Bienville readily granted their request, and dispatched his brother, Chateaugué, with thirty soldiers, to escort them. He was successful in his mission, and returned to Mobile without having met with any serious adventures.

The colony of Louisiana still remained in a precarious situation. It is true, the inhabitants had to some extent begun the cultivation of tobacco, the first samples of which were supposed to be superior to the quality raised in Virginia. Wheat came up most luxuriantly, but the damp atmosphere destroyed it when it commenced maturing.[2] Notwithstanding the long war which had existed between France and England, no attacks of the enemy had

[1] The new wooden fort—Fort Louis de la Mobile—was a five-hundred-forty-feet square structure with a bastion at each corner. The name of this fort was changed to Fort Condé by order of the Company of the Indies in October 1720. As noted before, the original Fort Louis was constructed near Twenty-Seven Mile Bluff on the Mobile River. *MPA: FD*, 3: 18 n. 2, 304 n. 1; Peter J. Hamilton, *Colonial Mobile*, ed. Charles G. Summersell (1897; reprint, Tuscaloosa: University of Alabama Press, 1976), 153; Waselkov, "French Colonial Archaeology," 4.

[2] As early as 1709, there were reports of wheat being grown successfully in Louisiana, but, generally, there were more reports that the wheat grew well in the blade until the "fogs came up that made it completely wither away"—greatly impacting yield. In

been directed against any part of the Louisiana colony, until about this time, when a pirate ship from Jamaica disembarked on Dauphin Island, and plundered the inhabitants of nearly all which they possessed.[3] Not long afterwards, this first and last act of hostility during the present war, was succeeded by the arrival of a ship which came upon a more agreeable mission. She brought large supplies for the colony, and when she hoisted her sails to return to France, D'Artaguette, the commissary general, an accomplished man, who well understood his business, became a passenger on board of her, to the regret of all the inhabitants, who ardently desired him to remain longer with them.[4]

The following is a statement of the colonial disbursements of the year 1711:[5]

PAYMENTS.

To 12 workmen on the fortification	4,480	*livres.*
" 23 naval officers, soldiers and cabin boys	4,572	
" superior officers	19,988	
" medicine chest	506	
" wax candles in the chapel	270	
" presents to the Indians	4,000	
" maintenance of military companies	27,688	
	61,504	*livres.*

D'Artaguette, the colonial commissary, had a prosperous voyage to France, and arrived there "at the time," to use the eloquent language of Gayarré, "when the star of Louis XIV, which had shed such brilliant glory around for half a century, was almost extinguished, and the doors of the old cathedral of St. Denis had already opened in expectation of receiving the great monarch, whom age and misfortune urged rapidly towards the tomb." The country, too, over which he had so long reigned, was then groaning under the effects of the long, bloody and expensive wars which he had waged.[6] The report which D'Artaguette now made of the unhappy condition of the colony of Louisiana, induced the French government to number that fruitless and extravagant bantling among its other misfortunes. It determined to hand the colony over to the care of a company, or to some rich merchant, with a grant of its exclusive commerce and other important privileges. Accordingly, an opulent merchant, named Antoine Crozat, entered into a contract with the king of France. The king granted to him, for the term of fifteen years, the exclusive commerce of all the country known as the colony of

October 1713, Lamothe Cadillac reported tobacco growing well in the colony, and in 1718, the Company of the Indies purchased the right to control France's tobacco trade. *MPA: FD,* 2: 50, 53, 59, 61, 68, 166–67; Barnett, *Natchez Indians,* 81, 101.

[3] According to Bienville, an English privateer from Martinique attacked Dauphin Island on 9 September 1710 and deceived the inhabitants by flying a French flag. The raiders pillaged and set fires before departing on the third day—losing only one, killed by a man returning from a hunt. *MPA: FD* 2: 69, 69 n. 3, 164, 164 n. 2.

[4] In November 1711, D'Artaguette returned to France aboard the *Renommée* with the results of his investigation into the complaints against Bienville—clearing him of the major charges raised by his critics—and to report on the status of Louisiana. *MPA: FD,* 3: 161, 168; Hamilton, *Colonial Mobile,* 92.

[5] The 1711 disbursements for Louisiana cited here by Pickett came from Bénard de la Harpe's *Journal Historique de l'Établissement des Français à la Louisiane,* published at New Orleans and Paris in 1831. However, La Harpe or his printer made an error in the total—printing "52,478" instead of 61,478 *livres.* Pickett or his printer transposed two entries in the column of expenses—printing 506 for the original "500" for "*médicamens*" and 27,688 for the original "27,668" for "*des companies.*" But, Pickett's column has a correct total for the numbers cited.

Louisiana, embracing the country upon the Alabama and Tombigbee, with their various tributary streams; of all the islands at and near their entrance to the sea; of all the lakes, rivers and islands connected with the lakes Pontchartrain, Maurepas, Borgne, &c.; of all the country upon the Mississippi and its numerous tributaries, from the sea as high up as the Illinois River, together with that of Texas. He also ceded to him "*forever*" all the lands which he could establish himself upon, all the manufactures which he could put into operation, and all the structures which he should erect. The king also granted to him the proceeds of all the mines which he might find and work, and agreed to appropriate fifty thousand livres annually toward the payment of his officers and troops in Louisiana.[7]

For all these privileges, Crozat obligated, on his part, to appropriate one-fourth of the proceeds of the mines of precious metals to the king's use; to forfeit the lands which were granted to him "forever," if the improvements or manufactures which he placed upon them should be abandoned by him or should cease to exist; to send a vessel annually to Guinea for slaves for the colony, and to send every year two ships from France, with a certain number of emigrants to Louisiana; and, at the expiration of nine years, to pay the salaries of the king's officers in the colony during the remainder of his time, with the privilege of nominating those officers for his majesty's appointment. All this country was to be a dependency upon the government of New France. The ordinances and usages of the provost and viscount of Paris were to rule the colony, in connection with a council similar to that which then existed in Santo Domingo. About the time that France thus abandoned our soil and the few white inhabitants upon it, to the wealthy Parisian merchant, the king, by the Treaty of Utrecht, ceded to England the country of Nova Scotia, with its ancient boundaries.[8]

The population of Louisiana, now turned over to Crozat, consisted of twenty-eight families, twenty Negroes, seventy-five Canadians, and two companies of infantry of fifty men each, the whole numbering three hundred and twenty-four souls. They were scattered over the colony, and separated by large rivers and expansive lakes, protected by only six forts of miserable construction, built of stakes, trees and earth, and portions of them covered with palm leaves. These forts were situated as follows: one upon the Mississippi, one upon Ship Island, one upon Dauphin Island, one at Biloxi, one at the old and the other at the new settlement of Mobile.[9]

Bénard de la Harpe, *Journal Historique de l'Établissement des Français à la Louisiane* (Nouvell-Orleans: A. L. Boimare, Libraire-Editeur, 1831), 112.

6 Despite the quote from Gayarré, King Louis XIV lived another three years, dying at Versailles on 1 September 1715. His aggressive foreign policy caused France to fight a series of wars which proved costly in treasure and blood from 1667 through 1714. John A. Lynn, *The Wars of Louis XIV, 1667–1714* (New York: Routledge, 1999), 105–360, 377–84.

7 Antoine Crozat, Marquis du Châtel (1655–1738), served as Louis XIV's counsellor and financial secretary and received the commercial monopoly over Louisiana because of his wealth and numerous colonial and maritime connections. He organized the Company of Louisiana with two associates, Lamothe Cadillac, who was appointed governor, and Le Bart, who served as comptroller of the company. Giraud, *Reign of Louis XIV*, 1: 249–51.

8 The Peace of Utrecht was a series of treaties negotiated between France and other European countries from 11 April 1713 through 7 September 1714, ending the War of Spanish Succession. In North America, France made numerous concessions to Great Britain, which included restoring territory to the Hudson Bay Company and ceding all claims to Newfoundland. Lynn, *Wars of Louis XIV*, 348–51, 355–58, 361–68.

9 The garrison at Fort Maurepas on Biloxi Bay was moved

to Fort Louis near Twenty-Seven Mile Bluff in 1702, and the latter post was abandoned for the new Fort Louis de la Mobile in 1711. Fort de la Boulaye on the Mississippi was abandoned in 1707, and the Dauphin Island installation was little more than a fortified battery in 1712. The Ship Island battery installation—Ile aux Vaisseaux—was constructed in 1720. *MPA: FD*, 3: 162, 264, 316; Chartrand, *Forts of New France*, 53–7.

[10] Jean-Baptiste du Bois du Clos (Duclos), who became the director of the colony's accounts, and Cadillac clashed constantly over company policies and fair treatment for the inhabitants. While Marc-Antoine de la Loire des Ursins and his brother, Louis-Auguste de la Loire Flaucourt, had a fairly long tenure in Louisiana and Illinois, Pierre Dirigoin was replaced as a director in 1714 by Raujon. *MPA: FD*, 2: 74–162; ibid., 3:177–78, 212–13; Giraud, *Reign of Louis XIV*, 1: 251, 305; Pénicaut, *Fleur de Lys and Calumet*, 166, 173, 173 n.7.

[11] Although appointed governor of Louisiana in May 1710, Antoine de Lamothe Cadillac did not arrive at Dauphin Island until 5 June 1713 with the other officers of Louisiana and the Company of Louisiana on board the *Baron de la Fauche*. In his first major correspondence with Pontchartrain on 26 October 1713, he either attacked the character or questioned the service of many who reported to him as governor, especially Bienville. His contentious, confrontational, and often combative tenure ended on 3 March 1716. *MPA: FD*, 2: 162

At length, a vessel of fifty guns disembarked, on Dauphin Island the officers intended for the government of Louisiana under Crozat's charter. Among them were Lamothe Cadillac, the new governor; Duclos, the commissary general; Le Bart, the comptroller; and Dirigoin and La Loire de Ursins, directors of the affairs of Crozat in the colony.[10] Governor Cadillac had served with distinction in the wars of Canada, and brought with him to the colony of Louisiana his daughter, whom he attempted, as we shall see, to marry to Bienville. He was a man of poor judgment, of weak feelings, and much selfishness. To interest him in the deepest manner, in accomplishing his various schemes of colonial aggrandizement, Crozat had promised him a portion of his profits. But Cadillac, in his first dispatch to the minister, began to complain of everybody and of everything appertaining to the colony; and all his other documents to that high functionary were, likewise, filled with carping epithets, which could only emanate from a selfish and childish mind like his. Dauphin Island, which, he said, had been represented to him as a terrestrial paradise, he assured the minster, was a poor and miserable spot, supporting but a few improvements, with a few fig trees and sapless vines of the grape and lemon.[11] Wheat did not grow upon the whole continent, having been abandoned upon the borders of Lake Pontchartrain and at Natchez, where one Lavigne had endeavored to raise it.[12] Other colonial officers, also, hastened to complain. Duclos wrote to the minister that twelve girls had lately arrived from France, who were too ugly and badly formed to secure the affections of the men, and that but two of them had yet found husbands. He was afraid that the other ten would remain on hand a long time. He thought proper to suggest that those who sent girls to the colony in future should attach more importance to beauty than to virtue, as the Canadians were not scrupulous as to the lives which their spouses may have formerly led. But if they were only to be offered girls as ugly as these, they would rather attach themselves to Indian females, particularly in the Illinois country, where the Jesuit priests sanctioned such alliances by the marital ceremony.[13]

Duclos again wrote to the minister, accusing Cadillac with having appropriated the presents intended for the Indians, to his own use, and recommended that the governor should, in future, be required to confer with Bienville in relation to the distribution of those presents; the latter, he remarked, having for so many years, by justice, honor and good advice, so happily conciliated the different tribes.[14] On the same day Cadillac wrote to the minister, the Count Pontchartrain, that the inhabitants knew nothing of the culture of silk, tobacco and indigo, but confined their attention to the production of Indian corn and vegetables. That the commerce of the colony consisted merely in skins of deer, bear, and other animals and lumber. That the *coureurs de bois* hunted for peltry and slaves, which they brought to Mobile and sold, and that the peltry was then re-sold, together with vegetables and poultry, to the Spaniards at Pensacola, or to ships which touched upon the coast, while the Indian slaves were employed to saw out lumber and till the earth. But the very next day Cadillac made another dispatch, in which he pronounced the country to be good for nothing, and the inhabitants "a mass of rapscallions from Canada, a cut-throat set, without subordination, with no respect for religion, and abandoned in vice with Indian women, whom they prefer to French girls." He complained that upon arriving at Mobile he found the garrison dispersed in the woods and Indian villages, where they went in search of bread; that Bienville, his brother Chateaugué, and their cousin Boisbriant, the major of Mobile, came to the colony too young to know how to drill soldiers, and had not since learned anything of proper discipline; and that the soldiers all had Indian wives, who cooked for them and waited upon them—all of which he pronounced to be intolerable. He believed that the colony presented but two objects of commerce—trade with the Spaniards of Mexico and the working of precious mines, if the latter could be discovered; but that, unfortunately, Dirigoin, one of Crozat's directors, was a man of no capacity, while Le Bart, the comptroller, was extremely dissipated. He desired more tradespeople, sailors, Canadians and artisans to be sent out, and a church to be erected at Mobile. But the latter the inhabitants would be delighted not to have. Indeed, a majority of the gentlemen, priests and missionaries, had not taken sacrament for eight years, the soldiers had not kept Palm Sunday, but followed the example of Bienville and his adherents, that the sea captain who brought out the twelve girls had seduced more than half of them upon the passage, which was the cause of their not having married respectable persons in the colony, and he contended that it was best, under the circumstances, that the *soldiers* should be allowed to marry them, for fear that their poverty would drive them to prostitution.[15]

In relation to the council which was to co-operate in the government of the colony, Cadillac said that it had not convened for the want of suitable members. To this string of complaints were added many others

n. 1, 162–204; ibid., 3: 178–80, 191–213.

[12] Apparently Lavigne (La Vigne) had settled at Natchez prior to 1713 and planted wheat to market in the colony. In October 1713, Cadillac reported to Pontchartrain that Lavigne's effort to grow wheat had failed "without ever having been able to gather a handful." Dumont de Montigny in his *Memoir* reported a Lavigne family with "a fine farm" living on the Bayou Saint John who are listed in the Louisiana census for 1722. *MPA: FD,* 2:166; Dumont de Montigny, *Memoir,* 148, 149 n. 19, 430.

[13] Despite his negative comments on the twelve young women who traveled to Louisiana with Cadillac and the other officials, Duclos wrote a detailed report on the condition of Louisiana and projected a detailed budget which included support "for twelve girls or boys sent every year to the colony, at 5 sous per day for each." *MPA: FD,* 2: 79–162.

[14] By October 1713, Duclos had developed an enmity for Cadillac, an alliance with Bienville, and a desire to be relieved of his position in Louisiana and return to France. Ibid., 74 n. 1.

[15] In his extensive report of 26 October 1713 to Pontchartrain on the condition of the colony, Cadillac referred to Fort Louis as "a little fort of poor cedar piles" and proposed building an impregnable stone fortification on Dauphin Island with appropriate housing for himself as governor. While he condemned Bienville's leadership, he also reported on

in a subsequent dispatch, among which were the following: that Bienville had governed the colony for years without having discovered any mines, which he (Cadillac) could have done in a short time; that Duclos was guilty of great impudence and presumption in censuring his official acts; that the French government was entirely too lenient to its colonial officers and soldiers, who threatened to revolt and burn up Crozat's establishment; and libertinism was carried to such an extent, that even the boys had Indian mistresses! In again alluding to the council, he stated that Duclos had nominated for attorney general a storekeeper; for councilor, the chief surgeon; for secretary, doorkeeper and notary, one Raguet, a low soldier; and that the assembly, which for the present was to meet at his house, wanted nothing but the bonnet and robe to make it perfect! He said that if the minister did not crush the cabals formed against him by Bienville and his clan, who kept up an intercourse with the inhabitants of Pensacola, to whom they sold and from whom they bought, that Crozat would be compelled to abandon his colonial project. He denied that he had withheld grants of land to the inhabitants, but admitted that his requirement that such grants as he had given should be subject to the ratification of the king, gave great dissatisfaction. He concluded this remarkable dispatch with the assertion that none of the lands were worth granting![16]

In the meantime, a ship had arrived from the mother country with a large supply of provisions and considerable merchandise. She was followed by the *Louisiana*, owned by Crozat, also laden with provisions for the colony. Delegations of chiefs of different tribes visited Mobile and smoked the pipe with Cadillac and Bienville, who received them with friendship, gratified them with presents, and dismissed them under pledges that they would abandon the interests of the English of Carolina and Virginia. But even after this, twelve Englishmen came among the Choctaws with a large number of Creeks or Muscogees, and were graciously received by the inhabitants of all save two towns, who fortified themselves, and, while besieged by the Creeks, one night made their escape to Cadillac at Mobile.*

During the reign of Charles I of England, the region south of the Chesapeake Bay was granted by that monarch to Sir Robert Heath, but the projected colony was neglected, and the grant was forfeited. Charles II decreed that this territory should assume the name of Carolina, and embrace the region from Albemarle Sound southward to the river St. Johns and westward to the Pacific, forming a province vast in extent, which was conveyed to eight joint proprietors. In the meantime, some adventurers from New England

* Charles Gayarré, *Historie de la Louisiane*, 1: 91–112; Bénard de la Harpe, *Journal historique de bétablissement des Français à la Louisiane*, 78–115.

the disorderly monks, men addicted to vice "with Indian women whom they prefer to French women," and land covered with "pine woods and pure sand." Ibid., 162–70.

[16] In his letter to Cadillac, Duclos recommended Chauvin de la Frénière—Cadillac's "storekeeper"—for attorney general and Des Lauriers, "the chief surgeon," for a council position. Cadillac proclaimed in his October 1713 report to Pontchartrain "the first learned how to write his name four months ago" and disqualified Des Lauriers because he was being called as a witness in a criminal case. Sieur de la Frénière was apparently something of an entrepreneur, selling timber to the Company of the Indies in 1723, purchasing sheep from the Company in 1725, and leasing slaves to the Company to complete work on a levee at New Orleans in 1728. In his memoir of 26 October 1717, Sieur Hubert, commissary general under Governor L'Epinay, recommended that Raguet, who was "well qualified for such an office" and had also served as a notary, be appointed clerk of the Superior Council of Louisiana. Ibid., 144, 204, 244, 236, 236 n. 1, 283, 287, 465, 547.

had planted a little colony at the mouth of the Cape Fear River. From that time emigrants gradually settled upon the coast now known as that of North Carolina, and extended their enterprises to South Carolina, where they formed a settlement several miles above the mouths of the Ashley and Cooper Rivers, and at length established themselves upon the site of the present city of Charleston.*

From the time that South Carolina was thus colonized, down to the period of 1714, to which we have brought the history of the French colony of Louisiana, forty-four years had passed. During much of that time, Carolina and Virginia traders had penetrated portions of the great Muscogee Nation, which extended from the Savannah nearly to the Warrior, in Alabama. They also carried their merchandise further west into the heart of the Chickasaw Nation, among whom they established trading shops, in defiance of the French settlements upon the Mobile. Notwithstanding that the French were the first, since the invasion of De Soto, to discover and occupy the country where the Tombigbee and Alabama lose themselves in the sea—and although the indefatigable Bienville had explored those rivers to their highest navigable points, at a very early period, freely interchanging friendly assurances with the Chickasaws living upon the one, and the Muscogees and Alabamas upon the other—yet the grasping English government attempted, through its enterprising traders and special emissaries, to occupy this region, and to induce the inhabitants to expel the French, not only from the headwaters of those streams, but from their very mouths. These fearless British traders conveyed, upon the backs of pack-horses, such goods as suited these Indians, from distant Charleston to the remote Chickasaw Nation, over creeks without bridges, rivers without ferries, and woods pathless and pregnant with many dangers. They did not, however, establish any permanent trading shops upon the Coosa, Tallapoosa or Alabama, at the period under review, but occasionally traded with the Indians upon these streams, dwelling in their towns no longer than sufficed to dispose of their goods, and receive, in return, valuable peltries, which they conveyed back to Charleston. But their intercourse with these tribes was vastly pernicious to the French below, and to the Spaniards inhabiting the provinces of Florida. The Creeks, in conjunction with their British allies, invaded the latter provinces, as we have already seen.[17]

* Hildreth, *History of the United States*, 2: 25–36; Coxe, *A description of the English province of Carolana* (London: 1741), 2; Stevens, *History of Georgia*, 1: 58, 59, 140, 141; Simms, *History of South Carolina*, 56–57; Carroll, *Historical Collections of South Carolina*, 1: 42–52: Ramsay, *History of South Carolina*, 1: 2–3; Hewatt, *A Historical Account of the Rise and Progress of the Colonies of South Carolina and Georgia.*

[17] The unstable relationship between the Chickasaw and Choctaw combined with the English-inspired attacks by the Alabamas and others on the Spanish at Presidio Santa María de Galve—especially from 1704 through 1715—delayed the French move north from Mobile. Judith A. Bense, ed., *Presidio Santa María de Galve: A Struggle for Survival in Colonial Spanish Pensacola* (Gainesville: University Press of Florida, 2003), 7, 28, 31, 268–74.

[18] Pickett's timeline for the establishment of a French fort—Fort Toulouse—near the juncture of the Coosa and Tallapoosa Rivers was off by three years. While Pontchartrain and the king had approved several new posts in 1714, the colonial officials and the Company of Louisiana did not have the resources—money, supplies, and men—to develop all of them. However, in his letter to Pontchartrain on 15 June 1715, Bienville reported that the "Alabamas are beginning to come here [Mobile] to trade and I am sending some Frenchmen to them." Despite Cadillac's opposition to building a fort above Mobile, Bienville reported to Pontchartrain on 2 January 1716 that a majority supported making "the establishment on the upper part of the river of the Alabamas . . . to

Bienville had repeatedly suggested to the French government the necessity of establishing a fort and trading post upon the Alabama River, in the immediate stronghold of the powerful Creeks, to counteract the influence of the Carolinians; but a war ensued between him and the Creeks, with whom he had an engagement, as we have seen, and against whom he found it imperative, for the preservation of his colony, to incite the Choctaws and other tribes. About the commencement of the year 1714, and when Crozat's charter had been in operation for near a twelve-month, Bienville, who was still retained high in authority as royal lieutenant, only second to the governor, was most fortunate in making peace with the Creeks. Having obtained from them their consent for the erection of a fort high up in their country, he was authorized by the colonial council at Mobile, to immediately establish it. Crozat's directors deemed the location a most suitable one for the advancement of his commerce, besides the barrier it would interpose to the enemies of that commerce.[18]

Accordingly Bienville embarked at Mobile, with eight iron cannon, many fire arms, a large supply of ammunition, merchandise suitable for the Indians, and a liberal supply of provisions, on board two small sailing vessels. With these vessels also went a number of canoes of various descriptions. The expedition was composed of soldiers, Canadians, and Mobile and Choctaw Indians. Bienville sailed up the Mobile River to the confluence of the Tombigbee and Alabama. Here, passing with his singular fleet into the latter stream, he slowly ascended it. After a long and tedious voyage, he arrived at one of the Alabama villages, not far above the site of the modern town of Selma. Continuing the voyage up the river, he successively passed the towns of Autauga,* Pauwacta and Ecunchata;† and at length moored his boats at the beautiful Indian town of Coosawda. These towns were inhabited by the Alabamas, who, as we have seen, were members of the great Creek Nation, which was composed of several different tribes, whom they had conquered and incorporated into their confederacy. Many of these people joined the fleet on its passage up the Alabama, and joyfully greeted Bienville, who was popular with all the savages, and who, with wonderful facility, acquired a perfect knowledge of their different dialects. He was met at Coosawda by some of the most prominent chiefs; and here, leaving his fleet, he embarked in a canoe, and explored the Coosa and Tallapoosa rivers for several miles up. He then resolved to erect his fort at the town of Tuskegee, which was then

* Now the site of Washington.

† Now the site of Montgomery.

prevent the English from regaining the alliance with the Indians by means of a good trade." *MPA: FD*, 3: 183, 192–93, 204; Thomas, *Fort Toulouse*, 6–10.

[19] Actually, Lieutenant Vitral (Vitrac) de la Tour—who was married to a Bienville cousin, Marie Le Sueur—led the French expedition up the Alabama in July 1717. Although sources differ on the size of his party, he apparently had twenty to twenty-five men, an interpreter, and possibly a Jesuit priest. Thomas, *Fort Toulouse*, xxxii n. 11, 9–10; J. E. Kaufmann and H. W. Kaufmann, *Fortress America: The Forts that Defended America* (Cambridge, MA: De Capo Books, 2004), 27–28; "Record of Mobile Marriages," trans. and ed. Jacqueline Olivier Vidrine, Center for Louisiana Studies, University of Southwestern Louisiana (online).

[20] Lieutenant de la Tour constructed a palisaded quadrilateral that measured about one hundred and fifty feet between the bastions on each corner, with an iron cannon in each, and was surrounded by a moat. It was constructed on the east bank of the Coosa, four miles up from its confluence with the smaller Tallapoosa River. He used Alabamas from nearby villages to supplement his construction crew and requested

situated on the east bank of the Coosa, four miles above the junction of that stream with the Tallapoosa.[19]

Bienville displayed much judgment in the selection of this place. It was at the head of a peninsula formed by the windings of these rivers, which here approached within six hundred yards of each other; after which they diverged considerably before they finally came together. It was in this neighborhood of some of the most populous towns, the inhabitants of which could easily bring down to the fort their articles of commerce by either river. Returning to Coosawda, Bienville now advanced his fleet from thence to the junction, where, entering the Coosa, he arrived at Tuskegee, where the voyage terminated. The crew left the boats, ascended the bluff, formed themselves in religious order, and surrounded a cross which had been hastily constructed. Two priests, who accompanied the expedition, chanted praises to the Most High, and went through other solemn ceremonies, in presence of a number of the natives, who contemplated the scene with calmness and respect, and who preserved the most profound silence. With the assistance of the natives, Bienville began the erection of a wooden fort with four bastions, in each one of which he mounted two of the cannon.[20] As the history of these cannon is rather singular, and may interest some of our readers, we must be allowed to digress a little from the main narrative, by a brief reference to it. These cannon remained upon the entrenchments of Fort Toulouse from 1714 to 1763. Then the French commandant spiked them, broke off the trunnions, evacuated the fort, and left the cannon there in that situation. The English, who, in 1763, succeeded to the possession of this country, threw a garrison into Fort Toulouse, but in a very short time also evacuated it and it fell into rapid decay; but still the French cannon remained there.[21] A few years after Col. Hawkins had been stationed among the Creeks, as their agent, he induced the government, as a means of encouraging agriculture, to send some blacksmiths to the nation. One of these men succeeded in filing away the spikes from two of the cannon. These the Indians used to fire with powder for amusement. Afterwards, the army of Jackson occupied the site of the old fort. In due time they marched away, and still these French pieces remained there.

Finally, the town of Montgomery, now our capital, began to be settled, and the inhabitants went up to old Fort Toulouse, then Fort Jackson, and brought down two of these cannon, which they fired at 4th of July festivals, and upon other extraordinary occasions. When it was known that John Quincy Adams had been elected president of the United States, his warm friends in Montgomery determined to make the forests resound with the noise of powder. One of the cannon was over-charged, and when touched off

permission to give presents for their labor and loyalty. Thomas, *Fort Toulouse*, xi, 9–11; Chartrand, *Forts of New France*, 58; *MPA: FD*, 2: 250.

[21] While the French formally ceded Fort Tombecbé on 22 November 1763, the evacuation of Fort Toulouse had been delayed and occurred between 14 November 1763 and 15 January 1764. Thomas, *Fort Toulouse*, 66; *Mississippi Provincial Archives: English Dominion, 1763–1766*, comp. and ed. Dunbar Rowland (Nashville: Brandon Printing Company, 1911), 97–100. [Hereafter cited as *MPA: ED*].

[22] According to Matthew Blue, the Fort Toulouse cannon had been discharged several times "without incident" on 25 February 1825 off Market Street, "opposite the present Artesian Basin." When Judge Ebenezer Pond (1799–1878)—an Adams supporter—accepted a challenge to light the cannon, "it bursted around the light-hole," sending particles of the cannon flying, striking Pond who recovered "in a short time... but has since borne powder marks in his face." Blue, *Works of Matthew Blue*, 48, 94.

[23] Despite Pickett's claim regarding Bienville's presence on the

upper Coosa, the people of the Upper Creek Towns made trips to Mobile to meet with Bienville and his successors. Bienville confirmed a peace with the Alabamas—the French name for the people of the upper Coosa and Tallapoosa Rivers—at Mobile in 1712. *MPA: FD,* 3: 139, 144, 161; David H. Corkran, *The Creek Frontier, 1540–1783* (Norman: University of Oklahoma Press, 1967), 56–57.

[24] Although Fort Toulouse was named in honor of Admiral Louis-Alexandre de Bourbon, Count de Toulouse (1678–1737), the French in Louisiana and France commonly referred to the fort as "Post aux Alibamons" or "Fort des Alibamons." Lieutenant de la Tour remained in command at Fort Toulouse through 1720, when he returned to Mobile because of poor health. He was replaced by Captain François Marchand de Courselle. Captain François de Mandeville, Sieur de Marigny, commanded a company at Fort Condé, and returned to France in 1720 to marry Madeleine Le Maire in Paris. Thomas, *Fort Toulouse,* xxxii n. 11, 11. See John Fortier, "François Phillippe de Hautmesnil de Mandeville," *DCB* (online).

[25] In a letter to the Naval Council dated 2 January 1716, Governor Cadillac identified a

by Ebenezer Pond, burst into pieces and mangled that gentleman in such a horrid manner, that he was a long time recovering.[22] The breech of the other cannon was, some years afterwards, burst off by heavy charges, and the portion which remains now stands at Pollard's Corner in Montgomery, being there planted in the ground, the muzzle up, for the purpose of protecting the corner of the sidewalk. About the year 1820, another of these cannon was carried to the town of Washington, then county seat of Autauga, where the inhabitants used to fire it upon the celebration of the 4th of July, and whenever a steamboat arrived, but at length it was also burst, by a party rejoicing one night at the result of a county election. Another of these old French pieces was carried to Wetumpka when that town was first established, and was fired upon like occasions. It is now at Rockford, in Coosa County, in the possession of the same Ebenezer Pond who was so badly wounded at Montgomery by the explosion of one of its mates. What became of the other four cannon we do not know, but have understood that they, together with a fine brass piece, are in the river opposite Fort Jackson.

But to return to Bienville and his romantic expedition. Around the stockading the governor cut entrenchments, and one hundred years afterwards, Jackson placed an American fort upon the ruins, which assumed his name. Bienville occupied the summer and fall in completing the fort and out-houses, and in exploring the surrounding country. He visited Tuckabatchee, upon the Tallapoosa, and extended his journey among the Lower Muscogees, upon the Chattahoochee—even crossing that river, and conferring with the chiefs in the towns of Coweta and Cusseta, within the present limits of Georgia. Upon all these dangerous excursions he was accompanied by only a few faithful Canadians, and always performed his journeys on foot. Was not this whole expedition most interesting—nay, romantic? Here was the former governor of Louisiana, and now the lieutenant governor, in the center of Alabama, in the deepest depths of her forests, among people with whom he had been at war, and who were yet tampered with by the English, visiting their towns, distributing presents, and exhorting them to form alliances with the French colony of Louisiana, and to expel the English who should attempt to form posts among them. Yes! Citizens of the counties of Montgomery, Coosa, Tallapoosa, Macon and Russell, reflect that one hundred and thirty-seven years ago* the French governor of Louisiana—the great and good Bienville—walked over your soil, and instituted friendly relations with its rude inhabitants—among whom not a solitary white man had a permanent abode—and established a small colony upon the east bank of the Coosa![23]

* This being now 1851.

Giving the fort the name of "Toulouse," in honor of a distinguished French count of that name, who had much to do with the government of France and her colonies, and leaving in command Marigny de Mandeville with thirty soldiers, and one of the priests, Bienville turned his boats down the river, and, after a prosperous voyage, arrived at Mobile with the Indians and Canadians who had accompanied him.* Thus, we see, that although the French had been residing upon the Mobile River since 1702, and the Canadians had several times explored central Alabama, yet no attempt was made to form permanent settlements in this region, until twelve years afterwards, when it was so successfully accomplished by Bienville.[24]

Governor Cadillac, in a dispatch to the minister, attempted to acquire all the credit for the peace which had been made with the Creek Nation, and boasted, generally, of the important services which, he contended, he had rendered the colony. But he was the same inefficient, selfish and faultfinding officer. A large majority of the inhabitants relied solely upon Bienville, whose most prominent friends were Duclos, Boisbriant, Chateaugué, Richebourg, and Dutisné, and the larger number of the priesthood. The friends of Cadillac were Marigny de Mandeville, Bajot, Blondel, Latour, Villers and Terrisse.[25] Thus this handful of men were at daggers' points with each other, instead of uniting for their own preservation and prosperity, and that of the feeble settlements over which they had charge. A tyrannical ordinance was issued in France, upon the petition of Crozat, which further embarrassed affairs. All persons were forbidden to bring any merchandise into Louisiana, or to carry any out of it, under penalty of confiscation to the profit of Crozat. No person in the colony was allowed to have a vessel fit to go to sea, and all subjects of the king were prohibited from sending vessels to the colony to carry on commerce. Crozat was determined to avail himself of the monopoly which had been granted him, and this ordinance was based upon the representations of Cadillac, who had, more than once, complained to the minister, that the inhabitants of the colony were *making a little for themselves*, in a commerce with the Spaniards, which was deemed a very unwarrantable thing by that illiberal man.[26]

Cadillac hated Bienville for several reasons, the most prominent of which were, that he was too popular with the Canadians and Indians, too much respected and obeyed by the inhabitants generally, and had absolutely refused to become his son-in-law. Cadillac's daughter, who had been educated in France, and who, like her father, thought much of the blood and honor

* MS letters obtained from Paris.

clique that needed to be "broken up for a while" which included: Bienville, "the King's Lieutenant," Major Pierre Sidrac Dugué de Boisbriant, Captain Antoine Le Moyne de Chateaugué, Captain Louis Poncereau de Chavagne de Richebourg, Adjutant Jacques Barbazon de Pailloux, and Ensign Claude-Charles Dutisné (Du Tisné). He also reported his satisfaction with "Sieurs Bajot [and] Mandeville, captains; Blondel [and] La Tour, lieutenants; Villers, Prades and Terrisse, Ensigns." *MPA: FD*, 2: 44 n. 1, 209–10; Dumont de Montigny, *Memoir*, 417, 420, 424, 434, 437.

[26] In his lengthy report on the condition of the colony to Pontchartrain on 25 October 1713, Jean-Baptiste Duclos, Louisiana's commissary general, reported that Crozat's commercial policy of restricting trade had not only hampered the economy and the people of the colony, but would negatively impact Crozat's development of Louisiana. Duclos also reported that Cadillac had made promises regarding prices and other products contrary to the company's trade policies. *MPA: FD*, 2: 74–142.

[27] The enmity between Cadillac and Bienville started with the appointment of Cadillac as governor of Louisiana in 1710

of the family, fell in love with Bienville, soon after her arrival in Mobile. The proud governor could not, at first, brook the idea of an alliance with a Canadian, but he saw, as he supposed, the strong attachment of his daughter, who now began, like many other hypocritical girls, to pine away and sicken in consequence of his refusal. Believing that Bienville's great influence with the inhabitants, as well as with the various Indian tribes, would materially strengthen his administration and advance the commerce of Crozat, the profits of which he was to share, if he could but once secure his friendship and obedience, he resolved to sacrifice his family dignity by gratifying the wishes of his daughter. One day he accosted Bienville, with much respect and suavity of manner, and invited him into his closet. He there disclosed to him his entire willingness to sanction the contemplated match between him and his daughter, charged him to treat her with affection, and concluded his conversation with a very patronizing air. Bienville, much surprised at the whole affair, as he had never alluded to marriage in the few visits which he had paid the daughter, gravely assured Cadillac that he had "determined never to marry." This was too bad; and, from that moment, Bienville found, in the persons of the governor and his daughter, two most cordial haters.[27]

The redoubtable Curate de la Vente continued to declaim, not only against the colonial government, but against everybody except his friend Cadillac. In his dispatches to the minister, he said that the Canadians particularly "did not wish to connect themselves with any women by marriage, much preferring to carry on scandalous concubinage with the young Indian squaws, who were hurried by their nature into all kinds of irregularities." That they scarcely ever saw a church, never performed mass, and never partook of the sacraments; that, while a few of the inhabitants did celebrate Sundays and festival days, the large majority resorted to taverns and to public game—"whence it is easy to comprehend that they are almost all drunkards, gamesters, blasphemers of the holy name of God, and declared enemies of all good, making a matter of ridicule of our holy religion and of the persons who perform its exercises." They corrupted the soldiers by such horrid examples; and even officers, who wore the sword and plume, had children by Indian females. The missionaries found themselves useless to a people who were led away by such vices, and to the Indians, who were corrupted by the sins of the latter, and consequently they would be forced to leave a land so accursed. La Vente suggested to the minister two plans "to rectify the affairs of the past and those of the future": —either to solely colonize Louisiana with Christian families, or permit the French

over Bienville. It grew when D'Artaguette's investigation of charges of malfeasance against Bienville lead to no indictment or punishment. While they tried to avoid contact with each other, Bienville accused Cadillac of sending word "that I was a simpleton and a conceited fool" and not making "any visits for more than two years, not even New Year's Day." Bienville also admitted in his letter of 20 January 1716 to Raudot: "Finally, my lord, I have displeased him by refusing his daughter in marriage." Ibid., 2: 199.

[28] Like his ally Governor Cadillac, the seminary priest La Vente found little to his liking in Louisiana, complaining about his own discomforts and demanding supplies to meet his needs, including brandy and a billiards table. When he was not launching personal attacks on Bienville, he focused on the unmarried officers and Canadians who used Indian servant girls as house keepers and sex partners. On one occasion, he warned Bienville about having "too great a familiarity" with Madame Catherine Cloquinet, and he refused to baptize the daughter of Jean-Baptiste Saucier if Bienville was to be the child's godparent. Higginbotham, *Colonial Mobile,* 246–62.

[29] In his letter of 15 June 1715 to Pontchartrain, Bienville reported Cadillac's search for silver in the Illinois country, and in a second letter of 1 September 1715, he reported

to marry the Indian women by religious rites. Or, if these plans could not be carried into effect, that a large number of girls, "better chosen than the last, and especially some who will be sufficiently pleasing and well-formed to suit the officers of the garrisons and the principal inhabitants," should be sent over from France as a partial remedy.[28] Verily, the worthy curate's head appeared to run much upon women of various grades!

According to the orders which he had received, De la Loire des Ursins made a settlement at Natchez, to promote the commerce of Crozat. Cadillac set off on an expedition to discover mines of gold and silver in the Illinois country, and did not return from his chimerical excursion until October, when he wrote to the minister that he had everywhere set the Indians upon the English; but, in truth, he had aroused the anger of the savages against himself wherever he had appeared among them; and, in descending the Mississippi, upon his way to Mobile, he had refused to smoke with the powerful and war-like Natchez chiefs, which was highly resented on their part, and afterwards led to a war with the French.[29]

An English officer from Carolina, named Hughes, who had passed through the Creek and Chickasaw nations, came into the territory of the Natchez. From thence he began the descent of the Mississippi, to form alliances with the tribes below. But Des Ursins, who had gained intelligence of his movements, pursued him in a boat, captured him near Manchac, and carried him to Mobile. From thence Bienville sent him to Pensacola; but having determined to reach Carolina by land, he was killed upon the route by a Thomez Indian. A large canoe, containing seven Alabamas, an Englishman and a Canadian named Boutin, arrived at Mobile.[30] They reported that the Indians, bordering upon Carolina, had risen in war against the inhabitants of that province, had killed those upon the frontiers, and that even Port Royal and several other towns had been destroyed. The war extended to the distant Chickasaw Nation. There, fifteen English traders, who had taken shelter in one cabin, were instantly slain in the presence of De St. Helene, a Frenchman, who was then among the tribe, and who, a few minutes after the massacre, was killed himself, through mistake, by two young Chickasaws, engaged in the bloody scene, they supposing him to be one of the enemy. His death was regretted by all the Chickasaws who were present.[31]

To profit by this intelligence, so agreeable to the French colony, Bienville immediately dispatched emissaries among the Alabamas and Muscogees, to renew the alliances which he had formed with them, and to engage them to turn their whole commerce into French channels. He sent messengers

that Cadillac had been gone eight months "for the said Illinois without speaking to anybody about it." Bienville received support from Duclos, who reported that Cadillac had failed on his journey to "receive the calumet of the Natchez either when ascending or descending the St. Louis [Mississippi] River." Despite the latter attack, the first Natchez War occurred when a small party of Natchez killed five Frenchmen to steal their guns and ammunition. *MPA: FD*, 2: 181, 186, 208–09.

[30] According to Bienville's letter of 1 September 1715 to Pontchartrain, the first English captive, Price Hughes (Hutchey), was delivered by the Choctaws to Mobile. Hughes, a Welsh trader who mixed in slave buying, was planning to lead an English settlement to the Mississippi. Within a few days, Marc Antoine de la Loire des Ursins and four Canadians brought in two other Englishmen—one with a commission from his governor—captured on the Mississippi "who were visiting the country and making presents to the Indians." Based on orders left by Cadillac, Bienville released them to return to Carolina. Ibid., 186–87; Crane, *The Southern Frontier*, 105–06; Barnett, "The Yamasee War," 18.

[31] The Yamasee War 1715–1716 erupted on the Carolina frontier in April 1715 when Yamasee warriors struck English slave traders and isolated English settlers. They

to the Choctaws, demanding the head of Outactachito, who had introduced the English into their nation, and who had driven off the inhabitants of the two Choctaw towns that were faithful to the French and who still lay around Mobile, anxious to return home. The messengers returned to Mobile with the head of this warrior, which had been reluctantly stricken off by the chiefs, who were afraid to disobey Bienville. They bore an invitation to those Choctaws whom they had forced to leave their homes, to return in peace.[32]

The store ship *Dauphin* came to anchor in Mobile Bay, where she landed two companies of infantry, commanded by Mandeville and Bajot, which increased the expenditures of the colony to the amount of thirty two thousand livres a year.[33] One of the passengers, named Raujon, came to fill the place of Dirigoin, one of the directors of Crozat, who had been removed from office.[34] At the same time a frigate from Rochelle, and a brigantine from Martinique, arriving in the bay, requested permission to dispose of their cargoes to the inhabitants; but the authorities, anxious to perfect the monopoly of Crozat, refused them the privilege.

In the meantime, Cadillac had not forgotten how to fill the sheets, which he sent to Count Pontchartrain, with gloomy pictures of the colony, and the licentiousness of its inhabitants. In one of these dispatches he denominated Louisiana "a monster which had neither head nor tail." He complained of the manner in which the council unscrupulously altered the decrees of the French government. He said that the whole country was the poorest and most miserable upon the globe, the people of which would sooner believe a lie than the truth. He recommended that a stone fort be erected at Mobile, but immediately interposed an obstacle to the project by saying that the topographical engineer was a man without firmness and judgment, and was always drunk. He was violently opposed to the establishment of a colony upon the Mississippi, on the ground which sustains New Orleans, a measure now contemplated by Crozat, through the recommendation of Bienville. He asserted that the Mississippi River was too crooked, too rapid in high tides, and too low in the dry season, for the navigation of canoes![35]

At length Cadillac went to reside on Dauphin Island, where he had formerly spent much of his time. It was fortified with four barracks of palisades, covered with rushes, and a guard-house, with a prison of the same style—the whole surrounded with palisades very irregularly arranged.[36] From this island he immediately issued the following singular ordinance:

ORDINANCE OF M. DE LAMOTHE CADILLAC.

"As we have obtained certain knowledge of several cabals and conspiracies which tend to revolt and sedition, and on account of some disturbances

were soon joined by others—especially Alabamas and Choctaw—who resented the double-dealing by the Carolina traders but did not share the Yamasee's concern over the encroaching settlements. Barnett, "The Yamasee War," 18–19; Crane, *The Southern Frontier,* 162, 165–84.

[32] Bienville had demanded the head of Outactachito (Oulactichiton) to stamp out the pro-English party among the Choctaw, and the pro-French Choctaw complied by delivering his head as proof of their loyalty. Crane, *The Southern Frontier,* 105–06. See Bénard de la Harpe, *Journal Historique de l'Établissement des Français à la Louisiane* (Nouvelle-Orléans: A. L. Boimare, 1831), 121.

[33] The *Dauphin* landed with one hundred twelve of the one hundred twenty soldiers who boarded at Nantes. The two old companies only had twenty-two men each, bringing the total in the colony to less than one hundred fifty men, including seven or eight who were old and infirm. Cadillac reported that twenty-four men had deserted within two months and blamed Bienville and Raujon for the lack of meat and supplies. *MPA: FD,* 2: 205, 214–16.

[34] Sieur Raujon is referred to as "Crozat's clerk" and he also served as comptroller for the colony. Soon after arriving, the Curate Le

from which evil consequences may ensue, in order to abolish and obviate the misconduct caused by drunkenness, and also disturbances fomented by women of irregular life, or by the instigation of other persons who excite to vengeance those who are so unfortunate as to expose themselves by evil discourse, and as everyone takes it upon himself to carry a sword and other weapons without having any right to do so, we most positively prohibit to all persons of low birth, to all clerks of M. Crozat, sailors and strangers lately arrived from France, if they are not provided with his majesty's commission, from carrying a sword or any other weapons, either by day or night on Dauphin Island, or at any other settlements where there is an actual garrison, under the penalty of three hundred *livres* fine, to be applied to the erection of a church on Dauphin Island; and in default of payment, the offender shall be confined in prison for the space of one month, and the penalty shall be greater for each repetition of the offence. We grant to all gentlemen the privilege of wearing a sword after having proved their nobility, and presented their titles to the secretary of the council for examination, and not otherwise, under the same penalties. We grant, also, to all civil and military officers, actually serving in the country, permission to wear a sword, &c."[37]

Thus, while this ridiculous governor was establishing himself in a court of heraldry, in a miserable cabin of palm logs on Dauphin Island, and pronouncing upon titles of nobility, Bienville was in the interior of the immense wilds of Louisiana, establishing trading posts and advancing the interests of the colony. Cadillac, whom the excellent commissary, Duclos, pronounced to be "an avaricious, cunning and obstinate man, who kept for himself everything which the court sent to the savages," was fast losing ground with the authorities in France. Crozat, in one of his last communications to him, used this language: "It is my opinion that all the disorders of which M. Cadillac complains in the colony proceed from the mal-administration of M. Cadillac himself." The minister added this postscript: "Messrs. Cadillac and Duclos, whose characters are utterly incompatible with each other, and who, at the same time, lack the intelligence necessary to the performance of their duties, are recalled, and their places are filled by others." It was unjust that Duclos should have been made to lose his station because his views of colonial policy clashed with those of the governor.[38]

The king of France had ordered Bienville to form several establishments upon the Mississippi, and to commence with that among the Natchez, with eighty soldiers. As soon as possible he began the construction of large canoes to be used as transports. Cadillac refused to place at his disposal the number of soldiers designated by His Majesty, and Bienville, when all things

Maire accused him of giving shelter to a woman who "led a scandalous life" in France and "pretended to be" married to Sieur de la Varenne at Mobile. In his report to the Council of the Navy on 2 January 1716, Cadillac happily reported Raujon's improprieties and criticized his handling of the supplies for the soldiers. Ibid., 210 n.3, 210–16.

[35] The quote about the monster without a head or tail is found in Cadillac's letter of 1 July 1716 to the ministry. He also reported the poor condition of the structures on Dauphin Island, where he had resided for three years. The Council duly noted: "It is his fault that he has not put it in a better condition." Ibid., 219–20, 220 n. 2. See "Memoire de M. de Lamothe Cadillac" in Charles Gayarré, *Histoire de la Louisiane,* 2 vols. (Nouvelle Orléans: Magne & Weisse, 1846–1847), 1: 125–27.

[36] In his letter of 1 July 1716, Cadillac described the structures on Dauphin Island as "fourteen poor huts of stakes, a guard-house, and prison, all of them covered with reeds." *MPA: FD,* 2: 220.

[37] Pickett's quote of Cadillac's "ORDINANCE" is found in Charles Gayarré, *Histoire de la Louisiane,* 1: 128.

[38] By the end of 1715, Crozat was urging that Cadillac and Duclos be recalled

were ready, departed with only thirty-four soldiers under the command of Richebourg. To these were added fifteen sailors. Bienville advanced to a town of the Tunicas, eighteen leagues below Natchez, and there learning from Father Davion, still a missionary among those people, that they were not to be trusted, and would probably become allies of the Natchez, he established himself temporarily upon an island in the Mississippi, where he erected three barracks, which he enclosed with piles. His object was to obtain possession of the persons of those chiefs and prominent warriors of the Natchez, who had recently murdered some Frenchmen, in consequence of the refusal of Cadillac to smoke with them, which they viewed as a declaration of war. He intended, after he had made an example of a few chiefs, and had intimidated the common people, to proceed to their towns and there construct a fortification in obedience to the orders of the king. Father Davion further informed Bienville that the Natchez chiefs did not suspect that the murders which they had committed were known to the French authorities, and were anxious to keep them concealed. Bienville then dispatched messengers up the river, who were instructed to pass by the Natchez during the night, and proceed toward the Wabash settlements, and inform all Frenchmen, whom they met descending, to be upon their guard, for that he was stationed at the Tunicas, and that he was preparing to be revenged upon the murderers of the Frenchmen, which would probably produce a serious war with that tribe.[39]

Three Natchez, who were sent by their chiefs to Bienville, arrived with the pipe of peace, but the latter declined to receive it, and stated that the messengers might smoke with his soldiers, but that he would only smoke with the Great Sun chiefs, for he was the Great Chief of the French. He affected indifference about establishing a trading post among them, and intimated an intention to give the Tunicas the benefit of his merchandise, as the Natchez chiefs had exhibited such a want of respect and friendship, in not coming themselves to greet him.[40]

The three savages speedily returned home with this startling message, and with a French interpreter, who could further explain the reply of Bienville. One morning, Bienville saw four magnificent canoes descending the river, and bearing toward the island. Eight warriors stood erect and sung the pipe-song, while three chiefs, in each canoe, sat under immense umbrellas. They were the Natchez chiefs, allured thither by the snare which the royal lieutenant had laid for them. Concealing one-half of his soldiers, and advancing, with apparent friendship, he conducted them within his rude military works, which they entered singing the song of peace, and holding the pipe over his head. Afterwards, they passed their hands over his stomach without rubbing, and

by the Council of the Navy, which was headed by Admiral Louis Alexandre de Bourbon, Comte de Toulouse. Crozat had learned that internal dissensions had increased since the arrival of Raujon, his new company director, who also had the title of comptroller of the navy. Cadillac's role in the events surrounding Bienville's expedition against the Natchez discredited him completely and the Council stood with Bienville. Marcel Giraud, *A History of French Louisiana*: vol. 2, *Years of Transition, 1715–1717*, trans. Brian Pearce (1958; reprint, Baton Rouge: Louisiana State University Press, 1993), 1, 72–76, 79–81.

[39] On 15 February 1716, Bienville's Natchez expedition left Dauphin Island with approximately forty men. About two weeks before his departure, he had dispatched a small detachment with a convoy of supplies under Ensign François du Tisné and agent François Derbanne. Although Bienville gives contradictory dates for his departure—15 March—and arrival among the Tunicas—23 April—he wrote a "Mémoire" to Richebourg from "au fort Saint-Joseph des Tonics" dated 15 April 1716. Ibid., 78–79, 79 n. 26.

[40] While the Natchez Sun chiefs generally advocated a closer alliance with the French, The Bearded and others—Alahofléchia and Oylape—sought to replace their slave trading with the English by raiding the

then over themselves, Bienville refused the pipe with contempt, and desired, first, to know the nature of their visit. Much disconcerted, the chiefs went out and presented their pipes to the Sun. The high priest, with his arms extended and his eyes fixed upon the bright luminary which he daily worshipped, invoked it to soften the temper and change the resolution of the stern Bienville. Again entering the works, he presented the pipe to Bienville, who scornfully refused it. At that moment the chiefs were seized, ironed, and placed in the prison.[41]

At night, Bienville informed the Great Sun, and his brothers, the Tattooed Serpent and the Little Sun, whom he had caused to be separated from the others and brought into his presence, that nothing would satisfy him but to be placed in possession of the heads of the chiefs who advised the murder of the five Frenchmen, and of those who executed the horrid deed; that he knew that they were not concerned in the transaction themselves, and, consequently, he did not desire to take their lives, unless they failed to comply with his demands. He gave them until morning to determine upon his requisition, and by daylight the three brothers appeared before him, and implored him to remember that no one now remained in their town of sufficient authority to chop off the heads of the men whom he demanded, and requested that the Tattooed Serpent might be permitted to return home to accomplish the dangerous mission. Bienville refused, but sent the Little Sun in his place, with an officer and twelve soldiers, who conveyed him in a canoe within six miles of Natchez, where he was placed on shore.[42] The Little Sun returned to Bienville, with three heads, two of which the French commander recognized as those he had demanded. The other head was that of an innocent person, the brother of one of the murderers, who had fled to the forests. Bienville expressed his deep regret to the chiefs, that they had thus caused an innocent person to suffer, and assured them that nothing would compromise his resentment but the possession of the head of the chief, White Earth. Notwithstanding the Little Sun had acted with so much promptness, and had brought with him a Frenchman and two Illinois Indians, whom he found tied to stakes in one of the Natchez towns, ready to be burned to death, yet Bienville caused him to be ironed and remanded to prison with the others.[43]

The next day he dispatched to the Natchez the high priest of the temple and two chiefs of war for the head of White Earth. They were conducted by a detachment almost to their villages. In the meantime, by a confession of the imprisoned chiefs, Bienville ascertained that the sEnglish had been encouraged, and the Frenchmen had been killed, at the instance of White

French *voyageurs* and the merchandise in their canoes. The Natchez chiefs knew Bienville's location when they dispatched the three warriors to his camp to offer their calumets—perhaps earlier than 27 April 1716, as written by Richebourg. Barnett, "The Yamasee War," 20–21; Swanton, *Indian Tribes of the Lower Mississippi Valley*, 196.

[41] The Natchez diplomatic party that arrived at Bienville's makeshift Fort Saint Joseph included eight chiefs: The Great Sun, Tattooed Serpent, Little Sun, The Bearded, Old Flour Chief, Old Hair, Yakstalchil, and Alahofléchia. According to Richebourg's narrative, Bienville commanded that the eight chiefs who he knew by name be "admitted into his tent only." They were later placed in the guard house in irons. Barnett, *Natchez Indians*, 68; Chavagne de Richebourg's narrative, quoted in Swanton, *Indian Tribes of the Lower Mississippi Valley*, 199.

[42] In his narrative, Richebourg says that Bienville told the Great Sun, Tattooed Serpent, and Little Sun that he expected to have satisfaction from them by receiving "not only the heads of the murderers, but also those of the chiefs who had given the order for it." Swanton, *Indian Tribes of the Lower Mississippi Valley*, 200–201.

[43] Before dispatching the Little Sun for the heads of the murderers, Bienville told the

Earth, Grigras, and two chiefs and two warriors then in his custody. The Indians whom he had sent to the Natchez having returned without the head of White Earth, who had made his escape, and the inundation of the Mississippi having caused much sickness on the island, Bienville determined to end the affair by a treaty with the chiefs, who willingly acceded to his terms, and were grateful that he had spared their lives.[44] They bound themselves to kill White Earth whenever he could be captured, to restore all the goods which they had seized, to cut two thousand five hundred piles of acacia wood, thirty feet long and ten inches in diameter, and to deposit them at the spot, at Natchez, where it was contemplated to erect a fort; and to furnish the bark of three thousand cypress trees, for covering the houses, by the end of July.*

Adjutant Pailloux departed, with two soldiers, to the town of the Natchez, with the chiefs and other warriors; Bienville, however, retained the Tattooed Serpent and his brother, the Little Sun, as hostages, and also kept the four murderers, who now rent the prison with their doleful death songs and loud speeches of defiance. Pailloux, upon arriving among the Natchez, found them assembled in council, and learned, with pleasure, that they were satisfied with the compact which their chiefs had made with Bienville. He selected an eminence, near the Mississippi, advantageously situated for that purpose, for the site of a fort.[45] In the meantime, Bienville had been visited at the island by nine old Natchez men, who came with much show of solemnity, and invited him to smoke the pipe of peace with them, which he now no longer refused to do. He sent them home with the Little Sun and four soldiers, who conveyed, in a large canoe, axes, spades, pickaxes, nails and other irons, to construct the fort. The next day, the soldiers, at the

* Charles Gayarré, *Histoire de la Louisiane*, 1: 114–44; Bénard de la Harpe, *Journal historique* de l›établissement des Français à la Louisiane, 115–28.

Great Sun, Tattooed Serpent, and Little Sun that he would recognize the heads of the guilty by their tattoos. Consequently, when the Little Sun returned with the heads of only two of the guilty chiefs, he immediately demanded the head of White Earth, also known as Oylape. Ibid., 201–02.

[44] By early May 1716, the spring flooding of the Mississippi had started to inundate the island where Bienville had built his post. Richebourg reports that the rising water "caused us much fever, illness in the legs, and colic." When the Tattooed Serpent caught the fever, Bienville took off his irons and allowed him to join him and his brothers in his tent and "passed all his days with these chiefs, reproached them for their evil practices." They confessed that the three war chiefs of the Hickories, White Earth, and Grigras "had brought the English into their village" and "at their orders the Frenchmen had been killed." Ibid.; *MPA: FD*, 3: 209–11.

[45] Richebourg writes that Jacques Barbazon de Pailloux "had found near the river a hill situated very advantageously for construction of our fort." The first Fort Rosalie was a simple rectangular stockade completed in early August 1716, with small bastions at each corner added in 1719. Swanton, *Indian Tribes of the Lower Mississippi Valley*, 203–04; Chartrand, *Forts of New France*, 49; Barnett, *Natchez Indians*, 70–71.

[46] According to Richebourg's narrative, The Bearded was one of the two chiefs that Bienville sent down the Mississippi with the Canadian *voyageurs* "and gave orders to break their heads when they were 10 to 12 leagues off." He added that The Bearded stopped "singing his death song and sang that of war. . . . He named the five Frenchmen whom he caused to die, and said that

island, struck off the heads of the two warriors. Afterwards Captain Richebourg was obliged to depart for Mobile, on account of sickness. A number of Canadian *voyageurs*, whom Bienville detained at the island, while on their way from the Illinois country, with peltries and supplies for the people of the lower part of Louisiana, now that the difficulty with the Natchez had ended, were permitted to proceed down the Mississippi; the royal lieutenant caused them to take with them the two chiefs, whose heads he ordered to be struck off twelve leagues below, which was faithfully executed.[46]

The Natchez, directed by the French officer and assisted by a few soldiers, labored upon the fort and ditches with great assiduity, and soon brought the works to a state of completion. Bienville had arrived a few days before, in company with the Tattooed Serpent, whom he had retained about his person until every seeming obstacle was overcome. Before the gate of the fort, six hundred Natchez warriors appeared, unarmed, and joined three hundred women in a dance in honor of Bienville; afterwards the chiefs crossed the threshold and smoked the pipe of peace with him. Such was the end of the first Natchez war.[47]

Leaving Pailloux in command of the post at Natchez, Bienville descended the Mississippi, and sailed to Mobile for the purpose of reporting to Governor Cadillac. Here he received a packet from the Marine Council, in which he was ordered by the king of France to govern as chief of the colony, until L'Epinay, the successor of Cadillac, should arrive. He was thus saved the disagreeable necessity of reporting to his old enemy, who had, in advance, denounced his conduct to the minister, as fraught with cruelty and the deepest treachery towards the Natchez chiefs. We are not prepared to defend Bienville from these charges, although his course was approved by the government and by all the colonial authorities, with the exception of Cadillac and his junto.[48]

The king of France, acceding to the request of Crozat, allowed one hundred salt-makers to be sent annually to Louisiana, who, after laboring there for three years, were to receive land. He also consented to send thither eight companies of soldiers, with permission to two, out of each company, to settle in the country, together with a hundred hospital girls, annually, to

he died with regret at not killing more." Based on Alahofléchia's prominence among the Grigas, he was probably the other chief sent with the *voyageurs*. Swanton, *Indian Tribes of the Lower Mississippi Valley*, 203–04; Barnett, *Natchez Indians*, 70–71.

[47] Richebourg tells us that on the same day—25 July 1716—the Natchez saluted Bienville and smoked their pipes: "30 men of the Yazous (Yazoos) and Offagoulas (Ofagoulas) came to sing the calumet song to M. de Bienville, who received them very well," perhaps validating the respect and/or fear that Bienville had established with an inferior French military presence in the Lower Mississippi Valley. Swanton, *Indian Tribes of the Lower Mississippi Valley*, 204.

[48] The Council of the Navy ignored Cadillac's attacks on Bienville and endorsed his tactics in dealing with the Natchez as "appropriate to the offense." Although Crozat did not endorse him for governor, he and the council understood his value to Louisiana. Giraud, *Years of Transition, 1715–1717*, 80–81, 90–91.

increase the colonial population. The king refused to adopt the suggestion of the Curate La Vente, of permitting Frenchmen to marry Indian women.[49]

For the payment of colonial expenses, for the year 1716, now nearly brought to a close, Duclos, the commissary-general, required of the French government an appropriation of the following amounts:[50]

"A Governor	6000	*livres.*
A commissary	6000	
A royal lieutenant	2000	
An adjutant	900	
Four captains of companies	4800	
Four lieutenants	3600	
Ensigns	2400	
A secretary	1000	
A storekeeper	800	
A surgeon	800	
A chaplain	800	
Incidental expenses	80,992	
	110,092	*livres.*"*

[49] **In his memoir to Lamothe Cadillac on 13 May 1710, King Louis XIV expressed his concerns regarding La Vente's conduct and that he had "given an order to the Superior of the Foreign Missions to send another curate" to replace him. He commended Cadillac on the efforts to establish a peace with the Alabamas and "the opportunity to make use of a salt-mine . . . on the river that leads to the Alabamas." *MPA: FD,* 3:144, 148; Higginbotham, *Old Mobile,* 403–12.**

[50] **The expenses outlined here for 1716 are a summary of the actual budgeted expenses submitted by Duclos. Gayarré, *Histoire de la Louisiane,* 1: 238–39.**

* Charles Gayarré, *Histoire de la Louisiane,* 1: 148–52.

Chapter VI

THE INDIA OR MISSISSIPPI COMPANY

L'Epinay, the new governor, and the fourth which had been placed over the colony of Louisiana, Hubert, the new commissary-general, three companies of infantry and fifty colonists, arrived from France, on board three vessels, which belonged to Crozat.[1] Among the colonists were Roi Dubreuil, Guenot, Tréfontaine and Massy, men of worth and intelligence, who had formed themselves into an association to settle some portion of the almost boundless country of Louisiana.[2]

To prevent the struggle for power which had never failed to display itself between the former governors, commissaries and officers of the colony, the king of France, by written instructions, defined the duties of each. He declared that all military regulations, and the "dignity of command," should pertain to the governor alone; but in the building of public houses and fortifications, the marching of expeditions, and the means of raising funds, he was to confer with the commissary, whose joint views were to be presented for the ratification of his majesty. The administration of the funds, provisions, merchandise and everything which related to the warehouses was confided to the commissary, who, however, could make no bargain or sale without the consent of the governor. The administration of the hospitals was also confided to the commissary, with the supervision of the governor. The administration of justice was committed to the commissary in his function of first councilor and chief judge. The affairs of the police, and the power of conferring grants of land were given jointly to these officers. Letters patent established a Superior Council of Louisiana, the meetings of which his majesty authorized to be held either at Fort Louis, of Mobile, or upon Dauphin Island.[3] The king granted to Bienville, for his numerous services, the Island of Corne, not as a fief, but in villanage, and instructed L'Epinay to present him with the Cross of St. Louis.

[1] Jean-Michel L'Epinay (c. 1665–1721) had a long naval career, reaching the rank of lieutenant commander before his appointment as governor of Louisiana. He arrived on 9 March 1717 and was recalled on 9 February 1718. Marc Antoine Hubert was appointed *commissaire ordonnateur,* making him the chief financial officer of Louisiana. While Crozat nominated L'Epinay, the Council of the Navy selected Hubert and confirmed Crozat's choice for governor on 12 March 1716. Giraud, *Years of Transition, 1715–1717,* 81.

[2] Vincent Dubreuil, Claude Guenot, Jean-Baptiste Massy, and Pierre and Phillipe de Tréfontaine reached an agreement with Crozat to engage in commercial ventures in Louisiana, which included trading with the Indians and the Spaniards. They made contributions in leadership roles, farming, timber and naval stores, and trade. Pickett's source here—Bénard de la Harpe—lists a M. Roi but he remains unidentified. Ibid., 120; La Harpe, *Journal historique* , 132; *MPA: FD,* 2: 322, 357, 393, 523, 583, 637, 667; ibid., 3: 360, 453, 779.

These marks of favor did not reconcile Bienville, who considered himself, beyond all others, entitled to the government of Louisiana. Consequently jealousies and disputes soon created a disagreeable and unhappy state of things, arraying the friends of Bienville on one side, and those of the governor and commissary on the other.[4]

As Crozat attempted to bribe Cadillac, in order to attain his most vigorous and successful exertions in advancing his commerce, so, for the same end, he entered into a contract with L'Epinay, engaging to give him two thousand livres a year, and diverse other advantages. The great monopolist had designed to establish a large contraband trade with the Spanish possessions if he could not carry on a legitimate one. But he succeeded in neither, and next, turning his attention to a commerce with the various Indian tribes upon the Mississippi, Alabama, Tombigbee, and their tributaries, he found that so far from being remunerated, he had to encounter the heaviest losses. At length, aware that he had assumed a burthen beyond his strength, he humbly offered to return to the king that charter, the extensive privileges of which he had once imagined would make him the richest man in the world! The proposition was accepted, and the council of state transmitted orders to L'Epinay to transfer the colonial government to Bienville, and to return to France. The gubernatorial career of the former gentleman was of short duration, and remarkable for nothing, except a proclamation, in which he forbade the sale of brandy to the Indians—at that period a very unpopular measure.[5]

During the five years of the existence of the colony, under the charter of Crozat, commerce and agriculture had not prospered, yet the population had slowly increased, and now numbered about seven hundred souls. The colonists, also, possessed some four hundred horned cattle. The inhabitants had devoted themselves to a trade in provisions and Indian slaves, and to a commerce with the Spaniards, who, despite of the watchfulness of Crozat's agents, had managed to carry off, annually, about twelve thousand piastres.

The Marine Cabinet of France, composed of De Bourbon and D'Estrées, came to the conclusion that as the enterprise which Crozat had assumed had proved itself of too gigantic a character for any one man, and as it would not be proper for the king to take charge of Louisiana, and embarrass himself by entering into its thousand cares and commercial details, it would better comport with the welfare of France and her colony, to turn the latter over to the management of

[3] Although the Superior Council—*Conseil Superieur*—had been established by the Letters Patent of 1712, it was never organized or convened by Lamothe Cadillac. Under the Council of the Navy, the Superior Council was made "perpetual and irrevocable, as in other colonies." The membership remained the same as prescribed in 1712: the governor and intendant of New France presiding *ex officio*, the "special governor" of Louisiana, a first councilor (i.e., *commissaire-ordonnateur*), the *lieutenant de roy* (i.e., king's lieutenant), two councilors, an attorney general, and a registrar. This body served primarily as a civil and criminal tribunal. Giraud, *Years of Transition, 1715–1717,* 87–88; Jerry A. Micelle, "From Law Court to Local Government: Metamorphosis of the Superior Council of Louisiana," *Louisiana History* 9 (Spring 1968): 85, 90–97.

[4] Actually Jean-Baptiste Le Moyne de Bienville was granted the prestigious Cross of St. Louis in September 1717, but he did not receive word of the award until March 1718. At the same time he had been promoted to *commandant-general,* making him the highest ranking official in Louisiana with the recall of L'Epinay. Pickett's Island of Corne is the L'Île de la Corne (Horn Island), located west of Cape Sanalo and part of the Archipelago of Sulcis off the coast of Sardinia. *MPA: FD,* 3: 227; Gayarré, *Histoire de la Louisiane,* 1: 155; Lawrence N. Powell, *The Accidental City: Improvising New Orleans* (Cambridge: Harvard University Press, 2012), 41–42.

[5] Crozat's resignation was accepted as a "conditional decision" on 23 August 1717. Ironically, it was Crozat who recommended that

an association of men.[6] Accordingly, the Western or India Company, with a capital of one hundred thousand livres, was allowed to take the unhappy people of Louisiana under their charge, and to expose them, once more, to an arbitrary and grinding monopoly. The members of this company were not required to be solely subjects of the king of France, but might be foreigners. The charter, which was registered in the Parlement, at Paris, gave this company the exclusive privilege of carrying on all commerce in Louisiana, for the long period of twenty-five years. It also gave them the exclusive privilege, extending from the 1st January 1718 to the 31st December 1742, of purchasing beaver skins from Canada—the king reserving the right of regulating their price, and of determining the quantity to be sold. The company possessed the power of conferring grants, making war or peace with the Indians, establishing forts, levying troops, appointing governors, or other officers, for the colony, upon the recommendation of the directors of the company; building vessels of war, casting pieces of artillery, and of nominating the inferior judges, and all the other officers of justice, the king reserving to himself only the right of appointing the members of the Superior Council.[7]

It was further provided by the charter that the military officers could enter into the service of the company without losing their rank in the army or navy, but they were not allowed to seize, either in the hands of the directors, or in those of its cashier or its agents, the effects, shares or profits of the stockholders, except in case of failure or open bankruptcy or death of said stockholders. The merchandise of the company was to be free from all charges either of entry or departure, and to those portions of the territory where they made permanent improvements, the company was to have durable rights, which were to extend also to the mines, which they might discover and work. The only thing which savored of liberality toward the inhabitants, was their exemption from taxation during the existence of the charter. The ecclesiastical jurisdiction was still to form a part of the diocese of Quebec, while the company was to build churches and pay the clergy. It was to transport to the colony, during the term of its charter, six thousand whites and three thousand Negroes; but it was prohibited from sending Negroes or whites to other French colonies, without the permission of the governor of Louisiana.[8] The directors were to be appointed by the king, for the first two years, and afterwards they were to be elected every three years, by the

Council of the Navy entrust Louisiana to another trading enterprise, which led to the emergence of the Company of the West. As noted above, L'Epinay was recalled on 9 February 1718. Giraud, *Years of Transition, 1715–1717,* 67–68.

6 Pickett's "Marine Cabinet" was the Council of the Navy which was led by Louis Alexandre de Bourbon, Comte de Toulouse, and its chairman Marshal d'Estrees, the Vice-Admiral of France, who worked closely with the King's Regent. Giraud, *Years of Transition, 1715–1717,* 1–4.

7 The Company of the West, headed by the Scottish financier John Law, took over Louisiana through a charter granted to his company by Parlement in Paris on 6 September 1717. In 1719, John Law reorganized the French trading companies, merging the Company of the West, the Company of the East Indies, and the China Company—creating the Company of the Indies. Henceforth, this new organization became known as the Mississippi Company. Antoin E. Murphy, *John Law: Economic Theorist and Policy-Maker* (Oxford, UK: Oxford University Press, 1997), 188–89, 193.

8 Law's company surpassed its first quota, transporting 7,020 European immigrants to Louisiana between 25 October 1717 and May 1721. The second quota of supplying 3,000 African slaves was met in 1727 or 1728. Paul Lachance, "The Growth of Free and Slave Populations of French Louisiana," in *French Colonial Louisiana and the Atlantic World,* ed. Bradley G. Bond (Baton Rouge: Louisiana State University Press, 2005), 210.

9 Upon the death of Louis XIV on 1 September 1715, his

stockholders, each of whom had a vote for every fifty shares. In short, the India Company was granted all manner of powers and privileges.[9]

A celebrated Scotchman, named Law, who was now director of the Bank of France; [10] D'Artaguette, receiver-general of the finances of Auch; Duché, receiver of those of Rochelle; Moreau, commercial deputy of the city of Saint-Malo; Piou, deputy of the city of Nantes; and Castaignes and Mouchard, merchants of Rochelle, were nominated by the king of France as the first directors for the colony of Louisiana, under the new charter.[11] The company then sent over three companies of infantry, and sixty-nine colonists. The three vessels which bore them arrived at Dauphin Island, and the inhabitants were revived with pleasing anticipations of better times, especially as the great and good Bienville, whom they almost idolized, was made governor with a salary of six thousand livres. He, who had been twenty years in this wild and inhospitable country, and who, amidst the deepest gloom and the greatest suffering of the colonists, had never once left them, but had sustained them with his fearless spirit, mighty arm and benevolent heart, was eminently deserving the high post to which he was now elevated. The first thing he did was to seek a suitable place for the location of the principal settlement of the colony. He selected the site of New Orleans, which had long been a favorite point with him, as we have seen. He proceeded there with fifty persons, carpenters and galley slaves, whom he set to work to clear away the woods and erect houses.[12] He next sent a detachment of fifty soldiers, under Chateaugué, to build a fort upon the bay of St. Joseph, situated between Pensacola and St. Marks, which, being completed, De Gousy was left there in command. From him Captain Roka, a Spaniard, induced twenty-five soldiers to desert and flee to St. Augustine. The post of St. Joseph was soon abandoned by the French, who had no right to settle any part of Florida, and it was immediately occupied by the Spaniards.[13]

In the vessels which arrived on the 9th of February came Major Boisbriant, who had paid a visit to France, and who was now commissioned a royal lieutenant, with a salary of three thousand livres. Hubert was retained as commissary general with a salary of five thousand livres. These vessels

great-grandson succeeded him as Louis XV at the age of five. However, his maternal great uncle, Phillip II, Duke of Orleans, served as Regent of France until 1723. Colin Jones, *The Great Nation: France from Louis XV to Napoleon* (London: Penguin Books, 2002), 36–39.

[10] John Law (1671–1729), a native of Edinburgh, Scotland, was a money reformer, economic policymaker, and political strategist. He wrote *Money and Trade Considered: With a Proposal for Supplying the Nation with Money,* which was first published at Edinburgh in 1705. He established a moderately successful banking system in France—*Banque Générale Privée*—using paper notes and merged several French trading companies into a holding conglomerate that was known popularly as the Mississippi Company. Murphy, *John Law,* 150–55, 162–71.

[11] While Duché directed the military affairs of the company, Castaignes and D'Artaguette had responsibility for the purchase of provisions and food in France. Moreau was appointed to buy and provision ships, and Piou was to act as the purchasing agent for Negro slaves. Mouchard was to act as the liaison for the Canadian part of the company's business. The document signed by the Duke of Orleans listed two other directors, De La Barr and Crozat. De La Barr was made responsible for the beaver account and the sale of beaver pelts to Parisian hat makers. Crozat was jointly listed with Law with responsibility for international remittances and the purchase of foreign provisions for Louisiana. Ibid., 172.

[12] Bienville acknowledged his promotion to *commandant-general* and the award of the Cross of St. Louis in his letter of 12 June 1718 to the Council of the Navy. He also reported on the start of work to establish New Orleans "thirty leagues above the entrance to

were succeeded by another, having on board sixty passengers for the grant belonging to Paris-Duverney, which embraced the old Indian village of Pascagoula, where they were presently located.[14] Three more ships arrived at Dauphin Island, which brought out Richebourg, now Chevalier of the Order of St. Louis; Grandval, intended to act as major of Mobile; Lieutenants Noyan and Mélique, and Daniel, major of New Orleans.[15] At the same time there arrived forty commissioners, with Legac, sub-director; seventy persons for the grant of Houssayes, and sixty for that of La Harpe.[16]

It was wisely determined to encourage agriculture, as the best means of increasing the wealth and importance of Louisiana; and for that purpose extensive grants of land were made to the richest and most powerful persons of the kingdom of France. Four leagues square were ceded to the Scotch financier, Law, on the Arkansas River, where he was to settle fifteen hundred Germans, whom he was to protect by a small body of cavalry and infantry.[17] The other persons to whom grants were made, likewise bound themselves to furnish a certain number of emigrants. But the experiment did not succeed. These great proprietors did send to Louisiana a few colonists, but a majority of them fell victims to the climate, and those who survived did not devote themselves to any useful occupation. Among the grants were several upon the Yazoo River, near Natchez, upon Red River, at Baton Rouge, and at other points upon the Mississippi River. Failing in the scheme to make the colony an agricultural country, by the importation of colonists who were to have settled upon these grants, the company next turned its attention to slavery, as a means of effecting that which was so much desired.*

The following regulation of the company fixed the price the colonists were to pay for the Negroes, which they imported from Africa: "The Company considers every Negro of seventeen years of age, and over, without bodily defect, also every Negress from fifteen to thirty years of age, as worth *piece d'Inde*.†

Three little Negroes, from eight to ten years old, are valued at two of the same coins.

* Charles Gayarré, *Histoire de la Louisiane*, 1: 148–66; Bénard de la Harpe, *Journal historique de l'établissement des Français à la Louisiane*, 131–44.

† Piece d'Inde was 660 livres.

the Mississippi". *MPA: FD*, 3: 227–28.

[13] After dispatching forces to seize St. Joseph's Bay, Bienville received a letter from Juan Pedro Matamoros de Isla, the Spanish governor at Pensacola, protesting that the bay belonged to the king of Spain. Captain Juan Manuel Roka had first discovered the French at Fort Crevecoeur sailing along the coast from St. Marks. In his letter of 25 September 1718 to the Council of the Navy, Bienville reported that he had withdrawn the garrison from St. Joseph's Bay and burned Fort Crevecoeur, "the little stockade fort that had been built there." Ibid., 228–29, 232–33; Chartrand, *Forts of New France*, 58.

[14] The Paris-Duverney concession was granted to Joseph Paris-Duverney, his two brothers and two other partners. Although one of the smaller concessions, it survived through 1731 with forty-eight adult slaves, their children, and five indentured servants. Marcel Giraud, *A History of French Louisiana*: vol. 5, *The Company of the Indies, 1723–1731*, trans. Brian Pearce (Baton Rouge: Louisiana State University, 1991), 128, 139, 161, 172–73, 303.

[15] Gilles-Augustin Payen de Noyan was a nephew of Bienville's. Pierre Mélique served at Fort de Chartres and established a habitation on the Kaskaskia River. Ibid., 36, 458.

[16] Charles Legac was an active member of the Council of Commerce for Louisiana. Bénard de la Harpe, a former captain general of the coast guards, arrived in Louisiana in August 1718 with forty colonists to develop his concession on the Red River. *MPA: FD*, 2: 264 n. 1; ibid., 3: 239–42, 255–68, 275–304.

[17] Jacques Levens established John Law's concession with a group of eighty indentured servants, skilled workmen, and craftsmen in August 1721 on the

Two Negro children, over ten years of age, are valued at one *piece d'Inde*.

One year's credit will be given to the old inhabitants for half the price. The other half must be paid immediately.

Those colonists who have been settled here two years are called old inhabitants.

The new settlers shall be entitled to one and two years credit."[18]

In a dispatch to the minister, Bienville complained that the colonists recently sent to Louisiana, were not the kind desirable; that among them were to be found scarcely any carpenters or laborers, "notwithstanding laboring people employed in the country are paid ten or fifteen livres per day, which delays improvement and causes great expense to the company."[19]

Two vessels arrived from the mother country, and brought the startling intelligence that Spain and France had gone to war with each other.[20] A council, composed of Sérigny, Bienville, Hubert, Larcebault and Legac, determined upon the necessity of immediately possessing the important post of Pensacola. None of the military officers were consulted in this movement, as they should have been, especially upon the plan of attack.

Bienville assembled, at Mobile, some Canadians and four hundred Indians. His brother, Sérigny, sailed from Dauphin Island, with three men-of-war, on board of which he embarked one hundred and fifty soldiers. Bienville embarked in a sloop, with twenty men, made the mouth of the Perdido, and went up that river to meet the Canadians and Indians, whom he had instructed to march across the country from Mobile, and whom he found already at the place of rendezvous. Placing himself at their head, he marched to Pensacola. In the meantime, the fleet stood before that place, and at four o'clock, in the evening, Governor Matamoras surrendered to the French, when he found that he was invested both by sea and land. According to the terms of the capitulation, Bienville embarked the Spanish garrison on board two of the men-of-war, with directions to convey them safely to Havana. Arriving at that place, the governor of Cuba ordered all the French forces to be landed and imprisoned, seized the two men-of-war, manned them with sailors and soldiers, and sent them back to attack Pensacola. This was a most shameful disregard of the terms of the capitulation.[21]

The Spanish fleet, comprising the two French vessels and a Spanish

Arkansas River at Little Prairie, Arkansas County, Arkansas. Law paid the expenses for 200 German families to populate his twelve-square-mile concession, but after hearing of Law's bankruptcy, they settled on land near New Orleans. Caty Henderson, "John Law's Concession," *The Encyclopedia of Arkansas History & Culture*, http://www.encyclopediaofarkansas.net.

[18] Near the end of 1722, the Company increased the cost of a *piece d'Inde* from 600 *livres* to 1,000 *livres*. The price for an individual black male with a trade could increase to 1,200 *livres* and an exceptional female might bring 1,300, 1,600, or more. Giraud, *Company of the Indies, 1723–1731*, 125.

[19] In his letter of 25 September 1718 to the Navy Council, Bienville stated clearly that the company needed to send farmers, carpenters, and joiners, and not all the "useless mouths in the companies of almost all the holders of concessions, among whom one can scarcely find one man suitable for the most urgent work." *MPA: FD*, 3: 235.

[20] The War of the Quadruple Alliance resulted from the efforts by Spain's King Philip V to retake territories in Italy and renew his claims to the French throne. An alliance of Great Britain, France, Austria, and the Dutch Republic defeated Spain and ended the conflict by the Treaty of The Hague in 1720. Jack D. L. Holmes, "Dauphin Island in the Franco-Spanish War, 1719–22," in *Frenchmen and French Ways in the Mississippi Valley*, ed. John Francis McDermott (Urbana: University of Illinois Press, 1969), 112–13.

[21] Using company ships and the *Philippe*, Bienville launched his

man-of-war, with nine brigantines and eighteen hundred men, invested Pensacola, and the next day made their attack. Bienville had returned to Mobile, and had left his brother, Chateaugué, in command. Seeing the superior force of the enemy, fifty soldiers deserted from the fort and joined the Spaniards, which forced Chateaugué to capitulate. He was allowed to march out of the fort, with the honors of war and to be carried to old Spain. The store ship *Dauphine* was accidentally destroyed by fire, and the *St. Louis* was captured by the Spaniards.[22] The commander of the Spanish squadron next turned his eyes to Dauphin Island, and presently sent thither two well manned brigantines. To the captain of the French ship, *Philippe*, which lay at anchor at Dauphin Island, he sent a summons to surrender, but the captain referred the messenger to Sérigny, who commanded the fort; the latter declined to surrender the island. During the night two brigantines entered the bay of Mobile, and half way between Dauphin Island and the town of Mobile, landed thirty-five men to burn and plunder the inhabitants. While they were here destroying the improvements of a settler, they were suddenly attacked by a detachment of Canadians and Indians, whom Bienville had hastened to send from Mobile, to support his brother, Sérigny. Five Spaniards were slain, whose scalps the Indians immediately secured; six were drowned in the endeavor to reach the brigantines, while eighteen were made prisoners; among the latter were some of the French soldiers, who had deserted from Chateaugué, and who were now promptly beheaded for their treason.* Two days afterwards the remainder of the Spanish squadron stood before Dauphin Island, and continued for four days to cannonade the *Philippe* and the town. Sérigny, with one hundred and sixty soldiers and two hundred Indians, aided by the gallant officers and men of the *Philippe*, which was anchored within pistol shot of the fort, succeeded in repulsing the Spaniards, who sustained considerable loss. The ships of the enemy then set sail for Pensacola.[23]

Three ships of the French line, under command of Champmeslin, convoying two of the company's ships, arrived off Dauphin Island, direct from France. The two Spanish brigantines, which were cruising

* La Harpe states (page 155), that eighteen French deserters, who were made prisoners, were bound by the Indians and carried to Bienville, at Mobile, who caused seventeen of them to be decapitated, and that the remaining one was hung on Dauphin Island.

assault of Pensacola on 13 May 1718. While Sérigny and Larcebault, a company director, led a force of 166 officers and men, Bienville left Dauphin Island with four vessels carrying eighty soldiers and forty-five volunteers. Chateaugué led a force of sixty soldiers and some four hundred Indians who marched overland from Mobile. After three hours of cannon fire from the French ships in Pensacola Bay, Governor Matamoras de Isla surrendered on 17 May, shaken by the knowledge that he did not know war had broken out between Spain and France. Contrary to the articles of capitulation, Gregorio Guazo Calderon, governor of Havana, seized the French ships *Maréchal de Villars* and the *Comte de Toulouse* bearing the Spanish prisoners under a flag of truce. Ibid., 113–14; *MPA: FD*, 3: 269–70, 272; Dumont de Montigny, *Memoir*, 104–05.

[22] The Spanish expedition under the command of Admiral Alfonso Carrascosa de la Torre, including the two captured French ships, a Spanish flagship, and nine coastal schooners carrying 1,200 to 1,800 men, arrived on 4 August 1719. Chateaugué was badly outnumbered with only 250 men and some company officials when the bombardment started on 6 August. He suffered 40 to 90 deserters on the first day, and he surrendered unconditionally the next day. Chateaugué, Chambeau, Richebourg, La Marque, Larcebault, and other officers and men were sent to Havana as prisoners. Holmes, "Dauphin Island in the Franco-Spanish War," 115–16; *MPA: FD*, 3: 242–44, 270; Dumont de Montigny, *Memoir*, 105–06.

in the bay, between this island and Mobile, escaped to sea and sailed to Pensacola, as soon as the French fleet was discovered. Bienville and Sérigny repaired on board of the ship of Champmeslin, where was presently convened a council, composed of all the sea captains in port, who decided to capture the Spanish squadron and to take the fort of Pensacola. Time was allowed the vessels to discharge their freight and to take in wood and water, and Bienville to assemble the savages and prepare them for the expedition. When all things were ready, the *Philippe* and the *Union*, vessels belonging to the company, were joined to the squadron, together with two hundred and fifty of the new troops, lately arrived, while Bienville, with the soldiers and volunteers, sailed in sloops to the river Perdido, where he was joined by five hundred Indians under the command of Longueville, who had marched with them from Mobile. From this point Bienville sent a detachment of French and Indians to invest the principal fort at Pensacola, to prevent all egress from it and to harass the enemy as much as possible. In the meantime, Champmeslin entered the harbor of Pensacola, and, after a conflict of two hours' duration, captured four ships and six brigantines, which were anchored before Santa Rosa, and reduced the small fort situated at the point of that island.[24]

Bienville, having marched across the country from the Perdido, had advanced in the rear of the town with his whole force. He made a resolute attack upon the fort, which was surrendered two hours after the victory at Santa Rosa Island. The Indians fought with great courage, often attempting to pull up the palisades of the fort. The plunder was divided among them, but they were prohibited by Bienville from taking any scalps. The pillage being ended, Champmeslin returned the sword which Don Alfonso, commander of the Spanish fleet, had presented to him as his conqueror, assuring him that he was worthy of wearing it. But Matamoras, the governor of Pensacola, who had acted with so much perfidy towards the French victors who conveyed him to Havana, was suffered to be disarmed by a common sailor, and was severely reproached for his conduct. The loss of the French in these engagements was only six men; that of the Spaniards was much greater. Champmeslin dispatched the *St. Louis*, one of the Spanish vessels, to Havana, with three hundred and sixty of the prisoners. The commander was instructed to demand an exchange of the French prisoners, at the head of whom was Chateaugué, who had not been carried to Spain, according to the capitulation, but had been closely confined in Moro Castle.[25]

A Spanish brigantine from Havana, laden with corn flour and brandy for the garrison, entered the bay of Pensacola, supposing the fleet to belong

[23] The Spanish task force commanded by Captain Antonio de Mendieta arrived off Dauphin Island on 13 August 1719 and demanded the French surrender, but Sérigny refused. Bombardment from the Spanish ships and the attacks by three separate landing parties were thwarted under Bienville's leadership and by Indian and Canadian forces led by François Trudeau, Louis Juchereau de St. Denis, and Sieur de Villainville. While several French deserters participated in the Spanish assault, eighteen were captured and seventeen were dispatched by the Indian allies and one was hanged on Dauphin Island. After a twelve-day siege, Mendieta's ships returned to Pensacola on 25 August. Holmes, "Dauphin Island in the Franco-Spanish War," 118–21; *MPA: FD*, 3: 244–51, 270–71.

[24] On 17 September 1719, Commodore Desnos de Champmeslin launched an attack on Pensacola with five ships and eight small boats carrying some 250 men under the command of Sérigny and Villardeau. Bienville had moved up the Perdido River in a sloop with about 100 soldiers and volunteers, where he met 500 Indians commanded by Sieur de la Longueville. Meanwhile, Champmeslin's guns overpowered Spanish batteries on Santa Rosa Island. Holmes, "Dauphin Island in the Franco-Spanish War," 122–23; *MPA: FD*, 3: 262, 272–74.

to Spain, into whose hands it was now believed the whole of Louisiana had fallen, and was immediately captured by the French squadron. On the same day forty-seven French deserters were tried, twelve of whom were hung at the yard-arms of the *Count de Toulouse*, and the remainder condemned to serve the company as galley slaves. Thus ended the expedition against Pensacola, the command of which was given to DeLisle, a lieutenant of the navy.[26]

Since the commencement of this year, vessels from France had constantly brought over to Louisiana liberal supplies of provisions, merchandise, and not unfrequently distinguished persons and emigrants, thus adding to the number and giving character to her population, and causing her slowly to emerge from the supineness and insignificance of former times. For this reason, and also on account of the war with Spain, it became necessary to re-organize the colonial government in several respects. A royal ordinance decreed that a Superior Council should be composed of those directors who were residents in the colony, the governor, the two royal lieutenants, four councilors, an attorney general, and a secretary. Three members for civil affairs, and five for criminal cases, could constitute a quorum. Its jurisdiction was to be the highest in the colony, and its sessions were to be monthly. The former council had been the only tribunal in the colony, but it was now decided to establish inferior courts, of which the directors of the company, or their agents, were to be judges, in the places where they resided. These, with two respectable citizens of the neighborhood, were to have cognizance of civil business. They were required, in criminal cases, to add four more citizens to their number. An appeal from their decisions could be had to the Superior Council—the members of which were not allowed to charge for their final opinions.[27]

Bienville, the governor; Hubert, commissary general and first councilor; Boisbriant and Chateaugué, royal lieutenants; Larcebault, Villardeau and Legac, other councilors; Chartier de Baulne, the attorney-general; and Couturier, secretary, composed the first Superior Council, which met under the auspices of the Western or India Company. Although the governor occupied the place of honor in this body, Hubert, the first councilor, was the real president, who took the vote, pronounced judgment, affixed the public seals, and filled the station of chief judge.[28]

Bienville was opposed in his long cherished desire of removing the government to the site of New Orleans, by Hubert and the directors, who dreaded the inundations of the Mississippi, and who contended that the colony was not in a situation to oppose levees to the floods at that point. Hubert suggested the location of Natchez; but as he owned large

[25] Bienville's siege force convinced Governor Matamoras to surrender Fort San Carlos. According to Bienville, his forces captured "possibly fifteen hundred Spaniards" and a large number of French deserters and privateers. Champmeslin captured twelve Spanish vessels, sent 625 prisoners to Havana, and kept the Spanish officers as hostages pending the release of French prisoners taken in August 1719. Holmes, "Dauphin Island in the Franco-Spanish War," 123; *MPA: FD,* 3:273.

[26] Bienville reported Champmeslin had captured thirty-seven French deserters aboard the Spanish ships, who were brought before a naval court martial which condemned twelve "to be hanged and the others to serve as convicts." On 12 October 1719, the French naval forces at Pensacola captured a Spanish ship which arrived from Veracruz "loaded with troops and provisions" and letters promising a squadron to seize French Louisiana. *MPA: FD,* 3:274.

[27] The council as a court served several basic functions: administering civil and criminal justice, serving notarial and registry functions, and acting as general legal counsel for the colonists. The specific powers assigned to the council were primarily judicial. However, most of their activity involved general legal administration, such as wills, property deeds, and marriage and business contracts. James

grants there, his motives were suspected. It was decided to adopt the views of Larcebault, Villardeau and Legac, who inclined more towards commerce than agriculture, and who recommended that a new establishment should be formed east of the bay of Biloxi, which should be called New Biloxi. A detachment was sent there to build barracks and houses.[29]

The cultivation of rice, indigo and tobacco had already occupied the attention of the colonists to some extent, who found the lands extremely productive for those profitable plants. But the climate was too warm and unhealthy for European labor, and hence one thousand of the "Children of the Sun," from Africa, had been introduced into the colony, and from that moment Louisiana began to prosper. But many things yet impeded its advancement. Among other impediments, the company, to secure the exclusive commerce of Louisiana, issued an edict forbidding any vessel to enter the colony under penalty of confiscation. This was followed up by a proclamation, regulating the price of merchandise, which the colonists were compelled to buy at the company's warehouses, and *nowhere else*. It also arbitrarily fixed the price which the colonists were to receive for their products, skins, and for everything which they had for sale.* Gayarré says: "At the present day, we can hardly discover how the whites, whom the company transported from Europe, differed from the blacks, who were bought from Africa, at least as to their relation to the company; for these two classes of men belonged both to one master—the all-powerful company!"

The Royal Squadron, intended to protect the commerce of Louisiana, arrived with two hundred and thirty passengers, among whom were several girls, and a considerable quantity of provisions and merchandise. Several months elapsed when two vessels of the Royal Navy bore the intelligence that a treaty of peace had been concluded with Spain. These were succeeded by three other vessels of war, which anchored at Dauphin Island, and which brought with them a contagious malady, contracted at Santo Domingo, which killed many of the crew, and filled their bodies, as it was ascertained by *post mortem* examination, with horrible worms! At the same time, the ship *Hercules* came with one hundred and twenty Negroes from Guinea, and a brigantine from Havana arrived at Mobile with Chateaugué and others, who had been

* Goods were to be obtained in the company's stores at Mobile, Dauphin Island, and Pensacola. To these prices, an advance of five percent was to be added on goods delivered at New Orleans, ten at Natchez, thirteen at the Yazoos, twenty at Natchitoches and fifty at the Illinois and on the Missouri. The produce of the country was to be received in the company's warehouses in New Orleans, Biloxi, Ship Island and Mobile. Martin, *History of Louisiana*, 1: 218–19.

D. Hardy, Jr., "The Superior Council in Colonial Louisiana," in *Frenchmen and French Ways*, 87–91.

[28] Attorney General Pierre Chartier de Baulne held a concession at the former village of the Colapissas and served to about 1724. Couturier arrived in March 1717, but the council and L'Epinay decided he was not qualified for his position, keeping Jean-Baptiste Raguet as registrar and notary. Couturier kept his commission and was assigned "to keep a canteen at Mobile." Giraud, *Company of the Indies, 1723–1731*, 291; Giraud, *Years of Transition, 1715–1717*, 96–97; *MPA: FD*, 3: 451; Henry P. Dart, "Criminal Trials: Louisiana, 1720–1766 French Colonial Period," *Louisiana Historical Quarterly* 3 (July 1920): 281–83.

[29] On 20 December 1720, the Council of Commerce met at Old Biloxi to discuss the pros and cons between Old Biloxi and a New Biloxi. They issued a memoir, "Parallel Between the Old and New Biloxi," and decided to begin work at once on New Biloxi, "and that the old fort shall cease." *MPA: FD*, 3: 298–302.

[30] On 16 June 1720, Bienville's brother Chateaugué and the "remaining prisoners from Pensacola" arrived from Havana,

made prisoners at Pensacola, and who were now released in pursuance of the treaty of peace.[30]

So long as the French colony of Louisiana remained in a feeble and thriftless condition, the English of Carolina were content only to annoy it occasionally; but now that it gave signs of durable vitality, under the auspices of a powerful company, they began to oppose it with the fiercest hostility. Rivalry in trade, together with national jealousy, fomented quarrels, and caused blood to flow between the *coureurs de bois* and the English. The French traders also met the latter in all parts of the Indian nations, within the limits of the present states of Alabama and Mississippi. Each contended for the patronage of the savages, and each endeavored to expel the other from those situations where they had established themselves. The Carolina traders, many of whom had quartered themselves in the Chickasaw towns, arrayed that tribe in war against the French, and they committed the first act of hostility, by the murder of Sorvidal, a French officer, whom Bienville had posted among them to cultivate their friendship. This war greatly embarrassed Bienville, who, with difficulty, brought to his assistance the larger body of the Choctaws. At this time, the forces of the colony had been augmented to twenty companies, of fifty men each, who were required to defend the province of Louisiana, the inhabitants of which were scattered from Fort Toulouse, upon the Coosa, to La Harpe's station, upon Red River. The Alabamas could barely be kept neutral, for they complained that their peltries brought lower prices at the French ports, than at those of the English, and that the goods which they received for them, were also held at a dearer rate.[31]

Vessels with emigrants and provisions, continued to cast their anchors upon the sands of Mobile Bay. A store ship brought out two hundred and sixty persons for the grant of Sainte-Catherine, in the vicinity of Natchez.[32] Another arrived at Ship Island with two hundred and forty emigrants, for the grant of Louvre, and was succeeded by still another, on board of which was Delorme, new director general, with a salary of five thousand livres, together with other vessels laden with provisions, laborers and merchandise.[33] In the meantime, the public houses had been completed at New Biloxi, and thither the government of Louisiana was, unwisely, transferred. It had remained at old and new Mobile since January 1702, but during this trying period, of eighteen years, the governors occasionally resided at Dauphin Island.

A vessel, belonging to the company, furled her sails in the splendid bay of Mobile, and disembarked three hundred colonists for the grant of Madame Chaumont, at Pascagoula, whom the colonial government soon placed there, but whom they forbade to enter into any branch of trade, such as that which would result from the culture of hemp, flax, and the vine, or which would

bringing word that there had been a suspension of hostilities between France and Spain. Ibid., 297.

[31] Bienville and the council attempted to counter the English intrusion among the Choctaws by removing obstacles "to the transportation of their peltries and other products to Mobile" and to establish a warehouse "near their villages" to facilitate trade and to adjust prices. They also agreed to pay the Choctaws for each Chickasaw scalp that they brought in with "one gun, one pound of powder, and two pounds of bullets." In addition, they agreed to pay for slaves and goods at the "rate of eighty livres each." The French soldier—Sorvidal—killed by the Chickasaw is identified in Francois-Xavier Martin's *The History of Louisiana, From the Earliest Period.* Ibid., 303; Martin, *History of Louisiana,* 1: 136.

[32] The Sainte-Catherine's concession was located near White Apple Village, which was pro-English and became a source of conflict in October 1722. Several shots were fired at the director of the concession, and before the violence called the Second Natchez War ended, three Frenchmen, one slave, and six Natchez had been killed. Martin, *History of Louisiana,* 1: 360; Giraud, *Company of*

compete with the commerce of the company.[34] A ship arrived with twenty-five girls, taken from a house of correction, in Paris, called the Salpêtrière. They had been sent over in consequence of the great complaints made to the minister, by various officers of the colony, on account of the want of wives, and they had been confided, by the directors in France, to Sister Gertrude, and, under her, to Sisters Louise and Bergere, who were authorized to conduct to Louisiana, "such girls as were willing to go thither and remain under the care of Sister Gertrude, until they shall marry, which they must not do without her consent." The directors or the minister in sending these prostitutes to Mobile, where they soon took up their abode, did not act consistently with a previous ordinance, which they had passed, that "hereafter, no more vagabonds shall be sent to Louisiana, but that any French and foreign families and laborers might go."[35] Much contention now arose between the stockholders and the directors. The latter were reproached for their enormous outlays, and for the appointment of persons to govern the colonies, who appeared to have their exclusive interest to subserve; and Bienville was written to, and informed that the regent complained that his services were not effectual. But to arouse all his exertions, the same letter promised the governor the rank of brigadier, with the ribbon of St. Louis, if his future conduct should merit them.[36]

The *Africaine*, a ship of war, arrived at Mobile, with one hundred and twenty Negroes, out of the number of two hundred and twenty-four, who had embarked at Guinea. She was succeeded by the *Duc du Maine*, with three hundred and thirty-eight more, who were, for the present, all quartered at Mobile, and where they remained in a state bordering upon starvation, from the famine which now universally prevailed in the colony. The *Néréide* also came with two hundred and thirty-eight Africans, the remainder of three hundred and fifty who sailed from Angola. She had put to sea, with the frigate *Charles*, laden with Negroes, which took fire and was consumed, more than sixty leagues from land, a large majority of her crew perishing in the flames. The whites escaped in the boats, with a few of the Africans, but tossed for many days at the mercy of the waves, and suffering for subsistence, the unhappy Negroes were killed, one after another, for food![37] The present population of France are *abolitionists*, and denounce the Southern states for their mild and beneficial system of domestic slavery, and yet their ancestors, in the manner we have described,

the Indies, 1723–1731, 133; Barnett, *Natchez Indians*, 86–89; Dumont de Montigny, *Memoir*, 177–79.

[33] Delorme arrived on the *Alexandre* in 1720 and served as a director of the Company of the Indies until December 1723. *MPA: FD*, 2: 299; ibid., 3: 298–304, 325–27, 334–42, 408; Dumont de Montigny, *Memoir*, 196–98, 422.

[34] The Chaumont concession struggled for several years without financial support from Antoine Chaumont and his wife. Following the death of its manager in 1729, the concession collapsed and reverted to the Crown. Giraud, *Company of the Indies, 1723–1731*, 161–62.

[35] More recent studies state that this group that accompanied three Grey Sisters in February 1721 numbered eighty-eight women from Salpêtrière, technically a hospital in Paris but in practice a women's prison. Marcia Zug, "Lonely Colonist Seeks Wife: The Forgotten History of America's First Mail Order Brides," *Duke Journal of Gender Law & Policy* 20 (Fall 2012): 122; Emily Epstein Landau, *Spectacular Wickedness: Sex, Race, and Memory in Storyville, New Orleans* (Baton Rouge: Louisiana State University Press, 2013), 33; Ned Sublette, *The World That Made New Orleans: From Spanish Silver to Congo Square* (Chicago: Lawrence Hill Books, 2008), 52.

[36] In his letter of 8 August 1721, Bienville defended his service in the colony to the King's Regent. He reasoned that despite all his efforts "to secure for the state the firm establishment of this country" that there had been little progress because of the lack of boats, workmen, merchandise, and the authority given by the company to the directors in Louisiana. He expressed his disappointment at not receiving the rank of brigadier of the

put these slaves into our possession. So did England with her men-of-war, at the same period, plant her American colonies with slaves, also captured in Africa. The Puritan fathers of New England received them, paid for them, put them to hard labor, sold and re-sold them for many years, and yet their descendants profess to be shocked at the sight of a Southern slaveholder, and denounce Southern slavery as a "damning sin before God!"

With two hundred German emigrants, who were sent over to occupy the grant of Law upon the Arkansas River, came also a woman, whose adventures in Europe and America are related in the histories of that period. She was believed to be the wife of the Czarewitz Alexis Petrowitz, son of Peter the Great, emperor of all the Russians.[38] Her resemblance to that princess was so striking as to deceive those who knew the latter intimately. The story ran, that to escape the brutal treatment of the prince, her husband, she pretended to die, and was actually entombed, but when taken from the tomb in a few hours afterwards put herself beyond the reach of persecution by flying to a foreign land. The Chevalier D'Aubant, one of the officers of the Mobile garrison, who had been at St. Petersburg, had seen the princess, and had heard of her strange escape, now believed that this woman who was then in Mobile was the beautiful and accomplished lady herself. He was sure he recognized her beneath the incognito which she had assumed, and which she appeared desirous to retain.[39]

The Chevalier married her, and after a long residence in Louisiana, most of which was passed in Mobile, she followed him to France, and thence to the Island of Bourbon, whither he was sent with the rank of major.[40] In 1765 she became a widow, and went to Paris with a daughter born in Mobile. In 1771 her mysterious and romantic life was terminated in the midst of the most abject poverty.*

* Judge Martin, in his *History of Louisiana*, 1: 231–32, states that this woman was an imposter, and that she imposed on the credulity of Chevalier D'Aubant and many others; that she had once been attached to the wardrobe of the princess whom she assumed to represent, and that a few years before the declaration of American Independence a similar imposition was practiced upon the people of the southern British provinces by a female, driven by her misconduct from the post of maid of honor to Princess Matilda, sister of George III. She was convicted at Old Bailey and transported to Maryland. Before the expiration of her time she affected her escape, traveled through the provinces of Virginia and the Carolinas, personating the princess, and

king's armies and "Commander of the Military Order of St. Louis," but not as much as "the misfortune of being out of favor with your Royal Highness." ***MPA: FD*****, 3: 307–09.**

[37] Departing from Whydah, a slave-trading post on the Gulf of Benin, the ***Africaine*** **with 182 slaves and the** ***Duc du Maine*** **with 349 slaves arrived in Louisiana in March 1721. The** ***Néréide*** **arrived with 294 slaves from Cabinda (Angola). While Bienville and Delorme praised the captain of the** ***Néréide*** **for the quality of his cargo, they complained that the captains of the other two ships had purchased adults who were old and sick. Of the 825 who arrived on these three ships, 537 were sold to individuals and 35 died after landing—leaving 253 to the company. Some were put to work on boats on the river, and some were sent to New Orleans for construction projects and were gradually sold. Gwendolyn Midlo Hall,** ***Africans in Colonial Louisiana: The Development of Afro-Creole Culture in the Eighteenth-Century*** **(Baton Rouge: Louisiana State University Press, 1992), 59–64.**

[38] In 1718, Peter the Great declared his son Alexis Petrowitz "unworthy of succession we do deprive him, our said son Alexis, for his crimes and unworthiness, of the succession after us to the throne of Russia." Sir John Barrow, ***The Life of Peter the Great*** **(Edinburgh: William P. Nimmo & Co., 1883), 401–14. See Alexis Petrowitz, et al,** ***The tryal of the Czarewitz, Alexis Petrowitz, who was condemn'd at Petersbourg, on the 25th of June 1718, for a design of rebellion and treason against the life of the Czar his father*** **(London: Printed for James Crockett, 1725).**

[39] Despite the romanticism associated with this story, there is no evidence to support its accuracy.

An ordinance decreed that the council should meet daily at New Biloxi; that merchandise should be sold at that place, Mobile, and New Orleans, at fifty per cent profit on the manufacture of France, seventy per cent among the Natchez and Yazoos, one hundred per cent among the Arkansas, and fifty per cent among the Alabamas and Muscogees, on account of the proximity of Fort Toulouse to the English influence, with which the French company were anxious successfully to compete. Another ordinance declared that Negroes should be sold to the inhabitants at the price of the *piece de Inde*, or six hundred and sixty livres,* in three annual installments, to be paid in tobacco or rice. If, after the second year, the debtor failed to pay, the company could take the Negro if not paid for during the third year. If the effects of the debtor failed to discharge the whole debt, the company could then take his body. It also declared that leaf tobacco delivered at the warehouses of New Biloxi, New Orleans and Mobile should command the price of twenty livres per quintal; rice, twelve livres per quintal; wine, one hundred and twenty livres a hogshead; and a quarter of brandy, the same price. It also declared that Louisiana should, hereafter, be formed into nine divisions—New Orleans, Biloxi, Mobile, Alabama, Natchez, Yazoo, Natchitoches, Arkansas, and Illinois; that in the chief town of each there should be a commandant and a judge, from whose decisions an appeal could be had to the Superior Council of New Biloxi.[41]

STATE OF THE COLONY AT THE CLOSE OF 1721.

"In the vessels which the India Company has sent thither from the 25th October 1717 to May 1721, there have emigrated, on the forty-three belonging to it, and in the squadron of M. de Saujon,[42] 7020

These, with the 400 who were already there, ... 400

7420

Of this number those who have died, deserted, or returned to France, ... 2000

5420

To them the number of colonists is added, to which may be set down about 600 Negroes."[43]

From this statement it appears that the colony of Louisiana had really begun to prosper, but many impediments still retarded its more rapid advance, among which may be enumerated its expenses, which, for the year 1721, amounted to 474,274 livres. The company, too, issued an ordinance

levying contributions upon the credulity of the inhabitants. She was at length arrested in Charleston, prosecuted and publicly whipped.

* Equal to one hundred and seventy-six dollars.

Captain Jean-Baptiste Benoist Aubert is Pickett's Chevalier d'Aubont and served as commandant at Fort Toulouse in 1759. Jean-Bernard Bossu encountered Aubert at Mobile, and he was present at Toulouse when Montault de Montberaut turned over command of the post to Aubert in April 1759. Bossu, *Travels in the Interior of North America,* 130, 151–54; Thomas, *Fort Toulouse,* xxxii.

[40] Peter Hamilton's exhaustive research on colonial Mobile refutes this marriage scenario of Aubert (D'Aubont) and the fake princess in Mobile. His research in the Mobile church records verify that Aubert's wife was Louise Marguerite Bernoudy—not someone posing as Charlotte Christine of Brunswick-Lüneburg (1694–1715). She died in Mobile in 1759 and was buried "in the church." Hamilton, *Colonial Mobile,* 194.

[41] Pickett continues to paraphrase from Charles Gayarré's *Histoire de la Louisiane,* published in 1846. However, the Company increased the basic cost of a *piece d'Inde* (i.e., a black male slave) from 600 *livres* to 1,000 *livres* near the end of 1722. Gayarré, *Histoire de la Louisiane,* 1: 183–85; Giraud, *Company of the Indies, 1723–1731,* 125.

prohibiting the inhabitants from selling their Negroes to the Spaniards, or to other foreigners, or taking them out of the colony, under a severe penalty, besides their confiscation.

Bienville, writing from Mobile, acquainted the minister with the difficulty of discharging the cargoes of vessels upon the low shores of New Biloxi, and again brought to his consideration the superior advantages of New Orleans, for the capital of the colony. One more councilor was added to the Superior Council, which now consisted of Buslé, Fazende, Perry, Guillet, and Masclary.[44] Two hundred and fifty Germans, commanded by the Chevalier D'Arensbourg, a Swedish officer, arrived at Mobile, with whom came Marigny de Mandeville, who had obtained, in France, the Cross of St. Louis and the command of Fort Condé, in Mobile.[45] This was by far the best fort in the colony, and was now rapidly drawing to a state of completion; it was built of brick, with four bastions, and a great many casements for soldiers.† The vessel which brought over these Germans bore the distressing news that the great royal bank, which Law, the Scotch financier, under the auspices of the Duke of Orleans, had established in France, had utterly failed; that Law had left the country in disgrace, and that the people whom he had induced to take stock, found it worthless and themselves ruined. All Paris was in a ferment, and no one could anticipate an end to the long train of commercial evils which the scheming ability of this Scotchman had engendered.[46] The company which had charge of Louisiana, and indeed the chief inhabitants of the province, were soon made to feel the explosion of this once powerful and popular institution. Louisiana, herself, was deeply involved in the failure, and her inhabitants now feared that the government of France would abandon them. But some supplies continued to arrive, in spite of the panic which pervaded the mother country. Duvergier, who had been appointed director-general and commander of the marine, disembarked at Pensacola, bearing the Cross of St. Louis for Boisbriant, St. Denis and Chateaugué.[47]

The failure of the Royal Bank of France, and the distress which it produced in all parts of that kingdom, caused Louisiana, for a time, to be so neglected, that the inhabitants became destitute of provisions. The officers were obliged to dismiss the garrisons of Mobile and Biloxi, and send them to the Choctaw

† Mr. E. T. Wood, of Mobile, who wrote a history of that place, embodied in a directory, which he published, says that when Fort Condé (which was also called Fort Charlotte by the British after they took possession of it) was pulled down by the Americans some years after the place fell into their hands, that the corner-stone was found with the date of 1717, distinctly engraved upon it.

[42] Bienville reported to the Council of the Navy in April 1720 that De Saujon (also Saugeon) had attempted to confront a Spanish fleet that threatened the Louisiana colony. *MPA: FD,* 3: 294–95.

[43] The 1721 census numbers are from Charles Gayarré's *Histoire de la Louisiane.* Gayarré, *Histoire de la Louisiane,* 1: 185.

[44] Apparently Sieur Guillet died sometime after arriving in Louisiana. Jacques de la Chaise, special commissary of the king, blamed Bienville and Delorme for causing his death "by subjecting him to ridicule." Bienville refused to accept Sieur Masclary as councilor to the Superior Council because he struck Sieur Desbrosses, "formerly keeper of the warehouse," with a stick. *MPA: FD,* 2: 305, 330–32.

[45] Charles Frederick D'Arensbourg (1694–1777), a native of Stettin, Pomerania (Poland), enlisted in the Swedish military in 1711 and reached the rank of captain before resigning in May 1719. He originally signed up with the Company of the Indies on 9 January 1721 and was commissioned a "reform captain"—a captain at half-pay. However, in March 1721 he was chosen to lead a contingent of 300 German settlers to Louisiana,

arriving aboard the *Portefaix* at Biloxi on 4 June 1721. Reinhart Kondert, *Charles Frederick D'Arensbourg and the Germans of Colonial Louisiana* (Lafayette: Center for Louisiana Studies, University of Louisiana-Lafayette, 2008), 1–2, 7, 9, 11, 14–17.

[46] John Law's bank, now France's national bank, had issued more and more paper money to fund purchases of Mississippi Company stocks. At the height of the stocks' value, investors started selling their shares for gold and this inflation bubble burst in May 1720 when the Royale Bank did not have the specie to support the paper money in circulation. By November the shares were worthless and Law fled France in December. This fiasco became known as the "Mississippi Bubble." James Howard Kunstler, *The Long Emergency: Surviving the End of Oil, Climate Change, and Other Converging Catastrophes of the Twenty-first Century* (New York: Grove, 2005), 196–99.

[47] Pickett's timeline and disembarkation port—Pensacola—for Sieur Duvergier appears to be incorrect. Duvergier and Delorme write Bienville on 20 August 1721 from New Biloxi asking him to protect them from the colonists who have refused to acknowledge their authority as commissaries and directors on behalf of the king. Without his assistance, they threaten to resign from their offices "that we may not be exposed to the insults and fury of those who publicly inveighed against us." *MPA: FD*, 3: 309–10.

[48] In his letter of 15 December 1721 to the Council of the Navy, Bienville gives a different version of the revolt at Fort Toulouse. He reported that three sergeants and five soldiers had deserted at Mobile and traveled to Fort Toulouse "where they corrupted two-thirds of the garrison who rose in revolt, seized

Nation to procure subsistence among the Indians, while many of the colonists abandoned their homes and betook themselves to the sea-side to procure a scanty living upon fish and oysters. It was even worse at some of the more distant posts, particularly at Fort Toulouse, upon the Coosa, now in Alabama. There, the soldiers were tortured by famine, and corrupted by some British traders, who induced them to desert and fly to Charleston. The command consisted of a captain, a lieutenant, an ensign, a corporal and twenty-six soldiers. When the latter had perfected their mutiny, the planning of which had occupied several days, they rose upon the officers, one morning, about breakfast. Captain Marchand was instantly slain. Lieutenant Villemont and Ensign Paque made their escape through a port-hole of one of the bastions, and fled to the Hickory Ground, a town of Creek Indians, three miles above, on the east bank of the Coosa, and embracing the lower suburbs of the modern city of Wetumpka. Here Villemont made irresistible appeals to the warriors to march against the mutineers. He, at the same time, dispatched Paque across the river to the town of Coosawda, where then lived the great chief, Big Mortar, whom the ensign succeeded in enlisting in the cause of the king. In the meantime, the mutineers, having killed the captain, intimidated the corporal, who now joined them in a general pillage of the fort. They appropriated to themselves the money and clothing of the officers, leaving only the sacred wardrobe of the priest, a Jesuit father, whom they did not molest. The magazine, constructed of brick, was forced open, and arms and ammunition taken from it.* The storeroom was plundered of its contents, consisting of a very limited supply of flour and meat. The mutineers, after partaking of a hearty repast, marched off to the Red Warrior's Bluff, †where they crossed the Tallapoosa and took up the line of march for Charleston. Villemont, with the Indian force which he had speedily raised, marched against them. A battle ensued at the ford of Line Creek, which now divides the modern counties of Montgomery and Macon. Sixteen of these

* Some of the brick of this magazine are yet to be seen lying about the ruins of old Fort Toulouse, now called old Fort Jackson, and I have several of them in my house, taken from that place.

† The Red Warrior's Bluff of that day is the present Grey's Ferry.

deserters were slain. They all fought with the desperation of tigers.* The others, except two who escaped, were taken prisoners, and Villemont, who was wounded in the action, marched with them back to Fort Toulouse. Here the fort was found to be in a very solitary condition, being inhabited only by the Jesuit father, who had resolved to remain until he could get a favorable opportunity of going to Mobile, not believing that the brave and indefatigable Villemont could subdue the deserters; the body of the unfortunate Captain Marchand had already been interred by him and some Indians. Villemont, the next day, obtained some canoes and placed the deserters in them, in charge of an Indian guard, at the head of which was Ensign Paque, who conveyed them to Mobile, where they were shortly afterwards executed.[48] Villemont and the priest were solitary inmates of Fort Toulouse for several months, until another garrison was sent up the river. The lieutenant had, however, many Indian warriors lying around the fort, who were ready to aid him if he had been attacked by the English, who were anxious to occupy this post.†

Fortunately, a vessel arrived with provisions for the king's troops. She brought the news that the Regent had entrusted the affairs of the colony to the management of three commissioners: Ferrand, Faget and Machinet.[49] A detailed account of a great hurricane which swept along the coast of Louisiana, of the desertion of soldiers, sailors and workmen, and a recommendation to allow free passage to all who might choose to return to France, as a remedy for desertions generally, formed the subjects of a communication addressed by Delorme to the minister.[50] While the distressing situation of the colony rendered the offices of the three commissioners by no means sinecures, embarrassments were further produced by a war

* The bones of these sixteen Frenchmen lay, for many years, very near the house which Walter B. Lucas afterwards erected, and where he for a long time kept entertainment.

† The revolt of the garrison of Fort Toulouse, upon the Coosa, is mentioned by Gayarré, in his *Histoire de la Louisiane*, 1: 190; by La Harpe, 261; by Judge Martin, 2: 239; but I have derived the chief facts from Indian traditions handed down by General Alexander McGillivray, a very great Indian chief of mixed blood, who was the grandson of the unfortunate Captain Marchand, who was killed upon this occasion.

the officers whom they bound, and set off for Carolina." They had unbound the officers before they left, who pursued them with "two hundred and fifty men," attacked them and killed eighteen, "and took the rest alive, whom the officers tried before a court martial." The surviving sergeant was "tomahawked immediately and all the others were to be convicts for life." Captain François Marchand de Courcelle was not killed, served at Mobile, and appears in French documents for years after this event. Ibid., 316–17, 400, 475; Thomas, *Fort Toulouse*, 19–20.

[49] Pickett's three commissioners cannot be identified. The minutes of the Superior Council are signed by Bienville, Puslé, Fazend, Fleuriau, and Perry into June 1724. They are joined by Jacques de la Chaise as commissary general and by Du Saunoy as a commissary before his death in 1724. *MPA: FD*, 2: 325; ibid., 3: 345–85, 392–413.

[50] The first recorded hurricane to strike New Orleans occurred at about 10:00 p.m. on 23 September 1722, causing wide spread damage and destroying thirty-four houses and public buildings, including a church, parsonage, and hospital. Although the Mississippi River was low, the storm surge raised the river by eight feet, flooding much of the four-year old community. Ten flatboats were broke up "and sunk together with launches, canoes, and pirogues." Two ships—the *Santo Christe* and the *Neptune*—and two smaller boats were badly damaged and driven ashore. "Journal of Diron D'Artaguiette," in *Travels in the American Colonies*, ed. Newton Mereness (New York: Macmillan Company, 1916), 24; David M. Ludlum, *Early American Hurricanes, 1492–1870* (Boston: American Meteorological Society, 1963), 60–61

[51] Pierre Michel was an employee of the Superior Council who was approved to convert the company's paper notes to cards that would be accepted in payments at company warehouses. In 1725 he demanded an

which the Natchez had begun, and the worthlessness of the paper money hitherto used in the colony, to remedy which *cards* were substituted after the notes were suppressed. One Michel, of Mobile, was the person appointed to engrave these cards.[51]

The new commissioners who had succeeded to the directorship of the company, readily acceded to the long cherished wish of Bienville, to remove the seat of government to New Orleans and it was accordingly established at that place.* The population of New Orleans, at that period numbered only two hundred souls, who occupied a hundred huts and cabins![52]

The commissioners of the company, in a new code of regulations, declared that Negroes should hereafter be sold at six hundred and seventy-six livres,† payable in one, two or three years, either in rice or tobacco. The province was divided into nine districts, civil and military, as follows: Alabama, Mobile, Biloxi, New Orleans, Natchez, Yazoo, Illinois, Wabash, Arkansas and Natchitoches. There was a commandant and a judge appointed for each of these districts. Three great ecclesiastical districts were also formed. The first was entrusted to the Capuchins, and extended from the mouth of the Mississippi River to Illinois. The barefooted Carmelites were stationed at Fort Toulouse, upon the Coosa River, at Mobile and at Biloxi, while the Jesuits labored upon the Wabash and Illinois. Churches and chapels were ordered to be constructed, for many of the colonists had been forced to worship in the open air, around crosses, the bottom parts of which were buried in the ground![53]

Bienville restored Pensacola to the Spaniards in pursuance of orders from his government; for Spain and France had concluded a peace. In a dispatch to the minister, he stated that his allies,—the Choctaws,—had destroyed three towns of the Chickasaws, and had brought to him one hundred prisoners and four hundred scalps! Bienville communicated this intelligence with much apparent *gusto*, accompanied with the remark that "this important result was obtained without risking the life of a single Frenchman."[54]

Although the colonists often existed in a state of penury and want, they did not abandon their passion for *gambling*, which was

* Charles Gayarré, *Histoire de la Louisiane*, 1: 166–93; Bénard de la Harpe, *Journal historique de l'établissement des Français à la Louisiane*, 144–289; Martin, *History of Louisiana*, 1: 218–44.

† Equal to one hundred and sixty-nine dollars.

increase in salary or permission to return to France, and the Council granted him a salary increase to one thousand livres per year. *MPA: FD*, 3: 335–36, 482

[52] Writing from Fort Louis on 12 June 1718, Bienville had reported to the Council of the Marine on the founding of New Orleans and clearing the entrance to the Mississippi. Nearly five years later—1 February 1723—he declared the successful transfer of the capital from New Biloxi to New Orleans and proclaimed: "It appears to me that a better decision could not have been made." Ibid., 228, 343.

[53] The Carmelite order had a center at Mobile with responsibility at large for the Alabamas, but a new ordinance issued in December 1722 partitioned the colony into two ecclesiastical jurisdictions. The district assigned to the Carmelites was added to the district of the Capuchins. However, for the most part, the Jesuits served the missions at the interior posts from about 1725 through 1763. Thomas, *Fort Toulouse*, 39–42; Jean Delanglez, *The French Jesuits in Lower Louisiana, 1700–1763* (1935; reprint; New York: AMS Press, 1974), 95–100.

[54] In April 1722, Bienville acknowledged the order to restore the fort at Pensacola to the Spaniards, and seven months later he confirmed that the formal transfer took place on 26 November 1722. In the same letter of 1 February 1723, he reported the Choctaw successes over the Chickasaw. *MPA: FD*, 3: 321–22, 342–43.

[55] In his extensive report of 6 September 1723 to the Directors of the Company of the Indies, Commissary General Jacques de la Chaise declared the Swiss company useless to the company. They were characterized as "mutinous and difficult" troops and only 80 remained in 1725 out of the

carried to such an extent that the government issued an ordinance against all games of chance. An ordinance was also promulgated against the trade which many of the colonists were illicitly conducting with the Natchez Indians. The month of September terminated with a dreadful tornado, which prostrated the church, the hospital, and thirty houses in New Orleans; destroyed the crops upon the Mobile and Pearl rivers; dismantled the shipping in the different ports, and left the whole colony in a condition of wretchedness and famine. Added to all this, a whole company of Swiss infantry, which had embarked at Biloxi for New Orleans, rose upon the captain of the vessel and compelled him to carry them to Charleston.[55] Yet, in the midst of all these calamities, the indefatigable Bienville departed from New Orleans with seven hundred men to punish the Natchez, who had recently killed several Frenchmen. He returned after having terminated the second war with them, by procuring the heads of the principal offenders.[56] Notwithstanding the important services which this great man was continuing to render the colony, his relentless enemies sought every opportunity to make him odious to the ruling powers of France. Aspersed in dispatches, which were speedily borne across the ocean, he was at the same moment insulted at home by libellous placards in the streets. At length he received orders to sail for France, to answer the charges against him, leaving the command to Boisbriant until his return.[57]

But before Bienville embarked upon the broad Atlantic, he issued the celebrated "Black Code," in the name of the king. It declared that all Jews should leave the colony; that all slaves should be instructed in the Roman Catholic religion; that no other religion should be tolerated in the colony; that if the owners of Negroes were not true Catholics, their slaves should be confiscated; and that the white inhabitants should not enter into marital relations with Negroes, nor live with them in a state of concubinage.[58]

The "Black Code" contained many other articles in relation to the government of slaves—some of which were precisely like those now in force in the southwestern states of the present confederacy. The year 1724 was remarkable for arbitrary edicts; but there was one which was beneficial. The inhabitants had become so accustomed to rely upon France for all the necessaries of subsistence, that valuable cattle, sent to Louisiana for purposes of propagation,

original 145 recruits. An ordinance for the dismissal of the Swiss company was issued on 26 July 1725. Ibid., 310–11, 535; Giraud, *Company of the Indies, 1723–1731*, 231–32, 232 n. 100.

[56] The Third Natchez War occurred in the fall of 1723 when friction over attacks on livestock and resentment over the French concept of land ownerships caused a harsh reaction by Bienville. On 29 September 1723, Bienville left New Orleans with four boat loads of soldiers and rendezvoused with Choctaw and Yazoo warriors. His force burned the huts and temples in the White Apple, Jenzenaque, and Grigra districts in two days, and he demanded the heads of six—including Old Hair of White Apple—and a free black man. Apparently, the head of Old Hair was taken back to New Orleans as proof of a successful expedition. *MPA: FD*, 2: 374, 421–22; ibid., 3: 385–87; Barnett, *Natchez Indians*, 90–94.

[57] Bienville and his brother Chateaugué, the King's Lieutenant, sailed to France aboard the *Gironde*, arriving at Lorient on 20 August 1725. Both brothers were effectively removed from their offices by the Company of the Indies. Their cousin Boisbriant was dismissed from his office in 1726, and their nephews, Gilles-Augustin and Pierre Benoit de Noyan, were deprived of their infantry ranks. *MPA: FD*, 3: 494; Giraud, *Company of the Indies, 1723–1731*, 33–37, 51–52.

[58] The Code Noir promulgated by Bienville in 1724 was an extension of the 1685 edict issued by King Louis XIV. While some articles provided elementary protection for slaves, they provided for capital punishment for striking a master, corporal punishment for thefts, and even allowed for mutilation for certain repeated acts. The slaves were "regarded as moveable property"

were always killed and devoured. An ordinance was issued by the king, at the request of the Superior Council, punishing with *death* every person who should intentionally kill or severely wound any horse or horned animal which did not belong to him. De la Chaise, nephew of the famous father of that name, who was the confessor of Louis XIV, presided over the council, which was now held monthly in the town of New Orleans.[59]

But to return to Bienville. That brave man appeared at Paris, after a prosperous voyage, and submitted an eloquent memoir to the king in justification of his official conduct. It also contained a history of the services to which he had, from the commencement of the colonial establishment, devoted a period of twenty-five years. But, in spite of his true exposition of his arduous labors spent in the insalubrious forests of America, among savages and reptiles, and in spite of the exertions made by his friends, both in France and Louisiana, to re-establish him in the confidence of the king, he was removed from office, and Périer nominated governor of Louisiana. The government did not stop here. Chateaugué, the brother of Bienville, lost the post of royal lieutenant, while two nephews of Bienville, named Noyan, one a captain and the other an ensign, were cashiered without any just cause. Thus the influence of Bienville was overthrown in Louisiana. In the meantime the new governor arrived in New Orleans.[60]

Governor Périer, in a dispatch to the minister, employed this language in reference to the encroachments of the English of South Carolina:[61] "The English continue to urge their commerce into the very heart of the province. Sixty or seventy horses, laden with merchandise, have passed into the country of the Chickasaws, to which nation I have given orders to plunder the English of their goods, promising to recompense them by a present. As yet I have heard nothing from that quarter. It appears that a league was formed among all the Indian nations of their neighborhood to attack the Spanish settlements. Whereupon the governor of Pensacola requested assistance from me. Having no news from Europe, I thought it was for our interest not to have the English so

to be divided at their master's death to his lawful heirs. Giraud, *Company of the Indies, 1723–1731*, 322–26.

[59] In the minutes of the "Council of War" on 23 November 1723, Bienville and others agreed that if anyone was "bold enough in the future to kill any horned cattle or horses belonging to the French" the commandant of the post "shall bring the heads of those who have killed them." *MPA: FD*, 3: 387.

[60] Bienville produced a lengthy "Memoir on Louisiana" which summarized his service in the colony and was apparently completed after his return to France. Although basically exonerated, Bienville remained in France for nearly seven years. Ibid., 495–540.

[61] Although Etienne de Périer arrived at New Orleans on 15 March 1727 without advance notice, he first presented his credentials to the Superior Council and then "had myself received by the troops and the inhabitants." On his first exposure to a calumet ceremony, he reported the Indians showed "great satisfaction at my arrival" and "have told me in their harangues that Mr. Bienville deceived them, that they were glad that he had not returned." Ibid., 2: 542–43, 545.

[62] Charles Gayarré first proffered this story in his *Histoire de la Louisiane* published in 1846. Based on modern research, it appears the shipment of a group of chaste *filles à la cassette* —casket girls—is more legend and myth than fact. Elizabeth Shown Mills, a renowned Southern genealogist, states: "I have never found evidence of the alleged 1728 shipment that is widely bandied about as the 'first' to come." Further she notes that after 1724 the only ship to Louisiana in that decade with single women aboard landed in 1727 and carried Ursuline nuns. She adds that a more accurate translation of cassette is small trunk and not casket. "Were They Really Casket Girls?" *Ancestry Magazine* 27 (November-December 2009), 26; Zug, "Lonely Colonist Seeks Wife," 115, 122–23; *MPA: FD*, 2: 553.

near us, and in consequence, informed the Tallapoosas,* who were before Pensacola, that if they did not immediately retire I should attack them with those nations who were friendly to us. I also gave notice to the Alabamas, that if they attacked the Spaniards, who were our friends, I should be compelled to assist the latter. But I should have taken care not to have interfered with the natives who were friendly to us, in order that I might not commit myself with regard to the English. This had a good effect. The governor thanked me, informing me that war was declared in Europe. Notwithstanding, I shall indirectly assist the Spanish until I receive other orders from your highness, at the same time taking the liberty to represent that our sole effort should be to prevent the English from approaching us.

"I have caused all the nations, from the Arkansas to the mouth of the river, to make peace with each other. There remain at variance only the Choctaws and Chickasaws, who have a discussion concerning a chief of the latter nation who was killed by the former. I shall go to Mobile to settle their affairs, and shall take measures with them to prevent the English from entering our territory during the ensuing year, and by degrees to abolish the custom which they have formed, of trading for all the deer skins obtained by the Indians, in order that the latter may not be obliged to trade with the English to get rid of them."

A vessel belonging to the company arrived with quite a number of young girls, who, unlike many others who had been sent to Louisiana, had not been taken from the house of correction. They were each provided with a little chest, containing articles of apparel, and from this circumstance they were called girls *de la cassette*—girls of the chest.[62] They were placed under the surveillance of the Ursuline nuns until they could be disposed of by marriage.†

* Meaning the Creeks, who lived upon the Tallapoosa River.

† Charles Gayarré, *Histoire de la Louisiane*, 1: 193–235.

Chapter VII

TERRIBLE MASSACRE AT NATCHEZ

The colony of Louisiana was now in a flourishing condition; its fields were cultivated by more than two thousand Negroes; cotton, indigo, tobacco and grain were produced; skins and furs of all descriptions were obtained in a traffic with the Indians; and lumber was extensively exported to the West India islands. The province was protected by eight hundred troops of the line; but the bloody massacre of the French population of Fort Rosalie, at the Natchez, arrested these rapid strides of prosperity, and shrouded all things in sadness and gloom.[1] Our library contains many accounts of this horrible affair, which harmonize very well with each other; but in reference to the causes which led to it, more particularly, we propose to introduce the statement of Le Page Du Pratz, who was residing in Louisiana at the time.[2] We give his account, in his own faithful style:[3]

"Chépart had been commandant of the post of the Natchez, from which he was removed on account of some act of injustice. Governor Périer, but lately arrived, suffered himself to be prepossessed in his favor, on his telling him that he had commanded that post with applause, and thus he obtained the command from Périer, who was unacquainted with his character.[4] This new commandant, on taking possession of his post, projected the forming of one of the most eminent settlements of the whole colony. For this purpose he examined all the grounds unoccupied by the French, but could not find anything that came up to the grandeur of his views. Nothing but the village of the White Apple, a square league, at least, in extent, could give him satisfaction, and there he resolved immediately to settle.[5] This ground was distant from the fort about two leagues.* Conceited with the beauty of his

* "The site of the White Apple village was about twelve miles south of the present city of Natchez, near the mouth of Second Creek, and three miles east of the Mississippi. The site was occupied by the plantation of Colonel Anthony Hutchins, an early emigrant to

[1] Fort Rosalie had been constructed in 1716, and Bienville in his "Memoir on Louisiana" reported that it needed repairs. The former commandant Charles Henri Desliettts di Tonti told the administrative council on 23 March 1725 that the Natchez fort was "completely decayed" and needed to be replaced. *MPA: FD*, 2: 381–82, 419–21; ibid., 3: 512.

[2] Antoine-Simone Le Page Du Pratz spent eight years among the Natchez. Arriving in January 1720, he had been authorized to secure two large concessions for Marc-Antoine Hubert and the Company of the West. He also purchased a cabin and six acres from a Natchez Indian, who remained his neighbor during his residence. After his departure in 1728, he served as the director of the royal plantation until the post was abolished and he returned to France in May 1734. His *Histoire de la Louisiane,*

project, the commandant sent for the Sun of that village, to come to the fort; upon his arrival, he told him, without ceremony, that he must look out for another ground to build his village on, as he, himself, resolved, as soon as possible, to build on the village of the Apple, and that he must directly close the huts and retire somewhere else. The better to cover his design, he gave out that it was necessary for the French to settle on the banks of the rivulet, where stood the great village and the abode of the Great Sun. The commandant, doubtless, supposed that he was speaking to a slave, whom we may command in a tone of absolute authority. But he knew not that the natives of Louisiana are such enemies to a state of slavery that they prefer death itself; above all, the Suns, accustomed to govern despotically, have still a greater aversion to it.

"The Sun of the Apple made answer, that his ancestors had lived in that village for as many years as there were hairs in his double cue, and, therefore, it was good they should continue there. Scarce had the interpreter explained this answer to the commandant, when the latter fell into a passion, and, threateningly, told the Sun, that if he did not quit his village, in a few days, he might repent it. The Sun replied: 'When the French came to ask us for land, to settle on, they told us there was land enough still unoccupied for them, and that the same sun would enlighten them all, and all would walk in the same path.' He wanted to proceed further, in justification of what he alleged, but the commandant, in a passion, said he was resolved to be obeyed. The Sun, without discovering any emotion or passion, then withdrew, only observing that he was going to assemble the old men of his village to hold a council upon the affair.

"In this council it was resolved to represent to the commandant, that the corn of all the people of their village was already shot a little out of the earth, and that all their hens were laying their eggs. That if they quitted their village now, the chickens and corn would be lost both to the French and to themselves. The commandant turned a deaf ear to these views, and threatened to chastise the chiefs if they did not comply with his orders, in a very short time, which he named. The Sun reported this answer to his council, who debated the question. But the policy of the old men was, that they should be allowed to stay in their village until harvest, and until they had time to dry their corn and shake out the grain. In consideration of this

Florida. All vestiges of Indian industry have disappeared except some mounds in the vicinity." Monette, *History of the Discovery and Settlement of the Valley of the Mississippi*, 1: 258.

published in 1758, provides the most accurate details of the events leading up to the Natchez rebellion of 1729. Barnett, *Natchez Indians*, 78–82; Le Page du Pratz, *History of Louisiana*, xx-xxiii.

[3] Apparently Pickett used a copy of first English translation of Le Page du Pratz' *The History of Louisiana, or of The Western Parts of Virginia and Carolina*, published in London in 1774. It was originally published in French in three volumes. Antoine-Simon Le Page Du Pratz, *Histoire de la Louisiane*, 3 vols. (Paris: Chez de Bure, 1758).

[4] Chépart arrived in Louisiana in 1719 as a lieutenant, and he was promoted to captain in 1723 and named commandant at Fort Rosalie in 1728. Contrary to Du Pratz, he had not been removed, but he had been reprimanded by Périer in New Orleans for mistreating Lieutenant Dumont de Montigny. Dumont de Montigny, *Memoir*, 213–24, 421; Barnett, *Natchez Indians*, 101.

[5] White Apple village was one of five Natchez districts after 1700 that also included Flour, Tiou, Grigra, and Jenzenaque (also called The Hickories or The Walnuts). It was also called White Earth or White Apple village by different sources. Barnett, *Natchez Indians*, 41–43.

privilege, they each proposed to pay the commandant, in so many moons, a basket of corn and a fowl. The cupidity of the commandant made him accept the proposition with joy, and blinded him with regard to the consequences of his tyranny. He, however, pretended that he agreed to the offer out of favor, to do a pleasure to a nation so beloved, and who had ever been good friends of the French. The Sun appeared highly satisfied to have obtained a delay sufficient for taking the precautions necessary to the security of the nation, for he was by no means the dupe of the feigned benevolence of the commander.

"The Sun, upon his return, again caused the council to be assembled. He stated to them that it was necessary to avail themselves of this time, in order to withdraw themselves from this proposed payment and tyrannic domination of the French, who grew dangerous in proportion as they multiplied. That the Natchez ought to remember the war made upon them, in violation of the peace concluded between them. That this war, having been made upon their village alone, they ought to consider of the surest means to take a just and bloody vengeance. That this enterprise being of the utmost importance, it called for much secrecy, for solid measures, and for much policy. That it was proper to cajole the French chief more than ever, and that the affair required reflection before it was proposed to the Grand Sun.[6]

"In the meantime, the old men had come to the determination, not only to revenge themselves, but to engage in the entire destruction of all the French in the province. When, therefore, the council again met, the most venerable man rose and delivered the following speech:

"'We have a long time been sensible that the neighborhood of the French is a greater prejudice than benefit to us. We, who are old, see this—the young see it not. The wares of the French yield pleasure to the youth, but to what purpose is it, except to debauch the young women, and taint the blood of the nation, and make them vain and idle? The young men are in the same condition—they must work themselves to death to maintain their families and please their children. Before the French came among us, we were men, content with what we had, and walked with boldness every path. Now we go groping about, afraid of meeting briars. We walk like slaves, which we shall soon be, since the French already treat us as if we were such. When they are sufficiently strong, they will no longer dissemble. For the least fault of our young people, they will then tie them to a post and whip them. Have they not already done so to one of our young men, and is not death preferable to slavery? What wait we for? Shall we suffer the French to multiply till we are no longer in a condition to oppose them? What will the other nations say of

[6] Le Page Du Pratz's Grand Sun is the new Great Sun of the Natchez, succeeding his uncle the Great Sun who died in 1728. Young and inexperienced, he was overwhelmed and controlled by the anti-French forces determined to wreak vengeance on the French occupying their homeland. George Edward Milne, "Picking up the Pieces: Natchez Coalescence in the Shatter Zone," in *Mapping the Shatter Zone: The Colonial Indian Slave Trade and Regional Instability in the American South*, ed. Robbie Ethridge and Sheri M. Shuck-Hall (Lincoln: University of Nebraska Press, 2009), 404–06.

the Natchez, who are admitted to be the greatest of all Red men? Let us set ourselves at liberty. From this very day let our women get provisions ready, without telling them the reason. Go and carry the pipe of peace to all the nations of this country. Tell them that the French, being stronger here than elsewhere, enslave us the more; but when they spread out, they will treat all nations in like manner. That it is their interest to join us to prevent so great a misfortune. That they have only to join us, to cut off the French to a man, in one day and in one hour!'"

Here the speaker continued his address and exhorted them to be prepared to fall upon the French at nine o'clock, on the morning of the day when they were to deliver to the commandant the corn and chickens, and that the warriors were to carry with them their arms, as if going to hunt. They unanimously approved of his views, and pledged themselves to carry them out. Du Pratz continues: "Notwithstanding the profound secrecy observed by the Natchez, the council held by the Suns and aged nobles gave the people great uneasiness, unable, as they were, to penetrate into the matter. The female Suns had alone, in this nation, the right to demand why they were kept in the dark in this affair. The young grand female Sun was a princess scarce eighteen. None but the The Stung Arm [Tattooed Arm], a woman of great wit, and no less sensible of it, could be offended that nothing was disclosed to her.[7] In effect, she made known to her son her displeasure at this reserve with respect to herself. He replied that the several deputations were made in order to renew their good intelligence with the other nations, to whom they had not, in a long time, sent an embassy, and who might imagine themselves slighted by such neglect. This feigned excuse seemed to appease the princess, but not quite to rid her of all her uneasiness, which, on the contrary, was heightened upon the return of the embassies, when she saw the Suns assemble in secret council together. She was filled with rage, which would have broken out, if her prudence had not set bounds to it. Happy it is for the French that she imagined herself neglected. I am persuaded that the colony owes its preservation to the vexation of this woman, rather than to any affection she entertained for the French, as she was now far advanced in years, and her French gallant long since dead. In order to get to the bottom of the secret, she prevailed on her son to accompany her on a visit to a relation that lay sick at the village of the Meal, and leading him the most distant and retired route, took occasion to reproach him with the secrecy he and the other Suns observed with regard to her. She insisted on her right, as a mother, and her privilege as a princess, adding, that although the world and herself, too, had told him he was the son of a Frenchman, yet her own blood was much dearer to her than

[7] In his original narrative, Pickett used Le Page Du Pratz's "Stung Arm" in referring to the female Sun who attempted to warn the French. Modern scholars have identified her as Tattooed Arm. Her brothers—Tattooed Serpent and Great Sun—had died in 1725 and 1728, respectively, putting much younger Suns in power and allowing the unchecked aggression of the anti-French factions. Barnett, *Natchez Indians,* 88, 95–98, 100, 104; Milne, "Picking up the Pieces," 388–90, 404–07.

[8] The young Great Sun (Grand Sun) may have been the son of the Jesuit Jean-Francois Buisson de Saint-Cosme, who had been murdered by Chitimachas in 1706. Milne, "Picking up the Pieces,"388–90, 396.

that of strangers; that he need not apprehend she would ever betray him to the French, against whom, she said, you are plotting.[8]

"The son, stung with these reproaches, told her it was unusual to reveal what the old men of the council had once resolved upon, and as he was Grand Sun, he ought to set a good example in this respect; but seeing you have guessed the whole affair, I need not inform you further. You know as much as I do myself, only hold your tongue."

"She replied that she was in no pain to know against whom he had taken his precaution, but as it was against the French, this was the very thing that made her apprehensive he had not taken his measures aright, in order to surprise them, as they were a people of great penetration, although their commandant had none. Her son told her that she had nothing to apprehend as to the measures taken; that all the nations had heard and approved their project, and promised to fall upon the French in their neighborhood on the same day with the Natchez; that the Choctaws had resolved to destroy all the French lower down and along the Mississippi, up as far as the Tunicas, to which last people, he said, we did not send, as they and the Oumas are too much wedded to the French. He at last told her that the bundle of rods* lay in the temple, on the flat timber. The Stung Arm [Tattooed Arm], being informed of the whole design, pretended to approve it, and leaving her son at ease, henceforward was only solicitous how she might defeat this barbarous design. The time was pressing, and the term fixed for the execution was almost expired. Unwilling to see the French cut off to a man in one day, she resolved to apprise them of the conspiracy through some young women who loved them, enjoining them never to tell from whom they had their information.†

* By all ancient and modern Indians, rods or sticks were used to assemble the nation together. A chief was accustomed to send forth a warrior with a bundle of sticks, and as he journeyed towards the towns to which he was dispatched he would throw away one of these sticks at the close of each day. When he gave them to the party to whom he was bearing them, the latter also continued, at the close of every day, to throw away a stick. The chiefs who sent these sticks also kept a duplicate number, and each day threw away one, so that those at a distance and those at the council house would meet together on the same day, when the last stick had been thrown away. In modern times sending sticks was called "sending out the broken days."

† "The Sieur de Massé, ensign of the garrison of the fort at Natchez, received advice by a young Indian girl who loved him. She told him, crying, that her nation was to massacre all the French. M. de Massé, amazed at this discourse, questioned his mistress. Her simple answers and her tender tears left him no room to doubt of the plot. He went immediately to give Chépart intelligence of it, who put him under arrest for giving false alarm." Bossu, *Travels Through . . . Louisiana* (London: 1771), letter 3, addressed to the Marquis de L'Estrade, 1: 62.

She desired a soldier, whom she met, to tell the commandant that the Natchez had lost their senses, and to desire him to be upon his guard. The soldier faithfully performed his commission, but the commandant treated him as a coward and a visionary,—caused him to be placed in irons, and declared he would never take any steps towards repairing the fort, as the Natchez would then imagine he was a man of no resolution.

"The Stung Arm [Tattooed Arm] fearing a discovery, notwithstanding her precaution and the secrecy she enjoined, repaired to the temple and pulled some rods out of the fatal bundle. Her design was to hasten the time fixed, to the end that such Frenchman as escaped the massacre might apprise their countrymen, many of whom had informed the commandant, who placed seven of them in irons. The female Sun, seeing the time approaching, and many of those punished whom she had charged to acquaint the governor, resolved to speak to the under-lieutenant, but to no better purpose. Notwithstanding all these warnings, the commandant went out into the night before on a party of pleasure, with some other Frenchmen, to the grand village of the Natchez, without returning to the fort till break of day, where he had no sooner arrived than he was admonished to be upon his guard. Still stimulated with his last night's debauch, he added imprudence to neglect, and dispatched his interpreter to demand of the Grand Sun whether he intended to kill the French. The Grand Sun, though but a young man, knew how to dissemble, and spoke in such a manner to the interpreter as to allay his suspicions and fears."*

We propose now to introduce the statement of Father Le Petit, who at the time of its occurrence was residing in New Orleans, respecting the massacre itself. He was a learned and pious Jesuit priest.[9] The following is his letter to Father D'Avaugour, procurator of the missions in North America.[10]

"AT NEW ORLEANS, 12TH JULY, 1730.[11]

"My Reverend Father,—the Peace of our Lord be with you:

After having given you an imperfect idea of the character and customs of the Natchez Indians, I proceed, my reverend father, as I have promised you, to enter upon a detailed account of their perfidy and treason. It was on the second of December of the year 1729, that we learned they had surprised the French, and had massacred almost all of them. This sad news was first brought

Bossu also states that Chépart, becoming enraged at Dumont de Montigny, the second in command, for remonstrating with him against his tyranny towards the Natchez in the commencement of the spring, placed that excellent officer and faithful historian in irons. Bossu, *Travels*, 1: 48.

* Le Page Du Pratz, *Louisiana*, 79–90. In copying this author's statement, I have occasionally omitted some redundancies and uninteresting detail.

[9] Father Mathurin Le Petit played an important role in the life of the church in Louisiana. He served among the Choctaws until he was promoted as the Jesuit Superior at New Orleans. He delivered the sermon at the dedication of the new convent of the Ursuline nuns in New Orleans on 17 July 1734. Delanglez, *French Jesuits in Lower Louisiana*, 150–51, 247, 321, 453–56; Marie Madeline Hachard, *Voices From an Early American Convent: Marie Madeline Hachard and the New Orleans Ursulines, 1727–1760*, ed. Emily Clark (Baton Rouge: Louisiana State University, 2007), 124–26.

[10] Father D'Avaugour served as the Jesuit Procurator in Paris for the missions of the Society of Jesus in North America, taking care of their material needs by sending them food, clothing, money, and other supplies. He signed a contract in August 1724 with the Company of the Indies that provided for the maintenance of Jesuit missionaries in their new district in Louisiana. Delanglez, *French Jesuits in Lower Louisiana*, 99–100.

[11] While Pickett does not cite his source of Father Mathurin Le Petit's letter, it can be found in *The Jesuit Relations and Allied Documents: Travels and Explorations of the*

Jesuit Missionaries in New France, 1610–1719, **ed. Reuben Gold Twaites, 73 vols. (Cleveland: Burrows Brothers, 1896–1901), 68: 121–223.**

[12] Father Philibert de Vianden, a Capuchin missionary, provided a register of the French massacred at the post of the Natchez, dated 6 June 1730, which listed 144 men, 35 women, and 56 children. Other documents gave slightly different totals. ***MPA: FD,*** **1: 122–26; "Data Concerning the Natchez Massacre, 1729–1730,"** ***Louisiana Historical Quarterly*** **1 (January 1918): 126–31.**

to us by one of the planters, who had escaped their fury. It was confirmed to us on the following day by other French fugitives, and finally, some French women, whom they had made slaves, and were forced afterwards to restore, brought us all the particulars.

"At the first rumor of an event so sad, the alarm and consternation was general in New Orleans. Although the massacre had taken place more than a hundred leagues from here, you would have supposed that it happened under our own eyes. Each one was mourning the loss of a relative—a friend—or some property; all were alarmed for their own lives, for there was reason to fear that the conspiracy of the Indians had been general. This unlooked for massacre began on Monday, the 28th of October, about nine o'clock in the morning. Some cause of dissatisfaction which the Natchez thought they had with the commander, and the arrival of a number of richly laden boats for the garrison and the colonists, determined them to hasten their enterprise, and to strike their blow sooner than they had agreed with the other confederate tribes.* First they divided themselves, and sent into the fort, into the village, and into the two grants, as many Indians as there were French in each of these places. Then they feigned that they were going out for a grand hunt, and undertook to trade with the French for guns, powder and ball, offering to pay them as much, and even more, than was customary; and, in truth, as there was no reason to suspect their fidelity, they made, at the time, an exchange of their poultry and corn for some arms and ammunition, which they used advantageously against us. It is true that some expressed their distrust, but this was thought to have so little foundation that they were treated as cowards, who were frightened at their own shadows. They had been on their guard against the Choctaws; but as for the Natchez, they had never distrusted them, and they were so persuaded of their good faith that it increased their hardihood. Having thus posted themselves in different houses, provided with the arms obtained from us, they attacked, at the same time, each his man; and in less than two hours they massacred more than two hundred of the French. The best known are M. De Chépart, commander of the post; M. Du Codère, commander among the Yazoos; M. Des Ursins; Messieurs De Kolly, father and son; Messieurs De Longraye, Desnoyers, Bailly, &c.[12]

"The Father Du Poisson had just performed the funeral rites of his associate, the Brother Crucy, who had died very suddenly of a sunstroke; he was on his way to consult Governor Périer, and to adopt with him proper measures

* Father Le Petit is mistaken as to the causes which hastened the massacre. It will be recollected that Le Page Du Pratz told us that Stung [Tattooed] Arm pulled out several sticks from the bundle, and it was this which brought on the time sooner.

to enable the Arkansas to descend the banks of the Mississippi, for the accommodation of the voyagers.[13] He arrived among the Natchez on the 26th of November, that is, two days before the massacre. The next day, which was the first Sunday of Advent, he said mass in the parish, and preached in the absence of the curé. He was to have returned in the afternoon to his mission among the Arkansas, but he was detained by some sick persons, to whom it was necessary to administer the sacraments. On Monday, he was about to say mass, and to carry the holy sacrament to one of those sick persons whom he had confessed, the evening before, when the massacre began. A gigantic chief, six feet in height, seized him, and having thrown him to the ground, cut off his head with blows of a hatchet.[14] The father, in falling, only uttered these words: 'Ah, my God! Ah, my God!' M. Du Codère drew his sword to defend him, when he was himself killed by a musket ball from another Indian, whom he did not perceive.

"The barbarians spared but two of the French, a tailor and a carpenter, who were able to serve their wants.[15] They did not treat badly, either the Negro slaves or the Indians who were willing to give themselves up; but they ripped up the abdomen of every pregnant woman, and killed almost all those who were nursing their children, because they were disturbed by their cries and tears. They did not kill the other women, but made them their slaves, and treated them with every indignity during the two or three months that they were their masters. The least miserable were those who knew how to sew, because they kept them busy in making shirts, dresses, &c. The others were employed in cutting and carrying wood for cooking, and in pounding the corn of which they made their *sagamité*. But two things, above all, aggravated the grief and hardness of their slavery; it was, in the first place, to have for masters, those same persons whom they had seen dipping their cruel hands in the blood of their husbands; and in the second place, to hear them continually saying that the French had been treated in the same manner at all the other posts, and that the country was now entirely freed from them.

"During the massacre, the Sun, or the Great Chief of the Natchez, was seated quietly under the tobacco shed of the company. His warriors brought to his feet the head of the commander, about which they ranged those of the principal French of the post, leaving their bodies a prey to the dogs, the buzzards, and other carnivorous birds.* When they were assured that no other

* Dumont de Montigny, in his *Mémoires historiques sur la Louisiane*, 2: 145–46, thus speaks of Chépart: "In the midst of this general massacre of the French, Chépart revived, as if Providence had wished to reserve him as a witness of the destruction of so many inhabitants who would not have perished but for his folly. He recognized it, at last, but

[13] Brother Crucy traveled from France with thirteen Ursuline nuns and several Jesuits, including Father Doutreleau and Father Tartarin. After a five month voyage on the *Gironde*, they arrived at Dauphin Island on 23 July 1727. He and Father Paul Du Poisson served a mission on the Arkansas River, where he died of a sunstroke. Delanglez, *French Jesuits in Lower Louisiana*, 234, 251, 251 n. 14, 379; Hachard, *Voices From an Early American Convent*, 52–53, 63, 65–7.

[14] Father Paul Du Poisson (1692–1729) and Brother Crucy served as missionaries among the Indians on the Arkansas River, where he had conducted Crucy's funeral service. He was returning from New Orleans, where he met with Périer, when he stopped at Fort Rosalie on 26 November 1729. Delanglez, *French Jesuits in Lower Louisiana*, 250–52, 251 n. 14.

[15] The two Frenchmen spared were Mayeux—identified as a carter—and Le Beau, a tailor. Mayeux and his oxen and wagon transported the booty ransacked from the fort and French habitations, and Le Beau was employed in altering the pilfered clothing to fit the new owners. Barnett, *Natchez Indians*, 105.

[16] Madame Desnoyers and her children were held as captives by the Great Sun. Her husband Laurent Desnoyers managed the Terre Blanche concession before his death. Dumont de Montigny, *Memoir*, 234, 243, 246.

Frenchmen remained at the post, they applied themselves to plunder the houses, the magazines of the Indian company, and all the boats which were still loaded by the banks of the river. They employed the Negroes to transport the merchandise, which they divided among themselves, with the exception of the munitions of war, which they placed, for security, in a separate cabin. While the brandy lasted, of which they found a good supply, they passed their days and nights in drinking, singing, dancing, and insulting, in the most barbarous manner, the dead bodies and the memory of the French. The Choctaws and the other Indians being engaged in the plot with them, they felt at their ease, and did not at all fear that they would draw on themselves the vengeance which was merited by their cruelty and perfidy. One night, when they were plunged in drunkenness and sleep, Madame Desnoyers wished to make use of the Negroes to revenge the death of her husband and the French, but she was betrayed by the person to whom she confided her design, and came very near being burned alive.[16]

"Some of the French escaped the fury of the Indians by taking refuge in the woods, where they suffered extremely from hunger and the effects of the weather.* One of them, on arriving here, relieved us of a little disquietude we felt in regard to the post we occupy among the Yazoos, which is not more than forty or fifty leagues above the Natchez by water and only fifteen to twenty by land. Not being able to endure the extreme cold from which he suffered, he left the woods under cover of the night, to go and warm himself in the house of a Frenchman. When he was near it he heard the voices of Indians, and deliberated whether he should enter. He determined, however,

too late, and raising himself from his seat, instead of taking his gun and placing himself on the defense, he fled to his garden, where he gave a whistle, in order to call the soldiers of the garrison. But they were no more. He could see all around him, by the sides of the palisades, which enclosed his garden, the earth strewn with their carcasses. At the same time he was surrounded by the savages, who breathed nothing more than his death, while none of them wished to lay hands upon him. They considered him as a "dog," unworthy of being killed by a brave man, and they made the chief stinking-man come, who killed him with the stroke of a club."

* In a dispatch made by Governor Périer to the Minister in France, dated the 18th March, 1730, he says: "A general assassination of the French ensued, which occupied but little time; one single attack terminated it with the exception of the house of M. la Loire des Ursins, in which there were eight men, six of whom were killed, and the remaining two escaped during the night—the Indians having been unable to seize them during the day. M. la Loire des Ursins was mounted on a horse when the attack commenced, and being unable to regain his house, he defended himself until he fell, having killed four Indians. Thus it has cost the Natchez only twelve men to destroy two hundred and fifty of our people." Gayarré, *Histoire de la Louisiane*, 1: 242–43.

to do so, preferring rather to perish by the hands of these barbarians than to die of famine and cold. He was agreeably surprised when he found these savages ready to render him a service, to heap kindness upon him, to commiserate him, to console him, to furnish him with provisions, clothes and a boat to make his escape to New Orleans. These were the Yazoos, who were returning from chanting the calumet, at Oumas. The chief charged him to say to M. Périer that he had nothing to fear on the part of the Yazoos, that 'they would not lose their spirit,'—that is, that they would always remain attached to the French, and that he would be constantly on the watch with his tribe, to warn the French boats that were descending the river, to be on their guard against the Natchez.

"We believed, for a long time, that the promises of this chief were very sincere, and feared no more Indian perfidy for our post among the Yazoos. But learn, my reverend father, the disposition of these Indians, and how little one is able to trust their words, even when accompanied by the greatest demonstrations of friendship. Scarcely had they returned to their own village, when loaded with presents they received from the Natchez, they followed their example and imitated their treachery. Uniting with the Corroys, they agreed together to exterminate the French.[17] They began with Father Souel, the missionary of both tribes, who was then living in the midst of them, in their own village. On the 11th of December, Father Souel was returning in the evening from visiting the chief, and while in a ravine, received many musket balls, and fell dead on the spot. The Indians immediately rushed to his cabin to plunder it. His Negro, who composed all his family and all his defense, armed himself with a woodcutter's knife to prevent the pillage, and even wounded one of the savages. This zealous action cost him his life, but happily less than a month before he had received baptism, and was living in a most Christian manner.[18]

"These Indians, who even to that time seemed sensible of the affection which their missionary bore them, reproached themselves for his death, as soon as they were capable of reflection; but returning again to their natural ferocity, they adopted the resolution of putting a finishing stroke to their crime, by the destruction of the whole French post. 'Since the Black Chief is dead,' said they, 'it is the same as if all the French were dead; let us not spare any.' The next day they executed their barbarous plan. They repaired, early in the morning, to the fort, which was not more than a league distant, and whose occupants supposed, on their arrival, that the Indians wished to chant the calumet to the Chevalier de Roche, who commanded that post, in the absence of M. de Codère.[19] He had but seventeen men with him, who had

[17] Father Le Petit's Corroys are the Koroas (also Coroas), a small tribe located on the Yazoo River near the Tunica and Yazoo. Swanton, *Indian Tribes of the Lower Mississippi Valley*, 330–32.

[18] Father Jean Souel (1695–1729) was the Jesuit missionary at the Yazoo post. While Le Petit records his death on 11 December, a Frenchwoman taken prisoner by the Yazoos reported he was killed the week before Christmas, putting his death on 18 December 1729. Delanglez, *French Jesuits in Lower Louisiana*, 252–54, 252 n. 21.

[19] Chevalier de Roche had been left in charge of Fort St. Pierre, a small French post among the Yazoo villages. His death and the slaughter of the other soldiers at the post occurred on 18 December 1729. *MPA: FD*, 1: 99; Mary Ann Wells, *Native Land: Mississippi 1540–1798* (Jackson: University Press of Mississippi, 1994), 123–24.

[20] Father Doutreleau traveled to French Louisiana with Brother Crucy and other Jesuit priests, arriving at Dauphin Island on 23 July 1727. He departed New Orleans in September 1727 for his assignment to begin a mission on the Wabash. Delanglez, *French Jesuits in Lower Louisiana*, 161, 255–57; Hachard, *Voices From an Early American Convent*, 43, 53, 63, 65–67.

no suspicion of any evil design on the part of the savages, and were, therefore, all massacred, not one escaping their fury. They, however, spared the lives of four women and five children, whom they found there, and whom they made slaves. One of the Yazoos having stripped the missionary, clothed himself in his garments, and shortly after announced to the Natchez that his nation had redeemed their pledge, and that the French, settled among them, were all massacred. In this city, there was no longer any doubt on that point, as soon as they learned what came near being the fate of Father Doutreleau. This missionary had availed himself of the time when the Indians were engaged in their winter occupations, to come and see us, for the purpose of regulating some matters relating to his mission. He set out on the first of this year, 1730, and not expecting to arrive at the residence of Father Souel, of whose fate he was ignorant, in time to say mass, he determined to say it at the mouth of the Little Yazoo River, where his party had cabined.

"As he was preparing for the sacred office, he saw a boat full of Indians landing; they demanded from them of what nation they were. 'Yazoos, comrades of the French,' they replied, making a thousand friendly demonstrations to the voyagers, who accompanied the missionary, and presenting them with provisions. While the father was preparing his altar, a flock of bustards passed, and the voyagers fired at them the only two guns they had, without thinking of reloading, as mass had already commenced. The Indians noted this, and placed themselves behind the voyagers, as if it was their intention to hear mass, although they were not Christians. At the time the father was saying the *Kyrie Eleison*, the Indians made their discharge; the missionary, seeing himself wounded in his right arm, and seeing one of the voyagers killed at his feet, and the four others fled, threw himself on his knees to receive the last fatal blow, which he regarded as inevitable. In this posture he received two or three discharges, but although the Indians fired while almost touching him, yet they did not inflict on him any new wounds. Finding himself then, as it were, miraculously escaped from so many mortal blows, he took to flight, having on still his priestly garments, and without any other defense than entire confidence in God, whose particular protection was given him, as the events proved. He threw himself into the water, and after advancing some steps, gained the boat, in which two of the voyagers were making their escape. They had supposed him to be killed by some of the many balls which they had heard fired on him. In climbing up into the boat, and turning his head to see whether any one of his pursuers was following him too closely, he received, in the mouth, a discharge of small shot, the greater part of which were flattened against his teeth, though some of them entered his gums and remained there for a long time. I have myself seen two of them. Father Doutreleau, all wounded as he was, undertook the duty of steering the boat, while his two companions placed themselves at the oars; unfortunately one of them at setting out had his thigh broken by a musket ball, from the effects of which he has since remained a cripple.[20]

"As soon as they found themselves freed from their enemies, they dressed their wounds as well as they could, and for the purpose of aiding their flight from that fatal shore they threw into the river everything they had in their boat, preserving only some pieces of raw bacon for their nourishment. It had been their intention to stop, in passing, at the Natchez, but having seen that the houses of the French were either demolished or burned, they did not think it advisable to listen to the compliments of the Indians who, from the bank of the river, invited them to land. They placed a wide distance between them as soon as possible, and thus shunned the balls which were ineffectually fired at them. It was then that they began to distrust all the Indian nations and, therefore, resolved not to go near the land until they reached New Orleans; and supposing that the savages might have rendered themselves masters of it, to descend even to the Balize, where they hoped to find some French vessel provided to receive the wreck of the colony. I cannot express to you, my reverend father, the great satisfaction I felt at seeing Father Doutreleau, his arm in a scarf, arrive (in New Orleans) after a voyage of more than four hundred leagues, all the clothes he had on having been borrowed, except his cassock. I placed him immediately in the hands of Brother Parisel, who examined his wounds and who dressed them with great care and speedy success.[21] The missionary was not yet entirely cured of his wounds when he departed to act as chaplain to the French army, as he had promised the officers, in accordance with their request.

"Knowing as you do, my reverend father, the vigilance and the oversight of our governor, you can well imagine that he did not sleep in this sad crisis in which we now found ourselves. We may say, without flattery, that he surpassed himself by the rapid movements he made, and by the wise measures he adopted to revenge the French blood which had been shed, and to prevent the evils with which almost all the posts of the colony were threatened. As soon as he was apprised of this unexpected attack, by the Natchez Indians, he caused the news to be carried to all the posts, and even as far as the Illinois, not by the ordinary route of the river, which was closed, but on one side by the Natchitoches and the Arkansas, and the other by Mobile and the Chickasaw. He invited the neighbors, who were our allies, and particularly the Choctaws, to avenge this outrage. He furnished arms and ammunition to all

[21] Apparently, the Jesuit Brother Parisel (also Parizel) was considered a surgeon or had some medical training. He served as the master of ceremonies at the dedication of the new convent of the Ursuline nuns in New Orleans on 17 July 1734. Delanglez, *French Jesuits in Lower Louisiana,* 257; Hachard, *Voices From an Early American Convent,* 43, 124–26.

the houses of the city and to the plantations. He caused two ships, that is, the *Duc de Bourbon* and the *Alexandre*, to ascend the river as far as the Tunicas. These ships were like two good fortresses against the insults of the Indians, and in case of attack, two certain asylums for the women and children. He caused a ditch to be dug entirely around the city, and placed guardhouses at the four extremities. He organized for its defense many companies of city militia, who mounted guard during the whole night. As there was more to fear in the grants and in the plantations than in the city, he fortified them with the most care. He had good forts erected at Chapitoulas, Cannes, Brules, Altemands, Bayogoulas, and Pointe Coupée.

"At first, our governor, listening only to the dictates of his own courage, adopted the design of placing himself at the head of the troops, but it was represented to him that he ought not to quit New Orleans, where his presence was absolutely necessary; that there was danger of the Choctaws determining to fall upon the city, if it should be deprived of its troops; and the Negroes, to free themselves from slavery, might join them, as some had done with the Natchez. Moreover, he could feel perfectly easy with regard to the conduct of the troops, as the Chevalier De Loubois, with whose experience and bravery he was well acquainted, had been appointed to command them.[22] Whilst our little army was repairing to the Tunicas, seven hundred Choctaws, mustered and conducted by M. Le Sueur, marched towards the Natchez.[23] We were informed, by a party of these people, that the Natchez were not at all on their guard, but passed all their nights in dancing. The Choctaws took them, therefore, by surprise, and made a descent on them, the 27th of January, at the break of day. In less than three hours they had delivered fifty-nine persons, both women and children, with the tailor and carpenter, and one hundred and six Negroes or Negro women, with their children. They made eighteen of the Natchez prisoners, and took sixty scalps.[24] They would have take more, if they had not been intent on freeing the slaves, as they had been directed. They had but two men killed and seven or eight wounded. They encamped, with their prizes, at the grant of St. Catherine, in a mere park enclosed with stakes. The victory would have been complete, if they had waited the arrival of the French army, as had been agreed upon by their deputies.*

"The Natchez, seeing themselves attacked by the formidable Choctaws,

* Monette, Martin, and other modern authors, state that Le Sueur advanced from the Tombigbee, with six hundred warriors, and near Pearl River increased his force to twelve hundred. Arriving near Natchez, and learning the unguarded condition of the Indians of that place, the Choctaws fell upon them, in spite of the entreaties of Le Sueur, who urged them to await the arrival of the French army.

[22] Chevalier de Louboey (Loubois) was in command of a detachment of troops and colonists at Point Coupée, forty leagues above New Orleans, when Périer ordered him to coordinate an attack on the Natchez with the Choctaws on 19 February 1730. *MPA: FD*, 1: 65–66.

[23] Apparently Jean Paul Le Sueur had organized the Choctaw force of five hundred warriors who struck the Natchez in January 1730. His mother was Bienville's first cousin. Diron d'Artaguette wrote to Count de Maurepas and recommended that he be granted a lieutenancy based on this expedition. Ibid., 60–61, 60 n. 2.

[24] In his letter of 9 February 1730 to Count de Maurepas, Diron d'Artaguette gives slightly different numbers. He reports the Choctaw "killed or captured about one hundred and fifty Natchez," recovered fifty-four French women and children, and found "about fifty Negroes." Ibid., 61.

regarded their defeat as certain, and shutting themselves up in two forts, passed the following nights in dancing their death dance. In their speeches, we heard them reproaching the Choctaws for their perfidy in declaring in favor of the French, contrary to the pledge they had given, to unite with them for our destruction. Three days before this action, the Sieur Mesplet landed at the Natchez with five other Frenchmen; they had volunteered to M. De Loubois, to carry to the Indians negotiations for peace, that they might be able, under this pretext, to gain information with regard to their force and their present situation. But, in descending from their boat, they encountered a party who, without giving them time to speak, killed three of their men and made the other three prisoners. The next day they sent one of these prisoners with a letter, in which they demanded, as hostages, the Sieur Broutin,[25] who had formerly been commander among them, and the chief of the Tunicas. Besides, they demanded, as the ransom for the women, children and slaves, two hundred guns, two hundred barrels of powder, two thousand gun flints, two hundred knives, two hundred hatchets, two hundred pickaxes, five hogsheads of brandy, twenty casks of wine, twenty barrels of vermilion, two hundred shirts, twenty pieces of limbourg, twenty pieces of cloth, twenty coats with lace on the seams, twenty hats bordered with plumes, and a hundred coats of a plainer kind. Their design was to massacre the French, who should bring these goods. On the very same day, with every refinement in cruelty, they burned the Sieur Mesplet and his companion.

"On the 8th February, the French, with the Tunicas and some other small tribes from the lower end of the Mississippi, arrived at the Natchez, and seized their temple, dedicated to the Sun. The impatience and impracticability of the Choctaws, who, like all these Indians, are capable of striking only one blow and then disperse—the small number of French soldiers, who found themselves worn down by fatigues—the want of provisions, which the Indians stole from the French—the failure of ammunition, with which they were not able to satisfy the Choctaws, who wasted one part of it, and placed the other in reserve to be used in hunting—the resistance of the Natchez, who were well fortified, and who fought in desperation—all these things decided us to listen to the propositions which the besieged made, after the trenches had been opened for seven days. They threatened, if we persisted in the siege, to burn those of the French who remained; while, on the other hand, they offered to restore them, if we would withdraw our seven pieces of cannon. These, in reality, for want of a good gunner, and under present circumstances, were scarcely in a fit state to give them any fear.[26]

"These propositions were accepted, and fulfilled on both sides. On the 25th

[25] Ignace François Broutin, a captain who came to Louisiana in 1720, served under the engineers, designed the Ursuline Convent in New Orleans, and worked on the defenses around New Orleans following the Natchez rebellion in 1729. He later became engineer-in-chief for Louisiana and served in this position until his death in 1751. Samuel Wilson, Jr., "Colonial Fortifications and Military Architecture in the Mississippi Valley," in *The French in the Mississippi Valley*, ed. John Francis McDermott (Urbana: University of Illinois Press, 1965), 115–18.

[26] According to Perier's report to Count de Maurpas, Louboey (Loubois) arrived at Natchez on 12 February 1730 and his troops did not finish their trenches in front of the Natchez positions until the twentieth. Louboey negotiated the surrender of "most our wives and children and our Negroes who were two essential points" and "ended the siege of the Natchez after six days of open trench and ten days of cannonading." *MPA: FD*, 1: 68–70.

of February, the besieged faithfully restored all that they had promised, while the besiegers retired with their cannon to a small fort which they had hastily built on the Escore, near the river, for the purpose of always keeping the Natchez in check, and ensuring a passage to the voyagers. Governor Périer gave the command of it to M. D'Artaguette, as an acknowledgement of the intrepidity with which, during the siege, he had exposed himself to the greatest dangers, and everywhere braved death.[27]

"Before the Choctaws had determined to fall upon the Natchez, they had been to them to convey the calumet, and were received in a very novel manner. They found them and their horses adorned with chasubles and drapery of the altars; many wore patterns about their necks, and drank, and gave to drink, of brandy in the chalices and pyx. And the Choctaws themselves, when they had gained these articles by pillaging our enemies, renewed this profane sacrilege, by making the same use of our ornaments and sacred vessels in their dances and sports.[28] We were never able to recover more than a small portion of them."*

Here Father Le Petit discontinues his detail of the Natchez War, and ends his letter with some remarks upon the character of the Illinois and several other tribes of Indians. He appears to have deemed it a very great outrage that the Natchez thus prostituted their holy vessels and priestly robes, yet he announces that the French army "arrived at the Natchez and seized their temple, dedicated to the Sun," which they, no doubt, also destroyed. The religion of the Natchez was as sacred to the Natchez, as the religion of the Roman Catholics was to the good Father Le Petit.[29]

The Natchez chiefs proposed to surrender more than two hundred prisoners, if the French commander would remove his artillery and withdraw his forces, or else all the prisoners would be consumed by fire. Loubois, to save the lives of these miserable captives, consented, yet with the secret intention of wreaking his vengeance upon the Indians as soon as the prisoners were in his possession. But he was sadly disappointed, for the Indians, suspecting treachery on his part, took advantage of the suspension of hostilities, and one night evacuated the fort, and succeeded in gaining the opposite shore of the Mississippi with all their women and children. The prisoners were found in the fort, agreeable

* *The Early Jesuit Missions in North America*, compiled and translated from the letters of the French Jesuits, with notes by the Reverend William Ingraham Kip, M. A., Corresponding Member of the New York Historical Society (New York: 1846). See part 2: 267–300.

[27] Louboey constructed a fort on the bank of the Mississippi as a position to regroup and to deliver a final blow against the Natchez. Périer praised the service of D'Artaguette in "detached service" and the volunteers led by Charles Frederick d'Arensbourg and "Mr. De Laye." He also reported the "surprising valor" of fifteen Negroes who had been "permitted to take arms." Ibid., 70.

[28] Actually this was only a party of twenty Choctaw under the chief from Cushtusha, who had been given "a letter last autumn" by Diron d'Artaguette in Mobile "to carry to the French chief of the Natchez." When the Choctaw arrived at the Natchez villages, they discovered the slaughter of the French, and they were given booty and urged to attack the French. Returning to Cushtusha, they encountered the Choctaws with Le Sueur and told what they had encountered. Ibid., 96–99.

[29] Father Mathurin Le Petit's letter reflects his deep bitterness at the "dark treachery" of the Indians who assaulted and slaughtered the French at Natchez. He was writing Father D'Avaugour to make him aware of "the character of these perfidious savages." Twaites, *Jesuit Relations*, 68: 203.

to the treaty. Loubois was astonished at the dexterous maneuver, but he saw the folly of pursuing the foe, who had now secreted themselves in the vast swamps. He began the erection of a terraced fort upon the verge of the bluff, and leaving there a garrison of one hundred and twenty men, returned with his troops and the rescued prisoners to New Orleans.[30]

The largest portion of the Natchez, conducted by the Great Sun, established themselves "upon the lower Washita [Ouachita], on the point between the Little River and the Washita,[31] just below the mouth of Little River, where the Washita assumes the name of Black River."* Here the Natchez placed about four hundred acres of land in a state of defense by the erection of large and small mounds and extensive embankments. Other portions of this tribe sought an asylum among the Chickasaws, while others wandered still further east, and took up their abode upon a portion of the territory now embraced in Talladega County, Alabama. The English traders in Carolina, it is said, rejoiced in the destruction of the French, and many of them, then residing among the Chickasaws, urged those people and the refugee Natchez to engage in a vigorous warfare, and not only to defend their soil but to exterminate the French. In the meantime Governor Périer made preparations to follow up the Natchez upon the Ouachita, but his exertions were, to some extent, defeated by a serious Negro insurrection, which occurred upon the plantations in the vicinity of New Orleans.[32]

However, upon the 10th of August one of the company's ships arrived at the Balize with some troops and supplies. Although mortified that the reinforcement was so small, Périer added them to the colonial troops, and, procuring a Choctaw force at Mobile, left New Orleans with an army of six hundred and fifty, which was increased on the way to one thousand by Indian allies. Reaching the mouth of the Black River, they at length came in sight of the enemy's stronghold. The troops were disembarked, the fort invested, and for three days the besieged made a spirited resistance, when they made propositions which Périer rejected. At length the Indians consented to surrender the Great Sun and one war chief, which the governor refused. They then consented to surrender sixty-five men and about two hundred women and children, upon condition that their lives be spared. Périer once more opened his artillery upon them, but a heavy rain, which continued until night, silenced his batteries. When night set in the Natchez began to escape from their defenses, and make their way up the river in the midst of a tempest of wind and rain. The Indian allies went in pursuit, and returned with one

[30] During the night of 25–26 February 1730, the Natchez escaped their fortified positions and crossed the Mississippi into Arkansas. Le Page Du Pratz claims the Natchez had retreated "about sixty leagues from the mouth of the Red River." Barnett, *Natchez Indians*, 116–17; Le Page Du Pratz, *History of Louisiana*, 92–93.

[31] The Ouachita (Washita) River runs south and east through Arkansas into Louisiana where it joins the Tensas River to form the Black River near modern Jonesville, Louisiana. Glen Gore, "Ouachita River," *The Arkansas Encyclopedia of History and Culture*, http://www.encyclopediaofarkansas.net.

[32] In his letter of 10 April 1730 to Count de Maurepas, Périer gives a follow-up scenario of the Third Natchez War, their escape across the river, and his military preparations around New Orleans. He does not mention a slave insurrection but reports that "all the settlers in general have been inclined to do all that I have ordered them to do, both for their security and for the public works." *MPA: FD*, 1:117–22.

* Monette, *History of the Discovery and Settlement of the Valley of the Mississippi*, 1: 267.

hundred prisoners. The next day Périer demolished the outworks of the fort and began his voyage to New Orleans, where he arrived, in due time, with four hundred and twenty-seven captives of the Natchez tribe.[33] At the head of them were the Great Sun and several principal chiefs. Soon afterwards they were all shipped to Santo Domingo and sold as slaves.* Those of the Natchez who escaped during the stormy night rallied again and collected in one body near the French settlements on Red River. They then marched and attacked the post in a most furious manner, but St. Denis, the commandant, an intrepid officer, repelled them with the loss of ninety-two braves, including all their chiefs. The remnant escaped by flight.[34] This was the closing scene in the Natchez drama, and ended the existence of these brave Indians as a distinct tribe.†

* "The French army re-embarked and carried the Natchez as slaves to New Orleans, where they were put in prison; but afterwards, to avoid the infection, the women and the children were disposed of on the King's plantation and elsewhere. Among these women was the female Sun, called the Stung [Tattooed] Arm, who then told me all she had done in order to save the French. Sometime after, these slaves were embarked to Santo Domingo, in order to root out that nation in the colony; and thus that nation, the most conspicuous in the colony and the most useful to the French, was destroyed." Le Page Du Pratz, 95.

† In relation to the massacre at Natchez, and the final defeat of those Indians, I have carefully consulted the following authorities: Le Page Du Pratz, *Louisiana* (London: 1774); Bossu *Travels Through . . . Louisiana* (London: 1771), vol. 1; *Mémoire historique et politique sur la Louisiane, par m. de Vergennes, ministre de Louis XVI* (Paris: 1802); [Baudry des Lozières], *Voyage à la Louisiane et sur le continent de l'Amérique septentrionale, fait dans les années 1794 à 1798* (Paris: 1802); M. Dumont de Montigny, *Mémoires historiques sur la Louisiane* (Paris: 1753); Kip, *Early Jesuit Missions* (New York: 1846); Gayarré, *Histoire de la Louisiane*; Martin, *History of Louisiana* (New Orleans: 1827); Stoddard, *Sketches, Historical and Descriptive, of Louisiana* (Philadelphia: 1812); Monette, *History of the Discovery and Settlement of the Valley of the Mississippi* (New York: 1846).

[33] Pickett's dates are off by one year. Périer's army made contact with the Natchez on 20 January 1731 west of Fool River, a tributary of the Tensas River near modern Sicily Island, Louisiana. The French soldiers laid siege to their fortification, referred to as Fort Valeur in Périer's official report of his campaign, using muskets, cannons, and wooden mortars to launch grenades. On 25 January, Périer received the surrender of four hundred and fifty women and children and forty-five men as a steady downpour continued into the night. Finally on 29 January, Périer loaded his boats with his prisoners and returned to New Orleans. An untold number of Natchez had escaped during the siege. Barnett, *Natchez Indians*, 122–25; John A. Green, "Governor Perier's Expedition Against the Natchez Indians: December 1730-January 1731," *Louisiana Historical Quarterly* 19 (July 1936), 547–77; Le Page Du Pratz, *History of Louisiana*, 94–95.

[34] On 5 October 1731, a band of approximately one hundred Natchez attacked the Natchitoches settlers, forcing them to seek refuge at Fort Jean Baptiste. Messengers were sent out to the surrounding villages and some three hundred and fifty Caddos came to aid the French. The siege was broken on 14 October and the Caddos pursued the Natchez east of the Ouachita River, killing forty and capturing a similar number. *MPA: FD*, 4: 105; Burton and Smith, *Colonial Natchitoches*, 11.

Chapter VIII

THE ENGLISH IN GEORGIA

We have shown that South Carolina had been established as a colony for some years, that its seat of government was at Charleston, and that its inhabitants, in endeavoring to extend the English trade to all the western Indian nations as far as the Mississippi River, had many conflicts and difficulties with the French, who occupied the territory of Alabama. They were also constantly opposed by the Spaniards of the Floridas. In order to interpose a barrier to these foes, as well as to protect the citizens from the attacks of the Creek Indians, the king of England and the British Parliament listened to a proposition of a great philanthropist, to plant a colony upon the western bank of the Savannah River. His motives, purely noble and disinterested, originated in a desire to ameliorate the condition of many unfortunate people in England. To carry out his plans of humanity, he was willing that the king should blend with them politic measures for the advancement of this, his most Southern province, and it was determined that "silk, wine and oil should be cultivated most abundantly."

James Oglethorpe, a descendant of one of the oldest and most influential families of England, was born on the 22nd of December 1696, and after graduating at Oxford University, was commissioned an ensign in the British army. In 1713, he accompanied the Earl of Petersburg, then ambassador to the Italian states, in the capacity of aide-de-camp. Returning to England, a year afterwards, he was promoted to a captaincy in the first troop of Queen Anne's Guard, and was soon an adjutant-general of the queen's forces. He was next transferred to the post of aide-de-camp to Prince Eugene, the first general of the age, and was with him amid all the sanguinary battles fought between the Austrians and the Turks, upon the frontiers of Hungary. When these wars were over, Oglethorpe returned to England, and in 1722 was elected a member of the British Parliament, where he soon became useful and influential.[1]

[1] James Edward Oglethorpe (1696–1785) attended Corpus Christi College at Oxford University but dropped out to pursue a military career during the war with the Ottoman Empire in 1714–1718. He returned to Corpus Christi but never graduated, receiving a special M.A. in 1731. He was elected to Parliament in 1722, following in the footsteps of his father and brothers. Phinizy Spalding, *Oglethorpe in America* (Chicago: University of Chicago Press, 1977), 2–7.

Oglethorpe caused an investigation to be made into the state of the English prisons, and it was ascertained that they groaned with thousands of poor wretches who had been imprisoned many years for debt. That the kingdom of England also contained thousands, "descended from good families," who were in destitute circumstances, and that hundreds of German exiles, driven from their native country by religious persecution, were starving among them. He brought this unhappy state of things before the king and Parliament, and, by his zeal and ability, succeeded in procuring a charter for the colonization of Georgia, the inhabitants of which were to consist of these distressed people.[2] He resolved, himself, to embark with the first emigrants. They consisted of thirty families, numbering, collectively, one hundred and twenty-five souls. Entering the sea from the Thames, the vessel, after a long voyage across the Atlantic, furled its sails in the harbor of Charleston. Oglethorpe landed, and was received with attention by the governor and council of South Carolina. The king's pilot carried the ship into Port Royal, while small vessels were furnished to convey the emigrants to the Savannah River. Leaving his people at Beaufort, and accompanied by Colonel Bull of South Carolina, Oglethorpe ascended the Savannah, and launched his boat at the splendid bluff, which now forms the site of the commercial emporium of Georgia.[3] At the northern end of this bluff, the great philanthropist came upon an Indian town, called Yamacraw, the chief of which was named Tomochichi, and where Musgrove, a Carolina trader, married to a half-breed named Mary, had established himself.*

This Indian, Mary, was born in the year 1700, at the town of Coweta, upon the Chattahoochee, in Alabama. Her Indian name was Coosaponakeesa, and by maternal descent she was one of the queens of the Muscogee Nation, and the Indians conceded to her the title of princess. When ten years of age, her father took her to Ponpon, in South Carolina, where she was baptized, educated and instructed in Christianity. Afterwards, she fled back to her forest home, laid aside the civilization of the British, and assumed the ease and freedom of the happy Muscogee. In 1716, Colonel John Musgrove was dispatched to the Chattahoochee, by the government of Carolina, to form a treaty of alliance with the Creeks, with whom that colony had been at war. It was there stipulated that the Creeks were to remain the free

* Stevens, *History of Georgia*, 1: 58–89; *Collections of the Georgia Historical Society*, 1: 9–12, 167–74; McCall, *History of Georgia*, 1: 9–32.

[2] Following the death of his friend Robert Castell in debtor's prison, Oglethorpe became involved in prison reform in 1729. His humanitarian efforts led him to partner with others to explore creating a new colony in America for England's "worthy poor." In 1732 King George II granted a charter for a new colony to twenty-one trustees, including Oglethorpe, between the Carolinas and Spanish Florida. Ibid., 3–4, 6–7; Julie Anne Sweet, *Negotiating for Georgia: British-Creek Relations in the Trustee Era, 1733–1752* (Athens: University of Georgia Press, 2005), 11–15.

[3] Oglethorpe met with Robert Johnson, governor of South Carolina, in mid-January 1733, who provided Oglethorpe with supplies and promises of future support. Johnson also sent Colonel William Bull, a South Carolina council member, and fifteen rangers to serve as scouts and guards. Moving up the Savannah River, Oglethorpe had his first meeting with Tomochichi near his Yamacraw village on 1 February 1733. Spalding, *Oglethorpe in America*, 9–11; Sweet, *Negotiating for Georgia*, 24–25.

[4] Coosaponakeesa—Mary Griffin Musgrove (c. 1700–1765)—was the niece of Brims, chief of Coweta, and the daughter of Edward Griffin, a Charles Town trader. She received a rudimentary education in a small community near Charlestown where she became known as Mary Griffin and successively married three times: John Musgrove, Jacob Mathews, and her third husband, the Reverend Thomas Bosomworth in 1744.

occupants of all the lands east, as far as the Savannah River. The son of the British negotiator, John Musgrove, had accompanied his father to Coweta, and falling in love with the Princess Mary, made her his wife. After remaining in the nation several years, and after the birth of their only child, they removed to South Carolina. There residing seven years in much happiness, they afterwards established themselves upon Yamacraw Bluff, at the head of an extensive trading house, and where Oglethorpe found them, as we have just observed. By his alliance with this remarkable woman, who was well versed in the Indian and English languages, Musgrove obtained considerable influence over the natives, and became exceedingly wealthy. Mary was, afterwards, the warm friend of Oglethorpe, and several times saved the early colonists of Georgia from savage butchery.[4]

Oglethorpe returned to Beaufort, and, collecting his colonists, sailed up the Savannah, and landing at the bluff, where now stands the beautiful city, immediately disembarked and pitched four large tents. Here the emigrants spent their first night in Georgia. The Indians received them with hospitality, and gave pledges of future friendship. Oglethorpe marked out the streets and squares; all was bustle and activity, and it was not long before Savannah assumed something of the appearance of a town. A small fort was established at the edge of the bluff, as a place of refuge, and some artillery was mounted upon it. Fort Argyle was built at the narrow passage of the Ogeechee, above the mouth of Canoochee, to defend the inhabitants against inland invasion from the Spaniards of St. Augustine.[5]

Soon after his arrival, Oglethorpe dispatched runners to the Lower Creek Nation, and having assembled eighteen chiefs and their attendants, at Savannah, he formed a treaty with them, in which they relinquished to the British government the lands between the Savannah and the Altamaha. It was also stipulated, among other things, that English traders should be allowed to establish themselves in any part of the Creek Nation. Their goods were to be sold at fixed rates—thus, a white blanket was set down at five buckskins, a gun at ten, a hatchet at three doeskins, a knife at one, and so on.[6] Returning to Charleston, after this important treaty, a dinner was given to the philanthropist by the legislative bodies, which he returned by a ball and supper to the ladies.

A company of forty Jews, acting under the broad principles of the charter, which gave freedom to all religions, save that of the Romish Church, landed at Savannah. Much dissatisfaction, both in England and

As Mary, an Englishwoman, and Coosaponakeesa, a Creek woman in colonial Georgia, she played a critical role in helping the English to establish the colony of Georgia and the Creek/Muscogee people to enjoy a period of relative peace and prosperity. Michael D. Green, "Mary Musgrove: Creating a New World," in *Sifters: Native American Women's Lives*, ed. Theda Perdue (New York: Oxford University Press, 2001), 29–37, 46.

[5] The first Fort Argyle was constructed by Captain James McPherson and a detachment of rangers on Thunderbolt Creek in August 1733, but it was abandoned in favor of the second site on the Ogeechee River, twenty miles from Savannah. The second Fort Argyle was completed by Captain McPherson and his rangers in February 1734 and contained twelve houses. It had palisaded walls six inches thick and eight feet above the ground. Sarah Gober Temple and Kenneth L. Coleman, *Georgia Journeys: Being an Account of the Lives of Georgia's Original Settlers and Many Other Early Settlers* (1961; reprint, Athens: University of Georgia Press, 2010), 42–44.

[6] The headmen from eight towns of the Lower Creeks, led by Youhowlakee, the mico of Coweta, came to Savannah in May 1733 to negotiate trade relations with Oglethorpe's new colony. They were joined by Tomochichi, Mary Musgrove, and her husband John Musgrove, who served as the interpreter. The treaty was consummated on 21 May, with the Creeks allowing

America, arose in consequence of the appearance of these Israelites, and Oglethorpe was solicited to send them immediately from the colony. He, however, generously permitted them to remain, which was one of the wisest acts of his life, for they and their descendants were highly instrumental in developing the commercial resources of this wild land. There also came, in the months of September and October, three hundred and forty-one Salzburgers, driven from Germany for their religious opinions, and Oglethorpe settled them above Savannah, on the river of that name, where they formed a town and named it Ebenezer. These people were succeeded by many Highlanders, from Scotland, who, being brave and hardy, were located upon the banks of the Altamaha, the most exposed part of the colony, where they founded the town of Darien.[7]

In the meantime Oglethorpe had made a voyage to England, taking with him Tomochichi, the chief of Yamacraw, Senauki, his wife, Toonahowi, their nephew, Hillispilli, the war captain, and five chiefs of the Cherokees. He was most graciously received by the ruling powers of England and by her citizens; and his noble and disinterested exertions were universally approved. In due time he returned to Georgia, with his Indian friends.[8]

The lands, between Ebenezer and Briar Creek, belonged to the Uchees, who refused to dispose of them. But to secure this part of the country, two forts were built on the South Carolina side of the river, which answered the purpose. Establishments were also made at Silver Bluff, and at the falls of the Savannah, where the town of Augusta was laid out, warehouses erected, and a garrison thrown into a small fort. Augusta immediately became a general resort for Indian traders, where they purchased annually about two thousand pack-horse loads of peltry. Six hundred white persons were engaged in this trade, including townsmen, pack-horse men and servants. Boats, each capable of carrying down the river a large quantity of peltry, were built, and four or five voyages were annually made with them to Charleston. A trading highway was opened to Savannah on which few of the creeks were bridged, or marshes and swamps causewayed.[9]

He who became the wealthiest and most conspicuous of all these Indian traders, was George Galphin, a native of Ireland. When quite a young man, he established himself upon the site of De Soto's ancient Cofitachequi, where that remarkable adventurer first discovered the Savannah River in 1540.[10] Upon the site of this old Indian

settlements between the Savannah, Altamaha, and Oglethorpe; agreeing to send traders to their towns; and to provide a list of prices to be charged in exchange for deerskins. Corkran, *Creek Frontier*, 84.

[7] Although he received criticism within Georgia and from the trustees, Oglethorpe welcomed those who suffered economic and religious oppression, including Jews, Salzburgers, and Moravians. It is speculated that a group of Jews had been allowed to land at Savannah because there was a Jewish doctor onboard, and he helped with illness in the colony. The German Salzburgers first settled at Ebenezer, but finding the land was poor, Oglethorpe grudgingly allowed them to migrate to Red Bluff at the confluence of the Ebenezer River and the Savannah, founding New Ebenezer. Hugh McKay led the Scots Highlanders who settled Darien and later defended the colony against the Spanish. Spalding, *Oglethorpe in America*, 4, 20, 22, 26–31; Harold E. Davis, *The Fledgling Province: Social and Cultural Life in Colonial Georgia, 1733–1776* (Chapel Hill: University of North Carolina, 1976), 14–21.

[8] Pickett is citing William Bacon Stevens, *A History of Georgia: From Its First Discovery by Europeans to the Present Constitution in MDCCXCVIII*, 2 vols. (New York: D. Appleton and Company, 1847–1859), 1: 117–21. Modern scholars agree that Oglethorpe's 1733 delegation was made up of eight Creeks, including Tomochcichi, Senauki, Toonahowi, Hillispilli, Tomochichi's brother-in-law and war chief of the Lower Creeks, Umpichi, Tomochichi's brother-in-law and a Euchee (Uchee, Yuchi) chief, and

town, on the east bluff of the Savannah, in Barnwell District, South Carolina, now called Silver Bluff, and at present the property of Governor Hammond, young Galphin first begun to trade with the Creek Indians.[11] Although he made Silver Bluff his headquarters, he had trading houses in Savannah and Augusta. He was a man of fine address, great sense, commanding person, untiring energy, and unsurpassed bravery. His power was felt and his influence extended even to the banks of the Mississippi. Among the Upper and Lower Creeks, Cherokees, Chickasaws and Choctaws, he sent forth numerous pack-horse men, with various merchandise, who brought back to Georgia almost countless skins and furs, kegs of bears' oil, hickory-nut oil, snake root and medicinal barks, which he shipped to England. He often went himself into these nations, fearlessly trading in the immediate vicinity of the French Fort Toulouse, upon the Coosa. Commercial policy and an amorous disposition led him to form connections with several females, who were called his wives, and from whom descended many intelligent and influential persons, now inhabiting Georgia, Alabama and the Arkansas Territory.[12]

Among the passengers who came out with Oglethorpe, upon his return to America, were the celebrated Methodists, John and Charles Wesley, who eat at the table of the philanthropist, and who received from him much kindness and courtesy, during a stormy and dangerous voyage. Their object was to make religious impressions upon the minds of the Indians. Among the colonists, with whom they resided many years, they became not only unpopular, but very obnoxious. They finally returned to England much mortified and much disappointed.[13] Stevens thus speaks of these talented and pious men: "The proceedings of the Wesley's in Georgia have, indeed, been violently assailed; and even writers, who can offer no excuse for their ignorance, accuse them of immorality and blame. But it was not so. They were men delicately brought up, of fine sensibilities, of cultivated minds, of deep learning and of ardent devotion. Accomplished, though reserved in their manners—associating from childhood with refined and learned society—they could not conform at once to the tastes and habits of communities like those of Savannah and Frederica, but were rather repelled by the gross immoralities and offensive manners of the early colonists. Their error was, especially in John, of holding too high ideas of ecclesiastical authority, and the being too rigid and repulsive in their pastoral duties. They

three attendants: Apokutchi, Santachi, and Stimaletchi. Helen Todd, *Tomochichi: Indian Friend of the Georgia Colony* (Atlanta: Cherokee Publishing Company, 1977), 62–75; Jace Weaver, *The Red Atlantic: American Indigenes and the Making of the Modern World, 1000–1927* (Chapel Hill: University of North Carolina Press, 2014), 20–23.

9 Oglethorpe understood that the success of the Georgia colony depended on trade and good relations with the Indians, especially the Creeks. He used his relationship with Tomochichi, Mary Musgrove, and her husband John Musgrove to negotiate a treaty with the Creeks in 1733 which would open up land to expand the Georgia colony peacefully. Spalding, *Oglethorpe in America*, 22–23, 49–59, 76–80.

10 As noted earlier, modern archaeological and ethnohistorical research places Cofitachequi on the Wateree River and not on the Savannah River at Silver Bluff. Hudson, *Knights of Spain*, 464; Chester B. DePratter, "Cofitachequi: Ethnohistorical and Archaeological Evidence," *Anthropological Studies* 9 (1989): 139–44.

11 James Henry Hammond (1807–1864), politician, slave owner, and plantation manager, served his native South Carolina as a U.S. Congressman (1835–1836), U.S. Senator (1857–1860), and governor (1842–1844). He abandoned his legal practice and editorial writing in 1830 to manage his plantation at Silver Bluff on the Savannah River. "James Henry Hammond," *Biographical Directory of the U.S. Congress, 1774-Present* (online). See Drew Gilpin Faust, *James Henry Hammond and the Old South: A Design*

stood firmly on little things, as well as on great, and held the reins of church discipline with a tightness unsuitable to an infant colony. But no other blame can attach to them."*

The colony of Georgia had prospered under the wise guidance of Oglethorpe. Five principal towns had been surveyed and settled: Augusta, Ebenezer, Savannah, New Inverness and Frederica, besides forts and villages. More than one thousand persons had been sent to Georgia, on the account of the trustees alone, while hundreds of other emigrants came at their own expense. The colonists being from different nations, were various in their characters and religious creeds. Vaudois, Swiss, Piedmontese, Germans, Moravians, Jews from Portugal, Highlanders, English and Italians were thrown together in this fine climate, new world and new home. With all these people, in their various costumes, were often intermingled different tribes of Indians. What a field for a painter the colony presented! What materials for a scribbling tourist![14]

Having thus colonized the northern, southern and eastern borders, Oglethorpe returned to England, and presented to his majesty and the Parliament an account of the affairs of Georgia. He asked, at their hands, a sufficient supply of military stores and men to defend the province from an invasion contemplated by the Spaniards of the Floridas. The colonization of Georgia had given great offense to Spain. That power claimed the whole of Georgia, but made no serious opposition so long as the English settlements were confined to the Savannah River, but when Oglethorpe planted his Highlanders upon the Altamaha, the Spaniards resolved upon their expulsion. A long succession of border wars and difficulties ensued, which, having but little connection with the history of Alabama, are omitted. It should be observed, however, that Oglethorpe succeeded in his applications to the court, and was appointed general of the forces in South Carolina and Georgia. In September, he was made colonel of a regiment to be employed in defense of the colony, which he had so successfully established. He returned to Georgia, with his army, and disembarked his artillery at St. Simon's Island.[15]

No sooner had Gen. Oglethorpe placed his feet upon Georgia soil than he saw the necessity of renewing his treaty with the Creeks, and of cultivating their alliance, for fear that they might form a dangerous

* Stevens, *History of Georgia*, 1: 339–49.

***for Mastery* (Baton Rouge: Louisiana State University Press, 1982).**

[12] George Galphin (1709–1780), a native of County Armgah, Ireland, arrived in 1737 and joined the Augusta based trading company of Brown, Rea, and Company in the 1740s. Through the trade and his relations with his Muscogee wives, Metawney and Nithchuckey, he became influential among the Lower Creeks and served as an interpreter and diplomat for the governors of South Carolina and Georgia. He purchased land at Silver Bluff in 1752, ran a successful trading house, and developed an expansive plantation with a number of slaves. During the American Revolution, he tried to keep the Creeks neutral and opposed the British efforts on the southern frontier. Michael P. Morris, *George Galphin and the Transformation of the Georgia–South Carolina Backcountry* (Lanham, MD: Lexington Books, 2015), 24–56.

[13] Charles Wesley came in the second wave of Georgia immigrants and served as both an Anglican clergyman and a secretary to Oglethorpe. They fell out over claims of inappropriate conduct by Oglethorpe with two women and a charge that Wesley was urging colonists to leave Georgia. Charles left Savannah for England in July 1736, and his brother John Wesley left in December 1737 after he became identified with "malcontents" who opposed Oglethorpe's domineering control of the colony. Harvey H. Jackson, "Parson and Squire: James Oglethorpe and the Role of the Anglican Church in Georgia, 1733–1736," in *Oglethorpe in Perspective: Georgia's Founder after Two Hundred Years*, ed. Phinizy Spalding and Harvey H. Jackson (Tuscaloosa: University of Alabama Press, 1989), 57–62.

connection with the Spaniards. He went immediately to Savannah, where he had an interview with the chiefs of four towns, and succeeded in strengthening their fidelity to the English. But in order to accomplish a complete alliance with the brave Creeks, he resolved to attend the great council of that nation, which was to assemble at Coweta, in July and August following. It was a long and perilous journey. Coweta lay upon the west bank of the Chattahoochee River, three miles below the falls, at which the city of Columbus is now situated, and within the limits of the present Russell County, Alabama. The distance from Savannah to that point was not only considerable, but lay over extensive pine forests, dismal swamps, and rapid and dangerous rivers, while the solitary trail was not unfrequently beset by Indian banditti. However, when the time arrived he, who had so courageously fought under Prince Eugene upon the frontiers of Hungary, was not to be dismayed by obstacles like these. With only a few attendants, and some pack-horses laden with goods, designed as presents for the Indians, Oglethorpe set off on his journey. He crossed the Ogeechee, Oconee, Ocmulgee, and the Flint, carrying over his effects in canoes, and sometimes upon rafts. Finally he halted upon the banks of the Chattahoochee. He had camped out every night in the woods, exposed by day to the heat of the sun, and often to pelting showers of rain. Crossing the Chattahoochee, and ascending its western bank, the great and good Oglethorpe soon arrived in the town of Coweta, upon Alabama soil. Forty miles in advance the Indians had met him and at various points upon the route had deposited provisions for his subsistence. They now received him in their capital with every demonstration of joy.[16]

Making Coweta his headquarters, Oglethorpe occasionally rode to some of the towns in the vicinity, the most prominent of which were Uchee, Cusseta and Ositche, conversing with these people through his interpreters, and engaging their affections by his liberality and irresistible address. He drank with them the black drink—smoked with them the pipe of peace—and lounged with them upon the cool cane sofas with which their ample public houses were furnished. In the meantime, the chiefs and warriors from the towns of Coweta, Cusseta, Ufaula, Hitchitee, Ositche, Chehaw, Oconee and Swagles, assembled in the great square.[17] After many ceremonious preliminaries, they made a treaty of alliance with Oglethorpe. It was declared that all the lands between the Savannah and the St. John's, and from the latter to the Apalachee Bay, and thence to the mountains, by ancient right, did belong to the

[14] Although the various ethnic and religious groups presented challenges to Oglethorpe's rule, they made significant contributions to the stability of the Georgia colony during its early years, especially the Salzburgers and Highlanders. Spalding, *Oglethorpe in America,* 18–32, 71.

[15] Oglethorpe played a major role during the War of Jenkins Ear, a struggle between British Florida and Spanish Florida and part of a larger conflict—the War of Austrian Succession. Oglethorpe led successful raids on Spanish outposts in January-May 1740 but failed in his siege of St. Augustine in June-July 1740. He redeemed himself at the battle of Bloody Marsh on 7 July 1742 by defeating Spanish forces that tried to seize the British Fort Frederica and St. Simons Island. Rodney E. Baine, "General James Oglethorpe and the Expedition against St. Augustine," *Georgia Historical Quarterly* 84 (June 2000): 197–229; Margaret Davis Cate, "Fort Frederica and the Battle of Bloody Marsh," *Georgia Historical Quarterly* 27 (June 1943), 111–74.

[16] Actually, Oglethorpe and his entourage of twenty-five set out for Coweta on 15 June 1739, following a trail from an Uchee (Yuchi) town above Ebenezer. At his meeting with Chigelli and other Creek headmen, the Creeks confirmed an earlier treaty giving land to King George II for his Georgia colony and promising Oglethorpe their assistance in time of war. From Coweta, Oglethorpe's party traveled to Augusta, arriving on 5 September 1739, where he met with Squirrel

Creek Nation. That neither the Spaniards nor any other people, excepting the trustees of the colony of Georgia, should settle them. That the grant on the Savannah River, as far as the river Ogeechee, and those along the seacoast, as far as the St. John's River, and as high as the tide flowed, with the islands previously granted to the English at Savannah, should now be confirmed. The chiefs again reserved all the lands from Pipe Maker's Bluff to the Savannah, with the islands of St. Catherine, Ossabaw and Sapelo.[18]

After signing the treaty, Oglethorpe left with the chiefs, for their protection against English encroachments, the following singular paper:

"By James Oglethorpe, Esquire, General and Commander-in-Chief of all His Majesty's forces in South Carolina and Georgia, &c.: To all His Majesty's subjects to whom these presents shall come, greeting: –

KNOW YE, that you are not to take up or settle any land beyond the above limit, settled by me with the Creek Nation, at their estates held on Saturday, the eleventh day of August, Anno Domini, 1739, as you shall, through me, at your peril answer.

Given under my hand and seal, at the Coweta town, this, the 21st day of August, Anno Domini, 1739.

JAMES OGLETHORPE."[19]

We desire it to be borne in mind, by the reader, that none of the Upper Creek Indians, who lived upon the Alabama, Coosa, and Tallapoosa Rivers, were present at this treaty. They never recognized any of the treaties made in the Lower Creek Nation with the Georgians. At this time, they were under the influence of the French; afterwards, they placed themselves under the wing of the Spaniards. Although the English built a fort and occupied it for many years, with a garrison, in the town of Okfuskee, on the east side of the Tallapoosa River, within forty miles of the French fortress, Toulouse, and partially succeeded in alienating some of the Upper Creeks from the French, yet the great body of these people forever remained the implacable enemies of the Georgians.[20]

Oglethorpe departed from Coweta, and after a disagreeable journey, reached Savannah. He there assisted in the funeral ceremonies of his friend, Tomochichi, who died at Yamacraw Bluff.[21] The body, brought down the river in a canoe, was received by Oglethorpe, and was interred in Percival Square, amid the sound of minute guns from the battery.*

* Stevens, *History of Georgia*, 1: 89–158; McCall, *History of Georgia*, 1: 32–142; *Collections of the Georgia Historical Society*, 1: 18–22, 182, 262.

King and a delegation of Chickasaw headmen and a day later with a Cherokee delegation. Edward J. Cashin, *Guardians of the Valley: Chickasaws in Colonial South Carolina and Georgia* (Columbia: University of South Carolina Press, 2009), 42–43; "Oglethorpe's Treaty with the Lower Creek Indians," *Georgia Historical Quarterly* 4 (March 1920): 5–8.

17 While Pickett generally uses Hawkins in discussing the Lower Creek towns, modern scholars use the following names: Yuchi (Uchee), Ooseoochee (Ositche), Eufaula (Ufaula), Hitchiti (Hitchitee), and Sauwoogelo (Swagles). Most of these towns were located in close proximity to each other in the Chattahoochee River valley near modern Columbus, Georgia. Foster, *Archaeology of the Lower Muskogee Creek Indians*, 55–71; Ethridge, *Creek Country*, 55, 62–66.

18 The Carolina treaty with Brims in 1717 and Oglethorpe's treaty in August 1739 with Chigelli and the assembly of Lower Creek headmen established the Savannah River as the border between British

and Indian occupied lands. Cashin, *Guardians of the Valley*, 42, 51; "Oglethorpe's Treaty with the Lower Creek Indians," 5–8.

[19] For the complete treaty negotiations with the Lower Creeks in August 1739 and approval of the treaty by the Georgia Trustees, see "Oglethorpe's Treaty with the Lower Creek Indians," *Georgia Historical Quarterly* 4 (March 1920): 3–16.

[20] As noted earlier, Captain Patrick McKay, Georgia's Indian agent, received approval from the Okfuskees to construct a small post at Okfuskee in May 1735. A contingent of Georgia rangers constructed the fort and a small garrison remained there until 1743 when the fort was abandoned. Piker, *Okfuskee*, 30–35.

[21] London's *The Gentleman's Magazine* published a lengthy obituary dated "Savannah in Georgia, Oct. 10, 1739" regarding Tomochichi's death and funeral: "King Tomo Chichi died on the 5th at his own town 4 miles from hence, of a lingering illness, being aged about 97. He was sensible to the last minutes . . . He expressed the greatest tenderness for General Oglethorpe." *The Gentleman's Magazine*, 10 (March 1740), 129; Sweet, *Negotiating for Georgia*, 136–38.

Chapter IX

JESUIT PRIESTS OR MISSIONARIES

Since the revolt of the French garrison at Fort Toulouse, upon the Coosa, things at that place had remained in rather an undisturbed condition. It is true that the English had given them much uneasiness, and had occasionally cut off some of the *couriers de bois*. In order to cultivate a better understanding with the Lower Creeks, a Jesuit priest, Father de Guyenne, went to Coweta, upon the Chattahoochee, and succeeded in building two cabins, one at that place, and the other at Cusseta. His object was to learn the language of the Indians, and to instruct them in the Christian religion; but the English of the province of Georgia prevailed upon the Indians to burn up these houses. The zealous father was therefore forced to retreat to Fort Toulouse.[1] Father Morand had been stationed, some years, at Fort Toulouse, and used to live occasionally at Coosawda.[2]

"The impossibility, however, of exercising his ministry there, for the benefit of either the Indians or the French, has induced the superior to recall him, that he might be entrusted with the direction of the nuns, and of the royal hospital, which is now under our charge. The English trade, as well as the French, among the Alabama Indians. You can easily imagine what an obstacle this presents to the progress of religion, for the English are always ready to excite controversy."* Among the Choctaw there were several missionaries, besides those stationed at Mobile. "The reverend Father Baudouin, the actual superior-general of the mission, resided eighteen years among the Choctaws.[3] When he was on the point of reaping some fruits from his labors, the troubles which the English excited in that nation, and the peril to which he was evidently exposed, obliged Father Vitry,[4] then superior-general, in concert with the governor, to recall him to New Orleans."†

* Letter of Father Vivier, of the Society of Jesus, to a father of the same company.
† Letter of Father Vivier, of the Society of Jesus, to a father of the same company.

While the English of Carolina and Georgia engaged in various schemes to rid the territory of the present states of Alabama and Mississippi of its French population, by unscrupulous intrigues with the natives, the French were but little behind them in similar enterprises. The Jesuits were adventurous and brave, and men of captivating address, and obtained much influence over the leading chiefs, wherever they appeared. An account of the artful intrigues of a German Jesuit, named Christian Priber, as related, in his singular style, by James Adair, an old British trader, who lived forty years among the Cherokees and Chickasaws, will now be introduced.[5]

"In the year 1736, the French sent into South Carolina one Priber, a gentleman of a curious and speculative temper. He was to transmit them a full account of that country, and proceed to the Cherokee Nation, in order to seduce them from the British to the French interest. He went, and though

[1] Father Alexis-Xavier de Guyenne served as a missionary to the Alabamas near Fort Toulouse from 1727 through March 1729. He left the Alabamas dressed in plain clothing to make contact with the Cowetas on behalf of France and later built a cabin among the Tallapoosas. It was destroyed in 1730. Delanglez, *French Jesuits in Lower Louisiana*, 480–83; Giraud, *Company of the Indies, 1723–1731*, 367–68.

[2] Father Guillaume François Morand (1701–1761) came to Louisiana in 1736 and served as chaplain at Fort Toulouse. He was recalled because of the difficulties he faced in carrying out his ministry and died in New Orleans in 1761. *MPA: FD*, 4: 210, 210 n. 2; Delanglez, *French Jesuits in Lower Louisiana*, 483–85; Thomas, *Fort Toulouse*, 41, 84 n. 12.

[3] Father Michel Baudouin (1692–1768), a native of Quebec, was the first Jesuit to arrive in Louisiana after the division of spiritual jurisdiction between the Jesuits and Capuchins in 1725. He served as a missionary to the Choctaws for eighteen years with the Chickasawhays near modern Enterprise, Mississippi. He served as vicar-general of Louisiana from 1757 until the Jesuits were expelled from the colony in 1763. *MPA: FD*, 1: 155–63; Delanglez, *French Jesuits in Lower Louisiana*, 456–60; John Gilmary Shea, *History of the Catholic Church in the United States: Colonial Days, 1521–1763* (New York: D. H. McBride & Co., 1886), 583–84

[4] Father Pierre de Vitry (1700-c.1750) arrived in Louisiana from France in 1732. He established the Catholic mission at Fort St. Jean Baptiste des Natchitoches in 1734, and he served as the chaplain on Bienville's second expedition against the Chickasaws. In 1739, he was appointed vicar-general of Louisiana and served until his death on 5 April 1749 (al. 1750). Delanglez, *French Jesuits in Lower Louisiana*, 316–19; Burton and Smith, *Colonial Natchitoches*, 14; Thwaites, *Jesuit Relations*, 71: 126.

[5] Contrary to James Adair and other writers, Christian Gottlieb Priber (1697-c.1744) was not a Jesuit priest or an agent of the French. Priber, a native of the German province of Saxony, fled his native country, first seeking refuge in England and then traveling to South Carolina in 1735. He filed a petition for land, "setting forth that he has a family of six persons in the province and also a wife, four children, and one servant in Saxony and praying he may have a warrant of survey for his whole family." There is no indication that Priber ever settled on the land granted to him, but he did advertise the sale of his personal possessions in three weekly issues of the *South Carolina Gazette* in December 1735. Priber traveled into the Cherokee Overhill country, reaching Great Tellico sometime in 1736. Adair, *American Indians*, 258–61; Verner W. Crane, "A Lost Utopia on the First American Frontier," *Sewanee Review* 27 (January 1919): 54; Knox Mellon, Jr., "Christian Priber's Cherokee 'Kingdom of Paradise,'" *Georgia Historical Quarterly* 57 (Fall 1973): 321–23; Knox Mellon, Jr., "Christian Priber and the Jesuit Myth," *South Carolina Historical Magazine* 61 (April 1960): 75–81.

he was adorned with every qualification that constitutes the gentleman, soon after he arrived at the upper towns of this mountainous country, he exchanged his clothes and everything he brought with him, and by that means made friends with the head warriors of the Big Tellico River. More effectually to answer the design of his commission, he ate, drank, slept, danced, dressed and painted himself with the Indians, so that it was not easy to distinguish him from the natives; he married, also, with them. Being endowed with a strong understanding and retentive memory, he soon learned their dialect, and by gradual advances, impressed them with a very ill opinion of the English, representing them as a fraudulent, avaricious and encroaching people. He, at the same time, inflated the artless savages with a prodigious high opinion of their own importance in the American scale of power, on account of the situation of their country, their martial disposition, and the great number of their warriors, which would baffle all the efforts of the ambitious and ill-designing British colonists.[6]

"Having thus infected them by his smooth, deluding art, he easily formed them into a nominal republican government. He crowned their old Archi-Magus, emperor, after a pleasing new savage form, and invented a variety of high sounding titles for all the members of his imperial majesty's *red* court and the great officers of state. He himself received the honorable title of his imperial majesty's principal secretary of state, and as such he subscribed himself, in all the letters he wrote to our government, and lived in open defiance of them.[7] This seemed to be of so dangerous a tendency as to induce South Carolina to send up a commissioner, Colonel Fox, to demand him as an enemy to public repose. He took him into custody in the great square of their state house. When he had almost concluded his oration on the occasion, one of the warriors rode up and bade him forbear, as the man he intended to enslave was a great beloved man, and had become one of their own people. Though it was reckoned our agent's strength was far greater in his arms than in his head, he readily desisted, for, as it is too hard to struggle with the Pope in Rome, a stranger could not miss to find it equally difficult to enter abruptly into a new emperor's court and there seize his prime minister by a foreign authority, especially when he could not support any charge of guilt against him. The warrior told him that the red people well knew the honesty of the secretary's heart and would never allow him to tell a lie, and the secretary urged that he was a foreigner, without owing any allegiance to Great Britain.[8] That

[6] In October 1722, Priber published his dissertation, *The Use of the Study of Roman Law and the Ignorance of that Law in the Public Life in Germany,* at Erfurt University. Sometime after completing his doctorate in jurisprudence, Priber developed his grandiose scheme to found a utopian commonwealth, and it was these ideas that caused him to flee the authorities in Saxony. It is not clear when he decided to pursue his "Kingdom of Paradise"—a utopian society—among the Cherokee. He settled at Great Tellico, where his most important convert was the young war chief Oconostota. Adair, *American Indians,* 258; Mellon, "Christian Priber's Cherokee 'Kingdom of Paradise,'" 319–21; Rennard Strickland, "Christian Gottlieb Priber: Utopian Precursor of the Cherokee Government," *Chronicles of Oklahoma* 48 (Autumn 1970): 265, 267–78.

[7] Apparently Adair's "Archi-Magus" is a reference to Moytoy (Amo-adawehi), who had been given the title of "Emperor of the Cherokee" by Alexander Cuming, a Scottish adventurer, in 1730. Adair, *American Indians,* 259; Williams, "Journal of Sir Alexander Cuming," 123–26, 136; Ludovick Grant, "Historical Relation of Facts Delivered by Ludovick Grant, Indian Trader, to His Excellency the Governor of South Carolina," *South Carolina Historical Magazine* X (January 1909): 57.

[8] Based on a letter written in 1734 to the Lords Commissioners for Trade, Adair's Colonel Joseph Fox was apparently a naval officer in Charleston, South Carolina. In

he only travelled through some places of their country, in a peaceable manner, paying for everything he had of them. That in compliance with the request of the kind French, as well as from his own tender feelings for the poverty and insecure state of the Cherokees, he came a great way, and lived with them as a brother, only to preserve their liberties, by opening a water communication between them and New Orleans. That the distance of the two places from each other proved his motive to be the love of doing good, especially as he was to go there and bring up a sufficient number of Frenchmen, of proper skill, to instruct them in the art of making gunpowder, the materials of which, he affirmed, their lands abounded with.[9] He concluded his artful speech by urging that the tyrannical design of the English commissioner towards him appeared plainly to be levelled against them, because, as he was not accused of having done any ill to the English before he came to the Cherokees, his crime must consist in loving the Cherokees. An old war leader repeated to the commissioner the essential part of the speech, and added more of his own similar thereto. The English beloved man had the honor of receiving his leave of absence and a sufficient passport of safe conduct, from the imperial red court, by a verbal order of the secretary of state, who was so polite as to wish him well home, and ordered a convoy of his own life-guards, who conducted him a considerable way, and he got home in safety.[10]

"From the above, it is evident that the monopolizing spirit of the French had planned their dangerous line of circumvallation, respecting our envied colonies, as early as the before mentioned period. The choice of the man, also, bespoke their judgment. Though the philosophic secretary was an utter stranger to the wild and mountainous Cherokee Nation, yet his sagacity readily directed him to choose a proper place, an old favorite religious man, for the new red empire, which he formed by slow and sure degrees, to the great danger of our Southern colonies. But the empire received a very great shock, in an accident that befell the secretary, when it was on the point of rising into a far greater state of puissance by the acquisition of the Muscogee, Choctaw, and the Western Mississippi Indians.[11]

March 1739 the South Carolina Commons House of Assembly appropriated ₣402 for the expenses of Fox and two men to seize Priber and bring him to Charleston. Adair, *American Indians,* 259–60; Joseph Fox to Lords Commissioners for Trade, [Charlestown], 27 March 1734, "List and Abstract of Letters in the State Paper Office London, relating to South Carolina . . . 1857," *Collections of the South Carolina Historical Society,* vol. 3 (Charleston: South Carolina Historical Society, 1859), 305.

[9] Adair's assertion that Priber was in the service of the French and planned to develop an alliance was the talk of an English trader who opposed the French inroads among the Chickasaw and Choctaw. The only documented connection between Priber and the French on the Gulf Coast was Antoinne Bonnefoy, a French captive of the Cherokees, who expressed admiration for his linguistic skills and utopian ideas. Adair, *American Indians,* 259–60; Mellon, "Christian Priber's Cherokee 'Kingdom of Paradise,'" 321–22; Antoinne Bonnefoy, "Journal of Antoinne Bonnefoy, 1741–1742," in Mereness, *Travels in the American Colonies,* 239–55.

[10] Before Colonel Fox's attempt to remove Priber, South Carolina officials had contacted Ludovick Grant (c.1696–1758), the resident trader at Great Tellico, urging him to capture Priber and bring him to Charleston. According to his letter to Governor James Glen, Grant had challenged Priber's activities with the Cherokee, but he feared losing his trade and his position among the Cherokee. Grant, "Historical Relation of Facts," 58–61; Mellon, "Christian Priber's Cherokee 'Kingdom of Paradise,'" 323–24.

[11] Other than the false charges of Priber's service to the French, his proposal to "settle a Town there [Cherokee Nation] of fugitive English, French, Germans, & Negroes" seemed to threaten the existence of South Carolina and Georgia. Mellon, "Christian

"In the fifth year of that red imperial era, Priber set off for Mobile, accompanied by a few Cherokees. He proceeded by land as far as the navigable part of the Tallapoosa River, and arriving at Tuckabatchee, lodged there all night. The traders of the neighboring towns soon went there, convinced the inhabitants of the dangerous tendency of his unwearied labors among the Cherokees, and of his present journey.[12] They then took him into custody, with a large bundle of manuscripts, and sent him down to Frederica, in Georgia. The governor committed him to a place of confinement, though not with common felons, as he was a foreigner, and was said to have held a place of considerable rank in the army.[13] Soon after, the magazine took fire, which was not far from where he was confined, and though the sentinels bade him make off to a place of safety, as all the people were running to avoid danger from explosion of the powder and shells, yet he squatted on his belly upon the floor, and continued in that position without the least hurt. Several blamed his rashness, but he told them that experience had convinced him it was the most probable means of avoiding danger. This incident displayed the philosopher and the soldier.[14] After bearing his misfortunes a considerable time with great constancy, happily for us, he died in confinement, though he deserved a much better fate. In the fifth year of his secretaryship I maintained a correspondence with him. But the Indians, becoming very inquisitive to know the contents of our papers, he told them that in the very same manner as he was their great secretary, I was the devil's clerk, or, an accursed one, who marked on paper the bad speech of the evil ones of darkness. Accordingly, they forbade him to write any more to such an accursed one. As he was learned, and possessed of a very sagacious, penetrating judgment, and had every qualification that was requisite for his bold and difficult enterprise, it is not to be doubted that, as he wrote a Cherokee dictionary, designed to be published at Paris, he likewise set down a great deal that would have been very accessible to the curious, and serviceable to the representatives of South Carolina and Georgia, which may be readily found in Frederica,[15] if the manuscripts have had the good fortune to escape the despoiling hands of military power."*

* James Adair, *History of the American Indians* (London: 1775), 240–43.

Priber's Cherokee 'Kingdom of Paradise,'" 319.

[12] The *South Carolina Gazette* on 30 May 1743 reported in a dispatch from Frederica, Georgia, dated 28 February: "The Creek Indians, who are Governor Oglethorpe's fast friends, have taken one Priber, a foreigner. He was an inhabitant of South Carolina; was going to the French and from thence the Spaniards." Quoted in Knox Mellon, Jr., "Christian Priber's Cherokee 'Kingdom of Paradise,'" *Georgia Historical Quarterly* 57 (Fall 1973): 326, 330 n. 36. Note: Another source claims that Priber was on his way to St. Augustine to seek assistance from the Spaniards. See Americus, "Jesuit Missionary in Georgia," *The London Magazine* 29 (September 1760), 443.

[13] Pickett's timeline appears to be off by twelve to thirteen months. Governor James Oglethorpe wrote the trustees of Georgia about Priber's incarceration at Frederica on 22 April 1743. Priber never held a military office, and the manuscripts in his possession included a Cherokee dictionary and a lengthy manuscript detailing his plans and concept for his utopian society. Apparently Oglethorpe read the latter manuscript and interrogated Priber on several occasions, which he commented upon at length in his letter to the Georgia trustees. Adair, *American Indians*, 260; Mellon, "Christian Priber's Cherokee 'Kingdom of Paradise,'" 327–28, 329 n. 1.

[14] Adair is making reference to the explosion of a large magazine at Fort Frederica on St. Simons Island on 22 March 1744. All the prisoners were released to seek shelter and to escape the exploding shells and gunpowder. Priber "politely refused" the offer to leave his cell and "put forth his head under his feather bed." Adair, *American Indians*,

William Bacon Stevens, formerly professor of belles lettres and history in the University of Georgia, and now an Episcopalian minister in Philadelphia, has published one volume of the *History of Georgia*, in which we find the following interesting account of Priber, which we copy, at length, in his own style. In alluding to the arrival of Oglethorpe at Frederica, Dr. Stevens says, "On the return of the general from Florida, he ordered his strange prisoner to be examined, and was not a little surprised to find, under his coarse dress of deer-skins and Indian moccasins, a man of polished address, great abilities, and extensive learning. He was versed not only in the Indian language, of which he had composed a dictionary, but also spoke the Latin, French and Spanish fluently, and English perfectly. Upon being interrogated as to his design, he acknowledged that it was 'to bring about a confederation of all the Southern Indians, to inspire them with industry, to instruct them in the arts necessary to the commodities of life, and, in short, to engage them to throw off the yoke of their European allies of all nations.' He proposed to make a settlement in that part of Georgia which is within the limits of the Cherokee lands, at Cusseta,* and to settle a town there of fugitive English, French and Germans, and they were to take under their particular care the runaway Negroes of the English. All criminals were to be sheltered, as he proposed to make his place an asylum for all fugitives, and the cattle and effects they might bring with them. He expected a great resort of debtors, transported felons, servants, and Negro slaves from the two Carolinas, Georgia and Virginia, offering, as his scheme did, toleration to all crimes and licentiousness, except murder and idleness. Upon his person was found his private journal, revealing, in part, his designs, with various memoranda relating to his project. In it he speaks not only of individual Indians and Negroes, whose assistance had been promised, and of a private treasurer in Charleston, for keeping the funds collected; but also, that he expected many things from the French, and from another nation, whose name he left blank. There were also found upon him letters for the Florida and Spanish governors, demanding their protection of him and countenance of his scheme. Among his papers was one containing articles of government for his new town, regularly and elaborately drawn out and digested. In this volume he enumerates many

260–61; Americus, "Jesuit Missionary in Georgia," 444–45.

[15] Unfortunately Priber's Cherokee dictionary and his longer manuscript on his utopian society were lost and never published. Because of his fluency and knowledge of early eighteenth century Cherokee, James Mooney, an American ethnologist, referred to Priber's Cherokee dictionary manuscript "which he had prepared for publication—the first, and even yet, perhaps the most important study of the language ever made." James Mooney, "Myths of the Cherokees," *Nineteenth Annual Report, Bureau of American Ethnology 7, 1897–1898* (Washington: GPO, 1900), Part 1, 37.

* If Doctor Stevens means the "Cusseta," on the east side of the Chattahoochee and opposite old Fort Mitchell, it was within the limits of the Creek lands, and never belonged to the Cherokees. I am not aware of any town named "Cusseta" in any part of what formerly was the Cherokee Nation, although there may have been, for by reference to page 119 of the *History of Alabama* it will be found that the Cherokees had towns named "Tallase" and "Tuskegee," and such towns were also in the Creek Nation.

[16] **Apparently William Bacon Stevens had access to *The London Magazine* article by the anonymous author Americus about Christian Priber, and he loosely paraphrased the account of Priber's incarceration and the exchanges between Oglethorpe and the utopian dreamer. See Americus, "Jesuit Missionary in Georgia," 443–45.**

rights and privileges, as he calls them, to which the citizens of this colony are to be entitled, particularly dissolving marriages, allowing a community of women, and all kinds of licentiousness. It was drawn up with much art, method and learning, and was designed to be privately printed and circulated. When it was hinted to him that such a plan was attended with many dangers and difficulties, and must require many years to establish his government, he replied, 'Proceeding properly, many of these evils may be avoided; and as to length of time, we have a succession of agents to take up the work as fast as others leave it. We never lose sight of a favorite point, nor are we bound by the strict rules of morality in the means, when the end we pursue is laudable. If we err, our general is to blame; and we have a merciful God to pardon us. But believe me,' he continued, 'before the century is passed, the Europeans will have a very small footing on this continent.'[16]

"Indeed, he often hinted that there were others of his brethren laboring among the Indians for the same purpose. Being confined in the barracks at Frederica, he exhibited a stoical indifference to his fate; conversed with freedom, conducted with politeness, and attracted the notice and favorable attention of many of the gentlemen there. His death in prison, put an end to all further proceedings, and his plans died with him. Such was the strange being whose Jesuitical intrigues well-nigh eventuated in the destruction of Georgia. A thorough Jesuit, an accomplished linguist, a deep tactician, far-sighted in his plans, and far-reaching in his expedients, he possessed every qualification for his design, and only failed of bringing down great evil upon the English, because he was apprehended before his scheme had been matured."*

There were many curious characters roving over the territory of Alabama and Mississippi at this period. Traders from South Carolina and Georgia, were found in almost every Indian village; while the French from Mobile and New Orleans and the Spaniards from the Floridas continued to swell the number of these singular merchants. They encountered all kinds of dangers and suffered all kinds of privations to become successful in their exciting traffic. Adair, one of these British traders, thus describes the mode by which difficult streams were passed:

"When we expect high rivers, each company of traders carry a canoe, made of the tanned leather, the sides overlapped about three fingers' breadth, and well sewed with three seams. Around the gunnels, which are made of saplings, are strong loopholes, for large deerskin strings to hang down both the sides. With two of these is securely tied to the stem and stern, a well-shaped sapling

* Stevens, *History of Georgia*, 1: 165–67.

for a keel, and in like manner the ribs. Thus they usually rig out a canoe, fit to carry over ten horse-loads at once, in the space of half an hour. The apparatus is afterwards hidden with great care on the opposite shore. Few take the trouble to paddle the canoe, for, as they are commonly hardy, and also of an amphibious nature, they usually jump into the river with their leathern barge ahead of them, and thrust it through the deep part of the water to the opposite shore. When we ride with only a few luggage horses, we make a frame of dry pines, which we tie together with strong vines well twisted. When we have raised it to be sufficiently buoyant, we load and paddle it across, and afterwards swim our horses, keeping at a little distance below them."*

* Adair, *American Indians*, 272.

Chapter X

THE FRENCH BATTLES UPON THE TOMBIGBEE

When we suspended our review of the operations of the French upon the territory of Alabama and Mississippi, for the purpose of bringing to the notice of the reader the early colonization of Georgia by Oglethorpe, it will be borne in mind that the horrible massacre at Natchez had occurred. The tribe of that name had crossed the Mississippi, and fortified on Black River, near the Ouachita. Governor Périer, attacking them at that point, had captured many of the men, women and children, whom he conveyed to New Orleans, and from thence shipped to the island of Santo Domingo, where they were sold to work upon the plantations. Some of those who escaped the hands of the French at Black River, retreated to the vicinity of the fort at Natchitoches, upon which they presently made a furious assault. The brave St. Denis, the commandant, successfully repulsed them. A remnant of this warlike but unfortunate tribe had fled to the Chickasaw Nation, while another small band sought a home among the Creeks, upon the Coosa.[1]

[1] Following the punitive expeditions by the French and their defeat near Fort St. Jean Baptiste des Natchitoches, the Natchez scattered across the Southeast. Some settled near their historic towns while others were absorbed into small tribes in the Lower Mississippi River Valley. However, the largest remnant populations found refuge among the Chickasaw, Cherokee, and Creeks, even establishing independent towns within these coalescent societies. Barnett, *Natchez Indians,* 128–33; Mooney, "Myths of the Cherokee," 234, 498–99; Swanton, *Early History of the Creeks,* 251, 312–16; James R. Atkinson, *Splendid Land, Splendid People: The Chickasaw Indians to Removal* (Tuscaloosa: University of Alabama Press, 2003), 65, 74–75.

Governor Périer was guilty of excessive cruelty to many of these poor fugitives who fell into his hands. In the streets of New Orleans, he publicly, and without any hesitation, caused four of the men and two of the women to be burned to death. He also cheerfully permitted the Tunicas, who brought down a Natchez woman whom they had discovered in the woods, to put an end to her existence in the same manner. A platform was erected near the levee. The unfortunate woman was led forth, placed upon it, and, surrounded by the whole population of New Orleans, was slowly consumed by the flames![2] What a stigma upon the character of the early inhabitants of the Crescent City! Gayarré says:—"The victim supported, with the most stoical fortitude, all the tortures which were inflicted upon her, and did not shed a tear. On the contrary, she upbraided her torturers with their want of skill, flinging at them every opprobrious epithet she could think of."*

* Charles Gayarré, *Louisiana: Its Colonial History and Romance* (New York: 1851), 444–45.

As a nation, the Natchez were thus entirely destroyed. Great sympathy was felt for them by all the tribes in Mississippi and Alabama; even the Choctaws, who were so wedded to the French, being sad on account of their fate, and annoyed at the unparalleled cruelties which they experienced at the hands of their vindictive conquerors. The noble Creeks, upon the Coosa, received some of the refugees with open arms, while the still nobler Chickasaws not only welcomed others to their doors, but swore to shed the blood of their pursuers, in a protracted war. These things made the condition of the French colony a very critical one. The English of Carolina did not fail to fan the fire which, they imagined, would soon consume their ancient colonial enemies. An expedition was fitted out in Charleston, composed of many traders and adventurers, with seventy pack-horses laden chiefly with munitions of war. Whether it was at the instance of the British government, or not, is unknown. They took the well-beaten path for the Chickasaw Nation, and passing by the town of Coosa, then situated in the territory of the present county of Talladega, they prevailed upon some of the refugee Natchez to accompany them, and to assist in repelling the French invasion, which, it was known, was then contemplated. Arriving in the Chickasaw Nation, they dispersed over the country, and not a few of them found their way to the towns of the Choctaws.[3] Soon the whole Indian sky was crimsoned with flashing meteors, and then made dark with angry clouds.

France, apprised of the precarious situation of her distant children, once more resolved to send the veteran Bienville to take care of them. The king began to see that his services could not be dispensed with, and after he had passed eight years in Paris, he sailed for the colony. His arrival at Mobile was hailed with joy and acclamations by the inhabitants.[4] Diron d'Artaguette, a man of nerve and much ability, who had been longer absent from the colony than Bienville, accompanied him. He was presently stationed at Mobile as the king's commissary.[5] Bienville, at first, occupied much of his time in visiting Mobile and New Orleans, for the purpose of giving quiet to the inhabitants and preparing them for a war of invasion. On one occasion, while he was in New Orleans, Diron d'Artaguette aroused all the French settlers towards the east by dispatches which he sent

[2] Marc-Antoine Caillot, a clerk for the Company of the Indies, not only discussed this incident in his hand-written manuscript—*"Relation du Voyage de la Louisianne ou nouvelle France fait par le Sr. Caillot en l'année 1730"*—but added an in-text drawing of the Natchez woman tied to the poles awaiting her torture. The Historic New Orleans Collection purchased Caillot's manuscript at auction in 2004. Although his residence in New Orleans was brief, he witnessed the arrival of wounded French refugees and had access to first-hand reports and documents about Natchez and other French outposts. Sophie White, *Wild Frenchmen and Frenchified Indians: Material Culture and Race in Colonial Louisiana* (Philadelphia: University of Pennsylvania Press, 2012), 224–25; Chris Waddington, "Scalawag French clerk stars in New Orleans exhibit and long lost historic text," *The Times-Picayune*, 11 June 2013.

[3] English traders had been trading in the Chickasaw towns under official sanctions since the passage of the Indian Trade Regulation Act of 1707 and unofficially since at least 1698. The French failed to aggressively establish trade with the Chickasaw while the English traders traveled to their towns with pack-horses loaded with a large array of goods—including guns, blankets and fabrics, kettles, glass beads, knives, hatchets, tools, and ornaments made of copper, brass, and silver. By the early 1720s, warfare with the French allied Choctaws and the English trade influenced small parties of Chickasaw under Squirrel King to establish a town on the Savannah River, with movement back and forth between the western villages and Savannah Town. In 1741, a village known as "Breed Camp" was established on the Coosa River among the Upper Creeks as a base between Savannah Town and the western villages. Atkinson, *Splendid*

among them in relation to the arrival of the English expedition, to which allusion has just been made, and of the determination of the Choctaws to act, in future, against the French. He warned everybody to be upon their guard, for it was probable they might be butchered at any hour. The people of Mobile were in a state of extreme terror; they never went to mass without carrying their guns in their hands. Indeed, they at one time resolved to retire to New Orleans; but Bienville arriving commanded them to remain and fear nothing. He highly disapproved of the excitement which Diron d'Artaguette had produced, and thought there was no occasion for such officious watchfulness on the part of the commissary. This produced unpleasant feelings between them, and they indulged in recriminations of each other in official reports to the government. Bienville was mortified at the conduct of D'Artaguette in rebuking the Choctaw chiefs, who had recently paid him a visit, for permitting the English to come among them. Further, he dismissed them without presents, upon which they returned home highly offended.[6] These things were represented to the government by Bienville, while D'Artaguette, on the other hand, stated in one of his dispatches that Bienville's opposition to him arose from the fact that he had reported the "misconduct of his protégés or favorites, Le Sueur, and the Jesuit, Father Baudouin, who, to the great scandal of the Choctaws, seduce their women."*

It is pleasant to us to be able to state that only a few of the missionaries, of the order of Jesuits, thus abused the holy offices with which they were entrusted. The great body of them led the most pious lives and suffered the greatest privations in their efforts to redeem the savages from heathenism.[7]

In the meantime small parties of Natchez, with their generous allies, the Chickasaws, sought all occasions to annoy their enemy. From ambuscades on

* Gayarré, *Louisiana: Its Colonial History and Romance*, 469.

***Land, Splendid People*, 18–23, 25; Cashin, *Guardians of the Valley*, 1–3, 10–14, 20–23.**

[4] King Louis XV signed a royal memoir of instruction to Bienville at Marly on 2 February 1732 confirming his appointment as "Governor of the Province of Louisiana" and outlining his powers and responsibilities. Bienville sailed to Louisiana in late 1732, arriving at Cape Français, Saint-Domingue, on 22 January 1733, where he was greeted by "the chiefs of the Natchez who are slaves." While D'Artaguette had returned to Mobile in 1732, Bienville did not arrive at New Orleans until late February 1733 with orders to replace Périer as governor. *MPA: FD*, 3: 540–83; Giraud, *Company of the Indies, 1723–1731*, 364.

[5] Actually Diron d'Artaguette had been back in France for less than a year, leaving Louisiana because of an open conflict with Périer and suspecting that Périer's tenure was about to end because of the Natchez revolt and his failed Indian policies. Bienville had been absent from Louisiana for eight years. Giraud, *Company of the Indies, 1723–1731*, 32–37, 363–64, 371–77, 427–30.

[6] Pickett is relying on Gayarré's *Louisiana; Its Colonial History and Romance,* which provides no documentation for the phantom English expedition, unless Gayarré believed the English traders to be a significant military threat. Bienville and D'Artaguette, commandant at Mobile, had conflicts over Indian affairs, especially over controlling trade and blocking the English traders among the Chickasaw and Choctaw. Bienville visited Mobile in August-September 1735, revoked D'Artaguette's orders relative to the English traders, restored calm, and met with Choctaw chiefs who affirmed their loyalty to the French. *MPA: FD*, 3: 681–84.

[7] The Jesuit priest Jean-Francois Buisson de Saint-Cosme was also caught up in a scandal surrounding a Natchez chief named Saint-Cosme, a son of the female Sun, Tattooed Arm. In an interview with Le Page Du Pratz as a prisoner at New Orleans in 1731, she disclosed that her son's father was a Frenchman. Barnett, in his *The Natchez Indians: A History to 1735,* denies the relationship, but George Edward Milne presents them as a couple in his "Picking Up the Pieces: Natchez Coalescence

the hilltops and banks of the rivers, along the Indian paths in the interior, and from dark valleys in the mountains, they sprang upon the French trappers, hunters, and traders with the impetuosity of lions and the agility of tigers, and drank their hot blood with the voraciousness of wolves.[8]

But Bienville was straining every nerve to complete his preparations for the invasion of the Chickasaw Nation. He visited Mobile once more, and having assembled at that point a large delegation of Choctaw chiefs, he, in a great measure, accomplished his object in gaining them over to his side. It was important that he should do so, for Red Shoes, a potent chief of that tribe, had already declared in favor of the English.[9] Bienville freely distributed merchandise, and promised a much larger amount if they would assist him in the war, to which they finally consented. Indeed, ever since his arrival from France, he saw the necessity of inspiring the Indian nations with awe and respect, by a bold and successful strike at the Chickasaws. Nor had he failed to demand the necessary men and military supplies from the mother country.[10]

In the midst of these precarious times, a most unfortunate affair occurred in the bay of Mobile. A smuggling vessel, from Jamaica, cast her anchor twelve miles from the town. Diron d'Artaguette ordered her commander to leave the French coast; he refused. The commissary, then, placed Lieutenant Develle in a boat, armed with thirty men, and ordered him to capture the smuggler. When he approached near her, the latter opened an effective fire; seventeen Frenchmen were immediately killed. Before D'Artaguette could reinforce Develle, the smuggler had made her escape to sea.[11] This affair again enraged Bienville, and the war of recrimination was fiercer than ever between him and the commissary. What a pity it was, that men of such worth and character did not better appreciate each

in the Shatter Zone" in *Mapping the Mississippian Shatter Zone: The Colonial Indian Slave Trade and Regional Instability in the American South,* edited by Robbie Ethridge and Sheri Shuck-Hall (Lincoln: University of Nebraska Press, 2009), 388–424. Barnett, *Natchez Indians,* 55–56, 148 n. 197; Le Page Du Pratz, *History of Louisiana,* 87.

[8] While there may have been some isolated strikes by Natchez warriors, most of the Natchez refugees by 1735 had sought safety with the Chickasaw or asylum with the Cherokee and Creeks, out of the reach of the French. Barnett, *Natchez Indians,* 127–32.

[9] Scholars refer to this Choctaw leader as Red Shoes or Red Shoe, who lived at Couëchitto. He served the French during the Natchez and Chickasaw conflicts of the 1730s and was rewarded with a medal as a principal war chief. He gradually became pro-English between 1734 and 1738. "Red shoe"—*soulouche oumastabé* or "red shoe killer"—was a war title and many Choctaw towns had a "red shoe or red shoes" chief or warrior. The French expressed the title as *soulier rouge,* or "red shoe." Galloway, "Choctaw Factionalism," 127–31, 154 n. 38; *MPA: FD,* 1: 34, 257, 296, 300, 371; ibid., 3: 711; ibid., 4: 139, See also Richard White, "Red Shoes: Warrior and Diplomat," in *Struggle and Survival in Colonial America* (Berkeley: University of California Press, 1981): 49–68.

[10] After his arrival in 1733, Bienville began an assessment of the Indian trade and immediately made requests for supplies and a 30 per cent increase in the annual allotment of 20,000 livres for Indian presents and merchandise. He traveled to Mobile in October 1734 where he met with Choctaw leaders who reported "the want of grain . . . forcing them to go live in the woods" and could not "go to war in the spring [1735]." He also hosted six Alabama chiefs who brought a request from four Chickasaw chiefs to meet with him in Mobile. He refused their request pending the receipt of the heads of the Natchez who had taken refuge with them. *MPA: FD,* 1: 254–60; Patricia Dillon Wood, *French-Indian Relations on the Southern Frontier, 1699–1762* (Ann Arbor: UMI Research Press, 1980), 116–17.

other. In olden times they had been great friends.

The commissary had a younger brother, who had behaved with distinguished gallantry in expeditions against the Natchez. He had recently been promoted to the command of the French fort in the district of Illinois. With him Bienville corresponded, respecting the invasion; he was ordered to collect the disposable French forces, and all the Indians in that country who would join him, and with them to march in a southern direction to the Chickasaw towns, while Bienville would march from the south, and meet him in the country of the enemy, on the 31st March 1736. Afterwards the governor informed young D'Artaguette that he had been unable to make his arrangements to join him at that time, but he would meet him at another time, which was also appointed.[12]

Bienville, nine months before this period, had dispatched M. De Lusser, with a company of soldiers and artisans, to a place upon the Tombigbee, which is now called Jones' Bluff, with orders to erect there a fort and cabins to be used as a depot for the army, and, afterwards, to serve as a permanent trading post. That fearless officer had reached these wilds in safety, and it was not long before the forest resounded with the noise of axes and the heavy falling of timber. He was assisted in his labors by many of the Choctaws.[13]

At length the army left New Orleans, and, passing through the lakes, reached Mobile. The vessels containing the supplies having entered the Gulf by way of the Balize, were retarded by winds, and did not arrive until six days afterwards; and then it was discovered that a cargo of rice was destroyed by the salt water. To replace this loss, Bienville set his bakers to work, who made a large supply of biscuits for the army. He sent a dispatch to De Lusser at Fort Tombecbé, ordering him to build ovens, and to have made an abundant supply of biscuits by the time of his arrival at that place. When all things were ready, Bienville embarked his troops at Mobile, and turned his boats up the river of that name. Never before had such a large and imposing fleet of the kind disturbed the deep and smooth waters which now flow by our beautiful commercial emporium. Every kind of up-country craft was employed, and they bore men nearly of all kinds and colors. The crews were composed of genteel merchants,

[11] The Jamaican smuggler incident remains a mystery. Pierre Annibal Develle served as post commander at Fort Toulouse in 1734, and in 1736 he served as a lieutenant under Gilles Austin Payen de Chavoy de Noyan in Bienville's first Chickasaw campaign. Develle had a successful career: commander at Fort Tombecbé in 1747, recipient of the Cross of St. Louis in 1750, major at Mobile in 1752, and named the king's lieutenant in 1759. *MPA: FD*, 1: 318; ibid., 4: 310 n. 10, 312, 314 n. 1.

[12] Pierre d'Artaguette served against the Natchez and was placed in command of the Illinois District and Fort de Chartres in October 1732. Following Bienville's order, he left the Illinois post on 22 February 1736 with a French force of "thirty soldiers, one hundred voyagers and colonists and almost all the . . . Kaskaskias." D'Artaguette expected warriors from the Cahokias, Michigamias, Miamis, and "forty Iroquois" to join him giving him over three hundred Indian auxiliaries. His force floated down the Mississippi River to Prudhomme Bluffs, north of modern Memphis, Tennessee, where he constructed a small outpost. Leaving a garrison of twenty-five men under Captain Jolibois, he led his force toward the Chickasaw towns on 5 March 1736. Ibid., 1: 74, 79, 311–12; ibid., 3: 615–16, 667; Atkinson, *Splendid Land, Splendid People*, 43.

[13] In January 1736, Bienville dispatched Joseph Christophe de Lusser, a Swiss captain in the French service at Mobile, to construct a fort with housing and ovens on the Tombigbee River above its confluence with the Black Warrior. If Bienville followed his 1735 plan for this military depot, De Lusser had forty French soldiers and twenty Swiss troops under his command. He selected a site on an eighty foot white limestone—Demopolis chalk—bluff

gentlemen of leisure and fortune, loafers and convicts, rough but bold mariners, veteran soldiers, sturdy and invincible Canadians, monks and priests, Choctaws and Mobilians, and a company of Negroes commanded by Simon, a free mulatto. The fleet comprised more than sixty of the largest pirogues and bateaux.[14] Entering the main Tombigbee, Bienville made his way up that stream to the confluence of the Warrior, and there, passing into the Little Tombigbee, he at length arrived at the fort.* Heavy rains and much high water had retarded his passage.

The governor found that the fort was unfinished, and only some cabins, surrounded by stockades and covered with leaves, could be occupied. The bakers had prepared but few biscuits, for the fire cracked the prairie soil of which the ovens were made. After various unsuccessful efforts to make suitable ovens, they succeeded by mixing sand with the earth. Bienville was surprised to see, at the fort, four persons in irons—one Frenchman, two Swiss, and Montfort, a sergeant. They had formed the design of assassinating the commandant of the fort, M. De Lusser, and also the keeper of the storehouse, and of carrying off Du Tisné and Rosalie, who had recently been rescued from the Chickasaws, among whom they had been held in slavery. They intended to convey these unfortunate men back to their masters, in order to gain favor with the tribe, who would therefore be induced, after a time, to facilitate their escape to the British provinces. But these assassins were defeated in their plans; for Lieutenant Grondel, with the rapidity of action and the bravery which had ever distinguished him, arrested Montfort with his own hands.[15] The prisoners were tried by a court martial,[16] and being sentenced to be shot, were "presently passed by the arms at the head of all the troops."†

When all the allied Choctaws had arrived, Bienville reviewed his troops upon the plain in the rear of the fort. He found that his army was composed of five hundred and fifty men, exclusive of officers, together with six hundred Indians. He now assumed the line of march for the country of the enemy. The larger number of the French troops embarked in the boats. Some of the Indians

* Now Jones' Bluff.

† Dumont de Montigny, *Mémoires historiques sur la Louisiane*, 216.

referred to as Jones' Bluff after the creation of Sumter County, Alabama, in 1832. *MPA: FD*, 1: 258, 278–79, 316.

[14] In building his army, Bienville withdrew all the officers and soldiers from the garrisons at Natchez, Natchitoches, and Balize without leaving them defenseless. He formed a volunteer company of young men and voyagers at New Orleans and recruited another company of militia from the unmarried men near the city. He departed for Mobile on 4 March 1736, leaving orders for De Noyan to bring four French companies to Mobile when other boats were available. At Mobile he also stripped the Fort Condé garrison of its French and Swiss soldiers, leaving only a token force and a volunteer militia company. After arriving at Fort Tombecbé, Bienville formed a company of forty-five Negroes out of some one hundred slaves, commanded by free Negro officers and led by Simon. Ibid., 298–99.

[15] Jean Philippe Goujon de Grondel came to Louisiana as an officer in Karrer's Swiss regiment in 1732. His wife was Captain Dutisné's (Du Tisné's) daughter. Chevalier de Karrer's regiment had one hundred and fifty men, and he had agreed to furnish their clothing, arms, and wages. Ibid., 306 n. 1; ibid., 3: 548–50, 558.

[16] Bienville scheduled a council of war on 30 April 1736 that found the two French soldiers "guilty of conspiracy against the lives of officers of the post and of plotting desertion." The Swiss also held a council and found the two Swiss soldiers guilty of the same charges. Ibid., 1: 301.

proceeded in their own canoes, while many hardy Canadians, called *couriers de bois*, marched with other Indians, sometimes along the banks, where the swamps did not intervene; and then again a mile or two from the river. It was truly an imposing scene to be exhibited in these interminable wilds.[17] After encountering many difficulties, the redoubtable Bienville at length reached the spot where now stands the city of Columbus, in Mississippi; and pursuing his tedious voyage, finally moored his boats at or near the place now known as Cotton Gin Port. Here disembarking, he immediately began to fell the trees in the forest, and soon stockaded a place ample enough to secure his baggage and provisions, together with the sick; while the side fronting the river was arranged with loopholes for muskets, to protect his boats, which were all unladen and drawn up close together. He was twenty-seven miles from the towns of the enemy, which lay in a western direction. He left twenty men here under Vanderek, besides the keeper of the magazine, the patroons of the boats, and some of the soldiers who were sick. With some difficulty he hired a sufficient number of the Choctaws to transport the sacks of powder and balls, for the Negroes were already laden with other things.[18]

Taking provisions with him to last twelve days, the governor began the march in the evening, and that night encamped six miles from the depot. The rains which incommoded him in his voyage up the river, did not forsake him on his march upon the present occasion; for scarcely had he formed his camp when a violent storm arose. The next day he passed three deep ravines—the soldiers wading up to their waists—and after gaining the opposite banks, slipping and falling constantly upon the slimy soil. Great difficulties were surmounted in transporting the effects of the army over these angry torrents. The banks on either side were covered with large canes, but Bienville took the precaution always to send spies in advance, to prevent surprise from ambuscades. Soon, however, the French were relieved by the appearance of the most beautiful country in the world. The prairies were stretched out wide before them, covered with green grass, flowers and strawberries, while forests of magnificent trees were to be seen in the distance.[19] A breeze gently played over the surface of the lovely plains, and a May day's sun warmed all nature into life. The sleek cattle were everywhere grazing upon these sweet meadows of nature. The nimble deer bounded along, and droves of wild horses, of every variety of color, with lofty tails and spreading manes, made the earth resound with their rapid tread. Alas! Alas! To think that the inhabitants, whom the Great Spirit had placed in a country so lovely and

[17] Pickett and Gayarré are not on the same page with Bienville. On 1 May 1736, Bienville met with an assembly of Choctaw chiefs who agreed to have their warriors in fourteen days at the Octibia (Oktibbeha)—now Tibbee Creek—"that forms the frontier between the Choctaws and Chickasaws forty leagues above Tombekbé." Two days later—3 May—Bienville's army of approximately 600 men began to move up the Tombigbee. Ibid., 301–02.

[18] Bienville's forces departed from Octibia (Tibbee) Creek on 16 May 1736 and moved up to their final portage "situated on a fine bluff ten leagues from the Chickasaw Indians." At this place, he was joined by the Choctaws—"from six to seven hundred men including their chiefs." After constructing a fortification to store "munitions, provisions and merchandise," he distributed ammunition and rations for twelve days. Bienville left Sieur Vanderek, a sergeant, eighteen soldiers, and "the masters of the boats and pirogues, who amounted to thirty-five men." Ibid., 301–02, 317.

[19] Since leaving Fort Tombecbé on 3 May, Bienville's army had suffered through nine days of rain, and on the 24th his encampment was doused by a violent storm throughout the night. After slogging through ravines and thick cane, his men arrived on 25 May in "the finest country in the world, and camped at the edge of a prairie two leagues from the villages." Ibid., 303.

so enchanting, were soon to be assailed by an army of foreigners, assisted by their own neighbors.[20]

Drawing nearer and nearer to the enemy, Bienville finally encamped within six miles of their towns. His camp was formed upon the border of a delightful prairie, the view across which was not interrupted by trees, until it had reached far beyond the Indian houses. He had previously sent spies in all directions, to look for D'Artaguette and his troops, who were to have joined him there. The bands, chiefly composed of Indians, returned without having heard anything of that unfortunate officer. The governor was sorely disappointed, and could no longer hope for aid from that source, and he resolved to rely upon his own forces. His intention, at first, was to march to a circuitous direction, around the Chickasaw villages, in order to attack the Natchez town which lay behind them, and which had recently been erected. But the Choctaws had become very impatient to assail an advanced village of the Chickasaws, which, they insisted, could be easily taken, and which, they stated, contained a large amount of provisions. Their importunities were disregarded until strengthened by the entreaties of the Chevalier Noyan, the nephew of the governor, and many other French officers, whose impetuous disposition made them eager for an immediate attack. The house of the enemy stood upon a hill, in the prairie, and spread out in the shape of a triangle. After some consideration, Bienville resolved to give the French an opportunity of gratifying a long sought revenge, especially when it was made known to him that his camp was then pitched near the last water which his men could procure for miles in a western direction. At two o'clock, in the afternoon, the Chevalier Noyan was placed at the head of a column consisting of a detachment of fifteen men drawn from each of the eight French companies, a company of grenadiers, forty-five volunteers and sixty-five Swiss.[21]

The Chickasaws had fortified themselves with

[20] The romantic prose added by Pickett and Gayarré cannot be found in Bienville's correspondence on this expedition or in his "Narrative of the War against the Chickasaws." Such a large army would have spooked all the deer for miles, and there is little evidence that the Chickasaw had herds of cattle. However, the Chickasaws were known to be great horsemen, but their horses were not wild. They would have grazed freely on the prairies near their villages. Ibid., 316–20.

[21] Bienville's army was first exposed at daybreak by Choctaw scouts who were discovered by a party of fifteen Chickasaws. The Great Chief pressed him to attack Chukafalaya (Choukafalya) before striking the Natchez town because it had given the Choctaws "more trouble than all the others." Contrary to his plan of attack, Bienville gave into their arguments and ordered an attack at two o'clock under Chevalier de Noyan. Ibid., 304–05.

much skill, and were assisted by Englishmen, who had caused them to hoist a flag of their country over one of their defenses. The French troops, as they advanced, were not a little surprised to see the British Lion, against which many of them had often fought in Europe, now floating over the rude huts of American Indians, and bidding them defiance. The Chickasaws had fortified their houses in a most defensive manner, by driving large stakes into the ground around them. Many loopholes were cut through the latter, very near the ground. Within the palisades, entrenchments were cut, deep enough to protect the persons of the Indians as high as their breasts. In these ditches they stood, and when the battle began, shot through the loopholes at the French. The tops of these fortified houses were covered with timbers, upon which was placed a thick coat of mud plaster, so that neither ignited arrows nor bombshells could set the houses on fire. What added still more to the security of the Chickasaws, was the position of some of their houses, which stood in nearly opposite directions, so as to admit of destructive cross-firing. Bienville having previously learned that there were several of the British in the village, had, with much humanity, as it may at that time have seemed, directed the Chevalier Noyan to give them time to retire before he brought on the attack.[22]

The division then marched briskly on. It was protected by movable breastworks, called mantelets, which were now carried by the company of Negroes. As their lives appear not to have been esteemed of as much value as those of the French, these Negroes were used in the same manner as *shields* are in battle. When the troops advanced within carbine shot of the village of Ackia, where waved a British flag, one of the Negroes was killed, and another wounded. They all now threw down their mantelets and precipitately fled.[23] The French, with their usual impetuosity, rapidly advanced. They entered the village. The grenadiers led. And now, no longer protected by the mantelets, they received a severe fire from the Chickasaws, which killed and wounded many. Among the former was the gallant and accomplished Chevalier de Contrecoeur; and when he fell dead it produced an unpleasant feeling among those around him, by whom he was greatly esteemed. Upon his right and left soldiers lay dead, discoloring the green grass with their hot blood. But the troops carried three fortified cabins, and reached several smaller ones, which they presently wrapped in flames. The chief fort and other fortified houses lay some distance in the rear of those they had in possession.[24]

The Chevalier Noyan was eager to advance upon them, but turning

[22] Bienville's force began their attack against three of the ten Chickasaw towns—Chukafalaya, Ackia, and Apeony—located on a hill or ridge that were well fortified and relatively close together. He ordered Chevalier de Noyan to strike Ackia, the town opposite Apeony, which was flying the British flag over a trader's cabin, perhaps thinking the Englishmen would take the opportunity to escape. Ibid., 305; Gregory A. Waselkov, "Indian Maps of the Colonial Southeast," in *Powhatan's Mantle*, 481–86.

[23] According to Bienville's journal of the Chickasaw campaign, the men moving the mantelets—a mobile wooden shield—suffered casualties and "threw down the mantelets on the spot and ran" as the French troops approached Ackia. *MPA: FD*, 1: 305. See Figures et plan du mantelet servant à l'attaque du fort des Chicachas [1739], Bibliothèque et Archives Canada, FR CAOM 3DFC308C (online).

[24] Bienville had sent Chevalier de Contrecoeur in July 1735 at the head of a convoy to deliver a load of gun powder to Fort Chartres to replace that which a combined Chickasaw and Natchez force had seized the previous fall. Since Bienville does not list him with a rank in 1736, he apparently was an ensign or one of his trusted Canadian militiamen. *MPA: FD*, 1: 266–67, 292, 318.

[25] De Noyan, Develle, and Grondel have been identified earlier. Renault de Hauterive (c. 1696–1741) was criticized by Périer for his lack of courage in the assault on the Natchez

round to take a rapid survey of his forces he was mortified to perceive that only the officers, a dozen of the volunteers, and some grenadiers remained with him. Dismayed by the fall of Captain de Lusser,* who was now killed, and seeing a popular sergeant of grenadiers and several soldiers also fall, the troops retreated to the cabins which were first taken. In vain did the officers, who belonged to the rear, endeavor to drive them on to the scene of action. A panic had seized them, and no exhortation, threats, promises of promotion, or hopes of military glory could induce them to make the slightest advance from their cowardly position. But the officers, resolved more than ever to do their duty, and placing themselves at the head of a few brave soldiers, essayed to storm the fort. But just at the moment of their contemplated charge the brave Chevalier Noyan, Grondel, an invincible lieutenant of the Swiss, D'Hauterive, a captain of the grenadiers, Monbrun, Develle, and many other officers and soldiers received severe wounds. The balls of the Chickasaws came thick and whizzed over the prairies.[25]

The bleeding De Noyan stood his ground, and dispatched his aid to assist in bringing up the soldiers, who still screened themselves behind the cabins; but as he left to perform the order a Chickasaw ball put an end to his existence. The death of this officer, whose name was De Juzan, increased the panic which had so unfortunately seized upon the larger number of the troops.[26] A party of Indians at this moment rushed up to scalp Grondel, the Swiss officer, who had fallen near the walls of the fort. A brave sergeant, with four fearless soldiers, rushed to the rescue. Driving off the savages, they were about to bear him off in their arms when a fire from the fort killed every one of these noble fellows! But the bleeding Grondel still survived, although those who came to protect his head from the blows of the hatchet lay dead by his side. Another act of heroism is worthy of record. Régnisse now rushed out alone, and making his way to the unfortunate Grondel, who still lay bleeding from five wounds, dragged him out from among the bodies of those who had fallen in his defense, placed him on his back, and returned to the French lines, without receiving a solitary wound from the showers of Chickasaw balls.[27] The almost lifeless Grondel received, however, another severe wound as he was borne off by the noble Régnisse.†

* It will be recollected that De Lusser, who was now killed, was the officer whom Bienville sent to construct Fort Tombecbé, upon the site of the present Jones' Bluff.

† This Grondel was an officer of indomitable courage. His life was full of romantic events. He had fought several duels at Mobile. He recovered from the wounds which

villages in 1730. However, Bienville appointed him as commandant at the Natchez post after his return to Louisiana, and he was one of the oldest captains in the first Chickasaw campaign, leading a company of grenadiers. Sieur Monbrun, a Canadian, and Sieur de Léry were sent by Bienville with Red Shoe's scouting party on 25 April 1736 to verify his report. Ibid., 119, 282, 299, 303, 306, 318–19, 362; Dumont de Montigny, *Memoir*, 267, 436.

[26] Pierre Gabriel Juzan came to Louisiana as a half-pay lieutenant in 1730, served as an adjutant at Natchez, and worked successfully with the Tunica. By 1733, he was serving at Mobile when he captured an English smugglers ship off Dauphin Island on 4 November 1733. He served as an adjutant to De Noyan against the Chickasaw when he was mortally wounded. *MPA: FD*, 1: 306, 319; ibid., 4: 111–13, 113 n. 1, 131–32; Dumont de Montigny, *Memoir*, 266, 268 n. 18, 428.

[27] According to Jean-Francois-Benjamin Dumont de Montigny, an unidentified Swiss soldier found Grondel in a cabin and carried him on his shoulders to safety. However, he maintains that they were struck by a single ball that hit Grondel's calf, passed through his leg, and struck the soldier between his shoulders—requiring several men to carry them to safety. Dumont de Montigny, *Memoir*, 268.

But where were the six hundred Choctaws, while the French were thus expiring in agony upon the prairie? Painted, plumed, and dressed in a manner the most fantastic and horrible, they kept the plain, on either side of the French lines, at a distance where the balls of the enemy could not reach them, sending forth yells and shouts, and occasionally dancing and shooting their guns in the air. The brave Chickasaws maintained their positions in the fortified houses, and, from loopholes, riddled the French with their unerring rifles. They, too, yelled most awfully. The scene was one calculated to excite deep interest, for, added to all this, the looker-on might have viewed the flames rising up from the burning cabins, and sending above them volumes of black smoke, which a May breeze wafted to the far off forests.[28]

The Chevalier De Noyan now ordered a retreat to the advanced cabins, and when he had arrived there, he dispatched an officer to Bienville, bearing an account of their critical condition. Noyan sent him word that, although severely wounded himself, he was determined to keep the position which he had just taken. He requested that a detachment should be sent to his assistance, to bear off the dead and wounded, and assist those who were alive to make a retreat, as, now, no further hope remained of storming the fortifications of the Chickasaws. Bienville was hastened in his determination to send aid, by observing that a Chickasaw force on the flank, which had not yet participated in the battle, was about to sally from their houses and immolate the French officers and the few soldiers who had remained with them. He then immediately dispatched Beauchamp, with eighty men, to the scene of action. Arriving there he found the French officers huddled together, keeping their ground at the imminent peril of their lives. Beauchamp, in advancing, had already lost several men. The Chickasaws now redoubled their exertions, and made the plains resound with their exulting shouts. Beauchamp began the retreat, carrying off many of the wounded and the dead, but unfortunately was forced to leave some behind, who fell into the tiger clutches of the Chickasaws.[29] When the French had retreated some distance towards Bienville's headquarters, the Choctaws, by way of bravado, rushed up to the Chickasaw fortifications, as if they intended to carry them by storm, but receiving a general volley from the enemy, they fled in great terror over the prairie.[30]

he received in this battle, and was promoted to high military stations.

[28] The Choctaws were arrayed on the outer flanks of the French force that made the initial assault on 26 May 1736 against Ackia around "three o'clock in the afternoon . . . with drums beating and flags flying." When the French and Swiss troops began falling back, Bienville sent Jadart de Beauchamp, commandant at Fort Condé, to direct an orderly retreat. At this point, the Choctaws, who had taken up a position "under cover on the slope of the hill waiting the outcome, then rose and fired several volleys," aiding the French retreat and losing twenty-two men, killed and wounded. *MPA: FD,* 1: 306–07, 318–20.

[29] In Bienville's letter to Minister Maurepas, he reported that he dispatched Jadart de Beauchamp with eighty men to assist with the retreat, but in an anonymous "Narrative of the War against the Chickasaw" in the Ministry of the Colonies files, the author reports that Beauchamp was in command of one hundred and fifty men. When Beauchamp arrived "at the place of the attack," he found mainly officers who had been abandoned by their men and who were "holding their ground." Ibid., 306–07, 319.

[30] Contrary to Pickett and his sources, Bienville reported the Choctaws under cover of the hill and on the flanks of the retreating soldiers "rose and fired several volleys" and suffered twenty-two casualties. In the "Narrative of the War against the Chickasaw," the anonymous author reported: "We were obliged to retire under the protection of our allies . . . about three hundred

The battle of Ackia had lasted three hours, and resulted in glory to the Chickasaws, and disgrace to the French. When the French troops arrived at the camp, proper attention was paid to the wounded and the dying.[31] It was not long before this brilliant and exciting scene was made to give place to one which presented an aspect at once quiet, calm and beautiful. The sun, in his retirement for the night, had just sunk to the tops of the trees in the far off distance. A cool and delicious breeze was made sweet with the odor of wild flowers. The Chickasaws were as quiet as the boa constrictor after he has gorged upon his prey.[32] The cattle and horses, much disturbed during the fight, now began to move up and feed upon their accustomed meadows. What a contrast had been produced by the lapse of only two hours!

During this quiet scene, a collection of French officers were on one side of the camp, summing up the misfortunes of the day. Among them stood Simon, the commander of the Negroes who fled from the field. Simon was a favorite with the officers, and had resolutely maintained his ground during the engagement. Some of them rallied him upon the flight of his company, which annoyed him excessively. At that moment, a drove of horses came down to the stream to slake their thirst, not far from the fortified houses of the Chickasaws. The desperate Simon, in reply to those who made sport of his company, seized a rope and ran off towards the horses saying, "I will show you that a Negro is as brave as anyone." He passed around the horses in full range of the Chickasaw rifles, from which balls were showered upon him, and making his way up to a beautiful white mare, threw a rope over her head, and thus securing her, passed it around her nose, mounted upon her back with the agility of a Comanche Indian, and pressed her with rapid speed into the French lines.[33] He did not receive a wound, and he was welcomed with shouts by the soldiers, and was no more jeered on account of the cowardice of his company.*

Bienville, pleased with the gallantry which Régnisse had displayed in bearing off the wounded Grondel, immediately from under the guns of the Chickasaws, had him brought to the marquee, complimented him upon the generous and heroic act which he had performed, and proposed to promote him to the rank of an officer. The brave Régnisse modestly replied that he had done nothing more than what could have been accomplished by any of his brother grenadiers, and stated that

* Dumont de Montigny, *Mémoires historiques sur la Louisiane.*

men in number who lost many of their men. They aided our retreat. . . . Our allies escorted us back to our boats and did not leave us until they saw us all embarked in our boats and pirogues, and we returned to our capital city." Ibid., 307, 319–20.

[31] In his *Mémoires historiques,* Jean-Francois-Benjamin Dumont de Montigny writes that "a big pit" was dug for a common grave for the bodies of their dead comrades and "a fire lit on top to conceal from the Indians the location of the grave." Dumont de Montigny, *Memoir,* 271.

[32] Jean-Francois-Benjamin Dumont de Montigny gives us a very different scenario emanating from the Chickasaw villages: "While our men shot off these fires of celebration, or rather of sadness, the Indian women in the village were beating on the great pot that they used as a drum, yelling insults and taunts at us in their songs, describing how ten of our men were worth less than one of theirs." Ibid., 270.

[33] Neither Bienville in his report to Minister Maurepas or the anonymous writer of the "Narrative of the War against the Chickasaw" name Simon as the commander of the Negro company, and they do not relate the rash incident of riding the white mare in front of the Chickasaw guns. *MPA: FD,* 1: 297–314, 316–20.

[34] Again, neither of the two reports to the Ministry of the Colonies—Bienville's or the anonymous "Narrative"—gives the name of Régnisse, the Swiss soldier credited with saving

as he could not write, he was unfitted for an officer; therefore he declined the intended honor.[34]

Night now shrouded the scene with its sable mantle, and the French troops reposed behind some trees which had been felled for their protection. The Chickasaws remained quiet within their entrenchments. At length day dawned, and exhibited to Bienville a painful sight. On the ramparts of the Chickasaws were suspended the French soldiers and officers, whom Beauchamp was forced to leave upon the field. Their limbs had been separated from their bodies, and thus were they made to dangle in the air, for the purpose of insulting the defeated invaders. Many of the officers wished to rush again upon the villages, but Bienville determined to retreat, as the Choctaws were of no assistance to him, and he was without cannon to batter down the fortifications. In the afternoon, at two o'clock, he began the retrograde march. The soldiers, worn down with fatigue produced by the battle and the mortifications arising from its disgraceful termination, were unable, in addition to their heavy loads of baggage, to carry the wounded, who were placed in litters. Consequently night set in by the time Bienville had marched only four miles; here the camp was again made.[35]

The Choctaws were highly exasperated on account of this slow movement, and Red Shoes, who had long endeavored to wean his people from the French interest, now vociferously threatened to take with him the greater portion of the Choctaws, and thus leave the French to the mercy of the Chickasaws in this wild and distant region. Bienville was startled when he was informed of this determination. He sent for the main chief of the Choctaws, and by his eloquence and the force of that mysterious influence which he possessed, he succeeded not only in getting the Choctaws to remain with the army, but made them consent to assist in the transportation of the wounded. Red Shoes rebuked the head chief, for consenting to such terms, in a manner so insulting, that the latter drew his pistol from his belt, and was in the act of shooting him, when Bienville seized his arm, saved the life of Red Shoes, and, for a while, put an end to an affair which threatened the most serious consequences. The next morning Bienville put his troops upon the march, and he arrived at the depot, upon the Tombigbee, on the 29th May, after he had buried two of his men, on the way, who had died of their wounds.[36]

Bienville was astonished to observe how much the river had

Grondel's life, or the meeting with Bienville. However, Dumont de Montigny in his *Memoir* relates how his height and weight caused his porters to abandon his stretcher. The surgeons were called back to examine him and they declared "his wound was fatal and untreatable," virtually condemning him to death. Father Baudoin, chaplain of the army, heard his confession, and he "was buried alive in a hole and covered with dirt." This story does not appear in Dumont de Montigny's *Mémoires historiques sur la Louisiane,* published in 1753. Ibid.; Dumont de Montigny, *Memoir,* 272, 272 n. 23.

[35] While Bienville's report and the anonymous "Narrative" are both silent about the dismembered bodies, Dumont de Montigny records that the Chickasaws had cut the bodies of the fallen "into quarters and hung them up in the air so as to make us see the spectacle." Bienville reports departing the camp near the Chickasaw villages "at one o'clock in the afternoon" and marching only "a league and a half" because of fatigue, baggage, and the wounded. *MPA/FD,* 1: 308; Montigny, *Memoir,* 271.

[36] Bienville met with the Great Chief of the Choctaws and several others and reminded them that he had altered his original plan to attack the Natchez village "to please them and to avenge them" on Chukafalaya. The chiefs agreed that each village would provide men to carry one wounded man to the portage on the river—reached on 29 May 1736. Both Bienville and the anonymous "Narrative" fail to give details of a confrontation between Red Shoes and the Great Chief. *MPA: FD,* 1: 308–09; 319–20.

fallen, and he hurried his effects into the boats, for fear that the delay of a day longer would leave him without a stream sufficient to convey him to Mobile. When the troops had embarked, the ropes which bound the boats to the banks were untied, and then the discomfited French party passed down the stream. The channel of the Little Tombigbee was here so crooked and narrow, that the boats had frequently to stop until logs and projecting limbs were cut out of the way. If the Chickasaws had followed up the French, they could easily have destroyed Bienville's army at this time. At length the army reached Fort Tombecbé, now Jones' Bluff. Bienville, sending on a portion of the troops, and the sick and wounded to Mobile, disembarked at the fort. He remained there, however, but one day, which he consumed in planning upon paper, and tracing upon the ground additions which he directed to be made to the defenses.[37] Then, leaving Captain De Berthet in command of Fort Tombecbé, with a garrison of thirty Frenchmen and twenty Swiss, provisions to last for the remainder of the year, and an abundance of merchandise intended to be used in commerce with the Indians, the governor entered his boats, and continued the voyage until they were moored at the town of Mobile.[38]

But where was the brave and unfortunate D'Artaguette? Why did not his army join Bienville at the Chickasaw town? The reader will presently see. That officer had assembled the tribes of the Illinois at Fort Chartres, and had made them acquainted with the plans of Governor Bienville. With these Indians, and others which De Vincennes had collected upon the Wabash, together with thirty soldiers and one hundred volunteers, D'Artaguette floated down the Mississippi River until he reached the last of the Chickasaw Bluffs.[39] He had expected to have been joined by De Grand-Pré, who commanded at the Arkansas, and that officer had sent twenty-eight warriors of that tribe to ascertain whether D'Artaguette was at Ecores à Prudhomme. These scouts were instructed to return with the necessary information;

[37] Before launching his attack on the Chickasaw, Bienville had drawn a plan of a completed Fort Tombecbé and promised Count Maurepas, minister and secretary of state, that he would send him the plan when he returned from the expedition. However, the only existing plan of Fort Tombecbé was drawn in pen, water colored on paper, and signed by Ignace-François Broutin (1690–1751), engineer-in-chief for Louisiana, and François Saucier, draftsman and engineer, at New Orleans on 20 May 1737—*Plan du Fort de Tombecbé, tel qu'il etoit au mois de mars 1737.* Ibid., 295, 297; ibid., 4: 191 n. 1; Wilson, "Colonial Fortifications," 115–18; Walter J. Saucier and Katherine Wagner Seineke, "Francois Saucier, Engineer of Fort de Chartres, Illinois," in *Frenchmen and French Ways,* 199–227; *Plan du Fort de Tombecbé, tel qu'il etoit au mois de mars* 1737, http://rla.unc.edu/emas/local-settl.html.

[38] Bienville departed Fort Tombecbé on 3 June 1736 and arrived back in Mobile on 8 June. On 7 June, he stopped at a Tohome village where he received "the first news of the disaster" suffered by Pierre d'Artaguette and his Illinois army. *MPA: FD,* 1: 309.

[39] After withdrawing most of his garrison at Fort de Chartres, recruiting volunteers and all the available Indians, D'Artaguette and François-Marie de Vincennes (1700–1736) floated down the Mississippi to the Prudhomme Bluffs—modern Memphis, Tennessee—arriving on 4 March 1736. They had a force of one hundred and forty-five French soldiers and volunteers and over three hundred Indians, including Arkansas, Illinois, Miami, and Iroquois. Vincennes served as commandant of the posts at Ouyatanons and Oüabache (Wabash). Ibid., 311; Yves F. Zoltvany, "François-Marie de Vinsenne (Vincennes)," *DCB* (online).

[40] Joseph Louis Boucher de Grand-Pré served as commander of the posts at Pointe Coupée and Tunica before being appointed commandant at the Arkansas post in 1734. He received a promotion to lieutenant in 1736 and, through his influence with the Arkansas, raised two parties to support D'Artaguette's advance on the Chickasaw. Unfortunately there was a breakdown

but upon arriving at that place, and finding that D'Artaguette had set out upon his expedition, they hastened to follow him into the enemy's country.[40] Disembarking at the Chickasaw Bluffs, D'Artaguette marched across the country, at a slow pace, hoping to be overtaken by De Grand-Pré, and also by Monchervaux, who had been ordered to bring on his Cahokias and Michigamias.[41] Pursuing the march in an eastward direction, D'Artaguette advanced among the sources of the Yalobusha and there encamped on the 9th May. He was but a few miles east of the site of the present town of Pontotoc, in Mississippi, near the place where he and Bienville were to have met each other, and not more than thirty miles from the spot where the latter, afterwards, moored his boats,—near the present Cotton Gin Port.[42]

D'Artaguette sought, in vain, for intelligence of the commander-in-chief. He was assisted by Lieutenant Vincennes, the young Voisin, and Sénat, a holy father of the order of Jesuits, in arranging and conducting the spy companies, who roamed the forests in search of Bienville.[43] But nothing could be heard of him until a courier brought to D'Artaguette a letter, in which he was informed that unexpected delays would prevent Bienville from reaching the Chickasaw towns before the last of April. The red allies had become impatient, for, by this time, D'Artaguette had occupied his camp for eleven days. He now resolved to advance upon the Chickasaws, as his allies had threatened to abandon him if he did not soon bring on the attack. They represented to him that the advance town was inhabited by the refugee Natchez, and by taking it they could return to their encampment with an abundance of provisions, where they might remain entrenched until Bienville's arrival. This plausible proposition found advocates in the French officers. The allied forces consisted of one hundred and thirty Frenchmen, and three hundred and sixty Indians. The French advanced within a mile of the village, on Palm Sunday. Frontigny was here left at the camp, with thirty men, in charge of all the baggage. D'Artaguette advanced rapidly to the attack, which he presently brought on with his accustomed gallantry. At that moment, thirty Englishmen and five hundred Indians, who were concealed behind an adjacent hill, rose up and fell upon the invaders with such impetuosity that the Miamis and the Illinois fled from the battlefield. Indeed, all the Indians took to their heels, except a few Iroquois and Arkansas, who behaved in the bravest manner.[44]

The guns of the enemy brought to the ground Lieutenant St.

in communication and he and his main party abandoned the expedition. *MPA: FD*, 1: 313–14; ibid., 4: 96 n. 12; Atkinson, *Splendid Land, Splendid People*, 43.

[41] Much like Grand-Pré, Jean-François Tisserant de Monchervaux failed to make the rendezvous with D'Artaguette at the Prudhomme Bluffs. In a letter to Count Maurepas on 8 May 1737, Diron d'Artaguette was very critical of both "on account of the little diligence that they used in order to join my brother." *MPA: FD*, 1: 337; ibid., 4: 307 n. 3; Arnold, *Colonial Arkansas*, 128.

[42] D'Artaguette feared losing many of his Indian auxiliaries and was operating under the schedule set by Bienville. He had not received Bienville's dispatch telling him to wait because of the delays he had encountered leaving New Orleans and later Mobile. *MPA: FD*, 1: 298, 300–01.

[43] Most sources report that young Voisin was sixteen years-old when he joined D'Artaguette's army. Father Antoine Sénat was a Jesuit missionary at Kaskaskia in the Illinois country. Ibid., 1: 312–13, 331–32; Atkinson, *Splendid Land, Splendid People*, 44.

[44] On Palm Sunday, 26 March 1736, D'Artaguette's forces struck Ougoula Tchetoka, a village of some thirty cabins, some distance from the larger Chickasaw villages, and located at modern Belden, Mississippi. When the Chickasaw force swept down a nearby hill, his Illinois and Miami allies gave way almost immediately. D'Artaguette and his French forces fought valiantly but the bravery and tenacity of the some forty Mission Iroquois and the twenty-eight Arkansas probably

Ange, Ensigns De Coulange, De La Graviere and De Courtigny, with six of the militia officers. By this time the French were almost surrounded, but they still continued to keep their position.[45] Presently, Captain Des Essarts was seen to fall, and also Lieutenant Langlois and Ensign Levieux.[46] So great was the loss of the French, in this short, but desperate conflict, that D'Artaguette determined to retreat to the camp, for the double purpose of saving his baggage, and of being reinforced by the men he had left there. But the retreat could not be conducted with the least order, for the Chickasaws were close upon their heels, and at length again surrounded them. D'Artaguette now fell, covered with wounds, and was taken prisoner, together with Father Sénat, Vincennes, Du Tisné, an officer of the regulars, a captain of the militia, named La Lande, and some soldiers, making nineteen in all. Not one man would have escaped the clutches of the brave Chickasaws if a violent storm, which now arose, had not prevented further pursuit. It was a great victory; all the provisions and baggage of D'Artaguette fell into the hands of the Chickasaws, besides eleven horses, four hundred and fifty pounds of powder and twelve hundred bullets. With this powder and these bullets they afterwards shot down the troops of Bienville, as we have already seen.[47]

Voisin, a youth of only sixteen years of age, conducted the retreat for many miles, without food or water, while his men carried such of the wounded as they were able to bear. This noble youth, - one of the bravest that ever lived, - stood by the side of D'Artaguette in all this bloody engagement.[48] At length, on the second day of his painful retreat, he halted his men at a place where Monchervaux, who was following D'Artaguette with one hundred and sixty Indians, had encamped. The latter, collecting the fragments of the army, fell back to the Mississippi River.[49]

At first, the unfortunate D'Artaguette and his

prevented a complete massacre. *MPA: FD*, 1: 312–13; Claiborne A. Skinner, *The Upper Country: French Enterprise in the Colonial Great Lakes* (Baltimore: John Hopkins University Press, 2008), 129–30.

[45] Pierre Groston de Saint-Ange (1693–1736), son of the former commander at Fort de Chartres, served under D'Artaguette at that post. Pierre de Coulange served under Grand-Pré at the Arkansas Post. Louis Drouet de la Graviere (1713–1736), a native of Quebec, was trading at Mackinac in 1731 before his service against the Chickasaw. Arnold, *Colonial Arkansas*, 177; John Francis McDermott, "Robert Groston de Saint-Ange," *DCB* (online); Donald Chaput, "The Family of Drouet de Richerville: Merchants, Soldiers, and Chiefs of Indiana." *Indiana Magazine of History* 74 (June 1978): 103–116.

[46] All but three of D'Artaguette's officers were killed in the initial engagement led by Mingo Ouma or burned alive following the battle. D'Artaguette's army suffered some forty to fifty killed and wounded, including twenty-five to forty French soldiers or militia and ten to fifteen Indian auxiliaries. Both D'Artaguette and Father Sénat were offered horses to escape capture, but both men refused to abandon the men who continued to resist the Chickasaw. *MPA: FD*, 1: 312–13; ibid., 4: 141; Skinner, *Upper Country*, 130–31; Atkinson, *Splendid Land, Splendid People*, 47.

[47] Apparently the Chickasaw took some twenty-two prisoners, including D'Artaguette, who had suffered three gunshot wounds—one to his hand that took off three fingers, one in a leg, and one in the abdomen—and two Indians, one identified as a Chickasaw slave. *MPA: FD*, 4: 141; Atkinson, *Splendid Land, Splendid People*, 47.

equally unfortunate companions in captivity were treated with kindness and attention by the Chickasaws, who dressed their wounds. Hopes of a high ransom prompted this conduct, so unusual with Indians.[50] They expected not only to receive money from Bienville, who was known to be approaching, but imagined that by holding these men as prisoners, the governor would consent to leave their towns unattacked. But at length they received intelligence that Bienville had been defeated, and they now resolved to sacrifice the prisoners.[51] They led them out to a neighboring field, and D'Artaguette, Father Senat, Vincennes, and fifteen others were pinioned to stakes and burned to death![52] One of the soldiers was spared to carry the news of the triumph of the Chickasaws,[53] and the death of these unhappy men, to the mortified Bienville.*

The Chickasaws have never been conquered. They could not be defeated by De Soto with his Spanish army in 1541; by Bienville, with his French army and Southern Indians, in 1736; by D'Artaguette, with his French army and Northern Indians; by the Marquis De Vaudreuil, with his French troops and Choctaws, in 1752; nor by the Creeks, Cherokees, Kickapoos, Shawnees and Choctaws, who continually waged war against them.[54] No! They were "the bravest of the brave"; and even when they had emigrated to the territory of the Arkansas, not many years ago, they soon subdued some tribes who attacked them in that quarter.

Young Men of Northwestern Alabama and Northeastern Mississippi! Remember that the bravest race that ever lived, once occupied the country which you now inhabit—once fished in your streams, and chased the elk over your vast plains. Remember, that whenever that soil, which *you* now tread, was pressed by the feet of foes, it was not only bravely defended, but drenched with the blood of the invaders. Will you ever disgrace that soil, and the memory of its first occupants, by submitting to injustice and oppression, and finally to invasion? We unhesitatingly give the answer for you—"No—no—never!"

* MS letters obtained from Paris. I have also consulted Gayarré, *Histoire de la Louisiane*, 1: 311–31, which contains the dispatches of Bienville to the French court in relation to these battles. Also, Dumont de Montigny, *Mémoires historiques sur la Louisiane*; Bancroft, *History of the United States*, vol. 3; *The Southwest* by Alexander B. Meek, of Mobile; Martin, *Louisiana*; Stoddard, *Louisiana*; Monette, *History of the Discovery and Settlement of the Valley of the Mississippi*, 1: 283–88; Charles Gayarré, *Louisiana: Its Colonial History and Romance* (New York: 1851), 476–95.

[48] The sixteen-year-old Voisin claimed that he had rallied some of D'Artaguette's fleeing troops and Indians, assisted with carrying off the wounded while marching for 100 miles without food and continuing to fight off the Chickasaws. Bienville investigated Voisin's story but he could not find anyone who remembered seeing any of his heroic deeds. Bienville dismissed his claims as "a pure fable" and attempted to have his promotion withdrawn. *MPA: FD*, 1: 331–32; Skinner, *Upper Country*, 130.

[49] Ensign Monchervaux had arrived too late with the Cahokia and Peoria Indians to join D'Artaguette, but he had remained at Fort Prudhomme and organized the retreat back to the Illinois country. *MPA: FD*, 1: 31–14; ibid., 4: 307 n. 3; Delanglez, *French Jesuits*, 303–04.

[50] Pickett's romantic version of the captives being treated kindly and having their wounds treated is not supported by eyewitness accounts or the documentary record. At least nineteen Frenchman—some dead, unconscious, and conscious—were burned to death the same day of the battle between three o'clock and midnight. Three Frenchmen—Claude Drouet de Richarville, Louis Gamot, and Pierre dit Courteoreille—were spared, either to be exchanged for a captured Chickasaw chief, Courserai, or ransomed. *MPA: FD*, 4: 141–42, 142 n. 4; Atkinson, *Splendid Land, Splendid People*, 48–49; "Account by Sieur Drouet de Richarville," [10 June 1739], Folio 256, *Report Concerning Canadian Archives, For the Year 1905*, 3 vols. (Ottawa: S. E. Dawson, 1906), 1: 457.

[51] While Pickett understood that D'Artaguette was defeated before Bienville made his assault on Ackia, he used "May" or "1736 May 20" for his marginal dates for D'Artaguette's attack and defeat instead of March or 1736 March. His primary source for this engagement was the memoir published by Dumont de Montigny in 1753, and he mistakenly reported this battle as taking place on 20 May 1736, leading to confusion in many accounts—including Pickett's *History*. See Jean-François-Benjamin Dumont de Montigny, *Mémoires historiques sur la Louisiane,* ed. Jean Baptiste Le Mascrier, 2 volumes (Paris: C. J. B. Bauche, 1753), 2: 229; Dumont de Montigny, *Memoir,* 273–74, 274 n. 24.

[52] Pickett tells us that eighteen captives were burned, but more recent research, eyewitness accounts, and documentary evidence raises the number to nineteen or twenty. The captives—either unconscious or dead—were consumed by two fires built by the Chickasaw women on a hill in the center of Chuckalissa. Several accounts speak about the bravery of several victims, especially Vincennes and Father Sénat. Most describe how Father Sénat led the captives in prayers or songs before they were tied to stakes or frames or thrown into the fires. Mingo Ouma is quoted as saying ". . . the black robe, who sang from the time he arrived in the village with all the others until the last breath." *MPA: FD,* 4: 141, 149; Atkinson, *Splendid Land, Splendid People,* 48; "Account by Sieur Drouet de Richarville," *Report Concerning Canadian Archives,* 457.

[53] Actually there may have been as many as five Frenchmen still living in the Chickasaw towns three days after the battle. Claude Drouet de Richarville, Louis Gamot, and Pierre dit Courteoreille were captured and later escaped or were ransomed after a manner of over a period of eighteen months. Sieur de Courceras had been left with the ammunition and baggage, became disoriented in the battle or retreat, and wondered into Chuckalissa three days later. He was tortured and burned along with an Iroquois from Sault St. Louis. An unnamed captive who was being escorted to Georgia with other French captives became ill and his Chickasaw escorts ended up hanging him. *MPA: FD,* 4: 141–42, 142 n. 4, 153 n. 17; Atkinson, *Splendid Land, Splendid People,* 48–49; "Account by Sieur Drouet de Richarville," *Report Concerning Canadian Archives,* 457.

[54] Pierre François Rigault (Riguad), Marquis de Cavagnal et Vaudreuil (1698–1793), a Canadian, was appointed governor of Louisiana in 1742, arrived 10 May 1743, and served until 1753. Unfortunately, several sources give Vaudreuil credit for leading a third expedition against the Chickasaw in 1752 that never happened. There was a major Choctaw assault on the Chickasaw on 6 September 1752 that may have included a small group of Frenchmen, but Governor Vaudreuil was far away in New Orleans. Pickett's source for this phantom expedition is François-Xavier Martin, *The History of Louisiana, From the Earliest Period,* 2 volumes (New Orleans: Lyman and Beardslee, 1827–1829), 1: 322. *MPA: FD,* 4: 210 n. 1; Atkinson, *Splendid Land, Splendid People,* 78, 257 n. 18; Dawson A. Phelps, "The Vaudreuil Expedition, 1752," *William and Mary Quarterly* 15 (October 1958): 483–93.

Chapter XI

BIENVILLE LEAVES THE COLONY—HIS CHARACTER

In our investigations of the French colonial history of Alabama and Mississippi, for a period of sixteen years from the conclusion of the campaigns of Bienville and D'Artaguette, in the Chickasaw Nation, we find but little to interest the reader. The same difficulties as heretofore continued to exist with the Indian tribes, with the colonial authorities, and with the English of Carolina. Bienville began, soon after his defeat near Pontotoc, to lose favor with the king and the West India Company.[1] To recover the ground which he had lost in their confidence, he exerted himself to organize another expedition against the Chickasaws; and having perfected it, he sailed up the Mississippi to Fort St. Francis, and disembarking, brought his army to a place near the mouth of the Margot or Wolf River.[2] Here his troops remained a long time, until, reduced by death from various diseases, and by famine, he was left with but few soldiers.

Finally, with these M. Céleron was ordered to march against the Chickasaw towns. As he advanced, the Chickasaws, supposing that a large French army had invaded their country, sued for peace. Celeron took advantage of their mistake, and immediately came to terms with them. The Chickasaws promised to expel the English traders from their country, and, from that time, to remain true to the French interest.[3]

When the result of this expedition, which terminated forever the military operations of Bienville, became known in France, the governor began to receive dispatches dictated in a spirit of much harshness and censure. The pride of Bienville was wounded—his spirit was humbled; and, being too sensible a man to retain a position the duties of which it was believed he had failed creditably to perform, he now requested to be recalled. He wrote to the minister as follows:[4]

1 Bienville's defeat in the Battle of Ackia on 26 May 1736 occurred in modern Tupelo, Lee County, Mississippi, and not in Pontotoc, Pontotoc County, Mississippi. See James R. Atkinson, "The Ackia and Ogoula Tchetoka Chickasaw Village Locations in 1736 during the French-Chickasaw War," *Mississippi Archaeology* 20 (June 1985): 53–70.

2 Bienville's expedition stopped briefly at Fort Saint Francis (Saint-François) near modern Helena, Arkansas, in November 1739 before moving up river to Fort Assumption (de L'Assomption) at the mouth of the Wolf (Margot) River on the southernmost of the four Chickasaw Bluffs—at modern Memphis, Tennessee. *MPA: FD*, 1: 390; Chartrand, *Forts of New France*, 50; "Journal of the Chickasa War," in J. F. H. Claiborne, *Mississippi, As a Province, Territory*

"If success had always corresponded with my application to the affairs of the government and administration of the colony, and with my zeal for the service of the King, I would have rejoiced in devoting the rest of my days to such objects; but, through a sort of fatality, which, for some time past, has obstinately thwarted my best concerted plans, I have frequently lost the fruit of my labors, and, perhaps some ground in your excellency's confidence:— therefore have I come to the conclusion, that it is no longer necessary for me to struggle against my adverse fortune. I hope that better luck may attend my successor. During the remainder of my stay here, I will give all my attention to smooth the difficulties attached to the office which I shall deliver up to him; and it is to me a subject of self-gratulation that I shall transmit to him the government of the colony, when its affairs are in a better condition than they have ever been."*

Bienville was, unquestionably, not only a great and good man, but a modest one. We find in this letter none of that disgusting cant indulged in by American politicians and American officeholders, when they lose their places. In these days it is common for such men to say that they have been treated with ingratitude by the government, if they are removed from an office—or by the people, if an opposing candidate is elected to Congress, and to whine and complain about having "grown gray in the service of their country," when, in truth, they have lived at their ease and feasted upon the contents of the public treasury, time out of mind. Some of these men have received over a hundred thousand dollars for occupying seats in the Senate and the House of Representatives, and much larger sums for filling the office of president, and for foreign missions; and yet, after all these favors, from the government and the people, they complain of being treated with ingratitude, if they lose their position. The people who permitted them so long to hold these trusts, often to their own injury, should never be charged with the crime of ingratitude; but the recipients of all these political favors should ever feel grateful, and retire with dignity and grace, like the good and wise Bienville.†

* Charles Gayarré, *Louisiana: Its Colonial History and Romance*, 526–27. See also Bienville's letter in French, contained in *Histoire de la Louisiane*, par Charles Gayarré.

† If Alabama should, hereafter, change the names of any of her present counties, or form new ones, we very respectfully suggest that one be named "DE SOTO," and another "BIENVILLE." The former was the first to discover our territory, and the latter was the French governor of it for forty years! We have a sufficient number of counties, rivers, creeks and towns bearing Indian names to preserve a remembrance of the former residence of the Red Men here. We have counties also named for politicians and warriors, but unlike Mississippi, Louisiana and Georgia, we have not one named for a person whose name would lead us to think of the history of our country.

and State, With Biographical Notices of Eminent Citizens **(1880; reprint, Baton Rouge: Louisiana State University Press, 1964), 71–72; James Patrick, *Architecture in Tennessee, 1768–1897* (Knoxville: University of Tennessee Press, 1981), 56.**

[3] Bienville's army had suffered sickness and delays from rain, flooding, and the elements since ascending the Mississippi, and it had become mired down while trying to decide on the best route to attack the Chickasaw. He finally selected Pierre Joseph Céleron de Blainville (1693–1759), a native of Montreal, to move against the Chickasaw in March 1740 "with drums beating and flags flying." Apparently the Chickasaw thought that Celeron's force represented only the first wave of Bienville's army, and, fearing a devastating assault by the entire French force, they raised a white flag, smoked the calumet, and agreed to peace terms. *MPA: FD*, 1: 412–13, 439, 443–45, 447–58; "Journal of the Chickasa War," 82–85; Dumont de Montigny, *Memoir*, 287–89.

[4] Pickett is quoting the first paragraph of a letter written by Bienville to Count de Maurepas, Minister of the Colonies, on 26 March 1742. While he gives a brief report on the state of the colony,

The successor to Bienville, the Marquis de Vaudreuil, arrived at New Orleans, and shortly afterwards the former sailed for France.[5] Although sixty-five years of age when he left the colony, Bienville lived to the advanced age of ninety. What a constitution for a man who had passed through such trials and hardships! In the whole of the twenty-five years that he passed in France, he never, for one moment, forgot the colony in Alabama, Mississippi and Louisiana. He nursed it in his remembrance, as does the aged grandfather who is far off from his beloved descendants. He sympathized with its misfortunes, and exulted in its triumphs and prosperity. Whenever a vessel, from the colony, reached the shores of France, Bienville was the first to go on board, and learn tidings of his beloved bantling. And when the French king, towards the last of Bienville's days, ceded the colony of Louisiana to Spain, the good old man implored him with tears in his eyes, not to place the French subjects of the colony under the control of the tyrannical Spaniards.[6]

Another distinguished person departed from our country about the time that Bienville sailed for France—Diron d'Artaguette, the royal commissary, who had lived so long at Mobile. As we have seen, he came to our country in 1708, where he filled several high offices until 1742. It was his younger brother whom the Chickasaws burned to death, near Pontotoc, in the present state of Mississippi. It is not known whether the royal commissary and Bienville ever again became friends. They ought, really, never to have disagreed, as they were both men of ability, honor and fidelity.[7]

The colony, at length, became prosperous. Capitalists embarked in agriculture and commerce, after the restrictions upon the latter had been set aside by the king. Cargoes of flour, hides, pork, bacon, leather, tallow, bear's oil and lumber found their way to Europe. These articles came chiefly from the Illinois and Wabash counties, and the inhabitants of that region, in return, received from New Orleans and Mobile, rice, indigo, tobacco, sugar and European fabrics. But a war broke out between France and Great Britain, and the Chickasaws, again becoming the allies of the English, the Marquis de Vaudreuil determined to invade their country. He organized his army, and embarking in boats, at Mobile, made his way up the Tombigbee River. After resting a few days at Fort Tombecbé, he renewed his voyage until he reached the place where Bienville, sixteen years before, had disembarked his army. Marching from this point with his troops,

Bienville closes his letter by assuring Maurepas that he has sacrificed his resentment against those who had opposed him and by thanking Maurepas for granting him letters of exchange worth sixty thousand livres. *MPA: FD*, 3: 763–65.

5 Although appointed governor of Louisiana on 1 July 1742, Pierre François Rigault (Rigaud), Marquis de Cavagnial et Vaudreuil (1698–1778), a native of Quebec, did not arrive in the colony until 10 May 1743, and served until the arrival of Louis Billouart de Kerlérec in 1753. W. J. Eccles, "Pierre de Rigaud de Vaudreuil de Cavagnial, Marquis de Vaudreuil," *DCB*.

6 Bienville had talked about his poor health for some time and volunteered to depart by the summer of 1742. Count Maurepas granted his request to retire in October 1741, but Vaudreuil's arrival in May 1743 delayed his farewell from Louisiana until 17 August 1743. He arrived in France on 19 October and resided in Paris for over two decades in relative obscurity. Bienville's Louisiana passed into Spanish hands in 1766, and he died on 7 March 1767 in Paris. O'Neill, "Jean-Baptiste le Moyne de Bienville," ibid.; *MPA: FD*, 3: 738–39.

7 Diron d'Artaguette (also d'Artaguiette) had come to Louisiana in 1708 at the age of thirteen with his older brother, Jean-Baptiste Martin d'Artaguette Diron. While he never received the acclaim of his former friend Bienville, he had a successful military and administrative career in Louisiana until 1742. He was appointed the king's lieutenant in Saint-Domingue and died there on 13 August 1742. *MPA/FD*, 1: 56 n. 1; ibid., 4: 16 n. 1.

composed of French and Choctaws, he reached the Chickasaw towns, and endeavoring to storm them, lost many of his men; and was finally beaten, and compelled to retreat to his boats near Cotton Gin Port. All he accomplished was to destroy the fields and burn some cabins of the enemy.[8] Arriving at Fort Tombecbé, he caused it to be enlarged and strengthened—leaving there a strong detachment to prevent the incursions of the Chickasaws.[9] Like Bienville, the Marquis returned to Mobile not at all satisfied with the laurels which he had won in his expedition against the Chickasaws.*

[8] Pickett is repeating a narrative about an expedition led by Governor Vaudreuil in 1752 that did not take place. His source, as noted elsewhere, is Francois-Xavier Martin, who described the undocumented campaign. Martin, *History of Louisiana*, 1: 322; Atkinson, *Splendid Land, Splendid People*, 82–83, 257 n. 18.

[9] Bernard Deverges, engineer-in-chief for Louisiana, designed new buildings for Fort Tombecbé in 1751 and 1759. The commandant at Fort Tombecbé had complained that the fort and buildings were "falling into ruins" in 1741. However, it was not enlarged and the garrison remained small and prone to desertion. *MPA: FD*, 5: 190; Wilson, "Colonial Fortifications," 118–19.

* It has been stated to me, by several persons, that cannon have been found in the Tombigbee, at or near Cotton Gin Port, and it has been supposed that they were left there by De Soto. De Soto brought from Cuba but one piece of artillery, and that he left behind him in Florida. If any such cannon have been found in the Tombigbee, they belonged to the Marquis De Vaudreuil. He carried with him a few pieces to operate against the Chickasaws upon the occasion just referred to. After he had fought the Chickasaws, and returned to his boats, he found that the Tombigbee had fallen considerably, and it is probable he threw these cannon into the river to lighten his boats.

Chapter XII

HORRIBLE DEATH OF BAUDREAU AND THE SWISS SOLDIERS

In 1757, Kerlérec was the governor of the colony. He had succeeded the Marquis De Vaudreuil, who had been transferred to the government of New France.[1] Some of the officers, stationed at the different posts, were great tyrants. One of them, named Duroux, was sent to command a detachment of troops of the Swiss regiment of Hallwyll,[2] who were stationed at Cat Island, which, we believe, is now within the jurisdiction of the state of Alabama. He forced his soldiers to work his gardens, and to burn coal and lime, which he disposed of in trade for his own emolument. Some of them, who refused to work for him, he caused to be arrested, stripped and tied naked to trees, where, for hours, the mosquitoes tortured them with their poisonous stings. These soldiers, repairing to New Orleans, received no satisfaction from Governor Kerlérec, who presently sent them back to Duroux.[3] That officer was now still more tyrannical, and in addition to his other severe usage, gave them no meat to eat, and fed them upon stale bread. One day he entered a boat, and was rowed to an adjacent island, for the purpose of hunting deer. Returning in the evening, a party of the soldiers prepared themselves to kill him, and, as soon as he put his foot upon shore, he was instantly dispatched, by the discharge of several guns. His body, stripped of its apparel, was contemptuously thrown into the sea. They then rifled the king's stores, and, for once in a long while, fared sumptuously.[4]

Becoming masters of the island, the soldiers set at liberty an inhabitant, named Baudreau, who had been unjustly imprisoned by Duroux.[5] He had been long in the colony, and was often employed upon dangerous missions in the Creek Nation. Indeed, he well understood the language of these Indians, besides that of neighboring tribes. Often had he made journeys to Fort Toulouse, upon the Coosa, both in boats and upon foot. He was a great favorite of Bienville. Baudreau was a powerful man, as to strength, and almost a giant

[1] On 31 January 1753, Louis Billouart de Kerlérec (1704–1770) arrived at forts St. Leon and St. Marie on board the store ship *Chariot Royal* with his wife, nephew, sister-in-law, secretary, and servants. He was greeted by Vaudreuil, who gave him a tour of the forts and carried his party into New Orleans. Donald E. Pusch, *The Logs of the Chariot Royal, 1752–1753* (Seabrook, TX: Petite Presse du Lac, 2010), 8–14.

[2] The Swiss Marine Regiment of Hallwyll served in the French service and fought against the English during the French and Indian War. F. H. Tyrell, "Swiss Regiments à L'Étranger," *Journal of the Royal United Service Institution* 41 (April 1897): 467.

[3] Pickett is using Bossu's *Travels in the Interior of North America, 1751–1762,* as his main source for this narrative.

in size, and these qualities, together with his bravery and prowess, endeared him to the Indians. The soldiers, who now released him from prison, compelled him to conduct them towards Georgia. Advancing rapidly through the woods, after they had touched the main land in their boats, the veteran Baudreau led them around Mobile, up the Tombigbee, and, crossing that stream, and afterwards the Alabama, in canoes which belonged to the Indians, Baudreau conducted them from thence to Coweta, upon the Chattahoochee. Here he was dismissed by the fugitives, whom he compelled to give him a certificate, stating that he had been *forced* to act as their guide, and was not in any way concerned in the killing of Duroux.[6]

Some of these soldiers, who pursued their journey, made safe their retreat to the English in Georgia; but others loitered in Coweta and Cusseta, enjoying the hospitality of the Indians. In the meantime, Montberaut, who then commanded at Fort Toulouse, had been made acquainted with the murder of Duroux and the flight of the soldiers.[7] Hearing that some of them were upon the Chattahoochee, a small detachment of soldiers and some Indians, under Baudin, were sent across the country, to arrest them. Baudin returned with three of the men, who, after being chained in the prison for a week, were put in canoes, and conveyed down the Alabama River, to Mobile, and there thrown into the dungeon, to await trial.[8]

Baudreau arrived in Mobile, and was quietly living in his hut, when two of his sons, who had just arrived from New Orleans, were the innocent cause of his arrest. Governor Kerlérec sent by them a sealed package to Develle, the commandant at Mobile, authorizing his imprisonment.[9] The poor fellow knew nothing of the arrest of the soldiers, until his eyes fell upon them in prison. Notwithstanding that he exhibited, upon the trial, his certificate, which declared his innocence of the murder, and which stated that he was compelled to facilitate the escape of the authors of it, a court martial condemned him to die. The soldiers, of course, were also condemned to share the same fate. As soon as Governor Kerlérec confirmed the judgment, the innocent and unfortunate Baudreau was led forth and broken upon a

Sieur Duroux arrived in January 1756 aboard the *St. Esprit* and had been dispatched as an ensign to Cat Island. Bossu, *Travels in the Interior of North America*, 178–79; *MPA: FD*, 5: 185, 188 n. 3.

4 Three soldiers involved in Duroux's murder who were eventually captured and found guilty included Joseph François Bazille from Captain Trant's company, François Vidou from Captain Murat's company, and a Swiss soldier. *MPA: FD*, 5: 187.

5 In his chapter title and original narrative, Pickett used "Beaudrot" from Bossu's account, but the settler involved in this incident was Jean Baptiste Baudreau. He had been imprisoned by Duroux for recovering food and other provisions from a Spanish shipwreck off Dauphin Island in 1757. Ibid., 5: 185–86; Bossu, *Travels in the Interior of North America*, 179–80.

6 Unlike Bossu's account of this incident, Governor Kerlérec blamed Baudreau for "inciting the garrison at Cat Island to insurrection" to avoid being arraigned before him and being punished for "his piracy." His friendship with the Choctaw had helped him escape punishment and imprisonment for robbery, "for which he had been condemned to the galleys." *MPA: FD*, 4: 322 n. 1; ibid., 5: 186.

7 Captain Henri Montault de Montberaut served as commandant at Fort Toulouse from 1755 to 1759. Thomas, *Fort Toulouse*, xxxii, 42; Montault de Montberaut, *The Mémoire Justificatif of the Chevalier Montault de Monberaut*, ed. Milo B. Howard, Jr., and Robert R. Rea (Tuscaloosa: University of Alabama Press, 1965), 16–20, 70 n.

8 Based on Bossu's account, Ensign Baudin was apparently stationed at Fort Toulouse and captured the two French soldiers - Joseph François Bazille and François Vidou—and the unnamed Swiss soldier who were delivered to Mobile. Bossu, *Travels in the Interior of North America*, 180; *MPA: FD*, 5: 187.

9 While Bossu provides the background

regarding Baudreau's sons, Governor Kerlérec in his report credits Sieur Roussève—the "King's interpreter at Mobile"—who led some Indians and "some picked inhabitants" in capturing Baudreau about six weeks after Duroux's murder. Bossu, *Travels in the Interior of North America,* 180; *MPA: FD,* 5: 187.

[10] Contrary to Pickett and his sources, Kerlérec reported that Baudreau and the guilty soldiers were brought to New Orleans, where they were examined by the "council of war" on 7 June 1758. Baudreau and the French soldier Joseph François Bazille were "condemned to be broken, alive, to death upon the wheel." *MPA: FD,* 5: 187.

wheel! The people of Mobile were shocked at the spectacle, for some of their lives had been saved by the sufferer.[10] Not many years before that, Baudreau, while trading in the town of Autauga among the Alabamas, ransomed a French boy who had been captured near Mobile by the Lower Creeks of the Chattahoochee, and who had sold him to those Indians. Baudreau paid away all his profits for the boy, and immediately carried him to Mobile and restored him to his uncle.

On another occasion, a party of the Lower Creeks had taken a Frenchman, who had gone up to his little plantation on the Tensaw River. They stripped the man, and, having pinioned him well, took the trail for the Chattahoochee. It so happened that Baudreau was returning upon that trail from Fort Toulouse, whither Bienville had some weeks before dispatched him with a letter to the French commandant. Night drew apace, and the wearied Baudreau sought repose upon the pine straw, behind a log, without a spark of fire. It was his custom, when alone, to sleep in the dark, for fear of being discovered by Indian enemies. He lay quietly, with his head resting upon his knapsack. Presently three stout warriors made their appearance, with the Frenchman to whom we have just alluded. They presently collected lightwood, which lay in profusion around, and kindled a large fire. Ten of the party, after the capture of the Frenchman, went in another direction, to see if they could not do more mischief in the French settlements, and, entrusting the prisoner to the three warriors who now guarded him, had not yet overtaken them. The fire threw a glare over the woods, and Baudreau would have been discovered had he not, fortunately, been behind a log. The warriors eat their supper, and, tying the Frenchman to a tree, where he would have been compelled to stand all night upon his feet, they dropped off to sleep. The heart of the generous Baudreau beat quick; he longed to rescue the man, whom he well knew, but endeavored to compose himself.

After a while, when the wearied warriors snored in profound sleep, he cautiously approached. His first intention was to unloose the prisoner and place a pistol in his hand, when they would both instantly fall upon the Indians; but a moment's reflection warned him that, if he approached the prisoner first, the latter would be startled and cry aloud, which would arouse the savages. This reflection altered his plans, and he now crept up to the camp, keeping a large pine tree between him and the warriors. Two of them lay together. Baudreau's carbine was heavily charged, and, raising himself suddenly, he fired, and the warriors were both killed. The third one rose up and rushed at Baudreau with his hatchet, having in his haste forgotten his gun. Baudreau had already a pistol in his hand, and now discharged its contents into the stomach of the Creek, who whooped and fell dead. Rushing to the tree, he untied his friend, who immediately sank in the arms of his generous deliverer. But they had no time to tarry here. The rescued prisoner informed Baudreau that the other party were probably upon their trail. They immediately left the spot, and, reaching the Alabama River, Baudreau constructed a raft, on which he now placed the prisoner, and they both floated down the river some distance, and landed on the western side. He tore the raft to pieces, and set the fragments adrift. Baudreau took all this precaution to keep the Indians from tracking him. About this time it was daylight, and he and the Frenchman were in a swamp, and quite secure. Baudreau now drew forth his bottle of brandy, and gave his companion a drink, which did much to revive him. They also shared some bread and dried venison. After they had rested here some hours, Baudreau and his companion arose, and, after a tedious march through the woods, subsisting upon what game Baudreau could kill, he arrived safe in Mobile, with the Frenchman.[11]

Such a man was Baudreau, whom the French authorities in Mobile broke upon a wheel! His life was worth a thousand such lives as that of the tyrannical wretch whom he was accused of having killed. On the same day that he was thus made to suffer death, in the most barbarous and excruciating manner, one of the fugitives, a French soldier, was also broken upon a wheel, while two poor Swiss soldiers were subjected to a still more horrible fate.[12] The authorities placed each one of them in a long narrow box, like a coffin, nailed it up, and then cut the box in two with a cross-cut saw.*

[11] Pickett's narrative of Baudreau's life and service is based on Bossu's *Travels in the Interior of North America* and manuscript letters in his possession. Bossu had a very strong enmity towards Kerlérec because he felt mistreated by him regarding the loss of a boat and its contents in 1753. Bossu, *Travels in the Interior of North America,* 91–92.

[12] As noted before, Joseph François Bazille of Trant's company was sentenced to death "upon the wheel." However, only one of the two Swiss soldiers were executed in New Orleans. Kerlérec had identified a Swiss corporal, a second Swiss soldier, and a French soldier—Joseph François Bazille—as the murderers. When the culprits were captured, the Swiss corporal "stabbed himself and died in the same instant." The other Swiss soldier was condemned to death and turned over to "M. Volant," commander of the Swiss troops, "to be axed, his head and his hand cut off, both to be displayed on a gallows for a week." *MPA: FD,* 5: 186–87.

* French MS letters in my possession, obtained from Paris. See also Bossu, *Travels*, 1: 320–25. But Bossu *incorrectly* states that these men suffered death in New Orleans. Some years previously, Fort Condé, a large brick fortress, had been built at Mobile, and it was in front of the gate of that fort that these men met such a terrible death.

Chapter XIII

BOSSU'S VISIT TO THE FRENCH FORTS UPON THE ALABAMA AND TOMBIGBEE RIVERS

Governor Kerlérec having ordered Bossu, a captain of the French Marines, to depart from New Orleans with a detachment, destined for Fort Toulouse, among the Creek Indians, that officer reached Mobile, and was there received by Aubert, adjutant of that place. The latter, the same officer who married the Russian princess, and lived with her in Mobile, as we have seen, had recently been appointed to the command of Fort Toulouse, and was instructed to accompany Bossu to that point; but sickness, for a while, detained him in Mobile.[1] In the meantime, Bossu embarked his soldiers and Choctaws in several boats. After a tedious voyage of fifty days, up the Alabama River, he moored his boats at the French fort, upon the Coosa. Here he had the pleasure of meeting Aubert, who, having recovered from his indisposition, had come from Mobile on horseback, across the vast wilderness. Montberaut, who was still in command of the fort, received Aubert with politeness, and, for three months previous to his departure to Mobile, instructed him in regard to the condition of the fort, and of the policy which it was necessary for him to pursue with the tribes around.[2]

Montberaut was an officer of high reputation among the Creeks and Alabamas, and "was remarkable for the spirited speeches which he delivered, in a manner analogous to the way of thinking of these nations."* He despised the Jesuits, and, as they were formally stationed at Fort Toulouse, he always lived upon bad terms with them. Father Le Roy, one of these missionaries, wrote a letter to the governor, in which he abused Montberaut in unmeasured terms, and advised his removal. The soldier to whom the letter was delivered, and who was to convey it to Mobile, handed it to Montberaut, who noted its contents. When the Jesuit met him the next morning, he showed him many

* Bossu, *Travels*, 1: 228.

[1] In this chapter, Pickett continued to refer to Jean Baptiste Benoist Aubert as "D'Aubant" and returned to reference the legend of the "Russian princess" and her marriage to "D'Aubant." In his account, Bossu refers to Aubert, who served as adjutant at Mobile before his appointment as commandant at Fort Toulouse. Despite Pickett's narrative, Aubert was married to Louise Bernoudy, daughter of the king's attorney at Mobile, François César Bernoudy, and there are no church records that connect him in marriage to Pickett's "Russian princess." *MPA: FD*, 4: 204, 205 n. 5; ibid., 5: 125–27, 127 n. 3; Montberaut, *Mémoire Justificatif*, 21; Bossu, *Travels in the Interior of North America*, 128; Hamilton, *Colonial Mobile*, 194.

[2] Bossu wanted the post of commander at Fort Toulouse, and he questioned

civilities, as Bossu says, "according to the political principles of these good fathers." The commandant asked him if he had written anything against him. The Jesuit, not suspecting that his letter was in the officer's hands, assured him, by all that was sacred, that he had not. Montberaut then called Father Le Roy an impostor and cheat, and fixed his letter at the gate of the fort.[3] Since that time no Jesuits have been among the Creeks and Alabamas.*

When Bossu visited Fort Toulouse, upon the Coosa, he found that the Creeks and Alabamas were happy people. They lived with ease, had an abundance around them, and were at peace with the surrounding savages. While at the fort, Bossu heard a chief deliver the following beautiful speech:

"Young men and warriors! Do not disregard the MASTER OF LIFE. The sky is blue—the sun is without spots—the weather is fair—the ground is white—everything is quiet on the face of the earth, and the blood of men ought not to be spilt on it. We must beg the MASTER OF LIFE to preserve it pure and spotless among the nations that surround us."[4]

Not only were the Creeks and Alabamas at peace with other nations, at this time, but gave evidences of warm and generous hospitality. They thronged the banks of the river, which now meanders along the borders of the counties of Autauga, Montgomery, Dallas, and Lowndes—as Bossu slowly made his way up the beautiful stream, greeted him with friendly salutations, and offered him provisions, such as bread, roasted turkeys, broiled venison, pancakes baked with nut oil, and deer's tongues, together with baskets full of eggs of the fowl and the turtle. THE GREAT SPIRIT had blessed them with a magnificent river, abounding with fish; with delicious and cool fountains, gushing out from the foot of the hills; with rich lands, that produced without cultivation, and with vast forests, abounding in game of every description. But now the whole scene is changed. The country is no longer half so beautiful; the waters of Alabama begin to be discolored; the forests have been cut down; steamers have destroyed the finny race; deer bound not over the plain; the sluggish bear has ceased to wind through the swamps; the bloody panther does not spring upon his prey; wolves have ceased to howl upon the hills; birds cannot be seen in the branches of the trees; graceful warriors guide no longer their well-shaped canoes, and beautiful squaws loiter not upon the plain, nor pick the delicious berries. Now, vast fields of cotton, noisy steamers, huge rafts of lumber, towns reared for business, disagreeable corporation laws, harassing courts of justice, mills, factories, and everything else that is calculated to destroy the beauty of a country and to rob man of his quiet and native independence, present themselves to our view.

* Ibid, 229.

Kerlérec's authority to appoint Aubert "against the King's orders forbidding adjutants and assistant adjutants to serve in any place but at their assigned stations." Bossu, *Travels in the Interior of North America*, 128, 130; Montberaut, *Mémoire Justificatif*, 21.

[3] Bossu claims that Montberaut disliked Jesuit priests and had open disputes with them. Apparently Father Maximilian Le Roy not only challenged Montberaut's leadership at Fort Toulouse, but he had also taken a hard stand against the sale of brandy to the Creeks. Bossu, *Travels in the Interior of North America*, 130; Delanglez, *French Jesuits in Lower Louisiana*, 486–88; Thomas, *Fort Toulouse*, 41–42.

[4] Bossu was at Fort Toulouse when the Coweta Emperor visited the post prior to Montberaut's departure in May 1759. At Montberaut's direction, Bossu gave him "a blue coat, a waistcoat with gold braid, a plumed hat, and a white shirt with embroidered cuffs." Bossu, *Travels in the Interior of North America*, 151–55.

The heart yearns to behold, once more, such a country as Alabama was the first time we saw it, when a boy. But where can we now go, that we shall not find the busy American, with keen desire to destroy everything which nature has made lovely?

Fort Toulouse, at various times, had many commandants, who filled each other's places according to the will or whim of the colonial governor and the different companies. At one time, the Chevalier D'Erneville commanded here, when a young warrior killed a French soldier, and fled to the forests. According to an agreement formed between the French and the Indians, when the fort was first established, the killing of a person was to be atoned for by the immediate execution of him who committed the deed, whether he was a Frenchman or an Indian. D'Erneville demanded the Indian of the chiefs, who stated that they were unable to find him. He next required that the mother of the guilty warrior should be made to expiate the crime.[5] They replied that the mother had not killed the Frenchman; but the officer only reminded them of the agreement, and further, of the previous customs of their country. Deeply embarrassed, in consequence of the escape of the criminal, and unwilling that the old woman should be put to death, the chiefs, to compromise the case, offered the French officer furs and horse-loads of booty. But D'Erneville was unyielding, and had the mother brought out before Fort Toulouse, to suffer death. Her relatives followed her with sad countenances, one of them exclaiming, in a loud voice, "My mother-in-law dies courageously, as she has not struck the blow." In a few minutes the son rushed through the canebrake, boldly walked up to D'Erneville, gave himself up, saved the life of his mother, and was then—killed![6]

One day it was announced at Fort Toulouse that the Emperor of Coweta, a town on the Chattahoochee, was advancing to pay the French a visit. Bossu walked some distance upon the pathway, towards the present Gray's Ferry, which was, at that early day, a great crossing place for the Indians.[7] He was accompanied by some soldiers, and, to surprise the emperor, they fired their muskets as soon as Bossu took him by the hand, which was also the signal for a general discharge of the artillery of the fort. The woods presently resounded with the noise of the cannon, and the emperor felt that he was greatly honored. He was mounted on a Spanish horse, with an English saddle, which was bordered with a beautiful spotted skin. He alighted from his horse, and advanced to the fort with an air of great dignity and importance. His costume was so singular as to excite the subdued risibilities of the Frenchmen, who marched behind him. He wore on his head a crest of black plumes; his coat was scarlet, with English cuffs, and beset with tinsel lace; he had neither

[5] Pierre Henri d'Erneville (1711–1788) served as commander of Fort Toulouse in 1736–1738 and was promoted to captain in 1740. He briefly served as commander at Fort Tombecbé in 1742 and returned as commander in 1744–1746. *MPA: FD,* 1: 371; ibid., 4: 96 n. 13.

[6] Bossu did not arrive in Louisiana until 1751, and he did not arrive at Fort Toulouse until April 1759. Consequently, his account of Pierre Henri d'Erneville's demand for the killer of a French soldier sometime during 1736–1738 was based on secondary sources or hearsay from soldiers at Fort Toulouse in 1759. Bossu, *Travels in the Interior of North America,* 142–43.

[7] Parker Gray established a ferry operation at Red Warriors Bluff on the Tallapoosa River near Fort Toulouse. It was later known as Hatchett's Ferry and even later as Hughes' Ferry. George Vernon Irons, "River Ferries in Alabama Before 1861," *Alabama Review* 4 (January 1951): 25.

waistcoat nor breeches; under his coat he wore a white linen shirt. His attendants were naked, and painted in a variety of colors. Being only eighteen years of age, the emperor was accompanied by his regent, a noble and wise old man, who ruled the Lower Creeks during his minority. When they reached the fort, the old man delivered a speech to Aubert, which was reported by Laubène, the king's interpreter, who had been long stationed at that place.[8]

Being anxious to alienate the Lower Creeks, upon the Chattahoochee, from the relations which they had formed with the Georgians, Aubert paid the visitors unusual attention. The next day, at ten o'clock, he received the emperor, his war chief, regent, doctor, and followers, in considerable state. They were marched before the officers and soldiers, who were all drawn up in full uniform. At noon they were conducted to the dining table, where they and the officers took seats together. The emperor was much puzzled in what manner to employ the knife and fork, and was extremely awkward and embarrassed. But the old regent seized the backbone and breast of a turkey, and broke them in two with his fingers, saying, "The MASTER OF LIFE made fingers before knives and forks were made."[9]

Towards the end of the repast, a servant of the emperor, who stood behind his chair, perceived that the French ate mustard with their boiled meat. He asked Bauodouin what it was that they relished so much? This officer, the same who went to the Chattahoochee, and arrested the soldiers who fled from Cat Island, and who lived forty years in the Creek Nation, replied that the French were by no means covetous of what they possessed. He handed the Indian a spoonful of the mustard, who swallowed it. He thereupon made many ridiculous contortions, giving several whoops, and affording the whole company much merriment. The Indian imagined himself to be poisoned, and Aubert, the commandant, could only appease him by a glass of delightful brandy.*

About this time the celebrated Russian princess, whom, as we have seen, Aubert had long since married, at Mobile, becoming tired of his protracted absence, determined to join him, which, indeed, had been planned when the chevalier left her at Mobile. Going on board a boat which was starting for Fort Toulouse, this remarkable and romantic woman, after a long voyage, arrived at this place with her little daughter and a female servant. She was affectionately received by Aubert, and had many lively adventures to relate of her passage up the Alabama. Not having pleasant quarters in the fort, a cabin

[8] Bossu's narrative of this event is included in a postscript to his letter (i.e., "Letter XVI") to the Marquis de l'Estrade dated 2 May 1759. Bossu, *Travels in the Interior of North America*, 141, 151–55.

[9] Pickett continues to loosely paraphrase from Bossu's narrative of his stay at Fort Toulouse, which is described in his letter to the Marquis de l'Estrade. Ibid., 153.

* *Travels Through That Part of North America Formerly Called Louisiana*, by M. Bossu, Captain in the French Marines, 1: 226–78.

[10] Pickett continues his account of the mythical "Russian princess" and her undocumented relationship to Jean Baptiste Benoist Aubert.

[11] Bossu's voyage up the Tombigbee to Fort Tombecbé and his adventure with the alligator is described in his letter to the Marquis de l'Estrade dated 19 September1759. Bossu, *Travels in the Interior of North America,* 156–62.

was built for her in the field, not far from the fort, to which was attached a brick chimney, the fragments of which still remain there.[10] Here this gay woman was accustomed to converse with the Indians and prattle with their pickaninnies. So, then, citizens of Wetumpka, there was once living, within three miles of your city, a Russian princess—so represented to be—who had married the son of Peter the Great!*

While at Fort Toulouse, Bossu received an order to repair to Mobile, for the purpose of serving under the orders of Develle, the king's lieutenant, stationed at that place. He entered a boat, and, after a prosperous voyage, reached Mobile. Sometime afterwards he was ordered to command a convoy to Fort Tombecbé. He left Mobile with three boats, in which were soldiers and Mobile Indians. He entered the Tombigbee River after a voyage of seven days, which now can be performed in four hours. Mooring his boats near some land, a little elevated above the water, he pitched his camp, and prepared to pass the night on shore, as was the custom of all voyagers of that day. While wrapped in a corner of his tent cloth, and reposing upon his bear's skin, with a string of fine fish, which he designed for his breakfast, lying at his feet, he was awakened from a profound sleep by finding himself suddenly carried away by an extraordinary force. Terribly alarmed, he cried out for help. An enormous alligator, intent upon seizing the string of fish, had caught in his teeth a portion of the tent cloth, and was hurrying Bossu, tent cloth, bear skin, fish and all, rapidly to his accustomed element. Fortunately, just before the alligator plunged into the river Bossu saved himself and the bearskin, but the fish and the tent cloth disappeared with the monster.[11]

The voyage up the river was remarkably tedious, for, it being at a low stage, Bossu was often compelled to drag his boats over the bars. He camped upon the banks every night, and, to protect himself as much as possible from the mosquitoes, he placed canes in the ground, and, making their tops meet by bending them over, formed an arch. Over this rude frame he threw a linen sheet, and slept under it most comfortably, reposing on his bearskin. On one occasion provisions got so scarce that Bossu sent out some of his men to procure game in the forests. Discovering the nest of a large eagle, built in the branches of a lofty tree, the Indians soon prostrated the latter with their axes. They obtained from this immense nest several fawns, rabbits, wild turkeys, partridges and wild pigeons, together with four young eaglets.† The

* French MS letters in my possession, obtained from Paris.

† Bossu must be mistaken as to the number of eaglets. According to my reading of natural history, I am under the impression that not more than *two* eaglets are ever found in the same nest.

old eagles fought desperately for their young, but the famished party bore off the nest and the abundance of game which it contained, all of which had recently been taken for the eaglets to devour. Bossu and his party lived sumptuously during the remainder of their voyage, which was at length terminated at Fort Tombecbé, the site of which is now familiarly known as Jones' Bluff. De Grand-Pré, a Canadian of much bravery, and possessed of much experience in relation to the habits and customs of the Indians, commanded the garrison at this post.[12]

Bossu's journal, kept at this place, is wholly occupied with the manners and customs of the Choctaws. As we have already referred to him, upon this subject, in our description of that tribe, we will omit here what would be a mere repetition, only submitting to the reader the following extract:[13]

"I saw an Indian of the Choctaws who had lately been baptized. As he had no luck in hunting, he imagined himself bewitched. He went immediately to Father Lefevre, the Jesuit missionary, who was stationed at Fort Tombecbé, and who had lately converted him.[14] He told him that his *medicine* was good for nothing, for, since he had practiced it upon him, he could kill no deer. He therefore desired the priest to take off his enchantment. The Jesuit, in order to avoid the resentment of this Indian, acted as if he had annihilated the baptismal ceremony. Sometime after this, the Indian killed a deer, and, thus thinking himself forever free from the enchantment, was a most happy fellow."*

But the colony of Louisiana, so vast in extent, and embracing within its limits the territory of our own state, and that of Mississippi, was soon to be taken from the French. It has been seen that the English and the French had long been competitors for the commercial patronage of the Indians, in Lower Louisiana, and also for the right to the soil. Far more bitter were their jealousies, and far more bloody their feuds upon the borders of Ohio, Virginia and Pennsylvania. For some time, a serious colonial war had been raging between the North American provinces of France and those of England. The French lost post after post. The victorious Britons garrisoned them with troops, and then captured others. In this manner, the king of France lost all his Louisiana possessions, and, with them, the soil of Mississippi and Alabama. Spain, too, had allied herself with France in the war. At length the three belligerent powers concluded a peace, the conditions of which are stated in the commencement of our next volume.[15]

* Bossu, *Travels*, 226–318.

[12] Actually, Pierre Chabert was the commander of Fort Tombecbé when Bossu's party arrived, and he surrendered the post to the English in November 1763. Governor Vaudreuil appointed Joseph Louis Boucher de Grand-Pré commandant at Fort Toulouse in 1749, and he successfully ended the Choctaw civil war and restored peace between the French and the Choctaw. Vaudreuil recommended Grand-Pré for the Cross of St. Louis as a reward for his service. *MPA: FD*, 5: 27, 32, 60–65, 97–98, 105 n. 10, 291.

[13] Bossu describes this incident in his letter (i.e., "Letter XVIII") to the Marquis de l'Estrade dated 30 September 1759. Bossu, *Travels in the Interior of North America*, 163, 168–69.

[14] Father Nicholas Lefevre had assisted Father Michel Baudouin among the Chickasawhay before being sent to Fort Tombecbé. Delanglez, *French Jesuits in Lower Louisiana*, 476, 527, 543; B. J. Bekkers, "The Catholic Church in Mississippi During Colonial Times," in *Publications of the Mississippi Historical Society*, vol. 6 (Oxford: Mississippi Historical Society, 1902), 354.

[15] The Peace of Paris of 1763 formally ended the French and Indian War—known as the Seven Years' War in Europe—between France, Great Britain, and Spain. France surrendered all her possessions in North America east of the Mississippi, except for the city of New Orleans, creating a new order

Agreeably to the provisions of that treaty, Pierre Annibal Develle, lieutenant of the king, commandant at Mobile, and René Jean Gabriel Fazende, *d'ordonnatuer*, delivered that town and its dependences to Major Robert Farmer, commissary of His Britannic Majesty.[16] Pierre Chabert, captain of infantry and commandant of Fort Tombecbé, and Valentine Dubroca, keeper of the magazine, delivered that post to Captain Thomas Ford, who garrisoned it with English troops.[17]

The Chevalier Lanouë, commanding Fort Toulouse, upon the Coosa, not being relieved by the appearance of any British officer, spiked his cannon, broke off the trunnions or ears, and left them in the fort.[18] The river being shallow, during a dry fall, and having his soldiers and all the provisions and military effects to convey to Mobile, in boats, he caused to be cast into the Coosa all which the magazine contained, among which was a large quantity of powder.*

* Charles Gayarré, *Histoire de la Louisiane*, 2: 108–09.

in the eighteenth-century Gulf South. Colin G. Calloway, *The Scratch of a Pen: 1763 and the Transformation of North America* (New York: Oxford University Press, 2006), 3–25, 30, 112–13, 133–36.

[16] Major Robert Farmar, commanding His Britannic Majesty's 22nd and 34th Regiments, accepted the surrender of Mobile and Fort Condé on 20 October 1763. *MPA: ED*, 1: 11–12, 78; Robert R. Rea, *Major Robert Farmar of Mobile* (Tuscaloosa: University of Alabama Press, 1990), 34–36.

[17] On 6 November 1763, Major Farmar dispatched Lieutenant Thomas Ford, commanding thirty troops of His Britannic Majesty's 34th Regiment, up the Tombigbee River to take possession of Fort Tombecbé. A brief surrender ceremony was concluded before sunset on 22 November, and Chabert and his soldiers retreated down river to Mobile in early December 1763. *MPA: ED*, 1: 23–24, 37–39.

[18] Lieutenant de Lanouë (also La Nouë) Bogard had been commandant of Fort Toulouse since 1760, and the evacuation of his post in 1763 was delayed until late November or December by British indecision in Mobile. No garrison was ever dispatched to Fort Toulouse, and Major Farmar gave James Germany, a trader, permission to occupy the fort on 10 January 1764, requiring him to maintain good relations with the Creeks. Ibid., 18; *MPA: FD*, 5: 280 n. 4; Rea, *Major Robert Farmar*, 38; Thomas, *Fort Toulouse*, xxxii, 66.

HISTORY

OF

ALABAMA,

AND INCIDENTALLY OF

GEORGIA AND MISSISSIPPI,

FROM THE EARLIEST PERIOD.

BY

ALBERT JAMES PICKETT,

Of Montgomery.

IN TWO VOLUMES.

VOL. II.

THIRD EDITION.

CHARLESTON:

WALKER AND JAMES,

1851.

Ancient Indian Fortifications, at Little River Falls, Cherokee County, Alabama, from a sketch by A. J. Pickett, who visited that place, in October, 1850.

BALDWIN.

CONTENTS OF VOLUME II.

CHAPTER XXIX.

CHAPTER XXX.

CHAPTER XXXI.

CHAPTER XXXII.

CHAPTER XXXIII.

CHAPTER XXXIV.

CHAPTER XXXV.

CHAPTER XXXVI.

CHAPTER XXXVII.

CHAPTER XXXVIII.

CHAPTER XXXIX.

CHAPTER XL.

CHAPTER XLI.

CHAPTER XLII.

CHAPTER XLIII.

Chapter XIV

THE OCCUPATION OF ALABAMA AND MISSISSIPPI BY THE ENGLISH

We mentioned, at the conclusion of the preceding chapter, that France had surrendered all of her North American possessions. Before finally doing so, however, she made a secret treaty with Spain, her ally, in which she ceded to that power the territory on the western side of the Mississippi, extending from the mouth of that river to its remotest sources, and including the island of New Orleans, which lay on the eastern side of the great river, and south of the Bayou Iberville or Manchac.[1]

Afterwards, a general peace between the three powers was concluded at Paris. France ceded to England all her Canadian possessions, and all that portion of Louisiana which lies on the eastern side of the Mississippi River, from its sources down to Bayou Iberville, which bayou, with a portion of the Amite, and a line through Lakes Maurepas and Pontchartrain, to the sea, was to form the southern boundary. France also ceded to England the port and river of Mobile. Spain ceded to Great Britain her provinces of Florida.

The king of England decreed that Florida should be formed into two governments, called the provinces of East and West Florida; that the northern line of West Florida should be the line of 31°, to run from the Chattahoochee to the Mississippi. But afterwards, understanding that this line did not embrace the valuable settlements at Natchez and above there, he again decreed the boundaries of West Florida to be as follows: a line, to begin at the mouth of the Yazoo, where that stream joins the Mississippi, and to run east to the Chattahoochee; thence down the Chattahoochee, to the mouth of the Apalachicola; thence westward, along the coast of the Gulf, and through Lakes Borgne, Pontchartrain and Maurepas, up to the river Amite; then along Bayou Iberville, to the Mississippi River, and up the middle of that river, to the mouth of the Yazoo.[2]

The territory within these lines, which was known for a period, dating

[1] France and Spain had long and secret negotiations that culminated in the signing of a "Family Compact"—linking the two Bourbon monarchies—in Paris on 15 August 1761. The agreement brought Spain into the Seven Years' War, which ultimately cost Charles III Florida. The war did allow him to regain Havana and acquire French Louisiana east of the Mississippi—including New Orleans—as compensation in the Peace of Paris of 1763. Arthur S. Aiton, "A Neglected Intrigue of the Family Compact," *Hispanic American Historical Review* 11 (August 1931): 387–93; Fred Anderson, *Crucible of War: The Seven Years' War and the Fate of Empire in British North America, 1754–1766* (New York: Alfred A. Knopf, 2000), 484–88, 504–06.

[2] George III's Royal Proclamation of 1763 established an Indian

from 1764 to 1781, as West Florida, embraced a large portion of the present states of Alabama and Mississippi. The northern line of the British province of West Florida, thus constituted, was that of 32° 28'. While a large portion of Alabama fell *below* this line, and was incorporated into British West Florida, more than half of our state, in a northern direction from the line of 32° 28', was embraced in the British province of Illinois.[3]

The province of Illinois was not only made to embrace more than the half of our state, and more than half of Mississippi, but also the western portions of Tennessee, Kentucky, and the country from thence to Lake Michigan. The province of West Florida, which was made to embrace the southern portion of Alabama, extended from the line of 32° 28', southward, to the Gulf of Mexico. We are thus particular in elucidating the British division of our state, because, hereafter, the reader will be made acquainted with the contentions which arose with the Spaniards, Georgians, and the federal government, in relation to it.[4]

To enable the reader still better to understand this matter, the line of 32° 28', which divided the Illinois portions of Alabama and Mississippi from the Florida portions of those states, was a line which commenced at the mouth of the Yazoo, and thence ran eastward, to the Tombigbee, striking that river a little below the present town of Demopolis, continuing east, touching the Alabama River a short distance below the junction of the Coosa and Tallapoosa, and terminating on the west bank of the Chattahoochee, between the present city of Columbus and old Fort Mitchell. During the British occupation of our state, its Illinois portion was uninhabited by Europeans,

reserve west of the Appalachian Mountains and colonial governments for East Florida, West Florida, Québec, and Grenada. East Florida included Spanish Florida from the Atlantic to the Apalachicola River and governed from St. Augustine. West Florida governed from Pensacola, included the panhandle of the modern state of Florida, approximately half of the present states of Alabama and Mississippi, and part of Louisiana east of New Orleans. Calloway, *Scratch of a Pen*, 92–100, 116–20, 152 ; Dennis H. McPherson and J. Douglas Rabb, *Indian from the Inside: Native American Philosophy and Cultural Renewal* (Jefferson, NC: McFarland & Company, Inc., 2011), 27–30; "The Royal Proclamation, October 7, 1763," https://primarydocuments.ca/documents/RoyalProc11763Oct7.

[3] In 1764, Governor George Johnstone requested the Board of Trade to issue a supplementary commission to extend the boundary of West Florida to "be bounded on the North by a line drawn from the Mouth of the River Yasons [Yazoo], where it unites with the Mississippi due East to the River Appalachicola." Between 26 March and 4 April 1765, Johnstone negotiated a treaty with the Choctaw confirming the new boundary. *MPA: ED*, 251–52; D. Clayton James, *Antebellum Natchez* (Baton Rouge: Louisiana State University Press, 1968), 13; Lawrence H. Gipson, *The British Empire Before the American Revolution*, vol. 9: *The Triumphant Empire: New Responsibilities within the Enlarged Empire, 1763–1766*, 15 vols. (Caldwell, ID: Caxton Printers; New York: Knopf, 1936–1970), 9: 203.

[4] Contrary to Pickett's references to the "province of Illinois," the Royal Proclamation of 1763 did not provide for any government administration outside the thirteen seaboard colonies and the three new provinces of East Florida, West Florida, and Québec. In effect, the Proclamation declared that American Indians held aboriginal title to their lands, prohibited the private sale of land from Indian to non-Indian, and reasserted the royal privilege for dealing with the Indians west of the Appalachians on the basis of nation to nation. Calloway, *Scratch of a Pen*, 94, 96–97; McPherson and Rabb, *Indian from the Inside*, 27–30.

[5] When the boundary line between U.S. and Spanish territory came into question in 1794–1795, George Chalmers of the British Office of Trade provided a detailed response to questions regarding the 32°30' line of north latitude—and the 32° 28' line—raised by Samuel Bayard. George Washington appointed Bayard in 1794 to prosecute American claims before the British admiralty courts,

excepting a few traders, who lived among the Upper Creeks, Cherokees and Chickasaws. It is rather singular to reflect that, during this period, the site of Montgomery was in British West Florida, while the site of Wetumpka was in British Illinois. These sister cities are within fifteen miles of each other.[5]

Between the Mississippi and the Wabash, a population of five thousand French and five hundred Negroes existed. But when the French commandant at Fort Chartres—the capital of the Illinois province, opposite St. Louis—surrendered the country, in the spring of 1765, to Captain Stirling, of the British army, who came by way of Detroit, at the command of his king, to take charge of it, then the French, generally, retired across the river, into Spanish territory.[6]

Captain George Johnstone, of the royal navy, was the first British governor of West Florida. He came to Pensacola, the seat of government, and brought with him a British regiment, and many Highlanders, from Charleston and New York. He issued his proclamation, defining the limits of his jurisdiction, and proclaiming the laws which he was instructed to enforce. The civil government was organized under military commandants and magistrates. The superior courts were formed under English judges.[7] The governor immediately proceeded to garrison Fort Condé, at Mobile, which he now named Fort Charlotte, in honor of the young queen of Great Britain. Soldiers were also thrown into the forts at Baton Rouge, and Panmure, at Natchez. A detachment went up to the Coosa, and occupied Fort Toulouse; but it was, in a short time, withdrawn, when the works, in a few years, went to ruins.[8]

When Governor Johnstone arrived in West Florida, there came with him a Major Loftus,

and Bayard asked Chalmers a series of questions on behalf of U.S. Attorney General William Bradford. Chalmers began by addressing Lieutenant Thomas Hutchins' "map of the west parts of Virginia, Carolina, Georgia, & c. . . states erroneously the junction of that river [Yazoo] with the Mississippi to be in the latitude 32°30', which is nine minutes too far southward, as indeed, all the maps place the junction of the Yazoo too far to the southward. Mr. [William] Faden, the King's geographer, assures me that it appears, from an accurate observation made by the late George Gaul, who surveyed West Georgia for the British Government, that the junction of the Yazoo with the Mississippi is in latitude 32°39'." Chalmers provided specific references regarding the lack of documentation on the boundaries of Georgia and South Carolina and that the northern boundary for West Florida was actually up to the 32°39' line of north latitude. George Chalmers to Samuel Bayard, Office of Trade, Whitehall, 25 September 1795, *American State Papers: Public Lands*, ed. Walter Lowrie and others, 8 vols. (Washington: Gales & Seaton, 1834–1861), 1: 55–58. [Hereafter cited *ASP: PL*].

[6] Captain Thomas Stirling (1731–1808) left Fort Pitt for the Illinois country on 24 August 1765 with about one hundred troops of the 42nd Royal Regiment of Foot—the Black Watch. Arriving at Fort de Chartres on 9 October, Stirling received the formal surrender of the post from Captain Louis St. Ange the next day, terminating French control of the region. James E. Davis, *Illinois Country* (Bloomington: Indiana University Press, 1998), 58–59; Clarence E. Carter, ed., "Documents Relating to the Occupancy of the Illinois Country by the British," in *Transactions of the Illinois State Historical Library for the Year 1907* (Springfield, Ill.: Phillips Bros., 1908), 201–21.

[7] Governor George Johnstone (1730–1787) landed at his capital of Pensacola on 21 October 1764—a full year after British military occupation of the former Spanish and French territory that was now British West Florida. While Johnstone was authorized to appoint "necessary Officers and ministers," the civil officers of West Florida were appointed in England based on an established patronage system. Robin F. A. Fabel, *Bombast and Broadsides: The Lives of George Johnstone* (Tuscaloosa: University of Alabama Press, 1987), 29, 31.

[8] Actually, Captain Robert Farmar received the formal surrender of Mobile and Fort Condé on 20 October 1763 when the grenadier companies of the 34th and 22nd regiments landed at Mobile and raised the Union Jack over the

who had been appointed to take charge of the Illinois country. Early in 1764, that officer sailed from Pensacola to New Orleans, and from thence to Manchac, where he joined his detachment, which had been some time exploring that bayou. With four hundred men he began the ascent of the Mississippi, in boats and canoes. Reaching the heights of La Roche à Davion, where Fort Adams was afterwards built, he was suddenly attacked by armed Indians, from ambuscades on both sides of the river. In this skirmish he lost several men and had many wounded. He returned to Manchac, and dispatched a captain, with twenty men, to Mobile, through the lakes, who arrived safe at that place. Major Loftus, with the residue of his command, dropped down to the Balize, and from thence went to Pensacola.[9] Thus was the occupation of the Illinois country, for a time, prevented by the fierce and successful hostility of these Indians.*

The French population along the east side of the Mississippi to the Walnut Hills was considerable, and, when they ascertained that British laws had been extended over them, many retired across the river, south of Manchac. Others, assured that they would not be disturbed, either in the enjoyment of the Catholic faith or in their rights or property, remained in the country. The English authorities encouraged emigration, and many availed themselves of their liberal offers.[10] The first Anglo-American colony came from Roanoke, in the province of North Carolina, and established themselves between Manchac and Baton Rouge. They were followed by others, from North and South Carolina, who crossed the mountains to the Tennessee, there constructing flat-boats, descended that river into the Ohio, and thence passed down the Mississippi. Others, from Georgia, even cut through the wilderness to find the Natchez country, which had become so favorably known. Emigrants from Virginia came down the Ohio. They all received, upon their

* French and Spanish MS; Martin, *History of Louisiana*; Gayarré, *Histoire de la Louisiane*; and Charles Gravier, Comte de Vergennes, *Mémoire historique et politique sur la Louisiane, par M. de Vergennes, Ministre de Louis XVI.*

former French settlement. Farmar renamed the crumbling post Fort Charlotte to honor King George III's queen. Farmar reported that he sent no British troops to occupy Fort Toulouse, because "I have not Men sufficient for that Service." Instead, Farmar granted James Germany, a trader, permission to reside at the abandoned French fort and required him to report to him on the activities of the Creeks in the region. *MPA: ED*, 12, 18–19; Rea, *Major Robert Farmar*, 35, 38.

9 Major Arthur Loftus of the 22nd Regiment joined Major Robert Farmar at Jamaica and met with Farmar and the French officers in a conference at Fort Condé on 18 October 1763. Farmar assigned Loftus and the 22nd Regiment the task of ascending the Mississippi River and occupying Fort de Chartres. With approximately 350 men under his command, Loftus's expedition departed from Fort Charlotte on 12 January 1764 only to be attacked on 20 March by belligerent Tunicas at La Roche à Davion—200 miles north of New Orleans. After a precipitous retreat and descent down the Mississippi, Loftus and his command arrived back in New Orleans on 22 March and ended their campaign at Pensacola on 7 April 1764. *MPA: ED*, 233–34, 267; Rea, *Major Robert Farmar*, 33, 35, 45.

10 West Florida had two distinctive waves of immigrants, one in the mid-1760s and a second in the 1770s, when word spread about the quality of the land near the Mississippi River. While the first period of immigration attracted European and American settlers, the second wave was primarily made up of Americans, which continued until the early years of the American Revolution. Free "family right" land grants, grants to veterans of the Seven Years' War, and mandamus grants up to 20,000 acres made to politically connected nonresidents and residents attracted Britons on both sides of the Atlantic as well as German, French, Irish, and Highland Scot settlers to West Florida. *MPA: ED*, 151, 281–82, 464; Robin F. A. Fabel, *The Economy of British West Florida, 1763–1783* (Tuscaloosa: University of Alabama Press, 1988), 6–16.

arrival, liberal and extensive grants. After a while emigrants came from Great Britain, Ireland and the British West Indies. During the three succeeding years, many flocked from Georgia, the Carolinas and New Jersey, and established themselves upon the soil drained by the Bayou Sara, the Homochitto and Bayou Pierre. All these settlements extended from the Mississippi, back, for fifteen or twenty miles. A few years afterwards, the Scotch Highlanders, from North Carolina, arrived, and formed a colony upon the upper branches of the Homochitto, thirty miles eastward of Natchez, and their numbers were, at a late period, increased by others from Scotland. This region afterwards assumed the name of New Scotland. They still retain much of their national character, and not a few of the old ones speak the Gaelic. In 1770, emigrants came from New Jersey, Delaware and Virginia, by the way of the Ohio, and, three years afterwards, a much greater number advanced by that state.[11]

West Florida continued to be governed by the general commandant at Pensacola. With the exception of some futile attempts to form a colonial legislature, like those of the Atlantic provinces, it remained, the whole time, a mere military government.[12] It was strengthened by garrisons at the places mentioned, and also at Manchac, where Fort Bute was erected, in 1765, for the purpose of monopolizing the trade of the Lower Mississippi.[13] England constantly introduced, through the lakes and by this fortified outlet, Africans obtained from their native country. These were purchased by the French, Spanish and British settlers, in defiance of the laws of Spain. Through Manchac, the English also supplied the Spanish subjects with all kinds of merchandise. To arrest this illicit trade, Don

[11] The year 1773 was a watershed year for immigrants and settlements, legal and illegal. Many of the immigrants who traveled overland became squatters on unoccupied land between Manchac and Natchez. In May-June 1773, the Company of Military Adventurers under Colonel Israel Putnam scouted for a site on the Mississippi—from Manchac to the junction of the Yazoo and Mississippi—for a potential 20,000 mandamus grant sought by General Phineas Lyman of Suffield, Connecticut. This group encountered only "tolerable" houses at Manchac and found the main building at Natchez was Fort Panmure, which had not housed any troops since 1768. They had contact with settlers from Redstone, Pennsylvania; migrants from the Holston River in East Tennessee; and Captain Amos Ogden's New Jersey settlers. On their descent down the Mississippi in June 1773, they met a North Carolina party of thirty-three looking to settle on the river. Fabel, *Economy of British West Florida,* 165–76.

[12] Except for its first year under military control (August 1763-October 1764), the administration of West Florida remained in the hands of royal governors from George Johnstone (October 1764-January 1767) through Peter Chester (August 1770-May 1781) and a bicameral legislature that included an appointed Council and an elected Commons House of Assembly. By 1778, the Commons House had members elected from several districts, including Pensacola, Mobile, Campbell Town, Manchac, and Natchez. In addition, West Florida had a court system modeled on those in the older colonies and England. Ibid., 138–42, 151; Herbert James Lewis, *Clearing the Thickets: A History of Antebellum Alabama* (New Orleans: Quid Pro Books, 2013), 28–32. See Robert R. Rea and Milo B. Howard, *The Minutes, Journals, and Acts of the General Assembly of West Florida* (Tuscaloosa: University of Alabama Press, 1979).

[13] At a meeting on 7 January 1765, Farmar, Major Arthur Loftus, Captain James Campbell, and Ensign Archibald Robertson decided on plans for a fortification at Point Iberville which Governor Johnstone named Fort Bute—after his benefactor John Stuart, Earl of Bute, and first lord of the treasury. Robertson of the Royal Engineers was assigned to build Fort Bute, "the least expensive . . . a Blockhouse with a Stockaded Fort fit to receive Stores and Provisions, and to contain two hundred Men on an emergency, and lodging comfortably a Captain and fifty Men, and a Detachment of Artillery, mounting six pieces of cannon." *MPA: ED,* 262, 282, 358; Fabel, *Bombast and Broadsides,* 14, 43–44.

Ulloa, the governor of Louisiana, constructed a fort on the south side of the Iberville, or Manchac, four hundred yards from Fort Bute; but with little effect.[14] Negroes continued to be imported, and sugar, indigo, cotton and tobacco were extensively cultivated.*

Discord made her appearance in the councils of the province of West Florida soon after its organization. The colonists became very much dissatisfied with Governor Johnstone. He was succeeded by the Honorable Montforte Brown, in the capacity of lieutenant governor. Governor Eliot came in the place of Brown; but, when the latter died, Brown again came into power. He was, however, a second time replaced, when the Honorable Peter Chester assumed the government of the province,[15] and under whose auspices it flourished for a long time. Governor Chester was universally esteemed.†

The year 1765 was fatal to the inhabitants of Mobile. The ravages of death gave it a reputation for unhealthiness, which, for years, kept it from increasing in population. In that year, the 21st British Regiment brought from Jamaica a contagious disease. Upon their arrival in Mobile, the officers and soldiers rioted in intemperance, and drank the water of stagnant pools. Death hovered over these imprudent people, until none remained. Indeed, the English population, generally, lived too fast, converting day into night, and sporting their lives away in dissipation.[16]

Far otherwise was it with the French inhabitants. Among them were exhibited instances of greater longevity than could be found in any other part of North America. In the family of the Chevalier de Lucere this was particularly the case. Its members were all extremely aged, and the mother of all died a few years previous to that period, from the snapping of her legs—the effect of the last stages of the gout. M. François, who then lived five miles above Fowl River, stated his age to be above eighty-three, and that the old woman, who was in the kitchen, cooking, and walking with activity and cheerfulness from one house to another, was his mother. She was one

* Monette, 1: 405–07.

† Romans, *Florida,* 4.

[14] Don Antonio de Ulloa, a captain in the Spanish royal navy, was commissioned as governor of Louisiana by King Charles III on 21 May 1765. In his "Extraordinary Expenses" for 1767, Ulloa proposed a fortification "opposite Manchac, to prevent the English, who have one there, from coming over to the south bank of the Iberville River, and to protect our convoys up the river." John Thomas, deputy commissioner for Indian affairs at Fort Bute, admitted that illegal trade in furs and other products flowed through the post at Manchac. Fabel, *Economy of British West Florida,* 91; Lawrence Kinnaird, ed., *Spain in the Mississippi Valley, 1765–1794,* in *Annual Report of the American Historical Association for the Year 1945,* 4 vols. (Washington: GPO, 1946–1949), 2: 1, 16, 17.

[15] The Earl of Shelburne recalled Governor Johnstone in February 1767 because of his mishandling of Indian affairs and "the spirit of disunion which has weakened and distracted the colony." Lieutenant Governor Montfort Browne served as the interim governor until the arrival of John Eliot, appointed in 1767 to replace Johnstone. However, Eliot did not arrive at Pensacola until 2 April 1769 and his tenure ended on 2 May 1769 when he "hung himself in his study." In the confusion following Eliot's death, Browne reassumed the role of interim governor until his commission was revoked in August 1769 and Elias Durnford replaced him as acting governor. Peter Chester arrived at Pensacola on 10 August 1770 and served as governor until he and General John Campbell formally surrendered West Florida to General Bernardo de Gálvez on 10 May 1781. J. Barton Starr, *Tories, Dons, and Rebels: The American Revolution in British West Florida* (Gainesville: University Presses of Florida, 1976), 13–23, 27, 210–11.

[16] Contrary to Pickett's indictment of the English for intemperance and living fast, Mobile and Pensacola presented challenges to the British military during the "sickly

of the first females that came to Mobile from France. At the age of sixty-five, François fell from a pine tree, which he was climbing, to disengage some game, which had lodged in the branches. If this accident had not occurred, he would not have felt the hand of time. Although now over eighty-three years of age, he was accustomed, almost daily, to walk five miles to the bay, angle there for hours, and, at night, walk home with a mule's load of fish upon his back, some of which his affectionate mother would instantly prepare for the supper of herself and her dutiful child![17]

They lived comfortably, on a small farm, subsisting upon its products, and those of a large herd of cattle. Many other cases of protracted life were witnessed by travelers to this country. The French assimilated their constitutions to the climate by a regular, abstemious life, refraining from spirituous liquors in the summer, and obtaining pure drinking water from a rivulet, three miles back of the town. It was also the custom of many to spend the fatal months upon their plantations, up the Tensaw and Mobile Rivers, where the air appears, at that day, to have been far more salubrious than in Mobile.* The plantation of the Chevalier de Lucere was on the first island, below the confluence of the Tombigbee and Alabama. Many of the islands on the Tensaw and Mobile rivers were well cultivated, by the French, and also by the English, who worked them in summer, and withdrew their laborers, in winter, to their settlements, hard by among the hills, where they engaged extensively in making tar and pitch for exportation.

The first plantation, after that of the Chevalier de Lucere, passed in descending the Mobile River, was that of Campbell. Then followed those of Stuart, Andry, McGillivray, Favre, Chastang, Strother and Narbonne.[18] Five miles below the latter was the site of an old French fort, which was once occupied a short time. Six miles further down, was, at one time, a splendid plantation,

* Bernard Romans, *Florida,* 4–13.

season" when their men died of "putrid bilious fever," "Jail or Hospial fever" (typhus), and the flux. The 21st Regiment—Royal North British Fusiliers—probably brought yellow fever from Havana, and Mobile became identified with "Quotitian Agues" and "Mobile Fever." Excessive heat and mosquito-borne illnesses added to the lack of wholesome drinking water, while dilapidated barracks and hospitals exacerbated the soldier's poor health and high death rates. *MPA: ED,* 169; Rea, *Major Robert Farmar,* 45; Michael N. McConnell, *Army and Empire: British Soldiers on the American Frontier, 1758–1775* (Lincoln: University of Nebraska Press, 2004), 122–23.

[17] Except for the last two paragraphs in this chapter, Pickett paraphrases liberally from Bernard Romans, *A Concise Natural History of East and West Florida.* Some of his page citations are incorrect or printer errors. Romans, *Concise Natural History,* 90–95, 173–74, 267, 283–84.

[18] While completing his descent down the Tombigbee and Alabama Rivers to Mobile on 17–19 January 1772, Romans encountered the plantations of Chevalier de Lucere, John Campbell, Charles Stuart, Simon Andry (also André), John McGillivray, Louis Favre, Chastang, Arthur Strother, Narbonne, and Henry Lizard. Henry Lizard was murdered after Bernard Romans's trip and his property was purchased by John McGillivray. Ibid., 283–84, 408 nn. 266 & 267; Hamilton, *Colonial Mobile,* 138, 287, 305, 323, 330, 494, 504–05, 510.

the property of the French Intendant of Mobile, but which now belonged to M. Lizard.*

The articles exported from Mobile and Pensacola, in 1772, were—indigo, raw hides, corn, fine cattle, tallow, rice, pitch, bear's oil, tobacco, tar, squared timber, indigo seed, myrtle wax, cedar posts and planks, salted wild beef, pecan nuts, cypress and pine boards, plank of various woods, shingles, dried salt fish, scantling, sassafras, canes, staves and heading, hoops, oranges, and peltry.

Cotton was not enumerated among the articles of export, but it is mentioned as having been, at that time, cultivated to some extent, and machines, for separating the lint from the seed, were in use. One of these is thus described by Captain Romans:

"It is a strong frame, of four studs, each about four feet high, and joined, above and below, by strong transverse pieces. Across this are placed two round well-polished iron spindles, having a small groove through their whole length, and, by means of treadles, are put in opposite motions. The workman sits behind the frame, with a thin board before him, upon which is placed the cotton, thinly spread, which the rollers receive. The lint goes through the rollers, and the seed falls down in a separate pile. The French population have much improved upon this plan, by a large wheel, which turns two of these mills, with so much velocity, that seventy pounds of clean cotton can be made every day."[19]

Mr. Krebs, upon the Pascagoula River, owned one of these improved machines, and claimed the invention of it.[20] He suspended canvas bags between pine trees, and packed in his cotton by treading, making them almost three hundred weight.†

Mobile, in common with the whole of West Florida, was visited with the most awful storms. Vessels, boats and logs were driven up into the heart of the town. The violence of the winds forced the salt water over the gardens, which

* Ibid.

† Bernard Romans, *Florida*, 211–12.

[19] For this quote, Pickett ran together two paragraphs from Bernard Romans, *A Concise Natural History of East and West Florida*, and changed some of the wording, such as "every day" for "*per diem*." In addition, the quoted material is found on pages 140 and 141 in the 1776 edition. See Bernard Romans, *A Concise Natural History of East and West Florida* (New York: R. Aitken, Bookseller, 1776).

[20] In his original narrative, Pickett refers to Hugo Krebs as Mr. Crebs—perhaps a printer error. Krebs was obviously raising cotton on his land near the Pascagoula River and using a crude cotton ginning machine as described by Bernard Romans. Romans, *Concise Natural History*, 90, 173–74; Hamilton, *Colonial Mobile*, 348.

destroyed the vegetables. The spray rose in the air, and fell again, at the distance of a half mile, like rain. All the houses were filled with water, several feet deep, and the one inhabited by a joiner was run entirely through by a schooner, which had broken from her moorings.[21]

Upon the Pascagoula, the storm was equally furious. The plantation of Mr. Krebs was almost entirely destroyed. A large crop of rice and corn was completely swept off. His dwellings were unroofed, his outhouses blown down, and his smith's shop washed away.[22] For thirty miles, up that river, the cypress trees were prostrated and the pines twisted into ropes. At Batereaux's cow-pen, the herdsmen were six weeks collecting and bringing home their cattle.[23] A colony of Germans up the Pascagoula, fearing that another Noah's flood was at hand, were about to set out for the Choctaw Nation; but the abatement of the waters preceded their usually slow movements. The whole west coast was ravaged. A schooner, with a detachment of the 16th British Regiment on board, was driven to Cat Island, and, when under the west point, parted her cables, and was carried entirely over the island, and stranded upon another, which bore the name of Free Mason. There the crew remained six weeks, and would have perished, but for their discovery by a hunting smack.[24] The different directions of the currents of wind were passing strange. That from the southeast drove the water, in immense volumes, up all the bays, rivers and bayous to the west, being here counteracted by the winds from the northeast. A body of water was violently forced into the Bay of Spirito Santo, behind the Chandeleur, Grand Gosier and Breton Isles, and, not finding sufficient vents up the rivulets, nor down the outlets of the bay, forced a number of deep

[21] Bernard Romans published the first account of this devastating Gulf Coast hurricane that was part of a storm system that swept across West Florida on 30 August to 3 September 1772. Modern meteorologists have named this storm the Bernard Romans Hurricane of 1772. Romans, *Concise Natural History*, 70. See Charles L. Sullivan, *Hurricanes of the Mississippi Gulf Coast* (Biloxi: Gulf Publishing, 1985), 5.

[22] As the result of extensive archaeological investigation, the Hugo Krebs plantation has become an important interpretive historic site in Mississippi as it features an original two-room structure—La Pointe-Krebs House—built between 1772 and 1780. Romans, *Concise Natural History*, 70. See Gregory A. Waselkov and Diane E. Silva, *Archaeology at the Krebs House (Old Spanish Fort), Pascagoula, Mississippi* (Mobile: University of South Alabama Center for Archaeological Studies, 1995).

[23] Romans spelled "Batereaux's" name as Botereaux's in his 1776 publication, and this may be a correction by Pickett or a printer's error. See Bernard Romans, *A Concise Natural History of East and West Florida* (New York: R. Aitken, Bookseller, 1776), 5.

[24] On 21 August 1772, Captain Edward Wild, in command of the *Mercury*—a converted merchant vessel—took on board sixteen troops of the 16th Regiment of Foot assigned to duty at Fort Charlotte, Mobile. He took on two artillery men at Red Cliffs and sailed to the bar outside Mobile Bay, but the *Mercury* could not enter the bay and anchored on and off the bar for seven days—fighting squalls, heavy winds, and swells. He anchored off Ship Island on the 31st, but the winds forced him to cut his masts on 3 September and drive his ship across the inundated island. Thomas Piggott, an artilleryman, was washed overboard by one of the stronger gusts. About mid-afternoon on the 4th, Wild realized his ship rested high and dry on a sandy island, later identified as one of the Sampshire Islands off the coast of Louisiana. Lieutenant Thomas Hutchins discovered the *Mercury* castaways on 30 September and departed for Pensacola that afternoon with Wild and thirteen men. By November 1772, he had recovered the *Mercury* and returned the eight remaining men to service. Robert R. Rea, "'Lieutenant Hutchins to the Rescue!' The Wreck and Recovery of the *Mercury*, 1772," *Gulf Coast Historical Review* 5 (Spring 1990): 56–59.

[25] Bernard Romans claimed that the hurricane of 1772 cut the two Chandeleur Islands into five islands and plotted the changes on a map that accompanied his book.

channels through these islands, thus forming many new islands.[25] The Chandeleur, being higher than the others, had all its surface washed off, and, but for the roots of the black mangrove and myrtle, which held much of the earth together, not a vestige of it would have been left. All the shipping at the Balize was blown into the marshes. A Spanish vessel there parted, and the whole crew were drowned.[26] The most extraordinary effect of this hurricane was the production of a second crop of leaves upon all the mulberry trees, which had never happened before. This tree budded, foliated, blossomed, and bore ripe fruit, within the brief space of four weeks after the terrible gusts had passed away. Other trees remained naked, until the following spring.*

At this time, Governor Chester was at the head of the government of West Florida. He was universally esteemed, and, under his auspices, the people prospered, and their valuable products continued to increase. Slavery was in existence, and the government of the mother country was active in transporting Africans into this country. The freeholders assembled in Mobile, Pensacola, and other parts of the province, to elect representatives to a colonial legislature; but, finding that the writs required the continuance of members for three years in office, they added the condition to their votes, that the elected members were to serve but one year. The governor, disliking this arrangement, declined to accept it.[27] The freeholders remained inflexible, and, rather than be deprived of annual elections, chose to remain without representatives.† In 1771, Pensacola contained about one hundred and eighty houses, built of timber, in good taste, and arranged with much convenience. The town formed an oblong square, near the foot of an eminence, called Gage Hill, named in honor of the great British officer,[28]

* Romans, *Florida,* 4–13.

† Romans, *Florida,* 4–13.

However, George Gauld, a British cartographer and surveyor, had counted five islands in 1768. John D. Ware and Robert R. Rea, *George Gauld: Surveyor and Cartographer of the Gulf Coast* (Gainesville: University Presses of Florida, 1982), 109–10.

[26] The Spanish merchant brigantine *Nuestra Señora del Amparo* sailing from New Orleans to Vera Cruz was struck by hurricane force winds on 2 September 1772 near Balize at the entrance to the Mississippi. The ship was quickly torn to pieces and only six men survived the devastating storm. Robert F. Marx, *Shipwrecks in the Americas* (revised edition; 1971, New York: Dover Publications, Inc., 1987), 187.

[27] While Peter Chester enjoyed general popularity and public support early in his tenure, his authority was challenged in 1779 when 130 citizens signed a petition calling for his removal as governor. Fabel, *Economy of British West Florida,* 132–34.

[28] Gage Hill was named for General Thomas Gage (c.1719–1787), who served as commander-in-chief of British forces in North America from 1763 through 1775. From his headquarters in New York, Gage showed a sincere interest and concern for his forces on the American frontier, including West Florida. Rea, *Major Robert Farmar,* 40, 43, 46, 55–56, 60–61; McConnell, *Army and Empire,* 51–52, 62, 90, 99, 123, 140; John R. Alden, *General Gage in America* (Baton Rouge: Louisiana State University Press, 1948), 25–30, 60–75, 280–81.

[29] Because of pressure from Augusta merchants and traders like George Galphin, Governor Wright and John Stuart convened the Augusta Congress with representatives of the Cherokee, Creeks, and Catawbas in late May 1773. While the Catawbas came seeking the services of a missionary, the Cherokee and Creeks agreed to participate to extinguish trade debt and to receive presents. John Richard Alden, *John Stuart and the Southern Frontier* (1944; reprint, New York: Gordian Press, Inc., 1966), 304, 304 n. 47; J. Russell Snapp, *John Stuart and the Struggle for Empire in the Southern Frontier* (Baton Rouge: Louisiana State University Press, 1996), 130–31.

[30] While the Cherokee had a large trade debt, the Creeks had a much smaller debt and were reluctant participants in the Augusta Congress. Despite a warning from Stuart, Wright made an agreement to assume the outstanding debt owed by the Creeks for 500,000

well-remembered by the Whigs of America.*

Turning our eyes towards the British province of Georgia, we find that the Cherokees and Creeks had assembled at Augusta, at the instance of Sir James Wright, the governor, and John Stuart, superintendent of Indian affairs.[29] These Indians there ceded to Great Britain a large area of territory, upon the headwaters of the Ogeechee, and northwest of Little River. The object was to compensate the Honorable George Galphin, and some other traders, for large debts due them by these nations. The governor, having no power to accept this cession, but seeing the influence it would enable him to wield, in behalf of the tottering power of his king, to whom he was devotedly attached, he had already obtained the consent of the ministry to make the treaty.[30] But Galphin never obtained any of these lands, or the proceeds of the sales thereof, on account of his boldly expressed patriotic opinions; and Governor Wright, with a vindictive partiality, paid the *loyal* traders, in preference, keeping the larger portion of the proceeds, to strengthen his government, and perhaps to add to his own coffers.[31] Galphin was wealthy; he sacrificed thousands in defense of American liberty, and, to this day, his descendants remain without remuneration.† It is said that Governor Wright received the order of knighthood, for the unjust direction which he gave these funds. In the meantime, land offices had been established

* Ibid, 303.

† Since I have written this paragraph, some of the heirs of Galphin have received a large amount of money, from the United States government, on account of this claim. They had previously applied to Georgia, Great Britain, and the United States, without success. The claim of the heirs of Galphin was just upon one of these powers; but many have contended that it was not a just claim upon the federal government, but one upon Georgia, while others have contended that it was a just claim upon Great Britain.

acres of pine barrens between the Ogeechee and Altamaha rivers. The Cherokee debt was extinguished for a cession of 1,616,298 acres above the Little River in the Upper Savannah watershed. Edward J. Cashin, *Lachlan McGillivray, Indian Trade: The Shaping of the Southern Colonial Frontier* (Athens: University of Georgia Press, 1992), 278–80; Edward J. Cashin, *The King's Ranger: Thomas Brown and the American Revolution on the Southern Frontier* (New York: Fordham University Press, 1999), 10–12.

[31] Despite Pickett's comments, none of the traders—including George Galphin—had been promised a share of the "Ceded Lands" surrendered by the Cherokee and Creeks in 1773. However, the traders who had remained loyal to the king were compensated by the British government in 1790. Galphin's heirs were paid through an act passed by Congress that permitted Zachary Taylor's secretary of the treasury to hear the original claim of £10,000. The heirs received a full payment and $191,000 in interest in 1850. Alden, *John Stuart,* 305 n. 49.

at Augusta, and at the confluence of the Broad and Savannah Rivers, where a town was laid out, called Dartmouth, but which was subsequently changed to the name of Petersburg.[32]

This newly ceded territory began to be rapidly settled, when a party of Creeks attacked Sherrill's Fort, killed seven persons, and forced the others to barricade an outhouse, where they would have been butchered, but for the timely arrival of Captain Barnard, with forty men, who dispersed the enemy. Other attacks by the Indians succeeded, and the settlers abandoned their new homes, and retired into the old British settlements, lower down, upon the Savannah.[33] The noble Galphin, who had great influence with the Indians, dispatched runners to the nation, who induced the chiefs to put a stop to the effusion of blood, which afforded the settlers the opportunity of coming back,[34] and of renewing their abandoned improvements.*

* McCall, *History of Georgia,* 2: 11–12.

[32] On 11 June 1773, Governor Wright issued a proclamation announcing the sale of the "New Purchase" lands. He also issued an order to establish a fort and the town Pickett mentions—Dartmouth, named for Lord Dartmouth, secretary of state for the colonies. During his tenure as royal governor of Georgia, Wright tripled Georgia's domain by adding 5,500,000 acres through negotiations with Indian neighbors. Cashin, *King's Ranger,* 11–12.

[33] William Sherrill, his wife, and nine slaves had settled on 200 acres on the south fork of the Little River in late 1773. By December 1773, parties of young Creek warriors angered by the land cessions began to attack the isolated settlers. On 14 January 1774, a party of seventeen Lower Creeks killed Sherrill and a nearby family, killing thirteen settlers and losing five warriors at Sherrill's Fort. Captain James Grierson's militia regiment and Edward Barnard's rangers searched for the Creek war parties. The militia was badly routed on 25 January, and the Creek war parties soon cleared everyone off the ceded lands. Alden, *John Stuart,* 306; Cashin, *Lachlan McGillivray,* 281–82.

[34] While Galphin exercised some influence in the Lower Creek towns, John Stuart and his deputy, David Taitt, asked John McGillivray and his cousin, Charles Stuart, to instigate a Choctaw attack on the Creeks. He also dispatched Lachlan McGillivray to serve as an advisor to Governor Wright and to advise him to stop trade to the Creeks. This strategy gave the peace chiefs the leverage to bring their "mad young men" under control. At a conference in Savannah, Stuart and Wright met with 137 Creeks who agreed to a peace treaty on 20 October 1774. Cashin, *Lachlan McGillivray,* 282–85.

Chapter XV

HARDSHIPS OF THE EARLY EMIGRANTS

Taking the reader with us, to the settlements of the distant Natchez region, he will find that emigrants continued to pour in, upon those fertile hills and alluvial bottoms, from all parts of "His Majesty's Atlantic plantations." Many were the hardships and perils they encountered, in reaching this remote and comparatively uninhabited region. It is believed that the history of one party of these emigrants will enable the reader to understand what kind of hardships and deprivations all the others were forced to undergo.

Major General Phineas Lyman, a native of Durham, a graduate of Yale, a distinguished lawyer, and a member of the legislature of the commonwealth of Massachusetts, became commander of the Connecticut forces in 1755.[1] He served with so much distinction, during the Canadian war, that he was invited, by persons high in office, to visit England. He had formed an association, composed of his brothers in arms, called the "Military Adventurers," whose design was the colonization of a tract of country upon the Mississippi. He sailed to England, as agent for this company, with the sanguine, yet reasonable hope, that the king would make the grant. Arriving there, he found, to his astonishment, that land in a wilderness was refused to those who had fought so valiantly for it, and whose contemplated establishment would have formed a barrier against enemies, who might seek to acquire it. In his own country, Lyman had never solicited favor, otherwise than by faithful public services. The coolness which he now experienced deeply mortified him—his spirits sank, and he lost all his former energy. Shocked at the degradation which he imagined he should sustain by returning home unsuccessful, he made up his mind to bury his bones upon an ungrateful soil. There he remained for eleven years, a neglected man.[2] His wife, a lady of superior endowments, distressed at his long absence, sent her son to solicit his return. The sight of his boy called up the remains of his resolution, and he resolved to go back

[1] Phineas Lyman (1716–1774) graduated from Yale College in 1738. In 1755 he left a successful law practice to accept an appointment as major general and commander-in-chief of Connecticut militia forces. Lyman led provincial troops in several campaigns during the French and Indian War, including the capture of Crown Point and Ticonderoga in 1759, Oswego and Montreal in 1760, and Havana in 1762. Franklin Bowditch Dexter, *Biographical Sketches of the Graduates of Yale College: With Annals of the College History*, 6 vols. (NY: Henry Holt and Company, 1885–1911; New Haven: Yale University Press, 1912), 1: 603–08.

[2] In England, Phineas Lyman encountered resistance from Lord Hillsborough, who opposed all settlements in the West. However, instead of moping for eleven years, he busied himself advancing his own personal interests,

and in 1770 he received a personal grant of 20,000 acres in West Florida. Hillsborough resigned in 1772 and was replaced by the more sympathetic Lord Dartmouth. Lyman returned to Connecticut confident that the Company of Military Adventurers would soon be approved for land grants in West Florida. Bernard Bailyn, *Voyagers to the West: A Passage in the Peopling of America on the Eve of the Revolution* (New York: Vintage Books, 1986), 485.

[3] Actually, upon General Lyman's return, the Company was reconvened on 18 November 1772 and a formal roster of members was drawn up, including old and new members. They appointed a committee to "explore and reconnoitre" the land in West Florida which included Colonel Israel Putnam, Lieutenant Rufus Putnam, Captain Roger Enos, and Thaddeus Lyman. Col. Putnam's thirteen-year old son Daniel and William Davis—a "hired man"—joined them at New London. They sailed on the sloop *Mississippi,* arrived at Pensacola on 5 March 1773, explored up the Mississippi to the Yazoo in April and May, and returned to Connecticut in August 1773. Ibid., 485–86; Israel Putnam and Rufus Putnam, *The Two Putnams, Israel and Rufus: in the Havana Expedition 1762 and in the Mississippi River Exploration 1772–73, with some account of the Company of Military Adventurers,* comp. Albert C. Bates (Hartford: Connecticut Historical Society, 1931), 27, 115–38, 144–232, 237–62; Robin F. A. Fabel, "Encounters on the Mississippi, Yazoo, and Big Black Rivers: The Explorers of the Company of Military Adventurers," *Gulf Coast Historical Review* 8 (Fall 1992): 98–101.

[4] The first party of about 30 settlers left Middletown, Connecticut, on 19 December 1773. General Lyman and his son Phineas Lyman, Jr., departed a few days later with a second party. Some sources report a third contingent left from Massachusetts in the summer of 1774, but Captain Matthew Phelps writes that Eleanor Dwight Lyman, her children, and other kinsmen left with him on 1 May 1776. Bailyn, *Voyagers to the West,* 486; Dexter, *Biographical Sketches of the Graduates of Yale College,* 3: 35–36; Matthew Phelps, *Memoirs and Adventures of Captain Matthew Phelps: Formerly of Harwington in Connecticut, now Resident in Newhaven in Vermont. Particularly in Two Voyages, from Connecticut to the River Mississippi, from December 1773 to October*

to America, as the grant upon the Mississippi had at last been made.* He reached home in 1773. But the grave had closed over most of his original associates, while others had arrived at an age unsuitable to bold enterprises.[3] In company with his eldest son, a man of rare attainments, but who had become subdued and listless, in consequence of the deep distress and mortification of his father, while so long absent, General Lyman sailed from New England with a number of emigrants, in two vessels, bound for New Orleans.[4]

It is deemed proper that an enumeration of these emigrants be here made, as the eyes of some of their descendants, still living in Mississippi, may perhaps rest on these pages. On board of these vessels were:[5]

General Lyman, of Suffield.

Captain Ladley, of Hartford.

Thomas and James Lyman, Durham.

Hugh White, Middletown.

Captain Elsworth, Ira Whitmore and — Sage, Middletown.

Major Early, Weatherford.

Thaddeus and Phineas Lyman, with eight slaves, Suffield.

Moses and Isaac Sheldon, Roger Harmon and — Hanks, Suffield.

Seth Miller, Elisha and Josiah Flowers, Springfield.

Moses Drake, Ruggles Winchel and Benjamin Barber, Westfield.

— Alcott, Windsor.

Daniel and Roswell Magguet, Hartford.

Thomas Comstock, — Weed, New Hartford.

Captain Silas Crane, Robert Patrick, Ashbell Bowen, John Newcomb and James Dean, of Lebanon.

Abram Knapp and Matthew Phelps, of Norfolk.

Giles and Nathaniel Hull, James Stoddart and Thaddeus Bradley, Salisbury.

* *Travels in New York and New England,* by Theodore Dwight, S.T.D., L.L.D., late President of Yale College, 1: 306–16.

Ephraim Case and Hezekiah Reu, Sheffield.

John Fisk and Elisha Hale, Wallingford.

Timothy and David Hotchkiss, Waterbury.

John Hyde, William Silkrag, Jonathan Lyon, and William Davis, Stratford or Derby.

James Harman and family, and Elnathan Smith, Suffield.

William Hurlbut and Elijah Leonard, with a number of slaves, Springfield.

General Lyman and these emigrants at length saw the mouth of the Mississippi, passed up to New Orleans, there obtained boats, and after a laborious ascent of that powerful stream, arrived upon the Big Black River. He settled his grant, but was too old to cultivate it. In a short time his son died, and, before he could arrange his own affairs, to return home, for the purpose of bringing out his family, the grave also closed over him, terminating a life, first, of honor and military glory, and then of sadness and misfortune.[6] But the half has not yet been told of the troubles of his family, the last of whom were miserable sufferers in the Creek Nation, as will hereafter be narrated.

Captain Matthew Phelps, one of the companions of General Lyman, returned to Connecticut, and his representations of the fertility of the new country excited many of the citizens, who resolved to return with him to occupy it. But various causes prevented their departure. At length, however, they sailed from Middletown.[7] Among these emigrants were Madame Lyman, the wife of the late general, with three sons and two daughters; Major Timothy Dwight, his wife and one child; Sereno and Jonathan Dwight, of Northampton;[8] Benjamin Day and his family; Harry Dwight and three slaves; Joseph Leonard and Josiah Flowers, with their families, from Springfield; the Reverend Jedediah Smith and his family, from Granville; Mrs. Elnathan Smith and children; and John Felt and his family, from Suffield; together with

1780, comp. Anthony Haswell (Bennington, Vt.: Press of Anthony Haswell, 1802), "Appendix": 56, 62–63.

5 Pickett's list is from Captain Matthew Phelps's first voyage to West Florida on a ship "commanded by Capt. Porter of Lebanon." The list is found in the "APPENDIX" of his *Memoirs and Adventures.* Phelps, *Memoirs and Adventures of Captain Matthew Phelps,* "Appendix," 60–62.

6 General Lyman established himself on Bayou Pierre prior to his death on 10 September 1774. His oldest son Phineas Lyman Jr., a 1763 Yale graduate, had died earlier but no date can be confirmed. Ironically, after receiving approval from King George III, his 20,000 acre land grant was confirmed by a patent issued under the great seal of West Florida on 2 February 1775. Mary Wilson McBee, ed., *The Natchez Court Records, 1767–1805: Abstract of Early Records* (1953; reprint, Baltimore: Clearfield Company, Inc., 2003), 356–57.

7 Pickett is using the dates from Matthew Phelps's *Memoirs and Adventures* and the narrative for his second voyage to West Florida. Other sources report that a third party of Military Adventurers departed from Massachusetts in the summer of 1774 that included Eleanor Dwight Lyman. Phelps, *Memoirs and Adventures of Captain Matthew Phelps,* 56–69; ibid., "Appendix," 62–63. See Bernard Bailyn, *Voyagers to the West: A Passage in the Peopling of America on the Eve of the Revolution* (New York: Vintage Books, 1986), 486, and Israel Putnam and Rufus Putnam, *The Two Putnams, Israel and Rufus: in the Havana Expedition 1762 and in the Mississippi River Exploration 1772–73, with some account of the Company of Military Adventurers,* comp. Albert C. Bates (Hartford: Connecticut Historical Society, 1931), 45.

8 Sereno Edwards Dwight (1754–1783) and Jonathan Edwards Dwight (1759–1800) were sons of Major Timothy Dwight and Mary Edwards Dwight (1734–1807), daughter of Rev. Jonathan Edwards (1703–1758). Jonathan Edwards, Sereno Edwards Dwight, and David Brainerd, *The Works of President Edwards: With a Memoir of His Life,* 10 vols. (New York: G & C & H. Carvil, 1829–1830), 1: 763–64.

Captain Phelps, wife and children, with many others.*

After a voyage of three months, attended with many dangers, the party reached New Orleans, on the 1st August. Here, obtaining boats, they began to stem the muddy current of the Mississippi. Mrs. Flowers, an estimable lady, who was too sick to continue the voyage, was left at Point Coupee, where she soon died. The eldest daughter of Captain Phelps was seized with a violent fever, and, in a few days after, the enterprising father became sick with the same disease. Many of the emigrants suffered with fever, and the boats were moved slowly up the river, by the feeble efforts of those who were less debilitated. Captain Phelps and all his children becoming prostrated with disease, his boat was tied to the willows, while the others continued the voyage. His intimate friend, Leonard, who had messed with him at sea, arrived at Natchez, where he buried his wife. The boat containing the Lymans and the Reverend Smith reached Natchez about the same time, a few days after which the worthy minister closed his earthly career, and was soon followed to his long home by the refined and estimable Major Dwight.[9] At length, those of this party who were left reached the Big Black, and the improvements made by General Lyman. Here Madame Lyman soon died, and was buried by the side of her husband and son!

The unfortunate Phelps remained in his boat, which was anchored fifteen miles above Point Coupee, when his daughter, Abigail, died. He was compelled to bury her with his own hands. All this time, it was only at intervals that his family were able to assist each other in the severe fits of the ague which afflicted them.

The Disposer of Events removed from this distressed man an infant, born on the ocean, whom the sailors had named "Atlantic." Phelps again had to perform the melancholy task of digging a grave, and burying the boy by the side of his lovely sister. Mr. Flowers, the other members of whose family had died below, came, with his child, in a small boat, to the gloomy habitation of Phelps. They now both obtained a larger boat, and, placing in it their joint effects, began again to ascend the river. The Phelpses were worn to skeletons, but, struggling forward, against singular adversity, and buoyed up with the hope of brighter scenes, they finally arrived at

[9] The Reverend Jedediah Smith served as pastor of the East Granville (Massachusetts) Church in 1755–1776 before being pushed out because of his loyalty to the British crown. He died near Natchez on 2 September 1776. Major Timothy Dwight, a 1744 Yale graduate, was a prominent merchant and public servant at Northampton, but his loyalty to the British government had compromised his position in his community, leading him to pursue a land grant in West Florida. He died on 10 June 1777, and his sister Eleanor Dwight Lyman had died two months earlier. His son Timothy Dwight IV, a 1769 Yale graduate, served as the twelfth president of Yale College in 1795–1817. Dexter, *Biographical Sketches of the Graduates of Yale College,* 1: 757–58; ibid., 3: 321–33; Lorenzo Sabine, *Biographical Sketches of Loyalists of the American Revolution, With An Historical Essay,* 2 vols. (Boston: Little, Brown and Company, 1864), 2: 311–12.

* *Memoirs and Adventures of Captain Matthew Phelps*, 18–72; also his "Appendix," 60–63.

the landing of Natchez. Advancing, after a few days, they reached the Petit Gulf, where lived Philip Alston, a gentleman of wealth and humanity. Mrs. Phelps, worn down with trouble and disease, was rapidly approaching dissolution. In a few days she died, and Alston had her remains decently interred. He did all in his power to alleviate the sorrows of the unhappy husband, and sheltered him and his two remaining children under his hospitable roof. A few days afterwards, the fated Phelps began again to move up the river, and, upon gaining Grand Gulf, entered the hospitable abode of an old acquaintance. Leaving this place, he came in sight of the mouth of the Big Black River, having consumed nearly one hundred days in performing a voyage from New Orleans, which can now be accomplished in a few hours. Near this place, three years before, he had purchased some improvements. Captain Phelps was so debilitated, that he hired a lad, of fourteen years of age, and a man, by the name of Knapp, to propel his boat.[10]

Upon entering the Big Black, the captain and the boy, disembarking, walked along the bank, dragging the boat after them with a long line, while Knapp remained on board, to steer, in company with the children, a boy of five and a girl of ten years of age. The children were quietly sitting upon the bed on which they had suffered so much. Presently the boat entered a whirlpool, which forced the stern under a willow. Knapp jumped out and swam ashore. The terrified Phelps secured the end of the rope around a tree, and rushed to the spot where his all remained in such imminent peril. Unable to swim, he crawled into the river upon the willow, imploring his daughter to remain quiet, until he could get out her little brother. While the little fellow was wading the water in the bottom of the boat, endeavoring to reach his unhappy father, the willow began to sink, with the additional weight upon it, and, at that moment, an angry billow came rushing down, the boat suddenly went under, and the poor children were swept rapidly off. "Oh, God, save them!" was all that the miserable Phelps could utter. Standing upon the unsteady willow, he saw them rise again to the surface, locked in each other's arms, and then sink forever. The bereaved man stood upon the tree in mournful silence—wet, cold, emaciated—without property, without friends, and without children, and with no wife to encourage him and sympathize with him in his misfortunes.

[10] Pickett continues to paraphrase and follow closely the narrative of Matthew Phelps. The Petit Gulf was a bend on the Mississippi River. Phelps, *Memoirs and Adventures of Captain Matthew Phelps,* 70–83.

But Phelps was a Christian, and he bore up with astonishing fortitude. The calamities which had befallen him had been unavoidable, and yet he tortured his imagination, for some time, with reproaches upon himself. In addition to his weighty troubles, he found that, during his absence, his improvements had been taken from him by a wretch who availed himself of the customs of the country. Phelps, however, survived *all* this, and lived to be an old man, surrounded, in New England, with a wife, children and plenty.[11] He was long accustomed to relate to the sober Yankees the horrors which he experienced in the "Natchez country," with perfect composure; always, however, avoiding the last terrible affair, when his two children, whom God had spared him, and with whom he had expected yet to see much happiness in the wilderness, rose up to his view, from their watery bed, for one short moment, locked in each other's arms, and then went down forever.*

[11] Following his devastating personal losses and financial setbacks, Matthew Phelps (1746–1817) returned to Harwington, Connecticut, in the fall of 1779. He married the widow Thankful Phelps Moore in January 1781 and soon thereafter settled in Norfolk, Connecticut, where they had three children — two lived to adulthood. He removed to New Haven, Vermont, in 1788 where he operated a hotel, wrote his memoirs, and died in 1817. Ibid., 208–09; Henry Perry Smith, ed., *History of Addison County Vermont: With Illustrations and Biographical Sketches* (Syracuse, NY: D. Mason & Co., 1886), 529; Oliver Seymour Phelps and Andrew T. Servin, comp., *The Phelps Family in America and Their English Ancestors*, 2 vols. (Pittsfield, Mass.: Eagle Publishing Co., 1899), 1: 253–54.

* *Memoirs and Adventures of Captain Mathew Phelps*, 56–100.

Chapter XVI

JOURNEY OF BARTRAM THROUGH ALABAMA

William Bartram, the botanist, who has been mentioned in our remarks upon the aborigines of the country, passed through the Creek Nation, and went from thence to Mobile.[1] He found that that town extended back from the river nearly half a mile. Some of the houses were vacant, and others were in ruins. Yet a few good buildings were inhabited by the French gentlemen, and others by refined emigrants from Ireland, Scotland, England, and the northern British colonies. The Indian trade was under the management of Messrs. Swanson and McGillivray. They conducted an extensive commerce with the Chickasaws, Choctaws and Creeks. Their buildings were commodious, and well arranged for that purpose.[2] The principal houses of the French were of brick, of one story, of a square form, and on a large scale, embracing courts in their rears. Those of the lower classes were made of strong cypress frames, filled in with plaster.

Major Farmar, one of the most respectable inhabitants of West Florida, who formerly had much to do with the colonial government, resided at Tensaw, in sight of the present Stockton, where once lived the tribe of Tensaw Indians. The bluff sustained not only his extensive improvements, but the dwellings of many French families, chiefly his tenants, while his extensive plantations lay up and down the Tensaw, on the western side. Indeed, all up that river, and particularly on the eastern branch, were many well cultivated plantations, belonging to various settlers, while others were in ruins, having been abandoned by the French when the English took possession of the country.[3] The plantations on the Mobile River, as seen five years before, have already been mentioned. At one of these Bartram stayed all night, in company with Dr. Grant, a physician of the garrison of Fort Charlotte. The occupant, who was an old gentleman and a famous hunter, annually killed three hundred deer, besides bears, panthers and wolves.[4]

[1] Contrary to Pickett's timeline, William Bartram arrived in British West Florida in late July 1775. Bartram, *William Bartram on the Southeastern Indians*, 94.

[2] Peter Swanson and John McGillivray operated trading partnerships in Mobile and Pensacola, and the members of their trading enterprises changed from time to time. In addition, they often were connected to more than one partnership in different locations. Amos Wright, Jr., *The McGillivray and McIntosh Traders on the Old Southwest Frontier, 1716–1815* (Montgomery: NewSouth Books, 2001), 119–25.

[3] William Bartram left Mobile on 5 August 1775 for Major Robert Farmar's plantation Farm Hall, where he obtained the use of a canoe and explored further up the Mobile River. He also used a sailboat to explore the islands in the Mobile-Tensaw

Arriving at Pensacola, Bartram received from Dr. Lorimer, one of the honorable council, much politeness and attention.[5] Mr. Livingston, the government secretary, took him to the department in which he did business.[6] Shortly afterwards, Governor Chester rode by in his chariot, having been upon a morning ride to his farm. He received the learned botanist with cordiality, invited him to remain some time in the country, to make his house his headquarters, commended his laudable pursuits, and offered to defray his expenses in traveling over the country under his jurisdiction.[7]

Pensacola, at this period, contained several hundred habitations. The governor's place was a large stone building, erected by the Spaniards, and ornamented with a tower. The town was defended by a large stockade fortress, of wood, on the plan of a tetragon, with a salient angle at each corner, where stood blockhouses a story higher than the curtains. Upon these, light cannon were mounted. Within this fortress was a council chamber, where the records were kept, also houses for the officers and barracks for the garrison, together with arsenals and magazines. The secretary resided in a handsome and spacious house, as did some eminent merchants and professional gentlemen.*

Returning to Mobile, the botanist presently embarked in a trading vessel, manned by three Negroes, and set sail for Pearl River. Passing along the western coast, and reaching the mouth of Dog River, he there landed, and entered the woods for recreation. Here he saw the remains of the old Fort Louis de la Mobile, with a few pieces of iron cannon, and also vast iron kettles, for boiling tar into pitch. Pursuing his voyage, he again came to the shore, a few miles beyond, where resided a Frenchman, eighty years of age, who was active, strong and muscular; his mother, who was present, and who appeared to be brisk and cheerful, was one hundred and five years of age. Fifty years previous to this period, she had landed in Mobile, from la belle France.[8] Arriving at Pearl Island, Bartram took up his quarters at

* Bartram, *Travels*, 402–07, 412–14.

delta, north of Mobile Bay. Bartram, *William Bartram on the Southeastern Indians*, 95–96; Rea, *Major Robert Farmar*, 135.

4 Bartram may have visited with Dr. William Grant, a retired British military physician, for several reasons. He had made a quick trip to Pensacola in early September 1775, and when he returned to Farmar's, he continued to suffer from "feverish symptoms" and had "a smart fit of fever" on his descent to Mobile. He also questioned Grant about honey bees, who replied that there was one hive in Mobile brought from Europe. Harper, *Travels of William Bartram*, 261; Rea, *Major Robert Farmar*, 135.

5 Dr. John Lorimer, a member of the Council of West Florida, came to Pensacola in 1765 as a surgeon to the 31st Regiment. He had been selected as an early member of the American Philosophical Society, and he and Bartram shared a common interest in the flora and fauna of the area. Harper, *Travels of William Bartram*, 555; Edward J. Cashin, *William Bartram and the American Revolution on the Southern Frontier* (Columbia: University of South Carolina Press, 2000), 183.

6 Philip Livingston, a member of the prominent Livingston family of New York, served as secretary to Governor Peter Chester from 1770 through 1778. He became deeply involved in land speculation and acquired 150,000 acres, primarily on the Mississippi. Rea, *Major Robert Farmar*, 123–24; Fabel, *Economy of West Florida*, 142, 168–69, 171; Cashin, *William Bartram*, 185–86.

7 Bartram met with Governor Chester on 5 September 1775, who gave Bartram a permit which granted him explicit freedom to travel throughout the province and permission to collect "Rare and useful Productions in Botany and Natural History." Bartram, *William Bartram on the Southeastern Indians*, 95; Harper, *Travels of William Bartram*, 406.

8 Returning from Pensacola, Bartram returned to Major Farmar's plantation, where he found himself "very ill . . . an excessive pain in my head, attended with a high fever, this

the house of a generous Englishman, named Rumsey, with whom he passed a month.[9] Leaving this place in a handsome boat, navigated by three Negroes, he coasted along the northern shore of Lake Pontchartrain, entered Lake Maurepas, and proceeded up the Amite River for thirty miles to the large plantation of a Scotch gentleman, who gave him a hospitable reception. Bartram, still ascending the Amite, next entered the Iberville on the left, and it was not long before he reached a landing, at which was situated warehouses for depositing English merchandise.[10]

A beautiful road, overhung with evergreens, led from this place to Manchac, upon the Mississippi. Here, also, the English had mercantile depots, the chief establishment of which was that of Swanson and McGillivray, who were Indian traders. The Iberville was now dry, its channel being higher than the Mississippi, which had receded from it. It was, however, navigable in winter and spring, for the "Father of Waters" then disgorged some portion of his tide through this channel into the lakes. It also separated, as before observed, the English colony of West Florida and the Spanish province of Louisiana. On one side of this bayou was an English fort, at Manchac, and just across, on the south point, was a Spanish fort. A slender wooden bridge connected the two establishments, and, strange to say, they were, at this time, peaceable, although such near neighbors. The next day Bartram began the ascent of the Mississippi, and, two miles above Manchac, stopped at an Indian town. The inhabitants were a portion of the Alabamas, who had once lived upon the river of that name, but who, when the French evacuated Fort Toulouse, followed them to Louisiana, and here had formed an establishment. The botanist visited Baton Rouge, now called by the English New Richmond, and various plantations on both sides of the great river. He was particularly pleased with the French planters, who had long tilled these superior lands. They were ingenious, industrious, and lived in ease and great abundance.[11]

About the middle of November, Bartram returned to Mobile, by the same route, arranged his specimen plants and flowers, and left them in the hands of Swanson and

disorder soon settled in my eyes." Despite his ill health he traveled west, where he encountered the French octogenarian on the Pearl River who tried for three days to cure his illness. Bartram, *William Bartram on the Southeastern Indians*, 95–96; Harper, *Travels of William Bartram*, 265–66; Cashin, *William Bartram*, 191.

[9] James Rumsey had a plantation on an island near the Rigolets, an eight mile long strait that connects Lake Pontchartrain and Lake St. Catherine to Lake Borgne and then to the Gulf of Mexico. Bartram referred to the island as Pearl Island, but it is known as Prevost Island in St. Tammany Parish, Louisiana. During his first night at Rumsey's, Bartram came close to death: "I sincerely thought it would be my last." He remained "four or five weeks" and could not expose his eyes to sunlight for "several weeks." "The Rigolets," *USGS Geographic Names Information System*; Bartram, *William Bartram on the Southeastern Indians*, 96; Harper, *Travels of William Bartram*, 266–68, 616; Cashin, *William Bartram*, 191–92.

[10] James Rumsey not only helped Bartram regain his health, but he provided him with his trading vessel and a three-man crew. He traveled the Tangipahoa River, entered Lake Maurepas, and then traveled some thirty miles up the Amite River, where he encountered the twenty-six year old Scot William Dunbar at Manchac in October 1775. Harper, *Travels of William Bartram*, 268–70; Cashin, *William Bartram*, 192–94.

[11] William Dunbar accompanied Bartram to Manchac and served as his guide as they navigated up the Mississippi River. He pointed out the displaced Indians in the lower Mississippi valley and introduced Bartram to settlers and planters along the river. He took Bartram to the French settlement at Point Coupée and then back to his plantation near Baton Rouge before returning Bartram to Manchac, where he had encountered "Messers. Swanson & Co." Harper, *Travels of William Bartram*, 270–76; Cashin, *William Bartram*, 194–98.

McGillivray, to be shipped to Dr. Fothergill, at London.[12] He then entered a boat and went to the mansion of Major Farmar, at Tensaw. The next morning he set out for the Creek Nation with a caravan of traders, who transported their merchandise upon pack-horses. The road, like all others in an Indian country, was narrow and well beaten. The pack-horses were arranged one after the other, the oldest and best trained in the lead. At night they were belled and turned out to graze in the woods. In the morning so much time was occupied in collecting them, arranging their packs, and preparing breakfast that the sun was high when a start was made. Then these faithful animals fell into line on the trail, like regular soldiers, and began a brisk trot, which was continued all day, amid the ringing of their bells and the whooping and cursing of the drivers.[13]

When near the site of the present city of Montgomery, the caravan met a party of Georgians, consisting of a man, his wife, a young woman, several young children, and three stout young men, with a dozen horses laden with their effects. These fearless people had passed through the Creek Nation, then very extensive, and were on their way to settle upon the Alabama, a few miles above the confluence of that river and the Tombigbee.[14] They are believed to have been among the first Anglo-Americans who settled in the present Baldwin County.*

[12] Bartram arrived back in Mobile on 16 November 1775 and spent the next ten days completing drawings and preparing his specimens to be shipped to Dr. John Fothergill (1712–1780) in London. Fothergill, a noted Quaker physician, subsidized Bartram's travels and cultivated plants from throughout the world. He became one of the first foreigners to be elected as a member of the American Philosophical Society in 1770. Bartram, *William Bartram on the Southeastern Indians*, 9–12, 18–19; Harper, *Travels of William Bartram*, 277, 509–10; Cashin, *William Bartram*, 126, 128.

[13] On 27 November 1775, Bartram traveled by boat from Mobile up the Tensaw River to Major Farmar's Farm Hall, where he met John Adam Tapley's caravan. Tapley, a Georgia trader, two pack-horsemen, Bartram, and "between twenty and thirty horses, sixteen of which were loaded" left Farm Hall the next day for Georgia. Bartram, *William Bartram on the Southeastern Indians*, 97; Harper, *Travels of William Bartram*, 278; Cashin, *William Bartram*, 201–02.

[14] The party of Georgians encountered by Bartram and his fellow travelers in the Creek Nation in December 1775 were Loyalists seeking refuge near Mobile. By late 1775, West Florida had been designated an official asylum for Loyalist refugees from the seaboard colonies. Bartram, *William Bartram on the Southeastern Indians*, 98; Usner, *Indians, Settlers, and Slaves*, 112.

* Bartram, *Travels*, 416–41.

Chapter XVII

AN ACCOUNT OF THE McGILLIVRAY FAMILY—THE REVOLUTIONARY WAR

War had now raged between the mother country and her colonies of North America for more than three years. It had become fierce and sanguinary along the Atlantic. But the people of West Florida, whose government was composed chiefly of military dependencies, had hitherto enjoyed peace. They were mostly loyal subjects of the king. But now, even in this remote region, the contest began to be felt. The Creek Indians were relied upon, mainly, by the British authorities, to harass the Whig inhabitants of Georgia and Carolina. They had stationed at Hickory Ground, the site of the lower suburbs of the modern Wetumpka, Colonel Taitt, an English officer, of captivating address, for the purpose of influencing the Creeks in behalf of the king. There, he soon became acquainted with the most gifted and remarkable man that ever was born upon the soil of Alabama, the history of whose family will now be given.[1]

A Scotch boy, of sixteen years of age, who had read of the wonders to be seen in America, ran away from his wealthy and respectable parents, living in Dunmaglass, and entered a ship which was bound for South Carolina. He arrived, without accident, at the port of Charleston. Young Lachlan McGillivray there first set his foot upon American soil. He then had no property, except a shilling in his pocket, a suit of clothes upon his back, a red head, a stout frame, an honest heart, a fearless disposition, and cheerful spirits, which seldom became depressed.[2] About this period, the English were conducting an extensive commerce with the Cherokees, Chickasaws and those of the Creeks who were not in the interest of the French. Young McGillivray repaired to the extensive quarters of the traders, in the suburbs of Charleston. There he saw hundreds of pack-horses, pack saddles, and curious looking pack-horsemen, in demi-civilized garbs, together with packs of merchandise, ready to be carried to the wilderness. The keen eyes of one of these traders soon fell upon

[1] David Taitt (also Tate), a Scot, had served as assistant surveyor in West Florida from 1764 to 1767. In 1772, John Stuart, superintendent of the southern district, appointed him as deputy superintendent and the last British commissary to the Upper Creeks. While Stuart wanted the Creeks to maintain their neutrality, he declared that Taitt's most important duty was "to frustrate the machinations of Mr. [George] Galphin and his associates." Alden, *John Stuart*, 297, 297 n. 18; Jim Piecuch, *Three Peoples, One King: Loyalists, Indians, and Slaves in the Revolutionary South, 1775–1782* (Columbia: University of South Carolina Press, 2008), 67.

[2] Pickett's romantic notion of a sixteen-year old runaway from Dunmaglass, Inverness, Scotland, is incorrect in many aspects. In the summer of 1735,

the smart Scotch boy, who, he saw at a glance, would be useful to him. The next day, Lachlan might have been seen, in the pine woods, several miles distant from Charleston, mounted upon a horse, and driving others before him, in company with a whole caravan of traders. Arriving upon the Chattahoochee, his master, as a reward for his activity and accommodating spirit, gave him a jack knife, which he sold to an Indian, receiving in exchange a few deer skins. These he sold in Charleston, upon his return, and the proceeds of this adventure laid the foundation of a large fortune. In the course of a few years, he became one of the boldest and most enterprising traders in the whole country. Whether it was owing to a superior address, a fearless disposition, or, which is more probable, a leaning towards the French, for personal interests, he even extended his commerce, without interruption, to the very neighborhood of Fort Toulouse.[3]

At the Hickory Ground, a few miles above that fort, he found a beautiful girl, by the name of Sehoy Marchand, whose father once commanded at Fort Toulouse, and was there killed, in 1722, by his own soldiers, as we have already seen. Her mother was a full-blooded Creek woman, of the tribe of the Wind, the most aristocratic and powerful family in the Creek Nation. Sehoy was an Indian name, which had attached to many persons of the family, time out of mind.[4]

Sehoy Marchand, when first seen by young Lachlan McGillivray, was a maiden of sixteen, cheerful in countenance, bewitching in looks, and graceful in form. Her unfortunate father, Captain Marchand, was a Frenchman, of dark complexion, and, consequently, this beautiful girl scarcely looked light enough for a half blood; but then, her slightly curled hair, her vivacity, and peculiar gesticulation, unmistakably exposed her origin. It was not long before Lachlan and Sehoy joined their destinies in marriage, according to the ceremony of the country. The husband established a trading house at Little Tallassee, four miles above Wetumpka, on the east bank of the Coosa, and there took home his beautiful wife.[5] The Indian tradition ran, that, while pregnant with her first child, she repeatedly dreamed of piles of manuscripts, of ink and paper, and heaps of books, more than her eyes had ever beheld in the fort, when, a child, she used to visit her father. She was delivered of a boy, who received the name of Alexander, and who,

Captain William Dunbar and Hugh Mackay traveled to Inverness to recruit settlers for Oglethorpe's Georgia colony. Lachlan McGillivray was one of some 165 men who took passage on Dunbar's *Prince of Whales* for Savannah, including McGillivray and his Mackintosh kinsmen. It appears that his twenty-four year old cousin John Mackintosh of Holme paid for their passage, as did seventeen others, while the Georgia trustees paid for 146 men. Cashin, *Lachlan McGillivray*, 6–13.

[3] Lachlan McGillivray's involvement in the Indian trade never depended on the exchange of a pocket knife for a few furs. Following Oglethorpe's failed siege against Spanish St. Augustine in 1740, a large number of the Scots Highlanders left their Darien settlement and relocated to Charleston (Charles Town until 1776), including his cousin John Mackintosh. Another factor that influenced Lachlan's removal was the prominence of Archibald McGillivray, who managed the largest trading company in the Creek Nation, which provided him opportunities to become fluent in the Muskogean language. Ibid., 30–36; Wright, *McGillivray and McIntosh*, 42–43.

[4] Pickett continues his erroneous account regarding the death of Captain François Marchand de Courtel (also Courcelles or Courcel) at Fort Toulouse. Marchand appears in Mobile baptismal and marriage records as a captain in 1723, commandant at Fort Toulouse in 1727, and a captain of the Mobile garrison in 1730. He also signed as a witness for marriage banns on 16 April 1732 in Mobile, and he wrote to Governor Périer on 15 September 1732 as the captain commanding at Natchez. *MPA: FD*, 4:124, 125 n. 2; Vidrine, *Mobile Marriages Recorded in French* (online).

when grown to manhood, wielded a pen which commanded the admiration and respect of Washington and his cabinet, and which influenced the policy of all Spanish Florida.[6]

Lachlan McGillivray, assisted by his alliance with the most influential family in the Creek Nation, continued to extend his commerce. He became wealthy, and owned two plantations, well stocked with Negroes, upon the Savannah, besides stores filled with Indian merchandise, in the towns of Savannah and Augusta.[7] When his son, Alexander, was fourteen years of age, he carried him to Charleston, by the consent of his wife, for we have seen that, among the Creeks particularly, the children always belonged to the mother. He was placed at school in that town, and, after a few years, was transferred to a counting house at Savannah. But Alexander had a distaste for business, and, while the other clerks were delving among the goods, and squabbling with the pack-horse traders, he was accustomed to steal to some corner, and there pore over the histories of European nations. Having an inordinate thirst after knowledge, his father, through the advice of his friends, again carried him to Charleston, and placed him with a clergyman of his name, with whom, in a short time, he mastered the Greek and Latin tongues, and became a good belles lettres scholar.[8] But Alexander was now a man. He had a thousand times thought, and dreamed, of his bow and arrows, his blow-gun, his mother's house, by the side of the clear and beautiful Coosa, in which he used to fish and bathe with the Indian lads of his own age—of the old warriors, who had so often recounted to him the deeds of his ancestors—of the bright eyes of his two lovely sisters, Sophia and Jeanette—yes, he remembered all these, and, one day, he turned his back upon civilization, and his horse's head towards his native land.[9]

About this time, the chiefs of the Creek Nation were getting into much trouble with the people of Georgia, and with anxiety they had awaited the time when Alexander McGillivray could, by his descent from the Wind family, assume the affairs of their government. His arrival now was most opportune, and the first we hear of him, after he had so suddenly left Charleston, he was presiding at a Grand National council, at the town of Coweta, upon the Chattahoochee, where the adventurous Leclerc Milfort was introduced to him, as we have seen.[10] He was, at this time,

5 Lachlan McGillivray held a traders license to the "Old Town on the Coosaw River" that dated from 1744, and he made his headquarters at Little Tallassee among the Okchoys (Hookchoie) on the Coosa, about nine miles above Fort Toulouse. While the records are silent, McGillivray and Sehoy Marchand became a couple sometime before 1748. Cashin, *Lachlan McGillivray,* 42, 46–51, 58–61.

6 Lachlan and Sehoy's famous son—Alexander McGillivray—was born on 15 December 1750, as recorded in Lachlan McGillivray's will. Thomas Woodward, in a letter to Pickett on 21 June 1858, claimed that Alexander's sister Sophia was born first. Lachlan's will is silent on the births of his daughters, Sophia and Jeanette. Ibid., 73, 257; Wright, *McGillivray and McIntosh Traders,* 183; Thomas S. Woodward, *Woodward's Reminiscences of the Creek or Muscogee Indians, Contained in Letters to Friends in Georgia and Alabama* (Montgomery, Ala.: Barrett & Wimbish, 1859), 60.

7 In applications for land in December 1757, McGillivray referred to himself as an "inhabitant and planter." He now owned a corner lot in Augusta and had eight hundred acres under cultivation. On his applications for the additional land, he reported owning eleven hundred acres and more than forty slaves. His status had changed from merchant trader to merchant planter. Cashin, *Lachlan McGillivray,* 156–57; Wright, *McGillivray and McIntosh Traders,* 85–90.

8 Alexander McGillivray's education started when his father Lachlan became a merchant planter in 1757–1758 and left his home on the Coosa River. One McGillivray family source cited by Edward J. Cashin in his *Lachlan McGillivray, Indian Trader* claims Alexander

started his education in the home of his uncle, Farquhar McGillivray, and with his cousins in Charleston when he was seven-years old. However, most modern studies place him under his uncle's tutelage at the age of fourteen and report his apprenticeships as a clerk for Samuel Elbert's mercantile firm and with Inglis and Hall. Cashin, *Lachlan McGillivray*, 75, 155, 257–58, 263; John Walton Caughey, *McGillivray of the Creeks* (Norman: University of Oklahoma Press, 1938), 15; J. H. O'Donnell, "Alexander McGillivray: Training for Leadership, 1777–1783," *Georgia Historical Quarterly* 49 (June 1965): 172–74.

[9] Pickett's romantic imagery of Alexander McGillivray as a child of the woods and streams is not supported by modern scholars. He traveled to Augusta as a six-year old, spent time in Charleston with his cousins, moved to Savannah with Lachlan as a ten-year old, and received more education in Charleston as a teenager, followed by his tenure as an apprentice. He grew to manhood in the company of Scots merchant traders and planters in Savannah and Charleston. He spoke English fluently, with little fluency in the Muskogean of his mother, Sehoy. Cashin, *Lachlan McGillivray*, 257, 263; Wright, *McGillivray and McIntosh Traders*, 85–95.

[10] Despite Pickett's effort to make McGillivray the head of the Creek Confederacy, he actually returned to Little Tallassee in 1777 with credentials as an assistant commissary to the Creeks in the British service —a post he held until 1783. Instead of presiding over a national council meeting, he was sent to maintain and build British relations in the Upper Creek towns. His clan kinship, his father's prestige among the Creeks, and his uncle Red Shoes—one of the most powerful headmen—gave him access to and instant influence among the Creeks. Michael D. Green, "Alexander McGillivray" in *American Indian Leaders: Studies in Diversity*, ed. R. David Edmonds (Lincoln: University of Nebraska Press, 1980), 42–45.

[11] In 1777, McGillivray, in his twenty-seventh year, returned to the Upper Creek country in the British service but with a commitment to the Creeks at a time of confused alliances and divided leadership among his mother's people. From August 1777 through December 1778, pro-American and neutralist factions in Upper Creek and Lower Creek towns threatened the lives of Creeks loyal to Britain and British agents, such as David Taitt, Alexander Cameron, and William McIntosh. McGillivray acted quickly by calling a meeting of headmen to prevent a civil war and promising John Stuart to restore British prominence in the nation. Although he emerged as the leader of the pro-British faction, McGillivray could not control all the Creek headmen and their divided loyalties. Corkran, *Creek Frontier*, 301–19; Martha Condray Searcy, *The Georgia-Florida Contest in the American Revolution, 1776–1778* (Tuscaloosa: University of Alabama, 1985), 74–75, 109–12, 114–16, 132–33, 137, 154–57.

[12] Alexander McGillivray did not hold the rank of colonel during the Revolutionary War. Thomas Brown, superintendent of British Indian affairs, signed a "Return of Extra Officers, interpreters and war conductors appointed and commissioned by Lord Earl Cornwallis and Sir Henry Clinton" that named McGillivray as "Commissary and Captain." Murtie June Clark, comp., *Loyalists in the Southern Campaign of the Revolutionary War*, 3 vols. (Baltimore: Clearfield Publishing Co., 1981), 3: 388.

[13] Unfortunately, Pickett had few sources other than Louis Leclerc Milfort's *Mémoire*—shaped by his faulty memory and ego—when writing this chapter on McGillivray. Despite Milfort's claims, McGillivray took an active role leading Creek warriors, especially after December 1778. In March 1779, McGillivray and Emisteseguo led war parties toward Augusta, and McGillivray broke off with a party of eighty Creeks and Loyalists to strike south of Augusta. On 2 April, near the Little River, McGillivray's party was overwhelmed by an American force of two hundred men, with several losses. Later McGillivray joined David Taitt and moved against Savannah with about seventy warriors, striking Whig plantations and stealing slaves. McGillivray and his warriors remained in the Augusta area for nearly a year. In April 1780, he and William McIntosh, with 1,500 warriors, responded to a British request to repulse a Spanish threat against Pensacola that did not occur until May 1781. It appears that McGillivray was present when Creek warriors forced the American withdrawal from Augusta in September 1780, and at Savannah, where Emisteseguo was killed during the American siege in the winter of 1781–1782. Corkran, *Creek Frontier*, 317–22; Wright, *McGillivray and McIntosh Traders*, 219–20.

about thirty years of age. He was then in great power, for he had already become an object of attention, on the part of the British authorities of the Floridas. When Colonel Taitt was stationed upon the Coosa, they conferred upon Alexander McGillivray the rank and pay of a colonel, and associated him with Taitt, for the purpose of procuring, through them, the alliance of the Creek Nation in the war of the Revolution. McGillivray, throughout the whole war, was devoted to their interests, and it was natural that he should have pursued that course towards those who first honored him; besides, his father, a man of great influence, was also a Royalist.[11]

Colonel McGillivray was tall, rather slender, and of a constitution by no means robust. To be a leader in war was not his *forte*, and was unsuited to his tastes and habits. His great power lay in diplomacy, and in the controlling of men, as the reader will often see, in perusing this history at a later date.[12] In 1778, he carried on an extensive correspondence with the British colonial governments of Florida, and also with that of the province of Georgia, and was indefatigable in co-operating with Taitt, in confederating the Indians against the Whigs. During the war, he led, in person, several expeditions with that officer; but his chief reliance was upon Leclerc Milfort, a man at once bold, daring, enthusiastic, possessed of an iron constitution, and every way qualified to lead Indians into battle. He often did so, while Col. McGillivray remained at home, controlling the arbitrary chiefs, and compelling them to raise warriors for his king.[13] All the while, McGillivray was not unmindful of the aggrandizement of himself and his nation, for it must be borne in mind that the blood which coursed his veins was Scotch, French and Indian. During the desperate struggle for human liberty, he acted in concert with many royalists, who had fled to East Florida, among the most conspicuous of whom were Colonel Daniel McGirth, and his brother, Captain James McGirth. They were bad men, but were brave and enterprising, and well suited to the times. Colonel McGirth commanded the "Florida Rangers," whose sudden and sanguinary attacks the Whigs of Georgia were often severely felt.[14] Leaving Colonel McGillivray, with his red army and white allies, engaged in expeditions most harassing to the Georgians, on their western frontier, we hasten to portray the exciting scenes about Natchez.*

Here, also, the Revolution began to be felt. James Willing, of Philadelphia, with a small body of American soldiers, arrived at Natchez, by way of the

* MS in my possession. Also information derived from conversations with the intelligent niece and nephew of Colonel McGillivray, still living; also with old Indian traders, who knew him in those times. See also Milfort, *Mémoire ou coup d'oeil rapide sur mes différens voyages et mon séjour dans la nation Crëck,* and McCall, *History of Georgia.*

[14] Originally Daniel McGirth and his brother James McGirth joined a patriot unit in Georgia, but when Daniel was disciplined for striking an officer, they deserted, stealing the company's horses. They joined Georgia Loyalist forces under Colonel Thomas Brown, known as the King's (also Florida) Rangers, that conducted a campaign of harassment and coordinated operations with British regular forces in Savannah and at Augusta. Brown appointed Daniel as a lieutenant colonel and James as a captain. Daniel at various times led a gang of twenty or more men who developed a reputation as plunderers and murderers, stealing slaves, horses, cattle, and other property. Searcy, *Georgia-Florida Contest,* 66, 138, 143; Leslie Hall, *Land and Allegiance in Revolutionary Georgia* (Athens: University of Georgia Press, 2001), 150–57.

[15] James Willing, a failed Natchez merchant, used his connections in Philadelphia to receive a navy captain's commission and congressional permission to raid Loyalist plantations and towns on the lower Mississippi River. David Narrett, *Adventurism and Empire: The Struggle for Mastery in the Louisiana-Florida Borderlands, 1762–1803* (Chapel Hill: University of North

Ohio.[15] The ports upon that river, and the Upper Mississippi, had fallen into the hands of the Americans, and had been supplied, for more than a year, by shipments from New Orleans, in consequence of a private arrangement between Don Gálvez and Oliver Pollock, the American agent at New Orleans.[16] Willing was now sent to further that end, and he was supplied with blank commissions, and authorized to recruit for the American service. Knowing that the inhabitants of this part of West Florida were loyal subjects of Britain, to allay their opposition to his schemes, he first sought to place them in a neutral position. A man of ingenuity and address, he made speeches, eloquently depicting the justice of our cause, and the certainty of final success, asserted that five thousand troops were then on their way to protect these inhabitants from the aggressions of the British government. He generally prevailed on them to take an oath of strict neutrality. Also enlisting a hundred men, whose officers he commissioned, he continued his voyage to Manchac, and was equally successful there. By stratagem, he made himself master of an English armed ship, which he conveyed to New Orleans, sold to the Spaniards, and wasted the avails in debauchery. With two subalterns, and forty of his original party, he returned to Manchac, plundered the plantations, without distinction, and rioted upon the booty.[17]

In the meantime, the Natchez people, hearing of these outrages, formed a large armed association, for their protection, and stationed themselves about the mouth of St. Catherine, not far below Natchez, to prevent the ascent of Captain Willing. He was presently seen to approach, but turned his boats to the opposite side of the Mississippi. Through the effects of a flag, and upon his professions of friendship, and assurances that he intended no injury to this section of the country, he received permission from the "settlers" to come over to them, across the river. After

Carolina Press, 2015), 80; Allan Reed Millett, *Semper Fidelis: The History of the United States Marine Corps* (New York: Free Press, 1991), 20.

[16] Bernardo de Galvez (1746–1786) was sent to Louisiana as a colonel and interim governor in late 1776. Despite his youth, Galvez understood the need to assist the American rebels against the British and began cooperating with Oliver Pollock, the American agent and money-raising merchant ensconced in New Orleans. With Pollock's encouragement, he secretly corresponded with many of the patriot leaders, such as Patrick Henry, governor of Virginia. David J. Weber, *The Spanish Frontier in North America* (New Haven: Yale University Press, 1992), 267; Robert L. Gold, "Governor Bernardo de Galvez and Spanish Espionage in Pensacola, 1777," in *The Spanish in the Mississippi Valley, 1762–1804*, ed. John Francis McDermott (Urbana: University of Illinois Press, 1974), 95–96.

[17] Pickett's source, Matthew Phelps, transposed the sequence of some events. Willing's raiders plundered the house of John Watkins on 18 February 1778 at Walnut Hills (Vicksburg) and struck Anthony Hutchins's plantation below Natchez, taking Hutchins as a prisoner on 19 February. Later, on the 19th, Willing's main force landed at Natchez, rounded up its inhabitants, extracted oaths of neutrality, and recruited several men. Near Manchac on 23 February, Thomas McIntire's group seized the British brig *Rebecca*, its captain, and crew without firing a shot. Willing's "banditti" laid waste to the settlements downriver, looting and extracting loyalty oaths at Point Coupée, Baton Rouge, Manchac, and at plantations along the river to New Orleans. Although Galvez forced the return of the British ship *Neptune*, several slaves, and other property, Pollock auctioned off seventy-four slaves, raising a total $62,500. Willing and his men proceeded to waste much of their ill-gained money in New Orleans brothels and grog houses. Starr, *Tories, Dons, and Rebels*, 84–92; William R. Nester, *The Frontier War for American Independence* (Mechanicsburg, PA: Stackpole Books, 2004), 210–11; Robert V. Haynes, *The Natchez District and the American Revolution* (Jackson: University Press of Mississippi, 1976), 59–67, 73.

some consultation, he dispatched Lieutenant Harrison, with a command, in a boat. In the meantime, the "associated settlers," reposing confidence in the promises of Willing, had abandoned their defensive positions, and now sat and lay upon the banks, at their ease. When the boat approached near enough, the gunner, by the orders of Lieutenant Harrison, fired a swivel upon the settlers, by which many were wounded. The latter instantly rose up, in great confusion, returned the fire with their guns, riddled the boat, and killed Lieutenant Harrison and seven of his men. The others came ashore, and surrendered.[18] Willing, with his remaining banditti, fled to Manchac, sailed over to the Tensaw settlements, above Mobile, and endeavored, in vain, to enlist the people in his cause. He was eventually made a prisoner of war, and kept in the British camp, in chains, and was not released until the close of 1779.[19]

The inhabitants now considered themselves absolved from their oath of neutrality, by the baseness of Captain Willing, and they all swore to defend the government of the king. They elected officers, repaired old Fort Panmure, and occupied it with a regular garrison. They also marched, in April, to the relief of the people in the neighborhood of Manchac, from which place Willing had already fled.[20] Thus, by the indiscretions and outrages of the first American command sent here, our glorious cause was materially injured.*

* *Memoirs and Adventures of Captain Matthew Phelps*, 107–20. This author was one of the "associated settlers," and appears to have been a conscientious and truthful man. He is sustained by Judge François-Xavier Martin, in his *History of Louisiana*, 2: 42–43, in regard to the outrages of Willing. It is, however, due to the descendants of that officer, to observe, that John Monette, in his *History of the Discovery and Settlement of the Valley of the Mississippi*, represents him as a brave and honorable man, and severely censures the "associated settlers" for the perfidy which they displayed in the fire upon Harrison and his command. I, however, after a careful and

[18] Reuben Harrison, a Natchez resident who joined Willing, commanded an armed bateaux and about thirty men that landed at White Cliffs below Natchez on 15 April 1778. He had sent word to Anthony Hutchins that he had no hostile intentions. However, after a brief meeting, Hutchins's followers opened fire, killing Harrison and four others, wounding three, and taking twenty-eight as prisoners. Hutchins boasted that the colors "of His Britannic Majesty most splendidly appear in triumph." Starr, *Tories, Dons, and Rebels*, 111–12, 118 n. 89; Haynes, *Natchez District*, 84–87; Ethan A. Grant, "Anthony Hutchins: A Pioneer of the Old Southwest," *Florida Historical Quarterly* 74 (Spring 1996): 409–10.

[19] By summer 1778, Governor Galvez and Oliver Pollock were ready for Willing and his men to leave Louisiana. With Galvez's approval, Lieutenant Robert George led Willing's men north through Spanish territory and joined his uncle, Colonel George Rogers Clark, on his march to Kaskaskia. On 15 November 1778, Willing and nine companions departed New Orleans aboard the *Morris*—the rechristened *Rebecca* —which was intercepted by the British, taking Willing as a prisoner to New York. After spending three months in irons, he was classified as a prisoner on parole and finally exchanged on 3 September 1781 "for a British officer named Rogers." Kinnaird, *Spain in the Mississippi Valley*, 1: 303–04; Starr, *Tories, Dons, and Rebels*, 116–17; Haynes, *Natchez District*, 95–99.

[20] William Dunbar (1750–1810), a Scotsman, immigrated to Philadelphia in 1771 and formed a partnership with John Ross, a Scot merchant in Philadelphia, in 1773 in West Florida. In his diary he reported on the settlers on the Mississippi: ". . . if we consider that one half of the inhabitants were in the American interests, which circumstances being well known to the loyal part of the people, was the means of tying up their hands and preventing their attempts to oppose the Banditti." Starr, *Tories, Dons, and Rebels*, 118; Eron Rowland, ed., *Life, Letters and Papers of William Dunbar* (Jackson: Mississippi Historical Society, 1930), 62.

[21] Governor Peter Chester had responded by dispatching forces to Manchac and Natchez, including Captain Michael Jackson and his company of Loyal Refugees, who occupied a partially restored Fort Panmure. He was known locally as a scoundrel and

Fort Panmure, at the Natchez, in a short time, received as a commander, Michael Jackson, a native of New England, an abandoned horse thief, who had been driven from the borders of civilization. During the whole of the fall and winter, this man, now a captain in the British service, produced great dissatisfaction by his oppressions and extortions.[21] Colonel Hutchins, an influential citizen of Natchez, placed himself at the head of the malcontents, arrested and confined Jackson, and placed Captain Thaddeus Lyman in command.[22] On promising to leave the country, he was released, but the first night after his dismission from the fort he was joined by thirty deserters, who were as abandoned as himself. Jackson now stationed himself "under the hill," where he seized some military stores and artillery. Sending runners to the Choctaws, they returned with a considerable force of these savages. Jackson now exultingly fired his artillery upon the fort; but his Indian allies, seeing the British flag flying from the ramparts, and learning the nature of the dispute, refused to be made the instruments of the rascal, and retired peaceably to their homes. Seeing himself abandoned, Captain Jackson requested a parley, which was agreed to, and he was suffered, with his men, to enter the fort, and there peaceably to remain until the whole affair should undergo an investigation. Here he soon raised a mutiny, and, one night, caused the drums suddenly to beat to arms, and, seizing Captain Lyman, placed him in close confinement. His tyranny caused many to desert, who were pursued by a detachment under Lieutenant Pentecost. An engagement took place, when Pentecost was killed, and the deserters made their escape to the Spanish garrison at Manchac, across the Iberville.[23] Again Jackson was overthrown and forced to retire; but before doing so he robbed the fort of all the valuables which he could transport.* In this manner the Royalists were divided, and in the midst of their dissensions, a large number of Whigs were scattered about the country, anxiously awaiting the time when they should be joined by aid from a distance, under Colonel Clark, of Virginia.[24]

Although Spain had long experienced evasions of her revenue

dispassionate examination, believe the statement of Phelps. See Monette, 1: 434–36. Monette quotes *The Journal of Andrew Ellicott,* 131–32.

* *Memoirs and Adventures of Captain Matthew Phelps,* 121–97.

horse thief, and his leadership was challenged by Anthony Hutchins, Thaddeus Lyman, and Matthew Phelps, which led to his removal in 1779. Phelps, *Memoirs and Adventures of Matthew Phelps,* 122–23; Starr, *Tories, Dons, and Rebels,* 111–12; Haynes, *Natchez District,* 94–95.

[22] The West Florida Council voted their thanks to Anthony Hutchins for his actions in stopping Reuben Harrison and recommended that Governor Peter Chester appoint him a brevet lieutenant colonel. Chester rewarded Thaddeus Lyman with appointment as captain of an independent company for his efforts to oppose Willing's raiders. Starr, *Tories, Dons, and Rebels,* 112, 112 n. 74, 124; Fabel, *Economy of British West Florida,* 188–89.

[23] One of the deserters, John Felt, is identified by Matthew Phelps, and Phelps reports that Felt inadvertently fired the shot that killed Lieutenant George Pentecost when the deserters resisted arrest. Phelps, *Memoirs and Adventures of Matthew Phelps,* 189–90; Fabel, *Economy of British West Florida,* 186–89.

[24] Willing's raiders or "banditti" had damaged the American cause in the Lower Mississippi Valley. Instead of moving south into the Natchez District, Colonel George Rogers Clark marched his poorly equipped army of less than two hundred men into the Ohio River Valley and turned north into the Illinois country, reaching Kaskaskia on 4 July 1778. Lowell H. Harrison, *George Rogers Clark and the War in the West* (Lexington: University Press of Kentucky, 1976), 17–24.

[25] Before learning of the declaration of war between Spain and England in mid-August 1779, Gálvez had decided to attack Manchac. He set out for Manchac on 27 August with a force of 1,427 men. The British had abandoned Fort Bute in July 1779 and concentrated their forces in a new redoubt at Baton Rouge.

laws, on the part of the British, and had been compelled to establish a fort at Manchac to prevent them, nevertheless she had, up to this period, maintained a neutrality in the war waging between England and the united American colonies. But France had not been an indifferent spectator, and the leaning of that power towards us brought about a collision with arbitrary John Bull. Spain interposed her friendly efforts to effect a reconciliation; but the canine propensities of England were aroused, and that ungenerous government declared war against Spain, as well as France. His Catholic Majesty, fired at the ruthless manner in which he had been treated for a friendly act, now resolved to dispossess England of every foot of land in the Floridas. According to his directions, Don Gálvez, the governor of his province of Louisiana, stood before Fort Bute, at Manchac, with a force of fourteen hundred men. After a resistance of five days, it was carried by storm and utterly demolished. Reinforced by a number of militia, including American patriots, Gálvez marched up and invested Baton Rouge. After a severe cannonade of two hours and a half, Colonel Dickson, the British commander, surrendered the fort and a garrison of four hundred regulars and one hundred militia. Fort Panmure, at the Natchez, a small fort and garrison on the Amite, and another, at Thompson's Creek, were also surrendered at the same time.[25]

Leaving Don Grand-Pré in command, at Baton Rouge, and, sending Spanish detachments to the other forts, which had already yielded to his arms, Gálvez returned to New Orleans, and there began extensive preparations for the reduction of Mobile.[26] After encountering a terrible storm, which came near destroying his transports and stores, he landed his army a little below Mobile, early in March 1780. Fort Charlotte refused to surrender, and Gálvez planted his six batteries. A severe cannonade opened a breach in the fort, when the British officer capitulated, by the surrender of Mobile, and all its dependencies, extending from the Perdido to the Pearl River. Thus, the Spaniards were now in possession of all West Florida, except Pensacola, and the country as far as the Chattahoochee.[27] Knowing the great strength of Pensacola, Gálvez determined to be well prepared for a siege. He put in requisition all his disposable regular forces and militia, both of Louisiana and of the country

Gálvez's force easily seized Manchac on 7 September and forced the capitulation of Lieutenant Colonel Alexander Dickson and his British forces at Baton Rouge on 21 September 1779. Kinnaird, *Spain in the Mississippi Valley,* 1: xxviii, 355–56; Starr, *Tories, Dons, and Rebels,* 148–57; Jack D. L. Holmes, *Honor and Fidelity: The Louisiana Infantry Regiment and the Louisiana Militia Companies, 1766–1821* (Birmingham: n.p., 1965), 29–31; W. James Miller, "The Militia System of Spanish Louisiana, 1768–1783," in *The Military Presence on the Gulf Coast,* ed., William S. Coker (Pensacola: Gulf Coast and Humanities Conference, 1978), 47–48.

[26] Carlos Luis Boucher de Grand-Pré (1746–1809), a Spanish officer of Arcadian origin, seized two small British posts on Thompson's Creek and the Amite River prior to Gálvez's march on Manchac and Baton Rouge in September 1779. Grand Pré and his Point Coupée militia also cut the communications between Baton Rouge and Natchez. Kinnaird, *Spain in the Mississippi Valley,* 1: 158–59; Haynes, *Natchez District,* 122–23; Holmes, *Honor and Fidelity,* 126; Miller, "Militia System of Spanish Louisiana," 49.

[27] Although Gálvez launched his campaign from New Orleans against Mobile on 18 January 1780, his forces did not begin their assault until 28 February. After a series of delays, the Spaniards began a heavy cannonading of Fort Charlotte on 12 March, which prompted the British commander Elias Durnford to request a truce. The British forces marched out of Fort Charlotte on the morning of the 14th, and the Spaniards raised their flag over Mobile. Kinnaird, *Spain in the Mississippi Valley,* 1: xxviii-xxix, 369–73; Starr, *Tories, Dons, and Rebels,* 168–73; Holmes, *Honor and Fidelity,* 32–33.

which he had conquered, and, in the meantime, sailed to Havana to obtain more troops and heavier artillery. With a large number of well-equipped troops, and an abundance of stores and ordnance, he entered the bay of Pensacola with his fleet, while his Louisiana and Mobile forces marched across the country, from the mouth of the Perdido.[28]

Being invested, both by sea and by land, General Campbell, after a vigorous defense, in which he was assisted by the Creek Indians, finally surrendered. The Creeks, on this occasion, were commanded by William Augustus Bowles, an interesting person, who will figure in our narrative hereafter. The town of Pensacola, the fortress and seaport, with eight hundred men, as prisoners of war, and the whole of West Florida, thus fell into the hands of the king of Spain.[29] The victorious Gálvez received many honors for his brilliant services.*

* Spanish MS.

[28] While Gálvez wanted to immediately attack Pensacola, he did not receive timely assistance from Havana and the British sent additional ships to reinforce the city. Despite delays and false starts, the Spanish finally moved against Pensacola on 9 March 1781. The Spanish fleet crossed the bar at Pensacola on 21–22 March and disembarked 1,600 Spanish regulars, 725 French regulars, and 1,504 seamen. Gálvez's army now numbered 7,686 men, compared to the fewer than 2,000 defenders commanded by General John Campbell. Kinnaird, *Spain in the Mississippi Valley*, 1: 421–23; Starr, *Tories, Dons, and Rebels*, 193–204.

[29] After Gálvez rejected the surrender terms proposed by General John Campbell and Governor Peter Chester on 8 May 1781, the British completed the formal surrender of Pensacola on 10 May—marching out to beating drums and flying their colors. Spain now controlled all of West Florida. Starr, *Tories, Dons, and Rebels*, 211.

Chapter XVIII

Extreme Perils and Sufferings of the Natchez Refugees

During the siege of Pensacola, a series of events, of an interesting and romantic character, began at Natchez, and afterwards ended, with unparalleled sufferings, in the vast Indian wilderness, which extended from thence to the Ogeechee River, in the distant province of Georgia. Some citizens of the Natchez district, the most prominent of whom were Philip Alston, Colonel Hutchins, John Alston, Captain Thaddeus Lyman, Thompson Lyman, John Blommart, and Jacob Winfree, put themselves at the head of a large party of royalists, for the purpose of seizing Fort Panmure, and expelling therefrom the Spanish troops, who had held it since September 1780. They had learned that a powerful British fleet was off the Florida coast, whose object was the re-occupation of the country, and, believing that Don Gálvez had already been defeated at Pensacola, they resolved immediately to anticipate what they supposed would be the desire of their king.[1] Having assembled a large body of Choctaws, the insurgents assumed a position upon an eminence, above the town of Natchez, in full view of the fort. At night they advanced and planted their artillery so as to bear upon the works; but, when day approached, the Spanish cannonade compelled them to retire.[2]

During the succeeding twenty-four hours, the firing continued between the parties. The commandant sent a flag to Colonel Hutchins, representing the danger of rebellion, and promising the clemency of his government, if the people would disperse, after they should have surrendered the ringleaders. An answer was promised, to be returned the next day. During the interval, the malcontents arrested a man bearing a dispatch to the Spanish commandant. It was from Captain McIntosh, a warm friend of the Spaniards, who lived in the neighborhood, and who wrote, entreating the commandant to hold out a little while longer, when he would be supported by friends from the country. His letter was destroyed, and another substituted, written by one who could

[1] **With the Spanish forces advancing on Pensacola in March 1781, General John Campbell attempted to get the Natchez Loyalists to revolt against Spanish control on the Lower Mississippi and to distract the Spanish military in the Gulf. He sent five blank captain's commissions to Natchez to be completed by the men who would raise a militia company. However, many of the Natchez insurgents wanted to use the Loyalists to overthrow Spanish rule but seek annexation to the United States. Haynes, *Natchez District*, 134–35; Starr, *Tories, Dons, and Rebels*, 213, 216–17.**

[2] **On 22 April 1781, John Blommart launched the attack on Fort Panmure with a force of 200 men, including settlers and Indians. Haynes, *Natchez District*, 135–36; John W. Caughey, *Bernardo de Galvez in Louisiana*,**

imitate the autograph of McIntosh.[3] It was conveyed to the Spanish commandant, and disclosed the astounding news, that the insurgents, by means of a deep ravine, which was at the base of the fort, had formed a cavern, leading directly under the fort, in which a vast quantity of powder had been placed, ready to be exploded by a train; that the people of the country were flocking to the standard of the enemy, and he, consequently, suggested an honorable surrender. Not suspecting the fraud, the Spanish commandant, in his confusion and alarm, surrendered the fort, and marched his garrison to Baton Rouge.[4]

But the exulting insurgents were, in a few days, deprived of the fruits of their victory. The news reached them, that General Campbell was defeated, and that the whole of West Florida had been surrendered to Spain. Consternation seized everyone. They knew that they should receive no mercy at the hands of those whom they had harassed by rebellion and conquered by stratagem. Abandoning the fort, they fled to the cane swamps, with their wives, children, horses, and movable effects, with the determination of cutting their way to the British settlements on the Savannah.* The avenues by the Mississippi were closed against them by the Spaniards below and the American Whigs above. In a short time, more than one hundred individuals, besides slaves, mounted upon horses, and with other horses laden with their effects, set off to avoid the Spaniards, whom they had expected hourly to arrive at Natchez. Many of the children were small, and some were at the breast. They began their painful and distressing flight by striking towards the prairie country in the present state of Mississippi. Wishing to avoid the Chickasaws and Choctaws, into whose power they feared to fall, a circuitous route was wholly unavoidable, and they wandered from point to point, as their desperate circumstances led them. It was during an unusually dry spring, and the prairies, which they had now reached, afforded them no water.[5]

At one time they suffered from the want of it with an intensity more than ordinary human beings, it would seem, could bear. Bordering upon desperation and becoming bewildered, the general direction, which they had endeavored to keep, was abandoned, and they now strolled over the country, with parched lips, under the burning rays of the sun, and amid the heart-rending cries of the children. Ever and anon their eyes fell upon distant clumps of trees, and their spirits revived, in the hope that there certainly would be found the sweet beverage of nature. Pushing on to the delusive spot, they found it as moisture less as the land over which they had traveled. Mrs. Dwight, a heroine upon

* *Memoirs and Adventures of Captain Matthew Phelps,* "Appendix," 4–5; Monette, 2: 462–63.

Notes (margin):

1776–1783 **(Berkeley: University of California Press, 1934), 216–17.**

[3] Alexander McIntosh, a planter and former member of Stuart's Rangers, had been a captive of Willing's raiders and had resisted their efforts to seize Natchez in 1778. He had warned Juan de la Villebeuvre, commander of Fort Panmure, of the insurgents' plot. Haynes, *Natchez District,* 62–63, 88, 135–36.

[4] The Spaniards held out for two weeks, but the Natchez rebels' ruse of threatening to blow up the fort worked. Juan de la Villebeuvre surrendered Fort Panmure to Captain John Blommart on 4 May 1781. The Spanish commander and his troops were conducted to Point Coupée. Ibid., 136–37; Jack D. L. Holmes, "Juan de la Villebeuvre: Spain's Commandant of Natchez During the American Revolution," *Journal of Mississippi History* 37 (February 1975): 108–09.

[5] The residents of the Natchez District that fled fearing reprisals by the Spanish included American patriots and British Loyalists. One group of eighty pro-American refugees settled around the Chickasaw Bluffs—modern Memphis: "We got safely to the Chickasaws." Spanish records indicate that this frontier colony may have

this eventful march, was descended from one of the best families of New England. She exhorted the miserable caravan to persevere in their efforts to find water, although more than thirty-six hours had passed since they had wet their mouths. They now halted and erected a small camp. The men, leaving the women and children in the camp, hunted, for hours, for water, but, towards evening, returned with their tongues exposed and fell down in despair. The noble Mrs. Dwight now set out, in company with several men and women. Fortune led her to the foot of two adjoining hills. The surface of the ground was spongy, and here, by her directions, they began to dig. Hitherto they had not resorted to this plan, but had wandered from point to point, expecting to find running streams. The signs of moisture increased, and presently slow drippings commenced. Redoubling their exertions, they struck a fountain. "Thank God!" was the shout of all.[6]

A messenger rapidly bore back the tidings. The miserable wretches rose from the ground and rushed to the spot. Dr. Dwight, the husband of the lady mentioned above, stationed a guard over the spring, until, by bathing the temples and the palms of the hands, they could drink a few drops, without fatal consequences. With their horses, also, who seemed as if they would tear up the very earth, and destroy everything that obstructed their passage to the water, they adopted the prudent course of allowing small quantities at a time. All night a continual drinking went on. The next day, filling their vessels from this spring, they continued northeast, and, on that day, happily reached some of the sources of the Tombigbee. But now their provisions were exhausted. They killed and devoured the few things which crossed their route, and the meat of a large terrapin, divided into small pieces, once saved their lives. They had but little ammunition, which was reserved for defense alone. Having lost their compass, they could only follow the sun, which was sometimes obscured by clouds. It rained occasionally, now that they had crossed the prairies. Now and then they came across small hunting parties of Indians, who, at night, robbed them of their pack-horses and plundered their effects. In addition to all these misfortunes, a loathsome disease spread in the camp.[7]

Finally, after wandering nearly to the Tennessee River, and then marching in a nearly southern direction, they reached the Tombigbee, about the site of the present town of Aberdeen, where they crossed upon rafts, constructed of dry logs. They next made the Warrior, at the Tuscaloosa falls, which they crossed, by alternately wading and swimming, from rock to rock. Unfortunately, from this point, they assumed an improper direction. Fearing to follow any trail, they, after a long time, found themselves

numbered three hundred by early 1782. The Choctaws provided refuge to another thirty refugees, and another group of some twelve families started off to reach Georgia or South Carolina. Kinnaird, *Spain in the Mississippi Valley*, 2: xi, 16–17; Haynes, *Natchez District*, 137–38, 141–42.

6 While narrating the travails of these British Loyalists, Pickett depends on Matthew Phelps' memoir. Their "Mrs. Dwight" was twenty-five year old Cynthia Pomeroy Dwight (1755–1790), the wife of Sereno Edwards Dwight. She made the journey through Indian country with her husband and nearly three-year old daughter Martha, born 10 August 1777 in the Natchez District. Benjamin Woodbridge Dwight, *The History of the Descendants of Elder John Strong, of Northampton, Mass.*, 2 vols. (Albany, NY: Joel Munsell, 1871), 2: 1278; Benjamin Woodbridge Dwight, *The History of the Descendants of John Dwight of Dedham, Mass.*, 2 vols. (New York: John F. Trow & Sons, 1874), 1: 212–16.

7 Dr. Sereno Edwards Dwight (1754–1783) was a graduate of Yale, but it is not clear where he received his medical training. One family genealogical source reports that he served as a physician and surgeon in the British army during the Revolutionary War. Dwight, *History of the Descendants of John Dwight*, 1: 212–13.

among the mountains of Blount County, Alabama. Having come thus far, again, towards the Tennessee, they thought that they might reach Georgia, by way of the Cherokee Nation, and they continued in that direction, until, one day, in a distant valley, they saw some persons approaching. All was breathless suspense. Presently an old Indian-trader, with two Chickasaw Indians, rode up, for they were now upon a trail. Shocked at the condition of the miserable caravan, the trader generously gave them all the provisions he had, and shared among them his last gallon of taffai.* He warned them not to attempt to reach Georgia through the Tennessee mountains, for they would meet with insurmountable obstacles, and be cut off by the Cherokees, many of whom were now in the interest of the Whigs; but advised them to assume a southern direction, and enter the Creek Nation, the inhabitants of which were entirely under the influence of Colonel McGillivray, who was a man of humanity, and a friend of King George. Turning immediately southward, they once more struck through the woods, re-crossed the mountains, and, after incessant toil and hunger, passed over those which border the Cahaba. Most of them had to walk, and lead their horses over the perilous rocks, while their naked feet bled at every pore. Finally, the caravan arrived upon the banks of the Coosa, in the upper part of the present county of Autauga, a few miles below the Big Island. Here the river was wide and deep, and its bottom rocky. But occasionally it was partially obstructed by small clumps of rocks, between which rushed the rapid current.

The feeble wanderers lay down upon the wild banks, without energy to construct a raft. Indeed, some believed that a raft would be torn to pieces by the rocks. Mrs. Dwight, who continued to infuse a spirit of resolution into the party, which had, thus far, overcome all difficulties, put herself forward, and declared that, if but one man would accompany her, she would attempt the passing of the river, when, perhaps, on the other side, they might find a canoe, or some better crossing place. Her husband, roused by her intrepidity, swore that he would not suffer his wife to risk her life for the good of the company without sharing in her perils. These two, with one other, then plunged their horses into the river, and the current carried them some distance down to a dry bed of rocks. Proceeding over these, to the farther end of the ledge, the two horsemen plunged from a steep rock and disappeared under the water, but presently arose, and their faithful horses carried them to the opposite shore. Mrs. Dwight, shutting her eyes, then made the fearful leap, and arose

* A mean New England rum, the only spirituous liquor drunk, in those days, by the Indians.

[8] Pickett's narrative of the adventures and travails of the Lyman and Dwight families and their fellow travelers is drawn heavily from Timothy Dwight's *Travels in New York and New England* and Matthew Phelps' *Memoirs and Adventures*. While Dwight does not name his kinsmen, both Pickett and Phelps refer to Doctor Dwight and Mrs. Dwight. Phelps, *Memoirs and Adventures of Captain Matthew Phelps*, "Appendix," 7–17; Timothy Dwight, *Travels in New England and New York*, 4 vols. (New Haven: Published by Timothy Dwight, 1821–1822), 1: 311–16.

[9] The British cartographer Joseph Purcell, in his 1770 map, located the Hickory Ground village near the mouth of Weoka Creek on the east bank of the Coosa River, placing it twenty miles north of Wetumpka, Elmore County, Alabama. Later maps place Hickory Ground below modern Wetumpka. Amos J. Wright, *Historic Indian Towns in Alabama, 1540–1838* (Tuscaloosa: University of Alabama Press, 2003), 84.

[10] The original quote from Timothy Dwight's *Travels* reads as follows: "If they are Englishmen, as they profess, they can make the paper talk." Dwight, *Travels in New England and New York*, 1: 314.

with her hands hold of the horn of her saddle. She, too, happily reached the opposite shore. Then the fearless party gave a whoop, to encourage their anxious friends, whom they had left behind. A mile above this they found a large, old Indian canoe, which had been stove against the rocks. Stopping the seams with whatever they could obtain, the two men went over the river in it, to their comrades, leaving the spirited Mrs. Dwight with the horses. Then the wide and angry Coosa roared and lashed its shores, separating her from every friend she had upon earth.[8]

In the course of that day and the next, the whole party were safely boated over. Proceeding some twenty miles farther, they approached the Creek town, called by the traders the "Hickory Ground," embraced in the southern suburbs of the present Wetumpka, on the east bank of the same river which they had crossed.[9] It is impossible to imagine a more forlorn band, or one more agitated by hopes and fears. This was the first Indian town which they had had the boldness to approach, since they left Natchez, for, indeed, during the whole of their travels, they expected, every moment, to be tracked out, and all suddenly butchered. They now held a consultation, and it was decided to dispatch three of their most plausible men, as ambassadors, to implore the compassion and hospitality of the inhabitants. With palpitating hearts, these men rode on, leaving their companions behind to await the issue. As they rode up to the square, the squaws were hoeing their green corn, and the warriors reposed by the sides of their cabins. The reader has often seen the fierce mastiff, as he slumbered in the yard, or the tiger of a menagerie, as he dozed in his cage, arouse out of his sleep, erect his ears, move his tail, and throw his fiery eyes upon strangers as they entered. He can then imagine the sudden and fierce looks which the lusty warriors bestowed upon these haggard, way-worn and miserable men.

Colonel McGillivray, unfortunately, was from home, for this place was one of his residences. The Indians scanned their saddles closely, and, as they were like those of the Georgians, they believed they were Whigs. In vain they asserted that they were royalists, and good friends of the Creeks. About seventy of the savages formed a circle around them. In vain did they allege the defenseless state of themselves, their company behind, with their wretched women and children, their destitution of provisions, and the frank and friendly manner in which they had entered their town. The expedition appeared to be mysterious, the motives which led to it inexplicable, and the unfortunate saddles, upon which they rode, contradictory to all their professions. A vehement debate

[11] In a footnote, Timothy Dwight refers to the person with the old letter: "This was my eldest brother." This is a reference to Dr. Sereno Dwight. Ibid.

[12] Pickett's narrative of the meeting with the Creeks is taken entirely from Timothy Dwight's *Travels in New York and New England,* with one exception. Dwight refers to "a black servant of Col. McGillivray" and does not use the name Paro. Apparently Pickett's "conversations with several Indian traders" provided the slave's name and some details missing from Dwight's narrative. Ibid.

[13] Dr. Sereno Edwards Dwight, his wife Cynthia Pomeroy Dwight, and their daughter Martha returned to Northampton. He died in a shipwreck off the coast of Halifax, Nova Scotia, on 10 October 1783. His wife married John Lyman in 1789 but died giving birth to their daughter, Cynthia Lyman, on 28 May 1790. Martha Dwight (1777–1826) married Austin Denison, a New Haven merchant, on 23 September 1798. Dwight, *History of the Descendants of John Dwight,* 212–16; Dwight, *History of the Descendants of Elder John Strong,* 2: 1278.

[14] Family genealogy records indicate Captain Thaddeus Lyman, Oliver Lyman, and Thompson Lyman returned to Connecticut after their flight from the Natchez District. However, the two Lyman daughters—Eleanor and Experience—both died in 1776 or 1777 and did not make the treacherous journey from Natchez to Georgia. Timothy

began among the Indians, of which only a few ill-boding words were understood, such as *Virginians! long knives! no good!* From all appearances, the fate of the wanderers was sealed. Instantly every warrior seized his knife, every face became distorted with wrath, every eye lighted up with fierce and gloomy vengeance.

Colonel McGillivray had a body servant. He was a smart black fellow, named Paro, who understood the English language as well as he did the Indian tongue. He had been off on a journey, and, at this moment, rode up among the excited throng. He demanded the cause of the tumult. They replied that these strangers were Georgians, were bad men, no friends to them or to their father, the king of Great Britain, and ought to be put to death. The ambassadors now appealed to the Negro, and gave him an account of the nature of their journey. He expressed himself fully satisfied, and endeavored to disabuse the minds of the savages. But they remained inflexible, when Paro called them fools and madmen. On account of their fear of McGillivray, they did not resent his offensive language, but assured him that the death of the strangers, and their friends behind, was resolved upon. A warrior, more moderate than the rest, said to the white men, "IF YOU TELL THE TRUTH, MAKE THE PAPER TALK."[10] The ingenious Paro caught the idea, and asked the men if they had not kept a journal of their travels. They replied, No! He then asked if they had any paper about them, with writing on it, and said anything would do. One of them found an old letter in his pocket,[11] which, according to the directions of Paro, he pretended to read, *slowly* and *solemnly*, giving a complete history of their flight from Natchez, and the cause of it. Paro, all the time, interpreted it to the Indians, with great animation. As the recital went on, their countenances gradually softened, and, before it was finished, the gloom gave way to a smile, and the ferocity was succeeded by friendship. The whole body put up their knives, and coming, one by one, to the ambassadors, shook them cordially by the hand, and welcomed them to the town. They presently brought in the whole caravan, lodged them in their houses, fed them at their tables, and "poured oil upon their wounds."[12]

When this party of royalists had sufficiently recruited, they proceeded on their route, crossed the Tallapoosa, Chattahoochee and Flint, and then divided their company, and separated. One of the parties shaped their course down towards East Florida, and finally reached Savannah in safety. The other party were taken prisoners by the Whigs, but shortly afterwards were released. Strange to say, not one died, or was killed, upon

Dwight referred to Thaddeus as the eldest who disposed of the remains of his father's estate and the Lymans as "the Unhappy Family." Dwight, *Travels In New England and New York*, 1: 315; Lyman Coleman, *Genealogy of the Lyman Family in Great Britain and America: The Ancestors & Descendants of Richard Lyman, from High Ongar in England, 1631* (Albany, NY: J. Munsell, 1872), 205–06.

[15] Fearing reprisals from the Spanish, Anthony Hutchins and John Ogg fled the Natchez District between November 1781 and March 1782. While there were reports of his being killed by Indians, Hutchins made his way to Georgia and spent two years in England before returning to his property south of Natchez. He corresponded with Esteban Miró, governor and intendant general of Louisiana, and he actually added to his land holdings while being nominated as a Spanish commissary. A 1792 census of the Natchez area lists Hutchins as the second largest landowner, with 8,512 acres, the most livestock, and 59 slaves. Grant, "Anthony Hutchins," 413–15; Haynes, *Natchez District*, 141–42, 175 n. 19; Kinnaird, *Spain in the Mississippi Valley*, 2: 142–43.

[16] Actually, John Alston, his son, and ten slaves were captured on the Yazoo River. Grand-Pré pardoned Alston's son, confiscated his slaves, and dispatched Alston under guard to New Orleans. The Spaniards imprisoned several leaders of the Natchez rebellion and confiscated the property of

the whole route from Natchez, which was accomplished in one hundred and forty-nine days.[13]

Several of the Lyman's, called the "unhappy family," were in this singular expedition. Two of the daughters of the late General Lyman died after reaching Savannah. Three of his sons were also in company. When the British evacuated Georgia, one of them went to New York, another to Nova Scotia, and the third to Providence. They all died with broken hearts.[14] Few have been born to higher hopes; few have begun life with a fairer promise of prosperity than their honorable father, and, for a time, no American possessed a more extensive reputation.*

Colonel Hutchins, with some of his friends, also fled from Fort Panmure to the swamps. Receiving information that the Indians were in pursuit of him, he set off, with twenty men, upon horses, intending to overtake the larger party, whose peregrinations we have just described. They left their families and most valuable effects. Hutchins abandoned an excellent plantation, with twenty workers upon it, an immense body of land, and seventeen hundred head of cattle. The Spaniards confiscated the whole of it, except a bare support for his wife. On the second night of their flight, the Choctaws overtook them, and killed all of them but Hutchins and one other man, who fled towards Georgia and arrived there naked, sunburnt, starved, and worn down with fatigue.[15] John Alston, and another small party, escaping to the Creek Nation, were there arrested by the Indians, carried to Mobile, and from thence to New Orleans, where, after being tried for rebellion, they were condemned to die. But the governor pardoned them.[16] During the fall of 1781, the property of all these unfortunate people was confiscated.†

In the meantime, the wild region upon the Cumberland River was explored, and some temporary establishments formed at the bluff, on which is now situated the city of Nashville. Captain James Robertson was the hero of these bold adventures, and had

* *Travels in New York and New England,* by Theodore Dwight, S.T.D., L.L.D., late President of Yale College, 1: 306–16; *Memoirs and Adventures of Captain Matthew Phelps,* "Appendix," 2–17. I also held conversations with several old Indian traders, of the Creek Nation, two of whom, when youths, were at the Hickory Ground when these retreating royalists arrived there.

† *Memoirs and Adventures of Captain Matthew Phelps,* "Appendix," 17–19.

twenty-one, including Philip Alston, John Blommart, Parker Carradine, William Eason, John Turner, and Jacob Winfree. Haynes, *Natchez District,* 142–43; "Sale of Property Belonging to English Prisoners," 6 May 1782, in Kinnaird, *Spain in the Mississippi Valley,* 2: 12–13.

[17] Richard Henderson, a North Carolina land speculator, recruited James Robertson and John Donelson to establish a settlement on land in Middle Tennessee—hunting land claimed by several Indian nations—acquired through his purchase agreement with the Cherokee at Sycamore Shoals in 1775. In the spring of 1779, Robertson led an eight-man exploring party through the Cumberland Gap via the Kentucky Path and to French Lick on the Cumberland River. Four men remained behind to clear land and to plant corn. Finger, *Tennessee Frontiers,* 50–51, 77–79; Harriette Simpson Arnow, *Seedtime on the Cumberland* (1960; reprint, Lexington: University Press of Kentucky, 1983), 210–12.

[18] James Robertson's overland party left the Watauga settlements in late October 1779 with wagons loaded with household goods and equipment while driving horses, cattle, hogs, and sheep. Robertson's party encountered several groups on their way to Middle Tennessee, including the Buchanans and Eatons, who arrived ahead of Robertson's party. Despite snow and below freezing temperatures, they crossed the frozen Cumberland River on 30 December 1779. Arnow, *Seedtime on the Cumberland,* 217–32; Richard Douglas Spence, "John Donelson and the Opening of the Old Southwest," *Tennessee Historical Quarterly* 50 (Fall 1991): 163–64.

[19] Unlike the overland party led by James Robertson, John Donelson's flotilla had several stops and starts along

several times, with a small party of men, cut his way from extreme East Tennessee to that country, passing over the lofty Cumberland Mountains and through dangerous Indian settlements.[17] Returning to the Holston, after having made several of these trips, he raised a large company of emigrants, and built boats at Long Island. When they were nearly ready to be launched, he placed himself at the head of a horse party, and set out, over the mountains, for the Cumberland, intending to leave signs upon the trees at the head of the Muscle Shoals, after going from Nashville to that place. These signs he intended for the purpose of letting the voyagers know whether it would be practicable for them to disembark at the Muscle Shoals and go to the Cumberland by land.[18]

A large number of flat boats, filled with emigrants and their effects, began the voyage from Long Island, upon the Holston. Those recollected will be mentioned, for the gratification of descendants. The large Donelson family, who, after reaching the Cumberland, settled upon Stone's River, and became connected, by affinity, with General Andrew Jackson, all embarked on this occasion. Among the others were Robert Cartwright, Benjamin Porter, Mary Henry, Mary Purnell, James Cain, Isaac Neely, John Cotton, Isaac Rounsever, Jonathan Jennings, William Crutchfield, Moses, Joseph and James Renfroe, Solomon Turpin,—Johns, Francis Armstrong, Isaac Lanier, Daniel Dunham, John Boyd, John Montgomery, John Cockrill, Mrs. Robertson, the wife of Captain Robertson, John Blackman and John Gibson. These persons had families with them, besides slaves.[19]

In consequence of great difficulty in descending the Holston, and many unavoidable delays, the rude fleet did not reach the mouth of the French Broad until March 2nd. It was then the habit to tie up at sunset, encamp upon the banks and around large fires, and to make the wild forests resound with noise and merry peals of laughter. All were now happy and filled with the most pleasing excitement. But when they approached the Cherokee towns below they observed great caution. When near Nickajack they were fired upon, from both banks of the river, by the savages, but, keeping in the middle, received no material injury. However, unfortunately, a boat belonging to Stuart, containing his family and Negroes, amounting to twenty-eight souls, who had been compelled to keep behind a few miles, on account of the small pox which they had taken, were all killed by the Indians, while their companions, in advance, could afford them no assistance. In passing the celebrated "Suck," the boats were again fired upon, when several of the voyagers were severely wounded.[20]

their river routes to Middle Tennessee. The Donelson family navigated a large flatboat that measured one hundred feet long and twenty feet wide—christened *Adventure*—that carried fifteen whites and thirty blacks. Andrew Jackson's future wife, fifteen-year old Rachel Donelson, was one of its passengers. They were joined by as many thirty other vessels of varying sizes. It has been estimated that these river craft carried as many as two hundred would-be settlers, and those that survived did not arrive until 24 April 1780. Arnow, *Seedtime on the Cumberland*, 235–37; Spence, "John Donelson," 164–65; Samuel Cole Williams, *Tennessee During the Revolutionary War* (1944; reprint, Knoxville: University of Tennessee Press, 1974), 110–16.

[20] According to John Donelson's journal, the attack on the Thomas Stuart (Stewart) family occurred on 8 March 1780. The twenty-eight people lost to smallpox and the attack by the Chickamaugas apparently included extended family members and several slaves. Williams, *Tennessee During the Revolutionary War*, 112, 112 n. 9; John Donelson, "Voyage of the Donelson Party (1779–1780)," in *Early Travels in the Tennessee Country*, ed. Samuel C. Williams (Johnson City, Tenn.: Watauga Press, 1928), 235–36.

[21] On 8 March 1780, the boat carrying Jonathan Jennings's family and others lodged on a rocky ledge in the Tennessee River, forcing its passengers

In the midst of the dismay and confusion a young woman, named Nancy Glover, seized the oar of her father's boat and steered it safely through the narrows, exposed to all the firing, and receiving a severe wound, of which she never complained. When the terrified voyagers had passed this place, they entered a wide and smooth sheet of water, and were out of danger. But, just at the termination of the narrows, the boat of Jonathan Jennings was stove upon a large rock. The voyagers were forced to leave these unhappy people. The Indians coming upon them, all the effects were thrown out of the boat in great haste, and it was shoved off, with Mrs. Jennings and Mrs. Peyton in it, who singularly made their escape. The Indians captured Jennings, his son, a Negro, and a young man with them, and carried them to Chickamauga, where they soon burned the latter to death by a slow fire. They knocked Jennings down with a club, but his life was spared by Rodgers, a trader, who ransomed him.[21] After being again attacked, near the head of the Muscle Shoals, they finally reached those cataracts, where a consultation was held. Being unable, upon a diligent search, to find the signals of Captain Robertson on the north bank, they resolved to trust their boats to the angry waves below.[22] Fortunately, the swollen state of the river carried them safely over the extended shoals. Reaching the mouth of the Tennessee on the 20th of March, an affecting and painful separation took place—Colonel Donelson and more than half of the voyagers going up the Cumberland, and the remainder to Natchez and the Illinois.*

to jump out to lighten the boat and dislodge it. They were attacked by a Chickamauga party that had been following the Donelson flotilla, which wounded a young slave and an unidentified young man. While Jennings's slave drowned and his son and the other young man were taken captives, he and his other passengers escaped. His young son was ransomed by the trader Rodgers, a relative of Cherokee humorist Will Rogers. Donelson, "Voyage," 237–38; Arnow, *Seedtime on the Cumberland*, 236; Spence, "John Donelson," 165.

[22] James Robertson became lost and ended up far west of the Tennessee before he discovered his mistake and missed leaving a sign noting safe passage overland to French Lick. Donelson's flotilla passed through the Muscle Shoals of the Tennessee on 12 March 1780 and entered the Cumberland River on the 24th. Donelson, "Voyage," 238–39; Arnow, *Seedtime on the Cumberland*, 237.

* Haywood, *Civil and Political History of the State of Tennessee,* 85–94. Mrs. Rachel Jackson, the wife of General Jackson, and the daughter of Colonel Donelson, who was then but a little girl, was with this party.

Chapter XIX

THE SPANIARDS IN ALABAMA AND MISSISSIPPI

England, having lost her West Florida provinces by the victories of Gálvez, and having the American Whigs, as well as the natives of France, Spain and Holland, arrayed against her, was finally forced to retire from the unequal contest. A preliminary treaty of peace was signed at Paris. England there acknowledged our independence, and admitted our southern boundary to be as follows: A line beginning at the Mississippi, at 31° north of the equator, and extending due east to the Chattahoochee River; down that river to the mouth of the Flint, and thence to the St. Mary's, and along that river to the sea. Great Britain also expressly stipulated, in that treaty, our right to the navigation of the Mississippi River, from its mouth to its source. Great Britain and Spain entered into a treaty.[1] The former warranted and confirmed to the latter the province of West Florida, and ceded to her East Florida.*

But although England, by the treaty of 1782, assigned to the United States all the territory between the Mississippi and the Chattahoochee, lying between the parallels of latitude 31° and 32° 28', embracing the same portion of the territory of Alabama and Mississippi, which lay in the British province of West Florida, yet it was not surrendered to us, by Spain, for years afterwards. Spain occupied it, contending that Great Britain, in the treaty with her, in 1783, warranted the province of West Florida to her, not defining its northern limits, and that England had no right to restrict her limits, even if she had attempted it, for Spain had, before the negotiations commenced, acquired all of West Florida, by conquest, through the victorious arms of Don Gálvez.[2]

Turning to Georgia, with which this history will now be much connected, we find that that province continued to consist, as at the time of its colonization by Oglethorpe, of a narrow strip of country, between the

[1] **Under the preliminary nine articles of peace signed on 30 November 1782, Great Britain recognized the independence of the thirteen American states and the 31° of north latitude as their southern boundary (2nd article). However, under a secret article number ten, the American representatives agreed that, should Great Britain retain possession of West Florida, "the Line of North Boundary between the said Province and the United States, shall be a Line drawn from the Mouth of the River aYassous where it unites with the Mississippi due East to the River Apalachicola." With existing control over Louisiana and by giving West Florida back to Spain, the United States could not exercise navigation down the Mississippi to the sea. "Preliminary Articles of Peace," [Paris], 30 November 1782, avalon.law.yale.**

* Thomas B. Wait, comp., *State Papers and Publick Documents,* Boston edition, 10: 132.

Savannah and Ogeechee Rivers, until 1773, when, as we have already seen, Governor Wright acquired from the Creeks and Cherokees a strip of country north of this, extending above Broad River. The legislature of Georgia elected commissioners, who met a delegation of Cherokees at Augusta. The latter ceded to Georgia the country upon the western side of the Tugaloo, including the headwaters of the Oconee. A small delegation of the Creeks also assembled at Augusta, and agreed to the boundary made with the Cherokees. Thus, as Georgia supposed, the lines between her and those tribes were, for a while, determined. But the treaty made with the Creeks was denounced by a large majority of that nation, as obtained unfairly, and with the representation of scarcely any of the towns.*

But, before entering upon these exciting topics, it will be necessary to recur once more to the close of the war. It has been observed, that Lachlan McGillivray, previous to the Revolution, owned extensive trading houses in Savannah and Augusta, and plantations upon the river. He was an active and influential royalist, and the Whigs of Georgia and Carolina sensibly felt his weight. When the British were forced to evacuate Savannah, he sailed with them to his native country, having scraped together a vast amount of money and movable effects. His plantations and Negroes he abandoned, in the hope that his son, Alexander, his two daughters, and his Indian wife, Sehoy, then living upon the Coosa, might be suffered to inherit them. But the Whigs confiscated the whole of this valuable property, with the exception of a few Negroes, who fled to the nation, and were added to those already at the residence of Sehoy.[3] Thus, Colonel Alexander McGillivray was deprived of a large patrimony, while his affectionate father was forced to flee the country. Another Scotchman, remarkable for his great commercial enterprise and capital sense, must also be introduced.

William Panton was born in Aberdeenshire, Scotland, and, at an early period, sailed for America, and landed in Charleston. He became an extensive Indian merchant, and owned large estates, in South Carolina and Georgia; but, at an early period of the war, was driven from these provinces, and his estates confiscated. He then established himself upon the St. Mary's.[4] In 1781, when the Spaniards took Pensacola, he was residing there, owning an extensive trading house. He soon formed a commercial treaty with Spain, which enabled him to become enriched,

* *American State Papers: Indian Affairs,* 1: 23.

edu/18th_century/prel1782.asp; Richard B. Morris, *The Peacemakers: The Great Powers and American Independence* (New York: Harper & Row, 1965), 351, 552.

2 Under the articles of peace signed on 3 September 1783 at Versailles, Great Britain surrendered East Florida and West Florida to Spain without reference to boundaries. Based on its conquest of British posts on the Mississippi, Spain claimed lands east of the river, north to the Ohio and Tennessee Rivers. Weber, *Spanish Frontier in North America,* 276–78; Samuel Flagg Bemis, *Pinckney's Treaty: America's Advantage From Europe's Distress, 1783–1800* (1926; reprint, New Haven: Yale University Press, 1965), 37–44.

3 Lachlan McGillivray sailed for England in May 1782. The Georgia General Assembly seized his land and property on 4 May and sold them for £23,084. After a residence in Inverness, he returned to his boyhood home of Dunmaglass, where he served his clan. He also corresponded with Alexander and sent him mementos of Scotland. Cashin, *Lachlan McGillivray,* 298–302.

4 William Panton arrived in Charlestown in 1765 and worked as a clerk for John Gordon and Company until 1772. In the early 1770s, he developed a partnership with Philip Moore in Savannah and a second with Thomas Forbes known as Panton, Forbes and Company. In January 1776, the Georgia Council of Safety seized 2,000 pounds of Panton's gunpowder destined for the

while the government of Florida was strengthened by his influence with the Indian tribes south of the Tennessee.[5] He had formed an acquaintance with Colonel McGillivray, and was struck with the power of his mind. Knowing that he had been deserted by the British, he sought to place him under the wing of Spain, for the personal advancement of the great chieftain himself, who he expected would, in return, promote his Indian commerce. He introduced him to the Spanish authorities of West Florida.[6] According to arrangement, Colonel McGillivray went to Pensacola, and entered into a treaty of alliance with Spain.[7] Spain was represented by Don Miró, of New Orleans, governor of West Florida; Don Arthur O'Neill, commandant of Pensacola; and Don Martin Navarro, intendant-general of Florida. Colonel McGillivray represented the whole Creek and Seminole nations.[8] It was stipulated that the Creek and Seminole Indians should defend and sustain the cause of His Catholic Majesty, and obey his orders, through his captain-general of the provinces of the Floridas and Louisiana, in those points which are compatible with Indian character; that Spain should proportion among the Indians a desirable and permanent commerce, at the most judicious places; that the Creeks should establish a general peace with the Chickasaws, Choctaws and Cherokees; that all strangers, introducing themselves among the Indians, for the purpose of stirring up rebellion against the king of Spain, should immediately be seized and conveyed to the governor of Pensacola; that the Indians should admit no white person into their country who did not bear a Spanish permit; that they should abandon the practice of taking scalps, if engaged in war; that they should deliver up all white prisoners, subjects of the United States, and not admit into their nations fugitive slaves from the provinces of Louisiana and Florida,[9] but should apprehend and deliver them to the commandants.*

* *State Papers and Publick Documents,* Boston edition, 10: 223–27.

Indian trade in East Florida and later declared Panton "dangerous to the liberties of America." Coker and Watson, *Indian Traders,* 15, 17–18, 24–30.

[5] Actually, Panton was a resident of St. Augustine, East Florida, where he was listed as an attorney-at-law in 1779 and served as a justice of the peace in 1783. He had also formed a new partnership—Panton, Leslie and Company—in late 1782 or early 1783, before the end of British control of East Florida. Ibid., 39–42.

[6] In the spring of 1783, Alexander McGillivray became the head warrior of the Creek Nation, and soon after he learned that the British intended to evacuate East Florida. William Panton advised him to seek Spanish protection and to promote Panton, Leslie and Company for the Spanish Indian trade. Ibid., 53–54.

[7] McGillivray opened a correspondence with Arturo O'Neill in January 1784, and he asked for Spanish protection and requested that Panton, Leslie and Company be allowed to continue their Indian trade. Ibid., 56; Green, "Alexander McGillivray," 46–47; Caughey, *McGillivray of the Creeks,* 64–67.

[8] Esteban Rodriquez Miró (1744–1795) served as governor of Louisiana from 1782 through 1792, and Martin Antonio Navarro (1738–1793) served as the first Spanish intendant-general of Louisiana between 1784 and 1788. The Irish-born Arturo O'Neill (1736–1814) was the first Spanish governor of West Florida from 1782 through 1792. Gilbert C. Din, "Esteban Rodriquez Miró Colonial Governor, 1782–1791," in *Louisiana Governors,* 61–62; Eric Beerman, "Arturo O'Neill: First Governor of West Florida During The Second Spanish Period," *Florida Historical Quarterly* 60 (July 1981): 29–41; José Montero de Pedro, Marqués de Casa Mena, *The Spanish in New Orleans and Louisiana,* ed. Richard E. Chandler (Gretna: Pelican Publishing Company, 2000), 113–14.

[9] The Pensacola congress and treaty with Alexander McGillivray and the Creeks on 31 May—1 June 1784 was the first of four Indian congresses hosted by Governor Miró. The other three were held in Mobile with the Alabamas,

Colonel McGillivray was induced to form an alliance with the Spaniards for various reasons, the chief of which were that the Whigs, as he contended, had confiscated his estates, banished his father, threatened him with death and his nation with extermination, and were constantly encroaching upon Creek soil. The Spaniards wanted no lands—desired only his friendship, and had not encroached upon him or his people. Besides, they were the first to offer him promotion and commercial advantages. When he had signed the treaty, they made him a Spanish commissary, with the rank and pay of colonel.[10]

Great dissatisfaction arose, as has been stated, in consequence of the treaty at Augusta and the occupation of the Creek lands. Border war commenced. The Spanish authorities fomented these discords between the Creeks and Georgians, for the purpose of monopolizing the entire commerce of the nation. Colonel McGillivray exerted himself to defeat all attempts at peaceable negotiation, now undertaken by those who had charge of our national affairs.[11]

The provisional Congress appointed Benjamin Hawkins, Andrew Pickens, Joseph Martin and Lachlan McIntosh, commissioners, to treat with the Southern Indians.[12] Pickens addressed a letter to Colonel McGillivray, urging him to meet them at a convenient place, at the head of all the chiefs of the nation, to enter into treaties of friendship. The Alabama Talleyrand replied, and we will publish his able and ingenious letter, as the reader can better understand from it the character of the man, and of the times of which he writes, than by a narration from the author.[13]

"LITTLE TALLASE,* 5th Sept. 1785.

"*Sir:* — I am favored with your letter by Brandon,

* Little Tallase (Tallassee), four miles above Wetumpka, on the east bank of the Coosa, was one of the residences of Colonel McGillivray, and from that point he wrote most of his able letters. Colonel Howell Rose now owns the site of Little Tallase, which is embraced in a cotton plantation.

Chickasaw, and Choctaw in June and July 1784. *Documents of American Indian Diplomacy: Treaties, Agreements, and Conventions, 1775–1979*, ed. Vine Deloria, Jr. and Raymond J. DeMallie, 2 vols. (Norman: University of Oklahoma Press, 1999), 1: 123–30.

[10] In a letter on 7 June 1784, Governor Miró appointed McGillivray as commissary to the Creek Nation with "all the honors, exceptions and privileges attached to the office, and the salary which his majesty . . . accords him." Other sources credit Vicente Manuel de Zéspedes, first Spanish governor of East Florida (1784–1790), with making McGillivray a colonel in the Spanish service. Caughey, *McGillivray of the Creeks*, 77; Cashin, *King's Ranger*, 169.

[11] Contrary to Pickett's assertions, the Spanish officials and McGillivray did not promote war with the Georgians. In the 1784 Treaty of Pensacola, McGillivray and the Creeks agreed to "establish a general peace with all nations . . . ceasing all kinds of hostilities," "renounce the taking of scalps, or making slaves of whites, and in case of an unexpected war against enemies of his Catholic Majesty" treating prisoners "with hospitality . . . of the civilized nations." However, McGillivray did authorize Creek warriors to drive American settlers off disputed lands in Tennessee in cooperation with the Cherokee and against Georgia settlers who moved into lands gained by fraudulent treaties in the mid-1780s—cessions considered unauthorized and illegal by the Creek national council. Green, "Alexander McGillivray," 47–48; "Treaty with the Creek, May 31–June 1, 1784," in *Documents of American Indian Diplomacy*, 1: 122–24.

[12] On 21 March 1785, the Confederation Congress appointed Andrew Pickens, Benjamin Hawkins, Daniel Carroll, William Perry, and Joseph Martin as a commission to treat with the Southern Indians. When Carroll and Perry refused to serve, Lachlan McIntosh was added to the commission. Alice Noble Waring, *The Fighting Elder: Andrew Pickens, 1739–1817* (Columbia: University of South Carolina, 1962), 130–31.

[13] By a letter of 14 September 1785, McGillivray notified Governor Arturo O'Neill that

he had been invited to meet with the American commissioners and that he planned to attend the conference to settle and fix the "Limits & boundary of the Lands between the Indians & the States of America." When O'Neill advised McGillivray not to meet with the Americans, he requested assurances that Spain would provide support if the Americans started a war. Caughey, *McGillivray of the Creeks,* 97–98, 98 n. 46.

who, after detaining it near a month, sent it by an Indian, a few days ago. He, perhaps, had some reasons for keeping himself from this region.

"The notification you have sent us is agreeable to our wishes, as the meeting is intended for the desirable purpose of adjusting and settling matters, on an equitable footing, between the United States and the Indian nations. At the same time, I cannot avoid expressing my surprise that a measure of this nature should have been so long delayed, on your part. When we found that the American independence was confirmed by the peace, we expected that the new government would soon have taken some steps to make up the differences that subsisted between them and the Indians during the war, to have taken them under their protection, and confirmed to them their hunting grounds. Such a course would have reconciled the minds of the Indians, and secured the states their friendship, as they considered your people their natural allies. The Georgians, whose particular interest it was to conciliate the friendship of this nation, have acted, in all respects, to the contrary. I am sorry to observe that violence and prejudice have taken place of good policy and reason, in all their proceedings with us. They attempted to avail themselves of our supposed distressed situation. Their talks to us breathed nothing but vengeance, and, being entirely possessed with the idea that we were wholly at their mercy, they never once reflected that colonies of a powerful monarch were nearly surrounding us, to whom, in any extremity, we might apply for succor and protection, and who, to answer some ends of their policy, might grant it to us. However, we yet deferred any such proceeding, still expecting we could bring them to a true sense of their interest; but still finding no alteration in their conduct towards us, we sought the protection of Spain, and treaties of friendship and alliance were mutually entered into—they guaranteeing our hunting grounds and territory, and granting us a free trade in the ports of the Floridas.

"How the boundary and limits between the Spaniards and the states will be determined, a little time will show, as I believe that matter is now on foot. However, we know our limits, and the extent of our hunting grounds. As a free nation, we have applied, as we had a right to do, for protection, and obtained it. We shall pay no attention to any limits that may prejudice our claims, that were drawn by an American, and confirmed by a British negotiator. Yet, notwithstanding we have been obliged to adopt these measures for our preservation, and from real necessity, we sincerely wish to have it in our power to be on the same footing with the states as before the late unhappy war, to effect which is entirely in your power. We want nothing from you but justice. We want our hunting grounds preserved from encroachments.

They have been ours from the beginning of time, and I trust that, with the assistance of our friends, we shall be able to maintain them against every attempt that may be made to take them from us.

"Finding our representations to the state of Georgia of no effect, in restraining their encroachments, we thought it proper to call a meeting of the nation, on the subject. We then came to the resolution to send out parties, to remove the Georgians and their effects from the lands in question, in the most peaceable manner possible.

"Agreeably to your requisition, and to convince you of my sincere desire to restore a good understanding between us, I have taken the necessary steps to prevent any future predatory excursions of my people against any of your settlements. I could wish the people of Cumberland showed an equal good disposition to do what is right. They were certainly the first aggressors since the peace, and acknowledged it in a written certificate, left at the Indian camp they had plundered.

"I have only to add, that we shall meet the commissioners of Congress whenever we shall receive notice, in expectation that every matter of difference will be settled, with that liberality and justice worthy the men who have so gloriously asserted the cause of liberty and independence, and that we shall, in future, consider them as brethren, and defenders of the land.*

"I am, with much respect, sir,

"Your obedient servant,

"ALEXANDER MCGILLIVRAY.

"HON. ANDREW PICKENS."

This well-written communication affords the first evidence of the consummate diplomacy of this great native Alabamian. The history of this remarkable Indian will be found to be full of interest.

The commissioners of Congress, elated by the conciliatory tone of Colonel McGillivray, arrived at Galphinton.† The latter failed to appear, and only the chiefs from two towns, with sixty warriors, met them. Disappointed and mortified, the commissioners declined to treat with so few.[14] In the meantime, the Georgia commissioners protested against those proceedings which the agents of Congress had intended to adopt; but the latter declined to do anything further than to explain to the Indians the policy which the Congress intended to pursue towards them, thanked them for their attendance, and afterwards departed. No sooner had they left than the commissioners representing Georgia made a treaty with the Creeks who were present, which

[14] Pickens, Hawkins, Martin, and McIntosh arrived at Galphinton between 24 and 28 October 1785 expecting to meet with McGillivray and representatives of all the Creek towns. On 8 November, they distributed presents to the Creeks present and explained that they had expected to treat with representatives of about one hundred towns and not two towns. Waring, *Fighting Elder*, 131–32; *ASP: IA*, 1: 16–18.

* *American State Papers: Indian Affairs*, 1: 17–18.

† This town was named in honor of George Galphin, the great Indian trader.

confirmed the treaty of Augusta of 1783, and granted to the state of Georgia the territory lying on the east side of a line, to run from the junction of the Oconee and Ocmulgee to the St. Mary's River, including all the islands and harbors, and which now constitutes more than half the coast of Georgia. What considerations induced the Indians to divest themselves of so much territory is not stated. The commissioners of Georgia laid before the legislature a copy of the articles intended to have been proposed to the Creeks by the agents of Congress, had a sufficient number been present, which that body declared, by resolutions, to be subversive of the rights of the state. They instructed their members in Congress to insist on the abolition of the powers of the commissioners, while they adopted measures for the preservation of the rights of the citizens of Georgia. Edward Telfair, John King and Thomas Glasscock received the thanks of the General Assembly, for their vigilance and patriotism, and particularly for the treaty which they had made.[15]

The Georgia legislature established a county called Houston, embracing the territory extending from Nickajack, below the Muscle Shoals, out of which are now formed the modern Alabama counties of Lauderdale, Limestone, Madison and Jackson. Sevier, Downes, Heard, Donelson and Lindsay were appointed commissioners to organize the county of Houston. With eighty men, in flat boats, they arrived at the Muscle Shoals, and, in the western part of the present Lauderdale County, established a land office, appointed military officers and magistrates, and elected Valentine Sevier to be a member of the Georgia legislature.[16] This remarkable government existed but two weeks, when the colonists were driven off by the Indians.*

Congress appointed James White as superintendent of the Creek Indians, who immediately proceeded to the town of Cusseta, upon the Chattahoochee.[17] He addressed a letter to Colonel McGillivray, and received the following reply:

"Little Tallase, 8th April 1787.

"*Sir*: — It is with real satisfaction that I learn of your being appointed by Congress for the laudable purpose of enquiring into and settling the differences that at present subsist between our nation and the Georgians. It may be necessary for you to know the cause of these differences, and our discontents, which, perhaps, have never come to the knowledge of the honorable body that sent you to our country.

"There are chiefs of two towns in this nation, who, during the late war, were friendly to the state of Georgia, and had gone, at different times, among those people, and once, after the general peace, to Augusta. They there demanded of them a grant of lands, belonging to and enjoyed as hunting grounds by

* Haywood, *Civil and Political History of the State of Tennessee,* 157–58.

[15] Fat King (Eneah Mico) of Cusseta and Tame King (Hopoithle Mico) of Tallassee led the delegation of some sixty Creeks to Galphinton in October 1785. On 12 November 1785, these two pro-American headmen and fifteen other non-Muskogees agreed to the treaty of Galphinton, which confirmed the boundary lines of the 1783 Treaty of Augusta and the extension of the new boundary line to the sources of the St. Mary's River. *ASP: IA*, 1: 17; Caughey, *McGillivray of the Creeks*, 101 n. 49; Green, *Politics of Indian Removal*, 32–34.

[16] Initially the state of Georgia appointed a seven member commission to organize Houston County, Georgia, in the Muscle Shoals area of the Tennessee River: Lachlan McIntosh, Jr., William Downes, Stephen Heard, John Morell, John Donelson, Valentine Sevier, and John Sevier. Although Valentine Sevier was selected to represent the new county, he was not seated by the Georgia legislature. While land speculators from North Carolina, Georgia, and the would-be State of Franklin supported this first land scheme at the Shoals, the Chickasaw, Creeks, and Chickamaugas prevented a permanent settlement. Zella Armstrong, *The History of Hamilton County and Chattanooga, Tennessee*,

the Indians of this nation, in common, on the east of the Oconee River. The chiefs rejected the demand, on the plea that these lands were the hunting grounds of the nation, and could not be granted by two individuals; but, after a few days, a promise was extorted from them, that, on their return to our country, they would use their influence to get a grant confirmed. Upon their return, a general convention was held at Tuckabatchee, when these two chiefs were severely censured, and the chiefs of ninety-eight towns agreed upon a talk, to be sent to Savannah, disapproving, in the strongest manner, of the demand made upon their nation, and denying the right of any two of their country to make cession of land, which could only be valid by the unanimous voice of the whole, as joint proprietors in common. Yet these two chiefs, regardless of the voice of the nation, continued to go to Augusta, and other places within that state. They received presents and made promises; but our customs did not permit us to punish them for the crime.[18] We warned the Georgians of the dangerous consequences that would certainly attend the settling of the lands in question. Our just remonstrances were treated with contempt, and these lands were soon filled with settlers. The nation, justly alarmed at the encroachments, resolved to use force to maintain their rights; yet, being averse to the shedding of the blood of a people whom we would rather consider as friends, we made another effort to awaken in them a sense of justice and equity. But we found, from experience, that entreaty could not prevail, and parties of warriors were sent, to drive off the intruders, but were instructed to shed blood, only, where self-preservation made it necessary.

"This was in May 1786. In October following, we were invited by commissioners, of the state of Georgia, to meet them in conference, at the Oconee, professing a sincere desire for an amicable adjustment of our disputes, and pledging their sacred honors for the safety and good treatment of all those that should attend and meet them. It not being convenient for many of us to go to the proposed conference, a few, from motives of curiosity, attended. They were surprised to find an armed body of men, prepared for and professing hostile intentions. Apprehensions for personal safety induced those chiefs to subscribe to every demand that was asked by the army and its commissioners. Lands were again demanded, and the lives of some of our chiefs were required, as well as those of some innocent traders, as sacrifice, to appease their anger. Assassins have been employed to effect some part of their atrocious purposes. If I fall by the hand of such, I shall fall the

2 vols. (1940; reprint, Johnson City, Tenn.: Overmountain Press, 1993), 2: 287–88; Kevin T. Barksdale, *The Lost State of Franklin: America's First Secession* (Lexington: University Press of Kentucky, 2009), 83–90, 145–46.

[17] James White (1749–1809), a native of Philadelphia, attended the College of St. Omer in France and completed his medical studies at the University of Edinburgh in Scotland. The Confederation Congress appointed him as the first superintendent of Indian affairs for the southern district in October 1786. Barksdale, *Lost State of Franklin*, 146–47.

[18] McGillivray is referring to Fat King from Cusseta of the Lower Creeks and Tame King from Tallassee of the Upper Creeks. They were pro-American, with close relationships with George Galphin and his traders, which influenced their acceptance of the treaties negotiated at Augusta in 1783, at Galphinton in 1785, and at Shoulderbone in 1786. They also strongly resented and opposed McGillivray's efforts to dominate the Creek Nation. Green, "Alexander McGillivray," 49–50; Green, *Politics of Indian Removal*, 33–34; Coker and Watson, *Indian Traders*, 80, 83–84.

victim of the noblest of causes, that of maintaining the just rights of my country.[19] I aspire to the honest ambition of meriting the appellation of the preserver of my country, equally with the chiefs among *you*, whom, from acting on such principles, you have exalted to the highest pitch of glory. And if, after every peaceable mode of obtaining a redress of grievances proved fruitless, a recourse to arms to obtain it be a mark of the savage, and not of the soldier, what savages must the Americans be, and how much undeserved applause have your Cincinnatus, your Fabius, obtained. If a war name had been necessary to distinguish that chief, in such a case, the Man-Killer, the Great Destroyer, would have been the proper appellation.

"I had appointed the Cussetas, for all the chiefs of the Lower Creeks to meet in convention. I shall be down in a few days, when, from your timely arrival, you will meet the chiefs, and learn their sentiments, and I sincerely hope that the propositions which you shall offer us will be such as we can safely accede to. The talks of the former commissioners, at Galphinton, were much approved of, and your coming from the White Town (seat of Congress) has raised great expectations that you will remove the principal and almost only cause of our dispute, that is, by securing to us our hunting grounds and possessions, free from all encroachments. When we meet, we shall talk these matters over.[20]

"Meantime, I remain,

"With regard, your obedient servant,

"Alexander McGillivray.

"Hon. James White."

Dr. White met McGillivray at Cusseta, with a large number of Lower Creeks, when the superintendent desired them to ratify the treaties of Augusta, Galphinton and Shoulderbone, and to make arrangements for running the boundary line around the ceded territory. The chiefs boldly opposed the proposition, and declared that their "lands were their life and breath, and if they parted with them they parted with their blood." The two chiefs, who conveyed away these lands, being severely censured, stated that the Georgians compelled them to make the grant by threats and the flourish of long knives.[21]

McGillivray startled the superintendent with a new proposition. He said: "Notwithstanding I prompt the Indians to defend their lands, I look upon the United States as our most natural ally. Two years I waited, before I would seek the alliance I have formed.

[19] In a letter of 15 August 1786, John Habersham, chairman of the Georgia commissioners, invited McGillivray and other Creek headmen to attend a conference at Shoulderbone Creek on the Oconee River "to remove all causes for discontent" and establish a permanent peace. Fat King and Tame King responded by leading a small contingent of Lower Creeks and even fewer Upper Creeks to this meeting. They were greeted by the commissioners, who had an escort of 1,500 armed Georgia militiamen, and concluded an agreement on 3 November 1786. Under duress, they agreed to fix boundaries, restore plunder, and atone for the lives of slain Georgians—a "death proviso" demanding the assassination of tribal members. The Georgians left little doubt that they expected the lives of McGillivray and his supporters as the appropriate payment to settle Creek affairs. Caughey, *McGillivray of the Creeks*, 129–30, 133, 138, 143; Coker and Watson, *Indian Traders*, 83–84; Randolph C. Downes, "Creek-American Relations, 1782–1790," *Georgia Historical Quarterly* 21 (June 1937): 154–58.

[20] The "former commissioners" at Galphinton was a reference to the actions and talks by Andrew Pickens, Benjamin Hawkins, Joseph Martin, and Lachlan McIntosh, Jr., who chose not to negotiate with representatives from only two Creek towns. Waring, *Fighting Elder*, 131–32; *ASP: IA*, 1: 16–18.

[21] According to McGillivray's letter to Arturo O'Neill of 18 April 1787, the meeting with James White took place in the public square of "Oussitche Town." The Hollowing King of Coweta was appointed speaker for the Lower Creeks, and White reported that he spoke eloquently,

I was compelled to it. I could not but resent the greedy encroachments of the Georgians, to say nothing of their scandalous and illiberal abuse. But I will now put it to the test, whether they or myself entertain the most generous sentiments of respect for Congress. If that honorable body can form a government to the southward of the Altamaha, I will be the first to take the oath of allegiance, and, in return to the Georgians, for yielding to the United States that claim, I will obtain a regular and peaceable grant of the lands on the Oconee, on which they have deluded people to settle, under the pretense of grants from the Indians, and which you, yourself, (Dr. White), have seen are most ill-founded. I will give you till the first of August for an answer."[22]

Thus terminated the council, and the superintendent found himself baffled and perplexed by the ingenuity of McGillivray, who always managed to defeat any scheme of the federal government.

The Georgians, on the other hand, denied the charges of violence and fraud, contended that a sufficient delegation of Indians were present to make the grants, and that they were procured from them fairly and honorably, without threats or the display of knives. They contended that the Upper Creeks, who never occupied the Oconee lands, had no right to have a voice in the matter. They admitted that, at the treaty of Shoulderbone, in 1786, they had armed troops present; but they were there for the purpose of suppressing hostilities, should they show themselves. They also admitted that, for enforcing a compliance of the treaty, they carried hostages to Augusta,[23] which had been customary in all former negotiations with savages.*

predicting that Congress and the Creeks could settle their affairs amicably, "but there was third party (Georgia) who had no mind to do justice." Caughey, *McGillivray of the Creeks*, 149–50; *ASP: IA*, 1: 20–23

[22] In a letter to General Henry Knox on 24 May 1787, James White reported on the state of affairs with the Creeks and quoted McGillivray's comments. *ASP: IA*, 1: 20–21.

[23] The Creek hostages taken at the Shoulderbone treaty grounds were from Cusseta, a pro-American town that had participated in the Augusta and Galphinton treaty conferences and land cessions. James White reported in his report of 24 May 1787 that they had been "dismissed, all but a youth, who, in his impatience of confinement, put himself to death." Ibid.

* *American State Papers: Indian Affairs*, 1: 18–23.

Chapter XX

BLOODY SCENES IN ALABAMA AND GEORGIA

At this period, some exciting scenes occurred in the region now known as North Alabama. We have already followed a party of emigrants to the Cumberland. Many others flocked to that country, and it soon became well settled, for a wild country. The Upper Creeks and Cherokees continually made war upon these Cumberland people. The French, upon the Wabash, had, for a long time, carried on a commerce, near the sites of the present towns of Tuscumbia and Florence. So long as M. Viez was at the head of this trade, the Cumberland people were not harassed; but, recently, he had been succeeded by others, who supplied the Indians with arms, and encouraged them to attack the American settlements.[1] The latter had only acted upon the defensive, but it was now determined to advance upon the frontier towns of the Indians. One hundred and thirty men assembled, from different parts of the Cumberland region, and marched, under Colonel James Robertson, to the Tennessee River, piloted by two Chickasaws. David Hay was dispatched from Nashville with boats, laden with provisions, destined for the Muscle Shoals. Descending the Cumberland, he was furiously attacked by the Indians, at the mouth of Duck River, and, after some of his men had been killed, and others wounded, he returned to Nashville with his boats. Owing to this, the horsemen were without food during the greater part of the expedition.[2]

Striking the Tennessee at a point very near the present town of Florence, Colonel Robertson concealed his men. A well-beaten path was discovered, leading down the banks, and on the south side of the river stood some cabins, in view. Seven men were placed in the canes, to observe the movements of the Indians. A canoe was seen to move to an island, filled with natives, who there plunged into the river and engaged in bathing. They then returned to the south bank, evidently watching for the Americans, of whose approach they had gained some vague intelligence. Captain Rains had set out up the river, with fifteen men, with orders to capture an Indian alive; but, after marching

[1] When James Robertson and John Donelson led the Watauga settlers to Middle Tennessee in the winter of 1779–1780, they were welcomed to the area by Jacques Thimote de Monbruen, who had established his fur trading post at French Lick in the Nashville Basin in the mid-1760s. M. Viez may have been an employee of Monbruen or one of the many *coureurs de bois* who operated along the major interior rivers in the Gulf South. Harriette Simpson Arnow, *Flowering of the Cumberland* (1962; reprint, Lexington: University Press of Kentucky, 1984), 32, 86, 242; J. G. M. Ramsey, *The Annals of Tennessee to the End of the Eighteenth Century* (1853; reprint, Knoxville: East Tennessee Historical Society, 1967), 473.

[2] While James Robertson led the mounted overland force of approximately 130 men, David Hay was in command of three boats,

to the mouth of Blue Water, he returned, without having made any discovery. When the shadows of twilight began to darken the wilderness, the troops assembled, in the most noiseless manner, upon the low grounds. The seven men, who had watched all day, plunged into the mighty river early in the night, and swam to the opposite shore, where they discovered that the cabins were unoccupied. Finding a tremendous canoe, with a hole in the bottom of it, they brought it over to the north bank. Stopping the leak with their shirts, Colonel Robertson placed in it all the fire-arms, and forty men; but they soon paddled back, in a sinking condition. The party made no further attempt to cross, until daylight; then fifty men, with the arms and ammunition, went over in the boat, which had now been rendered seaworthy, by a piece of linn-bark. The rest of the party swam their horses over.[3]

A heavy rain coming on, as soon as they reached the southern shore, they took shelter in the cabins. When the clouds had dispersed, they came forth, and began the march upon a plain path, leading westwardly. At about the distance of five miles, they reached cornfields, and, further on, they came to Coldwater Creek, the same which runs by the modern Tuscumbia. The larger portion of the command immediately crossed over, and entered upon the low grounds, among a number of cabins, distant from the river about three hundred yards. The people of the town ran down to their boats. Some, in endeavoring to escape, crossed over the creek, to the east side, where they were shot down by Captain Rains and a few men stationed there to intercept them. Colonel Robertson charged to the river, and his troops committed havoc on all sides. They killed many of the Indians, who got into the boats, and others who had plunged into the stream. Three French traders, and a white woman, who would not surrender, fled to a boat, and entered it, along with twenty-six Indians. The Americans, with one volley, killed them all. The chief French trader, and six others, were captured. In this town were stores of taffai, and all kinds of Indian merchandise, arms and ammunition. Colonel Robertson brought all the boats up the creek, had a strong guard placed over them, and then burned the town, killing the fowls and hogs. Next morning, giving to Toka, the Chickasaw guide, and his companion—who presently set out for their nation—a liberal supply of merchandise and arms, Colonel Robertson buried the whites, loaded several of the boats with goods, and placed them in charge of three men, who departed down the river, with the French prisoners.[4]

Robertson marched by land, and, near Colbert's Ferry, overtook the boats, and they all encamped there together. To their great joy, they found that not a soul had received a wound. In the morning, the French prisoners, with a squaw, were permitted to depart in one of the boats. They were liberally

variously described as a piragua and two canoes. Moses Shelby was in command of the larger boat that was struck in mid-June 1787 by a small war party near the mouth of Duck River on the Tennessee, suffering one man killed and eight wounded. Arnow, *Flowering of the Cumberland,* 335; Ramsey, *Annals of Tennessee,* 471.

[3] On 12 June 1787, James Robertson wrote a letter to North Carolina Governor Richard Caswell asking for permission to remove "a disorderly set of French and Spanish traders . . . on the Tennessee" who he thought were supplying and encouraging Indian attacks on the Cumberland settlements. After his brother Mark Robertson was killed on the 13th, he reported to Governor Caswell on 2 July that he assembled his militia force "and followed their tracks near the lower end of the Muscle Shoals . . . and alarmed a small town of Cherokees." Ramsey, *Annals of Tennessee,* 465, 470.

[4] When Robertson's militia arrived at the Muscle Shoals area of modern Tuscumbia, the Coldwater town had a population of some thirty Chickamaugas, nine or ten French traders, and a small Creek war party. With the element of surprise and numbers, the Tennesseans under Robertson and Captain John Rains

supplied with provisions, and their trunks of clothing were given up to them. The sugar and coffee, taken at the town, were articles of great luxury in those days, and were now equally divided among the troops. Robertson marched across the country to the Cumberland, and thus terminated a fatiguing expedition of nineteen days. The boats, with the merchandise, proceeded down the Tennessee River, in charge of Denton and others. On their way, they met a party of French traders, destined for the town which they had destroyed, who, in their enthusiasm, fired off their guns in a fit of joy, supposing the voyagers were also traders of their people. The Americans took advantage of the discharge, and before they could reload, captured the whole party, with all their goods. Arriving in the Cumberland settlements, the merchandise was sold at Eaton's Station, and the proceeds divided among the troops.[5]

This expedition produced a short respite from Indian attacks. The savages, however, rallied, and began a warfare fiercer than ever. At length, in the fall, Captain Shannon, with a mounted party, pursued some Creeks from the Cumberland to the northern bank of the Tennessee, in the present county of Lauderdale, and engaged in a severe fight with Black Foot and his clan. Victory at length declared for the daring Cumberlanders. The chief was killed, with a number of his warriors. During this fall, the settlers engaged in numerous military excursions, upon Duck and Elk Rivers, in pursuit of Indians, who were retreating from fresh scenes of pillage and blood.[6] The magnificent forests of North Alabama were scoured, in all directions, by these intrepid Americans.*

At the same time, the Creeks were active upon the Georgia frontier. Enraged at the settlement of the Oconee lands, they reduced to ashes the new town of Greensboro, together with the court house, killed many inhabitants, on various portions of the frontier, and carried to the nation white captives, Negroes, and all sorts of plunder.† Georgia urged the Congress to punish these depredators by sending against them an army; but the national agents were reluctant to enter into another war. However, Secretary Knox did plan upon paper a Southern army, which was not raised, while the Georgians were left to defend themselves, to the best of their ability.[7]

* Haywood, *Civil and Political History of the State of Tennessee,* 217–25.

† *American State Papers: Indian Affairs,* 1: 23–24.

killed some twenty Indians, three French traders, and a Frenchwoman, and burned the town. They took six or seven French traders as prisoners and confiscated a large cache of trading supplies. Ibid., 468, 470–71; Dale Van Every, *Ark of Empire: The American Frontier, 1784–1803* (New York: William Morrow and Company, 1963), 94.

[5] On their return to the Cumberland settlements, Robertson's force released the French traders, with their personal effects and one canoe, to return to their base in Detroit. A few days later, the flotilla under Johnathan Denton encountered French traders with several boats ascending the Tennessee, seized their merchandise, and released them below Nashville to descend the river. The French goods were auctioned off at Eaton's Station and the proceeds used to pay Robertson's troops. Ramsey, *Annals of Tennessee,* 468–71.

[6] Writing to Arturo O'Neill on 10 July 1787, McGillivray reported hearing that "the Americans of Cumberland had attacked and killed most of the French traders . . . together with some of our Indians & Cherokees are likewise killed. In consequence of this affair I have sent off between five & six hundred warriors . . . to go & ravage the settlement of Cumberland." The war party intercepted by Captain John Shannon was one of several small mobile war parties stealing horses and harassing Middle Tennessee. Caughey, *McGillivray of the Creeks,* 155.

[7] In his letter of 24 May 1787 to Secretary of War Henry Knox, James White reported that Georgia had extorted their most recent treaty with

Congress, again seeking to interpose by a treaty, appointed Richard Winn, Indian superintendent, with whom was associated George Mathews, on the part of Georgia, and Andrew Pickens, on the part of South Carolina. They opened a negotiation with Colonel McGillivray, but he refused to meet them, unless they first removed the Georgians from the Oconee lands, within the bounds of the old British government. Hostilities, of course, continued, for it was now impossible to comply with the bold demands of McGillivray, who stood upon an enviable and independent footing. Caressed by Panton, with whom he was a co-partner in an extensive commerce, paid by the Spanish government, obeyed by his own people, and many of the Cherokees and Choctaws, and supplicated by the American Congress, the chieftain could well afford to dictate arbitrary terms, and continue to advance against the Georgians with hundreds of his prowling warriors.[8]

At length, Governor Thomas Pinckney, of South Carolina, entered into a correspondence with McGillivray, to endeavor to bring about a peace and the settlement of the boundary, and elicited from him several letters.[9] A portion of one of them runs as follows:

"The third invitation which was sent to us to treat, was from the Georgians only, through their commissioners, at the head of whom was Mr. Habersham, President of the Executive Council, and he proposed the Oconee as the place of meeting. They pledged their sacred honors for the safety and welfare of every Indian that should attend; but I, being so often threatened, and having the worst opinion of the back people, as they are called, did not go, but sent a few Coweta warriors, to report to me on their return.[10] During the conferences of the Oconee, an additional cession was demanded, which was strongly opposed by the Cowetas and others, for which they were violently insulted by a Colonel Clarke, which the commissioners could not prevent. Though their sacred honors were pledged for maintaining good order, several warriors, of different towns, were forcibly seized upon by armed men and conveyed to Augusta, more as prisoners than hostages, to be kept as a pledge that my life, and six more of the leading men, should be taken.[11] Such conduct convinced the whole nation that it was

the Creeks by threats and the "general consent of the nation was wanting" and "white people on the frontier continuing their encroachments." Washington's administration wanted to minimize conflict with the Southern Indians and opposed aggressive encroachments on Indian lands. Knox projected the cost of waging war on the Creeks would cost $450,000 and require 2,800 troops, for nine months, raised in Georgia, North Carolina, and South Carolina. *ASP: IA*, 1: 20–21, 25; Daniel H. Usner, Jr., "Remapping Boundaries in the Old Southwest, 1783–1795," in *George Washington's South*, ed. Tamara Harvey and Greg O'Brien (Gainesville: University Press of Florida, 2004), 26–28.

[8] Richard Winn (1750–1818), a native of Virginia, was appointed superintendent of Indian affairs for the Creek Nation in October 1787 to negotiate a settlement of their boundary dispute with Georgia. The American commissioners set a meeting date for the spring of 1789, but the adoption of the Constitution disrupted their plans. They were replaced by Henry Osborne and Andrew Pickens, who also failed to convince McGillivray to support a general conference. *ASP: IA*, 1: 23–24, 26–38.

[9] Thomas Pinckney served as governor of South Carolina from 1787 to 1789, minister to Great Britain (1792–1794), and negotiated the Treaty of San Lorenzo el Real in 1795. "Thomas Pinckney," *Biographical Directory of the United States Congress, 1774—Present* (online); Bemis, *Pinckney's Treaty*, 267–83; Caughey, *McGillivray of the Creeks*, 38, 215–16.

[10] John Habersham held the rank of major in the First Georgia Continental Regiment, served as a member of Congress in 1785–1786, and as collector of customs at Savannah in 1789–1799. On

15 August 1786, he sent McGillivray a letter on behalf of the Georgia commissioners requesting a meeting with the Creek "Kings, Head men, and Warriors" to be held on the Oconee River, at the mouth of Shoulderbone Creek, on 15 October. McGillivray responded on 18 September declining the invitation "until we see the sincerity of your proposals fully verified and proved in the way we desire." Caughey, *McGillivray of the Creeks*, 129–31, 130 n. 69.

[11] Colonel Elijah Clarke (1742–1799), a noted veteran of the Revolutionary War, led some 1,500 Georgia militiamen to the conference at Shoulderbone Creek in October 1786. Under an atmosphere of threats and intimidation with the lives of Creek leaders threatened, the small Creek delegation confirmed the treaties of Augusta and Galphinton. At the conclusion of the conference, six Creeks—including Fat King and Tame King—were taken as prisoners to coerce compliance with the land cessions and demands of the commissioners. *ASP: IA*, 1: 15, 18–21; Robert S. Davis, "Elijah Clarke," *New Georgia Encyclopedia* (online).

[12] Colonel Joseph Kirkland, a former Loyalist from South Carolina, his son, another young man, John Linder, and a young Negro boy made up the traveling party that received passports and a guide from Alexander McGillivray. Benjamin Hawkins, *Letters of Benjamin Hawkins, 1796–1806, Collections of the Georgia Historical Society*, 21 vols. (Savannah: Georgia Historical Society, 1916), 9: 79.

[13] The packhorse party encountered by Joseph Kirkland's party included "John Catt of Holston, a Negro, Bob, belonging to Stephen Sullivan, Catt's wife, an Indian woman of the Fish Ponds, and Indian man called the murderer" (Pickett's Istillicha). Ibid.

[14] Contrary to Pickett's sources, journal entries by Benjamin Hawkins dated 11 February 1797 intimate that it was Daniel McGillivray who became involved in the seizure and execution of John Catt for the murders at Murder Creek—originally called Aloochahatcha Creek—near modern Brewton, Alabama. Ibid., 79–81; Wright, *McGillivray and McIntosh*, 134–35.

full time to adopt measures for the general safety."*

About this time, a bloody transaction occurred in the territory of the present county of Conecuh. During the Revolutionary War, Colonel McGillivray formed an acquaintance with many conspicuous royalists, and, among others, with Colonel Kirkland, of South Carolina. That person was at McGillivray's house, upon the Coosa, in 1788, with his son, his nephew, and several other gentlemen. They were on their way to Pensacola, where they intended to procure passports, and settle in the Spanish province of Louisiana. When they determined to leave his hospitable abode, McGillivray sent his servant to guide them to Pensacola. The presence of this servant would assure the Indians that they were friends, for it was dangerous to travel without the chieftain's protection. Colonel Kirkland and his party had much silver in their saddle-bags.[12] Arriving within a mile of a large creek, which flows into the Conecuh, they met a pack-horse party, about sunset, going up to the nation. They had been to Pensacola, on a trading expedition. This party consisted of a Hillabee Indian, who had murdered so many men, that he was called Istillicha, the *Man-slayer*—a desperate white man, who had fled from the states for the crime of murder, and whom, on account of his activity and ferocity, the Indians called the *Catt*—and a blood-thirsty Negro, named Bob, the property of Sullivan, a Creek trader of the Hillabees.[13]

As soon as Colonel Kirkland and his party were out of sight, these scoundrels formed an encampment. The former went on, crossed the creek, and encamped a short distance from the ford, by the side of the trading path. Placing their saddle-bags under their heads, and reclining their guns against a tree, Kirkland and his party fell asleep. At midnight, the bloody wretches from the other side, cautiously came over, and, seizing the guns of Kirkland and his men, killed every one of them, except three Negroes, one of whom was the servant

* *American State Papers: Indian Affairs*, 1: 19–20.

of the great chieftain, as before stated.[14] Dividing the booty, the murderers proceeded to the Creek Nation, and, when the horrid affair became known, Colonel McGillivray sent persons in pursuit of them. Catt was arrested; but the others escaped. Milfort was directed to convey the scoundrel to the spot where he had shed the blood of these men, and there to hang him, until he was dead. Upon the journey to that point, Milfort kept him well pinioned, and, every night, secured his legs in temporary stocks, made by cutting notches in pine logs, and clamping them together. Reaching the creek where poor Kirkland and his men were murdered, Catt was suspended to the limb of a tree, the roots of which were still stained with the blood of the unfortunate colonel and his companions. While he was dangling in the air, and kicking in the last agonies, the Frenchman stopped his motions with a pistol ball.[15] Such is the origin of the name "MURDER CREEK."*

[15] According to Benjamin Hawkins's journal, Robert Walton, with Robert Grierson (also Graison or Grayson), Red Shoes, "and another Indian . . . carried him [John Catt] within 15 miles of Pensacola." When Governor Enrique White refused to act because the murders did not occur in Spanish Florida, Daniel McGillivray directed John Forbes and Louis Leclerc Milfort (Milford) to hear Catt's defense and if the "evidences of his guilt was sufficient and they should hang him." Afterwards, they returned with Catt "over the English line and hung him on the first convenient limb over the path." Hawkins, *Letters*, 80–81; Wright, *McGillivray and McIntosh*, 134–35; Louis LeClerc de Milford [Milfort], *Memoir or A Cursory Glance at My Different Travels & My Sojourn in the Creek Nation*, trans. and ed. Geraldine De Courcy and John Francis McDermott (Chicago: R. R. Donnelley & Sons Company, 1956), 108–09, 109 n. 112.

* Conversations with Lachlan Durant, and two old traders, named Abram Mordecai and James Moore.

Chapter XXI

THE DEEP INTRIGUES OF MCGILLIVRAY

Occasionally, the Spanish authorities at Pensacola and Mobile were guilty of consummate folly in imposing restrictions upon the Creeks, which frequently offended them, creating a prejudice, which it required the compromising spirit of Panton and the authority and ingenuity of McGillivray to remove. We will here introduce a letter of the chief, in relation to the Spanish outrages. It was written to Panton, and dated at Little Tallassee.[1]

"I had written to you, during the great hubbub at Pensacola, by Frank Leslie.[2] I gave, then, a sketch of my idea of the times. The sudden flight of Cornells and Walker ought not to surprise you. The cowardice of the former is proverbial, and Walker fled, being my servant. When Linder and the others were taken up, a little Irishman, living at Tensaw, was in Pensacola. He became frightened, ran out to Walker, and informed him that the governor, in very severe terms, threatened to seize him, understanding that he was recruiting men for my service. Upon which, says Cornells, 'I am his interpreter, therefore my chance to escape is small.' The idea of the mines operated so strongly upon their imaginations, that they precipitately fled.[3] This custom, of taking up traders ignorant of the language, laws and customs of Spain, upon frivolous reports, if persevered in, will have effects of the most pernicious tendency. You were lucky that the American stores were broken up by us, upon the Altamaha; or else, after paying you some part of their skins, the whole of the Lower Creeks and part of the Upper Towns would have, in future, gone to them for supplies, so greatly have the traders been alarmed by the late proceedings at Pensacola. If our friends, the Spaniards, knew how very delicate it was to awaken the suspicions and fears of my people, by harsh measures, they would use none in future. All the traders that have already gone to you, I was positively obliged to *drive down*, or you would not have seen one, for they would rather have gone to St. Marks or St. Johns. I hope all this is now subsided in Pensacola, for I am ashamed and sorry for it. I can see no reason

[1] McGillivray's letter to William Panton was dated at Little Tallassee (Tallase), 20 September 1788. By the same date, he wrote Governor Esteban Miró a long letter regarding efforts by American commissioners to negotiate a peace treaty and his support of the Cherokees to resist North Carolina's intrusions on their lands. Caughey, *McGillivray of the Creeks,* 199–202; Coker and Watson, *Indian Traders,* 113 n. 90.

[2] In July 1788, West Florida's Governor Arturo O'Neill had questioned a group of drunken Creeks and harassed and incarcerated several, including McGillivray's relatives and followers. He had decided to investigate the plans of Panton and McGillivray for the control and operation of the Indian trade, such as the possible closing of Panton's Pensacola store and the development of a free port to escape Spanish regulations. Coker and

for all this bustle.[4] If the Grand Turk, or any other power, chooses to make me a present, provided they are not at war with Spain, they cannot be reasonably offended with me for accepting it. We are a free people, and mean to continue so.

"Your letter of the 2nd runs in the same strain of advice as your others, advising and exhorting me to be guarded in treating with the Americans, and to reserve our trade wholly to Spain. Governor Miró has instructed me to the same purpose, and which I am fully resolved to do, that is, if I have power to offer and insist upon any stipulations, and so I have answered his Excellency. But I was apprehensive that our late royal orders (concerning our treaty with the Americans), now strictly operating, would embarrass our affairs, if not altogether frustrate our intentions, regarding trade: because, if I comprehend the order right, it is that I must treat of peace, and measures which I have found fault with, to enforce it. It must be, of course, allowed that every power to insist upon an article of that kind, or, indeed, any other, is wholly taken from me—for experience has proved that such matters are only to be attained by the longest fire and point of sword, particularly with the Americans. So, as our affairs now stand, I cannot see a chance of our resisting any conditions which they may choose to dictate to us, and we all can foresee these will be no means favorable to our present condition. In the meantime, I have thrown some obstacles in the way of the present treaty, and have written to Governor Miró, stating these matters in a strong point of view, which he mentions he has referred to the Captain-General Ezpeleta, of Havana.[5] The letter is dated 28th August, and sent by one Nolan, a genteel young Irishman, whom the governor desired me to forward to Cumberland, with some propositions towards a commercial treaty.[6]

"The present interregnum in the American government, and the commissioners putting off the treaty until the next spring, will afford us all time to look around us. Whitefield's letter will show you the dispositions of the Georgians.[7] The United States commissioners wanted the Assembly to co-operate, in a treaty of peace, and the House would not assemble. The Georgians proclaimed a truce of arms with us, on the 31st July. A Coweta Indian gave me, lately, a wretched, dirty and scandalous scrawl, on foul paper, which he found on a tree, near Flint River. It

Watson, *Indian Traders,* 107–113.

3 Joseph Cornells (also Cornell) served as an interpreter and messenger for Alexander McGillivray, and he later served as the official interpreter for the treaty negotiations in New York in August 1790. Abraham Walker served as McGillivray's overseer on his plantation. John Linder, Jr., owned a plantation on the Tensaw River and was killed by John Catt's party on Murder Creek. Caughey, *McGillivray of the Creeks,* 41, 68, 212, 278, 357; Wright, *McGillivray and McIntosh Traders,* 264, 266–67; Kappler, *Indian Affairs: Laws and Treaties,* 2: 29.

4 Without mentioning their names, McGillivray does not hesitate to express his anger to his business partner William Panton over the duplicity of Governor Arturo O'Neill and Vicente Folch, commandant at Mobile. Wright, *McGillivray and McIntosh Traders,* 224–26.

5 José Manuel de Ezpeleta (1739–1823) served as captain general of Cuba from 1785 to 1789, and he advocated that Spanish officials in West Florida should act "so as neither to displease the Indians nor exasperate the commissary [McGillivray]." Caughey, *McGillivray of the Creeks,* 62 n. 3, 209 n. 166.

6 Philip Nolan (1771–1801), a native of Belfast, Ireland, became noted as a horse trader, filibuster, and protégé of General James Wilkinson. He delivered a letter from Governor Miró to McGillivray in September 1788, and McGillivray provided him with a horse to deliver a commercial proposal to the Cumberland settlements. Ibid., 199–200, 199 n. 151, 226; "Philip Noland," *Dictionary of Louisiana Biography,* http://www.lahistory.org/site16.php.

7 George Whitefield, a South Carolina trader, delivered a letter on

proved to be a threatening talk to me and my savage subjects; that we (the Creeks) should have no establishment of peace until they (the Georgians) shall have full satisfaction of all their desires, etc. Signed, James Alexander, the 15th August. The chap that signs is Colonel Alexander, who murdered the Cussetas. He and Clarke sway Upper Georgia.[8]

"The impolicy of certain late measures, in tying us up, is evident. If we could have followed up our blows, those fellows, ere this time, would have been effectually humbled; but we have all our work to do over again.

"I observe, with much satisfaction, that the Governor and Intendant of New Orleans have relinquished their claim of one-fourth of the profits of your trade. Such a procedure is extremely generous, and, as for my part, I now repeat to you what I told you more than twelve months ago, when we were talking upon the subject of the trade. I then observed that my nation was much benefited by the honorable and liberal manner in which you supplied them with goods; that, as my attention was wholly occupied about my people, it could not be in my power to be of any essential service to your business: therefore I could not, and ought not, to claim or hold a share of your industry and risks. In the meantime, I am thankful for the generous credit of necessaries which you offered me, and if I conclude a peace with the Americans, which I expect to do, it will be in my power and ability to settle my account with you. These gentry will probably restore me my property now among them.

"Our Indian news is in the old strain. The Congress, on the one hand, pretends to hold out the white wing to all the Southern nations; on the other, the back settlers of North Carolina are overrunning the Cherokees, driving them into the woods, murdering women and children, as if they wished to extirpate these poor wretches. A party of my warriors lately went among the Cherokees, collected some of them from their hiding places, and attacked a body of the Franklin troops, that were laying all waste before them, and completely routed them. Only three Americans escaped. This is the first check they ever got in that country, and it has revived the drooping spirits of the Cherokees.[9]

"During our present suspense and half truce, I have encouraged a considerable party of the Upper Creek warriors to go to the assistance of these poor devils, for a few more checks will be of great

12 April 1788 from Andrew Pickens and George Mathews, commissioners for South Carolina and Georgia, who were seeking to bring about a peace between Georgia and the Creeks. Caughey, *McGillivray of the Creeks*, 175, 180–81, 184.

[8] James Alexander and Elijah Clarke had taken an aggressive stand against any compromise over the Oconee lands disputed by McGillivray and other Creek leaders, who refused to accept the cessions made at Augusta in 1783 and Galphinton in 1785, which were confirmed under duress at Shoulderbone Creek in 1786. In the spring of 1786, Alexander was implicated in an attack on a Cusseta hunting party and the death of six Cussetas. Ibid., 154, 171, 200–01.

[9] The illegal State of Franklin under John Sevier had basically declared war on the Cherokee Nation and pressured the Overhill Cherokee into signing the Treaty of Coyatee in 1787. Sevier's out of control militiamen killed Old Tassel, Old Abram, Fool Warrior, Long Fellow, Tassel's son, and two sub-chiefs under a white flag in June 1788. *CSRNC*, 22: 695–96, 718; Pate, "The Chickamauga," 182–83.

[10] Daniel McGillivray, a fluent speaker in Muskogean, became a trusted messenger and representative in trade and meetings with the Indians. He received a land grant in West Florida in 1773 and by 1775 worked with the trading company Miller and Swanson in Pensacola. He was either McGillivray's nephew or cousin. Caughey, *McGillivray of the Creeks*, 84, 84 n. 32, 100, 132, 361–62; Wright, *McGillivray and McIntosh Traders*, 131–35.

[11] Upon close scrutiny of

service to their affairs with the Americans. I have instructed Daniel McGillivray concerning the skins he carries down, of the Wewocoe store. This specimen of the troubles of trade has sickened me with it.[10]

"Farewell, my dear sir, may every good attend you.

"Yours most truly,

"ALEXANDER MCGILLIVRAY."

"To WILLIAM PANTON, Pensacola."

The perusal of this letter has revealed the motives of its author. McGillivray had offended the Spanish authorities, and this letter appears to have been written chiefly for their eyes. He affects, also, to be under great obligations to Panton, and of little service to him in their commercial connection, which he pretends to desire shall terminate. This was all done for the purpose of alarming Panton, whom he informs he hopes to be able to pay up, if he should make a favorable treaty with the Americans. The wily chieftain well knew that both Spain and this distinguished merchant would make *any* sacrifices, before they would permit him to be bought up by the Americans, and that his letter would go to extort from them further favors and emoluments.[11]

During the succeeding twelve months, the federal government seized upon every occasion to gain the friendship of McGillivray, and to put an end to the excitement in Georgia. Henry Osborne and Andrew Pickens were all the time upon the frontiers, representing the general government, and writing to McGillivray to meet them, with a delegation from the entire Creek Nation, at Rock Landing, upon the Oconee, to settle the serious matters in dispute. The chieftain at length arranged to meet them; but, just before the time of joining them, wrote the following letter to Panton, which he requested should *privately* be exhibited to the Spanish authorities:[12]

"LITTLE TALLASE, 10th August, 1789.

"*Dear Sir*:—There being no pack-horses going to Pensacola for a long time past, I have had no opportunity to answer your last letters. The bearer, on my promising him two kegs of taffai, has undertaken to convey these to you.

"Galphin, whom I sent to the Rock Landing with a talk, declining the treaty of June last, returned about a fortnight since, and I find that they are resolved upon making a treaty.[13] In order to accommodate us, the commissioners are complaisant enough to postpone it till the 15th of next month, and one of them, the late Chief Justice

McGillivray's correspondence, printed in John Walton Caughey's *McGillivray of the Creeks*, it is apparent that McGillivray was an astute politician and that his lack of transparency caused Miró, O'Neill, Folch, and others to employ spies and informants and to question his loyalty. While many of his actions directly benefitted his personal goals, his ultimate goal was to protect his Creek clan and their general welfare. See John Walton Caughey, *McGillivray of the Creeks* (Norman: University of Oklahoma Press, 1938), 61–353.

[12] Pickett's version of this letter—written in English in McGillivray's own hand—differs in content, sentence structure, and format from the same letter found in John Walton Caughey's *McGillivray of the Creeks*. In his footnotes, Pickett acknowledges that he received copies of McGillivray's letters dated 20 September 1788 and 10 August 1789 from Colonel John A. Campbell and Alfred Hennen, found in papers filed in a lawsuit in the District Court of Louisiana. Caughey's principal sources for McGillivray's correspondence were the Spanish repositories in Seville and Madrid. See John Walton Caughey, *McGillivray of the Creeks* (Norman: University of Oklahoma Press, 1938), 245–49, 365, and James Lamar Appleton and Robert David Ward, "Albert James Pickett and the Case of the Secret Articles: Historians and the Treaty of New York of 1790," *Alabama Review* 51 (January 1998): 16–17, 17 n. 24.

[13] McGillivray sent John Galphin, a métis Creek son of George Galphin, to Rock Landing on the Oconee with a response to the invitation he had received from Andrew Pickens and Henry Osborne, which

Osborne, remains all the time at Rock Landing. Pickens returned for the Cherokee treaty; but in this I took measures to disappoint him, for those chiefs would not meet.[14] In this do you not see my cause of triumph, in bringing these conquerors of the Old, and masters of the New World,[15] as they call themselves, to bend and supplicate for peace at the feet of a people whom, shortly before, they despised and marked out for destruction.*

"My people being all at home, and the grand ceremony of kindling the new fire being just over, I deem it the fittest time to meet these commissioners, and have accordingly made the broken days, of which nine are left, to set out in. In conducting the business of the treaty, I will, as you observe, confine it to the fixing of our limits and the acknowledgment of the independence of my nation. This I deem very necessary, as the Americans pretend to a territorial claim and sovereignty over us, in virtue of the late peace made with England. This being settled will, in a great measure, be doing away with any cause of future quarrel between us. You well know how customary it is, in all treaties with the Indians, to agree to a commercial one also, it being absolutely necessary, as it more firmly attaches them to friendships formed for, without stipulations of that sort, in a treaty of peace, none will be lasting. However, in this instance, I will agree to none, as you have a prospect of being able, by the favor of the Spanish government, to supply this trade on as moderate terms as the Georgians can do. Here let me observe to you, that, in the affair of trade, the Americans will push hard for it, and it will be for us the most difficult part of the negotiation. But I will risk the breaking of the conference before I will give in to it. On the whole, if I find that the commissioners insist upon stipulations that will, in their operation, clash with those already entered into with Spain, I shall not hesitate to cut short the negotiation, and support the connection which we have with Spain, it being more safe and respectable than the republicans can make one. But, at the same time, I must insist upon an equal resolution in our friends, the Spaniards, to afford us their decided support by every means in their power, and not, under any pretenses, to repeat their conduct of last summer, in the very moment of vigorous exertion, to refuse a further aid, and incense

* I can well imagine how McGillivray looked when he wrote this strong and eloquent sentence. At that moment he evidently felt his power, and his face must have been expressive of much pride, exultation and scorn.

requested a meeting on 15 September 1789 in an effort to establish a peace. In their letter of 30 June 1789 to President Washington regarding McGillivray's response, they referred to John Galphin as "a chief speaker of the lower Creeks." Caughey, *McGillivray of the Creeks*, 245; *ASP: IA*, 1: 34–38.

[14] Henry Osborne (1751–1800), a native of Ireland, served in the Georgia Assembly (1786–1788), as Georgia's chief justice (1787–1789), and as superior court judge for the Western District. He and Andrew Pickens served as U.S. commissioners for Indian affairs in the Southern District in the late 1780s. "Henry Osborne," *Biographical Directory of the United States Congress, 1774-Present* (online); Caughey, *McGillivray of the Creeks*, 245, 251, 263.

[15] Pickett seems to have blended McGillivray's letters to Miró and Panton, both dated 10 August 1789, but the letters cited here came from papers found in New Orleans that were written in English. This sentence is in McGillivray's letter to Miró but not in his letter to Panton as printed in John Walton Caughey's *McGillivray of the Creeks*. See Caughey, *McGillivray of the Creeks* (Norman: University of Oklahoma Press, 1938), 244–49.

[16] The Spaniards had withheld the delivery of guns and munitions to pressure McGillivray and the Creeks to stop their attacks on the American frontier settlements—especially in Georgia—and to seek a permanent peace. O'Neill and Folch had decided that McGillivray was not fully committed to his alliance with Spain and West Florida. Ibid., 191, 193–98, 206–07.

and menace us to make a peace, right or wrong, with the Americans, which, if we had done at the time, we should have been driven into hostility with Spain before this day. I repeat to you what I have frequently done to Governor Miró, that, if we are obliged, for want of support, to conclude an unconditional peace with the Americans, it will prove essentially hurtful to the King's interest.[16]

"The ammunition and arms, given us by the King, we have not yet been able to fetch away. It is a good store in hand, to make ourselves firm in treating with the Americans. But I am miserably disappointed in the guns. These, my people, who have ever been accustomed to the best English guns, find the greatest difficulty to use, being entirely unfitted either for the purposes of hunting or war. They may say they have no other; but I pointed out where they may be got, and, if our friends resolve to support us, they might do it with that which is good.[17]

"A chief of the Coosawdas, named Red Shoes, has lately returned from New Orleans, very well satisfied with the reception and treatment there, and has brought a very good talk with him, and I am equally satisfied that the western horizon is again cleared up, and looks fair, and so it will always continue, if the intention of adopting, as good Spaniards.[18] The restless American is entirely given up, I mean in our neighborhood, between us and the Choctaws. I have observed to Governor Miró, that the reasons he gave me for settling Americans on the west side of the Mississippi are founded in real political principles, and I truly wish it was in the compass of our power to drive them all from the Cumberland and Ohio, to seek the new asylum, so, being moved out of our way, our warriors would never follow them there. The Coosawda chief, Red Shoes, being disgusted with Captain Folch, of Fort "Tombecbé," resolved to go to Governor Miró, who satisfied him. Between you and I, believe me, that Folch is a madman.[19] If he had spoken to an assembly of the Creek chiefs, as he did to the Alabamas, challenged them to war, and exhibited to them his swivels, etc., he would have been directly taken at his word. He has been heard to declare that any person who would murder me should be protected in Spanish limits. I do not doubt his evil intention, as he has already given a specimen of it, in having assassins to murder a poor fellow, Lawrence, in the house of

[17] Miró had promised to deliver 1,200 high-quality English muskets, which was 300 less than McGillivray had requested. Miró even authorized Panton to trade for additional weapons with the British West Indies. However, by November 1789, the Creeks had only received half of the promised muskets. Coker and Watson, *Indian Traders,* 124; Caughey, *McGillivray of the Creeks,* 225, 235.

[18] While McGillivray had an uncle named Red Shoes who died around 1784, it is unclear about his relationship to Red Shoes chief of Coosada. On 22 June 1788, he sent a letter to O'Neill by a Red Shoes, who he identified as "brother of one of my Uncles." In 1793, Red Shoes of Coosada led a migration to the Red River in Louisiana and eventually to the Trinity River in Texas. Caughey, *McGillivray of the Creeks,* 62, 63, 66, 68, 72, 158, 185, 230, 240, 343, 351; Wright, *McGillivray and McIntosh Traders,* 185–86.

[19] In a copy of this letter found in John Walton Caughey's *McGillivray of the Creeks,* Folch was on the "Tombegbe," not at Fort Tombecbé, and "that "Folk [Folch] acts rashly," not "Folch is a madman." Caughey, *McGillivray of the Creeks,* 247.

my sister, Sehoy Weatherford.* Such men, in official stations, do great injury to their country, at one time or another.[20] This has been proved.

"My friend, the governor, is likewise possessed with the belief that all the damage done the settlers below is done by us; but it is wrong. The whole was a few horses and men taken, and my sister Durant took back the greater portion of these from the Coosawdas.[21] But, at present, the Choctaw is the favorite, and all the outrages which they commit are carefully turned upon us by their partisans. It is notorious that the Choctaws are discontented, and Indians never fail to manifest it, either in taking scalps or committing depredations, which last they do, for it is common for them to kill horses and cattle, etc., on "Tombecbé," and this summer even about Mobile. But all this is concealed from Governor Miró. Ben James, who is so much confided in, is privately an American agent, and has actually a commission, which he received from Georgia, to act with Davenport, and I know, could he be supported with any necessaries by the Americans, he would throw off the mask. He was even weak enough to address me for leave to open a trade with the States, which I refused him, as well as his application.[22] As a proof of my assertions respecting the Choctaws, Folch sent them a talk this summer, menacing them with a stoppage of their trade, until they made satisfaction. I am ever ready to make allowances for a momentary impression, caused by false reports; but it would be better that they were more guarded against, and not made the grounds of making differences, which might produce a serious effect. The late menaces which were thrown out to me created no great anxiety in my mind, because I could have directly opened the eastern door, where large magazines of goods, etc., have been stored, for some time past, awaiting it to be opened, but, for peace and quietness sake, I hope that there will be no occasion now for it—as everything is fallen into a calm, so let it remain; and all that I have said or done was solely to discover and show the means to prevent it, I hope forever, between us.

"The Chickasaw Nation are content (whatever Diego Mingo may say

* Lawrence was killed in the house of Sehoy Weatherford, then situated upon the spot where Colonel Charles Hooks formerly lived, and which is now owned by Maurice Connolly. In those days, a man and his wife seldom lived in the same house. The husband, Charles Weatherford, lived at his racetrack, a few miles above, on the Alabama. Lawrence and others were accused of stealing horses from the Spaniards, near Mobile, and Captain Folch sent some equally bad men in pursuit of them. The accused took refuge in Sehoy Weatherford's house. It was surrounded, and Lawrence was killed in the middle of the floor. The others escaped. It is this circumstance to which McGillivray alludes. I derived these facts from Lachlan Durant, who was at the house of his aunt Weatherford when Lawrence was killed. Durant was then a boy.

[20] In an exchange of letters—22 May and 14 June 1789—printed in John Walton Caughey's *McGillivray of the Creeks,* McGillivray and Folch refer to the "Murder" or "death of Laurence" and both identify "Dyer and Johnson" as the other parties involved in his demise. Online genealogy sources citing Spanish records link John Lawrence and Thomas Betts together as horse thieves who also stole slaves in Georgia and in the Tensaw District. Ibid., 231, 237. See Jennifer Mieirs, "attempting to connect the dots," www.genealogy.com.

[21] McGillivray's sister Sophia married Benjamin Durant at Tallassee in 1779. They lived on one of Lachlan McGillivray's plantations until they were confiscated by the state of Georgia in 1782. Wright, *McGillivray and McIntosh Traders,* 206–07.

[22] William Davenport, Benjamin James, and others had been involved in the abortive attempt by Georgia to organize the Natchez District of Spanish West Florida as Bourbon County, Georgia, in February 1785. Although McGillivray never fully trusted James, William Panton recommended him to Governor Barón de Carondelet as Spanish agent to the Choctaws in 1792. Ironically, at the same time James was providing information

to the contrary), to put up with the loss of that chap's brother and son, for having fallen in bad company.[23] This will be a warning, and convince them that they will not be permitted, with impunity, to act or encourage hostile designs against us, in concert with any people.

"Now, let me talk a little upon my private affairs. I wish I could lay my hand on that last letter, to send you, and a very curious, and, to you, not an uninteresting Carolina newspaper, just received; but they are both swallowed up in a multitude of papers. You know how it is with me, in the paper way. The commissioners of the United States say it would give them great pleasure to have a private conversation, previous to our entering into the business of the treaty, as it would tend to make it go on agreeably, and with more ease. I need not interpret this paragraph to you, when you already know that I have, for some time past, been endeavoring to recover my house and lands, with my family estate, which, to your knowledge, is more than £30,000 sterling, the offer of which is now, I expect, to be pressed upon me. And there has, since I saw you last, arisen considerable conflict in my mind, in resolving these matters over. Here am I, an absolute heavy tax upon you, for years, and, in fact, not only for my private support, but for all the extra expenses of this department; and although, my dear sir, I know that I can still depend upon your generosity, and in your friendship, that you overlook the heavy expense that I put you to, yet you well know how hurtful it is to the feeling heart, to be beholden to subsist on the bounty of private friendship. Thus situated, I ask—I wish you to give me your opinion. On the one hand, I am offered the restoration of my property, of more than one hundred thousand dollars, at the least valuation; and on the other, not wherewithal to pay an interpreter. And I find that letters are still addressed to me, as agent for His Catholic Majesty, when I have some time ago renounced the pittance that was allowed, as being a consideration disgraceful to my station. If they want my services, why is not a regular establishment made, as was done by the English, with a competent salary affixed, and allowance for two interpreters, one among the Upper and one among the Lower Towns, for hitherto I have had to maintain them myself; or shall I have recourse to my American estate, to maintain them and myself? I wish you to advise me what I had best do.[24]

"Although I have no solid ground to hope a complete adjustment of our dispute with the Americans, I am resolved to go, if it is only to wipe off the suggestion made to me by our friends, that I am actuated by unjust motives and an unreasonable prejudice against the Americans, as the ground of hostility against them. But if they, on the other hand, should find a body of people approaching their mines, would not they say, what business have

to William Blount, governor of the territory south of the Ohio River. Caughey, *McGillivray of the Creeks*, 169, 247, 343; Coker and Watson, *Indian Traders*, 77, 83, 85, 167–68.

[23] In another version of this letter printed in John Walton Caughey's *McGillivray of the Creeks*, the Chickasaw war chief Piomingo is identified as "pio Mingo," versus "Diego Mingo" in Pickett's copy of the letter. Caughey, *McGillivray of the Creeks*, 248.

[24] McGillivray had not forgotten O'Neill's accusations of duplicity and the insulting actions and rhetoric of Folch, which had caused him to resign his commission as commissary and Spanish agent in a letter to Miró on 20 August 1788. The Treaty of New York gave him the leverage to force the Spanish to raise his "pension" of "2000 pesos annually, by 1500 pesos" during his meeting with Governor Barón de Carondelet in New Orleans in July 1792. Ibid., 195–96

you here? Do not you know that there are grounds from which we draw the chief source of our conveniences and happiness, and we cannot suffer you to participate in, or deprive us of them; and these encroachers should refuse to withdraw, would they not commence and support an inveterate hostility, until they should expel them?

"The fellow, Romain, whom Madame Villar writes of, was a great liar. He came here from the Choctaws, with a quantity of silverware and a few goods, and wanted Nick White to join him in purchasing Negroes, to carry and sell in New Orleans. After roving about for some time, he had a difference with Milfort,* who threatened to send him, in irons, to New Orleans, which terrified him, apparently, and he went off to the Creek town, Chehaw, and, from thence, either to Detroit or to the States.[25]

"A copy of this letter you can send to the **** Miró, as I intended the former one.

"I expect our treaty will be over by the middle of September. If we return safe, expect a visit early in October, from

"Dear Sir, yours, most truly,

"ALEXANDER MCGILLIVRAY."

"To WILLIAM PANTON, Pensacola."

William Panton was under great obligations to McGillivray, for the power of the chieftain had enriched him beyond measure. He now had large trading establishments at all the prominent posts of Florida. His chief store was at Pensacola. It usually contained a stock of goods to the value of fifty thousand dollars, and he employed fifteen clerks to attend to it. Here he had extensive "skin-houses," where his valuable skins and rich furs were assorted, and packed up, for foreign markets. Besides his stores at St. Johns, St. Marks, St. Augustine, Pensacola and Mobile, he had trading establishments at the Chickasaw Bluff, upon the Mississippi. It is said that fifteen schooners, owned by himself, were constantly employed by him, in his business. How alarming to him, then, was the preceding letter of McGillivray, and how anxious was he that no treaty should be made with the Americans that would affect his extensive commerce. McGillivray, on the other hand, was in a situation the most favorable to obtain honors and emoluments, and he could well threaten the Spaniards with "opening the eastern door"—the Americans with support from the king of Spain—and alarm Panton with the idea of a new commercial treaty. This able and ingenious Indian, Scotchman or Frenchman, (for who can tell which blood most influenced his disposition), kept Panton, Spain and the

* The French officer who lived so long in the nation.

[25] According to Benjamin Hawkins, Nicholas White was "a native of Marseilles" and a trader in the Creek Nation for thirty years, mainly at Fusihatchee. Much less is known about the Choctaw trader "Romain" or McGillivray's Madame Villar in Pickett's letter (Vallin elsewhere). Hawkins, *Letters,* 168; Caughey, *McGillivray of the Creeks,* 249.

[26] Despite Pickett's narrative about William Panton's fears of McGillivray's turning to the Americans, Panton's wealth and business success did not depend entirely on the trade with the Creek Nation. Panton, Leslie and Company owned 72,820 acres of land in East Florida before the Pensacola store was fully operational in 1785–1786. Panton's business survived the Treaty of New York, McGillivray's death in 1793, and the Treaty of San Lorenzo el Real in 1795. Prior to his death in 1801, his company controlled most of the Chickasaw and Choctaw trade and one-third of the Creek trade. Coker and Watson, *Indian Traders,* 36, 198–202, 250.

[27] On 29 August 1789, George Washington appointed David Humphreys, Benjamin Lincoln, and Cyrus Griffin "to negotiate and establish peace between the State of Georgia and the Creek nation."

United States in a state of feverish excitement, while Georgia was horribly harassed, and made to feel his malignant resentments, for the banishment of his father and the confiscation of his patrimony.[26]

Washington was now president. He associated with General Pickens, David Humphreys, Cyrus Griffin and Benjamin Lincoln, as commissioners, to treat with McGillivray. These three gentlemen, sailing from New York, arrived at Savannah, with abundant provisions to feed the Indians, while at the treaty ground.[27] In a few days, they reached Rock Landing, upon the Oconee, where McGillivray, at the head of two thousand warriors, had been encamped for more than a week, on the western bank of the river. The commissioners pitched their camp on the eastern bank. The first two days were spent in private conferences with McGillivray, much to the satisfaction of the commissioners, for they were treated by him with great courtesy and politeness. The latter also visited most of the chiefs, who all appeared friendly, and glad to make their acquaintance. The commissioners crossed the river, to the western side, and, after partaking of the black drink, were conducted, by the chiefs, with great pomp and ceremony, to the place of council. One of them made a speech to the Indians, promising much liberality on the part of the United States, which was well received. Impressed with the favorable turn of things, as they supposed, they immediately read to the chiefs a copy of the treaty, which they had drawn up. It stipulated that the boundary made at Augusta, Shoulderbone and Galphinton should remain; that the United States would guarantee the territory, west of that boundary, forever to the Creeks; that a free trade should be established with the Indians, from ports upon the Altamaha, through which the Indians could import and export, upon the same terms as the citizens of the United States. That all Negroes, horses, goods and American citizens, taken by the Indians, should be restored.[28]

The commissioners then retired to their encampments, and that night McGillivray and his chiefs went into a grand private council. The next morning the chieftain informed the commissioners, by letter, that the terms they proposed were not satisfactory, and that the Indians had resolved to break up and go home. He promised to meet them again at some future time, and to keep his warriors from acts of hostility during the ensuing winter.[29] The commissioners were astounded, for they had imagined that everything was in a proper train. But the terms they proposed were unaccompanied with a solitary equivalent, and exhibited an extremely niggardly spirit, from which the high-minded Andrew Pickens wholly dissented. He knew that a treaty could not be made without liberal compensation for the valuable lands which the Georgians were then cultivating. The federal powers also knew this, and

While Griffin had served as president of the Confederation Congress, Lincoln had been one of Washington's most trusted generals. Humphreys served as aide-de-camp to Washington during the Revolutionary War and as secretary to the American delegation in London and Paris in 1784–1786. *ASP: IA*, 1: 65–68; Caughey, *McGillivray of the Creeks*, 252 n. 224.

[28] On the morning of 24 May 1789, Benjamin Lincoln addressed the "Kings, Head-Men, and Warriors of the Creek Nation," offering them peace and telling them that "justice shall be done to the nations of Indians," "it will be more natural for you to be allied with us," and "a secure port in our country will be much more convenient for you than a port in any other country." After his speech, the commissioners presented a draft of a proposed treaty that protected Georgia's territorial claims to the disputed Creek lands. *ASP: IA*, 1: 73–74; Caughey, *McGillivray of the Creeks*, 251–52.

[29] McGillivray sent a brief note to the commissioners on the morning of 25 September 1789 stating his chiefs were unhappy with the "boundary marked out in the talk" and "they resolve to break up to depart; it would be proper to give some presents, that

had instructed the commissioners to pay the Creeks a fair equivalent for this territory. They now sought every means to induce McGillivray to remain, and begged him to state his grounds of objection to the draft of the treaty.[30] But he broke up his encampment and retreated to the Ocmulgee, from which place he addressed the commissioners the following letter:

"Ocmulgee River, 27th Sept., 1789.

"*Gentlemen*:—I am favored with your letter of yesterday, by Weatherford. I beg to assure you that my retreat from my former camp, on the Oconee, was entirely owing to the want of food for our horses, and at the earnest entreaty of our chiefs. Colonel Humphreys and myself, at different interviews, entered deeply and minutely into the subject of the contest between our nation and the State of Georgia. I observed to him that I expected ample and full justice should be given us in restoring to us the encroachments we complained of, in which the Oconee lands are included; but, finding that there was no such intention, and that a restitution of territory and hunting grounds was not to be the basis of a treaty between us, I resolved to return to the nation, deferring the matter, in full peace, till next spring. Many of the principals have gone hunting—nothing further can be done. I am very unwell, and cannot return. We sincerely desire a peace, but cannot sacrifice much to obtain it. As for a statement of our disputes, the honorable Congress has long since been in possession of, and has declared that they will decide on them on the principles of justice and humanity.[31] 'Tis that we expect.

"I have the honor to be, etc.,

"Alexander McGillivray.

To the Hon. Commissioners, Rock Landing."

The commissioners repaired to Augusta with their fingers in their mouths. They drew up a series of questions for Governor Walton, of Georgia, who answered them. He stated that the lands between the mountains and the old Ogeechee line, north of the Oconee, were equally the property of the Creeks and Cherokees; that, before the Revolution, the lands in the territory of Wilkes County were ceded by these tribes to Georgia; that, during the war, the province had been attacked by these Indians, and, at the close of it, they were respectively called upon to make some satisfaction; that, in the spring of 1783, the Cherokees came to Augusta and signed a treaty, and the Lower Creeks came, in the autumn, and performed the same act, thus ceding to Georgia their respective rights to lands specified in these treaties. These treaties were

they may not complain of losing their time." *ASP: IA*, 1: 74.

30 Andrew Pickens attended the Rock Landing conference as a representative of Georgia, but McGillivray respected him and considered him "a worthy moderate man." Pickens, "Cols. Few & Sanders," and Hollowing King overtook McGillivray at Ocmulgee: "We had a long conversation, but I would not consent to return to Rock Landing, without they would pledge themselves that the Commissioners would consent to treat as we wanted on equal terms." Caughey, *McGillivray of the Creeks*, 253.

31 After the commissioners received McGillivray's letter announcing he was departing on 25 September 1789, David Humphreys met with McGillivray "to argue me out of my objections" and continued to pursue his arguments for another two days using the "arts of flattery, ambition, and intimidation." In his letter to William Panton on 8 May 1790, McGillivray referred to Humphreys as "that puppy Humphries." Ibid., 39, 253, 260; *ASP: IA*, 1: 75.

32 George Walton (c. 1749–1804), a signer of the Declaration of Independence, served in the Revolutionary War; as chief justice of Georgia; two terms as governor (1779–1780; 1789–1790); and as a U.S. senator (1795–1796). "George Walton," *Biographical Directory of the United States Congress, 1774-Present* (online); *ASP: IA*, 1: 76–77.

laid before the legislature. These lands were surveyed, sold, settled and cultivated in peace; that the Indians made these cessions voluntarily, and received presents, in return, of value, and that, at the treaty of Galphinton, no unworthy use was made of the force which was sent upon the ground.[32] Governor Walton appended to this statement, a list of the Georgians who had been killed, and of the property stolen, during the recent hostilities, which was alarming in magnitude.*

The first impulse of President Washington, upon the return of the commissioners to New York, was to wage a war of invasion against the Creeks and compel them to make a peace, and relinquish the Oconee lands. He was influenced to this course, against his judgment, by the urgent demands of the Georgia delegation in Congress. But when he found, from an estimate, that the expenses of the war would amount to fifteen millions of dollars, he abandoned the project, believing that the general government could not sustain such an expense, while it was still struggling with that incurred by a long war with England. He believed that the difficulties could yet be settled by negotiation, if he could once get Colonel McGillivray into his presence.[33] Colonel Marinus Willett, a native of Long Island, New York, and a distinguished officer in the Canadian war, and the American Revolution, was selected by Washington, as a secret agent, to visit the Creek Nation, by a circuitous route, and to endeavor to return, with McGillivray, to the seat of the federal government.[34] He was strictly enjoined to keep his mission a profound secret from every one, except General Pickens, to whom he bore a letter. Colonel Willett sailed from New York, with a servant and two horses, and, after a passage of fourteen days, arrived in Charleston. Leaving this place, he had not proceeded far, before the servant, manifesting much fear, was ordered back to New York, while a German, of doubtful character, supplied his place. Colonel Willett reached the residence of General Andrew Pickens, on the Seneca River. General Pickens was a gentleman who had been engaged extensively, as we have already seen, in negotiations with the Indians, and one in whom Washington reposed great confidence. Obtaining from General Pickens an Indian guide for the Cherokee country, and purchasing two additional horses, he set out, to complete his lonely and difficult mission, after having enjoyed, for several days, the hospitality and kindness of that distinguished Revolutionary character.[35]

* *American State Papers: Indian Affairs*, 1: 65–78.

[33] Despite intensive pressure from Georgia, and contrary to Pickett's narrative, President Washington had little interest in launching a war against the Creeks, and Secretary of War Henry Knox expressed the same sentiment in his letter to Washington on 15 February 1790: "The serious crises of affairs . . . with the Creeks requires that every honorable and probable expedient that can be devised should be used to avert a war with that tribe." Henry Knox to George Washington, War Office, 15 February 1790, http://founders.archives.gov/documents.

[34] George Washington met with Marinus Willett (1740–1830) and impressed upon him the importance of his mission to the Creek Nation, getting their chiefs and McGillivray to come to New York, and conveying the message from Senator Benjamin Hawkins warning of the dire consequences of an open rupture with the United States. Willett received passports from Washington for McGillivray and the principal chiefs if they agreed to seek a peace in New York, and he received written instructions from Secretary of War Knox regarding the principal points to be negotiated. Ibid.; George Washington to Henry Knox, [New York], 8 March 1790, http://founders.archives.gov/documents.

[35] Pickens not only hosted Willett for several days, but he also hired Young Corn, a Cherokee, to guide him on his circuitous route to the Creek Nation. Young Corn led him through the Cherokee country, but Willett

Pursuing his journey leisurely, the Cherokee town of Santee, containing eighteen houses, and surrounded by mountains, was first reached. The route lay through Little Chota, and the town of Huntoweekee, which embraced both sides of a branch of the Coosa, and contained about fifty houses.[36] Along the banks of the Etowah, Colonel Willett entered Neueconoheta, or Long Swamp, where he met Mr. Thomas Gogg, to whom he bore a letter from General Pickens.[37] This gentleman accompanied him to Pine Log, where he had long resided, as a trader among the Cherokees, and introduced him to Yellow Bird, the chief, who not only received him with unaffected hospitality, but invited him to witness the novel and exciting game of the ball play.[38] On the banks of the river, they reached Euestenaree, a city of refuge, to which the guilty were wont to fly and be safe from punishment. No blood could be shed within the bounds of its sacred corporation.[39] Here resided two Indian chiefs, Badger and Jobberson, who gave him a warm reception, induced by the letters of General Pickens. The next morning, Jobberson and the interpreter, Mr. Carey, having agreed to accompany him to the Creek Nation, the party all proceeded to Hihotee, the last of the Cherokee towns in this direction, crossed the Etowah in a canoe, swam the horses, and ascended the Pumpkin Posk Mountain, which is nearly a day's travel from the river.[40]

The wealthy Mr. Scott, a European, who had long been a trader in the nation, resided in the first Creek settlement, which they now entered.[41] Here, learning that McGillivray was then on a visit to Okfuskee, on the Tallapoosa River, Colonel Willett determined to join him at that place. Since he had left the borders

recorded he "lagged behind the day [1 May 1790] on which I arrived at the Killebees [Hillabees] and I have heard nothing from him since." Willett had problems spelling and translating place names. William Marinus Willett, *A Narrative of the Military Actions of Colonel Marinus Willett: Taken Chiefly From His Own Manuscript* (New York: G. & C. H. Carvill, 1831), 103.

[36] On 22 April 1790, Willet reached Huntoweekee, a town not found on any historical maps. While he described it as a new town with fifty houses on each side of the Coosa River, the town had to be located on the Etowah River or a tributary, because the Coosa River is not located in that area of Georgia. Willett, *Narrative of the Military Actions of Colonel Marinus Willett*, 98.

[37] Neueconoheta (*Long Swamp*) was located on the west side of Long Swamp Creek near its juncture with the Etowah River in northeast Pickens County, Georgia. John H. Goff, *Placenames of Georgia: Essays of John H. Goff*, ed. Frances Lee Utley and Marion R. Hemperly (Athens: University of Georgia Press, 1975), 105.

[38] Thomas Gogg (also Gagg) was a long time Indian countryman and trader at Pine Log, and Benjamin Hawkins wrote on 30 November 1796: "I lodged in the house of Mrs. Gagg" at Pine Log. Yellow Bird or Chesecotetona signed the 1785 Treaty of Hopewell. Ibid., 252; Hawkins, *Letters*, 20; Kappler, *Indian Affairs: Laws and Treaties*, 2: 11.

[39] Willett apparently turned northwest to reach the village of Euestenaree on 24 April 1790, which would have put him near modern Calhoun, Georgia, and near the Coosawattee River, not the Coosa. Euestenaree does not appear on any of the historic maps or lists of Cherokee towns. Willett may have encountered Badger and Jobberson (also Jobber's Son) at Ustanali or Oostanaula. Willett, *Narrative of the Military Actions of Colonel Marinus Willett*, 99.

[40] James Carey (c. 1770–1845) was appointed by President Washington as an official interpreter for the Cherokee. Willett's Hihotee was probably Etowah, near modern Hightower, Georgia. Willett's Pumpkin Posk Mountain was probably Dugdown Mountain, which is cut by Pumpkin Pile Creek—both near Cedartown, Polk County, Georgia. *ASP: IA*, 1: 245, 327–29, 436–39.

[41] Thomas Scott, a Scotsman, came into the Upper Creek towns as a trader around 1775 and may have worked at Robert Grierson's trading post at Hillabee. Don C. East, *A Historical Analysis of the Creek Indian Hillabee Towns: and Personal Reflections on the Landscape and People of*

of South Carolina, more than ten days had been consumed in his solitary march, over a wilderness country, which was the constant scene of murder and robbery. The expenses of the expedition, chiefly for provender, were paid for in ribbons and paints. At the house of Mr. Graison, in the Hillabees, the secret agent had the good fortune to meet Colonel McGillivray.[42] He describes him as a "man of an open, generous mind, with a good judgment and very tenacious memory." Delivering the important letter of General Washington, two days were passed in conversation with this distinguished Indian personage, and here Colonel Willett, for the first time, witnessed the religious ceremony of the black drink. The party, accompanied by Colonel McGillivray and his servant, took leave of the hospitable mansion of Graison, and, after ten miles travel, approached the Fish Pond Town, where, in the evening, they were honored with a dance by the inhabitants. They soon arrived at the Hickory Ground, a large town, and one of the residences of Colonel McGillivray.[43] Here, it was understood that the Indians of Coosawda were engaged in a grand busking for mulberries.

It was not long before Colonel McGillivray sent out ten broken days, for the chiefs of the Lower Towns to meet at Ositchy, to consult on public business; and, during this time, Colonel Willett amused himself in riding about the vicinity.[44] He visited the old French fort, "Toulouse," the remains of which were scarcely visible. He tarried several days at Little Tallassee, the birthplace of McGillivray, which was also called the "Apple Grove," situated on the east bank of the Coosa, five miles above the Hickory Ground, a most delightful and well-improved place. Here he fared sumptuously on fish, venison, strawberries and mulberries.[45] On the 12th May, the agent and McGillivray, with their servants, set out eastwardly, and arrived at the great town of Tuckabatchee at four o'clock, in

Clay County, Alabama (New York: iUniverse, Inc., 2008), 88.

[42] Robert Grierson, Willett's Graison (also Grayson), became involved in the Upper Creek trade at Hillabee in 1775. When Benjamin Hawkins visited the Scotsman's home in December 1796, he had a successful farming operation that produced cotton, and he owned forty slaves, three hundred cattle, and thirty horses. Ibid., 87–91, 93; Hawkins, _Letters_, 29–32.

[43] Hickory Ground, known as Otciapofa to the Creeks, was located "one mile below the falls of the Coosa." Hawkins, "Sketch of the Creek Country," 39–40.

[44] Willett's Ositchy, Bartram's Hooseche, and McGillivray's Oussitche was located on the west bank of the Chattahoochee River, in Russell County, Alabama. Other sources and modern scholars more commonly refer to the town as Ooseoochee. Bartram, _William Bartram on the Southeastern Indians_, 109; Caughey, _McGillivray of the Creeks_, 108, 125, 148; Ethridge, _Creek Country_, 50, 55, 62; _ASP: IA_, 2: 852.

[45] Little Tallassee (Tallase) was located three miles above the falls of the Coosa River and several miles above modern Wetumpka, Alabama. Lachlan McGillivray referred to his settlement as "Weetomkee Old Town," but it became more commonly known as Little Tallassee. The old French Fort Toulouse was located about nine miles from the town. Cashin, _Lachlan McGillivray_, 59; Swanton, _Early History of the Creeks_, 242.

the evening, and passed the night with Mr. Cornells, the interpreter.[46] Crossing the Tallapoosa, in company with their host, they went by the house of the Tallassee King, and saw a Scotchman, named James McQueen, who had been a trader for sixty years, in the nation.[47] The next day, they passed the residence of the Hollowing King, and reached Coweta, upon the Chattahoochee River, where Mr. Durouzeau, the interpreter, sheltered them for the night.[48] Many of this numerous population were engaged in drinking taffai, and the night was spent in much noise and carousal. Passing down to Ositchy the next morning, these distinguished gentlemen remained there, awaiting the arrival of the chiefs, when, at 11 o'clock a.m., Colonel Willett, the secret agent, delivered to the assembled wisdom of the Creek confederacy an address, the substance of which was, that he had been sent an immense distance, by our great chief, George Washington, to invite them to his council-house, at New York, where he, with his own hand, wished to sign, with Colonel McGillivray, a treaty of peace and alliance. He stated to them that the United States wanted none of their lands, and that Washington would take effectual measures to secure their territory to them, according to the treaty which he and Colonel McGillivray would conclude; that the president was ready to promote their trade, by affording them means to procure goods in a cheap and easy manner, and intended to perform other acts, which would promote the welfare and happiness of the Creek Nation. Colonel Willett concluded his speech by earnestly inviting them to embrace these terms, and to select such chiefs as they chose to accompany Colonel McGillivray to the great council-house of New York, where Washington would make a treaty with their great chief, "as strong as the hills and lasting as the rivers."

Retiring for an hour from the vast assembly, whom he left to deliberate upon his overtures, Colonel Willett was again called in, when he received the following speech, from the Hollowing King, a fine looking man and great orator:[49]

"We are glad to see you. You have come a great way, and, as soon as we fixed our eyes upon you, we were made glad. We are poor, and have not the knowledge of the white people. We were invited to the treaty at the Rock Landing. We went there. Nothing was done. We were disappointed, and came back with sorrow. The road to your great council-house is long, and the weather is hot; but our beloved chief shall go with you, and such others as we may appoint. We will agree to all things which our beloved chief shall do. We will count the time

[46] Alexander Cornells (also Oche Haujo), a métis Creek, worked closely with Benjamin Hawkins as an interpreter. He lived on his farm on the Tallapoosa River below Tuckabatchee. Caughey, *McGillivray of the Creeks*, 357; Ethridge, *Creek Country*, 16, 79, 189, 207.

[47] McGillivray uses both Tallassee King and Tame King (Hopoithle Mico) in his correspondence, accusing him of being pro-American and creating confusion. According to several sources, James McQueen, a Scots trader, had lived among the Creeks since 1716. Caughey, *McGillivray of the Creeks*, 133, 136, 139–40, 197, 214; Woodward, *Reminiscences*, 10, 16, 95.

[48] Hollowing King was the chief of Coweta. In a letter to Governor Arturo O'Neill of 8 October 1786, McGillivray referred to him as "a brave good chief & His towns are determined enemies to the Americans." James Durouzeaux (Dourouzeaux) served as an interpreter for the Lower Creeks and lived at Coweta. Caughey, *McGillivray of the Creeks*, 123, 134, 308, 347; *ASP: IA*, 1: 23; Kinnaird, *Spain in the Mississippi Valley*, 3: 146–47, 163, 200.

[49] Although he quotes liberally from Willett's journal, Pickett cites only part of the speech made by the Hollowing King as recorded by Willett and he also changed its structure. Willett, *Narrative of the Military Actions of Colonel Marinus Willett*, 106–07.

he is away, and, when he comes back, we shall be glad to see him, with a treaty that shall be 'as strong as the hills and lasting as the rivers.' May you be preserved from every evil."

Having negotiated this business, to the mutual satisfaction of himself and the warrior, Colonel Willett returned to Coweta that evening, and the next morning assumed the retrograde march for Tuckabatchee, where he arrived on the 21st, partook of the ceremony of the black drink, and received a speech from the venerable White Lieutenant, as the voice of the Upper Creeks, breathing sentiments similar to those delivered at Ositchy.[50] Late in the evening of the next day, McGillivray and the agent arrived at the Hickory Ground. From this place Colonel Willett dispatched a letter to the secretary of war, by the hands of Mr. Carey, the Cherokee interpreter.

Finally, Colonel McGillivray, with his nephew and two servants, accompanied by the secret agent, set out from Little Tallassee for New York. They were all mounted on horseback, and accompanied by several pack-horses. Taking a northeastern direction through the wilderness, they arrived at the Stone Mountain, in the present state of Georgia, and were there joined by the Coweta and Cusseta chiefs. Reaching the house of General Pickens, the party received the warmest welcome, and, after being joined by the Tallassee King, Chinnabee, the "great Natchez warrior," and other chiefs, the expedition again set out, with three wagons, in which rode twenty-six warriors, while four were on horseback. Colonel McGillivray and suit were mounted on horses, and the agent rode in a sulky. At Guildford Court House, North Carolina, a truly affecting scene occurred. Some years before this, the Creeks had killed a man, named Brown, and captured his wife and children, whom they brought to the nation. Colonel McGillivray, moved at their unfortunate situation, redeemed them from slavery, by paying the price of their ransom, as he had done many others, and maintained them at his house over a year. Mrs. Brown, hearing of the arrival of Colonel McGillivray, rushed through the large assembly at the courthouse, and, with a flood of tears, almost overpowered him with expressions of admiration of his character, and gratitude for his preservation of her life, and that of her children, while alone in a land of savages.[51] The party passed through Richmond and Fredericksburg, where they were treated with much kindness, while Colonel McGillivray was received by the most prominent citizens with distinguished consideration.

Arriving at Philadelphia, Colonel Willett and his party were there

[50] White Lieutenant, the métis chief of Okfuskee, supported McGillivray but expressed a low opinion of Louis Leclerc Milfort as a "nobody" with a heart and tongue that was "not straight." Although James Seagrove, an American agent to the Creeks, made some inroads with the Upper Creeks, the White Lieutenant declared his loyalty to Spain as late as November 1793. Caughey, *McGillivray of the Creeks,* 132, 360–62; Kinnaird, *Spain in the Mississippi Valley,* 3: 375–77; Carolyn Thomas Foreman, "The White Lieutenant and Some of His Contemporaries," *Chronicles of Oklahoma* 38 (Winter 1960): 425–440.

[51] Jane Brown wrote to McGillivray from the Cumberland settlements on 4 June 1792 to let him know she had settled there with four of her children. She expressed her "many obligations . . . for the many kindnesses you have done for me." In a postscript to her letter, she asked McGillivray to write her on the prospects of her son being returned to her. There is no response in McGillivray's printed letters. Caughey, *McGillivray of the Creeks,* 325.

[52] Secretary of War Henry Knox dispatched two letters regarding the Creek delegation: one on 3 July 1790 to Thomas Mifflin, governor of Pennsylvania, and a second on 15 July to Marinus Willett. In his letter to Mifflin, Knox expressed President Washington's wishes that McGillivray and his chiefs "experience every proper civility and kindness." In the second letter to Willett, Knox

entertained, for three days, in a manner which could not fail to please.[52] Entering a sloop at Elizabethtown Point, they landed in New York, where the Tammany Society, in the full dress of their order, received them in splendor, marched them up Wall Street, by the Federal Hall, where Congress was then in session, and next, to the house of the president, to whom they were introduced with much pomp and ceremony.[53] Then, visiting the minister of war, and Governor Clinton, a sumptuous and elegant entertainment, at the City Tavern, finished the day.*

When it became known that McGillivray had departed for New York, great excitement arose in Florida and Louisiana. A correspondence began with the captain-general at Havana, and ending by his dispatching, from East Florida, an agent with a large sum of money, to New York, ostensibly to buy flour, but really to embarrass the negotiations with the Creeks. Washington, apprised of the presence of this officer, had his movements so closely observed, that the object of his mission was defeated.[54]

Washington, communicating with the Senate, advised that the negotiations with McGillivray should be conducted informally, as all the overtures hitherto offered by the commissioners had been rejected. Embarrassments existed, because the commerce of the Creeks was in the hands of a British company, who made their importations from England, into Spanish ports. It was necessary that it should be diverted into American channels; but McGillivray's treaty, at Pensacola, in 1784, could not be disregarded, without a great breach of faith and morals on his part.[55]

But finding, from the informal intercourse with them, that McGillivray and the chiefs were ready to treat, upon advantageous terms, Henry Knox was appointed to negotiate with them, and a treaty was concluded by him, on the part of the United States, and, on the other side, by McGillivray and the delegation, representing the whole Creek Nation. It stipulated that a permanent peace should be established between the Creeks and the citizens of the United States; that

* *A Narrative of the Military Actions of Colonel Marinus Willett*, 95–113.

expressed his approval of Willett's efforts to ensure that the Creeks were fully clothed when they arrived in New York. Henry Knox to Thomas Mifflin, War Office, 3 July 1790, http://www.wardepartmentpapers.org; Henry Knox to Marinus Willett, War Office 15 July 1790, ibid.; "Thomas Mifflin," *Biographical Directory of the United States Congress, 1774-Present* (online).

[53] McGillivray and his delegation were celebrities throughout the city. On 8 August 1790, Abigail Adams wrote about the Creeks to her sister Mary Smith Cranch: ". . . my Neighbors the Creeck Savages . . . are lodgd at an Inn at a little distance from us. They are very fond of visiting us as we entertain them kindly, and they behave with much civility. . . . MacGillvery, dresses in our own fashion speaks English like a native, & I should never suspect him to be of that Nation, as he is not very dark he is grave and solid, intelligent and much of a Gentleman, but in very bad Health." *Founding Families: Digital Editions of the Winthrops and the Adamses*, ed. C. James Taylor (Boston: Massachusetts Historical Society, 2016) [http:www.masshist.org/apde2/].

[54] Vicente Manuel de Zéspedes, governor of East Florida, dispatched his secretary Carlos Howard to Philadelphia, where he met with McGillivray and handed him letters from John Leslie and others reminding him that Spain was the true friend of the Creeks. Despite being watched by American agents, Howard followed McGillivray's delegation to monitor the negotiations and found opportunities to present "large presents" to the Creeks. Caughey, *McGillivray of the Creeks*, 263–65, 270–77, 276 n. 254; Duvon Clough Corbitt, "The Administrative System in the Floridas, 1783–1821, II," *Tequesta* 1 (July 1943): 57, 66–67.

[55] On 4 August 1790, President Washington proposed to the Senate the approval of a "Secret Article" to allow the importation of "any quantity of goods, wares, and merchandise" into the Creek Nation "free from

the Creeks and Seminoles should be under the protection, solely, of the American government, and that they should not make treaties with any state, or the individuals of any state; that they should surrender, at Rock Landing, white prisoners and Negroes, taken during the recent hostilities, in default of which the governor of Georgia was authorized to send persons in the nation to claim and demand them; that the boundary line between the Creeks and Georgia was to be that claimed by the latter, in the treaties which she had made at Augusta and Shoulderbone.[56]

Thus did Alexander McGillivray at last surrender the Oconee lands, about which so much blood had been shed, and so much negotiation wasted. And for what? For fifteen hundred dollars, to be paid annually to the Creek Nation, with also some goods, to be distributed among the Indians, which were then in the warehouses of Augusta.[57] The federal government also guaranteed to them their territory free from future encroachments.*

Did the proud, the powerful, the shrewd Alexander McGillivray surrender these valuable lands for the pitiful amount already mentioned? Ah!—but the reader must not be too fast. There was a *secret* treaty between him and Washington, which now, for the first time, comes to light, in history. It provided that, after two years from date, the commerce of the Creek Nation should be carried on through the ports of the United States, and, in the meantime, through the present channels; that the chiefs of the Okfuskees, Tuckabatchees, Tallassees, Cowetas, Cussetas, and the Seminole Nation, should be paid annually, by the United States, one hundred dollars each, and be furnished with handsome medals; that Alexander McGillivray should be constituted agent of the United States, WITH THE RANK OF BRIGADIER GENERAL, AND WITH THE PAY OF TWELVE HUNDRED DOLLARS PER ANNUM! that the United States should feed, clothe and educate Creek youth at the North, not exceeding four at one time.[58]

Thus Colonel McGillivray secured to himself new honors, and a good salary, by a secret treaty, which left him in a

* *American State Papers: Indian Affairs,* 1: 81–82.

any duties or impositions whatsoever." Two days later, he proposed that Henry Knox "be appointed and authorized to treat with" the Creek chiefs. *ASP: IA,* 1: 80–81.

[56] On 7 August 1790, Henry Knox, Alexander McGillivray, and "twenty-three chiefs and warriors" of the Creek Nation "set their hands and seals" to "A Treaty of peace and friendship . . . in the city of New York." Washington submitted the Treaty of New York to the Senate for its "advise and consent" on the same day, receiving approval by a vote of 15-4 five days later, with the two Georgia senators voting against approval. Ibid., 81–82; Joseph J. Ellis, *American Creation: Triumphs and Tragedies at the Founding of the Republic* (New York: Alfred A. Knopf, 2007), 156.

[57] Actually, McGillivray planned to use the new government under George Washington to stop the Yazoo land sales by the state of Georgia that threatened to eliminate the Creek hunting lands and rob McGillivray's people of their independence and sovereignty. Prior to his departure for New York, McGillivray acknowledged to Miró in a letter dated 2 June 1790 that he knew that Georgia had agreed to make land grants to the South Carolina Yazoo Company, Virginia Yazoo Company, and Tennessee Yazoo Company. By the first Yazoo Land Act of 21 December 1789, Georgia granted 25,400,000 acres to the three companies for $207,580 with a preemption for two years. Caughey, *McGillivray of the Creeks,* 266–67; Farris W. Cadle, *Georgia Land Surveying History and Law* (Athens: University of Georgia Press, 1991), 107–08.

[58] Washington and Knox negotiated six secret articles with McGillivray. The first granted unfettered trade up to $60,000 per year, which was designed to shift Creek trade through American ports. Article two allowed "the great medal chiefs," such as Tallassee King, "a commission, a great medal," and $100 annually for "themselves and the other beloved men of their towns."

position to return home and intrigue with Spain. Even in the presence of Washington and his able cabinet, the chieftain pushed hard for favorable terms,[59] and received them.*

Receiving half of his salary in advance, McGillivray left New York, with the chiefs, for the bright waters of the Alabama. A veil of silence covers the acts of the august chieftain, for several months, and we hear nothing more of him, until he was visited, in the nation, by Lieutenant Heth, who bore with him two thousand nine hundred dollars, in gold, the balance due to the chiefs, agreeably to the treaty. He brought this money, on pack-horses, from New York around by Virginia and East Tennessee. Heth was instructed to remain with McGillivray a long time, and endeavor to get him to carry out the provisions of the treaty, in regard to the restoration of prisoners and Negroes, and the running of the line between the Creeks and Georgians.[60]

* I am indebted to Colonel John A. Campbell, an eminent lawyer of Mobile, and to Mr. Alfred Hennen, a distinguished member of the New Orleans bar, for placing in my hands papers filed in the District Court of Louisiana containing the letters of Alexander McGillivray to Panton, dated at Little Tallase, September 20, 1788, and August 10, 1789, which have been copied, in this *History,* at length. I also found, among this file, the "secret treaty," written upon sheepskin, and signed by Washington, Knox, McGillivray and the chiefs. A celebrated lawsuit, brought in this court, by Johnson and other claimants, under the heirs of McGillivray vs. the heirs of Panton, was the means of the preservation of these important historical papers.

Under article three, McGillivray received an annual payment of $1,200 as a brigadier general "on his taking the usual oaths required by law," and McGillivray agreed to cultivate "friendship" between the Creek Nation and the U.S. under article four. By article five, the U.S. agreed "to educate and clothe" up to four young Creeks regularly, and McGillivray's nephews David Tate and David Moniac, the first Native American graduate of West Point, were among the first recipients. Article six provided for the enactment of these secret articles following ratification by President Washington and the Senate. *ASP: IA*, 1: 80–82; James Lamar Appleton and Robert David Ward, "Albert James Pickett and the Case of the Secret Articles: Historians and the Treaty of New York of 1790," *Alabama Review* 51 (January 1998): 25, 27, 29, 31, 33–34.

[59] While the Senate had given formal approval of the Treaty of New York on 12 August 1790, with the secret articles, Washington held a formal signing ceremony on 13 August at Federal Hall with the entire Congress present. The treaty was read aloud using the interpreter Joseph Cornells. Washington presented beads and tobacco to the Creeks, and McGillivray, wearing a full military uniform of blue trimmed in red, responded with a speech and gifts. Each Creek exchanged handshakes, Indian style with Washington locking arms while grasping elbows. The Creeks closed the ceremony with a song of peace. After McGillivray signed his oath of allegiance before Justice John Blair of the U.S. Supreme Court on 14 August, the Creek delegation left New York on 19 August 1790. Appleton and Ward, "Albert James Pickett and the Case of the Secret Articles," 9–11, 33, 35; Ellis, *American Creation*, 158; *Gazette of the United States* (New York), 21 August 1790. NOTE: Pickett discovered McGillivray's copy of the Treaty of New York—"the Creek original"—with the secret articles through Alfred Hennen, a New Orleans attorney, who directed him to the Panton-McGillivray papers in the files of the District Court of Louisiana. Pickett's copy of the secret articles can be found in his History Notebooks in the Pickett Papers in the Alabama Department of Archives and History in Montgomery, Alabama. See James Lamar Appleton and Robert David Ward, "Albert James Pickett and the Case of the Secret Articles: Historians and the Treaty of New York of 1790," *Alabama Review* 51 (January 1998): 11–18, 12 n. 14.

[60] While Lieutenant John Heth was assigned to deliver the gold to McGillivray, Secretary of War Henry Knox also instructed him "to impress upon McGillivray . . . the necessity for delivering up all prisoners, whether whites or negroes" and "to run the boundary line agreeably to the treaty." *ASP: IA*, 1: 125–26, 127; Caughey, *McGillivray of the Creeks*, 299, 299 n. 285; Appleton and Ward, "Albert James Pickett and the Case of the Secret Articles," 31.

Chapter XXII

THE FIRST YAZOO SALE—BOWLES, THE FREEBOOTER

Georgia claimed, under a charter of Charles II, all the territory, from the Savannah to the Mississippi River, lying between 31° and 35°. She had, as early as February 1785, established, by legislative enactment, the county of Bourbon, embracing the settlements along the Mississippi, above and below Natchez; but the occupation of this country by the Spanish government prevented its occupation and settlement.[1]

Governor Telfair approved an act of the General Assembly, at Savannah, which authorized a conditional sale of the larger portion of this wild domain, for the purpose of peopling it, and enriching the treasury of the state.[2] For a little upwards of sixty thousand dollars, five millions of acres, now embracing the territory of the middle counties of Mississippi, were sold to a "South Carolina Yazoo Company." Seven millions of acres, now embracing the territory of the northern counties of Mississippi, were sold to the "Virginia Yazoo Company," for a little over ninety-three thousand dollars. Three million, five hundred thousand acres, now embracing the territory of the northern counties of Alabama, were sold for something over forty-six thousand dollars to the "Tennessee Company."[3]

Spain claimed much of this territory, by conquests made towards the close of the Revolutionary War, as we have already seen, and that power and the United States were now negotiating to settle the boundaries; but Georgia took the matter into her own hands, as she has ever done with whatever concerned her, and as she always will do, as long as her soil is inhabited by its present enterprising, brave and restless population.

Washington, becoming alarmed at the collision which he supposed would take place between the federal government, Georgia, Spain and the Indians, in consequence of this extraordinary sale of territory, issued a proclamation against the whole enterprise.[4] But the "Tennessee Company" heeded him not.

[1] After receiving a petition from Thomas Green, and possibly others from residents of the Natchez District, the Georgia Assembly passed an act dated 7 February 1785 creating Bourbon County, Georgia, on the Mississippi River. Four days later, the Assembly formally adopted "Instructions to the Justices of Bourbon County." Distance, land ownership restrictions, and Spanish resolve defeated this effort to expand Georgia's boundary, and the state repealed the act creating Bourbon County in 1788. Edmund C. Burnett, ed., "Papers Relating to Bourbon County, Georgia, 1785–1786, I," *American Historical Review* 15 (October 1909): 68, 70–76.

[2] Governor Edward Telfair signed the Yazoo Land Act on 21 December 1789, setting off public protests and a fiasco referred to as the "Yazoo Land Fraud."

Its head and front, Zachariah Cox, with a number of his friends, floated down on flatboats from East Tennessee to the Muscle Shoals. Here, upon an island, they built a block-house, and other works of defense, intending to sell out much of the best lands, north and south of the river.[5] But the Cherokees, under the chief, Glass, probably set forward by Governor Blount, of Tennessee, who was the active agent of Washington, advanced upon this establishment, drove Cox and his adherents out of the block-house, and consumed it by fire.[6] Other efforts were afterwards made to colonize this region; but were defeated by the opposition of the Chickasaws, the Cherokees, and the federal government.*

The "South Carolina Yazoo Company" also attempted to colonize their lands, and, for that purpose, constituted Dr. James O'Fallon their agent-general, who went to Kentucky, raised troops, and issued commissions, in an illegal manner, with the design of taking the Natchez country from the Spaniards, and peopling the territory.[7] At the same time, Edmond Phelan, the sub-agent of the company, was piloted through the Creek and Choctaw country, to Natchez, by an old Indian countryman, named Thomas Basket, who was to have been their interpreter. But Washington caused O'Fallon to be arrested, and ordered General St. Clair to put down, by military force, all attempts to colonize the Natchez country, against which the Spanish minister had vehemently remonstrated. Great excitement existed; Washington was much embarrassed and much abused. The "Virginia Yazoo Company" made no attempts to settle the lands which they had purchased.[8]

These companies all failed to meet the payments due Georgia for these lands, and that state, by subsequent enactments, rescinded the whole bargain, having, in the meantime, withheld grants from the purchasers, which was a condition of sale, until the debt was fully

* Haywood, *Civil and Political History of the State of Tennessee*, 249–56; *American State Papers: Indian Affairs*, 1: 116.

ASP/IA, 1: 114; Cadle, *Georgia Land Surveying History and Law*, 107–08; Daniel K. Richter, *Facing East from Indian Country: A Native History of Early America* (Cambridge: Harvard University Press, 2001), 227; Charles H. Haskins, "The Yazoo Land Companies," *Papers of the American Historical Association* (New York: G. P. Putnam's Sons, 1891), 5: 399–400.

[3] Under the Yazoo land act, Georgia sold 25,400,000 acres to the South Carolina Yazoo Company, Virginia Yazoo Company, and Tennessee Company for $207,580, with the lands reserved as a preemption for two years. The purchase price owed by each company: South Carolina - $66,964; Virginia - $93,741; and Tennessee - $46,875. If the companies had paid these amounts after two years, Georgia agreed to issue grants to the companies "as tenants in common in fee simple." Cadle, *Georgia Land Surveying History and Law*, 107; Haskins, "The Yazoo Land Companies," 400.

[4] Actually, President Washington issued a general proclamation on 26 August 1790 "to warn the citizens of the United States against a violation of the treaties" made with the Cherokee, Choctaw, and Chickasaw. He warned "all officers of the United States, as well as civil as military, and all other citizens and inhabitants thereof, to govern themselves according to the treaties and act aforesaid, as they will answer the contrary of their peril." "By the President of the United States: A Proclamation, 26 August 1790," www.avalon.law.yale.edu.

[5] Zachariah Cox (c.1765–1838) and his partners—John Strother and Thomas Gilbert—announced plans to settle the Muscle Shoals area in September 1790 and advertised land bounties up to 500 acres for families. Despite Washington's proclamation and warnings from Governor William Blount, Cox led a party of seventeen down the Tennessee to the Shoals in January 1791. Finger, *Tennessee Frontiers*, 133; Ramsey, *Annals of Tennessee*, 549–51.

[6] While most secondary sources repeat the scenario given by Pickett, McGillivray in a letter to Governor Barón de Carondelet dated 10 April 1792 writes: "I sent off Partys from the Country & dispersed them [Tennessee Company settlers], since which no further attempts have been made

by the Americans to establish New Settlements in those parts." The party led in 1791 by Glass may well have been a combined Chickamauga/Creek war party. McGillivray also acknowledges in the same letter that he had been alerted to the Muscle Shoals intrusion by Governor William Blount. Caughey, *McGillivray of the Creeks*, 318.

[7] On 14 February 1791, Washington's Attorney General Edmund Randolph issued an opinion to the district attorney of Kentucky to take measures to prosecute James O'Fallon for treason, if applicable, or prosecute him for "disturbances of the peace." While planning the organization of his "Yazoo Battalion," O'Fallon opened a correspondence with Governor Miró in 1790, asserting his company wanted to ally with Spain and create an independent government in the Yazoo country. "Opinion of Attorney General on the Case of James O'Fallon," 14 February 1791, http://founders.archives.gov/documents; *ASP: IA*, 1: 115–17; Kinnaird, *Spain in the Mississippi Valley*, 2: 357–64.

[8] In a letter to Edward Phelan on 17 December 1790, O'Fallon wrote that he expected to arrive on 10 March 1791 with a "Regiment of Regulars" 750 strong, "with about 3000 Militiamen," and 19,000 colonists. He also reported that George Rogers Clark would command the regulars and militia with John Sevier as second in command. On 19 March 1791, President Washington issued a proclamation aimed at O'Fallon "for levying an armed force in that part of the State of Virginia which is called Kentucky, disturbs the peace, and sets at defiance the treaties of the United States." Kinnaird, *Spain in the Mississippi Valley*, 2: 395; "By the President of the United States: A Proclamation," 19 March 1791, http://founders.archives.gov/documents.

[9] Although President Washington appointed Andrew Ellicott to run the boundary line between the Creek Nation and the state of Georgia, he had been "detained a few weeks on public service" and sent his brother Joseph Ellicott in his place. On 8 September 1791, Secretary of War Knox wrote to Joseph Ellicott, authorizing him to commence running the boundary line with the anticipation that his brother might eventually join him. On the same date, Knox sent letters to Major Richard Call, Governor Edward Telfair, and Brigadier General McGillivray, asking them to help Joseph Ellicott "commence the operation." *ASP: IA*, 1: 128–29.

[10] Bowles's regiment was so racked by disease at Pensacola that there was talk of merging it with the Pennsylvania Loyalist Regiment. While it is unclear what provoked his resignation, the sixteen-year old ensign discarded his uniform and joined a party of Lower Creeks who had come to Pensacola to trade and receive presents. J. Leitch Wright, *William Augustus Bowles: Director General of the Creek Nation* (Athens: University of Georgia Press, 1967), 11–12.

[11] After staying for several months among the Creeks, Bowles wandered back to Pensacola, where he worked for a baker and developed contacts that helped him enter the Indian trade. On one of his trips among the Lower Creeks on the Chattahoochee, he may have taken the first of several wives, possibly a young Cherokee refugee who gave him one or two children. Later Bowles took a second wife named Mary, who was the daughter of Thomas Perryman, a métis Creek, whose village was located above the forks of the Apalachicola River. There may have been a third wife and more children. Ibid., 12–13; William C. Sturtevant, "The Cherokee Frontiers, the French Revolution, and William Augustus Bowles," in *The Cherokee Nation: A Troubled History*, 71–72.

[12] Bowles returned to Pensacola sometime in 1780 and participated in its defense against the successful Spanish assault and capture in May 1781. He may have had his commission as an ensign restored before the fall of Pensacola and received a parole from the Spanish, going to Havana and eventually to New York. By 1783, he reappears in the Bahamas with other Loyalist refugees. Sturtevant, "Cherokee Frontiers, the French Revolution, and William Augustus Bowles," 72.

discharged. A great deal of recrimination and abuse passed between the authorities of Georgia and these companies, and the people who had innocently suffered, in fitting out private enterprises, to settle the new region. So ended the *first* Yazoo sale, by the legislature of Georgia. An account of another, and a more important and extensive one, will hereafter be introduced.*

A Quaker of Pennsylvania, named Andrew Ellicott, appointed by the federal government to run the line between the Creeks and Georgians, arrived at Rock Landing, upon the Oconee, in company with James Seagrove, an Irishman, who was appointed superintendent of the Creek Nation. At this place the government erected a strong fort, and threw into it a large garrison. McGillivray was constantly urged, from this point, to cause the Indians to consent to the running of the boundary line, and to assist in its execution; but the chieftain delayed, and threw all the blame upon the hostile efforts of an extraordinary man, who must now be introduced to the reader.[9]

William Augustus Bowles, a native of Maryland, at the age of fourteen, entered the British army, as a foot soldier, and, after a year's service against his countrymen, sailed with a British regiment to Jamaica, in 1777, as an ensign, and, from thence, went to Pensacola. Here he was deprived of his rank, for insubordination. Disgusted with military discipline, and fond of a roving life, he contemptuously flung his uniform into the sea, and left Pensacola in company with some Creeks.[10] He lived upon the Tallapoosa for several years, and acquired the Muscogee language to great perfection. He visited the Lower Towns, and there married the daughter of a chief. His elegant and commanding form, fine address, beautiful countenance of varied expression, his exalted genius, daring and intrepidity, all connected with a mind wholly debased and unprincipled, eminently fitted him to sway the bad Indians and worse traders among whom he lived.[11]

Bowles led a party of Creeks to Pensacola, in 1781, and assisted General Campbell to defend that place from the attacks of Don Gálvez.[12] He went to New York, joined a company of comedians, and sailed to New Providence, of the Bahamas. Here he alternately acted upon the stage, and painted portraits, for which he had taste and genius. Lord Dunmore was then the governor of the Bahamas. Panton, Leslie & Co. dispatched to John Forbes, one of their associates, living at New Providence, a schooner, in which were six thousand piastres. Lord Dunmore seized upon this money, as contraband property. Panton instituted a complaint to the British Court, when the money was

* *American State Papers: Indian Affairs,* 1: 116–17; *American State Papers: Public Lands,* 1: 120–21, 163.

[13] Between 1783 and 1788, Bowles seems to have made several trips between the Bahamas, Georgia, and East Florida. During this period, he developed a relationship with John Miller, a Loyalist merchant in Nassau, and with the Earl of Dunmore, governor of the Bahamas, who were commercial and political rivals of the Bahamian based Panton, Leslie and Company. He made two or three trips into the Creek country in 1788 with gifts of guns and munitions from an anonymous source, which McGillivray accepted from this "Stranger" who he met in the Lower Creek towns. When he returned to the Lower Creeks in January 1789, Bowles promised the arrival of a large shipment of goods from Nassau, but, when they did not arrive, McGillivray became suspicious of his motives and alerted Robert Leslie. Caughey, *McGillivray of the Creeks*, 192–98, 202–05, 208–09, 221–23; Milfort, *Memoir*, 80–81.

[14] Under pressure from Panton, Miró, and O'Neill, McGillivray sent Milfort to intercept Bowles and to monitor his activities. By February 1789, McGillivray was aware of the plans to plunder Panton's stores at St. Marks and St. Johns, but he did not believe Bowles capable of coordinating the affair without support from the Lower Creeks, especially after most of his accomplices had deserted him. McGillivray does not mention anything about Milfort cutting off Bowles's ears in any of his correspondence, but he was willing to "dismiss him from this country for ever." Caughey, *McGillivray of the Creeks*, 217–25; Milfort, *Memoir*, 81–82; Coker and Watson, *Indian Traders*, 118–20.

[15] Following a circuitous route from Florida to Nassau to Canada, Bowles, three Cherokee, and two Creek delegates arrived at Portsmouth in October 1790. Since Bowles dressed as a Creek, they were often referred to as six Indians by the print media in London. The English government rejected their "views of hostility against the United States" but did offer access to free ports "in His Majesty's West Indian Islands . . . should find themselves in a situation to avail themselves of this indulgence." Frederick Jackson Turner, ed., "English Policy Toward America in 1790–1791," *American Historical Review* 7 (July 1902): 708, 726–27; Paolo Adreani, *Along the Hudson and Mohawk: The 1790 Journal of Count Paolo Adreani*, ed. Cesare Marino and Karim M. Tiro

ordered to be returned. Dunmore ever afterwards hated Panton and his co-partners. He selected Bowles as an agent, to establish a commercial house upon the Chattahoochee, which would check the prosperous commerce of these merchants. Bowles shortly appeared among the Lower Creeks, and threw the weight of his influence against Panton, and against McGillivray and the Georgians, all of whom he despised.[13] But Milfort was sent to the Chattahoochee, with an order for Bowles to leave the nation in twenty-four hours, on penalty of losing his ears.[14] He fled to New Providence, and, from thence, was sent to England, by Dunmore, in company with a delegation of Creeks, Seminoles and Cherokees, to enlist the English government in the cause of these nations by repelling American aggression.[15]

The British Court treated him with kindness, and heaped upon him valuable presents.[16] He soon returned to New Providence, and began a piratical war upon the coasting vessels of Panton, having taught his warriors to navigate the Gulf. He captured some of these vessels, laden with arms and ammunition, ran them up in bayous, where he and an abandoned set of white men from the prisons of London, together with hosts of savages, engaged in protracted debaucheries, and, day and night, made the woods echo with horrid oaths and panther screams. Panton's boxes of merchandise were torn open, distributed among the Indians, and carried to all parts of the nation. Such piratical successes soon gave him popularity in the Creek country.* He now boldly advanced to the heart of it, denouncing General McGillivray as a traitor to his people, and sought to overthrow him and place himself in power.[17] He had many bad men,

* Francois Marie Perrin Du Lac, *Voyage dans les deux Louisianes, et chez les nations sauvages du Missouri, par les États-Unis, l'Ohio et les provinces qui le bordent, en 1801, 1802 et 1803*, 458–60; Milfort, *Mémoire ou coup d'oeil rapide sur mes différens voyages et mon séjour dans la nation Crëck*, 116–24.

of influence with the Indians, who endeavored to stir up rebellion. The most conspicuous of these were Wellbank, a native of New York and a refugee Tory, and a half-breed Cherokee named Moses Price. His emissaries contended that neither the Americans nor Spaniards had any right to control the Indians, for that England had not ceded any of their country to either power, and that General McGillivray had endeavored to sell his people, first to Spain, and, next, to the federal government.[18]

Indeed, at this period, McGillivray, for the first time in his life, began to lose the confidence of many of the chiefs and common Indians, who were indignant at the provisions of the New York treaty, which they openly disavowed. The Spanish authorities were angry with him, and Panton was deceived by him. Bowles even boarded him in his den. All this time, the federal government was annoying him with urgent solicitations to comply with the treaty. Truly, one might suppose that General McGillivray was an unhappy man, and was soon to fall from his high position. At length he departed for New Orleans, when Bowles and his emissaries exultingly declared that he had fled, never again to show his face upon the Coosa. He went frequently to New Orleans, Mobile and Pensacola during the winter, and was treated with great attention by the Spanish authorities, notwithstanding the Treaty of New York. The *secret* one, of course, they knew nothing of, nor did Panton. He professed to be sick of his trip to New York, and requested not to be given the title of general.[19] Here he arranged for the capture of Bowles, and soon the freebooter was brought to New Orleans in chains, and from thence sent to Madrid, in Spain, where we must leave him for the present.[20]

It was not long before measures were adopted

(Philadelphia: University of Pennsylvania, 2006), 97–98.

[16] Contrary to Pickett's statement, the audience with King George III was canceled, and Lord Grenville, George III's foreign secretary, was very discreet in his contacts and communications with Bowles, who styled himself as the Director General of the Muskogee Nation. Bowles and his companions enjoyed the sights of London and many social engagements. Thomas Hardy painted Bowles's portrait, and William Hodges painted portraits of two métis Chickamauga-Cherokees—Richard Justice (Unatoy) and Moses Price (Wossee-o). Turner, "English Policy Toward America in 1790–1791," 708, 748–49; Anthony A. Pearson, "John Hunter and two Cherokee Indians: History through art," *Annals of the Royal College of Surgeons of England* 58 (September 1976): 374–79.

[17] In the fall of 1791, Bowles put his plans into action, addressing a grand council attended by Upper and Lower Creeks at Coweta, promising to protect them against their enemies and accusing McGillivray of betraying them to the United States. In January 1792, Bowles, Major William Cunningham, and his Creek auxiliaries plundered Panton's St. Marks store and used the merchandise as gifts and supplies to maintain his influence, especially among the Lower Creeks and Seminoles. Caughey, *McGillivray of the Creeks*, 305–09, 346; Coker and Watson, *Indian Traders*, 150–52.

[18] George Wellbank served as Bowles's second in command and constructed a make-shift port facility for the State of Muskogee at the mouth of the Ochlockonee River to receive shipments from Nassau. Moses Price lived at Lookout Mountain Town and was one of three Chickamauga-Cherokees that accompanied Bowles to England. Caughey, *McGillivray of the Creeks*, 305–06, 346–48; Coker and Watson, *Indian Traders*, 151, 153–54; Pearson, "John Hunter and two Cherokee Indians," 378.

[19] McGillivray visited New Orleans in June 1792, where he repudiated the Treaty of New York and signed a treaty of "reciprocal union" on 6 July 1792 with Spanish Governor Francisco Luis Hector, Barón de Carondelet. Carondelet also increased McGillivray's pension to $3,500 annually. Caughey, *McGillivray of the Creeks*, 329–30; Coker and Watson, *Indian Traders*, 163.

[20] Actually, Bowles had preceded McGillivray's visit to New Orleans in March 1792, where he attempted to discredit McGillivray and William Panton to Barón de Carondelet. Bowles proposed that Spain recognize his State of Muskogee and the right of free trade with the

to expel the American inhabitants, principally traders, from the Creek Nation. Governor Carondelet decreed that they were all to take the Spanish oath of allegiance, and "fight for the King, from the headwaters of the Alabama to the sea." James Leonard, who had recently arrived at Tensaw, refusing to take the oath, was stripped of his property, and, while arrangements were making to send him to Moro Castle, in Havana, he made his escape to Rock Landing, upon the distant Oconee.[21]

McGillivray returned to the banks of the Coosa, still in power and authority. It was suspected that he had intrigued with the Spanish authorities. Not long afterwards, one Captain Don Pedro Olivier, who was a Frenchman, but wore the Spanish military uniform, made his appearance in the nation, and was stationed at the Hickory Ground, upon the Coosa. His pay was one hundred dollars a month, and he was accompanied by an interpreter named Antonio. These things looked very suspicious to the federal agents upon the Oconee. It was believed by many that General McGillivray did not openly act against the American government, but that he was doing it secretly, through Captain Olivier and others.[22] It was certain that, upon the representations of Carondelet to the court of Spain, respecting the Treaty of New York, and the remonstrances of Panton to that power, in regard to its neglect of the chieftain, His Catholic Majesty made McGillivray superintendent general of the Creek Nation, with an annual salary of two thousand dollars! In July, to this amount was added a salary of fifteen hundred dollars by the same power.* He was, at this time, the agent of Spain, with a salary of thirty-five hundred dollars; the agent of the United States, with a salary of twelve hundred dollars; the co-partner of Panton; and the emperor of the Creek and Seminole nations.[23] He was almost unrivalled in intrigue, and

* Papers filed in the District Court of Louisiana.

Bahamas. Carondelet convinced Bowles to sail to Havana to negotiate further with Captain General Luis de Las Casas, where he was briefly imprisoned before being incarcerated in Spain and later exiled to the Philippines. *ASP: IA*, 1: 296; Kinnaird, *Spain in the Mississippi Valley*, 3: 17, 27–29; Caughey, *McGillivray of the Creeks*, 316–18; Coker and Watson, *Indian Traders*, 153–54, 156.

[21] James Seagrove, U.S. agent for Indian affairs, deposed James Leonard on 24 July 1792 at Rock Landing on the Oconee River in Georgia. In his deposition, Leonard claimed that the "French and English people" of Louisiana were "ripe to revolt against the Spanish government," "five Spanish regiments . . . between five and six hundred men arrived as reinforcement to the posts on the Mississippi," and "that the Spaniards are doing everything in their power to engage the Indians in a war with the United States." At this same time, Spanish colonial officials were more concerned with maintaining the status quo and urged McGillivray to maintain peace with Georgia. *ASP: IA*, 1: 307–08; Caughey, *McGillivray of the Creeks*, 332–46.

[22] In February 1792, Governor Carondelet sent Lieutenant Pedro Olivier as the "King's Commissary in the Creek Nation" to prevent the running of the Oconee boundary line and to monitor McGillivray's relations with the Americans. McGillivray realized that Olivier was sent as Carondelet's spy and to disrupt his leadership of the Creek Nation, which prompted McGillivray's trip to New Orleans in June 1792. Caughey, *McGillivray of the Creeks*, 307, 313–14, 317, 319–20; Coker and Watson, *Indian Traders*, 158–59; Kinnaird, *Spain in the Mississippi Valley*, 3: xiii, 21–22; *ASP: IA*, 1: 259.

[23] Actually, McGillivray was recognized as the "General & principal Chief of the Creek Nation" in the Treaty of New Orleans, which was signed by McGillivray and Governor Carondelet on 6 July 1792. The treaty reaffirmed the 1784 Treaty of Pensacola, signed by McGillivray, which had reestablished relations between Spain and the Creek Nation, and a separate document which named McGillivray as Spanish commissary to the Creeks at an annual pension of 600 pesos. In addition, by signing this new treaty, McGillivray repudiated the Treaty of New York and his emoluments accrued by

we doubt if Alabama has ever produced, or ever will produce, a man of greater ability.* We wish we could defend his conduct with a clear conscience, but we cannot. It was eminent for treachery, intrigue, and selfish aggrandizement. However he may have been wronged by the Americans, he ought to have acted in good faith with them, after he had made the treaty with Washington. But McGillivray was like many ambitious and unscrupulous Americans of our day, who view politics as a trade. But, notwithstanding he displayed eminent selfishness in his relation towards these rival powers, he was generous to the distressed, whom he always sheltered and fed, and protected from the brutalities of his red brethren. He had many noble traits, and not the least of which was his unbounded hospitality to friends and foes.

During the summer and fall of 1792, General McGillivray secretly caused large meetings to be held over the Creek and Cherokee nations, at which he appeared to be only a visitor, while Panton and Captain Olivier, in speeches, forbid the running of the line between them and the Georgians, in the name of the king of Spain, and decreed that no American trader should enter the nation.[24] Governor Carondelet was also active in endeavoring to defeat the provisions of the New York treaty. He sent to the Creek Nation a large body of bloody Shawnees, armed and equipped, who took up their abode at Sawanogi, upon the Tallapoosa.[25] McGillivray moved his Negroes to Little River, gave up his house to Captain Olivier, whom he had so well established in the affections of his people, and was gone, a long time, to New Orleans and Pensacola.[26] The Spaniards not only had in view the prevention of the advancement of the Americans on the east, but determined to oppose the settlements upon the

* I have only introduced a few of McGillivray's letters, to show the order of his mind. The *American State Papers: Indian Affairs* contain many of his ablest letters, addressed to Congress and to the secretary of war.

that document. On the same day, Carondelet notified McGillivray that he was increasing his annual pension, which had been adjusted over time to 2000 pesos by another 1500 pesos. Kinnaird, *Spain in the Mississippi Valley*, 3: 57–58; Caughey, *McGillivray of the Creeks*, 321–22, 327–28, 329–30; Saunt, *New Order of Things*, 75–76, 78–79.

24 William Panton made a trip to the "Cherokee Country" in April 1792 "to look after his affairs," as reported by McGillivray in his letter to O'Neill on 12 May 1792. There is no indication in the Spanish correspondence in Lawrence Kinnaird's *Spain in the Mississippi Valley, 1765–1794* or in John Walton Caughey's *McGillivray of the Creeks* that Pedro Olivier traveled into the Cherokee or Chickamauga towns with Panton. Caughey, *McGillivray of the Creeks*, 321–22.

25 Carondelet had no direct connection with the Shawnee warriors who resided in the Chickamauga or Creek towns. Sawanogi—Souvanoga in Pickett's original narrative—was historically a Shawnee town, and Benjamin Hawkins recorded that they spoke Shawnee and retained "the manners of their countrymen" in the Ohio country. The Shawnee delegation that came into the Creek country in February 1793 pressured the Creeks to coordinate attacks against the United States, especially against the Cumberland and Kentucky settlements. Kinnaird, *Spain in the Mississippi Valley*, 147–48, 306; *ASP: IA*, 1: 381–82; Ethridge, *Creek Country*, 82, 97; Saunt, *New Order of Things*, 104–05, 116; Gregory Evans Dowd, *A Spirited Resistance: The North American Indian Struggle for Unity, 1745–1815* (Baltimore: Johns Hopkins Press, 1992), 102, 104–05, 108–11.

26 McGillivray placed Lieutenant Pedro Olivier in his home at Hickory Ground so he could monitor his activities, not out of some misguided kindness or deference. He had no intentions of letting him or Carondelet undermine his authority in the Creek Nation. In his letter to Panton on 28 October 1791, McGillivray disclosed his determination to retire to his wife Vicey Cornells, a daughter of Joseph Cornells, who lived on his plantation on the Little River near Tensaw above Mobile. McGillivray traveled to New Orleans in June 1792, where he and Carondelet signed a new treaty of union. Kinnaird, *Spain in the*

Mississippi; to effect all of which, they attempted to unite the four nations of Indians on their side. They strengthened all their forts, and authorized Captain John Linder, of Tensaw, and other active partisans, to raise volunteers.

Carondelet gave Richard Finnelson and Joseph Dergue passports to go through the Spanish posts to the Cherokee Nation, as emissaries to incite those Indians to make war upon the Cumberland people.[27] John Watts, a half-breed of Willstown, was also an active agent. There was, suddenly, great excitement produced over the whole Indian country. One chief declared, at Willstown,* that he had taken the lives of three hundred Americans, but that now he intended to "drink his fill of blood." The Cumberland people fell victims on all sides, while the settlers upon the frontiers of Georgia shared the same fate.[28] During all this time, McGillivray and the federal authorities at Rock Landing were engaged in fruitless correspondence—the former professing his willingness to carry out the provisions of the New York treaty, but never doing it. Everything conspired to defeat the hopes of Washington. Even Captain Olivier had become intimate with Wellbank, and the rest of the adherents of Bowles, and used them against the American interests.[29] McGillivray also carried on a correspondence with the secretary of war, in which he displayed his usual powers of diplomacy.†

* Willstown, named for a half-breed chief called Red Head Will, whose father was a British officer, was an important Cherokee village. The grave of Red Head Will is within two hundred yards of the residence of Jesse G. Beeson, who owns the entire site of Willstown, situated in Little Will's Valley, DeKalb County, Alabama.

† *American State Papers: Indian Affairs,* 1: 288–90, 305–15, 432.

Mississippi Valley, 3: 57–58; Caughey, *McGillivray of the Creeks*, 300, 318–19, 327, 328, 341–42; Cashin, *Lachlan McGillivray*, 77; Saunt, *New Order of Things*, 70–71, 87–88; Waselkov, *A Conquering Spirit*, 39.

[27] John Linder, Sr., held a Spanish land grant of 491 acres on the east side of the Tombigbee River, beginning at the mouth of Tensaw Lake, on the Alabama River. Richard Finnelson, a métis Cherokee, and Joseph De'rague (Deraque), a French Canadian, traveled with John Watts, a métis Chickamauga chief, to Pensacola in the summer of 1792. In a letter written by Finnelson in September 1792 and enclosed in a letter from Governor William Blount to Henry Knox, Finnelson discussed in detail the efforts of Carondelet to persuade the Southern Indians to reject their treaties with the United States. *ASP: PL*, 1: 737–38; *ASP: IA*, 1: 276–77, 288–92, 327–28.

[28] John Watts (also Young Tassel) became the leading war chief of the Chickamauga following the death of Dragging Canoe on 1 March 1792. Watts moved to Willstown to be closer to his Spanish ally Governor O'Neill in Pensacola. Cheeseekau (Pepquannake, Shawnee Warrior), older brother of Tecumseh, was the chief at the Willstown conference who said "I will now drink my fill of blood." He was killed in the Chickamauga/Creek/Shawnee attack on Buchanan's Station on 30 September 1792. *ASP: IA*, 1: 327–28; Brown, *Old Frontiers*, 347, 359; John Sugden, *Tecumseh: A Life* (New York: Henry Holt, 1997), 57–60, 67–76, 421–22 n. 1.

[29] Following the incarceration of Bowles, George Wellbank tried to maintain the Nassau trade through the Ochlockonee River port but to no avail, and he returned to his friends at the Chickamauga's Lookout Mountain Town. In May-August 1793, he led a party of Chickamauga, Creeks, and Shawnees to Detroit and Niagara to confer with northern Indians and to meet with John Graves Simcoe, lieutenant governor of Upper Canada and to convince him to open trade to the Southern Indians. *ASP: IA*, 1: 297, 420, 439, 454; Wright, *William Augustus Bowles*, 83–84; Benjamin Lincoln, "Journal of a Treaty held in 1793, with the Indian Tribes North-West of the Ohio, by Commissioners of the United States," *Collections of the Massachusetts Historical Society, Third Series*, v. 5 (Boston: John H. Eastburn, Printer, 1836), 169, 172.

Chapter XXIII

SINGULAR INHABITANTS OF ALABAMA

The territory now called Alabama was but sparsely settled in 1792, except by the natives, and they occupied only some of the principal water-courses. Fort Charlotte, at Mobile, was garrisoned with Spanish troops. The old French "Tombecbé," which, in Spanish times, was called Fort Confederation, contained also a Spanish garrison.[1] The English trading post, near the present Stockton, then called Tensaw, was repaired and occupied. A Spanish garrison occupied Fort St. Stephens, which was built upon a bluff on the Tombigbee, called, by the Choctaws, Hobuckintopa.[2] A considerable Spanish garrison held the fortress at Pensacola. West Florida and Louisiana were governed by the Captain-General at Havana. The next person in authority was the governor of Louisiana, to whom all the commandants of the posts in Alabama and Mississippi were subordinate.[3] The whole territory of Alabama was then an immense wilderness, with American trading-posts on the east, upon the Oconee, and those of Spain upon the south and west, while it was uninhabited, by whites, as far as the distant Cumberland settlements on the north.

The most populous settlement, with the exception of Mobile, was upon the Tensaw River and lake of that name. It was composed of both Whigs and Royalists. The latter had been driven from Georgia and the Carolinas. Added to these, were men, *sui generis*, appropriately called old Indian countrymen, who had spent much of their lives in Indian commerce. The most conspicuous and wealthy inhabitant of this neighborhood was Captain John Linder, a native of the Canton of Berne, in Switzerland. He resided many years in Charleston, as a British engineer and surveyor. There General McGillivray became acquainted with him, and, during the Revolution, assisted in bringing here his family and large Negro property.[4]

In February 1791, a party of emigrants, consisting of Colonel Thomas Kimbil, John Barnett, Robert Sheffield, Barton Hannon, and [Hiram] Mounger,

[1] The Spanish did not construct Fort Confederation on the site of the old French Fort Tombecbé near present-day Epes, Alabama, at Jones' Bluff, until April 1794. See James P. Pate, "The Fort of the Confederation: Spain on the Upper Tombigbee," *Alabama Historical Quarterly*, 44 (Fall-Winter 1982): 171–186.

[2] Governor Esteban Miró ordered the construction of Fort San Esteban de Tombecbé (also St. Etienne), located on Hobuckintopa (also Hoe Buckintoopa) Bluff in 1789 to protect settlers along the lower Tombigbee and Tensaw Rivers. Josef Deville Degoutin Bellechase established San Esteban in 1789, and Fernando Lisoro replaced him as commander in 1791. Pedro de Rola was commandant from September 1794 through the spring of 1795. On 5 February 1799, Lisoro surrendered San Esteban to Richard Brashear and

with a wife and children, three of whom were grown, set out from Georgia for the Tombigbee. Entering the Creek Nation, one of the children was injured by a fall, which compelled the elder Mounger and his younger family to stop upon the trail. They were afterwards robbed, by the Indians, of everything they possessed, and had to make their way back to Georgia on foot. The three young Moungers, and the other emigrants, continued to the Tensaw, passing the creeks and rivers upon rafts. They found, upon their arrival at Tensaw, the Halls, Byrnes, Mimses, Kilcreases, Steadhams, Easlies, Linders and others. Crossing the Alabama and Tombigbee upon rafts, they found, residing below McIntosh Bluff, the Bateses, Lawrences and Powells. Above there, on the Tombigbee, they discovered the Dandleys, Wheats, Johnsons, McGrews, Hockitts, Freelands, Talleys and Bakers. Among these few people, Colonel Kimbil and his little party established themselves, and began the cultivation of the soil with their horses, upon the backs of which they had brought a few axes and ploughs.

The garrison at St. Stephens was composed of one company, commanded by Captain Fernando Lisoro. The block house, the residence of the commandant, and the church, were good buildings, of frame-work, clay and plaster. The other houses were small, and covered with cypress bark. All the inhabitants of this place, and of the country, were required to labor so many days upon the public works, to take the oath of allegiance, and to assist in repelling the depredations of the Creeks, who stole horses and other property. Some French farmers also lived upon this river, who dwelt in houses made almost entirely of clay, while those of the Americans were constructed of small poles, in the rudest manner. They all cultivated indigo, which was worth two dollars and fifty cents per pound. The burning of tar engaged much of the time of the Spaniards, still lower down.

Upon Little River, dividing the modern counties of Baldwin and Monroe, lived many intelligent and wealthy people, whose blood was a mixture of white and Indian.

evacuated his troops below the 31st parallel to Mobile under the terms of the Treaty of San Lorenzo el Real. Jack D. L. Holmes, "Spanish Military Commanders in Colonial Alabama," *Journal of the Alabama Academy of Sciences* 37 (January 1966): 60, 62–63; Jack D. L. Holmes, "Notes on the Spanish Fort San Esteban de Tombecbé," *Alabama Review* 18 (October 1965): 281–90.

[3] Francisco Luis Héctor, Barón de Carondelet (1747–1807), a native of Noyelles, Flanders, was appointed governor of Spanish Louisiana and West Florida in 1791. He arrived in New Orleans in January 1792, replacing Esteban Rodríguez Miró and served as governor until his appointment as President of the Royal Audiencia of Quito in 1797. Carl A. Brasseaux, "Francois-Louis Hector, Baron de Carondelet et Noyelles, Colonial Governor, 1791–1797," in *Louisiana Governors: Iberville to Edwards*, 64–69.

[4] Captain John Linder Sr., had received Spanish land grants that were confirmed by Vicente Folch and Esteban Miró in 1788. Pedro Favrot, commandant at Mobile, was so impressed with Linder's character and loyalty to Spain that he recommended that he be appointed commandant of the Tensaw post in 1785. He was actually appointed "Justice of the Peace for the district of Tensaw and Tombigbee," and his duties were similar to Spanish military commanders at frontier posts in West Florida and Louisiana. Linder's heirs were forced to prove their rightful ownership to his Spanish land grants under an act passed by Congress on 3 March 1803. Jack D. L. Holmes, "Alabama's Forgotten Settlers: Notes on the Spanish Mobile District, 1780–1813," *Alabama Historical Quarterly* 33 (Summer 1971): 89–90; *ASP/PL*, 1: 736–37.

This colony was formed at an early period, for the benefit of their large stocks of cattle, for the wild grass and cane were here never killed by the frost. A most remarkable woman, a sister of General McGillivray, lived occasionally among these people. Sophia McGillivray, a maiden beautiful in all respects, was living at her native place, upon the Coosa, when Benjamin Durant, a man of Huguenot blood, came from South Carolina, to her mother's house. A youth of astonishing strength and activity, he had mastered all who opposed him at home. Being informed by the traders that a man in the Creek Nation was his superior, he immediately set out for that region, to which he had long before been inclined to go. He was handsome, and his complexion was almost as brown as that of the pretty, dark-eyed Sophia. She went with him to the Hickory Ground, only a few miles distant, where many Indians collected, to see the antagonists meet. They encountered each other, and a tremendous fight ensued. Durant felled his antagonist to the ground, where he lay, for a time, insensible. The conqueror was proclaimed the champion of the nation. He soon married Sophia, and went to reside upon one of the estates of her father, the wealthy Lachlan McGillivray, situated upon the Savannah River. During the siege of Savannah, she was there with her father, her husband, and her little boy, Lachlan Durant, who is now favorably known to many of our modern citizens, and is yet a resident of Baldwin County. When the city was surrendered to the Americans, she parted from her father, amid a flood of tears, and set out for her native Coosa, while he, as we have seen, sailed with his British friends, to Scotland.[5]

Sophia Durant had an air of authority about her, equal, if not superior, to that of her brother, Alexander. She was much better acquainted with the Indian tongue, for he had long lived out of the nation. When, therefore, he held councils in the vicinity of her residence, she was accustomed to deliver his sentiments in a set speech, to which the chiefs listened with delight. Her husband became a wealthy man, and "Durant's Bend,"* and other places upon the Alabama, still preserve his memory.[6] In the summer of

* The most remarkable bend upon the Alabama, embracing a large tract of land lying between Montgomery and Selma, formerly the property of the late Honorable William Smith, and now owned by John Steele, of Autauga. It was cultivated by Benjamin Durant as early as 1786.

[5] Benjamin Hawkins visited Sophia McGillivray and Benjamin Peter Durant on 20 December 1796 near Little Tallassee. While Arturo O'Neill referred to Durant in 1783 as "an Indian half-breed . . . whose father was French," Hawkins described Durant as "a man of good figure, dull and stupid, a little mixed with African blood," and totally under the control of his wife. Hawkins, *Letters*, 43; Caughey, *McGillivray of the Creeks*, 62.

[6] When Hawkins visited Sophia Durant in December 1796, he wrote, "I found her poor, and dirty in a small hut. . . . She is in possession of near eighty slaves, near 40 of them capable of doing work in or out doors. Yet from bad management they are a heavy burthen to her and themselves, they are all idle." Hawkins, *Letters*, 43.

1790, while McGillivray was at New York, the Creeks threatened to descend upon the Tensaw settlers and put the whole of them to death. Mrs. Durant mounted a horse, with a Negro woman upon another, and set out from Little River, camped out at night, and, on the fourth day, arrived at the Hickory Ground, where she assembled the chiefs, threatened them with the vengeance of her brother upon his return, which caused the arrest of the ringleaders, and put a complete stop to their murderous intentions. Two weeks afterwards, this energetic and gifted woman was delivered of twins, at the Hickory Ground. One of them married James Bailey, who was killed at the fall of Fort Mims, in 1813, and the other lived to be an old woman. At a later period, Mrs. Durant will again appear in this history.[7]

The territory of the present county of Montgomery contained a few white inhabitants in 1792. Among others, there was a white woman, who had lived with her husband at Savannah. He was there a foot soldier in one of the British regiments, but deserted from the army, when she fled with him to the Chattahoochee. He died at Cusseta, and his bold and adventurous wife continued to wander through the Creek Nation, and finally settled in the territory of the present county of Montgomery, upon the eastern side of a creek, which still bears her name, for she was called by no other than that of "Milly." Here, among the Cuwalla Indians, she established herself, without husband, father, children, or even a single friend.[8] Espousing one of the sons of the forest, she soon began to have comforts around her. Her stock of cattle became large, to which was added, in a few years, a large drove of ponies. For many years, Milly lived alone upon this creek. The trading path leading from Pensacola to Tuckabatchee passed by her house.[9] But, at the period of 1792, her solitary hours were agreeably relieved by the prattle of a little white girl. In 1790, a party of Creeks advanced to the Georgia frontiers, and, surrounding the house of one Scarlett, killed him and his wife and children. A little girl, named Tempey Ellis, about eight years old, the child of a neighbor, was in the house at the time, and, when the attack was made, she concealed herself under the bed. After all the family lay upon the floor, in the sleep of death, a warrior discovered Tempey Ellis, and, dragging her out by the hair, raised his hatchet to kill her; but, reflecting that he could possibly obtain

[7] Benjamin Hawkins reported in 1796 that Sophia McGillivray and Benjamin Peter Durant had once had eleven children, with eight still living. Based on available genealogical records, it is not clear who the métis James Bailey married. Thomas Woodward gives the names of four daughters and their marriages: Rachel married Billy McGirth and, following his death, Davy Walker and "then a Brashears"; Mary (Polly) married "a full blooded Tallassee named Cochirny"; Sophia married "a Dr. Macomes [McComb]"; and Elizabeth (Betsy) married Peter McQueen. Ibid.; Woodward, *Reminiscences*, 98–99.

[8] According to George Stiggins, Euro-Americans referred to the Creeks at Hoithlewaule, located on the north bank of the Tallapoosa, as "Cluwallee" or Pickett's Cuwalla Indians. Stiggins, *Creek Indian History*, 37, 148 n. 27; Ethridge, *Creek Country*, 80–81.

[9] Milly operated a trading house, tavern, and toll-gate bridge at Milly's Creek (Norcoce Chappo Creek) on the Pensacola to Tuckabatchee trail east of modern Montgomery, Alabama. She may have had as many as three husbands, and her story is part of a Gulf South legend with little or no documented record. Peter A. Brannon, "The Pensacola Indian Trade," *Florida Historical Quarterly* 31 (July 1952-April 1953): 10–11; Henry deLeon Southerland and Jerry Elijah Brown, *The Federal Road Through Georgia* (Tuscaloosa: University of Alabama Press, 1989), 91–94, 119; Jessie Donaldson, "Genealogy or Chasing Our Tales," *Woodmere News* (Spring 2014), 5.

a handsome sum for her ransom, he placed her on his horse and carried her to Autossee, on the Tallapoosa. Here she was often beaten, and made to bring water from the springs. One day Milly heard that the Autossees had a white girl in slavery. She immediately mounted her pony, rode to Autossee, paid ten ponies and six head of cattle for Tempey, and, the next day, carried this unfortunate child to her house. For several years she acted the part of a most affectionate mother. Subsequently, the child was delivered to Seagrove, the Creek agent, at St. Mary's, and was sent from thence to her friends in Georgia.[10] Old Milly was exceedingly attached to Tempey, and gave her up with great reluctance.*

Near the prairies, within a few miles of this solitary woman, lived William Gregory, a native of one of the states, who had resided for years among the Indians. He was now a stock keeper, and lived in a cabin, which contained his Indian family. As far as the eye could reach, over the beautiful and gently rolling plains, his cattle and horses fed, undisturbed by man or beast. It is said that William Gregory was a kind-hearted man, who fed the wanderer "without money and without price," and who, even in a lawless land, possessed a heart which prompted him to be honest.[11]

In 1785 came, also, into this neighborhood a Jew, named Abram Mordecai, a native of Pennsylvania, and who established a trading house at the spot where now stands the house of Mrs. Birch, two miles west of Line Creek.[12] Here, also, lived James Russell, another trader, who, being a Tory, had sought this place to be rid of Whig persecution.[13] A Tory, named Love, and Dargan, a Dutchman and notorious horse thief, lived near the site of Mount Meigs, where they carried on a small commerce.[14] All these traders had Indian wives, except Mordecai, whose faithful spouse was Indian, considerably darkened with the blood of Ham.

At Ecunchate, *Red Ground*, now embracing the southern suburbs of the city of Montgomery, lived several white traders. Charles Weatherford established a trading house upon

* I have conversed with Tempey (Tempy) Ellis. She is now a respectable old woman, the wife of Mr. Thomas Frizzle, residing in Pike County, Alabama.

[10] Tempy or Temperance Ellis (c. 1783–1865) survived the attack on the James Scarlett family by a Creek war party in modern Greene County, Georgia. As a captive, she was eventually released through the efforts of the mysterious Milly and returned to Georgia by the federal Indian agent James Seagrove. Ironically, she returned to Alabama as the wife of Thomas Frizzle (Frazell) and was listed on the 1850 federal census of Pike County, Alabama. James Harold Evans, "Temperance Ellis, Child Captive of the Creeks," (online); "An Ellis Family Story," Delmar Historical and Art Society, January 22, 2016 (delmahas@yahoo.com).

[11] Benjamin Hawkins, federal agent to the Creeks, first met William Gregory when he worked for Nicholas White as a "hireling" in the Upper Creek town of Fusihatchee in 1797. He referred to him as a man "of a good character." Hawkins, *Letters*, 168.

[12] In 1797, Hawkins viewed Abram M. Mordecai as "a Jew of bad character; in debt to Mr. Panton, Mr. Clark and the factory." However, he thought Mordecai's "hireling" William McCart "to be honest." Pickett interviewed Mordecai some fifty years later at the age of ninety-two and judged him less harshly. Ibid.; "A Sketch of Old Mordecai," *Flag and Advertiser*, [5 October 1847], in Pickett Scrapbook, Pickett Papers, ADAH; Notes taken from the lips of Abram Mordecai, ibid.

[13] Hawkins met James Russell at the Upper Creek town of Hoithlewaule in 1797 and wrote he "has the character of a good trader." Hawkins, *Letters*, 168.

[14] In 1797, Hawkins located Hendrick Dargin (Dargan) as the trader at Opilthlucco, an Upper Creek town that aligned with the Red Sticks in 1813–1814. Pickett's Tory trader named Love cannot be identified. Ibid., 170; Waselkov, *Conquering Spirit*, 173.

the first eastern bluff below the confluence of the Coosa and Tallapoosa, and laid out the first race-paths ever known in East Alabama. Often would the noted horse thief, fresh from the frontiers of Georgia, here, for the first time, try the speed of his stolen ponies.[15]

The most blood-thirsty, fiendish and cruel white man that ever inhabited any country was Savannah Jack, or, as he was universally called by this outlawed world, "*Savaner Jack*," who lived at Sawanogi, upon the Tallapoosa. He boasted that he had killed so many women and children, upon the Cumberland and Georgia frontiers, in company with his town's people, that he could swim in their blood, if it was collected in one pool.[16]

Thus we see that the territory of Montgomery County, now the focus of so much wealth and intelligence, was then a wilderness, inhabited by Indians and the few singular characters who have been named. Indeed, all over the territory of Alabama and Mississippi, wherever an Indian town of importance was found, white traders lived. Some of them became wealthy; but, like all property acquired in a commerce with Indians, it generally left the owner, in his old age. One of these up-country traders, "Woccocoie Clarke," living at Woccocoie, in the modern Coosa County, transported his merchandise and skins upon seventy pack-horses. His squaw, who was of great assistance to him, he called Queen Anne, for Clarke was an Englishman.[17]

Besides skins, of various kinds, the traders bought up beeswax, hickory-nut oil, snake-root, together with various medicinal barks, and transported them to Augusta and Pensacola on pack-horses, and to Mobile and New Orleans in large canoes. The pack-horses used in this trade were generally small ones, raised in the nation, but were capable of sustaining heavy loads and of enduring great fatigue. A saddle, of a peculiar shape, was first placed upon the pony. The load consisted of three bundles, each weighing sixty pounds. Two of these bundles were suspended across the saddle, and came down by the sides of the pony, while the third was deposited on top of the saddle. The whole pack was covered with a skin, to keep off the rain. Thus the pony

[15] Charles Weatherford married the widow Sehoy McPherson Tate, Alexander McGillivray's half-sister, in 1778. They had six children, including William, who became famous as the Creek chief "Red Eagle" in A. B. Meek's *The Red Eagle: A Poem of the South* published in 1855. However, in 1797, Benjamin Hawkins referred to Charles Weatherford as "a man of infamous character; a dealer in stolen horses; condemned and repreaved the 28th May." Wright, *McGillivray and McIntosh Traders*, 202–05; Hawkins, *Letters*, 170; A. B. Meek, *The Red Eagle: A Poem of the South* (New York: D. Appleton and Company, 1855).

[16] Savannah Jack is referred to as a "Shawnee mestizo" or métis by several writers, including J. Leitch Wright Jr., and Don Greene, who describe him as the son of John Hague (Haig or Haigue)—a captive raised by the Shawnee—and "an Uchee woman." Thomas Woodward claimed that he "was the most hostile and bitter enemy the whites ever had among the Creeks." He collaborated with Bowles, served with the Creek Red Sticks, and engaged in lawless killings "until he moved West." Hawkins, *Letters*, 169; Woodward, *Reminiscences*, 37–40; Wright, *Creeks and Seminoles*, 121–22; Don Greene, *Shawnee Heritage, I: Shawnee Genealogy and Family History* (Lulu.com, 2008), 272–73.

[17] In a journal entry for 1797, Benjamin Hawkins lists John Clark, John Gilliard, and James Simmons as traders at Woccocoie. From this entry, it would appear that John Clark is Pickett's "Woccocoie Clarke." Hawkins, *Letters*, 195.

sustained a load of one hundred and eighty pounds. Even liquids were conveyed in the same manner. Taffai, a mean rum, was carried on these horses in small kegs. Indeed, these hardy animals transported everything for sale, and even poultry, of all kinds, was carried in cages, made of reeds, strapped upon their backs. A pack-horseman drove ten ponies in a lead. He used no lines, but urged them on with big hickories and terrible oaths. Accustomed to their duty, they, however, seldom gave trouble, but jogged briskly along. The route and the stopping places became familiar, and, as evening approached, the little fellows quickened their trot, with new life and activity. When the sun retired over the hills, the caravan stopped; the packs were taken off, piled up in a heap, and covered with skins; the horses were belled, and turned out to find their food, which consisted of grass and young cane. It was usually late the next morning before the horses were collected and packed, for no person, in an Indian country, is fool enough to regard time. An attack from the natives, upon traders, was of rare occurrence. They imagined that they needed the supplies which they brought into their country, and regarding these singular merchants as their best friends, did not even rob them. A pack-horseman always drank taffai—it cheered him in the forest, and emboldened him in distress. With a bottle slung by his saddle, he often indulged, while those before and behind him followed his custom. Those going to Pensacola and other places were frequently in want of the stimulant, and it was customary for the traders, whom they met coming from the market, to halt, and treat, and interchange jokes. The trader who suddenly rushed by a thirsty party was long remembered as a mean fellow.[18]

Nothing stopped these men on their journey. They swam all swollen creeks, and rafted over their effects or produce. Where they had no canoes, rivers were crossed in the same manner. If they reached a stream having large cane on its banks, these were presently cut, ten feet long, and tied up into bundles, about three feet in circumference, which were placed in the water. Across these others were laid, which formed an admirable raft, capable of sustaining great weight.

[18] The trade in taffai or tafia, a cheap rum made from sugarcane juice, had a devastating impact on the American Indians. Writing to the colonial minister from New Orleans on 10 January 1763, Jean-Jacques Blaise d'Abbadie (1726–1765) wrote: "The savages of the different parts of the Illinois are reduced to a very small number; war and tafia have almost destroyed them." He could have added the impact of Indian slavery and included all the Indians of the Gulf South. Clarence Walworth Alvord and Clarence Edwin Carter, eds., *The Critical Period, 1763–1765, British Series,* vol. 1 of 3, *Collections of the Illinois State Historical Library,* vol. 10 (Springfield: Illinois State Historical Library, 1915), 10: 210.

Logs were, also, often employed in the construction of rafts. Guided by long grapevines, they were generally dragged safely across to the opposite side, where the wet ponies stood, ready to receive their packs again. Then all hands drank taffai, and journeyed on, with light hearts and laughing faces. The average travel was twenty-five miles a day. The route from Pensacola was a well-beaten path, leading up the country, and across the fatal Murder Creek, and thence to within a few miles of the Catoma, when it diverged into several trails, one of which led to Tuckabatchee, along the route of the old Federal Road, the other to Montgomery and Wetumpka, by the Red Warrior's Bluff, now Gray's Ferry, upon the Tallapoosa.[19] This trail continued to the Tennessee River.*

Northward, there were no white settlements between the Alabama River and the vicinity of Nashville. Here, in 1792, the Creeks committed many depredations. They pushed their hostilities to the very doors of Nashville. They attacked the house of Thompson, a wealthy and respectable man, killed the whole family, except his interesting daughter, just arrived at womanhood, whom they carried in captivity to Kialegee, upon the Tallapoosa, together with an amiable lady, named Caffrey, with her little son.[20] The unhappy prisoners found, in this town, a young woman, named Sarah Fletcher, who had, several years before, been captured in the Miró District, which was also called Cumberland District.[21] Miss Thompson was ransomed by Riley, a trader, for eight hundred weight of dressed deerskins, worth two hundred and sixty dollars, and was treated with kindness by her benefactor, and restored to her friends. Mrs. Caffrey was separated from her son, beaten with sticks, scratched with gar's teeth, and made to work in the fields. After two years, she was also carried to Nashville, but without her boy. The little fellow became an Indian in his feelings, and,

* Conversations with Abram Mordecai, James Moore, and many other old traders; also conversations with Hiram Mounger, of Washington County, Mrs. Sophia McComb, Mrs. Howse and Lachlan Durant. In many things, they are supported by the reports contained in *American State Papers: Indian Affairs*, volume 1.

[19] The Pensacola Trail running to near Montgomery was a branch off the Camino Real, which connected Spanish St. Augustine, through St. Marks and Pensacola, to New Orleans, and west to the Spanish settlements at Nacogdoches, and then southward to Mexico City. Other ancient Indian trails crisscrossed Alabama, such as the Great Indian Warpath that connected to the Upper Creek Path. Myer, "Indian Trails of the Southeast," 828–29; Eddie Wayne Shell, *Evolution of the Alabama Agroecosystem: Always Keeping Up, but Never Catching Up* (Montgomery: NewSouth Books, 2013), 260–62; Angela Pulley Hudson, *Creek Paths and Federal Roads: Indians, Settlers, and Slaves and the Making of the American South* (Chapel Hill: University of North Carolina Press, 2010), 11–27, 67–90.

[20] In the spring of 1792, Creek war parties struck the Middle Tennessee settlements around Nashville in cooperation with their Chickamauga and Shawnee allies. On 17 May 1792, William Blount, governor of the Territory South of the River Ohio, wrote Alexander McGillivray requesting his assistance to put a stop to the raids, as well as to retrieve the captives and some 200 stolen horses. *ASP: IA*, 269–70, 274.

[21] The Cumberland area of Middle Tennessee was named the Mero District of Davidson County by the North Carolina General Assembly in 1788 on the recommendation of James Robertson, and the clerk misspelled Miró's name when he entered it in the minutes of the cession. Robertson and others schemed with Governor Miró to open trade to New Orleans and to negotiate free access to the Mississippi River. For his part, Miró wanted to break away Kentucky and the Cumberland settlements from the United States as a Spanish province. Robertson and his associates continued their correspondence with Barón de Carondelet when he replaced Miró as governor of Louisiana and West Florida in 1792. John Allison, "The Mero District," *American Historical Magazine* 1 (April 1896): 116–22; Kinnaird, *Spain in the Mississippi Valley*, 2: 270, 279; ibid., 3: 3, 39, 52–53, 252–53.

when he had been in the nation five years, it was with difficulty that Mordecai could separate him from his Indian playmates, and carry him to Seagrove. That gentleman sent him to Governor Blount, and he finally reached his mother's arms.[22]

The bloody Coosawdas, who lived upon the Alabama, were frequently out upon the Cumberland, engaged in the massacre of the settlers and the plunder of their effects. Captain Isaacs, the chief of this town, returned, in 1792, with Elizabeth Baker, a young lady from Cumberland. How miserable and lonely must have been the journey, with these sanguinary warriors, who bore the scalps of her father, mother, brothers and sisters, daily suspended upon poles, before her eyes. When she arrived in Coosawda, the savages hung their trophies upon the council house, and danced around them with exulting shouts. But she found a friend in Charles Weatherford, who lived across the river. He ransomed Miss Baker, and placed her in charge of his wife, Sehoy, the half-sister of General McGillivray, and the mother of the celebrated William Weatherford, who will figure in this history hereafter. The unfortunate captive ultimately reached her friends.[23] It would be an endless task, to enumerate all the instances of murder and captivity which occurred upon the frontiers of Georgia and Tennessee.*

[22] On 16 June 1792, James Ore gave a deposition regarding the captives in Kialegee and recalled the name of "Elsey Thompson" but not the others. He also named John O'Riley as the trader at Kialegee. On 2 October 1794, Blount in a letter to Secretary of War Knox acknowledged the return of "Miss Alice Thompson and Mrs. Caffrey" from captivity with the Creeks through the efforts "by a white trader" named Riley. *ASP: IA*, 1: 274, 634.

[23] According to a letter from James Robertson to Governor Blount dated 22 August 1793, the raid by Captain Isaacs, son of the White Lieutenant, on the Baker family and the capture of Elizabeth Baker occurred on 21 August 1793. Ibid., 1: 467–68; Albert V. Goodpasture, "Indian Wars and Warriors of the Old Southwest," *Tennessee Historical Magazine* 4 (March 1981): 201–02.

* *American State Papers: Indian Affairs*, 1: 270–74, 431–33, 634.

Chapter XXIV

DEATH OF McGILLIVRAY—BLOODY SCENES

The Spanish authorities of Louisiana and the Floridas were accused of producing the bloody scenes, to which allusion was made in our last chapter. Great jealousies and difficulties existed between them and the southwestern people of the United States, and even between them and the federal government. John Jay, on the part of the latter, and Don Gardoqui, representing Spain, began a correspondence at New York, then the seat of the federal government, as early as 1785, for the purpose of settling the matters in dispute. Jay insisted upon the right of the people of the Union, now fast settling upon the head branches of the Tennessee, the Cumberland and the Ohio, to navigate the Mississippi to the Gulf, with their commerce, free of duty, and also the right to occupy, exclusively, all the territory east of that river, as low down as the line of 31°, all of which, he contended, was consistent with our treaty with England, made in 1782.[1] Gardoqui resisted these claims, with great show of reason.[2] He contended that Don Gálvez, in 1780, by his victories, took from England, Mobile, Baton Rouge, and Fort Panmure, at Natchez, with all their dependencies; that, at the same time, Captains Purré and Villiers, with Spanish troops, took formal possession of the English posts on the Upper Mississippi, east of that river, one of which was situated two hundred and twenty-two leagues above St. Louis; that, in 1781, Don Gálvez completed these conquests by the reduction of Pensacola; that the territories now in dispute were, at the time of the signing of the treaty between England and the United States, solely in the occupation of Spain, and that England had no right to negotiate in regard to them, and, in fact, did not really do so, but rather "tacitly left safe the territorial rights of His Catholic Majesty."[3]

These positions were met by Jay, by a reference to the treaty which Spain made with England, seven weeks after the latter had made the one with us. In the eighth article, Spain agreed to restore, without compensation, all the English territories conquered by her, except the Floridas, the northern limit

[1] John Jay served as plenipotentiary minister to Spain from January 1780 until May 1782, where he remained as the unrecognized agent for the United States. During this period, Jay dealt with the Spanish minister Conde de Floridablanca, who refused to acknowledge the 31st parallel as a boundary of the American states or the free navigation of the Mississippi River. In August 1782, Conde de Aranda presented a French edition of John Mitchell's *Map of North America* to Jay in Paris with a red line drawn that established Spanish territorial claims eastward to the Flint River, northward to the confluence of the Kanawha River on the Ohio, around the western shores of lakes Erie and Huron, and then around Lake Michigan to Lake Superior. Later, Aranda and Conrad Alexandre Gérard de Rayneval (1729–1790), who became the first French diplomatic

of which, he asserted, was 31°; that Spain was bound, by this article, to have delivered up to England (who was to deliver to the United States) all the territory claimed by Georgia, from the Chattahoochee to the Mississippi, between 31° and 35°. But there was the rub. Which was the northern boundary of Spanish West Florida? We have impartially examined this subject. The charter of Charles II, to the Lords Proprietors of South Carolina, under which Georgia claimed all the present states of Alabama and Mississippi, that monarch had no right to make.[4] The territory of these states was discovered (to say nothing of the conquest of De Soto) by the French, under Marquette and La Salle, and then by Iberville. Alabama and Mississippi were immediately occupied by France. That power continued to hold possession for sixty-two years. We have seen that she did not surrender these territories to England until 1763. These territories were occupied, then, by England, from 1763 until 1780 or 1781, when they fell, by conquest, into the hands of Spain, who immediately occupied them with her troops and extended over them her government. Well, now, where was the just claim of the United States for Georgia? Did England have any right to transfer to us, in a treaty, territories of which she had three years before been deprived by Spanish conquest? Nay, England not only had no right to do that, but she admitted she had no right when, seven weeks afterwards, she concluded a treaty with Spain, and confirmed to her West Florida, the British northern line of which was 32° 28', and not 31°, as contended for by Jefferson, Jay, and various American historians.

The negotiation between Gardoqui and Jay resulted in nothing, and the navigation of the Lower Mississippi remained closed against American citizens. In the meantime, Spain became alarmed. The treaty with McGillivray, at New York, and the movements of the first Yazoo companies, aroused her. She asked for a renewal of negotiations. The president responded by sending, to Madrid, Carmichael and Short, who entered into negotiations once more with Gardoqui, who had been recalled to Spain, and was then secretary of foreign affairs.* After much

* *State Papers and Publick Documents,* Boston edition, 10: 131–37; also *American State Papers: Foreign Affairs,* 1: 252–55.

representative to the United States, developed a compromise line south of the Ohio River. Bemis, *Pinckney's Treaty,* 24–34.

[2] Diego de Gardoqui (1735–1798) was appointed as a plenipotentiary diplomat in 1784 with clear instructions as to the boundary between the Spanish Floridas and the new United States. For the next four years, Jay and Gardoqui held meetings in formal and social settings, which produced agreements regarding trade and commerce but with no meaningful progress on the boundary or navigation of the Mississippi. Ibid., 60–148.

[3] On 22 November 1780, Captain Balthazar de Villiers crossed the Mississippi River from Fort Carlos Tercero de Arkansas and "took possession of the left bank of the Mississippi . . . as far as the district of Natchez" in the name of King Carlos III. On 2 January 1781, Captain Eugenio Purré set out from St. Louis with sixty-five militiamen and sixty Indian auxiliaries. He seized the British post at St. Joseph at modern Niles, Michigan, on 12 February 1781 and raised the Spanish flag, abandoning the fort after twenty-four hours. On 10 May 1781, Governor Bernardo Gálvez completed the Spanish takeover of British possessions in the Floridas with the capture of Pensacola. Kinnaird, *Spain in the Mississippi Valley,* 1: 401, 431–34; Bernardo de Gálvez, "Bernardo de Gálvez Diary of the Operations against Pensacola," *Louisiana Historical Quarterly* 1 (January 1917): 74–76.

[4] Charles II granted the land between the 31° to 36° of north latitude from the Atlantic to the Pacific to eight favorites, who became the Lords Proprietors of Carolina in 1663, and in 1675 extended the boundaries from 29° to 36 ½°. William Patterson Cuming, "Naming Carolina," *North Carolina Historical Review*

correspondence, in which both powers frequently accused each other of improper interference with the Indians inhabiting the disputed region, over whom they each exclusively claimed the superintendence, the negotiations terminated, without arrangement satisfactory to us.[5] All that Spain would admit, was the probability of her ultimately allowing the northern boundary of her West Florida possessions to be the line of 32° 28', while she was also disposed to allow the establishment of a warehouse at the mouth of the Yazoo, in which American citizens could deposit their produce, from their own boats, brought down the Mississippi. These productions were then to be taken to New Orleans in Spanish boats, and sold or exported, subject to Spanish duties.*

All this time, the agents of Spain, near the federal government, were constantly annoying Jefferson, the secretary, with a series of complaints against Governor Blount, of Tennessee, and Seagrove, the Creek agent, which were answered by similar complaints against the Spaniards, on the part of the latter.[6] Much ill feeling was elicited between these parties, while the people of Georgia were perfectly rampant, censuring the federal authorities for the weakness, irresolution and tardiness displayed in conducting the negotiations. They proclaimed that, if the United States much longer neglected to drive the Spaniards from their territory, they would undertake it themselves. The horizon of this vast Indian wilderness was still further darkened by the incessant border warfare between the Indians and the frontier Americans.† Spain assumed very high and unwarrantable grounds, in one respect. She even opposed the running of the line around the Oconee lands, and it was made the subject of remonstrance to the federal government. She claimed a surveillance over the affairs of the Creeks, by her treaty with them, at Pensacola, and avowed her determination to protect them against the encroachments of the Georgians. As none of the Oconee territory lay within the limits of West Florida, Spain certainly stepped beyond reason in seeking a quarrel with the Americans about it.[7]

General McGillivray continued to make visits to Governor

* *State Papers and Publick Documents*, Boston edition, 10: 159–62.

† *State Papers and Publick Documents*, Boston edition, 10: 185–86.

22 (January 1945): 34–42; "A Declaration and Proposals of the Lord Proprietor of Carolina," 25 August 1663, *CSRNC*, 1: 43–46.

5 President Washington sent William Short, resident minister to The Hague, to Madrid, where he joined William Carmichael on 1 February 1793. As joint commissioners, they had little stature before the Spanish court and made little progress over the next year. By the time Carmichael was recalled and Short was made a regular minister, the Spanish minister Manuel de Godoy had transferred the negotiations to his representatives in Philadelphia. Bemis, *Pinckney's Treaty*, 164–72, 192–97.

6 In an exchange of notes in May and June 1793, the Spanish agents to the U.S., Josef de Jaudenes and Josef de Viar, used an aggressive, hostile tone with Secretary of State Thomas Jefferson. They questioned the efforts of Governor William Blount to promote an alliance with the Chickasaw against the Creeks and his plan for a fort on the Mississippi at the Chickasaw Bluffs. Ibid., 182–86, 186 n. 35.

7 In February 1792, Governor-General Barón de Carondelet sent Pedro Olivier to reside among the Creeks to monitor McGillivray's loyalty to Spain and to stir up Creek opposition to the running of the Oconee boundary line. Caughey, *McGillivray of the Creeks*, 51, 307, 320.

Carondelet.[8] In returning from New Orleans, late in the summer of 1792, a violent fever detained him long in Mobile. Recovering, he went to Little Tallassee, where he wrote his last letter to Major Seagrove. He appeared to deplore the unhappy disturbances which existed, and ascribed them to the interference of the Spaniards with our affairs. He had often responded to the letters of the secretary of war, in relation to carrying out the provisions of the New York treaty, and, several times, assured him that he had explained that instrument frequently to the chiefs, and had urged them to comply, but that the Spanish influence had defeated his recommendations. In one of his letters, he says to the secretary: "You will recollect, sir, that I had great objection to making the south fork of the Oconee the limit, and, when you insisted so much, I candidly told you that it might be made an article, but I could not pledge myself to get it confirmed, or that of the restoration of the Negro property, which had so often changed owners."[9]

But this remarkable man was fast approaching dissolution. He had long been afflicted, and was always of a delicate constitution. He spent the winter upon Little River, which now divides the counties of Monroe and Baldwin. The account of his death is presented in the language of the great merchant, William Panton, in a letter, dated Pensacola, April 10 1794, and addressed to Lachlan McGillivray, the father of the chieftain, who was, at that time, still alive at Dunmaglass, Scotland.

"Your son, sir, was a man that I esteemed greatly. I was perfectly convinced that our regard for each other was mutual. It so happened that we had an interest in serving each other, which first brought us together, and the longer we were acquainted, the stronger was our friendship.

"I found him deserted by the British, without pay, without money, without friends, and without property, saving a few Negroes, and he and his nation threatened with destruction by the Georgians, unless they agreed to cede them the better part of their country. I had the good fortune to point out a mode by which he could save them all, and it succeeded beyond expectation.

"He died on the 17th February 1793, of complicated disorders—of inflamed lungs and the gout on his stomach. He was taken ill on the path coming from his cow-pen on Little River, where one of his wives, Joseph Cornells's daughter, resided, and died eight days after his arrival here. No pains, no attention, no cost was spared to save the life of my friend; but fate would have it otherwise, and he breathed his last in my arms.

"He died possessed of sixty Negroes, three hundred head of cattle, with a large stock of horses.[10]

[8] McGillivray had a great fear of traveling in a ship and made only two visits to New Orleans. In May-June 1786, he met with Esteban Miró in New Orleans and convinced him to supply the Creeks with guns, munitions, and other military supplies. On his second trip in June-July 1792, he signed the Treaty of New Orleans on 6 July 1792 with Barón de Carondelet. Caughey, *McGillivray of the Creeks*, 30–31, 125, 128, 328–32.

[9] Article four in the 1790 Treaty of New York provided for a survey by "an able surveyor on the part of the United States . . . assisted by three old citizens of Georgia . . . and three old Creek chiefs" to determine the boundary on the Oconee. The original surveyor, Andrew Ellicott, sent his brother Joseph Ellicott to start the survey but delays by the Creeks prevented its timely completion. Kappler, *Indian Affairs: Laws and Treaties*, 2: 26; *ASP: IA*, 1: 255, 256.

[10] In a letter to John Leslie on 28 August 1793, Panton wrote that he had convinced McGillivray's sisters to "divide the Negroes . . . and part of the Cattle, for his children." Caughey, *McGillivray of the Creeks*, 359–60.

"I advised, I supported, I pushed him on, to be the great man. Spaniards and Americans felt his weight, and this enabled him to haul me after him, so as to establish this house with more solid privileges than, without him, I should have attained. This being the case, if he had lived, I meant, besides what he was owing me, to have added considerably to his stock of Negroes. What I intended to do for the father, I will do for his children. This ought not to operate against your making that ample provision for your grandson and his two sisters which you have it in your power to make. They have lately lost their mother, so that they have no friends, poor things, but you and me. My heart bleeds for them, and what I can, I will do. The boy, Aleck, is old enough to be sent to Scotland, to school,[11] which I intend to do next year, and then you will see him."*

General McGillivray was interred with Masonic honors in the splendid garden of William Panton, in the city of Pensacola. He was a severe loss to that gentleman, and to the Spanish government. His death, among the Indians, everywhere, produced deep sorrow and regret. The great chieftain, who had so long been their pride, and who had elevated their nation, and sustained it in its trials, now lay buried in the sands of the Seminoles.[12]

General McGillivray was six feet high, spare made, and remarkably erect in person and carriage. His eyes were large, dark and piercing. His forehead was so peculiarly shaped, that the old Indian countrymen often spoke of it: it commenced expanding at his eyes, and widened considerably at the top of his head. It was a bold and lofty forehead. His fingers were long and tapering, and he wielded a pen with the greatest rapidity. His face was handsome, and indicative of quick thought and much sagacity. Unless interested in conversation, he was disposed to be taciturn, but, even then, was polite and respectful. When a British colonel, he dressed in the British uniform, and when in the Spanish service, he wore the military dress of that country. When Washington appointed him a brigadier general, he sometimes wore the uniform of the American army, but never when in the presence of the Spaniards. His usual dress was a mixture of the Indian and American garb. He always travelled with two servants, David Francis, a half-breed, and Paro, a Negro, who saved the lives of over a hundred royalists, in 1781, as we have seen.[13] He had good houses at the Hickory Ground and at Little Tallassee, where he entertained, free of charge, distinguished government agents, and persons travelling through his extensive

* I found Panton's letter among the bundle of papers in the District Court of New Orleans.

[11] William Panton sent young Aleck McGillivray at the age of 10–12 and David Tate (Taitt), McGillivray's nephew, to Banff Academy in Scotland to be educated, and John Innerarity Sr., who lived in London, agreed to serve as their guardian and dispense funds for their expenses. According to Innerarity in 1798, Aleck "bids fair to make a good scholar," but John Leslie wrote from London on 15 July 1802 that he had consumption and "has little hopes of surviving longer than three months." A Chipstead Parish burial record discovered by John Dagger in 1996 recorded his death on 25 July 1802. Wright, *McGillivray and McIntosh Traders*, 269–71, 275–76; Marie Taylor Greenslade, "William Panton," *Florida Historical Quarterly* 14 (October 1935): 116–19.

[12] While his white friends provided the honors of a Masonic ceremony and burial, a number of Creeks in Pensacola followed his body to the grave with "loud screams of real woe which they vented in their unaffected grief." McGillivray's obituary notice was printed in *The Gentleman's Magazine*, August 1793, and quoted in Caughey, *McGillivray of the Creeks*, 362, 362 n. 353.

[13] David Francis was described as "a young half breed, kinsman to Col. M'Gillivray" in the 29 July 1790 issue of the *Pennsylvania Packet and Daily Advertiser*. Francis and David Tate (Taitt),

dominions. Like all other men, he had his faults. He was ambitious, crafty, and rather unscrupulous; yet he possessed a good heart, and was polite and hospitable. For ability and sagacity, the reader will admit that he had few superiors. We have called him the Talleyrand of Alabama. Will not his political acts, but a few of which have been presented, for the want of space, entitle him to that appellation?

The Indian sky still remained darkened by scenes of murder and robbery. The Chehaw Creeks, upon the Flint, instigated by James Burgess, a trader in the Spanish interest, plundered the store of Robert Seagrove, at Traders Hill, upon the St. Mary's, killed Fleming, the clerk, and two travelers named Moffit and Upton, most cruelly beating, with sticks, a woman residing there, named Ann Gray.[14] Six miles from the hill, they killed a family of men, women and children, moving in their wagons, and made prisoners a woman and a child, whom they reserved for greater sufferings. The inhabitants of the new counties of Glynn and Camden often felt such attacks. At the Skull Shoals, of the Oconee, Richard Thrasher, two children and a Negro woman, were shot down, while his wife, plunging into the river, with a babe in her arms, received a ball in her head, turned over, and sank beneath the waves.[15] Governor Telfair determined, at once, to raise a large force for the invasion of the Creek country. Washington, at the solicitation of the Georgia delegation in Congress, sent to Augusta a large stand of arms and ammunition. He authorized Governor Telfair to enlist a few companies for the protection of Georgia, but remonstrated against the contemplated invasion, stating that it was unauthorized by law, would embarrass the negotiations still pending between the federal agents and the Creeks, and also those going on with Spain, and that the enemy had only killed some people upon the remote frontiers. But Governor Telfair, with the true spirit of a Georgian, heeded him not, and resolved to "carry the war into Africa." He disdained to accept of the troops which the president had authorized him to raise, but placed General Twiggs at the head of seven hundred mounted men. That gallant officer, of Revolutionary memory, marched to the Ocmulgee River, where a mutinous spirit and the want of provisions caused a retreat. This abortive attempt at conquest emboldened the Creeks to new scenes of pillage and blood. Although mortified at the failure of his first attempt at invasion, Governor Telfair did not relax in his exertions to protect the people, but constantly scoured the country between the Oconee and Ocmulgee, with a large force of mounted militia, which, for a time, stopped the Indian ravages.[16] These

McGillivray's nephew, attended a Quaker school at Philadelphia at government expense under a secret agreement made by President Washington and Henry Knox under the 1790 Treaty of New York. Waselkov, *Conquering Spirit*, 45, 285 n. 32.

[14] James Burgess lived among the Lower Creeks and operated a trading post on the Flint River near modern Bainbridge, Georgia. Burgess denied culpability in the attack at Trader's Hill but admitted his brother-in-law was one of the perpetrators of the attack. Robert Seagrove was the brother of the U.S. Indian agent James Seagrove. While John Fleming, Daniel Moffit, and James Upton were killed, James Allen, Robert Brown, John Galphin, and Ann Gray either escaped or survived the attack. Caughey, *McGillivray of the Creeks*, 359–60; *ASP: IA*, 1: 373, 374.

[15] William Urquhart, secretary in Georgia's executive department, received several depositions regarding the random Creek attacks in Washington, Wilkes, and Greene counties, including the Richard Thrasher (Thresher) family on 22 April 1793. Mrs. Thrasher "was found alive, scalped, wounded in both her thighs, and her right breast with balls, and stabbed in her left breast with a knife . . . She died in about twenty-four hours. *ASP: IA*, 1: 369.

[16] Georgia's Governor Edward Telfair declared that he saw "little expectation of avoiding a general war with the Creeks and Cherokees" and decided to

operations again called out the remonstrances of Washington, which had no effect whatever upon the Georgians, many of whom entertained for the president the most implacable hostility, and placed his effigies upon pine trees, and fired guns at them. It is a very common belief, with people of modern times, that Washington, during his extensive career, HAD NO ENEMIES. He received as much abuse, not only in Georgia, but in various portions of the Union, as any of our presidents.*

Although Seagrove had been superintendent over two years, he had never entered the Creek Nation, but had communicated with the chiefs through an honest and intelligent man, named Timothy Barnard, who had long resided among the red people. At Cusseta, that gentleman met a council of chiefs, the most prominent of whom were the White Lieutenant, John Kinnard, the Mad Dog, the Head King, and Alexander Cornells, representing the Upper and Lower Towns, who requested him to assure Seagrove that they desired to see him in their country, and promised to protect him while he remained with them.[17] But the efforts of the agent to restore peace, and to procure the marking of the boundary, were embarrassed by the military operations of Governor Telfair, who assured him that his contemplated mission to the Creek Nation would result in no good; that his mind was made up, to chastise the Creeks, until they restored the white prisoners, the Negroes, and other stolen property, and delivered up ten hostages from the Upper, and an equal number from the Lower Towns, together with thirteen principal hostiles, to be put to death by the people of Georgia; that he would submit to no treaty made with the Creeks, where Georgia agents were not allowed to participate. Such was the Treaty of New York. It is singular that this treaty, made by Washington, for the good of all parties concerned, should have been so violently opposed. The Spaniards, as was anticipated, denounced it, but it received equal opposition from the Creeks and *Georgians*.

Notwithstanding the high grounds assumed by Governor Telfair, Seagrove resolved to go into the nation; but was deterred by information which he received that a body of armed men, under Captain Peter B. Williamson,† intended to intercept and prevent him, and that the Georgia troops had destroyed Little Okfuskee, upon the Chattahoochee, which resulted in the death of six Indians, while eight others were carried

* *American State Papers: Indian Affairs*, 1: 362–68.

† Afterwards Judge of the County Court of Lowndes, Alabama.

take an aggressive response by building fourteen block-houses from the St. Mary's to the Tugaloo River. Major General John Twiggs commanded a force of 700 men that crossed the Oconee but failed to engage any Creek forces. However, at a council of war in Augusta on 8 August 1793, Twiggs and seven militia generals agreed that they would need "two thousand horse, and three thousand foot" for a fall campaign against the Creek towns. *ASP: IA*, 1: 368–371.

[17] Timothy Barnard, an Indian countryman with an Uchee (Yuchi) wife and a large family, served as a deputy agent to the Creeks under James Seagrove. Because of his long association with the Lower Creeks, he hosted a number of peace chiefs at the Cusseta Conference on 21 July 1793, where Mad Dog gave a "talk . . . to be forwarded to his Excellency General Washington, President of the United States." Ibid., 386–87, 390–91, 411–21; Coker and Watson, *Indian Traders*, 189, 191.

[18] The White Lieutenant was pro-American, and James Seagrove described his town of Little Okfuskee as one of the friendly towns among the Lower Creeks. On 21 September 1793, Georgia militia forces under Lieutenant Colonel William Melton "burnt the huts of one town," "killed and scalped six Indian men," and took three women and five girls as prisoners at Little Okfuskee. The attack caused the White Lieutenant to reach out to Governor Carondelet, and Seagrove accused "lawless whites" on the Georgia frontier of fomenting

prisoners to Greensboro.[18] Barnard was again sent to the Chattahoochee, who, after a council with the chiefs, returned, with another invitation for Seagrove to visit their country, and that, although they were much aroused against the Georgians for this attack upon a peaceable town, they imputed no blame to the federal authorities. Finally, the agent set out from Fort Fidius, escorted by a military guard, to "prevent," as he wrote to the secretary of war, "my being robbed by the frontier banditti, who, two days ago, stole ten of the horses upon which I had to carry goods for the Indians." Seagrove had the reputation of being a timid man, and of not entertaining a very high sense of honor. Arriving at the Ocmulgee, the escort was dismissed, when one hundred and thirty Indian warriors took charge of his person, from thence to Cusseta, upon the Chattahoochee. At this place, he was saluted by the Indians with the beating of drums and the roars of a piece of artillery. He advanced to Tuckabatchee, the capital of the nation, which lay upon the west bank of the Tallapoosa. He occupied one whole day in a speech to a vast assembly, and, although surrounded by Spanish agents and enemies, he rose above his character, boldly pointed out the aggressions of the Creeks, and their faithlessness in not complying with the New York treaty.[19]

The council sat forty-eight hours, without adjournment, and then rose, having stipulated, on the part of the Creeks, to deliver to Seagrove the Negroes, horses, cattle, and other property taken from the Georgians during the last twelve months. They further agreed to put to death two or more of the principals engaged in the late murders upon the frontiers. The Spanish agent, Captain Don Pedro Olivier, was present, and congratulated Seagrove upon what he was pleased to term his fortunate mission.[20]

Having remained at Tuckabatchee some weeks,

war. *ASP: IA*, 1: 362, 372–73, 411; Caughey, *McGillivray of the Creeks*, 360–61.

[19] James Seagrove's first face-to-face conference with "a full representation" of Upper Creek and Lower Creek leaders at Tuckabatchee on 23–24 November 1793 caused him to declare "peace and good understanding is again re-established between the United States and the said nations." Tuckabatchee was the home of the slain David Cornells, and Seagrove promised that his murderers would be apprehended and punished. He asked Secretary of War Knox to issue a proclamation to that effect and to facilitate the return of prisoners held by the state of Georgia. *ASP: IA*, 1: 471–72; Coker and Watson, *Indian Traders*, 191.

[20] Before ending the meeting, the Creeks appointed White Lieutenant, Mad Dog, and Hollowing King as commissioners to work with Seagrove "to settle all other matters" and "to carry into effect what was determined on." Ironically, Seagrove and Pedro Olivier shared the same house during the two day conference. *ASP: IA*, 1: 472.

arranging his business with the chiefs, Seagrove, one night, was attacked by the Tallassee King at the head of a party; his house was plundered, and he was forced to fly, for his life, to a pond, thick with trees and bushes. There he remained several hours, up to his waist in cold water, expecting every moment to be scented out, dragged forth, and put to death. In the morning the chiefs interposed, pacified the Tallassee King, and the trembling agent came out from his watery place of refuge.[21] The Tallassee King was one of those who had conveyed away the Oconee lands, at Augusta, and who, like the Georgians, entertained no good feeling for the federal agents.*

A spirited border war continued to be waged upon the northern frontiers. Captain Hadley, whose troops had been attacked upon the Cumberland Mountains, was brought to Willstown by the victorious party, composed of Creeks, Cherokees and Shawnees.[22] They debated, for several days, upon his life, which was at length saved, through the solicitations of Alexander Campbell and John McDonald, two old British traders, of Willstown, but now in the Spanish interest.[23] Great preparations were on foot, in this region, for the final extermination of the Cumberland people. John Watts, a Cherokee half-breed, had regularly organized three companies of mounted Indians, who had been furnished with the necessary arms by Governor Carondelet. A large deputation of Shawnees, from the north, had just completed a campaign through the Creek Nation, endeavoring to enlist recruits for that end, and had succeeded in collecting six hundred and seventeen warriors, who passed through Willstown on their way up.[24]

The people of East Tennessee, also, felt the

* *American State Papers: Indian Affairs*, 1: 305,412–22; 2: 471–72. Also conversations with old Indian countrymen.

[21] Pickett's source for the narrative of the Tallassee King attacking James Seagrove at Tuckabatchee must have come from his "conversations with old Indian countrymen." Seagrove's correspondence published in the *American State Papers: Indian Affairs* does not mention this confrontation.

[22] Captain Samuel Hadley and his mounted detachment of forty-two men had been ordered to the Mero District by Governor William Blount. On 23 September 1792, Handley's East Tennessee force was struck by a Chickamauga force of fifty-six men under Middle Striker at Crab Orchard and suffered three killed, several wounded, and Handley taken as a prisoner to Willstown. Clarence Edwin Carter, comp. & ed., *The Territorial Papers of the United States,* vol. 4: *The Territory South of the River Ohio, 1790–1796,* 28 vols. (Washington: GPO, 1934–1964), 4: 234–35 [Hereafter cited as *Territorial Papers/Territory South of the River Ohio*]; Pate, "The Chickamauga," 219.

[23] Alexander Campbell and John McDonald were traders and Loyalists who had a long residence among the Chickamauga towns. McDonald, a Scotsman and Indian countryman, had a trading post at Running Water and developed a trading relationship with William Panton which led to his working closely with governors Carondelet and O'Neill. After his release, Handley reported to Blount that both men treated him civilly given their situation. Kinnaird, *Spain in the Mississippi Valley,* 3: 164, 268–69, 334–37, 344–45, 366; *ASP: IA,* 1: 434; Brown, *Old Frontiers,* 246–47, 338–39, 345, 350.

[24] Following Dragging Canoe's death on 1 March 1792, John Watts had been elected as the war leader of the Chickamaugas and established his headquarters at Willstown. He also became the beneficiary of the alliances that Dragging Canoe had developed with the Creeks, Shawnees, and other nations in the Ohio country. As noted earlier, there was a significant Shawnee presence in the Chickamauga Five Lower Towns prior to Dragging Canoe's death, and their principal leader was Cheeseekau, Tecumseh's older brother. Pate, "The Chickamauga," 207–08, 210–13, 216–21; Sugden, *Tecumseh,* 53–81.

attacks of these marauding parties. They defended themselves with bravery, but sometimes were guilty of acts of great imprudence, which served to irritate the Indians who were friendly. Captain Beard, at the head of mounted militia, attacked the peaceable people of Hiwassee, wounded Hanging Maw, the chief, and killed his wife and a dozen others. The Indians rallied and repulsed the assailants.[25] Such was the state of feeling and alarm, that Governor Blount placed General Sevier at the head of six hundred mounted men. That officer, crossing the Tennessee below the mountains, marched for the Oostanaula, where he made some Cherokee prisoners. Proceeding to the site of the modern Rome, he discovered Indian entrenchments on the opposite bank of the Etowah. Plunging into that stream, the troops gained the southern bank, and, after a fight of an hour, the Indians gave way, bearing off their dead and wounded, but leaving their camp equipage, horses, Spanish guns and ammunition. General Sevier afterwards scoured this whole region, without opposition, and returned to East Tennessee.[26] It appeared that the evil one, himself, was stalking through this wild region, for, independently of the commotions upon the frontiers of Georgia and Tennessee, the Creeks and Chickasaws were engaged in a bloody war, while French emissaries were at work to estrange the affections of the Southwestern people from the federal government.*

* *American State Papers: Indian Affairs*, 1: 434–39, 441–54, 464–70.

[25] President Washington had requested that Governor William Blount bring a delegation of Cherokee and Chickamauga chiefs to Philadelphia to discuss a lasting treaty of peace. Doublehead, Hanging Maw, Otter Lifter, Scantee, Fool Charlie, and nine other chiefs had gathered at Hanging Maw's house at Coyatee, a peaceful Upper Cherokee town, in anticipation of making the trip east. Captain John Beard was pursuing a party of horse thieves when he attacked Coyatee on 12 June 1793, wounding Hanging Maw and a daughter of the Beloved Woman Nancy Ward. Beard's men killed Scantee, Fool Charlie, Hanging Maw's wife, Betty, a daughter of Kitegista, William Rosebury, a white man, and "eight or nine others." *ASP: IA*, 1: 459–60; Carter, *Territorial Papers/Territory South of the River Ohio*, 4: 259–60; Pate, "The Chickamauga," 233–34; Brown, *Old Frontiers*, 386–88.

[26] The unprovoked attack on the Cherokee peace delegates in June 1793 caused a number of Cherokee warriors to seek revenge on the East Tennesseans by joining the Chickamaugas. After Watts' failed Knoxville campaign in September 1793, General John Sevier's seven hundred mounted militia force pursued some four hundred Lower Cherokee and Upper Creeks who resided in towns in northern Georgia on the headwaters of the Coosa River. His army made contact with a Cherokee/Creek force at Etowah near the junction of the Coosawattee and Coosa Rivers on 17 October 1793 and Sevier's superior numbers carried the day. They proceeded to destroy Oostanaula, Turnip Mountain, and other smaller Cherokee towns, burning cribs of wheat, corn, and beans, and killing three hundred head of cattle and one hundred hogs. Although his scouts discovered the trail to the Chickamauga towns, Sevier and his victorious troops turned northward into the Tennessee River Valley with their captives and booty. *ASP: IA*, 1: 469–70; Pate, "The Chickamauga," 240–41; Brown, *Old Frontiers*, 392–97.

Chapter XXV

THE FRENCH MINISTER, GENET— HIS DESIGNS UPON THE SOUTHWEST

Louis XVI, the friend of America, had been beheaded at Paris, and Robespierre and other hyenas swayed unhappy France. Genêt was their American minister. Upon his arrival in the United States, he assumed unwarrantable grounds.[1] After failing to enlist Washington in his Jacobinical notions of liberty, he sought to disaffect the southern and western people, and to dismember the Union. He took advantage of the excited feeling of the population upon the Holston, Cumberland, Ohio, and other tributaries of the Mississippi, who had long denounced the federal government for allowing them no protection against the savages, and for not compelling the Spaniards, who held the Lower Mississippi, to grant them the free navigation of that river. Indeed, these brave and adventurous people had just grounds of complaint. They were cut off from the rest of the Union, and had to defend themselves, while their rich products of corn, flour and tobacco rotted at their doors, on account of the arbitrary laws of the Spanish provinces below them. They, naturally enough, entertained no love for a Union which was no advantage to them.[2] The Georgians, on the other hand, claimed all the territory between 31° and 35°, from the Savannah to the Mississippi, and, although independent of the navigation of the "Father of Waters," viewed its exclusive occupation by the Spaniards as a great outrage, not only against their rights, but those of their Northwestern brethren. Georgia was also irritated with the federal government for its irresolution and tardiness in adjusting her various rights, both in regard to the Spaniards and Creeks, as we have repeatedly seen.[3]

Again, Genêt was further encouraged in his nefarious schemes on account of the war which was then declared between France and Spain. He was led to believe, from all these circumstances, that it would be an easy matter to make the disaffected citizens of the United States allies of France,

[1] **Instead of traveling directly to Philadelphia to present his credentials to President George Washington, Edmond Charles Genêt, France's new minister to the U.S., arrived in Charleston, South Carolina, on 8 April 1793. While his primary assignment was to promote France's war with Spain, Great Britain, and other European nations, Genêt used his time in South Carolina to commission four privateering ships to attack British ships and to organize militia forces to attack Spanish possessions. Harry Ammon, *The Genet Mission* (New York: W. W. Norton, 1973), 44–45; George C. Herring, *From Colony to Superpower: U.S. Foreign Relations since 1776* (New York: Oxford University Press, 2008), 71.**

[2] **In an "interview" on 5 July 1793 with Thomas Jefferson, as "Mr. Jefferson" and not as secretary**

of state, Genêt presented his plan to appoint André Michaux, a French botanist, to go to Kentucky as a French agent to disseminate propaganda to encourage the people of Louisiana to overthrow the Spanish government. He would be authorized to raise a force of Americans in Kentucky to march on New Orleans. According to Jefferson, he warned Genêt of the consequences of these actions, but he did not tell President Washington about this conversation. Stanley Elkins and Eric McKitrick, *The Age of Federalism: The Early American Republic, 1788–1800* (New York: Oxford University Press, 1993), 349–50.

[3] When Genêt's plans were thwarted by his recall to France and replacement by Jean Antoine Joseph Fauchet in February 1794, Elijah Clarke and his followers who opposed federal Indian and land policies established the quasi-independent Trans-Oconee Republic on Creek lands southwest of the Oconee River. See Watson W. Jennison, *Cultivating Race: The Expansion of Slavery in Georgia, 1750–1860* (Lexington: University Press of Kentucky, 2012), 89–125.

[4] From Charleston and along the coast to Philadelphia, Genêt was warmly welcomed. On 17 May 1793, the day following his arrival in Philadelphia, he was welcomed by crowds of people who filled the streets and marched to his residence to greet him, giving him a false sense of how the Washington administration would view his presence and activities on behalf of the new French Republic. Ammon, *Genet Mission*, 52–59; Elkins and McKitrick, *Age of Federalism*, 341–42.

[5] Before Genêt left France, George Rogers Clark had developed a plan to seize Louisiana and West Florida, and on 12 July 1793, Genêt notified Clark that his plan had been adopted and appointed him commander-in-chief of the "Revolutionary and Independent Legion of Mississippi." Genêt selected Samuel Hammond, William Tate, and Elijah Clarke to organize the Revolutionary Legion of the Floridas. While Hammond moved into East Florida to capture St. Augustine, Clarke and his volunteers were to take West Florida. Tate was to take a force through the Appalachian Mountains, descend the Tennessee, and join George Rogers Clark to seize Louisiana. "Correspondence of Clark and Genêt: Selections from the Draper Collection in the State Historical Society of Wisconsin," *Annual Report of the American Historical Association for the Year 1896*, 2 vols. (Washington: GPO, 1897), 1: 571–74, 967–71, 977–82, 986, 995–96.

[6] Elijah Clarke resigned his commission in the Georgia militia, citing his health and age, in February 1794, but in the fall of 1793, he had accepted Genêt's appointment as a major general in the Revolutionary Legion of the Floridas at an annual salary of $10,000. Ammon, *Genet Mission*, 166; Jennison, *Cultivating Race*, 109–10.

[7] Major Peter B. Williamson served as "paymaster of Clarke's troops." His father Micajah Williamson served with Elijah Clarke during the Revolutionary War, and his sister Nancy married John Clarke, son of Elijah Clarke. According to some reports, agents had been sent out with as much as $10,000 to enlist men and buy military provisions. No further identification could be found for Colonel Carr and Captain Bird by this editor. E. Merton Coulter, "Elijah Clarke's Foreign Intrigues and the 'Trans-Oconee Republic,'" *Bulletin of the University of Georgia* 23 (December 1922), 3, 5; *American State Papers: Foreign Relations*, 1: 459–60 [Hereafter cited as *ASP: FR*]; William J. Northen, ed., *Men of Mark in Georgia: A Complete and Elaborate History of the State*, 2 vols. (Atlanta: A. B. Caldwell, 1910), 2: 157–58.

[8] In a letter written on 13 April 1794, Major Henry Gaither reported to Secretary of War Henry Knox the presence of the *Le Las Casas* of eighteen guns and 200 French troops off the coast of St. Mary's and that the French ship had saluted his fort. Henry Gaither to Henry Knox, St. Mary's, 13 April 1794, http://wardepartmentpapers.org/.

[9] On 28 July 1794, Governor George Mathews issued a proclamation prohibiting the unlawful actions of Elijah Clarke and his followers southwest of the Oconee River on Creek lands. However, his actions resulted from pressure from his fellow Georgians and federal authorities and not from Juan Nepomuceno de Quesada (1738–1798) as governor of East Florida. *ASP: IA*, 1: 495–96; Kinnaird, *Spain in the Mississippi Valley*, 3: 368–69, 375.

[10] On 22 April 1793, President Washington issued his Proclamation of Neutrality to dissuade and prohibit U.S. citizens from becoming involved in the

and, associated with the dissatisfied French population upon the Mississippi, he could overthrow the Spanish provinces of Louisiana and the Floridas, and establish a government dependent upon the republic of France.[4] Two expeditions were planned by him, in the West, while in Charleston. Several distinguished citizens had accepted commissions under him. The desire to invade the Floridas prevailed in Georgia to an alarming extent. From the frontiers of South Carolina and Kentucky, detachments, called the "French Legion," marched to places of rendezvous. They were to serve three months, and receive bounties of land.[5] Genêt was to have been commander-in-chief. His most influential and powerful assistant was General Elijah Clarke, of Georgia. That gentleman had dispatched an agent to Lexington, Kentucky, who purchased, upon his credit, two boats, powder and cannon ball, which were conveyed down the Ohio.[6]

An agent was furnished with ten thousand dollars, to purchase supplies for a Georgia army, to assemble at St. Mary's. Clarke had authority to issue military appointments, in the name of the French Republic, and he constituted Peter B. Williamson, major, _____ Carr, a colonel, and conferred the commissions of captain on _____ Bird and other citizens of Georgia.[7] The French sloop-of-war, *Le Las Casas*, direct from Charleston, anchored at St. Mary's, within musket shot of the American post, which was in command of Major Gaither. She was destined for Louisiana, and her officers asserted that thirteen sail, large and well-manned, were yet to follow, from different ports of the United States.[8] In the meantime, boat builders were vigorously employed upon the Ohio, and persons of character and wealth sold their property at auction, to facilitate their completion. A considerable body of Creeks and Cherokees had likewise been enlisted in the cause of the "French republic." The governor of East Florida, alarmed at these preparations, remonstrated with Governor Mathews, of Georgia, who immediately issued his proclamation, forbidding the people of Georgia to engage in such enterprises.[9] Shortly afterwards, Washington issued a proclamation against the whole project, and authorized Governor Mathews to employ all the United States troops, then in Georgia, to put down the contemplated invasion.[10]

Governor Carondelet was active in preparations for defense. He strengthened New Orleans, and added troops to the fort at Mobile, and other posts, while he erected new ones at several points below the mouth of the Ohio. The militia, throughout Louisiana and the Floridas, were completely organized.[11] It is strange that the Barón Carondelet should, at this time, have resorted to the same scheme contemplated by his enemy, Genêt. He, too, dispatched an emissary—an Englishman, named Powers—among the western American

war between France and Great Britain, Austria, Prussia, Sardinia, and the Netherlands. On 5 June 1794, Congress codified Washington's proclamation when it enacted the Neutrality Act of 1794. It specifically prohibited U.S. citizens from enlisting in the service of a foreign power and the outfitting of foreign armed ships in U.S. ports. U.S. Congress, "Neutrality Act, 1794," *United States Statutes at Large,* 3rd Cong., Sess. I., 381–84; "The Proclamation of Neutrality," http://avalon.law.yale.edu.

[11] Contrary to Pickett's narrative, Carondelet did not build any new fortifications on the Mississippi in 1793–1794, but he did strengthen the existing posts above New Orleans: Natchez, Nogales, Arkansas Post, New Madrid, and St. Louis. In early January 1794, he also dispatched three galleys, two galiots, and one cañonera under Pedro Andrés Rousseau with an additional 150 troops to New Madrid with orders to patrol to the mouth of the Ohio River. At the time, the Spanish Mississippi River fleet was the largest naval force to operate above New Orleans. Abraham P. Nasatir, *Spanish War Vessels on the Mississippi, 1792–1796* (New Haven: Yale University Press, 1968), 74–84, 90–91.

citizens, with offers of arms, ammunition, money, and free navigation, if they would join his standard, and separate themselves from the federal Union. But his plans, as well as those of Genêt, were defeated by the firmness of Washington and the loyalty of the states of Georgia and South Carolina.[12] The latter, too, came to the rescue of the federal government—the legislature adopting measures for the arrest of Genêt's agents.*

Seagrove remained at Tuckabatchee until the 1st of April. Then he departed for Georgia, with a delegation of chiefs, who visited Governor Mathews, who appears to have been a more conciliatory man than the fiery Telfair, who had now gone out of office. The chiefs expressed a desire for peace, and Governor Mathews sent them back to the nation, well pleased with their visit, and guarded by a detachment, under General Glascock.[13]

A new settlement, contemplated west of the Oconee, was now about to originate more trouble with the Creeks. The restless and enterprising General Elijah Clarke, who had fought with so much indomitable courage, and who had displayed such remarkable endurance, during the whole of the Revolutionary War, and was one of the best Whigs that ever lived, was at the head of this movement, and that, too, immediately upon the heels of the abortive attempt to invade Florida. After the Revolution, he continued to defend his state, and his resolute spirit and mighty arm beat off many a murderous savage band. But he was too impulsive and restless for times of peace. He now undertook to extinguish the Creek claims, in a very practical manner. With a large party of men, he began a settlement opposite Fort Fidius, on the west side of the Oconee, upon Indian territory. General Irwin, on the part of the state, ordered him to remove, which he refused to do. Mathews forbid, by proclamation, the contemplated settlement, and accused Clarke of an attempt to form a separate and independent government. The latter appeared at the Superior Court of Wilkes, and surrendered himself to the judge, who placed his case before the MAGISTRATES. These worthy and learned men went into a full history of the laws of the United States, those of Georgia, those of the world, called the "law of nations," those of the Creeks, and those of the Spaniards, and came to the very liberal decision, endorsed upon the indictment, "*that the said Elijah Clarke be, and is, hereby discharged.*"[14]

Many people now flocked to the standard of Clarke. His settlements were pushed with vigor, a town was laid off, and Forts Advance and Defiance were erected and garrisoned. Washington was uneasy at this movement,

* *American State Papers: Foreign Relations*, 1: 454–60; Martin, *History of Louisiana*, 2: 91–118, 122–23, 126–28; Monette, *History of the Discovery and Settlement of the Valley of the Mississippi*, 1: 469–85,492–96, 505–10.

[12] Thomas Power worked as an agent for Carondelet in his intrigues with General James Wilkinson, Spain's hired agent in Kentucky, to develop a separatist movement. Ibid., 286–87 n. 5; Kinnaird, *Spain in the Mississippi Valley*, 3: xxxv-xxxvi, 258; "General Wilkinson," *Niles' Weekly Register* 1 (February 29, 1812), 470; David E. Narrett, "Geopolitics and Intrigue: James Wilkinson, the Spanish Borderlands, and Mexican Independence," *William and Mary Quarterly* 69 (January 2012): 101–46.

[13] In May 1794, James Seagrove and "six principal Creek chiefs" met with Governor George Mathews in Savannah, but the conference was disturbed by a report that "two men, belonging to the militia, being killed and followed by threat from the people of the upper part of the State . . . to destroy the Indians who came with me." Apparently the perceived threat caused Mathews to send a detachment under Brigadier General Thomas Glascock as an escort for the Creek peace delegation. *ASP: IA*, 2: 486–87.

[14] In defiance of Georgia and federal law and treaties, Elijah Clarke and his followers had set up a separate colony dubbed the Trans-Oconee Republic on the southwest side of the Oconee on lands claimed by the Creek Nation. They established a committee of safety and began to set up land grants. Governor George Mathews had quietly allowed the creation of this rogue state until he began to receive pressure from the federal government and from his fellow citizens. When the Wilkes County court and local justices refused to indict Clarke, Mathews called out the Georgia militia forces under Generals Jared Irwin and John Twiggs. Ibid., 496–502; Coulter, "Elijah Clarke's Foreign Intrigues," 12–13.

and requested Governor Mathews to put down all attempts at the occupation of the Indian domain, and promising to furnish him with troops from South Carolina, if it should become necessary. Mathews directed Generals Twiggs and Irwin to break up these establishments. They approached them with Georgia militia, who acted with great firmness and moderation. Clarke, abandoned by all his men except twenty, surrendered, upon condition that his property, and that of the colonists, should be returned to them. The forts and houses were destroyed by fire, and the affair happily ended, without the shedding of a drop of blood.[15]

The northern frontiers were still disturbed by Indian marauding parties. Major James Ore advanced from Nashville, with five hundred and fifty mounted infantry, to the town of Nickajack, surrounded and attacked it by surprise, and killed many of its inhabitants, while nineteen women and children were made prisoners. On his march from thence up the river, he was attacked at the Narrows by the savages, who, after a few fires, gave way and retreated to Running Water, which was soon taken, and likewise destroyed. Ore recrossed the Tennessee, before night, and took up the line of march for Nashville, with his prisoners and a large quantity of effects, which had been taken by the Indians from various persons.[16] Andrew Jackson, afterwards president, was a private in this expedition.*

[15] Writing to Secretary Knox on 29 September 1794 from Fort Fidius, Constant Freeman, an agent for the war department, reported on the successful operation of the Georgia militia under Generals Jared Irwin and John Twiggs and the federal forces under Lieutenant Colonel Henry Gaither. On the 26th, Irwin had promised Clarke and his men safe passage if they would evacuate Fort Advance, which occurred the following day. On 28 September, Fort Advance was destroyed by fire, and Fort Defiance and other structures were destroyed over the next twenty-four hours. *ASP: IA*, 2: 500–501.

[16] Major James Ore's expedition against the Chickamauga Five Lower Towns was guided to Nickajack by Joseph Brown, who had once been held as a prisoner by the Chickamaugas. During Ore's one day blitz, his men burned and looted Nickajack and Running Water and seized a number of women and children as prisoners. Resistance was light, and by 17 September 1794 Ore's force had returned safely to Nashville. Most of the seventy casualties were old men, women, and children. Pate, "The Chickamauga," 248–49; "Col. Whitley's Narrative," Draper Manuscripts, 1542–1916, Wisconsin Historical Society, Madison Wisconsin, 9CC1-2.

* *American State Papers: Indian Affairs*, 1: 495–500, 632; Kendall, *Life of Andrew Jackson*, 89.

Chapter XXVI

THE SECOND YAZOO SALE

The winter of 1794 and 1795 was remarkable for the celebrated Yazoo speculation, or, as the more intolerant opponents of the measure termed it, the "Yazoo fraud." We have already seen how a prior sale of territory, lying in Alabama and Mississippi, by the Georgia legislature, ultimately terminated. We have said that we did not believe that Georgia, under the treaties made between Spain, Great Britain and the United States, in 1782 and 1783, had a right to the extensive territory lying between the Chattahoochee and the Mississippi, but, as the federal government contended that she had, it ought to have placed her in possession of the country, by the expulsion of the Spaniards. The Georgians felt much aggrieved by the conduct of the general government, in not only permitting the Spaniards to occupy what they really believed to be their soil, but in suffering them constantly to instigate the Creeks in killing and plundering their frontier population, and in interfering with their treaties. In truth, Georgia did not recognize the right, even in the federal government, to make treaties with the Indians, respecting the territory which she claimed—while the general government, on the other hand, did not admit any right in Georgia to make treaties. These, and many other things of a like nature, we are charitable enough to believe, chiefly prompted the Yazoo sale.[1]

The first bill which the legislature of Georgia passed, in regard to the Yazoo sale, at the session of 1794, was returned with the objections of Governor George Mathews. He contended that the time had not arrived for the disposal of the territory; that the sum offered for it was not enough; that the quantity reserved for the citizens was too small; that greater advantages were secured to purchasers than to citizens; that it would operate as a monopoly; and that at least one-fourth of the lands ought to be reserved for the future disposal of the state. The legislature became excited at the veto of the bill, and, in a few days, passed another, which Governor Mathews signed. Governor

[1] Under the U.S. Constitution, Georgia officials were operating on very tenuous grounds and, in some aspects, violating federal law. Article 1, Section 8, Clause 3 in the Constitution gave Congress the power "To regulate Commerce with foreign Nations, and among the several States, and with the Indian Tribes." In 1789–1791, Congress enacted four statutes that placed Indian affairs clearly under the president and Congress. For example, in 1789, Congress established a Department of War with full oversight of Indian affairs, set aside money to negotiate treaties, and appointed federal commissioners to negotiate treaties with the tribes. Article VI of the Constitution makes it clear that all treaties entered into by the U.S. "shall be the supreme law of the land." In 1790 and 1791, Congress passed statutes "to regulate trade and intercourse with the Indian

Mathews was a man of honor and integrity. He vetoed the first bill, not on account of any fraud which he supposed the legislature was committing upon the federal government, for, in common with many other prominent citizens of Georgia, he believed that the state had a right to sell its own lands; but he vetoed it for the reasons which we have enumerated.[2]

Governor Mathews was a native of Ireland, and landed upon the Virginia shore in 1737. Establishing himself in the county of Augusta, he immediately became a formidable and fearless defender of the country against the Indians west of the Ohio, who frequently made incursions into western Virginia. After many combats, in defense of his father's house, and those of his neighbors, he was appointed a captain, and participated, in the most gallant manner, in the great battle fought between the Virginians and Indians, at the junction of the Ohio with the Kanawha, on the 10th October 1774. In 1775, he was elected a colonel of the ninth regiment, and, for two years, he commanded it on the eastern shore of Virginia, after which he joined General Washington. Colonel Mathews commanded his regiment at Brandywine, and, at the Battle of Germantown, captured a regiment of the enemy. He received a very severe wound with a bayonet in another skirmish, was taken prisoner, and confined on board a British ship in the harbor of New York. He was not exchanged until the termination of the war, when he joined General Greene as commander of the third Virginia regiment. He removed to "Goose Pond," on Broad River, Georgia, in 1785, with his family. One year afterwards, he was elected governor of the state. Under the present constitution, he was the first representative of Georgia in Congress, and, in 1794, 1795, he was again governor.[3]

Governor Mathews was short in stature and compactly made. His hair was light, and his complexion was fair and florid. He wore a three-cornered cocked hat, a pair of top boots, a shirt full-ruffled in front and at the wrists, and, occasionally, a long sword at his side. He was a man of unsurpassed bravery, and of indomitable energy. His mind was of a strong and vigorous order, but wholly uncultivated, except by observation of men and things. His education was more limited than that of any other man of the same distinction. In consequence of his valuable military services, the legislature of Virginia has preserved his memory in the name of one of the counties of that state.

The preamble to the Yazoo bill declared that the articles of confederation stipulated that each state was to retain her territory; that, by the Treaty of Paris of 1783, the boundaries of Georgia, as well as those of other states, were confirmed; that they were consistent with all the former acts of Georgia, and with the convention held at Beaufort, in 1787, between South Carolina

tribes," providing for the licensing of traders and penalties for trading without a license and declaring the purchase of lands invalid unless made by a public treaty with the United States government. Robert J. Miller, "American Indians and the United States Constitution," http://ssrn.com/abstract=1573144, 4–6; Francis Paul Prucha, *American Indian Policy in the Formative Years: The Indian Trade and Intercourse Acts, 1790–1834* (Lincoln: University of Nebraska Press, 1962), 45–47.

[2] While Governor Mathews vetoed the first bill, he signed the second bill on 7 January 1795. He may have succumbed to political pressure or he may have received some inducements, like the legislators who voted for both bills. According to most sources, all but one member of the Georgia house who voted in favor of the second bill received financial inducements of $1,000 and possibly promises of land shares. Charles H. Haskins, "The Yazoo Land Companies," *Papers of the American Historical Association* 5 (October 1891): 414–15.

[3] Contrary to Pickett's narrative, George Mathews (1739–1812) was born in Augusta County, Virginia, in 1739 to Ulster immigrant parents Ann Archer and John Mathews. His service in the Continental

and Georgia; that the states had the right of pre-emption, as well as the full exercise of all territorial rights; that the legislature disapproved of the New York treaty with McGillivray; that the president had no authority to guarantee, therein, all the territory west of the Oconee to the Creeks; and that Georgia clearly had the right to convey fee simple titles to all her territories to individuals or companies. The act stipulated that one-fifth of the purchase money should be paid into the Georgia treasury previous to the passage of the bill. The remainder was to be paid on the 1st November following, secured, by a mortgage, to the governor. Payments were to be made in specie, United States Bank bills, or military warrants, drawn by the governor, from 1791 to 1795, inclusive.[4]

For the sum of two hundred and fifty thousand dollars, the legislature sold to James Gunn, Matthew McAllister, George Walker, and their associates, termed the "GEORGIA COMPANY," an immense area of territory, which now embraces the following modern counties:[5]

IN ALABAMA—Clarke, Marengo, Greene, Perry, Autauga, Bibb, Shelby, Tuscaloosa, Pickens, Fayette, Jefferson, St. Clair, the southern portions of Blount, Walker and Marion, and portions of Wilcox, Monroe, Dallas, Sumter and Baldwin.

army in Georgia and South Carolina had introduced him to the rich lands of the Georgia upcountry. In 1783, a failed Georgia land speculating venture with other Virginians led him to buy land in Wilkes County, Georgia, and he acquired additional lands for his Revolutionary War service. His service as a Continental officer and early political involvement led to his election to the Georgia Assembly in 1787, and his fellow legislators elected him governor in 1787–1788. After failing to win a Senate seat in Congress, he rebounded by being elected governor for a second term in 1793. Carol Ebel, "George Mathews," *New Georgia Encyclopedia* (online).

[4] Pickett has paraphrased and summarized certain elements of a lengthy five paragraph long preamble to "AN ACT supplementary to an act, entitled, 'An act for appropriating a part of the unlocated territory of the State for the payment of the late State troops . . .'" Although McGillivray's name is not mentioned, the authors of the act went to some lengths to challenge federal authority, citing specific articles of the U.S. Constitution which supported their states' rights and discounted the 1790 and 1791 trade and intercourse acts passed by the U.S. Congress and signed into law by President Washington. *ASP: PL*, 1: 139.

[5] In 1789, Matthew McAllister was appointed the first U.S. Attorney General for the District of Georgia, and George Walker, a member of the Georgia Assembly, voted for the Yazoo act. James Gunn, a U.S. senator from Georgia, led the movement for the second Yazoo land sale, and he and his partners used personal inducements to influence the Georgia legislators. Their other associates included Zachariah Cox, Jacob Waldburger, William Longstreet, Wade Hampton, Gideon Denison, and William Stith Jr. George R. Lamplugh, *Politics on the Periphery: Factions and Parties in Georgia, 1783–1806* (Newark: University of Delaware Press, 1986), 107–11; C. Peter Magrath, *Yazoo: Law and Politics in the New Republic. The Case of 'Fletcher v. Peck'* (Providence, RI: Brown University Press, 1966), 6; *Laws of the United States of America, From the 4th of march, 1789, To the 4th of March, 1815*, 5 vols. (Philadelphia: John Bioren and W. John Duane; Washington: R. C. Weightman, 1815), 1: 531–33; *ASP: PL*, 1: 182, 185.

IN MISSISSIPPI—The larger portions of Kemper, Neshoba, Leake, Madison, Yazoo and Issaquena, all of Washington, Holmes, Attala, Winston, Noxubee, Lowndes, Oktibbeha, Choctaw, Carroll, Sunflower, Bolivar, Tallahatchie, Yalobusha, Chickasaw and Monroe.[6]

For the sum of one hundred and fifty thousand dollars, the legislature sold to Nicholas Long, Thomas Glascock, Ambrose Gordon, Thomas Cumming, and their associates, called the "Georgia Mississippi Company," all the territory out of which has since been formed the following counties:[7]

IN MISSISSIPPI—The northern portions of Greene, Perry, Marion, Pike, Amite and Wilkinson, all of Adams, Franklin, Lawrence, Covington, Jones, Wayne, Jefferson, Copiah, Simpson, Smith, Jasper, Clarke, Lauderdale, Newton, Scott, Rankin, Hinds, Warren, Claiborne, and the southern portions of Yazoo, Issaquena, Madison, Leake, Neshoba and Kemper.[8]

IN ALABAMA—Nearly all of old Washington and Sumter, and the southwest corner of Greene.

For the sum of thirty-five thousand dollars, that body also conveyed to Wade Hampton, John B. Scott and John C. Nightingale, termed the "Upper Mississippi Company," the territory extending entirely across the extreme northern part of the state of Mississippi, twenty-five miles deep, now embracing the northern portions of the modern counties of De Soto, Marshall, Tippah, Tishomingo and a fragment of the northern part of Tunica.[9]

For the sum of sixty thousand dollars, the legislature of Georgia also sold to Zachariah Cox, Mathias Maher, and their associates, called the "Tennessee

[6] The limits of the Georgia Company purchase were described as follows: "Beginning on the United States line 31° at the Mobile River, extend up the Alabama and Coosa to latitude 34°, and on the Mississippi River extend from latitude 34° south to 32° 40." *ASP: PL*, 1: 139–40; Dunbar Rowland, ed., *Encyclopedia of Mississippi History: Comprising Sketches of Counties, Towns, Events, Institutions, and Persons*, 2 vols. (Madison, Wis.: Selwyn A. Bryant, 1907), 2: 1009.

[7] The directors of the Georgia Mississippi Company published a 39 page pamphlet, *Grant to the Georgia Mississippi Company,* aimed at "The Purchasers in Connecticut" which included its location, soil, climate, and navigable streams. *ASP: PL*, 1: 136–37; Robert Watkins and George Watkins, eds., *A Digest of the Laws of the State of Georgia: From Its First Establishment as a British Province Down to the Year 1798* (Philadelphia: R. Aitken, 1800), 561. See Georgia Mississippi Company and Thomas Hutchins, *Grant to the Georgia Mississippi Company, the constitution thereof, and extracts relative to the situation, soil, climate, and navigation of the western territory of the state of Georgia; and particularly of that part thereof in which the Company's lands are situated* (Augusta: John Erdman Smith, 1795).

[8] The Georgia Mississippi Company lands were located in the southwest between the Mississippi and Tombigbee rivers, bounded by latitudes 32° 40' and 31° 18'. Haskins, "Yazoo Land Companies," 416; Watkins and Watkins, *Digest of the Laws of the State of Georgia*, 561–62.

[9] The lands of the Upper Mississippi Company were located in the extreme northwestern corner of the modern state of Mississippi, southward twenty five miles from the Tennessee state line, and eastward to the Tennessee River in the northwest corner of the modern state of Alabama. Haskins, "Yazoo Land Companies," 416.

COMPANY," all the territory comprising the whole of North Alabama, out of which the following counties have since been formed: Lauderdale, Limestone, Madison, Jackson, DeKalb, Cherokee, Marshall, Morgan, Lawrence, Franklin, and the northern parts of Marion, Walker and Blount.[10]

The lands thus conveyed to the four Yazoo companies, for the gross sum of five hundred thousand dollars, contained twenty-one million five hundred thousand acres. A reserve of two millions of acres was made, from this purchase, for the benefit of the citizens who desired to become purchasers upon the original terms of sale. The four companies paid promptly into the treasury one-fifth of the purchase money, and obtained titles from the governor. During the progress of this bold measure, the members of the legislature were in the midst of the profoundest excitement, which extended to the "lobby members" and the whole community.[11]

The bill was signed by Thomas Napier, speaker of the house; Benjamin Taliaferro, president of the senate; and approved by His Excellency, George Mathews, governor. It was asserted that "bribery and corruption distinguished the proceedings of the members favorable to the Yazoo act." The public documents abound with affidavits, pro and con. It was asserted that members were bought up, to vote for the measure, by receiving, in advance, from the companies, certificates of large shares of the land which they were about to vote to sell. The public became aroused upon the subject.[12]

[10] The 1795 act described the limits of the Tennessee Company's purchase as follows: "... beginning at the mouth of Bear creek, on the side of the Tennessee river; thence up the said creek to the most southern source thereof; thence, due south to the latitude of thirty-four degrees ten minutes north of the equator; thence, a due east course, one hundred and twenty miles; thence, a due north course, to the Great Tennessee river; thence, up the middle of the said river, to the northern boundary line of the State; thence, a due west course, along the said line, to where it intersects the great Tennessee river, below the Muscle shoals; thence, up the said river, to the place of beginning ..." *ASP: PL*, 1: 141.

[11] Georgia's James Jackson resigned his Senate seat and returned to Georgia to oppose and annul the state's Yazoo land deal. He authored a series of letters under the name "Sicilius" that were published in the *Augusta Chronicle* and *Georgia Gazette*, presenting learned essays on civics, the role of the people, and constitutional rule. Using the writings of Vattel, Montesquieu, and Blackstone, he argued that Georgia had erred and had been deceived about their ownership and value of the Yazoo lands. He compared the sale of land in the Northwest Territory at one dollar per acre by Congress, while Georgia had agreed to sell the Yazoo lands for a cent and a half per acre. William O. Foster, *James Jackson: Duelist and Militant Statesman, 1757–1806* (1960; reprint, Athens: University of Georgia Press, 2009), 109–13.

[12] Under the leadership of U.S. Senator James Gunn, the speculators made brazen offers to engineer the passage of the Yazoo act. While Georgia senator Thomas Whylly was offered eight or ten "likely Negroes" for his vote, his fellow senator Burrell Pope was promised "five hundred silver dollars." Senator Clem Lanier was offered 50,000 acres for each senate vote he could deliver. Other legislators were offered cash bribes or shares of land to leave and not be present for the final vote. *ASP: PL*, 1: 131–35.

A majority of the counties, through their grand juries, pronounced against the act. Public meetings assembled all over Georgia, and the bitterest denunciations fell from the lips of every speaker. A large convention was held at Louisville, where hundreds of petitions were read, and evidence adduced, setting forth "the atrocious speculation, corruption and collusion, by which said usurped acts and grants were obtained." Although the tide of public sentiment swept over the state in angry torrents, destroying the popularity of the members who voted for the act, and elevating to power its most violent opponents, yet the four companies paid up the whole of the purchase money, and believed themselves secure in their vast fortunes, because the bill stipulated that the acts of no subsequent legislatures should affect their titles.[13]

Washington was astounded at the Yazoo sale, and laid before Congress copies of the bill, using this language in reference to it: "These acts embrace an object of great magnitude, and their consequences may deeply affect the peace and welfare of the United States." The two houses of Congress adopted a resolution instructing the attorney general to investigate the title of Georgia to the lands sold.[14]

The legislature of Georgia again convened, in the winter, with a new governor and new body of members, except those who voted *against* the Yazoo sale. General James Jackson, a distinguished partisan officer of the Revolution, was at the head of the new organization. He had canvassed the state, and, from the hustings, denounced the extraordinary measure, while, with his able pen, he produced several severe pamphlets upon the subject. He introduced a bill for the repeal of the Yazoo sale, which declared it "null and void." It was adopted, and received the signatures of Jared Irwin, the new governor, Thomas Stephens, speaker of the house, and Benjamin Taliaferro, president of the senate.[15] In the midst of the largest procession ever known in the land, the records of the Yazoo act were expunged, and, to show the indignation of its opponents, the bill itself was consumed, in the streets of Louisville, by fire from HEAVEN.*

But, in the meantime, hundreds had emigrated to the Tombigbee and the Mississippi, establishing themselves in those distant and isolated regions, intending soon to occupy the lands which the companies had proposed to grant them. In this respect, the Yazoo sale was a great blessing. It contributed to throw into that wild region a population of Georgians, whose activity, ability

* They held a sun-glass over the paper until it was consumed by the fire thus generated. The Yazoo act may be seen, together with all the votes upon it, and an account of the excitement which it produced, in *American State Papers: Public Lands*, 1: 120–44; *American State Papers: Indian Affairs*, 1: 551–55, 561; *Georgia Digest of 1798*, 557–58.

[13] In May 1795, Louisville, Georgia, officially became the state capital with the opening of the statehouse and the convening of a constitutional convention. Yulssus Lynn Holmes, *Those Glorious Days: A History of Louisville as Georgia's Capital, 1796–1807* (Macon, Ga.: Mercer University Press, 1996).

[14] Both houses of Congress responded to the copies of the Yazoo act submitted to them by President Washington. The House of Representatives passed a resolution urging the president to use constitutional and legal avenues to prevent any violations of the Indian treaties by U.S. citizens. The Senate responded with a resolution requesting the president to ask the attorney general to collect documentation regarding Georgia's western land claims. *Annals of Congress*, 3rd Cong., 2nd Sess., 844, 1251.

[15] Senator James Jackson circulated his essays as a pamphlet entitled *The Letters of Sicilius to the Citizens of the State of Georgia* and campaigned state-wide for seats in the 1796 Georgia Assembly. On 11 January 1796, Jackson and the other newly elected anti-Yazoo legislators convened in Louisville and elected Jared Irwin as governor. On 13 February 1796, the Georgia Assembly passed

and enterprise better fitted them to seize, occupy, and bring into cultivation a wilderness, mark out towns, people them, build female academies, erect churches, and hold courts, than any other people.

By an arrangement between the president and the Georgia authorities, Benjamin Hawkins, of North Carolina, George Clymer, of Pennsylvania, and Andrew Pickens, of South Carolina, repaired to Colerain, upon the St. Mary's River, where they met James Jackson, James Simms and James Hendricks, agents for Georgia. The object was the formation of a treaty of peace with the Creeks, and the cession, to Georgia, of the lands between the Oconee and the Ocmulgee. A full delegation of Indians, consisting of twenty kings and seventy-five chiefs, together with three hundred and forty warriors, soon arrived. Seagrove, the Creek agent, suggested the propriety of moving the council from Colerain to Muscogee, a short distance off, which was accordingly done.[16] There, the chiefs, after marching under the United States flag, performing the eagle-tail dance, smoking with the commissioners, and engaging in other ceremonious preparations, began the council. The first day was occupied with the speeches of the commissioners, who gave a full exposition of the views and wishes of the president. On the following day, General Jackson, on the part of Georgia, made a long speech, in which he pointed out the faithless observance of their treaties with his state, by the Creeks, and exhibited two schedules of the property which they had stolen, amounting to the value of one hundred and ten thousand dollars, which he demanded to be restored. The Indians listened with profound attention, and, when he had concluded, they adjourned for the day—the Big Warrior, who had lately become a prominent chief, facetiously remarking, "I can fill up more paper than Jackson has done, with a list of similar outrages of the Georgians upon my people."[17]

A treaty was concluded, between the chiefs of the *whole* Creek Nation and the federal commissioners, the former ratifying the New York treaty, and pledging themselves to carry out its provisions, and to assist Spain and the United States to run their line. They also stipulated to allow the government the right to establish posts upon the territory between the Ocmulgee and Oconee, allowing to each five miles square of land; but they positively refused to cede any of this territory to Georgia. The United States stipulated to allow the Creek Nation two blacksmiths and two strikers, with tools and iron, and to distribute, immediately, six thousand dollars' worth of goods among those who were present.[18]

The Georgia agents were offended with Seagrove, with the Indians, and with the federal commissioners. They presented to the latter a protest,

an act rescinding the Yazoo act and nullifying the land sales. Foster, *James Jackson*, 110, 113–18; Magrath, *Yazoo: Law and Politics*,12–15, 17–18; *ASP: PL*, 1: 142–44.

[16] If the treaty conference was removed to nearby Mus'cogee, it was not reflected in the treaty submitted for ratification by President Washington and confirmation by the U.S. Senate, which read "Done at Colerain, the 29th of June, one thousand seven hundred and ninety-six." Kappler, *Indian Affairs: Laws and Treaties*, 2: 49.

[17] Given his size and effusive personality, Big Warrior (Tustunnuggee Thlucco) of Tuckabatchee was not intimidated by Senator James Jackson's speech or his excessive demands. While Article 7 provided for the return of "white inhabitants, Negroes, and property taken since the signing of" the Treaty of New York, it did not contain Jackson's $110,000 figure. Ibid., 48; Green, *Politics of Removal*, 38–39.

[18] Article 8 of the Treaty of Colerain gave President Washington the option of opening a trading post in the Creek Nation, and in November 1795 he appointed Edward Price as the factor at the Creek Trading House at Colerain on the St. Mary's River in Georgia. The federal trading houses or factory system allowed the federal government to furnish the Indian tribes with quality merchandise at fair prices

in which they accused them of having disregarded the interests of Georgia. They brought charges against Seagrove, who, they contended, influenced the Creeks not to cede the lands as far as the Ocmulgee. The federal commissioners denied these allegations.[19] Seagrove and Jackson became great enemies, and afterwards fought a duel.*

Washington had dispatched Thomas Pinckney, as envoy extraordinary, to Madrid, who there concluded, with the Prince of Peace, a treaty, in which the king of Spain stipulated that the southern boundary of the United States should be the line of 31°, from the Mississippi to the Chattahoochee, thence, down the middle of that river, to its junction with the Flint, thence direct to the head of the St. Mary's River, thence down the middle of that stream to the Atlantic; that all Spanish posts and inhabitants, found north of this boundary, should be removed within six months after the ratification of the treaty, and the American posts and inhabitants living south of it should also be removed within the same period; that the navigation of the Mississippi, from its source to the Gulf, should remain free for the commerce of the subjects of Spain and the citizens of the American union;[20] that both powers should cultivate peace with the Indians for mutual benefit and protection; that, hereafter, Spain should not form treaties of alliance with Indians living upon American soil, nor the federal government with Indians living upon Spanish territory; and that Spanish and American commissioners should mark the boundary, before the expiration of six months, after the ratification of the treaty.†

Colonel Andrew Ellicott, who had remained upon the Oconee so long, to no purpose, awaiting a favorable opportunity to run the line according to the New York treaty, was now transferred, by Washington, to Natchez, as one of the commissioners to mark the boundary between Spain and the United States.[21] He reached Natchez, by way of the Ohio, and immediately commenced negotiations with Don Manuel Gayoso de Lemos, commandant of Fort Panmure, governor of the Natchez dependencies, and commissioner on the part of Spain. But Carondelet had determined not to comply with the treaty, affecting to consider it made by his sovereign as a "*court finesse*," until he could settle his European difficulties, when he would wholly disregard it, and hold on to his posts east of the Mississippi. He again began to intrigue with the

* *American State Papers: Indian Affairs,* 1: 586–616.

† *American State Papers: Foreign Affairs,* 1: 553–59.

and to accelerate the "civilization plan" started by Washington and Henry Knox in 1791. Kappler, *Indian Affairs: Laws and Treaties,* 2: 49; Prucha, *American Indian Policy,* 44–49, 86–87; Ray H. Mattison, "The Creek Trading House: From Colerain to Fort Hawkins," *Georgia Historical Quarterly* 30 (September 1946): 169–184.

19 Actually, James Seagrove played a minor role in the negotiations with the Creeks at Colerain. When the Georgia commissioners delivered their protest to the treaty proceedings at Colerain on 28 June 1796, they listed seven issues and aimed specific comments at Benjamin Hawkins as "Superintendent of Indian Affairs" in three of them. Their greatest complaint was that the state of Georgia should be asked to pay "any share of the enormous and unnecessary expenses attending the present treaty" and not receive any additional Creek lands. *ASP: IA,* 1: 613–14.

20 The Treaty of San Lorenzo el Real (Pinckney's Treaty) was signed by Manuel Godoy y Álvarez de Faria (1767–1851) as prime minister of Spain and El Principe de la Paz ("Prince of the Peace"). The treaty negotiated by Pinckney and Godoy ended the contentious border dispute and most of the intrigue over the southwestern border of the young American republic. Bemis, *Pinckney's Treaty,* 170–71, 267–93, 311, 343–62.

21 As noted earlier, Andrew Ellicott sent his brother Joseph Ellicott to represent him on the

western American population for the dismemberment of the Union, through his emissary, the notorious Power.[22] General James Wilkinson, then at the head of the western American army, who had long been the intimate friend of Carondelet, and had received from him private and exclusive privileges of trade, which were highly beneficial to him as a western planter, was suspected of secretly advancing these ends. Meanwhile, Lieutenant McCleary, with an American force, unfurled the federal flag upon the heights of Natchez. He soon afterwards marched to Fort Panmure, and demanded its surrender, agreeably to the treaty. But Gayoso, who had placed it in complete repair, and had strengthened it with artillery and men, refused to evacuate it.[23]

The Spanish posts at Walnut Hills and Baton Rouge were all strengthened, by the orders of Carondelet. An angry correspondence ensued, in which Ellicott remonstrated against this conduct, as conflicting with the letter and spirit of the treaty. Gayoso justified himself upon the ground that the Choctaws and Chickasaws, whom he had hired to surround Natchez and make threats, intended to attack the Natchez settlements, in consequence of the presence of the American troops.[24] While these things were going on, Lieutenant Percy Smith Pope arrived at Natchez with forty men, which were added to the American force. Gayoso remonstrated against the presence of these troops, entrenched within sight of Fort Panmure. Their flag was an eye-sore to the Spaniards.

Oconee boundary survey. Several factors prevented the running of the boundary as required under the 1790 Treaty of New York, including Genêt's French legions and Elijah Clarke's "Trans-Oconee Republic." On 16 September 1796, Ellicott left his home in Chester, Pennsylvania, traveled to Philadelphia and then to Pittsburg, and descended the Ohio. *ASP: IA*, 1: 128–29; Andrew Ellicott, *The Journal of Andrew Ellicott, Late Commissioner on behalf of the United States During Part of the Year 1796, the years 1797, 1798, 1799, and Part of the year 1800: For Determining the Boundary Between the United States and Possessions of his Catholic Majesty in America* (1803; reprint, Chicago: Quadrangle Books, 1962), 1–6.

22 Despite his Quaker background, Ellicott possessed an aggressive, overbearing personality and an obvious disdain and mistrust of the Spanish officials. Although he opposed the loss of Spanish territory east of the Mississippi, Governor Gayoso de Lemos tried to cooperate with Ellicott. Gayoso appointed Thomas Power to serve as secretary to Spain's boundary commission that worked with the American commission led by Andrew Ellicott. Ellicott, *Journal*, 41–105; Jack D. L. Holmes, *Gayoso; The Life of a Spanish Governor in the Mississippi Valley, 1789–1799* (Baton Rouge: Louisiana State University Press, 1965), 177, 233–34.

23 Lieutenant John McCleary (McClary) journeyed down the Mississippi with a detachment assigned as an escort for Ellicott's party and authored the drama reported by Pickett at Fort Panmure. While Ellicott makes reference to the arrival of his military escort, he only identifies Lieutenant Percy Smith Pope in his correspondence with Governor Gayoso in March—June 1797. Ellicott, *Journal*, 45–109; Claiborne, *Mississippi*, 160, 162, 172, 184, 197–98, 529.

24 Unfortunately, Pickett took Ellicott's conduct as beyond reproach and his *Journal* as a totally unbiased reflection of the events that occurred in Natchez and surveying the 31st degree boundary line between the U.S. and the Spanish provinces. Excerpts from a letter written by Captain Isaac Guion (1775–1823), commander of U. S. troops who occupied the former

He desired their removal to Clarksville; but Ellicott refused. Various reasons were given by the Spaniards for not evacuating the country, one of which had some foundation, and that was the descent upon New Orleans contemplated by western American citizens, who had joined the British of Canada for that purpose. One of these men was Governor Blount, of Tennessee, whom the United States Senate, of which he was a member, unanimously expelled for endeavoring to enlist western men in such an enterprise. Colonel Hutchins, Mr. Rapalje, and other prominent citizens of the Floridas, it is asserted, were also concerned in the contemplated invasion. But this soon blew over, and other excuses for delay were invented by Carondelet and his subordinate commandants. These things served to irritate the Natchez population, which had greatly increased, and desired the expulsion of the Spaniards.[25]

Ellicott constantly urged Gayoso to begin the running of the line, but never could get him to appoint a time. The people became tumultuous, and Gayoso, dreading the consequences of an outbreak, issued a proclamation, announcing that the treaty would ultimately be complied with. They refused to listen to his promises, and the excitement became alarming, when it was ascertained that Gayoso had imprisoned an American citizen, a Baptist preacher, named Hannah, who, having taken too much whiskey, had given the Spanish commandant some insulting language. The excitement was great in the country.[26] Public meetings advised violent measures. Gayoso was

Spanish posts, gives a different perspective on Ellicott's time in the Natchez District: ". . . I found Mr. Ellicott . . . Lieutenants Pope and McCleary and some forty or fifty men, who had been there a long time doing no good, but a great deal of harm. They had got the people, who before their arrival had dwelt together in amity, cut up into factions and very discontented. . . . In a short time, Ellicott and his assistants and escort, left Natchez (very much to my satisfaction and the satisfaction of the people) . . ." Isaac Guion to Daniel Carthy (1806) quoted in J. F. H. Claiborne, *Mississippi, As A Province, Territory, and State* (1880; reprint, Baton Rouge: Louisiana State University Press, 1964), 184.

[25] While Ellicott groused about delays and the lack of cooperation, Gayoso de Lemos attempted to cooperate with Ellicott, but he did not receive the royal order of 22 September 1797 to proceed with the evacuation as originally planned until January 1798. Despite the runaway conspiracy stories in Ellicott's *Journal*, there was no confrontation over the presence of flags by the Spaniards, only an effort to follow international protocol. Ellicott blatantly impugned the intentions of eighty-two year old Anthony Hutchins and George Rapalje (Rapalji), a successful trader and landowner, because they had been British Loyalists. Claiborne, *Mississippi*, 161–86; Ellicott, *Journal*, 139–55. See George Rapalje/Rapalji Notebook, Mississippi Department of Archives and History, Jackson, MS.

[26] Pickett follows Ellicott's story about a Baptist preacher named Hannah who had become drunk, received a thrashing by a group of Irish Catholics, and was locked up in Fort Panmure. However, the man involved in this incident was a Barton Hannon, a shoemaker and a Baptist by church affiliation. Ellicott was right in reporting that he was intoxicated because at his trial he forgot what he had done. Natchez, like most frontier settlements, did not have a jail, and Hannon had been placed in the stocks or the brig at the fort. Ellicott, *Journal*, 99–101; Jack D. L. Holmes, "Spanish Regulation of Taverns and the Liquor Trade

greatly alarmed, and issued another proclamation, exhorting the people to submit to the Spanish government until the difficulties could be settled, and promising pardon to all who should repent of their misdeeds. The Georgians had never been accustomed to such language as this, and their anger now knew no bounds. Gayoso skulked through the cane, and had an interview with Ellicott, whose room he approached by the back way. By his earnest entreaties, the American commissioner urged the people to become quiet, and he was greatly assisted by Colonel Hutchins, who had much influence with the old English population. He is the same gentleman, it will be recollected, whose property the Spaniards confiscated in 1781, and who made his escape, through the Creek Nation, to Georgia.[27]

In the midst of scenes like these, Ellicott was kept in suspense, until the 29th March, when the Spanish fort was evacuated, and all the Spanish troops sailed down the river. He then marched his own troops, and corps of woodmen and surveyors, to Tunica Bayou, and commenced his survey in a dense swamp, upon the eastern bank of the Mississippi, where the line of 31° strikes it.[28] In a few days, he was joined by Major Stephen Minor and Sir William Dunbar, commissioners on the part of Spain.* Gayoso was now governor of Louisiana, and he visited Ellicott's camp, with his military staff, and approved of the work, as far as it had progressed. Spain, as well as the United States,

* Monette, 1: 517–32; Stoddard, *Sketches, Historical and Descriptive, of Louisiana,* 89; Barbé-Marbois, *History of Louisiana*, 163–65; Ellicott, *Journal*, 26–176; *State Papers and Publick Documents*, Boston edition, 3: 335.

in the Mississippi Valley," in *The Spanish in the Mississippi Valley*, ed. John Francis McDermott (Urbana: University of Illinois Press, 1974), 167, 167 n. 151.

[27] Despite Pickett's assertion about Georgians and their anger without bounds, Ellicott does not attribute any of the excitement or unrest in the Natchez District to Georgians or any specific immigrant group. In reality, as Pickett has discussed elsewhere, most of the population in the Natchez District came from New England, from the former British colonies of East and West Florida, or from the American seaboard states down the Mississippi via the Ohio, Cumberland, and Tennessee rivers. Ellicott, *Journal*, 41–176; Claiborne, *Mississippi*, 103–37.

[28] Actually, the bank of the Mississippi River was under flood waters, and before the "Arrival of Spanish, Commissioner Ellicott had also established a due East and West line in the parallel of 31°. . . ." William Dunbar, the Spanish astronomer, recommended "that the American commissioner should continue his progress eastward, with the White laborers, 50 in number, reserving myself the task of pushing the line through the low grounds to the margin of the Mississippi with the assistance of 2 Surveyors, 22 black laborers and a White overseer." Report of William Dunbar to the Spanish Government at the Conclusion of His Services in Locating and Surveying the Thirty-First Degree of Latitude," in *Life, Letters and Papers of William Dunbar*, ed. Eron O. Rowland (Jackson: Mississippi Historical Society, 1930), 79–80.

[29] Gayoso de Lemos replaced Carondelet as governor-general of Louisiana and West Florida on 5 August 1797 and appointed Stephen Minor as interim governor of Natchez. Minor (1760–1815), a native of Mapletown, Pennsylvania, served with the

furnished troops to protect the surveyors from attacks of the Indians.[29] These, with the pack-horses, woodsmen and laborers, had the appearance of an army. The commissioners met with great difficulties, from thick swamps, creeks, marshes and rivers, all of which they had to go through. The trees were well blazed along the line, and a mound thrown up at the end of every mile.[30] They did not reach the Pearl River until the 19th November. There Ellicott left the surveyors, and went down that stream, in a canoe, to New Orleans.[31]

Arranging his business with Gayoso, and purchasing a small vessel, camp equipage and supplies, he sailed to Mobile, and thence up the river of that name until he reached the camp of the surveyors. They had passed entirely through the Choctaw Nation without opposition from that people. The line of 31° struck Mobile River six miles below the junction of the Tombigbee and Alabama, where several rivers run parallel, forming an immense swamp, several miles wide, which was now inundated. By means of boats, they erected signals upon the high lands of either side, and took the necessary observations and distances. These signals consisted of flags and tremendous lightwood fires.[32] Ellicott here again left the surveyors, sailed to Pensacola, and lodged

Spanish army in the Pensacola campaign and became a wealthy Natchez landowner. While Minor served as the Spanish commissioner on the boundary commission, William Dunbar, a noted scientist, served as the Spanish astronomer on the commission. Dunbar had made a three-month commitment and served from 26 May through 28 August 1798. Claiborne, *Mississippi*, 197–201; Holmes, *Gayoso*, 50–51, 147 n. 27, 129, 199, 233; "Report of William Dunbar to the Spanish Government," 78–82.

[30] In his report to Governor Gayoso, Dunbar reported that once "the east and west line was established, a line was carried due west, cutting a trace Sixty feet wide." On 17 July 1798, the line had been extended to the bank of the Mississippi River, where a square post ten feet high was erected and surrounded by an earthen mound eight feet high. Dunbar noted that the post erected at this point was "inscribed on the South Side a crown with the letter R underneath; on the North U.S., and on the West side fronting the River Agosto 18th, 1798, 31 Lat. N." "Report of William Dunbar to the Spanish Government," 80, 81.

[31] Actually, Ellicott did not leave the Pearl River encampment until 17 December 1798 and reached "the Bluffs on the tide water" on Christmas Day. Governor Gayoso de Lemos sent a vessel to carry Ellicott's party across Lake Pontchartrain on New Year's Day 1799. With the wind and tide working against them, they "arrived at the fort, at the mouth of Bayou St. John's" late on the 3rd. Gayoso's barge picked them up the morning of the 4th and they reached New Orleans "at ten o'clock in the forenoon, and was received by the Governor and officers of the government, in the most polite and friendly manner." Ellicott, *Journal*, 185–88.

[32] Between 17 March and 9 April 1799, Ellicott and his crew completed the 31° line "over the Mobile swamp," and although he does not mention the stone marker known as the Ellicott Stone, his crew installed the only known permanent monument on the 31st parallel between Spanish territory and the U.S. The sandstone marker—3 feet high, 2 feet wide, and approximately half a foot thick—is located west of the Mobile-Tensaw River Delta. Inscribed on the north side is "U.S. Lat. 31 1799" and on the south side "Dominos de S.M.C. CARLOS IV. LAT. 31 1799." In recent times, a shed cover has been added over the stone and the wrought iron fence that surrounds the boundary marker. Ellicott, *Journal*, 198–99; Gregory Spies, "A Line of Demarcation and Ellicott's Survey of

at the elegant quarters provided by the hospitable firm of Panton, Leslie & Co. Colonel Benjamin Hawkins, now a prominent Creek superintendent, left the nation, by appointment, and, reaching Pensacola, informed Ellicott that a large number of Creeks were then on their way down, to hold a council. It was decided to meet them upon the Conecuh, where the line would cross. This was in opposition to the suggestion of Governor Folch, who proposed Pensacola, where, it was supposed, he intended to intrigue with the Creeks to prevent the line being run. Indeed, the Spaniards generally were opposed to the surrender of so much territory.[33]

At Miller's Bluff, Ellicott, Hawkins, Minor, and Colonel St. Maxent, with several Spanish officers, met the Creeks.[34] These agents of the United States and Spain, addressing the Indians, urged them to assist in running the line, and not to oppose it, all of which they had stipulated to do at the treaty of Colerain. The Mad Dog, of Tuckabatchee, replied, on the other side, and assured the commissioners that their wishes would be complied with, as they now understood that the line was to be run through their territory, by the consent of Spain. The surveyors, to whose party were added two chiefs and

the 31st Parallel," *Backsights* 15 (January 1996), 4–10.

[33] Ellicott's survey crew had set up an encampment on the Conecuh River some forty miles north of Pensacola Bay at Miller's Bluff or Miller's Farm. William J. Morton, *Andrew Ellicott: The Stargazer Who Defined America* (Atlanta: Georgia History Press, 2015), 293, 297.

[34] Colonel Francisco Maximiliano de St. Maxent, commander of the Third Battalion at Pensacola, arrived on 4 May 1799 as Governor Vicente Folch's representative. He later served as interim governor of West Florida on four separate occasions from March 1809 through November 1816. Holmes, *Gayoso*, 252–53; Morton, *Andrew Ellicott*, 295; Joseph E. Caro, ed., "Governors of West Florida," *Florida Historical Quarterly* 6 (October 1927): 118–19.

[35] Ellicott did not have any presents to give the Upper Creeks except his limited supplies, so he gave them "two or three hundred dollars" in lieu of presents. Hawkins, in a letter to Secretary of War James McHenry, wrote that "180 Indians from the Upper Towns came on a visit to the Governor [Folch] on his invitation. The old chiefs complained of his conduct by leaving. I rebuked them for their conduct and directed them to return to their nation and I gave them a stipend of one hundred dollars." Morton, *Andrew Ellicott*, 298–99.

[36] Governor Folch had received instructions to be cooperative while maintaining security along the boundary line. Ellicott and Hawkins met with Folch in Pensacola after the meeting with Upper Creek chiefs at Miller's Bluff. They asked him to send an agent to the Lower Creeks and Seminoles to explain the work of the survey party. Folch gave his assurance that their request would be honored immediately. Morton, *Andrew Ellicott*, 299–300.

[37] Hawkins had warned Ellicott not to stay on the Chattahoochee beyond July and August—a time when the Creek towns were involved in traditional rituals and the Green Corn Ceremony. On the night of 17 September 1799, Hopoithle Mico (*Tallassee King; Tame King*) of Tallase—a Red Stick leader in 1813–1814—led a raid on the camp, stealing horses and other property without opposition from Ellicott. Instead of the Spanish, Hawkins blamed the constant harassment and violence on anti-American Upper Creeks and Bowles's influence with the Lower Creeks and Seminoles. He also criticized Ellicott for hauling too much baggage and moving too slowly. Henri Florett, *The Southern Indians and Benjamin Hawkins,*

twenty Creek warriors, had reached the Conecuh, and begun the line from thence to the Chattahoochee. Returning to Pensacola, Hawkins and Ellicott learned, to their surprise, that a large body of Creeks were on their way, by an arrangement of Governor Folch, and that the survey would be stopped. Encamping three miles north of Pensacola, these savages demanded presents of the American commissioner, which, from motives of policy, were granted, although he had no agency in assembling them.[35] It was soon ascertained that Folch was secretly using every exertion to defeat the plans of the American government. Ellicott left Pensacola, sailed for the mouth of the Apalachicola, and ascended that river. Reaching the surveyor's camp, he ascertained that the Creeks had been very insolent, hanging upon their rear in large bodies, and plundering their effects. Greatly discouraged by this news, he pushed the survey to the Chattahoochee, where he fortified himself. He sent a runner to the Ocmulgee, for Hawkins, who had left Pensacola.[36]

About this time, Captain Minor dismissed his military escort, discharged many of his laborers, according to the instructions of Gayoso, given in May, and became very importunate to set out for the St. Mary's. In the meantime, Hawkins had arrived, and advised the continuance of the work. But a party of Indians advanced, and declared their intention to plunder the camps. Resolutely marching up to them, with the military, Hawkins kept them at bay until 10 o'clock at night, when they promised to remain at peace till morning. All that night, however, the woods rang with their riotous yells, while they threw down the beef-pens, and stole cattle and horses. They cut all the rigging of Ellicott's schooner, and robbed the master and crew, stripping them to their shirts. Fortunately, the cargo had been taken to the camp. The commissioners determined to retreat from Governor Folch's savage banditti.[37] Captain Minor, who is believed to have been innocent of any participation in originating

_1796–1816_ (Norman: University of Oklahoma Press, 1986), 212–14.

[38] While the Upper Creeks under Hopoithle Mico harassed Ellicott's camp, Seminoles under Miccosukee chief Kinache—one of Bowles's closest friends—led the party that struck Ellicott's schooner and forced his retreat down the Apalachicola River. Ironically, Captain Stephen Minor had warned Kinache not to harass the survey party and that, should he not abide by his request, that he would not be admitted to Spanish posts in the future. Minor reported that a "treaty" had been concluded, but on the same day "they stole five horse from us." Wright, _William Augustus Bowles,_ 125; Morton, _Andrew Ellicott,_ 306–07.

these hostilities, set out for the St. Mary's, attended by the American military escort, with the surveyors, who now ceased to work. Ellicott entered his naked schooner, and propelled her, in the best way he could, down the Apalachicola, having saved all his papers and astronomical apparatus. Nearly three years had expired since he landed at Natchez, and he had only been able to mark the line from the Mississippi to the Chattahoochee, in consequence of the duplicity, treachery and opposition of the Spaniards. But the chief object was accomplished—*the establishment of the southern boundary of the present states of Mississippi and Alabama*. Colonel Hawkins, abandoned by the whole expedition, fearlessly remained several days among the Indians, endeavoring to reconcile them.[38]

Approaching the sea, Ellicott found, wrecked upon Fox Point, a schooner of the British navy, commanded by Lieutenant Wooldridge, among whose crew was the celebrated William Augustus Bowles.[39] We left that gifted but bad man in the prison of Madrid in 1792. Knowing his great influence with the Creeks, the king of Spain often sent persons of his court to the prison, with offers of military titles and pay, if he would abandon his allegiance to the English interest, join that of Spain, return to the Floridas, and contribute to strengthen the colonies with his warrior forces. But the proud and unyielding Bowles spurned these offers. The court then confined him in elegant quarters, and surrounded him with servants, sparkling wines and rich viands, with the hope of engaging his affections; but, this treatment answering no purpose, he was threatened with transportation to the island of Manila, in the distant Pacific. Still unyielding, he was ironed, and sent there, in a vessel, where he remained until February 1797. He was then dispatched back to Spain; but, on the way, hearing of the war between that power and England, he escaped at Ascension Island, and reached Sierra Leone, where the English

[39] Violent storms had driven the British schooner *Fox,* under the command of Lieutenant James Wooldridge, unto the east end of St. George's Island. Wooldridge, his crew, and William Augustus Bowles were stranded on the island until they made contact with one of Ellicott's sailors, who was passing by the island in an open boat. Bowles and Wooldridge wrote letters to Ellicott on 22 September 1799 requesting his assistance. In their conversations, Bowles told Ellicott that he opposed the Treaty of San Lorenzo el Real and planned to counter its impact on the Creeks. Ibid., 114–16, 124; Morton, *Andrew Ellicott,* 321, 323–24; *The Miscellaneous Documents of the Senate of the United States for the Second Session, Thirty-Third Congress, 1854-'55,* 3 vols. (Washington: Beverly Tucker, Senate Printer, 1855), 2: 311–12, 314–15.

[40] Actually, Bowles spent nine months in England trying to convince officials, including his old friend Lord Dunmore, that he could be of service to George III back in Florida. He finally received passage on the warship *Atlas* to Barbados, where he remained for two months. From Barbados he sailed to Jamaica, where he convinced the governor, Alexander Lindsay, Earl of Balcarres, that his Muskogee Republic could be helpful to England and profitable to Jamaica. Balcarres arranged his passage on the *Fox,* but Lieutenant Wooldridge made a brief layover at Nassau before returning to the sea for Florida and the Apalachicola River—and shipwrecking on St. George's Island. Wright, *William Augustus Bowles,* 99–116.

governor gave him a passage to London.* Mr. Pitt and the Duke of Portland provided for his necessities in a munificent manner. He left England in the schooner in which he was now wrecked, with which he had, for some time, preyed upon the commerce of Panton and Spain in the Mexican Gulf.[40] General Bowles addressed Ellicott a polite note, inviting him to the wreck, where the latter repaired and was entertained with kindness. He and Bowles were of mutual assistance to each other, the one supplying the perishing crew with some American stores, and the other giving him charts and valuable directions in relation to the navigation around the Florida peninsula. Bowles had repeated conversations with Ellicott, in which he avowed his hatred of the Americans ,and his hostility to Spain, and declared his determination to visit his vengeance upon the latter in incessant attacks upon the Florida posts at the head of the Creeks, whom he termed "My people."[41]

Ellicott sailed from the wreck to St. Marks, where he lodged in the house of the commandant, Captain Portell, and was agreeably entertained by his fascinating wife. Having repaired his schooner, he sailed around the peninsula, and went up the St. Mary's to the camp of the surveyors, where he found all had arrived safe, and where, in conjunction with Minor, he determined the point of the line of 31°, and there erected a large mound.[42] Thus ended this protracted and disagreeable business.†

[41] While Bowles escaped St. George's Island to his Lower Creek and Seminole followers, Ellicott wrote to Governor Vicente Folch on 9 October 1799 warning him that Bowles "intends immediately attacking your post at St. Marks if it is not evacuated, and to seize Mr. Panton's property at Appalacy." Ibid., 116, 118–19, 123–25; *Miscellaneous Documents of the Senate of the United States,* 2: 316.

[42] When Ellicott arrived at Fort St. Marcos (St. Marks) de Apalache, he warned the commandant Captain Thomas Portell that Bowles intended to attack his post momentarily. Ellicott left St. Marks on 18 October 1799 and departed the town of St. Mary's on 25 April 1800. Less than a month later, Captain Portell surrendered Fort St. Marcos after a five week siege on 19 May to Bowles and his Indian army of 400 Creeks and Seminoles and ten white men. Ellicott, *Journal,* 239–40, 279; Wright, *William Augustus Bowles,* 128–32; Gilbert C. Din, "In Defense of Capt. Tomás Portell: An Episode in the History of Spanish West Florida," *Revista española de estudios norteamericanos* 21–22 (2001): 143–47, 149–53.

* Du Lac, *Voyage dans les deux Louisianes*, 466–70.

† Ellicott, *Journal*, 180–278. Also his "Appendix," 83. The Indians who broke up the survey belonged to the towns of Tallase, upon the Tallapoosa, and Eufaula, upon the Chattahoochee.

Chapter XXVII

THE AMERICANS IN ALABAMA AND MISSISSIPPI

It has been seen that the legislature of Georgia promptly repealed the Yazoo Act. Congress, with the consent of that state, organized a large portion of the domain, which was conveyed under the Yazoo sale, into a territorial government, embracing the country between the Chattahoochee and Mississippi Rivers, extending from the line of 31° to that of 32° 28'. This government was not to impair the rights of Georgia to the soil.[1]

John Adams, now president of the United States, conferred upon Winthrop Sargent the post of governor of the "Mississippi Territory." John Steele was, at the same time, appointed secretary, while Thomas Rodney, of Delaware, and John Tilton, of New Hampshire, were constituted judges of the superior court. Four months after the evacuation of the country by the Spaniards, these officers arrived at Natchez.[2] They found the country in the occupation of the federal troops, under General Wilkinson. The governor, whose powers were extensive, commenced the organization of his government. He decreed, by proclamation, the formation of the Natchez District into the counties of Adams and Pickering. He established county courts, which were to be holden quarterly by associate justices. Six thousand inhabitants, including slaves, comprised the population, who lived upon the waters of Bayou Pierre, St. Catherine, Coles, Homochitto, and Buffalo creeks. There was also a settlement at the Walnut Hills, and one upon Big Black. It has been seen what kind of a population lived upon the Tensaw and Tombigbee in 1792. It was now much increased, but was composed of the same kind of people. An advance towards civilization had, however, been made, in that region, by the establishment of a ferry by Hollinger, an Indian countryman, across the Tombigbee, and another, by Samuel Mims, to convey people over the Alabama. The route lay across Nanna Hubba Island, and, in times of high water, passengers were ferried from one river to the other, the distance of ten

[1] The Georgia Assembly repealed the 1795 Yazoo land act on 13 February 1796, passing a bill referred to as the "Rescinding Act" by nearly unanimous votes in both houses. Congress passed an act on 7 April 1798 creating the Mississippi Territory. Foster, *James Jackson*, 115–18; U.S. Congress, *Organic Acts for the Territories of the United States: With Notes Thereon, Compiled from Statutes at Large of the United States* (Washington: GPO, 1900), 12–13.

[2] Winthrop Sargent, a native of Gloucester, Massachusetts, and a 1771 Harvard graduate, had served as secretary of the Northwest Territory prior to his appointment as governor of the Mississippi Territory. He arrived in Natchez on 6 August 1798 deathly sick, with no legal training, and faced with multiple challenges exacerbated by his Federalist politics and

miles.[3] Lieutenant McCleary had marched across the country, from Natchez, and had taken possession of Fort St. Stephens, when the Spanish garrison marched out and dropped down below Ellicott's line.[4]

This portion of the Mississippi Territory was utterly defenseless, entirely isolated, and surrounded by Indian nations, on the north, east and west, while the treacherous Spaniards were just below, at Mobile. To protect it, the federal government established a post upon the first bluff below the confluence of the Tombigbee and Alabama. Captain Schaumburg, of the 2nd regiment, marched from Natchez, with two companies, and built a stockade, with one bastion, which was called Fort Stoddert, and was situated on the site of the present arsenal landing of Mount Vernon.[5]

Governor Sargent issued another proclamation, defining the limits of Washington County, embracing the population upon the Tombigbee and Alabama. Of all counties that ever were established, it was by far the most extensive in territory. It extended to the Chattahoochee on the east and to Pearl River on the west, and was bounded on the south by the line of 31° and on the north by that of 32° 28'. Twenty counties in Alabama, and twelve in Mississippi, have since been formed out of the territory of the original county of Washington. The people of the territory, becoming dissatisfied with the arbitrary measures of the governor, remonstrated with the president. These things, together with a prodigious increase of population, induced Congress to establish a second grade of territorial government, which allowed a legislature. Four representatives from Adams, four from Pickering, and one from Washington, convened at Natchez. The governor held an unqualified veto power.[6]

General Wilkinson deserves to be remembered for many important public services, among which were the treaties which he made with Indian tribes, and the military organization of new counties. He wrote with astonishing ease, and always expressed himself well. He was, unquestionably, a man of genius, as well as of much

"frigid and sour" disposition. Robert V. Haynes, *The Mississippi Territory and Southwest Frontier, 1795–1817* (Lexington: University Press of Kentucky, 2010), 27–29.

[3] Samuel Mims started his ferry, located about eight miles above Fort Mims, in 1797. Mims' Ferry operated below the cut-off which joins the Alabama and Tombigbee Rivers and carried travelers over the Alabama to Nanna Hubba Island. From this island, Adam Hollinger's ferry carried them to the west bank of the Tombigbee. Irons, "River Ferries in Alabama," 24.

[4] Giving up on the arrival of U.S. forces, Fernando Lisoro surrendered the keys to Fort San Esteban (St. Stephens) on 5 February 1799 to Richard Brashears and withdrew his forces below the 31st parallel. Lieutenant John McCleary (McClary) arrived around 17 March 1799 with Andrew Ellicott's surveying party. A few days later, David Gillespie, Ellicott's assistant, set up the Hadley sextant to determine the latitude of the fort. Holmes, "Spanish Military Commanders," 63; Ellicott, *Journal*, 198–99.

[5] In July 1799, Captain Bartholomew Schaumburg (Schaumburgh) and the men of his 2nd U.S. Infantry Regiment began the construction of a bastioned stockade fort with blockhouses at all four corners of Ward's Bluff on the Mobile River. The oppressive summer heat and sickness caused the work to continue well into the fall of 1799. Named for Benjamin Stoddert, secretary of the navy, it is often referred to as Fort Stoddart or Fort Stoddard in official documents and modern studies. Jack D. L. Holmes, ed., "Fort Stoddart in 1799: Seven Letters of Captain Bartholomew Schaumburgh," *Alabama Historical Quarterly* 26 (Fall/Winter 1964): 231–52; Jack D. L. Holmes, "Thomas Humphrey Cushing," *Handbook of Texas Online*, http://www.tshaonline.org/handbook/online.

[6] While the voters in Adams and Pickering elected four representatives each, Washington County elected William McGrew, who missed the convening of the legislature because Governor Sargent's election proclamation arrived too late for the scheduled election day. Haynes, *Mississippi Territory*, 45.

usefulness; yet he had always been suspected of allowing personal considerations to control much of his military and official conduct. However, now acting with great zeal and fidelity, he stationed troops at different points on the line of demarcation, from Fort Adams, upon the Mississippi, to Pearl River, and caused, as we have seen, Fort Stoddert to be built. While his headquarters were at Natchez, he made an advantageous treaty with the Chickasaws, obtaining their consent, among other things, to the cutting of a road, to remain as a highway, extending from the Cumberland District to the American settlements of Natchez.[7] He made another treaty, with the Choctaws, for a road from Fort Adams to the Yazoo River. The old boundary between the British and Choctaws was also confirmed by him, and marked anew.[8] He likewise repaired to the distant Oconee, and, near a fort named in honor of him, made a treaty with the Creeks, by which the latter, for valuable considerations, ceded to the United States all the territory east of a line, to run from High Shoals upon Apalachee, thence down the Oconee to its junction with the Ocmulgee, and thence to Ellicott's mound, upon the St. Mary's.[9] The fearless, wise and patriotic agents, Benjamin Hawkins and Andrew Pickens, were associated with General Wilkinson in all these treaties, and, with him, travelled from the Chickasaw Bluff, upon the Mississippi, backwards and forwards, over this Indian world, encountering its dangers and sharing in mutual hardships.*

Mr. Jefferson, who was now president of the United States, appointed William C. C. Claiborne governor of the Mississippi Territory. Governor Sargent retired from office, and never afterwards filled a public station. The new governor, who was

* *American State Papers: Indian Affairs*, 1: 648–81.

7 While Pickett gives Wilkinson credit for the 1801 Treaty of Chickasaw Bluffs, Benjamin Hawkins and Andrew Pickens, as treaty commissioners, with the assistance of Samuel Mitchell, agent to the Chickasaw, made the arrangements and led the negotiations with the Chickasaw. On 24 October 1801, seventeen principal Chickasaw leaders placed their mark or signature on the treaty document. For acceding to a road right-of-way through their nation, the Chickasaw received merchandise valued at $700. Kappler, *Indian Affairs: Laws and Treaties*, 2: 55–56; James F. Barnett, Jr., *Mississippi's American Indians* (Jackson: University Press of Mississippi, 2012), 164–65.

8 Again Pickett credits Wilkinson for the 1801 Treaty of Fort Adams with the Choctaw, but Benjamin Hawkins and Andrew Pickens, as treaty commissioners, and John McKee, deputy superintendent and agent to the Choctaw, should be acknowledged as the principal negotiators. Under Article 3 of this critical treaty of 17 December 1801, the Choctaw surrendered 2,641,920 acres of Choctaw land in the southwestern corner of the Mississippi Territory, occupied by seven counties of the modern state of Mississippi. For this massive land deal, the Choctaw received three sets of blacksmith tools and merchandise valued at $2,000. Kappler, *Indian Affairs: Laws and Treaties*, 2: 56–57; Barnett, *Mississippi's American Indians*, 165.

9 On 16 June 1802, forty-three "Kings, Head men, and Warriors" of the Creek Nation placed their mark or signature to the Treaty of Fort Wilkinson negotiated by General Wilkinson, Benjamin Hawkins, and Andrew Pickens. They surrendered a strip of land adjoining the Oconee, Ocmulgee, and Altamaha rivers and received $25,000 in goods and merchandise and the satisfaction of "certain debts" owed at the Creek Trading House or "to satisfy claims for property taken . . . citizens of the United States." In addition, the treaty commissioners agreed to pay the Creek Nation a perpetual annuity of $3,000, $1,000 for ten years "to the chiefs who administer the government," and to furnish "two sets of blacksmith tools and men to work them" for three years. Kappler, *Indian Affairs: Laws and Treaties*, 2: 58–59; Braund, *Deerskins & Duffels*, 179.

descended from an ancient Virginia family, removed to Tennessee when a youth, was a member of the convention which formed the constitution of that state, a judge of the Supreme Court, and a member of Congress. A man of unquestioned talents, fine address, and strict probity and honor, he could not fail to make a popular and useful officer in the Mississippi wilderness. The territorial secretary was Cato West, and the bench of the superior court was filled by Daniel Tilton, Peter B. Bruin, and Seth Lewis.[10]

The counties of Adams and Pickering being sub-divided into five others, and the name of the latter changed, they were now called Adams, Jefferson, Wilkinson, Claiborne and Washington. A code of jurisprudence was adopted, and the seat of government removed six miles east of Natchez, to the town of Washington. Joshua Baker was speaker of the house, and John Ellis president of the executive council or senate.[11] About this period, Colonel Andrew Marschalk, of Wayne's army, established the *Natchez Gazette*, the first paper issued in our country, and, afterwards, was so long engaged in the occupation, issuing different journals for forty years, that he was styled the "Father of the Mississippi press." It was not long, however, before Timothy and Samuel Terrell published the *Mississippi Messenger*, at the seat of government, where, also performing the duties of public printers,[12] they published the first digest of the territory, compiled by Judge Harry Toulmin.*

Upon the Tombigbee and Lake Tensaw, the people still lived without laws, and without the rite of matrimony. For years, the sexes had been in the habit of pairing off, and living together, with the mutual promise of regular marriage, when ministers or magistrates should make their appearance in the country. An amusing incident will here be related, in which a young couple were united by a functionary not hitherto known as participating in such sacred rites. The house of Samuel Mims, a wealthy Indian countryman, was the most spacious in the country, and hither the young and the gay flocked to parties, and danced to the music furnished by the Creoles of Mobile and others, for

* Monette, 2: 345; *Notes on the War in the South*, by Nathaniel H. Claiborne, 91–102.

[10] On 23 October 1801, the twenty-six year old Claiborne, a Jeffersonian Republican, and his new wife, Eliza Wilson Lewis, arrived in Natchez, and, unlike his predecessor, he received more challenges from his would-be friends than his Federalist adversaries, especially Cato West and the Greens—Abner, Henry, and Thomas. Haynes, *Mississippi Territory*, 48–50, 62–63.

[11] In its 1801 session, the Mississippi territorial legislature changed the name of Pickering County to Jefferson, created a second county—Claiborne—out of the new county, and transferred all future sessions of the legislature to the town of Washington in Jefferson County. The legislature also divided Adams, creating the new county of Wilkinson, and made all these changes effective in 1802. John Ellis had also received appointments as a justice and as lieutenant colonel of the 5th militia regiment for Wilkinson County from Governor Claiborne. Ibid., 55; Claiborne, *Mississippi*, 220–25, 228.

[12] Most sources credit Andrew Marschalk with establishing the first printing press, a mahogany press, in the Mississippi Territory in 1799, but there is some disagreement over who first published the *Mississippi Gazette* in Natchez—Marschalk or Ben M. Stokes. Over more than two decades, Marschalk published several papers and earned respect as the first public printer in Mississippi, founder of the *Mississippi Herald* in 1802, and "father of Mississippi journalism." The Terrell brothers used their *Mississippi Messenger* to support the Mississippi Republican Society but later split over attacks on Governor Robert Williams. Haynes, *Mississippi Territory*, 43, 63, 77, 172–75, 189, 199–201, 325–29; Charles S. Sydnor, "The Beginning of Printing in Mississippi," *Journal of Southern History* 1 (February 1935): 49–55; "The Press of Mississippi, With a Cursory Glance at the Literature of the

the country abounded in fiddlers, of high and low degree. Daniel Johnson and Miss Elizabeth Linder had, for some time, loved each other. She was rich and he was poor, and, of course, the parents of the former objected to a *pairing*. On Christmas night, a large party was assembled at "Old Sam Mims's," and the very forests resounded with music and merry peals of laughter. In the midst of the enjoyment, the lovers, in company with several young people, of both sexes, secretly left the house, entered some canoes, paddled down Lake Tensaw, into the Alabama, and arrived at Fort Stoddert, an hour before daylight. Captain Schaumburg, who had risen early to make his eggnog, was implored to join the lovers in the bonds of matrimony. The proposition astounded the good-natured old German, who protested his ignorance of all such matters, and assured them that he was only a military commandant, having no authority whatever to make people man and wife. They entreated, telling him, with truth, that the federal government had placed him there as a general protector and regulator of affairs, and that the case before him demanded his sanction and adjustment.[13] After the eggnog had circulated pretty freely, the commandant placed the lovers before him, and, in a stentorian voice, pronounced the following marital speech: "I, Captain Schaumburg, of the 2nd Regiment of the United States Army, and commandant of Fort Stoddert, do hereby pronounce you man and wife. Go home! behave yourselves—multiply and replenish the Tensaw country!" The happy pair entered their canoes, rowed back to the Boat Yard, and were pronounced, by the whole settlement, "the *best* married people they had known in a long time."*

The federal government displayed much wisdom in the establishment of a factory, or trading house, at St. Stephens. It was well stored with such merchandise as suited the Choctaws, for whom it was particularly designed. It served to create a good feeling with those Indians, and to entice them from the control of Panton and the Spaniards, below the line. Joseph Chambers, a man of a well-cultivated mind, and of business capacity, a native of Salisbury, North Carolina, was made superintendent of this factory, with an assistant, Thomas H. Williams, also from North Carolina, who afterwards was secretary of the territory, collector of the port of New Orleans, and United States senator from Mississippi.[14]

* Conversations with old settlers.

State," in *Biographical and Historical Memoirs of Mississippi*, 2 vols. (Chicago: Goodspeed Publishing Co., 1891), 242–43.

[13] While Pickett cites "Conversations with old settlers" for this frontier love story, there are sources to support his narrative. Elizabeth Linder was the daughter of John Linder Jr., and the granddaughter of John Linder Sr., a recipient of Spanish land grants and an important community leader in early Washington County. Daniel Johnston (Johnson) was the son of John Johnston and the grandson of Daniel Johnston, who lived in the District of San Esteban de Tombecbé in 1796. "Census of the District of San Esteban de Tombecbé," comp. Jack D. L. Holmes, Louisiana Collection Series, Birmingham, AL (online); "Excerpts from Lawsuit of Daniel L. Johnston," Alabama Department of Archives and History, Montgomery, AL, http://vidas.rootsweb.ancestry.com/s002.html; "Will of John Linder Jr.," http://vidas.rootsweb.ancestry.com/w005.html.

[14] The Jefferson administration appointed Joseph Chambers, a native of Salisbury, North Carolina, factor of the Choctaw Trading House at the site of Fort San Esteban in 1802. Thomas Hill Williams (1780–1840) was appointed by Jefferson as register of the land office west of the Pearl River on 20 December 1805 and served as secretary of the Mississippi Territory. President James Madison appointed him collector of customs at the port of New Orleans in 1810, and he was the first elected U.S. senator from Mississippi (1817–1829). Gaines, *Reminiscences*, 3, 40–41, 48, 138–39, 156, 205 n. 28.

The Yazoo act had been repealed, the treaty of Madrid had been made, Ellicott's line had been run, and the Spaniards had been removed; still great difficulties had arisen between Georgia and the federal government in relation to lands granted under the Yazoo act, which the companies, and various purchasers under them, resolutely claimed and defended. Many plans were proposed, for satisfactory adjustment, which produced debate and contention of an angry character. Finally, Albert Gallatin, James Madison and Levi Lincoln, on the part of the government, and James Jackson, Abraham Baldwin and John Milledge, representing Georgia, made a final disposition of the matter. For the sum of one million two hundred and fifty thousand dollars, Georgia ceded to the United States all the territory within the following boundaries:[15] Beginning upon the Mississippi, at the line of 31°, thence continuing up that river to the line of 35°, thence along that line, due east, to Nickajack, thence southward to the mouth of Uchee Creek, thence down the Chattahoochee to Ellicott's line, thence along that line due west, to the Mississippi, the place of beginning. The purchase money was to be paid to Georgia out of the first net proceeds of the sales of these lands. The United States stipulated to recognize all good claims, to any of this territory, under Spanish and British grants, and also under the act of Georgia of 1785, creating the county of Bourbon; but it refused to admit any of the Yazoo claims.* The United States now held the right of jurisdiction, and the right of soil, to all the territory which forms the present states of Alabama and Mississippi. After this compromise, the money paid by the Yazoo companies was made over to the United States. Some of it had been drawn by the purchasers, under the law of Georgia; some of it had been lost, whilst in deposit at the treasury, from which the state had taken the precaution to be saved harmless, having declared, in good time, that the deposit should remain in the treasury at the risk of the depositors. The Yazoo grantees, or those claiming under them, were never suffered to hold lands in Alabama or Mississippi, in virtue of either the Yazoo act or the compromise. They might have held as much as they pleased, in virtue of the stock of five million scrip, created by an act of Congress.[16]

Emigrants flocked to the Mississippi Territory by various routes, all of which were difficult, and some of them very circuitous. A party set out from North Carolina, consisting of Thomas Malone, a young

* *American State Papers: Public Lands*, 1: 114.

[15] The two commissions had struggled for nearly two years to reach a consensus on Georgia's cession of its western land claims. When Jefferson replaced John Adams's commissioners with Madison, Gallatin, and Lincoln, the prolonged deliberations gained impetus, culminating in an agreement known as "The Articles of Agreement and Cession of 1802" or, more generally, the Georgia Compact. Carter, *Territorial Papers/Mississippi*, 5: 142–46; Foster, *James Jackson*, 135–39.

[16] While the bitterness and legal wrangling over the Yazoo lands continued, Georgia's cession of 54,500,00 acres between the 31st and 35th degrees of north latitude allowed the federal government to extend the northern limits of the Mississippi Territory to the Tennessee state line. On 27 March 1804, the U.S. Congress passed an act that provided under "Sec. 7. . . That the tract of country lying north of the Mississippi territory, south of the state of Tennessee, and bounded on the east by the state of Georgia, and on the west by Louisiana, shall be, and the same is hereby annexed to, and made part of the Mississippi territory." U.S. Congress, *Statutes at Large, 8th Congress, 1st Session*, 303–06.

clerk in the land office of Raleigh, John Murrell and his family, James Moore, Goodwin Myrick, George Norsworthy, Robert Caller, William Murrell, and sixty Negroes.[17] With great difficultly they ascended the Blue Ridge with their wagons, and descended, through its dark gorges, into the valley of the Tennessee. Constructing flatboats, at Knoxville, they floated down the river to the head of the Muscle Shoals, where they disembarked at the house of Doublehead, a Cherokee chief.[18] Placing their effects upon the horses, which had been brought down, by land, from Knoxville, they departed, on foot, for the "Bigby settlements," about St. Stephens, a great distance off, and to which not a solitary direct path led. After a fatiguing march, they reached the residence of Levi Colbert, a celebrated Chickasaw chief, who gave them the necessary directions.[19] Pursuing their journey, they came upon the Tombigbee, at the Cotton Gin, which had, not long before, been erected by the federal government to encourage the Chickasaws in the cultivation of the great staple.[20]

Desiring to lessen the fatigues of the long and painful trip, the party constructed two canoes at this point, each forty feet in length, and very large, but of miserable workmanship, being executed with no other tools than axes and grubbing hoes. These they placed in the river, in parallel positions, five feet apart. They were connected by a platform, made of cane, upon which were deposited the effects of the expedition, which were piled up high above the heads of the emigrants, who

[17] John Murrell (Murrel) survived his horrendous experience on the Tombigbee, and he began serving as a justice of the peace in Washington County, Mississippi Territory, in March 1804. His brother William Murrell (Murrel) filed a claim in March 1804 on 175 acres by "right of pre-emption" under an act of Congress on 3 March 1803. Thomas Malone also worked as a surveyor for several land claims filed in 1804. The Murrell brothers, Robert Caller, Thomas Malone, and Goodwin Myrick are listed on the 1803 tax roll for Washington County. *ASP: PL*, 1: 652, 655, 705, 770–77; 1803 Tax Roll, Washington County, Mississippi Territory, http://theusgenweb.org/al/washington/1803TaxRoll.htm.

[18] Doublehead (c. 1750–1807) had been a prominent Chickamauga leader with Dragging Canoe on the Old Southwest frontier. He participated in the Treaty of Philadelphia which was signed on 26 June 1794. He lived in the Muscle Shoals area of modern Lauderdale County, Alabama, near Brown's Ferry until 1802, when he moved to Shoal Town at the mouth of Blue Water Creek. Kappler, *Indian Affairs: Laws and Treaties*, 2: 33–34; Rickey Butch Walker, *Doublehead: Last Chickamauga Cherokee Chief* (Killen, Ala.: Bluewater Publications, 2012), 62–74, 76–141, 190.

[19] Levi Colbert (1759–1834), a métis son of James Colbert, became a prominent leader among the Chickasaw. He was also known as the Itawamba Mingo and operated an inn or stand on the Natchez Trace, south of Colbert's Ferry, on Buzzard Roost Creek in modern Colbert County, Alabama. Don Martini, *Who was Who Among the Southern Indians: A Genealogical Notebook, 1698–1907* (Falkner, MS: n.p., 1997), 142.

[20] The "Cotton Gin" had been built through the efforts of John McKee, agent to the Choctaw and Chickasaw, and George and Levi Colbert. It was located on the west side of the Tombigbee River, one mile south of the junction of Town Creek with the Tombigbee in modern Monroe County, Mississippi. In March 1810, Willie Blount, governor of Tennessee, referred to the gin as the "Colbert's Cotton Gin, at the head of navigable waters on the Tombigbee River." Atkinson, *Splendid Land, Splendid People*, 184–85; Rowland, *Mississippi: Compromising Sketches*, 1: 575–76.

now sat down in long rows in the two canoes. A few of the men went by land with the horses, towards St. Stephens, to make preparations for the arrival of the main party. This rude and singular craft, then quite common in savage regions, had proceeded but two miles down the rapid, crooked and swollen stream, when it struck, with great force, against a log, which extended half across the channel, and immediately disappeared. The cane ligament which bound the Siamese canoes burst asunder, and every soul was washed deep under the waves. Those who rose again were presently seen struggling with the torrent, amid the wreck, now tossed about in the fury of the waters. Murrell rose, but in his arms was the lifeless body of a daughter. His wife also came to the surface, with a babe at her breast, both happily alive. Malone and others, swimming ashore, became active in assisting many of the party in reaching limbs of trees by extending to them grapevines and canes. At length, all who survived huddled upon a small piece of land, surrounded by water.

It was now night. The north wind swept over the gloomy swamp. The ducks, in their rapid flight, whizzed through the air. The wolves howled upon the prairies. The owls screamed and hooted upon the lofty trees. The mighty timber crashed as the angry currents passed by. Such were the unwelcome sounds that fell upon the ears of this miserable party. No succor came. No encouraging voice saluted them. Benumbed with cold, they hovered together to keep alive, shivering and knocking their agitated limbs against each other, while their wet apparel froze fast upon them. Being without fire, they had no way to produce one. It was two miles back to the old camp, and the route lay over thick cane, water and small islands. A resolute young Negro man volunteered to find it. He plunged into the low grounds, and strangely made his way to the camp. In the meantime, the helpless pioneers, despairing of his return, bewailed their condition with deep moans and bitter lamentations. Beneath the shadows of one of the darkest nights ever known, they mournfully counted over the missing and the drowned. Two long hours passed away, when the cheerful halloo of the Negro was heard afar off. It was answered by a united and sympathetic shout. All eyes were turned in the direction from which the

[21] On 27 March 1805, John Murrell (Murrel) may have sold some of the heroes from Pickett's narrative to James Caller: "Know all Men by these presents that I John Murrell of Warren county state of North Carolina have Bargained sold and Delivered to James Caller of the County & State aforesaid the following property that is a negro man named [Mack] aged about forty Jim a Negro man aged about 25 a boy by the name of [Richard] aged about 14 a boy By the name of Peter aged about 12 a boy by the name of Henry aged about 3 a woman by the name of Judith aged about 20 a woman by the name of Nancy aged about 17 a girl by the name of [ ] aged about 5 a girl by the name of [ ] aged about 3 a girl by the name of Fanny aged about 3 also 1 waggon and team that is 5 horses one small mare one filly one bay horse two sorrel horses . . . the sum of 900 Pound Virginia Money. . . ." John Murrell to James Caller, Bill of Sale, 27 March 1805, ADAH, Montgomery, AL (online).

sound came, and in the darkness was seen an indistinct light, which shone over the tops of the distant canes like a far-off Aurora Borealis. It was fire, and the noble Negro had brought it from the old camp. At length he came, with a cracking, crashing noise, familiar only to the ears of those who have walked through the dense cane swamps of Alabama.

Fires were kindled with dry cane, and around them sat the sufferers until the morning sun dispelled the horrid night. It was now ascertained that one white child, and twenty-one Negroes, were entombed beneath the tide of the angry Tombigbee. The survivors groped their way to the Cotton Gin, without provisions, without hats, without tools, without firearms, without money, and with no clothes except those which drooped upon their limbs. They were friendless and alone in a savage country, far from their point of destination, and still further from their native land.

Who saved these people from starvation, and enabled them to reach Washington County, Alabama, after a journey of one hundred and twenty days from North Carolina? Not the Indians, for one of them stole a Negro from the brave Malone, for the return of whom he had to give his watch. Those animals, who cling to their unfortunate masters to the last moment, and are never once guilty of the crime of ingratitude—who hunted rabbits, opossums and raccoons for their famished owners. They saved the lives of these people.[21]

Several years previous to this period, two brothers, from New England, came to the Boat Yard, upon Lake Tensaw. William Pierce pursued the business of weaving—a profitable employment in those days. His brother, John, established the first American school in Alabama. There, the high-blood descendants of Lachlan McGillivray—the Taits, Weatherfords and Durants, the aristocratic Linders, the wealthy Mimses, and the children of many others—first learned to read. The pupils were strangely mixed in blood, and their color was of every hue. It was not long before these Yankee brothers engaged in mercantile pursuits. They established a cotton gin at the Boat Yard, the first in that part of the country.[22] Six months before this, Abram Mordecai, an Indian trader, procuring the consent of the Creek chiefs and the approbation

[22] John Pierce played an important role in creating community in the Tensaw District with his school, and it may have been in operation until the destruction of Fort Mims in 1813. After conducting his school for some seven years, he and his brother William Pierce were involved in several business interests, including trade, a saw mill, and a cotton gin. He also served as postmaster from 1811 to 1818, when a new community emerged further away from the river. David Mathews, *Why Public Schools? Whose Public Schools?: What Early Communities Have to Tell Us* (Montgomery: NewSouth Books, 2002), 53.

of Colonel Hawkins, had established a cotton gin at Weatherford's racetrack, on the first eastern bluff below the junction of the Coosa and Tallapoosa. It was built by Lyons & Barnett, of Georgia, who brought their tools, gin saws and other materials from that state on pack-horses. The same enterprising mechanics also built the one for the Pierces, and another, at McIntosh Bluff, upon the Tombigbee.[23]

Abram Mordecai was a queer fellow. He traded extensively with the Indians, exchanging his goods for pink root, hickory nut oil, and peltries of all kinds. These he carried to New Orleans and Mobile in boats, and to Pensacola and Augusta on pack-horses. The hickory nut oil was a luxury with French and Spanish epicures. It was manufactured by the Indians, in a simple manner—by boiling the cracked nuts in water, and skimming off the oil as it floated on the surface. Mordecai bought cotton of the Indians in small quantities, ginned it, and carried it to Augusta on pack-horses, in bags much smaller than those of the present day. He was a dark eyed Jew, and amorous in his disposition. Tourculla, (Captain Isaacs), the chief of the Coosawdas, hearing of his intrigues with a married squaw, approached his house with twelve warriors, knocked him down, thrashed him with poles until he lay insensible, cut off his ear, and left him to the care of his wife. They also broke up his boat, and burned down his gin-house.[24] A pretty squaw was the cause of the destruction of the first cotton gin in Alabama.*

General Bowles, quitting the island where Ellicott found him, boldly advanced into the Creek Nation, disturbed the mild and beneficial influence which Hawkins had begun to engender, declared his eternal hostility to Spain and the United States, and became an object of dread to all quiet minds, and a terror to all interests against which he acted. Among other outrages, he headed a party of Indians, advanced upon St. Marks, captured the fort, and plundered the store of Panton, Leslie & Co. Hawkins united with the Spanish authorities in a scheme to rid the country of a common enemy. A large secret reward was offered for his capture. A great feast was given by the Indians at the town of Tuskegee, where the old French Fort Toulouse stood, to which Bowles and the Miccosukee chiefs were invited.[25] They attended, and during the feast the unsuspecting freebooter was

* Conversations with Lachlan Durant, James Moore, Abram Mordecai, and many other old traders.

[23] The cotton gins operated by Abram (Abraham) Mordecai (1755–1850) on the Alabama River and by the Pierce brothers on Boat Yard Lake featured saw-toothed iron discs instead of the wire spikes used in Eli Whitney's gins. Edward Lyons, a mechanic from near Wrightsboro, Georgia, is generally credited with this improvement, and he was sued by Eli Whitney in 1795 for patent infringement. However, the lawsuit was settled in his favor and Whitney was denied a new trial. Karen Gerhard Britton, *Bale O'Cotton: The Mechanical Art of Cotton Ginning* (College Station: Texas A & M University Press, 1992), 18.

[24] After interviewing Mordecai in 1847, Pickett published a biographical sketch of "Old Mordecai" in the Montgomery *Flag and Advertiser* on 5 October 1847, in which he described Mordecai's eyes as being "a deep hazel" and not "a dark eyed Jew." He also recorded Mordecai's story of his horses getting loose in 1805 and eating the young corn of the town of Coosawda, resulting in his beating at the hands of Captain Isaacs and other Creeks. There is no mention of the "married squaw" and the loss of his ear for an amorous adventure. "A sketch of Old Mordecai," *Flag and Advertiser*, 5 October 1847, Pickett Scrapbook, Pickett Papers, ADAH; Notes from the lips of Abram Mordecai, ibid.

[25] Actually, representatives of the four major Southern nations had agreed to send representatives to the Hickory Ground in the Upper Creek country in May 1803 to meet with Benjamin Hawkins and other U.S. representatives for preliminary discussions of the terms of proposed treaties forthcoming from the Jefferson administration. In

suddenly seized by concealed Indians, who sprang upon him, securely pinioned him, and placed him in a canoe full of armed warriors. They then rapidly rowed down the river. Hawkins and John Forbes, of Pensacola, were in the town, but were concealed, until Sam Moniac, a half-breed, had caused Bowles to be made a prisoner.[26] Arriving at a point in the present Dallas County, the canoe was tied up, the prisoner conducted upon the bank, and a guard set over him. In the night the guard fell asleep, when Bowles gnawed his ropes apart, crept down the bank, got into the canoe, quietly paddled across the river, entered a thick cane swamp, and fled. At the break of day, the astonished Indians arose in great confusion, but fortunately saw the canoe on the opposite side, which Bowles had foolishly neglected to shove off. Swimming over to that point, they got upon his track, and by the middle of the day once more made him a prisoner. He was conveyed to Mobile, and from thence to Havana,[27] where, after a few years, he died in the dungeons of Morro Castle.*

While the inhabitants of the eastern section were disturbed by Bowles, a notorious robber named Mason, was a terror to the people of the western part of the Mississippi Territory. During the occupancy of the country by the Spaniards, the lair of this remorseless human tiger was in a cave upon the Ohio, where he secreted his banditti, and the booty which he had acquired in a long and bloody havoc upon the public. He had now stationed himself upon the highway, between New Orleans and Natchez, with his two sons and their desperate associates. The western people boated their produce down the Mississippi, sold it in New Orleans, purchased horses, and returned by this route to Natchez, and from thence to Nashville, laden with goods and money. This, therefore, offered the most extensive theatre for the operations of Mason and his banditti. Hence his sanguinary outrages were perpetrated one day in the Chickasaw Nation and the next upon Pearl River. At length, the people in all parts of the country were aroused by his inhuman murders, and every hand was raised against him. Governor Claiborne declared him an outlaw, and offered a large reward for his head.[28] The proclamation was widely distributed, and fell into the hands of Mason; and while he was reading it, with a smile of scorn and contempt, a blow from

* Conversations with old traders, who were present when Bowles was captured. See also *American State Papers: Indian Affairs*, vol. 1.

the background, there was a well-designed plot to capture Bowles that involved Hawkins, Stephen Folch, son of Governor Folch, and John Forbes, William Panton's successor in the Spanish trade. Henri, *Southern Indians and Benjamin Hawkins*, 234–35; Wright, *William Augustus Bowles*, 162–64; John Forbes, "A Journal of John Forbes, May, 1803: The Seizure of William Augustus Bowles," *Florida Historical Quarterly* 9 (April 1931): 279–87.

[26] Bowles appeared at the intertribal gathering with his followers and continued to maintain his ties to the British and his opposition to the Americans and Spanish. Doublehead pushed for consensus on capturing Bowles, and a group of Upper Creeks, including Sam Moniac, Mad Dog, and Charles Weatherford, seized Bowles, and he was placed in handcuffs. In his original narrative, Pickett identifies Sam Moniac, a metis Creek, as Sam McNac, but he was not alone in identifying this illiterate trader of Dutch ancestry as a Scotsman. His name was spelled in a variety of ways: McNac, Manac, Macnac, and Monyak. Waselkov, *Conquering Spirit*, 296 n. 30; Henri, *Southern Indians and Benjamin Hawkins*, 165–66, 235–37.

[27] While John Forbes recorded in his journal that Bowles had been manacled with handcuffs, it is not clear how he escaped briefly from his captors on the descent to Pensacola. At Pensacola, Governor Folch sent Bowles to New Orleans, and from there he was sent aboard the *Aguila* for Havana, where he died on 23 December 1805 in a military hospital. Forbes, "Journal," 289; Wright, *William Augustus Bowles*, 167–68, 171.

[28] Samuel Mason, his son John

behind felled him to the earth. His sons were out upon an expedition, and he was alone with two of his men, who, tempted by the reward, now cut off his head and bore it to Washington, to Governor Claiborne. Fortunately, on account of a temporary lack of funds in the treasury, the reward was not paid. In the meantime, hundreds flocked to the governor's quarters to see the head of Mason, and it was recognized by many who had seen him. Among others went two young men, whose respectable father Mason and his gang had waylaid and robbed while they were with him. They immediately recognized his two associates, who brought in the head. These men were thrown into prison, condemned and hung,[29] and the reward was thus saved to the territory, while Mason was also out of the way.*

Down to this period, no Protestant preacher had ever raised his voice to remind the Tombigbee and Tensaw settlers of their duty to the MOST HIGH. Hundreds, born and bred in the wilderness, and now adult men and women, had never even seen a preacher. The mysterious and eccentric Lorenzo Dow, one day, suddenly appeared at the Boat Yard. He came from Georgia, across the Creek Nation, encountering its dangers, almost alone. He proclaimed the truths of the gospel here, to a large audience, crossed over the Alabama, and preached two sermons to the "Bigby settlers," and went from thence to the Natchez settlements, where he also exhorted the people to "turn from the error of their ways." He then visited the Cumberland region and Kentucky, and came back to the Tombigbee, filling his appointments to the very day.[30] Again plunging into the Creek Nation, this holy man of God once more appeared among the people of Georgia.†

As early as the summer of 1799, the Reverend Tobias Gibson, a Methodist missionary, from South Carolina, visited the Natchez settlements, by way of the Cumberland and Ohio—organized religious societies in Washington and its vicinity, and then departed from the wilderness. In the fall of 1800, he again appeared, now as a missionary from the Tennessee Conference, and formed societies from Bayou Pierre to the Spanish line, numbering, collectively, two hundred church members. After performing the most arduous labor in the cause of our Divine Master, for three years, in this rude and savage land, he died.[31] The Reverend Mr. Brown, another Methodist missionary, came from Tennessee in 1802, and brought with him, to the Natchez country, a mind stored with a knowledge of science, and a heart fervent with piety. He labored in Natchez until 1807.[32] Montgomery and Hall, two reverend gentlemen of

* Monette, 2: 351–53. Conversations with aged persons in Washington County, Alabama.

† Lorenzo Dow, *History of a Cosmopolite,* 76–101.

Mason, and Wiley Harp (Harpe) were identified as the leaders of "a set of pirates and robbers" who attacked river traffic above Walnut Hills (Vicksburg) and menaced travelers on the Natchez Trace. In 1802, Governor William C. C. Claiborne issued a reward of $2,000 for their capture and requested assistance from the U.S. military. At some point, Wiley Harp, and possibly his brother or cousin Micajah Harp, separated from Mason and moved into Kentucky, where Micajah was killed in 1799. Claiborne, *Mississippi*, 225–26; Fred Rosen, *The Historical Atlas of American Crime* (New York: Facts on File, Inc., 2005), 33–42.

[29] Apparently, the two members of Mason's gang who killed Mason for the reward were Samuel Mays and Wiley Harp, using the alias of John Sutton (Setton). Harp and Mays escaped from the Natchez jail, but they were captured some twenty miles north near Greenville, where they were hung on 8 February 1804. Claiborne, *Mississippi*, 227–28; Rosen, *Historical Atlas*, 41–42.

[30] Lorenzo Dow, a native of Coventry, Connecticut, was twice denied a license before being licensed by Methodist Bishop Francis Asbury on 18 September 1798. He was dropped from the conference roll in June 1802 when he left New England for Georgia. He had not been ordained when he started his seven-month tour of the western settlements on the Tombigbee and at Natchez that ended back in Georgia on 23 October 1803. After his marriage to Peggy Miller on 3 September 1804 in Western Connecticut, Lorenzo and Peggy traveled to Kentucky and then to the Cumberland before making his return to Natchez, the Tombigbee, and Georgia. In 1805–1807, Dow toured Ireland and England before making his third trip to Georgia. Richard Nye Price, *Holston Methodism: From Its Origin to the Present Time*, 5 vols. (Nashville: House of the M.E. Church, South, 1912), 2: 39–50; Richard J. Stockham, "The Misunderstood Lorenzo Dow," *Alabama Review* 16 (January 1963): 20–30.

[31] In the spring of 1799, Tobias Gibson (1771–1804), an ordained Methodist minister, became the first Protestant missionary to the Mississippi Territory, preaching from Walnut Hills (Vicksburg) to Fort Adams. Before his untimely death in 1804, Gibson established sixty Methodist congregations in his five years as a missionary supported by Bishop Asbury and the Tennessee Conference. "Tobias Gibson: The Man who brought Methodism to Mississippi," *The Mississippi United Methodist Advocate* (November 27, 1974) [online].

[32] Pickett's "Reverend Mr. Brown" cannot be identified. Most of the printed sources that name early Methodist ministers name only Tobias Gibson, Lorenzo Dow, Nathan Barnes, and Learner Blackman at Natchez between 1799 and 1807. Ibid.; Waselkov, *Conquering Spirit*, 352 n. 10; Horace Mellard Du Bose, *A History of Methodism* (Nashville: Publishing House of ME Church, South, 1916), 426. See "Complete List Historic Methodist Churches and Landmarks in Mississippi" at http://www.millsaps.edu/library/library_cain_complete_list.php.

[33] In 1800, William Montgomery of Georgia and James Hall and James H. Bowman of South Carolina were sent to the Mississippi Territory by the Synod of the Carolinas to evangelize. From October 1800 to April 1801, they preached at nine settlements, including Natchez, and subsequently organized five churches. Montgomery returned and settled near Natchez, serving the churches of Ebenezer and Union for several years prior to his death in 1848. Alfred Nevin, ed., *Encyclopedia of the Presbyterian Church in the United States of America: Including the Northern and Southern Assemblies* (Philadelphia: Presbyterian Encyclopedia Publishing Co., 1881), 561–62; Henry G. Hawkins, "Beginnings of Churches and Christian Work in Mississippi," *New Orleans Christian Advocate* (August 21, 1924) [online].

[34] Reverend David Cooper (c. 1770–1830) came as a Baptist missionary and settled at Greenville in Jefferson County. He had studied medicine in Philadelphia and married the widow of General F. L. Claiborne after moving to the Mississippi Territory in 1802. He preached at churches in southwestern Mississippi and eastern Louisiana and was "an active promoter of missions." L. S. Foster, *Mississippi Baptist Preachers* (St. Louis: National Baptist Publishing Company, 1895), 159–60; Robert Lowry and William H. McCardle, *A History of Mississippi: From the Discovery of the Great River by Hernando De Soto* (Jackson: R. H. Henry & Co., 1891), 433; Will Book #1, Adams County Chancery Court, pages 453 & 454.

[35] The Episcopal minister Adam Cloud, a native of Virginia, preached a sermon in the Natchez District

the Presbyterian order, also preached in Natchez for several years.[33] The Baptists, too, sent a "laborer into the vineyard," in the person of the Reverend David Cooper, who arrived in 1802.[34] Dr. Cloud, of the Episcopal Church, was also sent to "proclaim the glad tidings."[35] The efforts of these various sects were highly salutary, serving to soften and refine the people, and to banish much sin and vice from the worst region that ministers ever entered.*

Congress established regulations respecting the English, Spanish and Georgia grants. Many of the inhabitants claimed extensive tracts of land under them. A land office was established at the town of Washington, and a board of commissioners formed, composed of Thomas Rodney[36] and Robert Williams,[37] who proceeded to consider all claims arising under these grants, in a district extending from Pearl River to the Mississippi. They continued in office until the 3rd July 1807, having recorded two thousand and ninety claims. Their acts were sanctioned by the president. Another board of commissioners, consisting of Joseph Chambers,[38] Ephraim Kirby[39] and Robert Carter Nicholas,[40] was formed at St. Stephens, upon the Tombigbee, whose district extended from Pearl River eastward. They adjourned on the 21st December 1805, having admitted to record two hundred and seventy-six claims, which the president likewise ratified. The inhabitants, living upon public lands about the time of Ellicott's survey, were afterwards allowed, by the government, a section of land; and those who came just before the board of commissioners was established, received a quarter section. Isaac Briggs was surveyor-general.[41] The territorial government was made to extend to the southern boundary of the state of Tennessee; but the extinguishment of the Indian

* Monette, 2: 354–57.

in 1792 while it was under Spanish control. On the following day, he was told not to persist in his preaching. Ignoring the warning, he was arrested, placed in irons, sent to New Orleans, and forced out of the country. He spent twenty years in South Carolina and Georgia and returned in 1816 to organize Christ Church in 1820, the first Episcopal parish in Mississippi. Claiborne, *Mississippi*, 528; Hawkins, "Beginnings of Churches."

[36] Thomas Rodney (1744–1811), a native of Delaware, was an associate justice of Delaware's Supreme Court when President Jefferson appointed him chief justice of the Mississippi Territory in 1803. He kept a remarkable journal of his seventy-one day journey—14 August-1 December 1803—down the Ohio and Mississippi rivers to Natchez. "Thomas Rodney," *Biographical Directory of the United States Congress, 1774-Present* (online); Claiborne, *Mississippi*, 283–84. See Thomas Rodney, *A Journey through the West: Thomas Rodney's 1803 Journal from Delaware to the Mississippi Territory*, ed. Dwight L. Smith and Ray Swick (Athens: Ohio University Press, 1997).

[37] Robert Williams (1773–1836), a native of North Carolina, was appointed by President Jefferson as a federal land commissioner in 1803 and governor of the Mississippi Territory in 1805, serving until the end of Jefferson's presidency in 1809. Claiborne, *Mississippi*, 242, 258, 260–62, 295, 300–02.

[38] While serving as factor of the Choctaw Trading House at St. Stephens, President Jefferson appointed Joseph Chambers as the registrar of the federal land office at Fort Stoddert. *ASP: PL* 1: 593–98; Claiborne, *Mississippi*, 242.

[39] In addition to his service as a federal land commissioner, Jefferson appointed Ephraim Kirby (1757–1804), a native of Connecticut, the first superior court judge of the Mississippi Territory in April 1804. He died of fever at Fort Stoddert on 20 October 1804. *ASP: PL* 1: 593–98; Lewis, *Clearing in the Thickets*, 60–63; Allen V. Briceland, "Ephraim Kirby: Mr. Jefferson's Emissary on the Tombigbee-Mobile Frontier in 1804," *Alabama Review* 24 (April 1971): 83–113.

[40] Robert Carter Nicholas, a native of Virginia, had moved to Kentucky when Jefferson appointed him as a federal land commissioner on 12 July 1803 with his headquarters at Fort Stoddert. *ASP: PL* 1: 593–98; Lewis, *Clearing in the Thickets*, 60–61.

[41] Isaac Briggs (1763–1825), a Quaker from

title had been obtained to no portion, except a strip seventy miles long, above and below Natchez, and extending back twenty miles, and the small district upon the Tombigbee. The balance of the territory was occupied by the Creeks, Cherokees, Chickasaws and Choctaws.

Colonel James Caller, of North Carolina, was one of the first representatives to the legislative council, from the county of Washington, Alabama.[42] The first county court of this county was held at McIntosh Bluff, where John Caller, Cornelius Rain and John Johnson presided, with great frontier dignity.[43] These justices had no code before them, and coming from different states, decided cases according to the laws of their native land, so that the most amusing differences of opinion often prevailed. This was the case all over the territory; but the justices from Georgia holding the laws of South Carolina, North Carolina, Virginia, and the whole of New England in great contempt, contended that the practice in the state from which they came, was alone correct. With their usual success, they generally managed to carry their points.

Pennsylvania, was a noted astronomer, surveyor, and mathematician who worked with Andrew Ellicott on surveying and laying out the District of Columbia. He had recently completed marking the land in the Northwest Territory into ranges and townships when Jefferson appointed him surveyor general of lands south of Tennessee in 1803. He replicated his efforts with the land of the Mississippi Territory. Haynes, *Mississippi Territory*, 60, 94, 98–100; "Isaac Briggs," *Thomas Jefferson Encyclopedia*, https://www.monticello.org/site/research-and-collections/tje.

[42] While James Caller emerged as a frontier hero in the Creek Indian War of 1813–1814, Ephraim Kirby launched an investigation into his filibustering activities against Spanish Florida but died in October 1804 before he could bring charges against Caller. Harry Toulmin replaced Kirby and continued Kirby's investigation of Caller and others and tried to restrain their efforts to move against the Spanish in Mobile. Hamilton, *Colonial Mobile*, 345–46; Lewis, *Clearing in the Thickets*, 62–67.

[43] On 29 January 1802, Governor William C. C. Claiborne appointed John Caller, John Johnson, James Fair, Joseph Thompson, John McGuire, Thomas Bassett, and John Brewer as justices of peace for Washington County. On 1 September 1801, Cornelius Rain, Flood McGrew, and Thomas Bassett had been commissioned on the court of common pleas. Dunbar Rowland, *The Official and Statistical Register of the State of Mississippi, 1908* (Nashville: Brandon Printing Company, 1908), 17.

Chapter XXVIII

GOVERNOR TROUP, OR THE MCINTOSH FAMILY: INCIDENTS IN THE MISSISSIPPI TERRITORY

At the close of our last chapter it was stated that the first American court held in Alabama was at McIntosh Bluff, which is situated upon the western bank of the Tombigbee, between its confluence with the Alabama and the town of St. Stephens. Connected with this bluff, there is, to us, a pleasing historical reminiscence. Alabama has the honor of being the birthplace of George M. Troup, late governor of Georgia, and who is one of the most vigorous and expressive political and epistolary writers of the age.[1] His grandfather, Captain John McIntosh, the chief of the McIntosh clan, was long attached to the army of West Florida, and his valuable services were rewarded, by the king of England, with the grant of McIntosh Bluff, and extensive tracts of land upon the Mississippi. He had a son, who was also a British officer, and a daughter, a native of Georgia. The latter, while on a visit to England, married an officer of the royal army, named Troup. She sailed from England to Mobile, and, arriving at the latter place, entered a barge, and went up the Tombigbee River to the residence of her father at McIntosh Bluff, where, in the wilds of Alabama, Governor Troup was born in September 1780. She had an uncle, named Roderick McIntosh, or "Old Rory," as he was familiarly called, a most extraordinary character—a kind of Don Quixote, old Arab chief, Scottish and Irish chieftain, the Saladin and Coeur de Leon of chivalry. He was long an officer of His Majesty's army in Georgia and East Florida. Thus the father, brother, uncle and husband of this lady, the mother of George M. Troup, were all British officers before the commencement of the Revolution.[2]

Being removed from the scenes of that Revolution, none of them may be said to have taken sides against it, except "Old Rory," who, during the war,

[1] George Michael Troup (1780–1856), a Princeton graduate, started his long political career in the Georgia House of Representatives, followed by a stint in the U.S. House of Representatives (1807–1815) and the Senate (1816–1818). Although defeated in his first gubernatorial campaign, he was elected governor in 1823 and in 1825, when he became the first Georgia governor elected by a popular vote of Georgia voters. He returned to the U.S. Senate in 1829 but retired due to poor health in 1833. Natalie D. Saba, "George Troup (1780–1856)," *New Georgia Encyclopedia*, http://www.georgiaencyclopedia.org/; George Michael Troup, *Biographical Directory of the United States Congress, 1774-Present* (online).

[2] John McIntosh (1715–1787) and his brother Roderick came to Georgia in 1736 with their cousin John Mackintosh Mohr

was frequently in Georgia and East Florida, and, although far advanced in years, was, at all times, ready to storm any Whig fortress that might present itself. Before he came to America, he had been the champion of his native glen in Scotland, and was strongly attached to the Stuart family. In 1777, he was over sixty-five years of age. He was tall. His form was admirably proportioned for strength and activity. His complexion was ruddy, and his hair was white, frizzled and bushy. In walking, or rather striding, his step ordinarily embraced the space of four feet. He was not rich, but lived in ease and comfort, when not engaged in the actual service of the king. He cared nothing for money. During the Spanish occupation of East Florida, he sold a drove of cattle in St. Augustine, and, receiving payment in specie, placed it in a bag on his horse and rode towards home. On the route, the canvas gave way, and many of the dollars fell upon the path. He secured those which were left and pursued his journey, giving himself no concern about those upon the ground. Some years afterwards, being in want of money, he recollected his loss, went to the place, picked up as many dollars as he wanted, and returned home. He was fond of dogs. He once laid a considerable bet that he could hide a doubloon, at three miles distance, and that his setter, which he had taught to take his back track, would find it. *Luath* presently went off on his trail, was gone some time, and returned panting, with his tongue out, but came without the doubloon. *"Treason!"* vociferated "Rory", and he walked rapidly to the place where he had hidden the money. He turned over the log, and found that Luath had torn up the earth in search of it. A man was seen, some distance off, engaged in the splitting of rails. Without ceremony, "Rory" drew his dirk, advanced upon him, and swore he would put him to death if he did not give up the doubloon. The man, very much alarmed, immediately handed him the coin, observing that, having seen McIntosh put something under the log, he had gone to the place and found the gold. "Rory", tossing him back the money, said, "Take it, vile caitiff; it was not the pelf, but the honor of my dog, I cared for."[3]

In 1778, a portion of the garrison of St. Augustine, under General Prévost, marched, by land, to join a force from New York to attack Savannah, then in the occupation of the Whigs.[4] "Rory" was a captain of light infantry, upon this expedition. On

(Mor) and his company of Highlanders. He married Margaret McGillivray and they lived in Savannah, and, through his military service, he received a land grant on the Tombigbee known as McIntosh Bluff. Their son William became a Tory captain during the Revolutionary War and an agent to the Creeks, and their daughter Catherine married George Troup, a British naval officer. Daniel McDonald Johnson, *Blood on the Marsh. The Adventures of Brigadier William Mackintosh, John Mackintosh Mor, Captain Aeneas Mackintosh, Colonel Anne Mackintosh, General Lachlan McIntosh, Roderick McIntosh, Colonel John McIntosh, Flora MacDonald, Sergeant Allen McDonald and Alexander McDonald* (Allendale, SC: Daniel McDonald Johnson, 2014), 41–49, 166, 230, 269–70, 290–91, 298, 303–04, 572–73; John Barlett Meserve, "The MacIntoshes," *Chronicles of Oklahoma* 10 (September 1932): 312–13.

[3] According to a letter written by John Couper (1759–1850) to Dr. James Troup in 1842, he first met Roderick "Rory" McIntosh (Mackintosh) in St. Augustine in 1777 and was acquainted with him through 1781. While it is not clear when McIntosh moved to Sunbury, Georgia, he apparently served as the "governor of Sunbury"—an early Highland settlement—and "later sailed to England" but died in 1782 before reaching Scotland. His dog Luath's name comes from the Scots Gaelic word "luath," an adjective meaning "quick, fast." Johnson, *Blood on the Marsh*, 164–65, 249–50, 318–19, 572; John Couper to Dr. James Troup, St. Simons Island, 16 April 1842, in George White, *Historical Collections of Georgia* (New York: Pudney & Russell Publishers, 1855), 470–74; T. Reed Ferguson, *The John Couper Family at Cannon's Point* (Macon: Mercer University Press, 1994), 1–4, 39, 41, 43, 52.

the march, they passed near a small Whig fort, commanded by captain, afterwards Colonel John McIntosh.[5] Early one morning, when "Rory" had made rather free with the morning glass, he insisted on sallying out to summon the fort to surrender. His friends were unable to restrain him, and he presently advanced, with claymore in hand, followed by his faithful Negro, Jim. Approaching the gate of the fort, he said, in an audible and commanding tone, "Surrender, you miscreants! how dare you presume to resist His Majesty's arms!" Captain McIntosh knew him, and, forbidding any of his men to fire, threw open the gate, and said, "Walk in, cousin, and take possession." "No!" said Rory, with great indignation, "I will not trust myself with such vermin, but I order you to surrender." A rifle was fired at him, the ball of which passed through his face. He fell, but immediately recovered. He retreated backwards, flourishing his sword. His servant, seeing his face covered with blood, and hearing the shot falling around him, implored his master to face about and run for his life. He replied, "Run yourself, poor slave, but I am of a race that never runs." In this manner, he backed safely into the lines, flourishing his sword in defiance, and keeping his face to the enemy.[6]

Upon a certain occasion, "Rory" rode from St. Augustine to Savannah, and applied to his friend, Couper, for money to defray his expenses from that place to Charleston. Couper saw that something of an extraordinary character agitated him, and with difficulty learned the cause of his excitement. "That reptile in Charleston, Gadsden, has insulted my country, and I will put him to death." "What has he done?" said Couper. "Why," said Rory, "on being asked how he meant to fill up his wharf, in Charleston, he replied, 'by importing Scotchmen, who were fit for nothing better.'" With great difficulty, the friends of Rory prevailed on him to return home.[7]

It would be an endless task to enumerate all the anecdotes in our possession in relation to this remarkable Highlander, the grand-uncle of Governor Troup. He was often in the Creek Nation, and was the father of Colonel William McIntosh, a half-breed Muscogee, of high character, whom the Upper Creeks killed for his friendship to the Georgians.[8] "Rory" always dressed in the Highland costume. He was perfectly fearless in spirit, while his broadsword, wielded by one of the most powerful arms, caused streams of human blood to flow in many desperate engagements. Although engaged in the rebellion of '45, King George was nevertheless much attached to him, and "Rory" was ready to die for that monarch, at any moment.[9]

There was another branch of the McIntosh family—all, however, close connections of Governor Troup, by consanguinity—who were conspicuous Whigs in the Revolution, citizens of Georgia, and men who occupied high

[4] Major General Augustine Prévost (1723–1786) received orders from General Henry Clinton to invade Georgia, but Lieutenant Colonel Archibald Campbell drove the American forces out of Savannah on 29 December 1778 before the arrival of Prevost's army. James W. Raab, *Spain, Britain and the American Revolution in Florida, 1763–1783* (Jefferson, NC: McFarland & Company, 2008), 119–22.

[5] Lieutenant Colonel John McIntosh was in command of Fort Morris, located south of Sunbury, Georgia, when British forces under Lieutenant Colonel Lewis V. Fuser demanded its surrender on 25 November 1778. McIntosh refused and reportedly replied: "Come and take it." After blustering and threatening to burn the houses of Sunbury, Fuser withdrew his forces, and Fort Morris remained in American hands until 1779. Johnson, *Blood on the Marsh*, 317–19; Charles Colcock Jones, *The History of Georgia: Revolutionary Epoch* (Boston: Houghton, Mifflin and Company, 1883), 308–11; "Revolutionary War hero John McIntosh to be reinterred Saturday," *The Augusta Chronicle*, 19 October 2010.

[6] Rory McIntosh joined the command of Captain Patrick Murray of the 4th Battalion, 60th Regiment, as a volunteer that was part of the force under Lieutenant Colonel Lewis V. Fuser that failed to seize Fort Morris in November 1778. The narrative of Rory's animated demonstration and the exchange between the two McIntosh cousins before Fort Morris is related by eighty-three year-old John Couper in his letter to Dr. James Troup, written from St. Simons Island on 16 April 1842. Johnson, *Blood on the Marsh*, 318–19; White, *Historical Collections of Georgia*, 472; Jones, *History of Georgia*, 309–10 n. 2.

[7] This is another reference to John Couper, a fellow Scotsman who had befriended Rory McIntosh since their first encounter in St. Augustine in 1777. Christopher Gadsden (1724–1805) was a successful businessman and became one of South Carolina's leading patriots. In 1767, he started the construction of a very long wharf on the Cooper River that was not completed until March 1774. While it is unclear whether he ever heard Rory McIntosh's threat, Gadsden called Scots "that detestable Stuart race! a race of pedants, pensioners and tyrants." E. Stanley Godbold, Jr. and Robert Woody, *Christopher Gadsden and the American Revolution* (Knoxville: University of Tennessee Press, 1983), 75.

[8] William McIntosh played a major role in negotiating the Treaty of Indian Springs in 1825, which surrendered Creek lands in Georgia and two-thirds of their lands in Alabama. Most of the fifty-two Creeks who made their marks on the treaty came from McIntosh's town of Coweta. For his duplicity in agreeing to this removal treaty, the Creek National Council declared McIntosh a traitor and passed a death sentence on him. On 30 April 1825, a large force under Menawa set McIntosh's plantation on fire and riddled his body with bullets when he stumbled out of the burning house. Kappler, *Indian Affairs: Laws and Treaties*, 2: 214–17; Green, *Politics of Indian Removal*, 88–93, 95–96.

[9] Roderick "Rory" McIntosh, his kinsmen, and other Highlanders participated in the Jacobite rebellion of 1745–1746 that attempted to restore the exiled House of Stuart to the British throne. The effort to make Charles Edward Stuart king of England ended in defeat at the bloody Battle of Culloden on 16 April 1746. Johnson, *Blood on the Marsh*, 97–156; John Leonard Roberts, *The Jacobite Wars: Scotland and the Military Campaigns of 1715 and 1745* (Edinburgh: Edinburgh University Press, 2002), 168–97.

ranks in the army. One of these was General Lachlan McIntosh, who came out to Georgia with Oglethorpe, when a little boy, and the other, Colonel John McIntosh, who also fought for liberty throughout the war.[10] In later times, Colonel James S. McIntosh, one of the same family, became a distinguished American officer, was in the wars of 1813 and 1814, and recently, in the Mexican War, was wounded at Resaca de la Palma, and afterwards, at Molino del Rey, and died in the city of Mexico.[11] The McIntosh family was composed of people of marked character, all whom were born to command. The blood always exhibited itself, even when mixed with that of the Indian. After the Revolution, the father of Governor Troup established himself in Georgia, became an American citizen, and was much esteemed and respected, to the day of his death. His body is interred at Belleville, McIntosh County, and that of his wife in the family vault of General Lachlan McIntosh, at Savannah.*

Napoleon Bonaparte had turned his eagle eye to the rich province of Louisiana, and it was ceded by Spain to France. He contemplated its occupation, with a large army, and probably entertained designs of conquest against portions of the United States; but, becoming deeply involved in wars with the whole of Europe, he reluctantly relinquished these intentions, and ceded Louisiana to the United States for sixty millions of francs. Governor Claiborne, with a large number of emigrants, who had already flocked to Natchez from all parts of the Union, for the purpose of occupying Louisiana, sailed down the Mississippi, with Wilkinson and his forces, and took formal possession of the city of New Orleans, in behalf of the United States. He had been appointed the governor of the Louisiana Territory. He left the people of the Mississippi Territory duly impressed with a deep sense of obligation for his valuable public services. Cato West, the territorial secretary, discharged the executive duties until his successor arrived.[12]

* MS notes in my possession.

[10] On 16 May 1777, Lachlan McIntosh (1727–1806) fought a duel with Button Gwinnett, signer of the Declaration of Independence, near Savannah. Although both men were wounded, Gwinnett died from his wound three days later, and McIntosh's reputation was so tarnished that he left Georgia and joined George Washington's Continental Army. With Washington's support, he was given command of forces in the Ohio Valley and in 1779 participated in the campaign to retake Savannah. He became a prisoner of war in the failed attempt to retake Charleston in 1780. Johnson, *Blood on the Marsh*, 254–55, 334–36, 503–04, 569–70; Harvey H. Jackson, *Lachlan McIntosh and the Politics of Revolutionary Georgia* (Athens: University of Georgia Press, 1979), 64–67, 85–93, 111–123.

[11] James Simmons McIntosh (1784–1847), son of Lieutenant Colonel John McIntosh, entered the U.S. Army in 1812, seeing action along the Canadian border and being wounded in the neck at Black Rock, New York, in 1814. He later served as commander of Fort Brooke at Tampa. In the Mexican War, he served as a brigade commander under Zachary Taylor and received three severe bayonet wounds at the Battle of Resaca de la Palma on 9 May 1846. He recovered from these wounds but was shot twice on 8 September 1847 at the Battle of Molino del Rey. Although he recovered from these wounds, he bled to death in Mexico City when his old neck wound from the War of 1812 reopened. James S. Robbins, *Last in Their Class: Custer, Pickett and the Goats of West Point* (New York: Encounter Books, 2006), 89–90, 91, 106–10; Zachary Taylor, *Letters of Zachary Taylor: From the Battle-Fields of the Mexican War* (Rochester, NY: n.p., 1908), 1–2, 2 n. 1.

[12] Initially, General James Wilkinson and Governor Claiborne were dispatched by Jefferson to New Orleans in December 1803 to serve as U.S. commissioners to accept the transfer of Louisiana from France. The formal transfer occurred on 20 December 1803 between the U.S. commissioners and Pierre Clément de Laussat for the French Republic. Technically, Claiborne was appointed administrator of the province of Louisiana and continued as governor of the

The distance of Natchez from the Tombigbee was so great that Congress authorized the president to appoint an additional superior court judge for the benefit of the people settled upon that river. The Honorable Harry Toulmin was selected. He was born at Taunton, in England, the 7th April 1766, and descended from a learned and respectable family. He became a pastor of the Unitarian Church, at Chowbert, in Lancashire, in 1788, where he occupied a prominent position, officiating before a congregation of a thousand hearers. Becoming an object of suspicion to the government, it determined to silence not only his efforts, but those of every other person who indulged in an independent expression of opinion. Frequently threatened with personal injury, and often surrounded by mobs, who extended their violence to his private residence, as well as his church, Mr. Toulmin determined to seek a land where all religious opinions are tolerated. Landing at Norfolk, Virginia, he proceeded to Winchester, where he had the misfortune to lose two of his children. The year following, he became the president of Transylvania University, of Lexington, the duties of which he discharged for four years. He was then secretary of state, of Kentucky, for the long period of eight years, and wrote most of the public documents of that day. Having pursued the study of law, and attained great proficiency in it, he compiled a code of laws for Kentucky, in the most satisfactory manner. A fine writer, an excellent scholar, an amiable man, and a delightful fireside companion, Judge Toulmin won upon the hearts of his friends and engaged the confidence of the public. He came to Alabama, by way of New Orleans, settled at a cantonment near Fort Stoddert, and afterwards removed to the court house, which he called Wakefield, in memory of Goldsmith's good vicar. His first court was held in the fall of 1804, he having been diligently engaged, for several months previous, in arranging the judicial department of Washington County.[13] There was no newspaper here, and Thomas Malone, the clerk, advertised libels against boats, for smuggling, in a New Orleans paper, published by Bradford and Anderson.[14]

Mississippi Territory until Congress created the Orleans Territory, and he was formally appointed governor on 1 October 1804. *ASP: PL*, 5: 289; Claiborne, *Mississippi*, 242, 244; Haynes, *Mississippi Territory*, 69.

[13] Harry Toulmin (1766–1823) was appointed by President Jefferson in 1804 to preside over the courts in Washington County. He published the *Statutes of Mississippi Territory* in 1807 and enforced the rule of law by issuing arrest warrants for Aaron Burr in 1807 and for several prominent filibustering residents of the Mississippi Territory in 1810. Although the Alabama legislature did not elect him as a judge in 1819, the legislature commissioned him in 1821 to write a digest of laws which was published in 1823—*A Digest of the Laws of the State of Alabama*. Paul M. Pruitt, *Taming Alabama: Lawyers and Reformers, 1804–1929* (Tuscaloosa: University of Alabama Press, 2010), 1–13.

[14] Thomas Malone, a surveyor and prominent land owner in the lower Tombigbee, served as the clerk of the superior court of Washington County, Mississippi Territory. He also worked as the assistant factor of the Choctaw Trading House at St. Stephens and later at Fort Confederation (1807–1817). Gaines, *Reminiscences*, 9–19, 48, 70, 164; Haynes, *Mississippi Territory*, 320.

Fort Stoddert was now a prominent post. Captain Schaumburg retired from the command, which was assumed by Captain Schuyler, of New York, who had the command of eighty men. Lieutenant Reuben Chamberlain, now of Mobile, arrived at this station in June, as paymaster. Edmund Pendleton Gaines was then a lieutenant, under Captain Schuyler.[15] Here the Court of Admiralty was held, for it was a port of entry.*

Robert Williams, of North Carolina, appointed to succeed Governor Claiborne, arrived at the town of Washington, Mississippi, and partook of a public dinner, at which the Honorable Thomas Rodney presided.[16] His staff consisted of William Scott, William B. Shields, William Wooldridge and John C. Carmichael, the first with the rank of colonel, and the others with that of major.[17]

Congress, having constituted the country upon the Tombigbee a revenue district, known as the "District of Mobile," the most vigilant and annoying system of searches commenced. The people, with just cause, considered it an unnecessary restriction upon a weak and defenseless territory. Not only did Spain exact heavy duties, at the port of Mobile, upon American merchandise, destined for the American settlements above, but the federal government, which ought rather to have fostered and protected her wilderness-children, also exacted duties from them, at Fort Stoddert. These arbitrary revenue laws of Spain and the United States were applied, with equal severity, also, to whatever the persecuted settlers of Alabama chose to *export*—so that a Tombigbee planter, sending his produce to New Orleans, by way of Mobile, and exchanging it there for goods and supplies, paid, by the time he

* I have consulted some biographical notices of the life and character of Judge Toulmin. Conversations with Major Reuben Chamberlain, of Mobile, and Thomas Malone.

[15] As noted earlier, Captain Bartholomew Schaumburg established Fort Stoddert in 1799 and was succeeded by Captain Philip Peter Schuyler in 1804. After a three-year residence, Shuyler, a member of the prominent New York family, asked for a transfer, citing the "unhealthfulness" of the fort. Lieutenant Edmund Pendleton Gaines replaced Shuyler in 1807. Later, in 1813, Captain Reuben Chamberlain helped Colonel John Bowyer construct Fort Bowyer at Mobile Point. Holmes, "Fort Stoddard in 1799," 231–52; Thomas McAdory Owen, "Burr's Conspiracy," in *Transactions of the Alabama Historical Society*, 1898–99, ed. Thomas McAdory Owen, vol. 3 (Tuscaloosa: The Society, 1899), 169–70, 169 n. 7.

[16] Williams and Rodney had worked together as land commissioners for the area west of the Pearl River. While Cato West, interim governor of the territory, expected to succeed Claiborne as governor, Jefferson appointed Ephraim Kirby ,who died unexpectedly in 1804. Jefferson then offered the position to Robert Williams, who quickly accepted the office. Haynes, *Mississippi Territory*, 60, 76–82, 96–99.

[17] Colonel William Scott died and was replaced by Major Isaac Guion in August 1805. Shields, a successful Delaware attorney, became a critic of Governor Williams and was elected to the territorial council from Adams County. William H. Wooldridge was promoted to lieutenant colonel in 1805 and assigned to the 5th Regiment in 1810. Prior to his militia appointment on Williams's staff, John F. Carmichael, an ex-army surgeon, had served as customs collector under Governor Sargent. Ibid., 38, 77, 158, 169, 182, 184, 188; Rowland, *Encyclopedia of Mississippi History*, 2: 243; Dunbar Rowland, *Seventh Annual Report of the Director of the Department of Archives and History of the State of Mississippi; From October 1, 1907, to October 1, 1908* (Nashville: Brandon Printing Company, 1909), 26.

reached home, an *ad valorem* duty of twenty-five per cent. Vessels were required to pass under the guns of Fort Charlotte, and to submit to insult and search. The Spaniards valued the goods themselves, and imposed a duty of twelve and a half per cent. The federal government remonstrated with Spain, in an extensive correspondence, but, we think, with a very ill grace, while restrictions were imposed by herself, upon her own people, at the port of Fort Stoddert.[18]

When the line of demarcation was established by Ellicott and the Spanish commissioners, those inhabitants—chiefly Spaniards, old British subjects and Tories—living in the Natchez District, retired below the line, within Spanish jurisdiction, as the reader has already seen. Notwithstanding that General Wilkinson then entered into a convention with the governor of Louisiana, for the mutual surrender of deserters, and both sides adopted wise measures to prevent border disturbances, yet much prejudice and ill-feeling continued to exist between the American settlers and Spaniards. No serious outbreaks, however, occurred until after Louisiana was surrendered to the United States. A controversy then arose, in relation to a strip of country lying between the line of 31° on the north, the Bayou Iberville on the south, the Mississippi on the west, and Pearl River on the east. This had been organized, by the Spaniards, into a district, called the "Government of Baton Rouge," and placed under the control of Don Carlos de Grand-Pré. It comprised the posts of Baton Rouge, Manchac, Thompson's Creek, and Bayou Sara. A controversy also arose, in relation to the country bounded by the Perdido on the east, Pearl River on the west, the line of 31° on the north, and the Gulf of Mexico on the south, which was the Spanish "Mobile District."[19]

The United States contended that these two districts should have been surrendered at the same

[18] While Governor Claiborne warned Governor Vicente Folch about interfering with American shipping, Judge Harry Toulmin wrote letters to Secretary of State James Madison complaining about the Spaniards levying duties on all American vessels coming from and going to Fort Stoddert. The resentment expressed by the residents of Washington County to the tariffs levied by the United States at Fort Stoddert and the Spaniards at Mobile did not deter Jefferson's administration. In his letter to Matthew Maury of 9 November 1805, Jefferson made it clear that he intended to appoint a customs collector at Fort Stoddert and a receiver of public monies at Fort Stephens. William C. Davis, *The Rogue Republic: How Would-Be Patriots Waged the Shortest Revolution in American History* (Boston: Houghton Mifflin Harcourt, 2011), 56–57; Thomas Jefferson to Matthew Maury, Washington, 9 November 1805, http://founders.archives.gov/documents/Jefferson.

[19] From the retrocession of Louisiana by Spain to France in the secret Treaty of San Ildefonso and then the purchase treaty negotiated by Jefferson's administration, Grand-Pré, Spain's administrator and commander of the Baton Rouge District, had no intention of deferring to the Americans north of the international boundary established by the 31st degree of north latitude. The proclamation to the citizens of Louisiana issued by Manuel de Salcedo, the last Spanish governor of Louisiana—who was unaware of the purchase treaty—on 18 May 1803 makes clear the boundary of the territory that remained under Spain after the delivery of Louisiana and the island of New Orleans: ". . . Consequently, the settlements from the Rivers Manchac or Iberville to the line which separate the American territory from the dominions of the king shall remain under the power of Spain and be annexed to West Florida." Robert D. Bush, *The Louisiana Purchase: A Global Context* (New York: Routledge, 2014), 139–41.

time that the island of New Orleans and the country west of the Mississippi were given up; that Bonaparte, in his treaty with Spain, acquired the whole of the Louisiana which belonged to France before 1762; that, when subsequently he ceded Louisiana to the United States, he ceded all which he had acquired from Spain, and, of course, the Baton Rouge and Mobile districts were included, for they once belonged to French Louisiana. Spain met these arguments by assuming the positions, that, just before the close of the American Revolution, she became herself engaged in a war with England; that she took from Great Britain, by conquest, the Baton Rouge district, and that of Mobile, which was then a part of West Florida; that, in 1783, Great Britain confirmed these to her by treaty; that, since then, she (Spain) had always considered these districts as a part of Spanish West Florida; that Bonaparte only ceded to the United States Louisiana, not embracing, of course, the Baton Rouge and Mobile districts.[20]

The people of the Mississippi Territory, believing that the American government was right in this controversy, were impatient to occupy the rich lands in the Baton Rouge district, and were loud and open in their denunciations of the Spaniards. Border troubles commenced. Lieutenant John Glascock, a subject of Spain, placed himself at the head of twelve Spanish light-horse, crossed over the line, two miles, into the Mississippi Territory, seized William Flanagan and his wife, and forcibly carried them fifteen miles, into Spanish territory. Here, finding that they were not the persons whom the authorities wanted, he turned them loose, to make their way back on foot, having retained their horse.[21] This first open violation of American rights was followed by one more serious. Many citizens of the Union had settled already in the Baton Rouge district, while others lived near the line, ready to enter it when a suitable opportunity offered. Among the most conspicuous of the latter class were Nathan, Reuben and Samuel Kemper, sons of a Baptist preacher, who emigrated from Loudon, Virginia, to Ohio.[22] They came to the Mississippi Territory in 1803, and established themselves at and near Pinckneyville, within a few miles of the Spanish line. Men of strong frontier sense, with a pleasing appearance and fine address, the Kempers were well suited to the times, and were dreaded by the Spaniards. They had acquired lands in the Baton Rouge district, under Spanish grants, which they knew would enrich them, could the country once be occupied by Americans.[23] Beginning to exert their influence, with an end to the expulsion of the Spaniards, Governor Grand-Pré determined to seize and imprison them. He dispatched a company of kidnappers to the house of Nathan Kemper. They arrived there at 12 o'clock at night. They were Lewis Ritchie, Minor Butler, Abraham Horton, James

[20] Despite President Jefferson's claims, the American diplomats—Robert Livingston and James Monroe—who negotiated the Louisiana Purchase treaty of 30 April 1803 with Napoleonic France did not add any specific language regarding the Province of West Florida, which had remained under Spanish control. While there are no specific boundaries outlined in the treaty articles, Article 1 specifically refers to the transfer of the "Colony or Province of Louisiana" from Spain to France, and Article 2 refers to the cession of the "adjacent islands belonging to Louisiana" and all public property to the United States. "Treaty between the United States of America and the French Republic" in *Treaties and Other International Acts of the United States of America*, ed. Hunter Miller, 8 vols. (Washington: GPO, 1931), 2: 498–505.

[21] The Spanish authorities had tried to extradite William Flanagan as the prime suspect in the premeditated murder of Joseph Sharp. When Governor Robert Williams refused, the small light horse force crossed into the Mississippi Territory and forcibly took Flanagan into Louisiana. He was eventually freed but was forced to surrender his horse and saddle. Haynes, *Mississippi Territory*, 113–14; *American State Papers: Foreign Affairs*, 2: 686, 688 [Hereafter cited *ASP: FA*].

[22] The Kempers were Presbyterians from Fauquier County, Virginia. Peter Kemper and his five sons—Reuben, Presley, Samuel, Nathan, and Stephen—followed his brother James Kemper, a Presbyterian minister, to Cincinnati and helped fund the building of his church. Pickett may have assumed the Kempers to have been Baptists because of Reuben Kemper's partnership with John Smith, the first Baptist preacher in Ohio. Smith, a native of Virginia, developed an extensive trade in the Mississippi Valley and entered into a three-year partnership with Reuben Kemper to sell his stock in Spanish Louisiana and West Florida. Davis, *Rogue Republic*, 1–10, 12–13.

[23] According to Marques de Casa Calvo, a representative of the king of Spain in New Orleans, the Kempers had already taken unlawful actions and violated the international boundary between the Mississippi Territory and West Florida. While Rueben was writing threatening letters, Nathan, Samuel, and their armed followers rode about the countryside threatening Spanish subjects, whipping others, and killing a constable on 3 August 1804. Four days later, they seized Vincente Pintardo, a militia captain, John O'Connor, a magistrate, and Champness Terry, a planter, and held them as prisoners. They raised a blue and white striped flag and attempted to capture Grand-Pré, creating disorder and dissension around Baton Rouge. Marqués de Casa Calvo to Governor Claiborne, New Orleans, 11 August 1804, in Claiborne, *Mississippi*, 262; Davis, *Rogue Republic*, 21–68.

Horton, Dr. Bonner, Henry Flowers Jr., and Bryan McDermott, who were in disguise, and were citizens of the Mississippi Territory, but accomplices in the schemes of Grand-Pré. Seven Negroes were also in company with them. The party were armed with guns and clubs, and provided with ropes. They forced the door, entered the room in which Reuben Kemper was sleeping, dragged him from his bed, beat him with clubs, and then tied him. Some of them, at the same time, dragged Nathan Kemper from the bed, in which he was sleeping with his wife, who received some blows from their clubs in the scuffle, one of the kidnappers crying out, "If she utters another word, I will kill her!"[24]

Nathan was also severely beaten and well secured with cords. The brothers begged to know what they had done. A voice answered, "You have ruined the Spanish country!" The party gagged them by placing large sassafras roots in their mouths. Then, tying a line around their necks, they were made to run before the horses of the kidnappers, and were conducted to the Spanish line. At the same time, a branch of this party had entered the tavern of Samuel Kemper, at Pinckneyville, the proprietor of which they seized, beat with clubs, gagged and pinioned. In running along, by the side of a horseman, this prisoner, unable to keep up, fell to the earth, and was cruelly dragged a hundred yards by a rope around his neck. He, too, was conducted to the Spanish line, where all three of the unhappy brothers were delivered to Captain Solomon Alston, who conveyed them, with a guard, to the Tunica Landing, where they were placed in a boat, also guarded, which was ordered to transport them to Baton Rouge. In the meantime, a Dr. Towles, who had been visiting a patient, hearing of the outrage early in the morning, galloped his horse to

Point Coupée, informed Lieutenant Wilson, the commandant at that place, who, with a file of soldiers, rescued the Kempers and captured the Spanish guard.[25] They were all sent to the town of Washington, and the affair was legally investigated by Judge Rodney, and the

[24] Contrary to Pickett's account, Judge Thomas Rodney declared that the party that seized the Kempers were residents of the Mississippi Territory and the others who attempted to take them to Baton Rouge—before being intercepted by U.S. troops—were residents in Spanish West Florida. Rodney released the Spanish residents and never mentions collusion or the involvement of Grand-Pré. Rodney directed Justice Joshua Baker to require the Kempers to post bail and to keep the peace "towards the subjects of the King of Spain." Instead of some convoluted plot, this incident appears to have been a personal conflict or feud between the Kempers and their neighbors on either side of the 31st parallel. *ASP: FA*, 2: 689; Davis, *Rogue Republic*, 78–79.

[25] Lieutenant William Wilson, U.S. commander at Point Coupée, had been alerted by shouts from the Kempers in a pirogue with their captors. He and his small troop used a boat to intercept the party of "Spanish subjects," taking all as his prisoners. *ASP: FA*, 2: 686; Davis, *Rogue Republic*, 76.

parties were discharged. It, however, created much excitement, and Governor Williams formed a strong patrol, composed of two companies, at the head of which was Colonel John Ellis.[26] After some sharp correspondence between the governor and Colonel Grand-Pré, the people became quiet, and border troubles ceased for a while.[27] However, this shameful treatment of American citizens produced some excitement in Washington City, and John Randolph, of the committee of foreign relations, reported a bill for the raising an army to repel and punish Spanish aggressors. But the friends of Jefferson's administration refused to adopt it.*

Nothing but an Indian trail led from the Oconee to the Alabama River at Lake Tensaw. The houses of accommodation were few, kept by Indians and half-breeds, and were of the most indifferent kind. None of the rivers were provided with ferryboats, nor were the creeks bridged. The federal government, desiring to open a better avenue to the new country, obtained, from a delegation of thirty Creek chiefs and warriors, then at Washington City, the right of using a horse-path through their country, along which the chiefs agreed to establish ferries and bridges, and to open good houses of accommodation.[28] The Cherokees, at Tellico Blockhouse, granted the right for a mail route, from Knoxville to New Orleans, by way of the Tombigbee.[29] The United States also acquired more territory from the Chickasaws, who ceded about three hundred and fifty thousand acres, lying in the bend of the Tennessee, a very small portion of which, in the shape of a triangle, fell into Alabama and was afterwards formed into the county of Madison.[30] At Mount Dexter, the Choctaws ceded to the government five millions of acres, commencing at the Cut-Off, at a point half way between the Alabama and Tombigbee, running north to the Choctaw Corner, west to Fulluctabuna Old Fields, thence across the Tombigbee to the Mississippi

* *State Papers and Publick Documents*, Boston edition, 5: 103–24. Also historical MS notes in the possession of E. T. Wood, of Mobile.

[26] In his letter of 1 October 1805, Governor Robert Williams ordered Colonel John Ellis of the 5th Regiment, Mississippi Militia, to patrol the border with Spanish West Florida and "to prevent or check irregularities of every kind . . . stopping and securing any armed parties." *ASP: FA*, 2: 687; Claiborne, *Mississippi*, 262.

[27] Actually, the correspondence between Williams and Grand-Pré printed in *American State Papers: Foreign Affairs* is very diplomatic and professional in tone, not accusatory or threatening. *ASP: FA*, 2: 687–88.

[28] Under the leadership of William McIntosh, five other Creek headmen signed the 1805 Treaty of Washington, ceding a tract of land between the Oconee and Ocmulgee rivers and giving the U.S. government "a right to a horse path, through the Creek country," which led to the construction of the Federal Road from Milledgeville, Georgia, on the Oconee, to Fort Stoddert (Stoddart), on the Mobile River. Kappler, *Indian Affairs: Laws and Treaties*, 2: 85–86; Andrew K. Frank, *Creeks and Southerners: Biculturalism on the Early American Frontier* (Lincoln: University of Nebraska Press, 2005), 106. See Raven M. Christopher and Gregory A. Waselkov, *Archaeological Survey of the Old Federal Road in Alabama* (Montgomery: Alabama Department of Transportation, 2012).

[29] On 25 October 1805 at Tellico, thirty-three "chiefs and head men" of the Cherokee Nation ceded lands between the Duck River and the Tennessee, over five million acres of their hunting grounds, and agreed to the opening of two roads: "one to proceed from some convenient place near the head of Stone's river, and fall into the Georgia road. . . . The other to proceed from the neighborhood of Franklin . . . crossing the Tennessee at or near Muscle Shoals, to pursue the nearest and best way to the settlements on the Tombigbee." The government agreed to pay \$3,000 in merchandise, an additional \$11,000 within 90 days of ratification, and a \$3,000 annuity. Kappler, *Indian Affairs: Laws and Treaties*, 2: 82–83; William G. McLoughlin, *Cherokee Renascence in the New Republic* (Princeton: Princeton University Press, 1986), 103–05.

[30] On behalf of the U.S. government, James Robertson and Silas Dinsmoor convinced ten

"Mingo chiefs and warriors of the Chickasaw Nation" to surrender their claims to land north of the Tennessee River in modern North Alabama. In exchange, the Nation received $20,000 "for the payment of their debts due to merchants and traders," plus bribes of $1,000 each to George Colbert and Okoye (Tisshumastubbee) "for services rendered their nation, and "an annuity of one hundred dollars" to Chinnubbee Mingo, "king of the nation . . . during his natural life." Kappler, *Indian Affairs: Laws and Treaties*, 2: 79–80; Atkinson, *Splendid Land, Splendid People*, 195–97.

[31] Over a period of ten days beginning on 6 November 1805, James Robertson and Silas Dinsmoor negotiated and argued with Choctaw leaders before convincing the three district chiefs—Puckshunubbee, Hoomastubbee and Pushmataha—and twenty other "Chiefs and warriors" to place their marks on the Treaty of Mount Dexter on the 16th. In return for surrendering 4,142,720 acres, the government representatives agreed to pay the Choctaws $48,000–$50,500, which was owed to "merchants and traders," $2,500 to John Pitchlynn "for certain losses . . . and as a grateful testimonial of the nation's esteem," and an annuity of $3,000 in goods. Under Article 3, Puckshunubbee, Hoomastubbee, and Pushmataha were to receive $500 each and an annuity of $150 "during their continuance in office." Kappler, *Indian Affairs: Laws and Treaties*, 2: 87–88; Arthur H. DeRosier, Jr., *The Removal of the Choctaw Indians* (Knoxville: University of Tennessee Press, 1970), 31–32.

[32] Even before the Chickasaw and Cherokee agreed to treaties in 1805, surrendering their land claims in the Tennessee River valley of modern North Alabama, there had been many Euro-Americans who had learned of the Big Spring in the Great Bend of the Tennessee. However, John Hunt is generally credited with stumbling onto a sixty-foot high bluff in the fall of 1804 that overlooked a natural spring and three acres of water. He returned to Tennessee for his family and cattle, and they were soon joined by the Criner brothers, Joseph and Isaac, and others at Hunt's Spring. Daniel S. Dupre, *Transforming the Cotton Frontier: Madison County, Alabama, 1800–1840* (Baton Rouge: Louisiana State University Press, 1997), 18–20.

[33] Under the leadership of Governor William C. C. Claiborne, the Mississippi territorial legislature established Jefferson College in 1802. Joseph Caldwell served as its head. Claiborne, *Mississippi*, 228, 258–59.

settlements, thence south to Ellicott's line,[31] and east along that line back to the Cut-Off.*

Thus the whole southern portion of the present state of Mississippi was thrown open to the Americans. The new purchase was soon formed into three counties—Marion, Wayne and Greene. A population from Georgia and Tennessee poured into the magnificent forest north of the Tennessee, about "Hunt's Spring," which had been obtained from the Chickasaws, as just mentioned.[32] The population of the Mississippi Territory had much increased, Natchez had become a large town, where boats going down and up the great river landed and traded, while the crews engaged in fights, drunkenness, gambling, and all kinds of debaucheries. It was the greatest thoroughfare in the whole forest world, and was decidedly a most abandoned place.

The subject of education was not neglected, and Jefferson College had been established at Ellicott Springs, in the vicinity of the town of Washington.[33] Many improvements, in the way of houses, farms and new towns, gave the territory an air of civilization.

* *American State Papers: Indian Affairs* and *American State Papers: Public Lands.*

Chapter XXIX

THE ARREST OF AARON BURR, IN ALABAMA

Aaron Burr—a descendant of learned ancestry, a native of New Jersey, a graduate of Princeton, a Whig colonel of the Revolution, a lawyer of ability, a leading member of the New York legislature, a state's attorney general, a senator of the United States, a vice president of the Union—at length found himself nominated, by the Republican Party of New York, as a candidate for the office of governor of that state. Among his most formidable enemies was Alexander Hamilton, whom he, not long after, killed in a duel.[1] The tide of public opinion set strongly against him in consequence of this unfortunate affair, and he was swept into exile upon the seacoast of Carolina. He, however, returned to Washington, and presided over the Senate, until the expiration of his term of office, as vice president.[2]

A warrant, for the killing of Hamilton, in the hands of the officers of justice, prevented Burr from returning to New York.[3] He had, likewise, become unpopular with the friends of Jefferson, with whom he had been a close competitor for the presidency.[4] Of course, he had no friends among the prominent Federalists, against whom he had always acted. These things combined to make him long for brighter prospects in the Southwest. In 1805, he traveled through Kentucky and Tennessee, enjoying the society of Clay[5] and Jackson, besides that of many other distinguished persons.[6] From January until August of the following year, his hours were passed in Washington and Philadelphia, consumed in revolving schemes, the consummation of which, he believed, would elevate him above his fallen condition.[7]

Burr had purchased a portion of the lands granted by the king of Spain to Baron Bastrop, which lay between the Sabine and Natchitoches. His designs appear to have been the colonization of these lands, the expulsion of the Spaniards, the conquest of Texas, and, ultimately, of Mexico. To effect these things, it was necessary to raise a large armed force in the West. He believed, also, that a war would soon ensue between the United States and ,Spain, and

[1] The Burr-Hamilton duel was the result of a long and bitter political rivalry going back to 1791, when Burr defeated Hamilton's father-in-law Richard Shuyler for a U.S. Senate seat, and exacerbated by Hamilton's role in Jefferson's election on the 36th ballot as president over Burr and Hamilton's journalistic attacks on Burr in the 1804 New York gubernatorial race, which Burr lost. The duel on the shore of Weehawken, New Jersey, ended in Hamilton's death and destroyed Burr's political career and reputation. Joseph J. Ellis, *Founding Brothers: The Revolutionary Generation* (New York: Alfred A. Knopf, 2000), 20–47; Joanne B. Freeman, "Dueling as Politics: Reinterpreting the Burr-Hamilton Duel," *William and Mary Quarterly*, 53 (1996): 290–95.

[2] Actually, Burr went to St. Simon's Island in August 1804, where he stayed at Pierce Butler's

plantation, explored Florida, and reached Savannah on 1 October 1804. In Savannah, he was warmly received and traveled to South Carolina, where he was greeted by Theodosia and his grandson. Burr resumed his duties in the U.S. Senate on 5 November 1804. Thomas Fleming, *The Duel: Alexander Hamilton, Aaron Burr, and the Future of America* (New York: Perseus Books, 1999), 355–58.

[3] Although Burr was charged with murder in New York and New Jersey, he never faced the charges in a trial. In fact, the New Jersey Supreme Court dismissed the grand jury indictment on a motion by his lawyer, Colonel Aaron Ogden. Ibid., 355, 358–59, 370–71.

[4] Ironically, Thomas Jefferson appointed three people with direct connections to Burr to positions in the newly purchased Louisiana country. In 1805 he appointed Dr. Joseph Bowne—Burr's late wife's brother-in-law—secretary of the Louisiana Territory and Burr's close filibustering associate General James Wilkinson as governor of the Louisiana Territory. Burr's stepson Bartow Prevost was appointed judge of the superior court of the Orleans Territory. Ibid., 359.

[5] Henry Clay and his partner John Allen successfully defended Burr in November 1806 against charges brought by Joseph Hamilton Daveiss, U.S. District Attorney for Kentucky, who accused Burr of planning an expedition into Spanish territory west of the Mississippi. Clay encountered Burr after his trial for treason and refused to shake his hand. Robert Vincent Remini, *Henry Clay: A Statesman for the Union* (New York: W. W. Norton, 1991), 42–53; Clement Eaton, *Henry Clay and the Art of American Politics* (Boston: Little, Brown and Company, 1957), 15.

[6] Burr visited with Andrew and Rachel Jackson at Nashville in 1805. He apparently talked about leading a force into Florida in case of war with Spain, and Jackson agreed to build five boats and provide supplies for them. Suspecting something more sinister, Jackson later wrote Jefferson and Governor Claiborne: "I fear there is something rotten in the State of Denmark." Jon Meacham, *American Lion: Andrew Jackson in the White House* (New York: Random House, 2008), 27.

[7] Burr departed Nashville on 3 June 1805, met with General Wilkinson at Fort Massac for several days, and floated down the Mississippi to New Orleans on a barge with an escort provided by Wilkinson. In New Orleans, Burr conferred with several prominent members of the Mexico Association and discussed the possibility of invading Mexico and perhaps his rumored plan to "liberate" New Orleans. He journeyed back up the Mississippi to Natchez, traveled the Natchez Trace to Nashville for a second visit with Jackson, and returned east through the Ohio Valley, spending November and December 1805 in Philadelphia and Washington. Robert V. Remini, *Andrew Jackson and the Course of American Empire, 1767–1821* (New York: Harper & Row, 1977), 144–48; Matthew L. Davis, *Memoirs of Aaron Burr. With Miscellaneous Selections from His Correspondence*, 2 vols. (New York: Harper & Brothers, 1836–1837), 2: 371–75.

[8] Felipe Enrique Neri, Baron de Bastrop, received the rights to a twelve-square-league section of land on the Ouachita River from Barón de Carondelet in 1795–1796 with the requirement that he attract 500 families as settlers. Colonel Charles Lynch of Kentucky acquired the mortgage to about six tenths for $100,000. Lynch sold Burr a half interest for $50,000, and it appears that this enterprise became part of Burr's scheme to create a separate western empire. Narrett, *Adventurism and Empire*, 160–61; Davis, *Memoirs of Aaron Burr*, 2: 379–81.

[9] Burr had recruited Harman Blennerhassett, who lived on Blennerhassett Island in the Ohio River, as a fellow conspirator, and his island became the staging base for the assault on Louisiana or Mexico in 1806. On 9 December 1806, Ohio Governor Edward Tiffin sent his militia to destroy Burr's boats at the Marietta boatyard, and two days later they raided Blennerhassett's Island, seized supplies, and ransacked Blennerhassett's mansion. Francis D. Cogliano, "Failed Filibusters: The Kemper Rebellion, the Burr Conspiracy and Early American Expansion" (2013), http://www.shca.ed.ac.uk/staff/supporting_files/fcogliano/failed-filibusters.pdf, 19, 32.

[10] While several people suspected that Wilkinson was involved in Burr's western schemes, Andrew Jackson was convinced of Wilkinson's involvement in treason and tried to convince Jefferson, who defended Wilkinson. Remini, *Andrew Jackson and the Course of American Empire*, 150–51, 156–58.

he expected, in that event, to cooperate with General Wilkinson, who had charge of the western and southern army.[8] Upon his deathbed, Burr denied that he had any intention of dismembering the Union, and, as he had then arrived at the age of eighty, and outlived both his descendants and his reputation, it would seem that there was no inducement to conceal any act of his life.

Burr again made his appearance in the western country, where his plausibility captivated the people, who made active preparations to carry out his designs. Boats were constructed and stored with provisions and concealed arms.[9] General Wilkinson was suspected of having countenanced his enterprise.[10]

Rumors had reached President Jefferson that Burr was raising troops for the purpose of dismembering the Union. He caused him to be arrested at Lexington, where Clay appeared in his defense. Burr was discharged, for the want of sufficient evidence to convict him.[11] Then, descending the Cumberland River, and the Mississippi, with thirteen boats and sixty men, he was met, some miles above Natchez, by Colonel F. L. Claiborne, whom the governor of the Mississippi Territory, influenced by the proclamations of Jefferson, had dispatched, at the head of a detachment of two hundred and seventy-five men, for the purpose of arresting him.[12] Burr surrendered his boats and men, and proceeded, with Claiborne, to the town of Washington, once more a prisoner of the United States.[13] The people, generally, sympathized with him, and thought him much wronged. He was honored with balls and parties in Adams County. He found no difficulty in giving bonds, in the sum of ten thousand dollars, for his appearance at court. When it convened, he appeared, with his counsel, and demanded a release from his bonds, as the attorney general stated that he was satisfied his offenses did not

[11] Without mentioning Burr, Jefferson issued a proclamation on 27 November 1806 warning "that sundry persons . . . are conspiring & confederating together" and preparing a military expedition against Spanish territory. Thomas Jefferson, "Proclamation on Spanish Dominion Expeditions," 27 November 1806, in Paul Leicester Ford, ed., *The Works of Thomas Jefferson*, 12 Vols. (New York: G. P. Putnam's Sons, 1904–1905), 10: 301–02.

[12] Burr's flotilla of ten vessels and some 60 to 100 men reached Bruin's Landing on 10 January 1807. His host, Judge Peter Bruin, showed him a copy of the *Mississippi Messenger* that contained Jefferson's proclamation and an edited version of the 29 July 1806 cipher letter that Burr had sent to General Wilkinson. Jefferson had alerted all the western military posts to intercept any expedition against Spanish territory. On 16 January, Colonel Thomas Fitzpatrick and sixty dragoons visited Burr at his camp on the Louisiana side of the Mississippi, where he offered to surrender to him and face a trial. Cogliano, "Failed Filibusters," 24–25, 28–29, 32–33; Haynes, *Mississippi Territory*, 152–58.

[13] Acting Governor Cowles Mead sent his aides, George Poindexter and William Shields, to meet with Burr on 16 January 1807, and he agreed to accompany them to Calvit's to meet with territorial officials and to permit his boats to be searched. On 23 November 1806, Colonel Ferdinand Claiborne had been dispatched to New Orleans by Mead because he thought "that General Wilkinson is the soul of the conspiracy." Haynes, *Mississippi Territory*, 155.

come within the jurisdiction of Mississippi, and insisted on his being sent to a competent tribunal. The motion of the attorney general was sustained, and Burr's application for a discharge was overruled by the judges.[14] The next morning the prisoner did not make his appearance in the court room, and it was soon ascertained that he had fled. A troop of cavalry was dispatched in pursuit of him, while the governor distributed proclamations over the country, which promised a reward of two thousand dollars for his apprehension. His destination was unknown.[15]

During a cold night in February, two young men—Nicholas Perkins, a lawyer, and Thomas Malone, clerk of the court—were sitting in their cabin, in the village of Wakefield, Washington County, Alabama. Before them was a backgammon board, and they were absorbed in the playing of that game. The hour was ten o'clock.[16] The distant tramp of horses arrested their attention. Two travelers presently rode up to the door, one of whom inquired for the tavern. It was pointed out to him, and then he asked the road to Colonel Hinson's. Perkins informed him that the route lay over difficult paths, the place was seven miles distant, and a dangerous creek intervened. The fire, being replenished with pine, now threw a light in the face of the traveler who propounded these questions. His countenance appeared to Perkins exceedingly interesting. His eyes sparkled like diamonds, while he sat upon his splendid horse, caparisoned with a fine saddle and new holsters. His dress was that of a plain farmer, but beneath his coarse pantaloons protruded a pair of exquisitely shaped boots.[17] His striking features, with the strange mixture of his apparel, aroused the suspicions of Perkins, and, no sooner had the two travelers ridden from the door, than he said to Malone, with the most earnest gesticulation, "That is Aaron Burr. I have read a description of him in the proclamation. I cannot be mistaken. Let us follow him to Hinson's, and take measures for his arrest." Malone declined to accompany him, remonstrating, at the same time, upon the folly of pursuing a traveler, at such a late hour of the night and upon the basis of the merest conjecture. Perkins now rushed to the cabin of Theodore Brightwell, the sheriff, and awoke him. Presently these men were seen riding off with a rapid pace. The night was bitter cold, and the pine trees of the forest sadly moaned.[18]

The travelers strangely made their way to the residence of Hinson, where they arrived about half past eleven o'clock. The moon had just risen, and enabled the lady of the house, whose husband was absent, to see that they were travelers, by their saddle-bags and tin cups, as she timidly peeped through a small window. She made no answer to their "halloo," but quietly closed the window. The strangers alighted and went into the kitchen, where

[14] On 2 February 1807, Burr and his attorneys, Lyman Harding and William B. Shields, appeared before judges Thomas Rodney and Peter Bruin of the Supreme Court of the Mississippi Territory, but without Attorney General George Poindexter, who was absent. Over the next two days, the judges and the attorney general generally agreed to disagree on procedures and jurisdiction. Poindexter called for the dismissal of the grand jury because he had nothing to lay before them, and the grand jury declared Burr not guilty "of any crime or misdemeanor against the laws of the United States or of this Territory." Rodney and Bruin were divided over rescinding Burr's bond and dismissing Burr. Cogliano, "Failed Filibusters," 33; Haynes, *Mississippi Territory*, 161–63.

[15] Following his court appearance on 4 February 1807, Burr went into hiding at the home of Dr. John Cummins, Judge Bruin's son-in-law, at Bayou Pierre. After Burr left Washington, Governor Robert Williams declared Burr to be a fugitive and offered "$2,000 for his delivery here to me." On 7 February, the Supreme Court reconvened, but when Burr failed to appear, Poindexter "ordered the Sheriff to call out Aaron Burr on his recognizance." With few options left, Burr met with his supporters, gave them permission to sell the boats and provisions, and bid them farewell sometime between the 10th and 12th of February. Haynes, *Mississippi Territory*, 163–65; Lemuel Henry to Nicholas Perkins, Washington M.T., 9 February 1807, in Lemuel Henry and others, "The Capture of Aaron Burr," *American Historical Magazine* 1 (April 1896): 140–41.

[16] When Nicholas Perkins (1779–1848) provided Attorney General Caesar A. Rodney with a detailed report on the capture of Aaron Burr, he stated: "I believe it was the 18th day of February last, about 12 o'clock in the evening or after, I was at the Court House for the County and District of Washington in the Mississippi Territory . . . when I heard the sound of horses' feet as if coming on the road that passed by the house in which we were." Trained as a lawyer, the twenty-eight year old Tennessean had been appointed a register of lands by Jefferson and served as attorney general for the East District in 1807–1809. Rowland, *Official and Statistical Register*, 2: 4; Henry, "Capture of Aaron Burr," 141–46.

[17] When Burr left Adams County, Mississippi Territory, and headed east, he rode on a horse provided by Colonel Benijah Osmun, a militia commander and an old friend from the Revolutionary War. His traveling companion was Major Robert Ashley, who had previous connections to Elijah Clarke, George Rogers Clark, and Philip Nolan, a protégé of General James Wilkinson. Haynes, *Mississippi Territory*, 61, 158, 165–66; Claiborne, *Mississippi*, 152 n. -153 n.; Ed Bradley, *"We Never Retreat": Filibustering Expeditions into Spanish Texas, 1812–1822* (College Station: Texas A & M University Press, 2015), 1–26.

[18] Contrary to Pickett's narrative, Perkins, in his lengthy letter to Attorney General Caesar A. Rodney, stated that he wondered what two strangers were doing out late at night looking for directions to "Maj. Hinson's" and "that they must either have some bad design upon Hinson or his property, or that it was Col. Burr making his escape through the country." Perkins did not have the authority to arrest Burr, and Sheriff Theodore Brightwell never attempted to arrest Burr. Henry, "Capture of Aaron Burr," 142–44.

a cheerful fire was yet burning. Perkins and the sheriff soon came in sight of the house. The former, recollecting that he had already been seen at Wakefield, thought it politic to remain in the woods, until Brightwell could go in the house, make the necessary discoveries, and return to him. Mrs. Hinson was a relative of the sheriff, and, recognizing his voice, felt relieved, by his appearance, from the fears she had felt in consequence of the strangers having come at such a late hour of the night. Brightwell repaired to the kitchen, and discovered one of these men sitting by the fire, with his head down, while a handkerchief partially concealed his face. His companion had gone to the stable to assist a Negro in taking care of the horses. It was not long before they went into the main building, where the hostess had hastily prepared supper. While the elder traveler was eating, he engaged her in a sprightly conversation, in which he often thanked her for her kindness. At the same time, he cast the keenest glances at the sheriff, who stood before the fire, evidently with the endeavor to read his thoughts and intentions. After he had finished his supper, he arose from the table, bowed to the lady, walked back to the kitchen and took his seat by the fire. Mrs. Hinson then turned to his companion, and said, "Have I not, sir, the honor of entertaining Colonel Burr, the gentleman who has just walked out?" He gave her no answer, but rose from the table, much embarrassed, and also repaired to the kitchen. Her question had been prompted by Brightwell. In the morning, after breakfast, the elder traveler sought an interview with the lady, took occasion again to thank her for the hospitable attentions, regretted the absence of her husband, inquired the route to Pensacola, and rode off with his companion.[19]

Perkins remained at his post in the woods, shivering with cold, and wondering why Brightwell did not return to him. His patience at length became exhausted, and, believing the person he was pursuing to be really Burr, he mounted his horse, and rode rapidly to the house of Joseph Bates Sr., at Nanna Hubba Bluff. Procuring from that gentleman a Negro and a canoe, he paddled down the river, and arrived at Fort Stoddert at the breaking of day. Rushing into the fort, and acquainting Captain Edmund P. Gaines with his suspicions,

[19] Burr had met Major John Hinson in Natchez, and he apparently knew that he would be welcome at Hinson's home near Wakefield in Washington County. While Sheriff Brightwell was making arrangements with Hinson's servants for the care of their horses, Perkins and Ashley were in the house "when the person who had been at the kitchen fire came in. . . . At length I got a glance of his eye as he looked aside at me, upon which I became confident that this was Col. Burr." Ibid., 142–43; Thomas Perkins Abernethy, *The South in the New Nation, 1789–1819*—volume 4: *A History of the South* (Baton Rouge: Louisiana State University Press, 1961), 292.

the latter made instant preparations to take the road.[20] After a hasty breakfast, about the rising of the sun, Gaines, placing himself at the head of a file of mounted soldiers, rode off with Perkins. About nine o'clock that morning they met the two mysterious travelers, on the descent of a hill, near a wolf pen, at the distance of two miles from the residence of Hinson.[21] The following conversation immediately ensued:[22]

GAINES.—I presume, sir, I have the honor of addressing Colonel Burr.

STRANGER.—I am a traveler in the country, and do not recognize your right to ask such a question.

GAINES.—I arrest you, at the instance of the federal government.

STRANGER.—By what authority do you arrest a traveler upon the highway, on his own private business?

GAINES.—I am an officer of the army. I hold in my hands the proclamations of the president and the governor, directing your arrest.

STRANGER.—You are a young man, and may not be aware of the responsibilities which result from arresting travelers.

GAINES.—I am aware of the responsibilities, but I know my duty.

The stranger now became exceedingly animated, and, with much eloquence and force, denounced these proclamations as documents which had emanated in malevolent feeling, without any just foundation, and endeavored again to frighten the young officer from discharging his duty, by ingeniously animadverting upon the great liabilities which he was about to assume. But Gaines sternly replied, "My mind is made up. You must accompany me to Fort Stoddert, where you shall be treated with all the respect due the ex-vice president of the United States, so long as you make no attempt to escape from me." The stranger, for a moment, gazed at him with earnestness, apparently surprised at the unusual firmness which the young officer exhibited. He then assented, by a gentle motion of his head, wheeled his horse around, and took the road to the fort, riding by the side of the captain.[23] His traveling companion rode back towards Wakefield with Brightwell, the sheriff, who

[20] After observing Burr in the Hinsons' house, Perkins reported to Attorney General Caesar A. Rodney: "Soon after, I got my horse and left the house, as if going back to the Court House. But after pursuing that road I turned and took the road down to Fort Stoddert where I arrived before sunrise and informed Lieutenant Gaines of what I had seen and heard the preceding evening, and of my suspicions that the person in the white hat was Col. Burr." Joseph Bates Sr., was an early settler in the Tensaw District. Henry, "Capture of Aaron Burr," 143.

[21] Lieutenant Edmund Pendleton Gaines selected a sergeant and three soldiers of his detachment at Fort Stoddert "and, reconnoitering with Major Perkins about 14 miles up the country, met with the Colonel and escorted him to this place." Perkins reported in his letter to Attorney General Caesar A. Rodney: "When we came within two or three miles of Maj. Hinson's, we met Col. Burr in company with Sheriff Mr. Brightwell." Ibid., 143; Edmund P. Gaines to General Wilkinson and Governor Williams, Fort Stoddart, Mobile River, 19 February 1807, ibid., 146–47.

[22] Since neither Nicholas Perkins nor Lieutenant Edmund P. Gaines recorded or discussed the specific exchange between Burr and Gaines, it appears Pickett is simply speculating what the content of the exchange might have been. See Lemuel Henry and others, "The Capture of Aaron Burr," *American Historical Magazine* 1 (April 1896): 141–47.

[23] In his lengthy letter to Attorney General Caesar A. Rodney, Perkins noted that "When we rode up to them Lieutenant Gaines asked if he was not Col. Burr, he answered in the affirmative, and then Lieutenant Gaines arrested him. Some conversation passed between Lieut. Gaines and Col. Burr on the subject of the arrest. At length, Col. Burr asked Lieutenant Gaines if he had authority to arrest any person

was in company with the two travelers when they were met by Gaines.*

The party reached the fort in the evening, and Colonel Burr, being conducted to his room, took his dinner alone.[24] Late in the night, he heard a groan in an adjoining room. He arose from a table, at which he was reading, opened the door, entered the room, and approached the bedside of George S. Gaines, the brother of the commandant, who was sick. He was kind to the sufferer, felt of his pulse, said he had traveled much and knew something of medicine, and offered his services. They now entered into an agreeable conversation. Burr asked the Choctaw factor many questions about the Indians and their commerce. The next day he appeared at the dinner table, and was introduced to the wife of the commandant, who was the daughter of Judge Harry Toulmin. In the evening, he played chess with that accomplished lady, and, during his confinement at the fort, was often her competitor in that intricate game.[25] Every night he sought the company of the invalid, who became exceedingly attached to him, and who felt deep regret on account of the downfall of so interesting and so distinguished a character. Often and often did the good heart of George S. Gaines grieve over the adversities and trials of this remarkable man, as they discoursed together. In all their conversations, maintained every night, the impenetrable Burr never once alluded to the designs which he had failed to carry out, to his present arrest, or to his future plans.[26]

In the meantime, Captain Gaines had been untiring in his exertions to fit out an expedition for the conveyance of his distinguished prisoner to the federal city.[27] At length he placed Burr in a boat, along with a file of soldiers, and he was rowed up the Alabama River and then into Lake Tensaw. Passing some houses on the banks, several ladies wept,

* It remains a mystery, to this day, why Brightwell did not keep his promise with Perkins, and I can only account for it by supposing that he became fascinated with Colonel Burr, was sorry that he had sought to arrest him, and was now conducting him to Mrs. Carson's ferry, upon the Tombigbee, on the route to Pensacola. Burr had seen Colonel Hinson at Natchez, who had invited him to his house, should he ever pass that way. When he escaped from Natchez, he was secreted, from time to time, at the houses of his friends, and he was hastening to Hinson's, with whom he had intended to pass a week. But when he found him absent, and himself discovered by Brightwell, who probably informed him of the intentions of Perkins, he determined to fly to Pensacola, and there take a ship for Europe. He intended to enlist wealthy and influential persons, both in England and France, in the scheme of making the conquest of the North American Spanish possessions, now that he had so signally failed to accomplish it in the United States.

with him. Lieutenant Gaines said he had not; then Col. Burr requested that Mr. Ashley should be informed that he wished him to come to Fort Stoddart which I agreed to do if I should see him . . ." Henry, "Capture of Aaron Burr," 143.

[24] In his letter of 19 February 1807 to General Wilkinson and Governor Williams, Gaines reported that Burr "is now in one of our best rooms with a sentinel at his door." Ibid., 147.

[25] Lieutenant Edmund P. Gaines's first wife was Frances Toulmin Gaines (1788–1811), the second oldest daughter of Judge Harry Toulmin and his first wife, Martha Johnson. Owen, *History of Alabama*, 4: 1677; Gaines, *Reminiscences*, 207 n. 47.

[26] Pickett's account of the capture of Burr and his interaction with George Strother Gaines, Edmund Pendleton Gaines, and Frances Toulmin Gaines at Fort Stoddert comes directly from his first interview with George Strother Gaines in 1847. "Notes taken from the lips of Geo. S. Gaines at his home at Spring Hill near Mobile," Pickett Papers, ADAH; Gaines, *Reminiscences*, 143–45.

[27] On the same day—19 February 1807—that he brought Burr to Fort Stoddert, Lieutenant Edmund P. Gaines discussed conducting Burr to "Washington City" with Nicholas Perkins, and, later that evening, he addressed a letter to Perkins asking for his advice and whether he or his brother "Captain Perkins and Mr. Murray" would be willing "to undertake the arduous task."

upon seeing the ex-vice-president a prisoner, and one of them named a son for him. Everywhere, in the Southwest, the ladies were attached to the man, and suffered their feelings to become enlisted in behalf of his unfortunate enterprises. It is a prominent and noble trait in the female character, to admire a man of daring and generous impulses, and to pity and defend him in his adversities!*

Arriving at the Boat Yard, Burr disembarked, and was delivered to the guard which was so long to be with him, in dangers and fatigues. It consisted of Colonel Nicholas Perkins, of Tennessee, who had, as we have seen, been the cause of his arrest, Thomas Malone, formerly a clerk in the land office at Raleigh, North Carolina, but who, at this period, was a clerk of the court of Washington County, Alabama, Henry B. Slade, of North Carolina, John Mills, a native of Alabama, John Henry, of Tennessee, two brothers, named McCormack, of Kentucky, and two federal soldiers. With the exception of the two soldiers, Perkins had chosen these men on account of the confidence which he reposed in their honor, energy and fidelity. He had been placed over them by Captain Gaines, who entertained a high opinion of his bravery and capacity. Perkins took his men aside and obtained from them the most solemn pledge that they would not suffer the prisoner to influence them, in any manner, in his behalf; to avoid which, they promised to converse as little as possible with him, upon the whole route to Washington. The character of Burr, for making strong impressions in his favor, upon the human mind, was well known to Perkins.[28]

When the prisoner fled from the Natchez settlements, he assumed a disguise-dress. He was still attired in it. It consisted of coarse pantaloons, made of homespun, of a copperas dye, and a roundabout, of inferior drab cloth, while his hat was a flapping, wide-brimmed beaver, which had, in times past, been white, but now presented a variety of dingy colors. When the guard was ready to depart, he mounted the same elegant horse which he rode when arrested. He bestrode him most gracefully, flashed his large dark eyes upon the many bystanders, audibly bade them farewell, and departed.† Perkins and his men were well provided with large pistols, which they carried in holsters, while the two soldiers had muskets. They left the Boat Yard, a quarter of a mile from which the terrible massacre of Fort Mims afterwards occurred, and, pursuing the Indian path, encamped the first night in the lower part of the present

* Burr was not only popular with the ladies, but the most prominent men in the Southwest favored his enterprise, as they had long been anxious for the expulsion of the Spaniards.

† Many persons who saw Burr in Alabama have told me that his eyes were peculiarly brilliant, and, to use the comparison of Malone, "they looked like stars."

Gaines went on to intimate that either Perkins or his brother and "four active, sober, confidential young men . . . with good horses" could complete the assignment and receive "the 2000 dollars reward." Henry, "Capture of Aaron Burr," 147–49.

[28] Actually, the five member guard recruited by Nicholas Perkins included John Mertes, Samuel McCormack, John Henry Jay, and Henry B. Slade. Each of them signed their names to a contract dated 23 February 1807, pledging "our lives, our honor, each to the other, for the safe conducting and delivery of Aaron Burr, a United States prisoner, to the President of the United States, under the direction of Nicholas Perkins." Gaines assigned "Sergeant Harris and Cyrus Jones" of his 2nd U.S. Infantry as part of the escort team and under the direction of Perkins. Ibid., 149–50.

county of Monroe. The only tent taken along was pitched for Burr, and under it he lay the first night by large fires, which threw a glare over the dismal woods. All night his ears were saluted with the fierce and disagreeable howling of wolves. In the wilds of Alabama, in a small tent, reposed this remarkable man, surrounded by a guard, and without a solitary friend or congenial spirit. He was a prisoner of the United States, for whose liberties he had fought, and an exile from New York, whose statutes and institutions bore the impress of his mind. Death had deprived him of his accomplished wife, his only child was on the distant coast of Carolina, his professional pursuits were abandoned, his fortune swept from him, the magnificent scheme of the conquest of Mexico defeated, and he was harassed from one end of the Union to the other. All these things were sufficient to weigh down an ordinary being and hurry him to the grave. Burr, however, was no common man. In the morning he rose, with a cheerful face, and fell into traveling order, along with the taciturn and watchful persons who had charge of him.[29]

Although guarded with vigilance, he was treated with respect and kindness, and his few wants were gratified. The trail, like all Indian highways, was narrow, which required the guard to march in single file, with Burr in the middle of the line. The route lay about eight miles south of the present city of Montgomery, then an Indian town, called Ecunchate.* Passing by the residence of "Old Milly," who, as we have seen, lived upon the creek in Montgomery County, which still bears her name, Perkins employed her husband, a mulatto, named Evans, to conduct the guard across Line Creek, Cubahatchee and Calabee, all of which they were forced to swim. It was a perilous and fatiguing march, and for days the rain descended, in chilling torrents, upon these unsheltered horsemen, collecting in deep and rapid rivulets at every point. Hundreds of Indians, too, thronged the trail, and the party might have been killed in one moment. But the fearless Perkins bore on his distinguished prisoner, amid angry elements and human foes. In the journey through Alabama, the guard always slept

* Ecunchate means *Red Ground.*

[29] On 27 February 1807, in a letter addressed to "Major Perkins" at "Tensaw, near Fort Stoddert," Lieutenant Gaines provided Perkins and his party with a "passport" and general instructions for conveying Burr to Washington City, including "strictest economy in the expenditures of your expedition" and "furnish your prisoner, Aaron Burr, Esq., with whatever his convenience, accommodation and comfort may require." Ibid., 149–51.

in the woods, near swamps of reed, upon which the belled and hobbled horses fed during the night. After breakfast, it was their custom again to mount their horses and march on, with a silence which was sometimes broken by a remark about the weather, the creeks or the Indians. Burr sat firmly in the saddle, was always on the alert, and was a most excellent rider. Although drenched for hours with cold and clammy rain, and at night extended upon a thin pallet, on the bare ground, after having accomplished a ride of forty miles each day, yet, in the whole distance to Richmond, this remarkable man was never heard to complain that he was sick, or even fatigued.[30] At the Chattahoochee was a crossing place, owned by an Indian named Marshall, where the effects of the expedition were carried over the river in canoes, by the sides of which the horses swam. In this manner they passed the Flint and Ocmulgee.[31] Arriving at Fort Wilkinson, on the Oconee, Perkins entered the first ferry-boat which he had seen upon the whole route, and, a few miles beyond the river, was sheltered by the first roof—a house of entertainment, kept by one Bivins.[32]

While breakfast was in a state of preparation, and the guard were quietly sitting before a large fire, the publican began a series of questions; and learning that the party were from the "Bigby settlement," he immediately fell upon the fruitful theme of "Aaron Burr, the traitor." He asked if he had not been arrested—if he was not a very bad man—and if everyone was not afraid of him. Perkins and the rest of the guard, much annoyed and embarrassed, hung down their heads, and made no reply. Burr, who was sitting in a corner near the fire, majestically raised his head, and flashing his fiery eye upon Bivins, said,

"I am Aaron Burr!—what is it you want with me?"

Struck with the keenness of his look, the solemnity of his voice, and the dignity of his manner, Bivins stood aghast, and trembled like a leaf. He asked not another question of the guard, but quietly moved about the house, offering the most obsequious attentions.[33]

When Perkins reached the confines of South Carolina, he watched the prisoner more closely than ever; for in this state

[30] When Perkins and his party started their journey, they were directed by Lieutenant Gaines to convey Burr safely to Washington City in the District of Columbia. At some point in their trip, they received a notice from Secretary of State James Madison—dated 23 March 1807—through Lewis Ford to deliver Burr to George Hay, U.S. District Attorney, in Richmond, Virginia. On the same date, Secretary of War Henry Dearborn sent an order "To the officer who has charge of Aaron Burr" to call on George Hay in Richmond and "punctually follow such instructions as you may receive from Mr. Hay or from C. A. Rodney, Esq., Attorney General of the United States." Ibid., 151–52.

[31] Apparently a reference to Benjamin Marshall, a métis son of Thomas Marshall who was a trader at Coweta in the 1790s. He became an important Coweta headman and was associated with William McIntosh. Green, *Politics of Indian Removal,* 181.

[32] The Perkins-Burr party crossed the Oconee River on one of two ferries, Holt's Ferry or Scott's Ferry, near Fort Wilkinson, and they found shelter at a small tavern operated by William Bivins. Bivins, a veteran of the Revolutionary War, was a successful businessman and land owner near Milledgeville, with land holdings in Hancock County and Baldwin County, Georgia. Several principal roads intersected at Milledgeville, one leading to Augusta, Georgia, and another developed as a stage route to Washington City. Anna Maria Green Cook, *History of Baldwin County Georgia* (Anderson, SC: Keys-Hearn Printing Co., 1925), 20, 23, 29–30; "For Sale. A Tract of Land," [William Bivins], *Augusta Chronicle,* 10 October 1807; "Died," [William Bivins], *Macon Telegraph,* 22 December 1828; "Executors' Sale," [William Bivins], *Southern Recorder,* 31 January 1829.

[33] Pickett's narrative of the interchange between Burr and the sixty-one year old Williams Bivins seems to be incongruent

lived Colonel Joseph Alston—a man of talents and influence, afterwards governor—who had married the only daughter, and, indeed, the only child of Burr.[34] Afraid that the prisoner would be rescued at some point in this state, he exhorted his men to renewed vigilance. Before entering the town, in which is situated the Court House of Chester District, South Carolina, he made a halt, and placed two men in front of Burr; two behind, and two on either side of him. In this manner they passed near a tavern, at the Court House, where many persons were standing in front of the portico, while music and dancing were heard in the house. Seeing the collection of men so near him, Burr threw himself from his horse, and exclaimed, in a loud voice, "I AM AARON BURR, UNDER MILITARY ARREST, AND CLAIM THE PROTECTION OF THE CIVIL AUTHORITIES!" Perkins, with several of the guard, immediately dismounted, and the former ordered the prisoner to remount. Burr, in a most defiant manner, said, "I WILL NOT!" Being unwilling to shoot him, Perkins threw down his pistols—both of which he held in his hands—and seizing Burr around the waist, with the grasp of a tiger, threw him into his saddle.[35] Thomas Malone caught the reins of the prisoner's horse, slipped them over his head, and led the animal rapidly on, while others whipped him up from behind. The astonished citizens saw a party enter their village with a prisoner, heard him appeal to them for protection in the most audible and imploring manner, saw armed men immediately surround him and thrust him again into his saddle, and then the whole party vanish from their presence, before they could recover from their confusion. The least timidity or hesitation on the part of Perkins would have lost him his prisoner, for the latter was still popular in South Carolina.[36]

Far in the outskirts of the town the party halted. Burr was in a high state of excitement, and burst into a flood of tears. The kind-hearted Malone also wept, at seeing the low condition to which this conspicuous man was now reduced. The bold attempt to escape, and the irresolution of the people to whom he appealed, suddenly unmanned him. Perkins held a short consultation with some of his men, and sending Burr on the route in charge of the guard, with Malone in command, he went back to the village, and purchasing a gig, overtook the party before night. Burr was placed in this vehicle, and driven by Malone, escorted by the guard. Without further incident, they arrived at Fredericksburg, where dispatches from Jefferson caused

given Burr's conduct with the Gaineses at Fort Stoddert and his respect for Revolutionary War veterans. In its 22 December 1828 issue, the *Macon Telegraph* reported the death of William Bivins "on the 18th inst. of Dropsy" at the age of 83 and noted his service in the Revolutionary War.

[34] Joseph Alston (1779–1816), a wealthy South Carolina planter, married Theodosia Burr in 1801, and they had one child, Aaron Burr Alston (1802–1812) who died of malaria. He served multiple terms in the South Carolina House of Representatives and served one term as governor (1812–1814). David Duncan Wallace, *South Carolina: A Short History, 1520–1948* (Chapel Hill: University of North Carolina Press, 1951), 358, 368–71, 416–23; Richard N. Côté, *Theodosia Burr Alston: Portrait of a Prodigy* (Mt. Pleasant, SC: Corinthian Books, 2002), 111–12, 162–70, 259–70.

[35] If this really happened, Perkins could have easily manhandled Burr, as described by Pickett in this incident. Judge George Adams, writing at the time of Burr's trial in Washington, Mississippi Territory, described Burr as "about five feet six inches; has a spare meagre form." George Adams, "Sketch of Aaron Burr," in Dunbar Rowland, *Third Annual Report of the Director of the Department of Archives and History of the State of Mississippi, From October 1, 1903, to October 1, 1904* (Nashville: Brandon Printing Company, 1905), 170.

[36] Pickett cites Thomas Malone as one of his sources for this chapter and portrays him here and elsewhere as one of Burr's guards. However, Malone's name is not listed on the "passport" issued to

them to take Burr to Richmond. The ladies of the latter place vied with each other in contributing to the comforts of the distinguished ex-vice president, sending him fruits, wine, and a variety of fine apparel. Perkins and his men repaired to Washington, reported to the president, and returned to Alabama by the distant route of Tennessee.[37]

Aaron Burr was arraigned for treason, and was tried and acquitted. He was then arraigned for misdemeanor, and was tried and acquitted. Thus ended the most expensive and extraordinary trial known to the country.[38] A part of the time that he was in Richmond the federal government caused him to be confined in the upper story of the penitentiary, where he was permitted to enjoy the company of his daughter.[39]

Sailing to Europe, Burr was, at first, treated with great distinction in England. The winter of 1809 found him in Edinburgh. Residing some time in Sweden and Germany, he, at length, arrived in France, where Bonaparte, influenced by letters from America, conceived a prejudice against him so immovable that he refused him passports to leave the country. At length, the Duke de Bassano procured him the necessary documents, when he sailed for America, and arrived at New York on the 8th of June 1812. Here he engaged again in the lucrative practice of the law, living in dignified obscurity, if such a position could be assigned to a man of his notoriety. He died, at Staten Island, on the 11th of September 1836, at the advanced age of eighty. His body, attended by his relations and friends, was taken to Princeton, New Jersey, and interred among the graves of his ancestors.[40]

With the private character of Burr, we conceive we have nothing to do, except to add that we believe him to have been a most profligate and licentious man. When the world put him down—when he received nothing but abuse and ingratitude from those who once sycophantically surrounded him, and whom he had helped to offices of honor and profit—when he was shunned by his old companions in arms, not invited into the society of the refined, but was pointed at, in walking Broadway, as the *murderer* and the *traitor*—he became disheartened and soured; and, being without those religious feelings which sustain the most

Nicholas Perkins and his fellow guards by Lieutenant Edmund P. Gaines, and there are no references to his presence in Richmond or Washington at the end of the journey. Henry, "Capture of Aaron Burr," 149–50.

[37] As noted above, the messages to Perkins to deliver Burr to Richmond originated from James Madison and Henry Dearborn. Perkins and his six traveling companions traveled to Washington, where he received a cash payment of $3,331.91 for "9 horses furnished transporting A. Burr to Richmond," arms, "One sulkey and harness," "Wages of 5 men and their sustenance as a guard," and "traveling expenses to Washington." Ibid., 153.

[38] The Perkins-Burr party received a message at Fredericksburg to deliver Burr to Richmond, where they arrived on 26 March 1807. Burr's trial opened at the Eagle Tavern on the 30th with John Marshall, Chief Justice of the U.S. Supreme Court, presiding. The trial attracted a massive crowd of spectators, and Marshall moved the proceedings to the Hall of Delegates in the Virginia capital building designed by Thomas Jefferson. On 20 October 1807, the trial ended when Marshall refused to find Burr guilty of treason. Davis, *Memoirs of Aaron Burr*, 2: 405; David O. Stewart, *American Emperor: Aaron Burr's Challenge to Jefferson's America* (New York: Simon & Schuster, 2011), 226–67, 302–03.

[39] Theodosia Burr Alston and her husband Joseph Alston traveled to Richmond and visited with Burr during his trial. Burr had three rooms on the third floor of the penitentiary and wrote "My jailor is a quite polite and civil man." Stewart, *American Emperor*, 247–48; Davis, *Memoirs of Aaron Burr*, 2: 409–10; Côté, *Theodosia Burr Alston*, 238–40.

[40] Burr sailed to England in June 1808 under the alias G. H. Edwards and was later ordered to leave England. He traveled through Denmark, Sweden, and Germany before arriving in France in February 1810 without a passport. The U.S. consul gave him no assistance, but he finally received permission to leave France and sailed from Amsterdam.

unfortunate, he threw off every restraint, and gave a loose rein to sentiments always unprincipled, and to passions always strong.*

One of the gravest facts proved against Burr, at his trial, at Richmond, upon the evidence of General Wilkinson, was that the prisoner, in a letter written to him in cipher, "avowed his design of seizing upon Baton Rouge, as a preliminary measure, and, afterwards, extending his conquests into the Spanish provinces." Admitting this to be true, it did not prove that he intended to dismember the Union.[41] Our readers have already seen that the federal government, and the people of the Southwest, desired the expulsion of the Spaniards from the Baton Rouge District, which was a part of the purchase from Napoleon, when he sold us Louisiana; and hereafter, it will be seen that these Spaniards were driven from the Baton Rouge District only *three* years after Burr's trial, when the governor of it, Colonel Grand-Pré, was killed.[42] In the citizens of the Southwest, who accomplished this end, it was not held to be *treason*—but Burr, for merely contemplating it, was tried for that crime. It was not considered *treason*, when President Jackson allowed hundreds of people of the Southwest to be shipped from Mobile and New Orleans, with arms in their hands, who presently landed upon the coast of Texas, and took that country from the Spaniards—but, for similar designs, Aaron Burr was hunted down, thrown into prison, and tried for *treason*.

The impartial reader must arrive at the conclusion that the faults of Burr, in a political and public capacity, were not such as ought really to have placed that odium upon him which still attaches to his name. One of the great secrets of his political

* In relation to Burr's arrest in Alabama, and his journey through the wilderness, I conversed with Mr. Thomas Malone, one of his guard; with Mrs. Hinson, now Mrs. Sturdevant, at whose house Burr passed the night when he was discovered; with Mr. George S. Gaines, who was at Fort Stoddert when he was brought there; and with Mrs. Howse, who saw him when they were conducting him up Lake Tensaw. I also corresponded with Major General Gaines, and have his testimony. All these witnesses are reputable and as respectable as any persons in Alabama.

On the subject of Burr's early life, and of his operations in the western country, I consulted *Memoirs of Aaron Burr*, by M. L. Davis; the various *American State Papers*; Daniel Clark, *Proofs of the Corruption of Gen. James Wilkinson*; James Wilkinson, *Memoirs of My Own Times*; William Sullivan, *Familiar Letters on Public Characters, and Public Events*; and many other works.

His ship was intercepted and he was held in England until March 1812 when he sailed to Boston in disguise. He finally reached New York in June 1812 and endured the tragic news of his grandson's death and later the devastating loss of his daughter Theodosia at sea. He practiced law with mixed success before his death in 1836. Davis, *Memoirs of Aaron Burr*, 2: 413–26, 429–30, 447; Côté, *Theodosia Burr Alston*, 246–59.

[41] Actually, Wilkinson's credibility as a witness was undermined by his own conduct in New Orleans when he appeared before the Burr grand jury in June 1807, and in the end, there were jurors who thought Wilkinson should have been indicted for his actions. When he was called to testify in October 1807, Burr had been acquitted on the treason and misdemeanor charges, and Burr's lawyers forced Wilkinson to admit that he had attempted to conceal his relationships with Burr. He was subsequently the subject of several investigations and a court martial related to his dealings with Spanish officials and the conduct of the army in Texas. His role as a paid Spanish spy—"Spy 13"—was not uncovered until several years after his death. Stewart, *American Emperor*, 60–66, 111–14, 191, 264–66, 273, 299–305; Charles F. Hobson, "The Aaron Burr Treason Trial," in Federal Trials and Great Debates in United States History (2006), http://www.fjc.gov/history/docs/burrtrial.pdf, 5–6, 12, 28.

[42] Lieutenant Luis de Grand-Pré, a son of the former commandant at Baton Rouge, was mortally wounded on 23 September 1810 when the filibusters under Thomas Philemon attacked Fort San Carlos at Baton Rouge. Carlos Luis Boucher de Grand-Pré, governor of the Baton Rouge District of West Florida, had been replaced by Don Carlos de Hault de Lassus (1767–1843) in 1808 and died in Havana in 1809

misfortunes lay in the prejudices and malevolence of politicians and fanatics. Somebody heard General Washington say that "Burr was a dangerous man"; thereupon, the world set him down as a "dangerous man."[43] He killed Hamilton in a duel, because Hamilton abused him; thereupon the world said he was a "murderer." He was a formidable rival of Jefferson in the contest for the presidency; thereupon, a majority of the Republican Party said he was a political scoundrel. He had always opposed the federal party; for that reason, the federal party hated him with exceeding bitterness. A blundering, extravagant man, named Harman Blennerhassett, sought Burr, while he was in the West, eagerly enlisted in his schemes, and invited him to his house; thereupon, William Wirt said, in his prosecuting speech, that Burr "was the serpent who entered the Garden of Eden."[44]

We do not wish to be considered as the defender of Aaron Burr. We do not admire his character, or that of many of his distinguished contemporaries who assailed him. But, as a historian, we are expected to write the truth, even if that truth is unpalatable to the prejudices of the age.

while awaiting trial for his pro-French activities in Baton Rouge. Davis, *Rogue Republic,* 121, 186–87; Rose Meyers, *A History of Baton Rouge, 1699—1812* (Baton Rouge: Louisiana State University Press, 1976), 81–82, 88–95.

[43] More recent scholarship has attributed this quote to Alexander Hamilton, and it became one of the issues that pushed Burr to the shores of Weehawken. Fleming, *The Duel,* 279–87.

[44] At one point in Burr's trial, William Wirt, one of the four prosecuting attorneys, drew an analogy between Burr, the planner and contriver of treason, and Harmon Blennerhassett, a naïve but willing participant in Burr's plot, as part of a long soliloquy that included the following: "Such was the state of Eden when the serpent entered its bowers." Stewart, *American Emperor,* 255–56; "Argument of William Wirt (excerpts)," U.S. Circuit Court, 25 August 1807, in *United States v. Burr,* 25 Fed. Cases 122–36.

Chapter XXX

St. Stephens—Huntsville—Indian Commerce—Kemper Expeditions

The military movements of Burr increased the population and wealth of the Mississippi Territory, for hundreds of his followers became permanent citizens. About this time the cultivation of indigo was much abandoned for that of cotton, and some salutary laws were enacted in relation to the toll for ginning the latter staple. The cotton receipts obtained from the owner of a gin were also made a legal tender, and passed as domestic bills of exchange.[1] St. Stephens was laid off into town lots. A road was cut out from thence to the city of Natchez. Notwithstanding the revenue exactions upon the settlers, which now subjected them, by means of the Spanish custom-house at Mobile, and the American at Fort Stoddert, to a duty of from forty-two to forty-seven per cent *ad valorem* for articles essential to family comfort, while, at the same time, their fellow-citizens about Natchez were entirely free from such exactions, paying only four dollars per barrel for Kentucky flour, when the Tombigbee planter paid sixteen—yet they remained loyal to the federal government; and both Whigs and Tories participated in an animated public meeting at Wakefield, pledging their support to the United States, to avenge the wanton attack of the British upon the American ship *Chesapeake*, in a string of eloquent and patriotic resolutions, drafted by James Magoffin.[2]

The little town of Huntsville, north of the Tennessee, continued to receive around it many wealthy emigrants from several of the Atlantic and western states. Governor Williams issued a proclamation, forming a county, of which this became the court house. The new county of Madison, where it joined the Tennessee line, was about twenty-five miles wide, and approached the Tennessee River in the shape of a triangle, not exceeding three miles wide at Ditto's Landing. It embraced all the territory that fell within Alabama, to which the Indian title was extinguished by the treaty with the Chickasaws in 1805.

1 In the Natchez area alone, cotton production increased from 36,351 pounds in 1794 to more than 1.2 million pounds by 1800. In 1797, Andrew Ellicott reported that the "making of indigo and raising tobacco . . . have both given way to the cultivation of cotton." Farmers in the territory experimented with different varieties of seed, including the Petit Gulf seed introduced by Dr. Rush Nutt after 1811. Nutt, a successful planter and noted scientist, also made improvements to the cotton gin and replaced the use of horse power with a steam engine in 1830. Claiborne, *Mississippi*, 140–42, 141 n.; Haynes, *Mississippi Territory*, 12–13; Ellicott, *Journal*, 133–34.

2 James Magoffin represented Washington County in the Mississippi Territory legislature and operated a store at Grove Hill after the Creek War

The Mississippi Territory continued to improve. The forests began to be extensively felled; houses were reared as if by magic; the preacher was zealous in the discharge of his divine mission; the "schoolmaster was abroad"; the medical and legal professions flourished; the merchants drove a good business; the mechanics received constant employment and high wages—while the farmer worked for them all, and received his due reward. These remarks apply more particularly to the section upon the Mississippi. A stock bank, with a capital of five hundred thousand dollars, was established at Natchez.[3]

The factory of the United States, located at St. Stephens, continued to be managed with advantage, so far as the friendship of the Choctaws depended, which was the chief aim of the government. When quite a young man, Mr. George S. Gaines, a native of Virginia, and then a resident of Gallatin, Tennessee, received the appointment of assistant factor, and arrived at St. Stephens in the spring of 1805.[4] The parsonage of the old Spanish church was used as a skin-house, and the old block-house served the purpose of the government store. In 1807, Gaines was made principal factor. He received a good salary, as also did the assistant clerk, the skinsman, and the interpreter. To this establishment the Indians—principally Choctaws—and sometimes the American settlers, brought bear's oil, honey in kegs, beeswax, bacon, groundnuts, tobacco in kegs, and all kinds of skins and peltries. To pay for which, the federal government usually kept a stock of coarse Indian merchandise, besides all kinds of iron tools, ploughs, arms and ammunition. In the summer the furs and hides, often overhauled by the skinsman for the purpose of keeping out the worms, were assorted. In the fall they were packed up in bales and shipped to the Indian agent at Philadelphia.[5] Mr. Gaines, at first, came often in collision with the revenue authorities of Mobile, who exacted duties—delayed his vessels—and, upon one occasion, came near putting him in the calaboose of that place for venturing to remonstrate. The federal government, to avoid the payment of these duties, and to prevent delays, instructed the factor to obtain the

of 1813–1814. On 22 June 1807, the USS *Chesapeake* was intercepted and fired on by the British warship HMS *Leopard* off the coast of Norfolk, Virginia. In a blatant act of impressment, a boarding party removed four Royal Navy deserters from the *Chesapeake*, including one British-born—Jenkin Ratford—and three others considered to be American citizens. Magoffin's resolutions were part of a firestorm of protests throughout the young nation. Owen, *History of Alabama*, 4: 1147; Bradford Perkins, *Prologue to War: England and the United States, 1805–1812* (Berkeley: University of California Press, 1970), 140–46.

[3] The Bank of Mississippi was chartered as a private corporation in 1809, and its ten founding directors were individually liable for any notes or bills issued "over three times the amount of their capital stock." In 1818, the legislature of the new state of Mississippi established it as the state bank. Claiborne, *Mississippi*, 300–301; Haynes, *Mississippi Territory*, 216–17.

[4] While George Strother Gaines (1784–1873) had a distinguished Virginia pedigree, he was born on 1 May 1784 in Surry (later Stokes) County, North Carolina. Prior to his arrival at St. Stephens in 1805, he gained important business acumen working for the merchant brothers John and Robert Allen in Gallatin, Tennessee, northeast of Nashville. Gaines, *Reminiscences*, 2–3.

[5] Appointed the assistant factor at the Choctaw Trading House at St. Stephens in 1805, he replaced Joseph Chambers as factor when Chambers resigned in 1806 and returned to North Carolina. He also became postmaster for St. Stephens in 1807. While the Choctaw were his principal customers, the trading house attracted Chickasaws from the upper Tombigbee, Creeks from the Black Warrior and Tombigbee rivers, and Euro-Americans from the lower Tombigbee and Tensaw settlements. Ibid., 3–4.

consent of the Chickasaws for a road from Colbert's Ferry to St. Stephens. The government resolved to send supplies down the Ohio and up the Tennessee, to the former point.[6] The faithful and enterprising Gaines was unable to procure the privilege of a road, but was allowed the use of a horse path. Upon the backs of horses he was accustomed to transport goods, hardware, and even lead, from Colbert's Ferry to Pitchlynn's, upon the Tombigbee. There, boats being constructed, the merchandise was floated down to St. Stephens.[7] It is singular that our ministers, in forming the treaty with Spain in 1795, by which we acquired all of West Florida above the line of 31°, and the right of free navigation of the Mississippi, neglected to insert an article for the free navigation of the bays and rivers of Mobile and Pearl.*

The Spaniards continued to occupy the Baton Rouge District and that of Mobile, and the daring Kempers, who had received such cruel treatment at their hands, together with many other persons, impatient at the irresolution of the federal government, resolved to expel them. They were assisted by the people of Bayou Sara, and others below Ellicott's line. Organizing at St. Francisville, the patriots, as they styled themselves, marched upon Baton Rouge—took it by surprise, after a small skirmish, in which Governor Grand-Pré was killed.[8] The town and other posts fell into their hands, and the Spaniards retired to Pensacola. As the Americans at this period, and for a long time previous, were fruitful in plans to form governments independent of the Union, so the patriots, many of whom were old Spanish subjects, now resolved to have one of their own. A convention assembled, which adopted a declaration of independence, very similar in tone and sentiment to that drawn up by Jefferson. They declared their right and intention to form treaties, and to establish commerce with foreign nations. Afterwards, however, this new republic was annexed to Louisiana, with the approbation of the inhabitants.[9]

The Kempers, apart from mercenary motives for engaging in this rebellion, desired to gratify a feeling of revenge. Reuben and Samuel captured Kneeland, one of the kidnappers, and inflicted upon his naked back one hundred lashes, then one hundred more for their brother Nathan, who was absent, cut off his ears with a dull knife, and permitted him to retire. These trophies of resentment were long preserved in spirits of wine, and hung up in one of the Kemper's parlor.[10] Reuben caught another of these wretches named Horton, and chastised him as long as the latter could receive it, and live.[11] Barker, seized by the Kempers at the court house at Fort Adams, under the nose of the judge, was dragged forth, and flayed till they were content.[12]

* Conversations with Mr. George S. Gaines.

[6] In July 1807, Secretary of War Henry Dearborn ordered Gaines's brother Lieutenant Edmund P. Gaines to explore the region between the Tennessee and Tombigbee rivers to find an overland route to solve their supply issues. He surveyed and marked four possible routes from Muscle Shoals to Cotton Gin Port on the Tombigbee, but George Colbert of the Chickasaw Nation protested that an overland route would ruin his ferry business on the Natchez Trace—effectively blocking a new wagon road for several years. Ibid., 5–6; Secretary of War to E. P. Gaines, 31 July 1807, Carter, *Territorial Papers/Mississippi*, 5: 558.

[7] Despite Colbert's protest against a new road, Gaines used one of the routes marked by his brother from near Colbert's Ferry to Major John Pitchlynn's home on Tibbee Creek as a pack-horse route in 1810. In 1813, he built a barge at Pitchlynn's at the mouth of Tibbee Creek on the Tombigbee to haul his trading house goods down to St. Stephens. He continued to use the pack-horse path and the Tombigbee River route until General Wilkinson seized Mobile. Gaines, *Reminiscences*, 49–50; Frank Lawrence Owsley Jr., *Struggle for the Gulf Borderlands: The Creek War and the Battle of New Orleans, 1812–1815* (Gainesville: University Presses of Florida, 1981), 23.

[8] The filibustering force under the command of Colonel Philemon Thomas (1763–1847) attacked Fort San Carlos on 23 September 1810. During the assault, Lieutenant Luis de Grand-Pré, son of Carlos Luis Boucher de Grand-Pré, the former governor of the Baton Rouge District, was mortally wounded. Meyers, *History of Baton Rouge*, 81–82, 88–95; William C. Davis, *The Rogue Republic: How Would-Be Patriots Waged the Shortest Revolution in American History* (Boston: Houghton Mifflin Harcourt, 2011), 185–86; Henry Eugene Sterkx and Brooks Thompson, "Philemon Thomas and the West Florida Revolution," *Florida Historical Quarterly* 39 (April 1961), 381–83.

[9] From June through September 1810, a series of secret meetings by several hundred residents of Feliciana, Baton Rouge, and other communities led to the election of representatives to a convention that declared their independence from Spanish control. The convention delegates signed a declaration of independence on 26 September, and John Rhea, president of the convention, wrote to President James Madison proposing a process for annexation and "immediate protection." Madison moved quickly, directing William C. C. Claiborne to take possession of the Republic of West Florida, who encountered a minimum of resistance from its president, Fulwar Skipwith, and General Philemon Thomas. Davis, *Rogue Republic*, 172–81, 191–93; Sterkx and Thompson, "Philemon Thomas," 383–86.

[10] Ira Cook Kneeland, a deputy surveyor in the jurisdiction of Baton Rouge, participated in the Kemper kidnapping. Arthur Cobb gave an affidavit stating that a pistol found in Reuben Kemper's tavern belonged to Kneeland. Arthur Cobb Affidavit, 3 September 1805, *ASP: FA*, 2: 683; Davis, *Rogue Republic*, xi, 69–70, 71–79, 104–06.

[11] This is apparently a reference to Abraham (Abram) Horton, who was the leader of the group that kidnapped the Kempers and attempted to deliver them to Spanish authorities in Baton Rouge. Reuben Kemper gave an affidavit on 5 September 1805 and identified Abraham Horton and three of his slaves—"William or Bill, Nat, and Moses"—as members of the group that invaded his house. Reuben Kemper Affidavit, 5 September 1805, *ASP: FA*, 2: 684–85; Davis, *Rogue Republic*, x, 69–73, 81, 103.

[12] William Barker was a member of Captain Solomon Alston's militia "stationed within a few paces of the line of demarcation on the Spanish side." At Alston's direction, he accompanied the group that attempted to take the Kempers to Baton Rouge for trial, but Lieutenant William Wilson and the American troops stationed at Point Coupée intercepted them, taking the entire party to Fort Adams. Cogliano, "Failed Filibusters," 7; William Barker Affidavit, 5 September 1805, *ASP: FA*, 2: 685; Davis, *Rogue Republic*, 69, 74–76, 78.

Captain Alston, who received the Kempers at the line, with a Spanish guard, and conducted them to Bayou Tunica,[13] died of the dropsy, contracted in lying, in an open boat, at anchor, every night, to avoid the attacks of the injured brothers.*

However, before the new republic was annexed to Louisiana, the convention dispatched its colonel, Reuben Kemper, to the Tombigbee River to enlist an army for the purpose of expelling the Spaniards from the Mobile District. The hatred of all these people for the Spaniards facilitated the movements of Kemper, who operated in conjunction with Colonel James Caller, a man of wealth and considerable frontier influence, at whose house he lodged. Troops were secretly raised.[14] Flatboats, with provisions, were dispatched down the Tensaw River to Smith's plantation. Major Kennedy and Colonel Kemper crossed over to the Boat Yard, where they were joined by Dr. Thomas G. Holmes and other fearless and ardent spirits, together with a company of horse under Captain Bernard.[15] Arriving at the White House, one mile above the present Blakeley, Kemper dispatched young Cyrus Sibley with a letter to Governor Folch—who had just taken command of Mobile—demanding the surrender of that place. A party, under Dr. Holmes, was also dispatched to scour the surrounding country for arms, ammunition and provisions, which the inhabitants generally secreted and withheld, because, being Spanish subjects, they were not dissatisfied with that government, which exacted no onerous duties of them. The command dropped down to the old fields of Minette Bay, opposite Mobile, where they appropriated to themselves, without scruple, forage and provisions, the property of Charles Conway Sr.[16]

Captain Goss arrived with a keel-boat laden with whiskey, corn, flour and bacon, which had been sent by the Baton Rouge Convention down the Mississippi through the lakes. The whiskey put the whole expedition in good spirits. Glowing speeches were made by Kennedy, who pointed them to the ancient Mobile, which, he said, they would shortly capture. But cold, rainy weather, which the troops were forced to encounter without tents or covering of any kind, now sat in. This circumstance, together with a personal difficulty which arose between Dr. Holmes and Dr. Pollard, in which the former was compelled, in self-defense, to severely wound the latter with a pistol, influenced Kemper to conduct the campaign on the other side of the bay.[17] With a portion of the party, Major Hargrave proceeded in the boat to Sawmill Creek, on the west side of Mobile River, twelve miles above the town.[18] With an abundance of whiskey and several fiddles, a frolic was there kept up, which was intended to last until Kemper and the horse company could go round by the Cut-Off and join them.[19]

* MS notes in the possession of Mr. E. T. Wood, of Mobile; Monette, 2: 86–90; *State Papers and Publick Documents*, Boston edition, 7: 479, 482–84.

[13] Captain Solomon Alston, a planter in Feliciana for several years, led a party of Spanish militia that encountered the kidnappers of the Kempers in Spanish territory. He directed the kidnappers to take them to Bayou Tunica and then down river to Baton Rouge to face charges. William Barker Affidavit, 5 September 1805, *ASP: FA*, 2: 685; Davis, *Rogue Republic*, 69–70, 73, 79–80.

[14] Much like the Kemper brothers east of the Pearl River, the Caller brothers—James and John—embraced the concept of a separate government for the Tombigbee settlements and the elimination of the Spanish presence in Mobile. They had been identified as members of the "Mobile Society" that planned to launch an expedition to capture Mobile. Carter, *Territorial Papers/Mississippi*, 6: 86–90, 129; Davis, *Rogue Republic*, 53–54, 153–54; Haynes, *Mississippi Territory*, 265–69.

[15] Major Joseph Pulaski Kennedy had become one of the chief spokesmen for the "Mobile Society" and a leading advocate of an expedition against Mobile. Although not identified by Spanish governor Maximilian de St. Maxent as one of the "villains" bent on seizing Mobile and Pensacola, Dr. Thomas G. Holmes was definitely one of the "firebrands of the Tombigbee." Carter, *Territorial Papers/Mississippi*, 6: 82, 130 n. 82, 132; Davis, *Rogue Republic*, 132–33, 152–54, 230–31; Isaac Joslin Cox, *The West Florida Controversy, 1798–1818: A Study in American Diplomacy* (Baltimore: Johns Hopkins Press, 1918), 583.

[16] On 12 September 1806, Charles Patrick Conway Sr., had received a Spanish land grant for 400 *arpents* on the eastern shore of Mobile Bay, near modern Blakeley. Reuben Kemper and his filibuster force used Conway's planation as the base for their attack on Spanish Mobile. While Kemper took command of a mounted party to cross the Alabama at Hollinger's Ferry, Major William Hargrave and his forces crossed the bay and camped at Sawmill Creek. *ASP: PL*, 3: 10; Davis, *Rogue Republic*, 232–33; "1787 Spanish Census of the Tensaw District," http://vidas.rootsweb.ancestry.com/1787cen.html; "Documents show area's intrigue," *Mobile Press-Register*, 4 April 2008.

[17] After receiving "a pistol shot thru his breast" from his altercation with Dr. Thomas G. Holmes on or about 6 December 1810, Dr. Pollard sought treatment for his wound at Fort Stoddert. After he was able to be questioned, Judge Toulmin had him arrested for participating in an illegal military enterprise. Carter, *Territorial Papers/Mississippi*, 6: 152–53; Davis, *Rogue Republic*, 231.

[18] Major William H. Hargrave (c.1758–1823), a Revolutionary War veteran from North Carolina, moved to Washington County, Mississippi Territory, around 1800. In 1803, he was appointed a justice of the peace for Washington County by Governor Claiborne. "Our Hargrave Family: The Children of William and Rebecca Bishop Hargrave," https://jeannehargrave.wordpress.com; Claiborne, *Mississippi*, 243.

[19] Kemper never made it to Sawmill Creek. Apparently, Kemper and James Caller stopped off at Fort Stoddert on Sunday, 9 December 1810, where Judge Toulmin had both men arrested for conducting an illegal military operation. In his letter of 12 December 1810 to President Madison, he noted that Caller, who "was a good deal intoxicated," admitted the general truth of the evidence in his arrest warrant. Carter, *Territorial Papers/Mississippi*, 6: 153, 155; Davis, *Rogue Republic*, 231–32.

An evil old man in the neighborhood, who often drank with them, went one night to Mobile and assured Governor Folch how easily they might be captured. The latter sent Parades, with two hundred regulars and citizens in boats, up the river, late one evening, who entered Sawmill Creek, ascended it to the American camp, and while the poor fellows were dancing and shouting, at 11 o'clock at night, fired upon them. Many of them fled in all irections. Four were killed, and others were wounded.[20] Major Hargrave rallied a few of his men and fought, but was overpowered. He and nine more were loaded with irons—carried to Mobile, thrown into the calaboose, and from thence conveyed to Havana and immured in the dungeons of Moro Castle. Cyrus Sibley, afterwards recognized as the bearer of the dispatch to Folch from Kemper, was seized, and also sent to Moro Castle.[21] These men remained Spanish prisoners, in the Castle, for FIVE YEARS.* This affair broke up the "Kemper expedition," which was further embarrassed by opposition from the federal authorities about Fort Stoddert. Subsequently, Wilkinson dispatched Colonel Cushing, with some troops, to Mobile, for the protection of the Spaniards from the designs of the patriots. They encamped three weeks at the Orange Grove. Cushing then marched up to Fort Stoddert,[22] and built a cantonment at Mount Vernon.†

* MS notes in the possession of Mr. E. T. Wood, of Mobile. Also, conversations with Dr. Thomas G. Holmes, of Baldwin County, Alabama.

†Conversations with Major Reuben Chamberlain, of Mobile, who came with Colonel Cushing.

[20] Shortly before midnight on 10 December 1810, a Spanish force of 200 soldiers and volunteers under Captain Cayetano Perez fell on the Kemper-Kennedy expedition at their camp on Sawmill Creek some twelve miles north of Mobile. While the whiskey flowed and the fiddles bowed, the surprised Americans had four killed, several wounded, and ten captured, including Hargrave and Sibley, who ended up in Havana's Moro Castle prison. Carter, *Territorial Papers/Mississippi*, 6: 157, 180; Davis, *Rogue Republic*, 233–34; Claiborne, *Mississippi*, 308; Cox, *West Florida Controversy*, 483–84; Thomas D. Clark and John D. W. Guice, *The Old Southwest, 1795–1830: Frontiers in Conflict* (Norman: University of Oklahoma Press, 1996), 59–60.

[21] With approval from the federal government, Governor William C. C. Claiborne made a concerted effort to obtain the release of the captives. The USS *Viper* carried an application to Havana requesting a pardon, but the request was rejected. Claiborne received permission to send money and clothing and the survivors were eventually released. In 1818, Hargrave was living in Marengo County, Alabama, when his Revolutionary War pension application was approved, paying him $240 annually. He died in Greene County, Alabama, in December 1823. Davis, *Rogue Republic*, 285; Claiborne, *Mississippi*, 308 n.; "Our Hargrave Family" (online); Thomas McAdory Owen, comp., *Revolutionary Soldiers in Alabama, Being a List of Names Compiled from Authentic Sources of Soldiers of the American Revolution Who Resided in the State of Alabama* (Montgomery: Brown Printing Co., 1911), 50.

[22] Secretary of War William Eustis ordered Colonel Thomas Cushing (1755–1822) to occupy any posts abandoned by the Spanish in West Florida and to maintain order along the line of demarcation. On 3 January 1811, Cushing arrived off Mobile Bay with two companies of U.S. troops and five gunboats. Judge Harry Toulmin declared that Cushing "has really saved this country from becoming a scene of plunder and desolation." Carter, *Territorial Papers/Mississippi*, 6: 162–63, 167–68, 174, 179; Cox, *West Florida Controversy*, 583; Jack D. L. Holmes, " Thomas Humphrey Cushing," *Handbook of Texas Online*.

Chapter XXXI

TECUMSEH—CIVIL WAR AMONG THE CREEKS

The United States and Great Britain were upon the verge of war. British agents, in Canada and Florida, sought to procure the cooperation of the whole southwestern Indian force. The Creeks, more powerful in numbers than the others, were particularly urged to join the English. Colonel Hawkins had managed them, with much wisdom and policy, for several years, but they always remained dissatisfied, and were particularly so now, in consequence of a portion of their chiefs having granted a public road through the heart of their country, which had been cut out by Lieutenant Luckett and a party of soldiers. This thoroughfare, called the "Federal Road," and which runs from Mims's Ferry, upon the Alabama, to the Chattahoochee, was filled, from one end to the other, with emigrants for the western part of the territory.[1] The Creeks, with their usual sagacity, foresaw that they should soon be hemmed in by the Georgians on one side, and the Tombigbee people on the other, and many of them contemplated the expulsion of the latter, at some day not very distant. The Spaniards also hated the emigrants, who had continued to drive them, inch by inch, from the soil which they claimed. With both them and the Indians the British agents began to operate, to make secret allies of the one and open ones of the other. But the most powerful British incendiary was Tecumseh. His father and mother, of the Shawnee family, were born and bred at Sawanogi,* upon the Tallapoosa, in Alabama.[2]

With several children, they removed to the forest of Ohio, where Tecumseh was born, in 1768. He had five brothers, who were all celebrated for the human blood which they spilt and for their indomitable courage. His only sister, Tecumapease, a woman of great sense and strong character, he devotedly loved, and was much influenced by her.[3] In 1787, he visited the Cherokees

* Old Augusta, now the property of Henry Lucas, on the railroad, where there are some mounds.

[1] In September 1810, Lieutenant John R. N. Luckett conducted a survey party that included a detachment of soldiers from the U.S. 2nd Infantry Regiment stationed at Fort Stoddert. While his men used axes to clear the existing horse path east from Holly Creek near Samuel Mims's ferry, Luckett used his compass and chains to produce a road survey, blazing trees with Roman numerals as mile markers. However, a Creek party ended his work near mile 123 on 5 October 1810 when they refused to let him continue his survey and path clearing project. Southerland and Brown, *Federal Road,* 34–38, 50, 95; Christopher and Waselkov, *Archaeological Survey,* 35–36.

[2] Tecumseh's mother and father—Methoataaskee and Pukeshinwau—grew up in separate Shawnee towns on the Tallapoosa. In 1811, Tecumseh is quoted as saying that he

came from Tuckabatchee—an Upper Creek town that on occasion was referred to as Spokogi or Ispokogi in a ceremonial context. In separate studies, John Swanton and John Sugden concluded that Ispokogi could easily be a corruption of Kispoko—one of the five historical divisions of the Shawnee. Swanton, *Early History of the Creek Indians,* 277–82; Sugden, *Tecumseh,* 13–15.

[3] Tecumseh and Tecumapease remained close, and, in 1795, she and her husband Wahsikegaboe moved to his village, where she served as a female peace chief and advisor. Sugden, *Tecumseh,* 19, 94, 99.

[4] Tecumseh followed his brother Cheeseekau and his people to the Five Lower Towns of the Chickamauga in 1789. They settled at Lookout Mountain Town while other Shawnee lived at Running Water and Nickajack. In the spring of 1791, Tecumseh returned to the Ohio and his brother remained with Dragging Canoe's Chickamaugas. However, Tecumseh returned to the Chickamauga towns in the fall of 1792 and participated in John Watts's campaign against Nashville, which ended tragically in the death of Cheeseekau during the assault on Buchanan's Station on 1 October 1792. Ibid., 57–62, 72–76; Pate, "The Chickamaugas," 219–22.

[5] In April 1792, Tecumseh's hunting party was attacked early in the morning by Kentucky rangers led by Simon Kenton, who were searching for a party of horse thieves. Tecumseh rallied his party and killed one of the Kentuckians. The engagement at Big Rock occurred in December 1792 when Tecumseh led a counter attack against a larger Ohio force under Robert McClellan, causing two casualties and capturing their baggage. Before dawn on 5 April 1793 at Paint River, Tecumseh's hunting party of less than ten men was attacked by thirty-three rangers under Simon Kenton. Tecumseh's party slipped out in the confusion when the Kentuckians divided into three divisions and one group started firing prematurely. Sugden, *Tecumseh,* 82–86.

[6] On 30 June 1794, Tecumseh was involved in the ill-advised attack led by Blue Jacket against Fort Recovery that started with a successful assault on drovers in charge of grazing pack animals. Failing to carry the fort, the allied Indian forces engaged Major General Anthony Wayne's superior force at the Maumee on 15 August 1794, where they were routed despite Tecumseh's efforts to rally those around him. Wayne's victory at the Battle of Fallen Timbers brought Blue Jacket to the treaty conference at Greenville in June-August 1795 but not Tecumseh. Ibid., 87–92; Richard C. Knopf, trans. and ed., *Anthony Wayne, A Name in Arms: The Wayne-Knox-Pickering Correspondence* (Pittsburgh: University of Pittsburgh Press, 1960), 345–47, 351–55, 442–43; John Sugden, *Blue Jacket: Warrior of the Shawnees* (Lincoln: University of Nebraska Press, 2000), 161–64, 165–68, 172–80, 200–07.

[7] Following the defeat of Blue Jacket's forces at Fallen Timbers in 1794, Tecumseh and his people moved from Ohio and finally settled on the west fork of the White River in modern Indiana in 1798. They suffered deprivations, land sales that reduced hunting lands, and epidemic sicknesses, while peace chiefs made more land cessions. In the midst of this turmoil, Tecumseh emerged as a persuasive orator who urged his people to unite and to reject white demands and his brother, Lalawéthika (Tenskwatawa), emerged as a healer who became known as "The Prophet" and who shared a social ethic revealed to him by the Great Spirit—a ministry that advocated a return to the old ways. Sugden, *Tecumseh,* 95–157, 166–88.

[8] Actually, Tecumseh had fewer than four personal visits with the British at Fort Malden or with Canada's Lieutenant-Governor Francis Gore prior to the 1812 U.S. declaration of war against Britain by the war hawks in Congress. Tecumseh's twenty-man delegation, which included six Shawnees, six Kickapoos, six Winnebagos, and two Creeks as guides, left Vincennes on 5 August 1811. Ibid., 164, 170–74, 212–13, 237; John Sugden, "Early Pan-Indianism: Tecumseh's Tour of the Indian Country, 1811–1812," *American Indian Quarterly* 10 (Autumn 1986), 279.

[9] Although Tecumseh passed through the Chickasaw country, he made no attempt to recruit the Chickasaws or to divulge his mission to Levi and George Colbert. He spent time with the Choctaw but again he did not discuss his mission, except to urge unity against the Americans. Some of his companions would not reveal their tribal identity. There are no contemporary accounts of Tecumseh's visit to the Choctaw, except for the recollections of Himonubbee, who was twelve-years old, and no evidence to corroborate a trip to Florida. Sugden, "Early

and Creeks, with whom he remained two years, engaging in their hunts, festivals and frontier wars.[4] Returning to the Ohio, he fought a battle with a party of whites, near Big Rock, and another, with the Kentuckians, on the Little Miami, and still another, at Paint Rock, in 1793.[5] He then engaged in the attack upon Fort Recovery, in 1794, and participated in the Battle of Maumee Rapids in the same year.[6] From that period, until that in which we propose to connect him with Alabama history, Tecumseh was engaged in British intrigues, in hunts and in skirmishes. Wherever he appeared, devastation and havoc ensued. He possessed a fine form, a commanding appearance, and had the endurance common to all Indians, together with a high degree of sagacity. He entertained the most relentless hatred of the Americans.[7]

After many conferences with the British, at Detroit, Tecumseh left that country, with a party of thirty warriors, mounted upon horses, and shaped his course to the south.[8] Passing through the Chickasaw and Choctaw country, he was unsuccessful in arraying these tribes against the Americans. He went down to Florida, and met with complete success with the Seminoles.[9] In the month of October he came up to the Alabama, crossed that river at Autauga, where he, for the first time, appealed to the Creeks, in a long speech. Continuing to Coosawda, he had, by this time, collected many followers, who went with him to the Hickory Ground. Having, from their boyhood, heard of his feats in the buffalo chase, the bloody wars which he had conducted, and of his fierce and transcendent eloquence, the warriors flocked to see him.[10] He went to Tuckabatchee, where Colonel Hawkins was then holding his grand council with the Indians.[11] This ancient capital never looked so gay and populous. An autumnal sun glittered upon the yellow faces of five thousand natives, besides whites and Negroes, who mingled with them. At the conclusion of the agent's first day's address, Tecumseh, at the head of his Ohio party, marched into the square. They were entirely naked, except their flaps and ornaments. Their faces were painted black, and their heads adorned with eagle plumes, while buffalo tails dragged from behind, suspended by bands which went around their waists. Buffalo tails were also attached to their arms, and made to stand out, by means of bands. Their appearance was hideous, and their bearing pompous and ceremonious. They marched round and round in the square; then, approaching the chiefs, they cordially shook them, with the whole length of the arm, and exchanged tobacco, a common ceremony with the Indians, denoting friendship, as we have already seen.[12] Captain Isaacs, chief of Coosawda, was the only one who refused to exchange tobacco. His

Pan-Indianism," 279–83; Sugden, *Tecumseh*, 241–43.

[10] Pickett's timeline for Tecumseh's tour of the southern Indian tribes is inaccurate, and his itinerary for Tecumseh is also flawed. Tecumseh's party arrived in the Chickasaw country around 27 August 1811 near Levi Colbert's house, and they arrived at Tuckabatchee on 19 September 1811. Sugden, "Early Pan-Indianism," 279, 284; Sugden, *Tecumseh*, 241, 244.

[11] In August 1811, Hawkins had sent invitations to the Cherokee, Chickasaw, and Choctaw to meet at Tuckabatchee during the Creek annual national council scheduled for 15 September 1811. Hawkins opened the council on the 20th, which featured three days of arguments over opening the wagon road—Federal Road—through the Creek domain and "told them, he did not come to there to ask their permission to open a road, but merely to inform them that it was now cutting." Sugden, "Early Pan-Indianism," 284–85.

[12] After Hawkins ended his business for the day on 20 September, Tecumseh and his party introduced themselves to the delegates present at Tuckabatchee. During the following days, the northern visitors shared songs and stories and introduced the war dance of the Shawnees that became known as the "dance of the lakes." Although

head, adorned with its usual costume—a pair of buffalo horns—was shaken, in contempt of Tecumseh, who, he said, was a bad man, and no greater than he was.[13]

Every day Tecumseh appeared in the square, to deliver his "talk," and all ears were anxious to hear it, but, late in the evening, he would rise, and say, "The sun has gone too far today—I will make my talk tomorrow." At length Hawkins terminated his business and departed for the agency, upon the Flint. That night a grand council was held in the great round-house. Tecumseh, presenting his graceful and majestic form above the heads of hundreds, made known his mission, in a long speech, full of fire and vengeance. He exhorted them to return to their primitive customs, to throw aside the plough and the loom, and to abandon an agricultural life, which was unbecoming of Indian warriors. He told them that, after the whites had possessed the greater part of their country, turned its beautiful forests into large fields, and stained their clear rivers with the washings of the soil, they would then subject them to African servitude. He exhorted them to assimilate in no way with the grasping, unprincipled race, to use none of their arms and wear none of their clothes, but dress in the skins of beasts, which the Great Spirit had given his red children for food and raiment, and to use the war-club, the scalping-knife and the bow. He concluded by announcing that the British, their former friends, had sent him from the Big Lakes to procure their services in expelling the Americans from all Indian soil; that the king of England was ready to reward handsomely all who would fight for his cause.[14]

A prophet, who composed one of the party of Tecumseh, next spoke. He said that he frequently communed with the Great Spirit, who had sent Tecumseh to their country upon this mission, the character of which that great chief had described. He declared that those who would join the war party should be shielded from all harm—none would be killed in battle; that the Great Spirit would surround them with quagmires, which would swallow up the Americans as they approached; that they would finally expel every Georgian from the soil, as far as the Savannah; that they would see the arms of Tecumseh, stretched out in the heavens, at a certain time,[15] and then they would know when to begin the war.*

* The British officers in Canada had told him when a comet would appear, and that he might use that as a sign to delude the Southern Indians.

he knew a war pipe had been sent to the Creeks, Hawkins left Tuckabatchee without hearing Tecumseh speak or learning any details of Tecumseh's mission. Ibid., 285; Sugden, *Tecumseh*, 244; Henri, *Southern Indians and Benjamin Hawkins*, 269.

[13] Other sources seem to contradict Pickett here. According to Thomas S. Woodward, Captain Isaacs, a shaman and medicine maker, embraced Tecumseh's pan-Indian confederacy and followed him to the northwest. Woodward, *Reminiscences*, 33; Martin, *Sacred Revolt*, 124–26.

[14] Pickett's narrative is speculative and his last sentence is probably a stretch. There are no first-hand eyewitness accounts of Tecumseh's speech to the Creeks and very few whites met Tecumseh during his southern tour. Although he had embraced the British as an ally, Tecumseh did not trust them, and he was not ready to declare war on the Americans. Tecumseh did not learn of Tenskwatawa's defeat at Tippecanoe on 7 November 1811 for several months, and President Madison did not sign the declaration of war until 18 June 1812—after Tecumseh's return to the northwest. Sugden, *Tecumseh*, 233–36, 271–72; Woodward, *Reminiscences*, 73–74; Martin, *Sacred Revolt*, 120–22, 214 n. 23; "An Act Declaring War Between the United Kingdom at Britain and Ireland and the Dependencies Thereof and the United States of America and Their Territories," http://avalon.law.yale.edu/19th_century/1812-0.

[15] The prophet at Tuckabatchee was Seekaboo, who may have been a Muscogee kinsman of Tecumseh's and who had lived for some

A short time before daylight the council adjourned, and more than half the audience had already resolved to go to war against the Americans, Tecumseh visited all the important Creek towns, enlisting all whom he could on the side of England. He had much to overcome, in the obstinacy of many of the prominent chiefs, who had become attached to the federal government, which had lavished upon them munificent presents. Yet he was, in a great measure, successful.[16] He made use of gifted and cunning Indians, to carry out his plans, after he should have left the country. One of these was Josiah Francis, the son of a Creek woman, by a trader, of'Scotch and Irish descent, named David Francis.* The Shawnee prophet, it was said, inspired him. He placed him in a cabin by himself, around which he danced and howled for ten days. He said that Francis was then blind, but that he would again see, and would then know all things which were to happen in future. When the ten days expired, the prophet led him forth, and attended him all day, for Francis stepped high and irregular, like a blind man. Towards night, the vision of Francis suddenly came to him, and after that he was the greatest prophet in the whole Creek Nation, and was empowered to make many subordinate prophets.[17]

Tecumseh, having made numerous proselytes, once more visited the Big Warrior, at Tuckabatchee, whom he was particularly desirous to enlist in his schemes, but whom he had hitherto entreated to no effect, although his house was his headquarters. The Big Warrior still remained true to the United States, more from fear of the consequences of a war than any love he entertained for the Americans. Tecumseh, after talking with him for some time, to no purpose, pointed his finger in his face and emphatically said: "Tustenuggee Thlucco, your blood is white. You have taken my red sticks and my talk, but you do not mean to fight. I know the reason. You do not believe the Great Spirit has sent me. You shall believe it. I will leave directly, and go straight to Detroit. When I get there I will stamp my foot upon the ground and shake down every house in Tuckabatchee." The Big Warrior

* This David Francis lived for many years in the Autauga town, where he had a trading establishment. He was also a silversmith and made buckles, ornaments and spurs, of silver, for the Indians. Josiah, his son, also learned the trade. David Francis was a great uncle to Dr. [James Carrington] Francis, an intelligent and highly respectable gentleman of Benton County, Alabama.

twenty years among the Shawnee. He spoke Shawnee, Muskogee, Choctaw, and English, and he apparently was conversant in Spanish, French, and the Mobilian trade jargon. With no eyewitness accounts, Pickett's narrative of his speech is speculative and perhaps based on hearsay recollections of old Indian countrymen. Sugden, "Early Pan-Indianism," 279; Sugden, *Tecumseh*, 237, 242, 246, 248, 320–21, 448–49 n. 22; Woodward, *Reminiscences*, 83.

[16] Again, Pickett is making a claim about Tecumseh's speech without documentation and from interviews decades later. However, Tecumseh certainly urged his listeners in the Creek domain to join his Indian confederacy, to embrace the old ways preached by Tenskwatawa and the prophets, and to resist the American takeover of their lands. Sugden, "Early Pan-Indianism," 286–87. See John Sugden, "Tecumseh's Travels Revisited," *Indiana Magazine of History* 96 (June 2000): 150–68.

[17] According to George Stiggins, Josiah Francis (Hillis Hadjo) was the métis son of David Francis, a Frenchman who worked as a trader, blacksmith, and possibly as a silversmith in the Upper Creek town of Coosawda. Some accounts have him accompanying Tecumseh on his travels west of the Mississippi to the Osage and the Missouri Indians. Stiggins, *Creek Indian History*, 91–93, 121; Sugden, *Tecumseh*, 247–48, 255; Frank L. Owsley Jr., "Prophet of War: Josiah Francis and the Creek War," *American Indian Quarterly* 9 (Summer 1985): 273–74, 277.

said nothing, but puffed his pipe and enveloped himself in clouds of smoke. Afterwards, he thought much upon this remarkable speech.[18]

The common Indians believed every word of Tecumseh's last speech, which was intended solely to intimidate the Big Warrior, and they began to count up the time it would take the Shawnee chief to reach Detroit, when he would stamp his foot, as he had declared. One day a mighty rumbling was heard in the earth; the houses of Tuckabatchee reeled, and tottered, and reeled again.* The people ran out, vociferating, "Tecumseh has got to Detroit! We feel the shake of his foot!"[19]

Josiah Francis made many prophets, and, among others, High-Head Jim, of Autossee. The Indians began to dance "the war-dance of the lakes," which Tecumseh had taught them. In the meantime, that chief had reached Canada, having carried with him the Little Warrior, of the Creek Nation, with thirty of his warriors.[20] The British agents sent back by them letters to their agents in Florida, with orders to allow the Creeks extensive supplies of arms and ammunition.[21] The Little Warrior, in returning, by way of the mouth of the Ohio, attacked seven families, living near each other, and murdered them in the most cruel manner.[22] They dragged Mrs. Crawley from the bodies of her bleeding children, and brought her, a prisoner, to the Tuscaloosa Falls.[23] Being made acquainted with these outrages by General Robertson, the Chickasaw agent, Hawkins, demanded the punishment of the guilty warriors. A council, at Tuckabatchee, secretly dispatched a party of warriors, headed by McIntosh, of Coweta, who marched to the Hickory Ground, where they separated into smaller parties. One of these went to the Red Warrior's Bluff, upon the Tallapoosa, now Gray's Ferry, and there surrounded a house, and began to shoot at five of the Little Warrior's party. They defended themselves with bravery, all the time

* This was an earthquake well known to the old settlers. In relation to the visit of Tecumseh to Alabama, I have consulted General Ferdinand L. Claiborne's MS Papers and Benjamin Drake's *Life of Tecumseh*. I have also conversed with Lachlan Durant, Mrs. Sophia McComb, Peter Randon, James Moore, and others, who were at Tookabatcha [Tuckabatchee] when Tecumseh arrived there.

[18] First, Tecumseh did not go to Detroit, which was under American control, but he did go to Fort Malden at Amherstburg, Canada, in June 1812. Second, since no eyewitnesses recorded Tecumseh's speeches or his meetings at Tuckabatchee and other Creek villages, Pickett's quote is speculative and not documented. In 1827, during a visit to Tuckabatchee, Thomas L. McKenney, Superintendent of Indian Trade, 1824–1830, had a story related to him that Tecumseh promised to stamp his foot on the ground and shake down every house in Tuckabatchee. In his memoir, George Stiggins (1788–1845), a métis Creek, claimed that Tecumseh promised "in about four moons" to climb to the top of a mountain, whoop three times, clap his hands, stamp his foot three times, and "make the whole earth tremble." Sugden, *Tecumseh*, 250–51; Sugden, "Early Pan-Indianism," 286–91; Stiggins, *Creek Indian History*, 85–86.

[19] Contrary to Pickett's timeline, the New Madrid earthquakes started about 2:15 a.m. on the morning of 16 December 1811 in modern northeast Arkansas, some sixty miles southeast of New Madrid, Missouri. Jared Brooks, a Louisville engineer and surveyor, recorded 1,874 shocks between 11 December 1811 and 15 March 1812, including 221 from 9 to 15 March. Sugden, "Early Pan-Indianism," 290; Jay Feldman, *When the Mississippi Ran Backwards: Empire, Intrigue, Murder, and the New Madrid Earthquakes of 1811–12* (New York: Free Press, 2005), 137, 146, 157, 178, 185, 191, 193.

[20] While there is evidence that Josiah Francis (Hillis Hadjo) traveled with Tecumseh's party, Little Warrior (Tastanagi Ooche) made two separate trips to Prophetstown. In November 1812, he led a party of fifteen Upper Creeks to meet with Tecumseh, reporting the deep division among his people but promising to return with a war party in the following spring. He returned with nine warriors in February 1813 to coordinate plans with Tecumseh and the Prophet. Sugden, *Tecumseh*, 320, 350.

dancing the dance of the lakes. Finally, they were all killed and burnt up. A party, headed by Captain Isaacs, pursued the Little Warrior into a swamp, above Wetumpka, and killed him. Others were killed at Hoithlewaule.[24] Although the chiefs, friendly to the United States, acted with so much justice upon this occasion, it did not prevent the commission of other murders, more immediately at home. An old chief, named Maumouth, killed Thomas Meredith, an emigrant, at Catoma Creek,[25] and wounded others.*

Having engaged in a war with England, the federal government, fearing to leave the port of Mobile longer in the hands of the Spaniards, who were the secret allies of Great Britain, resolved to occupy the whole of the district lying between Pearl and the Perdido Rivers, and below the line of 31°, which we had claimed since the treaty with Bonaparte, who ceded to us Louisiana, of which this was a part, as was contended. Accordingly, General Wilkinson, with six hundred men, of the third and seventh regiments, sailing from New Orleans, in transport vessels commanded by Commodore Shaw, provided with scaling ladders, and every necessary equipment, landed opposite the site of the Pavilion, on the bay of Mobile. He marched up to the town, and took a position in the rear of Fort Charlotte. After some correspondence, the Spanish commandant, Captain Cayetano Perez, capitulated, surrendered the fort, and all the cannon and military stores, the latter of which Wilkinson agreed the United States should pay for. The Spanish garrison retired to Pensacola, and the stars and stripes were hoisted upon the ramparts of Fort Charlotte, which was built of brick, with casements for five hundred men, and with four bastions. It was quite an acquisition to the United States, at the present time. General Wilkinson sent nine pieces of artillery to Mobile Point, which were there placed in

* *American State Papers: Indian Affairs*, 1: 843–45.

[21] After his return to Prophetstown, Tecumseh dispatched eight Shawnees, eight Winnebagos, and eight Kickapoos led by a Kickapoo "orator" to Fort Malden in February 1812, where his messengers requested supplies, including a keg of powder for each of the nations represented. However, Matthew Elliott, the British Indian superintendent at Amherstburg (Fort Malden), had received orders not to incite the Indians against the Americans; besides, he had little food and powder, and no shot to give. Writing from Amherstburg on 16 June 1812, Colonel William Clark reported to Major General Isaac Brock that "for the last six months, I find that in powder they have only received 1,211 pounds, making a difference of nineteen hundred and twenty-one pounds less than at former periods—of lead, not one ounce has been issued since last December." Sugden, *Tecumseh*, 264–65; *ASP: IA*, 1: 806; Earnest A. Cruickshank, ed., *Documents Relating to the Invasion of Canada and the Surrender of Detroit, 1812* (Ottawa: Government Printing Bureau, 1912), 32–33.

[22] Following his second trip to Prophetstown in February 1813, and contrary to Tecumseh's strategy, Little Warrior returned south along the Ohio River and brutally murdered seven white families near the mouth of the river. In a letter of 5 March 1813, James Robertson, U.S. agent to the Chickasaw, notified Benjamin Hawkins of the murders, and Hawkins called on chiefs in the Upper Towns to deliver the murderers to him. *ASP: IA*, 1: 839–40; Sugden, *Tecumseh*, 350.

[23] Pickett has combined two separate events. On 12 May 1812, Little Warrior and a party of Creeks attacked the home of Jesse Manley at McSims Bottom, near the mouth of Duck River in Humphreys County, Tennessee. They killed Mrs. Manley, five Manley and Crawley children, and a young man left to protect the two families. The wife of John Crawley—Martha Crawley—was taken as a captive. She was rescued by Tandy Walker, a blacksmith, who brought her to the Choctaw Trading House, where she was nursed to health by Anne Gaines and returned to Tennessee. Gaines, *Reminiscences*, 53–54; Tom Kanon, *Tennesseans at War, 1812–1815: Andrew Jackson, the Creek War, and the Battle of New Orleans* (Tuscaloosa: University of Alabama Press, 2014), 59–62.

[24] The Creek National Council had expelled Little

battery. He then marched to the Perdido, and on its western bank, on the main road to Pensacola, began the construction of a strong stockade, under the superintendence of Colonel John Bowyer, which was afterwards abandoned. Marching back to Mobile, he dispatched Captain Chamberlain, with soldiers, to Mobile Point, who began and, in two years, completed Fort Bowyer.* Thus the long period had arrived *when no Spanish government was found to exist upon a foot of the soil of Alabama or Mississippi.*[26]

The effects of Tecumseh's visit began to be realized in every corner of the Creek Confederacy. Even at the falls of Tuscaloosa, where a Creek town had for several years been established, the inhabitants were extremely belligerent. The chief, Ocheoce Emathla, with a few warriors, dropped down the Warrior River in canoes, paid Mr. Gaines a visit, and were insulting in their bearing and importunate in their demands for goods, upon a credit. They disclosed to Tandy Walker, an honest white man, formerly a government blacksmith, their intentions shortly to attack the settlers and seize upon the factory. In an eastward direction, the Alabamas were furious advocates of American extermination. The Indian executions, to which allusion has just been made, connected with the occasional shocks of the earthquake, filled the Indian world with excitement and fanaticism.[27]

Peter McQueen, a half-breed of Tallassee,[28] the venerable Hopoithle Mico,[29] and other prominent men, who had inclined to the talks of Tecumseh, now assumed decided attitudes. The hostile spirit increased fearfully, and the whole nation was soon agitated with quarrels, fights, murders and robberies, and everything foreboded a direful civil war. The prophets practiced their incantations in towns, fields, and in the woods, wherever they found Indians to influence. Alarmed at this unusual state of things, the chiefs friendly to the United States frequently dispatched runners to Hawkins, who urged them, in return, to adhere to the cause of the federal government, and to take all means to avert a civil war. The agent seems to have been strangely benighted, slowly allowing his mind to be brought to the conviction that anything serious would grow out of these difficulties. The Big Warrior, on the contrary, was much alarmed. He endeavored to assemble the chiefs of the neighboring towns,

* Wilkinson, *Memoirs*, 1: 507–20. Conversations with Major Reuben Chamberlain.

Warrior in March 1813 and on 16 April 1813 the council authorized William "Billy" McIntosh and Tustunnuggee Hopoi to take a party to find Little Warrior and the party that committed the murders on the Ohio and Duck River. They were joined by Captain Isaacs, Tallassee Fixico, Ispoakaeke Harjo, and the others who intercepted and killed the Tuskegee warrior—who admitted to the murders on the Ohio—two of his brothers, and two young men from Tuckabatchee, at the Hickory Ground. Little Warrior and the others who escaped were hunted down and killed at Hoithlewaule. On 26 April 1813, Big Warrior sent a message to Hawkins confirming the death of eleven since the 16th. *ASP: IA*, 1: 812–13, 839–41, 843.

[25] On 26 March 1812, Thomas Meredith and his extended family, including his wife Abigail, their children and their spouses, and their slaves, were traveling from the Fairfield District, South Carolina, to new opportunities in the Mississippi Territory. They were passing through the Creek Nation on the Federal Road when they reached Pinchona Creek near Pintala, Alabama, and met Maumouth, an old Creek chief, and his party. All the Meredith party had crossed the creek except Meredith, his nine-year old son, and another man when an intoxicated Maumouth killed Meredith. In a letter to Secretary of War Eustis, Hawkins reported that Maumouth had been "put to death on the 19th." *ASP: IA*, 1: 809, 812; Gary Burton, "Pintlala's Cold Murder Case: The Death of Thomas Meredith in 1812," *Alabama Review* 63 (July 2010): 164–66, 169, 178–79, 186–87, 189.

[26] Captain Reuben Chamberlain started construction on Fort Bowyer

but a majority refused to appear, and continued to give countenance to the prophets. He dispatched a runner to the Alabamas, with this talk: "You are but a few Alabama people. You say that the Great Spirit visits you frequently; that he comes in the sun, and speaks to you; that the sun comes down just above your heads. Now we want to see and hear what you have seen and heard. Let us have the same proof, then we will believe. You have nothing to fear—the people who did the killing upon the Ohio are put to death, and the law is satisfied." The messenger was seized, killed, and scalped, at the junction of the Coosa and Tallapoosa, where a portion of the war party were engaged in "the dance of the lakes." They then paddled down to Coosawda, pursued Captain Isaacs into the cane, across the river, and, being unable to find him,[30] returned, burnt up his houses, destroyed his stock and murdered two of his chief warriors.*

The Indians also commenced hostilities upon the Americans. Between Burnt Corn and the Escambia, Greggs, an American mail rider, was seized, most severely beaten, and left upon the Federal Road, after being robbed of his mail bags and horse. Without anything to eat, save the berries in the woods, the lacerated youth, after wandering ten days through the forests, reached Montgomery Hill. The mail was carried to Pensacola, and rifled of its contents, in a Spanish trading house.† General Wilkinson, with his lady, had reached Sam Moniac's, near the Catoma, with an escort, which had attended him from Mims's Ferry. He wrote back to Judge Toulmin, informing him of the dangers attendant upon a trip through the Creek Nation, but that he was resolved to go on to Georgia.[31] In a short time, Moniac, who, for some time, lived, upon the Federal Road, for the

* *American State Papers: Indian Affairs*, 1: 846.

† Conversations with Mr. George S. Gaines, of Mobile, and Dr. Thomas G. Holmes, of Baldwin County.

shortly after the surrender of Mobile in April 1813. In June 1813, General Thomas Flournoy ordered Colonel John Bowyer to complete the construction of the semicircular earthen and log redoubt at Mobile Point at the entrance of Mobile Bay in Baldwin County, Alabama. Flournoy abandoned the fort in July 1814, but it was reoccupied by Major William Lawrence in August 1814 under orders from Andrew Jackson. David S. Heidler and Jeanne T. Heidler, eds., *Encyclopedia of the War of 1812* (Santa Monica: ABC-CLIO, 1997), 59–60.

27 According to George Strother Gaines, Ocheoce (Oceoche) Emathla, chief of the town at the falls of the Black Warrior, came to the Choctaw Trading House in the fall of 1811 "with a fleet of large canoes and thirty or forty warriors bringing a cargo of peltries." He told Gaines that he needed supplies for his store and wanted $1,000 in debt until his next trip. Tandy Walker warned Gaines that the Black Warrior Creeks were about to ally with the British, and the next day Gaines limited Ocheoce (Oceoche) Emathla to an additional $100 in debt. Gaines, *Reminiscences*, 50–52, 131–33.

28 After Tecumseh's tour of the Creek Nation, Peter McQueen (c. 1780–1820), a métis Creek warrior of Tallase, became one of the many prophets that emerged in the Upper Creek towns, including Josiah Francis and High-Head Jim. McQueen took a leadership role in the Creek civil war and arming the Red Sticks. *ASP: IA*, 1: 846, 848, 849, 851; Sugden, *Tecumseh*, 247, 352; Green, *Politics of Indian Removal*, 41–42.

29 Hopoithle Mico, a prominent headman of Tallase, signed the 1790 Treaty of New York, opposed the Federal Road, and became a Red Stick leader among the Upper Creeks. Kappler, *Indian Affairs: Laws and Treaties*, 2: 28; Hudson, *Creek Paths and Federal Roads*, 85, 110; Martin, *Sacred Revolt*, 131, 135.

30 By June 1813, the Creek Nation was engaged in a full-blown civil war between the forces that opposed the civilization program pushed by Hawkins and the pro-American headmen. The Red Stick prophets—Josiah Francis, Peter McQueen, Paddy Walsh (Welch), and others—had gained control over twenty-nine Upper Creek towns by late July and threatened to eliminate Big Warrior (Tustenuggee Thlucco) and his supporters. *ASP: IA*, 1: 845–52.

purpose of accommodating travelers, was driven off, some of his Negroes stolen, while his cattle were driven to 'Pensacola for sale.[32] Other half-breeds, suspected of friendship for the Americans, were treated in the same manner. Remaining concealed for some time, upon his island in the Alabama, Moniac ventured to visit his place upon the road.

Here he suddenly encountered High-Head Jim, one of the prophets of Autossee, who, after shaking him by the hands, began to tremble all over, and to jerk, in every part of his frame, convulsing the calves of the legs, and, from the severe agitation, getting entirely out of breath. This practice had been introduced by the prophet Josiah Francis, the brother-in-law of Moniac, who said he was so instructed by the Great Spirit. Wishing to make terms for the moment, Moniac pretended that he was sorry for his former friendship for the whites, and avowed his determination to join the hostiles. High-Head Jim, led away by his artifice, disclosed to him all their plans; that they were soon to kill the Big Warrior, Captain Isaacs, William McIntosh, the Mad Dragon's Son, the Little Prince, Spoko Hauge, and Tallassee Fixico, all prominent chiefs of the nation; that, after the death of these traitors, the Creeks were to unite, in a common cause, against the Americans; those upon the Coosa, Tallapoosa and Black Warrior were to attack the settlements upon the Tensaw and Tombigbee; those near the Cherokees, with the assistance of the latter, were to attack the Tennesseans; the Georgians were to fall by the fierce sallies of the Lower Creeks and Seminoles; while the Choctaws were to exterminate the Mississippi population.[33]

The most extravagant delusions prevailed upon the Coosa, at this period. Nearly all these people moved out of their towns, into the woods, dancing and preparing for war. Letecau, a prophet, of eighteen years of age, a native of the town of Aubecooche, went, with eighteen subordinate prophets, to the old Coosa town, from whence they sent out runners, inviting all the unbelievers to come and witness their magical powers. A large assembly, of both sexes, congregated upon the banks of the river, and surrounded the prophets. Letecau, with his wand, drew a circle in front, and he and his subordinates began "the dance of the lakes." After powerful exertions, for some time, the war whoop was given by Letacau, who fell, with his men, upon three chiefs, whom they killed.[34] The other

[31] According to a deposition given by James Cornells on 3 August 1813, General Wilkinson was stopped on the Federal Road "by enemies of Big Warrior" who declared they were enemies of the U.S. and asked when Wilkinson "would be ready to fight them." Hudson, *Creek Paths and Federal Roads*, 205 n. 92.

[32] Moniac operated a stand on the Federal Road and owned a plantation and other property. While driving cattle to sell in Pensacola, Josiah Francis, his brother-in-law, his sister, Hannah Francis, his brother, John, his son, Sam, and others destroyed Moniac's livestock and burned all his buildings. He later sought reimbursement for the losses caused by the Red Sticks, which included 700 cattle, 200 hogs, 48 goats and sheep, a cotton gin, 2,000 pounds of cotton, 36 slaves, and several houses. The U.S. government reimbursed him $12,597.25 for his losses. Ibid., 106; Saunt, *New Order of Things*, 260, 260 n. 59; Waselkov, *Conquering Spirit*, 300 n. 48.

[33] Although Pickett does not acknowledge his source, he appears to be paraphrasing a deposition given by Samuel Moniac on 2 August 1813 which is quoted by Henry S. Halbert and Timothy H. Ball in their history of the Creek War of 1813–1814. Hudson, *Creek Paths and Federal Roads*, 106; Waselkov, *Conquering Spirit*, 83, 97–98. See Henry S. Halbert and Timothy H. Ball, *The Creek War of 1813 and 1814*, ed. Frank L. Owsley Jr. (1895; reprint, Tuscaloosa: University of Alabama Press, 1969), 91–93.

[34] While Hawkins reported in a letter of 28 July 1813 to the Secretary of War that Letecau's followers killed three chiefs and wounded a fourth, other sources put the total killed at nine. In some of his

friendly chiefs sprang into the river, made their escape to their towns, and, assembling their warriors, returned, and killed Letecau and his prophets. They proceeded to Little Okfuskee, where Tecumseh's talk had been taken, and there put a number of his deluded followers to death.[35]

The hostiles destroyed the stock of the friendly Indians, at the Hillabee towns, several of whom they killed. They carried off seventy Negroes, belonging to Robert Graison, and committed many other depredations.[36] The town of Kialegee was burned down, and several of the inhabitants shot. These things overwhelmed the Big Warrior with fear, and he entreated Hawkins to relieve him with the federal troops. He had collected a large supply of corn at Tuckabatchee, where he built a fort. Hawkins prevailed upon two hundred warriors, of Coweta and Cusseta, to march to Tuckabatchee, where they soon arrived, and, after some annoyance, from the attacks of a few of the war party, succeeded in carrying off the Big Warrior, and those who adhered to him, in safety, over to the Chattahoochee.*

later correspondence with the secretary of war, Hawkins refers to the militant Upper Creeks as "Red Clubs," but he generally identifies this faction as Red Sticks. *ASP: IA*, 1: 849–50; Sugden, *Tecumseh*, 351; Alfred A. Cave, *Prophets of the Great Spirit: Native American Revitalization Movements in Eastern North America* (Lincoln: University of Nebraska, 2006), 169–70.

[35] The headmen who escaped the attack by Letecau and his followers returned with a war party, killing and scalping Letecau and seven of his companions. The attack on the Red Sticks at Little Okfuskee was made to avenge the killing of five pro-American chiefs by Letecau's followers. *ASP: IA*, 1: 850; Sugden, *Tecumseh*, 351; Cave, *Prophets of the Great Spirit*, 170.

[36] Robert Grierson's (Graison's) daughter-in-law had been invited to Okfuskee to teach the women to spin and weave, where the Red Sticks destroyed "much of her stock, her loom, and web of cloth." At Hillabee, where she had lived for twelve-years, Red Sticks took all her clothing, "except for the shift and petticoat on her back, and all her cattle and hogs." *ASP: IA*, 1: 850.

* Upon the civil war among the Creeks, see *American State Papers: Indian Affairs*, 1: 849–51.

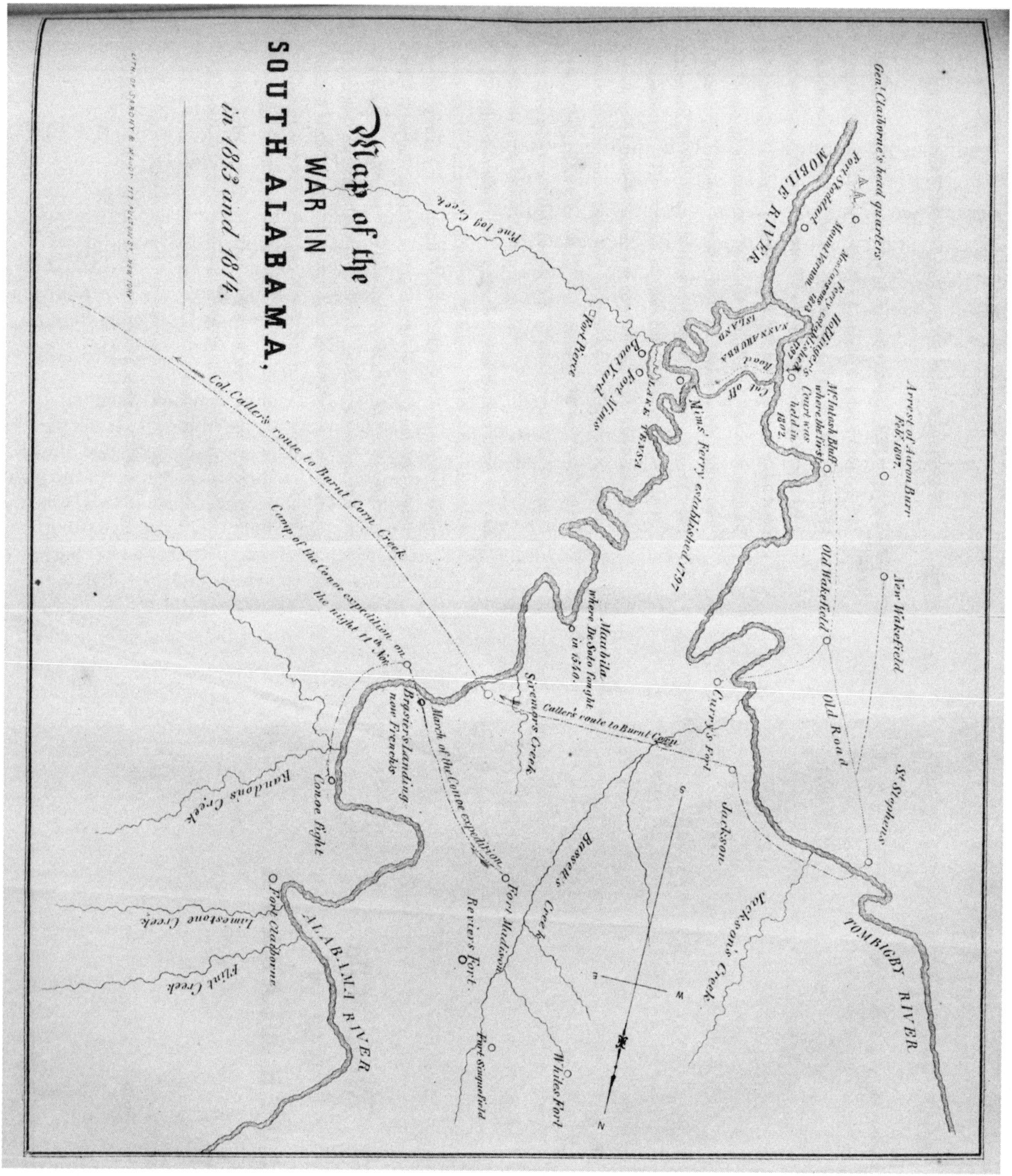
Map of the
WAR IN
SOUTH ALABAMA,
in 1813 and 1814.
Gen. Claiborne's head quarters
Fort Stoddart
Mount Vernon
MOBILE RIVER
Pine log Creek
Fort Pierce
Boat Yard
Fort Mims
NANNAHUBBA ISLAND
Road
Cut off
Mims' Ferry established 1797
McIntosh Bluff where the first Court was held in 1802
Arrest of Aaron Burr Feb. 1807.
Old Wakefield
New Wakefield
Old Road
St. Stephens
TOMBIGBY RIVER
Jackson
Jackson's Creek
Curry's Fort
Caller's route to Burnt Corn
Sizemore's Creek
Mauvila where De Soto fought in 1540
Col. Caller's route to Burnt Corn Creek
Camp of the Canoe expedition on the night 11 Nov.
Braziers Landing now Frenchs
March of the Canoe expedition
Randon's Creek
Canoe Fight
Fort Claiborne
Limestone Creek
Flint Creek
ALABAMA RIVER
Fort Madison
Reviers Fort
Bassett's Creek
Fort Sinquefield
Whites Fort

Chapter XXXII

Battle of Burnt Corn—
Arrival of General Claiborne's Army

Peter McQueen, at the head of the Tallassee warriors, High Head Jim, with the Autaugas, and Josiah Francis, with the Alabamas, numbering, in all, three hundred and fifty, departed for Pensacola, with many pack-horses.[1] On their way, they beat and drove off all the Indians who would not take the war talk. The brutal McQueen beat an unoffending white trader within an inch of his life, and carried the wife of Cornells, the government interpreter, a prisoner, to Pensacola.[2] The village of Hatchechubba was reduced to ashes.[3]

The inhabitants of the Tombigbee and the Tensaw had constantly petitioned the governor for an army to repel the Creeks, whose attacks they hourly expected. But General Flournoy, who had succeeded Wilkinson in command, refused to send any of the regular or volunteer troops.[4] The British fleet was seen off the coast, from which supplies, arms, ammunition, and Indian emissaries were sent to Pensacola and other Spanish ports in Florida.[5] Everything foreboded the extermination of the Americans in Alabama, who were the most isolated and defenseless people imaginable. Determined, however, to protect themselves, to the best of their means and abilities, they first sent spies to Pensacola, to watch the movements of the Indians there, under McQueen, who returned with the report that the British agents were distributing to them ample munitions of war.[6] Colonel James Caller ordered out the militia, some of whom soon rallied to his standard in the character of minute volunteers. He marched across the Tombigbee, passed through the town of Jackson, and by the new fort, upon the eastern line of Clarke, and from thence to Sizemore's Ferry, upon the Alabama, where, on the western bank, he bivouacked for the night. The object of the expedition was to attack the Indians as they were returning from Pensacola.[7]

The next morning, Caller began the crossing of the river, to the east side, which was effected by swimming the horses by the side of the canoes. It

1 The Creek Red Stick leaders received an invitation from West Florida Governor Mauricio Zuñiga to visit Pensacola, but Don Mateo González Manrique had replaced Zuñiga before McQueen's party arrived in July 1813. Owsley, *Struggle for the Gulf*, 24–26.

2 On their way to Pensacola, McQueen's party raided James Cornells's property near Burnt Corn Springs, taking his wife Betsy Coulter as a captive. A smaller party burned Samuel Moniac's plantation on the Little River and destroyed a house belonging to Leonard McGee. All three métis Creeks were punished because of their attachment to the "white people." Woodward and others report that the Red Sticks sold Betsy Coulter in Pensacola "to a French lady, a madame Barrone." *ASP: IA*, 1: 850, 851; Woodward, *Reminiscences*, 85; Waselkov, *Conquering Spirit*, 97–99; Saunt, *New Order of Things*, 259–62.

[3] In early July 1813, the Upper Creek town of Kialijee and its satellite village Hatchechubba were destroyed by part of McQueen's force, which killed several people and destroyed all their livestock. *ASP: IA*, 1: 849–50; Martin, *Sacred Revolt*, 135.

[4] In March 1813, Brigadier General Thomas Flournoy (1775–1857) replaced James Wilkinson as commander of the Seventh Military District with its headquarters in New Orleans. While Flournoy was slow to recognize the threat presented by the Red Sticks, the Creek Nation was located in two military districts and Secretary of War John Armstrong had given Major General Thomas Pinckney, commander of the Sixth Military District headquartered in Charleston, overall command of the armies. With the British blockade in the Gulf, communication between the two commands was slow and difficult. Owsley, *Struggle for the Gulf*, 45; Heidler and Heidler, *War of 1812*, 191–92.

[5] Contrary to Pickett's narrative, the first British contact with the Creeks was with a party from the Lower Creek towns—not affiliated with the Red Sticks—at Pensacola in September 1813. No high ranking British official aided the Creek militants until early January 1814. Moreover, the first British assault against Mobile did not occur until 12–15 September 1814, when an attack was repulsed by 158 men at Fort Bowyer at Mobile Point. Owsley, *Struggle for the Gulf*, 27–29, 109–12; Heidler and Heidler, *War of 1812*, 357–58.

[6] The commander at Fort Stoddert had sent David Tait (Tate), a métis Creek, and William Pierce from the Tensaw to Pensacola to gather information about the negotiations between the Red Sticks and the Spaniards. A third potential spy, Zachariah McGirth, may have simply arrived at Pensacola by happenstance. Whatever intelligence they gathered, there is no evidence of British agents providing supplies to the Red Sticks. In fact, John Innerarity, manager of the John Forbes store in Pensacola, was opposed to an Indian war and refused to provide supplies to McQueen's party. *ASP: IA*, 1: 854; Owsley, *Struggle for the Gulf*, 26–27; Waselkov, *Conquering Spirit*, 99–100.

[7] As the senior militia commander in Washington County, Colonel James Caller called out a militia force that included six small companies—about 180 men from the Tombigbee, Tensaw, and Little River settlements. Owsley, *Struggle for the Gulf*, 30; Waselkov, *Conquering Spirit*, 100.

[8] Captain Dixon Bailey, a prominent métis Creek, commanded a small company made up of 30 Tensaw and Little River métis Creeks. In notes furnished to Pickett, Patrick May commented that Bailey "was a man of intelligence and noble bearing and of unsurpassed chivalry . . . & displayed undaunted bravery." Waselkov, *Conquering Spirit*, 100, 337 n. 32.

[9] Wolf Trail, or Pensacola Trading Path, ran north out of Pensacola, across Burnt Corn Creek and intersected with the Federal Road at Burnt Corn Springs near James Cornells's plantation and cow pens. Waselkov, *Conquering Spirit*, 100, 282 n. 15; Halbert and Ball, *Creek War*, 130; Raven Christopher, Gregory Waselkov, and Tara Potts, *Archaeological Testing along the Federal Road: Exploring the Site of "Manack's Store," Montgomery County, Alabama* (Mobile: Center for Archaeological Studies, University of South Alabama, 2011), 8.

[10] On the morning of 27 July 1813, McQueen's party appears to have been spread out into two or three groups: one tending to the pack-horses near the creek, another group of about sixty, and perhaps a third of 20–30. Most were involved in eating or preparing food when Caller's force unexpectedly struck them, killing a Creek woman and a Negro man and causing the Indians to retreat. High-Head Jim, the party's war chief, later claimed "he did not start with a hundred men" and not all of them were in the fight. Owsley, *Struggle for the Gulf*, 31; Stiggins, *Creek Indian History*, 100, 102; Woodward, *Reminiscences*, 85.

occupied much of the early part of the day. When all were over, the march was resumed, in a southeastern direction, to the cow pens of David Tait, where a halt was made. Here Caller was reinforced by a company from Tensaw Lake and Little River, under the command of Dixon Bailey, a half-breed Creek, a native of the town of Autossee, who had been educated at Philadelphia under the provisions of the Treaty of New York, of 1790. Bailey was a man of fine appearance, unimpeachable integrity, and a strong mind. His courage and energy were not surpassed by those of any other man.[8] The whole expedition under Caller now consisted of one hundred and eighty men, in small companies. Two of these were from St. Stephens, one of which was commanded by Captain Bailey Heard, and the other by Captain Benjamin Smoot and Lieutenant Patrick May. A company, from the county of Washington, was commanded by Captain David Cartwright. In passing through Clarke County, Caller had been reinforced by a company under Captain Samuel Dale and Lieutenant Gerard W. Creagh. Some men had also joined him, commanded by William McGrew, Robert Caller, and William Bradberry. The troops of the little party were mounted upon good frontier horses, and provided with rifles and shotguns, of various sizes and descriptions. Leaving the cow pens, Caller marched until he reached the Wolf Trail, where he bivouacked for the last night. The main route to Pensacola was now before them.[9]

In the morning the command was reorganized, by the election of Zachariah Philips, McFarlin, Wood and Jourdan, to the rank of major, and William McGrew lieutenant-colonel. This unusual number of field officers was made to satisfy military aspirations. While on the march, the spy company returned rapidly, about 11 o'clock in the forenoon, and reported that McQueen's party were encamped a few miles in advance, and were engaged in cooking and eating. A consultation of officers terminated in the decision to attack the Indians by surprise. The command was thrown into three divisions—Captain Smoot in front of the right, Captain Bailey in front of the center, and Captain Dale in front of the left. The Indians occupied a peninsula of low pine barren, formed by the windings of Burnt Corn Creek. Some gently rising heights overlooked this tongue of land, down which Caller charged upon them. Although taken by surprise, the Indians repelled the assault for a few minutes, and then gave way, retreating to the creek.[10] A portion of the Americans bravely pursued them to the water, while others remained behind, engaged in the less laudable enterprise of capturing the Indian pack-horses. Caller acted with bravery, but, unfortunately, ordered a retreat to the high lands, where he intended to take a strong position. Seeing those in advance retreating from the swamp, about one hundred of the command, who had been occupied, as we have stated, in securing Indian effects, now precipitately fled, in great confusion and terror, but, in the midst of their dismay, *held on to the plunder*, driving the horses before them.[11]

Colonel Caller, Captain Bailey and other officers, endeavored to rally them, in vain. The Indians rushed forth from the swamp, with exulting yells, and attacked about eighty Americans, who remained at the foot of the hill. A severe fight ensued, and the whites, now commanded by Captains Dale, Bailey and Smoot, fought with laudable courage, exposed to a galling fire, in open woods, while McQueen and his warriors were protected by thick reeds. The latter, however, discharged their pieces very unskillfully.[12] Captain Dale received a large ball in the breast, which, glancing around a rib, came out at his back. He continued to fight as long as the battle lasted. At length, abandoned by two-thirds of the command, while the enemy had the advantage of position, the Americans resolved to retreat, which they did in great disorder. Many had lost their horses, for they had dismounted when the attack was made, and now ran in all directions, to secure them or get up behind others. Many actually ran off on foot.[13]

After all these had left the field, three young men were found, still fighting by themselves, on one side of the peninsula, and keeping at bay some savages, who were concealed in the cane. They were Lieutenant Patrick May, of North Carolina, now of Greene County, Alabama, a descendant of a brave Revolutionary family; a private, named Ambrose Miles; and Lieutenant Gerard W. Creagh, of South Carolina. A warrior presented his tall form. May and the savage discharged their guns at each other. The Indian fell dead in the cane; his fire, however, had shattered the lieutenant's piece, near the lock. Resolving also to retreat, these intrepid young men made a rush for their horses, when Creagh, brought to the ground by the effects of a wound which he received in the hip, cried out, "Save me, lieutenant, or I am gone!" May instantly raised him up, bore him off on his back, and placed him in his saddle, while Miles held the bridle

[11] When most of the startled Red Sticks fled their encampment following the first volley and charge, Caller's men apparently thought the fight was over, and most of his men began to secure the pack-horses and their loads, which included barrels of flour and corn, blankets, knives, gunpowder and shot, and four or five steers. High-Head Jim rallied his followers, who fired a few shots from cover, causing the militia to run from the encounter. Woodward, *Reminiscences*, 85; Waselkov, *Conquering Spirit*, 100; Halbert and Ball, *Creek War*, 134–35.

[12] Pickett seems to have forgotten that Caller's men were fighting Creek Red Sticks committed to old life ways. He continues to romanticize the role of the American militiamen and to denigrate the fighting ability of their Creek adversaries. According to George Stiggins, there were only sixty Red Sticks engaged in the fighting, and they were only armed with thirteen guns, bows and arrows, and hatchets and war clubs. Stiggins, *Creek Indian History*, 100; Woodward, *Reminiscences*, 84–85.

[13] According to Halbert and Ball, who inspected the battle site in the late nineteenth century, Caller's force had the advantage of position from a range of small hills that looked down on an acre of level ground occupied by the larger Red Stick contingent when the attack started. Samuel Dale recovered from his wound at Fort Madison in modern Clarke County, Alabama. Halbert and Ball, *Creek War*, 131–32; Herbert J. Lewis, "Samuel Dale," *Encyclopedia of Alabama* (online).

[14] Lieutenant Gerard W. Creagh suffered a wound at Burnt Corn Creek, but he continued his service in the Creek War, witnessing Dale's "Canoe Fight" and participating in the capture of Ecunchate. He later represented Clarke County in both houses of the Alabama legislature. Lieutenant Patrick May carried the wounded Creagh from the battle site and moved to Greene County, becoming its first state senator after it was established. Both men shared their "Notes" with Albert James Pickett. Brewer, *History of Alabama*, 179, 260; Waselkov, *Conquering Spirit*, 304 n. 12, 305 n. 14, 337 n. 32.

[15] While Pickett gives David Glass credit for firing the last shot for the Americans, Lieutenant

reins. A rapid retreat saved their lives.[14] Reaching the top of the hill, they saw Lieutenant Bradberry, a young lawyer of North Carolina, bleeding with his wounds, and endeavoring to rally some of his men. The Indians, reaching the body of poor Ballard, took off his scalp, in full view, which so incensed his friend, Glass, that he advanced and fired the last gun upon them.[15]

The retreat was continued all night, in the most irregular manner, and the trail was lined, from one end to the other, with small squads, and sometimes one man by himself. The wounded traveled slowly, and often stopped to rest. It was afterwards ascertained that only two Americans were killed and fifteen wounded. Such was the Battle of Burnt Corn, the first that was fought in the long and bloody Creek War. The Indians retraced their steps to Pensacola, for more military supplies. Their number of killed is unknown.[16] Caller's command never got together again, but mustered themselves out of service, returning to their homes by various routes. After many amusing adventures. Colonel Caller and Major Wood became lost, and wandered on foot in the forest, causing great uneasiness to their friends. When General Claiborne arrived in the country, he wrote to Bailey, Tait and Moniac, respectable half-breeds, urging them to hunt for these unfortunate men. They were afterwards found, starved almost to death, and bereft of their senses.[17] They had been missing fifteen days.*

General Ferdinand Leigh Claiborne, the brother of the ex-governor of the Mississippi Territory, was born in Sussex County, Virginia, of a family distinguished in that commonwealth, from the time of Charles I. On the 21st November 1793, in his twentieth year, he was appointed an ensign in Wayne's army, on the northwestern frontier. He was in the great battle in which

* Conversations with Dr. Thomas G. Holmes, of Baldwin County, Alabama, the late Colonel Gerard W. Creagh, of Clarke, and General Patrick May, of Greene, who were in the Burnt Corn expedition.

William Bradberry survived his wound at Burnt Corn Creek only to be severely wounded in the skirmish at Bashi Creek on 4 October 1813. He was brought back to St. Stephens, where he died. Halbert and Ball, *Creek War*, 219–21; Gaines, *Reminiscences*, 64, 185 n. 67.

[16] Several sources give different numbers regarding the killed and wounded on both sides. Pickett's sources led him to conclude the Americans suffered 2 killed—Ballard and Elijah Glass—and 15 wounded, including Dale, Creagh, Armstrong, William Bradberry, Jack Henry, Robert Lewis, Alexander Hollinger, William Baldwin, and seven others. The Red Sticks suffered 2 killed and 5 wounded. Stiggins reports that the "white people lost five killed and as many wounded. The Indians lost two and a Negro killed and five wounded." Creagh remembered the Americans losing "two killed and 18 to 20 wounded" and the Red Sticks lost "some 20 killed and a good many wounded." Stiggins, *Creek Indian History*, 101; Halbert and Ball, *Creek War*, 139; Owsley, *Struggle for the Gulf*, 31; Waselkov, *Conquering Spirit*, 100, 304 n. 12.

[17] When the Red Sticks under High-Head Jim counterattacked at Burnt Corn Creek, the American militiamen and their leaders panicked, became disoriented, and dispersed over a wide area. Caller and other militia leaders were ridiculed for their actions in the engagement where most agreed that they had the upper hand, with the element of surprise and superior weaponry. Caller's reputation suffered from the defeat and his wandering lost for more than two weeks simply added to the criticisms heaped on him, Wood, and others. Halbert and Ball, *Creek War*, 140–42; Owsley, *Struggle for the Gulf*, 31–32.

that able commander soon after defeated the Indians, and, for his good conduct, was promoted to a lieutenancy. At the close of the war, he was stationed at Richmond and Norfolk, in the recruiting service, and, subsequently, was ordered to Pittsburg, Forts Washington, Greenville and Detroit, where he remained, with the rank of captain and acting adjutant-general until 1805, when he resigned, and removed to Natchez. He was soon afterwards a member of the territorial legislature, and presided over its deliberations. We have already seen how active he was in arresting Aaron Burr, upon the Mississippi River, at the head of infantry and cavalry. On the 8th March 1813, Colonel Claiborne was appointed brigadier-general of volunteers, and was ordered, by General Wilkinson, to take command of the post of Baton Rouge. In the latter part of July, he was ordered, by General Flournoy, to march, with his whole command, to Fort Stoddert, and instructed to direct his principal attention to "*the defense of Mobile.*"[18]

On the 30th July, General Claiborne reached Mount Vernon, near the Mobile River, with the rearguard of his army, consisting of seven hundred men, whom he had chiefly sustained by supplies raised by mortgages upon his own estate.* The quartermaster at Baton Rouge had only provided him with the small sum of two hundred dollars. He obtained, from the most reliable characters upon the eastern frontier, accurate information, in regard to the threatened invasion of the Indians, an account of the unfortunate result of the Burnt Corn expedition, and a written opinion of Judge Toulmin, respecting the critical condition of the country generally. It was found that alarm pervaded the populace. Rumors of the advance of the Indians were rife, and were believed. In Clarke County—in the fork of the rivers—a chain of

* Upon the conclusion of the Creek War, General Claiborne returned to Soldier's Retreat, his home, near Natchez, shattered in constitution, from the exposure and hardships of the campaigns, and died suddenly, at the close of 1815. The vouchers, for the liberal expenditures which he made, were lost, and his *property was sold.*

[18] In a letter of 14 August 1813 to Benjamin Hawkins, Claiborne acknowledged that he had requested additional troops from Major General Flournoy "under whose orders I act, but I hope to strike at the heart of the Creek nation." Claiborne also urged Flournoy to call out the militia in the Mississippi Territory to defend the countryside, but Flournoy responded that he had not been authorized to use the militia forces. Claiborne, *Mississippi*, 334–35.

[19] Joseph Carney built Fort Carney at Gullett's Bluff, located six miles south of modern Jackson, Alabama. Easley's Station or Fort Easley was located at what became known as Wood's Bluff. Halbert and Ball, *Creek War*, 112, 114; Waselkov, *Conquering Spirit*, 103.

[20] Lavier's Fort was built by Captain Lawson Lavier and his neighbors. Zachariah Glass and his neighbors built Fort Glass. Fort Sinquefield was located on Sam Sinquefield's land on Bassett's Creek some five miles southeast of modern Grove Hill. Fort White, a small stockade, was located northeast of Grove Hill. Halbert and Ball, *Creek War*, 108, 109, 111, 112, 115; Waselkov, *Conquering Spirit*, 103.

[21] General Claiborne was so efficient at distributing his militia forces that he had no reserve forces. He requested reinforcements from Major General Thomas Flournoy, but Flournoy had no reserve forces and told him to assume a defensive posture, sending him additional equipment and armaments. Owsley, *Struggle for the Gulf*, 34; Waselkov, *Conquering Spirit*, 102–05.

[22] Although Pickett places Colonel Joseph Carson at Fort Glass in August 1813, he led the advance troops of General Claiborne's army to Fort Stoddert in July 1813, where he learned of the dire situation facing the outlying settlements. Carson dispatched Lieutenant Spruce McKay Osborne and sixteen volunteers to aid Samuel Mims and the families gathered there in constructing a stockade for their protection and safety. Waselkov, *Conquering Spirit*, 104, 106.

[23] After his service with the Mississippi volunteers, Captain Abram M. Scott served as a delegate from Wilkinson County to the 1817 Mississippi constitutional convention. He also

rude defenses had hastily been constructed by the citizens, and were filled, to overflowing, with white people and Negroes. One of these was at Gullett's Bluff, upon the Tombigbee, another at Easley's Station,[19] and the others at the residences of Sinquefield, Glass, White and Lavier.[20] They were all called forts. Two block-houses were also in a state of completion, at St. Stephens.

The first step taken by Claiborne was the distribution of his troops, so as to afford the greatest protection to the inhabitants.[21] He dispatched Colonel Carson, with two hundred men, to the fork, who arrived at Fort Glass without accident.[22] A few hundred yards from that rude structure, he began the construction of Fort Madison. He sent Captain Scott to St. Stephens, with a company, which immediately occupied the old Spanish block-house.[23] He employed Major Hinds, with the mounted dragoons, in scouring the country, while he distributed some of the militia of Washington County for the defense of the stockades.[24] Captain Dent was dispatched to Oaktupa,[25] where he assumed the command of a fort, with two block-houses, within a mile of the Choctaw line.*

served as lieutenant governor (1828–1832) and governor of Mississippi (1832–1833). Claiborne, *Mississippi*, 329, 352, 357, 395.

[24] Major Thomas Hinds and his dragoons were not happy with their assignment for frontier defense and as scouts, and Hinds wrote to Flournoy expressing their desire for military action against the Creeks. Flournoy considered their conduct "injudicious and unmilitary," ordering their release from service for insubordination and that they return to Governor David Holmes. Ibid., 327; Waselkov, *Conquering Spirit*, 151–52, 161.

[25] Captain Benjamin Dent, like Major Thomas Hinds, was part of the Regiment of Mississippi Territory Volunteers who were federalized under generals Claiborne and Flournoy. Dent was one of twenty-six officers who signed a statement in December 1813 opposing a winter offensive against the Red Sticks because their men were not properly equipped and their term of service had expired. However, when Claiborne ordered the troops to take to the field, Dent, his fellow officers, and the rank and file responded. Claiborne, *Mississippi*, 328–29.

* MS papers of General F. L. Claiborne.

Chapter XXXIII

TERRIBLE MASSACRE AT FORT MIMS

In the meantime, the wealthy half-bloods about Little River had dropped down the Alabama, in their boats, and had secreted themselves in the swamp about Lake Tensaw. Uniting with the whites, they soon began the construction of a fort around the residence of Samuel Mims, a wealthy Indian countryman, to whom we have often alluded, and who, originally, was one of the pack-horsemen of the Honorable George Galphin.[1]

Being about to relate a horrible affair, in which people of all ages and both sexes were subjected to savage butchery, a particular description of the place where it occurred is deemed necessary. Mims lived within four hundred yards of the Boat Yard, upon Lake Tensaw, a mile east of the Alabama River, and two miles below the Cut-Off. His house was a large frame building, of one story, with spacious shed-rooms. Around it pickets were driven, between which fence rails were placed. Five hundred port-holes were made, three and a half feet only from the ground. The stockading enclosed an acre of ground, in a square form, and was entered by two ponderous but rude gates, one on the east and the other on the west.[2] Within the enclosure, besides the main building, were various out-houses, rows of bee-gums, together with cabins and board shelters, recently erected by the settlers, wherever a vacant spot appeared. At the southwest corner a block-house was begun, but never finished. This defense was situated on a very slight elevation. A large potato field lay adjoining, on the south, in which were a row of Negro houses. Woods intervened between the picketing and the lake, while, in a northern direction, cane swamps, which grew denser as they approached the river, were hard by. On the east, the flat lands continued for several miles, interspersed with cane marshes and some ravines.[3] It was, altogether, a most ill-chosen place for a fort, as it ultimately proved.*

* Conversations with Dr. Thomas G. Holmes, of Baldwin.

[1] Samuel Mims (1742–1813) married Hannah Rains in Mobile on 23 January 1788; both were of English descent and residents of the Tensaw District of Spanish West Florida. According to Mobile baptismal records, they had six children, and they occupied a Spanish land grant on the Tensaw confirmed by the U.S. Congress. He was a prominent land owner and one of the largest slave owners east of the Pearl River in the Mississippi Territory. While many sources refer to Mims as an Indian countryman, it appears that is based on a relationship that predated his marriage to Hannah. Waselkov, *Conquering Spirit*, 20–21, 186, 277 n. 16, 278 n. 18, 278 n. 20; *ASP: PL*, 2: 87, 554–55, 575, 578–89, 591–92, 745–47, 763, 766.

[2] Recent research and archaeological investigations at the Fort Mims site by Gregory A. Waselkov question Pickett's

DRAWING OF FORT MIMS,

Found among Gen. Claiborne's manuscript papers.

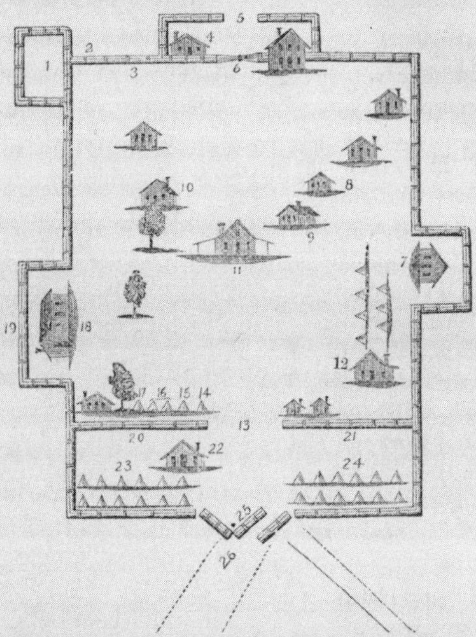

REFERENCES.

1 Block House.
2 Pickets cut away by the Indians.
3 Guard's Station.
4 Guard House.
5 Western Gate, but not up.
6 This Gate was shut, but a hole was cut through by the Indians.
7 Captain Bailey's Station.
8 Steadham's House.
9 Mrs. Dyer's House.
10 Kitchen.
11 Mims' House.
12 Randon's House.
13 Old Gate-way—open.
14 Ensign Chambliss' Tent.
15 Ensign Gibbs'.
16 Randon's.
17 Captain Middleton's.
18 Captain Jack's Station.
19 Port-holes taken by Indians.
20 21 Port-holes taken by Indians.
22 Major Beasley's Cabin.
23 Captain Jack's Company.
24 Captain Middleton's Company.
25 Where Major Beasley fell.
26 Eastern Gate, where the Indians entered.

description of the stockade walls of the fort—"pickets driven, between which fence rails were placed." The "pickets" at Fort Mims followed typical fort construction that featured upright side-by-side logs or split-posts, which were generally placed in trenches for greater strength. Pickett's five hundred port-holes also appear to be misleading for a fort with a perimeter of approximately 1,100 feet. Waselkov, *Conquering Spirit*, 120–21, 312 n. 14.

[3] The plantation that became Fort Mims was one of the most impressive and largest in the Tensaw District. In 1815, Joseph Mims filed a compensation claim seeking federal reimbursement for the estate of Samuel Mims with a total value of $7,220, which included ten buildings and other property. Ibid., 117.

[4] Major Daniel Beasley, a lawyer, former sheriff, and legislator from Jefferson County, Mississippi Territory, was appointed to the territorial volunteers on the request of General Claiborne. Beasley and his soldiers of the 1st Mississippi Regiment marched up from Mount Vernon Cantonment and arrived at Fort Mims on 3 August 1813. Lieutenant Spruce Osborne and his detachment were continuing their work to strengthen the fort's defenses. Ibid., 63, 106, 291 n. 24; James F. Doster, ed., "Letters Relating to the Tragedy of Fort Mims: August-September 1813," *Alabama Review* 14 (October 1961): 269–70.

[5] Captains William Jack (1786–1813) and Hatton Clark Middleton (1784–1813) were company commanders who were killed at Fort Mims on 30 August 1813. Pickett's "Batchelor" does not appear in more recent studies, but there was a Captain Samuel Batchelder in Lieutenant Colonel George H. Nixon's 13th Mississippi Regiment. Rowland, *Mississippi Territory in the War of 1812*, 38, 39, 48, 90, 165; Claiborne, *Mississippi*, 320, 324; Waselkov, *Conquering Spirit*, 107.

[6] Thomas Dunn, a métis Creek, resigned as an ensign in the Tensaw militia in August 1813. Plummer, a member of the Tensaw militia, was accused of cowardice at Burnt Corn Creek on 27 July and resigned as an ensign in August 1813. Both died at Fort Mims. Waselkov, *Conquering Spirit*, 227, 234, 249, 339 n. 60; Doster, "Letters Relating to the Tragedy of Fort Mims," 271.

[7] After his heroic efforts at Burnt Corn Creek, no one questioned the leadership of Dixon Bailey, but Alexander Crawford, a member of the Tensaw militia,

No sooner was Fort Mims partially finished than the citizens poured in, with their provisions and effects. Colonel Carson, who had reached Mount Vernon in advance of Claiborne, sent over Lieutenant Osborne, with sixteen men. Afterwards Claiborne dispatched one hundred and seventy-five more volunteers to Fort Mims, under the command of Major Daniel Beasley,[4] with Captains Jack, Batchelor and Middleton.[5] He found seventy militia upon duty, commanded, for the present, by Dunn and Plummer, two inexperienced officers.[6] Permitting them to elect their officers, the brave Dixon Bailey was unanimously chosen for the post of captain, and Alexander Crawford for ensign.[7] The next day, General Claiborne, arriving at Fort Mims and inspecting the works, addressed a general order of instruction to Beasley, charging him "to strengthen the picketing, build two more block-houses, respect the enemy, to send out scouts frequently, and allow the suffering people provisions, whether whites or friendly Indians."[8] Returning to his headquarters, at Mount Vernon, he, for the moment, directed his attention to other portions of the frontiers.* In the meantime, Major Beasley had extended the picketing on the east side, sixty feet deep, forming a separate apartment for the accommodation of the officers and their baggage. He greatly weakened his command by sending small detachments to Forts Madison, Easley, Pierce, and Joshua Kennedy's saw mill, where citizens had collected, and asked for assistance.† At this mill the government had a large contract for lumber, to put Fort Charlotte, of Mobile, in repair, and build a fort at Mobile Point,[9] and it was deemed necessary to strengthen it with troops to prevent the Indians from burning it down.‡

The whole population of Fort Mims, consisting

* Claiborne's MS papers.

† Conversations with Dr. Thomas G. Holmes.

‡ Claiborne's MS papers.

of whites, Indians, soldiers, officers and Negroes, now amounted to five hundred and fifty-three souls. Crowded together, in an Alabama swamp, in the month of August, much sickness prevailed.* In the meantime, Crawford was dismissed from the post of ensign, for having deserted from the regular army, and Peter Randon, a half-breed, was appointed in his place.[10] Beasley kept up a correspondence with Claiborne, several times acquainting him with alarms, which turned out to be false.†

The Creeks, whom we left returning to Pensacola from the battleground of Burnt Corn, were again liberally supplied with arms and ammunition.[11] Making their way back to the Tallapoosa ,without molestation, active preparations were made by them for immediate war. Warriors, from the towns of Hoithlewaule, Fooshatche, Cooloome, Ecunchate, Sawanogi, Mooklausau, Alabama, Oakchoieooche, Pockuschatchee, Ocheubofau, Puckuntallahasse, Wewocoe, and Woccocoie, marched in a southern direction,[12] while others, from Tallassee, Autossee and Okfuskee, formed a front of observation towards Coweta to conceal the movement.‡

Associated with McQueen and Francis was William Weatherford, the son of Charles Weatherford, a Georgian, who had lived almost a lifetime in the Creek Nation. His mother, Sehoy, was the half-sister of General McGillivray, and a native of Hickory Ground. William was uneducated, but was a man of great native intellect, fine form, and commanding person. His bearing was gentlemanly

* Conversations with Dr. Thomas G. Holmes.

† Claiborne's MS papers.

‡ *American State Papers: Indian Affairs*, 1: 858. The Spaniards and the British agents charged McQueen's party to "fight the Americans. If they prove too hard for you, send your women and children to Pensacola, and we will send them to Havana; and if you should be compelled to fly, yourselves, and the Americans should prove too hard for both of us, there are vessels enough to take us all off together." Ibid.

was dismissed as an ensign in August 1813 when it was discovered he was a deserter from the U.S. Army. He was replaced as ensign by Peter Randon. Waselkov, *Conquering Spirit*, 227, 233; Doster, "Letters Relating to the Tragedy of Fort Mims," 275.

[8] Despite Claiborne's general orders to Beasley, most sources indicate only one completed blockhouse at Fort Mims, and Beasley's lackadaisical command clearly demonstrates that he did not see the Red Sticks as a real threat to his post. When his scouting parties did not report signs of Creeks, Beasley dismissed all other reports, especially the reports of slaves. Waselkov, *Conquering Spirit*, 109; Owsley, *Struggle for the Gulf*, 35–36.

[9] Of his original force of 170 troops, Beasley had sent small detachments to Fort Pierce and to Hinson's and Kennedy's saw mills, leaving him about 120 at Fort Mims plus the local militiamen. Waselkov, *Conquering Spirit*, 109; Doster, "Letters Relating to the Tragedy of Fort Mims," 274–75.

[10] Lieutenant Peter Randon, a métis Creek, was a member of the Tensaw militia and the son of John Randon, a prominent Indian countryman killed at Fort Mims. Waselkov, *Conquering Spirit*, 227, 249, 250, 347 n. 173, 347 n. 174.

[11] Pickett bases his claim that the Red Sticks were liberally supplied after the Battle of Burnt Corn Creek in July 1813 on a letter from Benjamin Hawkins to Secretary of War Armstrong on 7 June 1814. While the British definitely raised their level of involvement in Spanish Florida and the Gulf, it did not involve British officials until after January 1814, and their early contacts were with Lower Creeks—not the Red Sticks. *ASP: IA*, 1: 858; Owsley, *Struggle for the Gulf*, 27–29.

[12] Pickett's spelling of the Red Stick towns comes from a Benjamin Hawkins letter of 30 September 1813 to General John Floyd in the *American State Papers: Indian Affairs*. These names may not have been transcribed correctly from Hawkins's manuscript letter, and the more appropriate names might have been, for example, Hookchoieoochee for Oakchoieooche, Pakan Tallahassee for Puckuntallahasse, and Pochusehatchee for Pockuschatchee. *ASP: IA*, 1: 854; Swanton, *Early History of the Creek Indians*, 201, 247, 276; Ethridge, *Creek Country*, 367.

and dignified, and was coupled with an intelligent expression, which led strangers to suppose that they were in the presence of no ordinary man. His eyes were large, dark, brilliant and flashing. He was one of "nature's noblemen," a man of strict honor and unsurpassed courage. He was now with the large Indian army, conducting them down to attack the Tensaw settlers, among whom were his brother and several sisters, and also his half-brother, David Tate.* How unhappily were these people divided! His sister, Hannah Moniac, with all her sons, belonged to the war party, while the husband was a true friend of the Americans, and had fled to them for protection. Weatherford led his army to the plantation of Zachariah McGirth, a little below the present Claiborne, where, capturing several Negroes, among whom was an intelligent fellow named Joe, from whom they learned the condition of Fort Mims, and the proper time to attack it, he halted for several days to deliberate. One of the Negroes escaped, and conveyed intelligence to the fort of the approach of the Indians.[13]

Major Beasley had continued to send out scouts daily, who were unable to discover traces of the enemy. The inmates had become inactive, free from alarm, and abandoned themselves to fun and frolic. The Negro runner from McGirth's plantation now aroused them for a time, and Fort Mims was further strengthened. But, the Indians not appearing, the Negro was pronounced to be a liar, and the activity of the garrison again abated. At length two young Negro men were sent out to mind some beef cattle that grazed upon the luxuriant grass within a few miles of the fort. Suddenly, they came rushing through the gate, out of breath, and reported that they had counted twenty-four painted warriors. Captain Middleton, with a detachment of horse, was immediately dispatched, with the Negroes, to the place; but, being unable to discover the least sign of the enemy, returned about sunset, when one of the Negroes, belonging to John Randon, was tied up and severely flogged for alarming the garrison, with what Major Beasley deemed a sheer fabrication.[14] Fletcher, the owner of the other, refused to permit him to be punished, because he believed his statement, which so incensed the major that he ordered him, with his large family, to depart from the fort by 10 o'clock the next day.[15] The next morning Randon's Negro was again sent out, to attend the cattle, but, seeing a large body of Indians,

* David Tate was the son of Colonel Taitt, a British officer, who was stationed at the Hickory Ground, upon the Coosa, in 1778, as we have seen.

[13] According to Thomas S. Woodward, Weatherford tried to delay the march of the Red Stick army to give the Fort Mims residents time to prepare for battle, and, for the slaves that brought the warning notices, it "was made convenient to let them escape." He also states that Weatherford knew "that an officer with troops had reached Fort Mims" and that he "had no expectation of taking it whatever, until the morning they got in view of the Fort." Woodward, *Reminiscences*, 85–86.

[14] John Randon, a wealthy métis Creek, lived in the Tensaw District with his extended family, including his wife Tura Dyer Randon, his brother James, five children, and five or six slaves. Waselkov, *Conquering Spirit*, 125–27, 141, 143, 231, 246, 249, 250, 347 n. 173.

[15] Josiah Fletcher, a wealthy Indian countryman, was married to Elizabeth Baily Fletcher, a métis Creek, who was killed at Fort Mims. He had ten slaves to be killed—including the slave tied up to be whipped—and two captured. Ibid., 127, 205, 231–32, 235–36, 238–39, 241–42, 245, 316 n. 41, 343 n. 113.

fled to Fort Pierce, being afraid to communicate the intelligence to those who had whipped him. In the meantime, Fletcher's Negro, by the reluctant consent of his master, was tied up and the lash about to be applied to his back; the officers were preparing to dine; the soldiers were reposing on the ground; some of the settlers were playing cards; the girls and young men were dancing, while a hundred thoughtless and happy children sported from door to door, and from tent to tent.

At that awful moment, one thousand Creek warriors, extended flat upon the ground, in a thick ravine, four hundred yards from the eastern gate, thirsted for American blood. No eyes saw them but those of the chirping and innocent birds in the limbs above them. The mid-day sun sometimes flashed through the thick foliage, and glanced upon their yellow skins, but quickly withdrew, as if afraid longer to contemplate the murderous horde. There lay the prophets, covered with feathers, with black faces, resembling those monsters which partake of both beast and bird. Beside them lay curious medicine bags and rods of magic. The whole ravine was covered with painted and naked savages, completely armed.[16]

The hour of 12 o'clock arrived, and the drum beat the officers and soldiers of the garrison to dinner. Then, by one simultaneous bound, the ravine was relieved of its savage burden, and soon the field resounded with the rapid tread of the bloody warriors. The sand had washed against the eastern gate, which now lay open. Major Beasley rushed, sword in hand, and essayed in vain to shut it. The Indians felled him to the earth, with their clubs and tomahawks, and, rushing over his body into the additional part of the fort, left him a chance to crawl behind the gate, where he shortly after expired. To the last, he called upon the men to make a resolute resistance.[17] The eastern part of the picketing was soon full of Indians, headed by five prophets, whom the Americans immediately shot down, while engaged in dancing and incantations. This greatly abated the ardor of the enemy, many of whom retreated through the gate, for the moment. They had been assured that American bullets would split upon the sacred persons of the prophets, and pass off harmless. The unhappy inmates of Fort Mims now made all efforts to defend the place, but their attempts were confused and ineffective. The assailants, from the old line of picketing, in the additional part of the fort, and from the outside stockading, commenced a general fire upon the Americans. Soldiers, Negroes, women and children, fell.[18]

Captain Middleton, in charge of the eastern section, was soon

[16] While Seekaboo was present at Fort Mims, the prophet covered with feathers "from top to toe" was another Shawnee prophet, who was killed by Dixon Bailey, along with other prophets who were killed very early in the assault. Woodward, *Reminiscences*, 86.

[17] Most of this chapter is based on Pickett's interviews or conversations with Dr. Thomas G. Holmes, but, in this particular instance, Pickett chose to alter Holmes's description and use the phrase "sand had washed against the eastern gate." As noted by Gregory A. Waselkov, "I can testify the soil there is heavy clay, not sand." Thomas S. Woodward, in his *Reminiscences*, wrote: "Maj. Beasley was drunk . . . The Fort gate was open and could not be shut." Waselkov, *Conquering Spirit*, 189, 329 n. 17; Woodward, *Reminiscences*, 86. See Notes of Doctor Thomas G. Holmes, Pickett Papers, ADAH.

[18] In his letter of 31 October 1858, reflecting on Billy Weatherford and Fort Mims, Thomas S. Woodward claims that Major Daniel Beasley was drunk when Jim Cornells warned him of the impending attack. Beasley apparently sloughed off Cornells's report of seeing the Red Stick army and replied that "he had only seen a gang of red cattle." Woodward, *Reminiscences*, 86.

dispatched, together with all his men. Captain Jack, on the south wing, with a company of riflemen, defended his position with great bravery. Lieutenant Randon fought from the guard-house, on the west, while Captain Dixon Bailey repulsed the enemy, to the best of his ability, on the northern line of pickets, against which much the largest number of Indians operated.[19] The number of savages was so great that they apparently covered the whole field, and they now rent the air with their exulting shouts. Many of the younger prophets surrounded the main building, which was full of women and children, and danced around it, distorting their faces, and sending up the most unearthly screams. The pickets and houses afforded the Americans some protection, where the young men, the aged, and even the boys, fought with desperation. Captain Bailey was the man to whom the eyes of all the settlers were turned, at this critical moment. He maintained his position, and was the only officer who gained the port-holes before they were occupied by the enemy. His repeated discharges made lanes through the savage ranks. Fresh numbers renewed their efforts against him, and often an Indian and an American would plant their guns across the same port-hole, to shoot at each other. Bailey encouraged the whole population in the fort to fight, assuring them that Indians seldom fought long at one time, and, by holding out a little while longer, many would be saved. Failing in his entreaties to prevail upon several to rush through the enemy, to Fort Pierce, only two miles distant, there procure reinforcements, and attack the assailants in the rear, he resolved to go himself, and began to climb over the pickets for that purpose; but his neighbors, who loved him dearly, pulled him back.[20]

About three o'clock, the Indians, becoming tired of the contest, plundered the additional part of the fort, and began to carry off the effects, to the house of Mrs. O'Neal, which lay three hundred yards distant, on the road to the ferry.[21] Weatherford overtook them, on a fine black horse, and brought them back to the scene of action, after having impressed them by an animated address. About this time, Dr. Osborne, the surgeon, was shot through the body, and carried into Patrick's loom-house, where he expired, in great agony.[22] The women now animated the men to defend them, by assisting in loading the guns and bringing water from the well. The most prominent among these was Mrs. Daniel Bailey,

[19] Despite their heroic resistance, Captains Hatton Middleton and William Jack were killed, while Dixon Bailey was mortally wounded near the end of the attack. Although he lost several family members, Lieutenant Peter Randon escaped the slaughter. Waselkov, *Conquering Spirit*, 128, 130, 230, 239, 244, 250; Owsley, *Struggle for the Gulf*, 37–38.

[20] In his memoir history of the Creeks, George Stiggins gives credit to Paddy Walsh (Welch), a leading prophet, for the intensive attack on Fort Mims, which was stirred by the unrestrained actions of several young prophets inciting their companions to believe they were invulnerable to bullets. Stiggins, *Creek Indian History*, 110–11.

[21] The home of Mrs. Benjamin O'Neal (O'Neil) was a cabin on the Federal Road a short distance from Fort Mims. Her husband was killed at Fort Mims and the Red Sticks burned her home. Waselkov, *Conquering Spirit*, 131, 247.

[22] Pickett's "Dr. Osborne" was Lieutenant Spruce Osborne, who Colonel Joseph Carson had sent with a detachment of sixteen men to strengthen Fort Mims in late July 1813. Based on his medical training at the University of North Carolina, Osborne had been appointed as surgeon of the garrison. Osborne received an appointment to the "Military Academy at West Point" on 15 June 1808, and he may have been the first West Point cadet killed in the War of 1812. Waselkov, *Conquering Spirit*, 104, 107, 247, 346 n. 162; Peter A. Brannon, "Spruce McCall Osborne: A Mississippi Territorial Volunteer at Fort Mims," *Alabama Historical Quarterly* 5 (Spring 1943): 68; *American State Papers: Military Affairs*, 1: 845 [Hereafter cited as ASP: MA].

who, provoked at the cowardice of Sergeant Mathews, severely punctured him with a bayonet, as he lay trembling against the wall.[23] Many instances of unrivalled courage could be enumerated, if our space permitted it. One of Jack's soldiers retreated to the half-finished blockhouse, after his commander and all his brothers-in-arms had fallen, and, from that point, discharged his gun at intervals, until he had killed over a dozen warriors. James and Daniel Bailey, the brothers of the gallant captain, with other men, ascended to the roof of Mims's dwelling, knocked off some shingles, for port-holes, where they continued to shoot the lusty warriors on the outside of the picketing. But the superior force of the assailants enabled them constantly to bring fresh warriors into the action. They now set fire to the main building, and many of the out-houses. The shrieks of the women and children went up to high heaven.[24]

To Patrick's loom-house had been attached some extra picketing, forming what was improperly termed a bastion.[25] Hither Captain Bailey, and those of his command who survived, entered and continued to pour upon the savages a most deadly fire. Many citizens attempted to reach that spot, now the only one of the least security. The venerable David Mims, attempting to pass to the bastion, received a large ball in the neck; the blood gushed out; he exclaimed, "Oh God, I am a dead man!" and fell upon his face. A cruel warrior cut around his head, and waved his hoary scalp exultingly in the air. Some poor Spaniards, who had deserted from the Pensacola garrison, kneeled around the well and crossed themselves, and, while interceding with the MOST HIGH, were dispatched with tomahawks. "TO THE BASTION! TO THE BASTION!" was now the fearful cry of the survivors. Soon it was full to overflowing. The weak, wounded and feeble, were pressed to death and trodden under foot. The spot presented the appearance of one immense mass of human beings, herded together too close to defend themselves, and, like beeves in the slaughter-pen of the butcher, a prey to those who fired upon them. The large building had fallen, carrying with it the scorched bodies of the Baileys and others on the roof, and the large number of women and children in the lower story. The flames began to reach the people in the bastion. Dr. Thomas G. Holmes, an assistant surgeon in the garrison, seized an axe, cut some pickets in two, but

[23] **Apparently, the "Sergeant Mathews" accused of cowardice was Private Samuel Mathews of the Mississippi Territorial Volunteers. Rowland, *Mississippi Territory in the War of 1812*, 182; Waselkov, *Conquering Spirit*, 242, 343 n. 116.**

[24] **James and Daniel Bailey, members of the Tensaw militia and brothers of Dixon Bailey, were both killed at Mims's house. Several members of their extended family also perished. Waselkov, *Conquering Spirit*, 118, 131, 133, 227, 229–31.**

[25] **"Patrick's loom-house" refers to the home of Patrick Mahoney, a weaver, who lived at Mims's compound prior to the outbreak of the Red Stick violence and depredations. Ibid., 119, 311 n. 9.**

did not take them down, suffering them to remain until a suitable opportunity offered to escape. The brave Dixon Bailey now cried aloud that ALL WAS LOST, that his family were to be butchered, and begged all to make their escape, if possible. His Negro man, Tom, (still living, at Sizemore's plantation) took up his favorite son, who was thirteen years of age, but feeble with the fever, and bore him through the pickets, which Holmes now threw down, and gained the woods in safety. But, strange to say, the infatuated Negro presently brought back the poor boy to a squad of hostiles, who dashed out his brains with war clubs. Little Ralph cried out, "Father, father, save me!" Of his HEAVENLY FATHER the poor little heathen had probably never heard.[26]

In front of the northern line of picketing was a fence, fifty yards distant, in every lock of which many warriors had placed themselves, to cut off all retreat; besides which, others stationed themselves, at various points, to shoot those who should run. Dr. Holmes, Captain Bailey, and a Negro woman named Hester, the property of Benjamin Steadham, were the first to escape through the aperture. Holmes, receiving, in his flight, several balls through his clothes, but no wounds, strangely made his way over the fence, gained the swamp, and concealed himself in a clay hole, formed by the prostration of an immense tree. Bailey reached the swamp, but, being badly wounded, died by the side of a cypress stump. Hester received a severe wound in the breast, but reached a canoe in the lake, paddled to Fort Stoddert that night, and was the first to give intelligence to General Claiborne of the horrible affair.[27]

Returning again to the fatal spot, every house was seen to be in flames. The bastion was broken down, the helpless inmates were butchered in the quickest manner, and blood and brains bespattered the whole earth. The children were seized by the legs and killed by beating their heads against the stockading. The women were scalped, and those who were pregnant were opened, while they were alive, and the embryo infants let out of the womb. Weatherford had, some time previous, left the horrid scene. He had implored the warriors to spare the women and children, and reproached them for their barbarity; but his own life was threatened, for interposing, many clubs were raised over his head, and he was forced to retire. In after years, he never thought of that bloody occasion without the most painful emotions. He had raised the storm, but he could not control it. The British agents, at Pensacola, had offered a reward

[26] As acknowledged in Pickett's notes, Dr. Thomas G. Holmes survived the slaughter at Fort Mims, and he also accompanied the burial detail led by Major Joseph P. Kennedy and Captain Uriah Blue to Fort Mims on 8 September 1813. Based on his exhaustive research, Gregory A. Waselkov has determined that Holmes, an assistant surgeon with the Mississippi Territorial Volunteers, was an African métis, being of African-Irish descent from Silver Bluff, South Carolina. See Gregory A. Waselkov, *A Conquering Spirit: Fort Mims and the Redstick War of 1813–1814* (Tuscaloosa: University of Alabama Press, 2006), 121, 134, 137, 149–53, 188–90, 226, 237–38, 341 n. 80.

[27] While Hester is given credit for being the first survivor to reach Fort Stoddert, she was one of five Africans who survived, while 30 were killed and 30 were taken as captives. She was later one of several survivors or eyewitnesses interrogated by Judge Harry Toulmin. Waselkov, *Conquering Spirit,* 134, 136, 228, 237; Doster, "Letters Relating to the Tragedy of Fort Mims," 283–84.

[28] Pickett seems to be reflecting unsubstantiated speculation about British influence on the Red Sticks prior to the attack on Fort Mims. If there had been a British presence in Pensacola during Peter McQueen's visit prior to Burnt Corn Creek, he would have apparently had more than thirteen guns, despite Governor Manrique's refusal to provide any guns. In addition, the John Forbes store in Pensacola managed by John Innerarity provided no guns or gun powder. The first official British contact with Creeks in Pensacola occurred in January 1814 with a party from the Lower Creeks who were not Red Sticks. Owsley, *Struggle for the Gulf,* 26–29.

of five dollars for every American scalp.[28] The Indians jerked the skin from the whole head, and, collecting all the effects which the fire had not consumed, retired to the east, one mile from the ruins, to spend the night, where they smoked their pipes and trimmed and dried their scalps. The battle had lasted from twelve to five o'clock.

Of the large number in the fort, all were killed or burned up, except a few half-bloods, who were made prisoners, some Negroes, reserved for slaves, and the following persons, who made their escape and lived:[29] Dr. Thomas G. Holmes; Hester, a Negro woman; Socca, a friendly Indian; Peter Randon, lieutenant of citizens' company; Josiah Fletcher; Sergeant Mathews, the coward; Martin Rigdon; Samuel Smith, a half-breed; A. J. Morris,[30] Joseph Perry, Mississippi volunteers;[31] Jesse Steadham; Edward Steadham; John Hoven; William Jones; and Lieutenant W. R. Chambliss, of the Mississippi volunteers.

Dr. Holmes lay concealed in the clay hole until nine o'clock at night. The gin-house, at the Boat Yard, had been fired, and the conflagration threw a light over the surrounding country, in addition to that still afforded by the ruins of Fort Mims. Hence, he was forced to resume his position, until twelve o'clock, when the flames died away. Remembering that he had never learned to swim, he abandoned the idea which he first entertained, of crossing the Alabama and making his way to Mount Vernon. He, therefore, bent his course towards the high lands. He frequently came upon small Indian fires, around which the bloody warriors lay in profound sleep. Bewildered and shocked, in every direction in which he turned, by unwelcome and fearful sights like these, he at length, after a great deal of winding and turning, fell back into the river swamp, hid in a clump of thick canes, and there subsisted upon water, mutton reed and roots. All this time he was in the immediate neighborhood of the scene of the tragical events we have described, and heard, distinctly, the Indians killing the stock of the citizens. When silence ensued, after the fifth day, he made his way to the race track, and from thence to Pine Log Creek, where he spent the night. Reaching Buford's Island the next day, and seeing the tracks of people and horses, he determined to fall in with them, although they should prove to be hostile Indians, so desperate had he become from starvation. At the Tensaw Lake, Holmes found the horses tied, and, rejoicing to find that they belonged to his friends, fired off his gun. John Buford and his party, supposing the discharge proceeded from the war party, fled up into a bayou, in a boat, where they remained two days. The disappointed

[29] According to the burial detail sent to Fort Mims, Major Kennedy and Captain Blue reported burying 247 men, women, and children and estimated the Red Stick dead "at least, one hundred." Stiggins, in his memoir, records that 303 occupants of Fort Mims died and that "28 escaped or were taken as prisoners." He placed the Red Stick losses at 202—"such as died of their wounds." Based on imprecise and incomplete records, Waselkov's modern evaluation has accounted for 210 individuals, excluding 14 Red Sticks: 130 killed, 37 escaped, and 43 captured. Stiggins, *Creek Indian History*, 112–13; Waselkov, *Conquering Spirit*, 149–53, 225–57.

[30] In his original narrative, Pickett identified A. J. Morris as "_____ Mourrice." However, he was one of the four privates—three named John or one named Joseph Morris—listed in the 1st Regiment of Mississippi Volunteers, and further identified by Gregory A. Waselkov in his definitive study of Fort Mims and the Creek War of 1813–1814. Rowland, *Mississippi Territory in the War of 1812*, 183; Waselkov, *Conquering Spirit*, 245, 345 n. 130.

[31] Although Pickett refers to Joseph Perry as one of the Mississippi volunteers, he does not appear on the rosters of the Mississippi Territorial Volunteers under General Claiborne in 1813. Gregory A. Waselkov's research places him with the Tensaw militia. Rowland, *Mississippi Territory in the War of 1812*, 174–88; Waselkov, *Conquering Spirit*, 134, 227, 248.

Holmes went to the abandoned house of Buford, where he fortunately obtained some poultry, which he devoured without cooking. Three days afterwards he was discovered by Captain Buford and conveyed to Mount Vernon, where the other fourteen who escaped had arrived and reported him among the slain.[32]

Martin Rigdon,[33] Samuel Smith,[34] Joseph Perry, A. J. Morris, and Jesse Steadham escaped through the picketing together. The latter was shot through the thigh, early in the action, and Morris in the shoulder. Leaping the fence in front of the bastion, over the heads of the squatting Indians, they reached the swamp, where they remained three days, when, finding an old canoe below the Boat Yard, they made their escape to Mount Vernon. Edward Steadham, who was wounded in the hand while flying from the bastion, entered the swamp, swam the Alabama, above the Cut-Off, and arrived at Mount Vernon four days after the massacre.[35] All the others who escaped so miraculously made their way, with success, through the Indian ranks, and had many similar adventures, reaching the American headquarters at the most imminent peril. Lieutenant Chambliss had received two severe wounds in the fort, and, in running across the field, received another. Reaching the woods, he crept into a log-heap. At night, a party of warriors set fire to it, for the purpose of smoking their pipes, and, when the heat was becoming intolerable, and he would soon have been forced to discover himself, they fortunately were called off to another camp-fire. He left that place immediately, wandered about, and, for a long time, was supposed to be dead.[36] He made his way, however, to Mount Vernon, and, from thence, went to Soldiers' Retreat, the residence of General Claiborne, near Natchez, where Dr. John Coxe, an eminent surgeon,[37] extracted two arrow-heads and a ball from his body.*

The day after the fall of Fort Mims, the Indians began to bury their dead, by laying their bodies between the potato rows and drawing dirt and vines over them; but, from the great number of the dead, it was abandoned. Many were also wounded, who were put in canoes and conveyed up the river. Others, wounded, started home on foot, and died at Burnt Corn Spring. Most of those who were unhurt remained in the neighborhood, to kill and plunder, while another party went to Pensacola, with the scalps suspended upon poles.†

* Claiborne's MS papers.

† I am indebted to Dr. Thomas G. Holmes, of Baldwin County, Alabama, for the prominent facts in the aforegoing narrative of the fall of Fort Mims. He made

[32] Pickett is continuing to quote almost verbatim from his interviews with Dr. Thomas Golphin Holmes. "Notes taken from the lips of Dr. Thos. G. Holmes," 1848, Pickett Papers, ADAH.

[33] Martin Rigdon, a private and drummer in the Tensaw militia, lost his brother John, parents, and sisters at Fort Mims. After prior service in the U.S. Army, he reenlisted at Mobile Point in November 1813 and died in 1816 after the Battle of New Orleans. Waselkov, *Conquering Spirit,* 107–08, 134, 227, 251–52, 307 n. 29, 348 n. 183.

[34] Samuel Smith was a member of the Tensaw Creek métis community and the Tensaw militia. Ibid., 134–35, 227, 248, 252–53, 349 n. 191.

[35] The brothers Jesse and Edward Steadham were both members of the Tensaw militia, and they lost their father Moses, three brothers, and six sisters at Fort Mims. Ibid., 134–35, 227, 253–54.

[36] William R. Chambliss was an ensign in Captain William Jack's rifle company, Mississippi Territorial Volunteers. He received three wounds before escaping and wandering down to Mount Vernon. Ibid., 134, 137, 226, 232; Claiborne, *Mississippi,* 320.

[37] Pickett's "Dr. John Coxe" does not appear on the list of officers under General Claiborne's 1st Regiment of Mississippi Infantry at Baton Rouge in January 1813. However, William R. Cox, a surgeon's mate, was assigned to General Claiborne's command in 1813, and he is

Zachariah McGirth was the son of James McGirth, who was, as we have seen, an unprincipled but brave man, and a captain of a company of Tories, during the Revolutionary War, called the "Florida Rangers," forming a part of a battalion commanded by his brother, Colonel Daniel McGirth. When the war terminated, Captain James McGirth fled to the Creek Nation, with his children, among whom was Zachariah. The latter married a half-breed Creek woman, named Vicey Cornells, had become wealthy, and was now an inmate of Fort Mims with his wife and eight children.[38] About ten o'clock, on the day of the massacre, McGirth entered a boat, with two of his Negroes, and went out of Lake Tensaw into the Alabama, with the view of ascending that river to his plantation, which was situated below Claiborne, for some provisions. Reaching the Cut-Off, he heard a heavy discharge of guns at Fort Mims. With pain and anxiety, he continued to listen to the firing, and, running his boat a mile down the river, in a small bayou, resolved to remain there, being firmly impressed with the belief that the Indians had attacked the fort. Late in the evening the firing ceased, and presently he saw clouds of black smoke rise above the forest trees, which was succeeded by flames. The unhappy McGirth now well knew that all was lost, and that, in all probability, his family had perished in the flames. Being a bold man, like his father, he resolved to go through the swamp, with his Negroes, to the fatal spot. When he came within a quarter of a mile of the fort, he placed the Negroes in a concealed place, and approached alone. All was gloomy and horrible. Dogs, in great numbers, ran all over the woods, terrified beyond measure. Seeing that the savages had left the ruins, he returned for his Negroes, and, a little after twilight, cautiously advanced. McGirth stood aghast at the horrible spectacle. Bodies lay in piles, in the sleep of death, bleeding, scalped, mutilated. His eyes everywhere fell upon forms half burned up, but still cracking and frying upon the glowing coals. In vain did he and his faithful slaves seek for the bodies of his family. Pile after pile was turned over, but no discovery could be made, for the features of but few could be recognized. He turned his back upon the bloody place, crossed the swamp to his boat, and paddled down the Alabama to Mount Vernon, with a sad and heavy heart.

McGirth, now alone in the world, became a desperate man, ready to brave the greatest dangers for the sake of revenge. During the Creek War, he was often employed in riding expresses from the Tombigbee to Georgia, when no one else could be found daring enough to go through the heart of the enemy's

notes of the horrible affair a few years after the massacre took place, while the facts were fresh in his memory. I also conversed with Jesse Steadham, of Baldwin, and Lieutenant Peter Randon, the latter of whom I found in New Orleans, who also escaped.

apparently Pickett's "Dr. Coxe". In early August 1813, Claiborne had sent "Surgeon Cox" to attend sick soldiers who had been left behind as Claiborne moved his forces to Mount Vernon Cantonment and Fort Stoddert. Rowland, *Mississippi Territory in the War of 1812*, 38; Claiborne, *Mississippi*, 334.

[38] Zachariah McGirth, a native of South Carolina, married Vicey Cornells, a métis Creek and the widow of Alexander McGillivray, sometime after 1793. After pursuing several enterprises, he settled his family on the Little River in late 1807 and ran a successful farming operation with a large slave labor force. Waselkov, *Conquering Spirit*, 56–59; Woodward, *Reminiscences*, 97.

[39] One of McGirth's relatives, Robert James, reported: ". . . he painted himself like a hostile warrior & shaved his head. Mounted a good horse with 3 pecks of shelled corn for his animal . . . solitary & alone pursued his journey." He made four rides to Georgia and back, and, on his first mission, he learned that his wife and daughters were still alive as Red Stick captives. Waselkov, *Conquering Spirit*, 160, 321 n. 2; "Notes from the lips of Col. Robert James (quote)," Pickett Papers, ADAH.

country.[39] After a long service, amid such dangers, a friend accosted him one day, in Mobile, and told him some people desired to see him at the wharf. Repairing there, he saw—a common sight in those days—some wretched Indians, who had been captured. He was asked if he knew them. Hesitating, his wife and seven children advanced and embraced him. A torrent of joy and profound astonishment overwhelmed him. He trembled like a leaf, and was, for some minutes, speechless.[40]

Many years before the dreadful massacre at Fort Mims, a little hungry Indian boy, named Sanota—an orphan, houseless and friendless—stopped at the house of Vicey McGirth. She fed and clothed him, and he grew to athletic manhood. He joined the war party, and formed one of the expedition against Fort Mims. Like the other warriors, he was engaged in hewing and hacking the females to pieces, towards the close of the massacre, when he suddenly came upon Mrs. McGirth and his foster-sisters. Pity and gratitude taking possession of his heart, he thrust them in a corner, and nobly made his broad savage breast a rampart for their protection. The next day he carried them off, upon horses, towards the Coosa, under the pretense that he had reserved them from death for his slaves. Arriving at his home, he sheltered them, hunted for them, and protected them from Indian brutality. One day he told his adopted mother that he was going to fight Jackson, at the Horseshoe, and that, if he should be killed, she must endeavor to reach her friends below.[41] Sure enough, the noble Sanota soon lay among the slain at Cholocco Litabixee.[42] Mrs. McGirth, now being without a protector, and in a hostile region, started off on foot, with her children, for Fort Claiborne. After much suffering, they reached their deserted farm, below Claiborne, where Major Blue, at the head of a company of horse, discovered these miserable objects, and carried them to Mobile, where the interview just related took place, with the astonished husband, who imagined that he had, some months before, surveyed their half-burnt bodies upon the field of Fort Mims. His son was the only member of his family who had perished upon that bloody occasion.*

General Claiborne dispatched Major Joseph P. Kennedy, with a strong detachment, to Fort Mims, from his headquarters at Mount Vernon, for the purpose of interring the dead. Upon arriving there, Kennedy found the air darkened with buzzards, and hundreds of dogs, which had run wild, gnawing upon the human carcasses.[43] The troops, with heavy hearts, succeeded in interring many bodies, in two large pits, which they dug. "Indians, Negroes, white

* Conversations with Colonel Robert James, of Clarke County, Alabama, who often heard McGirth relate these particulars. McGirth, in 1834, made the same statements to me.

[40] Based on the extensive research by Gregory A. Waselkov, it appears that McGirth greeted his wife Vicey, daughter Sarah McGirth, and four unnamed daughters. His son James McGirth had been killed at Fort Mims. Waselkov, *Conquering Spirit*, 243–44, 344 n. 121.

[41] Relying on his interview of Colonel Robert James, Pickett gives Sanota credit for saving Vicey McGirth and her daughters. However, using "Zach McGirth" as his source, Thomas S. Woodward, in his *Reminiscences,* credits Jim Boy (High-Head Jim) for saving Mrs. McGirth and her daughters and notes that "her only son, James, was killed." "Notes from the lips of Col. Robert James," Pickett Papers; Woodward, *Reminiscences,* 85–87, 97.

[42] Cholocco Litabixee is the Creek name for a bend in the Tallapoosa River in Tallapoosa County, Alabama, which translates to "Horse's Flat Foot." However, it became known as Horseshoe Bend after Andrew Jackson's army defeated the Creek Red Sticks there on 27 March 1814. William A. Read, *Indian Place Names in Alabama,* rev. ed. James B. McMillan (1937; reprint, Tuscaloosa: University of Alabama Press, 1984), 19; Sean Michael O'Brien, *In Bitterness and in Tears: Andrew*

men, women and children, lay in one promiscuous ruin. All were scalped, and the females, of every age, were butchered in a manner which neither decency nor language will permit me to describe. The main building was burned to ashes, which were filled with bones. The plains and the woods around were covered with dead bodies. All the houses were consumed by fire, except the block-house, and a part of the pickets. The soldiers and officers, with one voice, called on Divine Providence to revenge the death of our murdered friends."*

In drawing our account of this sanguinary affair to a conclusion, it is proper to observe that General Claiborne was in no way to blame for the unfortunate result. He corresponded with Beasley, heard from him almost every day, and in his dispatches constantly urged him to be prepared to meet the enemy. Claiborne, from every quarter, received distressing messages imploring assistance, and we have already seen how judiciously he distributed his forces, as far as it lay in his power, for their protection, contrary to the instructions of Flournoy, who endeavored to confine his operations chiefly to the defense of Mobile and the country below Ellicott's line. Just before the attack upon Fort Mims, he headed a large detachment of horse, and rushed to the defense of the people at Easley's Station, upon the Tombigbee, near the Choctaw line, whom he was induced to believe a large party of Choctaws and Creeks intended shortly to attack. They, however, did not appear, and, leaving a strong guard for the defense of that fort, he hastened back to Mount Vernon, and arrived there at twelve o'clock at night, after a march of seventy miles that day. He was there shocked to learn the fate of the garrison of Fort Mims. Supposing that he had already returned to Mount Vernon, Beasley addressed him a letter, *two hours, only, before the Indians entered the gate*, declaring his ability to maintain the post against any number of the enemy.† The major was as brave a man as ever lived, but neither he nor his officers, attached to the Mississippi division, believed that the enemy were at hand, so often had reports reached them, which they pronounced untrue, because they were not immediately realized, as in the case of the Negro who was whipped, and of the other who was killed by the Indians while tied up, ready to receive the lash.‡

Jackson's Destruction of the Creeks and Seminoles (Guilford, CT: Lyons Press, 2005), 141–51.

[43] As noted above, Major Joseph P. Kennedy and Captain Uriah Blue led a ten-man burial detachment to Fort Mims on 8 September 1813 and both men penned their observations to General Claiborne the next day. While they gave details of the deaths and body counts, they also reported that all the structures had been consumed by fire except the blockhouse and part of the stockade pickets. Waselkov, _Conquering Spirit,_ 149–150.

* Major Kennedy's MS report to General Claiborne.

† Beasley's letter, found among Claiborne's MS papers.

‡ The people at Fort Pierce, when the attack was made at Fort Mims, made their way, under Lieutenant Montgomery, to Mobile, where they safely arrived.

Chapter XXXIV

DARING OF HAYDEN—BLOODY SCENES—GAINES AND THE CHOCTAWS[1]

While the larger body of Creeks were destroying the people at Fort Mims, Francis, the prophet, at the head of a hundred warriors, was spreading his depredations in the fork of the Alabama and Tombigbee.[2] Abner James and Ransom Kimbell, with their large families, being inmates of Fort Sinquefield, and becoming dissatisfied at remaining among so many people, repaired to the house of Kimbell, situated two miles from the fort. Here they were living, when Francis suddenly surrounded the house, about three o'clock in the evening.[3] Abner James, his son Thomas, then fourteen years of age, and his daughter Mary, escaped, and fled to the fort. Isham Kimbell, then sixteen years of age, also safely reached Sinquefield, and is now the clerk of the Circuit Court of Clarke County.[4] All the others were dispatched with war clubs and scalped. After killing the stock and robbing the house, the Indians retired to the swamps. In the early part of the night, a slight rain commenced, which, it is believed, revived Sarah Merrill, the married daughter of James, whom the Indians had supposed to be dead. She felt among the bodies, which lay thick around her, and found her little boy, twelve months old, who also, fortunately, was alive. Some warm milk from her breast revived him more and more. Taking him in her arms, she, with difficulty, got upon her feet, and slowly walked towards the fort. Arriving within a half mile of that place, her bleeding wounds, weakening her at every step, forced her to place the babe by the side of a log, while she went on and communicated his hiding place to the anxious garrison. Some generous men boldly sallied out, found the boy, and brought him to the fort. They are both now alive. The young woman was severely beaten with large clubs, and the scalp of the entire top of her head was taken off. The savages slung the little fellow against the side of the house, and cut around his head, but his hair being too short, they did not pull off his scalp.[5]

Hearing of the murders, Colonel Carson dispatched from Fort Montgomery Lieutenant Bailey, with seven dragoons, and three men employed as spies, to bury the dead and ascertain if the Indians were numerous.[6] Twelve bodies were conveyed to Fort Sinquefield, in an ox-cart, and thrown into a pit dug fifty yards from the gate. About the time that the funeral ceremonies were closing, and while nearly the whole garrison were engaged therein, Francis suddenly rushed, with a hundred warriors, down a hill towards them. The men snatched up the children, and every one of them reached the gate in time, except about ten women, at the spring, who were engaged in washing. The Indians, failing to cut off the retreat of the main party, perceived with delight the helpless condition of these females, and rushed in that direction to secure them. Just at that moment, Isaac Hayden, who had been out cow-hunting,

[1] In his original chapter title, Pickett uses "DARING OF HEATON," but the hero at Fort Sinquefield was Isaac Hayden, not Isaac Heaton. He relied heavily on the "Notes" furnished by Gerard Walthall Creagh (1794–1848) and Jeremiah Austill (1794–1879) in writing this chapter. In his responses to Pickett, Creagh described the incidents at Fort Sinquefield and identified Hayden as "Isaac Heaton who had been out cow hunting." Austill identifies Pickett's Heaton as "Haden." "Notes furnished by Col. G. W. Creagh of Clarke County Alabama, In relation to the battle of 'Burnt Corn,' the 'Canoe Fight,' and other engagements in which he was concerned in 1813–1814," Pickett Papers, ADAH; "Notes furnished by Col. Jeremiah Austill in relation to the 'Canoe Fight' & other engagements in which he was concerned in the memorable years 1813–1814," ibid.; Halbert and Ball, *Creek War of 1813 and 1814*, 88–90.

[2] Most modern researchers agree that Josiah Francis (Hillis Hadjo) did not participate in the attack on Fort Mims because he feared it would be a failure. When it turned out to be successful, he participated in the attacks on the forks of the Alabama and Tombigbee rivers and at Fort Sinquefield to regain face and his place as the leading Creek prophet. However, George Stiggins, who had a very low opinion of Francis, identifies the Dog Warrior as the leader of the attack on Fort Sinquefield. Stiggins, *Creek Indian History*, 114–17.

[3] Fort Sinquefield is named for Samuel Sinquefield, a native of Georgia, who had a cabin near the stockaded fort. Abner James, a native of Georgia, and Ransom Kimbell, a native of South Carolina, were both outside the Kimbell house when the Red Sticks attacked. Kimbell later died at Fort Madison. Halbert and Ball, *Creek War of 1813 and 1814*, 177–78, 180–81; Waselkov and Christopher, *Archeological Identification of Creek War Sites*, Part 2: 29–30; Mary G. Bryan, *Passports Issued by Governors of Georgia, 1810–1820, Special Publication 28* (Washington: National Geographic Society, 1964), 106.

[4] Isham Kimbell (1797–1881) served as the circuit court clerk of Clarke County, Alabama—from 1833 to 1849—postmaster, and registrar in the chancery. Halbert and Ball, *Creek War of 1813 and 1814*, 177–79, 182.

[5] Sarah James Merrill and her infant son, William, survived their ordeal. According to Clarke County sources, her husband served under General Claiborne and was told that his wife and child had been killed in the Red Stick attack. They remarried, both not knowing the other had survived. Years later, when Merrill, traveling west to Texas, stopped off in Clarke County, he encountered his ex-wife, who had married Elijah Spencer Holtam. Charles Jackson, "Sarah Merrill's Miracle," *Clarke County Historical Quarterly* 2 (Summer 1977): 29–30.

[6] Actually, Colonel Joseph Carson commanded the Mississippi Territorial Volunteers at Fort Madison, and he dispatched Lieutenant James Bailey with eleven mounted riflemen to relieve Fort Sinquefield. Halbert and Ball, *Creek War of 1813 and 1814*, 185;

riding up, with his long whip and large pack of dogs, gave a tremendous crack, and, encouraging his canine army, charged upon the Indians. Such was the fury of the dogs, that the Creeks were forced to halt and fight them, which enabled Hayden to cover the retreat of the women until they arrived safely in the fort. His horse fell under him, from the wound of an Indian gun, but rose again, and followed into the fort his heroic master, who had received no other injury than the riddling of his coat with rifle balls.[7] Only one poor woman—a Mrs. Philips, who was in an advanced state of pregnancy—was overtaken and scalped.[8]

Hayden deserves to be remembered for this achievement—an eminent exemplification of bravery and presence of mind. The Indians now attacked the little stockade, but a brave resistance repelled them, with the loss of eleven warriors. Then, securing the dragoon horses, which had been tethered outside the walls, the savages rapidly retired. The Americans, having lost only one of their number, besides the unfortunate Mrs. Philips, the next day evacuated Sinquefield's fort, and marched to Fort Madison, for better security, where the inmates of Forts Glass and Lavier had also flocked, swelling the population to over one thousand souls, including the command of Colonel Carson of two hundred and twenty men.[9]

Occasionally, the farmers were accustomed to leave Fort Madison, for a few hours, to procure, from their fields, provisions for immediate use. A man, named Fisher, with three of his sons, set out for that purpose, and, arriving at the farm, one of the boys was shot in the back, while shelling some peas in the yard. Instantly rising up, he made his escape to the woods. His father, then in the cane, running out to learn the cause of the firing, was also severely wounded in the back, but likewise made his way to the forest. The other two sons, being in a different part of the field, fled to the fort, and reported the death of their brother and father. The next day, however, they came in, bleeding from their wounds,[10] and happily recovered.*

* Conversations with the late Colonel Gerard W. Creagh,

Waselkov, *Conquering Spirit*, 140, 317 n. 7.

[7] According to Henry S. Halbert and Timothy H. Ball, Isaac Hayden, a member of Bailey's detachment, rode out of Fort Sinquefield and drove about sixty dogs into the unsuspecting Red Sticks. The diversion caused by Hayden's "dogs of war" allowed the frightened washing party at the spring to find refuge within the stockade. Hayden's horse collapsed after he reentered the fort. Halbert and Ball, *Creek War of 1813 and 1814*, 186–90.

[8] Sarah Phillips, the wife of Charles Phillips Jr., and her unborn child lost their lives. Ibid., 186, 189, 199.

[9] After a two-hour battle, the Red Sticks withdrew from Fort Sinquefield, stealing horses and carrying away their dead and wounded. Stephen Lacey was mortally wounded in the neck while shooting at the Red Sticks from the upper floor of the blockhouse. Ibid., 193–94; Waselkov, *Conquering Spirit*, 141.

[10] Josiah Fisher, an Indian countryman, had a farm near Sizemore's Ferry on the Alabama River. When their father and brother Ben were shot, the other two sons, who were out in a field, ran to Fort Madison, where they reported the deaths of their father and brother. While Josiah and Ben both recovered, Josiah died a few years later when he ruptured a vessel near his old wound. Halbert and Ball, *Creek War of 1813 and 1814*, 206–07.

These things, following so closely upon the fall of Fort Mims, filled the whole population of the eastern section of the Mississippi Territory with the greatest panic imaginable, and every soul went into some kind of defensive work. Fort Hawn, at Gullett's Bluff, contained a mixed population of three hundred and ninety-one souls, including sixty men under Captain James Powell, of the eighth regiment of Mississippi militia.[11] At Mount Vernon were two forts, literally packed with people. Rankin's Fort contained five hundred and thirty persons—of whom only eighty-seven were capable of bearing arms, in consequence of the sickness which everywhere prevailed in these filthy stockades.[12] Fort Charlotte, of Mobile, was also daily receiving families. To this place Judge Toulmin and a number of his neighbors had repaired. Perhaps greater inquietude existed at St. Stephens than at any other point, if, indeed, any line of distinction can be drawn. Claiborne, all the time, was harassed by distressing messages, which hourly reached him, and his generous heart was racked, day and night, in revolving plans to assist them all; but he was unable to do more than he had already accomplished, on account of the smallness of his army and the restrictions put upon him by the commander-in-chief.

The enemy continued to spread their depredations, distributing themselves in all directions, burning the abandoned houses, driving off the cattle, and herding the hogs in the corn-fields, to fatten, that their flesh might be in good order for their feastings. Colonel Carson's condition was unknown to Claiborne, and, from the continued reports which he received, that a combined attack was soon to be made upon Fort Madison, the general transmitted him an order to abandon his post, and march to St. Stephens, which was deemed a more important point to defend. The order was *discretionary*, however, but Carson and his officers viewed it as rather *peremptory*. He started, with all his force, to St. Stephens, accompanied by five hundred settlers, of all ages and sexes. This created great consternation in the fork, and Claiborne was unjustly denounced for having abandoned the whole population of Clarke County. But if Carson had chosen to remain, it would have fully accorded with the views of the general.[13] The movement was unnecessary, and served to embolden the savages. When the evacuation took place, eighty citizens enrolled themselves,

of Clarke County, Colonel Jeremiah Austill, of Mobile, and others. See also Claiborne's MS papers.

[11] Pickett's Fort Hawn was known as Fort Carney in Clarke County and was located about four miles south of Gullett's Bluff on the Tombigbee River. By 1814, James Powell is listed as a lieutenant colonel in command of the 8th Regiment of Mississippi Territorial Volunteers (Baldwin County). Ibid., 114, 116; Rowland, *Mississippi Territory in the War of 1812*, 90.

[12] Rankin's Fort, located in Washington County, had a large stockade and was one of the most western forts built in the Tensaw District. It was possibly built on land owned by Richard Robert Rankin, a Virginia native, who lost two sons at Fort Mims: Joseph Rankin and Thomas Berry Rankin. Halbert and Ball, *Creek War of 1813 and 1814*, 114, 116; Waselkov, *Conquering Spirit*, 226–27, 250–51, 348 n. 179; "Colonel Robert Rankin," http://www.genealogy.com.

[13] Faced with uncontrolled panic and a growing refugee population, General Claiborne withdrew his Mississippi Territorial Volunteer companies from Forts Easley and Madison—leaving St. Stephens with a garrison—and reinforced Fort Stoddert with 100 troops from Captain Uriah Blue's 7th Regiment of U.S. Infantry. Of the twenty militia forts, only McGrew's Fort and Fort Carney continued as military outposts. Waselkov, *Conquering Spirit*, 142–44, 318 n. 15.

under Captain Evan Austill and Captain Sam Dale, (the latter still suffering from the desperate wound which he received at Burnt Corn), all of whom determined to stay within Fort Madison to protect a number of citizens, who preferred to remain.[14] A dispatch from Claiborne, dated the 8th of September, urging Carson "not to abandon the fort, unless it was clear that he could not maintain it," arrived too late, as that officer was already in the neighborhood of St. Stephens.*

The British were hovering along the coast to give their red friends countenance and aid. A British war schooner had anchored at Pensacola, with a large supply of munitions of war.[15] Afterwards, Mateo Gonzáles Manrique, the governor of Pensacola, addressed a letter to Weatherford and the chiefs, congratulating them on their late victory at Fort Mims, assuring them of his constant aid, but dissuading them from setting fire to Mobile, as that place properly belonged to the king of Spain,[16] which His Majesty would shortly reoccupy.†

While all was doubt and uncertainty as to the position which the Choctaws would assume, at this critical juncture, Pushmataha, the most enlightened and influential chief of that nation, rode to St. Stephens, and proposed to Mr. George S. Gaines to enlist several companies of his warriors in the American cause.[17] Gratified at the proposition, the latter hastened with the chief to Mobile, and had an interview with General Flournoy, in Fort Charlotte, who strangely declined to receive the Choctaws as United States soldiers. With deep mortification, Gaines and the chief returned to St. Stephens, and while the citizens, who had surrounded them when they rode up, were cursing Flournoy for his folly, a horse was seen at a distance, bearing a rider with

* Claiborne's MS papers.

† This letter was found in Weatherford's house, at the Holy Ground, several months afterwards, and is yet among the MS papers of General Claiborne. All these papers furnish the most indubitable evidence of the coalition between the Spaniards and English to exterminate the population of the Mississippi Territory.

[14] After Carson and some 500 settlers withdrew for St. Stephens, Captain Evan Austill (c. 1769–1819) and Captain Samuel Dale (1772–1841) designed a fifty-foot tall light fired by pine fat wood, which was kept burning at night and illuminated a wide area. Halbert and Ball, *Creek War of 1813 and 1814*, 202–04; Bud Hannings, *The War of 1812: A Complete Chronology with Biographies of 63 General Officers* (Jefferson, NC: McFarland & Company, Inc., 2012), 153.

[15] At this time, the British had not formulated a plan to use the Creeks or any Indian nation to attack the Gulf Coast of the U.S. In September 1813, Governor Charles Cameron of New Providence sent Captain Edward Handfield to gather information on the Southern Indians. He met with Lower Creeks and Seminoles and received requests for British arms and troops at their base at Apalachicola. On 28 October 1813, Cameron forwarded their requests to Earl Bathurst, secretary of state for war. The Red Sticks had suffered their devastating defeat at Horseshoe Bend before Captain Hugh Pigot sailed into Apalachicola in April 1814. Frank L. Owsley Jr., "British and Indian Activities in Spanish West Florida During the War of 1812," *Florida Historical Quarterly* 46 (October 1967): 114–115.

[16] Following the departure of Peter McQueen's Red Stick party in July 1813, Governor Gonzáles Manrique notified Captain General Ruiz Apodaca of his actions and requested his approval for arming the Creeks. Ruiz Apodaca gave his approval for arming the Indians and actually ordered Manrique to continue to provide the arms and supplies that he could spare. However, he warned him not to deploy any Spanish troops except to defend Pensacola. Ruiz Apodaca's decision received approval by royal order on 9 December 1813. Owsley, *Struggle for the Gulf*, 27; Owsley, "British and Indian Activities," 111–14.

[17] When Charles Juzan told Pushmataha about the attack on Fort Mims, the Choctaw chief immediately rode down to St. Stephens to see George Strother Gaines at the Choctaw Trading House and to offer his support against the Red Sticks. Gaines, *Reminiscences*, 57.

great speed. Flournoy had reconsidered the matter, and had sent a messenger, authorizing Gaines to go into the Choctaw Nation to raise troops. The people gave a shout, and all hearts were made glad. Everyone had feared that the Choctaws would join the Creeks, and now, through the influence of Pushmataha, it was believed they would actually assist the Americans. In company with Colonel Flood McGrew and the chief, Gaines departed immediately for the Choctaw country, with no other provisions than some jerked beef.[18] Colonel John McKee, agent of the Chickasaws, met them at Pitchlynn's, where they held a consultation, while Pushmataha went home to assemble his people in council.[19] They were living under three distinct governments: the eastern district was governed by Pushmataha, the western by Puckshunubbee, and the northwestern by Mushulatubbee.

In a few days Gaines reached the council-ground, where over five thousand Choctaws were encamped.[20] Pushmataha harangued them in a long speech, full of eloquence and ingenuity, in which he said, among many other things, "You know Tecumseh. He is a bad man. He came through our nation, but did not turn our heads. He went among the Muscogees, and got many of them to join him. You know the Tensaw people. They were our friends. They played ball with us. They sheltered and fed us, whenever we went to Pensacola. Where are they now? Their bodies rot at Sam Mims's place. The people at St. Stephens are also our friends. The Muscogees intend to kill them too. They want soldiers to defend them." (He here drew out his sword, and flourishing it, added:) "You can all do as you please. You are all freemen. I dictate to none of you. But I shall join the St. Stephens people. If you have a mind to follow me, I will lead you to glory and to victory!" A warrior rose up, slapped his hand upon his breast, and said: "I am a man! I am a man! I will follow you!" All of them now slapped their breasts, a general shout went up, and Gaines was filled with joy at the result.[21]

In the meantime, Colonel McKee was equally

[18] John Flood McGrew was a prominent landowner in the Tombigbee settlements. As a frontier leader, he had been appointed to the five member legislative council for the Mississippi Territory in 1808. Gaines, *Reminiscences,* 58, 183 n. 45.

[19] John McKee (1771–1832), a native of Virginia, had worked with the Cherokee on a boundary issue in 1792 and as a federal agent. He also served as the Choctaw agent from 1799 until Silas Dinsmoor's appointment in 1802. He was in Nashville when Gaines's letters were delivered to Andrew Jackson and Governor Willie Blount, requesting their help. Jackson directed McKee to "get out" as many Chickasaws and Choctaws as possible. McGrew, McKee, and Gaines met at John Pitchlynn's to coordinate their efforts. Ibid., 57–59, 183 n. 46.

[20] Flood McGrew and Gaines listened to Pushmataha deliver his speech before "several thousand Indians" at the Choctaw "Council Ground" at Kooncheto in Neshoba County, Mississippi. Ibid., 59, 183 n. 48.

[21] Pushmataha's speech quoted here comes from Pickett's interview with Gaines in 1847, and Pickett has shortened it and changed some of the wording. For example, while Gaines recalled Pushmataha saying "Their bones ly there now," Pickett uses, "Their bodies rot at Sam Mims's place." See "Conversation with George S. Gaines," in Gaines, *Reminiscences of George Strother Gaines,* 136.

successful with the Chickasaws, being greatly aided in his efforts by the influence of John Pitchlynn. McKee, at the head of a large force of Chickasaws, marched to the Tuscaloosa Falls, to attack the Creek town at that place, but found it reduced to ashes. The inhabitants had fled.[22] Returning to Pitchlynn's, at the mouth of the Oktibbeha, the force separated, one party going to their homes and the other to St. Stephens, to join General Claiborne, who had laudably exerted himself to procure the aid of these powerful tribes.*

[22] On 7 January 1814, McKee and Pitchlynn led nearly 600 Chickasaw and Choctaw warriors to Oceoche Emathla's Black Warrior Town. They found the town deserted, burned the deserted structures, and returned to their villages. Gaines, *Reminisces*, 63, 185 n. 65.

* Conversations with Mr. George S. Gaines. See Claiborne's MS papers.

Chapter XXXV

BATTLES OF TALLASEEHATCHEE, TALLADEGA AND AUTTOSEE

The arrival of an express, at Nashville, with letters from Mr. George S. Gaines to General Jackson and the governor, conveying the distressing intelligence of the massacre at Fort Mims, and imploring their assistance, created great excitement, and the Tennesseans volunteered their services to avenge the outrage.[1] General Jackson, at the head of a large force, passed through Huntsville, crossed the Tennessee at Ditto's Landing, and joined Colonel Coffee, who had been dispatched in advance, and who had encamped opposite the upper end of an island on the south side of the river, three miles above the landing. Remaining here a short time, the army advanced higher up, to Thompson's Creek, to meet supplies, which had been ordered down from East Tennessee.[2] In the meantime, Colonel Coffee marched, with six hundred horse, to Black Warrior's town, upon the river of that name, a hundred miles distant, which he destroyed by fire, having found it abandoned. Collecting about three hundred bushels of corn, he rejoined the main army at Thompson's Creek, without having seen an Indian.[3] Establishing a defensive depot at this place, called Fort Deposit, Jackson, with great difficulty, cut his way over the mountains to Wills' Creek, where, being out of bread, he encamped several days, to allow his foraging parties to collect provisions. The contractors had entirely failed to meet their engagements, and his army had, for some days, been in a perishing condition.[4]

Jackson dispatched Colonel Dyer, with two hundred cavalry, to attack the village of Littefutchi, situated at the head of Canoe Creek, twenty miles distant. They arrived there at four o'clock in the morning, burned down the town, and returned with twenty-nine prisoners, consisting of men, women and children.[5] Another detachment, sent out to bring in beeves and corn,

1 The letters from Gaines to Jackson and Governor Willie Blount were delivered by Samuel A. Edmondson. Gaines arranged for fresh horses to be made available each day to assure that the message of the debacle at Fort Mims would be delivered as quickly as possible. He was certain that Jackson's "Brigade of Mounted Volunteers" could end the Red Stick threat. Gaines, *Reminiscences,* 56–57.

2 When Jackson heard the news of Fort Mims, he was still recovering from wounds received in his confrontation with the Benton brothers and his left arm remained in a sling. He sent his trusted friend and business partner Colonel John Coffee and his cavalry ahead of his advance to the Huntsville area. Jackson took command of his West

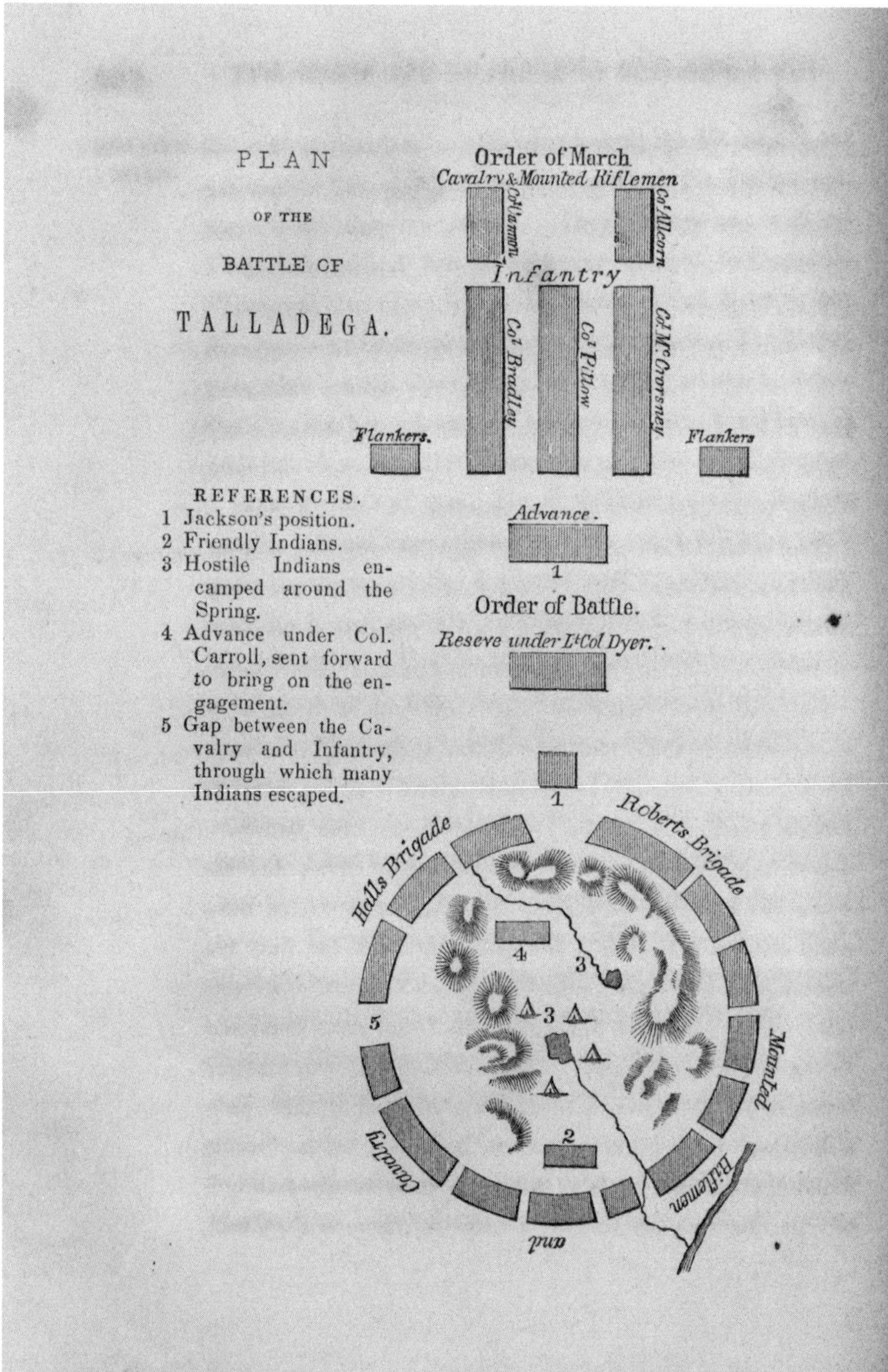
PLAN
OF THE
BATTLE OF
TALLADEGA.
Order of March.
Cavalry & Mounted Riflemen
Col. Cannon
Col. Allcorn
Infantry
Col. Bradley
Col. Pillow
Col. McCrorsney
Flankers.
Flankers
REFERENCES.
1 Jackson's position.
2 Friendly Indians.
3 Hostile Indians encamped around the Spring.
4 Advance under Col. Carroll, sent forward to bring on the engagement.
5 Gap between the Cavalry and Infantry, through which many Indians escaped.
Advance.
1
Order of Battle.
Reseve under Lt. Col Dyer.
1
Halls Brigade
Roberts Brigade
4
3
3
5
2
Mounted
Riflemen
and
Cavalry

returned with two Negroes and four Indians, of the war party. These prisoners, together with two others brought in by Old Chinnabee and his son, were sent to Huntsville.[6]

The Creeks having assembled at the town of Tallaseehatchee, thirteen miles from the camp, the commander-in-chief dispatched Coffee, now promoted to the rank of brigadier-general, with one thousand men, with one-half of whom he was directed to attack the enemy, and with the other half to scour the country near the Ten Islands, for the purpose of covering his operations.[7] Richard Brown, with a company of Creeks and Cherokees, wearing on their heads distinguishing badges of white feathers and deer's tails, accompanied the expedition.[8] Fording the Coosa at the Fish Dam, four miles above the islands, Coffee advanced to Tallaseehatchee, surrounded it at the rising of the sun, and was fiercely met by the savages with whoops and the sounding of drums—the prophets being in advance. Attacking the decoy companies, they

Tennessee army on 7 October 1813 at Fayetteville, Tennessee. Remini, *Andrew Jackson and the Course of American Empire,* 184–85, 191–92.

[3] Apparently, Coffee and his cavalry raided down the Black Warrior River into modern Walker County, Alabama, destroying deserted Creek villages—including Black Warrior Town—and confiscating 300 bushels of corn and beans. According to Davy Crockett, he was one of eight hundred men who raided as far south as modern Tuscaloosa, Alabama. Owsley, *Struggle for the Gulf,* 64; O'Brien, *In Bitterness and in Tears,* 69; David Crockett, *The Autobiography of David Crockett,* intro. Hamlin Garland (New York: Charles Scribner's Sons, 1923), 58.

[4] Jackson's supply depot, Fort Deposit, was constructed at the mouth of Thompson's Creek at the Tennessee River near modern Guntersville, Alabama, making it accessible to boats coming upriver. Remini, *Andrew Jackson and the Course of American Empire,* 192–93; O'Brien, *In Bitterness and in Tears,* 69.

[5] On 29 October 1813, Lieutenant Colonel Robert H. Dyer, commander of a regiment of Coffee's cavalry brigade, struck the Creek village of Littefutchi (Litafatchi) on Canoe Creek in modern St. Clair County, Alabama. Swanton, *Early History of the Creek Indians,* 285; O'Brien, *In Bitterness and in Tears,* 71.

[6] In his *Reminiscences,* Thomas S. Woodward identifies Old Chinnabee (Chennubby) as the chief of a band of Natchez who had settled in the old settlements of the Tallassees "in the Talladega country." His son Selocta Chinnabee provided Jackson with information on the Creek Red Sticks at Talladega. Woodward, *Reminiscences,* 67–68; Charles R. Burns, "Before the Battle of Horseshoe Bend: March to the Tallapoosa River and Destiny," *Journal of the War of 1812* 11 (Fall 2008): 7–8.

[7] Jackson's forces constructed Fort Strother near the Ten Islands of the Coosa River near Greensport, St. Clair County, Alabama. Tallaseehatchee (Tallushatchee), a Creek Red Stick town, was located some thirteen miles east of Fort Strother on Tallaseehatchee Creek. Tom Kanon, "Before Horseshoe: Andrew Jackson's Campaigns in the Creek War Prior to Horseshoe Bend," in *Tohopeka: Rethinking the Creek War & the War of 1812,* ed., Kathryn E. Holland Braund (Tuscaloosa: University of Alabama Press, 2012), 112.

[8] With a small detachment of twenty men, Richard Brown, a métis Cherokee, had been reconnoitering the Red Sticks ahead of Jackson's army. He was also commissioned a colonel by Jackson and given command of some 200 Cherokee and Creek warriors. Susan M. Abram, *Forging a Cherokee-American Alliance in the Creek War: From Creation to Betrayal* (Tuscaloosa: University of Alabama Press, 2015), 53, 59, 62.

were soon surrounded by the troops, who charged them with great slaughter. After a short but terrible action, eighty-four women and children were made prisoners, while the bodies of one hundred and eighty-six warriors were counted upon the field, where, unavoidably, some women also perished. Many other bodies lay concealed in the weeds. Five Americans were killed and eighteen wounded.[9] Late in the evening of the same day, Coffee re-crossed the Coosa and reached headquarters. Not a solitary warrior begged for his life, and it is believed none escaped to the woods. These prisoners were also sent to Huntsville. General Jackson, now forcing his way over the Coosa Mountain, arrived at the Ten Islands, where he began to erect a second depot for supplies, which was protected by strong picketing and blockhouses, and which received the name of Fort Strother.[10]

In Lashley's Fort in the Talladega town many friendly Creeks had taken refuge.[11] The war party, in strong force, had surrounded them so effectually that not a solitary warrior could escape from the fort unseen to convey to the American camp intelligence of their critical condition. One night, a prominent Indian, who belonged to the Hickory Ground town, resolved to escape to the lines of Jackson, by Indian stratagem. He threw over him the skin of a large hog, with the head and legs attached, and placing himself in a stooping position, went out of the fort and crawled about before the camps of the hostiles, grunting and apparently rooting, until he slowly got beyond the reach of their arrows. Then, discarding his swinish mantle, he fled with the speed of lightning to Jackson, who resolved immediately to relieve these people.[12] The commander-in-chief, leaving a small guard to protect his camp and sick, put his troops in motion at the hour of midnight, and forded the Coosa, here six hundred yards wide, with a rocky, uneven bottom. Each horseman carried

[9] While the prophets were "beating their drums," Coffee's superior force obliterated the Creek Red Sticks with a withering fire from their arms, and Coffee acknowledged the Red Sticks were primarily armed with bows and arrows. Virtually all the warriors were killed, along with several women and children, in this Battle of Tallaseehatchee (Tallushatchee) on 3 November 1813, and David Crockett observed, "We now shot them like dogs." This engagement confirmed Jackson's commitment to avenge the slaughter at Fort Mims and his strategy of total war against the Red Sticks. Ibid., 63–64; Crockett, *Autobiography*, 61; Kanon, "Before Horseshoe," 112; Owsley, *Struggle for the Gulf*, 64–65.

[10] Fort Strother, named for Captain John Strother, Jackson's topographical engineer, was erected on a bluff on the west side of the Coosa River below the current Neely Henry Dam, near modern Ohatchee, Alabama. It became Jackson's base of operations for his war on the Creek Red Sticks. Abram, *Forging a Cherokee-American Alliance in the Creek War*, 64; O'Brien, *In Bitterness and in Tears*, 76; E. J. Vernon, "St. Clair to acquire 80 percent of Fort Strother," *St. Clair News-Aegis*, 14 June 2012.

[11] Lashley's Fort (Leslie's Fort or Fort Leslie) at the Creek town of Talladega in modern Talladega County, Alabama, was actually the fortified home of Alexander L. Leslie, a métis Creek. However, it is misspelled by Pickett and in official correspondence—such as Andrew Jackson's letters—and it was often expressed as Lashley's Fort or Fort Lashley. Burns, "Before the Battle of Horseshoe Bend," 8; Owen, *History of Alabama*, 2: 1290; Vernon James Knight, Jr., "Fort Leslie and Upper Creek Ceramics of the Early Nineteenth Century," *Journal of Alabama Archaeology* 43 (June 1997): 37.

[12] According to Thomas S. Woodward, Selocta Chinnabee or "Sarlotta [Selocta] Fixico" was the warrior who left Fort Leslie to alert Jackson to their precarious situation. He also declares, "The story of the hog-skin over the Indian, is all a hoax." Woodward, *Reminiscences*, 68.

behind him a footman, until the whole army was over. Late that evening he encamped within six miles of Talladega. At four o'clock next morning, Jackson surrounded the enemy, making a wide circuit, with twelve hundred infantry and eight hundred cavalry. The hostiles, to the number of one thousand and eighty, were concealed in a thick shrubbery that covered the margin of a small rivulet, and at eight o'clock they received a heavy fire from the advance guard under Colonel Carroll. Screaming and yelling most horribly, the enemy rushed forth in the direction of General Roberts's brigade, a few companies of which gave way at the first fire. Jackson directed Colonel Bradley to fill the chasm with his regiment, which had not advanced in a line with the others; but that officer failing to obey the order, Colonel Dyer's reserve dismounted, and met the approaching enemy with great firmness. The retreating militia, mortified at seeing their places so promptly filled, recovered their former position, and displayed much bravery.[13]

The action now became general along the whole line, while the Indians, who had at first fought courageously, were now seen flying in all directions. But, owing to the halt of Bradley's regiment, and the cavalry under Alcorn having taken too wide a circuit, many escaped to the mountains.[14] A general charge was made, and the wood for miles was covered with dead savages. Their loss was very great, and could not be ascertained. However, two hundred and ninety-nine bodies were counted on the main field. Fifteen Americans were killed, and eighty-five wounded. The latter were conveyed to Fort Strother in litters made of raw hides. The fort contained one hundred and sixty friendly warriors, with their wives and children, who were all to have been butchered the very morning that Jackson attacked their assailants. Never was a party of poor devils more rejoiced at being relieved. General Pillow of the infantry,[15]

[13] Jackson used the advance guard under Colonel William Carroll to flush the Red Sticks, and he tried to overpower them with the fire power of General Isaac Roberts's brigade, only to see many of his militia break and run. Colonel Edward Bradley attempted to fill the breach with his regiment, but it was Lieutenant Colonel Robert Dyer's dismounted cavalry that solidified the line. O'Brien, *In Bitterness and in Tears*, 77–78; Remini, *Andrew Jackson and the Course of the American Empire*, 196–97; Tom Kanon, *Tennesseans at War 1812–1815: Andrew Jackson, the Creek War, and the Battle of New Orleans* (Tuscaloosa: University of Alabama Press, 2014), 77–79.

[14] Colonel John Alcorn commanded the 2nd Regiment of Volunteer Mounted Riflemen who had also followed Jackson to Natchez (December 1812–April 1813) and fought at Tallaseehatchee (Tallushatchee). O'Brien, *In Bitterness and in Tears*, 73–74, 77.

[15] Pickett's "General Pillow" was Colonel William Pillow (1772–1868), who had been promoted by Jackson on 26 September 1813. He commanded a regiment of cavalry or mounted riflemen at the Battle of Talladega, and, after he was seriously wounded, Colonel William Martin took command of the regiment. Kanon, *Tennesseans at War 1812–1815*, 74, 78–79; "Colonel William Pillow," *Columbia Herald*, 12 November 1869, www.oursoutherncousin.com.

Colonel Lauderdale of the cavalry,[16] Major Boyd of the mounted riflemen,[17] and Lieutenant Barton, were wounded—the last named mortally.[18] Colonel Bradley was arrested for disobedience of orders, but was released without a trial. Jackson buried his dead and marched back to Fort Strother as rapidly as possible, for he was out of provisions. Arriving there, he was mortified to find none at that point for him.*

About the time that the Middle and West Tennessee volunteers flocked to the standard of Jackson, a large body of volunteers from East Tennessee rendezvoused to march to the seat of war under Major General John Cocke.[19] Shortly afterwards, General White, commanding a detachment of one thousand men, belonging to Cocke's force, advanced to Turkey Town. From this place he reported to Jackson that he would, the next day, march in the direction of headquarters, and should, in the meantime, be glad to receive his orders.[20] The latter ordered him to march to Fort Strother, and protect that place during his absence to Talladega, where, he informed him, he intended immediately to march to the relief of the garrison of Lashley's Fort. While White was on the march to Fort Strother to comply with this requisition, he received a dispatch from General Cocke, ordering him to alter his route and form a junction with him at the mouth of the Chattooga. This order he obeyed, preferring to comply with

* A portion of the Talladega battlefield is now (1851) embraced within the limits of the beautiful and flourishing American town of that name, which contains a population of near two thousand, and is situated in a delightful valley, with magnificent mountain scenery in view.

[16] Lieutenant Colonel James Lauderdale (1768–1814), a native of Botetourt, Virginia, served in the cavalry brigade commanded by Brigadier General John Coffee at Talladega. He recovered from his wound and continued to serve under Jackson until his death near New Orleans on 23 December 1814. On 6 February 1818, the Alabama territorial legislature created and named Lauderdale County in his honor. Kanon, *Tennesseans at War 1812–1815*, 153; "Biography of the Late Lt. Col. James Lauderdale," *Niles Weekly Register, Supplement to Volume VII* (February 25, 1815), 82–84; Ken Johnson, "Lauderdale named for war hero," *Times Daily* [Florence, Alabama], 30 November 2003.

[17] Major Richard Boyd was a member of Colonel John Alcorn's 2nd Regiment of Volunteer Mounted Riflemen. Benson J. Lossing, *The Pictorial Field-Book of the War of 1812*, 2 vols. (1868; reprint, Gretna: Pelican Publishing Company, 2001), 2: 765.

[18] Lieutenant Samuel Barton was one of nineteen men killed at Talladega or who died from wounds received at Talladega. Ibid.; "1812 monument placed at Oak Hill Cemetary," *The Daily Home* [Talladega, Alabama], 18 March 1816.

[19] Major General John Alexander Cocke (1772–1854) served as the commander of the East Tennessee Division of the state militia at the beginning of the War of 1812. He had served in the Tennessee Senate (1799–1801) and House of Representatives (1796, 1797, 1807, 1809, and 1812), including as speaker in 1812. "John Cocke," *Biographical Directory of the United States Congress, 1774-Present* (online); Tom Kanon, "Glories in the Field: John Cocke vs. Andrew Jackson During the War of 1812," *Journal of East Tennessee History* 71 (1999): 49–51.

[20] Brigadier General James White led the advance of General Cocke's East Tennessee militia down the Tennessee River, and on 17 October 1813, he arrived at Ross's trading post at Lookout Mountain, near modern Chattanooga. A few days later, he marched down to Path Killer's Turkey Town on the Coosa River in modern Cherokee County, Alabama, and established a camp above Turkey Town that became Fort Armstrong. O'Brien, *In Bitterness and in Tears*, 70; Abram, *Forging a Cherokee-American Alliance in the Creek War*, 53, 61.

the commands of Cocke rather than those of Jackson, although the latter was generally considered the commander-in-chief of all the troops from Tennessee. Jackson was shocked at receiving an account of the retrograde march of White, and that, too, at a late hour of night, previous to the Battle of Talladega; and it determined him to attack the Indians forthwith, and rush back to Fort Strother, now left with a very feeble protection.[21]

However, before General White had reached Turkey Town, his advance-guard, consisting of four hundred Cherokees and a few whites under Colonel Gideon Morgan and John Lowrey, advanced upon the town of Tallaseehatchee on the evening of the 3rd November, and found that it had that morning been destroyed by Coffee. Collecting twenty of the wounded Indians, they returned with them to Turkey Town.[22]

The mischiefs of a want of concert between the East and West Tennessee troops—growing out of a jealousy of the former, and a strong desire to share some of the glory which the latter had already acquired in the few battles they had fought—were, in a very few days, made quite apparent. Through Robert Graison, an aged Scotchman, the Hillabees (a portion of whom fought Jackson at Talladega) made offers of peace, to which the general immediately and willingly acceded.[23] At that very time, and when Graison had hastened back with the favorable reply of Jackson, General White surrounded the Hillabee town early in the morning and effected a complete surprise, killing sixty warriors and taking two hundred and fifty prisoners. The Hillabees, it is asserted, made not the slightest resistance. At all events, not a drop

[21] On 6 November 1813, General Cocke sent General White a message ordering him not to join Jackson because of supply shortages, raising the possibility of defeat and taking "a different direction in which we can share some of the dangers and glories of the field." Jackson learned of White's reversal around midnight on the 8th. Kanon, "Glories in the Field," 51–52.

[22] Actually, the Cherokee forces under Colonel Gideon Morgan, an Indian countryman, and Lieutenant Colonel John Lowrey, a métis Cherokee, had been organized in early October 1813 and had been cooperating with Coffee's advance on Tallaseehatchee (Tallushatchee) before General James White's arrival at Turkey Town. Abram, *Forging a Cherokee-American Alliance in the Creek War*, 58–59, 64; Thurman Wilkins, *Cherokee Tragedy: The Ridge Family and the Decimation of a People* (Norman: University of Oklahoma Press, 1986), 66–69.

[23] Robert Grierson (Graison, Grayson) was a long-time resident, trader, and wealthy Indian countryman among the Hillabees. He and his extended family had become prisoners of the Red Sticks that dominated the Hillabee towns. Abram, *Forging a Cherokee-American Alliance in the Creek War*, 74, 191 n. 117; Owsley, *Struggle for the Gulf*, 67.

of Tennessee blood was spilt. The other Hillabee towns, viewing this as flagrant treachery on the part of *Jackson*, became the most relentless enemies of the Americans, and afterwards fought them with fiendish desperation. The destruction of this town was in pursuance of the orders of General Cocke. White, in marching down, had already destroyed Little Okfuskee and Genalga, both of which had been abandoned by the inhabitants, with the exception of five warriors, who were captured at the former.[24]

General Cocke, having given up the ambition of achieving separate victories, was now prepared to cooperate with Jackson, and for that purpose joined him at Fort Strother with fourteen hundred men. He was sent, by the commander-in-chief, back to East Tennessee, with a portion of his command, whose term of service had nearly expired, with orders to raise fifteen hundred men and rejoin him in the Creek Nation.[25]

Georgia, no less patriotic than Tennessee, soon came to the relief of her brethren of the Mississippi Territory. Brigadier General John Floyd crossed the Ocmulgee, Flint and Chattahoochee, and advanced near the Tallapoosa, with an army of nine hundred and fifty militia, and four hundred friendly Indians, piloted by Abram Mordecai, the Jew trader, of whom we have so often had occasion to speak.[26] Before sunrise, on a cold frosty morning, Floyd attacked the Creeks, who were assembled in great force at the town of Autossee, which was situated on the east bank of the Tallapoosa, at the mouth of the Calebee Creek. Booth's battalion, which composed the right column, marched from the center—Watson's composed the left, and marched from its right.[27] Upon the flanks were the rifle companies of Adams and Meriwether—the latter commanded by Lieutenant Hendon.[28] The artillery, under Captain Thomas, advanced in the road in front of the right column.[29] General Floyd intended to surround the town by throwing the right wing on Calebee Creek, at the mouth of which he was informed the town stood, and resting the left on the river bank below it; but the dawn of day exhibited, to his surprise, a second town,

[24] While Jackson had agreed to make peace with the Hillabees on 17 November 1813, General Cocke ordered White and his Cherokee auxiliaries under Colonel Gideon Morgan to attack the Hillabee towns on the 18th. The Cherokees led the attack and quickly overwhelmed the Hillabee Red Sticks, who thought they were through with fighting, killing some 60 warriors and taking 256 prisoners—mainly women and children. The perceived betrayal by Jackson and slaughter at the hands of the Tennesseans and Cherokees caused the surviving Hillabees to renew their resistance. O'Brien, *In Bitterness and in Tears*, 66–67; Abram, *Forging a Cherokee-American Alliance in the Creek War*, 65–66; Kanon, "Glories in the Field," 52–53.

[25] When Cocke arrived at Fort Strother on 12 December 1813, he learned that Jackson had been dealing with a near mutiny from his volunteers, whose three-month enlistments had terminated: "I found an almost deserted camp." To complicate matters further, the three-month enlistment for Cocke's East Tennessee volunteers had nearly expired. Kanon, "Glories in the Field," 55.

[26] While the Tennessee armies advanced on the Creek Red Sticks from the north, Major General John Floyd was expected to lead his Georgia militia forces to the Chattahoochee and to establish a base in the Creek Nation. In November 1813, he rendezvoused with allied Creek headmen at Coweta and constructed Fort Mitchell in modern Russell County, Alabama. According to James A. Tait, a private in Captain Smith's company, Floyd's army was "18 hundred strong, including 500 Indians, besides 8 hundred infantry, 200 cavalry, 200 riflemen and an artillery company of 100 men." James A. Tait, "Journal of James A. Tait For the Year 1813 [A Journal kept by Mr. Tait from the 25th of August, 1813, to the 21st of March, 1814]," ed. Peter A. Brannon, *Alabama Historical Quarterly* 2 (Winter 1940): 234; O'Brien, *In Bitterness and in Tears*, 93–95; Owsley, *Struggle for the Gulf*, 43, 51–54.

[27] Colonel David S. Booth, commander of the 4th Regiment in Floyd's First Georgia

about five hundred yards below. It was now necessary to change the plan of attack, by advancing three companies of infantry to the lower town, accompanied by Meriwether's rifles, and two troops of light dragoons commanded by Captains Irwin and Steele. The remainder of the army marched upon the upper town, and soon the battle became general.[30]

The Indians at first advanced, and fought with great resolution; but the fire from the artillery, with the charge of the bayonets, drove them into the out-houses and thickets, in rear of the town. Many concealed themselves in caves cut in the bluff of the river, here thickly covered with cane. The admirable plans of General Floyd for the extermination of the foe were not properly executed, owing to the failure of the friendly Indians to cross the Tallapoosa to the west side, and there cut off all retreat. The difficulty of the ford and the coolness of the morning deterred them, as they stated; but fear, in all probability, was the prime cause. They now irregularly fell back to the rear of the army. However, the Cowetas under McIntosh, and the Tuckabatchees under the Mad Dragon's Son, fell into the ranks, and fought with great bravery. The hour of nine o'clock witnessed the abandonment of the ground by the enemy, and the conflagration of the houses. From the number of bodies scattered over the field, together with those burnt in the houses and slain on the bluff, it is believed that two hundred must have perished, among whom were the kings of Tallassee and Autossee. The number of buildings burned, some of which were of fine Indian architecture and filled with valuable articles, amounted to about four hundred.[31]

The Americans had eleven men killed and fifty-four wounded.[32] The friendly Indians had

Brigade, led the right column, and Lieutenant Colonel James C. Watson and Meriwether's Rifle Company moved to the left to encircle Autossee. Tait, "Journal of James A. Tait," 234; O'Brien, *In Bitterness and in Tears,* 97; "Georgia Military—1812," http://www.rootsweb.ancestry.com/~gataylor/regim.htm.

[28] Captain William E. Adams and Captain James Meriwether were the commanders of the two rifle companies at the engagement at Calabee Creek. Apparently, Meriwether's company was commanded by Lieutenant Isham Hendon when the attack started on the morning of 29 November 1813. O'Brien, *In Bitterness and in Tears,* 96–97; "Georgia Military—Militia 1813 Drafted 3rd Division," http://files.usgwarchives.net/ga/military/warof1812/ros.txt.

[29] Captain Jett Thomas (1776–1817) commanded the Baldwin Volunteer Artillery Company from Milledgeville, Georgia. Private Tait reports that Thomas's artillery crews fired eighteen rounds, "shattering their miserable huts to pieces." Tait, "Journal of James A. Tait," 234; "Georgia Military—1812"; Gordon Burns Smith, *History of the Georgia Militia, 1783–1861,* 4 vols. (Milledgeville: Boyd Publishing, 2000), 1: 345.

[30] Captain Samuel S. Steele and Captain John Irwin commanded the two companies of light dragoons. "Georgia Military—1812"; O'Brien, *In Bitterness and in Tears,* 97.

[31] The attack on Autossee and the its satellite village did not go smoothly due to extremely cold weather, accompanied with a heavy frost and high water in the Tallapoosa that prevented the quick movement of the allied Creek forces under William McIntosh and Mad Dragon's Son. Thomas's two cannons and a charge by the dragoons had a devastating impact on the Red Stick forces, killing large numbers, including several prominent leaders. Although James A. Tait also records the death of the Tallassee King at Autossee, more recent research indicates that Hopoithle Mico—or Tallassee King—was not killed at Autossee. O'Brien, *In Bitterness and in Tears,* 97–100; Stiggins, *Creek Indian History,* 123–27; Tait, "Journal of James A. Tait," 235.

[32] According to James A. Tait, at least five officers were wounded, including "Capts. King, Little and Morise (sic)," Adjutant General Newnan "having his knee pan broken," and General Floyd receiving a leg wound. Tait, "Journal of James A. Tait," 234.

several killed and wounded. Important services were rendered by Adjutant-General Newnan,[33] the aides Majors Crawford and Pace, and the surgeons Williamson and Clopton.[34] Major Freeman, at the head of Irwin's cavalry and part of Steele's, made bold charges upon the Indians, completely routing them. [35]The companies led on by Captains Thomas, Adams, Barton, Myrick, Little, King, Broadnax, Cleaveland, Cunningham, Lee and Lieutenant Hendon, fought with gallantry.[36] Brigadier General Shackelford performed efficient services in successfully bringing the troops into action,[37] and Adjutants Montgomery and Broadnax exhibited activity and courage.[38] The battalion of Major Booth was properly brought into action, and that of Major Watson fought with commendable spirit.[39] The cavalry under Irwin, Patterson and Steele, charged with success when opportunities were afforded.[40] Great heroism was displayed by Quartermaster Terrill, who, though badly wounded, escaped after his horse was shot under him. The horse of Lieutenant Strong was shot under him, and he made a narrow escape.[41] In seven days the troops had marched one hundred and twenty miles, and fought this battle. Being now sixty miles from the depot of provisions, and the rations of the troops being nearly exhausted, Floyd, after the dead had been interred and the wounded properly attended, began the retrograde march to Fort Mitchell, upon the Chattahoochee. On ascending Heydon's Hill, a mile east of the battle-ground, many of the Creeks rallied and fiercely attacked his rear; but after a few rounds they were dispersed.*

* Upon the campaigns of the Tennesseans under Jackson and Cocke, and the Georgians under Floyd, I have consulted the various works and public documents upon the late war, such as the lives of Jackson by Kendall, Cobbett, Eaton and Waldo; Russell, *History of the War;* Brackenridge, *History of the Late War*; and the various *American State Papers.*

[33] At the outset of General Floyd's campaign, Private Tait referred to Colonel Daniel Newnan as the "most able, or skillful, commander in the southern country . . . delivering his orders with great precision, accuracy, and distinctness." While he continued to serve as Georgia's adjutant general (1806–1817), Newnan (1780–1851) served as a commander of Georgia Militia volunteers under General Floyd during the Creek War. Ibid., 231; O'Brien, *In Bitterness and in Tears*, 33–34, 94, 98, 126; Smith, *History of the Georgia Militia*, 1: 330; "Daniel Newnan," *Biographical Directory of the United States Congress, 1774-Present* (online).

[34] Major Joel Crawford (1783–1858) served as one of General Floyd's aides during the Creek War. Surgeon Charles Williamson was present at the battles at Autossee on 29 November 1813 and at Calabee Creek on 27 January 1814. Major Pace and Surgeon Clopton cannot be identified. I. J. Hofmayer and Harry S. Strozier, eds., *Report of Proceedings of the Thirty-Fifth Annual Session of the Georgia Bar Association, Held at Tybee Island, Georgia, June 7, 8, 1918* (Macon: J. W. Burke company, 1918), 63; "Joel Crawford," *Biographical Directory of the United States Congress, 1774-Present* (online); "Baldwin County War of 1812," http://theusgenweb.org/ga/baldwin/1812.html.

[35] Major Frederick Freeman commanded a reserve dragoon force that was called into action at a critical time, overwhelming and spreading panic through the Red Stick defenders. O'Brien, *In Bitterness and in Tears*, 97, 99.

[36] Pickett's captains who "fought with gallantry" may have been the following: Jett Thomas, William E. Adams, Willoughby Barton, John Myrick, John E. Little, Edwin D. King, John H. Broadnax, Benjamin Cleaveland, [John/Joseph] Cunningham, and Lewis Lee. Woodward, *Reminiscences*, 78–79; "Georgia Military—1812"; "Georgia Militia War of 1812: Harris Regiment," http://files.usgwarchives.net/ga/military/warof1812/harris.txt.

[37] On 23 August 1812, Edmund Meredith Shackelford (1786–1857) joined the rifle company of Captain William E. Adams as a second lieutenant. His future brother-in-laws John H. and Robert Broadnax, from Putnam County, Georgia, volunteered to serve as officers in Harris's Regiment of the Georgia Militia. On 19 September 1813, Shackelford was promoted to brigade inspector and served under General Floyd during the Creek War of 1813–1814. While Pickett refers to him as a brigadier general, it is not clear when he received this appointment from the state of Georgia. Glen Carew Beckwith, "General Edmund and Rebecca Power Broadnax Shackelford," http://www.genealogy.com/forum/; Woodward, *Reminiscences*, 7.

[38] Floyd's adjutants cannot be positively identified by this editor. Originally, a James Montgomery joined Floyd's Brigade in 1813 as a "wagon master" and was later identified as a "special commissary." Initially, Robert Broadnax volunteered with his brother, Captain John H. Broadnax, in Walton Harris's Regiment of Georgia Militia, and he is listed as "Adjutant." He also appears in later records as Colonel Robert Broadnax. Beckwith, "General Edmund and Rebecca Power Broadnax Shackelford"; "Georgia Militia War of 1812: Harris Regiment"; "Military Georgia 1812 Roster Surnames M," http://files.usgwarchives.net/ga/military/warof1812/rosterm.txt.

[39] Most sources cite David S. Booth with the rank of colonel and John C. Watson with the rank of lieutenant colonel. O'Brien, *In Bitterness and in Tears*, 97–98.

[40] Captain William Patterson commanded a company in Major Frederick Freeman's dragoon squadron. "Military Georgia 1812 Rosters Surnames N-P," http://files.usgwarchives.net/ga/military/warof1812/rostern.txt.

[41] Pickett's Quartermaster Terrill and Lieutenant Strong cannot be further identified by this editor, and they are not mentioned in Private James A. Tait's journal.

Chapter XXXVI

Remarkable Canoe Fight—Battle of Holy Ground—March to Cahawba Old Towns

Returning again to the seat of war, in the fork of the Tombigbee and Alabama, it will be seen that Colonel William McGrew advanced in pursuit of a party of the enemy, with twenty-five mounted militia. Coming upon them at Tallahatta, or Bashi Creek, a spirited action ensued. Colonel McGrew was killed, together with three of his company—the two Griffins and Edmund Miles—which put the remainder of the Americans to flight.[1]

General Flournoy, who had restricted the operations of Claiborne to those of a defensive character, now ordered the latter to advance with his army, for the purpose of defending the citizens while employed in gathering their crops; to drive the enemy from the frontiers, to follow them up to their contiguous towns, and to "kill, burn and destroy all their Negroes, horses, cattle, and other property that cannot conveniently be brought to the depots." General Flournoy, admitted, in the same order, that such usage was contrary to that of civilized nations, but stated that the conduct of Great Britain and the acts of her Indian allies fully justified it. On the same day that these instructions were received, Claiborne, at the head of Major Hind's Mississippi dragoons, a part of the twelve months volunteers, and some companies of militia, marched from St. Stephens, crossed the Tombigbee, and proceeded, by an indirect route, to the northern boundary, where Colonel McGrew had fallen. He found the body of that officer, and those of the privates, and interred them with military honors. On the march, small bodies of the enemy hovered around, but could not be brought into action.[2] A picket of infantry, was attacked from an ambuscade, and three of them wounded; but before Major Hinds, who was a little in the rear, could come up, the assailants leaped down a precipice and escaped the pursuit of Captain Foster's detachment.[3] Remaining two days at Fort Easley, upon Baker's Bluff, Claiborne scoured the whole country with detachments. In these expeditions he had five of his men severely wounded,

[1] On 12 October 1813, Colonel William McGrew's mounted unit rode out from St. Stephens to search for a Creek war party of 50 warriors reported near the deserted Easley's Fort. They were ambushed at Bashi Creek, and McGrew and three privates—Edmund Miles, David Griffin, and Jesse Griffin—were killed in a brief skirmish. George Strother Gaines wrote that this war party included "a few renegade Choctaws." Waselkov, *Conquering Spirit*, 161, 169; Rowland, *Mississippi Territory in the War of 1812*, 63; Gaines, *Reminiscences*, 64.

[2] On 16–20 October 1813, Claiborne's force of militia and dragoons scoured the Forks area, suffering more casualties and making little contact with the Red Stick war parties, who continued their hit-and-run tactics. Waselkov, *Conquering Spirit*, 161; Rowland, *Mississippi*

among whom was Capt. William Bradberry, who had acted so bravely at Burnt Corn. He was carried back to St. Stephens, and there died in great agony. Failing to bring the Indians to action, being convinced that they were in very inconsiderable force, and becoming destitute of subsistence, Claiborne marched to "Pine Level," in the neighborhood of some good farms, a mile east of the Tombigbee. From this point he sent spies to the Alabama.[4] He also sent a dispatch to Flournoy, requesting him to suffer all the disposable force to march immediately to the Creek country.*

The Indians were everywhere committing depredations, in small parties, and occasionally some of the settlers were killed. Tandy Walker, Benjamin Foster and Evans, a colored man, had been dispatched by the citizens of Fort Madison across the Alabama, in an eastern direction, as spies. Approaching the late battle-ground at Burnt Corn, they came upon a small camp of the enemy, upon whom they fired from a concealed position. The Indians fled with great precipitancy, while the spies seized some horses, plundered the camp, and retreated to Sizemore's Ferry. Here, late at night, while reposing in the cane, guns were fired upon them, and Evans was instantly killed. Walker escaped with a wound in the side and a broken arm, but the next day crossed the Alabama upon a cane raft and reached Fort Madison,[5] where Foster, having already arrived, had reported his death.†

Captain Samuel Dale, having now sufficiently recovered from his wounds, obtained the consent of Colonel Carson, who had returned to Fort Madison, to drive these small parties of the enemy from the frontiers. Dale was joined by a detachment of thirty of Captain Jones's Mississippi volunteers, under Lieutenant Montgomery, and forty Clarke County militia. Gerard W. Creagh, the same who was attached to his company at Burnt Corn, was his lieutenant upon this occasion. This expedition marched in a northern direction, visiting the abandoned plantations, and frequently discovering old traces of Indians.[6] Dale returned to the fort, and, the next day, marched southeastwardly towards Brazier's Landing, now French's, where an Indian Negro, named Caesar, who was in company, had two canoes concealed

* Claiborne's MS papers.

† Conversations with old settlers.

Territory in the War of 1812, 62–63.

3 Despite General Flournoy's objections, Major Thomas Hinds and his Mississippi dragoons continued their service under Claiborne. Captain James Foster served as a company commander in Claiborne's Mississippi Territorial Volunteers. Rowland, _Mississippi Territory in the War of 1812_, 38, 55–63, 157–62, 174.

4 While continuing to suffer losses—such as the death of Captain William Bradberry—in the guerilla warfare with the Red Sticks, Claiborne moved his base of operations in November 1813 from St. Stephens to Pine Level—now modern Jackson, Alabama—some ten miles east of the Tombigbee River. Waselkov, _Conquering Spirit_, 162; Halbert and Ball, _Creek War of 1813 and 1814_, 221–22; Justus Wyman, "A Geographical Sketch of Alabama Territory," _Transactions of the Alabama Historical Society, 1898–99_, vol. 3 (Tuscaloosa: The Society, 1899), 123–24.

5 Arthur Sizemore, a métis Creek, operated his ferry on the Alabama River at Gainestown in the Tensaw District. This is the same crossing place used by Colonel James Caller's militia on their way to Burnt Corn Creek in July 1813. George Strother Gaines visited Tandy Walker during his recovery at Fort Madison. Gaines, _Reminiscences_, 64; "Arthur Sizemore & Family," www.genealogy.com; Harvey H. Jackson, _Rivers of History: Life on the Coosa, Tallapoosa, Cahaba, and Alabama_ (Tuscaloosa: University of Alabama Press, 1995), 34.

6 The actions of Dale with the local militia forces, including Gerard W. Creagh and Lieutenant Andrew Montgomery, commanding part of Captain Randall Jones's company, were part of General Claiborne's strategy to search out and attack the Red Stick foraging and war parties. Rowland, _Mississippi Territory in the War of 1812_, 174, 183.

in the cane. In these they crossed the Alabama, at the close of the day, and bivouacked on the eastern bank. They were thinly clad, and the frost was severe. When the sun first made its appearance over the tall canes, Captain Dale put his command in motion and marched up the eastern bank, after having placed the canoes in charge of Jeremiah Austill, with six men, with orders to keep the boats parallel with those who marched on foot. Arriving opposite the farm of the late Dixon Bailey, who had heroically fallen at Fort Mims, as we have seen, Dale entered the boats, went over to the place, and discovered fresh signs of the mysterious foe, with whose habits he was so well acquainted. No sooner had he returned to his command on the eastern side than Austill discovered a canoe, occupied by Indians, descending the river, whom he immediately approached. They tacked about, paddled up the river, and disappeared in the thick cane, near the mouth of Randon's Creek. A few minutes only elapsed before a heavy firing ensued, up the creek, where the expedition had encountered some savages on horseback—Captain Dale's rifle, which unhorsed one of these Indians, having given the alarm. The yell was raised, and they made an attempt to charge; but the hot fire of the Americans compelled them to make a precipitate retreat, with one of their number killed and several severely wounded.[7]

In the meantime, Austill had reached Randon's plantation,[8] with the canoes, a quarter of an hour in advance of the main party.* When they came up, Dale ordered them to cross to the western side, as it was found impracticable to continue the route on the eastern, on account of the cane and thick vines. While the company of Captain Jones or Lieutenant Montgomery was being ferried over, Captain Dale, Jere Austill, Lieutenant Creagh, James Smith, John Elliott, a half-breed, Brady and six others occupied a position in a small field, between a sand bluff and the river, where, kindling a fire, they began to boil some beef and roast a few potatoes for their morning repast. When all the command had passed the river except these men, and immediately after the Negro, Caesar, had returned, with the smaller canoe, the men from the western side gave the alarm that the Indians were rapidly descending upon those who occupied the little field. They sprang up from their hasty meal, retreated to the river side, and were partially screened from the enemy's fire by a small bank. While in this perilous situation, hemmed in by the Indians and the river, their attention was directed to a large flat-bottomed canoe, containing eleven warriors.

* Randon was a wealthy Indian countryman, who was massacred at Fort Mims.

[7] The métis son of Louis Leclerc Milfort—Will Milfort—was the Red Stick killed in the skirmish in the thick canebrakes along the Alabama River, and Sam Dale claimed credit for taking his life. Waselkov, *Conquering Spirit*, 162, 282 n. 16, 322 n. 5.

[8] John Randon, a métis Creek, and most of his family had been killed at Fort Mims, and his plantation on the lower Alabama had been plundered and burned. Waselkov, *Conquering Spirit*, 137, 141, 143, 249–50.

Naked, and painted in a variety of fantastic colors, while a panther-skin encircled the head of the chief, and extended down his back, these Indians presented a picturesque and imposing appearance.[9]

For some reason, those in the rear now retired, leaving Dale and his little party free to attack those in the canoe. The red voyagers, apparently unapprised of their danger, glided gently down the river, sitting erect, with their guns before them. Dale and his party immediately opened a fire upon them, which they promptly returned. Several rounds were afterwards exchanged, resulting, however, in but little injury, as the Indians now lay flat in the canoe, exposing nothing but their heads. At length, two of the latter, cautiously getting into the water, swam for the shore, above the field, holding their guns dry above their heads. They swam near the land, above the mouth of a stream, over whose muddy bottom Austill and Smith crossed with difficulty, to pursue them. When near the Indians, the buckskin leggings of Austill, suspended by a band around his waist, fell about his feet, from the weight of water in them, causing him to slip and be precipitated down the bluff. At that moment, a ball from Smith's unerring rifle perforated the head of one of the Indians, who immediately turned over upon his back and then sunk. The other gained the bank and ascended it, keeping Smith off with his gun, which he pretended was charged. Austill, who had now gained the top of the bluff, pursued the Indian up the stream, when a gun was fired, the contents of which passed just over his head. Imagining himself among the enemy, and hesitating for a moment, the savage escaped. The fire proved to be from Lieutenant Creagh's gun, who, in the thick cane, supposed Austill to be the warrior, in whose pursuit he was likewise engaged.[10]

While these things were rapidly transpiring, Dale ordered the large canoe to be manned on the opposite shore, and to be brought over to capture the Indians who were still in their canoe. Eight men sprang into it, but having approached near enough to see the number of fierce warriors still alive, and ready to defend themselves to desperation, this cautious party rapidly paddled back to the western side. The exasperated Dale now proposed that some of his men should follow him, in the small canoe, which was immediately acquiesced in. Dale leaped down the bank, into the boat, and was followed by Smith and Austill. All the others were anxious to go, but it afforded room for no more. The noble Caesar paddled towards the Indians' canoe, and, when within twenty yards of it, the three resolute Americans rose to give them a broadside; but only the gun of Smith fired, for the other two had, unfortunately, wet their priming. Caesar was ordered to paddle up, and to place his boat side by side with that of the warriors. Approaching within ten feet, the

[9] Caesar (Jim Caesar) played a central role in the "canoe fight" and has been described as a free black and as a slave living with the Creek métis family of Josiah Fisher. While one narrative has him living out his life with Fisher's family, another has this hero being sold to Sam Dale and finally to the sheriff of Lauderdale County, Mississippi, and dying in Kemper County, Mississippi in 1866. Ibid., 208, 322 n. 5; Rowland, *Mississippi Territory in the War of 1812*, 65; Henry S. Halbert, "Creek War Incidents," *Transactions of the Alabama Historical Society, 1897–1898*, vol. 2 (Tuscaloosa: The Society, 1898), 98.

[10] Pickett's narrative of the events near the confluence of Randon's Creek and the Alabama does not explain how Sam Dale and eleven of his men became separated from his detachment of some seventy men that marched out of Fort Madison.

chief, recognizing Dale, exclaimed, "Now for it, Big Sam!"* At the same instant, he presented his gun at Austill's breast. That brave youth struck at him with an oar, which he dodged, and, in return, he brought down his rifle upon Austill's head, just as the canoes came together. At that moment, the powerful arms of Smith and Dale raised their long rifles, which came down, with deadly force, and felled the chief to the bottom of the canoe—his blood and brains bespattering its sides. Such was the force of the blow inflicted by Dale, that his gun was broken near the lock. Seizing the heavy barrel, still left, he did great execution with it, to the end of the combat. Austill, in a moment, engaged with the second warrior, and then with a third, both of whom he dispatched with his clubbed rifle. Smith, too, was equally active, having knocked down two Indians.[11]

Caesar had, by this time, got the canoes close together, and held them with a mighty grasp, which enabled Dale, who was in the advance, and the others to maintain a firm footing, by keeping their feet in both canoes. These brave men now mowed down the savages, amid the encouraging shouts of the men on both sides of the river, who had a full view of the deadly conflict. In the midst of this unparalleled strife, a lusty Indian struck Austill with a war-club, which felled him across the sides of the two boats, and, while prostrate, another had raised his club to dash out his brains, when Dale, by a timely blow, buried his heavy rifle barrel deep in the warrior's skull. In the meantime, Austill recovered his feet, and, in a desperate scuffle with another savage, knocked him into the river with the club which he had wrested from him. The only word spoken during the fight was the exclamation of the chief, upon recognizing Dale, and the request of Caesar for Dale to make use of his bayonet and musket, which he handed to him. Having laid all the warriors low, these undaunted Americans began to cast them into the bright waters of the Alabama, their native stream, now to be their grave. Every time a savage was raised up from the bottom of the canoe, by the head and heels, and slung into the water, the Americans upon the banks sent up shouts, loud and long, as some slight revenge for the tragedy of Fort Mims. Just as the last body found its watery grave, a ball, shot by the Indians from the eastern side, struck one of the canoes, and was followed by other discharges, but without effect. After the fight had ended, eight athletic Indians were thrown out of the canoe. It will be recollected that there were eleven in the boat when first seen, and that

[11] According to Sam Dale's biographer John Francis Hamtramck Claiborne (1809–1884), Dale had a personal relationship with Will Milfort and knew the chief he killed in the canoe fight as "Tar-cha-chee, a noted wrestler, and the most famous ball-player of his clan." J. F. H. Claiborne, *Life and Times of Gen. Sam Dale, the Mississippi Partisan* (New York: Harper & Brothers, 1860), 120–26.

* Dale had long been a trader among the Indians, and, on account of his prowess and large frame, was familiarly called by them "Big Sam."

two of them had swum ashore, and the other one Austill had knocked out before the conflict ended.[12]

The Indian canoe presented a sight unusually revolting—several inches deep in savage blood, thickened with clods of brains and bunches of hair. In this sanguinary bark, and the one paddled by Caesar, the nine Americans who had been left on the eastern side were now conveyed across to the opposite bank, where the heroes received the warm congratulations of their companions, who exultingly surrounding them.[13] The expedition then marched up to Cornell's Ferry, two miles distant, and, seeing no more of the enemy, and being out of provisions, returned that night to Fort Madison. It is remarkable that no one received the least injury, except Austill, whose head and arms were severely bruised.*

A short biographical sketch of these heroes may not be uninteresting, after a recital of their unsurpassed "hand-to-hand" fight, in the unsteady canoes, on the deep Alabama.

Jeremiah Austill was born near the Oconee Station, in Pendleton District, South Carolina, on the 10th August 1794. His father, Captain Evan Austill, has already been mentioned, as one of those who boldly remained to defend Fort Madison, after it had been evacuated by Colonel Carson. His mother was the only sister of Colonel David Files, who died in this state in 1820. At the time of the canoe expedition, Jere. Austill was nineteen years of age, and weighed one hundred and seventy-five pounds, without any surplus flesh. He was bold, active and strong, and had been raised upon the Indian frontiers, having lived some time at the agency, in the Cherokee Nation. He is still a resident of Mobile, and is regarded as a respectable gentleman. Since the canoe fight, he has filled several important offices, and represented the people of Mobile in the legislature. His countenance is open and manly, his eyes keen and piercing, of a dark brown color, his form is erect, and his step elastic. Even now, at the age of fifty-six Colonel Austill is capable of being a very troublesome adversary in a desperate encounter, although one of the most peaceable and amiable men in the country, in the ordinary pursuits of life.[14]

* Conversations with Colonel Gerard W. Creagh, who witnessed the canoe fight, while standing in full view, upon the eastern bank of the Alabama, and Colonel Jeremiah Austill, of Mobile, one of the heroes. Among the MS papers of General Claiborne I also found the report of Captain Randall Jones, of the first regiment of Mississippi Volunteers, respecting the "canoe fight," which fixes the date of the affair.

[12] Thomas S. Woodward, who knew all the participants in the "canoe fight," wrote that "the fight has been detailed by Col. Pickett to the best advantage for those engaged in it . . . it's a pity the eight big Indians killed in the canoe had not been taken to the shore for the landsmen to have looked at. . . . What Col. Pickett has written of Gen. Dale and others that I know, would do for a novel, but not history." The "canoe fight" described by Dale's biographer J. F. H. Claiborne places Dale in the middle of the large Indian canoe, slaying three Creeks single-handedly with his bayonet. Woodward, *Reminiscences*, 75–76. See J. F. H Claiborne, *Life and Times of Gen. Sam Dale, the Mississippi Partisan* (New York: Harper & Brothers, 1860), 124–26.

[13] Standing on the east bank of the Alabama, nine of Sam Dale's men watched the "canoe fight" as it unfolded: Lieutenant Walter Creagh, Drury Allen, Jonathan Embree, William Foster, John Bradley, John Campbell, John Elliott, John Graham, and John French. Halbert, "Creek War Incidents," 98.

[14] Evan Austill (1769–1818) moved his family to Washington County, Mississippi Territory, in 1812 from Georgia, where he worked with the Cherokee agency (1798–1812). Jeremiah Austill (1794–1879) worked as a clerk for his uncle in St. Stephens, served a one-year term in the Alabama legislature, and became a commission merchant in Mobile in 1824. Unfortunately, he would become a victim of the Panic of 1837. In 1840, he

James Smith was a native of Georgia, of low stature, well set, weighed one hundred and sixty-five pounds, and was twenty-five years of age at the period of the canoe fight. He was a brave, daring, frontier man, and died in East Mississippi several years ago. He was a man of great prowess, and had killed several Indians in former expeditions. He was admired by everyone for his courage, honesty, and willingness to defend his country, at all times and under all circumstances.[15]

Captain Samuel Dale, of Irish extraction, was born in Rockbridge County, Virginia, in 1772. In 1775, his father moved to Glade Hollow, on the Clinch River, in the county of Washington, Virginia, and was actively engaged in the border warfare of that day. In 1784, he removed, with his family, to the vicinity of Greensborough, Georgia, where he purchased a farm, but, in a short time was compelled to take refuge in Carmichael's Station, in consequence of the inroads of the Indians. Several desperate attempts were made to burn this fort, in one of which Captain Autrey was slain.[16] About this time, Mr. Dale and his wife died, leaving eight children. Samuel, the subject of this memoir, who was the oldest, placed the children upon the farm, and joined a company of troopers, raised by Captain Fauche, to watch the movements of the Creeks, which was soon after mustered into the federal service, and quartered on the Oconee, at a place called Fort Mathews.[17] Towards the close of 1794, this troop had several engagements with the savages, in which Dale displayed those traits which so distinguished his subsequent career—vigilance, perseverance, energy, and dauntless courage. At Okfuskee, on the Chattahoochee, he slew two Indians. Soon after, having been elected colonel, and stationed at the head of a separate command, at Fort Republic on the Apalachee River in Georgia, he rendered efficient services, until the troops were disbanded.[18]

Then he became a trader among the Creeks and Cherokees, purchasing his goods in Savannah, and exchanging them for cattle and ponies. He also acted in the capacity of guide to many parties emigrating to the Mississippi Territory. He finally established a trading house, in copartnership with a half-breed, in what is now known as Jones County, Georgia, where he remained for some time. He was at Tuckabatchee when Tecumseh appeared there, and assured Colonel Hawkins that the mission of that man would result in great evil, unless his efforts were immediately counteracted; but the agent did not concur with him in that opinion. His bravery has been seen at Burnt Corn, and in the canoe

purchased a plantation on the Tombigbee in Clarke County and moved there in 1844. Timothy H. Ball, *A Glance into the Great South-East, or Clarke County, Alabama, and Its Surroundings, From 1540 to 1877* (Grove Hill, Ala.: n.p., 1882), 459–67.

[15] While Dale, Austill, and Creagh are well known to Pickett, James Smith (c.1787–c.1850) played a critically important role in the "canoe fight" skirmish, especially in the recollection of Jim Caesar. Caesar's version of the "canoe fight" had James Smith doing most of the fighting. Halbert, "Creek War Incidents," 97–98; Halbert and Ball, *Creek War of 1813 and 1814*, 185, 193, 199, 209, 235, 236; A. B. Meek, *Romantic Passages in Southwestern History; Including Orations, Sketches, and Essays* (New York: S. H. Goetzel & Company, 1857), 309–10, 312–19.

[16] Pickett's sketch of Dale is loosely paraphrased from J. F. H. Claiborne's *Life and Times of Gen. Sam Dale*, indicating that he had access to Claiborne's early draft of the Dale biography. Captain John Autrey (Autry), a veteran of the Revolutionary War, was killed and scalped by Creeks on 2 February 1788 near Scull (Skull) Shoals on the Oconee River. Claiborne, *Life and Times of Gen. Sam Dale*, 15–45; "John Autrey," http://wc.rootsweb.ancestry.com; Lucien Lamar Knight, *Georgia's Roster of the Revolution* (Atlanta: Index Printing Co., 1920), 22.

fight. At the time of the latter, Captain Dale weighed one hundred and ninety pounds, was over six feet high, possessed a large muscular frame, without any surplus flesh, and was in the prime of life.[19] Although he will be mentioned hereafter, in connection with the Indian wars, we deem it proper, in further illustration of his character, to insert the following well-written obituary, published in the *Natchez Free Trader*, from the pen of John H. F. Claiborne, formerly a member of Congress from Mississippi, and the son of the general of that name, whose military services are now under review:

"I have not observed, in your paper, any notice of the death of our veteran friend, General Samuel Dale. He died at his residence, Daleville, Lauderdale County, on the 23nd ult., with the fortitude of a soldier and the resignation of a Christian. On his dying bed he repeated, as I am informed, a request which he made last summer, that I should make a memoir of his life, most of the particulars of which I wrote down from his lips. I design visiting Lauderdale, in a few weeks, to obtain all the materials that remain. Few men have run a career so full of benevolent actions and of romantic adventure, and no man was ever better adapted to the country and the period in which he lived—that *country* the frontiers of Georgia, Florida and the (then) Mississippi Territory, embracing all the present state of Alabama—the *period* including nearly all that bloody interval between the close of the Revolution and the termination of the last war. With the story of these times, the dreadful massacre at Fort Mims, the battle of the Holy Ground, General Jackson's Seminole campaigns, and the earlier events of the Georgia frontier, General Dale was closely connected. The most affecting of those scenes of murder and conflagration are as yet unwritten, and live only in the fading memorials of border tradition.

"In preparing the life of General Dale, I shall seek to put many of them on record. As a scout, a pilot to the emigrants who blazed the first path through the Creek Nation, from Georgia to the Tombigbee, with arms in their hands, and subsequently as a spy among the Spaniards, at Pensacola, and as a partisan officer during the most sanguinary epochs of the late war, present at every butchery, remarkable for 'hair-breadth 'scapes,' for caution and coolness in desperate emergencies, for exhibitions of gigantic personal strength and great moral courage, his story is studded over with spirit-stirring incidents, unsurpassed by anything in legend or history. His celebrated '*canoe fight*,' where, in the Alabama River, he, with Smith and Austill, fought nine warriors, with clubbed rifles,

[17] Captain Jonas Fauche commanded Georgia dragoons assigned to Fort Mathews and patrolled along the Oconee River. Private Samuel Dale was one of his troopers. George Gillman Smith, *The Story of Georgia and the Georgia People, 1732–1860* (Macon: G. G. Smith, 1900), 159–60; Dayna Gunter, "The Oconee Forts," *Athens Banner Herald,* 10 July 2002.

[18] Pickett's source is J. F. H. Claiborne's *Life and Times of Gen. Sam Dale,* but a Fort Republic on the Apalachee River cannot be located. However, there was a Fort Republic at St. Stephens. Claiborne, *Life and Times of Gen. Sam Dale,* 39–44.

[19] Pickett continues to follow J. F. H. Claiborne's *Life and Times of Gen. Sam Dale,* citing Dale's presence at Tuckabatchee during Tecumseh's visit and his warning to Hawkins. Most modern sources do not name Dale among the Euro-Americans present during Tecumseh's tour of the Upper Creek country. One contemporary, Thomas S. Woodward, declared that Pickett was "incorrect" when "he says Gen. Dale saw Tecumseh at the Council with the Creeks in 1811." If Dale provided Claiborne with the narrative in his biography, his recollection of events appears to have been based on hearsay and other sources after the Creek War. Ibid., 50–53; Woodward, *Reminiscences,* 77; Sugden, *Tecumseh,* 243–46.

killed them all, and rowed to shore, would be thought fabulous, if it had not been witnessed by many soldiers, standing upon the banks, who could render them no assistance. Some years before, he was attacked by two warriors, who shouted their war-whoop as he was kneeling down to drink and rushed upon him with their tomahawks. He knifed them both, and, though bleeding from five wounds, he retraced their trail nine miles, crept stealthily to their camp, brained three sleeping warriors and cut the thongs of a female prisoner who lay by their side. While in this act, however, a fourth sprang upon him, from behind a log. Taken at such a disadvantage, and exhausted by the loss of blood, he sank under the serpent-grasp of the savage, who, with a yell of triumph, drew his knife, and, in a few moments, would have closed the contest. At that instant, however, the woman drove a tomahawk deep into the head of the Indian, and thus preserved the life of her deliverer.

"Shortly after the treaty of Dancing Rabbit, our deceased friend settled in what is now known as Lauderdale County; and it is worthy of remark, that, at the first election, (1836, I believe) when he was chosen to the legislature, but *ten* votes were cast. *Now* the county could probably poll 750, and, in every direction, its fleecy fields, its fine flour-mills, its school-houses and churches, indicate a thriving, enlightened and moral population.

"One anecdote of the old general is so similar to an event in Roman history, that I cannot forbear relating it. The Consul Aquilius, returning from a campaign, was allowed a triumph, but shortly afterwards was arraigned for some misdemeanor, committed during his foreign service. He called no exculpatory evidence, nor deigned to court the favor of his judges, but when about to receive sentence, he tore open his vest and displayed the wounds he had received in the service of his country. A sudden emotion of pity seized the court, and unfixed the resolution which, a few moments before, they had taken to condemn the accused. Some time ago General Dale, being in Mobile, was held to bail as *endorser* upon a note. The debt was in the hands of a *stranger*. Accompanied by an officer, he sought the creditor, and found him in the saloon of Cullum's far-famed hotel. 'Sir,' said the general, 'I have no money to pay this debt. The principal has property—make him pay it, or let me go home and work it out.' The Shylock hesitated. '*Very well*,' said the veteran, in tones that rang indignantly through the apartment, '*Very well, sir! Look at my scars! I will march to jail down Main Street, and all Mobile shall witness the treatment of an old soldier!*' These simple words fell like electricity upon that high-toned people. In half an hour, a dozen of the brightest names of the city were on the bond, and before morning the debt was paid, and a full discharge handed to the general. I have seen the manly tears chasing down his

[20] Claiborne used this paragraph as his concluding pages in his *Life and Times of Gen. Sam Dale.* (232–33).

[21] Weatherford's Bluff, named for Charles Weatherford, was located about one mile below the confluence of the Coosa and Tallapoosa on the east bank of the Alabama. Wright, *McGillivray and McIntosh Traders*, 204; O'Brien, *In Bitterness and in Tears*, 105; Howell Tatum, "Major Howell Tatum's Journal: While Acting Topographical Engineer (1814) to General Jackson," ed. John Spencer Bassett, *Smith College Studies in History* 7 (October 1921-April 1922): 12.

cheek, as the aged warrior dwelt on these recollections of the generous citizens.

"In person, General Dale was tall, erect, raw-boned and muscular. In many respects, physical and moral, he resembled his antagonists of the woods. He had the square forehead, the high cheek-bones, the compressed lips, and, in fact, the physiognomy of an Indian, relieved, however, by a fine, benevolent Saxon eye. Like the Red Man, too, his foot fell lightly upon the ground, and turned neither to the right or left; he was habitually taciturn; his face grave; he spoke slowly and in low tones, and seldom laughed. I observed of him, what I have often noted as peculiar to border men of high attributes: he entertained the strongest attachment for the Indians, extolled their courage, their love of country, and many of their domestic qualities, and I have often seen the wretched remnant of the Choctaws camped around his plantation and subsisting on his crops. In peace, they felt for him the strongest veneration—he had been the friend both of Tecumseh and Weatherford—and in war the name of '*Big Sam*' fell on the ear of the Seminole like that of Marius on the hordes of the Cimbri."[20]

Captain Dale, with a scouting party, had effectually scoured the swamps of Bassett's Creek, and Major Hinds's horse had routed a small body of the enemy near Weatherford's Bluff, killing ten of their number, when an order from Flournoy permitted Claiborne to advance, with the Southern army, to the Alabama. His instructions confined him still to defensive operations, requiring him to establish a depot at Weatherford's Bluff, and not to advance further into the Creek Nation until he was joined by the Georgia and Tennessee troops.[21] Claiborne accordingly broke up his camp at Pine Level, marched across Clarke County with three hundred volunteers, the dragoons and some militia, flanked by detachments under Captains Kennedy and Bates and Lieutenant Osborne, and party of Choctaws, under Pushmataha and Mushulatubbee.[22] Arriving at the Alabama, the army encamped for the night upon the western bank, and the next day at 12 o'clock, had gained the other side, by means of rafts. Colonel Gilbert C. Russell, an accomplished and gallant commander in the regular army, marched the Third Regiment of federal troops from Mount Vernon, through Nanna Hubba Island, by Mims' Ferry, to the head of Little River, and thence to the encampment of Claiborne, with whom he had been instructed by General Flournoy to cooperate.[23]

In the meantime, Claiborne had made rapid progress in the construction of a strong stockade, two hundred feet square, defended by three block-houses and a half-moon battery, which commanded the river. Before the close of November it was completed, and received the name of Fort Claiborne, in honor of the commander. The town where it stood still bears his name. The

[22] Captain Joseph P. Kennedy, Captain William Bates, and Lieutenant Audley L. Osborne commanded Mississippi territorial volunteers and local militia forces. Osborne was the brother of Lieutenant Spruce Osborne, killed at Fort Mims. Most sources indicate that Lieutenant Colonel Pushmataha—dressed in a uniform purchased by Claiborne—alone commanded a party of Choctaws, estimated from 51 to 135. Rowland, *Mississippi Territory in the War of 1812*, 38, 71 .n, 90, 174, 224; Waselkov, *Conquering Spirit*, 149–52, 162, 336 n. 23; Griffith, *McIntosh and Weatherford*, 127.

[23] After General Flournoy released Major Thomas Hinds and his dragoons, Colonel Gilbert C. Russell (1782–1861) and his regular U.S. troops added critical strength to Claiborne's force. O'Brien, *In Bitterness and in Tears*, 107; Owsley, *Struggle for the Gulf*, 46–47.

general wrote to Jackson, congratulating him upon his victories, and giving him an account of the operations in the southern seat of war, and acquainting him with the fact that an abundance of corn and other provisions were to be obtained in the neighborhood of Fort Claiborne. He also wrote to Governor Blount, apprising him of the arrival of more English vessels in Pensacola, and added that he wished "to God that he was authorized to take that sink of iniquity, the depot of Tories and instigators of disturbances on the southern frontier." He had, a few days before, dispatched Major Kennedy and others to Mobile, to learn from Colonel Bowyer the particulars of the arrival of the British at Pensacola. They reported, giving satisfactory assurances that a large quantity of Indian supplies and many soldiers had arrived there;[24] and, in addition, that the Indians were committing depredations in Baldwin County, having recently burned down Kennedy's and Byrne's mills.[25]

Lieutenant Colonel George Henry Nixon had succeeded Russell in the command at Mount Vernon.[26] At his request, Claiborne permitted him, also, to man Fort Pierce, in the neighborhood of the disturbances.*

Claiborne, having determined to advance to the enemy's stronghold, the line of march was taken up by an army consisting of Colonel Russell's Third Regiment,

* Colonel Nixon was born in Virginia, and, living years in South Carolina, removed from thence, in 1809, to the Mississippi territory. He was among the first to offer his services in defense of his country. During the Creek War, Colonel Nixon, at the head of a considerable force, scoured the swamps of the Perdido and other streams, and frequently killed and captured Indians. After he had accomplished all he could, he marched to the head of the Perdido, where he divided his command, sending Major William Peacock, with the troops of the 39th, to the Boat Yard, on Lake Tensaw, while he marched with the remainder of his command to Fort Claiborne, He was an excellent officer, and served in the war until its final conclusion. He was a member of the convention that formed the constitution of the state of Mississippi, and was, afterwards, frequently a state senator. He died in Perlington, Mississippi, in 1824. He was a large and fine looking man, with fair complexion, and was very popular.

[24] Contrary to Pickett's assertion of the arrival of the British at Pensacola with "Indian supplies and many soldiers," there is no evidence of a British military presence at Pensacola in December 1813. In fact, when the British became militarily active on the Gulf Coast in May 1814, Captain Hugh Pigot sailed the HMS *Orpheus* to the mouth of the Apalachicola River, where he and Captain George Woodbine met chiefs from the Lower Creek and Seminole villages. On 25 May 1814, acting as the British agent to the Creeks, Woodbine seized John Forbes's store at Prospect Bluff on the Apalachicola. O'Brien, *In Bitterness and in Tears*, 166–67; Owsley, *Struggle for the Gulf*, 98–100; Dale Cox, *Nicolls' Outpost: A War of 1812 Fort at Chattahoochee, Florida* (Bascom, FL: Old Kitchen Books, 2015), 7–9, 21–22.

[25] The Kennedy brothers, Joshua and Joseph P., built tandem sawmills under the direction of Jesse Embree and Joshua's son-in-law Reese Smith. Construction of the mills started in 1811 and was completed in 1813. The mills were built on Rain's Creek, on land formerly owned by Robert Farmar, some two miles below the line of demarcation. Gerald and Thomas Byrne constructed their sawmill on the Tensaw River. The sawmills were abandoned after the attack on Fort Mims and burned by Red Stick war parties. Hamilton, *Colonial Mobile*, 362, 513; Robert Leslie Smith, *Gone to the Swamp: Raw Materials for the Good Life in the Mobile-Tensaw Delta*. (Tuscaloosa: University of Alabama Press, 2008), 101–07.

[26] On 15 November 1813, Lieutenant Colonel George Henry Nixon, commander of the 13th Regiment of Mississippi Militia, received orders from Governor David Holmes to march to Mount Vernon and to report to the commander of the post. Nixon's regiment arrived on 25 November with instructions to station troops at Mount Vernon, Pierce's Mill, St. Stephens, and Easley's. Governor Holmes to Lieutenant Colonel Nixon, Head Quarters, Fords, Pearl River, 15 November 1813, Mississippi Department of Archives and History, Jackson (online); Rowland, *Encyclopedia of Mississippi History*, 2: 341.

Major Cassells' battalion of horse, a battalion of militia, under Major Benjamin Smoot—Patrick May being adjutant, Dale and Heard captains, and Gerard W. Creagh one of the lieutenants—the twelve months' Mississippi Volunteers, under Colonel Carson, and one hundred and fifty Choctaws, under Pushmataha numbering, in the aggregate, near one thousand men.[27] A few days before, nine captains, eight lieutenants, and five ensigns, signed a remonstrance, in respectful language, against the march to the nation, and presented it to the general. They set forth that the time of service of many would soon expire, that the weather was cold, that they were too scantily supplied with clothing and food for such a campaign, and that the route to the enemy's towns was entirely a pathless one; but they stated their willingness to obey, if Claiborne should resolve to proceed.[28]

Claiborne moved in a northeastern direction, until he reached the high lands south of Double Swamp, at the distance of eighty miles, where he built a depot, called Fort Deposit, situated in the present county of Butler, and where he left the wagons, cannon, baggage and the sick, with one hundred men, as a guard. Thirty miles further brought him into the immediate neighborhood of the Holy Ground, which had been reached without the aid of a single path. The pork being exhausted, the troops were in a suffering condition, for they had only drawn, when leaving Fort Deposit, three days' allowance of flour. Econachtca (Holy Ground) had recently been erected by Weatherford, the prophets having assured the Indians that here no white man could approach without instant destruction.[29] It was strongly fortified in the Indian manner, and had for some months formed a point to which those who had been routed in battle retreated, and where a great amount of plunder had been stored. It was situated upon a bluff, on the eastern side of the Alabama River, just below the present Powell's Ferry, in the county of Lowndes. Here many of the white prisoners and friendly Indians were burned to death, by order of the prophets, and, when Claiborne was almost within sight

[27] While Major Henry Cassells commanded a cavalry unit in George Nixon's regiment, Captain Bailey Heard, Captain Sam Dale, Lieutenant Gerard W. Creagh, and Lieutenant and Adjutant Patrick May served in Major Benjamin Smoot's Battalion of Mississippi Militia. Colonel Joseph Carson also commanded a Mississippi militia regiment. "Compiled Service Records of Volunteer Soldiers Who Served During the War of 1812 in Organizations from the Territory of Mississippi," NARA M678 (online); Rowland, *Mississippi Territory in the War of 1812*, 73–74, 174, 213–15, 224–26.

[28] General Ferdinand Claiborne wrote a notice to the *Mississippi Republican* which was published after receiving the signed protest and after their successful campaign at the Holy Ground: ". . . when they were nine days without meat, and subsisted chiefly on parched corn, these brave men won an important battle, and endured without a murmur the exigencies of the service." Claiborne, *Mississippi*, 328–29.

[29] While Weatherford tried to rally his outnumbered forces to oppose Claiborne's army, Josiah Francis (Hillis Hadjo) had created Econachaca (Ikanatchka or Ecunchate) as a "Holy Ground," or sacred town, on the Alabama, under the influence of the "Master of Breath" and protected by a "enchanted death-dealing barrier" that could not be penetrated by Euro-Americans. Red Sticks from throughout the Upper Creek country sought refuge at Francis's Holy Ground and the nearby plantations of Weatherford and Sam Moniac. Most modern scholarship use Ecunchate or Econchata when discussing the Holy Ground. Stiggins, *Creek Indian History*, 116, 118; Owsley, "Prophet of War," 282–83; Waselkov, *Conquering Spirit*, 145, 165, 167; Ethridge, *Creek Country*, 51, 85–86, 149; Saunt, *New Order of Things*, 167.

of the town with his advancing army, Mrs. Sophia Durant, and many other friendly half-breeds, were mustered in the square and surrounded by lightwood fires, designed to consume them.[30]

The troops advanced toward the town in three columns, the center commanded by Colonel Russell, at the head of which was Claiborne himself, Lester's guards and Wells' dragoons acting as a corps of reserve. At noon Carson's right column came in view of the town, and was vigorously attacked by the enemy, who had chosen their field of action. The town was nearly surrounded with swamps and deep ravines, so that the enemy, who afterwards retreated, could not be successfully pursued. Major Cassells, who had been directed to form his battalion of horse on the river bank, west of the town, failing to effect such a movement, fell back on the head of Carson's regiment, who, however, advanced, and took his position. The third regiment, coming up in gallant style, did its duty. Major Smoot assumed his position in a proper manner, and all would have been right if Cassells' cavalry had not failed to obey orders, thereby permitting hundreds of the enemy to escape along the Alabama River, by the western border of the town. The Indians, headed by Weatherford, for a short time fought with considerable fury, but afterwards fled with great rapidity. The short engagement resulted in the death of thirty Indians and Negroes, whose bodies were afterwards counted upon the field. Many must have been severely wounded. Luckett, an American ensign, was killed, and twenty men were wounded.[31]

Several hours before the battle began the Indian women and children had been conveyed across the river, and were securely lodged in the thick forests of the region now familiarly known as the Dutch Bend of Autauga County. Here the retreating warriors, some of whom came over in boats, while others swam, joined them. Weatherford, seeing that his forces had deserted him, now pushed hard for his own safety. Coursing,

[30] Although the Holy Ground was located on high ground and fortified with stakes and fallen logs, most of its residents believed they were protected by the magical barrier or circle created by Josiah Francis under the influence or at the direction of the "Master of Breadth." Sophia McGillivray Durant and other family members may have been held against their wills at Econachaca (Ecunchate), but it is unlikely that her Red Stick sons John and Alexander Durant and other Red Stick kin would have allowed her or other family members to be burned. Owsley, "Prophet of War," 283; Waselkov, *Conquering Spirit*, 166–67; O'Brien, *In Bitterness and in Tears*, 110.

[31] While Francis and the prophets, women, and children escaped across the Alabama, Claiborne's force of some one thousand overwhelmed William Weatherford's force of less than 100 warriors. Some 30 Red Sticks were killed, which included 12 African slaves fighting as allies and a number of wounded. Claiborne's army lost one man killed—Lieutenant James Luckett—and 20 wounded. Rowland, *Mississippi Territory in the War of 1812*, 38, 73–76; O'Brien, *In Bitterness and in Tears*, 110–13; Waselkov, *Conquering Spirit*, 165–66, 168–69.

with great rapidity, along the banks of the Alabama, below the town, on a gray steed of unsurpassed strength and fleetness—which he had purchased a short time before the commencement of hostilities of Benjamin Baldwin, late of Macon County—came, at length, to the termination of a kind of ravine, where there was a perpendicular bluff, ten or fifteen feet above the surface of the river. Over this, with a mighty bound, the horse pitched with the gallant chief, and both went out of sight beneath the waves. Presently they rose again, the rider having hold of the mane with one hand and his rifle firmly grasped in the other.[32] Regaining his saddle the noble animal swam with him to the Autauga side.*

Claiborne reduced the town of the Holy Ground to ashes. He then dispatched the cavalry to Ward's place up the river, who, before reaching there, fell in with three Shawnees of distinction, retreating from the battle, whom they killed. The firing being heard at the camp, Claiborne struck his tents and marched in that direction during the night. Encamping at Weatherford's place in an open field, the cold rains descended in torrents upon the troops, and Christmas morning found them engaged in parching corn for breakfast, which was the only thing left to eat. After destroying some houses and farms, the army marched back to Fort Deposit, and from thence to Fort Claiborne, where, the term of service of Carson's Mississippi volunteers and cavalry having expired, they were mustered out of service.[33]

Colonel Russell, now left in sole command of Fort Claiborne, preferred charges against Major Cassells for disobedience of orders at the Holy Ground, and a court of inquiry, composed of Captain Woodruff,

* Extravagant tales have often been told of Weatherford's leap, and a bluff at or near the site of the Holy Ground town, which is probably eighty or a hundred feet high, is often pointed out as the one over which he charged. The account I have given is Weatherford's own statement of the affair.

[32] Weatherford's escape into the Alabama River took on legendary renown, with accounts that he leaped over a 60-foot or higher bluff and survived the plunge into the Alabama River. Thomas S. Woodward, who knew Weatherford, claims that Weatherford, instead of going down the river bank, followed the bluff near the river, rode down into a ravine near the river, and followed a footpath before crossing the river—totally out of sight of the Americans. George Stiggins, a brother-in-law of Weatherford, claims that the beast and man leaped thirty feet into the water and was followed by his McPherson cousin in the same manner. Woodward, *Reminiscences*, 87; Stiggins, *Creek Indian History*, 120; Halbert and Ball, *Creek War of 1813 and 1814*, 253–56; Owsley, *Struggle for the Gulf*, 47–48; Waselkov, *Conquering Spirit*, 165.

[33] Claiborne's Choctaw auxiliaries plundered Econachaca (Ecunchate) before burning over 200 buildings, and on Christmas Eve, the army moved up the Alabama, captured and killed three Shawnee prophets, and spent the night on Weatherford's plantation. On the next day, the American army burned the refugee camps at Weatherford and Moniac's plantations. O'Brien, *In Bitterness and in Tears*, 114–15; Waselkov, *Conquering Spirit*, 166; Rowland, *Mississippi Territory in the War of 1812*, 76–77.

president, Captain J. E. Dinkins and Lieutenant H. Chotard, decided that Sam Moniac, the guide, was chiefly to blame for the failure of Cassells to occupy the position which had been assigned him.[34] Another court of inquiry, composed of Colonel Carson and Lieutenant Wilcox, decided that the contractor of the army was solely to blame for the perishing condition of the expedition, as General Claiborne had given him ample instructions to furnish abundant supplies. The command had been entirely without meat for nine days.[35]

General Claiborne wrote to the secretary of war, from Mount Vernon, that he had been left with but sixty men, whose time lacked only a month of expiring; that his other volunteers, who had been disbanded, had gone home naked and without shoes, with eight months pay due them; and that his army, being thus broken up, he intended to return home as soon as he received permission from General Flournoy.*

Having planned an expedition against the enemy, Colonel Russell dispatched Captain Dinkins up the Alabama from Fort Claiborne in command of a barge, laden with provisions, and defended by a piece of artillery, with instructions to enter the Cahaba River, and to ascend it to the "Old Towns," where his army would shortly join him. Afterwards, marching the larger portion of his regiment to the crossroads, in Clarke County, four miles north of the present Suggsville, he was there joined by a company commanded by Captain Evan Austill and Lieutenant G. W. Creagh, and Captain Foster's horse company, both under the command of Major Samuel Dale.[36] Leaving this place, with six days rations, Colonel Russell reached the Cahawba Old Towns, where he was mortified to find that Captain Dinkins had not arrived—nor had he encountered, on the way, a solitary Indian. Dispatching Lieutenant Wilcox in a canoe, with five men, with directions to find Dinkins and hasten him on, that officer proceeded down the Cahaba, upset his boat the first night, wet his ammunition, and lost two of his guns. Recovering the canoe, however, and

* Claiborne's MS papers. Conversations with the late Colonel Creagh, General Patrick May, of Greene, and others.

[34] Captain Joseph Woodruff, Captain James E. Dinkins, and Lieutenant Henry Chotard were members of the 3rd Regiment of the U.S. Infantry assigned to Fort Claiborne under Colonel Gilbert C. Russell. By blaming the métis Sam Moniac for Major Henry Cassells's delayed arrival at his position in the battle formation at the Holy Ground, they were able to exonerate a fellow officer and cause no harm to Moniac. O'Brien, *In Bitterness and in Tears,* 131–32, 175; "Major Henry Chotard," http://www.wikitree.com/wiki/Chotard-16; William A. Gordon, *A Compilation of Registers of the Army of the United States, From 1815 to 1837* (Washington: James C. Dunn, 1837), 20.

[35] Lieutenant James M. Wilcox, a West Point graduate, served with Colonel Joseph Carson on the second court of inquiry, and they quickly reached a decision, blaming the contractor for failing to deliver the supplies as contracted. Like the decision involving Sam Moniac, they avoided placing blame on any officer, such as General Thomas Flournoy, who had demonstrated a less than enthusiastic support of General Ferdinand Claiborne. O'Brien, *In Bitterness and in Tears,* 105–06, 131–32; Waselkov, *Conquering Spirit,* 161–62, 164, 178.

[36] Captain Arthur Foster commanded a twenty-seven man mounted infantry company of Mississippi militia. Rowland, *Mississippi Territory in the War of 1812,* 163.

proceeding down the river, lying by in the cane in the daytime, he was, in the evening of the second day, fired upon by a party of Indians.[37]

The two Wilsons, who belonged to this expedition, made their escape, and reached the lower settlements many days after, in a starving condition. One of them, Mathew, was found by Hays Rodgers, on the ridge road of Clarke.[38] Lieutenant Wilcox and the other three were made prisoners by the Indians, who proceeded with them down the Cahaba, into the Alabama. In the meantime, Dinkins, unfortunately passing the mouth of the Cahaba by mistake, had ascended some distance up the Alabama, and was now returning to Fort Claiborne, knowing that the army could not wait for him, but would return to that place likewise. The Indians, going down the river also, descried the barge, and fearing to lose their prisoners, tomahawked and scalped Wilcox and his three companions, leaving them in their canoe. When the canoe and the barge came together Wilcox was still alive, but too far gone to give any account of the particulars of his capture, or of Russell's expedition. The body of this gallant young officer, being found upon the Alabama, where it meanders through the region between Canton and Prairie Bluff, the legislature appropriately preserved his memory, by giving the county his name.[39]

Colonel Russell remained two days at the Cahawba Old Towns, in which time one of his men was killed by some skulking savages. Despairing of the arrival of the barge, he began the return march, without any provisions; and setting the example himself, in having his best horse killed for subsistence, twelve animals of that kind were devoured by the perishing troops. At Bradford's Pond they were timely relieved by wagons, laden with abundant provisions,[40] and arriving again at the cross-roads, were disbanded, the regulars marching to Fort Claiborne.*

[37] Captain James Dinkins moved up the Alabama in two armed keel boats carrying seventy men and supplies. Russell's troops marched seven days overland to reach the Creek towns on the Cahaba only to find that they had been abandoned and to discover the supplies destined for General Andrew Jackson had not arrived. O'Brien, *In Bitterness and in Tears*, 132; Owsley, *Struggle for the Gulf*, 49–50.

[38] According to the roster of Major Sam Dale's battalion of Mississippi militia, the two privates sent with Lieutenant James Wilcox were Mathew Wilson and William Wilson. Mathew Wilson was found by Private Hays Rodgers (1783–1862), a native of Tennessee, who was also a member of Dale's battalion. Rowland, *Mississippi Territory in the War of 1812*, 224.

[39] Pickett's narrative of Lieutenant Wilcox's death appears to be primarily based on this event as described in J. F. H. Claiborne's *Life and Times of Gen. Sam Dale.* (143–45).

[40] Bradford's Pond is a rural community in modern Marengo County, Alabama. Kathryn Tucker Windham, *Spit, Scarey Ann, and Sweat Bees: One Thing Leads to Another* (Montgomery: NewSouth Books, 2009), 94.

* Conversations with Colonel Gerard W. Creagh, late of Clarke County.

Chapter XXXVII

BATTLES OF EMUCKFAU, ENITACHOPCO, AND CALEBEE

Since the battle of Talladega, Jackson had encountered innumerable difficulties and mortifications, owing to the failure of contractors and the mutiny of his troops, who were finally reduced to one hundred men, by the expiration of their time of service. He was now compelled to employ Cherokees to garrison Fort Armstrong, upon the Coosahatchie, and protect the stores at Ross's.[1] Almost alone, in a savage land, he yet constantly rode between Fort Strother and Ditto's Landing, to hasten supplies for the new army, which he had employed Governor Blount to raise for him. At last, two regiments, one of them commanded by Colonel Perkins, and the other by Colonel Higgins—numbering together eight hundred and fifty men, who had only enlisted for sixty days—reached Fort Strother.[2] Well understanding the character of minute men, like these, who must be constantly employed, Jackson immediately marched them across the Coosa, to the late battleground of Talladega, where he was joined by two hundred Cherokees and Creeks, who evinced great alarm at the weakness which the command presented.[3] Continuing the march towards the Tallapoosa, the army encamped at Enitachopco, a Hillabee village, and the next day, fell into many fresh beaten trails, indicating the proximity of a large force. Here Jackson determined to halt, for the purpose of reconnoiter. Before dark, his encampment was formed, his army thrown into a hollow square, his pickets and spies sent out, his sentinels doubled, and his fires lighted, some distance outside of the lines. About ten o'clock at night, one of the pickets, firing upon three of the enemy, succeeded in killing one, and at the hour of eleven the spies reported a large encampment, three miles distant, where the savages were whooping and dancing, and, being apprised of the approach of the Americans, were sending off their women and children.[4]

About six o'clock in the morning, the Indians suddenly fell upon Jackson's

1 The Coosahatchie Creek, located near modern Centre, Cherokee County, Alabama, is now called Terrapin Creek. Michael Tuomey, *Second Biennial Report on the Geology of Alabama* (Montgomery: N. B. Cloud, 1858), 90; "Terrapin Creek," http://www.placekeeper.com/Alabama/Terrapin_Creek-160732.html.

2 Colonel Nicholas Perkins (1779–1848) was the commander of the 1st Regiment of West Tennessee Volunteers, and Colonel William Higgins commanded the 2nd Regiment of Tennessee Mounted Volunteers. These were truly raw, untrained troops who had enlisted for sixty days. Kanon, *Tennesseans at War, 1812–1815*, 89; Tom Kanon, "Regimental Histories of Tennessee Units During the War of 1812," Tennessee State Library and Archives (online).

left flank, and upon the left of his rear, maintaining a vigorous attack for a half hour. General Coffee, Adjutant-General Sitler, and Inspector-General Carroll rode rapidly to the scene of action, as soon as the firing commenced, animating the men, who firmly kept the assailants at bay. Morning shed its light upon the exciting scene, enabling Captain Ferrill's infantry to reinforce the left flank, when the whole line was led to the charge by General Coffee, supported by Colonels Higgins and Carroll, and the friendly Indians, which forced the savages to abandon the ground in a rapid manner. They were pursued, with slaughter, for two miles. Coffee, being then ordered, with four hundred men and the friendly Indians, to burn up their encampment, advanced, and, finding it strongly fortified, returned for the artillery. Shortly afterwards, a body of the enemy boldly advanced and attacked the right wing of Jackson's encampment. Coffee again charged, but, through mistake, only forty-five men followed him, composing his own company of volunteer officers; but the friendly Indians were sent by Jackson to his support.[5] Dismounting his men, he now pursued the "Red Sticks" to the swamp of a creek.*

Jackson had ordered his left flank to remain firm, and now the Indians came rushing, with yells, against it. Repairing to that point, and ordering up Captain Ferrill to his support, the whole line received the enemy with intrepidity, and, after a few fires, advanced to the charge, under the impetuous Carroll. Again the Red Sticks fled before the bayonet, the Americans pursuing some distance, and marking their trails with blood. In the meantime, Coffee kept the enemy, who had now returned upon him from the swamp, at bay, until Jackson strengthened him, with a reinforcement of a hundred friendly warriors, at the head of whom was Jim Fife.[6] Coffee again charged, when the Red Sticks once more gave way, and the pursuit was continued for three miles, with the loss of forty-five savages.[7]

The brave Creeks had now been repulsed in every attempt, but they exhibited a ferocity and courage which commanded the serious consideration of Jackson, whose force was weaker than he desired. The horses had been without cane and without corn for two

* The Indian war-party were often called the "Red Sticks," because their war-clubs were invariably painted red.

[3] Most sources place Jackson's Indian allies at two hundred friendly Creeks and sixty-five Cherokee. Kanon, *Tennesseans at War, 1812–1815,* 89; O'Brien, *In Bitterness and in Tears,* 118.

[4] On 17 January 1814, Jackson's new army marched out of Fort Strother and, four days later, camped near the mouth of Emuckfau Creek, which flowed into the Tallapoosa River. Kanon, *Tennesseans at War, 1812–1815,* 89–90; O'Brien, *In Bitterness and in Tears,* 118–19; Remini, *Andrew Jackson and the Course of American Empire,* 207.

[5] While Colonel James W. Sitler served as Jackson's adjutant-general, twenty-five-year-old William Carroll served as his inspector-general. Together with General John Coffee and Captain Larkin Ferrill, they played a critical role in rallying Jackson's raw troops. Kanon, *Tennesseans at War, 1812–1815,* 88–90; O'Brien, *In Bitterness and in Tears,* 67, 118; Charles Kitchell Gardner, *A Dictionary of All Officers: Who Have Been Commissioned, Or Have Been Appointed and Served, in the Army of the United States* (New York: G. P. Putnam, 1853), 410.

[6] Jim Fife, a métis Upper Creek, led the Creeks who supported Coffee's final push at Emuckfau Creek. Fife is the Creek warrior who supposedly cloaked himself in a hog-skin to escape Fort Leslie to warn Jackson that the Red Sticks were about to overrun the outpost. Kanon, *Tennesseans at War, 1812–1815,* 91; Heard, *Handbook of the American Frontier,* 153.

[7] The Creek Red Sticks gave way when Coffee launched a final thrust which included twenty-five mounted Cherokee under the command of Colonel Richard Brown, who flushed a body of Red Sticks that had gained the cover of a large canebrake. Kanon, *Tennesseans at War, 1812–1815,* 91; O'Brien, *In*

days, and but few rations remained for the men. The wounded were numerous, and the enemy would, doubtless, soon be reinforced. Jackson determined to return to Fort Strother, with all possible dispatch.[8] The remainder of the day was employed in collecting and burying the dead, dressing the wounded, and fortifying the camp;[9] but the morning dawned without another attack.*

The army began the retrograde march about ten o'clock a.m., bearing the wounded, among whom was Coffee, in litters, constructed of the hides of the slain horses. Jackson reached Enitachopco before night, without molestation, and fortified himself at a place a quarter of a mile from the creek, around which the "Red Sticks" prowled, but refrained from attack. Dreading an onset at the ford of the creek, by which his army had passed a few days before, and which afforded great facilities for Indian ambuscades, the commander dispatched spies in search of a less exposed crossing place. Six hundred yards lower down was selected, and thither he advanced his troops in the morning. Carroll commanded the rearguard, Colonel Perkins the right column, and Colonel Stump the left. In case of attack, Carroll was to face about, display and maintain his position, while the other two colonels were to face outward, wheel back on their pivots, and attack the Red Sticks on both flanks.[10]

The wounded and the front guard had passed the creek, and, as Jackson was upon the eastern bank, superintending the crossing of the army, an alarm gun was heard, which was succeeded by a fierce attack of the savages upon the rearguard of Captain Russell's spies.[11] Colonel Carroll ordered the rearguard to halt and form, when the right and left columns, seized by a sudden panic, fled without firing a gun, drawing after them most of the center, with their officers foremost in the flight, at the head of whom was Colonel Stump, who came plunging down the bank, near the exasperated Commander-in-Chief, who made an unsuccessful effort to cut him down with his sword.[12] With only twenty-five men, under Captain Quarles, Carroll gallantly checked the advance of the Red Sticks. The artillery was under the command of Lieutenant Armstrong, in the absence of Captain Deadrick,

* The Battle of Emuckfau was fought near a creek of that name, which runs south, into the Tallapoosa River, in Tallapoosa County, Alabama.

Bitterness and in Tears, 119; John Alden Reid, "Prelude to Horseshoe Bend: The Battles of Emuckfaw and Enotochopco, January 1814," _Journal of the Indian Wars_ 1 (No. 2, 1999): 8–10.

[8] Pickett's description of the Battle of Emuckfau closely follows Amos Kendall's narrative in his _Life of Andrew Jackson_. See Amos Kendall, _Life of Andrew Jackson: Private, Military, and Civil_ (New York: Harper & Brothers, 1843), 253–56.

[9] Jackson's army had five men killed, including Major Alexander Donelson, Coffee's aide and brother-in-law, and twenty wounded, including Coffee, who was wounded in his right thigh. Kanon, _Tennesseans at War, 1812–1815_, 91, 94; O'Brien, _In Bitterness and in Tears_, 119; Reid, "Prelude to Horseshoe Bend," 9.

[10] Lieutenant Colonel John Stump and Colonel Nicholas Tate Perkins commanded regiments made up entirely of green volunteers who had signed up to serve sixty day enlistments. Kanon, "Regimental Histories of Tennessee," (online); Kanon, _Tennesseans at War, 1812–1815_, 88–90; Reid, "Prelude to Horseshoe Bend," 5.

[11] Captain William Russell (c.1762–1825), a native of North Carolina, led a company of spies throughout the Creek War of 1813–1814. David Crockett joined Russell's company prior to the engagement at Emuckfau. Kanon, "Regimental Histories of Tennessee," (online); Crockett, _Autobiography_, 66–67.

[12] Lieutenant Colonel John Stump and Colonel Nicholas Perkins lost control of their men, who were panicked by the fierce attack of the Red Sticks, and the two commanders fled across Enitachopco (Enotochopco) Creek along with most of their men. Jackson was enraged by their conduct, declaring: "They should be shot." Crockett,

who now ordered his company, armed with muskets, to advance to the top of the hill, while he, with Constantine Perkins, and a few others, dragged up the six-pounder from the middle of the creek. Instantly in their position, they maintained it against ten times their number, until Armstrong reached them with his piece. Discovering that, in the hurry of separating the gun from the limbers, the rammer and pricker had been left tied to the latter, with wonderful presence of mind, and while Indian bullets rattled like hail around them, Constantine Perkins and Craven Jackson, two of the gunners, supplied the deficiency. Perkins took off his bayonet, and rammed the cartridge home with his musket, and Jackson, drawing his ramrod, employed it as a pricker, priming with a musket cartridge.* The six-pounder was thus twice charged, pouring grape among the savages, then only a few yards distant. Several comrades of these men fell around them, and, after the second fire, the little artillery company furiously charged on the assailants, who became more cautious in their approaches.[13] Captain Gordon's spies, in front of the army when the alarm was given, made a circuit and attacked the left flank of the Indians. At the same time, a number of the rearguard and flankers, rallied by Jackson, re-crossed the creek and joined in the fight. The savages, finding that the whole army was now brought against them, fled, throwing away their packs and leaving upon the field the bodies of twenty-six warriors.[14]

One hundred and eighty-nine bodies of the enemy were counted upon the fields of Emuckfau and Enitachopco. The loss of the Americans was twenty killed and seventy-five wounded, several of whom afterwards died. Major A. Donelson was killed at Emuckfau. Captain Hamilton, Lieutenant Armstrong, Bird

* Constantine Perkins was born in Knox County, Tennessee, the 17th August 1792. He graduated at Cumberland College, in 1813, and was with Jackson, at the Battle of Talladega, in Carroll's advance guard, where he greatly distinguished himself. Refusing to abandon Jackson, in a hostile land, he remained, with the small number who adhered to him. In the two battles at Emuckfau, he fought side by side with the bravest. When the Creek War was at an end, he studied law at Nashville. He was elected solicitor of one of the Tennessee circuits, but, removing to Alabama in 1819, was elected solicitor of the third circuit, which office he held until 1826, when he was elected attorney general. In 1834, the people of Tuscaloosa County placed him in the state senate, of which he was a member until the 17th September 1836, when he died.

Autobiography, 67; Reid, "Prelude to Horseshoe Bend," 13, 17; Kanon, _Tennesseans at War, 1812–1815_, 94; "Letters from Gen. Coffee," _American Historical Magazine_ 6 (April 1901): 180–81.

[13] Lieutenant Robert Armstrong took command of Captain David Deadrick's artillery company at this critical juncture and, with the assistance of Constantine Perkins and Craven Jackson, provided the artillery cover so vital to Jackson's efforts to regroup. Even as Armstrong and others fell wounded, Perkins and Jackson managed twice to fire grapeshot at close range into the Red Stick warriors. Kanon, _Tennesseans at War, 1812–1815_, 93; O'Brien, _In Bitterness and in Tears_, 122; Reid, "Prelude to Horseshoe Bend," 13–15.

[14] Captain John Gordon and his company of spies had served with Jackson from the beginning of his command of the West Tennessee militia forces. His veteran troops and the leadership of John Coffee, who deserted his litter for his horse, helped preserve Jackson's army at Enitachopco (Enotochopco). Kanon, _Tennesseans at War, 1812–1815_, 78, 89, 93, 96.

Evans, Hiram Bradford and Jacob McGavock were severely wounded.[15] The first named afterwards died. Jackson, in his report, spoke in the highest terms of the bravery of these men, and also of that of Captains Sitler, Quarles, Elliott, and Pipkin, and Colonel Higgins.[16] He also mentioned the gallantry of the venerable Judge Cocke, who, at the age of sixty-five, was in the midst of these battles.[17]

The army continued its march to Fort Strother, where Jackson ordered the sixty day volunteers to march to Huntsville, for honorable discharge, at the same time granting to Coffee and his officers the privilege of returning home, until the government again demanded their services, to all of whom he addressed a kind letter, commending their patriotism and bravery. A court martial acquitted Colonel Perkins of the charge of cowardice, at the Battle of Enitachopco; but Colonel Stump was found guilty,[18] and cashiered.*

Such is the American account of these engagements. The brave natives of Alabama had no writers among them to record their achievements. Several chiefs and leading warriors, who were in the battles of Emuckfau and Enitachopco, have stated to us that they "whipped *Captain* Jackson, and run him to the Coosa River." The authors who have written upon these campaigns speak of the weakness of the American force. It consisted of seven hundred and sixty-seven men, with two hundred friendly Indians. We are enabled to state, with confidence, that the force of the Red Sticks, in these battles, did not exceed five hundred warriors, for the larger body had assembled below, to attack Floyd, while others were fortifying the Horse-Shoe, and various other places.[19]

It has been seen that the Georgia army, after the Battle of Autossee, retired to the Chattahoochee. There, for more than six weeks, it had reposed, for

* Kendall, *Life of Andrew Jackson*, 252–64; Waldo, Eaton, etc.

[15] Captain William Hamilton, whose enlistment had expired, was mortally wounded. Armstrong, Evans, Bradford, and McGavock survived their wounds from the Battle of Enitachopco. Reid, "Prelude to Horseshoe Bend," 15.

[16] Captains John B. Quarles, George Elliott, and Phillip Pipkin commanded companies in Colonel Nicholas Perkins's 1st Regiment of West Tennessee Mounted Volunteers. Captain Quarles's company, from its position in the center of Jackson's rear guard at Enitachopco, suffered heavy casualties, including Quarles, who died in the battle. Kanon, "Regimental Histories of Tennessee," (online); Reid, "Prelude to Horseshoe Bend," 16.

[17] Sixty-five year-old Judge William Cocke, father of Major General John Cocke, had joined Jackson's army as a private. Jackson credited Judge Cocke for killing a Red Stick and saving a fellow soldier. Kanon, *Tennesseans at War, 1812–1815*, 93.

[18] On 28 January 181, at Fort Strother, Jackson ordered the court martial of Colonel Perkins and Lieutenant Colonel Stump for disobedience of orders, cowardice, and abandoning their post. Colonel William Higgins presided over the court, which deliberated on the 28th and 29th and included six officers of Perkins's regiment. The court found Perkins not guilty of cowardice, but they found him guilty of disobeying orders and abandoning his post. They also found he did not retreat until abandoned by his men. Stump was not as fortunate, and he was found guilty of the charges and sentenced "to be cashiered and compelled to wear a wooden sword . . . marched and drummed a half mile . . . towards Fort Deposit . . . and that he be not permitted to wear any insignia of an officer in the service of the United States." William Philip Pipkin, "Philip Pipkin—A Tennessee Militiaman," http://files.usgwarchives.net/tn/davidson/military/pipkin01.txt; "Proceedings of Courts-Martials in the Creek War," *American Historical Quarterly* 6 (July 1901): 258–59.

[19] Throughout his narrative of Jackson's march and the battles at Emuckfau and Enitachopco, Pickett's prose closely parallels the descriptions found in Amos Kendall's *Life of Jackson* and S. Putnam Waldo's *Civil and Military History of Andrew Jackson*. Kendall, *Life of Jackson*, 253–64; S. Putnam Waldo, *Civil and Military History of Andrew Jackson: Late*

the want of expected supplies. When General Floyd recovered from his wound, he again marched to the seat of war, with a force of twelve hundred and twenty-seven, rank and file, besides a company of cavalry and four hundred friendly Indians. His destination being the town of Tuckabatchee, he established posts upon the route, for the purpose of keeping up a communication and facilitating the transportation of supplies. Marching from post to post, as they were established, he at length encamped on the Calebee Creek,[20] upon the high lands bordering its swamp.*

At twenty minutes past five o'clock in the morning, the Red Sticks, who had secreted themselves in the swamp during the latter part of the night, sprung upon the Georgians like tigers, driving in their sentinels, and taking the whole army by surprise. In twenty minutes, the action became general, and the front right and left flanks of the Americans were closely pressed; but the enemy was met at every point. The front line was preserved by the steady fire of the artillery, under Captain Thomas, aided by the riflemen of Captain Adams.[21] These troops suffered severely, for the enemy rushed within thirty yards of the cannon. Captain John Broadnax, who commanded one of the picket guards, maintained his post, until a party of Indians had cut off his retreat to the main army. In this desperate situation, his resolute band cut their way through to their friends, assisted by Timpoochee Barnard, a half-breed, at the head of some Uchees.[22] The other friendly Indians, with a few exceptions, taking refuge within the lines, remained alarmed and inactive while the battle lasted. When day appeared, the battalions of Majors Watson and Freeman were ordered to wheel up at right angles. Those of Majors Booth and Cleaveland, who formed the right wing, received the same order, while Captain Hamilton's

* This creek runs in a northwestern direction, through Macon County, Alabama.

Major-General in the Army of the United States, and Commander-in-Chief of the Southern Division **(New York: P. M. Davis, 1825), 113–24.**

[20] While Tuckabatchee was Floyd's primary objective, he wanted to eliminate all the Red Stick towns on the Tallapoosa River. On 11 January 1814, Floyd's army marched from Fort Lawrence, reached Fort Mitchell on the 17th, arrived at Fort Hull on the 20th, and made camp on Calebee (Calabee) Creek, a tributary of the Tallapoosa, on the 26th. His steady progress put him in striking distance of Tuckabatchee. Bunn and Williams, "Frontier in Flames,"122; Tait, "Journal of James A. Tait," 235–36.

[21] The attack, as planned originally by William Weatherford, called for an early morning attack on the officers' tents, killing them and seizing the two cannons commanded by Captain Jett Thomas. When Paddy Walsh (Welch) opposed his plan, Weatherford apparently left the Red Stick camp for his home. Thomas's artillery crew and Captain William E. Adams's rifle company held their ground amidst great confusion caused by the attacking Creeks in the early morning darkness. Stiggins, *Creek Indian History*, 129–32; Tait, "Journal of James A. Tait," 236–37; Woodward, *Reminiscences*, 88–89; O'Brien, *In Bitterness and in Tears*, 125–27.

[22] The quick strike by the Red Stick warriors cut off Captain Broadnax's small picket guard from the main body of the army during "Gen. Floyd's night fight." Fortunately, Major Timpoochee (Timpoochy) Barnard (c.1783–c.1834), a métis Uchee (Yuchi), rallied his men and helped Broadnax's men return safely within their lines. Woodward, *Reminiscences*, 36, 89; Griffith, *McIntosh and Weatherford*, 135.

cavalry was instructed to form in the rear of the right wing, to act as circumstances required. A charge was now made, and the Red Sticks gave way before the bayonet.[23] The cavalry, falling upon them, made considerable havoc, and, followed by the friendly Indians and the rifle companies of Merriweather and Ford, pursued them through Calebee swamp. From the traces of blood, and the number of headdresses and war clubs found in various directions, the loss of the enemy must have been considerable.[24]

In the commencement of the action, Colonel Newnan was wounded by three balls, which deprived the commander of the services of that gallant and useful officer.[25] Adjutant-General Narden, whose horse was wounded under him, performed important services, while the aide-de-camp of Floyd also had his horse killed under him. His additional aides, General Lee and Major Pace, acted in a manner highly honorable to themselves and useful to the army. The loss of the Americans was seventeen killed and one hundred and thirty-two wounded, to which must be added the loss of the friendly Indians, who had five killed and fifteen wounded.[26] The Georgians fought with great resolution; but, assailed before day, with no fortifications around them, the Indians, until the charge was made, had the advantage, and made use of it.* The large number of wounded Georgians, the proximity of the enemy, who continued to hover around them, indicating a disposition to renew the attack, were reasons deemed sufficient by Floyd for relinquishing the main object of the expedition,

* Zachariah McGirth, bearing a dispatch from General Claiborne to Floyd, passed through the Calebee swamp late in the night, while it must have been filled with the enemy, and strangely reached the American camp in safety.

[23] Majors John Watson and Frederick Freeman, Captain Benjamin Cleaveland, and Colonel David Booth were veterans of the Battle of Autossee. Captain Duke Hamilton's mounted dragoons had arrived the day before and were placed at the rear of Floyd's army as a reserve force. O'Brien, *In Bitterness and In Tears*, 127.

[24] While the rifle companies under Captains James Meriwether and William Ford made their charge with fixed bayonets, Private James A. Tait recorded in his journal that Captain Hamilton's dragoons "slew 15 in the charge." Tait referred to the Creek militants as "Red Clubs"—a term used occasionally by Benjamin Hawkins. Tait, "Journal of James A. Tait," 236, 237; Woodward, *Reminiscences*, 78–79; Thomas G Rodgers, "Night Attack at Calabee Creek," *Journal of the Historical Society of the Georgia National Guard* 4 (Spring 1995): 16–18; "Militia Draft—List of Field and Company Officers," *Georgia Journal*, [Milledgeville], 9 August 1813, http://www.usgennet.org/usa/ga/topic/military/militia.htm.

[25] Daniel Newnan (1780–1851) recovered from his wounds and had a long public career, serving Georgia as adjutant general (1806–1817) and secretary of state (1825–1827). He was elected to the U.S. House of Representatives (1831–1833) as a Jacksonian Democrat. Burns, *History of Georgia Militia*, 1: 330; "Daniel Newnan," *Biographical Directory of the United States Congress, 1774-Present* (online).

[26] Despite multiple references to "Adjutant General Narden" and to "General Lee and Major Pace," in various sources, this editor cannot verify their complete identity. See John Floyd to Major General Pinckney, Camp Defiance, 48 miles west of the Chattahoochee, January 27th 1814, in John Brannan, ed., *Official Letters of the Military and Naval Officers of the United States, During the War with Great Britain in the Years 1812, 13, 14, & 15* (Washington: Way & Gideon, 1823), 296–97.

retracing his steps, and awaiting further reinforcements. He accordingly marched from Calebee to Fort Hull, one of his newly-erected posts, and, the next night, the Indians were in possession of the battle field. Leaving at Fort Hull a small garrison, he returned to Fort Mitchell, upon the Chattahoochee, which he believed, from information, was soon to be attacked.[27] Although the Georgia army had gallantly maintained their ground, at the Battle of Calebee, the Indians stopped their further march into the nation, and caused them, in a few days, to retreat.*

General Jackson had employed the few militia who remained with him at Fort Strother, after the battles of Emuckfau and Enitachopco, in constructing flatboats, to descend the Coosa, with stores for the use of the new army, then being raised in Tennessee, which was to operate below. The Kialegee chiefs, whose neutrality Jackson had viewed with suspicion, becoming alarmed, paid him a visit, and disclosed that the Eufaulas, New-Yaucaus and Okfuskees, the remnant of the Hillabees, the Fish Ponds, and many Red Sticks from other towns, were then in a bend of the Tallapoosa, and on an island near Emuckfau, where they had resolved to defend themselves to the last extremity.[28] This information determined him to march upon them.

When the army arrived at Fort Strother, he embarked the stores in the flatboats, which were to proceed down the Coosa, in charge of the thirty-ninth regiment, and, leaving a garrison of four hundred and fifty men in Fort Strother, under the command of Colonel

* Russell, *History of the Late War*, 242–43; Waldo, *Civil and Military History of Andrew Jackson*, 124–26; Kendall, *Life of Andrew Jackson*, 240.

[27] James A. Tait recorded in his journal, "We were on the battle ground six days in an entrenched camp." The entrenched camp—known as Camp Defiance—gave Floyd and his staff time to regroup, bury their dead and tend to their wounded, and plan their retrograde back to Fort Hull on 1 February 1814. They marched out on the 16th, reached the Ocmulgee on the 26th, and arrived at Milledgeville on 7 March 1814, where Floyd's Georgia units began to discharge their men. Georgia's Red Stick War was over. Tait, "Journal of James A. Tait," 237–38; Griffith, *McIntosh and Weatherford*, 137–38.

[28] Kialigee (Kialejee), Eufaula, New-Yaucau, Okfuskee, Hillabee (Hillaubee), and Fish Ponds (Thlotlogulgau) were Upper Creek towns located in the Tallapoosa watershed and were generally aligned with the Red Sticks. Swanton, *Early History of the Creek Indians*, 249, 258–63, 272, 275–76; Ethridge, *Creek Country*, 36, 90–91, 114, 158, 170–72.

Steele, he began the march, for the third time, toward the seat of war.[29] Within five days, Jackson reached the mouth of Cedar Creek, having been retarded by the cutting out of thirty miles of the road. The boats, in descending the river, meeting with some obstructions, finally reached this point also, where a fort was immediately commenced, which Jackson called Fort Williams, in honor of the commander of the thirty-ninth regiment.[30] A detachment returned to the camp, and reported that they had burned two Indian towns, lower down, but had seen no Red Sticks.

[29] Colonel Robert Steele, commander of the 4th Regiment of West Tennessee Militia Infantry, was left in command of Fort Strother, but Jackson had also left him in charge of overseeing the construction of flatboats. Jackson needed the flatboats to move critical supplies and equipment to support his army. Kanon, "Regimental Histories of Tennessee," (online); Kanon, *Tennesseans at War, 1812–1815*, 97–98.

[30] Colonel John Williams, a Knoxville lawyer, was the commander of the thirty-ninth U.S. Infantry regulars who joined Jackson's army in March 1814. Williams and his troops floated down the river on flatboats carrying critical provisions, which became grounded within two miles of the new depot. Fort Williams was a stockade built near the mouth of Cedar Creek on the Coosa River in modern Talladega County, Alabama. Kanon, *Tennesseans at War, 1812–1815*, 96, 98–100; Owsley, *Struggle for the Gulf*, 78–79.

Chapter XXXVIII

BATTLE OF THE HORSE-SHOE: WEATHERFORD SURRENDERS HIMSELF AT FORT JACKSON

Leaving a guard at Fort Williams, General Jackson put his army, which consisted of two thousand men, upon the march. He opened a passage across the ridge which divides the Coosa and Tallapoosa, and, in three days, advanced to the immediate neighborhood of the enemy.

Cholocco Litabixee—the *Horse-Shoe*—where the Red Sticks had assembled, to make a desperate defense, was admirably adapted by nature for security, if well-guarded, but equally for destruction, if not well defended.[1] About one hundred acres of land was bordered by the Tallapoosa River, forming a peninsula. Across the neck of the bend, the Red Sticks had a breast-work of logs, so arranged as to expose assailants to a crossfire. The houses of the village stood upon some low grounds, at the bottom of the bend, where hundreds of canoes were tied to the banks of the river. The warriors of Hillabee, Okfuskee, Oakchoie, Eufaulauhatchee, New-Yaucau, Hickory Ground and Fish Pond towns, had concentrated upon the remarkable peninsula.[2] General Coffee, with a large body of mounted men, and the friendly Indians, forded the Tallapoosa, two miles below the breast-work, and, having gained the eastern side, extended his lines for a great distance, so as to encompass the bend.[3] As soon as Jackson saw, from signals which were made, that Coffee had taken his position, he marched the remainder of his force towards the breast-work, planted two pieces of artillery, eighty yards distant from the nearest part of the Indian defense, and, at ten o'clock in the morning, began to open them upon the enemy. These pieces, accompanied by occasional discharges from the muskets and rifles, effected but little. In the meanwhile, the Cherokees, under Coffee, swimming the river, took possession of the canoes, and, returning with them to the opposite bank, they were presently filled with friendly Indians and Americans, the latter headed by Colonel Morgan and Captain Russell. They reached the town and wrapped it in flames.[4]

[1] As noted above, "Cholocco Litabixee"—which can be loosely translated as "Horse's Flat Foot"—was the Muskogee name for the great bend in the Tallapoosa River in modern Tallapoosa County, Alabama. While modern scholars use the term Horseshoe Bend, most nineteenth century studies refer to the great bend or curve in the river as "The Horse Shoe" or the Horse-Shoe. Read, *Indian Place Names in Alabama,* 19. See Samuel Putnam Waldo, *Civil and Military History of Andrew Jackson* (New York: P. M. Davis, 1825), 131 (quote); John Bassett Spencer, *The Life of Andrew Jackson,* 2 vols. (Garden City, NY: Doubleday, Page & Company, 1911), 1: 114, 118.

[2] Pickett's Oakchoie (Oakchoy, Okchai) is generally referred to as Hookchoie after Benjamin Hawkins's list of Upper

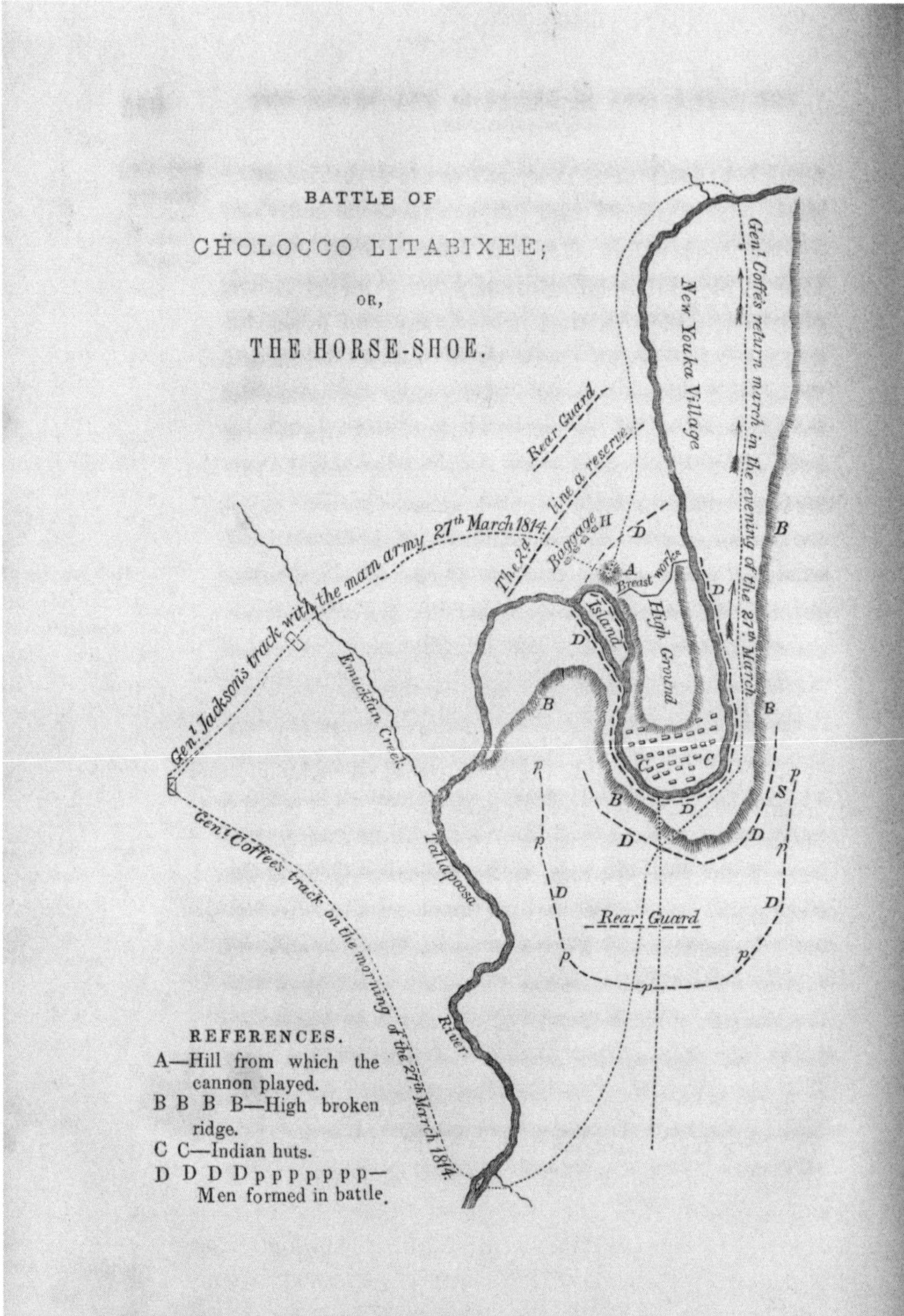
BATTLE OF
CHOLOCCO LITABIXEE;
OR,
THE HORSE-SHOE.
Gen.l Coffee's return march in the evening of the 27th March
New Youka Village
Rear Guard
The 2d line a reserve
Baggage H
Gen.l Jackson's track with the main army 27th March 1814.
A
Breast works
Island
High Ground
Emuckfau Creek
Tallapoosa
River
Gen.l Coffee's track on the morning of the 27th March 1814.
Rear Guard
REFERENCES.
A—Hill from which the cannon played.
B B B B—High broken ridge.
C C—Indian huts.
D D D D p p p p p p p—Men formed in battle.

Jackson then ordered his troops to storm the breast-work, behind which all the warriors had posted themselves. A short contest was maintained at the port-holes, but presently the impetuous Americans mounted the breast-work, and, dyeing the huge logs with their blood and that of the enemy, they finally, after a most desperate struggle, became masters of the interior. The Red Sticks, now assailed in front by Jackson, who had taken possession of their breast-work, and attacked from behind by a portion of Coffee's troops, who had just completed the conflagration of their village, fought under great disadvantages. However, none of them begged for quarter, but everyone sold his life at the dearest rate. After a long fight, many of them fled and attempted to swim the river, but were killed on all sides by the unerring rifles of the Tennesseans. Others screened themselves behind tree-tops and thick piles of timber. Being desirous not to destroy this brave race, Jackson sent a messenger towards them, who assured them of the clemency of the general, provided they would surrender. They answered by discharges from their guns and shouts of defiance. The artillery was then ineffectually brought to bear upon them. The Americans then applied fire to their retreat, which soon forced them to fly, and, as they ran, they were killed by American guns. It was late in the evening before the dreadful battle ended.[5]

The Red Sticks numbered about one thousand warriors, and, out of that number, five hundred and fifty-seven were found dead on the peninsula.* As many were killed in the river by Coffee's troops, while they were endeavoring to swim over, it may be safely stated that not more than two hundred survived. Some of them long afterwards suffered with the most grievous wounds. Menawa, one of the bravest chiefs that ever lived, was literally shot to pieces. He fought as long as he could. He saved himself by jumping into the river, where the water was four feet deep. He held to a root, and thus kept himself beneath the waves, breathing through the long joint of a cane, one end of which he held in his mouth, and while the other end came above the surface of the water. When night set in the brave Menawa rose from his watery bed, and made his way to the forest, bleeding from many wounds.†

* Kendall, Eaton, and Waldo's lives of Jackson.

† Known by the American settlers as "Old Manorway" [Menawa].

Creek towns. Swanton, *Early History of the Creek Indians*, 274–75; Ethridge, *Creek Country*, 84, 170.

[3] Around 6:00 a.m. on 27 March 1814, General John Coffee's brigade—consisting of approximately 700 volunteers and 600 Indian auxiliaries—began crossing the Tallapoosa and taking up positions to the rear of the Red Sticks on either side of the river. Kanon, *Tennesseans at War, 1812–1815*, 99–100.

[4] Believing that a white man should lead the Cherokee volunteers in the Red Stick War, Return J. Meigs, federal agent to the Cherokee, had selected Gideon Morgan, an Indian countryman, to lead the Cherokee who served with Jackson's army. Captain William Russell commanded a company of scouts and spies assigned to Coffee's brigade and worked in unison with the Cherokee. Abram, *Forging a Cherokee-American Alliance*, 59–60, 70–71, 77, 188 n. 67.

[5] Major William Bradford's artillery crews opened fire around 10:30 a.m. and had fired some seventy rounds by mid-day, with little impact on the breastworks. With his opponents outnumbered 3-to-1, Jackson unleashed his superior numbers and weaponry on the Red Stick defenders following a long drum roll by young Zachariah Turner at about 12:30 in the afternoon. Thomas Kanon, "'A Slow Laborious Slaughter': The Battle of Horseshoe Bend," *Tennessee Historical Quarterly* 58 (Spring 1999): 6–8.

Many years after the war, we conversed with this chief, and learned from him the particulars of his remarkable escape. His face, limbs and body, at the time we conversed with him, were marked with the scars of many horrible wounds. Another chief was shot down, among a number of slain warriors, and, with admirable presence of mind, saved his life, by drawing over him the bodies of two of them, under which he lay, till the darkness of the night permitted him to leave the horrible place.[6]

The loss of the Americans was thirty-two killed and ninety-nine wounded. The friendly Cherokees had eighteen killed and thirty-six wounded. The Tory Creeks had five killed and eleven wounded. Among the slain were Major L. P. Montgomery and Lieutenants Moulton and Sommerville, who fell in the charge upon the breast-works.[7]

Major Lemuel Purnell Montgomery was born in Wythe County, Virginia, in 1786. He was a relation, by consanguinity, of the gallant general of that name, who fell at the storming of Quebec. His grandfather, Hugh Montgomery, of North Carolina, a man of fortune and talents, commanded a Whig company during the Revolution, which he equipped and supported at his own expense. With this company he fought the British and Tories with great success. He was a member of the convention which formed the constitution of the state of North Carolina, and not long afterwards one of the counties of that state was named in honor of him. The father of Major Montgomery, also named Hugh, was a man of talents, and, having removed to Virginia, was a member of the senate of that state. At Snow Hill, in Maryland, he married a lady, whose maiden name was Purnell, which was the middle name of her son, the brave major, who fell at the Horse-Shoe. The father removed from Virginia to East Tennessee, near Knoxville.[8]

Major Montgomery completed his education at Washington College, Tennessee, studied law with Judge Trimble, of Knoxville, and established himself in that profession at Nashville, where, in four years, his attainments, eloquence, zeal, fearless independence and popular bearing, rendered him a formidable rival of the able Felix Grundy.[9] During this period, he was frequently placed at the head of parties of armed horsemen; and with them he scoured the dark gorges of the Cumberland Mountains in pursuit of desperate banditti, who had long pillaged the people in the valleys. At length

6 Menawa, a métis Creek of Okfuskee, had been slow to embrace the Red Stick faction, but he was generally acknowledged as a leading warrior and an opponent of land cessions to the Georgians. He openly clashed with the pro-American faction led by the métis Creek William McIntosh. Green, *Politics of Indian Removal*, 96, 98; Thomas L. McKenney and James Hall, *History of the Indian Tribes of North America, With Biographical Sketches and Anecdotes of the Principal Chiefs*, 2 vols. (Philadelphia: D. Rice & Co., 1872–1874), 1: 103–11.

7 Major Montgomery, First Lieutenant Robert M. Sommerville, and Second Lieutenant Michael C. Moulton (Molton) were members of the 39th U.S. Infantry, which included a large number of East Tennesseans recruited by Colonel John Williams. O'Brien, *In Bitterness and in Tears*, 147; Leota Driver Maiden, "Colonel John Williams," East Tennessee Historical Society's *Publications* 30 (1958): 18, 22–24; "Thirty-Ninth Regiment of Infantry," *Journal of the Executive Proceedings of the Senate of the United States of America*, vol. 2 (Washington: Duff Green, 1828), 399.

8 Colonel Hugh Montgomery Sr. (1720–1779), a native of Ireland, resided in Salisbury, North Carolina, where he served on the Committee of Safety and commanded the 1st Rowan County Regiment of Infantry (1776–1777). His only son was Hugh Montgomery Jr., who inherited his land in Virginia and was the father of seven sons—including Lemuel Purnell Montgomery—and two daughters. John H. Wheeler, *Reminiscences and Memoirs of North Carolina and Eminent North Carolinians* (Columbus, OH: Columbus

he was appointed by Madison first major of the Thirty-Ninth Regiment, which he gallantly led to the breast-works of the Indians at the Horse-Shoe. He was the first man that mounted the breast-work, and, while waving his sword and animating his men, a large ball, shot from the rifle of a Red Stick, entered his head and instantly killed him. When the battle was ended, Jackson stood over his body and wept. He exclaimed, "I have lost the flower of my army!"[10]

At the time of his death, Major Montgomery was only twenty-eight years of age. His eyes were keen and black; his hair was of a dark auburn color; his weight was one hundred and seventy-five pounds; his height was six feet and two inches; his form was admirably proportioned, and he was, altogether, the finest looking man in the army. A diversity of opinion prevails among the soldiers of this campaign as to the disposition of the body of Major Montgomery. Some contend that Jackson caused it to be sunk in the Tallapoosa River to protect it from Indian brutalities. We have in our possession the affidavit of two soldiers, now living in Tennessee—John Lovelady and Samuel Gearing—which states that they assisted to bury the body of Montgomery, and bore off the surplus dirt which remained about the grave upon the skin of a beeve and threw it into the river. They then burnt brush over the grave to conceal it from the keen eyes of the savages. Since then, and only a few years ago, the people of Tallapoosa County took up these remains, conveyed them to their courthouse and deposited them in the ground with military honors. The county of Montgomery, Alabama, was named in honor of Major Montgomery,[11] while the memory of his relation, who fell at Quebec, is preserved in the name of the city.[12]

The day after the terrible battle of the

Printing Works, 1884), 396–97; David B. Montgomery, *A Genealogical History of the Montgomerys and Their Descendants* (Owensville, Ind.: J. P. Cox Publisher, 1903), 346–47.

[9] James Trimble served as the first circuit judge of the second circuit in 1809, which included Knox County. He moved to Nashville in 1813 and became a law partner with Felix Grundy, and they served as legal counsel for the University of North Carolina. Samuel Dickens, a former congressman from North Carolina, wrote: "Grundy was the greatest orator and Trimble, the soundest lawyer." Kemp Plummer Battle, *History of the University of North Carolina: From Its Beginning to the Death of President Swain, 1789–1868*, 2 vols. (Raleigh, NC: Edwards and Broughton Printing Company, 1907–1912), 1: 382–83, 387–88.

[10] The day after the destruction of the Red Stick Creeks at Tohopeka, Jackson wrote letters to Major General Thomas Pinckney and Governor Willie Blount giving details of the bloody five-hour conflict. While neither letter is the source of Pickett's quote, Jackson, in his letter to Blount, specifically referred to Montgomery, Moulton, and Sommerville: "No men ever acted more gallantly or fell more gloriously." Brannan, *Official Letters of the Military and Naval Officers of the United States*, 319–20, 321–23.

[11] Montgomery County, Alabama, dedicated a bronze statue of Major Lemuel Purnell Montgomery on 10 May 1987. Clydetta Fulmer was the sculptor, and the statue was installed in front of the Montgomery County Courthouse at 251 South Lawrence Street where it intersects with Adams Street in Montgomery, Alabama. "Major Lemuel Purnell Montgomery (sculpture)," Inventories of American Painting and Sculpture, Smithsonian American Art Museum, Washington, DC.

[12] Major General Richard Montgomery (1738–1775), a native of Ireland and veteran of the British army, embraced the Patriot cause in 1775 and received a commission in the Continental Army. He led an invasion of Canada—capturing St. Johns and Montreal in November—and moved against Quebec in December, where he was killed on 31 December 1775. Several states have named counties in his honor, and there are six towns named for Montgomery, including Alabama's capital city. Hal T. Shelton, *General Richard Montgomery and the American Revolution: From Redcoat to Rebel* (New York: New York University Press, 1994), 133–50.

Horse-Shoe, General Jackson assumed the line of march, and reached Fort Williams on the second of April. Upon an examination of the Coosa River, it was found impracticable to transport the stores from Fort Williams to the termination of the falls, by water, and the reduced condition of the horses and the roughness of the country rendered it impossible to transport them by land in any quantity. However, with such provisions as the men could carry upon their backs, Jackson marched towards the Hickory Ground, relying upon the eastern army, whose advance guard was then under Milton, for supplies. Heavy rains retarded his march, but he reached Fusihatchee, where he captured a few prisoners. The Red Sticks fled from Hoithlewaule and other towns across the Tallapoosa.[13] Colonel Milton, with troops from the two Carolinas, had been a month at Fort Decatur, situated upon a commanding bluff, on the eastern side of the Tallapoosa, but took no steps to cooperate with Jackson in preventing the escape of the Indians.[14]

Prevented from pursuing the enemy by a flood in the river and the scarcity of provisions, Jackson marched to the head of the peninsula formed by the confluence of the Coosa and Tallapoosa, and planted his colors upon the spot where Governor Bienville, one hundred years before, had erected Fort Toulouse, so long garrisoned by French troops. Here the rivers approach within six hundred yards of each other, and diverging unite four miles below. The battle of the Horse-Shoe had nearly put an end to the war, and the dispirited Red Sticks made but few efforts to rally. Many came in and surrendered, while the larger portion escaped towards Florida. The old French trenches were cleaned out, and an American stockade with block-houses was erected upon the site, which received the name of Fort Jackson.[15]

Deputations of chiefs continually arrived, and submitted, in behalf of themselves and their people, to such terms as General Jackson thought proper to impose. Among the most conspicuous of these was William Weatherford, who led the Indians at Fort Mims, and at the battles of Calebee and Holy Ground. Jackson had directed that he should be captured, if possible, and brought to him, confined, to receive such punishment as his crimes merited. Weatherford, a man without fear, boldly

[13] Much like the other Red Stick-dominated Upper Creek towns, Fusihatchee, located some two miles below Hoithlewaule on the Tallapoosa, was abandoned after the Battle of Horseshoe Bend. John Swanton points out that Fusihatchee does not appear on the census list of 1832. Griffith, *McIntosh and Weatherford*, 150; Swanton, *Early History of the Creek Indians*, 269.

[14] Colonel Homer V. Milton commanded elements of the 3rd U.S. Infantry and General Joseph Graham's Carolina Brigade, which included militia units from North and South Carolina. His forces had crossed the Chattahoochee, searching and laying waste to the deserted towns south of the Tallapoosa. He constructed Fort Decatur in April 1814 as a base of operations and a supply depot to support Jackson's army. Gregory A. Waselkov, "Fort Jackson and the Aftermath," in *Tohopeka*, 159; Owsley, *Struggle for the Gulf*, 59–60.

[15] On 26 April 1814, General Joseph Graham's Carolina Brigade, consisting of the 7th Regiment of North Carolina Militia and a regiment of the South Carolina militia, established Camp Jackson on the Tallapoosa near the site of the old French Fort Toulouse and began construction of Fort Jackson. When the Carolina Brigade left in mid-June, they were replaced by Tennessee militia, who continued the fort's construction. Located near modern Wetumpka, Alabama, the fort featured four stockaded bastions, a demilune, earthen parapets, a moat, a powder magazine, and barracks to house two companies. Gregory A. Waselkov, Brian M. Wood, and Joseph M. Herbert, *Colonization and Conquest: The 1980 Archaeological Excavations at Fort Toulouse and Fort Jackson, Alabama*, Auburn University Archaeological Monograph 4 (Montgomery: Auburn University at Montgomery, 1982), 221, 241–44, 247–48, 251–73.

resolved to appear at the American camp voluntarily.[16] Mounting the same splendid gray steed which had borne him over the bluff at the Holy Ground,* he rode within a few miles of Fort Jackson, when a fine deer crossed his path and stopped within shooting distance, which he fired at and killed. Reloading his rifle, with two balls, for the purpose of shooting the Big Warrior, should he give him any cause at the fort, he placed the deer behind his saddle and advanced to the American outposts. Some soldiers, of whom he politely inquired for Jackson's whereabouts, gave him some unsatisfactory and rude replies when a gray-headed man a few steps beyond pointed him to the marquee.[17]

Weatherford rode up to it, and checked his horse immediately at the entrance, where sat the Big Warrior, who exulting exclaimed: "Ah! Bill Weatherford, have we got you at last!" The fearless chieftain cast his keen eye at the Big Warrior, and said in a determined tone: "You damned traitor, if you give me any insolence, I will blow a ball through your cowardly heart."[18] General Jackson now came running out of the marquee, with Colonel Hawkins, and, in a furious manner, exclaimed: "How dare you, sir, to ride up to my tent, after having murdered the women and children at Fort Mims?" Weatherford said:

"General Jackson, I am not afraid of you. I fear no man, for I am a Creek warrior. I have nothing to request in behalf of myself; you can kill me, if you desire. But I come to beg you to send for the women and children of the war party, who are now starving in the woods. Their fields and cribs have been destroyed by your people, who have driven them to the woods without an ear of corn. I hope that you will send out parties, who will safely conduct them here, in order that they may be fed. I exerted myself in vain to prevent the massacre of the women and children at Fort Mims. I am now done fighting. The Red Sticks are nearly all killed. If I could fight you any longer, I would most heartily do so. Send for the women and children. They never did you any harm. But kill me, if the white people want it done."[19]

At the conclusion of these words, many persons, who had surrounded the marquee, exclaimed, "Kill him! Kill him! Kill him!" General Jackson commanded silence, and, in an emphatic manner,

* The Weatherfords always had fine horses, and old Charles, the father, was a celebrated patron of the Alabama turf.

[16] In his letter of 25 April 1814 from Fort Williams, Jackson reported to Secretary of War John Armstrong the arrival of William Weatherford, "the King of the Hickory Ground tribe," "other distinguished leaders," and their followers, who were surrendering in large numbers. *ASP: MA*, 3: 790.

[17] In his *Reminiscences*, Thomas S. Woodward, a métis Creek and veteran of the Creek War of 1813–1814 who served under Jackson, refuted Pickett's narrative of Weatherford's arrival on a "grey steed" and delivering a recently killed deer. Woodward, *Reminiscences*, 80–81.

[18] Pickett's narrative of Weatherford's arrival and the confrontation with Big Warrior is not documented in Jackson's letters to Secretary of War John Armstrong. Again, Thomas S. Woodward, in his description of Weatherford's exchange with Jackson, does not mention the presence of Big Warrior or a confrontation with any of the allied Creek leaders. Ibid., 79–82.

[19] If there is an accurate or reasonably close documentation of Weatherford's speech and his interview with Jackson, it can be found in *The Life of Andrew Jackson* started by John Reid, Jackson's aide-de-camp who died in 1816, and completed and published by John H. Eaton in 1817. John Reid and John H. Eaton, *The Life of Andrew Jackson, Major-General in the Service of the United States: Comprising a History of the War in the South, From the Commencement of the Creek Campaign, to the Termination of the Hostilities before New Orleans* (Philadelphia: M. Carey and Son, 1817), 165–67.

[20] For his narrative of William Weatherford's appearance at Jackson's camp, Pickett cites his sources as Colonel Robert James and William Sizemore and bases his claims on their conversations with Weatherford. He also discounts the statements by John H. Eaton in *The Life of Andrew Jackson* as being based on camp gossip. However, John Reid, Jackson's personal aide, was present at the time of Weatherford's surrender and made notes of the encounter, which he used in the original draft of *The Life of Andrew Jackson,* first published by John H. Eaton in 1817 and revised and reprinted in 1824 and 1828. Griffith, *McIntosh and Weatherford,* 151–54; Remini, *Andrew Jackson and the Course of the American Empire, 1767–1821,* 172, 323–24.

[21] After returning to his home on the Little River, Weatherford had felt threatened and turned himself over to Colonel Gilbert C. Russell at Fort Claiborne. Russell secretly arranged for his safe return to Fort Jackson. Judith Knight, "Edited transcript of Case 1299: *Weatherford vs. Weatherford et al.*" in J. Anthony Paredes and Judith Knight, eds., *Red Eagle's Children: Weatherford vs. Weatherford et al.* (Tuscaloosa: University of Alabama Press, 2012), 67.

[22] An aide to Colonel Russell led Weatherford to Captain William Laval, who coordinated Weatherford's departure from Fort Claiborne to the safer confines of Fort Jackson. Griffith, *McIntosh and Weatherford,* 155.

said: "Any man who would kill as brave a man as this would rob the dead!" He then invited Weatherford to alight, drank a glass of brandy with him, and entered into a cheerful conversation, under his hospitable marquee. Weatherford gave him the deer, and they were then good friends. He took no further part in the war, except to influence his warriors to surrender.* He went to the place of his former residence, upon Little River, but soon had to leave it, as his life was in constant danger.[20]

He then went to Fort Claiborne, and the commanding officer of that place saved him from being killed, by placing him in a tent by himself, which was pitched very near the marquee, and which was constantly guarded by a file of soldiers. After he had been kept there ten or fifteen days, the commanding officer became still more uneasy, for fear he would be killed by persons who had lost relations at Fort Mims, and who were bent on his destruction. He now resolved to send him beyond the lines, during a dark night.[21] About midnight, he sent his aide, followed by Weatherford, to the station of Major Laval, who was then a captain, and the officer on guard.[22] He said, "Captain Laval, the commanding officer says you must take Weatherford to yonder tree, under which you will find a horse tied, and that he must mount the horse and make his escape." Captain Laval instantly told Weatherford to follow him. He passed by the guard, giving the countersign, and reached the tree.

* Such is the account of Weatherford's interview with Jackson, as related by the chieftain himself, to Colonel Robert James of Clark, William Sizemore of Little River, and many other persons. The incorrect statements of Eaton, in his *Life of Andrew Jackson*, are doubtless based entirely on camp gossip.

Weatherford eagerly seized the limb to which the horse was tied, threw the reins over the animal's head, shook Laval by the hand, and said, in earnest and grateful tones, "Good-bye! God bless you!" He then vaulted into the saddle and rode off rapidly. That was the last time he ever saw Weatherford. For the distance of one mile, at least, Laval heard the clattering of the horse's feet.*

After the war was over, Weatherford became a permanent citizen of the lower part of the county of Monroe, where, upon a good farm, well supplied with Negroes, he lived, maintained an excellent character, and was much respected by the American citizens for his bravery, honor and strong native sense. In 1826 he died from the effects of fatigue, produced by a desperate bear hunt.[23] Many persons yet living bear testimony to the bravery and honor of William Weatherford in private life, an instance of which we here take occasion to mention:

In 1820, many people assembled at the sale of the effects of the deceased Duncan Henderson, in the lower part of Monroe County, Alabama.[24] An old man, named Bradberry—the father of the gallant lieutenant, who fought at Burnt Corn, and who was afterwards killed in another action—was cruelly murdered upon this occasion by one Callier, who plunged a long knife into the back of his neck. The murderer had an accomplice, one Fisher, who was in pursuit of Bradberry at the same time, and who had, a few moments before, broken a pitcher over his head. These men were so desperate, and flourished their knives with such defiance, that Justice Henderson in vain called upon the bystanders to seize them, while the poor, unoffending old Bradberry lay weltering in his blood.[25]

Shocked at the cowardly and brutal act, and provoked at the timidity of the bystanders, William Weatherford, who lived in that neighborhood, now advanced towards Henderson, and said in a loud voice: "These, I suppose, are white men's laws. You stand aside and see a man, an old man, killed, and not one of you will avenge his blood. If he had one drop of Indian blood mixed with that which runs upon the ground there, I would instantly kill his murderers, at the risk of my life." Justice Henderson implored him to take them, and, being assured that the white man's law would not

* Conversations with Major Laval, a resident of Charleston, S. C.

[23] While Pickett refers to Weatherford's death in 1826, he actually died on 4 March 1824. He had participated in a deer and bear hunt near Lovett's Creek in Monroe County, Alabama, in late February 1824. Some days later he became ill and died. Ibid., 253.

[24] Duncan Henderson (1794-c.1821), a native of North Carolina, had served in the 3rd U.S. Infantry during the War of 1812. "Duncan Henderson," http://search.ancestry. com/cgi.

[25] Duncan Henderson and Justice Alexander Henderson appear in the 1816 census of Monroe County, Mississippi Territory (Alabama). Online genealogy records give the date of Duncan Henderson's death as 1821 and 23 August 1822. Ibid.; "1816 Census Index, Monroe County, Alabama," http://usgwarchives.net.

hurt him, but that he would be commended for the act, Weatherford now drew forth his long, silver-handled butcher-knife and advanced towards the murderers, who stood forty paces off, threatening to kill the first man who should attempt to arrest them. He first advanced to Callier, who, trembling at his approach, let his knife drop by his side, and instantly surrendered. Seizing him by the throat, he said to the bystanders, "Here, tie the damned rascal." Then, going up to Fisher, upon whom he flashed his tiger eyes, he also arrested him without the least opposition—Fisher exclaiming, "I will not resist you, Billy Weatherford."[26]

General Pinckney arriving at Fort Jackson, and being the senior officer of the Southern Army, assumed the command and approved of all the acts of Jackson. Learning that the Indians were generally submitting, he ordered the West Tennessee troops to march home. Two hours after the order was issued they were in motion. Arriving at Camp Blount, near Fayetteville, Jackson discharged them, after gratifying them with a feeling address. He then repaired to the Hermitage, from which he had been absent eighteen months, in a hostile land, and, a portion of the time, almost alone.

Pinckney remained at Fort Jackson with the troops from the two Carolinas and those from East Tennessee.[27] Four hundred of General Doherty's brigade of East Tennesseans were stationed at Fort Williams. General Johnson, at the head of five hundred men, had been dispatched to the Cahaba River, who proceeded to its source and joined Jackson before he reached the Tennessee River. Several detachments were sent forth from Fort Jackson, who scoured the country in all directions for the fugitive Red Sticks.[28] Colonel Hawkins performed several trips to the Chattahoochee, and exerted himself to induce the wretched Creeks to surrender and terminate a

[26] In his original narrative, Pickett referred to the murderers of Bradberry confronted by Weatherford as "C____r" and "F____r," while subsequent writers and family researchers have used the names of Callier, Collier, or Caller and Fisher. Thomas S. Woodward declares in his *Reminiscences* that "Col. Fisher and Jim Collier killed Bradberry." With all his contacts among older residents, it appears that Pickett may have chosen the unknown mysterious assailants over political conflict. Woodward, *Reminiscences*, 97; Meek, *Romantic Passages in Southwestern History*, 291–92; "Re: Fisher, Josiah & Simahoway—Monroe Co.—AL - 1816," http://www.genealogy.com/forum/general/topics/ai/13733/.

[27] Using the date 1 July 1814, Pickett refers to Fort Jackson, but, at this time, the military post on the Tallapoosa should be referred to as Camp Jackson. When Jackson returned in early July, he was very disappointed in the progress of the fort's construction: "I . . . found the Fort half finished . . . in fact it will take six months labour with the troops here to make the Fort capable of real defence." The fort was still a work-in-progress when Jackson hosted the treaty conference with the Creeks in August 1814. Waselkov, Wood, and Herbert, *Colonization and Conquest*, 247.

[28] Brigadier General George Doherty commanded an East Tennessee militia brigade that included Colonel Ewen Allison's 1st Regiment, Colonel Samuel Bunch's 2nd Regiment, and Colonel John Brown's East Tennessee Volunteer Mounted Gunmen. Brigadier General Thomas Johnson commanded a West Tennessee militia brigade that included Colonel Richard C. Napier's 1st Regiment, Colonel Stephen Copeland's 3rd Regiment, and Colonel Robert Steele's 4th Regiment. Although it appears that Bunch's 2nd Regiment of East Tennessee militia stayed beyond the expiration of their enlistment to June or July, the term of enlistment for these units ran from January through May 1814. O'Brien, *In Bitterness and in Tears*, 134, 136, 139; Kanon, "Regimental Histories of Tennessee" (online).

[29] Contrary to Pickett's narrative, the British did not have three hundred troops or a new fortification on the Apalachicola, and they had no military presence at Pensacola. However, they did land two vessels—HMS *Orpheus* and *Shelbourne*—at the mouth of the Apalachicola River on 11 May 1814 commanded by Captain Hugh Pigot and Lieutenant David Hope. Pigot delivered blankets, presents, 2,000 muskets, and ammunition, all

war which had proved so disastrous to them. But the British at Pensacola were endeavoring to rally them. Two vessels had anchored at the mouth of the Apalachicola, and had landed five thousand stand of arms and abundant ammunition, and three hundred British troops had commenced a fortification, under the command of a colonel. Runners were sent to all parts of the nation, inviting the Indians to rush to that point for provisions and military supplies, and thither many of the Red Sticks repaired.[29] The condition of the friendly Indians, too, was at this time most wretched, and upwards of five thousand of them were fed at the different American posts.*

supplied by Governor Charles Cameron of the Bahamas. He also conveyed a message to the Creek and Seminole chiefs from Admiral Alexander Cochrane, who had been appointed to coordinate the British campaign against the seaboard of the United States. Owsley, "British and Indian Activities in Spanish West Florida," 114–15; John Sugden, "The Southern Indians in the War of 1812: The Closing Phase," *Florida Historical Quarterly* 60 (January 1982): 279–81.

* *American State Papers: Indian Affairs*, 1: 857–60.

Chapter XXXIX

Treaty of Fort Jackson—Attack upon Mobile Point—March upon Pensacola

On the resignations of Generals Hampton and Harrison, Jackson had been promoted to the rank of major general.[1] Leaving the Hermitage once more, he proceeded with a small escort to Fort Jackson, where he safely arrived, and assumed the command of the Southern army. He had been empowered by the federal government to conclude a treaty of peace with the Creek Nation. After much opposition from the Big Warrior and other chiefs to the surrender of the territory which was demanded, a treaty was signed. It was stipulated that a line should commence upon the Coosa, at the southern boundary of the Cherokee Nation, and continue down that river to Wetumpka, and thence eastwardly to Georgia. East and north of that line, containing upwards of one hundred and fifty thousand square miles, remained to the Indians. West and south of it was secured to the United States. This territory was obtained as an indemnification for the expenses incurred by the government in prosecuting the war.[2] Before the treaty was signed the Big Warrior addressed Jackson and Hawkins in a long speech, and tendered them, in the name of the friendly chiefs, a reservation of three miles square of land each, "to be chosen where you like, from that we are going to give, as near as you can to us, for we want you to live by us and give us your advice." To George Mayfield and Alexander Cornells, their interpreters, they also gave one mile square each. Jackson accepted of this national mark of regard for him if approved by the president, who, he said, "would doubtless appropriate its value in aid of your naked women and children."[3] Colonel Hawkins said:[4]

"I have been long among you—I have grown grey in your service—I shall not much longer be your agent. You all know that when applied to by red, black or white, I looked not to color, but to the justice of the claim. I shall continue to be friendly and useful to you while I live, and my children, born among you, will be so brought up as to do the same. I accept your present, and

[1] With the resignations of Wade Hampton and William Benjamin Harrison, Secretary of War John Armstrong offered Harrison's vacant major generalship to Andrew Jackson on 28 May 1814. Jackson received Armstrong's letter in Nashville and accepted the appointment on 18 June. Remini, *Andrew Jackson and the Course of the American Empire,* 222.

[2] By the "Articles of agreement and capitulation" negotiated at Fort Jackson on 9 August 1814, "the chiefs, deputies, and warriors of the Creek Nation" surrendered some twenty two million acres to the United States. The allied Creeks who had fought beside Jackson and the other American forces were punished along with the Red Stick faction for failing to prevent the war. As compensation for ceding their lands west of the Coosa and along the

esteem it the more highly by the manner of bestowing it, as it resulted from the impulse of your own minds, and not from any intimation from the general or me."*

Among other gallant officers present upon this occasion was Colonel Arthur P. Hayne, who, after the peace, resided in Autauga County, Alabama, and was there much esteemed and respected.[5] He was born in Charleston, South Carolina, on the 12th March 1790, and descended from a family distinguished in the Revolution. Although not of age when the attack was made by the British upon the *Chesapeake*, he entered Colonel Wade Hampton's regiment of light dragoons as a first lieutenant. In 1809 he was stationed upon the Mississippi with Scott and Gaines, who then held the same rank with himself. When war was declared against England, Hayne was ordered to the North, and he presently participated in the Battle of Sacket's Harbor, in which he displayed so much gallantry and judgment that he was immediately promoted to the command of a squadron of cavalry, with the rank of major. He was with Wilkinson in 1813 on the St. Lawrence. General Hampton, who wanted Hayne to join his wing of the army, in one of his letters to the secretary of war, employed this complimentary language: "Send me Hayne; I want his constitutional ardor—it will add much to the strength of my army." After Major Hayne had been in several severe engagements at the North, he received the important appointment of inspector-general; and being ordered to join Jackson in the Creek Nation, we find him at the marquee of that officer when the treaty was made. Colonel Hayne, during the Battle of New Orleans, was constantly in his saddle, executing the many hazardous trusts confided to him by Jackson with promptness, bravery and ability. In later years, the duties of important offices abroad, emanating from the federal government, have been confided to him. He is now a resident of Charleston.[6]

In the meantime, General Jackson had been vigilant as to the movements of the British and their Indian allies upon the coast of the Floridas. He constantly dispatched spies to Pensacola and other points, who returned and confirmed the previous reports which had reached him. Provoked at the treachery of the Spaniards, he addressed a letter to Manrique, Governor of Pensacola, remonstrating against the attitude of the Spanish authorities towards the United States,

* *American State Papers: Indian Affairs*, volume 1.

Alabama and their claims to land in Florida, the United States promised to provide food rations for the destitute Upper Creek towns. Kappler, *Indian Affairs: Laws and Treaties*, 2: 107–10; *ASP: IA*, 1: 838.

3 On 18 January 1814, President Madison sent an "extract from the occurrences at Fort Jackson" regarding the donation of land to Jackson, Hawkins, Mayfield, and Cornells to the Senate and House of Representatives, recommending the grants be confirmed. *ASP: IA*, 2: 26.

4 Big Warrior (Tustunnuggee Thlucco) made his speech on 8 August 1814, and Alexander Cornells and George Lovett interpreted his comments and the responses by Jackson and Hawkins, including the quoted lines used by Pickett. Ibid., 1: 837.

5 While Pickett places Hayne at the treaty negotiations, he is not recorded in the officials present, which included Charles Cassedy, Return J. Meigs, Robert Butler, J. C. Warren, Hawkins, and the interpreters—George Mayfield, Alexander Cornells, and George Lovett. Kappler, *Indian Affairs: Laws and Treaties*, 2: 110.

6 Arthur P. Hayne (1788–1867) was appointed inspector general for the U.S. Army Division of the South on 12 April 1814 and resigned 30 September 1820. Hayne was brevetted a lieutenant colonel for his brave conduct at New Orleans. *ASP: MA*, 5: 102; "Arthur Peronneau Hayne," *Biographical Directory of the United States Congress, 1774-Present* (online); James B. Fry, *A Sketch of the Adjutant General's Department: U. S. Army, from 1775 to 1875* (New York: n.p., 1875), 68–69.

a power with which Spain professed to be at peace. Manrique, in his reply, denied that the fugitive Red Sticks were then with him, and that if they were he could not surrender them, upon the ground of hospitality, nor refuse them assistance at a moment when their distresses were so great; and, in admitting that the English had and still used the posts of Florida, he justified it on account of a treaty which existed between Great Britain and the Indians previous to the conquest of the Floridas by Spain. Jackson replied in strong terms to this letter, dispatching Captain Gordon with the document, who was instructed to gain additional information of the designs of the enemy.[7]

Having arranged all things at the fort which bore his name, Jackson, in company with Colonel Hayne, departed down the Alabama, in boats, with a portion of his troops, and arriving at Mobile, made that place his headquarters. He had been admonished that it was the design of the English soon to attack the city. He addressed a letter to Colonel Butler, which reached that officer, at Nashville, on the 9th of September, urging him to hasten the advance of the volunteers to protect that point and New Orleans. Soon General Coffee was on the march from Tennessee, at the head of two thousand men, while Colonel Butler hastened to press forward the militia under Colonel Lowry, which had been, heretofore, required for garrisoning posts in the Indian country. Captains Baker and Butler also commenced the march from Nashville to , with the regular forces lately enlisted.[8]

Colonel Nicolls, an Irishman by birth, now a British officer, arrived at Pensacola with a small squadron of his majesty's ships, immediately manned the Forts Barrancas and San Miguel, and hoisted the British flag upon their ramparts. Making the house of Governor Manrique his headquarters, Nicolls sought to draw around his standard the malcontents and traitors of the country, by issuing a proclamation, stating that he had come with a force sufficient to relieve them from the chains which the federal government was endeavoring to rivet upon them. This presumptuous appeal was even extended to the patriotic people of Kentucky and Louisiana. At the same time, in conjunction with Captain Woodbine, he employed himself in collecting and clothing, in British uniform, the Red Sticks and Seminoles, whom he publicly drilled in the streets of Pensacola. To these, and all the Red Sticks, he promised a bounty of ten dollars for every scalp, whether of men, women or children.[9]

[7] Despite Jackson's threats and his letter of 12 July 1814 delivered by Captain John Gordon, Governor Gonzáles Manrique could do little to prevent the migration of the Creeks into Florida, friendly or hostile. By June 1814, there were about 200 Red Stick warriors at Pensacola and by late summer perhaps as many as 800 had gathered in the vicinity of Pensacola. The estimates for those who remained in the Alabama watershed range upwards to another 1,500, which is probably high. Sugden, "Southern Indians in the War of 1812," 278; "The Blog of 1812: A Running Documentary of the War of 1812," http://www.blogof1812.com.

[8] In his letter of 27 August 1814, Jackson asked Colonel Robert Butler to urge John Coffee and "such officers as he may select" to join him and to write to "all the companies of horse that are ready." He also asked Butler to contact Return J. Meigs to get the "Brave Cherokees" under Colonels John Lowrey and Richard Brown to march "directly to Fort Jackson." Colonel Alexander Lowry commanded the 2nd Regiment of West Tennessee Militia but resigned on 20 November. Captain Isaac L. Baker and Captain William O. Butler were members of the 44th U.S. Infantry Regiment who joined Jackson in . Andrew Jackson to Robert Butler, Head Quarters 7th M. District, Murfreesborough, 27 August 1814, Daniel Feller, ed., *The Papers of Andrew Jackson Digital Edition* (Charlottesville: University of Virginia Press, Rotunda, 2015 –), 3: 83–84; C. F. Arrowood, ed., "The Journal of Captain Isaac L. Baker," *Southwestern Historical Quarterly* 30 (April 1927): 272–279, 282.

Fort Bowyer, at Mobile Point, had been dismantled by the orders of General Flournoy, who deemed it incapable of defense. Jackson, soon after arriving at , sailed to the Point, and after an inspection of this defense, resolved to garrison it. Sending from Mobile the artillery which was taken from it, and one hundred and thirty men, including officers, Major Lawrence, the commander, immediately prepared to resist the attacks of the enemy, should he make his appearance. At length a sentinel, stationed towards Lake Borgne, discovered six hundred Indians and one hundred and thirty British marines. In the evening, two English sloops of war, with two brigs, came to anchor on the coast, within six miles east from the fort. The next day, at twelve o'clock, the land force approaching within seven hundred yards, threw three shells and one cannon ball. The shells exploded in the air, but the ball carried away a timber of the rampart. The Americans, returning a few shots, forced the assailants to retire behind the sand hills, a mile and a half distant, where they began to raise entrenchments, but a few more discharges from the fort dispersed them. Some small boats were sent out from the ships to sound the channel, but the discharge from the battery drove them off. The ships now stood out to sea, but about two o'clock they bore down upon the fort in order of battle, the *Hermes*, on board of which was Commodore Percy, being in the advance.[10]

The Americans opened a fire upon her at four o'clock, but she came to anchor within musket shot—the other three taking their position behind her. The engagement became general, the ships discharging whole broadsides, while the American circular battery was destructive in its operations. Captain Woodbine opened a battery with a land force, from behind a sand bluff on the south-eastern shore, seven hundred yards distant, but the south battery of the Americans soon dispersed them. A furious cannonade of an hour filled the air with so much smoke, that Major Lawrence ceased for a moment, to ascertain the intentions of the English, seeing that the halyard of the commodore's flag had been carried away. The commodore raised a new flag, and, at that moment, all the guns of the American battery were discharged, sensibly shaking the earth around. After a short silence, the English renewed the action. The cable of the *Hermes* was cut and she was carried away by the current, keeping her head to the fort, which enabled

[9] After his arrival at Pensacola on 14 August 1814, Major Edward Nicolls had to combat the anti-British sentiments of the Spanish and the local population while recruiting 500 Creeks and 100 Negroes to supplement his 100 Royal Marines contingent. As the British agent to the Creeks, Captain George Woodbine had moved from the Apalachicola to Pensacola in late July 1814 in response to requests from the Creek refugees for food, clothing, and arms to oppose the raiding U.S. forces. Contrary to Pickett's narrative, Nicolls and Woodbine had received orders to prevent scalping and the mistreatment of prisoners by their Indian allies. Owsley, *Struggle for the Gulf*, 103–07; Sugden, "Southern Indians in the War of 1812," 283–88.

[10] Major William T. Lawrence, commander of Fort Bowyer, had 158 U.S. regular troopers who knew how to use their guns but only had eleven of his twenty cannon mounted when the British attack started on 13 September 1814. On the morning of 12 September, Captain William H. Percy landed Nicolls, 60 Royal Marines, and some 60 Indians with a howitzer nine miles east of Fort Bowyer. Nicholls became ill and turned his land force over to Captain Robert Henry, rejoining Percy aboard the *Hermes*. Percy's *Hermes* was joined by the HMS *Sophie* under Captain Nicholas Lockyer, but the HMS *Carron* and *Childers* could not maneuver into position due to the tide and unfavorable winds. Owsley, *Struggle for the Gulf*, 109–11; "Hon. William Henry Percy," in John Marshall, *Royal Naval Biography; Or, Memoirs of the Services of All the Flag-Officers, Superannuated Rear-Admirals, Retired-Captains, Post-Captains, and Commanders* (London: Longman, Rees, Orme, Brown and Green, 1829), 66–67.

Lawrence, for twenty minutes, to rake her, fore and aft.[11]

In the hottest of the engagement, Lawrence seized a sponge staff and hoisted upon the edge of the parapet another flag to supply the place of the one which had been carried away. The land force, under Woodbine, seeing the fall of the flag, rushed in triumph towards the fort; but some discharges of grape again dispersed them. The *Hermes* drifted a half mile, ran aground and was set on fire. The brig was so disabled that she could scarce retire to join the other two vessels, which now all put to sea.[12] At eleven o'clock at night the explosion of the magazine blew up the *Hermes*.*

The attack upon Mobile Point was a confirmation of the previous conjecture of General Jackson, and he determined to throw a force into Pensacola sufficient to expel the enemy, who had sailed to that place after their defeat at Fort Bowyer. He dispatched Colonel Hayne to Fort Montgomery, which was then in command of Colonel Thomas H. Benton, under whose superintendence it was erected, for the purpose of organizing the troops in that quarter.[13] Colonel Hayne discharged this duty with his usual promptness and decision. About this time, General Coffee had encamped on the western side of the Tombigbee, opposite the Cut-Off, with two thousand eight hundred men. Jackson reached his camp, and strained every nerve to afford supplies for the army, effecting loans upon his own credit and responsibility. The army crossed the Tombigbee, and proceeded across Nanna Hubba Island to Mims' Ferry. One thousand volunteers, hitherto mounted, left their horses in the care of keepers, to feed on the cane, and now cheerfully marched on foot. Reaching Fort Montgomery, the army reposed a short time, and again took up the line of march for Pensacola. It consisted of the Third, Thirty-Ninth and Forty-Fourth Regiments of Infantry, the militia of Tennessee, a battalion of volunteer dragoons of the Mississippi Territory and some friendly Indians.[14] Encamping within one mile and

* British loss—162 killed, 70 wounded; American loss—4 killed, 4 wounded. Latour, *Historical Memoir of the War in West Florida and Louisiana*, 32–42; Russell, *History of the War*, 279; Williams, *Florida*, 200; and Eaton, *Life of Andrew Jackson*, 236–37.

[11] In his report of the engagement against Fort Bowyer on 13 September 1814, Captain Percy commented: "At 5-30, the bow-spring being shot away, the *Hermes* swung her head to the fort and grounded, where she lay exposed to severe raking fire, unable to return it, except one cannonade and small arms from the tops." The land force under Captain Henry did not attack until the afternoon of 14 September 1814 but were repulsed, losing one man killed. Owsley, *Struggle for the Gulf*, 110; Marshall, "Hon. William Henry Percy," 67.

[12] Despite Pickett's claims for Woodbine, his Indians and the marines commanded by Captain Robert Henry had been repelled by the afternoon of 14 September. Although Captain Percy had maneuvered the *Hermes* out of range of the Fort Bowyer guns, it ran aground a second time and he combined the "storming parties" on board the *Sophie*. With his crew and wounded safely aboard the *Sophie*, Percy reported his final act on the *Hermes*: ". . . at 7-20 . . . I performed the painful duty of setting fire to H.M. ship . . . at 10 P.M. I had the melancholy satisfaction of seeing the *Hermes* blow up in the same spot in which I left her." Marshall, "Hon. William Henry Percy," 67–68.

[13] Under the command of Colonel Thomas Hart Benton, soldiers of the 39th U.S. Infantry Regiment constructed Fort Montgomery from August through October 1814 some two miles southwest of Fort Mims. Major Howell Tatum, a topographical engineer who visited the site of Fort Montgomery on 20 August 1814, referred to the location as Holmes's Hill. Christopher and Waselkov, *Archaeological Survey of the Old Federal Road*, 87–88; Bassett, "Major Howell Tatum's Journal," 49–50.

[14] Pickett's "friendly Indians" included six to eight hundred Choctaw and the "militia of Tennessee" included Captain

a half of Pensacola, Jackson sent a detachment of cavalry, under Lieutenant Murray, of the Mississippi dragoons, to reconnoiter. They captured a Spanish picket guard, but could perceive nothing. Lieutenant Murray was, unfortunately, killed by an Indian, while in a path somewhat separated from his command.[15]

Major Peire was dispatched from headquarters to the governor with a summons, preparatory to an attack upon the town, but was fired upon when he had arrived within three hundred yards of Fort San Miguel, although he held a white flag in his hand. Impelled by a feeling of humanity towards the oppressed Spaniards, whose fortifications were held by the English, Jackson sent a letter by a prisoner to the Governor, demanding an explanation for the insult offered to his flag. Through an officer, his Excellency disclaimed any participation in the transaction, and gave a pledge that American officers should in future be treated with respect. Major Peire being again sent at midnight, was unsuccessful in his negotiation with the Governor to allow Jackson to occupy Forts Barrancas and San Miguel, until Spanish troops should arrive in sufficient numbers to protect the Floridas from British outrages upon the neutrality of the nation. Major Peire then left the Governor, with the assurance that recourse would be had to arms.[16]

Zachariah McGirth, who has been mentioned in reference to Fort Mims and the battle of Calebee, was sent by Jackson into Pensacola, to ascertain the number and position of the enemy. About midnight he returned, and reported that a body of Indians, British and Spaniards, whom he estimated at over five thousand, occupied the heart of the town, and that some distance in advance of them, in the direction of the American camp, another party had erected a battery across the street.[17] Knowing that this battery commanded the only avenue by which he could reach the enemy, without passing under the guns of Fort San Miguel, Jackson determined to remove it. He sent for Captain Laval, of the Third Regiment, and informed him that he had selected him as the man to "lead the forlorn

David Deadrick's Nashville artillery company, a regiment from West Tennessee, and General John Coffee's brigade of mounted gunmen. Kanon, *Tennesseans at War, 1812–1815*, 127.

[15] While leading a small reconnaissance party in the vicinity of Pensacola, Lieutenant Alexander Murray, a member of Major Thomas Hinds's Mississippi Dragoons, was struck by an arrow and died from his wound. Dunbar, *Mississippi Territory in the War of 1812*, 98, 160.

[16] On 6 November 1814, Jackson sent Major Henry D. Peire of the 44th U.S. Infantry Regiment under a white flag to deliver a letter to Governor González Manrique announcing his intent to occupy the fortifications around Pensacola. After being fired upon, Peire made a second attempt and delivered Jackson's letter. Manrique responded that the British and their Indian allies had Pensacola and he could not surrender the city. However, as Jackson's forces began to move against Pensacola, Manrique met with Jackson and agreed to surrender Fort San Miguel and the other fortifications. Feller, *Papers of Andrew Jackson*, 3: 179–83.

[17] Contrary to Zachariah McGirth's report, Pensacola was not well defended or occupied by 5,000 Indians, British and Spanish soldiers, and seamen. Edward Nicolls and Captain James Gordon had evacuated the "600 warriors" and their families on 3–5 November, and the only significant British military personnel were on board British ships in the harbor and Pensacola Bay. The Spanish garrison numbered approximately 500 regulars, and the British took 200—basically as captives—from Fort Barrancas, which they destroyed when they evacuated Pensacola. In less than twenty-four hours, Jackson's forces moved against Pensacola with only minor resistance from the commander of Fort San Miguel and a few cannon rounds from the ships and armed barges in Pensacola's harbor. Owsley, *Struggle for the Gulf*, 112–19; Kanon, *Tennesseans at War, 1812–1815*, 127–32; Ruth Anna Fisher, "The Surrender of Pensacola as Told by the British," *American Historical Review* 54 (January 1949): 326–29.

hope." He ordered him to pick one hundred and twenty men, for the purpose of storming the battery. Laval commanded a company composing that number, and, although he had the option of selecting men from other companies, he first appealed to his own men, and stated to them the dangerous duty which had been assigned to him. They all responded by saying, "Wherever you go, Captain Laval, we follow." About eight o'clock in the morning Laval began his march. Captain Dinkins, who was ordered to support him with two pieces of artillery, if it should become necessary, marched some distance in the rear. Colonel Hayne, so anxious for the success of Laval, who was his warm friend, rode in the rear of the company. When Laval came near the battery Dinkins and his artillery were far behind, in consequence of the rapid march of the former and the heavy sand, which retarded the pieces of the latter. The enemy opened their cannon upon the "forlorn hope," while numerous assailants annoyed them by cross fires from the houses and gardens. The brave Laval, at the head of his company, however, marched steadily on. Colonel Hayne now dismounted and rushed upon the enemy on foot. Finally Laval reached the battery, and at that moment a large grape shot tore his leg to pieces, and he instantly fell to the ground. The troops rushed over the battery and secured the pieces of the enemy, all of whom presently fled, except the commanding officer, who bravely maintained his position and was taken a prisoner.[18]

Captain William Laval, now Major Laval, was born on the 27th May1788, in Charleston, South Carolina. His father, who had been an officer in France, came to America with the French army, in the legion of the Duke of Lauzun, to assist us in the struggle for our liberties. He was a cavalry officer, and participated in several of the American battles in Virginia, Delaware and New Jersey, and after peace was declared was, for many years, a sheriff of the Charleston district. The son entered the American army in October 1808, as an ensign. He was stationed at Forts Moultrie and Johnson, and at a recruiting encampment upon the Catawba. In 1812, he was appointed a first lieutenant. In January 1813, he advanced with his company, commanded by Captain Moore, from Fort Hawkins across the Creek Nation to Mobile and from thence to New Orleans. Very soon after, when the Creek War broke out, he was promoted to the post of captain, and marched with the Third Regiment, to which his company belonged, to Fort Claiborne, and from thence to the Holy Ground, in the battle

[18] Captain William Laval led an aggressive attack on the Spanish artillery battery on Palafox Street, a major north-south route in Pensacola. His U.S. infantry company quickly overwhelmed the gunners and captured the two cannons. In a letter to Rachel Jackson written on 15 November 1814, Jackson reported that Laval "got severely if not mortally wounded by a grape shot thro the thigh." Feller, *Papers of Andrew Jackson,* 3: 187–88; Kanon, *Tennesseans at War, 1812–1815,* 130.

[19] After his military service, William Laval (1788–1865) returned to his native South Carolina and took an active role in state and national politics. He supported South Carolina's nullification laws and in 1834 attempted to stop the construction of Fort Sumter in Charleston's harbor. Despite his anti-federal government stand, President James K. Polk nominated him to the Senate as assistant treasurer of the United States "at the city of Charleston" in 1846. In November 1857, the South Carolina House of Representatives elected Laval as treasurer of the Lower Division of South Carolina. *Journal of the House of Representatives of the State of South Carolina, Being the Session of 1857* (Charleston: n.p., 1857), 52; M. Patrick Hendrix, *A History of Fort Sumter: Building a Civil War Landmark* (Charleston: The History Press, 2014), 15–17; *Journal of the Executive Proceedings of the Senate of the United States of America; From December 1, 1845 to August 14, 1848, Inclusive,* vol. 7 (Washington: GPO, 1887), 140.

[20] In his letter of 15 November 1814 to Rachel Jackson, General

of which he participated. From the wound which he received upon the occasion of the siege of Pensacola, he was a severe sufferer for two years; but, although it has rendered him a cripple for life, he is now in fine health, and moves upon his crutches with ease and animation. Since the war, he has held various respectable offices, conferred by a people grateful for his military services. He has been a secretary of state of South Carolina, its comptroller general, a sheriff of Charleston, an officer in the custom house, assistant treasurer of the United States under Mr. Polk, and is now the treasurer of the state of South Carolina. Major Laval is near six feet high, very erect in person, and presents a very striking and military appearance.[19]

In the capture of the Spanish battery, seven Americans were killed and eleven wounded, among whom, besides Laval, was Lieutenant Flournoy.[20] Four Spaniards were killed, six wounded and several captured. After the storming of this battery, three thousand Americans, in three columns, advanced and proceeded along the beach, eastward of the town, to avoid the fire from San Miguel. A flag of truce from Governor Manrique produced a cessation of hostilities. The former terms of Jackson were now agreed to; but the commandant of San Miguel refused to obey the governor. Jackson now, leaving Major Peire, with eight hundred men, with orders to possess the fort before night, retired to his camp with the remainder of his troops, the British attempting to intercept his march by the fire of long guns from the shipping.[21]

It was important that the Americans should possess the fort before morning, for the British vessels, provided with spring cables, were, at any moment, ready to fire the town, or effect a landing. Indeed, by the aid of their boats, they had continued to fire upon our troops, as they passed along the principal streets; but Lieutenant Call, with a single piece of artillery, suddenly appeared upon the beach, and dispersed them.[22] Five hundred men were now placed upon the beach, to oppose the landing of the British, while Captain Dinkins, with two companies and three pieces of cannon, occupied Mount St. Bernard, which commanded Fort San Miguel. At six o'clock p.m., Colonel Soto, after having sent a verbal message that he would surrender, refused to receive Captain Dinkins and his command, which had been ordered to possess the fort, upon the pretense that they could not evacuate before morning. When Dinkins was about to commence an attack, Soto, aware of the consequences, surrendered, and at eleven o'clock at night the Americans took possession.[23] On the same afternoon the

Jackson reported that Lieutenant Alfred Flournoy (1796–1873) had "his leg broke above the ankle—is doing well & will soon recover." Feller, *Papers of Andrew Jackson*, 3: 187–88.

[21] Governor González Manrique met Colonel Thomas Williamson (1767–1825), who was leading dismounted troops of his 2nd Regiment West Tennessee Mounted Gunmen, and surrendered the town and Fort San Miguel unconditionally. For some reason, Lieutenant Colonel José de Soto, commander of the fort, continued to resist for several more hours. Ibid.; Kanon, "Regimental Histories of Tennessee" (online).

[22] Lieutenant Richard Call of the 44th Regiment took charge of the two Spanish cannons on Palafox Street and turned them on the British ships and armed barges in the harbor. The barges moved out of range quickly, and the ships under command of Captain James Gordon lifted anchor and moved out into Pensacola Bay, ending the exchange. Kanon, *Tennesseans at War, 1812–1815*, 130.

[23] Lieutenant Colonel José de Soto had been sent from Cuba after the fall of with 272 troops. He had challenged Governor González Manrique's leadership and resented the British presence at Fort San Miguel. Around 8 o'clock on 7 November 1814, Captain Henry Peire sent Jackson a message that Soto had agreed to deliver the fort over to Captain James Edward Dinkins: ". . . Spanish troops should remain for the night at the fort to avoid confusion . . . and the Spanish flag will

battery of Santa Rosa, opposite Fort Barrancas, was blown up by the Spaniards.[24]

The next morning the governor refused to give an order for the surrender of Fort Barrancas, and Jackson resolved to take it; but, while preparations were making to march down against it, it was blown up by order of the commandant. The British shipping, by this act, were enabled to pass by the ruins of Fort Barrancas and put to sea. Had Jackson possessed it in time, they would have been cut off from retreat.[25] Having effected the expulsion of the British from Pensacola, captured one of the forts, while the others were destroyed by the enemy themselves, and forced the Red Sticks to retreat to the forests in a perishing condition, and, being aware that his army could only be supported by tedious land transportation, that winter was setting in, and that the defense of New Orleans demanded his services, General Jackson took up the line of march for Fort Montgomery, where he arrived without accident.[26]

Placing a considerable portion of his army under Major Uriah Blue, of the Thirty-Ninth Regiment, the commander-in-chief visited Mobile, and then departed for New Orleans. Major Blue, at a period between the attack upon Pensacola and the battle of New Orleans, scoured the swamps of the Escambia and all the bays in West Florida with a large force of mounted men, consisting of Americans, Choctaws, Chickasaws and friendly Creeks. He killed many of the refugee Creeks, who fought him in their dense retreats, and captured a large number, besides women and children, whom he constantly sent to Fort Montgomery, guarded by strong detachments. We regret exceedingly that want of space forces us to omit a detailed account of this fatiguing and perilous expedition, taken from the lips of an intelligent surgeon. In some other work we hope to be able to record the brilliant achievements and valuable services performed on this occasion by Major Blue. We would remark, however, that he was the officer who brought the Creek War of 1813 and 1814 to a final termination. No official account of this march has fallen into our hands, and we believe none exists.[27]

In drawing our account of the Creek War to a close, we cannot refrain from indulging in some reflections upon the

remain hoisted. Tomorrow the conditions shall be written and signed." Feller, *Papers of Andrew Jackson*, 3: 182; Owsley, *Struggle for the Gulf*, 113 n.

[24] Actually, the Spanish soldiers did not blow-up or burn any of the military installations in and about Pensacola. British naval personnel under the command of Captain James Gordon set off the explosions destroying Fort Santa Rosa and Fort Barrancas before Jackson could move against them. The Fort Barrancas garrison of 200 Spanish black troops were taken as captives to Apalachicola, where they were used as a labor force. Owsley, *Struggle for the Gulf*, 117–19; Kanon, *Tennesseans at War, 1812–1815*, 130.

[25] By the morning of 8 November 1814, Fort Santa Rosa and Fort Barrancas, which guarded the entrance to Pensacola Bay, had been destroyed by British forces under orders of Captain James Gordon aboard the HMS *Sea Horse*. The control of the forts was beyond Governor González Manrique's control, and Jackson never had an opportunity to seize either fort. Owsley, *Struggle for the Gulf*, 116, 118.

[26] Before the attack on Pensacola, Jackson had been very ill, admitting in his letter of 15 November to Rachel "there was eight days on the march that I never broke bread—my health is restored but I am still very weak." Jackson had moved his headquarters from Fort Montgomery to Mobile—where he departed on 22 November—and arrived in New Orleans on 1 December 1814. Kanon, *Tennesseans at War, 1812–1815*, 143; Feller, *Papers of Andrew Jackson*, 3: 187, 192–94.

[27] Jackson ordered Major Uriah Blue with "about 1,000 volunteer horse" with available Choctaw forces "to scour the Escambia, Yellow Water, &c . . . to pursue the fugitive Creeks into the Seminole towns, and destroy them and their crops." Unfortunately, Blue's mission from late November 1814 through January 1815 was not very

bravery, endurance, self-sacrifice and patriotism of the Red Sticks. Let us, for a moment, recapitulate their achievements, never yet rivalled in savage life. They defeated the Americans at Burnt Corn, and compelled them to make a precipitate retreat. They reduced Fort Mims, after a fight of five hours, and exterminated its numerous inmates.[28] They encountered the large force under Coffee, at Tallaseehatchee, and fought till not one warrior was left, disdaining to beg for quarter. They opposed Jackson at Talladega, and, although surrounded by his army, poured out their fire, and fled not until the ground was almost covered with their dead. They met Floyd at Autossee, and fought him obstinately, and then again rallied and attacked him, a few hours after the battle, when he was leading his army over Heydon's Hill. Against the well-trained army of Claiborne they fought at the Holy Ground, with the fury of tigers, and then made good their retreat across the Alabama. At Emuckfau, three times did they charge upon Jackson, and when he retreated towards the Coosa they sprang upon him, while crossing the creek at Enitachopco, with the courage and impetuosity of lions. Two days afterwards, a party under Weatherford rushed upon the unsuspecting Georgians at Calebee, threw the army into dismay and confusion, and stood their ground in a severe struggle, until the superior force of Floyd forced them to fly, at daylight.[29] Sixty days after this, Jackson surrounded them at the Horse-Shoe, and, after a sanguinary contest of three hours, nearly exterminated them, while not one of them begged for quarter. At length, wounded, starved and beaten, hundreds fled to the swamps of Florida; others went to Pensacola, and, rallying under Colonel Nicolls, attacked Fort Bowyer. Fierce scouting parties, during the whole war, had operated against them, from point to point, and they were not finally overcome until Major Blue made the expedition just related.[30]

Thus were the brave Creeks opposed by the combined armies of Georgia, Tennessee and the Mississippi Territory, together with the federal forces from other states, besides numerous bands of bloody Choctaws and Chickasaws. Fresh volunteers and militia, from month to month, were brought against them, while no one came to their assistance, save a few English officers, who led them to undertake enterprises beyond their ability to accomplish. And how long did they contend against the powerful forces allied

successful because his troops suffered from severe weather, limited supplies and illness. Kanon, *Tennesseans at War, 1812–1815,* 134; Feller, *Papers of Andrew Jackson,* 3: 193, 208, 216; Brian R. Rucker, "In the Shadow of Jackson: Uriah Blue's Expedition into West Florida," *Florida Historical Quarterly* 73 (January 1995): 325–38.

[28] While a large number of defenders and occupants were killed in the attack on Fort Mims, Gregory A. Waselkov's *A Conquering Spirit: Fort Mims and the Red Stick War of 1813–1814* provides a detailed analysis of the participants who were killed, captured, or escaped during the devastating attack of 30 August 1813. Waselkov, *Conquering Spirit,* 225–57.

[29] Although William Weatherford provided the basic strategy for attacking Floyd's army, he left the Red Stick camp when his plan was opposed by Paddy Walsh (Welch) and High-Head Jim. George Stiggins and Thomas S. Woodward agree that Weatherford participated in three Red Stick battles—Fort Mims, Holy Ground, and Autossee. Woodward wrote that Weatherford "only heard the firing at Calebee from Pole Cat Springs." Stiggins, *Creek Indian History,* 128–32; Woodward, *Reminiscences,* 89–90.

[30] As noted earlier, Edward Nicolls had about 60 Red Sticks on board the HMS *Hermes* commanded by Captain William H. Percy who participated in the failed attack on Fort Bowyer on 12–15 September 1814 with some 60 Royal Marines. Muster rolls for the HMS *Hermes, Sophie, Caron,* and *Childers* from the British Admiralty for the first Battle of Fort Bowyer cited online list fewer than 120 Indians aboard the HMS *Hermes* and HMS *Caron.* Major Blue's expedition in late November 1814 through January may

have killed 50 hostile Creeks and Seminoles and captured 200 prisoners, but he did not eliminate the Red Stick faction. Marshall, "Hon. William Henry Percy, 66–67; "Fort Bowyer," https://en.wikipedia.org/wiki/Fort_Bowyer; Kanon, *Tennesseans at War, 1812–1815,* 126, 134; Owsley, *Struggle for the Gulf,* 109–12.

against them? From the 27th of July 1813, to the last of December 1814. In every engagement with the Americans, the force of the Creeks was greatly inferior in number, except at Burnt Corn and Fort Mims.

Brave natives of Alabama! to defend that soil where the Great Spirit gave you birth, you sacrificed your peaceful savage pursuits! You fought the invaders until more than half your warriors were slain! The remnant of your warlike race yet live in the distant Arkansas. You have been forced to quit one of the finest regions upon earth, which is now occupied by Americans. Will they, in some dark hour, when Alabama is invaded, defend this soil as bravely and as enduringly as you have done? Posterity may be able to reply.

Chapter XL

THE BRITISH TAKE MOBILE POINT—PEACE DECLARED—THE ALABAMA TERRITORY

The victory of the Americans at New Orleans forced the British to abandon the banks of the Mississippi and hover about Mobile Point.[1] Twenty-five of their vessels anchored in a semi-circular position five miles from Fort Bowyer. Thirteen ships of the line anchored two miles in the rear of it. Five thousand men landed and encamped. After several days of the most active preparations for the reduction of this little American defense, still under the command of the brave Major Lawrence, the latter assembled a council of his officers, who decided that it was impossible to contend with a powerful force, both by sea and land. The next day, according to previous negotiations, three hundred and sixty Americans, including officers, marched out of Fort Bowyer,[2] with colors flying and drums beating, and took up quarters on board of three British ships of the line, as prisoners of war.*

The treaty of peace between England and the United States, concluded at Ghent, did not reach General Jackson at New Orleans until the 13th March. A few days after this the latter informed Admiral Cochrane, of the British navy, of the joyous intelligence. But the latter, whose fleet still lay about Mobile Point, did not leave our shores immediately, in consequence of the exchange of prisoners constantly going on. Besides this, the great mortality from the wounds and disease which prevailed throughout his shipping, still further retarded his departure. Hundreds of British soldiers were entombed in the white sands of Mobile Point and Dauphin Island. At length, the first of April witnessed the departure of our enemies and the happiness of our people, now once more left to repose.[3]

At this period a large tract of country was still in possession of the Chickasaws, south and west of Madison County, but the American population began

* Latour, *Historical Memoir of the War in West Florida and Louisiana*, 207–16.

[1] Beginning with the early morning engagement at the Villeré plantation on 23 December 1814 through his victory at Chalmette on 8 January 1815, Jackson provided the leadership needed to defeat a much larger and better equipped British invading force commanded by Vice Admiral Alexander Cochrane. Kanon, *Tennesseans at War, 1812–1815*, 137, 146–49, 175–76, 181; Owsley, *Struggle for the Gulf*, 141–68.

[2] Embarrassed, but not humbled, Cochrane was intent on salvaging his Gulf campaign when he turned his attention east, ordering Major General John Lambert to move against Mobile and directing Edward Nicolls to strike the interior from Fort Stoddert to Georgia. On 8 February 1814, Lambert landed 600 troops east of Fort Bowyer supported by sixteen guns around the fort and a bomb vessel to

support this battery. Major Lawrence's force was no match for Lambert's superior numbers and firepower, and he surrendered his garrison of about 370 men, 20 women, 16 children, and three slaves four days later. Kanon, *Tennesseans at War, 1812–1815*, 181–82; Owsley, *Struggle for the Gulf*, 171–72.

[3] Although the U.S. Senate ratified the Treaty of Ghent, ending the War of 1812, on 16 February 1815 and word reached New Orleans by 21 February, Jackson would not lift martial law in the city until he received official notice on 13 March. Kanon, *Tennesseans at War, 1812–1815*, 182–83; Robert V. Remini, *The Battle of New Orleans: Andrew Jackson and America's First Military Victory* (New York: Penguin Books, 1999), 193–94.

[4] On 29 June 1815, Governor David Holmes issued a proclamation creating Monroe County, Mississippi Territory, out of lands ceded by the Creek Nation in the Treaty of Fort Jackson, 9 August 1814. The new county was named for James Monroe, secretary of state under President James Madison. Owen, *History of Alabama*, 2: 1032; Haynes, *Mississippi Territory*, 288, 312–13; Kappler, *Indian Affairs: Laws and Treaties*, 2: 107–10.

[5] Gabriel Moore, a native of North Carolina, served in the Mississippi territorial legislature from 1811 to 1817 and as speaker from 1815 to 1817. While Hugh McVay, a South Carolinian, served from 1815 until Mississippi became a state in 1817, William H. Winston, a Virginia native, had served from 1809–1810 before his election in 1815. Harriet E. Amos Doss, "Gabriel Moore," *Encyclopedia of Alabama* (online); Mary Jane McDaniel, "Hugh McVay," *Encyclopedia of Alabama* (online); David Byers, "Two Hundred Years—The Big Spring and John Hunt," *Huntsville Historical Review*, Special Issue (2008): 43.

[6] Following the unanimous ratification of the Treaty of Ghent by the U.S. Senate on 16 February 1815, British forces completed their withdrawal from the Gulf Coast in May 1815. Colonel Edward Nicolls remained at his outpost on the Apalachicola River, one mile below the confluence of the Flint and Chattahoochee rivers. He continued to advise the Lower Creeks and Seminoles who faced threats from Georgia filibusters and famine because of the thousands of Red Stick refugees in Spanish East and West Florida. Nicolls and his small retinue, which included his son, his interpreter, his servant, Josiah Francis, Earle Francis—the Prophet's son—and possibly Peter McQueen, departed the Apalachicola in late May or early June, arriving in England in early August 1815. Sugden, "Southern Indians in the War of 1812," 304–08; *Journal of the Executive Proceedings of the Senate of the United States of America*, 2: 619–21; Dale Cox, *Nicolls' Outpost: A War of 1812 Fort at Chattahoochee, Florida* (Bascom, FL: Old Kitchen Books, 2015), 82–83.

[7] On 20 September 1816, the Chickasaw Nation surrendered their land claims north and south of the Tennessee River, "due south course to the ridge path, or commonly called the Gaines's road," and southwest to Cotton Gin Port "and down the west bank of the Tombigbee to the Choctaw boundary." A month later, on 24 October 1816, thirteen Choctaw leaders, including Pushmataha, Mushulatubbee, and Puckshunubbee, placed their marks on a treaty at the Choctaw Trading House, ceding lands east of a boundary line running from the mouth of Oktibbeha (Tibbee) Creek down the Tombigbee until it intersected with the Mount Dexter treaty line of 1805. Kappler, *Indian Affairs: Laws and Treaties*, 2: 135–37; *ASP: IA*, 2: 99–107.

[8] From 7 July to 15 August 1817, forty-eight delegates elected from the fourteen counties east of the Pearl River met in a constitutional convention at a Methodist church on the Jefferson College campus. Under the leadership of George Poindexter and Governor David Holmes—serving as the president of the convention—they adopted a constitution that was approved and ratified by the citizens on 17 August. Frances Newton Thorpe, comp. and ed., *The Federal and State Constitutions, Colonial Charters, and Other Organic Laws of the States, Territories, and Colonies Now or Heretofore Forming the United States of America*, 7 vols. (Washington: GPO, 1909), 4: 2029–48.

[9] On 3 March 1817, Congress passed an Enabling Act creating the Alabama Territory, which continued under the officers of the Mississippi Territory until the appointment of a new governor and secretary. This act took effect with the admission of Mississippi to the Union on 10 December 1817. Limestone and Lauderdale were created on 6 February 1818 by the Alabama Territory Assembly. Ibid., 1: 89–92; Brewer,

to form settlements upon it. Hundreds went lower down, upon the Tombigbee, and others upon its headwaters. Governor Holmes extended, by proclamation, the jurisdiction of the Mississippi Territory over the country of the Black Warrior and Tombigbee, now acquired from the Chickasaws by treaty, and gave the whole the name of Monroe County.[4]

Madison, north of the Tennessee, at this time less than thirteen miles square, had, within six years, obtained a population of more than ten thousand souls, many of whom were wealthy and intelligent planters from the southern Atlantic states. Gabriel Moore, Hugh McVay, and William Winston were elected to the territorial legislature from this county in June.[5] Fifteen hundred and seventy votes were cast in Madison at the election for a delegate to Congress, while the aggregate vote of the counties of Jefferson, Claiborne and Adams, was only fourteen hundred and twenty. The Washington District, upon the Tombigbee, sent only two members to the territorial legislature.

The lands acquired by the treaty of Fort Jackson began to be only partially settled, as much of them was still in the occupancy of the Creeks, who had not removed, and, owing to the intrigues of British emissaries, still in Florida, the boundary lines had not been established. Indeed, even before the 16th October, the Creeks had again commenced hostilities upon the frontiers of Georgia, and had broken up the military cantonments on the line from Fort Jackson to Fort Mitchell. Again, settlements were still further retarded by the proclamation of the president, forbidding the settlement of this territory until it was surveyed.[6]

To facilitate the advance of population north and west of the Creek Nation, and to prevent encroachments upon the Choctaws, Chickasaws and Cherokees, commissioners of the United States obtained, by treaties, in the autumn of 1816, all the territory from the headwaters of the Coosa westward to Cotton Gin Port, and to a line running from thence to the mouth of Caney Creek, on the Tennessee.[7] After this, the Americans pressed forward, and, before the close of 1816, the population of the Mississippi Territory was more than seventy-five thousand, including slaves. Forty-six thousand of this population was distributed in the counties west of the Pearl River, the remainder in the Tennessee Valley, and upon the Tombigbee and the Mobile.

On the 1st March, Congress declared that the Mississippi Territory should be divided, by a line commencing at the mouth of Bear Creek, on the Tennessee, thence to the northwest corner of Washington County, and thence south, with the western limit of that county, to the sea. A convention, also upon the authority of Congress, composed of forty-four delegates, assembled at the town of Washington, near Natchez, and adopted the constitution of the state of Mississippi. None of the counties now lying in Alabama were represented in this convention. On the

10th December, the acts of the convention were ratified by Congress, and Mississippi became a member of the Federal Union.[8] The territory east of the new state of Mississippi, Congress erected into a territorial government, giving it the name of Alabama, from the great river which drained its center. Upon the first organization of this new government, seven counties only—Mobile, Baldwin, Washington, Clarke, Madison, Limestone, and Lauderdale—were formed within our limits, and they enjoyed the legislative and judicial powers which they possessed before the division, and the officers retained their places. The seat of government was temporarily fixed at St. Stephens.[9]

William Wyatt Bibb was appointed governor of the Alabama Territory. He was born in Amelia County, Virginia, October 2, 1781. His father, William Bibb, had held the commission of captain in the Revolutionary War, and was afterwards a respectable member of the legislature of Virginia. His mother, whose maiden name was Wyatt, a native of New Kent County, of the same state, was a lady of superior intellect, and was favorably known to the early settlers of Alabama. The family removed to Georgia at an early period, and settled in Elbert County, upon the Savannah. Captain Bibb died in 1796, leaving to his wife the care and responsibility of eight children, all of whom she lived to see in affluent and respectable positions in life. William, the subject of this notice, graduated at the College of William and Mary, returned to Georgia and established himself as a physician in the town of Petersburg. Shortly afterwards, he was elected to the legislature, where, for several sessions, he evinced considerable talents and usefulness. When scarcely twenty-five years of age, he took a seat in Congress, at the commencement of the session of 1806, where he was an active and efficient member. From the Senate of the United States to which he afterwards succeeded, he was transferred by President Monroe to the government of Alabama.[10]

The first territorial legislature convened at St. Stephens the 19th January 1818. James Titus was the only member of the executive council or senate. He sat alone, and decided upon the acts of the lower house, and adjourned and met again with a show of formality quite ludicrous.[11] Gabriel Moore, of Madison County, was the speaker of the house, which was composed of about thirteen members. Governor Bibb, on the 20th, presented his message, in which he recommended the advancement of education, the establishment of roads, bridges and ferries, the alteration in the boundaries of counties, and the formation of new ones, and many

***Alabama*, 294, 317.**

[10] On 6 March 1817, President James Monroe appointed William Wyatt Bibb, the former U.S. Senator from Georgia, governor of the Alabama Territory. He also appointed John W. Walker of Huntsville secretary of the new territory, but Walker declined the position, citing poor health. In place of Walker, Monroe turned to Henry Hitchcock of Washington County, who accepted the appointment. Harriett E. Amos Doss, "The State of Alabama," in *The Uniting States: The Story of Statehood for the Fifty United States*, ed. Benjamin F. Shearer, 3 vols. (Westport, Conn.: Greenwood Press, 2004), 1: 41.

[11] The journal of the last session of the Mississippi territorial assembly in November 1816 listed three residents of Alabama counties who were members of the legislative council: James Titus (Madison County), Joseph Carson (Washington County), and Robert Beatty (Madison County). However, before the first meeting of the General Assembly of the Alabama Territory in January 1818, Carson had died and Beatty had resigned his seat, leaving only Titus to serve. Titus (1775–1843) had served from 1812 to 1817, and he was president of the 1816 legislative council prior to the Mississippi Territory being authorized to call a constitutional convention. Dunbar, *Encyclopedia of Mississippi History*, 81; Cecil Harper, Jr., "James Titus," *Handbook of Texas Online*.

other things, calculated to promote the welfare of the territory. He brought to the serious attention of the assembly the petition from the Mississippi convention, recently addressed to Congress, praying that body to enlarge the limits of Mississippi, by restricting those of the Alabama Territory to the Tombigbee River. He opposed the project, and contended that the present line of partition had been deliberately fixed by the competent authorities and voluntarily accepted by the people of that state. Thomas Eastin was elected territorial printer.[12] George Philips, Joseph Howard, Mathew Wilson, Joseph P. Kennedy, John Gayle and Reuben Saffold were selected as nominees, from whose number the president of the United States should select three members for the next legislative council.[13]

The counties of Cotaco, Lawrence, Franklin, Limestone, Lauderdale, Blount, Tuscaloosa, Marengo, Shelby, Cahaba, Dallas, Marion and Conecuh were established.[14] In each, the superior courts of law and equity, and two county courts, and one intermediate court, were to be held annually. They were allowed one representative each in the legislature. The boundaries of Washington, Baldwin, Mobile and Marengo were altered and extended. Madison, the shape of which was formerly that of a triangle, was now made to assume its present form. The St. Stephens Academy was incorporated, and its trustees authorized to raise four thousand dollars by a lottery.[15] "The St. Stephens Steamboat Company" was also incorporated.[16] Hudson Powell, Robert Gaston, Joseph H. Howard, Howell Rose, and George Dabney were appointed commissioners to select a temporary place at which to hold the courts of Montgomery County, then of vast extent.

The legislature repealed the laws upon usury, and allowed any interest agreed upon between the parties, and expressed in writing, to be legal. The compensation of the members was fixed by themselves, upon a more liberal scale than at present. The

[12] Thomas Eastin (1790–1865), a native of Kentucky, served as a quartermaster under Andrew Jackson during the War of 1812. He published *The Halcyon* in St. Stephens in 1815–1819 before changing its name to *The Halcyon and Tombeckbe Advertiser* (1819–1823). He continued as publisher until the issue of 16 October 1820, when Joseph DeJeane became the publisher. Eastin married Lucinda Gayle, sister of John Gayle, in 1815. *Proceedings of the American Antiquarian Society*, New Series, Volume 23 (Worcester, Mass.: The Society, 1913), 252; "Thomas Eastin," https://familysearch.org/; Herbert James Lewis, *Lost Capitals of Alabama* (Charleston: The History Press, 2014), 26.

[13] On 17 April 1818, President James Monroe nominated George Phillips, Mathew Wilson, and John Gayle, a future Alabama governor, for approval by the Senate to serve on the legislative council of the Alabama Territory. Lewis, *Lost Capitals of Alabama*, 29; *Journal of the Executive Proceedings of the Senate of the United of America, From the First to the Termination of the Nineteenth Congress*, vol. 3 (Washington: Duff Green, 1828), 134.

[14] On 14 June 1821, the name of Cotaco County was changed to Morgan County in honor of American Revolutionary War General Daniel Morgan of Virginia. *Acts Passed at the Called Session of the General Assembly of the State of Alabama Begun and Held in the Town of Cahawba, on the First Monday in June, One Thousand Eight Hundred and Twenty One* (1821; reprint, Washington: Statute Law Book Co., 1913), 40.

[15] St. Stephens Academy evolved out of Washington Academy, established in 1811. After its incorporation under the auspices of the Alabama Territory, Reverend James Long Sloss, a Presbyterian minister, served as its head from 1818 to 1821. Ezra Hall Gillett, *History of the Presbyterian Church in the United States of America*, 2 vols. (Philadelphia: Presbyterian Publication Committee, 1864), 2: 389–90; Joel Campbell Du Bose, *Sketches of Alabama History* (Philadelphia: Eldredge & Brother, 1901), 152.

[16] The St. Stephens Steamboat Company successfully launched the first steamboat built in Alabama, which was named *Alabama*. In its maiden voyage, it traveled down to Mobile but did not have enough power to return upstream to St. Stephens. Lewis, *Lost Capitals of Alabama*, 29–30.

speaker and president were allowed seven and the members five dollars per diem, besides mileage. Clement C. Clay, Samuel Taylor, Samuel Dale, James Titus, and William L. Adams were elected commissioners to report to the next session the most central and eligible site for the territorial legislature.[17]

Madison, Limestone, Lauderdale, Franklin, Lawrence and Cotaco counties were erected into the "northern judicial district." Governor Bibb, on the 14th February, appointed Henry Minor attorney general of this district.[18] Clarke, Washington, Monroe, Conecuh, Baldwin and Mobile counties composed the "southern judicial district," and Mathew D. Wilson was appointed the attorney general thereof. Marion, Blount, Shelby, Montgomery, Cahaba, Marengo, Dallas and Tuscaloosa counties, composed the "middle judicial district," and Joseph Noble was appointed its attorney general.[19]

Before the division of the Mississippi Territory, and while the legislature sat at Washington, in Adams County, a stock bank had been established at Huntsville. A resolution adopted at the session of St. Stephens changed its name to that of "Planters' and Merchants' Bank of Huntsville."[20] The Tombeckbe Stock Bank was also now established, with a capital of five hundred thousand dollars.[21] Such were the only important acts of the first session of the legislature of the Alabama Territory.*

But Indian disturbances, as we have said, had commenced. Although the British army had sailed for Europe, yet there were still subjects of that nation in the Floridas, who originated the "Seminole War"; among the most active of whom were Captain Woodbine, Colonel Nicolls, Alexander Arbuthnot, and Robert C. Ambrister. They had adopted the opinion of Lord Castlereagh that the 9th article of the treaty of Ghent entitled the Creeks to a restoration of the lands which they had been compelled to relinquish at Fort Jackson.[22] Woodbine, entering upon the task of enforcing this ill-founded claim, had conducted to Florida a colony of

* State archives.

[17] The usury act, compensation act, and site selection committee were all confirmed by joint action of the house of representatives and the legislative council at the first session of the territory's first General Assembly, which ended in February 1818. *Acts Passed at the First Session of the First General Assembly of the Alabama Territory; In the Forty-Second Year of American Independence* (St. Stephens: Thomas Eastin, 1818), 149, 155, 158, 161, 163, 174, 176.

[18] Henry W. Minor (1783–1839), a native of Virginia, moved to Huntsville in 1816 and served as a member of the 1819 constitutional convention. When Chief Justice Clement C. Clay resigned his judgeship in 1823, Governor Israel Pickens appointed Minor to finish Clay's term on the fifth circuit court, effectively making him a supreme court justice (1823–1825). Although he went off the supreme court in 1825, he later served as clerk of the court. Daniel J. Meador, "The Supreme Court of Alabama—Its Cahaba Beginning, 1820–1825," *Alabama Law Review* 61 (Winter 2010): 898–99.

[19] While Mathew D. Wilson served on the legislative council, Joseph Noble served as Governor William Wyatt Bibb's personal secretary. He delivered Bibb's written messages during the first session of the Alabama Territory's first General Assembly. In September 1818, Noble moved from Jackson, Clarke County, to Tuscaloosa, which he felt had "more retail trade than Saint Stephens and Jackson put together." Lewis, *Lost Capitals of Alabama*, 29; *Acts Passed at the First Session of the First General Assembly of the Alabama Territory*, 9, 88, 114, 117, 132, 168, 172, 176, 178; William H. Brantley, *Three Capitals: A Book About the First Three Capitals of Alabama, St. Stephens, Huntsville & Cahawba* (1947; reprint, Tuscaloosa: University of Alabama Press, 1976), 25; Joseph Noble to Samuel B. Bidgood, Falls of the Tuskaloosa, 12th September 1818, ADAH.

[20] The Planters' and Merchants' Bank came under attack during the Panic of 1819 from

Negro slaves, which had been stolen by the British during the war from the Southern planters. He had ascended the Apalachicola, and had erected a strong fort, which was well supplied with artillery and stores. From this point he had presumptuously addressed Hawkins a letter, demanding the restoration of the ceded lands, and representing himself as commanding His Majesty's forces in Florida.[23]

Hostilities had already commenced upon the frontiers, and even the Big Warrior had declared that he had been deceived as to the extent of the lands which had been forced from him. Colonel Clinch, of Georgia, with detachments under Major Muhlenberg and Captain Zachary Taylor, had invested and completely destroyed Woodbine's Negro Fort, killing many of the inmates and burning a vast amount of military property.[24] Notwithstanding these difficulties, emigrants continued boldly to push through the Creek Nation, and to occupy portions of the Alabama Territory. A small colony had established themselves in the present Butler County. Among them was Captain William Butler, a native of Virginia, who had been a member of the Georgia legislature, and the commander of a company of volunteers at the Battle of Calebee;[25] Captain James Saffold, a lawyer, who had commanded a company of artillery, under Major McIntosh, while stationed at Fort Decatur,[26] besides William P. Gardner, Daniel Shaw, James D. K. Garrett, Britain M. Pearman, and others, all of whom came recently from Georgia. Most of these worthy settlers pitched their camps upon the ridge near the residence of the late Chancellor Crenshaw.[27] Two years previous to this, however, a few emigrants had settled on the Federal Road, near where Fort Dale was afterwards erected, in the present county of Butler, among whom were William Ogle, his wife and five children, with J. Dickerson. Another settlement had been formed in the "Flat," on the western border of that county.[28]

Sam Moniac, who still lived near the Pinchona, on the Federal Road, informed these emigrants that hostile Indians were prowling in that region, who meditated mischief. A temporary blockhouse was immediately erected at ——— Gary's, and those in the "Flat" began the construction of

William Long and his Huntsville *Democrat*, especially the "Royal Party," which included the bank's directors, speculators, and merchants. Long charged that the Royal Party had used their influence to repeal the usury law by the Alabama territorial assembly in 1818. Daniel S. Dupre, *Transforming the Cotton Frontier: Madison County, Alabama, 1800–1840* (Baton Rouge: Louisiana State University, 1997), 75–93; Thomas Perkins Abernathy, *The Formative Period in Alabama, 1815–1828* (1922; reprint, Tuscaloosa: University of Alabama Press, 1990), 111–15.

[21] On 13 February 1818, the Alabama territorial assembly passed an act chartering the Tombeckbe Bank at St. Stephens. Israel Pickens, a future governor of Alabama (1821–1825), served as its president and skillfully guided the bank through the Panic of 1819. As governor, Pickens became an advocate for banking reform and proposed the creation of the state-owned Bank of Alabama. *Acts Passed at the First Session of the First General Assembly of the Alabama Territory*, 169; Lewis, *Lost Capitals of Alabama*, 30, 79–80; Abernathy, *Formative Period in Alabama*, 96–101.

[22] While Captain George Woodbine played a minor role with the Lower Creeks and Seminoles, Colonel Edward Nicolls remained at his outpost on the Apalachicola through the withdrawal of British troops and signed his letters as "Commanding the British forces in the Floridas" or "Commanding H. B. M. forces in the Creek Nation." In March through May 1815 he exchanged a series of letters with Benjamin Hawkins, demanding that American citizens stop their attacks on the Seminoles and touting the application of Article 9 of the Treaty of Ghent to end hostilities "with all tribes or nations of Indians . . . and, forthwith to restore . . . all the possessions, rights and privileges which they may have enjoyed or been entitled to in 1811, previous to such hostilities." Cox, *Nicholls' Outpost*, 72–82, 119–22; "War Events: Or Things Incidental to the Late War," *Niles Weekly Register*, 10 June 1815, 261–62; "War Events/Indian

a fort, afterwards called Fort Bibb, enclosing the house of Captain Saffold, who had removed from the ridge to that place.[29] On the 6th March, William Ogle drove his ox-cart in the direction of Fort Claiborne for provisions, and he had not proceeded far before a chief, named Uchee Tom, and seventeen warriors, seized the rope with which he was driving, and gave other evidences of violence, but finally suffered him to proceed. Feeling much solicitude on account of his family, and purchasing corn at Sepulga Creek, he returned home, where the Indians had been in the meantime, and had manifested a turbulent disposition. On the 13th of March Ogle attended a company muster, and from thence there went home with him in the evening an old acquaintance, named Eli Stroud, with his wife and child. Meeting in a savage land, under sad apprehensions, these friends, having put their children to sleep, sat by the fireside of the cabin and continued to converse in undertones, ever and anon casting their eyes through the cracks to discover if Indians were approaching.[30]

Presently, by the dim light of the moon, Ogle saw a band of Red Sticks, who stealthily but rapidly approached the house. Springing from his seat he seized his gun, ran to the door, and set on his fierce dogs; but he was soon shot dead, falling upon the threshold which he was attempting to defend. Stroud and his wife sprang over his body into the yard, leaving their infant sleeping upon the hearth and ran off, pursued by a part of the savages. Paralyzed with fear, Mrs. Ogle at first stood in the floor, but recovering herself, ran around the corner of the house, and, protected by a large dog, escaped to a reed brake hard by, where she concealed herself. Here she heard the screams of Mrs. Stroud, who appeared to be running towards her, but who was soon overtaken and tomahawked. The savages entered the house, dashed out the brains of the infant, which was sleeping upon the hearth, and butchered the other children, whose shrieks and dying groans the unhappy mother heard, from the place of her concealment. After robbing the house, the wretches decamped, being unable to find Stroud, who lay not far off, in the high grass. The next morning some of the emigrants assembled, to survey the horrid scene. During the night, Mrs. Stroud had scuffled to the cabin, and was found in the chimney corner, sitting beside the body of her child, bereft of her senses. Ogle and four children lay in the sleep of death. His two daughters, Elizabeth and Mary Ann, were still alive, and were taken, with Mrs. Stroud, to the houses of the kind settlers, and, in a short time were sent to Fort Claiborne, with an escort furnished by Colonel Dale. On the way, Mrs. Stroud died, and, not long after reaching Claiborne, Mary Ann also expired. Elizabeth, through the kind attentions of Dr. John Watkins, survived her wounds, and is yet a resident of Butler County.[31]

One week after this massacre, Captains William Butler and James Saffold,

Affairs," *Niles Weekly Register*, 24 June 1815, 285–87.

[23] Pickett has conflated at least two separate and significant events. On 25 May 1814, Woodbine—a lieutenant of the Royal Marines at the time—arrived at Prospect Bluff on the Apalachicola, where he seized a trading store that belonged to John Forbes and the Company of Pensacola and eventually erected a British post near the store. When this well supplied fortification at Prospect Bluff was abandoned by the British in 1815, it became the "Negro Fort" and the center for African freedmen and former slaves. However, it was Colonel Nicolls who was placed in command of irregular operations on the Gulf Coast in July 1814, and in 1815, from his outpost north of the "Negro Fort," he demanded the restoration of Creek Nation lands under Article 9 of the Treaty of Ghent and exchanged letters with Benjamin Hawkins. Cox, *Nicholls' Outpost*, 47–48, 72, 119–22; Sugden, "Southern Indians in the War of 1812," 281–82, 285–89, 304–07; "War Events: Or Things Incidental to the Late War," *Niles Weekly Register*, 10 June 1815, 261–62; "War Events/Indian Affairs," *Niles Weekly Register*, 24 June 1815, 285–87.

[24] On 27 July 1816, Lieutenant Colonel Duncan Lamont Clinch—with two companies commanded by Major Peter Muhlenberg and Captain Zachary Taylor—William McIntosh, 150 allied Creeks, and U.S. Navy gunboats attacked the Negro Fort at Prospect Bluff on the Apalachicola River. When a cannon hot shot hit the fort's powder magazine, the explosion destroyed the post, killing 270 of the 330 African freedmen, runaway slaves, and Seminole and Choctaw defenders. Adam Wasserman, *A People's History of Florida, 15131876: How Africans, Seminoles, Women, and Lower Class Whites Shaped the Sunshine State* (Sarasota, Fla.: Adam Wasserman, 2009), 170–75.

[25] Captain William Butler, a veteran of the Red Stick War and a recent emigrant from Georgia, was killed by Creek or Uchee (Yuchi) dissidents in March 1818. When a new county was carved out of Conecuh County, it was named Butler in his honor. Brewer, *Alabama*, 145–46.

[26] Captain James Saffold, a former resident of Jones County, Georgia, commanded a volunteer company of artillery during the Red Stick War. He was appointed as one of twelve directors of the state bank of Alabama by a joint session of the General Assembly in 1824. Brantley, *Three Capitals*, 139; Stephen Franks Miller, *The Bench and Bar of Georgia: Memoirs and Sketches: With an Appendix*, 2 vols. (Philadelphia: J. B. Lippincott & Co., 1858), 1: 422.

[27] Judge Anderson Crenshaw (1783–1847), a native of South Carolina, was elected a circuit court judge for Monroe County in 1821, and, by this office, he also served as a justice of the Alabama Supreme Court until 1832. He resigned as circuit judge in 1838 to accept election as Chancellor of the Southern Division. Crenshaw County, Alabama, is named for him. Owen, *History of Alabama*, 3: 422; Meador, "Supreme Court of Alabama," 898.

[28] Between 1816 and 1818, William Ogle (Ogly, Ogley), John Dickerson, Thomas Gary, and others from Georgia and South Carolina had settled on the western edge of Butler County, first called Magnolia Flat and later Pine Flat, or simply "the Flats." John Buckner Little, *The History of Butler County, Alabama, 1815 to 1885: With Sketches of Some of Her Most Distinguished Citizens, and Glances at Her Rich and Varied Resources* (Cincinnati: Elm Street Printing Co., 1885), 26–29, 71–73.

[29] In 1818, Thomas Gary built a small stockade or blockhouse for protection from Indian attacks, but, when he tried to charge a fee, his indignant fellow settlers sought refuge at Fort Bibb—Captain James Saffold's home—and later at Fort Dale. Little, *History of Butler County*, 29–30, 72–73; Peter A. Brannon, "The Massacres," *Montgomery Advertiser*, 31 January 1943.

[30] The William Ogle home was located on the Federal Road about four miles from Fort Dale. Peter A. Brannon writes that Eli Stroud and his family were traveling through the country when they encountered William Ogle returning from his militia muster and received his invitation to stay overnight with his family. Little, *History of Butler County*, 26–27; Brannon, "The Massacres."

[31] In his letter of 25 April 1858 to Pickett, Thomas S. Woodward places the blame for the deaths of "Capt. Butler and the others" and the William Ogle and Elias Stroud family members on Savannah Jack and his embittered followers. The other culprit could be Pickett's Uchee Tom, who remains something of a mystery. Woodward, *Reminiscences*, 40; Brannon, "The Massacres."

in company with William P. Gardner, Daniel Shaw and young Hinson, set out from the fort, to meet Dale, who was then marching to that point with a party of volunteers, a portion of whom they desired to induce him to send to the Flat, to protect the citizens, while cultivating their fields. Advancing about two miles, Savannah Jack and his warriors—the same who had murdered the Ogles—fired upon them from a ravine. Gardner and Shaw, riddled with rifle balls, fell dead from their horses. Butler and Hinson, both being wounded, were thrown to the ground. The latter, regaining his seat in the saddle, fled back to the fort. Unable to reach his horse, Butler attempted, by running across the ravine, to gain the road in advance of the Indians; but he was pursued and shot at, from tree to tree, until he fell dead, but not before he had killed one of his pursuers. Captain Saffold escaped to the fort, receiving no injury, except the perforation of his clothes by rifle balls.[32] A detachment, sent by Dale the next day, buried the dead, whose heads were beaten to pieces, and their bodies horribly mutilated.* Not long after this affair, an emigrant, named Stokes, with his wife and children, was killed, fifteen miles below Claiborne. Great alarm pervaded the whole country, and the people moved upon the hills and began the construction of defenses.[33]

In the meantime, Governor Bibb, who had made several trips from Coosawda to St. Stephens, and who was well apprised of these depredations, resorted to prompt measures to afford protection to the settlers. By his directions, Colonel Dale had marched to the scene of the late murders. Bibb sent a dispatch to the Big Warrior demanding the withdrawal of all the Indians from the lands ceded at Fort Jackson, acquainting him with the murders committed upon unoffending white people, and requesting that the authors be pursued and punished by such warriors as he might think proper to send out.[34]

Dale advanced to Poplar Spring, erected a fort, which assumed his name, and assisted the people to finish Fort Bibb. Both of these forts were now garrisoned. Major Youngs, of the 8th Infantry, stationed at Fort Crawford, dispatched a detachment of whites and Choctaws, with orders to scour the Conecuh, and afterwards to join Dale.[35] The latter also scoured the surrounding country, but overtook none of

* In relation to the murders in Butler County, I must return my thanks to John K. Henry, Esq., of Greenville, who took the pains to procure correct statements of them from J. Dickerson and James D. K. Garrett. The late Reuben Hill, of Wetumpka, also furnished notes upon this subject.

[32] Butler, Saffold, Gardner, Shaw, and John Hinson left Fort Bibb to deliver a message to Colonel Sam Dale, who was constructing a fortification—later named Fort Dale—on the Federal Road at Poplar Springs some five miles north of modern Greenville, Alabama. They were attacked by a party of dissident Creeks—possibly Uchees (Yuchis)—led by the métis Uchee Savannah Jack on Pine Barren Creek. Little, *History of Butler County*, 29–32; Woodward, *Reminiscences*, 38–40.

[33] According to a Stokes family history, George Stokes (c.1772–1818), a native of South Carolina, was the only member of his family killed in the attack on his home in April 1818. While his wife Hester Ann Stokes was shot and left for dead, most of their children were elsewhere, except a son, who was placed under a barrel in a back room. Hester Stokes recovered and lived a long life, dying in Corsicana, Texas, around 1880. In his letter to Captain Richard Keith Call on 15 August 1818, Andrew Jackson asks Call to verify that the Indians were selling plunder in Pensacola from the Stokes family and "18 persons . . . killed on the Alabama." Wilford Perry Stokes Sr., *Stokes: A Family History* (Oakdale, LA: Wilford Perry Stokes Sr., 1987), 10–15; Feller, *Papers of Andrew Jackson*, 4: 230.

[34] Bibb had established his home at Coosawda (Coosada) in modern Elmore County in 1816, and he rode back and forth to St. Stephens, traveling by Fort Claiborne and crossing the Tombigbee at McGrew's Shoals. On 26 March 1818, Bibb sent a letter to Big Warrior referencing the attacks on the Federal Road and the eight people killed "by a party of red men." He advised him that he had

the Indians. Governor Bibb successfully cooperated with the United States officers stationed at Montgomery Hill and Fort Crawford for the protection of the citizens, and he visited in person all the newly erected stockades. On the 25th May he returned to Coosawda, and the next day rode up to Tuckabatchee and had a friendly interview with the Big Warrior. Leaving the Secretary of State, Henry Hitchcock, a young New Englander, of great ability, in charge of the government, his excellency returned to Georgia upon urgent business.[36]

The Red Sticks, in the meanwhile, had collected in a considerable band, and the country over which Dale had the command becoming too hot to hold them, they crossed the Alabama and marched through Marengo and Greene. In McGowan's settlement three children, named Hall, and a Negro woman, were murdered on 14 September. Suspicion falling upon Savannah Jack and his party they were pursued and trailed to Gun Island, or Gun Shute, on the Warrior, by Colonel Thomas Hunter, at the head of some settlers. Night coming on, the pursuit ceased. The next day a party under Major Taylor, and another under Captain Bacon, crossed the Warrior to the western side, and, in a dense swamp, came upon the savages. An action of an hour ensued. The officers, acting with bravery and prudence, were sustained by only a few of their men. A retreat was at length made, with the loss of two men killed and one severely wounded. The next day Colonel Hunter, with fifty men, followed upon the trail of the enemy, and came upon a small party, one of whom was killed.[37] The next morning he continued the pursuit for twenty miles, to the Sipsey Swamp, where, from the impracticability of entering it, the enemy was left to repose.*

* Report of Colonel Hunter to Governor Bibb, to be found among the state archives.

"ordered our soldiers to find and slay the hostile party . . . it is best your people should go home. They might be killed through mistake and I should be sorry for it." Unfortunately, Big Warrior exercised little control and no influence over the Creek dissidents, such as Savannah Jack and the Uchees (Yuchis), who bitterly resented the loss of their lands under the Treaty of Fort Jackson. Southerland and Brown, *Federal Road Through Georgia*, 57–58; Woodward, *Reminiscences*, 38–40; Brannon, "The Massacres."

35 Major White Youngs, a native of New York, had been commissioned as a captain of the 15th U.S. Infantry on 12 March 1812 and received a promotion to brevet major for his "gallant conduct" at the Battle of Plattsburg. On 15 May 1815 he was transferred to the 8th U.S. Infantry and was later appointed commander at Fort Crawford. Annie C. Waters, "A Documentary History of Fort Crawford," https://www.google.com, 17–26; Peter Force, *Register of the Army and Navy of the United States* (Washington: Peter Force, 1830).

36 Henry Hitchcock (1792–1839), a native of Vermont and grandson of Ethan Allen, immigrated to Mobile in 1816 and was appointed the first secretary of the Alabama Territory by Bibb in May 1818. He was a member of the 1819 constitutional convention and elected the first attorney general of Alabama by the General Assembly in December 1819. He was elected to the Alabama Supreme Court in 1835 and became chief justice in 1836. Meador, "Supreme Court of Alabama," 905; William H. Brantley Jr., "Henry Hitchcock of Mobile, 1816–1839," *Alabama Review* 5 (January 1952): 3–39.

37 In a letter of 22 September 1818 to the War Department, John M. Neel, a former lieutenant in the 43rd U.S. Infantry Regiment, identified the marauders as "a remnant of hostile Creeks" denied land among the Chickasaw and now determined to settle on land "over the Mississippi." The band of Indians consisted of "seventy warriors and their women and children" who had resolved "to fight their way through our settlements." They had killed "two white men and three Choctaws" before they reached the Black Warrior and continued to commit "outrages on our citizens." Major Samuel Taylor sent a similar report to Governor Bibb. On 16 September, Neel, Major Taylor, and Captain Bacon had pursued the Indian party below the falls of the Warrior, where they fought two skirmishes, killing

This expedition was followed up by several others upon the Warrior; but the Creeks had at length determined to leave the Americans in quiet possession of the lands, which were surrendered with such reluctance at the Treaty of Fort Jackson. The flood gates of Virginia, the two Carolinas, Tennessee, Kentucky and Georgia were now hoisted, and mighty streams of emigration poured through them, spreading over the whole territory of Alabama. The axe resounded from side to side, and from corner to corner. The stately and magnificent forests fell. Log cabins sprang, as if by magic, into sight. Never before or since, has a country been so rapidly peopled.[38]

14 to 18 and losing two killed and "one badly wounded." On the 19th, Colonel Thomas Hunter, "with 110 mounted men," pursued them and killed one of their warriors before the hostiles fled "toward the borders of the Choctaws." In its 26 September issue, the St. Stephens *Halcyon* reported that these Indians were Seminoles pushed out of Florida and were considered a threat to settlers on the Black Warrior and Cahaba. Carter, *Territorial Papers/Alabama*, 18: 419–20, 430–31; Rhoda Coleman Ellison, *Bibb County, Alabama: The First Hundred Years, 1818–1918* (Tuscaloosa: University of Alabama Press, 1984), 20.

[38] In the decade between 1810 and 1820, the Alabama-Mississippi area experienced remarkable growth. Mississippi's population increased from 16,600 whites and 14,706 blacks to 42,176 whites and 33,272 blacks. Alabama's population growth was even more spectacular, increasing from 6,422 whites and 2,624 blacks to 99,198 whites and 47,665 blacks. The Tennessee Valley—basically one county—saw unparalleled growth, growing from less than 5,000, free and slave, to encompass seven counties with 39,922 whites and 18,618 blacks. Georgia and Tennessee contributed the vast majority of these Euro-American emigrants, followed by the Carolinas. Charles D. Lowery, "The Great Migration to the Mississippi Territory, 1798–1819," *Journal of Mississippi History* 30 (August 1968): 184–86.

Chapter XLI

MODERN FRENCH COLONY IN ALABAMA, OR THE VINE AND OLIVE COMPANY

A colony of French sought Alabama as an asylum from Bourbon persecution. The winter of 1816 and 1817 found many of these distinguished refugees in Philadelphia. An ordinance of Louis XVIII had forced them from France on account of their attachment to Napoleon, who was then an exile upon St. Helena.[1]

The refugees dispatched Nicholas S. Parmentier to the federal city to obtain from Congress a tract of land in the wild domain of the West, upon which they had resolved to establish a colony.[2] On the 4th March 1817, Congress authorized the sale of four townships to them, at two dollars per acre on a credit of fourteen years, upon condition that they cultivated the vine and olive. In the meantime, the refugees had entered into a correspondence with intelligent persons of the West, in regard to the soil and climate of different regions.[3] Dr. Brown, of Kentucky, who had traveled in France, and had become much interested in these unhappy people, advised them to settle near the confluence of the [Black] Warrior and Tombigbee, which they determined to do.[4] Organizing in Philadelphia, the company was found to consist of three hundred and forty allottees, and the land was divided among them; some acquiring a full share of four hundred and eighty acres, and others half and quarter shares, and some not more than eighty acres. To each man was also assigned a lot in the town which they were to establish, and also one in the suburbs. Associated with them as assistants were Prosper Baltard,[5] A. Moquart[6] and J. Le François.[7] George N. Stewart, then a youth of eighteen, and now a distinguished lawyer of Mobile, was their secretary.[8]

The schooner *McDonough* was chartered, and the commissioners, with many French emigrants, set sail from Philadelphia. Late one evening, in the month of May, this vessel, bearing these romantic voyagers, was seen approaching Mobile Point, in the midst of a heavy gale. Governed by an obsolete chart,

[1] Napoleon Bonaparte (1769–1821) was initially forced into exile on the Mediterranean island of Elba in 1814 but escaped and returned to power. His devastating defeat at Waterloo in June 1815 gave his enemies the opportunity to overthrow him and place him in exile a second time in October 1815. Napoleon lived out his final years on St. Helena, a remote island in the South Atlantic, under British guards and with few companions. See Frank McLynn, *Napoleon: A Biography* (London: Pimlico, 1998) and Norwood Young, *Napoleon in Exile: St. Helena (1815–1821),* vol. 2 (London: Stanley Paul & Co., 1915).

[2] William Lee, vice president of the Colonial Society of French Emigrants, and Nicholas-Simon Parmentier, secretary of the Society, lobbied former President Thomas Jefferson, President Madison,

Secretary of State James Monroe, and Speaker of the House Henry Clay. Clay became an invaluable ally against pro-English Federalists who opposed the land grant bill. Rafe Blaufarb, *Bonapartists in the Borderlands: French Exiles and Refugees on the Gulf Coast, 1815–1835* (Tuscaloosa: University of Alabama Press, 2005), 47–48; Kent Gardien, "The Splendid Fools: Philadelphia Origins of Alabama's Vine and Olive Colony," *Pennsylvania Magazine of History and Biography* 104 (October 1980): 501–03.

[3] On 21 February 1817, the Senate passed the bill to grant lands to the French expatriates, and the House had a lively debate before passing the bill a day before the end of the session. On 3 March, his last day in office, President James Madison signed the act into law. Blaufarb, *Bonapartists in the Borderlands*, 48; Gardien, "The Splendid Fools," 502–03.

[4] While the French refugees actually explored several options for their American colony, Dr. Samuel Brown has traditionally been credited with recommending a location near the confluence of the Tombigbee and Black Warrior Rivers. Brown, an original grantee in the colony, received grant no. 152 of 240 acres, which was transferred on 26 October 1819 to Louis Bringier. Gardien, "The Splendid Fools," 500–01, 501 n. 21; Winston Smith, *Days of Exile: The Story of the Vine and Olive Colony in Alabama* (Tuscaloosa: W. D. Drake and Sons, Printers, 1967), 29.

[5] Prosper Baltard traveled with Parmentier in 1818, sold his grant in 1821, and moved to Mobile. Blaufarb, *Bonapartists in the Borderlands*, 189, 248 n. 117.

[6] Antoine-Marie Moquart traveled with Parmentier in 1818 and occupied his grant from 1818 to 1837. Ibid., 214, 248 n. 117.

[7] Brothers Jacques LeFrançois and Tougnet LeFrançois traveled with Parmentier in 1818 and lived on their grants from 1818 to 1827. Ibid., 211, 248 n. 117.

[8] George Noble Stewart traveled to his grant in 1818 with Parmentier, his mother, Helena Stewart, and his stepfather, Michel Leboutellier. When Leboutellier died in 1810, his mother married General Juan Rico. Admitted to the bar in 1821, Stewart had a long career in law and politics, serving as mayor of Tuscaloosa and in the state senate. Ibid., 223–24, 248 n. 117.

[9] The commander at Fort Bowyer, Second Lieutenant R. Beal, U.S. Corps of Artillery, had an active roster of twenty-eight men. *ASP: MA*, 1: 672; Gaius Whitfield Jr., "The French Grant in Alabama," in *Transactions of the Alabama Historical Society, 1899–1903*, ed. Thomas McAdory Owen, vol. 4 (Montgomery: The Society, 1904): 327.

[10] In his letter of 26 May 1817 from Mobile Bay to a friend in Philadelphia, Nicholas Parmentier gives a more circumspect report of the *McDonough* sailing under "a pleasant breeze" and becoming grounded in shallow water—"only two fathoms." He credits Captain John McCloud for saving "every person on board by his firmness and discretion" and for obtaining "succor from Fort Bowyer." With assistance from Lieutenant Beal, Captain Bourke, and four privates, the twenty or so passengers were carried to Fort Bowyer. The lightened *McDonough* suffered no damage and moved easily into the main channel. Smith, *Days of Exile*, 32–33; Whitfield, "The French Grant in Alabama," 327.

[11] Addin Lewis, an 1803 graduate of Yale, was the first collector of customs for the District of Mobile and also served as "inspector of the revenue for the port of Mobile." He supplied Parmentier's party with a "revenue cutter" that conveyed them up river to Fort Stoddert. He later served as mayor of Mobile in 1820–1822 and in 1823–1824. Blaufarb, *Bonapartists in the Borderlands*, 57; Smith, *Days of Exile*, 35–36; Dexter, *Biographical Sketches of the Graduates of Yale College*, 5: 724; "Mobile, Alabama 1838 Stampless Folded Letter from Edward Hall to Addin Lewis," http://www.mgjpostalhistory.com/node/385.

[12] On Sunday, 31 May 1817, when the revenue cutter arrived at Fort Stoddert, Judge Harry Toulmin sent horses to convey Parmentier and a small party to his residence. They traveled to Fort Montgomery, where Judge Toulmin introduced them to his son-in-law General Edmund Pendleton Gaines. Smith, *Days of Exile*, 36; Blaufarb, *Bonapartists in the Borderlands*, 58.

[13] According to George Strother Gaines, he had met General Charles Lefebvre Desnouettes "and several of his companions" prior to moving his family to the Choctaw Trading House near the site of the old French Fort Tombecbé (1736–1763) and Spain's Fort Confederation (1794–1797). After the French

the captain was fast guiding her into danger. Lieutenant Beal, commanding at Fort Bowyer, perceiving her perilous situation, fired an alarm gun.[9] Night coming on, and overshadowing both sea and land with darkness, he caused lights to be raised along the shore as guides to the distressed vessel. The wind continuing to increase, she was thrown among the breakers and immediately struck. Signals of distress being made, the noble lieutenant threw himself into a boat, with five resolute men, and with Captain Bourke, formerly an officer. Mounting wave after wave, they reached the wreck about one o'clock in the morning. The wind had somewhat abated, and Beal crowded the women and children into his boat and conducted them safely to shore. The larger number of the colonists remained on board the schooner, which was ultimately saved by being washed into deeper water. Bestowing upon the refugees every attention while they remained at the Point, Beal accompanied them to Mobile and partook of a public dinner, which they gave him in token of their gratitude.[10]

The commissioners remained a few days at Mobile, which was then a small place, with but one wharf, and proceeded up the river in a large barge, furnished by Addin Lewis, the collector of the port.[11] Stopping at Fort Stoddert, they were received with hospitality by Judge Toulmin, to whom they bore letters. They next visited General Gaines, then in command of a large force at Fort Montgomery, and the barge then cut across to the Tombigbee and landed at St. Stephens—a place of some size, with refined and lively inhabitants.[12] Discharging the government boat and procuring another barge, the refugees once more began their voyage up the winding and rapid current. Camping upon the banks occasionally, and exploring the country around, they at length established themselves temporarily at the White Bluff. A portion of them proceeded to old Fort Tombecbé, and near there visited Mr. George S. Gaines, who was still United States Choctaw factor, whose table fed the hungry, and whose roof sheltered the distressed. He advised them to make their location in the neighborhood of the White Bluff.[13] Jean A. Pénières and Basile Meslier, whom the association had dispatched to explore the Red River country now arrived.[14] Receiving favorable reports of the country in the Alabama Territory, the association at Philadelphia took measures to colonize it.[15]

The west side of the Tombigbee belonged to the Choctaws, and the east had recently been in possession of the Creeks. The region where the French emigrants had resolved to establish themselves was an immense forest of trees and canes, interspersed with prairie; and near the present town of Greensboro was Russell's settlement of Tennesseans, and some distance below the White Bluff were a few inhabitants.[16] However, the French continued to arrive in

refugees made their initial settlement at the White Bluff site, Desnouettes and others visited Gaines at the trading house and Desnouettes bought a pair of oxen from him. Gaines, *Reminiscences*, 78–79.

[14] Jean-Augustine Pénières-Delors had originally been appointed to explore "the southwestern part of the United States." He settled his allotment in Alabama but soon moved to Florida, where he died of yellow fever in 1821, serving as an agent for the Seminoles. Nicholas-Basile Meslier, a jeweler and watchmaker, became a recruiting agent and one of the early settlers at Demopolis in 1818, serving as the first justice of the peace. Sometime after 1825, he removed to Mobile, where he died in November 1849. Gardien, "The Splendid Fools," 495, 504, 506, 506 n. 31; Blaufarb, *Bonapartists in the Borderlands*, 217.

[15] Contrary to Pickett's comment here, the arrival of Parmentier with the first party of approximately twenty French immigrants at Mobile in May 1817 signaled the beginning of the French colony on the Tombigbee. Blaufarb, *Bonapartists in the Borderlands*, 57–58.

[16] The Russell settlement (Russell's Ridge) at modern Greensboro, Alabama, was made by three

boats by way of Mobile, and cabins were erected about the White Bluff in a rude and scattering manner. Having been accustomed to Parisian life, these people were very indifferent pioneers. Unprovided with wagons and teams, and unacquainted with the shifts to which pioneer people are often compelled to resort, they made but slow progress in subduing the wilds. Provisions of all kinds were remarkably high. They, however, slowly struggled against these difficulties, and endeavored to raise provisions upon small patches, without knowing upon what tract in the grant they were to live in future.

The meridian line was established, and the grant divided into townships and sections. A town was formed at the White Bluff, which, according to the request of Count Réal, of Philadelphia, was called Demopolis—the city of the people.* To secure the river front, two fractional townships were chosen by the commissioners, instead of two entire townships. Emigrants continuing to arrive, great confusion and controversy arose in the selection of lots and tracts of land, while the association at Philadelphia, unacquainted with the localities, were unwisely and arbitrarily planning their own forms of location.[17] By a new contract, made between Mr. Crawford, secretary of the treasury, and Charles Villar, agent of the association, the lands were sold and the tracts of each person designated. The allotments made at Philadelphia, and ratified by Mr. Crawford, being different from those already made by the settlers, forced the latter to abandon many of their hard-earned improvements, and to retire further into the forest. This wretched state of things caused General Lefebvre Desnouettes, who had opened a farm on his Tombigbee allotment, to proceed to Philadelphia to adjust these conflicting interests. He succeeded only in securing his own improvements, while the claims of the others were disregarded, and the contract made at Washington was ordered to be enforced. The settlers were then forced to retire upon the lands assigned them in township eighteen, range three east, and township eighteen, nineteen and twenty, in range four east.[18]

Among the French emigrants were many distinguished

* Afterwards it proved that Demopolis was not embraced in the townships of the French grant. An American company purchased it of the United States, at fifty-two dollars per acre.

brothers—Andrew, Caleb, and Isaac Russell—from Baldwin County, Georgia, in 1816. The settlers who joined them came from Georgia, Kentucky, Tennessee, and the Carolinas. After a few years, Caleb and Isaac moved to Mississippi, and, one or two years later, Andrew Russell moved his family to Perry County, Alabama. William Edward Wadsworth Yerby, *History of Greensboro, Alabama from Its Earliest Settlement* (Montgomery: Paragon Press, 1908), 1.

[17] Pierre-François Réal (1757–1834) became prominent during the French Revolution as an orator and criminal lawyer. He served as one of the four Counselors of State and later as chief commissioner of police during the Hundred Days. His royal pardon arrived in 1819, but he did not return to Paris until 1827, where he died on 7 May 1834. Blaufarb, *Bonapartists in the Borderlands*, 220; Gardien, "The Splendid Fools," 496, 496 n. 11.

[18] On 14 December 1818, Secretary of the Treasury William H. Crawford submitted a report to the House of Representatives on the progress of the French land grant containing four townships, along with maps and a list of shareholders. Charles Villars, agent for the "shareholders in the Tombeckbee Association," signed a contract with Crawford on 8 January 1819 that contained a list of shareholders and their allotments which may have altered some of the original allotments. *ASP: PL*, 3: 351–54; Ibid., 5: 23–28.

[19] Jacques Lafitte (1767–1844), a prominent French banker, served as governor of the Bank of France (1814–1820), as Napoleon's banker, and later as banker to King Louis XVIII and King Louis-Philippe. Virginie Monnier, *Jacques Laffitte: Roi des banquiers et banquier des rois* (Bruxelles: Peter Lang, 2013), 72–129, 160–76, 188–90,

characters. Count Lefebvre Desnouettes had been a cavalry officer, under Bonaparte, with the rank of lieutenant general. Accompanying Napoleon in his march to Russia, he rode with him in his carriage in his disastrous retreat over the snows of that country. He had served in Spain in many bloody engagements, and was an active participator in the dreadful Battle of Saragossa. Vivacious and active, handsome in person and graceful in carriage, he was the most splendid rider of the age in which he lived. His imperial master was so much attached to him, that when forced to abdicate the throne, and about to depart for Elba, and while addressing his weeping and sorrowing officers at Fontainebleau, said: "I cannot take leave of you all, but will embrace General Desnouettes in behalf of you all." He then pressed him to his bosom in the most affectionate manner. Napoleon frequently made him valuable presents, and influenced his cousin, the sister of the celebrated banker, Lafitte, to espouse him.[19] While he was at Demopolis, that lady made an attempt to join him in exile, but being shipwrecked on the coast of England, was forced to return to France. At length, she negotiated with the French government for his return, and, through the influence of her family, succeeded in obtaining permission for him to reside in Belgium. This induced Count Desnouettes, in 1823, to leave Alabama in the ship *Albion*, which was wrecked upon the coast of Ireland, at Old Kinsale, in view of an immense number of people, who were standing on the cliffs. The distinguished refugee was washed overboard, and the ocean became his grave.[20] While in Marengo County, he often received large sums of money from France, and was the wealthiest of the emigrants. Near his main dwelling he had a log cabin, which he called his sanctuary, in the center of which stood a bronze statue of Napoleon. Around its feet were swords and pistols, which Desnouettes had taken in battle, together with beautiful flags, tastefully hung around the walls.[21]

M. Pénières, another distinguished emigrant, was a republican member of the National Assembly, and voted for the death of the amiable Louis XVI. He remained about Demopolis, engaged in agriculture, but procuring an appointment of sub-agent for the Seminoles, died in Florida, in 1823. Distinguished in France, and honored with many civil appointments, he was at last expatriated for his adherence to the fortunes of Napoleon.[22]

Colonel Nicholas Raoul, a remarkable personage, had been a colonel under Bonaparte, and had accompanied him in his banishment to Elba. When his imperial master left that island, Raoul commanded his advanced guard of two hundred grenadiers upon the march from Cannes to Paris. When this small band was preparing to fire upon the king's troops, under Marshal Ney, who had come to capture the emperor, Bonaparte advanced to the front of

232–41, 256–58.

[20] Before leaving Alabama in 1823, Desnouettes visited George Strother Gaines at St. Stephens and asked Gaines to handle the sale of his real estate and the execution of title deeds under the power of attorney. He had loaned most of his personal property to friends near Demopolis. Gaines, *Reminiscences*, 81–82.

[21] George Strother Gaines was invited to a dinner party by Desnouettes and lodged for the night in his cabin with "a bust of Napoleon" and the walls "nearly concealed by the colors of France and several other nations." Ibid., 79–80.

[22] Jean-Augustine Pénières-Delors was one of several French regicides who voted for the execution of Louis XVI and found refuge in the United States. On 31 March 1821, Secretary of War John C. Calhoun appointed him as a "sub-agent to the Indians residing in the Floridas" under the supervision of Governor Andrew Jackson. David P. Jordan, *The King's Trial: The French Revolution vs. Louis XVI* (Berkeley: University of California Press, 1979), 178–94; Carter, *Territorial Papers/Florida Territory*, 22: 25–28.

[23] Nicolas-Louis Raoul (1788–1850) commanded

the lines, and gave the command to "order arms." Baring his breast to Ney's division, he exclaimed, "If I have ever injured a French soldier, fire upon me." The troops of Ney shouted "Vive la Empereur!" and Bonaparte marched at their head, through the gates of Paris. Colonel Raoul lived several years upon his grant, and, becoming much reduced in circumstances, was forced to keep a ferry at French Creek, three miles from Demopolis—being accustomed to ferry over passengers himself. Often would the American traveler gaze upon his foreign countenance, martial air and splendid form, and wonder what order of man it was who conducted him over the swollen stream. At this time Raoul, being in the prime of life, was a large, fine-looking man. He was firm and irascible in his disposition, and was a dangerous competitor in any controversy in which he might engage. His wife was a handsome woman, of the Italian style of beauty. She was a native of Naples, and had been Marchioness of Sinabaldi, and maid of honor to Queen Caroline, when Murat was king of that country. She brought with her to Alabama two children by a former husband. In 1824, she left her lonely cabin upon French Creek and followed Colonel Raoul to Mexico, where he engaged in the revolution, and fought with his accustomed fierceness and impetuosity. At length, once more reaching his beloved France, he there for a long time held an honorable commission in the French army.[23]

Jean Jerome Cluis, one of the refugees, cultivated a farm near Greensboro. He had been an aide to Marshal Lefebvre, the Duke of Rovigo, who was afterwards at the head of the police department of Paris. Colonel Cluis was then his secretary. At another time Cluis had the custody of Ferdinand VII, King of Spain, while he was imprisoned by Napoleon near the Spanish frontiers. Like all the other refugees, he found planting the vine and olive a poor business in Alabama, and, having become much reduced in fortune, kept a tavern in Greensboro. He died in Mobile not many years since.[24]

Jean Simon Chaudron, one of the Tombigbee settlers, formerly a resident of Philadelphia, where his house was a center of elegance and wit, was distinguished for his literary attainments. He had been the editor of the *L'Abeille Américaine*, and was a poet of considerable reputation.[25] He delivered a eulogy upon the life and character of Washington before the Grand Lodge of Philadelphia, which was pronounced a splendid effort, both in Europe and in America. He died in Mobile in 1846 at a very advanced age, leaving behind him interesting works, which were published in France.[26]

a corps in Mexico in 1832 when he learned of an order to reinstate him in the French army as a lieutenant colonel. He returned to France and subsequently received promotions to colonel in 1836, field marshal in 1845, and Commander of the Legion of Honor in 1848. Blaufarb, *Bonapartists in the Borderlands*, 218–19; Smith, *Days of Exile*, 78–81; Charles Mullié, *Biographie des Célébrités Militaires des Armées de Terre et de Mer de 1789–1850* (Paris: Poignavant, 1852), 2: 488–89.

[24] Jean-Jerome Cluis (1773–1834) farmed his allotment of 480 acres and kept a hotel-tavern at Greensboro. He and his wife Louise-Emilie de Mazières moved to Mobile, where they raised two children. Smith, *Days of Exile*, 54, 72, 88, 115; Blaufarb, *Bonapartists in the Borderlands*, 195.

[25] *L'Abeille Américaine* (The American Bee), a French weekly paper published by Jean-Simon Chaudron in Philadelphia, became the primary vehicle for recruiting immigrants for the French grant in Alabama. Blaufarb, *Bonapartists in the Borderlands*, 25, 43–47, 49, 120, 124; Gardien, "The Splendid Fools," 494–95, 498–99.

[26] Jean-Simon Chaudron (1758–1846), an accomplished silversmith, editor, orator, and poet, emigrated from Haiti to Philadelphia in 1793 and eventually owned 880 acres at Demopolis. When cataracts diminished his eyesight, he abandoned his farming

General Count Bertrand Clausel had been an officer of merit throughout Bonaparte's campaigns. During the Hundred Days he commanded at Bordeaux, and making the Duchess of Angoulême prisoner, released her, for some unknown cause. The general did not occupy his grant, but became a citizen of Mobile in 1821, living on the bay, furnishing the market with vegetables, and driving the cart himself. Returning to France in 1825, he was subsequently made, by Louis Philippe, governor and marshal of Algeria.[27]

Henri L'Allemand, who had been a lieutenant general, commanding the artillery of the imperial guard, was an officer of great merit and a man of high character. He married the niece of Stephen Girard. General Charles L'Allemand, his brother, had also been an officer of distinction in France. Filled with daring and ambitious projects, he employed the following language in writing to his brother: "I have more ambition than can be gratified by the colony upon the Tombigbee." This was literally true, for he soon made a hazardous expedition to Texas, collecting followers at Philadelphia and in Alabama. Arriving at Galveston Island, which was shortly afterwards submerged, his people suffered greatly for provisions, and were generously relieved by the pirate, Lafitte. Annoyed by the Indians, and prostrated by disease, in a short time most of the colonists perished, and the establishment failed.[28]

The celebrated Marshal Grouchy was one of the Philadelphia associates. He was a man of middle stature, and had very little, apparently, of the military about him. Not being popular with the refugees, in consequence of his conduct at Waterloo, to which they imputed the loss of that day, he became involved in controversies with them in the American gazettes. He never came to Alabama, but one of his sons, who had been a captain in the French army, settled his grant near Demopolis. The marshal afterwards returned to France and enjoyed honors under the Bourbons.[29]

operations for Mobile, where he died in 1846. His eulogy to George Washington—"Funeral Oration on Brother George Washington"—delivered in 1800 is one of his better known works. Smith, *Days of Exile*, 54–55, 73, 114, 119, 128; Blaufarb, *Bonapartists in the Borderlands*, 25–26, 144–45, 194; Harriet Smith, "Jean Simon Chaudron, "The Blind Poet of the Canebrakes, 1758–1846," *Bulletin de l'Institut Francais de Washington* 4 (1954): 111–119.

[27] Bertrand Clausel (1772–1842) had originally plotted with other prominent French refugees to accept their land grants and sell them to Philadelphia speculators to raise funds for a Napoleonic military refuge in Texas. He eventually received an allotment of 480 acres, but he withdrew to Mobile in 1820 where he learned of Napoleon's death in 1821 and that he had inherited 100,000 francs under his will. After his return to France in 1825, Clausel was elected to the legislature in 1829, named a marshal of France in 1831, and later became governor-general of Algeria in 1835–1837. Smith, *Days of Exile*, 40–41, 54, 68, 88, 96; Blaufarb, *Bonapartists in the Borderlands*, 194–95; Louis Antoine Fauvelet de Bourrienne, *Memoirs of Napoleon Bonaparte*, ed. R. W. Phipps, 3 vols. (London: Richard Bentley and Son, 1885), 3: 543, 543 n. 5.

[28] In March 1818, Charles-François-Antoine Lallemand (L'Allemand) and his younger brother Henri-Dominique Lallemand (1777–1823) attempted to establish a military colony—*Champ d'Asile* (Field of Asylum)—on the Trinity River in modern Texas. When Governor Antonio Maria Martinez began moving troops to the San Marcos, the French immigrants retreated to Galveston, and the Lallemands fled to New Orleans and became U.S. citizens. Charles Lallemand (1774–1839) inherited 100,000 francs under Napoleon's will, returned to France in 1830 under King Louis-Philippe, and served as military governor of Corsica in 1837–1838. Blaufarb, *Bonapartists in the Borderlands*, 209–10; Fauvelet de Bourrienne, *Memoirs of Napoleon Bonaparte*, 3: 543, 543 n. 2; Harris Gaylord and Betje Black Klier, "Charles Francois Antione Lallemand," *Handbook of Texas Online*.

[29] Emmanuel de Grouchy (1766–1847) joined Napoleon following his return from Elba and was made a marshal and a peer of France. Blamed for

M. Lakanal, a savant, and member of the academy at the head of the department of public education under the emperor, settled on the bay, near Mobile, in 1819. He was one of those members of the National Assembly of France who voted for the death of Louis XVI. After a long residence in Mobile, he went to France and there died in 1843.[30]

Among all the refugees who sought homes in Alabama, none had passed through more stirring and brilliant scenes than General Juan Rico, a native of Valencia, in Spain, who had been proscribed in that country, upon the return of Ferdinand VII, because he was a republican, and a supporter of the constitution of 1812. An eloquent member of the Cortes and a distinguished officer of the Spanish army, he resisted to the last the invasion of Napoleon. One day, an interesting scene occurred between General Rico and the elegant Desnouettes. Both being invited to dine at Demopolis, the conversation turned upon the campaigns in Spain, when allusion was made to the obstinate and sanguinary siege of Saragossa, where one of them had commanded the troops of France and the other those of Spain.[31] They were now assembled at a hospitable table in a humble cottage in the wilds of Alabama. They had met before, amid the din of arms, arraying their troops against each other, and pouring out rivers of blood, at the head of the best trained troops of Europe, who had figured in the most eventful times of France and Spain. Each had been expelled from his native country, and each had been blasted in his ambitious hopes. Nevertheless, good humor prevailed in the cabin, and the sorrows of all were drowned in wine, amid merry peals of laughter. In 1825, General Rico was recalled to Spain, and, arriving there, again became a member of the Cortes, under his favorite constitution. He met with singular reverses of fortune, was expelled from Spain the second time, became an inhabitant of England, and was again recalled to assist in the government of his country. When he lived in Alabama, he was fifty years of age, and was of a dark complexion. He possessed great energy

the defeat at Waterloo and exiled in 1816, he spent countless hours writing tracts defending his leadership in that pivotal battle. He received a royal pardon in 1819, returned to France, and regained some of his reputation when King Louis-Philippe returned his marshal's baton and restored him to the Chamber of Peers in 1830. His son settled briefly on his grant near Demopolis and returned to France a year later. Smith, *Days of Exile*, 84, 116; Blaufarb, *Bonapartists in the Borderlands*, 205–06.

[30] Joseph Lakanal (1762–1845), a French politician, educator, and regicide, came to the United States after the Battle of Waterloo in 1815. Although he received a land grant in Alabama, Lakanal lived in Kentucky and New Orleans, where he served as the president of the Collège d'Orleans (1822–1823). He traveled to Alabama in 1824, found the French settlements sadly dissipated, and settled near Bertrand Clausel in Mobile. He returned to France in 1834 and published his *Expos Sommaire des Travaux de Joseph Lakanal: Pour Sauver, Durant La Revolution, Les Sciences, Les Lettres, Et Ceux Qui Les Honoroient Par Leurs Travaux* in 1838. Smith, *Days of Exile*, 54, 87, 113, 119, 123; Blaufarb, *Bonapartists in the Borderlands*, 208–09.

[31] Napoleon's French forces laid siege to Saragossa (Zaragosa) on two occasions during the Peninsula War (1807–1812). General Lefebvre-Desnouettes launched the initial assault in June 1808 and yielded overall command to General Jean-Antoine Verdier, who arrived with reinforcements on 26 June 1808. The first siege ended on 14 August and a second siege commenced on 20 December under General Jean-Andoche Junot. Junot was replaced by Marshal Jean Lannes, who forced the surrender of Saragossa on 20 February 1809 at a terrible cost to both armies and the people of Saragossa. David Gates, *The Spanish Ulcer: A History of the Peninsular War* (Cambridge: Mass.: Da Capo, 2001), 73–78; Margaret Scott Chrisawn, *The Emperor's Friend: Marshal Jean Lannes* (Westport, Conn.: Greenwood Press, 2001), 187–212.

and decision of character, and was a most excellent farmer.[32] If our limits would permit it, many other interesting persons among the French emigrants might be described.

The principal portion of the French grant lay in Marengo County. This name was proposed by Judge Lipscomb, while a member of the legislature at St. Stephens, in honor of the great battle fought during the French Republic.[33] It also extended into the county of Greene, embracing some of the best lands in the vicinity of Greensboro. It has been seen that much difficulty arose among the French about their respective locations, and that three times they lost their improvements. Forced to abandon their settlements in Demopolis, they laid off the town of Aigleville, and erected cabins, but the drawing at Philadelphia not embracing this place, they were once more forced to go deeper in the forest.[34] The want of wagons and teams, and the great scarcity of water in the canebrake, induced them to dwell on small allotments, while their more valuable tracts were unoccupied. Owning no slaves, a number of German redemptioners were imported, through the enterprise of Desnouettes, but these people proved a burden and expense, and also disregarded their obligations.[35]

The French were less calculated, than any other people upon earth, to bring a forest into cultivation. The provisions which they raised were made at the expense of extravagant hire, and Desnouettes expended over twenty-five thousand dollars in opening and cultivating his farm. In this manner the whole colony, after a few years, became poor, and many were forced to sell their claims to Americans, who soon opened large plantations, and made the earth smile with abundant products. However, a majority of the French still held on to their grants, and, in good faith to the government, entered upon the cultivation of the grape and olive. Importations of plants were

[32] Before fleeing Spain, Juan Rico had served as vicar-general of the Spanish armies and as a deputy of the Cortes, Spain's national congress. He apparently left Spain in 1815, and his travels brought him to the French settlements on the Tombigbee in 1819, where he married George Noble Stewart's mother Helena Stewart Leboutellier. Although he was allowed to return to Spain, he remained a critic of the monarchy. *ASP: FR*, 4: 713, 725–26; Blaufarb, *Bonapartists in the Borderlands*, 223.

[33] Most sources give Judge Abner S. Lipscomb credit for recommending the name Marengo for the county organized by the Alabama Territory Assembly in February 1818. Brewer, *Alabama*, 372; Whitfield, "French Grant in Alabama," 330; Smith, *Days of Exile*, 45 n. 26.

[34] Under the act providing land grants to the Colonial Society of French Emigrants, Congress had granted four contiguous townships, but William H. Crawford, secretary of the treasury, had specified that the townships to be surveyed had to follow "the principal of contiguity . . . so as to avoid the creation of fractions of townships." Unfortunately, the French exiles established their first settlement at the White Bluff (Demopolis) on the Tombigbee and in a fractional township with its western portion across the river in modern Sumter County. The immigrants soon relocated to a new town, Aigleville (Eagleville), on the south bank of the Warrior River in the summer of 1818, clearly within their four townships but at some distance from most of the French allotments. In 1820, a group of West Indian refugees moved to Demopolis from Philadelphia under the leadership of Frédéric-Guillaume-Marie Ravesies, and they founded Arcola some fifteen miles northeast of Demopolis on the Black Warrior. Smith, *Days of Exile*, 47–53, 76–77; Blaufarb, *Bonapartists in the Borderlands*, 125, 129–31, 219; *ASP: PL*, 3: 351–54; Ibid., 5: 23–28; Carter, *Territorial Papers/Alabama*, 18: 190, 259–60, 392.

[35] According to some sources, General Lefebvre-Desnouettes recruited the Germans and other recent European immigrants as indentured servants. When they failed to produce, he and others made trips to Virginia and other states to purchase slaves to work their grants. Smith, *Days of Exile*, 60; Blaufarb, *Bonapartists in the Borderlands*, 120–21.

often made from Bordeaux, but the newness of the land and the ignorance of the colony in regard to their cultivation, were among the reasons why the experiment failed. The importations frequently arrived out of season, when the vines withered away and the olive seeds became defective. At length, with difficulty, grapes were grown, but they failed to produce even a tolerable wine, because the fruit ripened in the heat of summer. Before the vinous fermentation was completed the acetic had commenced. In 1821 the French planted three hundred and eighty-three olive trees upon the grant, and a large number in 1824. Every winter the frosts killed them down to the ground, but new shoots putting up were again killed by the succeeding winter. The usual mode of planting the grape was at the distance of ten feet in one direction, and twenty in the other. They were trained to stakes and cultivated with cotton.[36]

In addition to the ruinous failure of the vine and olive, the French were continually annoyed by unprincipled American squatters. Occupying their lands, without a shadow of title, they insultingly told the French that they intended to maintain their footing at all hazards. Several lawsuits arose, and although our supreme court decided in favor of the grantees, yet the latter became worn out with controversies, and allowed the intruders in many cases to retain possession for a small remuneration. On the other hand, many honorable Americans purchased their grants for fair considerations, and thus the French refugees were gradually rooted from the soil.[37]

But, in the midst of all their trials and vicissitudes, the French refugees were happy. Immured in the depths of the Tombigbee forest, where for several years want pressed them on all sides—cut off from their friends in France—surrounded by the Choctaws on one side, and the unprincipled squatters and land-thieves on the other—assailed by the venom of insects and prostrating fevers—nevertheless, their native gaiety prevailed. Being in the habit of much social intercourse, their evenings were spent in conversation, music and dancing. The larger portion were well educated, while all had seen much of the world, and such materials were ample to afford an elevated society. Sometimes their distant friends sent them rich wines and other luxuries, and upon such occasions parties were given and the foreign delicacies brought

[36] Many of the French refugees from Saint-Domingue who joined Frédéric-Guillaume-Marie Ravesies (1779–1857) in founding Arcola in 1820 may have been better equipped to till the Black Belt prairie than the earlier emigrants. Ravesies moved to Alabama to serve as the agent for the French Emigrants Association or Tombeckbee Association. He became a wealthy cotton planter and acquired large land holdings before moving to Mobile, where he died in 1857. Smith, *Days of Exile*, 76–78; Blaufarb, *Bonapartists in the Borderlands*, 21–32, 136–40, 142–46, 219; Whitfield, "French Grant in Alabama," 355; *ASP: PL*, 4: 675–85.

[37] While there were unscrupulous squatters and speculators, a number of prominent Black Belt planters and businessmen purchased lands from the French grantees, including Allen Glover, George Strother Gaines, Francis S. Lyon, James Manning, Robert Manning, and Elisha Young. Glover and Gaines also purchased lots at Demopolis at public land sales. Gaines, *Reminiscences*, 81; Smith, *Days of Exile*, 131–36.

back many interesting associations.[38] Well-cultivated gardens, and the abundance of wild game, rendered the common living of the French quite respectable. The female circle was highly interesting. They had brought with them their books, guitars, silks, parasols and ribbons, and the village, in which most of them dwelt, resembled, at night, a miniature French town. And then, farther in the forest, others lived, the imprints of whose beautiful Parisian shoes on the wild prairie, occasionally arrested the glance of a solitary traveler. And then, again, when the old imperial heroes talked of their emperor, their hearts warmed with sympathy, their eyes kindled with enthusiasm, and tears stole down their furrowed cheeks.*

[38] George Strother Gaines became a close friend of General Lefebvre Desnouettes and attended dinners in his home: "The dinner was excellent, cooked in the French style of course; and the wine was very good. . . . The General informed me that he had written a friend of his in Philadelphia for a few groceries, and also a few luxuries so as to enable him to give a dinner now and then. 'He took advantage of my confidence,' continued the General. 'He sent me wine and other luxuries to the amount of two thousand and five hundred dollars.'" Gaines, *Reminiscences*, 79.

* Conversations with George N. Stewart, Esq., of Mobile, who was the secretary of the French Vine Company; also conversations with Mr. Armand Pfister, of Montgomery, whose father was one of the French grantees.

Chapter XLII

LAST TERRITORIAL LEGISLATURE—STATE CONVENTION

The second session of the legislature of the territory of Alabama convened at St. Stephens, in the fall of 1818. John W. Walker was speaker of the house, and James Titus president of the legislative council. Among other acts, two new counties were formed—St. Clair, with the courts to be held at the house of Alexander Brown, and Autauga, with the courts to be held at Jackson's Mills, on Autauga Creek. The territory of the latter county was formerly attached to that of Montgomery. These new counties were added to the middle judicial district.[1]

The Bank of Mobile, with a charter extending to 1st January 1839, and with a capital stock of five hundred thousand dollars, was established. The banks at St. Stephens and Huntsville were empowered to increase their capital stock, by selling shares at auction. The profits, to the extent of ten per cent, were to be divided among the stockholders, and, if there proved to be an excess, it was to be applied to the support of Green Academy, in Madison County, and the academy at St. Stephens.[2]

Governor Bibb was constituted sole commissioner to lay off the seat of government at the confluence of the Cahaba and Alabama. He was required to have the town surveyed, expose maps of the same at public places, and give ninety days' notice of sale, out of the proceeds of which he was to contract for the building of a temporary capitol.[3] About the last of November the legislature adjourned, having determined to hold the next session at Huntsville.*

The territory of Alabama increased in population to such an extent that Congress authorized the people to form a state constitution.[4] The following persons were elected members of the convention:

* State archives.

[1] While there is a *Journal of the House of Representatives of the Alabama Territory at the Second Session of the First General Assembly,* there is no printed journal of the second session of the legislative council conducted by James Titus. See *Journal of the House of Representatives of the Alabama Territory at the Second Session of the First General Assembly; In the Forty-Third Year of American Independence* (St. Stephens: Thomas Eastin, 1818) and *Acts Passed at the Second Session of the First General Assembly of the Alabama Territory; In the Forty-Third Year of American Independence* (St. Stephens: James Eastin, 1818).

[2] On 25 November 1812, the Mississippi territorial assembly established Green Academy in Madison County, and, on 13 December 1816, the assembly appropriated

From the county of Madison—Clement C. Clay, John Leigh Townes, Henry Chambers, Samuel Mead, Henry Minor, Gabriel Moore, John W. Walker and John M. Taylor.

Monroe—John Murphy, John Watkins, James Pickens and Thomas Wiggins.

Blount—Isaac Brown, John Brown and Gabriel Hanby.

Limestone—Thomas Bibb, Beverly Hughes and Nicholas Davis.

Shelby—George Philips and Thomas A. Rodgers.

Montgomery—John D. Bibb and James W. Armstrong.

Washington—Israel Pickens and Henry Hitchcock.

Tuscaloosa—Marmaduke Williams and John L. Tindal.

Lawrence—Arthur F. Hopkins and Daniel Wright.

Franklin—Richard Ellis and William Metcalf.

Cotaco—Melkijah Vaughan and Thomas D. Crabb.

Clarke—Reuben Saffold and James Magoffin.

Cahawba[5]—Littlepage Sims.

Conecuh—Samuel Cook.

Dallas—William R. King.

Marengo—Washington Thompson.

Marion—John D. Terrell.

Lauderdale—Hugh McVay.

St. Clair—David Conner.

Autauga—James Jackson.

Baldwin—Harry Toulmin.

Mobile—S. H. Garrow.

These members convened at Huntsville on the 5th July 1819. John W. Walker was chosen to preside over the convention, and John Campbell was elected its secretary.[6] Being about to introduce biographical notices of some of these members,* we begin with the following well-written sketch, prepared by a college companion and intimate friend of the distinguished person of whom he writes.†

"John W. Walker was born in Virginia, and, while yet a child, accompanied his father, the Reverend Jeremiah Walker, who immigrated

* I regret to have occasion to observe that my application to the friends of many of the members of this convention, for information in relation to their birth, early life and political career, has not been responded to, and hence I have been unable to embody in this work any notice of them.

† From the pen of Richard Henry Wilde, formerly of Georgia, but afterwards of New Orleans, and now deceased.

$500 to Green Academy and Washington Academy in St. Stephens. It is not clear whether the bank charter legislation of 1818 produced any funds for the two schools. Brantley, *Three Capitals*, 214.

[3] After the first session of the Alabama territorial assembly, Clement Comer Clay had been appointed to chair a commission to select a site for the capital, and the commission made a report recommending Tuscaloosa. Governor Bibb ignored the report and used his influence in Washington to have land at the confluence of the Cahaba and Alabama set aside as a site for the capital. On 3 November 1818, Bibb communicated his decision and reasons for locating the capital at what became Cahaba to the General Assembly in a written message delivered by his private secretary. Brantley, *Three Capitals*, 31 n. 1, 31–35, 35 n. 1

[4] On 2 March 1819, Congress passed "An Act to enable the people of Alabama territory" to hold a constitutional convention to form a constitution and state government. *U.S. Statutes at Large*, 3: 489–92.

[5] On 4 December 1820, the Alabama General Assembly passed an act changing the name of Cahawba (Cahaba) County to Bibb County to honor William Wyatt Bibb. Brewer, *Alabama*, 135. Note: The modern spelling of Cahaba developed in the late 1850s.

[6] Following his service as secretary of the 1819 constitutional convention, John

to Elbert County, Georgia. His preceptor in the rudiments of education was the Reverend Moses Waddel, long accustomed, with an honest pride, to enumerate among his pupils many of the most celebrated jurists and statesmen of the South.[7] He graduated with distinguished honor at Princeton, preserving during his collegiate course an untarnished moral character, and acquiring, along with the reputation of an excellent scholar, a high relish for polite literature, which he ever afterwards retained. On leaving college he applied himself to the study of the law, and although more than once interrupted by illness, his quick and keen perception of the right and just, and the extent and variety of his previous attainments, speedily insured him clear and comprehensive views of a science not always enjoyed by more laborious, but less sagacious, students. Seeking the temple as a worshipper in spirit and in truth, who regarded jurisprudence not as a craft or mystery, but the noblest of sciences, he thus insured his future superiority over practitioners who treat their profession as an art and its principles as a mere collection of rules and codes.[8]

"In 1810 Mr. Walker, then a resident of Petersburg, Georgia, married Matilda, the daughter of LeRoy Pope, Esq., of the same village, and removed with his father-in-law and several of his neighbors to Alabama, then a territory, where they became the first settlers of Madison County, and founded the now flourishing town of Huntsville.[9] Here he began the practice of his profession, soon rose to eminence, and was repeatedly chosen a member of the territorial legislature. In 1819, he declined the office of district judge, tendered him by President Monroe, and in the same year was chosen to preside over the convention which formed the constitution of the state, an instrument indebted to him for many of its best provisions.[10]

"Immediately after its adoption and the admission of Alabama into the Union, he was elected a United States Senator, an office which he held until 1823, when ill-health compelled him to retire; and on the 23nd of April of that year he passed away from life, leaving behind him the memory of no fault and the enmity of no human being.

"In person Mr. Walker was tall, his figure slender but well formed, and his manners and address mild, graceful and prepossessing. He had blue eyes, brown hair, a fine complexion, handsome features, and a countenance whose expression, habitually pensive, kindled into animation with every lofty thought and generous feeling. Even to a stranger his appearance was highly engaging and attractive, while those who enjoyed his familiar conversation were charmed with the sweet, low tones of his colloquial eloquence, the intellectual music of a pure heart, a sound mind, a rich memory and brilliant imagination. Surrounded by friends who loved and honored, or in the bosom of a family who idolized him, how often hours vanished unconsciously in conversation, grave and gay, in the inexhaustible topics of art, science, literature, government and morals, to all of which his perfect urbanity, extensive reading, the refinement of his taste, and the delicacy of his feelings, gave interest and novelty. His letters, many of which have been preserved by the writer with reverential care, are models of the familiar epistolary style, correct and sparkling, yet free, cordial and unstudied—true to the feeling of the moment, and passing from the whimsical and excursive playfulness of Sterne to the pathos of McKenzie, with all the graceful negligence of Byron, or slip-shod gossip of Walpole.

"Before the higher aims or heavier burdens of life came upon him, he was, like most other men of genius, a rhymer, and the few specimens of his verse, which had currency in the circles of his love and friendship, were prized, not unreasonably, as jewels by their possessors.

"Mr. Walker's literary attainments, far from impairing, increased his efficiency as a jurist and orator. Many, it is true, believe that belles-lettres scholarship is usually an impediment to forensic eloquence; but the examples of Mansfield and Blackstone, Story and Legaro, stamp this as a vulgar error. The prejudices of ignorance and envy may, indeed, retard the success of the more thorough-bred and highly educated; but, in this case, as in every other, where industry and good sense are not wanting, all learning is useful, as well as ornamental, and ultimately tends to form the character of a perfect advocate. As might naturally be expected, therefore, Mr. Walker's contemporaries at the bar speak of his professional skill and knowledge with the highest praise, and assigned to him the palm for persuasive

Campbell left Madison County and moved back to his native Virginia. Pickett contacted him about his papers, and Campbell responded from Abingdon on 19 July 1847: "I kept no other journal [than] that of the proceedings of the convention which you will find of course among the records of the state department." "Literary Remains of Public Characters," in *Publications of the Alabama Historical Society: Miscellaneous Collections, Volume 1; Report of the Alabama History Commission to the Governor of Alabama, December 1, 1900*, ed. Thomas McAdory Owen (Montgomery: Brown Printing Co., 1901), 163.

[7] Moses Waddel (Waddell), an educator and Presbyterian minister, operated the famous Willington Academy (1804–1819), where he taught several prominent future American political leaders, including Andrew Jackson, John C. Calhoun, and William H. Crawford. Tom Horton, *The American Eton: Moses Waddel's Famed Willington Academy* (Bloomington, Ind.: Trafford Publishing, 2012), 62–104.

[8] John Williams Walker (1783–1823) died in Huntsville on 23 April 1823 in his fortieth year. The state recognized his many contributions by naming the new county created out of Marion and Tuscaloosa counties on 20 December 1824 Walker County. Owen, *History of Alabama*, 4: 1716–17; Brewer, *Alabama*, 571.

[9] Walker's father-in-law, Leroy Pope, was often referred to as the "father of Huntsville" who selected Twickenham as the original name for the town and acquired land that he set aside for a courthouse and public square. Pope was a wealthy land owner, leading member of the "Georgia faction" (Royal Party or Broad River group), and manager of the Merchants' and Planters' Bank of Huntsville. Brantley, *Three Capitals*, 213, 213 n. 1; Rogers, et al., *Alabama*, 61–62, 73, 76, 78–79; Thornton, *Politics and Power in a Slave Society*, 8–11.

[10] Walker led an eight-member delegation from Madison County that included two future governors—Clement C. Clay and Gabriel Moore—who also served terms in Congress as representatives and senators. Three of the Madison delegates served on the Alabama Supreme Court, including Henry W. Minor, John M. Taylor, and Clay, who served as the first chief justice (1820–1823). Meador, "Supreme Court of Alabama," 897–900; Rogers, et al., *Alabama*, 87–88, 137–40.

eloquence, readiness of resource and gentlemanly bearing.

"In the Senate, he was mainly instrumental in producing the passage of the first law for the relief of purchasers of the public lands, emphatically a bill of peace, which, while it saved the new state of Alabama from bankruptcy, preserved their affections to the Union, and led to the abolition of the credit system, thus preventing future evils.

"To this new theatre of usefulness and honor, Mr. Walker brought all the modest worth and unalloyed patriotism of Lowndes, with much of the easy and graceful manner of Forsyth, and, to his career as a statesman, only a longer life was wanting. But time, as it has been beautifully observed, is the indispensable ally of genius in its struggle for immortality, and, though death may have shut the gate on other aspirants as highly gifted, it has never closed on one more fondly loved or more deeply mourned."[11]

Arthur Frances Hopkins was born near Danville, in the state of Virginia. He was a descendent of Arthur Hopkins, an Englishman, and a physician of very high standing, who settled in the early part of the eighteenth century in the colony of Virginia. His grandmother was a Miss Jefferson, a relative of the president of that name. His father, James Hopkins, was in the severe Battle of Guilford Court House, a volunteer soldier of the United States at the age of fifteen, and died at his residence in Pittsylvania County, Virginia, in 1844.

In the pursuit of an education, Arthur Frances Hopkins studied in an academy at New London, in Virginia, in another at Caswell Court House, North Carolina, and at the University at Chapel Hill. He received his law education in the office of the Honorable William Leigh, of Halifax County, Virginia, who was a distinguished jurist, and the brother of the celebrated Benjamin Watkins Leigh. In December 1816, Mr. Hopkins, at the age of twenty-two, settled in the town of Huntsville, Alabama. Owning a plantation near Huntsville, and the price of cotton then being very high, and the practice of law in the valley of the Tennessee River worth but little, he relinquished his business at the bar in the spring of 1818. In January 1819, he moved to the county of Lawrence, was elected a member of the convention in May of that year, and took his seat in that

[11] As noted by Pickett, Richard Henry Wilde (1789–1847), a native of Dublin, Ireland, wrote this glowing, eulogistic biographical sketch of John Williams Walker. Wilde practiced law in Augusta and represented Georgia in Congress (1815–1817, 1827–1835). He moved to New Orleans in 1844, where he practiced law, taught constitutional law at the University of Louisiana in New Orleans, and died from yellow fever in 1847. He was a noted poet and literary critic, a founding member of the board of managers of the Smithsonian Institution, and was known "for his courtly manners and brilliant conversation, and in the world of letters as one of the most elegant scholars of the present day." Lee Ann Caldwell, "Augusta's First Poet," *Augusta Magazine* (June-July 2013), http://www.augustamagazine.com/Augusta-Magazine/June-July-2013-1/Augustas-First-Poet/; Edward L. Tucker, ed., "Richard Henry Wilde in New Orleans: Selected Letters, 1844–1847," *Louisiana History* 7 (Autumn 1966): 333–35, 352–53 n. 69.

[12] Joshua L. Martin (1799–1856), a native of Tennessee, served in the state house of representatives (1822–1828), as solicitor in the fourth judicial district (1827–1831), and later as judge on the circuit court (1834–1835). He was elected as a Jacksonian Democrat to Congress (1835–1839), but, in 1845, he was elected governor as an independent and proceeded to dismantle the state bank. Hugh C. Bailey, "Joshua L. Martin," in *Alabama Governors*, 58–62.

[13] James Jackson (1782–1840), a native of Ireland, moved to Lauderdale County in 1821 from Nashville, where he had been a successful businessman and the principal agent and partner of Andrew Jackson, who was not related. He also served as one of seven trustees of the Cypress Land Company—which included John M. McKinley, Leroy Pope, Thomas Bibb,and John Coffee—and was instrumental in the founding of Florence, Alabama. While he served in both houses of the Alabama

body, as we have seen. The people of Lawrence elected him to the state senate in August 1822. He immediately ranked with the most talented and influential men, and endeavored, with all his ability and ingenuity, to dissuade the legislature from enacting a measure which, it is believed by many, has inflicted much evil. We allude to the establishment of the state bank. His speeches upon that occasion were powerful efforts against the system of connecting bank and state, and the evils which he predicted have been, as many believe, most sensibly realized. His views were overruled by the legislature, only thirteen of the entire body, among whom were the Honorable Joshua L. Martin, afterwards governor of Alabama,[12] James Jackson, of Lauderdale,[13] and Nicholas Davis, of Limestone, concurring with him. The opposition of Mr. Hopkins to the state bank, which was called the People's Bank, diminished materially his popularity, which was shortly afterwards impaired still more by his opposition to the election of General Jackson to the office of president of the United States. He preferred Henry Clay to all other men, and supported him whenever he was a candidate for the presidency. He voted for Judge White in 1836, and for General Harrison in 1840, again for Henry Clay, and lastly for General Taylor; but, as he emphatically said to us one day, "never for General Jackson."[14]

In March 1825, Mr. Hopkins returned to Huntsville, and applied himself successfully to the profession of the law, without any interruption, until the summer of 1833, when he was returned a member of the legislature from Madison County. The most exciting measure before the legislature was the "Creek controversy," then waging between the national administration and Governor John Gayle.[15] Although personally friendly to the governor and opposed to General Jackson, the conviction of his judgment led Mr. Hopkins to take the side of the administration, and in support of his views he delivered in the house a speech of power and research, which was published and widely distributed, giving him great reputation as a constitutional lawyer and statesman. Since the close of the session of 1833 and 1834, he has not been a representative of the people of this state. In January 1836, he was elected by

General Assembly, he was recognized for his wealth, his plantation home "Forks of Cypress," and his success at raising and racing thoroughbred horses in the 1820s and 1830s. Steven Preston Brown, *John McKinley and the Antebellum Supreme Court: Circuit Riding in the Old Southwest* (Tuscaloosa: University of Alabama Press, 2012), 33–35; Joseph Frazer Smith, *Plantation Houses and Mansions of the Old South* (1941; reprint, New York: Dover Publications, Inc., 1993), 76–78; Curtis Parker Flowers, "Thoroughbred Horses at Muscle Shoals," *Alabama Heritage* 80 (Spring 2006): 26–32.

14 Despite his defeat in 1836 against Jackson's handpicked successor Martin Van Buren, Hugh Lawson White helped to solidify the Whig Party in the South and as a national party. William Henry Harrison's election victory over the incumbent Van Buren in 1840 was historic in many ways but his death less than a month into his presidency robbed the Whigs of political ascendency over the Democrats. Henry Clay, Arthur Hopkins's personal choice for president, was destined to always be the runner-up and not the victor, losing in 1824, 1832, and 1844. Robert V. Remini, *Henry Clay: Statesman for the Union* (New York: W. W. Norton & Company, 1991): 248–49, 409–11, 662–75; Jonathan M. Atkins, "Hugh Lawson White," *Tennessee Encyclopedia of History and Culture*, http://tennesseeencyclopedia.net/entry.php?rec=1497.

15 Under the Treaty of Cusseta approved by Creek leaders on 24 March 1832, the Creek Nation surrendered the balance of their lands east of the Mississippi River, virtually all Creek land located in east Alabama. President Andrew Jackson ordered army troops to remove all whites from the newly ceded lands until surveys were completed. Governor John Gayle took an aggressive states' rights stance against this federal action, which he interpreted as protecting the Creeks and a violation of

the legislature one of the judges of the supreme court without opposition, and at the solicitation of both political parties; and in 1837 he was appointed by his associates on the bench chief justice of Alabama. In December, 1836, the Whig members of the legislature did him the honor to vote for him, as a senator in Congress, against the Honorable John McKinley.[16] They conferred upon him the same unsolicited honor in January 1844, when Mr. Lewis was elected a senator of the United States.

In June 1837, Judge Hopkins resigned his seat upon the bench, returned to Huntsville, engaged in the practice of the law, and was soon tendered by Mr. Van Buren the office of commissioner, with others, under a late treaty with the Cherokees, which he declined. During the presidential canvass of 1840, Judge Hopkins was one of the Whig electors, and addressed many public meetings in North Alabama. At the Baltimore Whig convention in May 1844, he presided as chairman, until the convention was fully organized, and during that summer, he often addressed the people of Alabama, to induce them to vote for Mr. Clay, for the presidency. Judge Hopkins appears to have always been a great favorite with the Whig Party, for they ran him upon a two day's ballot, when William R. King[17] and Dixon H. Lewis[18] were candidates for the United States Senate, during the first session of the legislature held at Montgomery, and again, in the winter of 1849 and 1850, he was balloted for against Colonel King, to fill the vacancy which occurred in the Senate, and, when the latter succeeded over him, the Whig Party immediately ran him for the other vacancy in the Senate, against our excellent and much-admired friend, Governor Fitzpatrick. But the Whigs, being in a minority, have never been able to place him in the United States Senate.[19]

state sovereignty, especially over the settlement of land titles and due process for squatters. Thornton, *Politics and Power in a Slave Society*, 28–31; Kappler, *Indian Affairs: Laws and Treaties*, 2: 341–43.

[16] John McKinley (1780–1852), a native of Virginia, moved to Huntsville in 1818 where he practiced law and became active in land speculation, organizing the Cypress Land Company and founding Florence, Alabama. Closely allied with the Georgia faction (Broad River group), he became a circuit judge, lost a U.S. Senate race by one vote in 1822, and won the Senate seat vacated by Israel Pickens in 1826. Although defeated in his reelection bid in 1830, McKinley won an election as a state representative in 1831 and an election to Congress in 1832 but did not stand for reelection. He defeated Gabriel Moore for the Senate in 1836, but his second term ended in 1838 when Martin Van Buren appointed him an associate justice of the U.S. Supreme Court, the first Alabamian to serve on the court (1838–1852). Brown, *John McKinley and the Antebellum Supreme Court*, 33–43,

[17] William Rufus de Vane King (1786–1853), a graduate of the University of North Carolina, served as a congressman from North Carolina (1811–1816) before moving to Cahaba in 1818. He was elected as a delegate to the 1819 constitutional convention and served as a U.S. senator from 1819 to 1844, when he resigned to become minister to France. When Arthur P. Bagby resigned from the Senate in 1848, King was elected to fill the vacancy and resigned in 1852, citing his poor health. Thornton, *Politics and Power in a Slave Society*, 24, 92, 136 n. 32; "William Rufus King," *Biographical Directory of the United States Congress, 1774-Present* (online).

[18] Dixon Hall Lewis (1802–1848), a graduate of South Carolina College, moved to Autauga County in 1820 and served in the Alabama House of Representatives in 1826–1828. He served as a congressman from 1829 through 1844, when he resigned to accept appointment to fill the Senate vacancy caused by William R. King's resignation in 1844. Lewis was a powerful force in regional and national politics until his sudden death in 1848. Thornton, *Politics and Power in a Slave Society*, 136 n. 32, 169–77; "Dixon Hall Lewis," *Biographical Directory of the United States Congress, 1774-Present* (online).

[19] Benjamin Fitzpatrick (1802–1869), a Georgia native, moved to Alabama in 1816 and practiced law in

Judge Hopkins lives in Mobile, where he is regarded as a lawyer of ability, and as a gentleman of honor, benevolence and refinement. In person, he is compactly made, and rather large. He has an agreeable countenance, and is pleasant and affable in his manners.

William Rufus King is a native of North Carolina. He was born on the 7th April 1786. His father, William King, was a planter, in independent circumstances, whose ancestors came from the north of Ireland, and were among the early settlers on James River, in the colony of Virginia. He was highly esteemed for his many virtues, and was elected a member of the state convention which adopted the federal Constitution. The mother of Mr. King was descended from a Huguenot family, which had been driven from France by the revocation of the Edict of Nantes.

William Rufus King received his education at the University of North Carolina, to which he was sent at the early age of twelve years. On leaving that institution, where his attention to his studies, and uniformly correct and gentlemanly deportment, had commanded the respect and regard of his fellows, and the approbation of the professors, he entered the law office of William Duffy, a distinguished lawyer, residing in the town of Fayetteville, North Carolina, and in the autumn of 1805, obtained a license to practice in the superior courts of the state.[20] In 1806, he was elected a member of the legislature of the state, from the county of Sampson, in which he was born. He was again elected, the year following, but on the meeting of the legislature, he was chosen solicitor by that body, and resigned his seat.[21] Colonel King continued in the practice of his profession until he was elected a member of Congress from the Wilmington district, which took place in August 1810, when he was but little more than twenty-four years of age; but, as his predecessor's term did not expire before the 4th March 1811, Colonel King did not take his seat in the Congress of the United States until the autumn of that year, being the first session of the twelfth Congress. This was a most important period in the history of the country. The governments of England and France had for years rivalled each other in acts destructive of the neutral rights and ruinous

Montgomery (1822–1827) before retiring to his plantation in Autauga County. He pursued the Democratic Party's nomination for governor in 1837 when Clement Comer Clay resigned to enter the U.S. Senate, losing out to Arthur P. Bagby. He defeated Whig nominee James W. McClung in 1841 and won reelection unopposed in 1843. When Fitzpatrick's brother-in-law Dixon H. Lewis died in 1848, Governor Reuben Chapman appointed Fitzpatrick to fill the Senate vacancy, and, in 1853, Governor Henry Collier appointed him to replace William R. King, who had been elected vice president of the United States. In 1855, the Alabama Senate elected him to a full term, and, although he opposed secession, he resigned when Alabama seceded from the Union. J. Mills Thornton, "Benjamin Fitzpatrick," in *Alabama Governors*, 54–57; Owen, *History of Alabama*, 3: 582.

[20] William Duffy served as counsel and land agent for the University of North Carolina and was elected to represent Fayetteville in the North Carolina General Assembly in 1806. In 1803, he fought a duel with Duncan Cameron, a legal rival, for the hand of Rebecca Bennehan, receiving a serious hip wound and losing Rebecca in the exchange. Duffy was generally recognized as one of North Carolina's ablest lawyers, and his pupils included Archibald DeBow Murphey and William Rufus King. Mark F. Miller, "William Duffy" in *Dictionary of North Carolina Biography*, ed. William S. Powell, 6 vols. (Chapel Hill: University of North Carolina Press, 1979–1996), 2: 114.

[21] According to modern sources, King was elected to the North Carolina House of Commons in 1808 at the age of twenty-two. He was reelected in 1809 but resigned to become the fifth circuit's solicitor in Sampson County. Daniel Fate Brooks, "William Rufus De Vane King," in *Vice Presidents: A Biographical Dictionary*, ed. L. Edward Purcell, Fourth edition (New York: Facts On File, 2010), 130.

to the commerce of the United States. Every effort had been made, but in vain, to procure an abandonment of Orders-in-Council on the one hand and decrees on the other, which had nearly cut up the commerce of the country by the roots, and a large majority of the people felt that to submit longer to such gross violations of their rights as a neutral nation would be degrading, and they called upon their government to protect those rights, even at the hazard of a war.[22]

In this state of things, Colonel King took his seat in the House of Representatives, and unhesitatingly ranged himself on the side of the bold and patriotic spirits in that body, who had determined to repel aggression, come from what quarter it might, and to maintain the rights and the honor of the country. The withdrawal of the Berlin and Milan decrees by France,[23] while England refused to abandon her Orders-in-Council, put an end to all hesitation as to which of those powers should be met in deadly strife.[24] In June 1812, war was declared against England, Mr. King advocating and voting for the declaration. He continued to represent his district in Congress during the continuance of the war, sustaining, with all his power, every measure deemed necessary to enable the government to prosecute it to a successful termination; and not until the rights of the country were vindicated and secured, and peace restored to the land, did he feel at liberty to relinquish the highly responsible position in which his confiding constituents had placed him.[25] In the spring of 1816, Colonel King resigned his seat in the House of Representatives, and accompanied William Pinkney of Maryland, as secretary of legation, first to Naples and then to St. Petersburg, to which courts Mr. Pinkney had been appointed minister plenipotentiary.[26]

Colonel King remained abroad not quite two years, having, in that time, visited the greater portion of Europe, making himself acquainted with the institutions of the various governments and the condition of their people. On his return to the United States, he determined to move to the territory of Alabama, which determination

[22] While Pickett refers to "Colonel King," the military rank was purely honorific and had no connection with actual military appointment or service. Daniel Fate Brooks, "The Faces of William Rufus King," *Alabama Heritage* 69 (Summer 2003): 17.

[23] The Berlin Decree (1806) and Milan Decree (1807) were proclamations issued by Napoleon to blockade Europe from the importation of British goods and weaken the British economy. In the end, this "Continental System" caused more harm to the economy of France and contributed to Napoleon's downfall. Alexander Grab, *Napoleon and the Transformation of Europe* (London: Palgrave Macmillan, 2003), 29–33.

[24] From 1783 through 1812, Britain had issued a dozen or more blockade decrees collectively referred to as "Orders-in-Council" that impacted neutral trade and enforced by the Royal Navy. For the most part, American protests were ignored, as the British waged war against Napoleon until June 1812. On 16 June 1812, two days before the U.S. Senate declared war on Great Britain, Lord Castlereagh announced the suspension of the Orders-in-Council in Parliament. Donald R. Hickey, *The War of 1812: A Forgotten Conflict* (Urbana: University of Illinois Press, 2012), 15–30, 38–44.

[25] Becoming a strong supporter of Madison's administration, King had aligned himself with the young War Hawks led by Henry Clay and John C. Calhoun. He was reelected without opposition in 1812 and 1814. Brooks, "William Rufus De Vane King," 130.

[26] William Pinkney (1764–1822) was a veteran politician and diplomat when James Madison named him as minister plenipotentiary to Russia with a special mission to the Kingdom of Naples in 1816–1818. He had served with John Jay at the Court of St. James (1796–1804), returned to Britain as a joint minister with James Monroe (1806–1807), and continued as minister plenipotentiary until 1811. In between and after his international assignments, he served as a Maryland state

he carried into effect in the winter of 1818–19, and fixed his residence in the county of Dallas, where he still resides.[27] A few months after Colonel King arrived in the territory, Congress having authorized the people to form a constitution and establish a state government, he was elected a member of the convention. Colonel King was an active, talented and influential member of that body, was placed on the committee appointed to draft a constitution, and was also selected by the general committee, together with Judge Taylor, now of the state of Mississippi, and Judge Henry Hitchcock, now no more, to reduce it to form, in accordance with the principles and provisions previously agreed on. This duty they performed in a manner satisfactory to the committee. The constitution thus prepared was submitted to the convention and adopted, with but slight alterations.[28]

On the adjournment of the convention Colonel King returned to his former residence in North Carolina, where most of his property still was, and, having made his arrangements for its removal, set out on his return to Alabama. On reaching Milledgeville, in the state of Georgia, he received a letter from Governor Bibb, of Alabama, informing him that he had been elected a senator in the Congress of the United States, and that the certificate of his election had been transmitted to the city of Washington. This was the first intimation that Colonel King had that his name even had been presented to the legislature for that high position, and, injuriously as it would affect his private interests in the then condition of his affairs, he did not hesitate to accept the honor so unexpectedly conferred upon him; and, leaving his people to pursue their way to Alabama, he retraced his steps, and reached the city of Washington a few days before the meeting of Congress. His colleague, the Honorable John W. Walker, had arrived before him.

Alabama was admitted as a state, and her senators, after taking the oath to support the Constitution of the United States, were required to draw for their term of service, when Major Walker drew six years and Colonel King four. At the time that Alabama became a state of the Union, the indebtedness of her citizens for lands, sold by the United States under what was known as the credit system, was nearly twelve millions of dollars. It was perfectly apparent that this enormous sum could not be paid, and that an attempt to enforce the payment could only result in ruin to her people. Congress became satisfied that the mode heretofore adopted for the disposal of the public domain was wrong, and a law was passed reducing the minimum price from two to one dollar and twenty-five cents

legislator, Madison's attorney general, congressman, and senator (1819–1822). During the War of 1812, he served as a major in the Maryland militia and was wounded at the Battle of Bladensburg in August 1814. "William Pinkney," *Biographical Directory of the United States Congress, 1774-Present* (online).

[27] King became a prominent landowner in the Alabama Black Belt and built his home, Chestnut Hill, in a bend of the Alabama River known as King's Bend. He is credited with naming the nearby river community Selma. Brooks, "Faces of William Rufus King," 17.

[28] Judge John M. Taylor of Madison County served on the committee of fifteen at the 1819 constitutional convention that developed a draft constitution. He also served on a three-member subcommittee with King and Hitchcock charged with reducing and refining the rough draft for debate and adoption by the convention of the whole. He entered into a law partnership with Henry W. Minor and succeeded him on the Alabama Supreme Court in 1825. After serving on the court for eight years, he resigned and a year or two later moved to Mississippi. Lewis, *Clearing the Thickets*, 134–36; Brewer, *Alabama*, 352; Meador, "Supreme Court of Alabama," 898–99.

the acre, with cash payments. This change was warmly advocated by our senators, Walker and King.[29]

At the next session a law was passed authorizing the purchasers of public lands, under the credit system, to relinquish to the government a portion of their purchase, and to transfer the amount paid on the part relinquished so as to make complete payment on the part retained. At a subsequent session another law was passed, authorizing the original purchasers of the lands so relinquished to enter them at a fixed rate, much below the price at which they had been originally sold.[30] To the exertions of Senators King and Walker, Alabama is mainly indebted for the passage of these laws, which freed her citizens from the heavy debt which threatened to overwhelm them with ruin, and also enabled them to secure their possessions upon reasonable terms.

Colonel King was elected a senator in 1823, in 1828, in 1834, and in 1840. His firm but conciliatory course insured for him the respect and confidence of the Senate, and he was repeatedly chosen to preside over that body as president pro tem, the duties of which position he discharged in a manner so satisfactory, that, at the close of each session, a resolution was adopted, without a dissenting voice, tendering him the thanks of the body for the ability and impartiality with which he had discharged those duties.[31] In the spring of 1844, Colonel King was offered the situation of minister to France, which he declined, as he had, on previous occasions, refused to accept other diplomatic situations, which had been tendered to him, preferring, as he declared, to be a senator from Alabama to any office which could be conferred on him by the general government. At this time, the proposition for the annexation of Texas was pending, and there was but too much reason to believe that the British government was urging that of France to unite with her in a protest against such annexation. It was, therefore, of the highest importance to prevent, if possible, such joint protest, as, should it be made, must have inevitably resulted in producing hostilities with one or both of these powers; for no one, for a moment, believed that the government of the United States would be deterred from carrying out a measure which she considered essential to her interests, from any apprehension of consequences which might result from any combination of the powers of Europe.[32]

Colonel King was a decided advocate of the annexation of Texas,

[29] Under the Land Act of 1820, Congress attempted to eliminate the fraud associated with the credit sales of public lands by ending the purchase of public domain lands on credit or installments over a period of years. Under the new law, full payment was required, but the lawmakers reduced the minimum price from $2 to $1.25 and minimum size from 160 acres to 80 acres. Henry Clay, Speaker of the House, did not vote on this bill, and the advocates of preemption to legalize squatter's claims still faced strong opposition, especially in the Senate. However, King and Walker voted with the majority for passage 31 to 7. *Annals of Congress*, Senate, 16th Cong., 1st sess., 489; John R. Van Atta, *Securing the West: Politics, Public Lands, and the Fate of the Old Republic, 1785–1850* (Baltimore: Johns Hopkins University Press, 2014), 85–95, 256 n. 22.

[30] On 16 February 1821, Congress passed the Relief Act of 1821, which adjusted the debt repayment schedule for landowners who had purchased public lands prior to the Land Act of 1820. Van Atta, *Securing the West*, 143.

[31] In his reelection for a full six-year term in 1822, King defeated U.S. District Attorney William Crawford of Mobile by a vote of 38 to 35. As an acknowledged Jacksonian Democrat, he was reelected in 1828 and 1834 without opposition, and, in 1840, he defeated his Whig opponent—former Governor John Gayle. Brooks, "William Rufus De Vane King," 130.

and when urged by the president and many of his friends in Congress to accept the mission, he consented, under these circumstances, to give up his seat in the Senate. Colonel King, feeling the importance of prompt action, did not even return to his home to arrange his private affairs, but repaired at once to New York, and took passage to Le Havre. Arriving in Paris he obtained an audience of the king, presented his credentials, and at once entered upon the object of his mission. After frequent conferences with the king of the French, who had kindly consented that he might discuss the subject with him, without going through the usual routine of communicating through the foreign office, Colonel King succeeded in convincing His Majesty that the contemplated protest, while it would not arrest the proposed annexation, would engender on the minds of the American people a feeling of hostility towards France, which would operate most injuriously to the interests of both countries, now united by the closest bonds of friendship; and His Majesty ultimately declared that "he would do nothing hostile to the United States, or which could give to her just cause of offense." The desired object was accomplished. England was not in a condition to act alone, and all idea of a protest was abandoned. Colonel King remained in France until the autumn of 1846, dispensing a liberal hospitality to his countrymen and others, and receiving from those connected with the government, and a large circle of the most distinguished individuals in Paris, the kindest attention. He returned to the United States in November 1846, having requested and obtained the permission of the president to resign his office.[33]

In 1848, the Hon. Arthur P. Bagby was appointed minister plenipotentiary to Russia, and resigned his seat in the Senate of the United States.[34] Colonel King was appointed, by the governor of Alabama, to fill the vacancy thus created, and in 1849, the term for which he was appointed having expired, he was elected by the legislature for a full term of six years. In 1850, on the death of General Taylor, the president of the United States, Mr. Fillmore, the vice president, succeeded to that high office, and Colonel King was chosen, by the unanimous vote of the Senate, president of that body, which places him in the second highest office in the government. Colonel King has ever been a decided republican of the Jeffersonian school. He has during his whole political life opposed the exercise of implied powers on the part of the general government, unless palpably and plainly

[32] Actually, the issue of the annexation of Texas to the American Union was complicated by multiple issues, including mediation efforts by Great Britain, negotiations by Texans to remain part of Mexico but with greater self-governance, and strong opposition to annexation by Democrats and Whigs. While Texans were concerned about security should they pursue annexation, other forces in England and Europe were pressing to stop slave trafficking and the expansion of slavery. William W. Freehling, *The Road to Disunion: Volume I: Secessionists at Bay, 1776–1854* (New York: Oxford University Press, 1991), 368–71, 380–401.

[33] When King sailed from New York to Le Havre in June 1844, he was joined by his widowed niece Catherine Ellis, his nephews Alfred Beck and William Thomas King, and his personal servant John Bell. Although he encountered difficulties with the French foreign minister Francois Guizot, King apparently developed a cordial rapport with King Louis Philippe I in July 1844. King described the monarch's policy as "peace, and non-intervention as the best means of securing peace." Brooks, "Faces of William Rufus King," 21; Justin Harvey Smith, *The Annexation of Texas* (New York: Macmillan Company, 1919), 399–402.

[34] Arthur Pendleton Bagby (1794–1858), former Alabama legislator and governor, was elected to the U.S. Senate following the resignation of Clement Comer Clay in 1841. On 16 June 1848, he resigned from the Senate to become "Envoy Extraordinary and Minister Plenipotentiary" to Russia, replacing Ralph J. Ingersoll, who

necessary to carry into effect an expressly granted power, firmly impressed with the belief, as he has often declared, that the security and harmony, if not the very existence of the federal government, was involved in adhering to a strict construction of the Constitution.

In all the relations of life, Colonel King has maintained a spotless reputation; his frank and confiding disposition, his uniform courtesy and kindness, has endeared him to numerous friends, and commanded for him the respect and confidence of all who have had the pleasure of his acquaintance. Colonel King is about six feet high, remarkably erect in figure, and is well proportioned. Brave and chivalrous in his character, his whole bearing impresses even strangers with the conviction that they are in the presence of a finished gentleman. His fine colloquial powers, and the varied and extensive information which he possesses, render him a most interesting companion.[35]

Clement Comer Clay was born in Halifax County, Virginia, on the 17th December 1789. His father, William Clay, son of James Clay, and his mother, Rebecca, daughter of Samuel Comer, were Virginians by birth, and of English descent. His father, William Clay, entered the Revolutionary army as a private soldier at the early age of sixteen, and made several tours. He was in various engagements, and was present at the siege of Yorktown and the surrender of Cornwallis. At an early age, his father removed west of the Alleghenies to Grainger County, East Tennessee.

Clement Comer Clay completed his education at the East Tennessee University at Knoxville. Leaving college, he read law with the Honorable Hugh Lawson White, and obtained a license in December 1809. He remained in East Tennessee until 1811, when he removed to Huntsville, where he has resided ever since. With a determined self-reliance, he pursued the practice of his profession steadily, and with gradually increasing profit, until the spring of 1817, taking no other interest in political matters than such as might be expected in any intelligent private citizen. When hostilities were commenced by the Creeks in 1813, he performed military duty as adjutant of a battalion of volunteers, called into service from Madison County; but he had volunteered as a private soldier in one of the companies of that battalion. This battalion never joined the army of General Jackson in the Creek Nation, but, under his orders, was kept on the frontier, south of the Tennessee River, to watch the enemy, and repel any advance which might be made.

In the spring of 1817 the friends of Mr. Clay announced him as a candidate for the territorial council, and he was elected by more than two hundred votes above the next highest candidate who was returned. He went to St. Stephens, and discharged his duties during the two sessions held at that place

was "recalled at his own request." *Niles National Register* 74 (July 5, 1848), 2; "Arthur Pendleton Bagby," *Biographical Directory of the United States Congress, 1774-Present* (online); John M. Martin, "The Senatorial Career of Arthur Pendleton Bagby," *Alabama Historical Quarterly* 42 (Fall/Winter 1980): 124–56.

[35] King's "spotless reputation" did suffer significant scrutiny in Washington when he developed his friendship with James Buchanan of Pennsylvania. The two senators shared a residence in Washington, causing some to make jokes and refer to them as "the Siamese Twins." When newspapers began to talk about a possible Buchanan-King ticket in 1844, the defaming comments about King and Buchanan began to resurface in Washington, especially from supporters of James K. Polk, such as Andrew Jackson and Aaron V. Brown, Polk's former law partner. Brooks, "William Rufus De Vane King,"131–32.

[36] The thirty-one year-old Clay presided over an Alabama Supreme Court that included Abner Smith Lipscomb, Reuben Saffold, Henry Young Webb, Richard Ellis, and Anderson Crenshaw. When he resigned in 1823, Governor Israel Pickens appointed Henry W. Minor as his interim replacement.

in a manner creditable to himself and useful to his constituents and the territory. His absence, however, seriously interrupted a lucrative practice at the bar, and deprived him of the favorable opportunity of purchasing a valuable tract of land near Huntsville as a permanent home. When the convention was organized at Huntsville, Mr. Clay appeared as one of the delegates from the county of Madison. An active and assiduous member to its close, he was appointed chairman of the committee of fifteen to prepare and report a plan of government, and in that capacity brought forward a paper containing the main features of the constitution as it was originally adopted. When the convention terminated he resolved to devote himself exclusively to the practice of his profession and to planting; but in December 1819, before he had completed his thirtieth year, he was elected, without opposition, one of the judges of the circuit court. When the judges assembled at Cahaba, in May1820, although he was several years younger than any other one on the bench, he was elected by his associates the first chief justice of the state of Alabama. As judge he served more than four years, when he resigned, in December 1823, to resume the practice of his profession.[36]

On his return to the bar Judge Clay reentered upon the practice of his profession with his accustomed assiduity, energy and talents, and immediately obtained a highly lucrative business. But in 1828, he was elected to the legislature by the people of Madison, to advance their interests in the grant of four hundred thousand acres of land made by Congress for the improvement of the navigation of the Tennessee River. On his arrival at Tuscaloosa, then the seat of government, he was elected speaker of the house of representatives without opposition.[37] He performed the high and responsible duties of that post during the unusually long and exciting session of 1828–1829 in a manner very satisfactory to the house. He participated in the debates upon the most important questions, and earned a reputation as an able legislator. Upon his return to Huntsville his friends placed him in nomination for Congress. Captain Nicholas Davis, who had been a member of the senate, and its president, was his opponent.[38] The canvass was a most exciting one. Each candidate had numerous active and influential friends. The district then consisted of the counties of Madison, Jackson, Limestone, Lauderdale, and Lawrence.

In Jackson, and the eastern part of Madison, the public lands had never been offered for sale, and the great question was whether the right of pre-emption should be given to the pioneers. The government of the United States had sold all the lands in the other counties of the district in 1818–1819–1820 under the credit system, which then prevailed, at such enormous prices as, under

Meador, "Supreme Court of Alabama," 896–98.

[37] On 13 December 1825, the Alabama General Assembly voted to relocate the state capital from Cahaba to Tuscaloosa, and the first legislative session convened there on 20 November 1826 in the Bell Tavern. Brantley, *Three Capitals*, 167–70; Lewis, *Lost Capitals of Alabama*, 84, 108.

[38] Nicholas Davis (1781–1859), a native of Virginia, served in the 1819 constitutional convention and as a state representative from Limestone County. From 1820 to 1828, he served in the state senate and as president of that body through five sessions. He entered the race for Congress against Clay as a Whig who favored preemption and anti-nullification. Thornton, *Politics and Power in a Slave Society*, 24, 33, 133; Owen, *History of Alabama*, 3: 464.

the change brought about by the reduced price of cotton, rendered many unable, and nearly all the original purchasers, unwilling, to pay for them. Consequently, nearly all the lands in those counties had been relinquished and forfeited, including, in many instances, the dwelling-houses, gin-houses and other improvements, and the question was whether adequate relief should be obtained for the former purchasers, and those holding under them. Judge Clay and Captain Davis were both advocates of pre-emption rights to the settlers on public lands, and relief to the unfortunate purchasers, who had relinquished or forfeited. Judge Clay, the successful candidate, took his seat in Congress in December 1829, and devoted his best energies to the accomplishment of those great measures. He succeeded to his entire satisfaction, and the journals of Congress show the labor and talent which he employed in aiding in the passage of the "relief laws." On his return home, he was everywhere greeted with expressions of praise and gratitude.[39]

The tariff was one of the exciting questions then agitating the national councils. Judge Clay took the ground he has ever occupied, in favor of a revenue tariff and *ad valorem* duties, and delivered in Congress a creditable speech upon that subject. In another speech, he sustained General Jackson's policy and measures in opposition to the Bank of the United States and the removal of the deposits. He agreed with the administration, in the main, in regard to the tariff, and disapproved of the course taken by South Carolina to nullify the tariff laws, yet he could not be induced to vote for the "force bill," as it was familiarly called.[40] His regard for the sovereignty and rights of the states was such that he would not consent to give the federal executive additional power against any member of the confederacy, however much he condemned her action. Judge Clay's course in Congress was such that he never incurred opposition to his several reelections, and in 1835 he was nominated as the Democratic candidate for governor. At that time Judge White was placed in nomination by his friends as a candidate for the presidency, in opposition to Van Buren. Although Judge Clay's personal preferences were in favor of the claims of the former, and he would have preferred him as the nominee, he would not consent to divide the Democratic Party, to which he belonged, and, therefore, he gave his support to Van Buren. This brought out opposition to him, in the person of General Enoch Parsons, but Judge Clay was elected governor in

[39] After taking his seat in the Twenty-first Congress in December 1829, Clay became a member of the committee on public lands and worked on preparing relief legislation, which was introduced on the House floor in March 1830. With the passage of the 1830 relief act, Clay returned to Congress for his second session in December 1830 and pushed for the successful passage of the land relief act of 1831. Ruth Ketring Nuermberger, *The Clays of Alabama: A Planter-Lawyer-Politician Family* (Lexington: University of Kentucky Press, 1958), 32–36.

[40] The "Force Bill" was an act pushed by President Andrew Jackson entitled "An Act further to provide the collection of duties on imports" which was enacted on 2 March 1833 during the nullification crises with South Carolina. The controversial language was found in Section 5 that authorized the president to use force "to cause the said laws or processes to be duly executed." Three Alabama Jacksonians—Clement C. Clay, Samuel Mardis, and Dixon H. Lewis—joined with other Southern Jacksonians in opposing the bill, which passed the House 149–47. Ibid., 39–40; "Message: Gentlemen of the Senate and House of Representatives [President Andrew Jackson, 16 January 1833]," *The Evening Post* [New York], 19 January 1833; *Statutes at Large: 22nd Cong., Sess. II*, https://www.loc.gov/law/help/statutes-at-large/22nd-congress/session-2/c22s2ch57.pdf.

[41] Enoch Parsons ran for governor with the support of the Hugh Lawson White faction in Alabama, but he was handily defeated by Clay, who received sixty-five percent of the vote. His title of "General" may have been a carryover from service

August 1835, by the largest majority ever given any candidate for that office in the state, being upwards of thirteen thousand votes.[41] He was inaugurated as governor in November 1835.[42]

Governor Clay has been charged with inactivity and neglect of duty during the Creek War, in the spring of 1836. If we were writing a history of those times, we could vindicate him in a most successful manner, for we were then attached to the executive staff, and well remember what transpired. We cannot, however refrain from remarking that no man ever labored more assiduously to bring into the field a force sufficient to subdue the hostile Indians, and no one ever evinced more willingness to afford relief to his fellow citizens in the Creek Nation, or felt for them more anxiety. As soon as he learned, at Tuscaloosa, the alarming condition of the settlers in the Creek Nation, he addressed an order to Major General Benjamin Patteson, directing him to bring down a force from North Alabama, to hasten to the seat of war, and to assume the immediate command of all the Alabama troops intended to be employed against the hostiles.[43] At the same time, he addressed a letter to the commandant of the United States arsenal at Mount Vernon, making a requisition upon him for arms, munitions and tent equipage, directing them to be shipped forthwith to Montgomery. At the same time, he also issued an order to Brigadier General Moore, of the Mobile division, ordering him to send troops to Eufaula, upon the Chattahoochee. He then took a seat in the stagecoach, arrived at Montgomery, and temporarily established his headquarters at that place. It was during a period when provisions of all kinds were scarce and exorbitantly high,—when the whole country had run mad with speculations—and when even the elements were in commotion—tornadoes prostrating trees across the highways, and heavy rains swelling every stream and sweeping off every bridge.[44]

Yet, in spite of these things, he assembled a large force from North Alabama, from West Alabama, and from South Alabama. He caused a great quantity of arms, tent equipage and ammunition to be brought up the river from the arsenal at Mount Vernon. He made the most judicious arrangements with highly responsible contractors, who sent forward from New Orleans and Mobile an abundance of subsistence for the army. To meet some pressing necessities, he sold his own bill of exchange to the Bank of Montgomery for the sum of twenty-five thousand dollars. He exerted himself, in gaining over to

in the War of 1812. His brother, Silas Parsons (c.1800–1860), was elected to fill a vacancy on the Alabama Supreme Court in 1849. Thornton, *Politics and Power in a Slave State,* 33–34; Owen, *History of Alabama,* 4: 1323–24.

[42] Clay's administration faced two major challenges—the Creek War of 1836 and the Panic of 1837. Unfortunately, he gave undue attention to the dissemination of abolitionist publications and pushed the indictment and extradition of William Goodell, the editor of the New York-based *The Emancipator.* While demanding cooperation from New York, he also urged tighter slave regulations and the arrest and conviction of abolitionists. Nuermberger, *Clays of Alabama,* 49–50.

[43] Benjamin Patteson (1789–1862) served as a brigadier general on Andrew Jackson's staff and was elected major general of the Alabama militia. He commanded the 2nd corps of Alabama volunteers and militia under Major General Thomas S. Jesup of the U.S Army during the Creek War of 1836. He also served as U.S. marshal for the Northern District of Alabama for several years. "The Creek War," *Niles Weekly Register* 50 (July 30, 1836), 364; Owen, *History of Alabama,* 4: 1327; Garratt, *Reminiscences of Public Men in Alabama,* 81.

[44] Pickett's defensive posture regarding Governor Clay's administration during the Creek War of 1836 comes from his service as an aide-de-camp to Clay in 1836–1837. The state's newspapers printed a large number of orders that were signed by Pickett as Clay's aide or assistant adjutant. Owsley, "Albert James Pickett," 9–10.

[45] James E. Belser (1805–1859), a native of South Carolina, practiced law in Montgomery, represented Montgomery County in the legislature, and edited the *Planter's Gazette*. He served one term in Congress (1843–1845) as a Democrat, but he was elected to the Alabama House of Representatives in 1853 as a Whig and an advocate for internal improvements, especially railroads. Owen, *History of Alabama*, 3: 131–32; Blue, *Works of Matthew Blue*, 100, 133, 192, 230–31.

[46] Colonel John Archibald Campbell (1811–1889) attended West Point, the U. S. Military Academy in 1826–1828 and served as aide-de-camp to Governor Clay during the Creek War of 1836. Although he served two terms in the state legislature—one prior to his move to Mobile in 1837 and a second in 1842—his greatest achievements came as a lawyer and jurist, serving as an associate justice of the U.S. Supreme Court from 1853 to 1861. While the Civil War disrupted his life and professional career, he again became a nationally recognized lawyer in the 1870s, arguing several important cases before the Supreme Court through his retirement in 1886. Owen, *History of Alabama*, 3: 293–94; Robert Saunders Jr., *John Archibald Campbell, Southern Moderate, 1811–1889* (Tuscaloosa: University of Alabama Press, 1997), 9–13, 20–38, 105, 110–52, 210–33.

[47] George Washington Gayle, a South Carolina native, practiced law in Dallas County, where he was elected to the state legislature and served as a U.S. district attorney. He was indicted for conspiracy in 1865 along with two former editors of the *Selma Dispatch* for publishing a notice in the *Dispatch* on 1 December 1864 asking for "A million dollars wanted, to have peace by 1st of March." to be used to take "the lives of Abraham Lincoln, William H. Seward, and Andrew Johnson." On 27 April 1867, President Johnson issued a pardon to Gayle following a letter writing and lobbying effort that involved former governors and legislators as well as former U.S. Army officers. Owen, *History of Alabama*, 3: 646; *Impeachment Investigation: Testimony Taken Before the Judiciary Committee of the House of Representatives in the Investigation of Charges Against Andrew Johnson. Second Session, Thirty-Ninth Congress, and First Session Fortieth Congress, 1867* (Washington: GPO, 1867), 563–70.

[48] Major James J. Donegan was a banker and business leader in Huntsville. Major Jones Mitchell Withers (1814–1891) attended Green Academy in Huntsville and graduated from West Point, the U.S. Military Academy in 1835. In May 1836, he joined Major General Benjamin Patteson's staff and then transferred to Major General Thomas Jesup's staff. Prior to his service in the Mexican War, Withers practiced law in Mobile and became a commission merchant. At the beginning of the Civil War, he was commissioned a colonel in the 3rd Alabama and ended his Confederate service as a major general in command of Alabama reserves in North Alabama. He later edited the *Mobile Tribune*. Owen, *History of Alabama*, 4:1792–93; Ezra J. Warner, *Generals in Gray: The Lives of the Confederate Commanders* (Baton Rouge: Louisiana State University Press, 1959), 342–43.

[49] Opothleyahola (Opothele Yoholo) emerged as the political leader of the Creek Nation in 1828, dominating the Creek National Council. He was the principal signatory to the Treaty of Cusseta in 1832, providing for removal, and openly advocated removal by 1835. Greene, *Politics of Indian Removal*, 107–11, 117–25, 137–39, 183–84; Kappler, *Indian Affairs: Laws and Treaties*, 2: 341–43.

[50] In May 1818, Thomas Sidney Jesup was promoted to brigadier general and appointed Quartermaster General of the U.S. Army, a position he held for forty-two years. Secretary of War Lewis Cass dispatched Jesup as a brevet major general to put down the Creek conflict in east Alabama known as the Creek War of 1836. Greene, *Politics of Indian Removal*, 185; James M. Denham and Keith L. Huneycutt, eds., *Echoes from a Distant Frontier: The Brown Sisters' Correspondence from Antebellum Florida* (Columbia: University of South Carolina Press, 2004), 42, 42 n. 39; John C. Fredriksen, *The United States Army: A Chronology, 1775 to the Present* (Santa Clara, CA: ABC-CLIO, 2010), 89.

[51] Clay left the Senate because his personal finances had suffered dramatically during the depression years following the Panic of 1837. In his resignation letter of 12 November 1841 to the Alabama legislature, he confidently stated Alabama continued to embrace "the Republican faith" and principles. Nuermberger, *Clays of Alabama*, 64.

our side many of the prominent chiefs. Opothleyahola and eleven principal chiefs came down to Montgomery by his invitation, to whom he made an ingenious appeal in the ball-room of the Montgomery Hall in the presence of Colonel James E. Belser,[45] Colonel John A. Campbell,[46] Colonel George W. Gayle[47] and the author—who were his aides—and General Patteson, with his staff, among whom were Major J. J. Donegan, Major Withers,[48] and others, who, at this moment, are not recollected. Opothleyahola responded in a "talk" of an hour's length. He concluded, by tendering to Governor Clay his services and those of his people.[49] In short, an army of near three thousand men was organized, who reached the Creek Nation by the time that General Jesup, who had been sent by the federal government to assume the command, arrived there.[50]

In June 1837, Governor Clay was elected to the United States Senate, without opposition, and shortly afterwards resigned the gubernatorial office. He took his seat in the Senate in September 1837 (an extra session) and served the four succeeding regular sessions, and the extra session of 1841. The journals of the Senate contain evidences of his talent and industry. In consequence of the ill health of his family, he resigned his seat in the Senate.[51]

Governor Clay is of medium size. He is erect in figure, and walks with elasticity, presenting but few of the marks of age. His eyes are of a dark brown color, expressive and penetrating, and are ever in motion. Nothing escapes his observation; and while conversing with you, even upon a topic highly interesting to him, it is his custom frequently to cast his eyes upon someone who has entered the room, or who is passing the streets, and then upon you. He tells an anecdote well, and is an agreeable companion. He is a brave man, and is exceedingly punctual and honorable in all the relations of life.[52]

Nicholas Davis, a member of the convention from the county of Limestone, will next be noticed. He was born on the 23d of April 1781, in Hanover County, Virginia, in a region of country familiarly called the "Slashes," where, also, the great orator of Kentucky first saw the light. He descended from the Davis and Ragland families, whose names are preserved in the archives of Virginia, as among the earliest settlers of Yorktown. He was educated in the same county, and partly in the same school, with Henry Clay.

Captain Davis never studied any profession, but has been all his life a farmer. He removed to Alabama in March 1817, and established himself at "Walnut Grove," in the county of Limestone, where he has resided ever since. After the termination of the convention, he was elected a member of the first legislature of Alabama, which sat at Huntsville in the fall of 1819. In 1820 he was again a member, at Cahaba, where the legislature was permanently

[52] In June 1842, Clay received an interim appointment to the Alabama Supreme Court to replace Henry Barnes Goldthwaite, who had resigned to run for Congress. His salary of $2,250 was a short-lived financial windfall that eased his lagging finances. However, Goldthwaite lost his congressional race and defeated Clay in the election for a regular term. Ibid., 65.

established. The people of Limestone placed him in the senate in 1821, and when he arrived at Cahaba, in the beginning of the winter, he was selected to preside over that body. His impartiality, honesty, firmness, talents and efficiency caused him to be continued in the office of president of the senate for the period of ten years.[53]

In the preceding memoir, we have alluded to the congressional canvass in which Captain Davis was engaged in the summer of 1829. It was exceedingly spirited. Governor Clay found him to be a truly honorable and liberal competitor, but a very formidable one. Everywhere Captain Davis met him upon the stump, and exhibited decided evidences of a first-rate popular speaker. At that period, Captain Davis was a man in the prime of life, of commanding person, vigorous constitution, and an honest and generous heart. Possessing a handsome and expressive countenance, beaming with intelligence, and a clear and distinct voice, he might have been pointed out as one of the noblest specimens of an intelligent yeomanry. He was defeated for Congress, as we have seen, although every man in the district who voted against him was ready to acknowledge that, as a representative, he would have been honest, faithful and efficient; but the early opposition which he made to General Jackson in North Alabama has served to build up a barrier to his political success.[54]

The Whig party of Alabama, upon whose list the name of Nicholas Davis has ever been among the first and most prominent, placed him upon the electoral ticket in the memorable contest between Van Buren and Harrison. Again, when Clay and Polk were candidates for the presidency, Captain Davis was one of the Whig electors, and frequently addressed the people of North Alabama upon that occasion, in a zealous and eloquent manner, sometimes imploring them, even with tears in his eyes, to vote for the Whig candidate! It was a fine theme for this gentleman, which at once brought out all his warm and generous feelings, emanating from the recollections of his youth, and the unbounded admiration which he had ever since entertained for Henry Clay.

His party supported him for the office of governor of Alabama against the honorable John Gayle, but the Democratic Party being greatly in the ascendancy, the latter prevailed over him.[55] When the Honorable Reuben Chapman was nominated by the Democratic convention for governor, the Whigs again supported Captain Davis for that office, and he was again defeated from the same cause. As a legislator, Captain Davis was exceedingly sensible and useful. He manifested much firmness in his opposition to the state bank and its branches. He always preferred well regulated stock banks.[56]

Captain Davis is large and well proportioned. His eyes are deep blue, very expressive, and indicative of benevolence, or much of the "milk of human

[53] During his early career in the General Assembly, Nicholas Davis was a Jeffersonian Republican and held sway in the Alabama senate until the divisive issue of nullification pushed him into the anti-nullification faction that supported Hugh Lawson White. Thornton, *Politics and Power in a Slave Society*, 21–24, 30–33.

[54] Clay's principal issue was his advocacy of relief for land debtors, an obviously critical issue in Madison County, where he outpolled Davis with 2,029 votes to 443. However, he won the election with a majority of 336 votes out of more than 8,000 votes cast. Ibid., 29.

[55] John Gayle, a Jackson man, used the tariff issue in his 1831 campaign, declaring his strong anti-nullification commitment and his pro-Jackson sentiments, which reflected the positions of most Alabama voters. Ironically, after his election as governor, Gayle clashed with Jackson's policies and turned to the Whig Party. Rogers, et al., *Alabama*, 90–92.

[56] Despite his popularity and his legislative service, Davis could not defeat Reuben Chapman, who left his seat in Congress to seek election as governor in 1847. Chapman, a Huntsville lawyer and planter, received strong support

kindness." He is a man of great energy of character, and is remarkable for his physical strength and industrious habits. He has ever been a patron of the turf. His horses have run at New Orleans, Nashville, Mobile, and through the South generally. He was present at the celebrated contest between the horses of Andrew Jackson, of Tennessee, and James Jackson, of North Alabama, at Huntsville.

Captain Davis still lives at "Walnut Grove," esteemed and respected by all classes and parties. Many refined and intelligent gentlemen in Huntsville and its vicinity, and other portions of North Alabama, deem it their imperative, but most pleasing duty, to pay him two long visits every year. Often his large old log-house, which he erected when he first came to Alabama, and which he venerates so much that he would not exchange it for a palace, contains forty or fifty visitors at one time, who, for days together, are entertained by his agreeable conversation, fed from his abundant table, and delighted with the survey of his extensive groves, rich fields, happy Negroes, fine blooded horses, and sleek and well-formed cattle.[57]

Reuben Saffold was born in Wilkes County, Georgia, on the 4th September 1788. He received such an education as was usually imparted at a common academy, where he made some proficiency in the Latin language. He studied law with ——— Paine, of Watkinsville, Clarke County, Georgia, and in that place he entered upon the practice of his profession. In the spring of 1811, he married Mary Phillips, daughter of Colonel Joseph Phillips, then of Morgan County, Georgia, who soon after removed to the southern part of Alabama.

Mr. Saffold, in the spring of 1813, established himself at the town of Jackson, situated upon the Tombigbee River, then in the Mississippi Territory. Soon, thereafter, the Indian war broke out, and he at once became actively engaged in the protection of a suffering people and an exposed frontier. Holding at the time the rank of colonel in the militia, he nevertheless raised a company of sixty volunteers, and, as their captain, scoured the thickets from the mouth to the head of the Perdido River, upon which occasion several Indians were killed, while others were driven to the more remote parts of Florida. But before he made this tour he had been a participant, as a private, in the Battle of Burnt Corn, and was one of those who fought bravely and retreated among the last. During these early times he was also a member of the legislature of the Mississippi Territory at several sessions. When peace was restored he entered upon the practice of his profession, but in 1819 he was chosen a member of the convention. At the session of the legislature of the state of Alabama, held at Huntsville in the fall of 1819, he was elected, without opposition, one of the circuit judges, and in December of that year he

from Madison County and the Tennessee Valley. Ibid., 155.

[57] Even after his death in 1859, Davis's character was recognized by the Alabama novelist Jeremiah Clemens (1814–1865). He dedicated his 1857 book *Mustang Gray* to his friend Nicholas Davis Jr. and his parents: "But it is not these alone that move me to write your name on the first page of this volume. The last words your mother was ever heard to speak, were warm regard for me, and to the hour of his death your father honored me with a friendship which is among my proudest recollections. In the whole range of my acquaintance I have never known two persons more remarkable for unswerving integrity of thought and action or more distinguished for a lofty scorn of all that was low or vile in humanity." Owen, *History of Alabama*, 3: 348, 467; "Nicholas Davis, Jr.," http://huntsvillehistory-collection.org/hh/index.php?title=Person:Nicholas_Davis,_Jr.

removed to the residence at which he died, in the county of Dallas.[58]

Judge Saffold held the office of circuit judge, under various reelections, with distinguished ability and honor until January 1832, when the legislature authorized the organization of a separate supreme court. Then he was elected one of the three who were to constitute that court. Upon this new theatre of judicial labor he lost none of the high and deserved reputation which he had acquired in the "court below." At the January term of 1835 Judge Lipscomb resigned the office of chief justice, and Judge Saffold was selected in his place. He occupied this dignified position until the spring of 1836, when he resigned it and bid a final adieu to the bench, having held the office of judge for more than sixteen years. The reports of the Supreme Court of Alabama are enduring memorials of his strength of mind, patient investigation, deep research and profound learning. Before the separate organization, the people of the whole state had it in their power to scan his acts as a circuit judge. They remember him to have been firm and dignified, but not austere. Wherever he presided entire order and decorum prevailed, and he was respected and admired by both clients and attorneys. Such, indeed, was his reputation throughout the state, and such was the confidence reposed in him, that his retirement from the bench was a source of public regret.[59] When Judge Henry Goldthwaite resigned his seat upon the bench of the supreme court, Governor Fitzpatrick tendered the vacancy to Judge Saffold, who declined it.[60]

Judge Saffold, a few years after his resignation, resumed the practice of the law, and pursued it with distinguished success until his death. His political opinions, although he never sought political preferment, and engaged but little in the exciting contests of the times, were well known. He was a Democrat. He was warmly devoted to the interests of the South. The firm friend of Texan independence, he rejoiced in her annexation to the United States. A devoted husband and father, it was his fortune to raise a large family, and most nobly did he discharge his duty to them. As a master, he was kind, merciful and just. He never attached himself to any church, yet he was a firm believer in the atonement, and was accustomed to express the confident hope that he had nothing to fear beyond the grave. He died of apoplexy on the 15th February 1847. He was a large man, with an excellent face, and an exceedingly fine forehead. No man of distinction has ever died in Alabama

[58] On 16 December 1819, Saffold was one of five men—including Abner S. Lipscomb, Clement C. Clay, Richard Ellis, and Henry Y. Webb—commissioned as circuit court judges by the General Assembly. Six years later, on 27 December 1825, he was elected and commissioned as judge of the second circuit, and, when a separate state supreme court was created in 1832, he was elected as one of three justices, with Lipscomb serving as chief justice. Meador, "Supreme Court of Alabama," 896–99; Philip Phillips, *Digest of Cases Decided and Reported in the Supreme Court of the State of Alabama* (Mobile: R. R. Dade & J. S. Kellogg & Co., 1840), xv.

[59] In May 1838, Philip Henry Gosse, a young English zoologist and naturalist, encountered Judge Reuben Saffold aboard a steamboat traveling from Mobile up the Alabama River. Saffold offered Gosse a teaching position at the log schoolhouse that he and his neighbors were building near Pleasant Hill in Dallas County. Gosse spent eight months in his teaching position before departing for England from Mobile on 31 December 1838. He published articles and letters about his experiences in the English magazine, *The Home Friend,* and later in an 1859 book. Philip Henry Gosse, *Letters from Alabama, Chiefly Relating to Natural History,* intro. Harvey H. Jackson (1859; reprint, Tuscaloosa: University of Alabama Press, 1993), [8]-[13], 1, 25, 43, 303.

[60] Judge Henry Barnes Goldthwaite (1802–1847) resigned as chief justice to become the Democratic candidate for Congress but lost to his Whig opponent James Dellett. Owen, *History of Alabama,* 3: 675.

leaving behind more reputation for legal ability, and for honor, justice and probity.[61]

Israel Pickens was born on the 30th January 1780, in the county of Mecklenburg, state of North Carolina. He was the second son of Captain Samuel Pickens, a gentleman of French descent, who served his country in the Revolutionary War against the British and Tories in the two Carolinas. Israel Pickens received his academic education partly in South Carolina, but principally at a school in Iredell County, North Carolina, and finished his studies at Washington College, Pennsylvania, where he also completed his law education. He returned to his native state, established himself at Morganton in the practice of the law, lived there many years, and occasionally represented Burke County in the legislature. In 1811, he was elected to Congress from that district, and continued to represent it till the year 1817. He gave his vote for the war of 1812, and continued a firm supporter of all the prominent measures of President Madison's administration. Mr. Pickens removed to Alabama in 1817, and settled at St. Stephens, where he practiced law, and held the post of register of the land office.

After the death of Governor Bibb, Mr. Pickens was elected as his successor in 1821, and again in 1823, filling up the period allotted to him by the constitution. Very soon after the expiration of his last term as governor, a vacancy occurred in the Senate of the United States by the death of Dr. Chambers, and Governor Pickens was appointed by the executive to fill it. A few days after his departure to Washington City, a letter was received at Greensboro conveying a commission for him as district judge of the United States for Alabama, which he declined to accept. In the fall of 1826 he resigned his seat in the Senate and returned home, in consequence of a serious affection of the lungs. He died in the Island of Cuba on the 24th April 1827, at the early age of forty-seven years.[62]

Governor Pickens was six feet high, very slender and erect, with a fair complexion and blue eyes. In all the attributes of a moral nature he was, indeed, a remarkable man. His manners were easy, affable and kind—his temper mild, amiable and always the same. Benevolence was a predominant trait in his character. He had a finished education and talents of a high order—more solid than brilliant. As a public man, he was very popular, and, although mild and gentle in his deportment, no one was firmer in the discharge of his public duties. He possessed extraordinary mechanical ingenuity, and a great fondness for mathematics, natural philosophy and astronomy. While a student under Dr. Hale, of North Carolina,

[61] After resigning from the Alabama Supreme Court, Saffold lived in Mobile for a period of years before resuming his legal practice in 1843 from his office on the grounds of his plantation Belvoir. Owen, *History of Alabama*, 4: 1488; "Tribute of Respect to the Memory of Hon. Reuben Saffold," in *Reports of Cases Argued and Determined in the Supreme Court of Alabama, During the January Term*, 1848, J. J. Ormond, Reporter, vol. 13 (Tuscaloosa: M. D. J. Slade, 1848), 16.

[62] Dr. Henry H. Chambers (1790–1826), a Huntsville physician and planter, was elected to the U.S. Senate in March 1825, but he died on 24 January 1826 en route to attend the opening session of the 27th Congress. By appointing Israel Pickens to the vacant Senate seat in 1826, Governor John Murphy violated an unwritten understanding that Alabama's U.S. senators should be allocated on a north-south basis. Pickens—from Greensboro, in modern Hale County—joined William Rufus King from Dallas County in the Senate. Rogers, et al., *Alabama*, 83; Elbert L. Watson, "Henry Chambers," *Encyclopedia of Alabama*, http://www.encyclopediaofalabama.org/article/h-2943.

he invented the lunar dial, by which the time of night could be ascertained by the moon. While a member of Congress, the celebrated Reidheifer pretended to have discovered the perpetual motion, and exhibited a model in Washington City, to the inspection of which he invited the members of Congress. Mr. Pickens, with many others, attended and witnessed its performance; and being satisfied that there was deception in the matter, he returned the next day and gave it a more thorough examination. Finding the doors open, he entered, but there was no one within. During this second visit, he detected the fraud and exposed it, by inserting a card in the *National Intelligencer*, signed "A Member of Congress."[63] This brought forth a bitter reply from the impostor, and a rejoinder from the "Member of Congress," but, in a few days, Reidheifer, model and all, left the city never again to return.*

* A notice of James Jackson, a member of the convention from Autauga, will be found near the close of this volume.

[63] In 1812, Charles Redheffer (Reidheffer, Redhoeffer) set up his "perpetual motion machine" in his home near Germantown, Pennsylvania, charging up to $5 to see his machine. He repeated his fund raising scam in New York City in 1813, where Robert Fulton challenged his perpetual motion machine, declaring his machine was crank-driven. On 3 August 1816, a third documented presentation by Redheffer occurred in Philadelphia at a public meeting that he requested and was chaired by William Tilghman, chief justice of the Pennsylvania Supreme Court. However, when given the opportunity "to put his machine in motion, Mr. Redheffer replied that he could not with safety—but refused to give reasons or explanations." Israel Pickens was in Washington as a North Carolina congressman in 1811–1817 and may have encountered Redheffer between 1813 and 1817. However, Pickett does not document when Pickens confronted Charles Redheffer. "Israel Pickens," *Biographical Directory of the United States Congress, 1774-Present* (online); *Niles Weekly Register* 11 (September 7, 1816), 25–27; Robert Patterson to Thomas Jefferson, Philadelphia, 30 November 1812 [Enclosure: Drawing of Charles Redheffer's perpetual-motion machine], Looney, *Papers of Thomas Jefferson* 5: 474; Martin Gardner, *The New Age: Notes of a Fringe-Watcher* (Amherst, NY: Prometheus Books, 1991), 156–58.

Chapter XLIII

THE FIRST LEGISLATURE OF THE STATE OF ALABAMA—GOVERNOR BIBB

An election was held throughout the new state of Alabama for a governor and members of the legislature, in anticipation of the admission by Congress of the state as of a member of the American Union. William W. Bibb received 8,342 votes for governor, and his opponent, Marmaduke Williams, received 7,140.[1] The General Assembly of Alabama convened at Huntsville on the fourth Monday in October. The house of representatives was composed of forty-five members, and James Dellett, of Monroe, was elected speaker.[2] The senate had twenty-one members, and Thomas Bibb was elected president of that body.[3]

William W. Bibb was inaugurated as the first governor of the state before both houses of the legislature, in the presence of a large assemblage of citizens, to whom he made a handsome and appropriate address. He had previously presented an excellent message, in which he congratulated the people upon the abundant crops which it had pleased the Almighty to afford them, the health which they had universally enjoyed, and the fortunate termination of the convention, which had resulted in the establishment of an excellent constitution. He brought to the attention of the legislature the subject of the liberal donations by Congress in reserving for a seminary of learning seventy-two sections of land—the sixteenth section in every township for the use of schools—five percent of the net proceeds of the sales of the public lands (sold after the first of September 1819) for purposes of internal improvements—and sixteen hundred and twenty acres of land, at the confluence of the Cahaba and Alabama rivers, for a seat of government. He reported that he had laid off the town of Cahaba, and that one hundred and eighty-two lots had been sold, for $123,856—one-fourth of which, received in cash, had been deposited in the Planters' and Merchants' Bank of Huntsville, to be expended in the erection of a temporary state-house, which was then under

[1] Marmaduke Williams (1772–1850), a former North Carolina legislator and U.S. congressman (1803–1809), moved to Huntsville in 1810 and to Tuscaloosa in 1818. His brother Robert Williams served as governor of the Mississippi Territory. Although defeated by Bibb for governor in 1819, he served in the Alabama House of Representatives for eighteen years (1821–1839) and as judge of the Tuscaloosa county court from 1832 to 1842. Brantley, *Three Capitals*, 46–48, 52–53, 188; "Marmaduke Williams," Biographical Directory of the United States Congress, 1774-Present (online).

[2] James Dellett (1788–1848), a lawyer and graduate of South Carolina College, moved to Claiborne, Monroe County, Alabama Territory, in 1818. He was elected speaker of the house in 1819 and again in 1821, serving four

contract. The message concluded by recommending a revision of the statutes, the organization of the judicial department, the election of judges, and the appointment by law of an engineer to examine the rivers, who was to report in what manner their navigation might be improved.[4]

The legislature proceeded to elect two senators of the United States. William R. King and John W. Walker were elected upon the first ballot, over Thomas D. Crabb[5] and George Phillips.[6] During the session of the legislature, General Jackson visited Huntsville with his horses, and was enthusiastically engaged in the sports of the turf, then an amusement indulged in by the highest classes. Colonel Howell Rose, a senator from the county of Autauga, was also at Huntsville. Colonel Rose was then a young man of indomitable energy and fearless spirit, and possessed a native intellect of remarkable vigor and strength. He was ardent in his attachment to Jackson, and was the first to propose resolutions approbatory of his valuable services to the state performed during the late Creek and Seminole wars. Colonel Rose introduced joint resolutions of this character, together with one inviting the general to a seat within the bar both of the house and the senate on all occasions when it

terms in the General Assembly. William Travis, of Alamo fame, was his apprentice and later a law partner. Although he lost his first congressional race to John Murphy in 1833, Dellett was elected as a Whig to the Twenty-sixth (1839–1841) and Twenty-eighth (1843–1845) Congress. Brantley, *Three Capitals*, 190–91; Owen, *History of Alabama*, 3: 478; "James Dellett," Biographical Directory of the United States Congress, 1774-Present (online).

3 Thomas Bibb (1783–1839), a planter and merchant, moved from Georgia to Huntsville, Mississippi Territory in 1811 and later to a plantation in Limestone County. He was elected to the Alabama senate in 1819 where he was the presiding officer and next in line to the governor. When his brother William Wyatt Bibb died on 10 July 1820, he became governor and served out his term. He was a trustee of the Cypress Land Company and became one of the largest landowners in Alabama. Owen, *History of Alabama*, 3: 147; Brown, *John McKinley*, 34.

4 Bibb had used his influence with the Monroe administration to increase the land grant for the proposed "Seat of Government" to 1,620 acres. He contracted with Willis Roberts and Benjamin Clements to survey the town of Cahaba and conduct the sale of lots in May 1819. The sale of the 182 lots produced $30,000 in cash sales, giving Bibb the liquidity he needed to construct his proposed "State House." Brantley, *Three Capitals*, 60–63.

5 Thomas D. Crabb (1792–1829), a native of Maryland, served as a delegate to the 1819 constitutional convention from Cotaco (Morgan) County. Despite his defeat for a U.S. Senate seat in 1819, he was elected to the Alabama senate in 1822 and reelected in 1825. He operated a ferry at Crabb's Landing on the Tennessee River, and, in December 1820, the General Assembly passed an act authorizing "Thomas D. Crabb and his associates" to build a turnpike from a point west of Huntsville "to the falls of the Tuskaloosa river." Brewer, *Alabama*, 487; Harry Toulmin, comp., *A Digest of the Laws of the State of Alabama: Containing the Statutes and Resolutions at the End of the General Assembly in January, 1823* (Cahawba: Ginn & Curtis, 1823), 401–03.

6 George Phillips (1769–1835), a physician and planter, emigrated from Ireland to Delaware and later moved to North Carolina where he studied medicine and became a practicing physician. He moved to Georgia in 1803 and to Huntsville in 1815 before settling in Dallas County in 1819. Although defeated

should be his pleasure to attend those bodies, which were adopted. Colonel Rose, at the head of a committee, waited upon Jackson, with a copy of the resolutions, to which the latter replied in a letter full of the liveliest gratitude. Since that interesting occasion Colonel Rose has from time to time performed valuable services to the state, as a member of the General Assembly. He is a wealthy citizen of the county of Coosa. His mind, naturally one of the richest in the country, and improved by self-instruction, is still vigorous and clear, while his agreeable eccentricity of manner, and original ideas and sayings, engage the attention of all who are thrown in his way. His colloquial powers are of a very high as well as of a very peculiar order. He delivers his views with force and energy, and is never at a loss for a spicy repartee. While he was addressing the members of the legislature, he never failed to engage their attention. Colonel Rose was born in North Carolina, removed from thence to Georgia, and immigrated to Alabama soon after the Creek War.[7]

So soon as the judicial circuits were organized, the legislature proceeded to elect officers. Henry Hitchcock, the former territorial secretary, was elected attorney general over John N. S. Jones[8] and D. Sullivan.[9] Abner S. Lipscomb

for the U.S. Senate in 1819, Phillips represented Dallas County in both houses of the General Assembly (1823–1824, 1832–1834) and was a founder and trustee of the University of Alabama (1821–1833). Brewer, *Alabama*, 218, 233; Owen, *History of Alabama*, 4: 1357.

[7] Howell Rose (1791–1866), a lawyer and planter, emigrated from Georgia in 1816 and served three years in the first senate and became quite wealthy through his large landholdings and properties in Autauga, Coosa, Elmore, and Lowndes counties. His interest in business opportunities and markets led him to attend a "Free Trade Convention" in Philadelphia in September 1831 with ten other Alabamians, including John A. Elmore, Henry Goldthwaite, Enoch Parsons, and Benijah S. Bibb. Brewer, *Alabama*, 239; Owen, *History of Alabama*, 4: 1462; "Free Trade Convention," *Niles Weekly Register* 41 (October 29, 1831), 166.

[8] John N. S. Jones (1793–1853), a lawyer and planter, was practicing law at the time of his defeat for the office of attorney general. In fact, his law office was located in a small frame building that became the first library in Alabama—the Huntsville Library Company—opened in October 1819. According to the 1850 Alabama Slave Census for Limestone County, Jones was one of the largest slave owners in the county with 115 slaves. However, under an act of the General Assembly of 11 December 1820, he was "authorized and empowered to manumit and set free" a mulatto woman named Elizabeth, aged forty, and her children: Evelina, age thirteen; Ann, age six; and Shandy, age three. Shandy Wesley Jones served in the Alabama House of Representatives in 1868–1870 and President Grant appointed him to a position with the customs office in Mobile. Brantley, *Three Capitals*, 57; Sarah Huff Fisk, "Mapping 1819 Huntsville in Retrospect," *Huntsville Historical Review* 33 (Winter-Spring 2008), 23; 1850 Alabama Slave Census, Limestone County, District 3; *Acts Passed by the Second Session of the General Assembly of the State of Alabama* (Cahawba: Allen & Brickwell, 1820), 62; Richard Bailey, *Neither Carpetbaggers Nor Scalawags: Black Officeholders During the Reconstruction of Alabama*, 1867–1878 (Montgomery: NewSouth books, 2009), 46–48, 78, 109–110, 142.

[9] Despite losing his election for attorney general, William Dunklin Sullivan (1791–1837), a successful lawyer and planter, served two terms in the Alabama senate as Perry County's first state senator

was elected judge of the first judicial circuit over Harry Toulmin;[10] Reuben Saffold, judge of the second without opposition;[11] Henry Y. Webb, judge of the third without opposition;[12] Richard Ellis,[13] judge of the fourth over Beverly Hughes[14] and John McKinley; Clement C. Clay, judge of the fifth without opposition.[15] John Gayle was elected solicitor of the first judicial circuit without opposition;[16] Constantine Perkins, of the third,[17] over Sion L. Perry;[18] Peter Martin, of the fourth, without opposition;[19] James Eastland, of the fifth, over James W. McClung and Poladore Naylor.[20]

The legislature was exceedingly anxious to see the laws enforced; and, for that purpose, selected magistrates from among the most respectable and prominent men throughout the state. They discharged the same duties which

(1822–1824, 1825–1827). During his service in the senate, he opposed the efforts of Nicholas Davis, Thomas D. Crabb, and others to move the capital to Tuscaloosa. He also served as a probate judge in Perry County for a number years, was elected to the Alabama house in 1837, and died on 1 December 1837 while attending a session in Tuscaloosa. Brantley, *Three Capitals*, 57, 162, 164, 174–75, 187; Brewer, *Alabama*, 98; Owen, *History of Alabama*, 4: 1637.

[10] Abner Smith Lipscomb (1789–1856), a native of South Carolina, studied law under John C. Calhoun and George Bowie in Abbeville, South Carolina, before immigrating to Washington County, Mississippi Territory, in 1811. His first judicial circuit included Baldwin, Washington, Clarke, Monroe, and Conecuh counties in 1819. When the General Assembly created a separate supreme court in 1832, he became the first chief justice of the new court. In 1835, Lipscomb resigned from the court and moved to Mobile, where he was elected to the legislature in 1838. He moved to Texas in 1839, practiced law, served as secretary of state in 1840, and was a member of the 1845 constitutional convention before his appointment as an associate justice of the Texas Supreme Court in 1846. Meador, "Supreme Court of Alabama," 896–97; Owen, *History of Alabama*, 3: 1052; Mary J. Highsmith, "Abner Smith Lipscomb," Handbook of Texas Online.

[11] Reuben Saffold (1788–1847) emigrated from Georgia to the Mississippi Territory in 1813, where he served in the militia during the Creek War of 1813–1814 and represented Clarke County in the territorial assembly. He was practicing law in Dallas County when he was elected judge of the second judicial circuit, which included Henry, Butler, Wilcox, Dallas, Autauga, and Montgomery counties. He became one of three justices under the newly organized supreme court in 1832, and he served as chief justice in 1835–1836 before resuming his law practice in 1836. Meador, "Supreme Court of Alabama," 897; Owen, *History of Alabama*, 4: 1488.

[12] Henry Young Webb (1784–1823), a graduate of the University of North Carolina, served in the North Carolina legislature prior to his appointment as a judge of the Mississippi Territory by President James Monroe in 1818. He had moved to Greene County, Alabama, when he was elected judge of the third judicial circuit, which included Marengo, Greene, Perry, Cahawba (renamed Bibb), Tuscaloosa, and Jefferson counties. Meador, "Supreme Court of Alabama," 897; Owen, *History of Alabama*, 4: 1738.

[13] Richard Ellis (1781–1835) was admitted to the Virginia bar in 1806 and practiced law there before moving to Huntsville in 1817. He moved to Franklin County, where he continued his law practice and established a plantation. His fourth judicial circuit included Limestone, Lauderdale, Franklin, Lawrence, and Marion counties. Ellis moved his family and slaves to Pecan Point in 1834, settling on a land grant of 4,428.4 acres in modern Bowie County, Texas. In 1836, he was elected to the Texas constitutional convention and, as president of the convention, signed the Texas Declaration of Independence on 2 March 1836. Before retiring from public service, he served as a senator in the first, second, third, and fourth

congresses of the Republic of Texas between 1836 and 1840. Meador, "Supreme Court of Alabama," 897; Owen, *History of Alabama*, 3:536, 539; Joe E. Ericson, "Richard Ellis," Handbook of Texas Online.

[14] Beverly Hughes, a lawyer and planter, was an early immigrant to Huntsville in 1816, and he served as a superior court judge for the Mississippi Territory, replacing Obadiah Jones. He joined Thomas Bibb and Nicholas Davis as representatives from Limestone County to the 1819 constitutional convention, and he served on the committee of fifteen that drafted a proposed state constitution. Brewer, *Alabama*, 326; Lewis, *Clearing the Thickets*, 135; Owen, *History of Alabama*, 3: 867.

[15] Clement Comer Clay (1789–1866), a native of Virginia, graduated from East Tennessee University in Knoxville and read law with Hugh Lawson White before starting his long career as an Alabama public servant. He volunteered for service in the Creek War of 1813–1814 in Huntsville, which led to his election in 1817 to the Alabama Territory Assembly and in 1819 to the constitutional convention. His fifth judicial circuit included Shelby, St. Clair, Jackson, Madison, and Cotaco (renamed Morgan) counties, and he served as Alabama's first supreme court justice, resigning in 1823. Meador, "Supreme Court of Alabama," 897–98; Owen, *History of Alabama*, 3: 342–43.

[16] John Gayle (1792–1859), a graduate of South Carolina College in 1813, settled near Mount Vernon, Washington County, Mississippi Territory, and served in a local militia in the Creek War of 1813–1814. He completed law studies under Judge Abner Smith Lipscomb and opened a law office at Claiborne, Monroe County, in 1818. Gayle served in the Alabama territorial assembly prior to his appointment as solicitor in the first judicial district and the beginning of a long public life, including two terms as governor (1831–1833, 1833–1835). Sarah Woolfolk Wiggins, "John Gayle," in *Alabama Governors*, 37–40; Owen, *History of Alabama*, 3: 646–47.

[17] Constantine Perkins (1792–1836), a Tennessean and graduate of Cumberland College, served under Andrew Jackson during the Creek War and served as a Tennessee district solicitor. Shortly after moving to Tuscaloosa in 1819, he was elected solicitor of the third judicial district , followed by his election as attorney general in 1825. He was elected to the Alabama house in 1832 and to the senate in 1834. Owen, *History of Alabama*, 4: 1342; Brewer, *Alabama*, 553, 570.

[18] Sion (Simon) L. Perry (1793–1800), a native of Tennessee, started his law practice at Sevierville before volunteering in the Creek War of 1813–1814. He moved to Huntsville in 1815 and relocated to Tuscaloosa County in 1818, practicing law with Henry W. Collier. He served in the General Assembly (1821–1822) prior to serving as a district circuit court judge for six years (1828–1831). Owen, *History of Alabama*, 4: 1344; Brewer, *Alabama*, 553, 570.

[19] Peter Martin (1793–1863), elder brother of Joshua L. Martin, Alabama's eighth governor (1845–1847), started his law practice in Russellville, Franklin County, Alabama, before his election as solicitor for the fourth judicial circuit. He served a term in the Alabama house (1825–1826) from Franklin County and served as attorney general (1832–1836). Governor Clement C. Clay appointed Martin to the circuit court in 1836, and he was elected twice by the legislature before resigning in 1843. He served a term in the Alabama house (1844–1845) before resuming his law practice in Tuscaloosa. Owen, *History of Alabama*, 4: 1167–68; Brewer, *Alabama*, 560, 571.

[20] Unfortunately, this editor failed to find additional biographical information on James Eastland and Poladore Naylor. On the first vote by the combined houses of the General Assembly for solicitor of the fifth circuit, none of the candidates received a majority. On the second vote, Eastland was declared the winner, with 36 votes, over Naylor, with 23 votes, and James W. McClung, with 8 votes. Although defeated for solicitor, McClung (1798–1848), a graduate of the University of North Carolina in 1816 and nephew of Hugh Lawson White, practiced law in Huntsville and served multiple terms in the Alabama house. He served as speaker of the house in 1835, 1837, and 1838 and was reelected to the house in 1842 and 1844. McClung was defeated as an independent candidate for governor in 1841 by Benjamin Fitzpatrick but won a senate seat in 1845. Owen, *History of Alabama*, 4: 1094; House Journal, Annual Session 1819, http://www.legislature.state.al.us/aliswww/history/acts_and_journals/House_Journal_1819_Oct_25-Dec_17/Page44_Dec14.html, 174.

the judges of the county courts had done previous to the adoption of the present probate system, and as was the practice of Virginia. A few of those now selected must be mentioned merely to show the determination of our then infant state, to give tone and dignity to the administration of the laws, even in inferior courts. For the county of Autauga, for instance, John A. Elmore, John Armstrong,[21] Robert Gaston,[22] James Jackson and William R. Pickett were elected magistrates.

General John A. Elmore, one of these justices, was a native of South Carolina, of the legislature of which state he had often been a respectable member. Not long after his removal to Alabama, he represented the county of Autauga in our legislature, which then sat at Cahaba. He was a man of firmness and much good sense, and always delivered his opinions, even in common conversation, in a distinct and loud voice, with that candor and honesty which characterized his conduct through life. He had a commanding appearance, was large in person, and, altogether, an exceedingly fine looking man. He delighted in the sports of the chase, being a most successful and spirited hunter, and an agreeable companion in the many camp-hunts in which he engaged with his neighbors and friends. Towards the close of his life, we remember that he presented a dignified and venerable appearance, and we saw him preside as chairman of several large and exciting meetings in the town of Montgomery, during the days of nullification.[23]

James Jackson, another of these magistrates, was born in the county of Wilkes, Georgia. He had been a man of influence in that region. Upon his arrival, in 1818, in the territory of Alabama, he immediately ranked with the leading men of the county of Autauga. He was elected a member of the state convention, and assisted to give us the excellent constitution we now have. Afterwards, Mr. Jackson was several times an active and influential member of the house of representatives and of the senate of the state of Alabama. He died the 19th July 1832, at his residence in Autauga, within a few miles of that of General Elmore, who also died about that period. Mr. Jackson was a man for whom nature had done much. Although raised upon the frontiers of Georgia, among a rude population, and thrown upon the world with but little means and still less education, he was decidedly elegant in conversation and polite and polished in his manners. He had the faculty of adapting himself to all classes. In person he was of medium size, his face was handsome and expressive, and, when meeting a friend, was generally enlivened with a smile. He was a most excellent and liberal neighbor. Smooth and fluent in conversation, and conciliating in his general views, he was a most delightful fireside companion. He was shrewd and sagacious, and a close and correct observer of human nature.[24]

[21] John Armstrong (c.1769–1844), elected as a magistrate for Autauga County in 1819, was apparently an early settler, perhaps arriving before 1818. He married Nancy Kittle (1777–1852) of Effingham County, Georgia. "John Armstrong," http://listsearches.rootsweb.com/th/read/armstrong-gen-only/2001-01/0980486478.

[22] Robert Gaston (1774–1830), a native of North Carolina, was one of the five magistrates elected by the General Assembly for Autauga County. He had also been appointed by the final territorial assembly to a five member committee which included Zachariah Pope, Alex R. Hutchinson, Alsey Pollard, and Zaccheus Powell to select a site for the permanent county seat of Autauga County. Brewer, *Alabama*, 108; Owen, *History of Alabama*, 1: 77.

[23] John A. Elmore (1762–1834), a veteran of the American Revolution, emigrated from South Carolina to Autauga County in 1819 and served a term in the Alabama house (1821–1822). When Elmore County was created in 1866 from territory taken from Autauga, Coosa, Montgomery, and Tallapoosa counties, it was named for him. Brewer, *Alabama*, 109, 236; Owen, *History of Alabama*, 3: 540–41.

The author, being the son of William R. Pickett, another of the Autauga magistrates, is relieved from the delicate task of portraying his character by copying the following obituary, written by a friend for the gazettes:

"Colonel William Raiford Pickett died at his residence, in Autauga County, on the 20th September 1850, aged seventy-three years. Colonel Pickett was born in Anson County, North Carolina, upon the Pee Dee River, where his parents, James Pickett and Martha Terry, had removed some time before the Revolutionary War from their place of nativity, near Bowling Green, in Caroline County, Virginia. Their ancestors, whose extraction was Scotch, English and French, were among the earliest colonists of Virginia.[25]

"Soon after he became of age Colonel Pickett filled the post of sheriff of Anson County, and was afterwards elected to the legislature, which sat at Raleigh, where he served for several years. When the federal revenue was collected by direct taxation, he received from Mr. Madison, then president, the appointment of assessor and collector for a large district in North Carolina, the arduous and responsible duties of which he discharged to the end with zeal and fidelity.

"In the spring of 1818 he brought his family out to this country, and established himself as a planter and merchant in the present Autauga County, which then formed a portion of the county of Montgomery. Two years before this early period he had explored these southwestern wilds, in company with his near relative and friend, Tod Robinson, encountering dangers and hardships incident upon the close of a sanguinary war with the Creeks.[26]

"When the legislature of Alabama sat at Cahawba, Colonel Pickett took his seat in that body in 1821. In 1823 he was a member, and again in 1824, which term closed his duties in the lower house. In 1828 he was elected to the state senate, and entered that body in the fall of that year at Tuscaloosa, then the capital of Alabama. He was a senator for the period of five years, when, in the summer of 1834, he was beaten for that position by Colonel Broadnax, during an exceedingly high state of party excitement, the election turning solely upon party grounds, and many of his old friends voting against him with much reluctance.[27] In his legislative career, he was an active and very influential member, and was the originator of many salutary laws, some of which are still in force. In the meantime, he was three times placed upon the Democratic electoral ticket for president and vice president, and each time received overwhelming majorities.

[24] James Jackson (1773–1832), a lawyer and planter, served one term in the Alabama house (1820–1821) and one term in the senate (1825–1826). When he died in 1832, he provided for the division of his estate, which included forty-six slaves, between his wife, Temperance Motley, son, Crawford Jackson, son-in-law, Lunsford Long, and nephew, William Jackson, in Georgia. Brewer, *Alabama,* 112; "Probate Records for James Jackson, Autauga, Alabama," http://files.usgwarchives.net/al/autauga/court/jjackpro.txt; "James Jackson & Temperance Motley," http://archiver.rootsweb.ancestry.com/th/read/ALAUTAUG/1999-08/0934552271.

[25] Colonel William Raiford Pickett's obituary was published in the 10 October 1850 issue of the *Alabama Journal.*

[26] Tod Robinson (1766–1838), a native of Anson County, North Carolina, explored the future Autauga County with his first cousin, William Raiford Pickett, in 1816, purchased land in 1817, and moved his family to Alabama in 1819. He became a prominent planter in Autauga County and purchased additional land in Montgomery County. "Tod Robinson, Sr.," http://alabamapioneers.com/biography-tod-robinson-sr-born-1776/#sthash.n301QK0N.dpuf.

[27] Robert Broadnax (1792–1877), a lawyer and planter, immigrated to Autauga County from Georgia after the Creek War of 1813–1814. He won

"He was a man of sterling honor and integrity, and, perhaps, no one ever surpassed him in disinterested benevolence and charity, for he not only supported the poor and destitute around him, but freely dispensed to those upon the highway. In person, he was large, erect and commanding, with a face beaming with intelligence, a forehead bold and lofty, and eyes brilliant and expressive, to the last moments of his existence. He was peculiarly remarkable for his wit and originality, and the risible faculties of more men have been aroused, while in his company, than in that of almost any other person. And even to this day, in North Carolina, though thirty-two years have transpired since he left that state, his original sayings and anecdotes are often repeated. No man ever received more attention, during his protracted illness, from those in his immediate neighborhood, who deeply mourn his departure from their midst. Persons from all parts of the country visited him in his affliction."[28]

The legislature of Alabama, during its session at Huntsville, enacted many salutary laws, and judiciously arranged the districts. Six new counties were established, and were added to those already organized. They were Greene, Jefferson, Perry, Henry, Wilcox, and Butler. Wilcox was named in honor of the lieutenant, who, in 1814, was killed by the Indians upon the Alabama River, as we have seen, and Butler in memory of the captain, who was also killed by the Indians, near Fort Dale, on the 20th March 1818.[29] The legislature adjourned on the 17th December 1819.*

The land offices at Milledgeville and Huntsville were in active operation. Extensive surveys had been completed, sales had been everywhere proclaimed, and thousands of eager purchasers flocked into the country from every Atlantic and western state. Never before or since, did the population of any state so rapidly increase as that of Alabama from the period of 1820 until 1830.[30]

No sooner had the flourishing state of Alabama been thoroughly organized, than the citizens were called upon to mourn the death of their first governor. Riding in the forest one day, the horse of Governor Bibb fell with him to the ground, and he then received an injury from which he never recovered. He died at his residence, in the county of Autauga, in July 1820, in

* State archives.

consecutive terms in the Alabama house from 1825 through 1833. He served in the Creek War of 1836 and was generally referred to as Colonel Broadnax. He later moved to Mobile, spent two years in Cuba studying tobacco cultivation, and settled in Clarke County, where he raised tobacco. During the Civil War, he represented Clarke, Monroe, and Baldwin counties in the senate in 1863–1864. After the Civil War, he immigrated to Brazil in 1867, returning to Alabama in1874. Brewer, *Alabama*, 110, 112; Owen, *History of Alabama*, 3: 221.

[28] While Pickett quotes most of his father's obituary from the *Alabama Journal*, his mother's obituary had appeared in the same paper on 15 August 1850. Fanny Amelia Dickson Pickett died on 4 August 1850 "at Cedar Grove, Autauga County, Alabama, aged seventy years and four months." Her father, Colonel William Dickson (1739–1820), civic leader and public servant, served in North Carolina's colonial assemblies, provincial congresses, house of commons, and clerk of the court of pleas and quarter sessions (1777–1819). A veteran of the Revolutionary War, he served in the militia and saw significant action receiving at least one wound. *Alabama Journal*, 15 August 1850; Charles M. Ingram, "William Dickson," *Dictionary of North Carolina Biography*, 2: 68–69.

[29] In mid-February 1814, West Point graduate Lieutenant James M. Wilcox was killed by a Red Stick war party near the confluence of the Alabama and Cahaba rivers. On 20 March 1818, Captain William Butler was killed when Uchee (Yuchi) dissidents led by Savannah Jack attacked his small party between Fort Bibb and Fort Dale. Brannon, "The Massacres"; Brewer, *Alabama*, 145–46, 577; O'Brien, *In Bitterness and in Tears*, 131–32.

[30] In the decade from 1810 to 1820,

the fortieth year of his age—calm, collected, peaceful—surrounded by numerous friends and relations.[31]

Governor Bibb was five feet ten inches in height, with an erect but delicate frame. He was exceedingly easy and graceful in his bearing. His interesting face bore the marks of deep thought and great intelligence. His eyes, of a dark color, were mild, yet expressive. Whether thrown into the company of the rude or the refined, his language was pure and chaste. No one ever lived, either in Georgia or Alabama, who was treated with a greater degree of respect by all classes. This was owing to his high moral character, unsurpassed honor, excellent judgment, and a very high order of talents. Entirely free from that dogmatism and those patronizing airs which characterize many of our distinguished men, he invariably treated the opinions of the humblest citizen with courtesy and respect. He was, however, a man of firmness, swaying the minds of men with great success, and governing by seeming to obey.

In all the stations which he filled, Governor Bibb was eminently successful. When quite a young man his skill and attention as a physician, in the then flourishing town of Petersburg, Georgia, secured for him an extensive practice. He next went into the legislature from Elbert County, and, serving four years in that body, acquired a popularity rarely attained by one of his age. At the early age of twenty-five he was elected to Congress under the general ticket system, by a vote so large as to leave no doubt but that he was a great favorite with the people. He immediately became a leading member of the lower house of the national legislature—was an able and fearless advocate of the war of 1812, and a conscientious supporter of the administration of Madison. His contemporaries, at his first election, were Bolling Hall, George M. Troup, and Howell Cobb. He had not been long in Congress before his popularity caused him to come within a few votes of being elected to the office of Speaker of the House. Afterwards the legislature of Georgia elected him to the Senate of the United States.[32] He was thus a member of Congress from 1806 until 1816, when as we have seen in the preceding pages, he was appointed by the president, governor of Alabama Territory, and was afterwards elected by the people governor of the state of Alabama. In reference to his congressional career, we have often heard, from the lips of many of his distinguished contemporaries, that the practical order of his mind, the wisdom of his views, and the peculiar music of his voice, contributed to render him one of the most attractive and effective of speakers.

Alabama's population had increased more than 1,000 percent to 127,901, with the greatest growth occurring after 1815. From 1820 to 1830, the state's population grew by 142 percent, reaching 309,527—greater growth than any of the surrounding states. Rogers, et al, *Alabama*, 54.

31 Although he was only in his fortieth year, William Wyatt Bibb was not in good health, suffering from tuberculosis and a kidney injury. When thrown from his horse, he suffered a serious head injury and contusions that led to his death on 10 July 1820. Ibid., 72–73; Brantley, *Three Capitals*, 71; Daniel S. Dupre, "William Wyatt Bibb and Thomas Bibb," in *Alabama Governors*, 17–18.

32 William Wyatt Bibb, a native of Virginia, started his political career in the Georgia house of representatives in 1803–05. He was elected to Congress in 1807 to fill a vacancy caused by the resignation of Thomas Spalding and won re-election to the Tenth through Thirteenth Congresses. He resigned from the House of Representatives in November 1813 when he was elected to replace William H. Crawford in the U.S. Senate, serving from 6 November 1813 until his resignation on 9 November 1816 to become governor of the Alabama Territory. "William Wyatt Bibb," Biographical Directory of the United States Congress, 1774-Present (online).

When Governor Bibb first established himself as a physician he married Mary, only daughter of Colonel Holman Freeman, of Revolutionary memory, and then a citizen of Wilkes County. She was one of the most beautiful and accomplished ladies of her day, and has ever been esteemed and admired by the early inhabitants of Alabama. She is now residing in the county of Dallas, in the enjoyment of fine health. Governor Bibb left two children by this lady—a son and a daughter. The latter, the late Mrs. Alfred V. Scott, who died some years ago, was much like her father in the mildness of her disposition, the grace and ease of her manners, and the intellectual beauty of her face.[33] After the death of Governor Bibb his brother, Thomas Bibb, who was president of the senate, became the acting governor. He was a man of strong mind and indomitable energy.[34]

In the preceding pages we have alluded to the mother of Governor Bibb. She was one of the most remarkable women we ever knew, for energy, decision, and superior sense. When Captain Bibb, her husband, died, he left her with eight children, and an estate much embarrassed by debt. Benajah, the ninth child, was born a few months after the death of his father. Mrs. Bibb worked the estate out of debt—educated her children, and lived to see them all in affluence, and many of them enjoying offices of honor and profit. She was known to the early inhabitants of Alabama, by whom she was much esteemed, as Mrs. Barnett, having married a gentleman of that name.[35] Thomas Bibb resembled his mother more than any of the children, in the native strength of his mind and energy of his character. The memory of Governor William Wyatt Bibb is preserved in the name of a county in Georgia, and one in Alabama.

But here we lay down our pen. The early history of Alabama, as far as it rests in our hands, is ended, and our task is accomplished. To some other person, fonder than we are of the dry details of state legislation and fierce party spirit, we leave the task of bringing the history down to a later period.

THE END.

[33] The surviving children of William Wyatt and Mary Ann Freeman Bibb were George Bailey Bibb (1804–1866) and Mary William Bibb Scott (1809–1837), wife of Alfred Vernon Scott (1903–1860). Mary Bibb Scott gave birth to six children in eight year; one died in infancy and she died sometime after the birth of her last child. James Edmonds Saunders and Elizabeth Saunders Blair Stubbs, *Early Settlers of Alabama: With Notes and Genealogies,* 2 parts in 1 (New Orleans: L. Graham & Son, Ltd., 1899), part 1: 435–36; "Mary William Bibb Scott," http://www.ancestry.com; "George Bailey Bibb," http://wc.rootsweb.ancestry.com.

[34] Thomas Bibb completed the final eighteen months of his brother's term in 1821, fought with the senate, and refused to stand for reelection. He subsequently represented Limestone County in the Alabama house in 1828–1830 and served as director of the Huntsville branch of the state bank. Brantley, *Three Capitals,* 73–74, 84–85, 87, 91–92, 95–97; Brewer, *Alabama,* 327; Owen, *History of Alabama,* 3: 147; Daniel S. Dupre, "William Wyatt Bibb and Thomas Bibb," in *Alabama Governors,* 17–18.

[35] Sally Wyatt Bibb Barnett (1759–1826), a descendant of Virginia Governor Francis Wyatt, was the second wife of Captain William Bibb (1735–1796) of Prince Edward County, Virginia, and later of Elbert County, Georgia. On 21 March 1807, she married William Barnett in Elbert County, Georgia. "Queries," *William and Mary Quarterly* 12 (January 1904): 273; Saunders and Stubbs, *Early Settlers of Alabama,* part 1: 435–36.

Pickett's Bibliography

Adair, James. *History of the American Indians; Particularly Those Nations adjoining to the Missisippi [sic] East and West Florida, Georgia, South and North Carolina, and Virginia.* London: Edward and Charles Dilly, 1775. [Pickett Book Collection, ADAH].

American State Papers: Documents, Legislative and Executive, of the Congress of the United States. Edited by Walter Lowie and Mathew St. Clair Clarke. 38 vols. Washington, DC: Gales and Seaton, 1832–1861.

Archaeologia Americana. Transactions and Collections of the American Antiquarian Society. Vol. 2. Cambridge: The Society, 1836.

Bancroft, George. *History of the United States, From the Discovery of the Continent.* 8 vols. Boston: Charles Bowen, 1834–1848; Boston: Little, Brown and Company, 1844–1852.

Barbé-Marbois, François marquis de. *The History of Louisiana: Particularly of the Cession of that Colony to the United States of America: With an Introductory Essay on the Constitution and Government of the United States. Translated from the French by an American Citizen.* Philadelphia: Carey & Leo, 1830.

Barcía Carballido y Zúñiga, Andrés González de, ed. *Historiadores primitivos de las Indias Occidentales, que juntò, traduxo en parte, y sacò à luz, ilustrados con erudìtas notas, y copiosos indices, el ill.* 3 vols. Madrid: 1749. [Pickett Book Collection, ADAH].

Bartram, William. *Travels Through North & South Carolina, Georgia, East & West Florida, the Cherokee Country, the Extensive Territories of the Muscogulges, or Creek Confederacy, and the Country of the Chactaws: Containing an Account of the Soil and Natural Productions of Those Regions, Together With Observations On the Manners of the Indians.* Philadelphia: Printed by James & Johnson, 1791.

Baudry des Lozieres, Louis-Narcisse. *Voyage à la Louisiane et sur le continent de l'Amérique septentrionale, fait dans les années 1794 à 1798; Contenant un Tableau historique de la Louisiane, des observations sur son climat, ses riches productions, le caractère et le nom des Sauvages, des remarques importantes sur la navigation, des principes d'administration, de législation et de gouvernement propres à cette Colonie, etc. etc.* Paris: Dentu, 1802.

Biedma, Luis Hernandez de. *Relation de ce qui arrive pendant le voyage du Capitaine Soto par Luis Hernandez de Biedma.* Paris: Inédit, 1841.

Bossu, Jean-Bernard. *Travels Through That Part of North America Formerly Called Louisiana; By Mr. Bossu, Captain in the French Marines.* Translated by Johann Reinhold Forster. 2 vols. London: T. Davies, 1771.

Brackenridge, Henry M. *History of the Late War, Between the United States and Great Britain: Comprising a Minute Account of the Various Military and Naval Operations.* Pittsburgh: C. H. Kay & Co., 1839.

Bradford, Alexander W. *American Antiquities and Researches into the Origin and History of the Red Race.* New York: Wiley & Putnam, 1843. [Pickett Book Collection, ADAH].

Cabeza de Vaca, Alvár Núñez. *Naufragios de Álvar Nuñez Cabeza de Vaca, y Relación de la Jornada, que hizo a la Florida con el adelantado Pánfilo de Narváez.* In *Historiadores primitivos de las Indias Occidentales, que junto, truduxo en parte y sacó a luz.* Vol. 1. Edited by Andrés Gonzáles Barcia Carballido y Zúñiga. Madrid: 1749.

Carroll, Bartholomew Rivers, comp. *Historical Collections of South Carolina: Embracing many Rare and valuable Pamphlets, and Other Documents, Relating to the History of That State, from Its first Discovery to Its Independence in the Year 1776.* 2 vols. New York: Harper & Brothers, 1836. [Pickett Book Collection, ADAH].

Charlevoix, Pierre-François Xavier de. *Journal of a Voyage to North America, Undertaken by Order of the French King.* Translated from the French of P. de Charlevoix. 2 vols. London: R. and J. Dodsley, 1761. [Pickett Book Collection, ADAH].

Chateaubriand, François René, vicomte de. *Les Natchez, Oeuvres de M. le vicomte de Chateaubriand.* 2 vols. Paris: Lefevre, 1833.

_______. *Voyage en Amérique, suivi des Natchez.* Paris: Lefèvre, 1838.

Claiborne, Nathaniel H. *Notes on the War in the South; With*

Biographical Sketches of the Lives of Montgomery, Jackson, Sevier, the late Gov. Claiborne, and Others. Richmond: William Ramsay, 1819.

Clark, Daniel. *Proofs of the Corruption of Gen. James Wilkinson, and of His Connection with Aaron Burr, With a Full Refutation of His Slanderous Allegations in Relation to the Character of the Principal Witness Against Him*. Philadelphia: Wm. Hall, Jun. & Geo. W. Pierie, Printers, 1809.

Cobbett, William. *Life of Andrew Jackson: President of the United States of America*. London: Bolt-Court, 1834.

Compere, Lee, et al. "Supplementary Vocabularies of Muskhogee, Chocta, Caddo, Mohawk, Seneca, and Cherokee." In *Archaeologia Americana: Transactions and Collections of the American Antiquarian Society*. Vol. 2. Cambridge: The Society, 1836.

Coxe, Daniel. *A description of the English province of Carolana: by the Spaniards call'd Florida, and by the French, la Louisiane*. London: Olive Payne, 1741.

Crabb, George. *Universal Historical Dictionary, or, Explanation of the Names of Persons and Places in the Departments of Biblical, Political, and Ecclesiastical History, Mythology, Heraldry, Biography, Bibliography, Geography, and Numismatics*. 2 vols. London: Baldwin, Craddock, and Joy, 1825. [Pickett Book Collection, ADAH].

Darby, William. *A Geographical Description of the State of Louisiana: The Southern Part of Mississippi, and the Territory of Alabama; Presenting a View of the Soil, Climate, Animal, Vegetable, and Mineral Productions; Illustrative of the Natural Physiognomy, their Geographical Configuration, and relative Situation; With an Account of the Character and Manners of the Inhabitants; Together with a Map*. 2d Ed. New York: James Olmstead, 1817. [Pickett Book Collection, ADAH].

Davis, Matthew L. *Memoirs of Aaron Burr. With Miscellaneous Selections from His Correspondence*. 2 vols. New York: Harper & Brothers, 1836–1837.

D'Elvas, Fidalgo (Gentleman of Elvas). "A Narrative of the Expedition of Hernando de Soto into Florida, by a Gentleman of Elvas, translated from the Portuguese by Richard Hackluyt, in 1609." Vol. 2. In *Documents Relating to the History of Louisiana*. Edited by Benjamin Franklin French. New York: Wiley and Putnam, 1850.

Dow, Lorenzo. *History of a Cosmopolite; or the Four Volumes of the Rev. Lorenzo Dow's Journal, concentrated in One, containing his Experience and Travels from Childhood to 1814*. 5th ed. Wheeling, Va.: Joshua Martin, 1848.

Drake, Benjamin. *Life of Tecumseh, and His Brother the Prophet; With a Historical Sketch of the Shwanoe Indians*. Cincinnati: E. Morgan & Co., 1841.

Du Lac, Francois Marie Perrin. *Voyage dans les deux Louisianes, et chez les nations sauvages du Missouri, par les États-Unis, l'Ohio et les Provinces qui le bordent, en 1801, 1802 et 1803; avec un aperçu des moeurs, des usages, du caractère et des coutumes religieuses et civiles des peuples de ces diverses contrées*. Paris: Capelle et Renand, 1805.

Dumont de Montigny, Jean-Francois-Benjamin. *Mémoires historiques sur la Louisiane, Contenant ce qui y est arrivé de plus mémorable depuis l'année 1687. jusqu'à présent; avec l'établissement de la Colonie Francoise dans cette Province de l'Amérique Septentrionale sous la direction de la Compagnie des Indes; le climat, la natur & les productions de ce pays; l'origine & la religion des Sauvages qui l'habitent; leurs murs & leurs coutumes, &c*. Edited by Jean Baptiste Le Mascrier. 2 vols. Paris: C. J. B. Bauche, 1753.

Dwight, Timothy. *Travels in New England and New York*. 4 vols. London: W. Baynes and Son, and Ogle, Duncan & Co., 1823.

Eaton, John Henry. *The Life of Andrew Jackson, Major-General in the Service of the United States: Comprising a History of the War in the South, From the Commencement of the Creek Campaign, to the Termination of the Hostilities before New Orleans*. Philadelphia: S. F. Bradford, 1824. [Pickett Book Collection, ADAH].

Ellicott, Andrew. *The Journal of Andrew Ellicott, Late Commissioner on behalf of the United States During Part of the Year 1796, the years 1797, 1798, 1799, and Part of the year 1800: For Determining the Boundary Between the United States and Possessions of his Catholic Majesty in America*. Philadelphia: William Fry, 1814.

Flint, Timothy. *The History and Geography of the Mississippi Valley; To Which is Appended a Condensed Physical Geography of the Atlantic United States, and the Whole American Continent*. 3d ed. 2 vols. Cincinnati: E. H. Flint; Boston: Carter, Hendree and Co., 1833. [Pickett Book Collection, ADAH].

Force, Peter, comp. *Tracts and Other Papers Relating Principally to the Origin, settlement, and Progress of the Colonies in North America, From the Discovery of the Country to the Year 1776*. 4 vols. Washington: Peter

Force, 1836–1844; Washington: Wm. Q. Force, 1846. [Pickett Book Collection, ADAH].

French, Benjamin Franklin, comp. *Historical Collections of Louisiana: Embracing Translations of Many Rare and Valuable Documents Relating to the Natural, Civil and Political History of the State; Compiled with Historical and Biographical Notes, and an Introduction, by B.F. French.* 5 vols. New York: Wiley and Putnam, et al., 1846–1853. [Pickett Book Collection, ADAH].

Gallatin, Albert. "A Synopsis of the Indian tribes of North America," *Archaeologia Americana. Transactions and Collections of the American Antiquarian Society.* Cambridge: The Society, 1836. Vol. 2.

Gayarré, Charles. *Histoire de la Louisiane.* 2 vols. Nouvelle Orléans: Magne & Weisse, 1846–1847. [Pickett Book Collection, ADAH].

_______. *Louisiana: Its Colonial History and Romance.* New York: Harper & Brothers, 1851.

Georgia Historical Society. *Collections of the Georgia Historical Society.* Vols. 1–3. Savannah: Georgia Historical Society, 1840–1848.

Gravier, Charles, Comte de Vergennes. *Mémoire historique et politique sur la Louisiane, par M. de Vergennes, Ministre de Louis XVI, accompagné d'un précis de la vie de ce ministre, et suivi d'autres mémoires sur l'Indostan, Saint-Domingue, la Corse et la Guyane.* Paris: Lepetit Jeune, 1802.

Harris, Thaddeus Mason. *Biographical Memorials of James Oglethorpe, Founder of the Colony of Georgia in North America.* Boston: Freeman and Bolles, 1841. [Pickett Book Collection, ADAH].

Hawkins, Benjamin. "A Sketch of the Creek Country, In the Years 1798–1799." *Collections of the Georgia Historical Society.* Vol. 3, pt. 1. Savannah: Georgia Historical Society, 1848. [Pickett Book Collection, ADAH].

Haywood, John. *The Civil and Political History of the State of Tennessee From Its Earliest Settlement up to the Year 1796, Including the Boundaries of the State.* Knoxville: Heiskel and Brown, 1823.

_______. *The Natural and Aboriginal History of Tennessee: Up to the First Settlements Therein by the White People, In the Year 1768.* Nashville: George Wilson, 1823.

Herrera y Tordesillas, Antonio de. *The General History of the Vast Continent and Islands of America, Commonly Call'd, the West-Indies, From the First Discovery Thereof: With the Best Accounts the People Could Give of Their Antiquities, Collected from the Original Relations Sent to the Kings of Spain.* Translated by Captain John Stevens. 6 vols. London: Wood and Woodward, 1740.

Hewatt, Alexander. *A Historical Account of the Rise and Progress of the Colonies of South Carolina and Georgia.* 2 vols. London: Alexander Donaldson, 1779. [Pickett Book Collection, ADAH]

Hildreth, Richard. *The History of the United States of America, from the Discovery of the Continent to the Organization of the Government under the Federal Constitution, 1497–1789.* 3 vols. New York: Harper & Brothers, 1849.

Holmes, Abiel. *The Annals of America; From the Discovery by Columbus in the Year 1492, to the Year 1826.* 2 vols. 2nd edition. Cambridge: Hilliard and Brown, 1829. [Pickett Book Collection, ADAH].

Johnson, William. *Sketches of the Life and Correspondence of Nathanael Greene, Major General of the Armies of the United States in the War of the Revolution.* 2 vols. Charleston: A. E. Miller, 1822. [Pickett Book Collection, ADAH].

Joutel, Henri. *Journal Historique Du Dernier Voyage que feu M. de LaSale fit dans le golfe de Mexique, pour trouver l'embouchure, & le cours de la Riviere de Missicipi, nommeé à present la Riviere de Saint Loüis, qui traverse la Louisiane.* Paris: Estienne Robinot, 1713.

Kendall, Amos. *Life of Andrew Jackson: Private, Military, and Civil.* New York: Harper & Brothers, 1843.

Kip, William Ingraham. *The Early Jesuit Missions in North America; Compiled and Translated from Letters of the French Jesuits, with Notes.* Vol. 1, pt. 2. New York: Wiley and Putnam, 1846.

La Harpe, Jean-Baptiste Bénard de. *Journal historique* de l'établissement des Français à la Louisiane. Nouvelle Orléans: A. L Boimare, 1831.

Latour, Arsène Lacarrière. *Historical Memoir of the War in West Florida and Louisiana in 1814–15: With an Atlas.* Philadelphia: John Conrad and Co., 1816.

Lee, Richard H. *Memoir of the Life of Richard Henry Lee, and His Correspondence with the Most Distinguished Men in America and Europe, Illustrative of their Characters, and of the Events of the American Revolution.* 2 vols. Philadelphia: H. C. Carey and I. Lea, 1825. [Pickett Book Collection, ADAH].

Le Moyne de Morgues, Jacques. *Brevis Narration Eorum*

Quae in Florida, Americae Provincia Gallis acciderunt, secunda in allam Navigatione, duce Renato de Laudoniere. Pt. 2. Frankfurt: Theodor de Bry, 1591.

Le Page Du Pratz, Antoine Simon, *The History of Louisiana, or of the Western Parts of Virginia and Carolina.* London: T. Beckett, 1774.

McCall, Hugh. *The History of Georgia: Containing Brief Sketches of the Most Remarkable Events up to the Present Day.* 2 vols. Savannah: Seymour & Williams; William T. Williams, 1811–1816. [Pickett Book Collection, ADAH].

McCulloh, James Haines. *Researches, Philosophical and Antiquarian, Concerning the Aboriginal History of America.* Baltimore: F. Lucas, Jr., 1829. [Pickett Book Collection, ADAH].

Martin, François-Xavier. *The History of Louisiana, From the Earliest Period.* 2 vols. New Orleans: Lyman and Beardslee, 1827–1829. [Pickett Book collection, ADAH].

Meek, Alexander Beaufort. *The Southwest: Its History, Character, and Prospects.* Tuscaloosa: C. B. Baldwin, 1840.

Milfort, Louis Le Clerc. *Mémoire ou coup d'oeil rapide sur mes différens voyages et mon séjour dans la nation Crëck. Par le gal. Milfort, Tastenégy ou grand chef de guerre de la nation Crëck et général de brigade au service de la République française.* Paris: Giguet et Michaud, 1802.

Monette, John W. *History of the Discovery and Settlement of the Valley of the Mississippi, By the Three Great European Powers, Spain, France, and Great Britain, and The Subsequent Occupation, Settlement and Extension of Civil Government by the United States Until the Year 1846.* 2 vols. New York: Harper & Brothers, 1846. [Pickett Book Collection, ADAH].

Phelps, Mathew. *Memoirs and Adventures of Captain Matthew Phelps: Formerly of Harwington in Connecticut, now Resident in Newhaven in Vermont. Particularly in Two Voyages, from Connecticut to the River Mississippi, from December 1773 to October 1780.* Bennington, VT.: Press of Anthony Haswell, 1802.

Ramsay, David. *The History of South Carolina: From Its First Settlement in 1670, to the Year 1808.* 2 vols. Charleston: David Longworth, 1809. [Pickett Book Collection, ADAH].

Raynal, Abbé [Guillaume-Thomas-François]. *A Philosophical and Political History of the Settlements and Trade of the Europeans in the East and West Indies.* Revised, Augmented, and Published in Ten Volumes, by the Abbe Raynal. Newly Translated from the French, by J. O. Justamond, F.R.S. With a New Set of Maps adapted to the Work, and a copious Index. 2d ed. 6 vols. London: A. Strahan, and T. Cadell, jun. and W. Davers, 1798. [Pickett Book Collection, ADAH].

Rede, Leman Thomas. *Bibliotheca Americana; or, A Chronological Catalogue of the Most Curious and Interesting Books, Pamphlets, State Papers, &c. Upon the Subject of North and South America, From the Ealiest Period to the Present, in Print and Manuscript.* London: J. DeBrett, J. Sewell, R. Baldwin and J. Bew, and E. Harlowe, 1789. [Pickett Book Collection, ADAH].

Rich, Obadiah. *Bibliotheca Americana Nova: Or, A Catalogue of Books in Various Languages Relating to America, Printed Since the year 1700.* London: O. Rich; New York: Harper & Brothers, 1835. [Pickett Book Collection, ADAH].

Rich, Obadiah. *Bibliotheca Americana Nova: A Catalogue of Books Relating to America, in Various Languages, Including Voyages to the Pacific and Round the World, and Collections of Voyages and Travels Printed Since the Year 1700.* London: Rich and Sons, 1841. [Pickett Book Collection, ADAH].

Richelet, Pierre. *Histoire de la Conquete de la Floride: ou Relation, de ce qui s'est passé dans la Decouverte de ce païs, par Ferdinand De Soto, Composée en Espagnol, par L'Inca Garcillasso de la Vega, et traduite en Francois, par Sr. Pierre Richelet.* 2 vols. A. Leide: Pierre Vander, 1731.

Romans, Bernard. *A Concise Natural History of East and West Florida.* New York: R. Aitken, 1776.

Russell, John, Jr., comp. *The History of the War, Between the United States and Great Britain, Which Commenced in June, 1812, and Closed in Feb. 1815.* Hartford: William S. Marsh, 1815.

Simms, William Gilmore. *The History of South Carolina, From its First European Discovery to its Erection into a Republic: With a Supplementary Chronicle of Events to the Present Time.* Charleston: S. Babcock & Co., 1840.

Squier, Ephraim George and Edwin Hamilton Davis. *Ancient Monuments of the Mississippi Valley: Comprising the Results of Extensive Original Surveys and Explorations.* Smithsonian Contributions to Knowledge, vol. 1. Washington, DC: Smithsonian Institution, 1848.

Stevens, William Bacon. *A History of Georgia: From Its*

First Discovery by Europeans to the Present Constitution in MDCCXCVIII. 2 vols. New York: D. Appleton and Company, 1847–1859.

Stoddard, Amos. *Sketches, Historical and Descriptive, of Louisiana.* Philadelphia: Mathew Cary, 1812.

Sullivan, William. *Familiar Letters on Public Characters, and Public Events; From the Peace of 1783, to the Peace of 1815.* Boston: Russell, Odiorne, and Metcalf, 1834.

Ternaux-Compans, Henri, ed. *Voyages, relations et mémoires originaux pour servir à l'histoire de la découverte de l'Amérique, publiés pour la première fois en français.* Vol. 10: *Recueil de Pieces sur la Floride.* 20 vols. in 10. Paris: Arthus Bertrand, 1837–1841.

Timberlake, Henry. *The Memoirs of Lieut. Henry Timberlake: Who Accompanied the Three Cherokee Indians to England in the Year 1762.* London: J. Ridley, 1765.

Toulmin, Harry. *The Statutes of the Mississippi Territory, Revised and Digested by the Authority of the General Assembly.* Natchez: Samuel Terrell, 1807.

Vega, Garcilaso de la. *Histoire de la Conquěte de la Floride: ou Relation de ce qui s'est passé dans la Découverte de ce païs, par Ferdinand de Soto, Compossée en Espagnol, par L'Inca Garcilasso de la Vega, et traduite en Fracais.* Nouvelle Edition. Leide: Pieter van der Aa, 1731.

Transactions and Collections of the American Antiquarian Society. 12 vols. Worcester, Mass.: The Society, 1820–1911.

Wait, Thomas B., comp. *State Papers and Publick Documents of the United States From the Accession of George Washington to the Presidency, Exhibiting a Complete View of Our Foreign Relations Since That Time.* 10 vols. 2d ed. Boston, T. B. Wait and Sons, 1817.

Waldo, S. Putnam. *Civil and Military History of Andrew Jackson: Late Major-General in the Army of the United States, and Commander-in-Chief of the Southern Division.* New York: P. M. Davis, 1825.

[Wante, Charles Etienne, or Gilles Boucher de La Richarderie]. *Mémoires sur la Louisiane, et la Nouvell-Orléans, accompagnés d'une dissertation sur les avantages que le commerce de l'Empire doit tirer de la stipulations faite par l'article VII de traité de cession, du 30 avril 1803, M. ***; suivis d'une traduction de diverses notes sur cette colonie, publiées aux États-Unis peu de tems aprés la ratification du traité; terminés par un écrit traitan.* Paris: Ballard, 1804. [Pickett Book Collection, ADAH].

Warden, David Bailie. *A Statistical, Political, and Historical Account of the United States of North America; From the Period of Their First Colonization to the Present Day.* 3 vols. Edinburgh: Archibald Constable and Co., 1819. [Pickett Book Collection, ADAH].

Watkins, Robert and George Watkins, ed. *A Digest of the Laws of the State of Georgia: From Its First Establishment as a British Province Down to the Year 1798, Inclusive, and the Principal Acts of 1799.* Philadelphia: R. Aitken, 1800. [Pickett Book Collection, ADAH].

Wilkinson, James. *Memoirs of My Own Times.* 3 vols. Philadelphia: Abraham Small, 1816. [Pickett Book Collection, ADAH].

Willett, William Marinus. *A Narrative of the Military Actions of Colonel Marinus Willett: Taken Chiefly From His Own Manuscript.* New York: G. & C. & H. Carvil, 1831.

Williams, John Lee. *The Territory of Florida: or Sketches of the Topography, Civil and Natural History, of the Country, the Climate, and the Indian Tribes, from the First Discovery to the Present Time.* New York: A. T. Goodrich, 1837.

Winterbotham, William. *An Historical, Geographical, Commercial, and Philosophical View of the American United States, and of the European Settlements in America and the West Indies.* 4 vols. London: J. Ridgeway, 1795. [Pickett Book Collection, ADAH].

Wood, Edwin Thomas. "A Historical Sketch from the First Settlement of Mobile, and the adjoining Country to the Present." In *Mobile Directory and Register for 1844.* Mobile: Dade and Thompson, 1844.

Editor's Suggestions for Additional Reading

Adair, James. *The History of the American Indians*, ed. Kathryn Holland Braund. 1775; reprint, Tuscaloosa: University of Alabama Press, 2005.

Atkinson, James R. *Splendid Land, Splendid People: The Chickasaw Indians to Removal*. Tuscaloosa: University Alabama Press, 2003.

Barnett, James F., Jr. *The Natchez Indians: A History to 1735*. Jackson: University Press of Mississippi, 2007.

Beidler, Philip D. *First Books: The Printed Word and Cultural Foundation in Early Alabama*. Tuscaloosa: University of Alabama Press, 1999.

Blaufarb,Rafe. *Bonapartists in the Borderlands: French Exiles and Refugees on the Gulf Coast, 1815–1835*. Tuscaloosa: University of Alabama Press, 2005.

Braund, Kathryn E., ed. *Tohopeka: Rethinking the Creek War & the War of 1812*. Tuscaloosa: University of Alabama Press, 2012.

Bridges, Edwin C. *Alabama: The Making of an American State*. Tuscaloosa: University of Alabama Press, 2016.

Caughey, John W. *McGillivray of the Creeks*. Norman: University of Oklahoma Press, 1938.

Clayton, Lawrence A., Vernon James Knight Jr., and Edward C. Moore, eds. *The De Soto Chronicles: The Expedition of Hernando de Soto to North America in 1539–1543*, 2 vols. Tuscaloosa: University of Alabama Press, 1993.

Davis, William C. *The Rogue Republic: How Would-Be Patriots Waged the Shortest Revolution in American History*. Boston: Houghton Mifflin Harcourt, 2011.

Dupre, Daniel S. *Transforming the Cotton Frontier: Madison County, Alabama, 1800–1840*. Baton Rouge: Louisiana State University, 1997.

Ethridge, Robbie. *Creek Country: The Creek Indians and Their World*. Chapel Hill: University of North Carolina Press, 2003.

___. *From Chicaza to Chickasaw: The European Invasion and the Transformation of the Mississippian World*. Chapel Hill: University of North Carolina Press, 2010.

Galloway, Patricia, *Choctaw Genesis, 1500–1700*. Lincoln: University of Nebraska Press, 1995.

___. ed. *La Salle and His Legacy: Frenchmen and Indians in the Lower Mississippi Valley*. Jackson: University Press of Mississippi, 1982.

Haynes, Robert V. *The Mississippi Territory and Southwest Frontier, 1795–1817*. Lexington: University Press of Kentucky, 2010.

___. *The Natchez District and the American Revolution*. Jackson: University Press of Mississippi, 1976.

Henri, Florett. *The Southern Indians and Benjamin Hawkins, 1796–1816*. Norman: University of Oklahoma Press, 1986.

Holmes, Jack D. L "Alabama's Forgotten Settlers: Notes on the Spanish Mobile District, 1780–1813," *Alabama Historical Quarterly* 33 (Summer 1971): 87–97.

___. "Notes on the Spanish Fort San Esteban de Tombecbé," *Alabama Review* 18 (October 1965): 281–90.

___. "Spanish Military Commanders in Colonial Alabama," *Journal of the Alabama Academy of Sciences* 37 (January 1966): 55–67.

Hudson, Angela Pulley. *Creek Paths and Federal Roads: Indians, Settlers, and Slaves and the Making of the American South*. Chapel Hill: University of North Carolina Press, 2010.

Hudson, Charles. *Knights of Spain, Warriors of the Sun: Hernando de Soto and the South's Ancient Chiefdoms*. Athens: University of Georgia Press, 1997.

Kanon, Tom. *Tennesseans at War, 1812–1815: Andrew Jackson, the Creek War, and the Battle of New Orleans*. Tuscaloosa: University of Alabama Press, 2014.

Knight, Vernon James Jr., ed. *The Search for Mabila:*

The Decisive Battle between Hernando de Soto and Chief Tascalusa. Tuscaloosa: University of Alabama Press, 2009.

Lee, Harper. "Romance and High Adventure." In *Clearings in the Thicket: An Alabama Humanities Reader*. Edited by Jerry Elijah Brown. Macon, Ga.: Mercer University Press, 1985.

Lewis, Herbert James. *Clearing the Thickets: A History of Antebellum Alabama*. New Orleans: Quid Pro Books, 2013.

___. *Lost Capitals of Alabama*. Charleston: The History Press, 2014.

Milne, George Edward. *Natchez Country: Indians, Colonists, and the Landscapes of Race in French Louisiana*. Athens: University of Georgia Press, 2015.

Neeley, Mary Ann, ed. *The Works of Matthew Blue, Montgomery's First Historian*. Montgomery: NewSouth Books, 2010.

O'Brien, Greg. *Choctaws in a Revolutionary Age, 1750–1830*. Lincoln: University of Nebraska Press, 2002.

O'Brien, Sean Michael. *In Bitterness and in Tears: Andrew Jackson's Destruction of the Creeks and Seminoles*. Guilford, CT: Lyons Press, 2005.

Owsley, Frank L., Jr. "Albert J. Pickett: Historian of Alabama," *Alabama Review* 11 (January 1958): 31–43.

___. "Albert J. Pickett: Planter-Historian of the Old South," *Louisiana History* 8 (Summer 1969): 158–64.

___. *Struggle for the Gulf Borderlands: The Creek War and the Battle of New Orleans, 1812–1815*. Gainesville: University Presses of Florida, 1981.

Pate James P., ed. *The Reminiscences of George Strother Gaines: Pioneer and Statesman of Early Alabama and Mississippi, 1805–1843*. Tuscaloosa: University of Alabama Press, 1998.

Pattillo, Edward. *Carolina Planters on the Alabama Frontier: The Spencer-Robeson-McKenzie Family Papers*. Montgomery: NewSouth Books, 2011.

Rea, Robert R. *Major Robert Farmar of Mobile*. Tuscaloosa: University of Alabama Press, 1990.

Rogers, William Warren, Leah Rawls Atkins, Robert David Ward, and Wayne Flynt. *Alabama: The History of a Deep South State*. Tuscaloosa: University of Alabama Press, 2010.

Shields, Johanna Nicol. *Freedom in a Slave Society: Stories from the Antebellum South*. New York: Cambridge University Press, 2012.

Smith, Winston. *Days of Exile: The Story of the Vine and Olive Colony in Alabama*. Tuscaloosa: W. B. Drake and Son, Printers, 1967.

Thornton, J. Mills III. *Politics and Power in a Slave Society: Alabama, 1800–1860*. Baton Rouge: Louisiana State University Press, 1981.

Waselkov, Gregory A. *A Conquering Spirit: Fort Mims and the Redstick War of 1813–1814*. Tuscaloosa: University of Alabama Press, 2006.

___. and Kathryn E. Holland Braund, eds. *William Bartram on the Southeastern Indians*. Lincoln: University of Nebraska Press, 1995.

Wright, Amos J., Jr. *Historic Indian Towns in Alabama, 1540–1838*. Tuscaloosa: University of Alabama Press, 2003.

___. *The McGillivray and McIntosh Traders on the Old Southwest Frontier, 1716–1815*. Montgomery: NewSouth Books, 2001.

Wright, J. Leitch. *Creeks and Seminoles: The Destruction and Regeneration of the Muscogulge People*. Lincoln: University of Nebraska Press, 1986.

___. *William Augustus Bowles: Director General of the Creek Nation*. Athens: University of Georgia Press, 1967.

Index

Editor's Note: Spanish and French colonial period names like Jean-Baptiste Le Moyne de Bienville are indexed by their most familiar designations, such as Bienville; De Soto; Du Clos; etc. Many Indian towns were given various spellings by the sources Pickett used and also had the same names as the native people who occupied them; these are indexed like "Talase/ Talisi town, people, battle of." Similarly named counties or towns that developed into territorial or statehood locations are indexed like "Tallassee, Alabama" or "Chickasaw County, Mississippi." Indian names are indexed like "Menawa (chief)" or by the first letter of anglicized names like "Pouting Pigeon (warrior)."

C

E

I

M

O

S

T

U